P9-BHT-424

Twentieth-Century Literary Criticism

Guide to Gale Literary Criticism Series

When you need to review criticism of literary works, these are the Gale series to use:

If the author's death date is:

You should turn to:

After Dec. 31, 1959
(or author is still living)

CONTEMPORARY LITERARY CRITICISM

for example: Jorge Luis Borges, Anthony Burgess,
William Faulkner, Mary Gordon,
Ernest Hemingway, Iris Murdoch

1900 through 1959

TWENTIETH-CENTURY LITERARY CRITICISM

for example: Willa Cather, F. Scott Fitzgerald,
Henry James, Mark Twain, Virginia Woolf

1800 through 1899

NINETEENTH-CENTURY LITERATURE CRITICISM

for example: Fyodor Dostoevsky, Nathaniel Hawthorne,
George Sand, William Wordsworth

1400 through 1799

LITERATURE CRITICISM FROM 1400 TO 1800
(excluding Shakespeare)

for example: Anne Bradstreet, Daniel Defoe,
Alexander Pope, François Rabelais,
Jonathan Swift, Phillis Wheatley

SHAKESPEAREAN CRITICISM

Shakespeare's plays and poetry

Antiquity through 1399

CLASSICAL AND MEDIEVAL LITERATURE CRITICISM

for example: Dante, Homer, Plato, Sophocles, Vergil,
the Beowulf Poet

Gale also publishes related criticism series:

CHILDREN'S LITERATURE REVIEW

This series covers authors of all eras who have written for the preschool through high school audience.

SHORT STORY CRITICISM

This series covers the major short fiction writers of all nationalities and periods of literary history.

POETRY CRITICISM

This series covers poets of all nationalities and periods of literary history.

DRAMA CRITICISM

This series covers dramatists of all nationalities and periods of literary history.

ISSN 0276-8178

Volume 40

Twentieth-Century Literary Criticism

**Excerpts from Criticism of the
Works of Novelists, Poets, Playwrights,
Short Story Writers, and Other Creative Writers
Who Died between 1900 and 1960,
from the First Published Critical Appraisals
to Current Evaluations**

**Paula Kepos
Laurie DiMauro
Editors**

**David Kmenta
Jelena Krstović
Marie Lazzari
Thomas Ligotti
Joann Prosyniuk
Associate Editors**

 Gale Research Inc. • *DETROIT* • *LONDON*

STAFF

Paula Kepos, Laurie DiMauro, *Editors*

David Kmenta, Jelena Krstović, Marie Lazzari, Thomas Ligotti, Joann Prosyniuk, *Associate Editors*

Catherine Falk, Mary K. Gillis, Ian A. Goodhall, Tina N. Grant, Alan Hedblad, Elizabeth P. Henry, Grace Jeromski, Andrew M. Kalasky, Susan M. Peters, James Poniewozik, Mark Swartz, Bridget Travers, Debra A. Wells, Janet M. Witalec, *Assistant Editors*

Jeanne A. Gough, *Permissions & Production Manager*

Linda M. Pugliese, *Production Supervisor*
Maureen Puhl, Jennifer VanSickle, *Editorial Associates*
Donna Craft, Paul Lewon, Lorna Mabunda, Camille Robinson, Sheila Walencewicz, *Editorial Assistants*

Victoria B. Cariappa, *Research Manager*
Maureen Richards, *Research Supervisor*
Paula Cutcher-Jackson, Judy L. Gale, *Editorial Associates*
Jennifer Brostrom, Robin Lupa, Mary Beth McElmeel, Tamara C. Nott, *Editorial Assistants*

Sandra C. Davis, *Permissions Supervisor (Text)*
Josephine M. Keene, Denise M. Singleton, Kimberly F. Smilay, *Permissions Associates*
Maria L. Franklin, Michele Lonoconus, Shelly Rakoczy, Shalice Shah, Nancy K. Sheridan, Rebecca A. Stanko, *Permissions Assistants*

Patricia A. Seefelt, *Permissions Supervisor (Pictures)*
Margaret A. Chamberlain, *Permissions Associate*
Pamela A. Hayes, Keith Reed, *Permissions Assistants*

Mary Beth Trimper, *Production Manager*
Mary Winterhalter, *External Production Assistant*

Arthur Chartow, *Art Director*
C. J. Jonik, *Keyliner*

Contents

Preface   vii

Acknowledgments   xi

Preface

Since its inception more than ten years ago, *Twentieth-Century Literary Criticism* has been purchased and used by nearly 10,000 school, public, and college or university libraries. *TCLC* has covered more than 500 authors, representing 58 nationalities, and over 25,000 titles. No other reference source has surveyed the critical response to twentieth-century authors and literature as thoroughly as *TCLC*. In the words of one reviewer, "there is nothing comparable available." *TCLC* "is a gold mine of information—dates, pseudonyms, biographical information, and criticism from books and periodicals—which many libraries would have difficulty assembling on their own."

Scope of the Series

TCLC is designed to serve as an introduction to authors who died between 1900 and 1960 and to the most significant interpretations of these authors' works. The great poets, novelists, short story writers, playwrights, and philosophers of this period are frequently studied in high school and college literature courses. In organizing and excerpting the vast amount of critical material written on these authors, *TCLC* helps students develop valuable insight into literary history, promotes a better understanding of the texts, and sparks ideas for papers and assignments. Each entry in *TCLC* presents a comprehensive survey of an author's career or an individual work of literature and provides the user with a multiplicity of interpretations and assessments. Such variety allows students to pursue their own interests; furthermore, it fosters an awareness that literature is dynamic and responsive to many different opinions.

Every fourth volume of *TCLC* is devoted to literary topics that cannot be covered under the author approach used in the rest of the series. Such topics include literary movements, prominent themes in twentieth-century literature, literary reaction to political and historical events, significant eras in literary history, prominent literary anniversaries, and the literatures of cultures that are often overlooked by English-speaking readers.

TCLC is designed as a companion series to Gale's *Contemporary Literary Criticism,* which reprints commentary on authors now living or who have died since 1960. Because of the different periods under consideration, there is no duplication of material between *CLC* and *TCLC*. For additional information about *CLC* and Gale's other criticism titles, users should consult the Guide to Gale Literary Criticism Series preceding the title page in this volume.

Coverage

Each volume of *TCLC* is carefully compiled to present:

- criticism of authors, or literary topics, representing a variety of genres and nationalities

- both major and lesser-known writers and literary works of the period

- 12-16 authors or 4-6 topics per volume

- individual entries that survey critical response to each author's work or each topic in literary history, including early criticism to reflect initial reactions; later criticism to represent any rise or decline in reputation; and current retrospective analyses.

Organization of This Book

An author entry consists of the following elements: author heading, biographical and critical introduction, list of principal works, excerpts of criticism (each preceded by an annotation and followed by a bibliographic citation), and a bibliography of further reading.

- The **author heading** consists of the name under which the author most commonly wrote, followed by birth and death dates. If an author wrote consistently under a pseudonym, the pseudonym will be listed in the author heading and the real name given in parentheses on the first line of the biographical and critical introduction. Also located at the beginning of the introduction to the author entry are any name variations under which an author wrote, including transliterated forms for authors whose languages use nonroman alphabets.

- The **biographical and critical introduction** outlines the author's life and career, as well as the critical issues surrounding his or her work. References are provided to past volumes of *TCLC* and to other biographical and critical reference series published by Gale, including *Short Story Criticism, Children's Literature Review, Contemporary Authors, Dictionary of Literary Biography,* and *Something about the Author.*

- Most *TCLC* entries include **portraits** of the author. Many entries also contain reproductions of materials pertinent to an author's career, including manuscript pages, title pages, dust jackets, letters, and drawings, as well as photographs of important people, places, and events in an author's life.

- The **list of principal works** is chronological by date of first book publication and identifies the genre of each work. In the case of foreign authors with both foreign-language publications and English translations, the title and date of the first English-language edition are given in brackets. Unless otherwise indicated, dramas are dated by first performance, not first publication.

- **Criticism** is arranged chronologically in each author entry to provide a perspective on changes in critical evaluation over the years. All titles of works by the author featured in the entry are printed in boldface type to enable the user to easily locate discussion of particular works. Also for purposes of easier identification, the critic's name and the publication date of the essay are given at the beginning of each piece of criticism. Unsigned criticism is preceded by the title of the journal in which it appeared. Some of the excerpts in *TCLC* also contain translated material. Unless otherwise noted, translations in brackets are by the editors; translations in parentheses or continuous with the text are by the critic. Publication information (such as publisher names and book prices) and parenthetical numerical references (such as footnotes or page and line references to specific editions of works) have been deleted at the editors' discretion to provide smoother reading of the text.

- Critical excerpts are prefaced by **annotations** providing the reader with information about both the critic and the criticism that follows. Included are the critic's reputation, individual approach to literary criticism, and particular expertise in an author's works. Also noted are the relative importance of a work of criticism, the scope of the excerpt, and the growth of critical controversy or changes in critical trends regarding an author. In some cases, these annotations cross-reference excerpts by critics who discuss each other's commentary.

- A complete **bibliographic citation** designed to facilitate location of the original essay or book follows each piece of criticism.

- An annotated list of **further reading** appearing at the end of each author entry suggests secondary sources on the author. In some cases it includes essays for which the editors could not obtain reprint rights.

Cumulative Indexes

- Each volume of *TCLC* contains a cumulative **author index** listing all authors who have appeared in Gale's Literary Criticism Series, along with cross-references to such biographical series as *Contemporary Authors* and *Dictionary of Literary Biography.* For readers' convenience, a complete list of Gale titles included appears on the first page of the author index. Useful for locating authors within the various series, this index is particularly valuable for those authors who are identified by a certain period but who, because of their death dates, are placed in another, or for those authors whose careers span two periods. For example, F. Scott Fitzgerald is found in *TCLC,* yet a writer often associated with him, Ernest Hemingway, is found in *CLC.*

- Each *TCLC* volume includes a cumulative **nationality index** which lists all authors who have appeared in *TCLC* volumes, arranged alphabetically under their respective nationalities, as well as Topics volume entries devoted to particular national literatures.

- Each new volume in Gale's Literary Criticism Series includes a cumulative **topic index,** which lists all literary topics treated in *NCLC, TCLC, LC 1400-1800,* and the *CLC* Yearbook.

- Each new volume of *TCLC,* with the exception of the Topics volumes, contains a **title index** listing the titles of all literary works discussed in the volume. The first volume of *TCLC* published each year contains an index listing all titles discussed in the series since its inception. Titles discussed in the Topics volume entries are not included in the *TCLC* cumulative index.

A Note to the Reader

When writing papers, students who quote directly from any volume in Gale's Literary Criticism Series may use the following general forms to footnote reprinted criticism. The first example pertains to material drawn from periodicals, the second to material reprinted from books.

[1] T. S. Eliot, "John Donne," *The Nation and the Athenaeum,* 33 (9 June 1923), 321-32; excerpted and reprinted in *Literature Criticism from 1400 to 1800,* Vol. 10, ed. James E. Person, Jr. (Detroit: Gale Research, 1989), pp. 28-9.

[2] Clara G. Stillman, *Samuel Butler: A Mid-Victorian Modern* (Viking Press, 1932); excerpted and reprinted in *Twentieth-Century Literary Criticism,* Vol. 33, ed. Paula Kepos (Detroit: Gale Research, 1989), pp. 43-5.

Suggestions Are Welcome

In response to suggestions, several features have been added to *TCLC* since the series began, including annotations to excerpted criticism, a cumulative index to authors in all Gale literary criticism series, entries devoted to criticism on a single work by a major author, more extensive illustrations, and a title index listing all literary works discussed in the series since its inception.

Readers who wish to suggest authors or topics to appear in future volumes, or who have other suggestions, are cordially invited to write the editors.

Acknowledgments

The editors wish to thank the copyright holders of the excerpted criticism included in this volume, the permissions managers of many book and magazine publishing companies for assisting us in securing reprint rights, and Anthony Bogucki for assistance with copyright research. We are also grateful to the staffs of the Detroit Public Library, Wayne State University Purdy/Kresge Library Complex, and the University of Michigan Libraries for making their resources available to us. Following is a list of the copyright holders who have granted us permission to reprint material in this volume of *TCLC*. Every effort has been made to trace copyright, but if omissions have been made, please let us know.

COPYRIGHTED EXCERPTS IN *TCLC*, VOLUME 40, WERE REPRINTED FROM THE FOLLOWING PERIODICALS:

Agenda, v. 19, Summer-Autumn, 1981 for "Keith Douglas" by Jon Silkin. Reprinted by permission of the author.—*American Literature,* v. XLI, March, 1969. Copyright © 1969 Duke University Press, Durham, NC. Reprinted by permission of the publisher.—*American Quarterly,* v. XXIII, December, 1971 for "The Uses of Despair: The Sources of Creative Energy in George Santayana," by Lois Hughson. Copyright 1971, American Studies Association. Reprinted by permission of the publisher and the Literary Estate of Lois Hughson.—*Boston University Journal,* v. 24, 1976. Copyright © 1976 by the Trustees of Boston University.—*boundary 2,* v. V. Winter, 1977. Copyright © *boundary 2,* 1977. Reprinted by permission of the publisher.—*Canadian Literature,* n. 26, Autumn, 1965 for "Faust and 'Under the Volcano' " by Anthony R. Kilgallin; n. 84, Spring, 1980 for "The Myth of the Hero" by George Rhys Garnett. Both reprinted by permission of the respective authors.—*Commentary,* v. 10, 1950. Copyright 1950 by the American Jewish Committee.—*Contemporary Literature,* v. XIX, Winter, 1978. © 1978 by the Board of Regents of the University of Wisconsin System. Reprinted by permission of The University of Wisconsin Press.—*Critical Quarterly,* v. 6, Summer, 1964 for "The Sick Rhetoric of War" by George MacBeth. Copyright © by the author 1964. Reprinted by permission of Anthony Sheil Associates on behalf of George MacBeth./ v. 5, Spring, 1963 for "The Poetry of Keith Douglas" by Ted Hughes. Reprinted by permission of Faber and Faber Limited on behalf of the author. v. 7, Autumn, 1965 for "The Fearful Self: Henry James's 'The Portrait of a Lady' " by Tony Tanner. Reprinted by permission of the author.—*English Studies,* Netherlands, v. 50, February, 1969. © 1969 by Swets & Zeitlinger B. V. Reprinted by permission of the publisher.—*German Life & Letters,* v. XXXVI-II, April, 1984. Reprinted by permission of the publisher.—*The Henry James Review,* v. 7, Winter-Spring, 1986. © 1987 The Henry James Society. All rights reserved. Reprinted by permission of the publisher.—*Journal of European Studies,* v. XIX, March, 1979 for "Gabriele D'Annunzio and Thomas Mann: 'Venice, Art and Death' " by Giuliana Giobbi. Copyright © 1979 Seminar Press Limited. Reprinted by permission of the author.—*Journal of the History of Ideas,* v. XXXIV, January-March, 1973. Copyright 1973, Journal of the History of Ideas, Inc. Reprinted by permission of the publisher.—*Journal of the History of Philosophy,* v. XIV, July, 1976. Copyright 1976 by the *Journal of the History of Philosophy.* Reprinted by permission of the Editor.—*The Leo Baeck Institute of Jews from Germany Yearbook,* v. XXIII, 1978. © Leo Baeck Institute 1978. Reprinted by permission of the Editor of the Leo Baeck Institute Year Book, Dr. Arnold Paucker.—*The Literary Half-Yearly,* v. XIV, January, 1973. © 1973 *The Literary Half-Yearly.* Reprinted by permission of the publisher.—*The Nation,* New York, v. 217, October 22, 1973. Copyright 1973 *The Nation* magazine/The Nation Company, Inc. Reprinted by permission of the publisher.—*The New Criterion,* v. V, June, 1987 for "George Santayana and the Consolations of Philosophy" by Joseph Epstein. Copyright © 1987 by The Foundation for Cultural Review. Reprinted by permission of the author.—*The New York Review of Books,* v. XX, November 15, 1973. Copyright © 1973 Nyrev, Inc. Reprinted with permission from *The New York Review of Books.*—*The New York Times Book Review,* November 25, 1956. Copyright © 1956 by The New York Times Company. Reprinted by permission of the publisher.—*The New Yorker,* v. XXIX, May 2, 1953 for "Through the Collarbone of a Hare" by W. H. Auden. Copyright 1953 by the author. Reprinted by permission of the Literary Estate of W. H. Auden.—*The Pennsylvania Magazine of History and Biography,* v. CI, January, 1977. Reprinted by permission of the publisher.—*Russian Literature Triquarterly,* v. 7, 1973; v. 11, 1975. © 1973, 1975 by Ardis Publishers. Both reprinted by permission of the publisher.—*The Russian Review,* v. 22, July, 1963 for "Mikhail Kuzmin: Notes on a Decadent's Prose" by Andrew Field. Copyright 1963 by The Russian Review, Inc. Reprinted by permission of the author.—*The Saturday Review of Literature,* v. XXX, February 22, 1947. Copyright 1947, renewed 1975 *Saturday Review* magazine.—*The Sewanee Review,* v. LV, Summer, 1947. Copyright 1947, renewed 1974 by The University of the South. Reprinted by permission of the editor of *The Sewanee Review.*—*Slavic Review,* v. 38, September, 1979 for "Death and Resurrection of Mikhail Kuzmin" by Simon Karlinsky. Copyright © 1979 by the American Association for the Advancement of Slavic Studies, Inc. Reprinted by permission of the publisher and the author.—*South Atlantic Bulletin,* v. XLI, January, 1976. Copyright © 1976 by South Atlantic Modern Language Association. Reprinted by permission of the publisher.—***Stand Magazine,*** v. 6, 1964 for " 'I in Another Place.' Homage to Keith Douglas" by Geoffrey Hill. Copyright © 1963 by the author. Reprinted by permission of the publisher.—***Studies in the Novel,*** v. XII, Fall, 1980. Copyright 1980 by North Texas State University. Reprinted by permission of the publisher.—***The Times Literary Supplement,*** n. 3566, July 2, 1970. © Times Newspapers Ltd. (London) 1970. Reproduced from *The Times Literary Supplement* by permission.—***University of Toronto Quarterly,*** v. LVIII, Winter, 1988-89. © University of Toronto Press 1989. Reprinted by permission of University of Toronto Press.—***TSE: Tulane Studies in English,*** v. XVI, 1968. Copyright © 1968 by Tulane University. Reprinted by permission of the publisher.—***The Virginia Quarterly Review,*** v. 12, Spring, 1936; v. 13, Summer, 1937. Copyright, 1936, renewed 1963; copyright, 1937, renewed 1964, by *The Virginia Quarterly Review,* The University of Virginia. Both reprinted by permission of the publisher.—***Yale French Studies,*** n. 68, 1985 for "Sartre, Nizan and the Dilemmas of Political Commitment" by Patrick McCarthy. Reprinted by permission of the publisher and the author.

COPYRIGHTED EXCERPTS IN *TCLC,* VOLUME 40, WERE REPRINTED FROM THE FOLLOWING BOOKS:

Auchincloss, Louis. From ***Reading Henry James.*** University of Minnesota Press, 1975. Copyright © 1975 by Louis Auchincloss. All rights reserved. Reprinted by permission of the publisher.—Bergonzi, Bernard. From ***The Turn of a Century: Essays on Victorian and Modern English Literature.*** Barnes & Noble, 1973. © Bernard Bergonzi, 1973. All rights reserved. Reprinted by permission of the Peters Fraser & Dunlop Group Ltd.—Binns, Ronald. From ***Malcolm Lowry.*** Methuen, 1984. © 1984 Ronald Binns. All rights reserved. Reprinted by permission of the publisher.—Blackmur, R. P. From an introduction to ***The Portrait of a Lady.*** By Henry James. Dell, 1961. Copyright © 1961 by R. P. Blackmur. Renewed 1989 by Elizabeth Blackmur. Reprinted by permission of the Literary Estate of Richard P. Blackmur.—Bleiler, E. F. From an introduction to ***The Collected Ghost Stories of Mrs. J. H. Riddell.*** Edited by E. F. Bleiler. Dover Publications, 1977. Copyright © 1977 by Dover Publications, Inc. All rights reserved. Reprinted by permission of the publisher.—Chalmers, David Mark. From ***The Social and Political Ideas of the Muckrakers.*** The Citadel Press, 1964. Copyright © 1964 by David Mark Chalmers. All rights reserved. Published by arrangement with Carol Publishing Group.—Chandler, Frank W. from ***Modern Continental Playwrights.*** Harper & Brothers, 1931. Copyright 1931 by Harper & Row, Publishers, Inc. Renewed 1958 by Adele Walton Chandler. Reprinted by permission of HarperCollins Publishers.—Chase, Richard. From ***The American Novel and Its Tradition.*** Doubleday & Company, Inc., 1957. Copyright © 1957 by Richard Chase. Renewed 1985 by Frances W. Chase. All rights reserved. Used by permission of Doubleday, a division of Bantam Doubleday Dell Publishing Group, Inc.—Costa, Richard Hauer. From ***Malcolm Lowry.*** Twayne, 1972. Copyright 1972 by Twayne Publishers. All rights reserved. Reprinted by permission of the author.—Croce, Benedetto. From ***Philosophy, Poetry, History: An Anthology of Essays.*** Translated by Cecil Sprigge. Oxford University Press, London, 1966. Introduction and English Translation © Oxford University Press 1966. Reprinted by permission of the publisher.—Di Piero, W. S. From ***Memory and Enthusiasm: Essays, 1975-1985.*** Princeton University Press, 1989. Copyright © 1989 by Princeton University Press. All rights reserved. Reprinted with permission of the publisher.—Festa-McCormick, Diana. From ***The City as Catalyst: A Study of Ten Novels.*** Fairleigh Dickinson University Press, 1979. © 1979 by Associated University Presses, Inc. Reprinted by permission of the publisher.—Filler, Louis. From ***The Muckrakers.*** New and enlarged edition of ***Crusaders for American Liberalism.*** Pennsylvania State University Press, 1976. Copyright 1976 by Louis Filler. Reprinted by permission of the author.—Galloway, David. From ***Henry James: The Portrait of a Lady.*** Edward Arnold (Publishers) Ltd., 1967. © David Galloway 1967. All rights reserved. Reprinted by permission of the publisher.—Gass, William H. From ***Fiction and the Figures of Life.*** Knopf, 1970. Copyright © 1971 by William H. Gass. All rights reserved. Reprinted by permission of the author.—Geismar, Maxwell. From ***Henry James and the Jacobites.*** Houghton Mifflin Company, 1963. Copyright © 1962, 1963 by Maxwell Geismar. All rights reserved. Reprinted by permission of Houghton Mifflin Company.—Gilmore, Thomas B. From ***Equivocal Spirits: Alcoholism and Drinking in Twentieth-Century Literature.*** University of North Carolina Press, 1987. © 1987 The University of North Carolina Press. All rights reserved. Reprinted by permission of the publisher and the author.—Grunfeld, Frederic V. From ***Prophets without Honour: A Background to Freud, Kafka, Einstein and Their Worlds.*** Holt, Rinehart and Winston, 1979. Copyright © 1979 by Frederic V. Grunfeld. All rights reserved. Reprinted by permission of the Wallace Literary Agency, Inc.—Gumilev, Nikolai. From ***Nikolai Gumilev on Russian Poetry.*** Edited and translated by David Lapeza. Ardis, 1977. Copyright © 1977 by Ardis. Reprinted by permission of the publisher.—Krook, Dorothea. From ***The Ordeal of Consciousness in Henry James.*** Cambridge at the University Press, 1962. © Cambridge University Press 1962. Reprinted with the permission of the publisher.—Leech, Clifford. From ***The Dramatist's Experience: With Other Essays in Literary Theory.*** Chatto & Windus, 1970. © Clifford Leech 1970. Reprinted by permission of the author and Chatto & Windus.—Longley, Edna. From ***Poetry in the Wars.*** Bloodaxe Books Ltd., 1986. Copyright © Edna Longley 1986, 1987. All rights reserved. Reprinted by permission of the publisher.—Lowry, Malcolm. From ***Selected Poems of Malcolm Lowry.*** Edited by Earle Birney with Margerie Lowry. City Lights Books, 1962. © 1962 by Margerie Lowry. Reprinted by permission of the publisher.—Malmstad, John E. and Gennady Shamakov. From "Kuzmin's 'The Trout Breaking through the Ice'," in ***Russian Modernism: Culture and the Avant-Garde, 1900-1930.*** Edited by George Gibian and H. W. Tjalsma. Cornell University Press, 1976. Copyright © 1976 by Cornell University. All rights reserved. Reprinted by permission of George Gibian.—Markov, Vladimir. From a preface to ***Wings: Prose and Poetry.*** By

Mikhail Kuzmin. Edited and translated by Neil Granoien and Michael Green. Ardis, 1972. Copyright © 1972, by Ardis. Reprinted by permission of the publisher.—Matthiessen, F. O. From *Henry James: The Major Phase.* Oxford University Press, 1944. Copyright 1944 by Oxford University Press, Inc. Renewed 1971 by Mrs. Peters Putnam. Reprinted by permission of the publisher.—Pacifici, Sergio. From *The Modern Italian Novel: From Capuana to Tozzi.* Southern Illinois University Press, 1973. Copyright © 1973 by Southern Illinois University Press. All rights reserved. Reprinted by permission of the publisher.—Perella, Nicolas J. From *Midday in Italian Literature: Variations on an Archetypal Theme.* Princeton University Press, 1979. Copyright © 1979 by Princeton University Press. All rights reserved. Reprinted with permission of the publisher.—Poggioli, Renato. From *The Poets of Russia: 1890-1930.* Cambridge, Mass.: Harvard University Press, 1960. Copyright © 1960 by the President and Fellows of Harvard College. Renewed © 1988 by Sylvia Poggioli. Excerpted by permission of the publishers and the Literary Estate of Renato Poggioli.—Redfern, Walter. From "Nizan: A Matter of Death and Life," in *Socialism in France: From Jaurés to Mitterrand.* Edited by Stuart Williams. St. Martin's Press, 1983. © Association for the Study of Modern and Contemporary France 1983. All rights reserved. Used with permission of St. Martin's Press, Inc.—Russell, Bertrand. From "The Philosophy of Santayana," in *The Philosophy of George Santayana.* Edited by Paul Arthur Schilpp. The Library of Living Philosophers, Vol. II. Northwestern University, 1940. Copyright 1940 and 1951, renewed 1968 by the Library of Living Philosophers, Inc. Reprinted by permission of the publisher, Open Court Publishing Company, La Salle, Illinois.—Santayana, George. From "A General Confession," in *The Philosophy of George Santayana.* Edited by Paul Arthur Schilpp. The Library of Living Philosophers, Vol. II. Northwestern University, 1940. Copyright 1940 and 1951, renewed 1968 by the Library of Living Philosophers, Inc. Reprinted by permission of the publisher, Open Court Publishing Company, La Salle, Illinois.—Sartre, Jean-Paul. From *Situations, Vol. I.* Gallimard, 1948. © Gallimard 1948. Renewed 1975 by Jean-Paul Sartre. Reprinted by permission of the publisher.—Scott, Nathan A., Jr. From *The Poetics of Belief: Studies in Coleridge, Arnold, Pater, Santayana, Stevens, and Heidegger.* The University of North Carolina Press, 1985. © 1985 The University of North Carolina Press. All rights reserved. Reprinted by permission of the publisher and the author.—Scriven, Michael. From *Paul Nizan: Communist Novelist.* St. Martin's Press, 1988, Macmillan Press, 1988. © Michael Scriven 1988. All rights reserved. Used with permission of St. Martin's Press, Inc. In Canada by Macmillan, London and Basingstoke.—Shires, Linda M. From *British Poetry of the Second World War.* St. Martin's Press, 1985, Macmillan, 1985. © Linda M. Shires 1985. All rights reserved. Used with permission of St. Martin's Press, Inc. In Canada by Macmillan, London and Basingstoke.—Smith, Henry A. From "Gertrud Kolmar's Life and Works," in *Dark Soliloquy: The Selected Poems of Gertrud Kolmar.* By Gertrud Kolmar, translated by Henry A. Smith. The Seabury Press, 1975. Translation copyright © 1975 by The Seabury Press. All rights reserved. Reprinted by permission of the publisher.—Suleiman, Susan Rubin. From *Authoritarian Fictions: The Ideological Novel as a Literary Genre.* Columbia University Press, 1983. Copyright © 1983 Columbia University Press. All rights reserved. Used by permission of the publisher.—Thomas, Benjamin P. From *Portrait for Posterity: Lincoln and His Biographers.* Rutgers University Press, 1947. Copyright 1947, renewed 1974 by The Trustees of Rutgers College. All rights reserved. Reprinted by permission of the publisher.—Thornberry, Robert. From "Paul Nizan: Revolutionary in Politics, Conservative in Aesthetics," in *Literature and Revolution.* Edited by David Bevan. Rodopi, 1989. © Editions Rodopi B.V., Amsterdam - Atlanta, GA 1989. Reprinted by permission of the publisher.—Tifft, Stephen. From "Tragedy as a Meditation of Itself: Reflexiveness in 'Under the Volcano'," in *The Art of Malcolm Lowry.* Edited by Anne Smith. London: Vision Press, 1978. © 1978 Vision Press. All rights reserved. Reprinted by permission of the publisher.—Tomkins, Mary E. From *Ida M. Tarbell.* Twayne, 1974. Copyright 1974 by Twayne Publishers. All rights reserved. Reprinted with the permission of Twayne Publishers, Inc., a division of G. K. Hall & Co., Boston.—Wagenknecht, Edward. From *Eve and Henry James: Portraits of Women and Girls in His Fiction.* University of Oklahoma Press, 1978. Copyright 1978 by the University of Oklahoma Press. Reprinted by permission of the author.—Walker, Ronald G. From *Infernal Paradise: Mexico and the Modern English Novel.* University of California Press, 1978. Copyright © 1978 by The Regents of the University of California. Reprinted by permission of the publisher.—West, Rebecca. From *Henry James.* Henry Holt and Company, 1916.

PHOTOGRAPHS AND ILLUSTRATIONS APPEARING IN *TCLC*, VOLUME 40, WERE RECEIVED FROM THE FOLLOWING SOURCES:

Museum of Modern Art, Paris: **p. 12;** Gerra Collection: **p. 23;** Photograph by G. Civivini: **p. 48;** Editions Sociales Internationales, Paris: **p. 295;** Mrs. Daniel Cory, the Estate of George Santayana: **p. 351;** Harvard University Portrait Collection, Gift Harvard Alumni and Friends of Professors James, Royce and Palmer, 1920: **p. 397;** Photograph by Alfred Cheney Johnson: **p. 421.**

Gabriele D'Annunzio

1863-1938

(Also wrote under the pseudonyms Il Duca Minimo and Angelo Cocles) Italian novelist, dramatist, poet, short story writer, and journalist.

For further discussion of D'Annunzio's career, see *TCLC*, Volume 6.

D'Annunzio is one of the most flamboyant personalities in modern literature. While the popular press reported the romantic scandals of his life, many literary critics excoriated him as a moral delinquent, and in 1911 the Catholic Church placed his works on their Index of Forbidden Books. Nevertheless, he was renowned in his lifetime as Italy's leading author, a consummate stylist who combined the poetic grandeur of Dante and the classical writers with such contemporary trends as Naturalism, Symbolism, and Decadence.

The third of five children born to the mayor of Pescara, a small town in the Abruzzi region of Italy, D'Annunzio was educated by private tutors and studied Latin with priests of the local diocese. At the age of eleven, he was sent to Cicognini College at Prato, a prestigious boarding school run by Jesuits. There he excelled in his studies, particularly in Greek and Latin. Forbidden by his father to return home for two years in the hope that he would lose his provincial accent, D'Annunzio quickly adopted the more esteemed Tuscan dialect spoken at the school and developed an interest in archaic words. When he was sixteen, D'Annunzio published *Primo vere,* his first collection of poetry. Noted for its open treatment of sexual themes, *Primo vere* was a commercial and critical success. After graduating from Cicognini in 1881, D'Annunzio entered the University of Rome and began writing short fiction and society columns for local newspapers under both his own name and a variety of pseudonyms. The following year, he published *Terra vergine,* a collection of naturalistic regional tales, and *Canto novo,* a volume of poetry which incorporates details of his first romantic relationship. In 1888, finding that his journalistic writing occupied too much of his time, D'Annunzio quit his job as a reporter to finish his first novel, *Il piacere (The Child of Pleasure).*

Throughout the following decade D'Annunzio wrote a number of successful novels and in 1897 was elected as a deputy to the Italian Parliament. The events of his private life were widely reported, particularly his relationship with the noted actress Eleonora Duse, who frequently performed the leading roles in his plays and served as the model for the character Foscarina in the novel *Il fuoco (The Flame of Life).* While serving in the air force and army during World War I, D'Annunzio distinguished himself with several notable feats of heroism. After the war, believing that Italy had been cheated by the Allies in the division of land, D'Annunzio led several thousand irregular troops in the occupation of the town of Fiume

(now Rijeka, Yugoslavia) against the wishes of the Italian government. Deposed by Italian troops in 1921 shortly before a planned invasion of Rome, D'Annunzio was allowed to retire to his villa, where he continued writing until his death of a cerebral hemorrhage in 1938.

Commentators usually divide D'Annunzio's works into four overlapping phases, with each phase dominated by, but not exclusively devoted to, works in a particular genre. The first phase, which includes the naturalistic short stories of *Terra vergine* and *San Pantaleone,* is nevertheless chiefly noted for the poetry of *Primo vere* and *Canto novo.* Displaying the linguistic virtuosity that established his reputation, the works of this period are characterized by their regional settings, archaic language, and sensual lyricism. Most of the poems in *Primo vere* were strongly influenced by Giosuè Carducci's *Odi barbare* (1877), particularly in the use of ancient Greek and Latin meters. In the revised edition of *Primo vere,* D'Annunzio removed several poems that are considered directly imitative of Carducci's work. The second stage of D'Annunzio's career was primarily devoted to novels, beginning with the publication of *Il piacere* in 1889. The novels of this period feature contemporary urban settings, openly autobiographical elements, and subjects commonly associated with Decadent literature, most prominently the hedonistic pursuit of pleasure in a culture that is slowly declining. Viewed by some critics as thinly veiled representations of D'Annunzio, the protagonists of these novels frequently consider themselves beyond ordinary social constraints and reflect D'Annunzio's interest in Friedrich Nietzsche's concept of the "Superman," an individual who does not recognize the validity of conventional moral codes and values.

The beginning of the third phase of D'Annunzio's literary career coincides approximately with his election to the Italian Parliament in 1897. The prominent works of this period are his dramas, which became notorious for their sensational qualities. Exemplifying this aspect of D'Annunzio's dramatic works is *La Pisanelle ou la mort parfumée*, which concludes with the main character being slowly smothered to death by a shower of rose petals. While D'Annunzio's dramas have been praised for their innovative use of classical mythology, they are more often criticized for their excessive displays of murder, incest, and mutilation, and are generally regarded as D'Annunzio's least successful works. In the final stage of his career, D'Annunzio edited his earlier works for inclusion in a collected edition published by the Italian government and devoted his energies to autobiographical writings in which he frequently blurred the distinction between biographical fact and fictional embellishment. The most famous of these works, *Notturno*, was written while D'Annunzio was recovering from a 1916 plane crash in which he lost his right eye, and records the sensations he experienced from his injuries as well as his memories of the war. It has been suggested by some critics that D'Annunzio's inclusion of autobiographical elements throughout his works represents his attempt to examine and interpret his life by creating an elaborate personal mythology.

(See also *Contemporary Authors,* Vol. 104.)

PRINCIPAL WORKS

Primo vere (poetry) 1879; also published as *Primo vere* [revised edition], 1880
In Memoriam (poetry) 1880
Canto novo (poetry) 1882; also published as *Canto novo* [revised edition], 1896
Terra vergine (short stories) 1882
Intermezzo di rime (poetry) 1883; also published as *Intermezzo* [revised edition], 1894
Il libro delle vergini (short stories) 1884
Isaotta Guttadàuro ed altre poesie (poetry) 1886; also published as *L'Isottèo—La Chimera (1885-1888)* [revised edition], 1890
San Pantaleone (short stories) 1886; also published as *Le novelle della Pescara* [revised and enlarged edition], 1902
[*Tales of My Native Town,* 1902]
Il piacere (novel) 1889
[*The Child of Pleasure,* 1898]
Elegie romane (poetry) 1892

Giovanni Episcopo (novel) 1892
[*Episcopo and Company,* 1896]
L'innocente (novel) 1892
[*The Intruder,* 1898]
Il trionfo della morte (novel) 1894
[*The Triumph of Death,* 1896]
Le vergini delle rocce (novel) 1896
[*The Maidens of the Rocks,* 1898]
Sogno d'un mattino di primavera (drama) 1897
[*The Dream of a Spring Morning* published in journal *Poet Lore,* 1902]
La città morta (drama) 1898
[*The Dead City,* 1902]
Odi navali (poetry) 1898
Poema paradisiaco (poetry) 1898
Sogno d'un tramonto d'autunno (drama) [first publication] 1898
[*The Dream of an Autumn Sunset* published in journal *Poet Lore,* 1904]
La Gioconda (drama) 1899
[*La Gioconda,* 1901]
La gloria (drama) 1899
Il fuoco (novel) 1900
[*The Flame of Life,* 1900]
Francesca da Rimini (drama) 1901
[*Francesca da Rimini,* 1902]
Maia (poetry) 1903
Alcione (poetry) 1904
[*Alcyone,* 1978]
Elletra (poetry) 1904
La figlia di Iorio (drama) 1904
[*The Daughter of Jorio,* 1907]
La fiaccola sotto il moggio (drama) 1905
Più che l'amore (drama) 1906
La nave (drama) 1908
Fedra (drama) 1909
Forse che sì forse che no (novel) 1910
Le martyre de Saint-Sébastien (drama) 1911
Contemplazione della morte (meditations) 1912
Merope (poetry) 1912
Le chèvrefeuille (drama) 1913
[*The Honeysuckle,* 1915]
La Leda senza cigno (prose) 1913
La Parisina (drama) 1913
La Pisanelle ou la mort parfumée (drama) 1913
Notturno (meditations) 1921
Cento e cento e cento e cento pagine del libro segreto di Gabriele D'Annunzio tentato di morire [as Angelo Cocles] (meditations) 1935
Solus ad solum (prose) 1939
Tutte le opere. 9 vols. (poetry, short stories, novels, dramas, meditations, and prose) 1939-50
La crociata degli innocenti (drama) 1948
Roma senza lupa: cronache mondane, 1884-1888 (journalism) 1948
Taccuini (notebooks) 1965
Altri taccuini (notebooks) 1976

---

*These four collections comprise the series *Laudi del cielo, del mare, della terra e degli eroi.*

G. B. Rose (essay date 1897)

[*In the following essay, Rose discusses D'Annunzio's early works.*]

In the days of Queen Elizabeth most Englishmen of cultivation spoke Italian, the plots of most of the plays were taken from the works of Italian authors; and only the perfect sanity of Shakspere and the sturdy morality of the English nature prevented the Renaissance from following in England the downward course that it pursued in Italy. But since that time the breach between the Italian and the Anglo-Saxon has been constantly widening, and now there are few who speak our language that have any idea of the intellectual activity prevailing in Italy to-day, or of the new literature arising there, in which the realism of the French is so happily blended with something of the idealism of Dante and Petrarch. Yet it may be doubted whether the contemporary literature of any country will better repay the attention, especially of an age that is weary of French cynicism and German pedantry. And foremost among living Italian authors, for good or for evil, stands the name of Gabriele d'Annunzio.

Baudelaire's poetry has been aptly compared to a Parisian gutter, amongst whose filth and stench blossom strange flowers of a rare and delicate grace. The works of the young Italian genius who has flashed upon the world in the last few years may be likened to a beautiful tropical morass, filled with luxuriant vegetation and gorgeous flowers, peopled by birds of brilliant plumage and snakes with glittering scales, but whose air, so full of flashing butterflies and golden scarabs, is heavy with subtle poison. He is the most brilliant figure that has arisen in the last years of the dying century, and if he is a promise of what the next is to bring forth the outlook is as ominous as it is fascinating.

His chief characteristics are brilliancy and corruption. In all the range of Italian literature there is perhaps no such brilliant prose. It flashes like gems in the sunlight; it reminds one of the glories of summer sunsets, of strains of delicious music. It is always of crystaline clearness, but it is full of subtle harmonies, of rich cadences that haunt the memory. In the Italian language d'Annunzio has an instrument of marvelous capacities, and he strikes it with the hand of a master, drawing from it strains that were never evoked before.

Perhaps no writer of equal talent is so corrupt. A distinguished French critic has said of him that he is a pagan of the days of Nero, and he might have added, worthy of the imperial court, a fit leader of the revels in the Golden House. But he has none of the brutality of Zola. D'Annunzio is an aristocrat to the finger-tips, and his is the elegant and polished corruption of the declining days of Greece and Rome. We feel that at the banquets of the Corinthian hetaerae or of Heliogabalus he would have been the guest of honor.

He reminds one of Theophile Gautier, of the worship of pagan beauty in Mlle. de Maupin and Fortunio and Arria Marcella; but his style is more brilliant, more varied, more passionate, more highly colored. And his scope is wider. With an appreciation of classic beauty that is equal to Gautier at his best, he combines an unsurpassed feeling for the strange graces, the undefined charm of the early Italian painters, those delicious primitives who are caviare to the vulgar, but who have so intense a fascination for the elect. If the characteristics of Guy de Maupassant and Pierre Loti could be combined with something of Ruskin, it would give a better idea of his work.

Even to those accustomed to the plainness of speech common among the Latin races the plainness of d'Annunzio's language, the frankness with which he depicts all the mysteries of passion, is amazing. Unless it be Pierre Louys' *Aphrodite,* I know of nothing intended for public circulation where the fig-leaf is stripped so remorselessly from Nature's shame. But he is never coarse. He remains always the exquisite Sybarite, the refined voluptuary, and instead of the cold, glittering style in which Louys depicts the corruption of ancient Alexandria, we have one whose rich coloring reminds us of the glories of Venetian painting, with an immodesty surpassing that of the voluptuous queen of the Adriatic.

By reason of his immodesty as well as because the graces of his style cannot be reproduced in another language, he can be understood and appreciated only in his own tongue. Imagination fails to depict the indignation of Mr. Comstock should one of these books fall into his hands. Some of d'Annunzio's novels have been translated into English, but the reader need not imagine that he gets in them the brilliant colors, the graceful forms or the subtle perfume of these poisonous flowers.

Born upon the Adriatic and brought up in the wilds of the Abbruzzi, he has a sense of the beauties of nature, of the charms of the mountains and the sea, of hill and vale and tinkling rivulet, rarely to be found in one so profoundly versed in the artificial life of great cities. His descriptions are gems, whether he describes the unfolding of a lily or the turbulent scenes of the religious pilgrimage in the *Triumph of Death*—a description which he seems to have penned to show how such a subject could be handled without the ponderous dullness of Zola's *Lourdes.* And where will one find a description of music so powerful as his portrayal in the same book of Wagner's *Tristan and Isolde,* that supreme cry of the passion-laden soul?

He began as all who seek a purely literary distinction should begin, with poetry; for of all means of mastering language the struggle with the perplexities of versification is the most efficient. Great poets are always masters of an exquisite prose, and many who, like Southey, have no poetic inspiration, have in this way gained a felicity of prose diction that has given them a permanent place in literature. And while the cadences of verse should be avoided in prose, in no other way does one acquire so sensitive an ear for the harmony of words.

He was but fifteen years of age when in 1879 he published his first volume of poems, and compelled the world to recognize that in this boy a new force had arisen in literature with which the future would have to reckon. Since then his production in verse has been as constant as in prose, though different in character, and has won for him a place second only to Carducci among the living poets of Italy.

But while his prose is of crystalline clearness, his verse is often hazy, with vague and indeterminate outlines. He has expressed the idea that verse should be distinguished chiefly for sound and rhythm, that like music it should be suggestive, and not pictorial. He is an accomplished English scholar, and a worshiper of Shelley, and in the richness of his diction and the occasional vagueness of his meaning he reminds one of Shelley's verse, while the sensuous and often immoral turn of his thoughts makes one think rather of Swinburne. And like Swinburne, though a wonderful tamer of sounds, so that he seems to have all the words in the language at his finger tips, his vocabulary is really not particularly extensive, and his effects are produced not by its profusion, but by the skill with which it is handled.

When we were boys we were continually admonished in the old rhetorics that of all virtues of style clearness was under every circumstance the first. But now all that is changed. An impressionist picture is not worthy of note if one can tell in less than half an hour whether it is a girl or a kangaroo that he is looking at, and among the most exasperating elements in our *fin de siècle* literature is its vague, misty impressionism. Though d'Annunzio's verse is always exquisite, the outlines of the pictures which it draws before the mind's eye are often dim, though sometimes as clear-cut as a carved gem. It is frequently only a cadence of sweet sounds, a suggestion of beautiful things, unrealized visions such as float before our eyes as we lie half awake listing to the songs of the birds greeting the morning sun, dreaming of passionate loves and bitter disenchantments. But he is never so great a sinner as Swinburne. He never requires a torrent of words to express an almost infinitesimal idea. The trouble is that he frequently is content to suggest only the vaguest outlines of his thought; but often, with the fewest and best chosen words, he draws a picture as firm and distinct as a steel engraving. A steady improvement is noticeable in his verse, and he may yet attain to a perfection as great as that of Leopardi or Carducci, though necessarily in a different way.

In prose he is *facile princeps*. That he had no superior among his fellows became apparent upon the publication when a very young man of his **Piacere (Pleasure)**. It is a sad book showing the bitter lees that ever lie at the bottom of pleasure's tempting cup—the record of the career of a brilliant young man of the Roman aristocracy, going from one facile amour to another until there comes that hardening of the heart which Burns recognizes as the worst effect of immorality, so that he can no longer feel even for the one woman who loves him with a true though guilty love, while he is devoured with an unavailing desire for the most corrupt siren that he has known. And the book leaves him so, hungering vainly for one who has passed on to other embraces, incapable of any genuine feeling, disillusioned, blasted, wrecked, an empty hulk drifting aimlessly upon the sea of life.

His next work, **Giovanni Episcopo,** is a study of crime worthy of Dostoyevski. It is the story of a poor, weak creature, the *âme damnée* of a strong, brutal bully named Wanzer, at whose command he marries a beautiful and abandoned woman; of his shame, his degradation, his weak compliance, of his love for his poor child which at last stirs him to revolt and to the murder of his tormentors. It is a horrible book, a loathsome night-mare, but powerful and fascinating to an unusual degree.

But of all studies in criminal psychology *L'innocente* is perhaps entitled to the highest rank. There is probably no story in which the tortures of a damned soul are depicted with such realistic force. To be forever faithless to a wife forever faithful is the dream of the libertine "Tullio Hermil." The time comes when, stirred by jealousy, his old love revives, but it is too late. The noble woman whom he has betrayed, neglected, outraged, though still loving him with all her heart, in a moment of despairing weakness has yielded to another. The suspicion, the doubt, the fearful certainty, the long agony, the birth of the child which is not his but which must bear his name and usurp his titles, the bitterness, the despair and the last awful crime, are told with an utter disregard of the decencies of life but with a realistic power that stands unrivaled. It is morbid, unwholesome, revolting, but unspeakably vivid.

In **Il trionfo della morte (The Triumph of Death)** he turns again to the lees that lie at the bottom of passion's cup, but this time it is the hate that grows up in the breast of man as the flame of passion flickers to its socket against the woman who has dragged him down, whose Delilah charms have robbed him of his strength, the tomb's allurement for the shattered nerves of the exhausted voluptuary.

The last of his books, **Le vergini delle rocce (The Virgins of the Rocks)** is perhaps the most perfect, certainly the most charming. In it alone there is nothing to offend the reader's modesty.

Faithful to the exiled Bourbon King, an old nobleman has retired to his castle standing before a strange volcanic rock in remotest Sicily. With him are his insane wife, who bedecks her horrible form in the finery of the court and has herself carried about in a sedan chair, his two sons slowly following their mother into the gulf of insanity, and his daughters, Massimilla, the Saint, Vialante, the Venus, and Anatolia, the Heroine. Here the hero, whose chilhood had been passed on his neighboring estates, weary of the pleasures of Rome, comes for rest and peace. Toward him, the one young man of their own rank who enlivens their solitude, the only one who can break their bonds and lead them forth to liberty, to love, to life, the hearts of all three are turned. Which shall he choose? Massimilla attracts him by her blind devotion, by her yearning for self-surrender and obedience, for absolute absorption into the being of the man she loves. Violante—Palma Vecchio's Violante—stirs his senses profoundly by her glorious pagan beauty, her infinite capacity for pagan joy. But at last he wisely chooses the noble Anatolia, born to be the mother of heroes, to bear her husband ever upward on the path to glory and honor. Upon a mountain top, amid fantastic rocks, he asks her for her hand. Before her she sees love, freedom, happiness, an opening for her noble ambitions; but she thinks of her aged father, her insane mother, her brothers hanging upon the brink of the abyss, of the crumbling house of which she is the support and stay, and with a breaking heart she tells him no, as Violante, aflame with jealousy, breaks in upon them.

Here the volume, which is to be but the first of a trio, comes to an end. The motto of the book and the headings of each chapter are from the works of Leonardo da Vinci, and it must be owned that there is about it something of the subtle charm of the *Madonna of Rocks,* of the unfathomable smile of the *Mona Lisa.*

When d'Annunzio first appeared it was predicted that his unexampled precocity would be followed by a premature decay; but so far, both in his prose and in his poetry, there has been a steady improvement. The harmony of his verse has continually gained in richness, while its meaning has become clearer as he has won a fuller mastery over the instrument that makes his music. His prose has gained in strength, in flexibility, in warmth and brilliancy of coloring. The morbid and unwholesome tinge still hangs over his work, but his last book offers the hope that with his youth this dross may pass away, and the pure gold of exquisite diction and subtle thought alone remain. Whether he is to be merely a baleful comet or a fixed star in the literary heavens cannot yet be determined; but if he continues his progress toward higher ideals and perfection of form his position must soon be established. (pp. 146-52)

> *G. B. Rose, "Gabriele D'Annunzio," in* The Sewanee Review, *Vol. V, No. 2, April, 1897, pp. 146-52.*

Arnold Bennett (essay date 1910)

[*Bennett was an Edwardian novelist who is credited with bringing traditions of European Naturalism to the English novel. His reputation rests almost exclusively on* The Old Wives' Tale *(1908) and the Clayhanger trilogy (1910-16), novels which are set in the manufacturing district of Bennett's native Staffordshire and which tell of the thwarted ambitions of those who endure a dull, provincial existence. In the following excerpt, Bennett praises the first part of* Forse che sì forse che no, *but finds the remainder virtually unreadable.*]

One of the moral advantages of not being a regular professional, labelled, literary critic is that when one has been unable to read a book to the end, one may admit the same cheerfully. It often happens to the professional critic not to be able to finish a book, but of course he must hide the weakness, for it is his business to get to the end of books whether they weary him or not. It is as much his living to finish reading a book as it is mine to finish writing a book. Twice lately I have got ignominiously "stuck" in novels, and in each case I particularly regretted the sad breakdown. Gabriele d'Annunzio's *Forse che sì forse che no* has been my undoing. I began it in the French version by Donatella Cross, and I began it with joy and hope. The translation, by the way, is very good. Whatever mountebank tricks d'Annunzio may play as a human being, he has undoubtedly written some very great works. He is an intensely original artist. You may sometimes think him silly, foppish, extravagant, or even caddish (as in *Il fuoco*), but you have to admit that the English notions of what constitutes extravagance or caddishness are by no means universally held. And anyhow you have to admit that there is a man who really holds an attitude towards life, who is steeped in the sense of style, and who has a superb

passion for beauty. Some of d'Annunzio's novels were a revelation, dazzling. And who that began even *Il fuoco* could resist it? How adult, how subtle, how (in the proper signification) refined, seems the sexuality of d'Annunzio after the timid, gawky, infantile, barbaric sexuality of our "island story"! People are not far wrong on the Continent when they say, as they do say, that English novelists cannot deal with an Englishwoman—or could not up till a few years ago. They never get into the same room with her. They peep like schoolboys through the crack of the door. D'Annunzio can deal with an Italian woman. He does so in the first part of *Forse che sì forse che no.* She is only one sort of woman, but she *is* one sort—and that's something! He has not done many things better than the long scene in the Mantuan palace. There is nothing to modern British taste positively immoral in this first part, but it is tremendously sexual. It contains a description of a kiss—just a kiss and nothing more—that is magnificent and overwhelming. You may say that you don't want a magnificent and overwhelming description of a kiss in your fiction. To that I reply that I do want it. Unfortunately d'Annunzio leaves the old palace and goes out on to the aviation ground, and, for me, gradually becomes unreadable. The agonies that I suffered night after night fighting against the wild tedium of d'Annunzio's airmanship, and determined that I would find out what he was after or perish, and in the end perishing—in sleep! To this hour I don't know for sure what he was driving at—what is the theme of the book! But if his theme is what I dimly guess it to be, then the less said about it the better in Britain. (pp. 235-37)

> *Arnold Bennett, "Unfinished Perusals," in his* Books and Persons: Being Comments on A Past Epoch, 1908-1911, *George H. Doran Company, 1917, pp. 235-38.*

Ashley Dukes (essay date 1911)

[*Dukes was an important English dramatist and drama critic during the first half of the twentieth century. He is most noted for his writings on modern European theater, particularly poetic drama. He had a broad knowledge of continental drama and, both as a translator and as the manager of his own theater, introduced English audiences to the work of several important French and German dramatists, including Ernst Toller, Georg Kaiser, and Lion Feuchtwanger. In the following essay, Dukes discusses* La Gioconda *and* The Dead City.]

Given imaginative power, what are the essential conditions of the theatre? Psychology suggested rather than described; descriptive colour arising spontaneously in speech rather than plastered on in elaborate stage directions; impressionism together with good draughtsmanship;—an ever-watchful austerity far removed from the exuberance of the author with a hundred thousand words to spend and a whole language to choose them from; in a word, symmetry extended from form to content; the rhythmic instinct of the lyric poet combined with the verbal economy of the aphorist and the concentration of the painter in miniature.

D'Annunzio is poet, novelist, and playwright together. He has his place in the European chain, not far removed from

Maeterlinck and Hofmannsthal. Recall for a moment the quality which distinguishes these two dramatists (together, perhaps, with Tchekhov) from all the other authors of their time. It is their revolt, conscious or unconscious, against the *bourgeois* theatre, that theatre which is concerned mainly with the social conditions of a period, filled with moral indignation and designed to replace convention by an ethical standard. The theatre, typically, of Björnson, Shaw, Brieux, Heijermans, Hauptmann and Galsworthy. Maeterlinck rehabilitated symbolism. Hofmannsthal, revisiting renaissant Italy, became the leader of the New Romanticists; and his reconstruction of Greek tragedy was in itself an artistic challenge. Tchekhov rebelled against the "morality for household use," and sought in *The Seagull* and *The Cherry Orchard* to remould modern drama by uniting dignity of conception with beauty of stage setting. All three were pioneers. With the gradual decay of modern realism their originality begins to be understood.

There remains the case of D'Annunzio, no pioneer, but a superbly gifted imitator. "Imitator" may be too harsh. He is a magnificent virtuoso, if no composer of symphonies; a great artificer of words, a collector of sensational curios, a conjurer who would pass for a magician, a mixer of glorious colours, a swaggerer in the grand style. Superlatives are his vocabulary. He flings them prodigally right and left, with the air of one who inherits the Latin culture of a thousand years and exults in the mastery of the sweetest language that the world has known. He has no "tendency," no hatred of convention save in speech. A connoisseur of impressions, he calls every art to his aid: sculpture in *Gioconda* and *The Dead City,* where a woman suffers mutilation to save a statue, and another is likened to "the Victory unlacing her scandals"; architecture in every pillared setting, in the ruined walls of Mycenæ or the glimpse of San Miniato from a balcony; tragic verse, where two women read aloud from Sophocles and weep together over the death of Antigone; music in the folk-song of Francesca's playmates; handicraft in the heaped treasures of Greece excavated by Leonardo, and described with the collector's love of old, strange words. (The chords of speech in this passage have the timbre of long-forgotten instruments). Painting, again, in every scene: in the drooping posture of Bianca Maria as she stands upon the loggia steps; in the crushed, bleeding hands of Silvia, like those of some mediæval martyr-saint; in the dead body of Bianca lying by the fountain. All of these are fruits of reminiscence. The achievement of the world is swept for D'Annunzio's writing-table. Then the weaving, the embroidery, the word-painting begin. Most skilfully the impressions are arranged. About the dead city whirls "a tempest of flaming dust." Visions are recalled in flashes. "All the desert of Argos, behind us, was a lake of flame. The mountains were tawny and savage, like lionesses." A "thirsty plain" encircles the ruins. The atmosphere vibrates with heat. Then, in the cool of evening, a change, A description of Bianca: "The quiver of a thousand wings was in her voice." "The quiver of a thousand wings." A great virtuoso.

There is the first impression of his work. I pause to extricate drama from this tropical profusion of speech. Little

can be found. For D'Annunzio, not content with the spoils that he has gathered from the arts, and discovering, naturally enough, that his own gift of word-painting serves only a decorative purpose, has met the demands of the theatre by further borrowing in a meaner quarter. He has propped his structure with two unsteady supports, the one a peculiarly gross form of theatrical sensation, the other a bastard symbolism. Take for example the case of the notorious *Gioconda.* A sculptor is dragged this way and that by two women struggling for possession of his soul. Silvia, his wife, is a gentle, saintly creature, who possesses him completely in his calmer moments; Gioconda, his model, is the familiar "panther-woman" of modern drama, sex incarnate, lithe, passionate, dangerous. (I speak of intention only. D'Annunzio says that Gioconda is so disposed. She herself says so. But she remains unconvincing because she is only a decorative talker with one trapeze act to perform. These are the traps which the theatre lays for the virtuoso.) Gioconda inspires the sculptor's statue; Silvia nurses him through a long illness. Thus far D'Annunzio offers nothing new in subject or treatment. Many authors before him have dramatised the conflict of saintly devotion and sensual charm. But he has the instinct for sensation—a sensation in superlatives, a monstrous catastrophe—and he arranges a scene between the two women in the studio before the clay symbol of their war. Gioconda the passionate, the revengeful, endeavours to throw the statue to the ground. Silvia rushes to save it, and a struggle takes place behind a curtain. Then a thud, a cry of horror. Gioconda emerges madly and escapes. Silvia comes forward with both her hands crushed into pulp, wrapped in wet cloths that are soaked through and through with blood. The statue has fallen upon them. She staggers, is supported, recovers herself. The inevitable phrase is spoken: "But—the statue is saved!" Curtain. A sensation for all Europe. D'Annunzio outdoes Pinero. What was Mrs. Ebbsmith's rescue of the Bible from the flames compared with this?

Needless to say, the scene forms the pinnacle of the third act. The fourth, in accordance with the same base tradition, is steeped in sentimentality. It appears that, for some reason unexplained, Gioconda has carried off the sculptor, Silvia is left alone. A new effect is arranged, the convalescent mother without hands embracing her infant child. A double symbolism of martyred love and a mutilated life.

The same symbolic device is used from time to time in *The Dead City,* a play of far greater beauty. The blindness of Anna, the "thirsty plain" of Argos, Bianca's hair entangled by chance in Alessandro's ring, the golden pair of scales that lay upon Cassandra's breast—all of these have their part in the tragedy. The atmosphere is more completely rendered. The historian may discover less of Sardou than in *Gioconda,* and more of Maeterlinck; but there is also something of D'Annunzio, something more than words. If all the borrowed plumes can be removed, and all the moods realised with sympathy, it will be found that he is indeed a problem dramatist, not of custom or morality, but of sex itself. He lives, not in the everyday world, but in the exceptional moment. He portrays conditions of high nervous tension without the creative skill to make them develop convincingly. In characterisation, as in drama, he leaps directly from the positive to the superlative without a thought of all that lies between. The *bourgeois* theatre is concerned with problems of conduct and moral conventions; D'Annunzio passes in a flash beyond them to the last analysis of motive. He is meteoric, productive of much dust and little drama. But there is grace in his flight. Even the word-painting is brought, in ecstatic moments, into harmony with the conception of the play. The windy stage directions of *Gioconda,* with their sunlight and clouds and rain, convey very little. They belong to the art of the novelist. One is conscious that they are easily imagined and lightly set down upon the printed page, but seldom realised in the theatre. Then comes an inspiration of genius. Flowers are brought. Some one says, "There is a bee in the room." In a pause, all present listen for its hum. The sandpaper bee in the wings of the stage is unnecessary. Silence is music enough. There *is* a bee in the room. There is more,—all the streaming warmth of spring and the scent of flowers. The bald statements of scenic decoration become real; an atmosphere is created. Such an atmosphere is exhaled by the Dead City and by the gardens of the *Francesca da Rimini.* The conjurer is sometimes a magician. He has the will to illusion. Let us be grateful. (pp. 264-72)

> Ashley Dukes, "Italy," in his Modern Dramatists, *Charles H. Sergel, 1911, pp. 264-72.*

Mario Praz   (essay date 1922)

[*A prominent Italian educator and critic, Praz was best known as an authority on the literature of the Baroque and Romantic periods. His pioneer study,* The Romantic Agony (1933), *explored the tradition of sadism in literature, art, and music. In the following excerpt, Praz applauds* Notturno *as the high point of D'Annunzio's career.*]

While Futurism gives its last flashes at the bottom of the single Province of Sicily, where it has arrived after prudent delay; while the Futurists of yesterday, who have gone over to the tradition, are no longer able to produce anything that stirs the public; and while such new æsthetic formulæ as neo-classicism bear fruit enough for academic discussions, but of original works of art nothing it is natural that public and critic set to and read again the works of the writers of some years back and see the injustice of the unfavourable judgments hitherto passed upon them.

We are waiting for something. We feel that the literature of to-morrow will be different. We strain our eyes seeking new stars on the horizon; but meanwhile we turn to the past. We are again reading Ada Negri, Grazia Deledda and Giovanni Verga, whose complete works Bemporad is publishing; while writers formed in the school of d'Annunzio return to the light, and are greeted with sympathy. Thus among books published last year I saw favourable reviews of a novel by Milly Dandolo called *Il figlio del mio dolore,* and a volume of verses called *Evalga,* by Matteo Darzi, books so deeply influenced by d'Annunzio that they would have been pilloried when Futurism raged only a few years ago. Thus our state of mind explains why d'Annunzio's recently published *Notturno* has caused such enthusiasm.

To understand this book, which many think marks a turning-point in d'Annunzio's art, one must know its history. On January 16th, 1916, d'Annunzio's hydroplane collided near Grado with a sandbank. He was struck violently and suffered a partial displacement of the retina of his right eyeball, with hemorrhage. During the long weeks of healing, confined to his bed, threatened with blindness and suffering insomnia without respite, he had within his damaged eye

> A smithy of dreams which the will could neither guide nor break off.

Peril of madness was ever hanging over his bandaged head. Perhaps the will to externalise its interior tumult was the brain's attempt to remain sane. Thus it was that he decided to write down what he felt. But how with bandaged eyes? At this point he remembered

> The way of the Sibyls, who used to write short sentences on the leaves which were scattered in the wind by Fate.

He took narrow strips of paper only wide enough for one line and thus wrote his *Commentary of the Shadows.* Line by line it grew; and the strips, of which at last there were ten thousand, were copied down partly by his daughter Renata and later by himself. The book, therefore, although only now published, largely precedes *Licenza,* which formed Volumes II and III of *Leda senza Cigno,* and was published in 1916.

The priority of *Notturno* must be kept in mind in order to avoid the mistake of some Italian critics who have by oversight expressed their belief that it gives the first and most perfect expression of a new method of d'Annunzio's—a method which, suggested here and there in *Forse che sì, forse che no,* accentuated in *Contemplazione della morte* and *Faville del maglio,* in *Leda* and *Licenza,* reached its full development, they think, exactly in *Notturno.* True enough that it marks in d'Annunzio art the highest point of his new method; but equally true that in *Licenza,* a work written, as I have said, for the most part later, the characteristics of d'Annunzio, his style and the quality of his thoughts and images, return to the command. Before speaking of a new tendency in his art, one must hold fast that *Notturno* is an exceptional book, conceived in a state of grace, conditioned by an especial and momentary sensibility. It was written at a time when the optic nerve

> Drew from every strata of my culture and previous life, and projected in my vision innumerable figures with a rapidity of digression unknown to my most ardent lyrical moments.

It is as exceptional as *Kubla Khan,* which is said to have been created in a dream.

Notturno is conceived in the form of fragments composing a lyrical diary (which epithet "lyrical" we apply to-day to prose work in which the connection of thoughts and the vivacity of digression are as free as in works written in verse). It is a succession of impressions, of memories, of fancies, broken here and there by episodes of very precise and solid outline. Baudelaire, Rimbaud, Moréas were the first to use this mode of expression, as the best one to note the finest shades of a keen and copious sensibility. But it has become so common among the latest writers that the reaction against the decadents and Futurists is to some extent a reaction against this very form.

D'Annunzio belongs, of course, to an earlier generation. His art was born under the shadow of Carducci's rough, often solid, sometimes pretentious but always strong architecture. A desire to construct, to organise has always dominated him. When no architecture underlay some poetical fancy he arranged his images in a borrowed plan forcibly; perhaps it was the architectural preconceptions which he absorbed in his artistic education that drove him to employ the novel or dramatic form, for these are pretexts for him, not his necessity. His art has reached its highest only when he has been able freely to treat of his own experiences. Whoever has read his novels and dramas (and these are more widely known abroad than his poetry) can call to mind his descriptions of scenery, passages, images and sumptuous chorography, but not a single man's character, or any chain of events. His long and dangerous eye-trouble offered him the opportunity to diarise his peculiar and marvellous sensibility, without the need to invent a plot, or construct a psychology or a philosophy, two things he is incapable of doing.

From what I have said, it will be understood that *Notturno* is a work almost richer in value than any other of its author's. Under the shadow of suffering, and before the face of death, his sensibility grew refined and enriched; sounds translated themselves into colours, scents into sounds, and Pain was sculptured in plastic images of hallucinating solidity; colours were produced in a clime not apparently conditioned by earthly laws. It is as if d'Annunzio had acquired, beyond his five ordinary senses, a sixth sense, having its root not in this or that organ, but in something richer and stranger; a sixth sense which long ago irradiated him in his *Ore Paniche* with the feeling of a perfect fusion with the surrounding universe, but needed the purifying intermediation of sorrow to free itself from some opacity that hindered it.

This greater wealth of sensibility, however, must not deceive one as to d'Annunzio's nature, and when he signs his book with the motto *Vide cor meum* ["See my heart"], if we recall the contents of the book, we become convinced that once more the motto would be expressed more exactly thus: *Vide sensus meos* ["See my feelings"]. Because, although in this book he speaks to us not only of his wonderful senses and the things about him, but the men about him also, and his companions who died heroically fighting, yet he speaks chiefly of their horrible wounds, and his pity for them is a mere shuddering of the flesh. The terror-striking aspects of physical suffering still hold his imagination as fascinated now as when long ago he wrote *Novelle della Pescara.* But though he cannot draw the characters of men, those of animals he does wonderfully well. Perhaps the finest pages of the book are those where he recalls to life his horses. (pp. 644-46)

Mario Praz, "A Letter from Italy," in The London Mercury, *Vol. V, No. 30, April, 1922, pp. 644-46.*

Frank W. Chandler   (essay date 1931)

[*In the following excerpt, Chandler surveys D'Annunzio's dramas.*]

Essentially a lyric and descriptive genius [D'Annunzio] was led only late to the theater, beginning just before the turn of the century with dialogues from the *New Testament.* Herein he praised all that the religious would condemn, emphasizing, for example, the wisdom of the foolish virgins. In two *Dreams of the Seasons—The Dream of a Spring Morning* and *The Dream of an Autumn Sunset*—he set forth in rich colors and by impassioned rhetoric sensational situations. In the first, a crazed wife, whose lover, stabbed by her husband, has died in her arms, imagines the scene as recurring and grows madder still. In the second, the doge's wife, having slain her lord by sorcery in order to wed a lover, finds the latter enamored of a courtesan, and destroys this rival by the same black art she had employed against her husband, the action being merely suggested as the dogaressa raves to her servants and thrusts pins into the waxen image of her victim.

In *The Dead City,* his first full-length drama, d'Annunzio created an atmosphere heavy with the fragrance of morbid passion and of tombs freshly opened. An archeologist, in love with his sister, and delving for the remains of Agamemnon, is infected by the crimes of the ancient house of Atreus and ultimately drowns his sister that she and he may be saved from incest. "Who would have done for her what I have done?" he asks. "I closed her eyelids upon her eyes . . . ah, softer than a flower upon a flower! . . . And every stain is gone out of my soul: I have become pure, quite pure." A second motive to the slaying is confessed by Leonardo. He has drowned his sister that his married friend who has also loved her guiltily may no longer be separated from him by jealousy. "O my brother in life and death, . . . forever reunited to me by this sacrifice that I have made. . . . She is perfect; now she is perfect. Now she can be adored like a divine being." The wife of the friend is a blind girl, supremely unselfish, so much desiring that the husband shall possess Leonardo's sister that she is ready to take her own life to facilitate an amour that will make him happy for the moment. She obviously is a companion character to Maeterlinck's Sélysette,—a quiet, understanding, inexpressive soul. But here the sense of impending doom is deepened.

The artistic credo of d'Annunzio is proclaimed in *Gioconda,* which protests against the common association of art and morality. A sculptor, married to a charming wife, finds inspiration for his work in a beautiful mistress. Distraught by his struggle between duty and desire, he has tried suicide. Nursed back to health by his patient wife, he vows reform, yet can no longer create, and is tempted to revisit his studio where his model has been awaiting him, having kept wet against his return the clay of his unfinished masterpiece. In the meantime, the wife hastens to the studio, lies to Gioconda in declaring that Lucio would turn her out, but when Gioconda, in rage, seeks to overset and destroy the statue, saves it at the cost of her lovely hands—those of Duse, who suggested and played the part. But the wife's sacrifice proves futile, for a final act shows the maimed Silvia deserted by her husband, rallied by a beggar-maid on the loss of her hands, and unable therefore to take the flowers brought by her unsuspecting child. When Silvia affirms the beauty of her love, Lucio replies that his destiny requires him to think only of a beauty of body to be arrested and preserved in marble. "I was born to make statues," he declares. "When a material form has left me with the imprint of beauty, the office assigned me by nature has been fulfilled." Such, too, is the faith of the devoted model, whose features, supposed to be divinely fair, are veiled and thus left to be imagined by the fond fancy of each spectator. Says Gioconda of Lucio's studio: "Household affections have no part here; domestic virtues have no sanctuary here. This is a place outside laws and beyond common rights."

A play which exalts political rather than artistic egotism followed, its scene Papal Rome, its strong and ruthless heroine jilting one lover for another since he promises her greater power. But *Gloria* failed upon the stage, and when printed was dedicated "To the dogs that hissed it." *Francesca da Rimini* was more fortunate. Here, in his first drama after the turn of the century, d'Annunzio richly embroiders the famous episode from the fifth canto of Dante's *Inferno,* using it as an excuse for displaying passion and flamboyant poetry. Francesca, trapped into a marriage of convenience with the lame and ugly Gianciotto, mistakes his handsome brother Paolo for her bridegroom and thereafter loves him absorbingly. She aids him in repelling a siege, and, when peace is won, reads with him the story of Launcelot which prompts them to yield to their desire. Spied upon by a jealous younger brother, one-eyed and malignant, Francesca so rebuffs him that he informs her husband, who thereupon surprises the guilty pair, slays them both—Francesca because she intercepts his thrust at Paolo—and breaks his bloody sword across his knee. This husband, on the whole, is humanized, but the informer Malatestino is a melodramatic villain upon whom falls all the odium, enabling the lovers and even the husband to retain the spectators' sympathy. Every feature of the play is wrought out in elaborate detail. Attention is focused upon what is pictorial and emotional, rather than what is ethical. No greater contrast could be conceived than that between this rococo piece and Maeterlinck's misty *Pelléas and Mélisande* or Stephen Phillips' chaste and delicately chiseled *Paolo and Francesca* or the robust and captivating *Francesca da Rimini* of George Boker.

Peasants of the Abruzzi observed by d'Annunzio at first hand are the characters of his powerful tragedy, *The Daughter of Jorio,* perhaps the best of his plays as drama. The superstitious point to Mila di Codra, child of a sorcerer, as being herself a sorceress. Escaping from field hands who have lusted for her in drink, she bursts into the hut of a shepherd about to wed with pagan ceremonies a girl he does not love. Though he starts to drive Mila forth, he succumbs to her spell at one glance, and protects her from her pursuers including his own father. Then, when he has taken her up into the hills, Aligi, to save her from his drunken father who follows, kills the latter in a struggle. As a parricide, Aligi must suffer death, first losing a hand, then being sewn up in a sack along with a wild mastiff, and finally being tossed into deep water. His mother, forgiving

his sin, offers him before his execution a draught of forgetfulness to dull his mind. He is already dazed when Mila, distracted, rushes in to declare that it was she who did the murder and then bewitched him into believing himself the slayer. Now, even Aligi, convinced of the truth of her words, curses her, as he sees her dragged forth to be burnt as a witch. Here is brisk action, and a dramaturgic tightening of tension leading to a series of stirring climaxes. The local color is laid on with accurate knowledge of peasant psychology and peasant customs and beliefs. But Mila and Aligi are romantic figures, notwithstanding, living together platonically in their mountain cavern, Mila planning to leave him lest his bride suffer from his defection, and Aligi, who has earlier protected her by laying at the door of his hut a waxen cross that instantly curbs the passion of her pursuers, now wielding upon his imperious father the ax he had been using to carve his vision of Mila's guardian angel. As always with d'Annunzio, the favorite themes are lust and revenge.

So, in *The Light under the Bushel,* another violent tragedy of the Abruzzi, appears a she-devil to be contrasted with the noble Mila. This is Angizia, daughter of a snake-charmer, who, having found employment in the castle of a decadent nobleman, has caused the death of her master's wife, and proceeds to marry him and poison his son and make love to his brother. The nobleman's daughter, blaming herself for not having saved her mother from the unspeakable Angizia, commits suicide after a novel fashion, plunging her arms into a bag of vipers, part of the stock-in-trade of Angizia's father. In the mean time, the nobleman, rendered frantic by all that his family has endured from the she-devil, slays her, to the delight of the audience.

More than Love, which failed upon the stage, perhaps because the public had come to expect only the sensational from d'Annunzio, was better in dialogue than in plot. It told the story of an explorer embittered to find his discoveries stolen by an impostor. Refused government aid in his desire to return to Africa, he murders a gambler whose ill-gotten gains he will use for a good purpose, like the hero of Dostoyevsky's *Crime and Punishment.* But, being threatened with prosecution, he takes his life, comforted in dying by a mistress who assures him that she is to bear him a child, one to be worthy of its father, this self-justified superman.

Passion is again to the fore in *Fedra* and *The Ship,* the former revamping Euripides, whose Phædra becomes for d'Annunzio a luxury-loving nymphomaniac. Having falsely accused her cold stepson of making advances to her when he has actually rebuffed her, she feels in his ensuing death a certain purification for herself, but is slain by a moon-ray sent by Diana, guardian of the chaste Hippolytus. *The Ship* is all spectacle, a thing of pagan fume and fury, showing the revenge of the imperious Basiliola upon the doge who has blinded and slain her father and her brothers. To accomplish her ends, she comes from the Byzantine camp to Venice, ensnares the doge, secures from him the torture of her enemies, charms them even while shooting them with arrows where they wallow in a trench, and then allures the bishop, the doge's brother, and sets the two to fighting. But when the doge has killed the bishop, he declares that Basiliola shall be nailed as figurehead to the prow of the ship in which he will embark upon a voyage of expiation. As the ship is launched, Basiliola, perceiving that her game is lost, immolates herself upon an altar to naval victory, the people hymning her defeat and that of Byzantium. The period represented is the sixth century, and the scenic panorama is more appropriate to opera than drama, the verse pulsing with fluctuant rhythms in splendid vowel harmonies. It was not long, indeed, before d'Annunzio wrote two librettos for opera, **Parisina,** for the music of Mascagni, and **La Piave,** at the end of the War, for the music of Italo Montemezzi. The former piece, like **Fedra,** tells the story of a woman's love for her stepson, and, like **Francesca da Rimini,** shows that love as mutual and inducing the murder of the lovers by the outraged husband. The Duchess of Ferrara, who has accompanied her stepson Ugo to the shrine at Loreto, nurses him when he is wounded in repulsing the Saracens, and dies with him when her lord wreaks revenge upon them both.

It was natural, too, that d'Annunzio, who had given increasing attention to spectacle, should have attempted the moving picture scenario, accepting the doctrine of Gordon Craig that the stage should emphasize what is plastic, and in **Cabiria** turning the Second Punic War into a splendid show. D'Annunzio has affirmed that he sees in the cinema a new art of enlarged possibilities, thanks to its being no longer bound by the limitations of time and place and also to its supplementing the appeal to the ear by a greatly increased range of appeal to the eye.

In the mean time, just before the War, d'Annunzio had demonstrated his linguistic virtuosity by writing in perfect French two plays for the actress Ida Rubinstein. Both were couched in free verse. **The Martyrdom of Saint Sebastian,** the first and better of the two, imitates an ancient mystery in the somewhat archaic forms of a foreign tongue, and was aided in production by the designs of Léon Bakst and the incidental music of Claude Debussy. Its subject is the conversion and death of the young Roman archer, friend of Augustus Cæsar, drawn as a superstitious fanatic, converted when the arrow he has shot heavenwards fails to return to earth. His progress is attended by miracles, lilies blossoming from the hot coals over which he walks unharmed. His religious fervor leads him in an ecstasy of passion to destroy the idols of his old faith and to enjoy to the full the thrill of martyrdom as he bids his archers administer to him the sweet balm of death. Here may be noted the influence upon the Italian of French and Belgian mystics.

The second French play of d'Annunzio was **The Pisan Woman,** or **Perfumed Death,** another drama of lust and revenge. Again a father proves the rival of his son for love of a beauty. When the son has been killed by the father, King of Cyprus, the beauty is put to death by order of the jealous queen, and dies a fragrant death, smothered beneath a mountain of roses. In each act, the king dreams of an ideal love, and beholds her now as a beggar girl, now as a slave, now as a courtesan in the guise of a nun, and at last as a dancer in his palace.

Less luxuriantly sensational was a third play in French,

the prose **Honeysuckle,** a revenge-tragedy, feverish with suppressed passion. A girl of nineteen, suspecting that her father has been murdered by his friend and physician, now married to her mother, probes the mystery and extorts from the physician a confession of his crime. He alleges that he was justified, since, in slaying his sick friend by an injection of morphia, he but obeyed that friend's sacred injunction. The avenging daughter, however, will accept no such excuse. She endeavors to incite her brother to punish the murderer, whom she also suspects of intriguing with the brother's wife; but, failing here, she nerves her mother to the deed. The physician, protesting that he was but a servant of fate, true to his friend, is stabbed by his wife. He dies after praying to the soul of his victim as one who alone can understand the purity of his motive and his sacrifice. But the girl triumphantly kisses her mother's bloody hand. Setting and atmosphere add to the sense of impending doom in this drama, which echoes *Electra* and *Hamlet,* as to plot, and the tales of Poe and the early plays of Maeterlinck, as to mood and manner.

Although here and elsewhere d'Annunzio's criticism of life is of no value, he is a poet of the first order, and a dramatist of the second or third. It must be conceded that his plays are lacking in variety, harping always upon the same themes, and using the same general incidents and characters over and over. With the single exception of **Gioconda,** they are dramas of emotion rather than ideas, and even **Gioconda,** stresses merely the notion that for the artist beauty is an end in itself divorced from morality. Indeed, beauty and feeling constitute d'Annunzio's world. His people are but facets of his own personality. They are abnormal folk dominated by passion, unable to reason, or to defer response to the imperious calls of sense long enough to indulge in wit or humor. They cannot know the genial warmth of friendship or of pity. They are never kind or gentle or devoted. For them the only duty is to follow instinct. Passion thwarted generates jealousy and hate; hence for them revenge is the complement of lust, cruelty of desire.

D'Annunzio is the artist pure and simple, thrilled by lovely forms, by the flow of melodious language, by the ecstasy of high moments. He would render all that is voluptuous in love, sickness, and death. So distinguished is the poetic quality of his work that it will endure in spite of its persistent morbidity. As a playwright d'Annunzio prefers either the static or the spectacular; indeed, his genius is epic and lyrical rather than dramatic. He looks backward rather than forward, disclosing nothing of the new Italy of efficient Fascism. Idolized by his countrymen, especially after the adventure of Fiume, he stands apart in a time of optimistic social coöperation as a reactionary aristocrat, a Byronic individualist, a pagan loving freedom because, like Byron, devoted to it in his personal life. (pp. 548-56)

> *Frank W. Chandler, "D'Annunzio and the Minors," in his* Modern Continental Playwrights, *Harper & Brothers, 1931, pp. 547-72.*

Benedetto Croce (essay date 1935)

[*An Italian educator, philosopher, and author, Croce de-*

*veloped a highly influential theory of literary creation
and a concomitant critical method. Croce's literary theories had a profound impact on the criticism of the first
half of the twentieth century, particularly in his emphasis on judging the totality of a work within a context created by its own existence as a separate, independent entity. In the following essay, originally published in 1935,
Croce offers an unfavorable assessment of D'Annunzio's
later works, faulting their "lack of humanity."*]

As "late" works of D'Annunzio may be classed those after
1904, that is after the composition of the volume entitled
Alcione and of **La figlia di Iorio,** the last to exhibit some
sort of originality. What followed were works which repeated or exaggerated the old themes, the old forms, the
old devices: literary exercises of a routine order, the writer
being by now incapable of anything else.

To the pre-war decade belong the tragedies **La fiaccola
sotto il moggio** (**The Light beneath the Bushel,** 1905), **Più
che l'amore** (**More than Love,** 1906), **La nave** (**The Ship,**
1908), **Fedra** (1909), **Parisina** (1913) with music by Mascagni, and in French **Le martyre de Saint Sébastien**
(1911), **La Pisanelle ou la mort parfumée** (1912), **Le
Chèvrefeuille** (1913: Italian version entitled **Il Ferro**); further, the novels **Forse che sì forse che no** (**Perhaps Yes,
Perhaps No,** 1910) and parts of the series **Leda senza
cigno** (**Leda without Swan,** 1913); also, in verse, **Le canzoni d'oltremare** (**Songs of Overseas,** 1911), and in prose
La vita di Cola di Rienzo together with **Proemio** (1905)
and **Contemplazione della morte** (1912).

It would serve no purpose to scrutinize these works for
their shortcomings and badness. Contemporary criticism
has dealt with them destructively, indeed they pass criticism on themselves, so naked is the artifice of their composition, needing no definition beyond the indication of the
works themselves. Wantonness, incest, sadism, ferocity,
cruelty, delinquency, and a toying with the memories of
ancient Greek tragedy and mediaeval mysteries are the
means used in a vain attempt to excite violent and troublous moods. But for all the magnificence of the stylistic
devices the end is not achieved. The magnificence, instead
of reinforcing such feelings, weakens them, by trifling with
them for mere literary effect. As usually happens with
D'Annunzio, feelings supposedly heroic are contaminated
with the aforesaid, as for example in **La nave, Più che
l'amore,** and even **Canzoni d'oltremare**; feelings supposedly of affection and kindness are submerged by the sensuality which steadily prevails and dictates to the author, forcing him to delineate not persons but bodies, and not even
idealized bodies but bodies heavily fleshy, radiating attraction for the senses but also that disgust and recoil which
flesh does sometimes excite. These works contain occasional "Beauties of D'Annunzio" but even these special
pages are but repetitions of exhausted forms brought
under the false light streaming from a central, all-
embracing falsity.

All this was well known and undisputed in the year 1914,
four years after D'Annunzio had left Italy to reside in
France, where in virtue of a sensuality investing his very
gift of language—it was with the ear of sense that he heard
words and so was impelled to take sensual possession and

to make sensual use of them—he proceeded to write tragedies and other so-called dramas in both modern and archaic French. Serra, in the fine, witty, and at the same time
truthful account, which he penned at that time, of the condition of Italian literature, unhesitatingly described
D'Annunzio as an exhausted writer now devoid of personality, having become "a sort of sample of a language, an
aesthetic attitude, a stylized mechanical heroism available
for all uses". The last works, according to Serra, had
shown up the artifice in all its nakedness, "dispelling almost instantaneously his halo of illusion and prestige".
And Serra, exemplifying his judgement, continued:

> He [D'Annunzio] has quietly pitched his tent in
> Babylon, and set up shop there, ready to execute
> all orders whatsoever: to produce literary arti-
> cles or if occasion demands nationalist rhymes
> for the *Corriere della sera,* to turn out librettos
> for Mascagni, ballets for the Russian corps, mys-
> teries and dramas or what-will-you, for Italy or
> for France, for the oratory, the theatre, the cine-
> ma, it being now all one to him and all exhibited
> quite indifferently: the clichés are known to all,
> the themes used up and exhausted in the utter
> monotony of these products for the market. We
> are being invited to a sale—the contents of every
> drawer in the shop are included.

Here are more of Serra's observations:

> Consider this style compounded of the mea-
> sured, spicy classicism of the French nationalists
> and of the huge, unrhythmically panting utter-
> ance of Claudel with adjuncts of old dactylic and
> tragic scansion; consider these verses of antique
> style and modern stress—they are the fruit, not
> of the efforts, but rather of the indifference of the
> mechanic for whom all metals, all materials are
> good enough for his press—he collects and fires
> whatever scraps he finds to hand, left over from
> his former work, the drawing-room mysticism
> and decadent Latin in his Saint Sebastian, the
> palaces and paintings of Ferrara in **Parisina,** the
> Levant of the Crusades and some mariners' lore
> in **Pisanella.** Remnants of **Forse che sì** reappear
> in **Il ferro.** Everything he uses, careless altogeth-
> er whence he takes it and from what pretended
> diversity of ideals; anything is good enough to
> serve for the usual clichés of lust flowering in
> blood, of innocent ecstasy exuding from lust, of
> heroism and incest, the invariable conclusion of
> these literary artifices.

And yet this exhausted artist, with no poetry left in him
(though still trying to work himself up and to excite others
by the provocative force of imagery), retained in his arm-
oury of rousing imaginations certain ones which were not
indeed qualitatively different from the others, but were of
a different material order: imaginations of war, which took
on the colour of nationalistic patriotism, accompanied by
much greed of adventure, destruction, rapine, bloodshed,
such as filled his dreams already along with the other cravings aforesaid. Having departed to France for purely private reasons, it had amused him to strike an attitude as an
"exile" from home, on a level with those great exiles who
on foreign soil had worked for the creation of the new
Italy. He was, it seemed, awaiting the advent of an Italy

worthy of himself, author of **La nave,** pioneer enthusiast for the virtues of aeronautics (had he not himself coined an Italian word "velivoli" for the new flying machines?). From French territory he delivered hymns of celebration and triumph on the outbreak of Italy's war for Libya, directing his tirades verbally against the Turks, but really and substantially against the Austrians. Then came the European war to provide him with the outlets and the scope for action which he longed for. He was selected as the orator to deliver that commemorative celebration of Garibaldi's exploit with the Thousand, which heralded Italy's entry into the war. And soon he passed from political action in favour of Italy's intervention, to military service and departure for the front.

Thus began a six years' period (1915-21) in which the man who had for a quarter century been one of Italy's most brilliant artists, and then for a further ten years an indefatigable literary craftsman, broke into Italian political history as a combatant, an inspirer of combatants, an inventor and executor of bold enterprises, the culmination being his occupation of Fiume against the decisions of the governments of both hemispheres—an occupation on behalf of Italy which he protracted against the decisions of the treaty-makers and the will of the Italian Government itself, which was compelled to drive him out by force. This is no place, in an essay of poetic and literary criticism, to recount or pass judgement upon these deeds. What properly belongs here is, however, a mention of the efficacity of his rhetoric in the cause of war, for this derived not solely from the example he gave personally, but also from his prestige and skill as a man of letters and stylist, greatly superior to others as an intoxicating speechmaker even when become incapable of poetry. Nor is this all, for his success was owed also to intelligence, shrewdness, and sense of the due moment. After the rout of Caporetto he addressed a gathering of officers of all arms as follows: "Ours not to ask what has happened: useless for us would be such knowledge. At first some would fain have lost consciousness in order to know nothing of that horror, worse than the darkness of desperation, worse than a despairing death." But then, striking a note of hope: "If shame there was, it will be washed away. If there was infamy, it will be avenged. The spirit is already at work upon the brute mass rousing it from its misery." How well he found accents to move the hearts of the seventeen-year-olds summoned in 1917 to drive back the invader: "Only yesterday you were children with a mother to smooth your hair, put the lamp on your desk, turn down the sheets. From that you have been called away by the summons which must be followed, and all at once you were breathing a new air, that of the heights. You were caught up: and now you can understand better than from any fable the meaning of transfiguration and rapture. This is the moment of understanding, the moment, above all others, of the spirit" [*La riscossa,* speeches published by the Government Press Office]. In these talks to soldiers and simple folk the artful phrasing that was elsewhere shallow became efficacious. We ought to include in his best rhetorical performances, as a rhetoric of action and gesture, his flight with eight aeroplanes over Vienna, not to spread fear and fury with bombs, but to drop "a tricolour greeting in the three colours of liberty" in the spirit of Italian humanity. The sig-

nal seemed to proclaim victory and an end to war, with a new era of peace among the peoples heralded by Italy.

Yet neither during nor after the war did D'Annunzio revive as a writer. He might write of warlike exploits and deaths in battle, he might mourn lost friends, but the sentences were never pure from physical and carnal obsession. In cruel and acrid terms they illuminated the hateful and material features—never the inner life of thought and feeling. A troublous riot of sensations and images generated the **Nocturne,** a book composed as he lay in the dark with shaded eyes to recover from an injury to the eye, and designed to give outer shape to the countless visual impressions passing before him "with a definiteness of form and pungency of detail which vastly heightened the pathetic intensity". The **Faville del maglio (Sparks from the Anvil)** of 1924-8 are mainly autobiographical. When he sought lyrical elevation he resorted—which was nothing new for him and reflected French models—to forms of divine prayer and Franciscan praise, filling out these with the usual multitudinous adumbrations of whatever objects his eye rested upon.

D'Annunzio's final phase, his last thirty years and more, that is to say, seems to me to offer little scope to the critic who is not content with reiterating the obvious. Any critical problem which remains to be solved is more likely to concern the value and significance of his best work, which may be said to start with **Canto novo** or even some pages

The Comandante Gabriele d'Annunzio.

of *Primo vere* and to end with such works as *Alcione* and *Figlia di Iorio.*

Criticism at the beginning of this century found its most urgent and indeed inescapable preliminary problem, in dealing with D'Annunzio, to be the sorting out of a confusion (due in part to careless and superficial reading, in part to the author's deliberate craft) between the genuine and the bogus parts of his work, between the D'Annunzio who was really expressing himself and that imaginary, counterfeit D'Annunzio who so readily assumed the masks of a poet of goodness or piety, expiation or high tragedy, superhumanism, heroism, or gospel-utterance. For it was this bogus D'Annunzio who more than the real D'Annunzio won belief and praise and the flattery of imitation. But once the required surgical operation had been successfully performed, its results were lasting, for never again did the critics ascribe value or significance to the pseudo-D'Annunzio, author of projects and programmes: when he continued along this false line they were prepared in advance and could not be deceived. The very outlet which D'Annunzio as projector and programmatist discovered in the realities of war so that he could actually give vent to those tendencies in a partly beneficial way, served but further to mark off the limits of D'Annunzio as a genuine artist.

These limits were by the writer of the present notes defined in 1903 as those of a "dilettante of sensation" (limits, it was added, within which D'Annunzio was strongly entrenched and insuperable). Certain critics have subsequently sought to modify this definition but I hold to it as the simplest and truest. The discernment of this character was not an invention of mine, it had already been mooted by various readers and critics. It is mine only in that I selected it from among others and gave it preference as the basis of interpretation of D'Annunzio's works. One of the most responsible and attentive of recent critics, Francesco Flora, author of a critical monograph on the poet and of an admirable critical commentary on D'Annunzio's *Laudi,* offers the alternative delineation of a D'Annunzio carried away by lascivious excess, by a "constitutional lasciviousness", impairing a great part of his work by perverting it into a rhetorical means towards concupiscence. In other parts, however, according to Flora, the poet rises superior to this into a serene, airy lyricism. I myself question this diagnosis of a fierce lustfulness: what I find in him is rather detachment and curiosity, pursuit and savouring of experiences, not that whirlwind which seizes upon the lustful as in Dante's *Inferno,* not the delirium, anguish, fixation, folly belonging to that state of mind and its expression: I do not find in him the signs of the erotomane. I am equally unconvinced about that wrestling match between lust and lyricism allegedly played out with varying fortunes in D'Annunzio's work, nor can I accept that picture of an inferior D'Annunzio employing rhetoric to the ends of lust. The only inferior D'Annunzio I recognize is the one who seeks to evade his own limits by feigning spiritual interests which can never be his: likewise a rhetorical D'Annunzio I know—the one whose appearance signals the moments of weariness, mannerism, decadence in the artist. Flora's psychological delineation seems to me better to fit Gustave Flaubert, who was the author of *Tentations*

and *Salammbô* on the one hand, and of *Madame Bovary* and *Éducation sentimentale* on the other. It does not fit D'Annunzio, who never emerges from the world of sense, but is at home there, cultivating and governing this realm of his, drawing from it all the delights he wants, including the delights of cruelty which seem to offer him a singular enjoyment.

It was, I think, a proper conclusion worthy of retention, to ascribe D'Annunzio's best art to this inspiration, and to discard all that work in which he vainly laid claim to a higher inspiration. Such was the conclusion reached thirty years ago. Perhaps it rather overvalued the best work of D'Annunzio, a natural consequence of the great effort put forth to segregate it from the inferior work which infected and sometimes smothered it. And then too little attention was given to the character and origin of the poetry: a natural fault, because things have to be done by stages, and this was a further problem properly to be tackled only when the preceding problem had come fully to the surface of consciousness.

The ulterior problem for the critic of D'Annunzio's poetry is this. By common agreement there is a lack of "humanity" even in the best of it. This seems quite undeniable. All his work attests it, and indeed much of what has been discerned and rejected as false is simply a failed attempt to achieve this "humanity" through the medium of the human tragedy of terror and pity. The failure underlines the fact of the lack and of the limit. This limit is most evident in certain pages in which the quality of the argument seems to promise an irresistible appeal to the heart: yet the author, who sees and describes the scene with amazing clarity and perfection, watches it impassively, with but a heightened curiosity of the senses. Take for example the episode in *Trionfo della morte* when the mother of the drowned boy, desperate and distraught with grief, hastens to the scene and raises her lament:

> In the shadow of the rocks, over against the white sheet shaped to the stiff form of the corpse, the mother uttered her plaint in the form hallowed by all the past and present grief of her race. It seemed that the lament would never end.

In *La figlia di Iorio,* a pretty little piece unjustly handled by many critics, the sensual and sanguinary background seems to be relieved by goodness, purity, and the generous, expiatory sacrifice. But these are introduced in fairy tale style, which, if it excludes the falsity of tone of some other similar attempts by D'Annunzio, leaves them without solidity: if anything in the play is solid it is that background which impresses itself so strongly as to involve the whole work in the climax of the voluptuous death in the consuming flame. A perfectly clear tone, a response to sheer and simple feeling, is perhaps to be found only in some early compositions from the time before he had, simultaneously, perfected his technique and exhausted his vein. Flora, who rightly observes that D'Annunzio wholly lacks the sense of sin while correlatively his art is devoid of "cordiality", "domestic intimacy", "friendliness", has not hesitated to translate "non-humanity" into the positive term of animality or bestiality. "If a beast or a tree were to express itself, it would be in the D'Annunzian manner. Humanity in this art is nature: the colours, odours, tastes, sounds of things as they are humanly digested, and not the thoughts and feelings which a man forms, are here transcribed into a symbolic music. If Man is God coming to consciousness in us, then D'Annunzio is nature coming to consciousness—a beast, one might say, conscious of nature." For that matter all can see the consistency of D'Annunzio's culture, one in which all the *humaniora,* History, Philosophy, Religion, even the higher Poetry, are missing.

Now if in all solemnity we proclaim this absence of humanity and presence of bestiality in D'Annunzio (in justice to those very humane beasts the dogs and those highly spiritual beings the birds we must observe that the use of the words is metaphorical), we must perforce deny him any intimately poetical quality, for what else is poetry but humanity? Can "nature", can a beast, acquire consciousness without becoming aware of a limit, thereby passing beyond this into humanity? It avails nothing to hail D'Annunzio as a great poet "lacking inwardness" or as a great "lyrical landscapist" (according to the view of Gargiulo . . .). Inwardness and humanity are necessary to the painter and the landscapist, for it is the soul, not the eye, which paints. Flora noticed this difficulty and the need there was to resolve it and to reconcile the denial to D'Annunzio of needful qualities with the affirmation of value in his best work. So he proclaimed that humanity, totality, cosmic feeling could after all be ascribed to D'Annunzio, but not in the elect form displayed by other poets: rather, in a form special to himself, in which the distinction of spirit and nature fades, the spirit becomes concrete in nature, whereby the poet achieves, like other poets, a conjunction and harmony with the All. He adds that in the charge of want of humanity levelled against him there lurks "the shadow of the old transcendent, the shadow of the old Creator, the problem of the sense of eternity outside physical time" and other irrelevancies.

There is no complaint to be made against this judgement as regards its critical method, nor would there be as regards its content, were not the "humanity" which is found to be lacking in D'Annunzio one and the same thing as the harmony with the All, with the life of the Cosmos, lack of which is lack of the life of the Spirit. There are other poets who are strongly, almost wholly, absorbed in the senses, in mere vitality, in pleasure and pain, yet they redeem themselves in poetry through sheer suffering and its expression, whereby the animal is resolved into the man, the natural is spiritualized, or, to use my own philosophical terms, the lower stage of the spirit is dialectically surpassed in the higher stages. With D'Annunzio this never happens. Never, touching one string, does he awaken the whole human harmony to life. Frequently he wins our admiration for his artistic skill, but he never transports us by rising above himself and so raising us above ourselves.

That characterization of him as the "dilettante" here again proves useful, though some would have us discard it. For the dilettante of vital sensation would quite evidently be incapable of surrendering to that rapture of the universal which is the mystery of poetry. He could not shuffle off the interested hedonistic attitude which would check his self-surrender to the full contemplation of the mystery

of life. This accounts for the character of D'Annunzio's composition, from which there is never absent a certain self-satisfaction: the artist is aware, and makes the reader aware, of his skill and flourish, and the words he uses are continually reminding us of the fact of language and dictionary. The Odes of the book *Alcione,* his best artistic achievement, are admirable but never altogether convincing or spiritually satisfying. How should we not admire *Versilia* in its celebration of fresh fruit and foliage, young flesh and blood, through the songful medium of a woman's prayers and promises and invitations and yieldings? But even this poem is (though but lightly) shackled to the tyranny of dilettantism. How should one not greatly admire the ode on the death of a stag, *La morte del cervo,* unsurpassed and almost unrivalled in its marvellous conversion of lines, colours, odours, motions, sounds, savours, into well-shapen phrase and syllable, rhythm and metre? Yet this composition does not only display but also at the same time explicitly declares the skill of the craftsman who has moulded "in Corinthian bronze"—that is in the wealth of the Italian vocabulary possessed by him—"what his bright eyes saw". With the Centaur, man and beast, the poet's "soul surcharged with drafts of antique power" does indeed throb. But this is an exercise of rare and frantic pleasure rather than a true rapture finding its culmination and release in the joy of song.

And so, for all its luxuriant appearance, the world of D'Annunzio conveys a sense of poverty, the poverty of a Midas, if you will, condemned to convert into the gold of sensation whatever he touches. Hence what is called the "monotony" of his art. Now poetry is never really monotonous, even when a poet remains for ever within his own range of feeling or his own hierarchy of feeling, presenting it variously. But with D'Annunzio we have the repetition of the same proceeding, the same game, the same elaborate or indeed subtle tricks, with little poetic charm. The critics have accordingly attempted to rehabilitate this poetry by attributing to it recondite meanings and elaborate reasonings. In this connexion I would recommend that the *cliché,* originated, I think, by Borgese, but used by pretty well all critics, that D'Annunzio created "new myths", should be discarded. "Myths" are not objects of artistic creation, but formations thrown up in the course of men's intellectual experience: concepts still clouded or infected by imagery, signs not of the power but of the "poverty" of the human mind in its immaturity, as the first great thinker to formulate a theory of them pronounced. D'Annunzio's myths are not concepts or even would-be concepts: they are mere representations of the desire and life of the senses, or at most what old-fashioned rhetoric used to call "personifications".

As soon as D'Annunzio's art began to receive wide attention, its similarity to that of the Italian decadence, the Baroque school, the school of Marino, was observed: a many-sided and far from superficial likeness which I will not here illustrate, having done so [in *Saggi sulla letteratura italiana del seicento.* In *Storia dellvetà barocca in Italia*] I have also remarked upon the monotony, the propensity towards mere game-playing and the resort to extraneous artifice in the seventeenth-century artistic appeal to the senses. Not only should D'Annunzio be denied any comparison with the great, severe, austere poets, but he should not be compared either with those, like Tasso, and Foscolo in his *Grazie,* in whom there is a hot vein of sensuality and eroticism. For these poets lift themselves to the level of the heroic and religious drama of mankind whence D'Annunzio remains absent. A comparison with them could only emphasize his essential poetic aridity. He will remain a notable symbol of decadent art—common opinion (*vox populi vox Dei*) has already pronounced this judgement. (pp. 961-72)

> *Benedetto Croce, "Late D'Annunzio," in his* Philosophy, Poetry, History: An Anthology of Essays, *translated by Cecil Sprigge, Oxford University Press, London, 1966, pp. 961-72.*

D. A. Traversi   (essay date 1941)

[*In the following essay, Traversi examines the moral framework of D'Annunzio's writings, drawing parallels between the development of D'Annunzio's nationalistic philosophy and the roots of Italian fascism.*]

D'Annunzio is, in a peculiar sense, the adopted poet of Italian Fascism. This does not mean that he is widely read in modern Italy. Fascismo does not encourage reading, either in quantity or in quality, and the taste of those Italians who still read seriously tends to have been formed on other and more modern lines. But the "philosophy" of the movement, and the ritual by which it has sought to appeal to the imagination, both owe a great deal to a man who was in the details of his own life an embodiment of the dramatic principle. Himself an extensive borrower from many sources, D'Annunzio has lent much to a leader whose tastes are as eclectic as his own. When Mussolini affirmed that the destinies of Italy were fatally bound up with her fortunes on what he called *Mare Nostrum* ["Our Sea"], he gave political substance to a dream to which the poet had already given public expression; and when party gatherings are brought to a close with the invocation of the Duce and the legionary response of *"A Noi!"* ["To Us!"] his supporters are following in word and gesture the example set by D'Annunzio's picturesque and incongruous band at Fiume. But the Fascisti would be the first to assert that the influence of the poet lies in something deeper. They would call theirs, in the first place, a spiritual debt, and they would say that the importance of D'Annunzio lies not in this or that gesture or affirmation, but rather in the example of a life "heroically" lived, a life in which thought and action, fused in a common unity, were consecrated to the service of *La Patria.* It is by virtue of this conception of the poet as "hero", as highly conscious artificer of the pattern of his own life, that D'Annunzio has exercised in modern Italy a peculiar moral influence. This moral content—which bears witness, in its very weakness, to the inadequacy of attempts to define political behaviour solely in the light of economic motive—is worth defining, worth relating to its roots in the intellectual and spiritual conditions of Italian life; for it throws light upon aspects of Fascismo which are not generally understood, but which explain much in the present and need to be borne in mind in estimating the possibilities of the future.

English writers have attempted to define this "heroic" quality in D'Annunzio's work by referring to him as an "Elizabethan" born out of due time. It is a dangerous and, on the whole, a misleading parallel. D'Annunzio's vitality has about it a feverish quality, an unmistakable self-consciousness which no Elizabethan could have understood and which denotes something less than spiritual health. As much as any European writer he reflects in the variety and incoherence of his attempts to organize his experience the instability and vacillation of his own times; and his special interest lies in the fact that his reflection of them is distinctively Italian. The decisive features in his spiritual make-up are peculiar to the peninsula. In the first place, by virtue of his origin at Pescara in the Abruzzi—then, as now, one of the most backward provinces of Italy—D'Annunzio was a provincial. Secondly, provincial as he was, he was plunged into a world of wider interests, national and cosmopolitan, for which his birth and temperament had imperfectly prepared him; and here again he is typically, unmistakably Italian. Thirdly, he possessed an unusually acute sense of the continuity of Italian literary culture, a sense which his innate provincialism, his assumed nationalism, and the veneer of European speculation which he had rather haphazardly acquired were all unable to satisfy. Poised between these elements, which remained throughout his life distinct and conflicting, it was D'Annunzio's peculiar fate to sum up in his own nature the knot of spiritual incompatibilities from which Fascismo was eventually to spring. His very egoism reflects uneasiness. The self-emphasis which was always so marked in his work proceeds as much from isolation as from personal confidence. He leaned heavily upon himself because he had nothing else to lean on; and his final definition of his own nature might have been that which, in 1889, he put into the mouth of the hero of his first important novel [*Il piacere*]: "I am like the chameleon (*camaleontico*), chimerical, incoherent, inconsistent. Every effort of mine towards unity will always be vain. I must resign myself to this. The law of my nature is written in one word: NOW."

First of all, then, D'Annunzio was a provincial. Provincialism implies in Italy, where regional bonds are notoriously tenacious, a great deal more than the mild, intellectual and moral lethargy which Matthew Arnold used to regard as its main English characteristic. It implies a definite and deeply rooted allegiance independent of and sometimes cutting across the claims of national unity. Its effect upon the latter may be symbolized in those chains of high mountains which, throughout the long peninsula, run across from the Appenines to the sea, obstructing the main lines of communication and dividing Italy into so many separate and highly localized communities. There are signs that this provincial allegiance was in D'Annunzio very strong: so strong, indeed, that it inspired in the poetic drama of *La figlia di Iorio* some of his best writing. This tragedy of peasant life in the Abruzzi, pitilessly barbaric and sensual in its conception, shows remarkable feeling for the language and customs of the local peasantry. Its verse, simple, intensely dramatic and full of Abruzzese words and idioms, indicates what might under other circumstances have been the main inspiration of his career. As it was, however, *La figlia di Iorio* was no more than an incident in D'Annunzio's literary development.

The possibilities of Italian regionalism as a living force were, at the end of the last century, almost exhausted. A writer like Giovanni Verga, who still represented it with remarkable vitality, did so by turning his back deliberately upon the problems of his day. The characters of *I Malavoglia,* his great novel of life on the Sicilian coast, are so remote from the centre of things that the words "King" and "government" mean nothing definite to them. The special conditions of Sicily allowed Verga to do this with conviction, but for D'Annunzio to have settled down as an Abruzzese *novelliere* would have been to isolate himself in a world of fictitious simplicities. His was the position of the born provincial in a society where local allegiances, set against a new background of national and cosmopolitan interests, were no longer sufficient; and the novels which first brought him literary fame are largely an effort to overcome inherited provincial limitations and find his balance in a highly complex and largely decadent society. The adventures into which this effort brought him are, from the point of view of the slow and difficult formation of a united Italian consciousness, highly representative.

The effect upon D'Annunzio of his entry into sophisticated society can be deduced from his first important novel, *Il piacere,* which he published in 1889. It describes, through the character of the poet Andrea Sperelli, the immersion of the young provincial into aristocratic Roman life at the end of the last century. The matter is not put just like that. The element of naïve snobbery which was an essential feature of D'Annunzio's peculiar kind of provincialism would never have allowed him to present his hero in a position of social inferiority. Andrea Sperelli must be not only an aristocrat but also—and this is the vital point—an aristocrat distinguished by the highest qualities of detachment and intelligence. He was, we are told, the only heir to a long family tradition. His character, standing out against "the grey democratic deluge of our times"—this is the kind of opulent gesture that D'Annunzio loved—was that of "the ideal type of the young Italian Signore of the nineteenth century, the legitimate champion of a line of gentlemen and elegant artists, the last descendant of an intellectual race". Beneath the façade of pedigree, however, Sperelli's attitude is that of the *parvenu*. His eyes stray round the luxurious villas and Seicento palaces in open-eyed astonishment. He lingers over the trappings of a conventional aristocracy—the rare books, the sumptuous pictures, the period furniture—delighted and a little surprised to find that his taste in these things is so much like that of a real nobleman. Sperelli is never quite at home in Roman society. Born provincial that he is, whatever his lineage, he cannot simply accept the world he has entered, move in it spontaneously as an integral part; he must either dominate it by his excellence, or despise it. Like D'Annunzio himself he contrives, according to the impulse of the moment, to do both.

It is this ambiguous position of the hero that gives the novel its peculiar character. When Sperelli is in the mood of domination, his indefinable sense of social insecurity prompts him to build up, down to the last detail, an enthralling picture of his innate superiority and *signorilità* ["refinement"]. Nothing in these recurring scenes of triumph comes naturally. Every pose and every reaction is carefully studied, every possession carefully placed to produce the greatest effect. Our first meeting with Sperelli in his house near the Spanish Steps is typical. The sentences which introduce him read in themselves like a stage-direction: "Andrea Sperelli was waiting in his rooms for a lover. Everything around him revealed a special attention to love." The majolicas of Castel Durante, the heavy masses of roses, "like those which rise behind the Virgin in Botticelli's tondo in the Borghese Gallery"—the studied artistic reference is very typical—are so much scenery before which Sperelli is to act the highly self-conscious drama of his own superiority in passion. Even the famous immorality which so shocked many readers of this book when it first appeared is full of this naïve, theatrical element. It is, in the last analysis, yet another means whereby D'Annunzio asserts his superiority. If he is going to live the aristocratic life—so the argument might run—he will be extraordinary, domineering, irresistible even in his vices. The "ladies" of Roman society—about whose gentility he shows himself in *Il piacere* more than a little sceptical—shall be at his beck and call. The attitude is, all things considered, rather commonplace. There are pages, in this and other novels, where D'Annunzio tries to linger analytically over some of the refinements of romantic perversion, after the manner of French originals. They are not, even in their own kind, very convincing. The sadistic hobbies of Lord Heathfield described in detail at the end of *Il piacere* shocked D'Annunzio almost as much as they fascinated him; and the moral irregularities in which his heroes delight retain, beneath the veneer of analysis and elaboration, their essential character as manifestations of simple and even rather provincial sensuality. As such, they are mostly repetitive and dull.

But the provincialism which keeps Sperelli from entering fully into the world of aristocratic glitter, expresses itself quite as typically in shrewd criticism. Being essentially outside the world to which he has obtained a social entry, he is able to observe its failings with detachment and even a touch of cynicism. His picture of the spiritual vacancy of these Roman *salons* can be surprisingly precise, drawn clearly down to the realistic detail. Don Filippo del Monte, as Sperelli talks to him at a fashionable auction in the Via Sistina, is presented with malevolent objectivity. He is "a man of about forty, almost completely bald, a subtle weaver of epigrams", who bears on his face "a kind of Socratic mask in which the right eye shone with extreme mobility in a thousand different expressions whilst the left remained always immobile and almost glazed under its round lens, as though one served for expression and the other for seeing". The provincial D'Annunzio cannot refrain from this kind of comment on the world he is so anxious to enter; it inserts itself persistently into his descriptions of Roman society, adding an odd note of detachment to the aristocratic ecstasies.

More important still, D'Annunzio cannot help criticizing the character and the values of his own hero. He is not satisfied with the conquests of Sperelli. On the surface, *Il piacere* describes the gratification in endless triumphs of one man's physical desires and social ambitions; but behind his hero, with his repetitive sentiments, his bad taste and his monotonous immoralities, there is a genuine if unwilling boredom, an *ennui* which is the most sincere thing about him. This awareness of futility leads to a quantity of self-analysis, most of it pretty inconclusive. In D'Annunzio's efforts first to define and then to overcome it there is a good deal of patent insincerity, refinements and distinctions that clearly correspond to no reality; but this insincerity is as much his problem as his deficiency. Aware that much in the posturings of his heroes was without meaning, D'Annunzio tried to impart significance to their discontents by assimilating them to the spiritual self-dissections which foreign, and especially Russian, fiction had brought into vogue. No doubt there was a large element of opportunism and literary snobbery in this adherence to fashion; but there was a foundation of sincerity too. Sperelli is continually defining himself as a modern, as a man in whom excessive sensibility and analytic insight have destroyed the possibility of moral coherence and integrity. Not everything in this account, abstract and mannered though so much of it is, is false. "From the beginning," we are told, "he was prodigal of himself: since the great sensitive force with which he was endowed was never tired of furnishing treasures to his prodigality. But the expansion of this strength implied the destruction in him of another force, of the moral force which his own father had not been backward in debasing. And he did not perceive that his life was the progressive reduction of his faculties, of his hopes, of his pleasure; and that the circle was continually drawing in upon him, inexorably if with extreme slowness." So far at least the picture does substantially correspond to reality. The problem that presented itself to D'Annunzio, made more acute by his position in a society that attracted him but left him profoundly uneasy, was essentially *moral.* It concerned the organization of his fragmentary experience, the discovery of a force capable of bringing together his great sensitive gifts and ordering them in relation to an end that was necessarily outside and beyond them. In the field covered by *Il piacere* there lay only repetition and a growing sense of confinement to a meaningless circle of activity, from which he could only be released by contact with a wider range of society and by accepting a more human set of moral values. Nothing in the Italian life of the nineties seemed to offer these things.

At this point we touch upon the second distinctive element in D'Annunzio's make-up. His provincialism, which had made him a stranger—albeit a brilliant one—in the aristocratic and cultured world, helps to account for a curious naïvety in his attempts to assimilate the various spiritual attitudes which that world presented to him. He reproduces them with fluency, even with skill, but the central core of conviction is lacking. *L'innocente,* written two years after *Il piacere* and conceived in a similar spirit, is the novel in which the effort to lend moral and intellectual significance is most consistently made. It fails. The ethical problem which D'Annunzio would have us accept as the central issue of the book has no imaginative reality, no power to compel assent. Being unreal, indeed, it simply perverts his genuine inspiration, which was fundamentally sensual and unreflective, turning it into forms which are morally equivocal. It is in this perversion that the poet's real immorality lies. The imagination of the artist, set against an abstract framework of borrowed morality, is re-

pelled by it, struggles against it, seeks to dispose of it; and in so doing it exposes itself to the charge—which would have been irrelevant to a direct transcription of experience—of a definite immorality. There was nothing in D'Annunzio's make-up, essentially direct and positive, which corresponded to the introspective complexity of his models. The moral sanctions he needed, and which his environment did not offer him, were essentially straightforward and unambiguous. In the absence of such sanctions he was deflected from his natural sphere to speculations for which he was not adequately equipped; and the result is seen in these unsatisfactory, because ultimately insincere, novels. Unable to dedicate himself with conviction to the *now,* to the direct vision which was his positive gift, he was forced into subtleties with which he was unable to identify himself. His failure in *L'innocente* illustrates perfectly the moral weakness which he shared with a great part of contemporary Italian Society.

The kind of moral content which D'Annunzio intended to give his novel is apparent in the plot of *L'innocente.* It is, in essence, familiar. *L'innocente* is the story of yet another artist, Tullio Hermil, whose egoistic pursuit of personal triumphs has led him to betray his wife Giuliana. Moved by her illness, and by a deepening sense of futility which covers his whole life, he now desires to return to her. The resolution is taken too late. Giuliana, though still in love with her husband, has given herself during the long interval of his infidelity to a rival, and a new-born son who is not Hermil's stands between them at the very moment when both desire sincerely to return to the sanctified simplicities of married life. To end this intolerable situation, Hermil—acting, as he insists, in full awareness—determines to remove the obstacle to their happiness; and he causes the new-born child, the *Innocent* of the title, to die. Most of this story is clearly an elaborate fiction, a compromise between the moral and the sensational which reflects its author's instability. Ideas are systematically borrowed from other writers, taken up and brought to no definite conclusion. The notion of a murder premeditated and carried out in perfect "lucidity of conscience" recalls *Crime and Punishment.* So does the manner in which Hermil's opening statement raises the question of responsibility: "Human justice does not concern me. No earthly tribunal could judge my case. And yet I must accuse myself, confess. I must reveal my secret to someone. To whom?" But the resemblance to Dostoievsky is simply verbal. The spiritual drama of egoism and its clash with the moral law, the distinction between human justice and a superior conception is, for D'Annunzio, no more than an abstraction; just as the morality which he seeks to oppose to the conduct of his hero is simply a pale reflection of other Russian models. Hermil's brother, Federico, and his friend the simple peasant Giovanni di Scordio, whose integrity is meant to be contrasted with the chaotic futility of the poet, use the phrases of Tolstoy without convincing us that D'Annunzio is really interested in their content. Tullio, in one of his "spiritual" moments, asks the peasant to act as godfather to his new-born child. Finding him at work on his fields, they exchange what might be called a sacramental handshake—"We clasped those unwearied hands, sanctified by the seed which they were scattering, and by the good they had scattered"—and Giovanni, accepting the invitation, replies with words that belong palpably not to D'Annunzio but to his Russian model: "May God grant that my godson be as good as the bread which is born from this seed. So be it." It is not difficult to see the falsity beneath all this. The "spirituality" of *L'innocente* is a matter of phrases, not of feeling, and the problem we are asked to consider is as artificial as its solution.

The most vivid scenes in the book are, significantly enough, the least "moral". They are those in which D'Annunzio's sensual inspiration, denied direct expression, fulfils itself in the undermining of the artificial structure of morality. This, in effect, is what happens when Hermil takes Giuliana back to Villalilla, where they had once loved for the first time. Conceived as a scene of reconciliation and repentance, it ends on a note of sensual domination, almost of seduction. It is only fair to add, however, that this immorality is a consequence of the insincerity of the moral purpose which the novelist had imposed upon himself. Since he does not *feel* the reality of Hermil's penitence and confession of guilt, it is natural that he should instinctively seek to destroy their validity. The situation is developed with sufficient subtlety. The morning is hot with a "precocious" heat, the garden is "solitary" and the house "secret", the fruit-trees are "delicious", the roses "insinuate themselves" between the branches. Everything combines to create a mood which is certainly not of penitence, and which cannot—once the artificial moral purpose has been introduced—be simply and self-sufficiently conceived. A certain corruption, therefore, inevitably makes itself felt. The poet's first words, if a little strained and presumptuous, are indeed to the moral purpose: "The best part of me had always been yours, and a hope has always remained kindled there: the hope of freeing myself from evil and of finding again my first and only love intact." So far, so good; but it is not long before the poet's real inspiration, encouraged by his surroundings, begins to make itself felt. The egoist and the sensualist in him take charge. The flowers and the secrecy, the "triumphant smile, *too open,* of the Spring" are so many allies with whose help D'Annunzio sets about the destruction of his own moral fiction. Even Giuliana is not straightforwardly presented. The traces of her illness, still visible in convalescence, are emphasized by a number of realistic touches—"a small part of her bloodless gums appeared in her smile"—and the fact that she is with child, though still unrevealed, is suggested more than once. She becomes, in fact, not the wronged wife but the victim, herself tarnished, of circumstance; and it becomes easier for the hero to shift his emphasis from the sense of guilt to that of passionate, unrepentant devotion: "I have always loved you alone in life; I love you alone." And again, with a more direct flash of that egoism which is so inseparable from D'Annunzio's nature: "You are full of pain. But what creature in the world has been loved as you are loved." It is not surprising, after this, that the proposed scene of repentance merges into a description of the hero's sensual triumph: "It was a lover's kiss I gave her, a long, deep kiss which shook the whole essence of our two lives." The moral purpose with which D'Annunzio set out has been replaced by something not easily distinguishable, even in the expression, from the cheapest variety of "romantic" passion. Meanwhile the sense of prodigality and futility

which had demanded in *Il piacere* a definite moral resolution remains unsettled. It remained so—and this is the key to all D'Annunzio's later work—for the rest of the poet's life.

The moral framework of *L'innocente* is, in fact, a sham: not simply because D'Annunzio was insincere, but because the moral fashions which he had attempted to graft on to his own originally direct, clear-cut vision had no reality for him. The moral speculations which something in his nature seemed to find necessary were, as an artist, fatal to him; for, speaking from a strictly artistic standpoint, they only brought him to an immorality that was invariably dreary and generally vulgar. When his real inspiration, operating through gifts of sensual perception at levels where moral considerations have no place, occasionally attains to free expression we realize that D'Annunzio could be a writer of the first order. There is a remarkable instance of this in *L'innocente,* in the chapter we have just been considering. When Tullio Hermil has regained his ascendancy over Giuliana, his triumph is reflected in a vision, surprisingly clear and alive after the ambiguous ecstasies through which we have just passed, of the fertility of nature. The flowers, heavily and rather oppressively fertile, are replaced by the swallows nesting in the eaves of the villa. The new scene, beneath all its elaboration—elaboration is characteristic of all D'Annunzio's prose—is as limpid and exact in its perception of significant detail as it is delicate and, above all, *alive:*

> On the rustic façade, at every cornice and every projecting angle, along the drain-pipe and over the cross-beams, under the parapets of the windows and the paving-stones of the balconies, everywhere the swallows had nested . . . Some of the nesting birds remained for a few minutes suspended at the holes of their nests. Others supported themselves shining on their wings; others had slipped in half-way, leaving behind them the little forked tail which trembled eagerly, black-and-white against the yellow clay; others, who were already inside, leaned out half-way, showing a little of their bright breast and tawny throat; others, till then invisible, flashed into flight with a high-pitched cry, and sped away. And all that keen and joyful movement round the closed house, all that vivacity of nesting around our own nest of former times, was such a sweet spectacle, such a miracle of refinement and delicacy that we forgot ourselves for a few moments, as though in a pause of our own fever, in the contemplation of it.

"As though in a pause of our own fever". The phrase is, in a sense, symbolical of D'Annunzio's plight as a writer. The fever is the moral uneasiness which he cannot, being what he is, ignore, and yet which he cannot, in the form in which it presents itself to him, accept; and the "moment of forgetfulness" is the interval, necessarily brief and imperfectly realized in the absence of a co-ordinating vision, in which the true consciousness of the artist slips out of the toils and takes command.

After the failure of *L'innocente,* D'Annunzio's career is inevitably a matter of broken ends. A novel like *Il fuoco*—a dreary account, highly flattering to his self-esteem, of his relationship with Eleonora Duse—is still diversified, between the posturings and the sensationalism, by rich descriptions of autumnal splendour on the Venetian lagoon; but the impression of pointlessness, and the self-indulgence which goes with it, are noticeably on the increase. Yet the desire to justify his egoism by relating it to an outlook that transcends the selfish and the fragmentary remains. It was this desire that led D'Annunzio increasingly into Italian politics. In the last forty years of his life the poet lived in his own person the spiritual crisis that brought Italy, through Crispi's tentative imperialism and the Great War, to Fascismo, to a transformation of moral bankruptcy into fanatical voluntarism and the glorification of the pure and self-sufficient act. The stages of this transformation can be traced in that group of semi-political addresses and meditations which were collected into one volume under the specious title of *Il libro ascetico della Giovane Italia.* The first step was the borrowing from Nietzsche of the conception of the Superman. Thrown back once more upon the instability of impulses which had no logical centre, having realized—after the failure of *L'innocente* repeated in later writings—his fatal dependence upon the isolated *Now,* D'Annunzio sought in mere assertion the significance he could not found upon a coherent interpretation of reality. The idea of the Superman, as he used it, was no more than a rhetorical device to cover underlying emptiness: "Who condemns me to be a mere milestone? I was born to pass milestones or to overthrow them." The natural consequence of this outlook is the cult of action which D'Annunzio first formulated in Italy and which Fascism, assisted by the philosophic speculations of Gentile, has adapted to its own ends. The Superman became, in his Italian form, the Hero, and his heroism affirmed itself in the decisive quality of his actions. Actions, be it noted, not to an end clearly conceived and rationally defined—D'Annunzio's whole outlook presupposes that such action is inconceivable—but desired for its own sake and pursued until the various categories of human endeavor, philosophical, moral and political, are fused into an incoherent and undifferentiated activism: "Goodness for me is action, just as poetry is action." In a world where each moment of experience stands by itself, intensity replaces purpose as the criterion of human endeavour, and the Fascist conception of "living dangerously" becomes the only moral precept of the new age.

At bottom, however, D'Annunzio realized that the action which he proposed as his end in life was vitiated by its lack of purpose. He realized it sufficiently to devote a large part of his life to attempts at providing a purpose in terms of national and patriotic endeavour. He came to see the poet's particular activity, the means by which he asserted his value as an individual and escaped the barren circle of unrelated experiences, in his prophetic or incitatory influence upon the soul of the masses. Poetry, as much as the flying which so fascinated him, was thus essentially an *action:* "The work of the poet communicated to the crowd is *an act,* like the gesture of the hero." This belief in the civil function of his art he did not derive from the fashions of his youth, but rather evolved in reaction against them. Andrea Sperelli, indeed, had referred contemptuously to the massacre of Dogali, which so stirred the conscience of patriotic Italians, as the death of "four hundred brutes

brutally murdered"; but D'Annunzio, in his revulsion against the irresponsibility of *Il piacere,* repudiated that attitude too. Political themes inspired some of his attempts in the dramatic form. *La nave,* a spectacle—one can hardly call it a play—written to recall Italians to an awareness of their destinies in the Mediterranean, petered out in a succession of erotic spasms and empty rhetoric; but the political, civil purpose was there, though the strength to pursue it consistently was not. From the time of the Great War, in which he distinguished himself as an aviator, D'Annunzio's entries into politics became more frequent and more explicit. This was especially the case after his intervention at Fiume. Discerning in the incoherent beginnings of Fascism, which looked favourably upon his activities there, the birth of the "new Italy" he identified his own conception of the Superman with "L'Italiano nuovo", the new Italian. This identification expressed itself in a "dynamic" imperialism of which he, as the poet-hero, regarded himself as the prophet. D'Annunzio measured the vitality of the national conscience, like that of the individual, by its capacity for decisive action, for imposing its will upon the stream of circumstance. From this position followed, logically enough, the glorification of war, in which individual and state alike proved themselves and affirmed the temper of their will with an intensity which recalled that of the poetic emotion: "War is a lyrical event, an enthusiastic outburst of the will to create."

The Fascist debt to D'Annunzio, and the spiritual affinity which underlies it, is sufficiently apparent in this conception of the state as decisively extended in action. The detailed parallels are close and numerous. There is hardly a single conception in Mussolini's published speeches which is not at least suggested in the poet's writings. The emphasis upon the Great War in which Italy, acting for the first time as a nation with European significance, achieved not only her natural, her "sacred" frontiers, but also the consciousness of her political maturity, was as congenial to D'Annunzio as it was to the first Milanese *Fasci:* "I am an Italian who founds the new Italy upon the holiness of her war and on the integrity of her Victory." Like the Fascists, too, D'Annunzio combined this emphasis upon the war with an attack on what he called "the old greeds and the old jealousies of the Allies", and especially with denunciations of the "insatiability" of England, "intent only to reserve for herself the lion's share of every ill-gathered booty". And like the Fascisti again he spoke of those "who hold our Malta and have torn our Fiume from us". The claims are familiar, but we understand them better when we find them expressed by a poet in whom we can discern clearly the spiritual roots of the malady from which Fascist "dynamism" springs. Italian imperialism is the political manifestation of a baseless cult of action, of activity for its own sake, which can thrive only upon the existence of some irritation or grievance. The grievance, real or imaginary, is part of a doctrine which would without it simply collapse in the absence of solid foundations, which can only live by artificial stimulation of the desire to react. It was the absence of a coherent set of values, as we detect it in D'Annunzio's political writings, that brought the whole of Italy to Fascismo.

The truth is that D'Annunzio's nationalism matured at a

very unfortunate moment. The national tradition towards which he gravitated was decidedly tenuous in comparison with the provincialism upon which he had turned his back; and what there was of it was not in a healthy state. Italian nationalism itself, which had originated almost entirely in the aspirations of a restricted group of Liberal idealists, seemed unable to extend its convictions to the bulk of the population. It offered, in any case, no vision of adequate power to move a generation whose prevailing temper was more than a little coarsened. Power and a kind of sumptuousness were the watchwords of the time, and Italy, which had neither, had begun to share the common desire for both. The political systems of the day—and particularly the state capitalism of Bismarck by which many Italians, perhaps because they felt that Germany too could be called a young nation, were particularly impressed—were such as the men of the Risorgimento would have abhorred; but the scale of these new developments and their obvious capacity to make history, had a powerful appeal. Morally and materially, the modest nationalism of Italian tradition seemed to have lost much of its attraction. D'Annunzio's political aspirations reflect the spiritual failings of Italian imperialism from the days of Crispi: an imperialism without moral vision, based on facile rhetoric and concealing an uneasy sense of Italy's actual weakness. Behind his rather empty affirmation of the "will to power" there lies always the notion of "Italy deluded, Italy betrayed, Italy impoverished", a sense of inferiority which, as we have already seen, expresses itself in complaints against the treachery of others. More than once, it is ominous to note, D'Annunzio brackets defeated Germany with Italy in a common fate: "What was, and what is, the object of the evil conspiracy of the Allies? Not only the crushing of Germany, but also the annihilation of our victory." To read D'Annunzio in his nationalistic moments is to realize some of the motives, moral perhaps even more than political, involved in Italy's fatal dedication to the policy of the Axis.

To judge D'Annunzio, however, simply on the strength of his imperialistic writings is to see something less than his real stature. There was much in his work that transcended this rather spurious political energy. Politics, in D'Annunzio, is best regarded as the result of his inability—owing to circumstances beyond his control—to acquiesce in the sources of his true strength. In the first place, his provincialism, although he could not work consistently within its limitations, was genuine and alive and therefore a source of inspiration. Even in prose works whose purpose is political and imperialistic we find him writing: "I can never be uprooted from my native place, from the soil which is almost a quality of my corporal substance, from the living soil which can suffer and rejoice in me as my living flesh." This sensual, one might almost say *carnal* apprehension of place, this awareness of it as an extension of the flesh itself, inspired him to writing, notably in *La figlia di Iorio,* that was vivid, direct, and passionate; it is one of his most genuine sources of inspiration.

There were also others. His sense of national tradition, so weak politically, was remarkably strong in all that concerned the written word. This is not surprising when we consider that the national consciousness of Italy, from Pe-

trarch to Manzoni, had been confined for five hundred years almost exclusively to the written word. In D'Annunzio the sense of literary tradition allied itself to that keen apprehension of the individual moment of intense experience which was as strong in him as the power to synthesize was weak. This limitation to the *Now,* which we have seen confessed in *Il piacere,* accounts for the incoherence of his political vision, but is perfectly compatible with the writing of great lyric poetry. Andrea Sperelli, intent as he is upon the definition of his own weaknesses and frustrations, recognizes in himself the strength and purity of this feeling for the written word, which itself stands in the closest relationship to the intensity and delicacy of his perceptions. It is, in fact, at once his gift and his temptation: "His spirit was essentially formal. More than the thought he loved its expression." "He chose, in the exercise of his art, instruments that were difficult, exact, perfect, incorruptible . . . and it was his intention to renew with severity the traditional Italian forms, referring back to the poets of the *stil novo* and to the painters who preceded the Renaissance." On the occasions when this delicate apprehension of style expressed a genuine, unimpeded purity of vision, we can see D'Annunzio for what he was— the last great poet in the Italian literary tradition. In the four volumes of *Le Laudi,* which are the height of his achievement—and notably in the third of them, *L'Alcione,* published in 1903—extraordinary intensity of feeling is often linked with an equally extraordinary precision of phrase. The linguistic instrument in these poems is one refined by centuries of poetic tradition; the inspiration, limited to the vivid apprehension of single experiences, is in its kind often flawless. To deal adequately with D'Annunzio's poetry would need a separate essay, an essay whose tone would be notably more sympathetic, generally speaking, than what I have written above. In this one, meanwhile, I have attempted to set in its proper light D'Annunzio's relation to Italy in our times. (pp. 140-53)

D. A. Traversi, "D'Annunzio and Modern Italy," in The Dublin Review, Vol. 209, No. 419, October, 1941, pp. 140-53.

George MacBeth   (essay date 1964)

[*MacBeth is a Scottish poet whose work characteristically examines personal suffering in a macabre and satiric manner. His poetry is most often praised for its formal dexterity and criticized for its occasionally insubstantial themes. In the following essay, MacBeth examines D'Annunzio's response to World War I in his works and political speeches, arguing that it was strongly influenced by nineteenth-century Romanticism.*]

One of the most interesting facts about the Italian campaign in 1918 is that two writers crucial to the literature of war were engaged in action within a few miles and within a few months of each other on the same sector of the front near Venice. Hemingway, who had volunteered to serve as a driver with the Red Cross Ambulance Corps, was wounded while issuing chocolate to men in the trenches near Fossalta. D'Annunzio, who had enlisted in the Italian army but later fought with all three of the Italian services, for some years made his military headquarters in a palace on the Grand Canal. The difference between their responses to the war is the difference between the 19th and 20th centuries.

The year 1963 was the centenary of D'Annunzio's birth. His reputation has been constantly revalued in Italy and throughout Europe, but in England few critics have seriously considered his work since the eighteen-nineties, when some of his plays were translated by Arthur Symons. Continental views in centenary articles have differed widely in their re-assessments. Montherlant was enthusiastic in "Les nouvelles litteraires":

> En effet, ce qui est proprement unique en d'Annunzio, c'est son effort inégal mais inégalé pour integrer à la vie et à l'action quotidiennes les formes de l'art les plus hautes, dans la croyance que poésie et culture sont l'unique réalité.

> [Indeed, what is properly unique in D'Annunzio is his unequal, but unequalled, effort to integrate into daily life and activities the forms of the highest art, in the belief that poetry and culture are the sole realities.]

Moravia was dismissive in *L'Espresso:*

> His poetry breaks down under the slightest pressure. As a novelist, his characters are always false, superficial and common: they show a total absence of psychological insight, social observation and moral judgement. In my opinion, d'Annunzio is not a creative writer, but a man of letters.

In England there were no centenary articles. The most interesting assessment of D'Annunzio in English is still Hemingway's in *Across The River And Into The Trees,* where Colonel Cantwell (a fairly obvious persona for Hemingway himself) describes him as

> writer, poet, national hero, phraser of the dialectic of Fascism, macabre egotist, aviator, commander, or rider, in the first of the fast torpedo attack boats, Lieutenant-Colonel of Infantry without knowing how to command a company, nor a platoon properly, the great, lovely writer of *Notturno* whom we respect, and jerk.

Hemingway seems to have been fascinated both by the virtues and the vices of D'Annunzio. D'Annunzio was an old-fashioned Romantic and a rhetorician, as he himself was not. He enjoyed the war, even the horror, cruelty and pain of war, which he still saw in nineteenth century terms as a field of glory and honour. He still seems to have believed in all those large empty words which Hemingway's Lieutenant Henry in *A Farewell To Arms* had lost his faith in:

> I was always embarassed by the words sacred, glorious, and sacrifice and the expression in vain. We had heard them, sometimes standing in the rain almost out of earshot, so that only the shouted words came through, and had read them on proclamations that were slapped up on bill-posters over other proclamations, now for a long time, and I had seen nothing sacred, and the things that were glorious had no glory and the sacrifices were like the stockyards at Chica-

go, if nothing was done with the meat except to bury it.

In fact, Lieutenant Henry is almost certainly remembering the sort of speech by D'Annunzio himself which Hemingway may have heard, or at any rate heard of, while serving in the Piave sector. There is a long and bitterly ironic account in *Across The River And Into the Trees* of the Colonel as a platoon commander listening to D'Annunzio haranguing his troops in the rain:

> and D'Annunzio, with his lost eye, covered by the patch, and his white face, as white as the belly of a sole, new turned over in the market, the brown side not showing, and looking thirty hours dead, was shouting, "Morire non a basta", and the Colonel, then a lieutenant, had thought, "What the muck more do they want of us?"

This particular speech survives and has been translated into English by Magda Sindici in *The Rally:*

> Dying is not enough.
> If dying means to desist from fighting, then we cannot die. We must rise up again. The country gives constant birth to her strong sons: raises them up and hurls them forward. She gives back a living man for each dead man, a soldier for each one that falls. No place may stay empty today. Wherever there is room for a man, there a man must be—standing or kneeling, creeping or crawling, but ever with a rifle in his hand, ever at the service of some new weapon.

Despite the relative weakness of its phrasing, this is a passage which illustrates two of D'Annunzio's main themes, and is instinct with the violence and afflatus which most of us can sympathise with Hemingway for despising. The conception of living soldiers as a body of ant-like automata given unity and importance only through their subservience to an inanimate guiding force is a familiar piece of non-democratic political theology from Carlyle to Nkrumah. The theme of a constant generation of new men, thrown up by the mother country to replace the slain, has its echoes from Sulla to Franco.

Nevertheless, this rhetoric is not the closet-production of an armchair theorist. D'Annunzio's rhetoric, like T. E. Lawrence's, had been tested in battle. He had, in the words of Colonel Cantwell, "put the chips on the line". His speeches had already helped to bring Italy into the war on the Allied side in 1915. No-one would have blamed him, as his biographer Anthony Rhodes says in *The Poet As Superman,* if he'd sat back on his laurels and devoted the remainder of his life to his poetry. D'Annunzio believed, however, that he could no longer write poetry unless he got into the war and saw some action. For years he'd been living in exile in France, and his patriotism seems to have combined with his psychic energy to drive him towards active participation in the fighting. Despite considerable opposition from friends and statesmen, he enlisted in the Italian army. He was fifty-two years old. Anyone who has read the accounts of writers like Graves and Blunden who went through the war in their late teens or early twenties will be able to guess at its probable impact on the system of a man in advancing middle age. The difference between D'Annunzio and a younger volunteer like Wilfred Owen, however, was not in the crack-up of his physique, but in the rigidity of his sensitivity. Here is a specimen of this rigidity in a speech describing the slaughterous assault which took the twin heights of the Veliki and the Faiti in the Carso above Trieste:

> The men seemed to bite into the blue air. The light multiplied the effect from moment to moment. That impact itself was an ascension into the heavens. Strength seemed to rebound from death. Death was dragged upwards by ardour and clamour, like a peasant woman caught by the contagion of a tumult who should start singing a song of fury. The fallen were not encumbrance but an impulse. The wounded became the standard-bearers of the scarlet ensign. The summit was only a sublime feeling in the breasts of those who meant to reach it. There was nothing but rocks, shambles, crumbled trunks, iron spikes, things wrenched apart and smoke and corpses. But everywhere too there was the light of Italy, the noon-day of Italy.

As an account of an infantry charge this makes an interesting parallel with Owen's "Spring Offensive:"

> So, soon they topped the hill, and raced together
> Over an open stretch of herb and heather
> Exposed. And instantly the whole sky burned
> With fury against them; earth set sudden cups
> In thousands for their blood; and the green slope
> Chasmed and steepened sheer to infinite space.
>
> . . . . .
>
> Of them who running on that last high place
> Leapt to swift unseen bullets, or went up
> On the hot blast and fury of hell's upsurge,
> Or plunged and fell away past this world's verge,
> Some say God caught them even before they fell.

Owen goes on, of course, to set the tone of headlong excitement into sober perspective, as D'Annunzio does not. The interest lies in their similarity of source. The impact of Shelley on Owen has been noted by D. S. R. Welland in his critical study. Here the model for both Owen and D'Annunzio seems to be the storm section of the "Ode To The West Wind". We know from biographical evidence that D'Annunzio frequently read and admired Shelley as a young man, and there are stylistic parallels in his early poetry.

It was a later and sicker English Romantic, however, on whom D'Annunzio's maturer sensibility was more firmly modelled. In his own words

> A. Swinburne, author of "Laus Veneris" and of "Anactoria", in whom there seems to live again, with incredible violence, the criminal sensuality which fills primitive dramas with wild cries and desperate slaughters.

It wasn't, in other words, the political Swinburne who wrote so enthusiastically about the liberty of Italy, and who knelt to recite his *Songs Before Sunrise* at the feet of Mazzini in Winchester Road. It was the earlier, pre-flogging-block Swinburne, whose darker passions were still flowering in frustrated cruelty in his love poetry; the Swinburne who had shocked the eighteen sixties, and later

titillated the nineteen twenties, with the erotic violence of Chastelard:

> I know not: men must love you in life's spite;
> For you will always kill them; man by man
> Your lips will bite them dead; yea, though you would,
> You shall not spare one; all will die of you . . .
>
> Stretch your throat out that I may kiss all round
> Where mine shall be cut through: suppose my mouth
> The axe-edge to bite so sweet a throat in twain
> With bitter iron, should not it turn soft
> As lip is soft to lip?

This sort of Swinburne, the Swinburne of Dolores and Faustine, those whip-wielding fatal mistresses, is ever present in D'Annunzio, though with a new twist, a special kinkiness in his war speeches:

> In order to fight, one had to love and believe. One had to divine the features of Italy at each leap, beneath the alien crust. The jet of one vein was enough, sometimes, to alter the countenance of a place that had been fashioned by many causes in the fullness of time. We shed this mystic blood in a full tide, along stony valleys, up steep slopes, down squalid craters, in blackened woods, on heaps of ruined houses. We found once more the flint and the fever of Rome in the deadly marshes.

What D'Annunzio is doing here that is new and crucial in the history of the Romantic agony is to transform the fatal woman from a person into a country. If Kipling or Henley had done this in 1890 their patriotic poetry would have taken on real verve and power. Unfortunately, Victorian good taste supervened. It was left to D'Annunzio, though at a much later and more dangerous date, to make the crucial advance. His enlargement of the sado-masochistic fantasies of a few nineteenth century intellectuals into the guiding principle of a new, more consuming patriotism, a love of country which pinned the loyalty, and sapped the conscience, of millions, is what places D'Annunzio at the pivot-point of his age. If pacifism was bred in the First World War in the nausea and compassion of poets like Wilfred Owen, so was Fascism in the manic energy of D'Annunzio:

> Necessity cannot be abolished. The furnace cannot be quenched: it burns and roars and devours. What have we to throw into the great flame? We will throw all if need be: even our most sacred canvases.

When D'Annunzio wrote that "there is more ideal value for us today in a smooth metal helmet than in the head-piece of Benvenuto" he was already envisaging the aesthetic appeal of the jackboot. We all tend to remember that it was Hermann Goering who said: "When I hear the word culture I reach for my gun". What we easily forget is that for Goering as for D'Annunzio, reaching for one's gun was itself an aesthetic act. No-one can understand National Socialism who fails to see that it was based on, and owed much of its success to, an essentially Romantic approach to the normally prosaic and dreary problems of politics. Hitler was never against art; he was only against

Benito Mussolini and D'Annunzio, propaganda card.

art he didn't himself like. His ability to manœuvre art to his ends is recognised even by William L. Shirer in *The Rise and Fall of the Third Reich,* where he comments on Hitler's revival of the *hakenkreuz* as a Nazi symbol in the summer of 1920:

> This may not have been 'art', but it was propaganda of the highest order. The Nazis now had a symbol which no other party could match. The hooked cross seemed to possess some mystic power of its own, to beckon to action in a new direction the insecure lower middle classes which had been floundering in the uncertainty of the first chaotic postwar years. They began to flock under its banner.

This ability to translate art into action was at this time being exhibited most notably by D'Annunzio at Fiume. His emblems, mottoes and decrees would, of course, be familiar to Hitler from the newspapers.

There is internal evidence that Hitler's rhetoric was also influenced by the D'Annunzian example. Sometimes the Nordic mist and dazzle is there in the earlier Italian as it is in the later English of Sir Oswald Mosley:

> None knows what is before us, although all know that a magnificent destiny is in the process of formation, not only on the face of the earth, but in the vortex of man's being. The most perspicacious of seers cannot discern the modes of this troubled genesis, nor distinguish the marks

of its impression; but he can divine the rhythm—set ringing by passion and victory—of a lyrical force that is about to be made manifest at the apex of every future height.

There are also hints of the homosexual side of Nazi racialism, albeit in a more attenuated and Latin form, in D'Annunzio's praise of "gentil sangue latino" [gentle Latin blood] in the faces of the recruits of 1899:

> You are pure and spotless, unhurt by life, similar to those changing countenances that wind and light create on the sea's vicissitude. Our hopes breathe in from you the innocence of our new time, they grow wide within us and intoxicate us.
>
> > You are the aroma of battle to us.
> > You are the maidenhood of Victory.

This praise of youthful good looks is more reminiscent of pre-war German stamps, or of certain sequences in *The Triumph of the Will,* than of its more intoxicating and repellent inverse, the contempt for Jewishness towards which it seems to have led. It derives, of course, from the fascination with youth and innocence which characterised so much late nineteenth century Romanticism from Huysmans to Wilde. In this sense, it provides another excellent example of how D'Annunzio's rhetoric looks both back and forward.

The note of impassioned comradeship with the young and

dedicated is not new. It goes back in Italian literature at least to Abba, whose *Noterelle,* with their account of his service with Garibaldi in 1860, was published when D'Annunzio was at the impressionable age of 17. When Abba writes, after rejoining his fellow-soldiers in Naples

> I have found my brigade once more. Nothing, there is absolutely nothing in the world to compare with the sensation of feeling oneself absorbed into the life of a great body of youth, love, and valour

he is celebrating the same bond as Siegfried Sassoon does when he writes in England on sick leave:

> In bitter safety I awake, unfriended;
> And while the dawn begins with slashing rain
> I think of the Battalion in the mud.

There seems to be a dialogue on this theme between English and Italian literature which begins with Byron in *The Corsair* and perhaps ends for ever in the Western Desert with Keith Douglas's lament in "Aristocrats":

> How can I live among this gentle
> obsolescent breed of heroes, and not weep?

These elements of sexual sublimation and idealised friendship are allied in D'Annunzio with a deeper and ultimately more interesting obsession with the basic symbol of blood. This obsession gives the best of his rhetoric a peculiarly post-Freudian resonance. Mario Praz has praised D'Annunzio for his carnality of thought, for the "weight of blood" in his work, and indeed the concept of blood is a very rich one in his thinking. He manipulates it to link both divine right with physical pleasure, and pagan heroism with Christian sacrifice. Sometimes, as in the following passage about Easter, the blood of Catholic ritual becomes transmuted before our eyes into the heady ichôr of primitive cannibalism:

> Over there, blood is seething and glistening in the chalice of the air. It pours from the edgeless cup, overflows from the rimless bowl. It repeats one word only, as in the closed Coenaculum: "This is my blood.
> Let all drink of it". Again it exclaims: "Let all drink of it".
> Once more it repeats the words and cries: "Let all drink of it".
> For the third time it repeats the words and shouts: "Let all drink of it".
> It is the blood that coloured the Isonzo as far as Sdobba.
> The blood of San Michele of the four peaks.
> The blood of San Martino.
> The blood of Monfalcone.
> The blood of Vermigliano.
> The blood of Rubbia.
> The blood of Boscomalo.
> The blood of Doberdo.
> The blood of Merna.
> The blood of Debeli.
> The blood of Pecinka.
> The blood of the Veliki.
> The blood of the Faiti.
> The blood of all burning calvaries, of all infernal valleys.
> The blood of all our thirsty victories.

> The blood that made fruitful the forsaken road to Trieste, the barren road.
> The blood that was washed away at the springs of the Timavo.
> Soldiers, each one of you should drink of it. Your hearts should be filled with it. Your breast should widen to receive it. It will never suffocate you, but will give you power over death.
> Your country cries out to each one of you in the morning, as the Lord of Hosts cried out in the twilight: "Take up this cup filled to the brim with the wine of my wrath".
> She repeats and commands each one: "Take up this cup".
> She administers a sacrament that makes you all partakers of her divinity and her passion, of her miserable humanity and her immortal hope.

The sentiments here may be technically blasphemous: but the sense is not vague. D'Annunzio is suggesting that to be wounded or killed fighting for Italy is to be turned into a pagan divinity enjoying everlasting sexual satisfaction and into a saved Christian soul freed for ever from the fear of death. The appeal is to the mixture of carnal longing and morbid spiritual doubt which we may suppose to have characterised almost all poorly educated and underpaid conscripts in the First World War. Seen in this light, the rhetoric may be unscrupulous, but it could scarcely be called obtuse or irrelevant. Advertising has taken thirty years to catch up with D'Annunzio's insights. In an affluent society at peace, the symbol for sexual success and psychological poise is petrol, as in the Super-Shell campaign for "getaway people". In a Catholic society at war, the symbol for divine intervention was blood. The beautiful saviour would come, not smiling and windblown behind the wheel of a Jaguar, but suffering and crucified in the shape of an aeroplane:

> Our heroes know, the living and the dead know, that the shadow of the winged machine is like the shadow cast by the Sign of sacrifice and redemption.

> The similarity between the two shadows struck me on the field of Goras, one already far off day of that other war, when I saw the machine, all covered with blood, brought back by Oreste Salamone with its burden of death.

> Its double transverse wings, from prow to screw, formed a cross of blood.

According to Colonel Draper in *Christianity and War,* when the Pope blessed the standards of William of Normandy before his invasion of England in 1066, he made the conflict a just and pious war for the French armies. In the careful muddle of his blood-rhetoric, D'Annunzio was trying to do the same thing for the cause of Italy against Austria. Religion, of course, played a powerful part in the First World War. The angel of Mons is only one among many examples of divine visitations. D'Annunzio with his concrete sensibility was able to give this attractive myth a new look:

> Our Christ today is the one we saw at the crossroads under fire, that had lost its two feet like a

soldier caught by a large splinter. It is still there, nailed to the cross by the left hand, but it hangs forward against the enemy, its thorn-pierced brow held out to the shock, its outstretched right hand still sharp with its transfixing nail as with a desperate weapon.

The idea of a macabre resurrection which already seems hinted at in this passage acquires a more full-blooded and terrifying reality in D'Annunzio's speech to the recruits of 1900:

> In a hollow of the Carso, beyond the blood-soaked Vallone towards Nova Villa, is that skeleton still there which the landslip revealed, standing up against the red earth washed by the storm, with the holes of its cranium turned towards the enemy?
>
> And near the Observatory of the Bombarde, to the west of the Veliki, in that split reef of hell, is that raised arm among the stones still there with its closed fist: one single coil of cartilage and sinew and bone, turned towards the enemy?
>
> What if the rains of yesterday, the clear rains of an Italian April, have carried away the earth from our sloping cemeteries? What if the dead appear? What if their lonely, fleshless feet are bare? We took their hobnailed boots from them that we might march on further, beyond charnel-houses and graveyards, further and still further on. And we mentioned them in a votive song when we gathered them together on the altar of the roofless church of Doberdo, that was filled with wounded lying on straw.
>
> We had brought one of our men to the holy ground of Aquileia, to the tomb of our earlier dead, of our first martyrs. The cemetery was thronged, full of armed soldiers. The mounds of earth interrupted their lines. And the youth of the last call were there, your brethren older by one year, those of Ninetynine, with their clean-shaven faces in the sunshine, their feet between one grave and the next. It was in June, on the day of San Leone. A voice was speaking beside the sanctuary. And, as the words rose, faces bent down under the weight of checked tears. And then, one saw the shining bayonet surpassing the grey helmet, like a clear straight flame, like sharp, white fire. It was the Pentecost of the dead, the ardour of the dead crowning the peerless sacrifice.
>
> Your feet do not tarry among tombs today; they hasten along a straight road. But the subterranean flame is thick upon your heads as in that vision. And this year the fiery Pentecost precedes the third anniversary by five days. Five days and one night.
>
> And here is the prayer of your vigil, O initiates both of the next and of the far victory. The prayer of all free men:
>
> O dead who are in earth as you are in heaven, hallowed be your names,
> The kingdom of your spirit come,
> your will be done on earth.
> Give to our faith its daily bread.

> Keep alight within us your holy hatred, as we will not deny your love.
> Lead us not into any infamous temptation, deliver us from all vile doubt.
> And, if it be necessary,
> we will fight, not to our last drop of blood, but with you to our last grain of ashes.
> If it be necessary,
> we will fight until our just God
> shall come to judge the quick and the dead.
> So be it.

Here the corpse-love of Edgar Allan Poe and the Satanism of Baudelaire are given a deadly realistic twist. For a world so profoundly concerned with the horror of war as ours is, the idea of an army of the dead praying to a God of War may scarcely seem a strange one for a speech on the field of battle. The abnormal basis of blood-lust has perhaps never been so forcefully demonstrated as in such grim and chilling propaganda as this. The moral of all D'Annunzio's mature prose, though it was not one he chose to point himself, is that the ordinary man is a creature of bottomless evil, morbid appetites and atrocious cruelty, a creature eager for blood, and for the sublimation of his primitive impulses in brutal ritual. What may disturb us is that D'Annunzio could celebrate this homo sanguinis with a resounding cadence, and a Miltonic flair for names, worthy of Churchill:

> Those soldiers of the line whose feet left their imprint on the tawny clay of Oslavia, those who trampled underfoot the clotted mire of Podgora, those who were ensnared by the red slime of the Carso, all—from the San Michele to the Monte Nero, from the Vodice to the Ermada, from Tolmino to Pecinka, from Sagrade to Plezzo, from Plava to Doberdo, whose victorious names outnumber the record of Brescia—all, from the first ones who hacked away barbed wire with pincers and shears to the last who over-ran the passes opened up by the crushing bombardment, all are the heroes of the most laborious battle that has been fought for the cause of free man on the united front.

For D'Annunzio the human condition was epitomised by the torturing spiral of war. His attitude to amelioration of this condition took no account of decent feeling or rational motivation. His belief in the virtues of work and faith was shared by, and devalued by, the heirs of his rhetoric and panache, Mussolini and Hitler. We know today, as D'Annunzio did not, what thinking with the blood has led to in human suffering and degradation. The importance of D'Annunzio for the literary critic, as for the social historian, is that he was the last major writer who could use the Romantic ideal with its full political relevance before it went bad in the hands of the Fascists. Perhaps the last word should go to Valéry who wrote to D'Annunzio in the year when Hitler became Chancellor of Germany:

> Je garde la sensation que tu m'as donnée d'avoir connu la personalité absolue du Poète—l'Être qui est contre le temps. Tu es le dernier . . . et ton nom marquera un âge révolu de l'histoire de la terre.

> ["I keep the sensation that you have given me of

having known the absolute personality of the Poet—the Being who is against the times. You are the last . . . and your name will mark the end of an epoch in the history of the world."]

(pp. 154-63)

George MacBeth, "The Sick Rhetoric of War," in Critical Quarterly, *Vol. 6, No. 2, Summer, 1964, pp. 154-63.*

Sergio Pacifici   (essay date 1973)

[*Pacifici is an American educator, translator, and critic specializing in Italian language and literature. In the following excerpt, he discusses the role of the Nietzschean superman in D'Annunzio's early novels.*]

Whatever opinion readers and critics may have about Gabriele d'Annunzio, he is unquestionably one of the most controversial and most discussed literary personalities of modern Italian culture. In the early years of this century, Benedetto Croce put it clearly when he wrote: "It is beyond doubt that d'Annunzio occupies a large place in the modern soul and that, as a consequence, he will occupy [a similar place] in the histories that will be written about the spiritual life of our time." Certainly few other poets dominated the world of letters, and perhaps even fewer lived a life as daring, damning, and dramatic as he: poet premature at the age of sixteen, novelist of repute, scenario writer (he was among the very first novelists to become aware of the possibilities of the new medium), soldier, flier, political figure, polemicist, d'Annunzio lived a life full of scandals of most kinds—personal, financial, military, diplomatic, and political—all of which certainly helped to draw interest to his work. He was, this much is sure, a man of genius, of exceptional vanity and versatility, who had an uncanny ability to catch and retain public attention with a flair today's Madison Avenue advertising agencies could justifiably envy. In the words of the anonymous reviewer of the *Times Literary Supplement,* December 29, 1966:

> In the role of cultural fugleman to his country he was helped and not hindered by his extravagance of manner. That as a young man he was a dandy who sometimes overdressed with an appalling (and provincial) bad taste did not tell against him: most of his countrymen would have liked to own his well-publicized wardrobe (though irreverent little boys, seeing him in his carefully chosen white riding-habit on his white horse, would ask him if he were posing for his monument). His elopement with a duchess, his later appropriation of another man's wife, and his well-publicized life as sexual *condottiere* generated even more fame and admiration among his fellow-countrymen; he was, after all, living out the favourite myth of the Italian male.

His fame grew steadily from the time he was first published until the end of the first decade of this century. Mussolini himself, who was both fascinated and annoyed by D'Annunzio's egocentricity, shrewdly accorded him official recognition by sponsoring and financing a monumental, forty-nine-volume finely printed, deluxe edition of his *opera omnia.* Ironically enough, even such an unusual honor proved to be insufficient to enable the poet to keep a prominent place among his peers. D'Annunzio's star, which had risen so fast and so high, began declining steadily in an irreversible motion which neither the sympathy of the Fascist regime nor that of the faithful coterie of his critics-admirers could change. As he approached his death in 1938, he found himself almost forgotten, although still imitated, passé, as it were, in an era that both believed and practised the very cult of superman he had done so much to create. (pp. 32-3)

There are a couple of observations that should properly be made at this point: first, d'Annunzio's life was so extravagant and his position in matters of aesthetics, morality, and politics so extreme and, at least for his time so controversial, that it was and is still problematical for a literary historian to offer a reasonably unbiased view on d'Annunzio's creative work; second, so diversified was the man's genius, so numerous his interests, and so uneven his artistic performance, that an assessment of his creative writing is inevitably less than fair if reached through an analysis of only one of the genres he practised.

There is, in this paradoxical situation, at least one comforting side: the present generation of readers, brought up in a substantially less repressed awareness of sexuality, is no longer shocked by what at the turn of the century were considered to be obscene pages. Indeed, the emphasis on a more legitimate literary judgment requests that we focus our attention on more substantive questions: did d'Annunzio succeed in representing the decadence of his characters? How well was his sensuous view of life objectified by and through the plot of his novels and the actions of his heroes? What did the author contribute to changing a tradition he had inherited? To answer these fundamental questions, we may turn to *Il piacere,* the first novel d'Annunzio wrote, certainly his most representative, and probably his best.

The book tells a rather simple story. Andrea Sperelli of Ugenta, a wealthy Roman aristocrat, a *bon vivant,* connoisseur of art and himself a gifted artist, has been left by his mistress, Elena Muti. After challenging a rival to a duel, he is seriously wounded and leaves for Schifanoja, the villa of a cousin, in order to recover. It is there that he meets a gracious, introspective young matron, Donna Maria Ferres who is the wife of the Ambassador of Guatemala. The two fall quickly in love, and Andrea is given to understand that some day Maria will physically reciprocate his love. Back in Rome, Andrea once again sees his former mistress and hopes that, despite the fact that she is now married to Lord Heathfield, a wealthy English aristocrat, she will consent to resuming their love affair. Things, however, do not work out quite this way. Andrea, still yearning for Elena, gradually comes to love her through Maria. When Maria's husband, having contracted a large gambling debt he is unable to pay, flees from Rome, she gladly gives herself to him—only to be horrified when during their love-making he cries out the name of his former mistress. The book closes with Maria departing from Rome and Andrea more lonely and wretched than ever.

So much, or enough, for the story itself. As for the atmosphere of the novel, that admittedly is something else. Seldom before (or for that matter since) has another writer managed to match d'Annunzio's re-creation of the incredibly pretentious, sophisticated, and bored life of the Roman aristocracy in the 1880s. We move amidst the "beautiful people" of post-*Risorgimento* Rome; we hear their conversations about futile matters—mistresses, *objets d'art* being auctioned, the latest gossip—and we are privileged to be present as invisible observers of the gaiety of their drawing rooms and the intimacy of their bedrooms. There is nothing wrong, to be sure, with the milieu or with the special focus of d'Annunzio: indeed, the social and moral decadence he portrays could have been an immensely fascinating matter in other hands. The problem is not with the subject itself, but with the way the subject is treated. There is little, if indeed any irony in the book, and by and large (the single exception being toward the end of the novel) d'Annunzio is satisfied with skimming the surface, of giving us the picture but not its true flavor, concentrating on the colors and shapes of the things that constitute the milieu but not the essence of the souls that inhabit it.

This manner of treating a serious subject ends by being extremely damaging to it. Andrea Sperelli is nothing more than an effete intellectual, a sensitive but basically hollow aesthete who in some ways resembles Machiavelli's prince. Like the prince, Andrea is unreal, a figure with no depth, constructed for the sole purpose of illustrating the novelist's intention of giving form to the abstract ideal of a man seeking to make pleasure both a means and an end. To be sure, we do hear a good deal about various kinds of pleasures. Yet, the superlatives and refined language used to define such pleasure not once give us much of an insight into the experiences being described. Likewise, there is in the book a complacent, almost studious overindulgence in describing the "things," the physical habitat of the characters—something that probably inspired Mario Praz to state flatly in his excellent introductory essay to the anthological Ricciardi edition of d'Annunzio's work:

> If we really reflect about the impression d'Annunzio's novels make on us, we realize that what is positive [about them] comes not from [their] psychology, but from [their] atmosphere . . . we remember things, not people. As in Arcimboldi's paintings, we have nothing to do with men, but [only] with things. . . . Through atmosphere and things, d'Annunzio tries to create human beings: but as we draw closer to them we become aware of the stuff they are made of.

The problem of his art is directly traceable to a human flaw. As d'Annunzio's distinguished English biographer Frances Winwar remarks: "Essentially his genius lay in the acuity of those senses, to which he had given full play. He delighted in the things he saw, the emotions he felt, the music he adored and desired as through an extension of his eroticism. Yet the very force of his sensations dulled him to a human appreciation of the feelings of others." All throughout the novel, the author strives to present the intellectual side of Andrea: aside from being knowledgeable

in matters of art, he collects precious bric-a-brac and old furniture; he is a fine drawing artist and a gifted engraver; he delights in being able to discern the refined from the good with a sure, practical awareness of the monetary value of the things he purchases or admires. In addition, he is intimately acquainted with the classics, which he cites frequently: he is also at home in several European literatures and quotes liberally from Goethe, Byron, Shelley, Swinburne, and others. Music is another of his interests, and he is well versed in the works of Bach, Beethoven, Chopin, Schumann, Haydn, Mozart, Boccherini, and Cherubini, as well as the lesser-known Paisiello and Rameau. Finally, Andrea's encyclopediac knowledge extends to modern languages, particularly French, Spanish, and English, freely sprinkled throughout the book. Andrea is presented as an exceedingly well-informed gentleman, to be sure; but his knowledge, his intellectual equipment play no significant role in the development of his character. In the final analysis, culture appears as something merely superimposed on the persona of the story, to the point of existing for its own sake. Love itself is treated with the only dimension of libidinous appetite, as an insatiable appetite that reduces Andrea to a kind of sexual maniac so engrossed in sexuality that life passes him by without making much more than fleeting impressions upon him.

The Child of Pleasure is also a hopelessly romantic novel, romantic in the worst possible meaning of the term, both with respect to its theme and its style. Human relations are noted but never analyzed: thus, for example, Andrea's first mistress, Elena, breaks her affair with him for reasons that, since never explained, are for the reader to imagine. On the scant evidence offered by the novelist, we are to believe that Elena, however deep her love for Andrea may have been, decides to leave him on the grounds that her financial situation is so critical that she must marry a man of great means, Lord Heathfield, in order to continue living in the style to which she has become accustomed. After she has broken off with Andrea, she consents to visit him in their old love nest, Palazzo Zuccoli, where Andrea resides, for reasons that are never made clear since she gives no evidence of wanting to resume their liason. If we turn to Donna Maria, Andrea's second great love, we are no less baffled. Here is a woman of grace and sensitivity who, wretchedly married to a diplomat, falls in love with the hero of the novel in a matter of a few days, although it takes her considerably more time to bring herself to the physical consummation of her love. She does so, however, only when her husband is forced to depart in a hurry when he is unable to repay his gambling debts. Love itself, so fervently cherished in all of d'Annunzio's books, is pervasively thought of in incestuous terms (the highest form of love is described as a love between brother and sister), while, when consummated, it has the connotations of a religious experience (the bed is called "the altar"). Finally, there are the usual stock items of the romantic novel: aside from a sentimental kind of love, there is a duel, a serious wound, passionate love affairs, and a language that, at the crucially dramatic points, degenerates in clichés: "Adieu!" "Farewell!" "Love me forever!" While these sound like, and may even be touching words when properly and sparingly used, they lose their tension and impact by being over-stressed in d'Annunzio's work and confuse the reader in his effort to gain significant insights into what such "love" is about. Can love be nothing more than a masochistic or sadistic experience, a form of punishment inflicted upon another human being—an experience utterly devoid of any uplifting elements? "Each of these loves," comments d'Annunzio apropos of Andrea, "brought him to a new degradation; each inebriated him with evil rapture, without satisfying him; each taught him some special subtlety of vice yet unknown to him. He had in him the seeds of all infections. He corrupted and was corrupted." In a letter addressed to his friend Francesco Paolo Michetti, which serves as a preface to the novel, d'Annunzio claims that his work was essentially a study of corruption, depravity, and of "many other subtleties and falsities and vain cruelties." By focusing on Andrea's existence, the author's intention was to condemn, if only by implication, a decadent life-style that poisons the human character. What ultimately dissatisfies the reader is not the theme of the book but d'Annunzio's conception of how his theme is to be artistically realized. His constant "denunciation" of the debauchery of his hero is inconclusive and unconvincing because it is stated, discussed, but never really depicted in any depth. In short, the reader is asked to accept without seeing the degradation of Andrea Sperelli. To achieve his objective, d'Annunzio uses a technique based heavily on an inordinate accumulation of details of a merely external kind. The problem raised by such a technique must be seen from the larger perspective of just what it contributes, or fails to contribute, to the work as a whole. Here one can hardly take issue with Moravia's opinion that the obsession with objects is indicative of d'Annunzio's intention of "affixing a maximum attention and immobility to every detail as if it stood by itself and had no connection with what comes before and follows after. . . . Page follows page composed not structurally, but according to purely extrinsic demands."

No one, I suspect, would claim that *The Child of Pleasure* is a great, or even a good novel. By the same token, it can hardly be dismissed for it does reflect a break with the traditions of *verismo* and the historical novel. It is, in a very special way, a personal novel in which reality and imagination are fused in such a way that literature is transformed from the mirror of life into a "way of life." When pressed on this issue, d'Annunzio could affirm, as he actually did in discussing his work *The Triumph of Death* with the French writer Romain Rolland, "[My book] is in no sense a work of the imagination but a representation of life." Yet, when his mistress Barbara Leoni came upon the notes d'Annunzio had been writing about their love affair, the poet insisted, without batting an eyelash, that there was "no connection between reality and a work of art."

D'Annunzio was not only a writer but, as noted earlier, something of an ideologist who regarded his literary work, as well as his individual actions, as proper vehicles to define within their respective limitations his concepts of man and society. A closer look at Andrea Sperelli reveals that, much like the majority of Dannunzian characters, he embodies the qualities of Nietzsche's *Uebermensch,* the superman. The *Uebermensch* follows a cult of superiority achieved through cultural, racial, or physical strength, or

any combination of these and other expressions of the self. Similarly, the artist is assigned to a privileged position in society, set on a pedestal apart from the others, clearly contemptuous of the masses and any democratic political system of government. Military and political power has an important role to play in the world of superman, since presumably it alone can restore the former prestige and glory of the *patria.* Such nationalism of the most parochial sort is accompanied by a cheap, vulgar brand of patriotism (of the lurid kind we have seen lately in our own political wasteland) which stresses achievement of objectives through any means, usually violent, blood baths and complete elimination of those who, unable to share aspirations similar to ours, must be considered cowards, uninformed, naïve, and expendable.

If *Il piacere* foreshadows the figure of superman, *L'innocente (The Intruder)* d'Annunzio's third novel, brings *Uebermensch* to its fuller realization. Tullio Hermil is in love with his wife Giuliana, of whom he demands an absolute fidelity he himself does not feel obliged to return. In a moment of weakness, Giuliana has an affair with a novelist, Filippo Arborio. Upon learning that she will have a child, she and her husband, who knows of the extramarital relation, begin making plans to kill the offspring—a murder they eventually carry out by exposing the baby to the rigors of the weather. Theirs is a crime, but there will not be a punishment. As Tullio declares, at the beginning of what is essentially a confession-type novel, "I have committed a crime. . . . Man's justice does not touch me. No earthly court could ever judge me."

It is instructive to turn to d'Annunzio's fourth novel to perceive just how the superficial intellectualism that characterizes *The Child of Pleasure* evolves into a novel with regional, mystical, and anthropological excesses: *Il trionfo della morte (The Triumph of Death*). Less pretentious than d'Annunzio's earlier novels, *The Triumph of Death* is particularly rewarding in terms of its vivid sense of the primitive, hard existence in the Abruzzi region. Sections of the book, particularly those depicting the extreme poverty, superstitions, and abysmal number of illnesses afflicting the peasantry, surely rank among d'Annunzio's best pages. Once again the book's central theme is the love of Giorgio Aurispa for a married woman, Ippolita Sanzio, whose human flaw is her inability to conceive a child. Theirs is a highly sensual love, always striving to achieve a perfection possible only when Ippolita completely surrenders herself—her body and mind—to her lover. Her mission becomes that of catering to and satisfying the libido of her mate to the point that she changes into a kind of lustful animal, while Giorgio's own sensuality becomes intellectualized through his monologues and broodings. Unlike Andrea Sperelli's passion, which is mundane and refined, Giorgio's is savage and destructive. When he realizes that Ippolita's lust can no longer be satisfied, he concludes that he is no more a free man, freedom being equated to sexual superiority. He sees himself doomed to becoming slave to the woman he had sought to master, and realizes that such threat must ultimately be stopped by violence. One day, as he tries to push Ippolita down a precipice, he becomes locked in a brutish embrace. The couple plunge down to death and to a final liberation from an un-bearable existence.

Despite its dramatic moments and its occasional suspense, the novel is not an exciting, profound work, nor does it contribute much to a clarification and elaboration of its author's vision of the world. On the other hand, the novel shows an effort to move away from the standard treatment of a story. As reflected in their individual titles, the six parts of the work serve a dual purpose: to carry out the plot to its inevitable denouement and to give us some insights into the circumstances that went into the making of the character of the hero, for example, chapter two, "La casa paterna." The broader strategy of d'Annunzio is to develop and bring to fruition the theme of the protagonist's tendency toward murder and suicide, intimated at the beginning of the book.

Such brief synopses as I have given of d'Annunzio's novels give only a notion of the kind of world he depicted time and again in his narratives. A careful reading of his novels bring out what are their essential characteristics. Their beauty and effectiveness is at best sporadic, limited to a few pages, especially when they are descriptive. Only then does the poet's real genius emerge in full evidence: his formidable sensitivity (perhaps unmatched by any poet in Italian letters except Petrarch) of the musicality of words; his capacity to create subtle, if short-lived effects through the use of archaic, refined, or invented words; his occasional ability to suggest the temperament of his characters through the descriptions of their milieu. There is also evidence, however, that d'Annunzio, for all his eagerness to be at once the spectator, the reporter, the painter, *and* the judge of the decadent society of his tales, became himself caught in the web of the world he sought to portray. Even insofar as his expressive instrument is concerned, as Giuseppe Petronio points out in his monographic essay on the poet, "it is impossible to distinguish. . . . nature from fiction, honesty from falsehood, so closely and inextricably are they woven together." Hailed for the elegance of his style, to the modern reader d'Annunzio sounds artificial and precious: and while his stylistic resources and resourcefulness retain some of their magnetism, they are hardly sufficient to maintain our curiosity in his writings. His vision of life is seldom convincing and even more seldom profound: on the contrary, the textual evidence points to the fact that the world d'Annunzio saw and claimed to be true was the product of a fervid imagination and a distorted mind. His plots are farfetched, artificial, and contrived; his characters have little human and psychological depth and are rarely convincing as human beings. A master plagiarist, d'Annunzio borrowed freely from the works of classical antiquity as well as from the works of his own era and earlier periods. Perhaps he may ultimately be recognized as a superb technician of words rather than an "engineer of the soul"—Quasimodo's description of a true poet. He used language as an end in itself rather than an instrument to give form to his view of life. Never a visionary, he lacked the ideals, the artistic discipline, and the sense of purpose of a true artist, and he is thus remembered primarily for the way he wrote rather than *what* he wrote. The crowning irony of d'Annunzio's life is that, despite his exceptional bravery on the battle-field and his unusual sensitivity to the expressive values of art, he left his nation a legacy of words, not symbols; of conceits, not ideas; of images, not ideals. (pp. 39-48)

Sergio Pacifici, "Gabriele d'Annunzio: The Birth of Superman," in his The Modern Italian Novel: From Capuana to Tozzi, *Southern Illinois University Press, 1973, pp. 32-48.*

Diana Festa-McCormick   (essay date 1979)

[*In the following excerpt from her* The City as Catalyst: A Study of Ten Novels, *a study which attempts to "characterize the city as a protagonist in fiction, projecting visions and molding individuals," Festa-McCormick examines the influence of Rome on the thoughts and feelings of the characters in* The Child of Pleasure.]

D'Annunzio was born in the Adriatic town of Pescara, and he must have looked at the capital of his country with the eye of a provincial, both critical of and fascinated with the glitter of that large and cosmopolitan center. He is not well known to the American reader, for his gifts reside in the evocative and mostly untranslatable lyrical quality of his writing. He was above all a poet, but he also wrote dramas of merit (**Francesca da Rimini, Iorio's Daughter**) and was a much-acclaimed novelist. His better known novels include, aside from **The Child of Pleasure, The Intruder, The Triumph of Death,** and **The Virgin of the Rocks.**

D'Annunzio's life was one of daring and romantic intrigue, making him, along with his renown in the field of letters, one of the most notorious Italians of his times. His march over Fiume to reconquer the lost city for his country in 1919, made of him an almost legendary figure, and his turbulent relationship with the celebrated actress Eleonora Duse conferred on him the halo of the irresistible seducer. Loyal to the Fascist movement and passionately patriotic at the same time, he retired in disillusionment over the Rapallo Treaty in 1921, and lived to the end in the town of Gardone on Lake Garda.

D'Annunzio's literary career is varied, both in genre and in stylistic approach, and it is difficult to define him within any specific movement. He is generally labeled a "decadent" both because of the richness of his language and for the fascination that the image of death appeared to hold in his work. His writing seems to aim primarily at rendering, in poetic language, the reality of situations, without much effort at penetrating psychological depths. Both his first and his last novels deal with the irresistible power of the city, Rome in **The Child of Pleasure** and Venice in **The Fire.** Both cities are presented as infused with vague harmonies of mystical and sensuous aspirations. The first of these two works has been selected for analysis because here one finds the additional element of country life away from Rome, through which the role of the city emerges with greater clarity.

The "eternity" of Rome is such an old subject, explored and exploited in so many directions, that it has become something akin to a cliché. What "eternity?" one wonders, aside from the considerable age of the city, which has, all the same, undergone so many changes and is still supposed to be the same! The sameness is of course arguable, even if it eludes definition. Yet the descriptions "eternal Rome" and "eternal city" remain, echoed perpetually by novelists, poets, or travelers. D'Annunzio, himself the product of a provincial upbringing, was fascinated by the capital of his country and, at the age of twenty-five, set about to write a novel in which Rome would be a central force, a kind of mesmerizing siren holding irresistible attraction. The theme is precisely that of the "eternity" of the famous city, weighed against the passing follies and ephemeral struggles of its inhabitants.

Writing from Francavilla-a-Mare on the Adriatic sea, only a few miles away from where he was born and brought up, D'Annunzio presents a vision of Rome that is not merely one of recollection in tranquillity and away, in this case, from the actual bustle of the city. It is a poetic rendition in which romantic inventiveness and traditional—even conventional—views are at play. Sitting by the very sea and pine groves he often celebrated in his poetic works, the author evokes a setting disturbing to the senses and quite different from the one so familiar to him. He recalls another blue, more mysterious and ethereal than that of the limpid waters in front of him, more intense and more remote—not a simple nature with a clear sky and warm sand, but the image of something both primordial and complex like the one he thought he had detected in Rome, where spirit and matter are never separate from one another. What he envisaged was a complexity of elements that would dictate passion and a hedonistic surrender to refined pleasures, a cerebral desire indistinguishable from the most pervasive sensuality. *Il piacere,* as his work was called, connotes far greater sensuality in Italian than the English word *pleasure* suggests, a combination, perhaps, of *delight, enjoyment,* and *gratification.* Its setting could not be an uncomplicated town like Francavilla, nestled by the sea and in the shadow of a hill; it needed a place that would offer contrasts, alternatives, and admonitions against the vagaries of the senses.

The Rome of **The Child of Pleasure** is more than a spectator and less than a heroine. It is at once an energy that must be dealt with, and an unconcerned witness to the vicissitudes of the characters. Its power is undefinable and corrosive at once, in keeping, that is, with the decadent spirit of the society presented. Yet it would be too easy to absolve the hero of the story of his ultimate failure, of his betrayal of the ideals he had once cherished, and hold the city responsible instead. Rome is a catalyst here, more than it is a force of evil; it is the element of glittering distraction in the lives of those tempted by the monotony of vice. The people in the story are all too prone to look for asylum in the din and variety of city life, so that they can indulge the repetitive emptiness of acts that only have the illusion of variety; they feel secure within the city, protected from the temptation of self-analysis and harsh judgment.

In 1888, when Zola's theories of Naturalism were already reshaping literary views and the understanding of life's conditions, D'Annunzio was not quite certain yet about the direction his work would eventually take. Still imbued with romantic concepts and the traditions of the earlier

part of the century, he could not altogether renounce the appeals of poetry and lyric beauty; yet he could not stay with the illusion that man is a world unto himself, when an important segment of that world was in fact proclaiming that the human condition resided outside man. Unable perhaps to resolve the dilemma between the dictates of Romanticism and those of Naturalism, he combined the two. He thus made his main character's personality dependent upon his environment—the seductive quality of Rome or the peaceful restraint of the countryside—while endowing him at the same time with a dynamism of sensuality that is only inspired and incited by the city, but not altogether given by the city or culled from its presence.

The protagonist of the story is Andrea Spirelli, Count Fieschi D'Ugenta, a poet and, potentially at least, a refined artist. He has, however, a double personality and one that alternates with the changes of the environment. He is, on the one hand, a gifted and sensitive artist; on the other Andrea is a member of the rich Roman aristocracy, one of the many bored and restless elegant people for whom the city is merely the theater for savoring gossip, dances, dinners, and receptions. There they collect "objects d'art" or love intrigues without much appreciation for either. What distinguishes Spirelli from his circle of acquaintances is precisely his artistic sensitivity and the possibility, therefore, of going beyond the emptiness of a mundane society and the attraction of a hedonistic existence. His gifted nature has offered him the chance of defying the laws of heredity and of discerning the spirituality of Rome, rather than surrendering to its sensuous appeal. The choices offered to him are symbolized by the two women in his life: Helen and Mary, representing in turn desire and purity, the voluptuousness of the flesh and the lasting beauty of truth and sentiment. Yet the choice is a missed opportunity, one that can only be contemplated in retrospect when decisions are already irretrievable, for the story is a reliving of events that have taken place at an earlier date and are now beyond recall.

The story opens on a December afternoon in 1887, and it retraces its steps to two years earlier, filling gradually the gap from 1885 until the present. It advances at this point only very slightly in time from that early opening day, and it ends on a note of loss and emptiness. It is not so much the tale of a love as one of the possibility of love and missed opportunity, a love, that is, which is squandered instead, along avenues of insatiable appetites in the shadow of a city that is both tacitly encouraging and strangely aloof.

> The year was dying gracefully. A late sun filled the sky over Rome with a soft, mild, golden light that made the air feel almost spring-like. The streets were full as on a Sunday in May. A stream of carriages passed and repassed rapidly through the Piazza Barberini and the Piazza di Spagna, and from thence a vague and continuous rumble mounted to the Trinitá de' Monti and the Via Sistina and even faintly reached the apartments of the Palazzo Zuccari.

From the very first lines the reader is offered the vision of a city held within the languour of death ("the year was dying") and a renewed energy of life ("golden . . . almost spring-like"). The opening sentence presents the essence of the story through a city resplendent in wintry sun, soft and undulating with crowds and carriages mingling in continuous flow. The noise is only slightly audible, and yet it is a presence in Andrea's room; it blends with the smell of roses, delicate and pervasive. The themes of repetitiveness, perishability, tenderness, mobility, elusiveness, sensuality, and spirituality, which are the components of the entire work, are present in this initial paragraph. They are brought to the fore by the soft feeling in the air, the glorious steps of Trinitá de' Monti, the elegance of Via Sistina, the confused stirring of the crowd, and finally by the roses and the winter, the motifs of rebirth and death.

In his room carefully fitted to recapture the atmosphere of earlier days, Andrea waits for Elena. After two years of absence, this enchanting female who had held him captive to her sensuous beauty is coming to pay him a visit. The days of the past suddenly obliterate the two years' interval and fill the present with longing. The force of the imagination rekindles desire. The old passion, interrupted before it could run its course, stirs in Andrea, and he is filled with a kind of painful craving to hold, to possess, to relive. Everything is in place as in the past, the flames playing acrobatics in the fireplace, the tea table set with china, the big roses, open and inviting, filling the amphorae. Every detail is the same, evoked with care and culled from memory, with visions of nudity by the fire and petals of roses strewn on the rug.

Early in the story roses acquire the strength of a symbol voluptuously pervading the air with their perfume; they are both an ethereal presence and a stirring one inflaming the senses.

> The room began slowly to fill with the scent exhaled from numberless vases of flowers. Full blown roses hung their heavy heads over crystal vases that opened like diamond lilies on a golden stem, similar to those standing behind the Virgin in the *tondo* of Botticelli in the Borghese Gallery.

Flowers here stand as a parallel to the city, both to its mystical aspect ("similar to those standing behind the Virgin") and to the pagan connotations, suggested by the velvety touch and the insidious aroma of the petals. Roses reflect also the perishability of man's love and his ability to discover each time anew the joys of the senses; they have, as love does, only one day of blossoming, soon to fade before they live again. The endless sequence and perennial rebirth of both love and flowers are mirrored in the ageless presence of the city under its immutable sky. Implicit, too, is the theme of death that the very blossoming of a rose suggests. And death is already in the air, as the roses stand with their "heavy heads" reflected in the delicate transparency of the crystal vase that holds them. These roses recall as well other roses and other days, when the rituals of love beheld the naked body of Elena and the scattering of petals on the rug.

> She had a rather cruel habit of pulling all the flowers to pieces and scattering them over the carpet at the end of each of her visits and then stand ready to go, fastening a glove or a bracelet,

and smile in the midst of the devastation she has wrought.

Each love stands alone, briefly poised in the center of an existence as an undefined promise, a hope that soon becomes a fulfillment and hence approaches inevitably its own end. This image of love that repeats itself is echoed by the city; her life also runs in chapters through history, in successive motion, with the Imperial Rome followed by the Gothic, the Renaissance, the Baroque city, up to the present day. Each "new" Rome is unique in itself and simultaneously an echo of its past. The continuity and changeability of the city are reflected here in the motifs of flowers, women, and love, which are all equally perishable and renewable in time.

The present, so carefully built to evoke the past in Andrea Spirelli's room, is a stale imitation of it. When Elena arrives, she is strangely different from the woman he knew two years ago, resembling her only on the surface, but incapable of hiding now a kind of cold detachment; the illusion of warmth in their past intimacies no longer exists. "From Dreamland," reads an inscription on her purse, "a stranger here." Like the story of their love, Elena is both true and unreal, a creation reflected in the reality outside and trapped in the imagination. Her presence now, carefully anticipated as a vision of renewed seduction and expected surrender, acquires the magnetic quality of an unpredictable event and the fascination of mystery. "And in truth, she was even more desirable than in the former days, the plastic enigma of her beauty more obscure and more enthralling." Attitudes rehearsed ahead of time soon become authentic emotions, and the two acts, that of Andrea feigning love, and that of Elena feigning renunciation, are insinuated in the reality of the present and become the determining force in the life of Andrea. His desire, revived by a chance encounter and kept unsatisfied, will destroy, through its obsessive force, the precarious inner balance on which his salvation depends. In the room now pervaded by "an ineffable melancholy" the presence of Rome hangs as an inescapable fatality, deaf to the urgent call of desire and the appeal of the flesh.

> There was no sound but the dull deep inarticulate murmur of the city. Not a carriage passed across the piazza of the Trinitá de' Monti. As the wind came in strong gusts from time to time, she closed the window, catching a glimpse as she did so of the point of the obelisk, black against the starry sky.

The movement and the implied gaiety of two years ago give way to a forlorn image where the city appears suddenly as a desert, windswept and somber; yet there is a sense of vigilance in this Sphinx-like Rome, with its obelisk etched against the stars as a mute presence and a reminder of durability.

Andrea Spirelli is the last heir to a noble name, and he has cultivated the traditional refinement of his forefathers. Endowed with a keen intellect and impeccable taste, he had led a life absorbed by studies, the worship of beauty, and a penchant for sensuous pleasure, before meeting Helen. For a man ready for the experience of passion, the encounter seemed almost predictable; desire erupts and triumphs, while love is limited by a casual *"habere, non haberi"* ["to have, but not to be had"]. It is summertime, and Andrea waits. There is suspense in the air, as Rome waits too.

> It was a St. Martin's summer, a "Springtime of the Dead," calmly sad and sweet, in which Rome lay all golden, like a city of the Far East, under a milk-white sky, diaphanous as the firmament reflected in Southern seas.

The milky quality of the sky suggests a woman languidly dreaming and sensuously displaying her graces. She can be held in voluptuous surrender or cherished and contemplated as a "diaphanous" presence. The vision recedes in the background as Elena sighs "mi piaci, mi piaci," ("I like you, I like you"). It later echoes Andrea's exultation, as he leaves the hothouse atmosphere of his mistress's house.

> Thus began for them a bliss that was full, frenzied, for ever changing and for ever new; a passion that wrapped them round and rendered them oblivious of all that did not minister immediately to their mutual delight.

The sensuous correspondence of the two lovers explores all avenues of rapture: in the shade of Santa Maria in Cosmedin; at Villa Albani, Villa Medici, or Villa Ludovisi; by the statues in the Museo Borghese; or up the steps of Trinitá de' Monti. Each stone or step or road is an accomplice and a memory of their bliss, and the city echoes Goethe's cry, *"Lass dich, Geliebte, nicht reu'n, dass du mir so schnell dich ergeben!"* ("Have no regrets, my beloved, that thou didst yield thee so soon"). This could have been a beautiful parenthesis preceding a more complete and spiritual involvement. It could have led to new heights and the aspiration of sentiment. It was instead at the onset a culmination already, something that could only deteriorate with time. Because the reader looks at the events in retrospect and that day of summer wait is now but a memory in the wintry sun, one can only lament the spent youth, the fading of a dream, the decay, the emptiness ushered in by a brief period of orgy and pleasure.

Weeks and then months go by. Elena leaves, mysteriously, after a last meeting. Her carriage disappears by the Quattro Fontane, and the sentimental exaltation experienced only a few moments earlier "under the influence of a tumultuous sunset" fades with the noise of the wheels. Uneasily, the adventure is concluded, without explanation but without any sense of suspension either. It has—or it should have—run its course in the appeasement of the senses and the joys of the moment. Two or three months later a brief notice in the paper announces Elena's marriage to Lord Heathfield. Two years go by before the two lovers meet again, and only now, two years later, Andrea is for the first time shaken by a touch of jealousy. The name Heathfield assumes in his mind the shape of hands and lips that can hold and caress this woman who slips away from his arms. But jealousy or even sorrow, no less than boredom, are the province of the intellect with Andrea. Incapable of surrendering to spontaneity, mesmerized by the sensuous force of the city, he reduces all joys and pain alike to a manipulation of the imagination. Dictated through an assumed pose or a feigned interest, his

emotions are in a way seized by the intellect and given a new life. Love thus becomes a contrivance like a mechanical toy, which must run its course once it has been put into motion; to stop it at any point before it reaches its natural end is to put into motion yet another device that clings to the imagination and directs its course. A new "toy" is born, a dangerous one at times, with wheels turning in rusty fashion and wearing out the very fabric that gives them life.

With the fading of the nineteenth century, the concept that love might be a fatality decreed somewhere in the stratosphere of the soul became less valid. D'Annunzio, with Gide, Proust, and others, became intrigued instead with the role that the imagination plays in the life of all sentiment. They seemed to agree in the assumption that a reality created by the mind is endowed with strength comparable to that of matter and all other verifiable truths. Love, with all its exuberance, its tenderness or passionate feelings, can thus be inspired by a place or a mood in the air. The object of love in such a case, be it a pensive delicate face or the alluring movement of a figure in the sunshine, becomes subordinate to the initial force that had inspired love. D'Annunzio thus made Andrea Spirelli's yearnings and Elena's appeal dependent upon the presence of Rome, so that the very composition of his lust and pleasure, of his obsessive desire, and, eventually, of his crushing emptiness is that of the city's sky, roads, and buildings, its streets and its mysterious voice.

The richness of the Roman sky and the intensity of colors in the city have hidden from Andrea's sight the presence of more ethereal beauties and the sense of the divine that often hovers in the air.

> Rome was his passion—not the Rome of the Caesars, but the Rome of the Popes—not the Rome of the triumphal Arches, the Forums, the Baths, but the Rome of the Villas, the Fountains, the Churches. He would have given all the Colosseums in the world for the Villa Medici, the Campo Vaccino for the Piazza di Spagna, the Arch of the Titus for the Fountain of the Tortoises.

Not in the glory of its past but in the dizzying richness of its present does Andrea cherish the nearness of Rome; not in the spatial symmetry of its arches and its forums but in the intricate composition of the Tortoises' fountain and the shaded villas does he find an echo of his desires. The sounds of bells from the many churches touch his senses before they can ever provoke flights of the spirit. They disguise sensuous pleasures within a mystical mantle:

> These fallacious ideas of purity and loftiness of sentiment were but the reaction after more carnal delights, when the soul experiences a vague yearning for the ideal.

The sacred and the profane, the temporal and the eternal, become indistinguishable one from the other, and raptures of the flesh are imbued with something resembling a mystical experience. Back in Rome after an absence of travels and studies, Andrea has surrendered to the warm breath of the city, and he allows his drunken senses to distort his vision and the ideal he had contemplated in solitude.

After Elena's initial departure there is a kind of lull. Other adventures—vague interests, horse races, and flirtations—fill the time for a few intervening months. Eventually, an incident resulting from a duel provoked by a jealous lover suddenly menaces to change the game of love into one of death. Having casually bartered his life for a passing fancy, Andrea is wounded, and he leaves Rome for a rest in the country. The setting is here one comparable to D'Annunzio's own provincial past. In Schifanoia, away from the enticing forces of the city, and in contemplation instead of the sea and trees swaying in the wind, he regains not only physical health but a new spiritual stability. His convalescence is transformed into a period of reappraisal that could lead—or could have led—to a rebirth and a closer relation with his old ideals of beauty and life. Andrea's nostalgic reaching out for the values he had once held sacred is as genuine as the fever that had pushed him earlier in the pursuit of Elena. Yet this dual nature in him does not exist simultaneously but only in keeping with the elements of place and atmosphere in which he finds himself. Where the Rome of monuments and obelisks attesting to the vagaries of man's passions had prevented a continuity of feelings in Andrea and the search for a spiritual balance to the joys of the flesh, Schifanoia operates in reverse manner. Here, the pristine nature, the vastness of the distant sea, and the gardens laid out with care seem to point to a greater and more harmonious order than the one created by man. Here, his old passionate urges seem distant, and Andrea begins to cherish more lasting values. A new strength pervades him—a new goodness and different hopes.

There are three stages in the development of the novel, each corresponding to Andrea's initial stay in Rome, departure to the country, and final return to the city. The first comprises the meeting with Elena, the blossoming of their passionate relation followed by disorder after her departure, and ending with the foolishness of the duel. The second, in Schifanoia, witnesses fresh poetical aspirations and the birth of a new love, one that is tender, generous, and spiritual. Maria appears in Andrea's life and their relation seems enhanced by their renunciation of physical surrender in favor of a purity more in keeping with an image of duration. But back in Rome, all hope of redemption is abandoned in favor of a sensuality that soon becomes dissolution. The ensnaring quality of the city will have triumphed once again and crushed all expectations of virtue and harmony.

During the time spent in Schifanoia, Rome is hardly a memory. Paradoxically, however, its presence is felt by the reader through the intentional denial of its presence and the contrast that inevitably arises out of an invidious comparison between the serenity of the present and the turmoil of the past. Instead of the inscrutable Roman sky, the blue of the sea stretches to heaven so "that the two elements seemed as one, impalpable and supernatural"; not the stones of antiquity laden with man's passions, but "the wide amphitheatre of hills" gathers in the distance to meet the contemplative eye. "Where were now all his vanities and his cruelties, his schemes and his duplicities?" Andrea asks himself in the new peace that descends magically upon him. His very breathing becomes attuned to the

rhythm of the sea and the wind, while memories of youth and purity lull him to ineffable tranquillity. This new pantheistic relation with existence points to the sacred force of nature as opposed to the ephemeral qualities of the city. Man's vision of the eternal is now given life and substance by the vastness of the sea, while before, crowds of people and buildings only obscured Andrea's vision and led him to disarray.

Just as the expectation of love in Rome had soon been rewarded with the meeting of Elena, Andrea, now transformed in a "vas spirituale," is inspired in Schifanoia by the gentle beauty of Maria. The two women, with their symbolic names representing, in turn, seduction and purity, are themselves to be seen as expressions of outside forces—the corrupting power of the city and the assuaging elements of nature. Maria is the tender mother of a little girl and the chaste spouse of a coarse man; she is suffused with melancholy and spirituality. Her personality—the feeling of love gradually blossoming in her soul, her struggle with the temptation of surrendering to the man who has whispered such gentle words in her ear, her supreme vow of renunciation—comes movingly alive through her journal. She leaves, finally, having triumphed over the fascination of love, finding solace in her child and in the oppression of virtue. Her triumph and her spirituality are also the triumph of a land where the sun and the wind still hold a promise of heaven.

This second adventure is also concluded uneasily. If this were the end of the idyllic love, one might see a comforting element in the incorruptibility of a gentle soul, and the triumph of virtue in the face of the greatest temptation. One should perhaps wish it to be so, and thus retain the illusion that every man, even one who had come so close to being contaminated by vice, could nurture sentiment and a poetic image of life. But the role of Maria is not over; it must yet show the vulnerability of the purest of beings when exposed to the forces of the city. In the languid air of Rome, Maria's strength will be diminished; she will surrender, vanquished, another victim of the triumphant city.

The brief summer months at Schifanoia are an interlude, a parenthesis during which dreams, desires, and aspirations coincide and contribute to a depth of understanding and a measure of maturity in the hero. But the real story takes place in Rome, and there Andrea soon becomes engrossed in more frivolous pursuits and the fever of sensuality. It is the month of October when he returns to his Palazzo Zuccari overlooking Trinitá de' Monti. There is in him an immediate stirring, "a lively reawakening of his old love for Rome," which recalls his old love for Elena and the desire to hold and to forget oneself within the joys of the senses. Deceptively, both Rome and Elena offer an image of languid surrender, of enticing promises and the gift of happiness. The room where Andrea retires as if in hesitation before abandoning himself to the charms of the city lulls him to a kind of torpor. Culled by the mixture of profane and sacred images around him—the bed, which is a high baldaquin, altarlike, the faded red and gold of the church drapes and the Latin inscriptions, the sacrificial pictures of grapes and wheat—both Elena and Maria appear in his dream, the features of one overlapping the

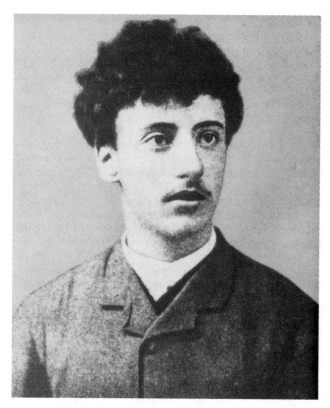

D'Annunzio at age eighteen.

other, blending and separating, confused at the end and indistinguishable from each other. As he awakens, the room becomes flooded by the golden luminosity of the Roman sun, suggesting the same diffused and enticing aura of the images in his dream.

> Rome appeared, all pearly gray, spread out before him, its lines a little blurred like a faded picture, under a Claude Lorrain sky, sprinkled with ethereal clouds, their noble grouping lending to the clear spaces between an indescribable delicacy, as flowers lend a new grace to the verdure which surrounds them. On the distant heights the gray deepened gradually to amethyst. Long trailing vapours slid through the cypresses of the Monte Mario like waving locks through a comb of bronze. Close by, the pines of Monte Pincio spread their sun-gilded canopies. Below, on the Piazza, the obelisk of Pius VI looked like a pillar of agate. Under this rich autumnal light everything took on a sumptuous air. Divine Rome!

Framed by the window, Rome appears as a painting in which artistic rendition has created a reality more engrossing than truth. The city presents an image that is at once its own reflection and that of an imitation of the self, immediate and tangible yet out of reach and removed. The "clear spaces" alternate with "blurred" pictures, the "trailing vapors" from the rain contrast with the starkness of the cypresses, while the closer view of the pines is shrouded in "sun-gilded canopies" and the obelisk on the square directly below acquires the transparency of agate. But after Andrea's eyes have roamed the spaces of distant

hills and the clusters of green, after they have taken in all the golden liquidity of the air and the sky, they finally rest on the pavement crossed by carriages and the movement of people. The regions of the spirit readily surrender to the appeal of the immediate, and Andrea's contemplative mood progressively shifts to the languid and the lascivious. Maria's purity is desecrated in his imagination, and he delights in falsifying the sentiment of love with the "refinements of sensuality." He catches one last glimpse of the sky before he surrenders completely to the spell of the street.

Life soon resumes its old mundane rhythm, full of masked balls alternating with dinners and concerts; but the intervening time between Andrea's first stay in the city and his return has created a psychological awareness that is itself only an imitation of the old one. The sense of wait and mystery that had conferred a certain youthful vigor to the earlier days is now missing. There are no longer any expectations or the illusion that a purifying presence might suddenly appear to arrest the decline of the spirit. There are hardly any hopes, in fact, outside the need for distraction and the urge for immersion into the social vortex. Gradually the opiate becomes a way of life, and only very rarely are vague memories of a distant past evoked by a starry night or the clear sight of pines against the sky. The story moves inexorably toward its unavoidable conclusion, as the link is made with the initial events at the beginning of the novel. The events introduced with the meeting with Elena in the room full of roses have retraced all the steps of the preceding two years and have come full circle back to that initial meeting. The presence of Elena is now disturbing to the senses yet devoid of the old passion so resembling love. What had been staged to imitate the old fervor in a traditional act of seduction, becomes, through Elena's capricious refusal, a consuming fever. Elena's decision, itself a calculated imitation of purity and friendship, becomes an irritant and a stimulus to Andrea's senses. When he meets Maria again, he is in the grip of the frustration and desire that Elena's return had kindled.

The character of Andrea is the only one in the novel that assumes substance and credibility. All the others—the passing image of his cousin silently in love with him or the various people in the numerous salons, and even the two ladies who play a major role in his life—are but dimensions of his own vision, answers to a need or the complement to an aspiration of the moment. It is Andrea's world that comes alive through the pages of the novel, as it is the rise and fall of his hopes and his ambitions that the reader witnesses, in the constant presence of a city that is both an uncaring observer and a molding force. Andrea is a typical end-of-the-century hero, Baudelairian, Gidean, or Nietzschean in turn, in his vague longings and assumed postures. He is bent upon the conquest of his nature, reshaping and redirecting his life, removing from it all that is instinctual and spontaneous, and placing in its stead culture, refinement, and artistry. But when these efforts are applied to sentiment and love, the results are not always happy. Pleasure ("Il Piacere," of which the title speaks) becomes an intellectual contrivance, a cerebral stimulus that must take firm possession of the mind before it can reach the nether regions of sensuality. Emotions themselves are summoned by fantasy and its power of inventiveness; only images that have been entertained by the imagination are capable of arousing feelings. Love as such, or what one generally means by it—a strong attraction, a longing, or a natural communion—becomes totally subservient to the same cerebral stimuli that direct lust. Andrea's inability to distinguish between sentiment and desire, his search for an impossible appeasement are the dominating themes in the third and final part of the story. It is here too that the presence of the city is most keenly felt, that Rome becomes a cooercive element of vice not only for those who, like Andrea, offer little resistance, but also for Maria, who had until now found the strength to resist. Never an innocent bystander, the city now appears as a force and a mirage, and as a hot breath that turns man's attention away from the ethereal beauty of the sky in order to bend it toward the pavement. The possibility of redemption suggested by the sound of bells echoing through the air and the purity of lines of the columns and arches is but a mirage, the chimerical blending of Elena's sensuality and Maria's chastity; the two faces, superimposed one upon the other, become contaminated and inseparable.

The fact that Elena had disappeared from Andrea's horizons before the adventure could pale of its own accord has left the note of suspension or of incompleteness that exacts a price and demands a conclusion. It is to be noted here that never has there been the slightest suggestion to crown this relationship with the vows of marriage when Elena was still a widow and thus perfectly eligible. Marriage and the traditional bourgeois concept of family never enter the picture here unless it be to show, indirectly at least, that legally sanctioned unions have hardly any bearing upon love, desire, or sentiment. Elena's sudden departure for England and the eventual notice of marriage in the newspaper are never even suspected to imply any sort of attraction for her new husband. She was pressed with financial problems, and marriage was simply a way of solving them. Andrea himself is the typical city dandy for whom marriage, usually at a late date, is reluctantly accepted in quest of wealth, purity, or both. One might speculate that Maria, had she been free, might more readily have inspired a wish for continuity in Andrea than any amount of availability in Elena, while it is this latter, or women in her image, who alone could persistently have stimulated desire.

Elena's visit to Andrea after two years of unexplained silence can only be seen as an act of provocation in keeping with the suggestive mellowness of the Roman air. One wonders otherwise why she would have troubled to come, with her act of renunciation and pretended piety, if not to play her role to the end according to the unwritten laws of love games. She might have simply refused to accept Andrea's invitation when she accidentally ran into him, but that might have aroused a kind of disdain, through which she would soon be shrugged off. More prone to keep intact her image of the irresistible siren, she chooses to affect languor and painful renunciation, submission to a mysterious fatality, while retaining the upper hand and a measure of domination in Andrea's life. "Could you suffer to share me with another?" she cries dramatically when her old lover comes near her. The answer should be: yes, of course, why not? But there is a strict if unwritten code that does not allow for truth to triumph here; it must first be molded by fiction and be given life through the imagination. Only in solitude can Andrea recognize the abyss that separates lust from love; but in the duplicity of his own words and thoughts resides the strongest element of corruption:

> So it was true—she had never really loved him. She had not scrupled to break with him in order to contract a marriage of convenience. And now she put on the airs of a martyr before him, wrapped herself round with a mantle of conjugal inviolability! A bitter laugh rose to his lips, and then a rush of sullen blind rage against the woman came over him. The memory of his passion went for nothing—all the past was one long fraud, one stupendous, hideous lie; and this man, who throughout his whole life had made a practice of dissimulation and duplicity, was now incensed at the deception of another.

Once Andrea recognizes that there are no truths or principles that can act as bulwark against his desire, he knows as well that all ideals have been renounced. "Impurity crept through his blood like a corroding poison," and consciously, almost calculatedly, he surrenders to the appeal of lust, foregoing all possibility of redemption. After one last effort to cling to a remnant of goodness in him ("suddenly the beauty of the night filled him with a vague but desperate yearning towards some unkown good"), he obstinately turns away from the temptation of purity, "he bent his head and entered the house without turning again to look at the night." Symbolically, he leaves behind, with the balmy light of the stars, the image of Maria and all that she represents.

The sublimation of desire and her renunciation had been difficult for Maria, but not altogether devoid of beauty. It had been the price exacted by a temptation born in a languorous summer by the sea, but a compensation, too, for a sentiment that transcended greed. When she comes to Rome, the reader is prepared already for Maria's surrender. The city has brought about by now the capitulation of Andrea's aspirations; how could the innocent woman resist or even detect the falsity of the situation! Maria does not have the strength to take flight once again before the attraction of love, and yet she is not unaware; she knows that only pain awaits her, and her surrender is a sacrificial act, one of self-immolation. "I cannot describe to you," she tells Andrea, "the strange foreboding that has weighed upon me for a long time past." When she is ready to promise that they would meet again soon, there is a din and an outcry in the air, as if the city itself could not watch unmoved its own victory.

> She rose abruptly, trembling from head to foot, giddy, paler still than on the morning when they walked together beneath the flower-laden trees. The wind still shook the panes; there was a dull clamour in the distance as of a riotous crowd. The shrill cries borne on the wind from the Quirinal increased her agitation.

It is the city of Rome that clamors with the wind from its

highest hill, for if it exacts evil, this Rome of D'Annunzio is not altogether evil. It is simply a city too complex and enigmatic to offer peace to those who are uncertain and perturbed, who lack strength and resiliency in the face of temptation.

The episodes that follow lead toward the unavoidable conclusion. Maria loves, but more in reminiscence of her idyll in Schifanoia than through the allurement of the present; yet it is the present that has undermined the strength she once had. Andrea takes her and whispers words of love in her ear, while he mentally superimposes the image of Elena on the madonnalike face he beholds. Maria must finally leave and join her husband in South America; in anguish and an oppressive sense of guilt, she prepares to leave the man she loves. Their last walk together is to the Protestant cemetery outside the walls where the poet Shelley is buried; "And forget me, for I can never be thine"—the verses come sadly to memory. Maria unwraps the black veil from her hat and ties with it the white roses she has brought for the poet.

> "How did you manage to get those roses?" he asked. She smiled, but her eyes were wet. "They are yours—those of that snowy night—they have bloomed again this evening. Do you not believe it?" The evening breeze was rising, and behind the hill the sky was overspread with gold, in the midst of which the purple cloud dissolved, as if consumed by fire. Against this field of light, the serried ranks of the cypresses looked more imposing and mysterious than before.

On "that snowy night," exasperated from a long and fruitless wait for Elena, Andrea had thrown a bunch of roses in front of Maria's door. She had spiritually retrieved them and nestled them in her heart, while the snowplow had mechanically buried them in any icy tomb. Could the roses of this last and mournful day be the same? In the allegorical meaning of the story, yes, they are the very same ones, nurtured by faith and love after being cast into the snow, and relinquished finally on a cold stone. They remain, on the tomb of the poet who had loved and died, the symbol of love and death, pervaded by the same golden light that had shined, at the beginning, upon rose petals strewn on the rug. More striking now, the theme of death is repeated in the dark cypresses, which are as ageless and imposing as the city in the distance and the chime of bells echoing from the Aventine.

The last scene is merely a reinforcement of what has already been suggested and developed. Maria abandons herself into Andrea's arms, mistaking the set expression upon his face for a pain similar to the one she suffers; but he is only consumed by jealousy and craving for Elena, and, in a last cruel irony, he murmurs her name.

> All at once, she struggled free of his embrace, her whole form convulsed with horror, her face ghastly and distraught as if she had at that moment torn herself from the arms of death.

The arms of death that, under the disguise of love, have wrecked her peace, now also claim her memories and the last shreds of illusion. Nothing will be left if not squalor, the sense of having surrendered all into an immensurable

void. After she will have left on the following day, her furniture is auctioned away, disposable as her feelings had been. Andrea walks in mechanically and buys a Buddha, the inscrutable God who seems to smile. The story closes as he finds himself following the porters up the stairs, an empty man behind meaningless objects, while "Rome, immense and dominated by a battle of clouds, seemed to illumine the sky."

This last image of the city that has borrowed the glow from the sky, shows a Rome that is triumphant and distant, perpetuating itself through the pages of history, watching generations of men, but remaining invulnerable, unheeding of their suffering and fleeting passions. D'Annunzio's Rome coincides, finally, with the image of the Buddha in the last pages—God-like, tangible, and remote at once, earthy and spiritual, seemingly fragile but immensely durable. (pp. 49-68)

> *Diana Festa-McCormick, "D'Annunzio's 'Child of Pleasure': A City's Power of Seduction," in her* The City as Catalyst: A Study of Ten Novels, *Fairleigh Dickinson University Press, 1979, pp. 49-68.*

Nicolas J. Perella   (essay date 1979)

[*In the following excerpt from his study* Midday in Italian Literature: Variations on an Archetypal Theme, *Perella discusses the various manifestations of the midday sun in D'Annunzio's works.*]

Few poets have paid tribute to the sun with a fervor, even frenzy, that can match that of Gabriele D'Annunzio, and for no one more than for him has midday been the hour par excellence of the secret of life. From the time of his precocious collection of verse, *Primo vere,* he presented himself as a passionate devotee of Helios, hymning at noon the glory of existence and, in keeping with the archetypal pattern, modulating his lyre to sweetly elegiac music at sunset:

> —O Sole, pronubo fulvo, di gioia datore,
> Sacro a gli aedi, a' pampini
>
> Caro, m'odi: se mai canzoni di gloria a' meriggi
> Ti dissi, e a' vespri placidi
> Meste elegie suavi, deh l'ala de 'l tempo fuggente
> Tu indugia . . .
>
> (—O Sun, tawny paranymph, donor of joy,
> Sacred to poets, dear to the vine,
>
> Hear me: if ever songs of glory at midday
> I sang to you, and in the calm evenings
> Sweet sorrowful elegies, ah, hold back the wing
> Of fleeing time . . .)

At the height of his fame (in the 1903 volume *Alcyone*) he declared his aggressive love of glory in terms of an allegorical representation in which glory is acclaimed as the vulture of the sun and himself the prey cruelly yet sweetly seized. As he is carried aloft he raises his face to the sun and, looking through the red membranes of his closed eyelids with a pain that is mixed with joy, he sees the world radiant with his blood. It is one of several occasions in which the poet suggests a kinship between himself (his "blood") and the sun (glory) and declares his identity as a solar poet:

> O Gloria, o Gloria, vulture del Sole,
> Che su me ti precipiti e m'artigli
> Sin nel focace lito ove m'ascondo!
>
> Levo la faccia, mentre il cor mi duole,
> E pel rossore de' miei chiusi cigli
> Veggo del sangue mio splendere il mondo.
>
> (Oh Glory, oh Glory, vulture of the Sun,
> You who swoop down upon me and claw me
> Even in the burning shore where I hide!
>
> I raise my face, while my heart is in pain,
> And through the redness of my closed eyelids
> I see the world radiate with my blood.)

Yet the earliest of D'Annunzio's poems using the midday motif suggest not triumph and glory so much as the sense of oppression and aridity, and a vision of a humanity vanquished or threatened with destruction. The representation of this theme is given, interestingly enough, in terms that reflect the veristic tendencies in Italian literature of the time. Thus the poem **"Pellegrinaggio"** (**"Pilgrimage,"** 1880) is very much like a veristic genre picture of a rural landscape in which a procession of mountain and country folk moves along a seemingly endless road, through fields of burnt stubble that lie beneath a pitiless midday sun fixed in a cloudless, birdless sky: "Sta il meriggio fiammante su l'aride stoppie . . . il sole da cieli deserti le fiamme saetta" ("Flaming midday hangs over the parched stubble . . . from empty skies the sun darts its flames,"). In this vein, the poem **"Solleone"** (**"Days of the Dog Star,"** 1880) is worth our attention for a number of reasons. It begins with the evocation of a vast silence of a midsummer noontide in which the sun, again from a cloudless blue sky, relentlessly pours its heat and light upon a parched land of endless fields. The creatures of the earth—a waggoner, his horse and dog—are weary and near collapse. Once more cicadas figure as a negative element in the description, their song being referred to as an irritant—"canta la cicala / La canzone de l'uggia" ("The cicada sings / Its monotonous song"). Curiously, however, in a long digression the poet apostrophizes them as symbols of the endless and joyous energy of nature, and as such they are contrasted with the lot of suffering humanity: "Niuna cura te persegue; a gli uomini / Le vane lotte ed il dolore" ("No care pursues you. Unto men / Vain struggle and grief "). The digression is followed by a brief return to the veristic description. Preceded by a calf and followed by a panting child, a passing peasant woman looks at the poet. This feature not only allows for the introduction of the poet into the scene, but, even as it does so, focuses our attention on him. And indeed it is precisely the figure of the poet himself that is of the greatest import here. For the poem closes with a view of him on the scene as a solitary figure emblematic of man overmastered by a hostile and drought-stricken world that offers no refuge (no shade) and no relief (no water). Before him, through the burnt fields, the white road stretches endlessly with no apparent destination:

> . . . . Ho sete:
> Il sole mi brucia orribilmente il volto.

> Non un ruscello mormorante intorno,
> Non un albero ombroso, nulla! Via
> Dritta si slancia la candida strada
> Fra le siepi riarse; sopra il capo
> Il vasto azzurro senza ombra di nube;
> A 'l guardo campi, campi, campi ancora.
>
> (. . . . . I am thirsty:
> The sun burns my face horribly.
> Not a murmuring stream around me,
> Not a shady tree, nothing! Far
> And straight the white road stretches
> Through the parched hedges; above my head
> The vast blue without the sign of a cloud;
> Before my gaze fields, fields, and still more
>   fields.)

We must be careful not to read too much into these verses, to see in them, for example, an existentialist sense of man's isolation (or lostness) or an Eliot-like picture of modern civilization as a spiritual wasteland. And yet, although the switch from the veristic depiction of the humble folk to the poet himself suggests that the humanitarian or social-minded impulse is simply a pretext for a literary exercise, it would be wrong to deny that the poem's closing lines in some way anticipate the modern use of the midday motif to emblematize the negativity of existence. For that matter, how frequent in veristic literature itself is the portrayal of a vast scorched landscape (where *stoppie riarse* ["parched stubble"] abound) and a mute suffering humanity under the fierce meridian sun of midsummer! The transposition of the motif from a realistic and humanitarian key to a psychological and existentialist one should hardly surprise us. (pp. 114-17)

[D'Annunzio's] poems of the immediately succeeding period in the volume *Canto novo* (1882) continue to show a fascination with the hostile Gorgon face of the midday sun, still painted to a degree in semiveristic terms, but not without features that anticipate the vision of, say, a Montale. Thus in the midst of an "immense burning" and an "immobile, virulent splendor," it is again the exhausted poet himself that we see in search of a shady refuge:

> Io cerco a bocca aperta, avidamente,
> Un po' di rezzo qui sotto le rame:
> Dinnanzi, l'Adriatico silente
> Ha barbagli terribili di lame.
>
> (With mouth agape I look, avidly,
> For a bit of shade here under the boughs:
> Before me, the silent Adriatic
> Has terrible flashes of blades.)

(p. 117)

But in [*Primo vere*], the poem **"Lucertole"** (**"Lizards"**) already reveals a relationship between the poet and midday that seems more authentically Dannunzian in character by virtue of its classically pagan inspiration and its erotic, sensualistic orientation. The poem evokes a midday scene in which the poet in faunlike fashion is about to complete his seduction of a nymph only to have her suddenly flee . . . in fright at the sound of a rustling in the bushes. The poet turns to see a number of lizards issue forth and then scamper away. In the volume *Canto novo* this midday eroticism acquires a richer context and a deeper significance, particularly in section VII of the poem **"Canto del**

Sole" ("Song of the Sun"). Again taking his cue from classical precedents (cf. Mallarmé's "Après-midi d'un faune"), the poet as faun prepares to ambush a nymph:

> Sta il gran meriggio su questa di flutti e di piante
> Verde-azzurrina conca solitaria;
> Ed io, come il fauno antico in agguato, m'ascondo,
> Platano sacro, qui fra le chiome tue.
> Quando vedrò la ninfa con pavido passo venire,
> Chiusa ne' suoi capelli l'agile corpo ignudo?

> (Great midday hovers over this solitary blue green basin of sea and forests;
> And I, like an ancient faun in ambush, conceal myself, oh sacred plane tree, midst your foliage.
> When will I see the nymph approaching with fearful step and her lithesome nude body enclosed within her hair.)

Beneath the rain of the golden light that pours down from the midday sun through the forest leaves and upon his head, the trembling expectation of the poet-faun is experienced as a Panic surge aiming at the possession of all of nature in a god-like sexual embrace with the nymph.

The same desire to merge sensually with nature, a merging to be experienced vicariously by sexual union in a noonscape setting, is the theme of section XII of **"Canto dell'ospite"** ("Song of the Guest"). But rather than being simply propitious, midday here figures as a demanding, even cruel, absolute lord that holds all of nature enthralled. Accordingly, the classical and Arcadian motif of the noontide retreat to a *locus amoenus* ["pleasant place"] is important to the poem which begins precisely on this note of finding relief from an apparently hostile force:

> Dolce godere e l'ombra e l'aura
> Sotto i ciliegi!—Lungi sta l'arido

> Giallore dei liti, e il fiammante
> Al sol di giugno tremulo mare.

> Lungi ed intorno le solitudini
> Regna il Meriggio, atroce despota,
> Mentre errano per gli orizzonti
> Cupe caligini di viola.

> Dolce godere e l'ombra e l'aura
> Sotto i ciliegi!

> (How sweet to enjoy the shade and the breeze
> Beneath the cherry trees!—Far from me is the arid
> Yellowness of the shores, and the tremulous sea
> Aflame in the sun of June.

> Afar and all around the solitude
> Midday reigns, cruel despot,
> While along the horizon wander
> Dark mists of purple.

> How sweet to enjoy shade and breeze
> Beneath the cherry trees!)

Here too, the midday sun finds its way through branches and leaves, now playfully arousing the lovers, now "wounding" them, until, in a paroxysm of sensual joy, the *locus amoenus* is expanded by desire to include all of na-

ture in its full sublimity as the setting for the enactment of the act of love:

> In alto! In alto! I cieli attingere
> Io voglio teco, aver per talamo
> La nube profonda.

> . . . Oh delizia
> Suprema! Il mare, il sole, gli alberi,
> I frutti, una chioma, l'amore,
> La giovinezza, fiamma del mondo.

> (On high! On high! To reach the heavens
> With you is my desire, to have for bridal bed
> A dense cloud.

> . . . Oh pleasure
> Supreme! Sea, sun, trees,
> Fruit, locks of hair, love,
> Youth, flame of the world.)

As though by the silent command of the midday despot (the sun at the zenith), the poet is, paradoxically, driven to the inebriating joy of Panic immersion.

This same motif appears in a slightly different guise in one of D'Annunzio's earliest prose works, the novella **"Fra' Lucerta"** ("Brother Lucerta") from the volume *Terra vergine* (1882). In the burning hours of noontide the protagonist, a monk, has the habit of seeking a sensually mystic union with nature by lying facedown upon the earth and appearing almost as part of the ground in a posture that suggests a coital embrace. While in this state, he feels himself to be a particle in the womb of immense nature. A tingling and quivering sensation is communicated to him by the earth, and he has the sensation that his blood, though flowing into infinity rather than to his heart, is yet constantly replenished as though by the fount of a god of Hellas. It is a midday delirium—"ubriacature del sole," as the author says.

The midday sun's exacting lordship is the underlying theme of yet another early poem. In fact the sonnet **"Panico"** (from the collection *Intermezzo*) is the most interesting and most promising of D'Annunzio's early poems on the midday motif insofar as it seeks to communicate a sense of Panic awe and terror in the description of a noontide calm that yet pulsates with life:

> A questo di salute alito enorme
> Che dal sen de la terra umida emana
> Mentre amata da 'l sol la terra dorme
> Ne la tranquillità meridiana;
> Io ne l'imo de l'essere un informe
> Viluppo sento che si schiude. Strana
> Un'angoscia mi preme. Or quali forme
> Partorirà la stanca pianta umana?
> E l'angoscia m'incalza. E l'infinita
> Vista de i piani, ed il profumo occulto
> Che si eleva da i piani, e lo splendore
> De l'aria, e queste immense onde di vita
> Che su 'l capo mi passano in tumulto,
> Or mi dànno io non so quale terrore.

> (At this huge breath of vigor
> That issues from the bosom of the damp earth,
> While loved by the sun the earth sleeps
> Midst the meridian tranquillity,
> Within the innermost of my being I feel

A formless, tangled knot unfold. A strange
Anguish presses upon me. To what forms now
Will the weary human plant give birth?
And the anguish keeps crowding upon me. And
 the infinite
Vista of the plains, and the hidden scent
That rises from the plains, and the radiance
Of the air, and these immense waves of life
That tumultuously pass over my head
Now cause me a nameless terror.)

The "strange anguish" that oppresses the poet is hardly to be mistaken for a Leopardian sentiment of metaphysical anguish. It refers rather to a new stirring and a call to life, felt by the poet in the very heart of a noontide languor and weariness after a period of excess in sexual luxury. (The poem is the third of fourteen sonnets under the general title of *Animal triste*.) It is as though the poet in the guise of a satiated faun is compelled even against his will to respond to the activation of life that the domineering midday sun as relentless lover demands from the earth and its creatures. But the curious thing here is that the analogy developed in the poem is between the impregnated languid earth (cf. Carducci's "Canto di marzo," "Song of March") as a feminine life-giving principle and the poet-faun. Hence the stirring within the poet is experienced as the urge of an embryo to take on form and issue forth. D'Annunzio is here in the role of generatrix (indeed, of womb) on the level of a purely phenomenal relationship with the sun at the zenith. This is true even if we interpret his experience as the sensation of an impulse to a metamorphosis into one of the many "forms" of nature. In the sonnet's sestet, this impulse gives way to an identification of the poet himself as a sort of human sounding board catching and vibrating with the sensually grounded intimations of a life force coursing through the whole of the landscape in the hour of Pan. But in seeking to convert the "anguish" into a sense of demonic dread, the sestet seems almost to belong to a different inspiration or level of experience until we realize that it is still the poet as generatrix who has been visited by the midday god Pan himself.

That the revelation of the midday god could have an ambiguous value and even prove a negatively perceived experience (at least for the weak) was a fact well known to D'Annunzio. The most fascinating example of such an encounter in his work occurs in *Il trionfo della morte* (*The Triumph of Death*), a novel in which the sun appears in its dual aspect of virile life-giving source and pitiless god raining cruel light and destructive heat on mankind. The novel's hero seems to have an atavistic kinship with this god, for at one time he even felt the sun to be at the core of his physical and psychic being. But this relationship has been undermined by a fatal flaw in the hero who has now lost the capacity to "revive the Panic delirium of the first day when he believed he had really felt the sun within his heart." Giorgio Aurispa, who has heard the voices of Wagner and Nietzsche, proves unable to rise to the heights of the superman, and as the crowning act of his failure he will descend into the night of Tristan, forcibly dragging his mistress Ippolita with him as an unwilling Isolde. Significantly, the full revelation of his failure is first made in the encounter with midday, which, as we have seen in the introduction, is the supreme Nietzschean test. The further

irony or ambiguity lies in the fact that the hero is fully cognizant of the implication of the encounter. The setting is a secluded beach on the Adriatic where Giorgio and Ippolita are bathing:

> Guardando [at Ippolita], egli aveva negli occhi a tratti scintillazioni quasi dolorose; e la gran luce meridiana gli dava un senso nuovo di malessere fisico misto a una specie di vago sgomento. Era l'ora terribile, l'ora pànica, l'ora suprema della luce e del silenzio, imminente su la vacuità della vita. Egli comprendeva la superstizione pagana: l'orrore sacro dei meriggi canicolari su la plaga abitata da un dio immite ed occulto. In fondo a quel suo vago sgomento si moveva qualche cosa di simile all'ansietà di chi sia nell'attesa di un'apparizione repentina e formidable. Pareva egli a sé stesso quasi puerilmente debole e trepido, come diminuito d'animo e di forze dopo una prova sfavorevole.

> (While looking at her, his eyes at times were filled with scintillations that were almost painful, and the intense midday light caused him a new sense of physical discomfort mixed with a kind of vague bewilderment. It was the terrible hour, the Panic hour, the supreme hour of light and silence, hovering over the emptiness of life. He understood the pagan superstition: the sacred horror of hot summer noontides in a region inhabited by a hidden and pitiless god. In the depth of his vague bewilderment there stirred something similar to the anxiety of one who is waiting for a sudden and formidable apparition. He felt himself almost childishly helpless and fearful, as though weakened in courage and strength after having failed in a challenge.)

This is a passage of remarkable insight into the very core of the secret of the midday encounter and the sense of being overmastered. There is in it, moreover, the rich but bewildering ambiguity peculiar to noonday. On the one hand, we find the intuition that this hour of crisis in which light and silence reign supreme contains the revelation of the emptiness or nothingness of existence; on the other, the sense of a mysterious force on the verge of self-revelation toward which the quasi-abulic hero is attracted but by which he ultimately feels diminished and defeated. And in all this there is the suggestion that the two impressions are one and the same.

There are in the novel several symbolically rich scenes in which the noontide sun figures as the overarching antagonist reigning in a terrible glory over human misery, madness, and death, but we may pass over these in order to consider briefly the meditation on Wagner's *Tristan and Isolde* because of its more immediate connection with the episode just discussed. Coming near the end of the novel, it is meant to serve as a prelude to the final scene of murder and suicide by establishing a sense of mystical *amor fati* in the hero who sees a parallel between his own desire for a return to origins (ultimately death) and Tristan's yearning for eternal night. In his reflection on the scene of Tristan's delirium and death, which includes occasional quoting and paraphrasing of Wagner's text, Giorgio equates the fatal love potion with the sun as an instrument and symbol of infinite yearning. This fusion of the two symbols is made clear by the attention given to the fact that the potion is drunk from a *golden* goblet and is felt as a *liquid fire* that roars through the lovers' veins. However, it is the sun that becomes the dominant libido symbol of the passion that burns and consumes Tristan:

> In nessun luogo, in nessun luogo, ahimè, troverò riposo. La notte mi respinge al giorno, e l'occhio del sole si pasce del mio perpetuo soffrire. Ah come il sole rovente mi brucia e mi consuma! E non il refrigerio d'un'ombra a questa divorante arsura
>
> (Nowhere, nowhere, alas, will I find peace. Night rejects me and drives me back to day, and the eye of the sun feeds on my perpetual suffering. Oh, how the fiery sun burns and consumes me! And not the relief of a shade for this devouring fire.)

The personification of both sun and passion in the image of the solar eye that cruelly feeds upon Tristan's suffering, even as it evokes the idea of the intensity of the passion (= suffering), deifies that passion by virtue of being itself a relentless, overmastering god. That it is a midday god (or demon) is suggested by the absence of any shade in which to find relief. Of course, this sun/passion burns *within* Tristan and so may be said to feed upon itself. Thus Tristan's cry against the sun is, like his curse of the love potion, really directed against himself:

> Questo terribile filtro, che mi danna al supplizio, io, io medesimo lo composi. . . . Io, io medesimo composi il tossico di questo filtro. E io lo bevvi, a lunghi sorsi di delizia . . . Maledetto sii tu, filtro terribile! Maledetto sia chi ti compose!"
>
> (This terrible philter which damns me to torment, it is I myself who have prepared it. . . . I myself have prepared the poison of this philter. And I have drunk it in long draughts of joy. . . . Be cursed terrible philter! Cursed be he who concocted you.)

The sun of passion, however, is also the source of the suprahuman joy Tristan has known. Its value had been declared earlier in his delirium when he stated that it was only since the sun had made its secret abode in their breasts that he and Isolde had experienced a paradisal (literally, a *stellar*) light of happiness: "Da che il sole s'è occultato nel nostro petto, le stelle della felicità diffondono il loro lume ridente." Now that it has completed its work of consuming Tristan from within, this sun is revealed for the supreme ecstatic libido symbol that it is, radiating a blinding light that floods the universe as music. This interpretation is inspired by the synesthetic image of Wagner's text (and its accompanying music) where Tristan, just before dying at the approach of Isolde, claims to *hear* the light. D'Annunzio emphasizes the synesthetic element:

> All'approssimarsi d'Isolda e della Morte, egli credeva *udire* la luce. "Non odo io la luce? Non odono i miei orecchi la luce?" Un gran sole interiore lo abbagliava; da tutti gli atomi della sua sostanza partivano raggi di sole e per onde luminose e armoniose si diffondevano nell'universo. La luce era musica; la musica ere luce.

> (At the approach of Isolde and of Death, he believed he *heard* the light. "Do I not hear the light? Do my ears not hear the light?" A great internal sun dazzled him; from all the atoms of his being rays of sunlight went forth and spread throughout the universe in luminous and harmonious waves. The light was music; the music was light.)

Here, the image of the sun and Tristan have merged. It is from *within* the hero that the solar rays irradiate as luminous music that permeates the universe. Tristan has become expanded into the All—the *Gran Tutto*. The paradox is that this "light" is the desired "night" of nothingness: "Tristano era entrato alfine nell'eterna notte." ("Tristan had entered at last into the eternal night.") Isolde too is now transfigured from poisoner and murderess (as D'Annunzio, or Giorgio, sees her) into a being of pure light and joy who, like her lover, dissolves into the mystic gulf—into the Great All. And the meditation closes with Isolde's words translated from Wagner's text: "Nell'infinito palpito dell'anima universa perdersi, profondarsi, vanire, senza conscienza: suprema voluttà!" ("To be lost in the infinite beating of the universal soul, to sink into it, dissolve, without consciousness: supreme pleasure!")

The episode from *Il trionfo della morte* in which Giorgio is overmastered by the sun has all the authenticity of a firsthand experience of an *échec* ["defeat"] in the encounter with the midday demon. But more often than not D'Annunzio shows himself equal to the encounter and "increased" or "expanded" in the tensive hour of Pan, sometimes with such intimations as we have found in his retelling of Tristan's death, although we are more likely to think of him in an aggressive pose. Whatever the case, the midday god ("atroce despota") will forever be a cruel god ("dio immite"), yet a beneficent god nonetheless, though in the joy he brings there can be no room for tenderness or nostalgia. This is the message of which D'Annunzio made himself the champion in introducing the several volumes of his *Laudi del cielo del mare della terra e degli eroi (Songs in Praise of the Sky, the Sea, the Earth, and Heroes)*. The introductory poem of 156 lines is pregnantly entitled "L'Annunzio," and the "announcement" is that the poet comes as a herald to proclaim the revelation made to him at midday that "great Pan is not dead":

> Uditemi! Udite l'annunziatore di lontano
> Che reca l'annunzio del prodigio meridiano
> Onde fu pieno tutto quanto
> Il cielo nell'ora ardente! V'empirò di meraviglia;
> V'infiammerò di gioia; vi trarrò dalle ciglia
> Il riso e il pianto.

> (Hear me! Hearken to the messenger from afar
> Who brings the tidings of the midday miracle
> Wherewith the heavens were completely
> Filled in the fiery hour! I will fill you with wonder;
> I will inflame you with joy; I will draw from your eyes
> Laughter and tears.)

At high noon when the revelation (*parola solare!*) was

made to him, all of nature was in an attitude of hushed devotion toward the sun. The description of this moment culminates in a stanza that equates the poet with the sun, and even, one may say, with the midday god himself from whom the announcement is heard:

> Tutto era silenzio, luce, forza, desìo.
> L'attesa del prodigio gonfiava questo mio
> Cuore come il cuor del mondo.
> Era questa carne mortale impaziente
> Di risplendere, come se d'un sangue fulgente.
> L'astro ne rigasse il pondo.
> La sostanza del Sole era la mia sostanza.
> Erano in me i cieli infiniti, l'abbondanza
> Dei piani, il Mar profondo.
>
> E dal culmine dei cieli alle radici del Mare
> Balenò, risonò la parola solare:
> "Il gran Pan non è morto!"
>
> (All was silence, light, force, desire.
> The wait for the miracle swelled my
> Heart like the heart of the world.
> This mortal flesh was anxious
> To shine forth, as if the sun had veined
> The heaviness [of my flesh] with a refulgent
>   blood.
> The Sun's substance was my substance.
> In me were an infinite sky, the abundance
> Of the plains, the deep Sea.
>
> And from the summit of the heavens to the roots
>   of the Sea
> There flashed, resounded, the solar word:
> "Great Pan is not dead!")

The title **"L'Annunzio"** is pregnant, of course, because it echoes the poet's real name. But his "Christian" name is no less significant here, and we may be sure that D'Annunzio expected his readers to understand that he was "correcting" an earlier Gabriel's annunciation as a false prophecy. By the same token, the general title *Laudi* echoes the Franciscan lauds of the Middle Ages in a defiantly pagan way. **"L'Annunzio"** is an exhortation to return to nature, and there is even a polemical thrust at Christianity for having made men deaf to nature's call. But our main concern is with the character of D'Annunzio's noontide as expressed in the foregoing verses. Silence and light pervade all of nature, but along with them, in the heart of all things, is the sense of a latent primal energy that seems on the very point of bursting into actualization. The sonnet **"Panico"** already suggested this same characteristic of noontide, and we shall meet with it again in other and greater verses of the poet. Here we may note that at the beginning of an essay on the painter Giorgione, D'Annunzio had referred to it specifically when he wrote that the sense of stasis at the hour of Pan derives from a concentrated passion and a repressed violence: "Soprastava a Venezia una di quelle ore che si potrebbero chiamar paniche, in cui la vita sembra sospesa ma non è, chè anzi la sua immobilità risulta da passione concentrata e da violenza repressa." ("Over Venice there hovered one of those hours that can be called Panic, in which life seems suspended but is not, for on the contrary, its immobility results from concentrated passion and repressed violence.")

The verses we have quoted from **"L'Annunzio"** bespeak a pantheistic sentiment. At the very least there is the sense of an identity of the self with the whole of nature. Though one may deny a theological interpretation to D'Annunzio's midday encounter, it is not possible to deny that it involves a clear case of a perception of a concentration of all energy and of all nature in the self. For a moment individual being has been transcended or has merged into a universal self. The poet is identified with Pan. With that identification, it is true, he is ready to plunge into multiplicity and to celebrate the infinite forms (or "members") of the god. In what Italian critics refer to as D'Annunzio's panism there is now a sense of confidence in which the self is declared to be commensurable with all the phenomenal world.

In connection with this last point it can be instructive and perhaps not as digressive as it might at first seem if at this point we pause to take note of a poem by the English writer with whom our poet shows the greatest affinity. Algernon Charles Swinburne's work was known, admired, and in some cases "imitated" by D'Annunzio, and the long noon piece entitled "A Nympholept" (1894) may well have influenced the latter's midday mythology, though it would certainly be wrong to think of it as having had a formative influence. But even if one prefers not to speak of a direct influence in this case, Swinburne's themes, images, mood, and, to a degree, the intonation and verbal excesses are, from an Italian point of view, quite "Dannunzian" and so may properly serve as an interesting touchstone in our consideration of the Italian poet.

Intended to describe the splendid oppression of nature, "A Nympholept" is an amazing nature poem by any standard. Besides bringing us as deep into the heart of midday as the texts of the most audacious sounders of that hour, it traces the whole arc of noontide (or man's reaction to it) from its negative to its positive pole. The first two lines of the poem refer to that midday phenomenon in which silence and light may be spoken of in terms of one another, and either or both may be seen and "heard":

> Summer, and noon, and a splendour of silence,
>   felt
> Seen, and heard of the spirit within the sense.

That the noontide stasis is highly charged with the tension of energy and latency is indicated in line 50, "But the silence trembles with passion of sound suppressed," which also confirms the experience of a midday silence so deep that it may create its own audible impression. The bewilderment experienced in the ambiguous atmosphere of midday which circles man round with "rapture or terror," with "hope" and "dread," is summarized in these two lines:

> Is it love, is it dread, that enkindles the trembling noon,
>   bling noon,
> That yearns, reluctant in rapture that fear has
>   fled?

Though noon "pervades, invades, appals," the presence of Pan is felt as a fear so "deep" and "sacred" that it is "wellnigh sweet." And here indeed is a feature that is also characteristic of D'Annunzio's noontide encounters. The fear or dread is not really dissipated entirely at any time, but rather becomes absorbed into what might ordinarily be thought of as its opposite. We are dealing, so to speak, with an experiential oxymoron. This important motif is also present in the treatment of the poet's attraction to the visionary maiden, a figure who is not so much a surrogate as an epiphany of Pan or of the noontide mystery itself. Noon, Pan, and the maiden are ultimately one and the same, a triune divinity that is nature revealing itself at midday. At the poem's climax, as he looks into the maiden's eyes, the poet notes that "her eyes embolden / Fear, till it change to desire, and desire to delight." The progression is typical of the mystical experience whether it be in an orthodox religious context or in an atheistic one such as that in Leopardi's inexhaustible "L'infinito."

All the lines we have quoted are pregnant and brilliant, but Swinburne's notorious obsession with words vitiates even this often admirable poem, and it would be tedious to follow him in all the verbal vagaries of his dithyrambic celebration of Pan. We need only observe further that in the end the feeling of dread and menace yields entirely to what is clearly an ecstasy:

> The terror that whispers in darkness and flames
> in light,
> The doubt that speaks in the silence of earth and
> sea,
> The sense, more fearful at noon than in mid-
> most night,
> Of wrath scarce hushed and of imminent ill to
> be,
> Where are they? Heaven is as earth, and as heav-
> en to me
> Earth: for the shadows that sundered them here
> take flight;
> And nought is all, as am I, but a dream of thee.

Though the second person pronoun *thee* (the very last word of the poem) is addressed specifically to the visionary maiden, it is an ambiguous referent that applies equally to Pan, noon, and, of course, to the all of nature that is implied therein. The ecstasy or the pantheistic experience of absorption of the self into the all is one in which the self is clearly annihilated—"And nought is all, as am I, but a dream of thee"—and as this most ambiguous of lines would seem to suggest, the all may indeed be nothingness or the Absolute perceived negatively. The atmosphere in which this revelation occurs is the epitome of noon. The absence of shadows and the equality of the light throughout obliterates the distinction between heaven and earth, creating the impression of an undifferentiated luminosity in which all things are transfigured in an immanent glory. And the whole, of course, is permeated with silence. It is a silent glory.

In returning directly to the Italian poet we can say that the sense of infinite latency and expectancy at the core of nature and the self is perhaps the most typical feature of D'Annunzio's midday encounters. It is connected with the sensation of an absolute suspension in which timelessness is experienced. This is the case especially in a passage from the long "hymn" *Laus Vitae* where the midday stasis is experienced as a "pausa infinita," and eternity actually

appears as a quality in things—a quality that is *seen,* as it were ("L'occhio solo / Era vivo e veggente"), and *felt.* In sight of Mount Parnassus, the boat in which the poet and his companions have been sailing over Grecian waters slackens as a vast noontide calm descends:

> Cadde il vento. Noi tutti
> Èramo senza parola
> Fissi alla gran maraviglia.
> Sospeso era il Giorno sul nostro
> Capo. Tutte le cose
> Tacevano con un aspetto
> Di eternità. L'occhio solo
> Era vivo e veggente.
> O tregua apollinea, Meriggio!
> . . . . Il silenzio
> Era come il silenzio
> Che segue o precede le voci
> Delle volontà sovrumane.
> Tutta la vita era a noi
> Quasi tempio lieve senz'ombra,
> Ch'entrammo non più morituri.
>
> (The wind fell. All of us
> Were speechless,
> Intent on the great prodigy.
> The Day was suspended above
> Our heads. All things
> Were silent with a look
> Of eternity. Only our eyes
> Were alive and perceiving.
> Oh Apollonian truce, Midday!
> . . . . The silence
> Was like the silence
> That follows or precedes the voices
> Of superhuman wills.
> All of life was for us
> Like the airy temple without shadows,
> Into which we entered no longer mortal.)

This representation of a deathlike suspension of all things, including all human faculties and sensations save for the eye alone which is said to live, is strikingly similar to Nietzsche's characterization of a noontide ecstasy as "a death with waking eyes," a death in which "the heart stands still, and only the eye lives." In Nietzsche's experience, too, all things are said to have been stilled and bear the "expression" of a silent luminosity that is eternity. One thinks also of the ecstasy recorded in "Sils-Maria" or, better yet, of the poem "Nach neuen Meeren" where the images of boat, voyage, and sea are all present, and as midday "sleeps" over space and time, only the vast eye of infinity looks upon the poet. . . . In D'Annunzio's verses the air of expectancy and infinite potency is an attribute of the all-pervading silence itself which is spiritually energized by the references to divine or suprahuman voices that may have preceded it or may follow it. The whole of the phenomenal world is transfigured, experienced as cosmos, and now appears as a shadowless, luminous temple of silent glory in which the poet and his companions move, feeling themselves shorn of mortality. Here too, then, the experience is clearly one in which there is a consciousness of *possession* of or participation in eternal life.

Although the last quoted passage gives an account of as mystical or spiritual a moment as one is likely to find in D'Annunzio, the highest poetic expression of his relationship with midday is connected with the naturalistic interpretation of existence that he unabashedly proclaimed. Three of his very best lyrics, **"Furit aestus," "Meriggio,"** and **"Stabat nuda aestas"** deal with the theme in this key. All three poems are from his finest volume of verse, *Alcyone,* which includes the sonnet **"Il vulture del sole"** referred to at the outset of this chapter. And it is that poem's image of a feral sun that is here dithyrambically hailed over and over by the poet, the tawny lion/sun as a fiery libido symbol that burns into the poet its own insatiable thirst:

> O fulva fiera
> O infiammata leonessa dell'Etra,
> Grande Estate selvaggia,
> Libidinosa,
> Vertiginosa,
> Tu che affochi le reni,
> Che incrudisci la sete—
>
> (Oh tawny beast
> Oh flaming lioness of the Ether,
> Great untamed Summer,
> Libidinous,
> Dizzy,
> You who set fire to our loins,
> You who exacerbate our thirst.)

It is a sun that is loved in its contrasting faces of Muse and Gorgon, an oxymoron or fusion of a Grace and a Bacchante, beautiful in its silent violence:

> Musa, Gorgòne,
>   . . . . .
> Grazia, Baccante,
>   . . . . .
> Bella nelle tue rabbie
> Silenziose, acre nei tuoi torpori.
>
> (Muse, Gorgon,
>   . . . . .
> Grace, Bacchante,
>   . . . . .
> Beautiful in your silent
> Fury, acrid in your languor.)

The poem **"Furit aestus"** is a dramatic representation of the repressed energy and infinite potency that exist in a midsummer noontide and of the intense, almost wild state of expectancy in the poet:

> Un falco stride nel color di perla:
> Tutto il cielo si squarcia come un velo.
> O brivido su i mari taciturni,
> O soffio, indizio del sùbito nembo!
> O sangue mio come i mari d'estate!
> La forza annoda tutte le radici:
> Sotto la terra sta, nascosta e immensa.
> La pietra brilla più d'ogni altra inerzia.
>
> La luce copre abissi di silenzio,
> Simile ad occhio immobile che celi
> Moltitudini folli di desiri.
> L'Ignoto viene a me, l'Ignoto attendo!
> Quel che mi fu da presso, ecco, è lontano.
> Quel che vivo mi parve, ecco, ora è spento.
> T'amo, o tagliente pietra che su l'erta
> Brilli pronta a ferire il nudo piede.
>
> Mia dira sete, tu mi sei più cara

> Che tutte le dolci acque dei ruscelli.
> Abita nella mia selvaggia pace
> La febbre come dentro le paludi.
> Pieno di grida è il riposato petto.
> L'ora è giunta, o mia Mèsse, l'ora è giunta!
> Terribile nel cuore del meriggio
> Pesa, o Mèsse, la tua maturità.
>
> (A hawk screeches in the color of pearl:
> The whole sky is torn like a veil.
> Oh shudder on the mute sea,
> Oh breath, sign of the sudden storm.
> Oh my blood, like the summer sea!
> A force knots together all the roots:
> It is under the ground, hidden and immense.
> The rock gleams more than all other inert forms.
>
> Light covers the abysses of silence,
> Like a motionless eye that conceals
> Wild multitudes of desires.
> The Unknown comes to me, the Unknown I
>   await!
> That which was near me, behold, now it is far
>   off.
> That which seemed alive to me, behold, now it
>   is dead.
> I love you, oh cutting rock that on the steep
> Glisten ready to cut the naked foot.
>
> My tremendous thirst, you are dearer to me
> Than all the sweet waters of the streams.
> In my wild peace there dwells
> Fever as in the midst of swamps.
> My stilled breast is full of cries.
> The hour has arrived, oh my Harvest, the hour
>   is here!
> Terrifying in the heart of midday
> Oh my Harvest, your ripeness weighs.)

From the opening image of the hawk's screech tearing the expanse of a bright yet hazy sky like the sudden tearing of a veil (and poetically here the sky *is* the pearl-colored veil), the highest pitch of tension is created. Though the sea is still, a tremor seems to course over it, caused by a breeze that announces a cloud. In an image that suggests a correspondence between the poet and nature that will be vital in the poem's conclusion, the blood coursing through the poet's veins is said to be like the waters of the sea that are apparently calm on the surface but are permeated with a mysterious current. It is the same energy, identified in lines 6-7, that pulsates secretly but with infinite potentiality beneath the surface of the earth. Line 8 identifies the mysterious force with light. All things appear inert in this charged stasis, yet that which would seem to be the most inert object of all, the mountain rock, glistens with more energy (reflected light) than anything else. The dazzling line (9) that follows—"La luce copre abissi di silenzio"— reveals that the midday light is master of all, filling heaven and earth and the space between with an absolute silence. Midday has imposed silence on all things. For the light *is* silence (or vice versa) in such a moment. The very substance of the universe is experienced as a luminous silence which is mysteriously (and paradoxically) pregnant with the desire and promise of life. This is made clear in the succeeding lines (10-11) by the simile that equates the silent light with a motionless eye that conceals a restless host of desires, i.e., life in an inchoate state yearning to burst into form.

How different then is this absolute light and silence of midday from that recorded by Leopardi in the second stanza of . . . "La vita solitaria!" Where Leopardi sought and found insentience and a primordial stillness or void, which can only be thought of as a state of nonbeing, D'Annunzio finds the intimation of original energy. At this point of the poem (and of the experience) where the light and silence are experienced at the deepest level, D'Annunzio appears as a passionate devotee hovering between anxiety and ecstasy, caught in the timeless moment of absolute latency—"L'Ignoto viene a me, l'Ignoto attendo!" In such a moment all things prized in the past lose their value and give way to the expectancy of the future present (13-14). Thus the timeless moment being experienced, which is objectified in the jagged granite mountainside bathed in the light of midday (suggesting a "cruel" side to the encounter), is what the poet desires fiercely (15-16). The midday despot is met on his own terms by the poet, and the terrible thirst of desire—"dira sete"—which the sun has burned into the very body of the poet is dearer to him now than all the quenching sweet waters of the streams would be. The attitude that dismisses D'Annunzio as a theatrical wordmonger is itself superficial. His choice of the word *dira* is as precise as it is significant. It is a numinously charged word that Rudolf Otto in his study on the holy connects with the concept of *tremendus*. As such "it may mean evil or imposing, potent and strange, queer and daemonic, and a source of *energy* [Rudolf Otto, *The Idea of the Holy*]." In the context of **"Furit aestus,"** the use of the term in the phrase *mia dira sete* expresses not merely the poet's subjective feeling but an awareness of and a positive response to original and infinite energy. The fierceness of midday's charged stasis, with its heat, light, and silence, pregnant with a repressed infinite potency, is matched by the poet in whom resides a violent peace ("selvaggia pace") vibrant with the fever of expectancy and potentiality. At this point, the expression *selvaggia pace* is followed by yet another oxymoron in which the midday silence is perceived as a wild howl. The poet's breast, apparently calm, barely represses a core of energy ready to explode into actualization. Now, in the very heart of noontide, is the eternally imminent moment of promise to be fulfilled, of latency on the verge of escaping into the infinite multiplicity of forms. In keeping with the poem's seasonal and diurnal context—a blazing summer midday—this repressed energy or latency is represented by the image of an awesome harvest heavy with ripeness (17-24). (And here we recall the "ripeness" and fullness that Nietzsche connected with the perfect hour of midday.) It is not too much to say that the poet has established an experiential equation between himself and the midday described by him in the first part of the poem, although the self has not been obliterated.

D'Annunzio has written that force is the primary law of nature and can neither be abolished nor destroyed ("la forza è la prima legge della natura, indistruttibile, inabolibile"). His poem **"Furit aestus"** reveals this energy as original power at the highest possible level of tension, existing

both in the heart of nature (midday) and in the human body.

On the other hand, the second great noon piece from *Alcyone,* entitled precisely **"Meriggio,"** evokes a profound midday calm that seems almost devoid of tension. Here the complete identification between nature (i.e., midday = Pan) and the poet is realized via an interchange or fusion in which, while the poet's self is happily surrendered to nature, nature itself acquires something of a human identity. During a midsummer midday in which the poet lies on a sandy beach of the Mediterranean Sea near the mouth of the Arno, a sultry calm weighs heavily upon the waters: "A mezzo il giorno / Sul Mare etrusco / . . . grava / La bonaccia." ("At midday / On the Etruscan sea / . . . a dead calm lies heavily.") A series of negatives (cf. Leopardi's second stanza of "La vita solitaria") describes the utter stillness of sky, sea, and land: "Non bava / Di vento intorno / Alita. Non trema canna / Su la solitaria / Spiaggia. . . . / Non suona voce." ("Not even a light breeze whispers around. / No reeds waver / On the solitary shore . . . / No voice sounds.") Once again, light and silence are apprehended as one and the same. Inasmuch as it belongs to the light, silence acquires a spatial dimension. All things are perceived as existing within this all-pervading luminous silence of midday ("Pel chiaro silenzio"): the white sails fixed in a motionless sea, cape and islands in an indefinable distance, jagged mountains that stand majestically above the waters, the mouth of the Arno which in the morning rippled sparkingly and now has the appearance of a lifeless pond that suggests a Lethean oblivion, the distant meeting point of the banks of the river where the reeds seem to enclose the waters of forgetfulness ("l'oblio silente"). Everywhere there is nought but a vast stillness, sultriness, absolute light and silence; and yet, for all that, there is the sense that summer has ripened to fullness around the poet like a promise of rich fruit to be picked and enjoyed by him alone:

> Bonaccia, calura,
> Per ovunque silenzio.
> L'Estate si matura
> Sul mio capo come un pomo
> Che promesso mi sia,
> Che cogliere io debba
> Con la mia mano,
> Che suggere io debba
> Con le mie labbra solo.

> (Dead calm, intense heat,
> Everywhere silence.
> Summer ripens
> Over my head like a fruit
> That is promised to me,
> That I must pluck
> With my hand,
> That I must suck
> With my lips only.)

As in **"Furit aestus,"** so too in these verses there exists a relationship of desire between the poet and nature, but here the potential wildness suggested by the imagery is magically absorbed and nullified by the placid, lulling rhythm of the verses. The tension of expectancy and latency gives way to appeasement and fulfillment. First the human form of the poet is transfigured by the midday light:

> . . . Ogni duolo
> Umano m'abbandona.
> Non ho più nome.
> E sento che il mio volto
> S'indora dell'oro
> Meridiano.

> (. . . All human
> Suffering leaves me.
> I have no name more.
> And I feel that my face
> Becomes gilded with the gold
> Of midday.)

There follows the sense of a dissolving of the self into the various objects of the vast surrounding landscape which calls to mind Leopardi's *meriggio* from "La vita solitaria," a comparison between the two noonscapes that has already suggested itself because of the use in both poems of a series of negatives to indicate the absence of motion. But there is some question as to whether D'Annunzio means to describe a Leopardian passing into absolute insentience. Certainly there is a sense of the poet's own life force flowing into and becoming one with the multiplicity of nature's forms, even with those that are only apparently inanimate, and a sense of nature as being the very body of the poet himself: "E il fiume è la mia vena, / Il monte è la mia fronte, / La selva è la mia pube, / La nube è il mio sudore" ("And the river is my vein, / The mountain is my forehead, / The forest is my pubis, / The cloud is my sweat.") Even as the poet has been released from his human form and limitations, so too the multiplicity of nature's forms is experienced—or, we may say, experiences itself by way of the poet—as a transfigured whole (an anthropomorphized body), a single greater self that can be identified as the one-in-all. Between the poet and the whole of the phenomenal world there obtains a state of *coinherence.* And because midday with its stasis and absolute light is the experiential revelation of this miracle, the name of the poet, as of all things, is taken from the blazing hour of Pan:

> Ardo, riluco.
> E non ho più nome.
> E l'alpe e l'isole e i golfi
> E i capi e i fari e i boschi
> E le foci ch'io nomai
> Non han più l'usato nome
> Che suona in labbra umane.
> Non ho più nome né sorte
> Tra gli uomini; ma il mio nome
> É Meriggio. In tutto io vivo
> Tacito come la Morte.

> E la mia vita è divina.

> (I blaze, I glitter.
> And I have no name more.
> And mountains and islands and gulfs
> And capes and lighthouses and forests
> And the outlets I have named
> No longer have their usual name
> That sounds on human lips.
> I have no name more or lot
> Among men; but my name

> Is Midday. In all I live
> Silent like Death.

> And my life is divine.)

"Meriggio" records the serene but triumphant actualization of the miracle that is anxiously, even violently, intimated in **"Panico," "L'Annunzio,"** and **"Furit aestus."** It goes beyond these poems in giving expression to a sentiment which, if not pantheistic in the strictest theological sense of the word, is nonetheless "pamphysistic" and born of a genuine mystical experience of nature. In it D'Annunzio describes the silent yet thrilling life of the self transcending human limitations ("Non più nome né sorte / Tra gli uomini") and realizing infinite identity. If this is so, then the last three lines of the poem are to be understood as proclaiming the abolition of all limits and of any division between life and death. While **"Meriggio"** is not in the dithyrambic mode common to much of *Alcyone,* it is not really far removed from the expansive manner in which the immanent glory of midday is sung by the poet on other occasions. D'Annunzio would seem to be all the more alive for being expanded into the calm "all" of nature where by virtue of possession (it is the poet who possesses and is all) the tension of desire is finally at rest. And yet a doubt or ambiguity remains, the suspicion that this divine quietude of fulfillment—the Nietzschean midday stasis of fullness—may somehow be the expression of still another desire, the secret desire for an absorption of the self into the silent light that is the night of nothingness. Nonetheless, the experience seems to me to remain on this side of the *antica quiete* of Leopardi's noonscape and the earlier poet's unambiguous absorption into nonbeing. The mood and "sensation" with which D'Annunzio concludes are perhaps nearer to what we found at the close of Swinburne's "A Nympholept."

There is no doubt that the principal direction of D'Annunzio's midday pamphysism or panism is toward a sensualistic identification of the self with the forms of nature, but this does not make his panism any less authentic. It is for this reason that among the most successful of his poems are several dealing with metamorphosis or the mythological representation of the fusion of the human and the natural, although **"Meriggio,"** which records the same experience, does without this device and supersedes all such poems. For D'Annunzio, to "know" nature does not mean to understand or to deduce an organizational principle in nature; rather it is to be immersed in a perception and sensation that is experienced not as annihilation but as an expansion of the self. This is the significance of his discovery and proclamation of joy and the abolition of sorrow in the concluding section of *Laus Vitae:*

> Ma il meridiano delirio
> Nel Deserto l'oblìo
> D'ogni cima più perigliosa
> Mi diede e d'ogni demenza
> Più lucida e d'ogni divieto
> Abbattuto.

> . . . . .

> E l'anima mia dalla culla
> Dell'eternità parve alzata
> In quell'ora.

. . . . .

Ed ella taceva, profonda
Del suo più profondo silenzio.
Ma parole erano dette
In lei, alla gran luce
Del mezzodì, chiare parole.

. . . . .

Felicità, non ti cercai;
Ché soltanto cercai me stesso,
Me stesso e la terra lontana.
Ma nell'ora meridiana
Tu venisti a me d'improvviso.

(But the midday delirium in the Desert
Brought me forgetfulness
Of all the most perilous peaks
And of all the most lucid
Follies and of every broken
Prohibition.

. . . . .

And my soul seemed raised
From the cradle of Eternity
In that hour.

. . . . .

And she [my soul] was silent, deep
With its deepest silence.
But words were spoken
In her, in the great light
Of midday, luminous words.

. . . . .

Happiness, I did not seek you;
For I sought only myself,
Myself and the far away land.
But in the midday hour
You came to me suddenly.)

Here *in nuce* is D'Annunzio's symbolic identification of midday with the epiphany of joy. Unsentimental, even cruel, joy is the fulfillment of the self. If one wishes, one may reverse the terms. In either case, joy or the unashamed realization of the self is the means by which man truly "knows" (and one may rightly keep the sexual connotation of the word) life and nature, and by which he rises above the ordinary class of humans. In the final verses quoted above, the personification of joy suggests a woman whose appearance and surrender to the poet in the *ora meridiana* is yet another variation of the poet-as-faun myth. It is, in fact, one of the more extraordinary versions of the ancient theme of midday nympholepsy to be found in world literature. Hour of "ripeness" and fullness, and, because of that, hour of crisis, midday is the time for the revelation or the advent of joy as a value of self-realization and the immanental sense of original power which lies stored at the heart of existence. (pp. 118-44)

> *Nicolas J. Perella, "Gabriele D'Annunzio," in his* Midday in Italian Literature: Variations on an Archetypal Theme, *Princeton University Press, 1979, pp. 114-44.*

Giuliana Giobbi   (essay date 1989)

[*In the following essay, Giobbi compares and contrasts D'Annunzio's* The Flame of Life *with Thomas Mann's* Death in Venice, *focusing on the recurrent topics of Venice, art, and death.*]

Because of its unique nature and atmosphere, Venice has traditionally been a favourite setting in the fiction and poetry of European authors. The architecture of Venetian buildings attracted the attention of art critics like John Ruskin, and the wealth of masterpieces contained in Venice's churches and museums were required study for scholars as well as the object of admiration for foreign tourists. But Venice was not only a city of Art; it was also a city of sickness, decay, death. For its very frailty, for the muddy waters of its canals and the endangered situation of many of its houses and monuments, Venice has always appeared a sad, a dying city.

I want to use the three topoi of Venice, Art and Death—with many correlated leitmotifs—to highlight the relationship between two apparently unrelated works: D'Annunzio's *Il fuoco* (1900, *The Flame*) and Thomas Mann's *Der Tod in Venedig* (1912, *Death in Venice*). Gabriele D'Annunzio, the leading figure of Italian *fin de siècle* literature, had already written some poems and novels,

D'Annunzio in 1928.

and was trying his hand at drama while sentimentally involved with the great actress Eleonora Duse.

He had been thinking about a Venetian novel for some time before beginning **Il fuoco** in June 1896. Two years earlier, he had stayed in this 'magic' city and had met for the first time Eleonora Duse—the 'Foscarina' of the novel. These two facts set in motion his imagination, and he often went back to Venice to 'capture' new motives and images for his 'frame'. The theme of the novel is the ardent desire for glory and for aesthetic and sensual pleasure with which the central character, Stelio Effrèna—*alter ego* but also Nietzschean *Übermensch* [Superman]—is virtually obsessed. Foscarina shares his dreams, reflexions and self-eulogy. The unique Venetian landscape, the canals, the old *palazzi* and the little islands in the lagoon are an integral part of the novel, whose 'plot' is practically nonexistent.

> "Conoscete voi, Perdita," domandò Stelio d'improvviso, "conoscete voi qualche altro luogo del mondo che abbia, come Venezia, la virtù di stimolare la potenza della vita umana in certe ore eccitando tutti i desideri sino alla febbre? Conoscete voi una tentatrice più tremenda?"

> ("Do you know, Perdita"—Stelio asked suddenly—"do you know any other place in the world, which could, as Venice does, stimulate the power of human life in certain hours and excite desires to a fever pitch? Do you know a more terrible temptress?")

In the case of Thomas Mann, too, there are autobiographical elements in the 'background' of *Der Tod in Venedig,* which follows some 'major' productions such as *Buddenbrooks* (1900) and other short stories (*Tristan*, 1902; *Tonio Kröger,* 1903). Thomas Mann had spent his holidays in Venice in June 1901 and May 1907. From the 26 May to the 2 June 1911, he stayed at the Lido in the Hotel des Bains, with his wife Katja and his brother Heinrich—after a short stay in the Adriatic isle of Brioni—and went through much the same experiences which his character Gustav von Aschenbach undergoes in *Der Tod in Venedig.* The novella tells the story of a mature German writer, who suddenly feels the need to interrupt his work and take a holiday in some southern, 'exotic' place: he travels from Munich to Venice, and finds himself staying at the Hotel des Bains in the Lido, where he meets—and falls in love with—a Polish boy of incredible beauty. Despite the spread of cholera in Venice, Aschenbach stays on at the hotel, his mind filled with adoration for the Apollonean Tadzio. He finally dies on the beach as he experiences an 'epiphanic' vision of the young man. As Mann himself wrote in the autobiographical 'piece', *Lebensabriss:*

> Nothing is invented in *Death in Venice* (. . .); all that and anything else you like, they were all there. I had only to arrange them when they showed at once and in the oddest way their capacity as elements of composition. Perhaps it had to do with this: that as I worked on the story—as always it was a long-drawn-out job—I had at moments, the clearest feelings of transcendence, a sovereign sense of being borne up such as I had never before experienced.

Other elements Mann would need for his tale also came to hand with almost uncanny convenience, like the death of the composer Gustav Mahler, whom Mann personally knew and admired.

Both in D'Annunzio's **Il fuoco** and in Mann's *Der Tod in Venedig,* Venice acts not only as landscape, but also as a proper 'character' in the story. The chiaroscuro of its *calli,* the magic of the sea 'inside' the city, the melancholy atmosphere—autumnal in the case of D'Annunzio, summer in the case of Mann—play a conditioning role in the development of both works.

The speech made by Stelio at the beginning of **Il fuoco,** "L'Allegoria dell'Autunno"—written by D'Annunzio on 8 November 1895 for the closing of the Art Exhibition in Venice—is an oratorical homage to Venice. The vitality and universality of the Venetian artistic tradition are emphasized in the great Venetian painters like Giorgione and Canaletto, and the harmony between art and atmosphere is symbolized by the union of Venice and Dionysus.

> Tutto il mistero e tutto il fascino di Venezia sono in quell'ombra palpitante e fluida, breve e pure infinita, composta di cose viventi ma inconoscibili, dotata di virtù portentose come quella degli antri favoleggianti, dove le gemme hanno uno sguardo.

> (The whole mystery and fascination of Venice reside in that palpitating, fluid shade, short and yet infinite, composed of living but unknowable things, endowed with wondrous virtues like that of the fabulous caves, where precious stones have eyes.)

Symbolism and Mythology, as well as the central concern with a possible balance between Art and Life, are also to be found in the complex, multi-layered structure of Mann's *Tod in Venedig.* More than one critic has pointed out several analogies with myths. The 'keys' offered by the patterns of Euripides's *Bacchae* and Plato's *Phaedrus* certainly provide insights into the characters and events of the novella. The influence of Nietzschean readings—especially *Die Geburt der Tragödie*—also helps in 'deciphering' symbolic presences.

But, as Vernon Venable remarks:

> In the process of trying to achieve the symbolic identifications which his irony demands, he (i.e. T. Mann) has created a new technique for the exploitation of poetic meaning, a technique in which no symbol is allowed univocal connotation or independent status, but refers to all the others and is bound rigorously to them by means of a highly intricate system of subtly developed associations.

This system of associations has its centre in Venice, whose alluring, exotic and dangerous nature—not to forget the cholera epidemic—mirrors the unearthly beauty of Tadzio and symbolizes the risks of an absolute love for beauty.

> Nur dieser Ort verzauberte ihn, entspannte sein Wollen, machte ihn glücklich.

> (Only this place charmed him, extended his will, made him happy.)

Mann himself fell under the charm of Venice, but he also realized—while Aschenbach does not—the ambiguity and the possible danger of the city. In a letter addressed to his children Erika and Klaus, who were staying in Venice in May 1932, Mann explains his peculiar relationship with Venice:

> . . . Weil mir der Ort so bedeutend ist und ich euch gern dort weiss und im Geiste mit euch das sonst nie vorkommende Leben zwischen dem warmen Meer am Morgen und der 'zweideutigen' Stadt am Nachmittag führe. Zweideutig ist wirklich das bescheidenste Beiwort, das man ihr geben kann . . . aber es passt in allen seinen Bedeutungslagen ganz wunderbar auf sie, und bei aller Albernheit und Verderbtheit, die sich ihrer bemächtigt hat (. . .) bleibt dieser musikalische Zweideutigkeitszauber eben doch lebendig oder hat wenigstens Stunden, wo er obsiegt.
>
> (Because the city is so significant for me and I am happy to know you are there, and in spirit I lead a life—normally never so pleasant—between the warm sea in the morning and the 'ambiguous' city in the afternoon. Ambiguous is really the simplest term one can use to define Venice . . . but it suits her in all its possible meanings, notwithstanding the fatuity and corruption which dominate her, this musical enchantment is still alive—at least, at moments.)

The reference to music in the description of the Venetian atmosphere has its own weight. D'Annunzio as well as Mann admired both the aesthetics and the works of Richard Wagner. Both authors wrote critical essays on him, and the Wagnerian presence can be perceived—more or less explicitly—in their works of fiction. D'Annunzio's *Il fuoco* ends with the tragic death of Wagner in Venice, and Stelio himself is present both to help the musician when he faints and to carry his coffin. The description of Wagner is that of a demigod, surrounded by a divine aura and by the admiration of the people.

> Tutti erano fissi all'eletto della Vita e della Morte. Un infinito sorriso illuminava la faccia dell'eroe prosteso: infinito e distante come l'iride dei ghiacciai, come il bagliore dei mari, come l'alone degli astri. Gli occhi non potevano sostenerlo; ma i cuori, con una meraviglia e con uno spavento che li faceva religiosi, credettero di ricevere la rivelazione di un segreto divino.
>
> (Everyone had his eyes fixed on the Elect of Life and Death. An infinite smile illumined the face of the hero: infinite and distant like the shining glaciers, like the glittering waves, like the halo of the stars. Human eyes could not bear it; but the hearts, made religious by astonishment and fear, appeared to have a divine secret revealed.)

D'Annunzio found in Richard Wagner a prototype for the role of the poet-leader. The Italian author interpreted Nietzsche's various attacks on Wagner as directed against his own literary and political ideals, the cultivation of the individual ego, and the 'aristocratic' and 'heroic' in music. D'Annunzio's reading of Nietzsche, as well as his defence of Wagner's theory of the 'Wort-ton-drama'—emphasized

in *Il fuoco*—are rather idiosyncratic, since he referred the whole question to himself. For D'Annunzio the kind of musical regeneration offered by Wagner implied an accompanying social regeneration, and such was his absorption in Wagner in the 1890s, that the Wagnerian influence became a crucial factor in his novels. As a consequence, the enormous popularity of D'Annunzio's novels may have made it easier for Wagner to be accepted in Italy.

> Riccardo Wagner, non soltanto ha raccolto nella sua opera tutta questa spiritualità e questa idealità sparse intorno a lui, ma, interpretando il nostro bisogno metafisico, ha rivelato a noi stessi la parte più occulta di nostra intima vita.
>
> (Richard Wagner not only has gathered in his works all the spirituality and ideality which were spread all around him, but, by interpreting our metaphysical needs, has also revealed to us the most hidden part of our own innermost life.)

The admiration Thomas Mann had for Richard Wagner was lifelong, and not limited to simple musical pleasure. He read Nietzsche's works when he was very young, and this had a lasting effect on him. But his judgement is independent of the philosopher's positions. Most critics recognize in Mann's works the use of the Wagnerian leitmotif, alongside references to performances of Wagner and the use of Wagnerian myths. Even though the name of Wagner is suppressed in *Der Tod in Venedig,* the surroundings evoke in Aschenbach's mind the figure of the German musician and his fatal association with Venice. Significantly, Aschenbach's mind censors the fact of Wagner's death in Venice, leaving only the suggestion that his art flourished there.

The apt jungle metaphors—as Aschenbach is lost in the labyrinth of Venice while following the Polish family—probably relate to the "Liebestod" music and can be seen as ironic in the sense that Aschenbach also meets both love and death in this very same labyrinth.

In D'Annunzio, too, there is a long, well-known scene set in the labyrinth of a villa in Strà, during one of the lovers' walks. Here Stelio cruelly hides himself from Foscarina, who calls to him more and more anxiously. It is interesting to compare the feelings of the two characters, lost in the labyrinth and full of passion for the person they are following. Here is Mann's Aschenbach:

> . . . Er verlor sie, suchte erhitzt und erschöpft nach ihnen über Brucken und in schmutzigen Sackgassen und erduldete Minuten tödlicher Pein, wenn er sie plötzlich in enger Passage, wo kein Ausweichen möglich war, sich entgegenkommen sah.
>
> (He lost them, and, sweating and exhausted, looked for them over bridges and along dirty alleys, and bore minutes of deadly pain, as he saw them suddenly coming towards him in narrow passages, where no way out was possible.)

And here is D'Annunzio's Foscarina:

> Ella si slanciò nell'intrico per trovarlo; andò diritta verso la voce e il riso, portata dall'impeto. Ma il sentiero si torse; una muraglia di busso

cieca le si parò dinanzi, l'arrestò, impenetrabile.
Ella segui la tortuosità ingannevole; e una svolta
succedeva all'altra, e tutte erano eguali, e il giro
pareva non aver fine.

(She plunged into the labyrinth in order to find
him; she headed straight for his voice and laughter, prey to her impulse. But the pathway suddenly turned; a wall of blind boxwood appeared
in front of her, brought her to a stop, impenetra-
ble. She followed the deceptive windings; and
one turn led to another, and they were all alike,
endless.)

In Mann's case the connotation of the alleys—
"schmutzig"—is negative, in line with his image of Venice
as a city in decay, which was to become the hotbed of a
terrible epidemic. The idea of twilight and pollution indeed, permeates—with obvious variations—both
D'Annunzio's and Mann's stories. D'Annunzio describes
in a dreamlike tone the emptiness and desolation of the lagoon:

La laguna e la caligine inghiottivano tutte le
forme e tutti i colori. Soli interrompevano la
grigia eguaglianza i gruppi dei pali, simili a una
processione di monaci per un cammino di ceneri.
Venezia in fondo fumigava come i resti di un
vasto saccheggio.

(The lagoon and the mist devoured all forms and
colours. Only the groups of piers broke into the
grey sameness, like a procession of monks along
a pathway of ashes. Venice, in the background,
lay smoking like the remains of a city laid
waste.)

On the other hand, Mann's vision tends towards pathology and sickness, an imminent spectre of cholera and death:

Das war Venedig, die schmeichlerische und ver-
dächtige Schöne—diese Stadt, halb Märchen,
halb Fremdenfalle, in deren fauliger Luft die
Kunst einst schwelgerisch aufwucherte und wel-
che den Musikern Klänge eingab, die weigen
und buhlerische einlullen (. . .) Er erinnerte
sich auch, dass die Stadt krank sei.

(This was Venice, the flattering and suspect
Beauty—this city, half fabulous, half foreign, in
whose unhealthy air Art once flourished luxuriously, a city which gave musicians melodies
which lulled sweetly (. . .) he also remembered that the city was sick.)

This link between art and sickness—and, indeed, between
art and death—is particularly common in Thomas Mann's
work. More generally it is part of the heritage of the Aesthetic period and of that feeling of end which was general
at the turn of the century.

Both *Il fuoco* and *Der Tod in Venedig* formulate, with different aims, statements about art. Stelio, in his speech
about Venice, proclaims a new Art and dreams of a national theatre, thus playing the role of a D'Annunzio
masked as an egocentric and ambitious *Übermensch.*
Mann's Aschenbach, on the other hand, gives up his discipline and is ensnared by an infatuation which excites, then
enervates and finally destroys him. Venice means for Asc-

henbach a regression to the wild and cruel aspects of the
primitive, the sensual, the irrational. If the substance of
creation is chaos, then this chaos can destroy its creator.

In both 'Venetian' novels, Art is seen as endangered by
corruption, passion, and decay. Foscarina's ageing makes
her love for Stelio fragile and hopeless. Aschenbach's piti-
ful use of make-up cannot hide the work of time on his
face. The spreading of cholera and the very filthiness
and precariousness of Venice are omens of death.
D'Annunzio's description of the villas on the river Brenta,
a prey to wilderness and decay, as well as the story of the
countess Glanegg, secluded in her *palazzo* once her youth
has passed, correspond—in Mann's novella—to the description of Venice's *calli* and to sinister apparitions such
as the singer and the beggar.

If some 'redemption' for Art is envisaged in D'Annunzio
through Stelio Effrèna—the supreme 'artifex' who gathers
together in his art the treasures of beauty and refinement
of the past, though on the verge of natural and commercial
destruction—Mann offers us through Aschenbach only ir-
rationality and self-destruction. In fact, it is intriguing to
see how the respective characters relate to their authors.

D'Annunzio was 37 when *Il fuoco* was published, and was
already a well-known and experienced writer: this is why
the novel may appear as a kind of confession, a form of
self-veneration in his identification with Stelio. Stelio is a
D'Annunzio without the slightest fault or weakness which
would be unworthy of a 'divine' poet: as a consequence,
Stelio appears too perfect and under-characterized. We do
not know his family or his home-town: his career is vague.
In Venice, he lives in the Hotel Danieli or in rented *palazzi,* and has a group of 'disciples' around him. We do not
even know his age, but we do know he is a writer of genius
and an eloquent speaker.

La sua voce limpida e penetrante, che pareva
disegnare con un contorno netto la figura musi-
cale di ciascuna parola, dava maggior risalto a
questa singolar qualità del suo dire. Talchè in
quanti l'udivano per la prima volta si generava
un sentimento ambiguo, misto di ammirazione
e di avversione, manifestando egli sè medesimo
in forme così fortemente definite che sem-
bravano risultare da una volontà costante di sta-
bilire tra sè e gli estranei una differenza profonda
e insormontabile.

(His limpid, penetrating voice, which seemed to
draw with a neat outline the musical picture of
every word, emphasized even more this singular
quality of his speech. So much so that in those
who heard him for the first time, an ambiguous
feeling of admiration mixed with aversion was
generated, because he manifested himself in
forms so strongly defined that they seemed to
come from a constant wish to define a deep, in-
surmountable difference between himself and
others.)

The characterization of Mann's Aschenbach is quite different. The reader of *Der Tod in Venedig* is given a good
deal of information about Aschenbach's youth, his aims
and motives, his private 'existential philosophy'. The
bourgeois morality in which Aschenbach believes, with its

strenuous discipline of work—his motto is *"Durchhalten* ['Hold fast']"—is superseded in Venice by his sensual passion for Tadzio, in whom Beauty—and its snares—are personified. As Hans Mayer infers, Mann might have let Aschenbach die in order to free himself from the conflicts and rules of his past artistic career: in other words, in order to go on writing. This cathartic purpose is confirmed by the similar conflict between bourgeoisie and *"Künstlertum"* in Aschenbach *and* in Mann, as well as by the irony implied in Aschenbach's lack of self-knowledge and moral stamina. Mann continually points to the writer's fragile resources: as Apter remarks—"Mann shows the artist's respectable, spiritual purpose being waylaid by his own imagination; he shows how the discipline necessary to art distorts, through detachment, the artist's human impulses". In his own view, Aschenbach is the distanced practitioner of noble art who—a little like D'Annunzio's Stelio—is able to transmute examples of physical beauty into the intellectual realm of formal perfection. But in fact, he succumbs to passion and renounces *"Ruhm"* and *"Würde"*—fame and dignity.

> Er hatte dem Geiste gefrönt, mit der Erkenntnis Raubbau getrieben, Saatfrucht vermahlen, Geheimnisse preisgegeben, das Talent verdächtigt, die Kunst verraten—ja, während seine Bildwerke die gläubig Geniessenden unterhielten, erhoben, belebten, hatte er, der jugendliche Künstler, die zwanzigjährigen durch seine Zynismen über das fragwürdige Wesen der Kunst, des Künstlertums selbst in Atem gehalten.

> (He had enslaved the Spirit, ransacked Knowledge, espoused its fruits, revealed secrets, made his talents suspect, betrayed Art—yes, while his creations entertained, elevated, revived his faithful readers, he, the young artist, through his cynicism on the questionable essence of Art, of the artist himself, had kept the twenty-year-old in suspense.)

On Mann's own admission the work is an attempt to obtain *"Erkenntnis"* about himself. But—in spite of many similarities between Mann and his 'hero'—it will not do to equate them.

The very ironic distance established by Mann—here as in the case of Serenus Zeitblom in *Doktor Faustus*—prevents us from attempting to do this. However, as in the relationship D'Annunzio-Effrèna, there is much of the author's own personality and ideas in the characters. But while D'Annunzio projects his 'better' self in the *'Wunschbild'* Stelio, Mann depicts in Aschenbach the artist he *could* have become if he had followed certain rules and had lacked true 'genius'.

The similarity between *Il fuoco* and *Der Tod in Venedig* is striking in the description of a momentary epiphany, as well as of a sensual urge. Let us first look at the final epiphanic scene in Mann's novella:

> Ihm war (. . .), als ob der bleiche und liebliche Psychagog dort draussen ihm lächle, ihm winke; als ob er, die Hand aus der Hüfte lösend, hinausdeute, voranschwebe ins Verheissungsvoll—Ungeheure.

> (The pale, charming Psychagogue appeared to be smiling at him there in the distance, gesturing at him; as though, moving his hand from his side, he could foreshadow and float towards the Mysterious and the Prodigious.)

A similar artistic impulse comes to Stelio from the sight of Foscarina on a staircase in firelight:

> L'ignota in quelle brevi ore aveva già vissuto entro di lui una vita fittiva così intensa che, vedendola avvicinarsi, egli provava un turbamento non dissimile a quello che avrebbe provato vedendosi d'improvviso venire incontro l'incarnazione spirante d'una delle creature ideali gènite dalla sua arte.

> (The unknown woman had already lived in him—in those short hours—such an intense unreal life that, while seeing her approaching, he was troubled as if he had suddenly seen coming towards him the breathing incarnation of one of the ideal creatures born from his art.)

In both cases, the person observed by the artist is transfigured and idealized, and provokes strong emotive reactions in the observer. Two similar visions of primitive, passionate disorder can be found in both works: both pictures symbolize the character's inner feelings and chaos. Here is D'Annunzio's image:

> Di lontano, di lontano gli veniva quel torbido ardore, dalle più remote origini, dalla primitiva bestialità delle mescolanze subitanee, dall'antico mistero delle libidini sacre.

> (From far, far away, that obscure longing came to him, from the remotest origins, from the primitive bestiality of sudden couplings, from the ancient mystery of sacred lusts.)

The same feelings, primaeval and instinctive, bestial and irrational, are present in Aschenbach's obsessions in his nightmare:

> Woher kam und stammte der Hauch, der auf einmal so sanft und bedeutend, höherer Einflüsterung gleich, Schläfe und Ohr umspielte? Weisse Feder-Wölkchen standen in verbreiteten Scharen am Himmel gleich weidenden Herden der Götter.

> (Where did this breeze come from, a breeze which was at the same time so sweet and so meaningful, similar to a celestial whisper, wafting around his temples and his ears? Light white clouds stood in enlarged rows in the sky, similar to herds of the Gods, at grass.)

Both 'heroes', though different in age and situation, strive for Beauty and formal perfection: both have a rich imagination and transfigure places and persons around them. As a consequence, Venice and the object of love—respectively, Foscarina and Tadzio—map out a series of descriptions, thoughts, and images which finally constitute most of the stories.

There are however obvious differences between Stelio and Aschenbach: the one is young, full of dreams and ambitions for his future artistic career, the other is old and accepts an unheroic death. But the authors are different from one another as well, in age, class, and—last but not least—nationality. Thomas Mann, on the threshold of the First World War, abhorred Nationalism and the defenders of War; he defined the Italians as *"die Heerscharen Gabriels* ('Gabriel's troops')"—'Gabriel' being D'Annunzio— and explicitly expressed his aversion to the Italian writer's political attitude in his writings:

> Aber woher nehme ich das Wort, um ein Mass von Verständnislösigkeit, Staunen, Abscheu, Verachtung zu bezeichnen, wie ich es angesichts des lateinischen Dichters Politikers und Kriegsrufers vom Typ des Gabriele D'Annunzio empfinde?"

> (But where shall I find the words to indicate the amount of incomprehension, amazement, horror, hate, which I feel for latin poets and politicians who call for war, such as Gabriele D'Annunzio?)

There are no signs of any kind of contact between the two contemporary authors, and we do not know whether Mann ever read D'Annunzio's works. But, notwithstanding the political enmity, more than one parallel can be drawn between the Aesthetics of the two writers, particularly in their respective 'Venetian' novels. Both authors choose Venice and a central artist-character in order to create a suitable atmosphere for a series of statements about Art and Life. Both 'heroes' are partly autobiographical and possess definite aesthetic rules. *Il fuoco* and *Der Tod in Venedig* have no complex plots, and consist mainly in descriptions and meditations, always in third-person narrative. The two artists portrayed in these novels have their respective 'Muses'—Foscarina and Tadzio—who inspire in them thoughts of Beauty, Art and Myth.

Venice plays—both for D'Annunzio and for Mann—a determining role in the structure of the story. The city of the lagoon is inevitably bound up—more or less overtly—with the memory of Richard Wagner, the idea of decay, the Italian artistic heritage, and impending death. Even though they are very different in opinions and culture, the two contemporary authors finally appear similar in their connection with this contemporary Aesthetic.

> Ah, Venedig! Eine herrliche Stadt! Eine Stadt von unwiderstehlicher Anziehungskraft für den Gebildeten, ihrer Geschichte sowohl wie ihrer gegenwärtigen Reize wegen!

> (Ah, Venice! A wonderful city! A city of irresistible attraction for cultivated people, because of its past history as much as for its present charm!)
>
> (pp. 55-66)

Giuliana Giobbi, "Gabriele D'Annunzio and Thomas Mann: 'Venice, Art, and Death'," in Journal of European Studies, *Vol. XIX, No. 73, March, 1989, pp. 55-68.*

FURTHER READING

Clyne, Anthony. "Two Italians: Da Vinci and D'Annunzio." *The London Quarterly Review* fifth series, XIX, No. 38 (April 1920): 162-74.
> Compares and contrasts the achievements, personalities, and politics of D'Annunzio and Leonardo da Vinci, criticizing D'Annunzio's flamboyant life-style and his occupation of the town of Fiume after World War I.

Cortesi, Salvatore. "D'Annunzio, America, and the War." In his *My Thirty Years of Friendships,* pp. 239-53. New York: Harper & Brothers Publishers, 1927.
> Includes several personal anecdotes, portions of a letter from D'Annunzio on the United States' entry into World War I, and an account of a trip to Fiume shortly before D'Annunzio surrendered the town.

Harrison, Thomas. "D'Annunzio's Poetics: The Orphic Conceit." *Annali d'Italianistica* 5 (1987): 60-73.
> Argues that inconsistencies exist between D'Annunzio's aesthetic theories and their expression in his works, focusing on several poems in *Alcyone.*

Huddleston, Sisley. "D'Annunzio: Prince, Poet, Politician." In her *Those Europeans: Studies of Foreign Faces,* pp. 180-92. New York: G. P. Putnam's Sons, 1924.
> Comments on D'Annunzio's significance in Italian politics.

Huneker, James. "Duse and D'Annunzio." In his *Iconoclasts: A Book of Dramatists,* pp. 320-49. New York: Charles Scribner's Sons, 1905.
> Discusses the romantic and professional relationship between D'Annunzio and the noted actress Eleonora Duse, who devoted a substantial portion of her career to acting in his plays. Huneker comments: "The wisdom of her choice in selecting only D'Annunzio's dramas is not altogether apparent."

James, Henry. "Gabriele D'Annunzio." In his *Notes on Novelists: With Some Other Notes,* pp. 245-93. New York: Charles Scribner's Sons, 1914.
> Reprints a 1904 essay discussing D'Annunzio's novels. James praises D'Annunzio's descriptive style and use of language but comments: "For the critic who simplifies a little to state clearly, the only ideas [D'Annunzio] urges upon us are the erotic and the plastic, which have for him about an equal intensity, or of which it would doubtless be more correct to say that he makes them interchangeable faces of the same figure."

Kibler, Louis. "Myth and Meaning in D'Annunzio's *La figlia di Iorio.*" *Annali d'Italianistica* 5 (1987): 178-87.
> Explores the unifying effect of pagan, Christian, and romantic myths on the structure of *La figlia di Iorio.*

Klopp, Charles. *Gabriele D'Annunzio.* Boston: Twayne Publishers, 1988, 138 p.
> A literary and biographical study of D'Annunzio. Dividing D'Annunzio's works into periods, Klopp briefly discusses each of the major works in separate sections interspersed with related biographical material.

——. "Form and Foam in D'Annunzio's *La nave.*" *Esperienze Letterarie* XIV, No. 1 (January-March 1989): 31-44.
> Interprets *La nave* as "a struggle between the fixed and

the formless, that is, between a defining male principle and a potentially engulfing female one."

MacClintock, Lander. "Gabriele D'Annunzio." In his *The Contemporary Drama of Italy,* pp. 94-134. Boston: Little, Brown, and Co., 1920.
An unfavorable assessment of D'Annunzio's dramas.

Meyers, Jeffrey. "Gabriele D'Annunzio (1888-1935)." In his *A Fever at the Core: The Idealist in Politics,* pp. 89-111. New York: Barnes & Noble, 1976.
Discussion of D'Annunzio's political activities.

Mosse, George L. "The Poet and the Exercise of Political Power: Gabriele D'Annunzio." In his *Masses and Man: Nationalist and Fascist Perceptions of Reality,* pp. 87-103. Detroit: Wayne State University Press, 1987.
Examines D'Annunzio's contributions to the development of fascism. According to Mosse, D'Annunzio "illustrates the importance a poet could take in the shaping of a new secular religion that became an all-embracing political style."

Ouida [pseudonym of Marie Louise de la Ramée]. "The Genius of D'Annunzio." *The Fortnightly Review* LXI, No. CCCLXIII (March 1897): 349-73.
Evaluates several of D'Annunzio's novels, generally praising them but criticizing the influence of foreign writers on his style and the "indecent" content of his works.

Radcliff-Umstead, Douglas. "The Artist's Role: Ibsen, D'Annunzio, Pirandello." *Canadian Journal of Italian Studies* 6, No. 2-3 (1983): 75-102.
Examines common elements in the role of the sculptor in Henrik Ibsen's *When We Dead Awaken,* D'Annunzio's *La Gioconda,* and Luigi Pirandello's *Diana e la tuda.*

Re, Lucia. "Gabriele D'Annunzio's Theater of Memory: Il Vittoriale degli Italiani." *Journal of Decorative and Propaganda Arts* 3 (Winter 1987): 6-51.
Excerpts a critical study of D'Annunzio's rhetoric that views his villa as a "text." Re writes: "Il Vittoriale was to be an architectural structure whose strategic arrangement of emblems, images, artifacts, objects, devices, and enigmatic inscriptions—intended to function as mnemonic keys—allowed the 'initiate' to recuperate in memory the substance and the possible interconnections of an encyclopedic discourse."

Schnapp, Jeffrey. "Nietzsche's Italian Style: Gabriele D'Annunzio." *Stanford Italian Review* VI, No. 1-2 (1986): 247-63.
Examines D'Annunzio's interpretation of Friedrich Nietzsche's philosophy. Schnapp notes that "in D'Annunzio's Italian transcription, Nietzsche's text is driven out of the unstable ground between philosophy and literature (which is its usual abode) into a lyrical

realm of dreams and philosophical fictions, where it finds itself animated and, indeed, transformed by certain ghosts from ancient and early-modern Italian literary history."

Sforza, Count Carlo. "D'Annunzio, or The Literary Origins of Fascism." In his *Makers of Modern Europe: Portraits and Personal Impressions and Recollections,* pp. 310-18. Indianapolis: Bobbs-Merrill Co., 1930.
A discussion by a former Italian Minister of Foreign Affairs on the development of fascist ideology among prominent Italian literary figures.

Spackman, Barbara. "Nietzsche, D'Annunzio, and the Scene of Convalescence." *Stanford Italian Review* VI, No. 1-2 (1986): 141-57.
Compares the rhetoric of sickness in works by Friedrich Nietzsche, D'Annunzio, and Charles Baudelaire, noting the significance of illness and recovery in the development of artistic consciousness.

Squire, J. C. "The Future Poet and Our Time: D'Annunzio in 1920." In his *Essays on Poetry,* pp. 197-209. London: Hodder and Stoughton, 1923.
Discussion of D'Annunzio in relation to the political climate of Europe after World War I.

Tintner, Adeline R. "Henry James's 'The Story in It' and Gabriele D'Annunzio." *Modern Fiction Studies* 28, No. 2 (Summer 1982): 201-14.
Examines D'Annunzio's influence on Henry James.

Valesio, Paolo. "Declensions: D'Annunzio after the Sublime." *New Literary History* XVI, No. 2 (Winter 1985): 401-15.
Meditations on various images and themes related to light and time in *Fedra.*

Woodhouse, J. R. "D'Annunzio's Election Victory of 1897: New Documents, New Perspectives." *Italian Studies* XL (1985): 63-84.
Analyzes recently discovered documents from D'Annunzio's 1897 campaign for office, noting that the poet later quoted verbatim from his own speeches in *Il fuoco (The Flame of Life).*

——. "Curiouser and Spuriouser: Two English Influences on Gabriele D'Annunzio." *Italian Studies* XLII (1987): 69-80.
Examines the influence of the aesthetic theories of Pre-Raphaelite artists and the poetic theories of Percy Bysshe Shelley on D'Annunzio's works.

——. "Gabriele D'Annunzio's Reputation and Critical Fortune in Britain." *Annali d'Italianistica* 5 (1987): 245-58.
Discusses D'Annunzio's personal and literary reputation, attributing current neglect of his works at British universities to political and social prejudices.

Keith Douglas

1920-1944

English poet.

Considered one of the foremost English poets of the Second World War, Douglas is best remembered for poems describing his experiences as a tank commander in North Africa during 1942 and 1943. These works are distinguished from those of most well-known poets of the world wars by their detached, reportorial style and avoidance of the traditional rhetoric of patriotism or protest. While largely unknown at the time of his death, Douglas's poetry has been praised by such prominent English poets and critics as Geoffrey Hill, Ted Hughes, and Roy Fuller, who declared Douglas "unarguably the finest English 'war poet' to come out of the Second World War."

Douglas was born in Tunbridge Wells, Kent. His parents separated when he was six years old, and Douglas spent much of his childhood in boarding schools. In 1931 he enrolled in Christ's Hospital, a charitable school with a strong literary heritage; its alumni included Samuel Taylor Coleridge and Charles Lamb. Douglas was considered a rebellious student by school officials, but he excelled in his studies and distinguished himself as an athlete and artist whose drawing and painting gained the praise of his teachers and classmates. He began writing poetry while a teenager, publishing his first poem at age sixteen. In 1938, while still a student at Christ's Hospital, he published the poem "Dejection" in the prestigious journal *New Verse*. Soon afterward Douglas was granted a scholarship and entered Merton College, Oxford. He participated fully in the school's literary life, editing the undergraduate weekly and studying under the renowned poet Edmund Blunden, who encouraged Douglas to publish a collection of his poetry.

With the advent of war in Europe in 1939, Douglas volunteered for military duty. He began his service in 1940 in the cavalry, and was eventually transferred to a tank regiment in North Africa. Desiring combat experience, he deserted an office assignment in defiance of his superiors to assume command of a tank troop at the beginning of the El Alamein offensive in October 1942. Douglas remained with his regiment until January 1943, when he was wounded by a land mine near Tripoli. During his recuperation he wrote several of his most famous poems based on his combat experiences, as well as *Alamein to Zem Zem,* a war memoir supplemented by his poems and drawings. Returning in late 1943 to England, where his regiment was readied to participate in the D day invasion of France, Douglas sought publication of *Alamein to Zem Zem* and a collection of poems he planned to title "Bête Noire." In June 1944 he sailed with the invasion fleet for Normandy, where he was killed three days after landing.

Most critics identify three major stages in Douglas's poetry, the first comprising his adolescent work, the second coinciding with his studies at Oxford, and the last beginning

with his military service. Some also contend that Douglas was entering a fourth stage with the "Bête Noire" poem fragments he wrote just before his death. His early poems are considered important primarily because they exhibit a precocious technical facility. Concerned largely with pastoral and mythic themes, these works are considered derivative in form and content. At Oxford, he wrote poems in which, as critics have observed, he began to develop an individual style, characterized by melancholy and economy of phrase.

Douglas entered military service believing battle experience would be beneficial to him as a writer. He considered the war the most relevant literary topic of his time, and maintained that only a soldier could write authentically about war. After experiencing battle, he abandoned the musicality and smooth rhythms that characterized his poetry in favor of a grim, often jarring voice that he considered better able to depict the carnage he had witnessed. He defended this stylistic departure to his friend and fellow poet J. C. Hall in a letter which many critics have understood as his poetic manifesto: "My rhythms, which you find enervated, are carefully chosen to enable the poems to be *read* as significant speech: I see no reason to be either musical or sonorous about things at present." Rather than using emotive language, as he had in his earlier poems, Douglas began utilizing understatement and juxtaposition for emotional effect, techniques for which critics have compared him to such metaphysical poets as John Donne. In perhaps his most acclaimed poem, "Vergissmeinnicht" ("forget me not"), he described in exacting detail his discovery in the desert of a dead German soldier carrying with him a photograph of his sweetheart. Commenting on war's threat to both life and personal identity, Douglas contrasted the woman's perception of her lover with the killer he had become, and concluded: "And Death who had the soldier singled / has done the lover mortal hurt." Unlike such earlier war poets as Wilfred Owen and Siegfried Sassoon, Douglas avoided moral judgments in his works. Detached and sometimes ironic, his battle poems are characterized by a visual sensibility that critics attribute to his training as an artist, notably in the three-poem sequence, "Landscape with Figures." Douglas also wrote about his internal conflicts, and commentators recognize in his more meditative poems a writer troubled by despairing moods and a premonition of death, which he openly treated in his poems "On a Return from Egypt" and "Simplify Me When I'm Dead."

Douglas was little known as a poet until after his death, and by the time *The Collected Poems of Keith Douglas* was published in 1951, critical and popular interest in war poets had subsided. However, Douglas attracted the notice of poets of the postwar generation, including Hughes and Lawrence Durrell, who saw his severe, unsentimental battle poetry as a precursor to their own reaction against English neoromantic poetry of the 1940s. Douglas's greatest achievement, they believed, was his invention of a new, anti-lyrical voice and aesthetic in which to render the horrors of the battlefield. With the revival of Douglas's poetry in the early 1960s came a renewed interest in *Alamein to Zem Zem,* which critics saw as a key to understanding Douglas, who, in contrast to the popular conception of the reluctant soldier-poet, enjoyed battle and fought well. Negative criticism of Douglas has focused on his detached approach, which Ian Hamilton compared to "the tight-lipped insensitivity of the officers' mess," and on what some critics consider an immaturity and morbidity in his work. Even Douglas's admirers have qualified their praise, describing him as a good poet with a great unrealized potential. Nevertheless, critics maintain that Douglas's work signalled changes in modern English poetry and remains valuable as an example of art undergoing radical adaptation to fit specific circumstances. As Hughes wrote, Douglas "invented a style that seems able to deal poetically with whatever it comes up against."

(See also *Dictionary of Literary Biography,* Vol. 27.)

PRINCIPAL WORKS

*Selected Poems (poetry) 1943
Alamein to Zem Zem (prose and poetry) 1946
The Collected Poems of Keith Douglas (poetry) 1951
Selected Poems (poetry) 1964
The Complete Poems of Keith Douglas (poetry) 1978
Keith Douglas: A Prose Miscellany (short story, letters, and essays) 1985

*This work also contains poems written by J. C. Hall and Norman Nicholson.

John Waller (essay date 1948)

[*A British poet and critic, Waller edited* The Collected Poems of Keith Douglas *and the 1966 edition of* Alamein to Zem Zem. *In the following excerpt, he examines Douglas's poetry and prose in* Alamein to Zem Zem.]

Gregorio Prieto in his collection of drawings "Students: Oxford and Cambridge" has one entitled "Poet," depicting a young man asleep on the grass with his head resting on a pile of books; as he breathes, small tinsel-like stars float softly out of the carrier basket attached to the handlebars of his bicycle, dropping over the young man's body, several hovering over his face and one even paused gently above his open lips as if the next breath will blow it upwards again. The poet's hair is untidy and seems almost to be growing into the books and into the ground. One can imagine a river passing alongside and its quiet murmuring. Indeed the whole scene is ominous in its peace-like quality. To look at it now is to remember an old Oxford friend, Keith Douglas, and that scorching ominous summer of 1940, when he wrote—before going into the army—his poem **"Canoe."**

> Well, I am thinking this may be my last
> summer, but cannot lose even a part
> of pleasure in the old fashioned art
> of idleness. I cannot stand aghast
>
> at whatever doom hovers in the background;
> while grass and buildings and the somnolent
>   river,
> who know they are allowed to last for ever,
> exchange between them the whole subdued
>   sound
>
> of this hot time. What sudden fearful fate
> can deter my shade wandering next year
> from a return? Whistle and I will hear
> and come another evening when this boat
>
> travels with you alone towards Iffley:
> as you lie looking up for thunder again,
> this cool touch does not betoken rain;
> it is my spirit that kisses your mouth lightly.

After joining the army and getting commissioned Keith Douglas was posted to the Middle East where he ran away from a staff job at base to join his regiment in the desert, fought in a Crusader tank from Alamein to Zem Zem, and returned safely to England—only to be killed a few days after the beginning of the Second Front, on his third day in Normandy. The vagaries and delays of modern British publishing have resulted in his first book—excluding group productions—being published in England only three years after his death, at a time when the things he wrote about have begun to be forgotten.

Alamein to Zem Zem is not just another soldier's diary to be sympathized over and given that sympathetic pat on the back that the critic symbolically gives to the dead; it is foremost a poet's diary in which the poet was only incidentally a soldier. The book also contains drawings, two of which in colour portray with stark force and jovial satire respectively a man burning to death in his tank ("cannot get out of the turret") and a Cairo Street scene—and a handful of poems written in the Middle East. (The latter are not . . . the whole of Douglas' Middle East poetry, for they omit at least three significant poems lying still in Middle East magazines or anthologies, but it is to be hoped that all will eventually be included in his forthcoming collection *Bête Noire*.)

The poems are of primary importance. It is late in the day now to discover a war poet, but when the publication of the work is so long delayed so also must be any acknowledgment. And to those who had previously read these poems—apart from the Editor of *Poetry London*, mainly other writers who had seen them in the Middle East—Keith Douglas appeared the finest or at any rate one of the three finest poets *in* the war, the other two being Alun Lewis and Sidney Keyes. As with Edward Thomas, Rupert Brooke, and Wilfred Owen in the 1914-18 war, it is a matter for sorrow that all three were killed in action. It is the last of these perhaps, Wilfred Owen, that Keith Douglas most nearly approximates.

But to return to Prieto's picture of the dreaming young man. That appearance of dreaming is the first impression to be received from Douglas's poetry, his earlier poems notably. I once said that he was an "ivory tower" poet and that he very rarely left his tower, at which another writer remarked wittily that by that he supposed me to mean that Douglas did not get brilliantly drunk at bottle parties. Yet I did not intend a criticism. There is nothing wrong in an ivory tower if you can get a good view from it and Douglas' view was always exact and comprehensive. "My object," he once wrote in a letter to a friend, "is to write true and significant things in words which work for their keep." So, he never shirked the true and significant things in warfare, he wrote only one poem and that satirical without actually having experienced a battle, he was like Owen an extremely efficient officer—and yet, with all this, his work gives an impression of an ivory tower being taken into action, of a dreamer on battlefields, and Douglas' pity is the more piercing for being that macabre and ghostly pity of dreams. "This is what I see," he seems to say, "yet why should I feel it when I shall wake up shortly?" And yet he does feel it, because there is no such awaking. It is a way of avoiding sentimentality, of never being caught out in the standardized war poem, Mark I, II, or III.

Compare the early **"Canoe"** with his **"Elegy to an 88 Gunner,"** written in Tripolitania in 1943.

> Three weeks gone and the combatants gone
> returning over the nightmare ground
> we found the place again and found
> the soldier sprawling in the sun.
>
> The frowning barrel of his gun
> overshadows him. As we came on
> that day, he hit my tank with one
> like the entry of a demon.
>
> And smiling in the gunpit spoil
> is a picture of his girl
> who has written: *"Steffi, Vergissmeinnicht"*
> in a copybook Gothic script.
>
> We see him almost with content,
> abased and seeming to have paid,
> mocked by his durable equipment
> that's hard and good when he's decayed.
>
> But she would weep to see today
> how on his skin the swart flies move,
> the dust upon the paper eye
> and the burst stomach like a cave.
>
> For here the lover and the killer are mingled
> who had one body and one heart
> and Death who had the soldier singled
> has done the lover mortal hurt.

It is as if the fact that Douglas was also an artist gave him always an artist's impersonal eye and enabled him to pass through scenes of bloodshed and death with a poetic disembodiment or unconcern that made the dead and the dying merely figures in a landscape. Where the décor is a horrible tracery of iron the dead men appear to wriggle in their dowdy clothes. And the question is raised: is this really pity or is it again that streak of sadism or delight in pain that pierces so often the poetry of Sidney Keyes? Yet it is pity,—my futile mercy that I drop from my tower, the poet might say, from the turret of my tank as I go by.

His method is clearly stated. When someone in his regiment had his leg destroyed by an 88 shell and was taken away to an ambulance where he died later, Douglas overheard him to cry petulantly: "It's most unfair—they've shot my foot off." And he wrote:

> How can I live among this gentle
> obsolescent breed of heroes and not weep?

Yet weeping does not help, for in weeping is sentimentality and in sentimentality is bad art and its inward squirm. It is better therefore to write it in another, more roundabout way, as if it was only another game at school.

> These plains were their cricket pitch
> and in the mountains the tremendous drop fences
> brought down some of the runners. Here
> under the stones and earth they dispose themselves
> in famous attitudes of unconcern.

So Douglas' becomes the famous pity of apparent unconcern, which is both elegiac and striking. Around it "the separative glass cloak" (which he had earlier mentioned in his first version of the poem **"Syria"**) protects it from shrillness and stillness and tears. He hated anything artificial. He liked emotion to happen, not to be raised. And strangely in this way he was able to couple so much stark reality with so much beauty and elegance.

Other poems in **Alamein to Zem Zem** lead off to the quietly descriptive and even to the quietly satirical. The sunlit idyll of Mersah Matruh is made ominous by the "logical little fish" who nip at the flesh of the soldier bathing in the sea:

> imagining I am one of the dead.

Christodoulos, who makes money out of the troops, is:

> the original wise one
> from whose experiments they told
> how War can be the famous stone
> for turning rubbish into gold.

There is a fine perfected description of the Garden Groppis between Sharia Adly Pasha and Sharia Malika Farida under the title **"Behaviour of Fish in an Egyptian Tea-Garden."** Yet all these are the background to that other world of the decaying figures and the fighting tanks, which is why a poem of Douglas' called **"Cairo Jag"** rings true where a similar poem by someone else strikes only faintly or does not ring at all. After all, there is no difference spiritually between a Cairo Jag and any other type of Jag if the desert does not follow it.

> Shall I get drunk or cut myself a piece of cake?

You think of the girls, the evening, the lights, the drinks in cafés, the friends who must be forced into becoming acquaintances. You are led to the slumbrous afternoon, then to the roaring shrieking evening streets of Cairo, the beggars, the women with brown paper breasts, dust and ordure, the cripples whose legs have been cut off by the trams. And "it is all one, all as you have heard." For a day's travelling brings you to a new world, there quietly to enjoy that macabre peace again or furious activity, among:

> the dead themselves, their boots, clothes and
>   possessions
> clinging to the ground. A man with no head
> has a packet of chocolate and a souvenir of Trip-
>   oli.

Keith Douglas was constantly a poet of naturalness. Although he himself appeared in *New Verse* at the age of fifteen while still a schoolboy at Christ's Hospital, he always attacked—perhaps unfairly—the trend towards obscurity which he felt *New Verse* represented. He allied himself more with the Georgians, their lyricism, their grace, and their elegance. Yet he had also this naturalness, this true view that the Georgian poets never had, the lack of which makes so much of their poetry artificial. Douglas could not only see clearly, he could also write clearly, and without throwing over completely that poetic tradition which so many young poets scorn. He belonged to no school and in his bookcase Edmund Blunden lay alongside T. S. Eliot, for he found merit in both. Where he uses intellect or philosophy it is to produce emotion or effect, not for their own ends. And so he wrote what is by any judgment a

poem and he was a natural poet, simply himself. I can say no more of anyone.

On almost the last occasion when I met him in Cairo Keith Douglas remarked that he thought Richard Hillary's *The Last Enemy* an overrated book because it was too exhibitionist. It seemed to him to be so obviously written for a general public, and yet at the same time wickedly desirous of seeming sincere. Remembering this is to turn to Douglas' own war-time journal, **Alamein to Zem Zem,** with a certain interest. But there is no attempt to emulate Hillary. Douglas may start at roughly the same point, but he travels almost at once in a different direction. There is no philosophizing which may not sound quite true to someone who has experienced the same ordeal; there is no easy flashiness or story; whatever Douglas has done he has not written a best seller. And yet I feel he may have written a work of literature about war.

He writes still as the observing dreamer. "I observed these battles partly as an exhibition—that is to say that I went through them a little like a visitor from the country going to a great show, or like a child in a factory—a child sees the brightness and efficiency of steel machines and endless belts slapping round and round, without caring or knowing what it is all there for. When I could order my thoughts I looked for more significant things than appearances; I still looked—I cannot avoid it—for something decorative, poetic or dramatic." He saw men living in an unnatural, dangerous, but not wholly terrible world, having to kill and be killed, and yet moved by a feeling of comradeship for their enemies who had experienced the same emotions and disasters. "It is tremendously illogical—to read about it cannot convey the impression of having walked through the looking-glass which touches a man entering a battle." And yet Douglas does manage to convey this feeling.

This De Quincey touch, this seeming to walk through that looking-glass, to seek out and find that illogicality which lies hidden in existence, has often seemed to produce the finest English prose where the writer has been writing about himself. "So, then, I said, I have found you at last," to take one very striking example. And so Douglas, and the house of Milena in Rouchdy Pasha, where his feet subtly led him on a short visit to Alexandria. "The odd face, with its delicate bones and nobility of line, the twisted smile and curious sad dishonest eyes; and her sinuous and cleanly made body, like a drawing made with an airbrush; her absurd accent; all beat down my fortitude when she confronted me." And yet Milena scarcely exists, slips into a few hundred words only, and then vanishes, as Anne does in *The Confessions of an Opium Eater.*

And on the extensions of this parallel, to hold up against all those odd illogical characters and episodes in De Quincey which critics have questioned the existence of and regarded as inspired by opium, there are in Douglas similar beings and incidents. Where others might only have seen an eccentric major or a martinet colonel, the first was to Douglas a feudal legend looking upon the men of his regiment as if they were his tenants, sub-tenants, and serfs, wearing a flannel shirt and brown stock pinned with a gold pin, a yellow suede waistcoat lined with sheep's wool, faun cavalry trousers, brown suede shoes, a highly polished peaked cap, the whole surmounted with a Boer War moustache which could be seen from the back, while the second appeared as a spruce, brave, pomaded figure, a man of astonishing tantrums known as "Picadilly Jim," whose only method of making an apology was to send by a messenger a quotation from Disraeli which he always attributed to Napoleon, and who was to die so typically, standing up in his tank and shaving under shell-fire. There are others too, the soldier whose spare issue of kit was always kept ready sewn up for those inspections which he confidently awaited in the glass-house for irregularities yet to be performed, the poor old hospital orderly who called out in a weak, quavering voice: "Oxo or tea, Oxo or tea," Willi, the young German prisoner who had lost his paybook, and the tank driver, standing nonchalantly against his tank and referring to his dead companions inside with the phrase, "Bit mucky in the turret," as if apologizing to an inspecting officer. (pp. 226-32)

The small illogicalities, the minor surrealisms of life, are always there if only one can see them and the discovery of their comforting presences on battlefields is what makes the difference between a correspondent's account which is boring as soon as it is out of date and that of a poet and an artist. Douglas' diary is full of these wistfully bright moments. Owing to the fact that battledress trousers are supplied with sharp tin buttons which begin to cut themselves off as soon as they are sewn on, his main concern in one battle is to keep up his trousers only to have them fall about his legs when he has to report to his colonel. Once, halted for the night, he reads aloud to his fellow officers from Sacheverell Sitwell's *Valse des Fleurs,* finding them fascinated by the costumes and regiments taking part in the march-past before the Imperial Palace until they realize that there is no story to hang their attention on. Somewhere else the morphia turns out to be a preparation for waking people up under anaesthetic. And just outside Sousse he falls among a group of French officers who insist on his spending the night drinking toasts comprised of tumblers two-thirds full of neat whisky, until all are unconscious and "the captain in the act of announcing another toast, fell backwards into a corner, where he lay, still crying his toast amiably, his eyes twinkling like harbour lights." Upon his return to his regiment the next morning, it is not surprising that a hen for which his driver has swapped a pair of khaki shorts lays two eggs without shells in the terrifying passage by truck over the hill roads.

Also in **Alamein to Zem Zem** will be found those nightmare yet dreamlike descriptions of the scenery of battle, which Douglas later translated into verse. The dead fascinated him. "The most impressive thing about the dead is their triumphant silence, proof against anything in the world." And he always described them differently. A dead Libyan soldier reminded him first of Paul Robeson and then of Rimbaud's "Le dormeur du val" and as he looked "a fly crawled up his cheek and across the dry pupil of his unblinking right eye." Dead Italians are described as lying about "like trippers taken ill." And a dead German appears in the form of a cleverly posed waxwork representing an orgasm of pain. "He seemed to move and writhe. But he was stiff. The dust which powdered his face like an

actor's lay on his wide open eyes, whose stare held my gaze like the Ancient Mariner's."

Always Douglas paints a scene with a clear accurate view and then drives the point home by relating it to something not at all horrific. This technique can sometimes be brutal. Take the phrases "huge yellow vegetable" and "child exhausted with crying" and note their effect in this passage from his nightmare progress over the open desert after his own tank has been hit, after he has suddenly discovered the friendly Sherman tanks around him to be all burnt out with not a living soul in any of them, after a corporal with no right foot has mounted his back like an old man of the sea, and when trudging wearily onward, trying to avoid the enemy guns and the trip wires of mines, he comes across two wounded crawling along the sand. "I looked at the second man. Only his clothes distinguished him as a human being and they were badly charred. His face had gone: in place of it was a huge yellow vegetable. The eyes blinked in it, eyes without lashes, and a grotesque huge mouth dribbled and moaned like a child exhausted with crying."

The question of courage does not enter into Douglas' writing. He was always so much something else first, an artist, before being a soldier or a person, that he can write about episodes in which he behaved heroically by normal standards with almost complete detachment. It is only afterwards that one thinks: that must have taken some doing. His descriptions of anything he did are so careful and yet at the same time so casual, that his diary reads for all the world like a new Alice gone to explore a new wonderland in which the scenery is unaccountably composed of strange flowers made by the dead and the dying and their broken machinery, and all the episodes have that surrealist glitter which seems to warn: "This is all a dream. Isn't it ridiculous?" And then reassuringly: "Remember all you can, for you'll wake up shortly." Douglas himself describes it as like being in a land unrelated to real life, like the scenes from *The Cabinet of Dr. Caligari.*

To Keith Douglas the battlefield was an experience that he wanted to have and he ran away from a staff job to get it, but it was for artistic, not for heroic reasons, and that is what makes him worth reading. He once told me, after all the incidents described in his diary: "I don't need to do it again. When you've been in one battle you've been in all." He would, I think, at this point have been perfectly content to have stayed in staff jobs or even in the Ministry of Information for the rest of the war. But an officer who can take a battle with such cold, efficient, and ruthless detachment as Douglas' diary shows him to have done was obviously too valuable to be used for anything else. The cold detached man is more reliable than the hot hero, or to take a bad parallel Ulysses achieves more than Ajax. A true artist is from this point of view probably the most successful soldier in modern warfare if only he is efficient as Douglas—most rare for an artist—was, and if only he will always remain inwardly more of an artist than a person. Significantly Douglas admired the bombs falling from a plane, "an isolated shower of rain, a succession of glittering drops" before realizing the necessity of taking cover. And so, he did not need courage as others would have done; if ever he mentions personal fear it seems added as an afterthought, a conventional modesty. The "true significant things" were so interesting, so engrossing, that the emotions normally raised by danger had nowhere to make their home.

In a long "Monologue for a Cairo Evening" written just before departure from the Middle East and remembering so many of those happy or fated shadows who passed through Cairo during the war years, G. S. Fraser has a verse:

> And Keith Douglas' shrewd and rustic eyes
> That had endured "the entry of a demon":
> His poems spat out shrapnel; and he lies
> Where all night long the Narrow Seas are
> screaming . . .

And I can discover no better epitaph, unless perhaps it be to remember that same sad serenity of Prieto's young poet by a river in Oxford in 1940, and the stars falling casually around. . . . (pp. 232-35)

> John Waller, "The Poetry of Keith Douglas,"
> in Accent, Vol. 8, No. 4, Summer, 1948, pp.
> 226-35.

Alan Ross   (essay date 1954)

[*An English poet, critic, and travel writer, Ross wrote extensively on English poetry of the post–World War II period. Ross himself served in the Royal Navy during the Second World War, and his first book of poems,* The Derelict Day *(1947), depicted occupied Germany, where he was stationed after the war. In the following excerpt, he offers an appreciative overview of Douglas's poetry.*]

The prose part of *Alamein to Zem-Zem* is informal, witty, and sharply evocative in a loose kind of way: it is the sort of journal only a poet could have written, direct and ironically compassionate, yet often hurried and formless, like a letter which presumed on friendship to fill in the gaps. It is written by someone who has found excitement not in the vocation of the soldier, but in the poetic opportunities provided by war. The style is drily pictorial, completely unaffected: the natural good prose of a painter, which Douglas was, too. He states his aims on the first page:

> I am not writing about these battles as a soldier, not trying to discuss them as military operations. I am thinking of them . . . as my first experience of fighting: that is how I shall write of them. I observed these battles partly as an exhibition—that is to say that I went through them a little like a visitor from the country going to a great show, or like a child in a factory—a child sees the brightness and efficiency of steel machines and endless belts slapping round and round, without caring or knowing what it is all there for. When I could order my thoughts I looked for more significant things than appearances; I still looked—I cannot avoid it—for something decorative, poetic or dramatic. . . . But it is exciting and amazing to see thousands of men, very few of whom have much idea why they are fighting, all enduring hardships, living

in an unnatural, dangerous, but not wholly terrible world, having to kill and to be killed, and yet at intervals moved by a feeling of comradeship with the men who kill them and whom they kill, because they are enduring and experiencing the same things. It is tremendously illogical—to read about it cannot convey the impression of having walked through the looking-glass which touches a man entering a battle.

The editors of the *Collected Poems,* a score or so of which appeared at the end of *Alamein to Zem-Zem,* have included two of Douglas's statements on poetry which offer, in the most profitable way, an insight into his methods and the nature of his achievements. The first contains this paragraph: "Writing which is poetry must say what the writer has himself to say, not what he has observed others to say with effect, nor what he thinks will impress his hearers because it impressed him hearing it. Nor must he waste any more words over it than a mathematician: every word must work for its keep, in prose, blank verse, or rhyme." The second, much longer, came in a letter to J. C. Hall, who shared a book of *Selected Poems* with Douglas and Norman Nicholson. In it Douglas, in similar manner to Owen a war earlier, defended the superficial roughness of his technique:

> I don't know if you have come across the word Bullshit—it is an army word and signifies humbug and unnecessary detail. It symbolizes what I think must be got rid of—the mass of irrelevancies, of "attitudes," "approaches," propaganda, ivory towers, &c., that stands between us and our problems and what we have to do about them. To write on the themes that have been concerning me lately in lyric and abstract form would be immense bullshitting. . . . I don't disagree with you if you say I am awkward . . . but my object is to write true things, significant things, in words each of which works for its place in a line. My rhythms, which you find enervated, are carefully chosen to enable the poems to be *read* as significant speech: I see no reason to be either musical or sonorous about things at present. . . . Certainly you will never see the long metrical similes and galleries of images again. . . . Perhaps all this may make it easier for you to understand why I am writing the way I am and why I shall never go back to the old forms. You may even begin to see some virtue in it. . . .

Douglas is often an elliptical poet, therefore of no interest to the slovenly reader who only wants to read what he (or she) expects: his instinctive understanding that poems have a form of their own, dictated by their subject-matter and purpose, which has nothing whatever to do with the outworn forms that some people seem to imagine constitute the essential difference between poetry and prose, makes him a visual rather than a musical poet—that is, a poet whose poems exist on the page with the abstract unity of a painting, a unity which is stronger and terser than that of sound. Poetry for Douglas was a necessity first, an art second, an exercise in verbal ingenuity never. That right order (which many self-satisfied performers to-day reverse) meant that every poem he wrote had a validity over and above its poetic success—if, which is doubtful, these can be separated. In fact, the writing of poems needs luck as well as application: there are good days and bad days as in racing, or cricket, or painting. Douglas's short life consisted almost entirely of good days: it is possible to trace in nearly all his poems the moment when the prose statement becomes a poetic one, when a fortunate rhyme fashions the earlier intractable sentences and creates an inevitable form. It is inevitability that indifferent poems lack, and which Douglas's poems always give the feel of: of course, in practice, no poem seems inevitable to its writer until, almost by accident, it suddenly clicks into rightness. But Douglas insures against luck by, in his own phrase, making every word "work for its keep"—there is no slack to be pulled in, each image is telling, definitive, but also an integral part of the poem.

He wrote very close to life, very idiomatically and naturally, so that there is no sense of strain in his poems, nothing absurd or intense which a man of sensibility would find himself unable to say to another man in ordinary conversation. "The poetry is in the pity": Owen's phrase applies obviously, but the poetry is also in the images through which Douglas's poems progressed—images that were beaten into the poem as into metal. The texture of his poems is beautiful in an off-hand, never moony kind of way, and they are affecting because they state direct experiences directly. Their comments are ironic but not detached, and they are involved in the poem as Douglas was involved in the experiences and events that led to them. "I never tried to write about war (that is battles and things, not London can Take it), with the exception of a satiric picture of some soldiers frozen to death, until I had experienced it. Now I will write of it, and perhaps one day cynic and lyric will meet and make me a balanced style." He wrote this in August, 1943. In fact, the balanced style had by then resolved itself, though cynicism was never a part of it.

One tends to think of Douglas exclusively in terms of that handful of desert poems, the writing of which must have given him a wonderful feeling of release before his death—the death he was prepared to expect. "I can't afford to wait," he wrote to his prospective publisher, Tambimuttu, "because of military engagements which may be the end of me." Yet he had appeared in *New Verse* at the age of sixteen and the pure accomplishment of these earlier poems—written before he joined the army—is unmistakable. For example, this passage from a poem called **"On Leaving School,"** written at seventeen:—

> This simple evening moment, when the shallow
> Echoes stagger against Big School, it is awkward
> Realizing happiness seems just to have started
> And now we must leave it, live like trees or charlock.
> One of us will be the kettle past care of tinkers,
> Rejected, one the tip-top apple, the winking
> Sun's friend. It will be that way, and Time on our ground
> Will sweep like a maid, and where we were be clean.
> Shall we find room to laugh, if turning round
> We see where we have walked, how wrong we have been?

A boy's poem, a little Rupert Brookeish, but with already greater sense of perspective, of human possibilities, and a quite different care over adjectives and imagery.

Time was one of Douglas's major poetic preoccupations and the concept of it appears over and over again, especially in the Middle East poems. "And Time will cage again, The devils we let run," "Time comes and eats," "Ravenous Time has flowers for his food," "Time's ruminative tongue will wash And slow juice masticate all flesh," "But Time, who ate my love, cannot make such another." It is a straightforward, not surprising obsession—how short is a man's life when he knows his number is likely to come up any day, and, no matter how many new men can be bred as quickly as they die, they will not be the same ones. Douglas wrote as that unique man who saw the sun going down and who knew that what he had observed would have to be noted immediately, for he would not be likely to last out the night. In Egypt he wrote:—

> I see men as trees suffering
> Or confound the detail and the horizon.
> Lay the coin on my tongue and I will sing
> Of what the others never set eyes on.

Most of the Middle East poems are on two levels and contrast what the eye sees with the soldier's reading of what it sees. In others the contrast is between Base life, with its shabby pleasures, and the real life of the desert, which, in spite of its litter of human débris, Douglas both preferred and found strangely beautiful:

> Shall I get drunk or cut myself a piece of cake,
> a pasty Syrian with a few words of English
> Or the Turk who says she is a princess
>   she dances
> apparently by levitation? Or Marcelle,
>   Parisienne
> always preoccupied with her dull dead
>   lover:
> she has all the photographs and his
>   letters
> tied in a bundle and stamped *Décédé* in
>   mauve ink.
> All this takes place in a stink of
>   jasmin. . . .
> But by a day's travelling you reach a new
>   world
> the vegetation is of iron
> dead tanks, gun barrels split like celery
> the metal brambles have no flowers or
>   berries
> and there are all sorts of manure, you
>   can imagine
> the dead themselves, their boots, clothes
>   and possessions
> clinging to the ground, a man with no
>   head
> has a packet of chocolate and a souvenir
> of Tripoli.

At El Ballah he wrote:

> And the pockmarked house bleached by
>   the glare
> whose insides war has dried out like
>   gourds
> attracts words. There are those who
>   capture them

in hundreds, keep them prisoners in black
bottles, release them at exercise and clap
   them back.
But I keep words only a breath of time
turning in the lightest of cages—uncover
and let them go: sometimes they escape
   for ever.

Appropriately enough, for his life ended with the neatness of art, his last poem was the most perfect that he wrote, and the mere act of copying it down says more about him as a poet, about what he wrote and how he wrote it, and what it meant, than anything else could:

On A Return From Egypt

To stand here in the wings of Europe
disheartened, I have come away
from the sick land where in the sun lay
the gentle sloe-eyed murderers
Of themselves, exquisites under a curse;
here to exercise my depleted fury.
For the heart is a coal, growing colder
when jewelled cerulean seas change
into grey rocks, grey water-fringe,
sea and sky altering like a cloth
till colour and sheen are gone both:
cold is an opiate of the soldier.

And all my endeavours are unlucky
   explorers
come back, abandoning the expedition;
the specimens, the lilies of ambition
still spring in their climate, still unpicked:
but time, time is all I lacked
to find them, as the great collectors
   before me.

The next month, then, is a window
and with a crash I'll split the glass.
Behind it stands one I must kiss,
person of love or death
a person or a wraith,
I fear what I shall find.

In the last resort, over and above techniques and themes, one judges poets—or, rather, likes them, because "judge" is a depressing verb to apply to poetry—by whether or not one finds them sympathetic. To me, Keith Douglas is the most sympathetic poet of his (which is my own) generation: he wrote the kind of poetry I should like to have written, which is the most any writer can say about another.

   Alan Ross, "The Poetry of Keith Douglas," in
   The Times Literary Supplement, *No. 2740,*
   August 6, 1954, p. xxii.

G. S. Fraser   (lecture date 1956)

[*A Scottish poet, critic, and translator, Fraser wrote a number of works on twentieth-century poets, including Dylan Thomas, Ezra Pound, and Lawrence Durrell. As a poet, Fraser was most closely associated with the New Apocalypse, a group of English poets of the 1940s whose works championed human imagination and often employed surrealist imagery. In the following excerpt from a lecture on Douglas, he outlines Douglas's development as a poet.*]

Douglas is remembered today (if, indeed, the English general reader remembers him with any vividness at all) as a war poet. He is remembered as one of three young English poets of great promise and early fame—the other two were Alun Lewis and Sidney Keyes—who all perished in the Second World War. Now, the attitude of the English public to war poets is an odd one. Poetry is what the English do best, but it is only, I think, in war-time that they remember that; it is only in war-time that they clamour for new poetry, that they ask, 'Where are the new young poets?', that they buy eagerly volumes and anthologies and periodicals devoted to new verse. Good young English poets, during a war, are published easily; so, I am afraid, are other young poets who are not so good; and in fact the sense of exile, the novelty of a foreign scene, the stress of action do, during a war, stir many young men into trying to express themselves in verse who, in quieter times, would never think of themselves as poets. And, in fact, so long as a war continues, so long as many of our young people are overseas, we find that we can read poetry by young men in the forces, even if it is not quite successful poetry, with sympathy. At the least, it will have a documentary interest; it will have the interest of an exile's letter home. That documentary and sentimental interest, alas, soon fades, once a war is over; and with it there tends to fade, however unfairly, our interest in the more genuine poetry which a was has produced. (p. 90)

It is true that, in 1951, Keith Douglas's *Collected Poems* were well received; Mr. Ronald Bottrall, I remember, wrote a particularly perceptive review in *The New Statesman*. Yet they appeared in an unfortunate year. The year 1951 marked something like a watershed between two movements in contemporary English poetry. The prevailing mood among the younger poets of the 1940's, or at least among a fairly coherent group of them, was what was often called the mood of neo-romanticism. It was a mood that owed a great deal to poets like Dylan Thomas and Mr. George Barker; it is carried on today by a poet like Mr. W. S. Graham. It was a mood that preferred evocation to description, images to statements, feeling to thought, colour, one might say, to line. It was a mood, also, to which Keith Douglas had almost nothing to offer. I remember a typical new romantic poet of the 1940's, Mr. Tom Scott, telling me that he found Douglas's poetry hard, cold, and dry. Since 1951, indeed, a whole new school of young poets has come into notice that does share Douglas's ideals of precise and disciplined statement in verse: I am thinking of poets like Mr. Philip Larkin, Miss Elizabeth Jennings, Mr. Philip Oakes, Mr. Kingsley Amis, Mr. Gordon Wharton, Mr. Bernard Bergonzi, Mr. John Wain. But these new young poets do not share Douglas's temperament. Their attitude to life is more negatively ironical than his, or at least more constrained and more hesitant. For in a sense, though not in the cant sense of the 1940's, Douglas *was* a romantic poet.

Keith Douglas's mother . . . wrote to me the other day, reminding me of an excellent short statement, called **'On the Nature of Poetry'** which Douglas, in 1940, contributed to *Augury*, an Oxford miscellany of prose and verse of which he was one of the editors. It is worth quoting in full. It was written, we must remember, by a boy of twenty; and the qualities that come out in it are, I think, not only Douglas's simplicity and sincerity, his remarkable lack of undergraduate pose, but also his penetration. It might be a statement by a very mature man. It owes, I think, here and there, just a little to Croce:

> Poetry is like a man, whom thinking you know all his movements and appearance you will presently come upon in such a posture that for a moment you can hardly believe it a position of the limbs you know. So thinking you have set bounds to the nature of poetry, you shall as soon discover something outside your bounds which they should evidently contain.

> The expression 'bad poetry' is meaningless: critics still use it, forgetting that bad poetry is not poetry at all.

> Nor can prose and poetry be compared any more than pictures and pencils: the one is instrument and the other art. Poetry may be written in prose or verse, or spoken extempore.

> For it is anything expressed in words, which appeals to the emotions either in presenting an image or picture to move them; or by the music of words affecting them through the senses; or in stating some truth whose eternal quality exacts the same reverence as eternity itself.

> In its nature poetry is sincere and simple.

> Writing which is poetry must say what the writer has himself to say, not what he has observed others to say with effect, nor what he thinks will impress others because it impressed him hearing it. Nor must he waste any more words over it than a mathematician; every word must work for its keep, in prose, blank verse, or rhyme.

> And poetry is to be judged not by what the poet has tried to say; only by what he has said.

These aphorisms seem to me to be true; and perhaps Keith Douglas's criticism of many of the new romantic poets of the 1940's might have been that they wanted to be judged by what they had tried to say, not by what they had said, that they did not make words work hard enough for their keep. His criticism of our immediate contemporaries, the poets of the 'New Movement' of the 1940's, might be perhaps that they are not sincere and simple enough; that they too often say what they have observed others to say with effect, or what they think will impress their hearers because it impressed them hearing it. That would apply, for instance, to the many attempts by young poets in the last few years to imitate Mr. Empson's attitudes and catch his tone. Thinking as he did about poetry, Keith Douglas could obviously belong, in the strict sense, to no 'school'. And when I say that he was essentially a romantic poet, I am referring not to his formal ideals about poetry, but to his personal temperament.

Thus, Douglas's attitude to war was, though humane and deeply compassionate, a heroic attitude. It had nothing in common with the humanitarian, pacifist attitudes of contemporaries of his like Nicholas Moore or Alex Comfort or Douglas's friend, John Hall. He was a good soldier, and in a sense he enjoyed his war. He enjoyed, at least, the ex-

ercise of the will in action. He was an officer, and an efficient officer, who enjoyed the company of his fellow officers, and accepted and enjoyed the responsibility that went with his rank. In that, among our poets of the last war, he was almost unique; Alun Lewis and Sidney Keyes were both also officers, and conscientious ones, but neither of them was a natural soldier in the sense that Keith Douglas was. And much more typically the soldier-writer of the last war tended to be, like myself, the sergeant-major's nightmare: the long-haired private, who could not keep step, who not only looked like a bloody poet, but turned out in the end to be one: a great nuisance to his superiors generally till he could be parked in an office with a typewriter. Douglas, on the other hand, was physically and temperamentally adapted to war. It was a rough game that he was good at playing. Again, he was a very intelligent man, as these aphorisms on poetry prove, but not a man, I think, who had much use for intellectual chatter. The two or three times I personally met him, I do not remember our exchanging a word on any abstract topic. Whatever else he may have pined for during the war years, it will not have been evening parties in Chelsea.

Douglas, in fact, was a cavalier. Riding was almost his favourite sport, and in war he thought of his tank as if it were a horse. There is a poem, written at Enfidaville, in Tunisia, in 1943, which gives us, I think, some leading clues to his temperament. . . .

Aristocrats

'I think I am becoming a God'

The noble horse with courage in his eye
clean in the bone, looks up at a shellburst:
away fly the images of the shires
but he puts the pipe back in his mouth.

Peter was unfortunately killed by an 88:
it took his leg away, he died in the ambulance.
I saw him crawling on the sand; he said
It's most unfair, they've shot my foot off.

How can I live among this gentle
obsolescent breed of heroes, and not weep?
Unicorns, almost,
for they are falling into two legends
in which their stupidity and chivalry
are celebrated. Each, fool and hero, will be an
    immortal.

The plains were their cricket pitch
and in the mountains the tremendous drop
    fences
brought down some of the runners. Here then
under the stones and earth they dispose them-
    selves,
I think with their famous unconcern.
It is not gunfire I hear but a hunting horn.

In that fine last line, as Sir John Waller remarks in his notes to the *Collected Poems,* there is an echo of Roncesvalles. And the aristocratic morality, evoked in this poem, was the morality to which in the depths of his nature Keith Douglas was most profoundly drawn. He was an aloof, gay, and passionate man. He loved risk. The state of the world, and perhaps the nature of man, and perhaps his own nature in its depths, filled him with profound sadness; nevertheless, for him the sadness of human existence was a kind of destiny that had to be bravely and lovingly embraced. He was as far as can be from a nagging or carping attitude to life. And this partly explains the obscurity of his present reputation. The new poetry of the last five years has in itself many virtues of reticence and control; but it does not express, in its spirit, precisely these generous, aristocratic virtues. (pp. 91-4)

Douglas had early joined the Oxford O.T.C., partly for the sake of the free riding it offered, and thus he was liable for service on the outbreak of war. He was not, in fact, called up, till fairly late in 1940. He trained in various places in Great Britain and in June 1941 was posted to the Middle East, transferred to the Notts Sherwood Rangers Yeomanry, but seconded to a staff job at base. He disliked this, and on the eve of El Alamein ran away to rejoin his old regiment, who welcomed him. He fought with them in a Crusader tank from El Alamein to Wadi Zem Zem in Tunisia, continuously, except for one interval of hospitalization and convalescence in Palestine, after he had been blown up by a land-mine. He kept a diary, and the book he made out of it, *Alamein to Zem Zem,* is probably one of the very few accounts, indeed, of fighting in the Second World War likely to rank, as literature, with classics of the First World War like Sir Herbert Read's *In Retreat,* the war chapters in Mr. Robert Graves's *Good-Bye to All That* or Mr. Siegfried Sassoon's *Memoirs of a Fox-Hunting Man* and *Memoirs of an Infantry Officer.* The book has two great qualities: visual immediacy, and an almost frightening emotional detachment. 'I observed,' Douglas says, 'these battles partly as an exhibition—that is to say, I went through them like a little child in a factory—a child sees the brightness and efficiency of steel machines and endless belts slapping round and round, without knowing or caring what it is all there for. When I could order my thoughts I looked for something more significant than appearances; I still look, I cannot avoid it, for something decorative, poetic, or dramatic.'

The qualities of Douglas's prose in *Alamein to Zem Zem*—the brutal vividness of presentation, combined with an apparent almost icy detachment—are to be found, of course, in even greater concentration, in the poems he wrote in the Western Desert and during periods of leave in Cairo or convalescence in Palestine. These he published almost as soon as he had written them, sending many of them on airgraphs to M. J. Tambimuttu's *Poetry London,* giving others to his friends Bernard Spencer and Lawrence Durrell to put into the excellent magazine they were bringing out in Cairo, *Personal Landscape.* At the end of 1943 Douglas was posted home to train for the invasion of Europe. And with that posting the history of his career, as a poet, really comes to an end. His last completed poem is called **'On a Return from Egypt'**. . . . [It] expresses very beautifully both a clear premonition of death, and a bitterness at the foreknowledge that he will not be allowed to survive, to write the poems he might have written:

> And all my endeavours are unlucky explorers
> come back, abandoning the expedition;
> the specimens, the lilies of ambition
> still spring in their climate, still unpicked:
> but time, time is all I lacked

to find them as the great collectors before me.

(pp. 95-6)

Douglas's poems fall into a number of distinct groups, and any later group is always more interesting and important than the group that immediately precedes it. The poems that he wrote at school are mainly important in that they show us a boy patiently learning his craft. The poems that he wrote at Oxford have more depth and subtlety, but they have something in common—both in their charm, and in their occasional weakness—with all undergraduate poetry. They are very 'literary' poems. In the poems which Douglas wrote during his period of military training in England, we begin to feel that he is biting deeper into experience; or that experience is biting deeper into him. Finally, the poems written in the Middle East are, of course, Douglas's most important achievement. If we take these groups in turn, we shall get a fairly accurate picture of his development.

There is, however, one more group still: the group of poems Douglas was never able to finish. The most important of these is a poem, or a set of frustrated beginnings of a poem, called **'Bête Noire'**. This, as it stands, is not anything achieved. It is a succession of hopeless attempts to grapple with an intractable subject, the subject of what Douglas called, in conversation and in letters, 'the beast on my back'. It is the subject of what any of us colloquially might call 'the black dog on my back': or in more ambitious language, it is the subject of what Freudian psychologists call, or used to call, the Death-Wish and Jungian psychologists call the Shadow. I imagine a Jungian psychologist would say that Douglas was very much aware of his Shadow, in a sense at times almost obsessed with it, but that he had never properly accepted it, or come to terms with it, and that therefore, in spite of the impression he gave of being far more mature than his years, he was not, when he died, yet a fully integrated personality. There was, as it were, a crucial and painful experience still to come, of which he had a kind of poetic premonition. The Shadow, in more homely terms than those of the psychologists, is the sudden awareness, which can be a blinding and shattering one, of all the nastiness, all the ulterior self-centredness, in our own motives and in those of others. To accept the Shadow is, in Christian language, to accept the possibility of Damnation and the reality of Original Sin. The Shadow, if we try to suppress our latent awareness of it—most people of a liberal morality and of progressive views try to do this, most of the time—can, as it were, irrupt upon us. And the moment of its irruption is the moment when we feel not only that we have never loved anybody properly, but that nobody has ever loved us, that love is a lie. (pp. 97-8)

Douglas, I think, found it excessively difficult to come to terms with his Shadow just because he was such an unusually good man. He had high principles, and he always acted on his principles. As a boy, his first thought was of what he owed to his mother; as a young man, of what he owed to his country. His personal interests he had concentrated on high and wholesome things, on love, and poetry, and comradeship, and adventure. So it seemed to him inexplicable, I suppose, that he should have these black despairing moods. What had he done to deserve them? He had certainly never shirked any duty or danger, he was incapable of a mean act, and yet his black beast was liable to pounce upon him at the most unexpected moments, like the sense of guilt of a very bad, or the sense of inadequacy of a very weak man. On his bad days, it could spoil everything:

> It's his day.
> Don't kiss me. Don't put your arm round
> And touch the beast on my back.

Had Douglas survived, given this obsession with the Shadow, and given also the strain under which he had laboured as a fighting soldier and the iron self-control which he had always exercised, given the roaring guns and the dead men and the buckled tanks in the Western Desert, I think that, a few years after the war, he might have had a bad breakdown. He would have emerged from that breakdown, I imagine, having come to terms with the Shadow, and with a new depth as a poet. **'Bête Noire'**, as I say, is an unfinished poem, a failure; but in its light, or against its darkness, all Douglas's other poems must be read.

I shall be fairly brief about the poems Douglas wrote while still a schoolboy. In a schoolboy's poems one does not look for originality of thought or feeling. One looks for adroitness in handling words, for signs that the handling of rhythms, the shaping of phrases, gives a young poet pleasure. Here is the poem which Douglas at sixteen sold to *New Verse,* a short poem which says nothing very much, but says it very agreeably:

Dejection

> Yesterday travellers in summer's country,
> Tonight the sprinkled moon and ravenous sky
> Say, we have reached the boundary. The autumn
>   clothes
> Are on; Death is the season and we the living
> Are hailed by the solitary to join their regiment,
> To leave the sea and the horses and march away
> Endlessly. The spheres speak with persuasive
>   voices.
> Only tomorrow like a seagull hovers and calls
> Shrieks through the mist and scatters the pools
>   of stars.
> The windows will be open and hearts behind
>   them.

The Oxford poems, written between 1938 and 1940, deserve, of course, much more attention. There are about thirty of them. They show, as contrasted with the school poems, a growing range and suppleness. But most of them are still very much what I would call 'literary' poems and also still very much 'occasional' poems. There is about them, occasionally, a slightly self-indulgent melancholy and a youthful romantic morbidity. One of the best of them, **'Leukothea'**, is about a beautiful dead woman. Her beauty was so supernatural that the poet imagines it has resisted corruption in the ground. A bad dream disillusions him:

> So all these years I have lived securely. I knew
> I had only to uncover you
> to see how the careful earth would have kept
> all as it was, untouched. I trusted the ground.
> I knew the worm and the beetle would go by

and never dare batten on your beauty.

> Last night I dreamed and found my trust be-
>   trayed
> only the little bones and the great bones disar-
>   rayed.

That is good partly because it is so beautifully phrased, but good partly also because, I think, one finds oneself, half consciously, reading into it a meaning far deeper than the fantastical surface meaning. One thinks of the parable, in the Bible, of the buried talent. One thinks of people who fling themselves, from some practical compulsion, into the thick of the world, but dream always of reaching a stage when they can afford to cultivate some gift, to pursue some vision, which meant much in their boyhood, and then, when they have their chance, find that the vision has faded, the gift has decayed. (pp. 98-100)

'Leukothea', however, is rather exceptional. More typically, Douglas's Oxford poems express a mood which most generations of undergraduates must have felt, and Douglas's own generation, waiting to go to war, particularly poignantly. There is the sense of magical years, soon passing, but for that reason to be treasured all the more highly; there is the special sense of the magic of Oxford as a place:

> This then is the city of young men, of beginning,
> ideas, trials, pardonable follies,
> the lightness, seriousness, and sorrow of
>   youth. . . .

Already, however, towards the end of Douglas's Oxford period, his concept of poetry was becoming more mature. He was trying to say more, and to friends who had liked his early lyrical smoothness it seemed that the new style he was developing was a rather harsh and rough one. Answering such a criticism from his friend, John Hall, Keith Douglas, when a soldier, wrote:

> In my early poems I wrote lyrically, as an inno-
> cent, because I was an innocent; I have (not sur-
> prisingly) fallen from that particular grace since
> then. I had begun to change during my second
> year at Oxford. T. S. Eliot wrote to me when I
> first joined the Army, that I appeared to have
> finished with one form of writing and to be prog-
> ressing towards another, which he did not think
> I had mastered. I knew this to be true without
> his saying it.

The nature of the change in style, and the degree of the progress towards mastery, can be seen in two poems, the two most successful ones, out of the comparatively small batch which Douglas wrote during his period of military training in England. One of these, called **'The Prisoner'**, is addressed to a Chinese girl called Cheng. There is in it a new depth, a new intimacy, a new painfulness:

> Today, Cheng, I touched your face
> with two fingers, as a gesture of love;
> for I can never prove enough
> by sight or sense your strange grace,
>
> but mothwise my hands return
> to your fair cheek, as luminous
> as a lamp in a paper house,
> and touch, to teach love and learn.

Douglas as a student at Oxford, 1939.

I think a hundred years are gone
that so, like gods, we'd occupy.
But alas, Cheng, I cannot tell why,
today I touched a mask stretched on the stone

person of death. There was the urge
to break the bright flesh and emerge
from the ambitious cruel bone.

The other important poem of this training period, **'Time Eating'**, might be described as metaphysical. This, like **'The Prisoner'**, gives us a hint about some of the deep sources of Douglas's *bête noire* obsession:

Ravenous Time has flowers for his food
In Autumn, yet can cleverly make good
each petal: devours animals and men,
but for ten dead he can create ten.

If you enquire how secretly you've come
to mansize from the smallness of a stone
it will appear his effort made you rise
so gradually to your proper size.

But as he makes he eats; the very part
where he began, even the elusive heart,
Time's ruminative tongue will wash
and slow juice masticate all flesh.

That volatile huge intestine holds
material and abstract in its folds:
thought and ambition melt and even the world
will alter, in that catholic belly curled.

But Time, who ate my love, you cannot make
such another; you who can remake
the lizard's tail and the bright snakeskin
cannot, cannot. That you gobbled in
too quick, and though you brought me from a
    boy
you can make no more of me, only destroy.

Nothing in Douglas's earlier writing had led us to anticipate the melancholy gusto, here, of his metaphysical wit:

That volatile huge intestine holds
material and abstract in its folds:
thought and ambition melt and even the world
will alter, in that catholic belly curled.

There is something of the passionate ingenuity of Donne in these four lines, combined with something of the eloquent directness of Dryden.

During the period of his army training in England, Douglas began, therefore, as it were, to reconnoitre himself in depth. But his main reputation will probably rest on the best of the thirty or so poems which he wrote while on active service in the Middle East. These are uneven; there are, in almost all of them, if we compare them to his Oxford poems, certain technical roughnesses, of which Douglas was quite conscious. For he is not seeking merely as in **"The Prisoner'** and **'Time Eating'** to probe new and painful depths of personal feeling, but to absorb into his verse raw material which might, of its very nature, seem intractable to poetry. **'Cairo Jag',** for instance, which I shall now read to you, will remain, to anybody who served in the Middle East during the last war, a vivid piece of documentation. It brings it all back, so to say. But is it, in the ordinary sense, a *poem,* is its painfulness resolved? Do its images merely pile up brutally or do they work, in the end, into some large reconciling pattern? It is a marginal case among Douglas's poems: certainly very memorable, but not certainly very good. I leave you to judge:

Shall I get drunk or cut myself a piece of cake,
a pastry Syrian with a few words of English
or the Turk who says she is a princess—she
    dances
apparently by levitation? Or Marcelle, Parisien-
    ne
always preoccupied with her dull dead lover:
she has all the photographs and his letters
tied in a bundle and stamped *Décédé* in mauve
    ink.
All this takes place in a stink of jasmin.

But there are the streets dedicated to sleep
stenches and sour smells, the sour cries
do not disturb their application to slumber
all day, scattered on the pavement like rags
afflicted with fatalism and hashish. The women
offering their children brown-paper breasts
dry and twisted, elongated like the skull,
Holbein's signature. But this stained white town
is something in accordance with mundane con-
    ventions—
Marcelle drops her Gallic airs and tragedy
suddenly shrieks in Arabic about the fare
with the cabman, links herself so
with the somnambulists and legless beggars:
it is all one, all as you have heard.

But by a day's travelling you reach a new world
the vegetation is of iron
dead tanks, gun barrels split like celery
the metal brambles have no flowers or berries
and there are all sorts of manure, you can imag-
　　ine
the dead themselves, their boots, clothes and
　　possessions
clinging to the ground, a man with no head
has a packet of chocolate and a souvenir of Trip-
　　oli.

So it was. And the only moral comment Douglas allows himself to make in the poem is that so it was:

it is all one, all as you have heard . . .

And, when we have read the poem carefully, we realize that he means by that not only that it is all one in Cairo, that the shrieking Marcelle is at one with the shrieking cabman and the legless beggars, the squalor is universal, but also that it is all one between Cairo and the Desert: moral death and disorder match physical death and disorder; Marcelle's photographs and letters of her dull dead lover exactly match the dead soldier's packet of chocolate and souvenir from Tripoli, are as futile, and pathetic, and meaningless, and ultimately enraging. It is the kind of poem which Pope or Dryden would have written in neatly antithetic heroic couplets, Cairo in one line, the Desert in the next. Douglas leaves it as a jumble, giving us one clue that will enable us to sort it out for ourselves. We *can* sort it out, but we still wonder if it is a good poem; it is, at least, a very bold and original experiment.

It is interesting to contrast **'Cairo Jag'** with the poem that immediately precedes it in Douglas's ***Collected Poems,*** **'Behaviour of Fish in an Egyptian Tea Garden'.** During the Middle East it was Cairo which focused all Douglas's negative emotions, which made a satirist of him. But **'Cairo Jag'** fails, if it does fail, because it lacks that 'coolness at the centre' which Saintsbury noted as the mark of a great satirist like Dryden; it is too near hysteria. **'Behaviour of Fish in an Egyptian Tea Garden'** is urbane, detached, even gay in tone. A single metaphor is brilliantly sustained, and in sustaining it Douglas can bring to bear all his powers of visual fantasy. Yet the effect is more properly satirical, more damaging to its object, than that of **'Cairo Jag'**:

As a white stone draws down the fish
she on the seafloor of the afternoon
draws down men's glances and their cruel wish
for love. Slyly red lip on the spoon

slips in a morsel of ice-cream; her hands
white as a milky stone, white submarine
fronds, sink with spread fingers, lean
along the table, carmined at the ends.

A cotton magnate, an important fish
with great eyepouches and a golden mouth
through the frail reefs of furniture swims out
and idling, suspended, stays to watch.

A crustacean old man clamped to his chair
sits coldly near her and might see
her charms through fissures where the eyes
　　should be

or else his teeth are parted in a stare.

Captain of leave, a lean dark mackerel,
lies in the offing; turns himself and looks
through currents of sound. The flat-eyed flatfish
　　sucks
on a straw, staring from its repose, laxly.

And gallants in shoals swim up and lag,
circling and passing near the white attraction;
sometimes pausing, opening a conversation;
fish pause so to nibble or tug.

Now the ice-cream is finished, is
paid for. The fish swim off on business
and she sits alone at the table, a white stone
useless except to a collector, a rich man.

One has no doubts that *that* is a good poem.

But Douglas's temperament was not that of the satirist; it was, as I have said, a romantic temperament, in its ardour, though without that passion for self-deception, that indignant refusal to see things as they are, which we sometimes associate with the idea of romanticism. In the desert, he could still find release, in poetry, for the positive ardour of his mind. He need not merely be a satirist. He could address his Muse, partly as a lost, cruel mistress, partly as the moon:

I listen to the desert wind
that will not blow her from my mind;
the stars will not put down a hand,
the moon's ignorant of my wound

moving negligently across
by clouds and cruel tracts of space
as in my brain my nights and days
moves the reflection of her face.

Skims like a bird my sleepless eye
the sands who at this hour deny
the violent heat they have by day
as she denies her former way:

all the elements agree
with her, to have no sympathy
for my tactless misery
as wonderful and hard as she.

O turn in the dark bed again
and give to him what once was mine
and I'll turn as you turn
and kiss my swarthy mistress pain.

One is very often aware of Douglas's reading—one is aware, there, of how well he knew Wyatt:

as she denies her former way—

without ever feeling that he is writing pastiche.

I earlier this evening read to you one of Douglas's poems of action, **'Aristocrats'.** It was not a mere poem of action, but a poem in praise of chivalry. He is never merely a descriptive poet: and his best poem of action, **'Vergissmeinnicht'**, is like the earlier **'The Prisoner'** essentially a poem about love and death:

Three weeks gone and the combatants gone,
returning over the nightmare ground
we found the place again, and found

the soldier sprawling in the sun.

The frowning barrel of his gun
overshadowing. As we came on
that day, he hit my tank with one
like the entry of a demon.

Look. Here in the gunpit spoil
the dishonoured picture of his girl
who has put: *Steffi. Vergissmeinnicht*
in a copybook gothic script.

We see him almost with content
abased, and seeming to have paid
and mocked at by his own equipment
that's hard and good when he's decayed.

But she would weep to see to-day
how on his skin the swart flies move;
the dust upon the paper eye
and the burst stomach like a cave.

For here the lover and killer are mingled
who had one body and one heart.
And death who had the soldier singled
has done the lover mortal hurt.

Always look in a poem like that, which moves you, and
which might seem to move you merely by its material, by
what it rawly presents, for the handling. Douglas, I think,
never wrote a more skilful poem than this; or one in which
his skill is more modestly subdued to the total effect he is
aiming at. What gives us the effect, for instance, in the first
stanza, of the tanks lumbering bumpily and relentlessly on
is a kind of wheeling motion in the stanza itself, repetitions
and a concealed rhyme:

Three weeks *gone* and the combatants *gone*,
returning over the nightmare *ground*
we *found* the place again, and *found*
the soldier sprawling in the sun. . . .

What saves the stanza about the dead soldier's appearance
from being merely repellent is, again, the deliberate formality of the syntax and the choice of a literary adjective—'the swart flies', not 'the black flies', and an objective
precision of statement, without emotional commentary,
that gives an effect of icy pity:

But she would weep to see to-day
how on his skin the swart flies move;
the dust upon the paper eye
and the burst stomach like a cave.

And in the last stanza the effect of aesthetic distance, of
the whole experience being held in control, is clinched by
the eighteenth-century antithesis:

And death who had *the soldier* singled
has done *the lover* mortal hurt.

I shall not attempt to 'place' Douglas as a poet: I think
that four or five of the poems I have read to you this evening would have to be considered very seriously indeed by
any anthologist attempting to produce a representative selection of the best poems, written by the younger English
poets, over the past twenty-five years; and I think it would
be hard, among poems by younger poets of the 1950's,
which have attracted much attention in the last few years,
to match these four or five poems. But what is specially

and sadly interesting about Douglas is the sense that his
development was continuous and steady; the sense that,
if he had been spared—he would be now in his middle thirties, if he were alive—he might well be, today, the dominating figure of his generation and a wholesome and inspiring influence on younger men. He had courage, passion, and generosity. These are three qualities that our age
generally needs. (pp. 101-08)

*G. S. Fraser, "Keith Douglas: A Poet of the
Second World War," in* Proceedings of the
British Academy, *Vol. XLII, 1956, pp. 89-
108.*

Ted Hughes   (essay date 1963)

[*An English poet, critic, dramatist, and short story writer, Hughes was appointed Poet Laureate of England in
1984. He is best known for poems in which he exalts both
the beauty and the violence of nature. Hughes believes
that Western rationalism has alienated people from
their physical nature, and seeks to reconcile this division
by writing in forceful, evocative language on natural,
mythic, and primitivist themes. The editor of the posthumously published work of his wife, the poet and novelist
Sylvia Plath, Hughes was also one of Douglas's principal
critical champions and the editor of his* Selected Poems.
*In the following essay, which was later reprinted as the
introduction to that volume, Hughes gives a laudatory
appraisal of Douglas's poetic development.*]

Keith Douglas was born in 1920 and killed in Normandy
in 1944. When his collected poems were first published in
1951, by Editions Poetry London Ltd, with notes and introduction, edited by John Waller and G. S. Fraser, he appeared primarily interesting to most of his readers as a
"war-poet", and as such seems to have been largely forgotten. Now, twelve years later and eighteen years after his
death, it is becoming clear that he offers more than just a
few poems about war, and that every poem he wrote,
whether about war or not, has some special value. His poetry in general seems to be of some special value. It is still
very much alive, and even providing life. And the longer
it lives, the fresher it looks.

Here is a poem, dated 1936, titled **'Encounter with a God'**:

Ono-no-komache the poetess
sat on the ground among her flowers,
sat in her delicate-patterned dress
thinking of the rowers,
thinking of the god Daikoku.

Thinking of the rock pool
and carp in the waterfall at night.
Daikoku in accordance with the rule
is beautiful, she said, with a slight
tendency to angles.

But Daikoku came
who had been drinking all night
with the greenish gods of chance and fame.
He was rotund standing in the moonlight,
with a round, white paunch.

Who said
I am not beautiful,

I do not wish to be wonderfully made,
I am not intoxicated, dutiful daughter,
and I will not be in a poem.

But the poetess sat still
holding her head and making verses:
"How intricate and peculiarly well-
arranged the symmetrical belly-purses
of Lord Daikoku".

It is quite limited in scope, and comes properly into the category of Juvenilia, but it accomplishes its job, not an easy one, as brilliantly and surely as anything Douglas ever did. And the qualities that create and distinguish his most important later work are already there.

It is not enough to say that the language is utterly simple, the musical inflexion of it peculiarly honest and charming, the technique flawless. The language is also extremely forceful; or rather, it reposes at a point it could only have reached, this very moment, by a feat of great strength. And the inflexion of the voice has a bluntness that might be challenging if it were not so frank, and so clearly the advance of an unusually aware mind. As for the technique, insofar as it can be considered separately, there is nothing dead or asleep in it, nothing tactless, and such subtlety of movement, such economy of means, such composition of cadences, would do credit to any living poet. Behind these qualities we feel the prevailing independence of temperament. And behind that, ordering its directions, the essentially practical cast of his energy, his impatient, razor energy.

In his nine years of accomplished writing, Douglas developed rapidly. Leaving his virtuoso juvenilia, his poetry passed through two roughly distinguishable phases, and began to clarify into a third. The literary influences on this progress seem to have been few. To begin with, perhaps he takes Auden's language over pretty whole, but he empties it of its intellectual concerns, turns it onto the practical experience of life, and lets a few minor colours of the late 1930 poetry schools creep in. But his temperament is so wholly modern he seems to have no difficulty with the terrible, suffocating, maternal octopus of ancient English poetic tradition.

The first phase of his growth shows itself in this poem titled **'Forgotten the Red Leaves':**

Forgotten the red leaves painting the temple in
    summer,
Forgotten my squirrel in his dark chamber
The great turtle and the catamaran;
Rivers, where the mosaic stones are found

That church, amputated by high explosive,
Where priests no more lift up their murmurous
    Latin,
And only the sun, a solitary worshipper,
Tiptoes towards the altar and rests there.

These and the hazy tropic where I lived
In tall seas where the bright fish go like footmen
Down the blue corridors about their business,
The jewelled skulls are down there. I have for-
    got,

Almost forgot. How slowly they return

Like princes into the rooms they once owned.
    How dimly
I see the imaginary moon, the magic painter
Of long, deserted acres with splendour and si-
    lence.

Once on Monte Nero in the spring
Some peasant girl fashioned for love and work
Taught me a smile that I had forgotten,
It is so hard to speak her language now.

Almost forgot. How slowly they return
Like princes into the halls they once owned.

He has lost nothing since **'Encounter with a God'**, but gained a new range of imagination, a new ease of transition from image to image. We begin to see what one of Douglas's genuine gifts, to us, is going to be: a poetic speech that is life-size without being extroverted, the language of a man speaking his mind with a flexibility and nonchalance that contrast hypnotically with the ritual intensity, the emblematic density, of what he is saying. Yet in this particular poem the fairyland images are being remembered by one still partly under their spell, indulging the dream, and this mode of immaturity is the mark of this first phase, which lasts until he leaves Oxford in 1940.

Before he leaves, a poem titled **'The Deceased'** heralds the next stage:

He was a reprobate I grant
and always liquored till his money went.

His hair depended in a noose from
a Corona Veneris. His eyes, dumb

like prisoners in their cavernous slots, were
settled in attitudes of despair.

You who God bless you never sunk so low
censure and pray for him that he was so;

and with his failings you regret the verses
the fellow made, probably between curses,

probably in the extremes of moral decay,
but he wrote them in a sincere way:

and appears to have felt a refined pain
to which your virtue cannot attain.

Respect him. For in this
he had an excellence you miss.

Here the picturesque or merely decorative side of his imagery disappears; his descriptive powers sharpen to realism. The impression is of a sudden mobilising of the poet's will, a clearing of his vision, as if from sitting considering possibilities and impossibilities he had stood up to act. Pictures of things no longer interest him much: he wants their substance, their nature, and their consequences in life. At once, and quite suddenly, his mind is whole, as if united by positive action, and he produces poetry that is both original and adult. Already, in this poem **'The Deceased'**, we can see what is most important of all about Douglas. He has not simply added poems to poetry, or evolved a sophistication. He is a renovater of language. It is not that he uses words in jolting combinations, or with titanic extravagance, or curious precision. His triumph lies in the way he renews the simplicity of ordinary talk, and he does this by infusing every word with a burning exploratory freshness of mind—partly impatience, partly exhilaration at speaking the forbidden thing, partly sheer casual ease of penetration. The music that goes along with this, the unresting variety of intonation and movement within his patterns, is the natural path of such confident, candid thinking.

There is nothing studied about this language. Its air of improvisation is a vital part of its purity. It has the trenchancy of an inspired jotting, yet leaves no doubt about the completeness and subtlety of his impressions, or the thoroughness of his artistic conscience. This poem titled **'Egypt'**, for instance, could be a diary note, yet how could it be improved as a poem?

> Aniseed has a sinful taste:
> at your elbow a woman's voice
> like, I imagine, the voice of ghosts,
> demanding food. She has no grace
>
> but, diseased and blind of an eye
> and heavy with habitual dolour,
> listlessly finds you and I
> and the table are the same colour.
>
> The music, the harsh talk, the fine
> clash of the drinkseller's tray,
> are the same to her, as her own whine;
> she knows no variety.
>
> And in fifteen years of living
> found nothing different from death
> but the difference of moving
> and the nuisance of breath.
>
> A disguise of ordure can't hide
> her beauty, succumbing in a cloud
> of disease, disease, apathy. My God,
> the king of this country must be proud.

The war brought his gift to maturity, or to a first maturity. In a sense, war was his ideal subject: the burning away of all human pretensions in the ray cast by death. This was the vision, the unifying generalisation that shed the meaning and urgency into all his observations and particulars: not truth is beauty only, but truth kills everybody. The truth of a man is the doomed man in him or his dead body. Poem after poem circles this idea, as if his mind were tethered. At the bottom of it, perhaps, is his private muse, not a romantic symbol of danger and temptation, but the plain foreknowledge of his own rapidly-approaching end—a foreknowledge he becomes fully conscious of in two of his finest poems. This sets his writing apart from that of Hemingway, with which it shares certain features. Hemingway tried to imagine the death that Douglas had foresuffered. Douglas had no time, and perhaps no disposition to cultivate the fruity deciduous tree of How to Live. He showed in his poetry no concern for man in society. The murderous skeleton in the body of a girl, the dead men being eaten by dogs on the moonlit desert, the dead man behind the mirror, these items of circumstantial evidence are steadily out-arguing all his high spirits and hopefulness.

Technically, each of the poems of this second phase rest on some single objective core, a scene or event or thing. But one or two of the latest poems, and one in particular,

start something different: the poems are **'On a Return from Egypt'** and **'Simplify Me When I'm Dead'**. Their inner form is characterised not by a single object of attraction, but a constellation of statements. In the second of these poems, more liberated than the first, Douglas consummated his promise.

> Remember me when I am dead
> and simplify me when I'm dead.
>
> As the processes of earth
> strip off the colour and the skin:
> take the brown hair and blue eye
>
> and leave me simpler than at birth,
> when hairless I came howling in
> as the moon entered the cold sky.
>
> Of my skeleton perhaps,
> so stripped, a learned man will say
> "He was of such a type and intelligence," no
>   more.
>
> Thus when in a year collapse
> particular memories, you may
> deduce, from the long pain I bore
>
> the opinions I held, who was my foe
> and what I left, even my appearance
> but incidents will be no guide.
>
> Time's wrong-way telescope will show
> a minute man ten years hence
> and by distance simplified.
>
> Through that lens see if I seem
> substance or nothing: of the world
> deserving mention or charitable oblivion,
>
> not by momentary spleen
> or love into decision hurled,
> leisurely arrive at an opinion.
>
> Remember me when I am dead
> and simplify me when I'm dead.

Here he has invented a style that seems able to deal poetically with whatever it comes up against. It is not an exalted verbal activity to be attained for short periods, through abstinence, or a submerged dream treasure to be fished up when the everyday brain is half-drugged. It is a language for the whole mind, at its most wakeful, and in all situations: a utility general-purpose style, as, for instance, Shakespeare's was, that combines a colloquial prose readiness with poetic breadth, a ritual intensity and music of an outstandingly high order with clear direct feeling, and yet in the end is nothing but casual speech. This is an achievement for which we can be grateful. (pp. 43-48)

> *Ted Hughes, "The Poetry of Keith Douglas,"*
> in Critical Quarterly, *Vol. 5, No. 1, Spring,*
> *1963, pp. 43-8.*

Geoffrey Hill   (essay date 1964)

[*Hill is considered one of the most important English poets of the post–World War II era. While working within traditional poetic forms, he has experimented with meter, rhyme, and language, producing poetry that ranges from simple to opulent. His frequent use of para-dox, irony, pun, and allusion contributes to the various layers of meaning in his verse. Hill's work is informed by a religious and mythic sensibility, through which he explores such themes as the relationships between sacri-fice and salvation, ritual and violence, doubt and faith, and the discrepancies between artifice and experience. In the following excerpt from a review of* Selected Poems, *Hill examines the various approaches to war in Douglas's prose and poetry.*]

Keith Douglas's **Collected Poems** were published, by Edi-tions Poetry London, in 1951, seven years after his death in action. **Alamein to Zem Zem,** his desert diary with an appendix of sixteen poems, had appeared already, in 1946. Now we are presented with a selection of the poems edited and introduced by Mr. Ted Hughes. One finds oneself un-expectedly in two minds about the venture. One would agree that some reminder was necessary. Douglas, who must count as one of the finest British poets of the last forty years, is still without security of tenure in the curious pantheon of our time. He is, for instance, unrepresented in the *Penguin Book of Contemporary Verse* which finds space for a fair number of his innocuous contemporaries and successors. The intention behind this present selection is clearly laudable: to introduce new readers to the best of Douglas, free from the distractions of poor or mediocre work, variants and fragments. On the other hand it can be argued that Douglas's ambivalent status—at once "estab-lished" and overlooked—presents certain problems of edi-torial logistics that have not been entirely overcome by the decision to select. It is difficult to avoid the impression that the subject is being chaperoned, or at least tidied-up to meet the public. One would be prepared to suggest that circumstances require not so much a selection as a re-issue of the **Collected Poems;** and one would add that such a volume might be further augmented into a *Collected Works.* Douglas was also a graphic artist and **Alamein to Zem Zem** contains several drawings of scenes of desert-fighting: a strafed jeep, dead gunners sprawled round a piece of artillery, a corpse with a hovering cloud of flies, etc.; and the whole diary is of the greatest relevance to any study of Douglas's poetry. This would obviously involve all kinds of pragmatic considerations for the publisher and put the book into quite another category from the one under review. There is a precedent, however, in the publi-cation, in 1937, of *The Collected Works of Isaac Rosen-berg,* a poet killed in the First War. Rosenberg's collected works comprise poetry, prose, letters and some drawings; and one has only to compare this volume with the later **Collected Poems** to recognize the superiority of the earli-er, comprehensive edition. Douglas, one would argue, presents a parallel case and should ideally be presented in the same way.

Few would deny the close correspondence between the tone and stance of Douglas's desert-poems and his presen-tation of aspects of that milieu in his prose and drawings. Some might feel, however, that in wishing to discuss the poems in the light of the diary and the sketches, one was threatening to diminish the stature of poetry. The great virtue of poetry, it might be said, is that is transcends envi-ronment. To set it "in context" presumes to reduce the

transcendent once more to the level of the ephemeral. Moreover, an individual poem is a precise identity; to treat it merely as an "equivalent" of another statement is to de-stroy its vital integrity. This is certainly an argument one would prefer to many others, and would employ oneself against any suggestion that the prime function of poetry is the dissemination of religious or political creeds. But there can be no appeal, in such a case, to absolute rules. (pp. 6-7)

There are failures in poetry because technique is unable to do justice to intention. There are also failures for quite the opposite reason: because artifice is only-too-adequate to engulf purpose. This is what Mr. Hughes [see excerpt dated 1963] . . . calls "the terrible suffocating maternal octopus of ancient English poetic tradition." His sugges-tion, with which one is in entire agreement, is that Doug-las dealt very satisfactorily, and from a very early stage in his poetic career, with the embraces of the octopus. But in order to establish the consistent brilliance of Douglas's efforts to form his own style, Hughes puts himself in a po-sition where he seems to under-value the special intensity of the war-poetry. His premises are basically right: he feels that the term "war-poet" has become a mere tag in a kind of literary lost-property office; that Douglas has been given this title so that he may be abandoned there, together with a heap of obscure memories and old embar-rassments. He would argue that to treat Douglas as a "war poet" has become an increasingly-lame excuse for not giv-ing him his proper due as a writer. It is open to suggestion, however, that Hughes's justifiable irritation at a cliché has swung his assessment too far the other way. When he says of Douglas:

> eighteen years after his death, it is becoming clear that he offers more than just a few poems about war . . .

he is really glaring out of the page at some hypothetical straw-man, some model cretinous reader or oafish review-er who can think only in terms of periods, trends and in-fluences. One would assert, and Mr. Hughes would doubt-less agree, that the crux of Douglas's achievement is to be found in those poems whose subject is war and the envi-ronment of war; and that he himself saw his own develop-ment as a poet to be bound up with his success, or failure, in creating an idiom capable of the most direct transmis-sion of his experiences in that war. This, at least, is what one gathers from the letter—printed in the notes to **Col-lected Poems**—to his friend and fellow-poet John Hall; and dated 10th August, 1943:

> . . . you say I fail as a poet, when you mean I fail as a lyricist. Only someone who is out of touch, by which I mean first-hand touch, with what has happened outside England—and from a cultural point of view I wish it had affected En-glish life more—could make that criticism. I am surprised you should still expect me to produce musical verse. A lyric form and a lyric approach will do even less good than a journalese ap-proach to the subjects we have to discuss now . . . I never tried to write about war (that is battles and things, not London can Take it), with the exception of a satiric picture of some

soldiers frozen to death, until I had experienced
it. Now I will write of it . . .

(*Collected Poems*).

This seems to say, quite unambiguously, that an idiom
which *was* relevant is no longer applicable to his experience. He makes a point of stressing the polarity between
the domestic, insular view of poetry and *his* view of it—as
seen in the light of his immediate situation. Mr. Hughes,
of course, points to the significance the war had for Douglas; but, again, it becomes a question of emphasis, and one
would suggest that Hughes gets the emphasis wrong. He
writes that:

> The war brought his gift to maturity, or to a first
> maturity. In a sense war was his ideal subject:
> the burning away of all human pretensions in the
> ray cast by death. This was the vision, the unify-
> ing generalization that shed the meaning and ur-
> gency into all his observations and particulars:
> not truth is beauty only, but truth kills every-
> body.

To say that "war was his ideal subject" implies a greater
scope of freedom-in-choice than is, perhaps, called-for. To
do justice to Douglas one has to acknowledge how the
virtù of his art arose from the necessity of his life as a soldier. "Unifying generalization" overlooks the fact that the
theme of much of Douglas's prose, as well as of his verse,
is the sense of the unique and alien existence of a man destined for, or engaged in battle:

> It is tremendously illogical—to read about it
> cannot convey the impression of having
> walked through the looking-glass which
> touches a man entering a battle.
> (*Alamein to Zem Zem*).

> We repeated over and over again in our thoughts
>   and
> conversation that the battle was over . . . it was
>   all
> over. We had made it. We stood here on the safe
>   side
> of it, like swimmers. (ib.)

> But by a day's travelling you reach a new world
> the vegetation is of iron
> dead tanks, gun barrels split like celery
> the metal brambles have no flowers or berries
> and there are all sorts of manure. . . .
> ("**Cairo Jag**")

> . . . . I in another place
> see the white dresses glimmer like moths. Come

> to the west, out of that trance, my heart—
> here the same hours have illumined
> sleepers who are condemned or reprieved
> and those whom their ambitions have deceived;
> the dead men. . . .
> ("**Dead Men**")

> The wires touch his face: I cry
> NOW. Death, like a familiar, hears
> and look, has made a man of dust
> of a man of flesh. This sorcery
> I do. Being damned, I am amused
> to see the centre of love diffused
> and the waves of love travel into vacancy.
> How easy it is to make a ghost.

("**How to Kill**")

"The impression of having walked through the looking-
glass"; "We stood here on the safe side of it"; "you reach
a new world"; "I in another place"; "the same hours":
each of these phrases, far from asserting a "unifying generalization" about experience, conveys a sense of alienation,
exclusion, of a world with its own tragi-comic laws, like
Alice with all the sinister suggestions exaggerated. And
much of the acuteness of the perception is in the recognition that not everyone has to go through with this; that
two absolutely different worlds co-exist at about a day's
journey from each other. And in "**How to Kill**," "being
damned" is without the aura of romantic suggestion that,
for example, surrounds a discussion of the "damnation"
of Baudelaire or Poe. Douglas speaks of himself as
damned since he has been put away into a sphere of trivial
and momentous logic: "How easy it is to make a ghost."

To say this is not to try to suggest that one should take
Douglas's attitude to the war as a one-dimensional plan.
He saw it in several ways: as a test of his courage as a man
and of his "negative capability" as a poet. And, allowing
for distinctions in emphasis, one takes Mr. Hughes's point
that "the war brought his gift to maturity, or to a first maturity." In early poems like "**Forgotten the Red Leaves**"
Douglas poses the dead in such a way that they become
icons of a somewhat-ornate sense of doom and loss:

> In tall seas where the bright fish go like footmen
> Down the blue corridors about their business,
> The jewelled skulls are down there . . .

It would seem that he possessed the kind of creative imagination that approached an idea again and again in terms
of metaphor, changing position slightly, seeking the most
precise hold. And in *Alamein to Zem Zem* there is a passage where one can sense theory fastening upon actuality:

> Silence is a strange thing to us who live; we de-
> sire it, we fear it, we worship it, we hate it. There
> is a divinity about cats, as long as they are silent:
> the silence of swans gives them an air of legend.
> The most impressive thing about the dead is
> their triumphant silence, proof against anything
> in the world.

In the chronology of the book this passage precedes Douglas's first sight of a dead man (though it might be naive to
suppose everything composed in the order in which we
read it). While "the silence of swans" looks back to the accomplished work of the adolescent translator of Horace
and *Le dormeur du val* the silence of the dead stands the
test of such subsequent passages as these:

> The Italians lay about like trippers taken ill

> Each time I dismounted I still skidded about on
> the metal of the tank, the soles of my boots being
> covered with half-congealed blood from the pool
> in the bottom of the turret. Flies hung above the
> tank in a cloud.

I have tried to suggest that Douglas approaches an idea
repeatedly through metaphor, as if seeking the absolute
definition of experience. This is revealed in his published
work in two ways: by a relation between the diary *Alamein
to Zem Zem* and the poems; and by verbal metamorphoses

between the poems themselves. Some of the poems are a little like palimpsests. And phrases and sentences in the diary read like notes of experiences which—perhaps simultaneously—became poems:

> Looking down for a moment at a weapon-pit beside us, I saw a Libyan soldier reclining there. . . . There were no signs of violence. As I looked at him, a fly crawled up his cheek and across the dry pupil of his unblinking right eye. I saw that a pocket of dust had collected in the trough of the lower lid.

compare:

> But she would weep to see today
> how on his skin the swart flies move
> the dust upon the paper eye
> and the burst stomach like a cave.
>   **("Vergissmeinnicht")**

> About two hundred yards from the German derelicts. . . . I looked down into the face of a man lying hunched up in a pit. His expression of agony seemed so acute and urgent, his stare so wild and despairing, that for a moment I thought him alive. He was like a cleverly posed waxwork, for his position suggested a paroxysm, an orgasm of pain. He seemed to move and writhe.

compare:

> On sand and scrub the dead men wriggle in their dowdy clothes. They are mimes who express silence and futile aims enacting this prone and motionless struggle at a queer angle to the scenery, crawling on the boards of the stage like walls, deaf to the one who opens his mouth and calls silently
>   **("Landscape with Figures II")**.

> The bodies of some Italian infantrymen still lay in their weapon pits, surrounded by pitiable rubbish, picture postcards of Milan, Rome, Venice, snapshots of their families, chocolate wrappings, and hundreds of cheap cardboard cigarette packets.

compare:

> Look. Here in the gunpit spoil
> the dishonoured picture of his girl
> who has put: *Steffi Vergissmeinnicht*
> in a copybook gothic script. . . .
>   **("Vergissmeinnicht")**

or:

> . . . . a man with no head
> has a packet of chocolate and a souvenir of Tripoli.
>   **("Cairo Jag")**

In **"Selected Poems"** Mr. Hughes prints one of the poems Douglas wrote in Palestine in 1942 and published later in Cairo, **"The Sea Bird."** In **"Collected Poems"** this is printed next to a poem called **"Adams,"** which has a number of phrases in common with **"The Sea Bird."** Hughes omits **"Adams"** and it is possible that he regards it as a rejected variant of the poem he prints. Messrs. Waller and

Fraser, in their notes to the **"Collected Poems"**, suggest that **"Adams"** may in fact be the later version "though dates (often unreliable) on MSS suggest otherwise". In my estimation, **"Adams"** is by far the finer of the two poems. In it, Douglas swings abruptly from a description of the bird to the evocation of a (supposed) acquaintance, a dominating personality:

> Adams is like a bird;
> alert (high on his pinnacle of air
> he does not hear you, someone said);
>
> in appearance he is bird-eyed
> the bones of his face are
> like the hollow bones of a bird . . .

It is conceivable that Douglas composed **"Adams"** first; and, for reasons best known to himself, decided later to break this almost-perfect poem down. The fine description of Adams's bird-like face occurs again in a poem called **"Words"** dated the following year, 1943:

> For instance this stooping man, the bones of
> whose face are like the hollow birds' bones, is
> a trap for words.

If there is the slightest chance that **"Adams"** is the more authentic text that chance should be seized. And, although a delicate point of ethics is involved, I would feel sympathy for any degree of casuistry that resulted in this poem becoming widely-known.

In this next instance of variant readings a much more involved casuistry would be necessary: but here too I am morally certain that Douglas's first intuition was the right one and that he spoiled it by over-emphasis later. *Alamein to Zem Zem* gives a version of **"Vergissmeinnicht** (there called **"Elegy for an 88 Gunner"**):

> And smiling in the gunpit spoil
> is a picture of his girl
> who has written. . . .

This the editors of *Collected Poems* reject (as they must) for the later version published in Egypt under Douglas's supervision:

> Look. Here in the gunpit spoil
> the dishonoured picture of his girl
> who has put. . . .

Perhaps Douglas felt that "smiling" was too sentimental. But "dishonoured" seems much too portentous for the occasion; it draws attention to itself instead of to the object. The editors of *Collected Poems* did the only thing open to them in this case: they printed the final draft, but gave the earlier reading in the notes. To me, this is one more argument for re-issuing the *Collected Poems* rather than publishing a selection. Both the Blunden and the Day Lewis editions of Owen provide appendices of variant readings; and this procedure is surely entirely proper in the case of a posthumous collection.

The publication of variants is particularly desirable in the present instance. For in his attitude to language Douglas is not unlike Rosenberg, whom he obviously admired ("Rosenberg, I only repeat what you were saying"). Mr. Siegfried Sassoon has written that Rosenberg's "experiments were a strenuous effort for impassioned expression . . . he *modelled* words with fierce energy and aspiration"; and the term "modelling" applies also to Douglas's methods. It is revealed in the way he shapes and re-shapes a phrase or an image through several poems. Between the two poets there are of course obvious differences, distinctions, of talent and circumstance. Douglas was an ex-public-schoolboy and officer; Rosenberg a private from London's East End. And, despite his sense of "useless pity" for the dead, the frequent irritation he felt at the ritualistic gallantries of the professional officers, the "aristocrats", Douglas clearly relished many of the techniques and some of the machinery of war:

> To see these tanks crossing country at speed was
> a thrill which seemed inexhaustible—many
> times it encouraged us, and we were very proud
> of our Crusaders; though we often had cause to
> curse them.
>
> **(Alamein to Zem Zem)**

There is, of necessity, none of this occasional professional excitement in Rosenberg. His lot was to endure, in the ranks, the most squalid miseries of the Flanders mud. What they do share is a fearlessness of the imagination and a scepticism that is not so much metaphysical doubt as the willingness to lay the mind completely open to experience. Mr. Hughes writes that Douglas, particularly in his later poetry, "invented a style that seems able to deal poetically with whatever it comes up against." Rosenberg wrote in one of his letters:

> I am determined that this war, with all its powers for devastation, shall not master my poeting; that is, if I am lucky enough to come through all right. I will not leave a corner of my consciousness covered up, but saturate myself with the strange and extraordinary new conditions of this life, and it will all refine itself into poetry later on."
>
> (*Collected Works*).

Neither Rosenberg nor Douglas had the "luck" to "come through"; but it is useless to brood over the loss to poetry caused by their early deaths. What each accomplished in his short life is sufficient for our constant gratitude. (pp. 7-13)

> *Geoffrey Hill, " 'I in Another Place.' Homage to Keith Douglas," in* Stand Magazine, *Vol. 6, No. 4, 1964, pp. 6-13.*

Bernard Bergonzi (essay date 1968)

[*An English novelist, scholar, and essayist, Bergonzi has written extensively on the works of H. G. Wells, T. S. Eliot, and other major figures in twentieth-century literature. In the following excerpt, Bergonzi focuses on technique, tone, and perspective in an examination of Douglas's literary response to warfare.*]

Reading through [Keith Douglas's] *Collected Poems* I made a number of discoveries. The first of them was that most of Douglas's poems about the Middle East were, indeed, as good as they are usually said to be, and as I remembered them as being from anthologies and the issues

of *Poetry London* where several of them first appeared in the late forties and early fifties. Douglas was, indeed, a poet of tremendous technical accomplishment, a quality already very evident in the first poems in the collection, which he wrote as a schoolboy at Christ's Hospital, and he had an impressive sense of economy. Yet although he wrote magnificently when on form, his form was only precariously maintained, and when he was off it his language could collapse into an awkward prattling. The process is remarkably apparent in the poem **'Simplify Me When I'm Dead'**. After the opening injunctions ["Remember me when I am dead / and simplify me when I'm dead."] it continues:

> As the processes of earth
> strip off the colour and the skin:
> take the brown hair and blue eye
>
> and leave me simpler than at birth,
> when hairless I came howling in
> as the moon entered the cold sky.

There is an admirable concentration about this, and a line like 'when hairless I came howling in' makes a splendid effect. The poem relaxes a little in the next three lines, with a dry, Eliotic wit:

> Of my skeleton perhaps,
> so stripped, a learned man will say
> 'He was of such a type and intelligence,' no
> more.

Then, in the following six lines, we have a disconcerting decline into clumsiness and rhythmic incoherence:

> thus when in a year collapse
> particular memories, you may
> deduce from the long pain I bore
>
> the opinions I held, who was my foe
> and what I left, even my appearance
> but incidents will be no guide.

It seems that Douglas's precociously formed technique had great bravura qualities but rather little staying power, although in making such a judgement one must remember that if he had lived and had continued developing as promisingly as he had between 1940 and 1944, then most of the poems in this volume would be regarded as no more than juvenilia in the perspective of a normal life's work.

If one aspect of the 'simplification' of Douglas's posthumous reputation has been to assume that he was a more evenly accomplished poet than was the case, another has overemphasised him as a dry, precise, intelligent poet, in sharp contrast to the sticky neo-romanticism that dominated English verse during the 1940s. Douglas had a rare intelligence, and a happy mastery of the rational virtues; but a reading of the *Collected Poems* shows how much literary romanticism he had absorbed, even if it was not of the shrill Apocalyptic variety; doubtless such currents of feeling were running strongly in Oxford in 1940, as we can see from the exactly contemporary work of Sidney Keyes and John Heath-Stubbs. Here, for instance, is the opening of Douglas's **'An Oration'**, written in that year:

> In this city, lovers beneath this moon,
> greater here than elsewhere and more beautiful,

> who loves conspiracies and lovers, here you
>   walked.
> It was you who spoke in the dark streets, stood
>   in the shadows
> or where the lamps lit your white faces and red
>   lips.

Douglas was acutely sensitive to prevailing influences, at least in his pre-Army days, and before this genteel romanticism he had shown himself very aware of Auden, or, at least, of that astonishingly homogeneous thirties idiom which was Auden's main legacy. It is conspicuous in **'Dejection',** written at school and published in *New Verse* in 1938:

> Yesterday travellers in summer's country,
> Tonight the sprinkled moon and ravenous sky
> Say, we have reached the boundary. The autumn
>   clothes
> Are on; Death is the season and we the living
> Are hailed by the solitary to join their regiment,
> To leave the sea and the horses and march away
> Endlessly. The spheres speak with persuasive
>   voices.

The prevalence of this manner means I can read Douglas's early poems with a peculiar pleasure that has little to do with their actual literary merit; it is simply that I find the possible variation of this idiom—well exemplified, for instance, in Robin Skelton's anthology of thirties poetry—exceedingly fascinating in a largely extra-literary way. Yet critical honesty constrains me to say that of all the poems that Douglas wrote at school and university the most exquisitely achieved is **'Encounter with a God',** dated 1936, which owes little to fashionable styles, and is an extraordinarily poised and mature composition for a boy of sixteen.

Douglas was always poised, but in battle his poise shifted from the knowing, carefully nurtured self-consciousness of the articulate schoolboy and undergraduate to something much tougher, the total preparedness for experience of the hardened young tank officer, although, as we see from the late poems and his journal, traces of the earlier attitude always persisted. Douglas's war poems inevitably invite comparison with the parallel work of the First World War, though the immediate effect of the comparison is to force me into somewhat oblique reflections about the relation between literary form and collective experience. It is, of course, true that in the desert Douglas was fighting a very different war from the trench poets of 1914-18, and that he knew far more than Owen, Sassoon or Rosenberg (who is alluded to sympathetically in Douglas's **'Desert Flowers'**), for their transmutation of experience was very much a part of what he knew. There is no sense of shock, of protest or anger, and not a great deal of pity, merely a calm, disdainful acceptance of the worst experience can offer, which does not strike a sufficiently emphatic attitude to be called stoical.

Yet Douglas's way of responding to war, it seems to me, could hardly have been expressed in the former war, not because people could not feel like that, but because there was no effective way for them to express their feelings in words. Thus, the best poetry of that war tends to be polarised between the pity of Owen and the anger of Sassoon; only Rosenberg, who had read Donne very thoroughly,

comes close in a few poems to a deeply felt complexity of attitude. Yet Douglas, though formally a fairly conservative poet, had grown up in the mainstream of modernist poetics, whose basic attitudes were to be found in Eliot's poetry and criticism, and enshrined in a more systematic way in the tenets of the New Criticism: the essential poetic qualities were wit, irony, ambiguity, complexity, tension, all that is implied in the capacity to treat of several different—even conflicting—aspects of experience at the same time. One of Douglas's best poems, though marred in some lines by his recurrent clumsiness, is **'Time Eating',** which begins:

> Ravenous Time has flowers for his food
> in Autumn, yet can cleverly make good
> each petal: devours animals and men,
> but for ten dead he can create ten.

It is a poem I have known for a long time, and these words never fail to call up in my mind a famous sentence from a critical essay of Eliot's: 'The poets of the seventeenth century, the successors of the dramatists of the sixteenth, possessed a mechanism of sensibility which could devour any kind of experience.' The resemblance is, no doubt, fortuitous, and merely brought to mind by the emphasis given to the verb 'devour' in both passages (in strictly poetic terms there may be a closer parallel elsewhere in Eliot: 'The tiger springs in the new year. Us he devours'). Yet the association can remind us how closely Douglas adhered to the concept of 'wit' and unity of thought and feeling that Eliot outlined in his writings on the Metaphysical poets, at least in the apparent intentions underlying the later poems, if not always with perfect success in their realisation. Such a poem as **'Dead Men',** for instance, is both a powerful crystallisation of his experience of the desert war and a textbook exercise in the use of 'serious wit'. The opening recalls the rather lax romanticism of Douglas's Oxford period, though sharply controlled by an astringent vocabulary ('inveigles', 'infer', 'tacit'); from there the poem moves steadily to a confrontation with the fact of death that recalls Eliot (and, perhaps, Donne behind him), with possibly a conscious echo of 'Oh keep the dog far hence':

> Tonight the moon inveigles them
> to love; they infer from her gaze
> her tacit encouragement.
> Tonight the white dresses and the jasmin scent
> in the streets. I in another place
> see the white dresses glimmer like moths. Come
> to the west, out of that trance, my heart—
> here the same hours have illumined
> sleepers who are condemned or reprieved
> and those whom their ambitions have deceived;
> the dead men whom the wind
> powders till they are like dolls: they tonight
>
> rest in the sanitary earth perhaps
> or where they died, no one has found them
> or in their shallow graves the wild dog
> discovered and exhumed a face or a leg
> for food: the human virtue round them
> is a vapour tasteless to a dog's chops.

The poem develops its opposition between love and death

until the last stanza, where two opposed attitudes are juxtaposed without resolution:

> And the wise man is the lover
> who in his planetary love resolves
> without the traction of reason or time's control
> and the wild dog finding meat in a hole
> is a philosopher. The prudent mind resolves
> on the lover's or the dog's attitude forever.

Elsewhere Douglas picks up this opposition between love
and death, as in **'Vergissmeinnicht'**, which is his best-
known poem, though not necessarily his best: 'And death
who had the soldier singled / has done the lover mortal
hurt.' Most of his late poems are filled with the presence
of death, though Douglas is capable of treating it with considerable coolness, as in the final lines of **'Mersa'**, which
is a finely chiselled piece of poetic description:

> I see my feet like stones
> underwater. The logical little fish
> converge and nip the flesh
> imagining I am one of the dead.

Arguably, Douglas carried the coolness too far, almost to
the point of callousness, but it must have been a very necessary fiction to preserve his psychic poise, a difficult business for a man of his evident sensitivity: as he wrote in
'Aristocrats', another fine poem: 'How can I live among
this gentle / obsolescent breed of heroes, and not weep?'
Doubtless many elements made up this characteristic
poise in Douglas, beyond his literary dedication to the poetics of complexity and irony; the ethos acquired at an English public school, perhaps as well as the pervasive attitude manifested in all the services during the Second
World War: anti-heroic, understating, consistently sardonic.

This tone and underlying state of mind also permeates

Douglas in the desert, 1942.

Alamein to Zem-Zem, which is an absorbing document
even though it falls short of the distinction of Douglas's
best poetry. Whereas the principal battle narratives of the
First World War described a war of immobility and largely passive endurance, broken by episodes of extreme and
often suicidal action, like the infantry assaults that opened
the Somme offensive, Douglas's book gives a graphic account of a highly mobile, wholly mechanised kind of fighting. Its stress on the intimate relation between the tank
soldiers and their vehicles reminded me a little of the Fu-
turist praise of the machine that was often expressed in the
years immediately before 1914. In the desert war the individual tank commander, although receiving orders by
radio, was very much on his own, and was able to determine his own actions and fate to a very large extent. It is
this freedom that makes **Alamein to Zem-Zem** so different
from the narratives of the earlier war, which were mostly
written by infantry officers who felt themselves to be part
of a vast predetermined process. In some ways Douglas recalls the gaily chivalric standards of the old days of heroic
warfare, although his tone is always realistic, and his sense
of the total confusion of a battle when seen from the point
of the participants recalls the classical descriptions of
Stendhal and Tolstoy and expresses a similarly anti-heroic
sensibility.

As one might expect from a journal, as opposed to a considered narrative written after the event, Douglas offers
vivid description, a great sense of immediacy and involvement, but not very much perspective. It does, in fact, possess all the journalistic virtues, and is likely to remain a
uniquely valuable narrative of the desert war. The poise,
the coolness and toughness do at times become a little
fixed, a little too much of a deliberate attitude. I do not
know whether Douglas had read Robert Graves's *Good-
bye to All That,* but in places he seemed to be aspiring to
a similar nonchalance in dealing with the unspeakable:

> That night we were issued with about a couple
> of wineglasses full of rum to each man, the effect
> of which was a little spoiled by one of our twen-
> ty-five-pounders, which was off calibration and
> dropped shells in the middle of our area at regu-
> lar intervals of seconds for about an hour. The
> first shells made a hole in the adjutant's head,
> and blinded a corporal in B Squadron. I spent
> an uncomfortable night curled up on a bed of
> tacky blood on the turret floor.

The difference is that Graves achieved his calm at great
cost, after war-time experience that was far longer and
more intense than Douglas's, followed by ten years of
learning to live with what he had undergone. Possibly if
Douglas, too, had survived he might have returned to his
experiences and produced an account that fully possessed
the literary power that **Alamein to Zem-Zem** promised.
(pp. 207-14)

Taken together, [the **Collected Poems** and **Alamein to
Zem-Zem**] form a fitting memorial to this extraordinarily
attractive and talented young man, who significantly developed the possibilities of literary response to modern
warfare. One would like to think that it will not fall to anyone else to develop them still further. (p. 214)

Bernard Bergonzi, "Keith Douglas," in his The Turn of a Century: Essays on Victorian and Modern English Literature, Barnes & Noble Books, 1973, pp. 206-14.

Antony Coleman　(essay date 1970)

[*In the following excerpt, Coleman considers the advice offered by T. S. Eliot in his correspondence with Douglas.*]

Keith Douglas in a letter to J. C. Hall of August 10, 1941, remarks that "T. S. Eliot wrote to me when I first joined the Army, that I appeared to have finished with one form of writing and to be progressing towards another, which he did not think I had mastered. I knew this to be true without his saying it." Eliot wrote to Douglas on February 15, 1941, as follows:

Dear Mr. Douglas,

I have been somewhat delayed by illness in considering your poems which Mr. Blunden sent me some time ago, but I have now read them several times and with continued interest.

They seem to me extremely promising, and I should like to keep in touch with you. I should much like to know whether circumstances permit you to keep on writing at the present, or whether we must expect a silence of indefinite duration.

My impression so far is that you have completed one phase which begins with the very accomplished juvenilia and that you have started on another which you have not yet mastered. Of the first phase I feel that, as might be expected, there is a certain musical monotony in the rhythms. That does not matter in itself because it is a good thing to go on doing one thing until you are sure that its use is exhausted. . . . I think you have definitely an ear.

What I should like to see is the second phase which you have begun developed to the point of formal mastery, and meanwhile I think it would be useful to get poems in periodicals outside of Oxford. There are not, of course, many periodicals now in which to publish verse, but I shall be very glad to draw the attention of the editors of *Horizon* to your work. If you are still writing I should like to see something.

I am keeping the poems which Blunden gave me until I hear from you.

Yours very truly

Douglas responded to this invitation. Eliot wrote to him again on June 24 enclosing copies of the poems with his marginal comments. He writes:

Dear Mr. Douglas,

I have now had time to brood over your new poems and have made some marginal comments. In spite of appearances, I like the poems and I think that the one called **"Song"** is very nearly [? typist's error for "neatly"] written. The others seem to me to need a good bit of work

with special attention to ineffective adjectives. I am least certain about the one called **"The House,"** It is obscure and I am not sure that its myth is wholly consistent. For instance, toward the end you spoke of exorcising the dead lady in the upper room. One does speak of exorcising ghosts from material houses but in this case, the lady to be exorcised seems to be very much more substantial than the house in which you have set her. That is that I mean by inconsistency.

With best wishes,
Yours sincerely

Douglas was posted abroad in June. Eliot wrote to Mrs. Douglas on July 9 to thank her for forwarding his letter. He added: "I hope that you have enclosed the copies of the poems which I returned as I feel that the remarks in my letter lose their point apart from the marginal notes."

These notes (British Museum Add. Mss. 53773) range from simple interrogatives to full sentences: together with the letters they are valuable for the evidence they provide of Eliot's encouragement of a young poet and for the light they throw, by implication, on his own poetic practice.

In lines 1-2 of **"The House"** (*Collected Poems*) Douglas describes himself as "a pillar of that house / of which it seems the whole is glass . . . ". Eliot has underlined "whole"; his note reads: "Do you mean you also are glass?" In line 7 Douglas has another self-comparison, "myself am like a mouse", which elicits the comment: "I don't think you should be a pillar and like a mouse in the same stanza." A number of adjectives and phrases are criticized as "weak" ("amazing walls", "hard to see", "unpleasant prompting"). Other comments query the choice of epithet (" 'narrow' porcelain"); or of noun, "refuse" ("litter" is the suggested alternative); or of verb, "my incredulous eyes / discern her" ("I don't think *discern* is the right verb"); or seek elucidation: "a voice by itself, a face traversing the stair" ("crossing" is suggested with the further questions, "going up? going down?"). Eliot's sensitiveness to this last point draws attention to the importance of the stair-symbol in his own work where it is used to chart a progress from erotic adventure to mystical ecstasy (cf. Gervais Jones, *Approaches to the Purpose,* 1964). Eliot seems to have decided that the *poet* was ascending, for a later emendation reads, "If I but raise there my incredulous eyes" (Douglas has written "them"). Eliot queries the line "whom I admit I knew once" with "why not admit it?" In the poem's concluding section Douglas refers to "this impermanent building". Eliot remarks: "The impermanence should have been clearly established earlier in the poem."

The cumulative effect of these criticisms bears heavily on **"The House"**. The overall impression left suggests that Eliot felt Douglas had not fully realized his object: redrafting, along the lines proposed, would have resulted in greater precision, and a more complex texture.

The comments on **"The Marvel"** (*Collected Poems*) follow the same pattern: "interesting waves" is queried ("Why?"); "bright Pacific" ("no force in this adjective here"); "dim water" ("was the water dimmer than most seawater?")—in the published version this last is given as "dim place"; "mariners who rotted into ghosts" is given the (surely playful?) gloss, "they might be ghosts before they rotted". The appropriateness of "spread-eagled" as an adjective for a swordfish is questioned ("Though it would do for a cuttlefish"). Douglas describes the cutting out of the fish's eye in the line "yielding to the sharp enquiring blade". Eliot comments: "The *surgeon's* blade is enquiring but I am not sure about this one." "East Coker," which was published at Easter, 1940, has the lines: "The wounded surgeon plies the steel / That questions the distempered part." Eliot's line may have prompted Douglas's choice of adjective; it is interesting that Eliot recalls the image at a time when *he* is engaged in using language as a scalpel, as a penetrative instrument. The necessary adjunct, *exactness* of analysis, may well have prompted his concluding recommendation (which is coupled with "A nice poem nevertheless"): "v. Marianne Moore on fishes, etc. (neater)". In his introduction to Miss Moore's *Selected Poems* (1935), Eliot praised the discriminating fineness of her observations and remarked her ability to find "the exact words for some experience of the eye." One does not place too heavy an interpretative burden on these marginal comments by arguing that they were also the qualities he sought in other verse. His criticisms pinpoint those moments in **"The House"** and **"The Marvel"** where the poet has relaxed control, and a blur replaces exact notation. Two general points emerge: an insistence on the mastery of *form* and internal imagaic coherence. These Eliot could legitimately demand: they are the qualities that distinguish his own verse.

Douglas's stated object was "to write true things, significant things in words *each of which works for its place in a line*" (**Collected Poems**, my italics). Had he lived he would doubtless have considered with care the remarks of the elder poet. This at least can be said. Eliot's specific commentary does honour to them both.

> Antony Coleman, "T. S. Eliot and Keith Douglas," in The Times Literary Supplement, No. 3566, July 2, 1970, p. 731.

Jon Silkin   (essay date 1981)

[*Silkin, an English poet and critic, edits the poetry review* Stand, *which he founded in the 1950s. In the following essay, Silkin praises Douglas's "metaphysical wit."*]

In 1971, six years after Alan Ross had published *The Poetry of War 1939-1945*, its editor, Ian Hamilton, told me that although I might consider Keith Douglas the best poet of the Second War, I was to go away and re-read Alun Lewis. I was, he said, wrong. Such certainty requires courage, but I reckon, after several re-readings, that not only had Keith Douglas needed to have greater courage than either myself or Ian Hamilton, but that he had greater talent as a *poet* than Alun Lewis. Lewis's prose fiction is another matter.

Douglas's courage, of which as his prose *Alamein to Zem Zem* indicates he had plenty—sufficient, that is,—no-one can have too much—is as inseparable from his talent as is his wit. The courage finds expression in the wit, and the

wit is the point at which the meaning becomes poetry. It is the poetry's expressive thrust. That's my thesis. I define wit, not only in the current sense of verbal sharpness that may induce amusement—the product of a mind that, as Ted Hughes put it [see excerpt dated 1963], 'reposes at a point . . . by a feat of great strength'; I also define it in the eighteenth-century sense of imagination, metaphysical imagination, which Pope makes use of in his 'Elegy to the Memory of an Unfortunate Lady':

> Most souls, 'tis true, but peep out once an age,
> Dull sullen pris'ners in the body's cage;
> Dim lights of life, that burn a length of years
> Useless, unseen, as lamps in sepulchres.

The deliberately-made vehicle of 'sullen pris'ners' and 'cage' has as much or even more *life* than what it stands for—body/soul. In the sense that Pope was affected by the metaphysicals Douglas, I think, was more affected by Eliot, and his metaphysics, than by Auden. Auden, for the most part, he left to his contemporaries Keyes and Lewis. It is Douglas's tough but not grimacing animation to which some of us respond.

This animation is best expressed in his facing death's foreshortening of life through war. But there are additional 'places' ('I in another place') where courage is in order love, for instance: and in love—or so I read the poems written from what was the Palestine of the British Mandate (Tel-Aviv and Jerusalem)—the voice grows lonely, aware of its loneliness:

> But among these Jews I am the Jew
> outcast, wandering down the steep road
> into the hostile dark square:
> and standing in the unlit corner here
> know I am alone and cursed by God
> like the boy lost on his first morning at school.
> **('Saturday Evening in Jerusalem')**

They are not the lines of a man afraid, but neither do they have the sheeing "wit" of the gun-barrel, such as we find in his "desert" poems. Once more from Palestine:

> your face, flower that draws down my lips
> our hands meet like strangers in a city
> among the glasses on the table-top
> impervious to envy or pity
> we two lost in the country of our eyes.
> **('Jerusalem')**

I wonder if for Douglas it might, at times, have appeared more difficult to endure the continuing pain of love, in survival, than the prospect of extinction in war.

I don't think a guess of that nature is much use to a biographer, or of any use to a literary critic, except in that it helps to distinguish between the morose, almost for Douglas lugubrious, verses of love, and this more alert poetry of war.

The poems I name, some of which I'll consider, are those the reader of Douglas might expect: **'Adams', 'The Knife', 'Mersa', 'Dead Men', 'Cairo Jag', 'Snakeskin and Stone', 'Desert Flowers', 'Enfidaville', 'Aristocrats', 'Vergissmeinnicht', 'How to Kill',** and **'Behaviour of Fish in an Egyptian Tea Garden';** enough poems, in my opinion, to ensure Douglas's reputation as a fine poet, if not the finest of the War. And what for me stands out, stands forth, is, as I have defined it, the wit. But it is the nature of the wit, and its type of recurrence, its thoughtful unselfprotecting energy which both interests me and compels my admiration.

In **'Enfidaville'**, for instance

> In the church fallen like dancers
> lie the Virgin and St. Thérèse
> on little pillows of dust.

'Like dancers' brings out, perhaps, gestures of the religious ecstatic—beatitude beamed from the uplifted face; 'fallen', however, 'like dancers' reminds us (as Owen reminded us in 'Le Christianisme'—'One Virgin still immaculate / Smiles on for war to flatter her')—reminds us that earthly manifestations of the sacred are as vulnerable in war as the profane. The wit continues its trajectory. The 'little pillows of dust' brings about the age-old conjunction of death with its likeness 'sleep'. We have of course tombstone clichés of this. But 'little' reminds us that this is illusion, and that 'dust' is indeed the aptest conjuration of death, in which we rest and into which we at length crumble. Who else is Douglas reminding if not, among others, himself ?

In the last line of the first stanza the 'detonations' *shivered the hands of Christ* (my italics)—'shivered' makes effective its pun on both the sacred (=frightened) and temporal (=shattered) levels. The second stanza reverses an earlier emphasis. Where the saints were 'like dancers' (temporal comparison) the 'men and women' of the town are now said to have 'moved like candles' (sacred comparison). Damaged by bombardment, 'The white houses are bare / black cages', but they let in more than they keep in— except for darkness. As 'cage' may associate with caged prisoners, so it may remind us of the body's 'cage'—that is, mortality. In all these I see wit, and in the wit an unflinching courage such as Rosenberg expressed when he wrote

> I am determined that this war, with all its powers for devastation, shall not master my poeting; that is, if I am lucky enough to come through all right. I will not leave a corner of my consciousness covered up, but saturate myself with the strange and extraordinary new conditions of this life, and it will all refine itself into poetry later on.

> (Letter to Laurence Binyon, Autumn 1916)

From **'Desert Flowers'** we know Douglas admired Rosenberg, and we can guess why. At the close of **'Enfidaville'** Douglas, operating wit, clashes the sacred with the temporal by evoking in the eyes of the saints those of the living:

> I seem again to meet
> the blue eyes of the images in the church.

Or is it the other way round—a temporary piety induced by suffering and seen in the eyes of the returning townsfolk?

In **'Cairo Jag'** he clashes two modes of life, of existence, and produces some third thing—a judgement. The *Marcelle* of civilian Cairo—where the fortunate spend their

leave—is provocative and, apart from her grace,—she 'dances . . . by levitation'—Douglas finds little to commend her to the poet-annalist. 'All this', the poem tells us, 'takes place in a stink of jasmin'. In reversing the expectation of the flower's lovely odour by means of the poem's giving us 'stink', instead, Douglas is able to focus his judgement—disgust. In the third and final stanza, a different reversal occurs. This is the desert, not its city; it is war, not a temporary release from it:

> But by a day's travelling you reach a new world
> the vegetation is of iron
> dead tanks, gun barrels split like celery
> the metal brambles have no flowers or berries
> and there are all sorts of manure, you can imagine
> the dead themselves, their boots, clothes and
> possessions
> clinging to the ground, a man with no head
> has a packet of chocolate and a souvenir of Tripoli.

The contrasting reference to Donne's sexual Elegy 19 'To His Mistress Going to Bed'—'O my America, my new found land'—is nothing compared to the 'dead tanks' and, more powerfully still, to 'gun barrels split like celery'. The power of the wit here depends on Douglas's ability to have the visual exactitude of 'guns split like celery' to neither outweigh nor be outweighed by the poised contrast with life in Cairo; which, among other dispensations, provides the relative luxury of—celery. And 'you can imagine' puts into mind something else, the sharp staccato voice of Sassoon, making his prose protest of 1917:

> I am not protesting against the conduct of the War, but against the political errors and insincerities for which the fighting men are being sacrificed. On behalf of those who are suffering now I make this protest against the deception which is being practised on them; also I believe that I may help to destroy the callous complacency with which the majority of those at home regard the continuance of agonies which they do not share, and which they have not sufficient imagination to realize.

> (*The Complete Memoirs of George Sherston*)

Douglas (and Sassoon) may as well remind us of the last stanza of Owen's 'Insensibility'—'By choice they made themselves immune / To pity'. It is to provoke our sympathetic imagination that Douglas, with wit, works in the double meaning of "you could perceive it if you cared" *and* "I'm sure you'll really have no trouble in imagining it". By how much this doubleness has been worked for may be appreciated if the last two lines of the stanza above are compared with the prose entry in **Alamein to Zem Zem**:

> The bodies of some Italian infantrymen still lay in their weapon pits, surrounded by pitiable rubbish, picture postcards of Milan, Rome, Venice, snapshots of their families, chocolate wrappings, and hundreds of cheap cardboard cigarette packets. Amongst this litter, more suggestive of holiday-makers than soldiers, there were here and there bayonets. . . . The Italians lay about like trippers taken ill.

The journal-entry has been sifted to make a point. One is reminded of the "rain" passage in Edward Thomas's *The Icknield Way,* and by how much Thomas re-shaped that in his poem 'Rain'.

A similar conjunction to that of **'Cairo Jag'** and its contrasting "lifes" is enacted in the last three lines of the first stanza of **'Dead Men'**:

> Tonight the white dresses and the jasmin scent
> in the streets. I in another place
> see the white dresses glimmer like moths. Come
>
> to the west

—to the almost entrancing desert war, that is. The ending of the poem is, clearly, not witty, yet wit of a different kind is as visible as that in **'Cairo Jag'**. The 'wise man' will settle for no less or more than love; the dog, wise as a philosopher, settles for *his* bone. If we are 'prudent', we will be like lovers and dogs. Thus is our temporal nature defined, humbled, and given a modest chance of a slightly more assured survival.

Douglas was an omniverous learner; from Pope as much as from Donne, or Eliot; from Owen as much as from Rosenberg. Owen in his poem 'Beauty' (unfinished) makes an extremely complex notation on the word—

> A shrapnel ball
> Just where the wet skin glistened when he swam.
> Like a full-opened sea-anemone.
> We both said 'What a beauty! What a beauty,
>   lad!'
> I knew that in that flower he saw a hope
> Of living on, and seeing again the roses of his
>   home.
> Beauty is that which pleases and delights
> 'Not bringing personal advantage'—Kant.

When Owen speaks of the soldier's wound being 'a beauty', he implies both a substantial wound (it was subsequently lethal) but one that, in the context, was desirable in that it served to transport him back to the safety of blighty. In **'Vergissmeinnicht'** ("Forget me not"—the lover's plea) Douglas says in stanza four:

> We see him almost with content,
> abased, and seeming to have paid
> and mocked at by his own equipment
> that's hard and good when he's decayed.

'Hard and good' works in contrast to the now 'decayed' soldier (and lover); but what is 'good' for the soldier is not so for the human being and lover. 'Good' has about it all the wit of of Owen's 'beauty' and, by bifurcating the two persons, 'killer' from 'lover', Douglas prepares us for the last stanza where the distinction becomes explicit which was implicit in stanzas three and four:

> For here the lover and killer are mingled
> who had one body and one heart.
> And death who had the soldier singled
> has done the lover mortal hurt.

Is the half-rime intentional? At any rate, 'singled' is another pun—the soldier in his death is separated from his love; but 'singled' also suggests "singled out for the full works" Instances of compression also occur in the poem (wit is

just one form of it); the sleek barrel of the gun is 'frowning' with one supposes death. The 'paper eye' is fragile, dry of its life; the 'burst stomach', cave-like, is now empty.

I wish to refer to two more poems—**'Desert Flowers'** and **'How to Kill'**. In the former there is again the reprise of Owen who in 'A Terre' speaks of

> The dullest Tommy hugs that fancy now,
> "Pushing up daisies" is their creed you know.

In Douglas's poem we get

> but the body can fill
> the hungry flowers . . .

The spoken, colloquial force of Owen has perhaps been sacrificed, but the savage voracity of nature (and of war) is much intensified by 'hungry flowers'. And in the artificial, theatre imagery with which stanza three opens

> Each time the night discards
>
> draperies on the eyes and leaves the mind awake
> I look each side of the door of sleep
> for the little coin it will take
> to buy the secret I shall not keep.

—in this theatre imagery, we are reminded by how much the mind "constructs" its perceptions, bringing together the unpalatable true meanings that lie about waiting for the poet's wit, and courage perhaps, to make a union of them in a poem. Johnson of course formulates this in his essay on Cowley, when he writes of the metaphysical poets:

> Of wit, thus defined, they have more than enough. The most heterogeneous images are yoked by violence together . . .

Johnson's judgement was adverse.

The 'secret' (in the stanza above) that Douglas will not keep consists in such memories of the horror of war which the mind, with wit, sets out. The coin, paid to Charon to ferry the dead across the Acheron, ought to purchase secrecy, for secrets are supposed to perish with the dead. And the dead, by drinking the waters of Lethe, were supposed to be blessed with forgetfulness. Douglas cleverly reverses these superstitions: the coin will not buy any collusion from him:

> Lay the coin on my tongue and I will sing
> of what the others never set eyes on.

Wit has its explicit task. It will tell the truth, it will 'sing' if with the irony of that word—to sing, *cantare*—the unsuitability of war for such song is understood. This will again be touched on in Douglas's letter to his fellow-poet John Hall, quoted below.

In **'How to Kill'** we take the most delicate of Douglas's cruxes

> I cry
> NOW. Death, like a familiar, hears
>
> and look, has made a man of dust
> of a man of flesh. This sorcery
> I do. Being damned, I am amused
> to see the centre of love travel into vacancy.
> How easy it is to make a ghost.

In his affirming essay ' "I in Another Place": Homage to Keith Douglas' [see excerpt dated 1963] Geoffrey Hill nevertheless indicates that

> Douglas clearly relished many of the techniques and some of the machinery of war

and then goes on to quote a passage concerning how proud 'we were . . . of our Crusaders' (tanks)—from *Alamein to Zem Zem.* He might as easily, though perhaps with more hurt, have quoted the stanza above. The wound, I suggest,—it is our wound—is located not only in the 'Being damned'; if that were all, the self-condemnation and the almost mawkish confessional of the 'killer would find no restraint in its self-pity; though even this we ought to find it hard in *ourselves* to condemn who are presently living 'at peace'. It is of course the unassailably clear 'I am amused' that pains, and who but Douglas would have the "nerve" to say this? Owen wrote in a letter to his mother dated 4th (or 5th) October 1918 and headed 'Strictly private', 'I lost all my earthly faculties, and fought like an angel'. Private indeed. And Rosenberg momentarily preened himself, 'I must be looking smart, for I was offered a stripe which I declined' (letter to Sydney Schiff, December 1915). Grenfell, in 'Into Battle', saw himself as combining the roles of Roland and Nimrod. But 'amused'? Is this the reposing point of the civilized ego? What terminus is this, one wonders.

It is the ease with which he can kill, as well as the sudden transformation of the victim, that amuses Douglas. 'Being damned' one has, has one (?), "earned" the right to amusement, for what else remains to one in combat but the perception of such lethal efficiencies? I don't justify, supposing, that is, that Douglas needs to be justified; but I do suggest that the skin which separates amusement from horror is, like the eye, 'paper' thin. And as Douglas's victim is vulnerable to 'the mosquito death' so was Douglas, killed three days after his D-day landing, June 9th, 1944. Douglas didn't not know his vulnerability. He knew.

In a by-now famous letter to his fellow-poet, John Hall, Douglas in 1943 wrote from Palestine:

> I don't know if you have come across the word Bullshit—it is an army word and signifies humbug and unnecessary detail. It symbolizes what I think must be got rid of—the mass of irrelevancies, of 'attitudes', 'approaches', propaganda, ivory towers, etc., that stands between us and our problems and what we have to do about them.

> To write on the themes which have been concerning me lately in lyrical and abstract forms, would be immense bullshitting . . . I never tried to write about war . . . until I had experienced it. Now I will write of it, and perhaps one day cynic and lyric will meet and make me a balanced style. Certainly you will never see the long metrical similes and galleries of images again . . . To be sentimental or emotional now is dangerous to oneself and to others.

> To trust anyone or to admit any hope of a better world is criminally foolish, as foolish as it is to

stop working for it. It sounds silly to say work without hope, but it can be done; it's only a form of insurance; it doesn't mean work hopelessly.

> *(The Complete Poems)*

No *cantare,* no cantata. The way from that *cantare,* from the *morbido* of poetry, such soft unctious lyric utterance, is wit. It took not merely physical courage to fight, but imaginative courage to take the route Douglas describes in the letter(s) quoted above—a route (with the possible exception of Webster and his verse) new to the matter of war and violence; the route of wit and its spoken poetry. Douglas took this route. No bullshit. (pp. 49-58)

> *Jon Silkin, "Keith Douglas," in* Agenda, *Vol. 19, Nos. 2-3, Summer-Autumn, 1981, pp. 49-58.*

Linda M. Shires (essay date 1985)

[*An American critic, Shires is the author of* British Poetry of the Second World War, *which was researched in part through interviews with surviving British poets and editors of that era. In the following excerpt from that work, Shires discusses Douglas's attempts to reconcile his military and romantic natures in his poetry.*]

'Dear Grandpapa', wrote Keith Douglas at the age of six, 'I went to a Fate yesterday and a consert too. I bought a gun for 4^d which was marked 6^d at the toy shop there.' In this fragment from a letter of childhood, Keith Douglas naively reveals what would become the most significant difference between himself and the other major poets of the Second World War. For, attracted to the military from his youth and schooled in its ways, Keith Douglas gave himself gladly to the excitements and dangers of war. In a schoolboy's analysis (possibly from 1932) he defined himself as a 'militarist' who 'like many of his warlike elders, built up heroic opinions upon little information'. While lamenting the brutality of war, he still remained devoted to the Officers' Training Corps and joined its Mounted Section for the free riding when he went up to Oxford in the autumn term of 1938. An aristocratic horseman and a courageous soldier by nature, Douglas also possessed the finely complex sensibility of the artist. Already a promising painter, he set out at fourteen to master the art of poetry. The war of 1939-45 proved his fittest subject, and he was its best poet.

More than Lewis or Keyes, Douglas was conscious of the given attitudes towards war and military life. Brought up on stories of combat, Douglas was known from his cadet days for his obsessive attention to cleaning and polishing the accoutrements of his trade—his uniform, saddle, bridle, boots, and so on. In a 1940 picture which shows him at ease in uniform, he stands tall with buttons and boots shining. Significantly enough, Douglas added an embellished decorative border to the picture with the caption: 'Dulce et decorum est pro patria mori'. The romantic hearts and flowers in the border suggest a certain sentimentality about the classically heroic line. Yet it can also be no accident that in his chosen caption Douglas should echo Wilfred Owen's sardonic use of Horace in his First World War poem, 'Dulce Et Decorum Est'. Even though he had not yet gone to battle, Douglas saw himself not only in the romantic tradition of great warriors, but also in the great chain of realistic modern war poets. (pp. 113-15)

Two images, expressed in various forms, weave in and out of Douglas' poems. The first is that of an uncaring father, a distanced God who governs men's lives and reduces them to puppets on the stage of life. The other major image is that of a beast 'so amorphous and powerful that he could be a deity. It seems clear that the two images of uncaring father and beast are related, outer and inner forms of the same ruling deity. Variously named as Devouring Time, Death, the beast, God, the power he describes is 'inefficient' or cruel. Implacably, this devilish manipulator breaks and severs the relationships that Douglas seeks. His strong response to its domination was exacerbated by his need for order, his attraction to justice, and the real absence of his father.

Douglas responded fully to the Second World War for complicated reasons. He loved the military order; he took pride in being a member of a group. But essentially he responded to the breakdown of structures and was drawn to the nobility inherent in the role of warrior. The reality of his youth and manhood was dominated by family severance and catastrophic national events. Even his poetic creed, found in an essay **'On the Nature of Poetry'**, which was printed in *Augury* (the Oxford anthology of 1940 that he edited with Alec Hardie), stresses the ideals of honour and order:

> In its nature poetry is sincere and simple. Writing which is poetry must say what a writer has himself to say, not what he has observed others to say with effect, nor what he thinks will impress his hearers because it impressed him hearing it. Nor must he waste any more words over it than a mathematician: every word must work for its keep in prose, blank verse, or rhyme.

The passage reflects Douglas' independent spirit and his desire for sincerity, but above all it records his interest in structure. The parts of a poem, each single element, must join to the larger whole and work significantly for it. In an earlier age, Douglas might well have been a Rupert Brooke patriot; however, the hierarchical empire was dissolving and a lonely waste land was replacing it. It is probably no accident that Douglas' work appealed to T. S. Eliot [see Coleman excerpt dated 1970], for both men were interested in tradition, fusion, and structure. Both were also seekers for belief in an age providing none.

Douglas did not move, like Eliot, towards faith—perhaps because his experience of the 'boredom, the horror and the glory' of battle outstripped any of Eliot's mental demons, more likely because scepticism and doubt dominated any leanings towards faith. A devil constantly rides on Douglas' back. In a drawing he made in 1944 for the cover of a book he planned to call *Bête Noire*, a black devil clings to Douglas as he rides his horse. In other sketches, the 'monster' grips, claws and fells him. Douglas' battles are not only with outer forces but with inner ones, for he feels cut off from half of himself. The war did not cause his self-division, but it provided him with the opportunity to face

the bestial landscapes of war in the Middle East and Europe and the monster within his aristocratic self. Like Keyes, he used war to explore the darker side of himself in personal terms, yet unlike Keyes he did not put faith in sacrifice. He responded fully to each experience, including death, and while moral, was not a moralizer.

Douglas' poetic development shows an increased understanding of these private struggles and a need to weld them to external events. The dualities noticed in **'Dead Men'** and **'Cairo Jag'**—dualities of landscape, and attitudes—were adumbrated in his earlier poems. From his Oxford days, in a poem such as **'Invaders'**, one detects a split in his psyche. There the duality is one of head and heart. 'Intelligences like black birds / come on their dire wings from Europe', threatening ominously to 'harden' sensitive hearts. Douglas warns an unidentified *you* who is himself as much as any reader: 'You will find, after a few tomorrows / like this, nothing will matter but the black birds.' Douglas comes out on the side of the heart, defending it against its struggle with trespassers who would rob it of the pleasures in beauty and order. The political allegory of this poem written in the eventful year of 1939 is overt; what is equally significant is the equation of foreign invaders with the mind's own scourging black birds. The birds are clearly forerunners of the black beast whom Douglas will describe as residing 'inside my mind'. His only defence against the invaders, however, is to incorporate their perpetrations, to become as 'intelligent' as they are and fight them on their own terms. Douglas exhorts, 'To keep the heart still sensitive as air will be our part, always to think'. Though written at Oxford, **'Invaders'** is a military poem. The black aggressors whom Douglas wants to repulse are, like the late enemy armies, already dimly perceived as integral elements of his own divided psyche.

In another early poem, **'Sanctuary,'** Douglas is more personal but again writes of invasion and the breakdown of the heart.

> Once my mother was a wall;
> behind my rampart and my keep
> in a safe and hungry house
> I lay as snug as winter mouse:
> till the walls break and I weep
> for simple reasons first of all.
>
> All the barriers give in,
> the world will lance at every point
> my unsteady heart, still and still
> to subjugate my tired will.
> When it's done they will anoint me,
> being kinder if they win.
>
> So beyond a desperate fence
> I'll cross where I shall not return,
> the line between indifference
> and my vulnerable mind:
> no more then kind or unkind
> touch me, no love nor hate burn.

The split between head and heart now is cast through the opposition of youth and age. One side of the speaker is the mother's child, the small and snug and loved 'mouse' who felt at one with his environment. But the child's safe world is destroyed. The child feels subjugated and as an adult grows more indifferent and unwilling to be as vulnerable as he once was. Yet though he crosses the fence and leaves the sanctuary behind, he does so reluctantly. For he still clings to the barriers which have fallen.

Two versions of the same poem, 'Soissons' and 'Soissons 1940', illustrate the duality in Douglas even more strongly. In the first version Douglas is as ironic and intellectual a speaker as the adult of 'Sanctuary' or the victim of 'Invaders'. He describes the religious sanctuary of Soissons as permeated by devils. The craftsman who would have made angels in 'the religious century' makes 'devils from the selfsame stone'. The poem is shot through with dark and sinister suggestions which go unexplained: 'Down the long hill snakes / the hard hot road into the town's heart' and 'How dark / seems the whole country we enter.' In this first version of 'Soissons' Douglas gives us a single tone and reality; yet his second version testifies to his realization that a single point of view is incorrect. He attempts to set right the first version: 'a simplified medieval view / taken from a Book of Hours'.

Douglas writes the second poem from a much more complex vantage point. By incorporating two points of view, he introduces what will become a hallmark of his war poetry. First he describes a real edifice:

> This town is no tower of the mind
> and the cathedral, not an edifice of air, stands
> dignified and sleepy with serenity—
> so I would have said, and that this solid city
> was built here close under the angels' hands,
> something we had no longer reckoned to find.

The cathedral is not airy but solid. Yet in stanza two, he admits that once it was insubstantial:

> Yet here something of the mind lived and died,
> a mental tower restored only to fall
> and we in England heard it come down
> as though of all, this was the most ominous
>   sound.
> The devils pilloried in that holy wall
> must smile to see our faith broke to the wide.

By the second stanza the main theme of the poem, the crisis of belief, comes into focus. The solid structure is just a hollow shell of former faith. Douglas feels the need for that solid structure informed by belief, but he is forced to document its destruction. Where earlier he was content to give a simple view, here he dwells on paradox and ambivalence. The last stanza leaves us undecided, as is the author, about the relationship among God, history, and believers:

> You who believe you have a kind creator
> are with your sire crowding into twilight,
> as using excellent smooth instruments,
> material man makes himself immense.
> Oh you may try, but can't deny he's right
> and what he does and destroys makes him great-
>   er.

No longer settling for one side, the poet accepts ambivalence and incomplete understanding.

In these early poems, Douglas records his self-divisions which took various forms: two aspects of the self in con-

flict, two realms such as heart and intelligence, two systems such as Catholic France and Protestant England. Not able to fuse the discordant opposites, Douglas nonetheless persists in his need for some kind of order. It is significant that many of his poems concern buildings or walls. Just as on the border of the 1940 picture of himself in uniform Douglas drew classical columns, so in these poems he expresses the same desire for a structure of belief which will survive. One of the key changes in 'Soissons 1940' from draft to final version is the deletion of the word *survived* in line 8, 'a mental tower restored only to fall' where it has been replaced by *restored*. Even the structure itself is fragile and may be rebuilt only to fall again.

War accentuated both the split that Douglas had come to feel and his need to integrate the dualities of his psyche. But at first he was sceptical about writing 'war poetry'. His gradual assumption of the role of war poet becomes clearer when we look at an article he wrote called 'Poets in This War', an important essay that develops an ideal also underlying his fine poem 'Desert Flowers'. Like 'Cairo Jag', this essay was probably written in 1943, after Douglas had experienced his first campaign of tank warfare. Here Douglas recalls Brooke, Owen, Sassoon, Sorley and Rosenberg and reminds us why they were able to capture in verse the unique nature of the First World War:

> Such was the jolt given to the whole conception
> men had had of the world and of war, and so
> clear was the nature of the cataclysm, that it was
> natural enough not only that poets should be
> stirred, but that they should know how to express themselves.

On surveying his own generation, however, Douglas finds no one to compare with the poets of that earlier cataclysmic war: 'I do not find even one who stands out as an individual'. Having dismissed various predecessors and contemporaries including recent colleagues who had 'sprung up among the horrors of wartime Oxford', Douglas tries to account for the dearth of poets writing about the war. The reasons he lists are psychological, military and strategic.

At the time Douglas wrote 'Poets in This War' he was experiencing some frustration in coming to terms with the war. For while he clearly felt a strong kinship with the First World War poets, he also recognized that all poets of the Second World War must inevitably be alienated from them. There *are* 'fighting' war poets among his contemporaries, he admits, but these 'do not write because there is nothing new, from a soldier's point of view about this war except its mobile character'. Given such a paucity of subject matter, it follows according to Douglas that 'almost all that a modern poet on active service is inspired to write would be tautological'.

Douglas' point of view was probably shared by other poets and helps to explain why some, like Keyes and Douglas himself, were driven to stress more personal issues. A despairing spirit, along with an awareness of the disjunction between poetry and politics, looms behind this essay. Such a separation may also explain the difficulties of a poet like Alun Lewis whose creative impulses were more social than personal. When Douglas closes his essay by referring to the poetry of this global war as 'civil and military', he refers to the bombing of Britain as well as to war abroad; yet he also calls attention to the key feature he shares with poets of the First World War, and also to a major difference. Like its predecessor, the Second World War involved a conflict between armed forces of hostile nations. Yet the average British soldier did not want to go to war; rather, like Alun Lewis, he felt torn by responsibility and desire. More than any previous war, the Second World War produced an internal 'civil' conflict, as the allied components within individual psyches often were drawn into friction and battles by a divided self. (In Douglas' case, self-division is apparent not only in the 1940 photograph and in poems discussed earlier, but also in drawings bordering on the schizophrenic.)

In setting down his generation's ideas about the relation between war and creativity and about the war poets who had preceded them, Douglas was not including himself among those who would shirk or postpone writing of the 1939-45 war. In fact, by his very authorship of the essay, he was dissociating himself from other poets. But by not publishing the essay he may possibly have indicated his doubt about its central point of view. *He* would write a poetry of war. While despairing of new themes, he was sharply aware of his own peculiar strengths—strengths that could and did allow him to write poetry capable of facing both the 'civil and military' conflicts without and within. In **'Desert Flowers'**, written like **'Poets in this War'** in 1943, he maintains that he has something fresh and distinctive to say. Though the speaker at first purports only to duplicate what Rosenberg had already chronicled in poems of war, it soon becomes obvious that he also wants to remove himself from his predecessor. The dependent 'I' of the second line has become independent in lines 10, 13 and 15. This speaker clearly assesses himself as doing much more than corroborating an earlier vision:

> Living in a wide landscape are the flowers—
> Rosenberg I only repeat what you were saying—
> the shell and the hawk every hour
> are slaying man and jerboas, slaying
>
> the mind: but the body can fill
> the hungry flowers and the dogs who cry words
> at nights, the most hostile things of all.
> But that is not new. Each time the night discards
>
> draperies on the eyes and leaves the mind awake
> I look each side of the door of sleep
> for the little coin it will take
> to buy the secret I shall not keep.
>
> I see men as trees suffering
> or confound the detail and the horizon.
> Lay the coin on my tongue and I will sing
> of what the others never set eyes on.

As the logical outcome of Douglas' independence of his predecessors and colleagues, **'Desert Flowers'** executes the main ideas of **'Poets in this War'**. Death on the battlefield promises a new vision for the poet whose eyes have been clouded. His new theme will be an honest exploration of his own relationship to war, battle and death.

Douglas was drawn magnetically to the stage of war 'where the incredible things happen'. In his *Journal* which

would become his prose account of war, *Alamein to Zem Zem,* Douglas confided that: 'When I could order my thoughts and look for more significant things than appearances, I still looked—I cannot avoid it—for something decorative, poetic or dramatic'. He describes many sights of the battlefield in romantic terms: 'This scene with the silhouettes of men and turrets interrupted by swirls of smoke and the sky lightening behind them, was to be made familiar to me by many repetitions'. Douglas gives an account of one of these common scenes, a tank in flames, mythologically: dark grey-blue smoke issues from the side of a turret 'like the Goddess Sin springing from the left shoulder of Satan'. Bombs and a fighter plane are likened to raindrops and a gliding bird: 'The silver body of the aeroplane was surrounded by hundreds of little grey smudges, through which it sailed on serenely. From it there fell away, slowly and gracefully, an isolated shower of rain, a succession of glittering drops.' In these prose passages, Douglas attempts to tame the fury and terror of war with similes involving comparisons to the familiar or beloved.

In his poetry of battle, however, he charts war's effect on himself. It is there that he sees remorseless cruelty as a condition not only of the physical landscape but also of man himself. **'Devils'**, written in 1942, most clearly shows Douglas' recognition of a single evil, without and within. This discovery occurs in a vast silence, a 'deceptive quiet' similar to that Douglas associated with the desert, a torn yet honest landscape. It also recalls his *Journal* description of tank warfare: 'The view from a moving tank is like that in a camera obscura or silent film'. The world seems silent but is not; yet the world within (inside the tank or inside the mind) is even noisier:

> Outside the usual crowd of devils
> are flying in the clouds, are running
> on the earth, imperceptibly spinning
> through the black air alive with evils
> and turning, diving in the wind's channels.
> Inside the unsubstantial wall
> these idiots of the mind can't hear
> the demons talking in the air
> who think my mind void. That's all;
> there'll be an alliance of devils if it fall.

Again Douglas struggles to keep apart two factions, but here instead of imagining angels in combat with devils, he views his mind as he had viewed his body: as a fortress infiltrated by devils. Earlier divided, body and mind are now joined by the fact that they are both attacked. Both are subjected to assaults by a group of devils and angels. **'Devils'** is a poem of confusion in which the speaker is alone and unable to help himself against powerful forces which now threaten to fell him for good.

In landscape poems '1', '2' and '3', Douglas attempts to define a direct relationship to the figures of war, dead and alive. In **'Landscape with Figures 1'** Douglas observes the battlefield from the vantage point of an airplane and sees the same insect world described by poets of the First World War. The plain is 'dotted': 'the sand vehicles / squashed dead or still entire, stunned / like beetles: scattered wingcases and / legs, heads, show when the haze settles'. Yet Douglas seems to reject as spurious any visions of battle which are too romantic or distanced.

In **'Landscape with Figures 2'** the spectator personally confronts dead bodies which 'wriggle' as mimes of life. They are 'stony actors' unable to conquer the reality of the play they perform. Douglas records his own creative struggles with the reality and unreality of war. He continues in **'Landscape with Figures 3'** to speak in theatrical terms but moves to centre stage from his position of spectator in '1' and from a figure on 'the back cloth' in '2':

> I am the figure burning in hell
> and the figure of the grave priest
> observing everyone who passed
> and that of the lover. I am all
> the aimless pilgrims, the pedants and courtiers
> more easily you believe me a pioneer
> and a murdering villain without fear
>
>   . . . . .
>
> I am all these and I am the craven
> the remorseful the distressed
> penitent: not passing from life to life
> but all these angels and devils are driven
> into my mind like beasts. I am possessed,
> the house whose wall contains the dark strife
> the arguments of hell with heaven.
>   ? April-September 1943

By splitting himself into actor and spectator in the drama, Douglas paradoxically is able to see himself in many more roles. He no longer pigeonholes himself or his poems into stereotyped combats of devils and angels, but forces a multiple point of view on himself, even as he had forced it on his reader in other poems. Now he is priest, penitent, killer, questor, victim; it bears noting that he will never again use *angel* in a poem.

Seeking to be more than an oracular poet—or one of the 'orators dropping down a curtain of rhetoric' (**'The Offensive 2'**)—Douglas chooses to pull back the self-imposed draperies of man's eyes, to move from background to foreground, and openly confront his own complicated feelings toward destruction and self-destruction. War enabled Douglas to develop a new stage in his work. As he wrote to J. C. Hall in the summer of 1943, the lyricism of his early days was no longer viable after his active participation in battle. While he was 'finished with one form of writing' and was 'progressing towards another', Douglas was grasping for a closer personal integration of conflicting internal impulses. He could no longer write in the lyrical 'old forms' Hall admired; he could write only 'true things'. Having faced war, he declared: 'Now I will write of it and perhaps one day cynic and lyric will meet and make me a balanced style'. Douglas could not succumb to a 'sentimental or emotional' reaction to war (though his very declaration proves how alluring lyricism was) but spoke passionately for 'honesty' and some kind of belief even if that belief had to be tempered:

> To be sentimental or emotional now is dangerous to oneself and to others. To trust anyone or to admit any hope of a better world is criminally foolish, as foolish as it is to stop working for it. It sounds silly to say work without hope, but it

can be done; it's only a form of insurance; it doesn't mean work hopelessly.

Like Lewis, Douglas was a realist, but like Keyes he was also a romantic who carried a beast within. In war, romantic and realist met. Douglas had realized that the new war poet could not be a patriotic national spokesman. Nor was there a need to teach the civilians about war or 'paint' specific war events. Rather, he understood that the Second World War poet carried his own demon into the realm of history and that his identity could be defined only by their interaction. Douglas looked upon war as a personal test and a battle with the devilish tormentor he called 'Bête Noire'.

Douglas dramatically documents the predominance of this beast in the drawings of February 1944 and in notes he made in connection with his volume of poetry called *Bête Noire.* In December of 1943, on leave to prepare for the invasion of Europe, Douglas had started work on a manuscript of his poems for Tambimuttu who had published some of them already in *Poetry (London)*. In February 1944 he received a contract with Editions Poetry London, and in March he had decided on the title. While rushing to select and order his poems, Douglas attempted versions of a new poem called by the same name as his volume. One draft names the beast 'my particular monster' and recognizes it as a permanent inhabitant for over ten years. Although Douglas fails to identify fully the nature of this beast, it seems to represent an asocial and destructive, or self-destructive, urge. In another version of this Ur-poem, Douglas feels the stifling power of the animal he cannot subdue or yield to:

> The beast is a jailer
> allows me out on patrol
> brings me back by telepathy
> is inside my mind
> breaks into my conversations with his own
>   words
>
> speaking out of my mouth
> can overthrow me in a moment
> writes what I write, or edits it (censors it)
> takes a dislike to my friends and sets me against
>   them
>
>   . . . . .
>
> If this is a game, it's past half time and the beast
>   is winning.

After five fragmentary attempts, *Bête Noire* proved to be intractable material. And yet . . . the black monster-devil of Douglas' mind had already had a positive influence. ' **"Bête Noire"**,' he wrote in a **'Note for the Jacket of *Bête Noire***', 'is the name of the poem I can't write: a protracted failure, which is also a protracted success I suppose. Because it is the poem I begin to write in a lot of other poems: this is what justifies my use of that title for the book.' (pp. 118-30)

The climax of Douglas' movement towards welding two sides of himself and integrating his personal struggles with history, is reached in his most famous poem **'Vergissmeinnicht'**. There he is able to project fully his own internal battles onto the outer landscape of death by identifying himself with the enemy. Written in Tunisia in 1943, when Douglas' regiment was resting, **'Vergissmeinnicht'** gains from being a poem of rediscovery and remembrance, a poem which moves from the common scenes of war to the more particularized and intimate instance of *one* dead man. Douglas discovers the body of a soldier, the same fighter who, like a demon, had fired at his tank in the warfare three weeks before. What remains of him now are the picture of his girlfriend and his utilitarian weapons, emblems of Eros and Mars:

> Three weeks gone and the combatants gone
> returning over the nightmare ground
> we found the place again, and found
> the soldier sprawling in the sun.
>
> The frowning barrel of his gun
> overshadowing. As we came on
> that day, he hit my tank with one
> like the entry of a demon.
>
> Look. Here in the gunpit spoil
> the dishonoured picture of his girl
> who has put: *Steffi. Vergissmeinnicht.*
> In a copybook gothic script.
>
> We see him almost with content,
> abased, and seeming to have paid
> and mocked at by his own equipment
> that's hard and good when he's decayed.
>
> But she would weep to see today
> how on his skin the swart flies move;

the dust upon the paper eye
and the burst stomach like a cave.

> For here the lover and killer are mingled
> who had one body and one heart.
> And death who had the soldier singled
> has done the lover mortal hurt.
>
> (Tunisia May/June 1943)

Like others of his complicated poems, **'Vergissmeinnicht'** refuses to allow the reader one reaction. It is not simply a recognition scene, nor is it carrying the message of a conciliatory Whitman: 'For my enemy is dead, a man as divine as myself is dead'. At first the speaker is glad to see the enemy abused by death, but this contentment is too easy. Gradually, tenderness develops in the poem with the introduction of the enemy's beloved who 'would weep' if she could see the broken body of her man. Yet dwelling only for a moment on the 'dishonoured' picture of the German girl, Douglas withholds expressions of direct compassion and uses sparingly any phrases or words which would elicit pity. 'She would weep' distances the speaker's and the reader's involvements by making the crying come from another person, and conditionally at that. The literary and half-romantic *swart* is a touch of beauty which saves stanza 5 from becoming totally disgusting. It is, nevertheless, reduced to objective realism by modifying *flies.* It is just such a cautious interweaving of romantic touches with realism that complicates our response. Like Douglas, we are deeply moved by the scene before us; yet we are not allowed any self-deceptions.

Douglas exercises strict control over the material and over our responses, from the first stanza to the final antithetical closing. At first we see the soldier with the sun falling on his body. Then in its decay, as we follow directions and 'look' closer, we confront a paper eye and a stomach burst open like a giant hole. Beside him likes the picture of his girl. Yet perhaps the most important point about **'Vergissmeinnicht'** is that the man is not a stereotype, even though the opening stanza with its slow and repetitive movement conditions us for a stereotyped war scene—the tank rolls slowly over ground travelled before. 'Look', which means 'look closer', is the most important single word in the poem. This enemy soldier is not just a German; he is 'Steffi', a man who loved a girl and who died in battle with Douglas.

Douglas fictionalizes the scene by his choice of words and by the progression of his images; he invests personal life with care into a common war occurrence. The fact that he understates his feelings, that all is given with the minimum of active involvement, stresses the power of his and our identification. The soldier is presented as killer, then as lover, but the last stanza shows the vulnerability of both such roles before Death. Douglas joins the personal with history here by his own self-projection; for in the last stanza, even as he speaks of the German soldier, he speaks primarily of himself:

> For here the lover and killer are mingled
> who had one body and one heart.
> And death who had the soldier singled
> has done the lover mortal hurt.

The killer and lover are yet another antithetical pairing of

Sketches by Douglas for the cover of Bête Noire.

Douglas' beast/devil and angel/romantic. By his understanding that they mingle inextricably, he acknowledges their relationship: by inflicting mortal hurt on another, one kills the essentially human part of oneself and becomes no better than the beast. The lover here represents all that is human, moral, and personal; the killer is the inhuman, immoral and impersonal. Yet they are one.

Douglas' earlier poem **'The Prisoner'** provides a valuable contrast to **'Vergissmeinnicht'**. Written in 1940 at Sandhurst, the poem is addressed to a woman Douglas loved at Oxford:

> Today, Cheng, I touched your face
> with two fingers, as a gesture of love
> for I can never prove enough
> by sight or sense your strange grace;
>
> but like moths my hands return
> to your skin, that's luminous
> like a lamp in a paper house,
> and touch, to teach love and learn.
>
> I think a thousand hours are gone
> that so, like gods, we'd occupy:
> but alas, Cheng, I cannot tell why,
> today I touched a mask stretched on the stone-
>
> hard face of death. There was the urge
> to escape the bright flesh and emerge
> of the ambitious cruel bone.

The poem illustrates rather startlingly the reverse of Douglas' superimposition of love on death, as in **'Vergissmeinnicht'**. Here he applies the face of death, a skull, to the face of a lovely living human. A sketch of a divided face, half-woman, half-skull and skeleton belongs with this poem. But in **'Vergissmeinnicht'** Douglas does not have to provide a mask of death, a corpse or skull. The battlefield provides the scene of death, and he is able to draw something vital from it—a poem of rediscovery (the body), discovery (the photograph), and remembrance. While the war scene is responsible for the reversal, Douglas' ability to divide himself into spectator and actor is equally important. He becomes that German, lying dead, in a far more personal way than he ever relates to Cheng. In the later poem, he realizes that he has killed a part of himself.

Douglas truly becomes, with **'Vergissmeinnicht'**, a poet for whom literary history and geo-political history match: stereotypical boundaries are broken down. In the poems of 1943 boundaries between himself and others are dissolved by his declaration of himself as outcast, killer, lover, victim, brother, Jew, German, corpse. **'Vergissmeinnicht'** is the culmination of that development towards a greater humanity. His poetry is not just that of a broken landscape or an exiled destroyed heart, but that of a civil war in which he sees and plays both sides. While Lewis could not commit himself to another and Keyes did not extend his poems of connection to the battlefield, Douglas recognizes that there is no enemy named Germany; its name is Death. (pp. 130-35)

> *Linda M. Shires, "No Enemy But Death: The Poetry of Keith Douglas," in her* British Poet-

ry of the Second World War, *St. Martin's Press, 1985, pp. 113-39.*

Edna Longley   (essay date 1986)

[In the following excerpt, Longley outlines the most important subjects, themes, and techniques in Douglas's poetry.]

In a recent poll [published in *Poetry Review,* April 1974] Keith Douglas's **Complete Poems** received heartening votes as one of the best books of poetry since 1939. However, the voters were mostly poets (compare the Edward Thomas lobby), and the "tradition", as manufactured by academies and anthologies, still leaves Douglas on the margin. What Geoffrey Hill, twenty years ago [see excerpt dated 1964], called his 'ambivalent status—at once "established" and overlooked' remains unresolved. And this, despite not only Hill's backing but Ted Hughes's splendid introduction to the **Selected Poems;** 'It is a language for the whole mind, at its most wakeful, and in all situations. A utility general-purpose style, as, for instance, Shakespeare's was, that combines a colloquial prose readiness with poetic breadth. . . . ' [An expanded version of Hughes's introduction is excerpted above.] Nor can all sins of omission be explained by Douglas's half-shunting into the 'war poetry' siding; although perhaps only in England would Michael Hamburger's point not be taken: 'In the era of total politics . . . war poetry has become continuous, ubiquitous and hardly distinguishable from any other kind of poetry' [In *Poetry Nation,* No. 4, 1975]. Roger Garfitt, reviewing Desmond Graham's helpful biography (1974), implies a deeper reason why English criticism and poetry lack the catholic belly' to digest Douglas: 'Critics have mistaken his masterly verse control for a cerebral detachment.'

It is certainly ironical that Ian Hamilton should find 'reticence stiffening into the tight-lipped insensitivity of the officers' mess' [see Further Reading], where Ted Hughes finds 'burning exploratory freshness'. Yet even studies of Hughes—far more abundant than of Douglas—make little room for an obvious ancestor and inspiration. That Douglas has not come through on Hughes's strong push may reflect an aesthetic conflict in England, not so much between Larkinians and Hughesians, as between the style-faction and the content-faction (which Hughes in this case straddles), cavaliers and puritans, Martians and down-to-earthers. At present battle-lines seem to be drawn up behind Craig Raine and Peter Porter, with Ulster poets sniped at in No Man's Land for not keeping their enviable raw material raw enough: '[The Ulster poets] . . . have more urgent matter to write about than most, but they commonly opt for style rather than message.' Garfitt exposes this kind of false polarisation when he castigates Hamilton for

> valuing [Alun] Lewis's theorising on integrity above Douglas's realisation of it through form. Douglas's poetry is almost an imitation of action in the vigour and compactness of its language, yet fully human in its response.

Such unity of creative being points back beyond Larkin,

Hughes and Hill to Yeats. And in a very precise sense. Yeats and MacNeice envied men of action. Edward Thomas put his life where his poetry was; Wilfred Owen his poetry where his life was. But the symbiosis between Douglas's literary and military careers—soldier, poet, horseman—uncannily acted out the heroic aesthetic which Yeats constructed around Major Robert Gregory:

> Some burn damp faggots, others may consume
> The entire combustible world in one small room
> As though dried straw. . . .

It is no sentimentality but well-documented fact that Keith Douglas conceived his short life-work in these terms, though without self-glorification. His 'terror of perishing into an ordinary existence', 'hatred for wasted time', desertion *to* the battle of Alamein (his batman commented 'You're shit or bust, you are'), are inseparable from his poetry's imaginative courage.

Douglas told J. C. Hall, in a significant metaphor:

> Your talk of regrouping sounds to me—if you will excuse me for exhibiting a one-track mind— like the military excuse of a defeated general. There is never much need to regroup. Let your impulses drive you forward; never lose contact with life or you will lose the impulses as well. Meanwhile if you must regroup, do it by re-reading your old stuff.

(The workshop advice is Yeatsian too.) All 'war poets' feel a special urgency to get things said: Owen to 'warn', Thomas 'to pack into that hour/ [His] unwilling hoard of song'. Douglas, with his absolute 'conviction . . . that he would be killed in the war' and compulsion from childhood to 'picture coming events' ('sing of what the others never set eyes on'), tried to concentrate into his poetry all the experience he would ever and never have: 'The entire combustible world in one small room', A to Z. His hungry fore-imagining resembles the older Yeats's insatiability: 'I feel constantly if I were but twenty years old and not over sixty all I ever wanted to do could be done easily. One never tires of life and at the last must die of thirst with the cup at one's lip.' For similar reasons, Douglas wanted to step on to 'the simple, central stage of the war' where 'the interesting things happen':

> To say I thought of the battle of Alamein as an ordeal sounds pompous: but I did think of it as an important test, which I was interested in passing . . . during two years or so of hanging about I never lost the certainty that the experience of battle was something I must have. . . .

> But it is exciting and amazing to see thousands of men, very few of whom have much idea why they are fighting, all enduring hardships, living in an unnatural, dangerous, but not wholly terrible world, having to kill and to be killed, and yet at intervals moved by a feeling of comradeship with the men who kill them and whom they kill, because they are enduring and experiencing the same things. It is tremendously illogical—to read about it cannot convey the impression of having walked through the looking-glass which touches a man entering a battle.

Hughes considers war 'in a sense [Douglas's] ideal subject: the burning away of all human pretensions in the ray cast by death'. Hill argues for a different terminology: 'To say that "war was his ideal subject" implies a greater scope of freedom-in-choice than is, perhaps, called for. To do justice to Douglas one has to acknowledge how the virtù of his art arose from the necessity of his life as a soldier.' Perhaps even this formulation omits Douglas's excitement and amazement, his theatrical sense, his 'lonely impulse of delight' or 'beast on my back'. And although Hill finally agrees with Hughes that 'the war brought his gift to maturity, or to a first maturity', Douglas himself anticipated a last or only maturity, not phases in any Yeatsian masterplan of development.

Douglas's lust to say everything gives his imagery its cosmic thrust:

> The hand is perfect in itself—the five
> fingers, though changing attitude, depend
> on a golden point, the imaginary true focal
> to which infinities of motion and shape are
>   yoked.
> There is no beginning to the hand, no end,
> and the bone retains its proportion in the grave.
>   **('The Hand')**

That microcosm might be an anatomy of his poetry. The love poems, for instance, progress from half-absorbed Donne ('You are the whole continent of love') to the true Donnean dimensions of **'The Knife'** (1942):

> And in your body each minute I died;
> moving your thigh could disinter me
> from a grave in a distant city. . . .

The body, the head, houses, cities, countries, the globe regularly metamorphose into each other. (In *Alamein to Zem Zem* Douglas first perceives the army 'as a body would look to a germ riding in its bloodstream'.) Also, the organic and inorganic fuse with particular power in the face of death: 'the pockmarked house bleached by the glare / whose insides war has dried out like gourds', 'the burst stomach like a cave'. Douglas constantly personifies the sun, moon, stars, time, death; and his cosmos includes angels and devils. The Shakespearean **'Time Eating'** suggests the nature as well as the scope of his imagination. Both a portrait of the artist (creator-maker), and of what the artist is up against, Time comprehends what Douglas sets out to comprehend:

> That volatile huge intestine holds
> material and abstract in its folds. . . .

All Douglas's images of art and the artist are on a large scale. His juvenilia yearn for 'The old free poets who talked to lustful kings', for Shelleyan 'unacknowledged rulers' who 'walk over the hilltop / Into their rarer climate'. Despite the Yeats-like disillusionment of **'The Poets'** (1940):

> For we are hated,
> known to be cursed, guessed to be venomous;
> we must advance for ever, always belated

'princely', if not regal, versions of the poetic activity persist. The poet 'lies in wait' for words 'by the white pillar of a prince', his ears 'admit princes to the corridors / into the mind'. And Douglas continues to celebrate the imagination as having a universal design behind it or before it. The theoretic recommendation of **'Extension to Francis Thompson'**—'Look in earth and air to catch / his mineral or electric eye'—becomes the practice of **'The Marvel'**, which affirms creation in more ways than one. Douglas's aristocratic 'baron of the sea, the great tropic / swordfish' survives in spirit both the removal of his eye and an astonishing metamorphosis from animal to mineral:

> which is an instrument forged in semi-darkness
> yet taken from the corpse of this strong traveller
> becomes a powerful enlarging glass
>
> reflecting the unusual sun's heat.
> With it a sailor writes on the hot wood
> the name of a harlot in his last port.

The 'glass' also conjures up 'the querulous soft voice// of mariners who rotted into ghosts'. A focal, focusing point for the elements, for sea and sky, for unconscious and conscious powers, for life and death, for life and art, 'the burning eye' concentrates all the energies of creation as the poet does:

> And to engrave that word the sun goes through
> with the power of the sea,
> writing her name and a marvel too.

This naming proclaims a unified if awesome cosmos. It also proclaims a marvellously unifying imagination.

Keith Douglas's and Ted Hughes's images of poetry diverge. Hughes's early poetry also identifies the eye with poetic vision. A surrogate eye, his 'Drop of Water', is a 'without heart-head-nerve lens / Which saw the first and earth-centering jewel / Spark upon darkness'. Meanwhile the created world stares back into the eye of the beholder. The hapless ratiocinator of 'Meeting' shrinks under the gaze of a cosmic-eyed goat, '[Watching] his blood's gleam with a ray / Slow and cold and ferocious as a star'. Or this too is the poet's eye, like that of 'The Thought-Fox': 'A widening, deepening greenness, / Brilliantly, concentratedly, / Coming about its own business'. Itself a flash of energy (ray, drill), Hughes's eye engages in an eyeball-to-eyeball exchange of sparks with the universe. He would not have detached the swordfish's eye. Douglas's eye, whether appropriated from a swordfish or not, does not go it alone but participates in a complex chain-reaction that includes 'heart-head-nerve':

> If at times my eyes are lenses
> through which the brain explores
> constellations of feeling. . . .
>
>   ('Bête Noire')

'The Hand' lengthens the chain. Although not mentioned, the eye's rigorous scrutiny governs the 'transmutations' of the poem, 'this making a set of pictures, this drawing / shapes within the shapes of the hand'. Douglas then moves from hand to brain, to 'arguments', to 'the centre of reason, the mainspring':

> To do this is drilling the mind, still a recruit,
> for the active expeditions of his duty
> when he must navigate alone the wild

cosmos, as the Jew wanders the world:

> and we, watching the tracks of him at liberty
> like the geometry of feet
> upon a shore, constructed in the sand,
> look for the proportions, the form of an immense
>   hand.

As the poem comes full circle it declares a humanistic confidence. The mind, in order to grapple with 'the wild / cosmos', learns from the body, but is not thereby devalued like Hughes's 'Egg-Head'. (Douglas commonly uses 'mind' for imagination.) The military and mathematical language too, the repetitions of 'proportion' and 'form' align the poem's perspective with Yeats's Greek-Renaissance 'Measurement began our might'. The 'measured' deliberation of the syntax dramatises an 'instrumentation' crucial to Douglas's concept of art: 'This perfection slips / through the hands to the instrument'; 'an instrument forged in semi-darkness'; 'Words are my instruments but not my servants'. Hughes, despite his brilliant summarising phrase, 'a language for the whole mind', might dispute the conclusion of **'Extension to Francis Thompson'**: 'analysis is worshipping'.

Keith Douglas does not always assert the order of creation. **'The Offensive'**, which echoes Owen's 'Spring Offensive', co-opts the constellations to express man's disorders: 'The stars dead heroes in the sky', 'The stars . . . are the heavenly symbols of a class / dead in their seats'. Nevertheless, another component here—anger—reclaims Douglas for the humanism that Hughes would deny him:

> The truth of a man is the doomed man in him
> or his dead body . . . Douglas had no time, and
> perhaps no disposition, to cultivate the fruity de-
> ciduous tree of How to Live. He showed in his
> poetry no concern for man in society. The mur-
> derous skeleton in the body of a girl, the dead
> man behind the mirror, these items of circum-
> stantial evidence are steadily out-arguing all his
> high spirits and hopefulness.

It all depends what you mean by society—a word Hughes narrows till it indeed shrinks 'to a trinket shape' as compared with 'the whole Sun-swung zodiac of light'. Hughes and his admirers also shrink humanism to a version of the Movement. Thus Keith Sagar:

> The poet is a medium for transmitting an occult
> charge from the non-human world into the psy-
> che and thence into consciousness . . . Most En-
> glish poets have drifted into a rational human-
> ism and arrogantly expect us to value their mea-
> sured musings.

Hughes's 'out-arguing', while acknowledging Douglas's dialectic, downgrades it even as a source of imaginative energy. Sagar's polarities accommodate neither dialectic nor 'the whole mind'.

Douglas of course radically criticised the socio-political emphases of thirties poetry, themselves worn out by 1939. Yet he also maintained much more continuity with the preceding generation than did Hughes with the Movement. *Autumn Journal* not only ended an era but inaugurated a new one, and a new poetry (for MacNeice himself too):

The New Year comes with bombs, it is too late
To dose the dead with honourable intentions.

At this time MacNeice (and Auden) was making amends
to Yeats, and insisting that the war enforced a new aesthetic:

> Some of the poets who renounced the Ivory
> Tower were ready to enter a Brazen Tower of
> political dogma; where the Ivory Tower repre-
> sents, isolation from men in general, the Brazen
> Tower represents isolation from men as individ-
> uals (witness the typical entowered politician)
> and also from oneself as an individual. Bad logic
> demanded a choice between the Towers, but sal-
> utary self-deceit allowed many of the Brazen
> school to leave the door open. The impact of the
> war with its terrible threat of genuine spiritual
> imprisonment has brought them again out of
> doors. The poet is once more to be a mouth in-
> stead of a megaphone, and poetry, one hopes, is
> to develop organically from the organic premises
> of life—of life as it is lived, not of life when it is
> dried into algebra.

Douglas's MacNeicean **'Invaders'** (1939) resolves 'always
to think, and always to indite / of a good matter, while the
black birds cry'. Although Douglas followed Yeats in re-
pudiating a populist view of art (hence his kings and
princes), he also followed him in not therefore abandoning
all interest in society. That magnificent letter (in 1943) to
Hall, which resembles MacNeice's aesthetic, includes a social and human agenda within war's imaginative imperative:

> I don't know if you have come across the word
> Bullshit—it is an army word and signifies hum-
> bug and unnecessary detail. It symbolises what
> I think must be got rid of—the mass of irrelevan-
> cies, of "attitudes", "approaches", propaganda,
> ivory towers, etc., that stands between us and
> our problems and what we have to do about
> them. . . . To be sentimental or emotional now
> is dangerous to oneself and to others. To trust
> anyone or to admit any hope of a better world
> is criminally foolish, as foolish as it is to stop
> working for it. It sounds silly to say work with-
> out hope, but it can be done; it's only a form of
> insurance; it doesn't mean work hopelessly.

Having absorbed First World War poetry ('hell cannot be
let loose twice . . . Almost all that a modern poet on active service is inspired to write, would be tautological')
Douglas addressed himself to the unfinished business that
had permitted the futility of one war to beget the illogic
of another. His short essay **'Poets in This War'** certainly
raises the issue of 'How to Live' as well as 'How to Write':

> During the period "entre deux guerres" we were
> listening alternately to an emphasis of the horri-
> ble nature of modern war and to the vague reme-
> dies of social and political reformers. The na-
> tion's public character remained, in spite of
> all, as absurdly ignorant and reactionary as
> ever . . . the poets . . . who were accustomed
> to teach politics and even supposed themselves,
> and were supposed versed in the horrors of the
> current struggles in Spain, were curiously unable

to react to a war which began and continued in
such a disconcerting way.

Michael Hamburger argues that **'Aristocrats'**, mourning
a 'gentle / obsolescent breed of heroes', writes off Keith
Douglas as well as Rupert Brooke: 'Perhaps Douglas . . .
knew in his heart that his own truthfulness in the face of
corporate experience owed a good deal to his upbringing,
to a liberalism and individualism that were no less in danger of becoming obsolete than the reliance on fair play
which the same institutions served to inculcate.' However,
in this sense too Douglas swallowed the lessons of the thirties along with those of the twenties, and thus enlarged
rather than abandoned the humane critique of war.

Yeats might have relished, not only a stance nearer to
'tragic joy' than to 'passive suffering', but also Douglas's
importation of a phantasmagoria into the theatre of war.
His poetry is much more populated than Hughes's, less
anonymously populated than Owen's, its inhabitants falling somewhere between thirties type and Yeatsian archetype. In addition to his own interior drama, where love as
well as life dices with death, the poetry, like *Alamein to
Zem Zem,* observes others closely. Nor does Douglas confine his observation to Cairo 'vignettes', although the
'stained white town' consummates his concern with the
city: not the socio-political laboratory of thirties poetry,
but a timeless ferment (like MacNeice's Greek city-state
in section IX of *Autumn Journal*). As sunlit landscape
haunts First World War poetry, 'golden age' Oxford-
Byzantium, home of 'leisurely immortals', haunts Douglas's:

> This city experiences a difficult time. The old
>   bells
> fall silent, or are bidden to silence. The buildings
>   lean
> inwards, watching the questionable sky,
> and across the meadows, where youth and age
>   inhabit,
> exchange an austere opinion of foreboding.

'Soissons' (1940) and **'Enfidaville'** (1943) also epitomise
'fallen' civilisation:

> Yet here something of the mind lived and died,
> a mental tower restored only to fall. . . .
>
> In the church fallen like dancers
> lie the Virgin and St Thérèse
> on little pillows of dust.

'An Oration', with its Yeatsian cast of 'lovers', 'hucksters',
'ballad-mongers', 'beggars', 'saints and national heroes',
opposes the vivid past to a living death: 'the people themselves are dead, / wakeful and miserable in their dark
graves'. Not to be fully alive (more horrifying to Douglas
than 'the skull beneath the skin') receives subtler diagnosis
in his Egyptian scenarios. For an Egyptian sentry 'There
is no pain, no pleasure, life's no puzzle / but a standing,
a leaning, a sleep between the coasts// of birth and dying'.
Cairo's 'stink of jasmin' symbolises all the sleeping sickness and corruption that allows the deaths 'in another
place'. Egypt is

> the sick land where in the sun lay
> the gentle sloe-eyed murderers
> of themselves, exquisites under a curse. . . .

Douglas's poetry concentrates less on compassion for death (Owen) than on a Shakespearean passion for the life which war highlights and destroys.

The image of a corrupt woman, Cleopatra, Dark Lady, Cressida (**'Time Eating'** also points to the influence of *Troilus and Cressida*) often accompanies rottenness in the state. The declaration of war coincided with Douglas's final rejection by his obsessively loved Yingcheng, 'Cressida could not match you':

> [Douglas] . . . visited the Cowley Road garage where Yingcheng had left the red sports car. Asking the girl there if she had news of Yingcheng, Douglas was told she was going to be married. Hatten remembers that he 'took this news with impassivity and then said to me, "Anyway, I had that week in Paris".' On 6 September Douglas reported to No. 15 Reception Unit, in Manor Road, to enlist in the 'Cavalry of the Line.'. . . . Afterwards . . . Douglas announced that he would join a good cavalry regiment and 'bloody well make my mark in this war. For I will not come back.'

'I listen to the desert wind' identifies Yingcheng's cruelty and hardness with that of the desert world. **'Syria II'**, echoing Isaac Rosenberg's 'Returning, we hear the Larks', presents war in terms of sexual betrayal: 'fair apples where the snake plays', 'a murderer with a lover's face'. **'Egypt'** personifies the country as a woman 'diseased and blind of an eye / and heavy with habitual dolour'. **'Behaviour of Fish in an Egyptian Tea Garden'** portrays decadent, commercial sex as a submarine region—often, for Douglas, symbolic of mortality. As in *Troilus and Cressida,* all this trafficking between love and war enriches a tragic perspective on perverted values:

> For here the lover and killer are mingled. . . .

'Snakeskin and Stone', with its sharp antithesis between how to live and how to die, spells out Douglas's credo:

> I praise a snakeskin or a stone:
> a bald head or a public speech
> I hate: the serpent's lozenges
> are calligraphy, and it is
> truth these cryptograms teach,
> the pebble is truth alone.

Together, the 'complication' and 'subtlety' of the snake, the age and cruelty of the stone sum up life and death, establish a site for Byzantium:

> all the buildings truth can make,
>
> a whole city, inhabited by lovers,
> murderers, workmen and artists
> not much recognised: all
> who have no memorial
> but are mere men. . . .

The human irreducibility of these citizens contrasts with the 'mask of words or figures' assumed by public life—like the bald head, 'a desert / between country of life and country of death'. Again, it is the 'bullshit' of inbetween states that Douglas scorns. His attack on lifeless, yet deathly,

rhetoric fuses, within another submarine vista, 'dead words' and dead bodies: 'Tangled they cruise / like mariners' bodies in the grave of ships.' **'Snakeskin and Stone'** confirms that Douglas's concept of death not only takes in 'dead bone', but attacks all that belies glowing skin. The end of the poem does not dismiss the social 'world' as separate and irrelevant, but hunts to their source, more ruthlessly than even Owen did, the origins of war:

> for you who think the desert hidden
> or the words, like the dry bones, living
> are fit to profit from the world.
> And God help the lover of snakeskin and stone.

'Landscape with Figures'—whether read as single poem or sonnet sequence—channels this love and hatred into a more inward assumption of responsibility. In a parallel with 'Dulce et Decorum Est', the speaker moves from observer to participant ('I am the figure writing on the back-cloth') to scapegoat-redeemer:

> all these angels and devils are driven
> into my mind like beasts. I am possessed,
> the house whose wall contains the dark strife,
> the arguments of hell with heaven.

The pun on 'contain' and Douglas's recurrent sense of the mind as a house define an intensely feeling, densely peopled imagination, convulsed by, yet controlling, Yeatsian antinomies. **'Devils'**, those inside the mind divided by an 'unsubstantial wall' from those outside, dramatises a similar tension. **'Enfidaville'** implicitly equates the poet's mind, desolated by 'the pain this town holds', with the war-emptied houses. Both beautifully fill up again at the end of the poem:

> But already they are coming back; to search
> like ants, poking in the débris, finding in it
> a bed or a piano and carrying it out.
> Who would not love them at this minute?
> I seem again to meet
> the blue eyes of the images in the church.

Antinomies or dualism? That reconciliation suggests the former. But dualistic himself, Hughes casts Douglas in the same mould—a mould which simplifies the reading of some poems. Thus the 'murderous skeleton in the body of a girl' may carry additional symbolic and dramatic layers. Addressed to Yingcheng **'The Prisoner'** contrasts not only life and death, but love and the death of love, and perhaps again peace and war:

> But alas, Cheng, I cannot tell why,
> today I touched a mask stretched on the stone
>
> person of death. There was the urge
> to break the bright flesh and emerge
> of the ambitious cruel bone.

'Mask' (critical in **'Snakeskin and Stone'**) and 'cruel', a word associated with Yingcheng, indicate that the skeleton may stand for her real character. Or conversely, the poet's *memento mori* may take a 'cruel' revenge. Again, the 'dead men being eaten by dogs' appear in a context where Douglas offers a choice of 'attitudes', his irony implying their dualistic inadequacy:

> And the wise man is the lover

who in his planetary love revolves
without the traction of reason or time's control
and the wild dog finding meat in a hole
is a philosopher. The prudent mind resolves
on the lover's or the dog's attitude forever.

'Dead Men', like 'Cairo Jag,' bears out Geoffrey Hill's
contention that war did not so much provide Douglas with
'a unifying generalisation', as introduce him to 'a world
with its own tragi-comic laws, like *Alice* with all the sinister suggestions exaggerated. And much of the acuteness
of the perception is in the recognition that not everyone
has to go through with this; that two absolutely different
worlds co-exist at about a day's journey from each other.'
At the end of 'Cairo Jag' these worlds collide: 'a man with
no head / has a packet of chocolate and a souvenir of Tripoli'. However, Cairo has its 'somnambulists and legless
beggars'. And while the whole gaze of Douglas's poetry
widens towards extremes, its effort is to comprehend—
though without squinting reconciliations—their 'coexistence'. Dualism would preclude 'the arguments of hell
with heaven'. Douglas's self-portrayal after reaching the
Alamein army, fits Hill's distinction: 'a scepticism that is
not so much metaphysical doubt as the willingness to lay
the mind completely open to experience':

> Perhaps betrayed by the spectacle of the stars as
> clear as jewels on black velvet into a mood of
> more solemnity, I suddenly found myself assum-
> ing that I was going to die tomorrow. For per-
> haps a quarter of an hour I considered to what
> possibilities of suffering, more than of death, I
> had laid myself open. This with the dramatic
> and emotional part of me: but my senses of pro-
> portion and humour, like two court jesters,
> chased away the tragic poet, and I drifted away
> on a tide of odd thoughts, watching the various
> signs of battle in the lower sky.

But if not dualism, double vision certainly shapes Douglas's perceptions and methods. 'Negative Information', a
poem about travelling to war, about passing through the
looking-glass, ends without reconciliation:

> To this there's no sum I can find—
> the hungry omens of calamity
> mixed with good signs, and all received with lev-
>   ity,
> or indifference, by the amazed mind.

As with Robert Frost, the question of 'seeing' is crucial to
any sceptical poetic procedure. However, in the absence
of 'metaphysical doubt' (whether *a priori* or *a posteriori*)
Douglas's eye differs from Frost's as well as Hughes's. It
does not so much look from alternative angles, as aim at
progressive penetration: 'lenses / through which the brain
explores. . . . ' (Exploration is another favourite idea.)
Different perspectives extend rather than qualify each
other, strive towards the total comprehension of a camera
obscura blended with a microscope: a kind of analytic synthesis. The early stages of *Alamein to Zem Zem,* particularly abundant in metaphors of visual display, outline an
aesthetic for the desert war: 'the spectacle of the stars', 'the
silhouettes of men and turrets', 'the view from a moving
tank is like that in a camera obscura or a silent film',
'Against a backcloth of indeterminate landscapes of

moods and smells, dance the black and bright incidents'.
Verbs of seeing had rehearsed in 'The House' (of the imagination): seems (3), inspect (2), ('like a conjured spectacle'), appear (3), see, scrutinising, prospecting, 'my incredulous eyes / discern her'. Such verbs function actively and
dramatically: 'I watch with interest, for they are ghosts';
'Look. Here in the gunpit spoil . . . '; 'I see my feet like
stones / underwater', 'I look each side of the door of
sleep'. Neither in prose nor poetry does this resemble the
'spectatorial' attitude condemned by Edward Thomas.
Douglas uses techniques—verbal as well as imagistic—of
montage, collage, silhouetting, juxtaposition, the two-way
telescope to elicit the incongruities and complexities of
what he perceives. 'Russians' (1940), written before he
had witnessed the 'triumphant silence' of the dead, suggests how experimental metaphors of mime, ballet and
tableau trained him for the desert theatre:

> How silly that soldier is pointing his gun at the
>   wood:
> he doesn't know it isn't any good.
> You see, the cold and cruel northern wind
> has frozen the whole battalion where they stand.

Later, anticipating an image in *Alamein to Zem Zem,* the
poem asks us to 'Think of them as waxworks'. The frozen
pose, sustained by a tone and syntax of faux-naif understatement, chills, then pains when emotional 'thaw' arrives in an injunction which ostensibly rules it out:

> Well,
> at least forget what happens when it thaws.

As double vision becomes single here, 'Russians' sets a
pattern for later poems where, in Roger Garfitt's words [in
Poetry Nation, No. 4 (1975)], 'the detachment is not cerebral but is rather a strategy deployed against the strength
of feeling'.

Three poems which proceed by still finer gradations of
focus are 'Syria II', 'How to Kill' and 'Landscape with
Figures'. Syria, 'this two-faced country', is presented in
terms not only of contradictory images and ambiguous
perspectives ('you think you see a devil stand / fronting
a creature of good intention'), but of linguistic surprise: 'a
movement of live stones / the lizards with hooded eyes /
of hostile miraculous age'. Oxymorons culminate in the
images of 'a mantrap in a gay house, / a murderer with
a lover's face'. Athough the poem in a sense remains dual-
istically unresolved ('devil and angel do not fight, / they
are the classic Gemini'). Douglas's final irony holds this
kaleidoscope in a single frame that partly 'accounts' for all
contradictions:

> Curiously
>
> though foreigners we surely shall
> prove this background's complement,
> the kindly visitors who meant
> so well all winter but at last fell
> unaccountably to killing in the spring.

What oxymoron is to 'Syria II', contracting, enjambed,
sometimes inverted sentences are to 'How to Kill':

> The wires touch his face: I cry
> NOW. Death, like a familiar, hears

and look, has made a man of dust
of a man of flesh. This sorcery
I do.

Everything in the poem helps Douglas to get death as accurately into his sights, 'my dial of glass', as the speaker his victim (for here the poet and killer are mingled). The exact hit, the instant proximity of life and death, are captured by radii towards a verbal centre, the delicate 'touch' of sounds and images:

> A shadow is a man
> when the mosquito death approaches.

Like the mosquito, Douglas's imagination hovers over the invisible point or frontier where extremes meet; where life becomes death; flesh, dust or bone; love, indifference; Cairo, the desert; man's creativity, destruction (the 'excellent smooth instruments' of war). In **'Desert Flowers'** he 'looks each side of the door of sleep'. In **'On a Return from Egypt'** he lays his whole life and poetry, his dark Muse, on the line:

> The next month, then, is a window
> and with a crash I'll split the glass.
> Behind it stands one I must kiss,
> person of love or death
> a person or a wraith,
> I fear what I shall find.

Does the incomplete rhyming of 'find' with 'window' stop just this side of the glass? The thinly dividing walls, doors, glass in Douglas's house of the imagination reflect a scrutiny as finely balanced as a coin on its edge; or the situation between wartime lovers who 'can never lean / on an old building in the past / or a new building in the future', but must

> balance tiptoe on a pin,
> could teach an angel how to stand.
>
>   **('Tel Aviv')**

Yet the amount of touching, meeting, sudden synchronisations at the end of poems—for good or ill—again suggests an ultimate integrity of vision. **'Landscape with Figures'** constitutes Douglas's most comprehensive desert panorama and two-way looking-glass, his sharpest etching of human puniness and lunacy against cosmic spaces. Before section III contains the whole situation, the poet's imagination swoops from being 'Perched on a great fall of air', to a close-up which traps the speaker into the picture as 'the figure writhing on the backcloth'. Just through the looking-glass from **'How to Kill'**, the poem catches death while it still mimics life. The particular visual tactic of section I uses distance to create a surreal pathetic fallacy. Military vehicles seem the *disjecta membra* of violated insects or plants: 'stunned / like beetles', 'the steel is torn into fronds / by the lunatic explosive'. After that 'eccentric chart', Douglas's metaphor of art fuses with his metaphor of theatre. Oxymoron again reinforces a life-death paradox: 'the dead men wriggle', 'express silence', 'this prone and motionless struggle', 'the one who opens his mouth and calls / silently', and climactically 'stony actors' (compare 'live stones'). In contrast with the violent action arrested in the past participles of section I (squashed, stunned, scattered, torn) the feeble active verbs of section

II (wriggle, express, enacting, crawling) have the shocking impact of life continuing as a reflex action. As the stage language moves in from 'scenery' to 'maquillage', the collisions between artifice and reality underline a terrifying unreality. Douglas's 'cosmetic blood and hectic / colours death has the only list of' wounds as deeply as Owen's 'hurt of the colour of blood'. The last line of section II—'I am the figure writing on the backcloth'—thaws like the end of **'Russians'**, since 'writhe' is a verb of emotion as well as motion, and prepares for the protean empathy of section III.

Some poems isolate a particular 'stony actor'. **'John Anderson'**, like **'How to Kill'**, expresses a life at the moment of death: 'his creative brain whirled'. But it is the enemy soldier of **'Vergissmeinnicht'** (how different a poem from 'Strange Meeting') who most completely characterises the unbridgeable nearness of life and death. His eloquent soliloquy indeed 'calls / silently':

> Look. Here in the gunpit spoil
> the dishonoured picture of his girl
> Who has put: *Steffi. Vergissmeinnicht*
> in a copybook gothic script.
>
> We see him almost with content
> abased, and seeming to have paid
> and mocked at by his own equipment
> that's hard and good when he's decayed.
>
> But she would weep to see today
> how on his skin the swart flies move;
> the dust upon the paper eye
> and the burst stomach like a cave.

By displacing his own feeling into the girl's hypothetical reaction, Douglas combines the intimate ('how on his skin') with the universalised: 'lover and killer' (which includes loved and killed). Hughes narrows Douglas's 'nightmare ground' in defining it as 'the burning away of all human pretensions in the ray cast by death'. Despite 'abased' and 'mocked', the poem's tone encompasses human waste and human dignity. Or Douglas 'burns away' in the sense of exposing essentials rather than of reducing to nothing. His imagination works in the way **'Simplify Me When I'm Dead'** demands of posterity. It is the difference between Hughes's 'Relic' and Douglas's **'Time Eating'**. Hughes's evolutionary, zoological perspectives— 'Time in the sea eats its tail, thrives'—are too long for grief. **'Time Eating'**, with its Shakespearean love story, inhabits historical and psychological time—if with fierce stringency: 'and though you brought me from a boy / you can make no more of me, only destroy'. The last two lines of **'Vergissmeinnicht'**, where double vision again becomes 'single', prove the indivisibility of 'mortal hurt' and Douglas's art:

> And death who had the soldier singled
> has done the lover mortal hurt.

'Vergissmeinnicht' also exemplifies Douglas's unusual blend of statement and mimesis. His technique is consistent with the philosophical refusal of **'The Hand'** to prefer mind over matter or matter over mind. On the side of statement, his debt to Yeats and Auden appears most strikingly in emphatic adjectives: 'That volatile huge intestine', 'The logical little fish', 'the querulous soft voice // of mariners'. **'The Marvel'** combines abstract polysyllabic adjectives—'one most curious device / of many, kept by the interesting waves'—with strong basic monosyllables: great, bright, sharp, dim, strong, hot, soft. As regards rhetorical demonstratives, 'this' outscores the Yeatsian 'that': 'This sorcery / I do', 'this prone and motionless struggle', 'this strong traveller', 'this making a set of pictures, this drawing / shapes within the shapes of the hand'. The structural role of 'this' in **'The Hand'** clarifies its function of uniting close-up and distance, distilling the essence of a phenomenon which it holds out for inspection. More broadly, by mixing in various strengths evocation and declaration, Douglas's syntax pursues his analytical synthesis. The first line of **'Devils'**, 'My mind's silence is not that of a wood' (for Keith Douglas the verb 'to be' is never weak) prepares for a dialectic, indeed a poem about dialectics. 'A baron of the sea', on the other hand, plunges us into physical experience. Yet there is no hard and fast distinction between the poems. **'Devils'** illustrates the link between Douglas's adjustment of sights and redefinition of images. In Geoffrey Hill's words: 'It would seem that he possessed the kind of creative imagination that approached an idea again and again in terms of metaphor, changing position slightly, seeking the most precise hold'. Thus **'Devils'** proceeds: 'not that of a wood', 'but this deceptive quiet', 'Only within they make their noise'. But **'The Marvel'** too moves over a track of argumentative Syntax, if more deeply embedded. Mimesis and statement, material and abstract, cooperate most delicately in the sphere of sound and rhythm. In **'Vergissmeinnicht'** Douglas not only consonantally imitates the thick intricacy of 'a copy book gothic script', or increases horror through dynamic assonance ('the burst stomach like a cave'), but in the 'mingled' r, l and t sounds of the last quatrain makes his final statement sensuously and musically incontrovertible.

The war governed Douglas's aesthetic as well as his content, and he saw it as conscripting music and imagery into the service of 'significant speech':

> my object (and I don't give a damn about my duty as a poet) is to write true things, significant things in words each of which works for its place in a line. My rhythms, which you find enervated, are carefully chosen to enable the poems to be *read* as significant speech: I see no reason to be either musical or sonorous about things at present. When I do, I shall be so again, and glad to. I suppose I reflect the cynicism and the careful absence of expectation (it is not quite the same as apathy) with which I view the world . . . perhaps one day cynic and lyric will meet and make me a balanced style. Certainly you will never see the long metrical similes and galleries of images again.

This, in 1943, was too modest. Give or take a few immaturities, a few incompletions ('time is all I lacked'), Douglas achieved syntheses, both thematic and stylistic, since unmatched in English poetry. And within his fine balances speech and music, cynicism and lyricism *do* meet. As an aesthetic his economical prescription of economy—'every word must work for its keep'—is not nearly as well known

as it should be, in comparison with many inflated twentieth-century poetic manifestoes. One of Douglas's rich wartime economies is a rigorous paring of phrase, clause and sentence to create a new kind of music as well as a 'sharp enquiring blade':

> A baron of the sea, the great tropic
> swordfish, spreadeagled on the thirsty deck
> where sailors killed him, in the bright Pacific,
>
> yielded to the sharp enquiring blade
> the eye which guided him and found his prey
> in the dim place where he was lord.

'The Marvel' begins with an apposition, a participial phrase, an adverbial clause, pivotal main verb ('yielded'), relative clause, adverbial clause, several prepositional phrases: a great deal of information and implication packed into six lines. Also, the last line of the second stanza reverses syntactically the last line of the first. This reinforces a temporal reversal that resurrects the fish, 'lord' restoring 'baron', and sets up its double role in the poem's cycles of destruction and creation. Douglas's syntax further works for its keep by levelling out historic sequence into a deceptively uniform past tense. His lean periodicity, like MacNeice's ampler rhetoric, may have benefited from classical studies. Not skeletal poetry, but poetry with no superfluous flesh, fighting fit, the cadence of energy. (pp. 94-111)

> *Edna Longley, " 'Shit or Bust': The Importance of Keith Douglas," in her* Poetry in the Wars, 1986. Reprint by University of Delaware Press, 1987, pp. 94-112.

Vincent Sherry   (essay date 1989)

[*An American critic, Sherry has written extensively on British and Irish poets of the post–World War II period, in particular the Welsh poet and painter David Jones. In the following excerpt, Sherry analyzes Douglas's dispassionate presentation of post-combat war scenes.*]

Since his death in 1944, Keith Douglas's reputation as a poet has grown considerably, but fitfully. Largely disregarded for his imaginative daring by the Movement writers, he appealed to poets a half-generation younger than himself, who found in him a stark vitality, a counterforce to what was, for them, the drably mechanical verse being written in the 1950s. Ted Hughes hailed Douglas's 'burning exploratory freshness of mind' [see excerpt dated 1963]; Geoffrey Hill praised a 'fearlessness of the imagination.' Yet Hill's assessment in 1964 of Douglas's ambivalent stature—'at once "established" and overlooked" [See excerpt dated 1964]—remains relevant today. 'Established,' one might say, and 'avoided,' for it is the particular ability of Douglas's art to disconcert. The best of the war poems exhibit a coolness, a bracing diffidence and restraint. The sort of stoic verve that Yeats captures in his 'Irish Airman' Douglas can match in the icy bravura of **'How to Kill'**

> Now in my dial of glass appears
> the soldier who is going to die.
> He smiles, and moves about in ways
> his mother knows, habits of his.

The wires touch his face: I cry
NOW. Death, like a familiar, hears

and look, has made a man of dust
of a man of flesh.

Some readers may relegate such composure to the tight-lipped insensitivity of the officers' mess; others may find his insouciance a powerful coadjutor to the brutalities it records. Yet the combination of realistic violence and emotional composure strikes me as the mark of Douglas's special achievement as a war poet. A pictorial as well as stylistic discipline informs his best poems; recognizing these components enables one not only to appreciate the verse, but to assess its complex effects and understand its place within the tradition of modern war poetry.

Alamein to Zem Zem, Douglas's diary-memoir of his experience in the North Africa desert campaign, is often a vivid narrative of combat action. However, most of his war poems offer post-combat settings. The dead are the figures in his warscapes. Yet these tableaux are as if alive; the dead are usually arrested in the gestures of life, and of life at its most intense in the instant of its extinction. The picture of a frantic mortuary is Douglas's visual signature, as in **'Landscape with Figures 2'**:

> On scrub and sand *the dead men wriggle*
> in their dowdy clothes. They are mimes
> who express silence and futile aims
> enacting this prone and *motionless struggle*
> at a queer angle to the scenery
> crawling on the boards of the stage like walls
> deaf to the one who opens his mouth and calls
> silently.
>
> (***Complete Poems,*** emphases added)

There is a kind of hectic stasis here; suspended in their frenzy, the figures are at once antic and grave. Similar images appear in **'Cairo Jag,'** a post-combat scene glimpsed from the imaginative distance of the Egyptian city:

> . . . you can imagine
> *the dead themselves,* their boots, clothes and pos-
> sessions
> *clinging* to the ground . . .
>
> (***Complete Poems,*** emphases added)

These scenes reveal more than a casually pictorial quality. Behind them likes the specific influence and model of Aubrey Beardsley, above all the graphic work he exhibited in the *Yellow Book.* Douglas wrote an essay on the *Yellow Book* in 1940 for the Oxford magazine the *Cherwell.* It is a revealing irony here that Douglas scolds a Beardsley who has 'postured away his life'; Douglas is himself posturing in this piece, putting on an adult probity that must censor the English 'decadents.' For Douglas is engaged far more deeply and imaginatively by the vivid particulars of Beardsley's art than by its moral issues. Indeed, as prelude to the double effects in his own warscapes, he appreciates the rival qualities of the florid and statuesque in the drawings. He observes these opposing traits in consecutive perceptions, however, not yet as a simultaneity in the art. First he notes the hectic whorl: 'The decadents who produced the *Yellow Book* became entangled in their own complications, as the eye is entangled by the involved patterns and turn of their drawings . . . '; and then he re-cords his sense of the instant arrested—a stasis featured not only in the freeze-frames of the visual arts but in the linear modes of fiction and poetry as well: 'Their stories end not with a moral but with a moment. A moment is caught in their poetry, in their illustration, poising a dancer in the air, or recording a fleeting impression. They sought thus to gain the essential virtue of life, working in a feverish hurry against Time and Death.

Douglas wrote another essay on the *Yellow Book* in 1943, just after his first experience of battle and his first attempt to write war poetry. The false notes of *superbia* are gone; the engagement is clean and direct. He now finds in the literature and graphic art of the *Yellow Book* 'the essential body . . . of a short, tremendously important epoch.' He notes again in the drawings the rival qualities of abundant energy and a nearly ascetic perfection of line, but he now understands these traits as a severe and perfect alloy, indeed as conditions of each other. He finds 'the madder music and stronger wine, inflaming the world to create a million lunatic structures of absolute perfection.' In 'the sinister convolutions of Aubrey Beardsley's pen,' in his 'hectic beauty,' Douglas extols a genius of design, an architectonic quality. The paradox Douglas perceives can be illustrated easily enough: in Beardsley's 'Peacock Skirt,' say, the manic traces and drapery are stylized and frozen within a firm bounding line, a nearly rigid and abstract and non-vital line. But Douglas required the experience of war—or the experience of writing war poetry—to crystallize the perception and see the visual riddle of Beardsley's art.

Hectic stasis in Douglas's war verse is chiefly a visual impression, too, but the riddle finds its resonance through a stylistic, tonal art. Against the agitation in **'Landscape with Figures,'** for example, he finds a point of composure in the wizened, dispassionate temper of the speaker. What drollery to talk of the dead men's 'dowdy clothes,' to mark the pitch of bodies in a mass grave only as a curio: 'at a queer angle to the scenery.' Similarly, in **'Cairo Jag,'** a terse, even elegant understatement contrasts with and defines the violence in the scene. The lunatic stasis in these landscapes, then, is more than a visual conceit; it signals the composure of the speaker in the face of such violence. For the control required to frame a scene of carnage as an aesthetic object offers 'composure'—in the double sense of aesthetic composition and emotional balance—as its shaping spirit. It is a profoundly unrhetorical, anti-rhetorical art; it is uncompelled, uncompelling. Yes, an anti-rhetoric may calculate its effects as surely as any oratory. Yet Douglas tends to avoid not only a direct address to the audience but the sentimental reactions that rhetoric typically targets and manipulates. Thus, as he builds a scene in his prose-memoir around that creative paradox of hectic stasis, he dismisses 'pity,' explicitly, as 'useless.' Douglas refuses to stoke the kinetic response through rhetoric, and sets about turning images of chaos into a grim but placid statuary.

The strong visual priority, the disgust at empathy, the neck of rhetoric wrung: these traits align Keith Douglas's art with the severe aesthetics of T. E. Hulme and the stream of literary modernism he helped to influence. Indeed, Douglas includes a line from Hulme, 'the old star-eaten blanket of the sky,' in a desert skyscape of *Alamein to Zem Zem.* Where Hulme and Ezra Pound could trust the Image as an aesthetic monad, as the irreducible 'what' of poetic experience, the same kind of faith enables Douglas to free his verse from discursive, rhetorical, and affective considerations; to let his pictures stand without building up the meaning of the poems from outside; to speak without 'the will doing the work of the imagination,' Yeats's phrase for the voice of rhetoric and its extroverted, kinetic rhythms. That rejection of the empathic and vital was incomplete, however, as Frank Kermode has demonstrated in *Romantic Image.* In the modernist (and in this sense symbolist) Image Kermode sees rival loyalties to the organic and the non-vital, to the life of action and the life of contemplation, to the kinetic and the static. The rivalry is consummated in the figure of the dancer, 'one of Yeats's great reconciling images, containing life in death, death in life, movement and stillness, action and contemplation, body and soul'; in the frozen but ecstatic mask of Jane Avril in Toulouse-Lautrec's work, reminiscent in many details of Beardsley's. That crafted paradox of hectic stasis in Douglas's verse, then, resonates strongly within the tradition of symbolism and modernism. Yet the issues most relevant to the poems I am considering are more tightly focused, I believe, in view of modern war poetry in particular.

'Useless pity': Douglas's phrase evokes the very tradition of modern war verse that it would suppress. 'My subject is War, and the pity of war,' Wilfred Owen had declared. 'The Poetry is in the pity.' Of modern war poets, Owen was perhaps best known to Douglas; it is wrong, however, to assume a line of direct succession between them. Both poets are working within the conventions of lyric realism, but Owen's use of poetic voice to declamatory purposes certainly jars against Douglas's more stringent, reserved speaking manner. (pp. 295-98)

'We,' to Wilfred Owen, are the audience responsible for total war: we are a civilian populace mobilized in a war effort. That effort has lost its moral authority, and 'we' must change things. 'We,' to Keith Douglas, are different. We are not to be dissuaded from the rightness of war; indeed its ideological rationale is so pat that it provides rhetorical opportunities only for politicians and ideologues. Thus the explicitly rhetorical poetry of World War II tends to be written from the capitals by non-combatants, but it is notably a non-ideological verse: 'Still Falls the Rain' and 'A Refusal to Mourn the Death, by Fire, of a Child in London.' The better soldier poets of the war—Sidney Keyes and Alun Lewis—avoid declamation. It is an aversion learned from that demagogic rhetoric of denunciation emanating daily from London and Berlin.

Douglas's distaste for rhetoric is also informed by a literary sensibility. He is alert to the contradiction implicit in Owen's art: that Owen seeks to deter the coercions of nationalist rhetoric through the coercions of his own oratory, more insidious in being a musical declamation. In a 1943 letter to J. C. Hall, Douglas makes this literary sensibility articulate. He is defending his new poetic manner of ironic lyric—running the rhythms of speech against song,

chastening his music by refusing to embellish it—to those, like Hall, who dislike its diffidence, its laconic character, its deadpan tones and sometimes enervated cadences. Thus he assumes a linkage between a conventional lyric music in war verse and the ideologies it has served to convey, all in the ethic and method of Owen's (or Brooke's) rhetorical lyrics:

> I am surprised you should still expect me to produce musical verse. A lyric form and a lyric approach will do even less good than a journalese approach. . . . It symbolizes what I think must be got rid of—the mass of irrelevancies, of 'attitudes', 'approaches', propaganda, ivory towers, etc., that stands between us and our problems and what we have to do about them.

> To write on the themes which have been concerning me lately in lyrical and abstract forms, would be immense bullshitting.

And so conventional declamation no less than conventional music is to be set aside. Douglas puts the morale-building rhetoric of a city under bombardment—'London can Take it'—in derogatory upper-case; that is not the method of his art, he claims, for 'To be sentimental or emotional now is dangerous to oneself and to others'. His wariness about rhetoric and its perfidious, urging rhythms is the active conscience, the ethical sensibility, in the best of his war writings. In those warscapes where the frenzy is statuesque, where the tone is accordingly composed, Douglas affirms his control in the face of violence—emotional as well as physical violence—and affords the reader the opportunity of an equally dispassionate response.

The images of hectic stasis in the final vignette of **'The Little Red Mouth,'** Douglas's short story, illustrate the speaker's own composure before the violence he records, here sculpted into the German's corpse:

> His left hand was raised, supported in the air apparently by rigor mortis, the fingers crooked as though taking hold. It was this seeming to be *arrested in motion,* which made the pose so vivid. . . . Pain, a climax or orgasm of pain, was expressed in his face and attitude as I would not have believed a motionless body and countenance could express it. It is not too much to say his position was a cry of pain.
>   *(Keith Douglas: A Prose Miscellany,*
>   emphases added)

The passage is based on the episode recounted in the diary entry alluded to earlier, where Douglas dismisses 'pity' as 'useless.' In this fictional version he checks that kinetic emotion through an anti-rhetoric. The speaker is dispassionate, tentative, a curious presence only. He offers conjectural explanations: 'this *seeming* to be arrested,' '*as if* he had seized it.' He shows a solid incredulity, a refusal to have common sense swept away: 'pain . . . in his face and attitude as I *would not have believed.*' He protects himself against overstatement: '*it is not too much to say* his position was a cry of pain.' Not that he creates no effect on the reader. Our reaction may be intense, but is not permitted to leap the bounds of the narrator's own manifest control. In the next sentence, the last of the story, Douglas makes such an intense but composed response the final one:

> I looked at him, trembling with horror, stunned
> into involuntary speech, saying over and over
> again, in an audible whisper, 'et la bouche ver-
> meillette.'

An inward monologue, self-directed speech rather than other-directed declamation: here is the vocal image of the author's own self-contained, non-inciting method.

The artistry is finer and the effects subtler in one of Douglas's best-known poems, **'Vergissmeinnicht.'** The poem recounts the discovery of a dead German soldier, a letter from his girlfriend spilling out of his pocket. Douglas's revision of a single line here shows him shaping that visual riddle of hectic stasis and, accordingly, arresting our imminently violent reaction to the savagery immanent within the scene. He addresses the dead German thus, in the first version: 'your stomach open in a stinking cave'. The adjective 'stinking' may be true as description but in the texture of the poem it is reactive, loaded, inciting. The kinetic effect of the rhetorician shows as a visual symptom in the image of a space left 'open,' sprawling, unbounded. Two minimal strokes work to maximum effect in the revision: 'your burst stomach like a cave'. The stresses in the line now settle naturally onto the two key words, 'burst' and 'cave'; the first word depicts the frantic disembowelling, the second surrounds the frenzy with a strong bounding line. The contained space of the cave pictures the very control he exercises in composing the image, in dropping the hotly scented rhetoric. The rhythm of the first version, by contrast, is wasteful; the line squanders its emphases; he spreads four stresses across its length—'your stomach open in a stinking cave'—and thus fails to point the descriptive image as he does in the finely etched revision; the surplus of stresses is again the messy hand-print of that heavy-handed orator. In the finished version, moreover, he is able to find rhythmical equivalents for that paradox of hectic stasis. He runs a splendidly expressive counter-rhythm as he envisions the dead soldier's girlfriend:

> But she would weep to see today
> How on his skin the swart flies move;
>   (*Complete Poems*)

The regular iambic tetrameter of the first line catches the rising rhythm of the girl's emotive response, which then runs down into the clogged cadence of three stressed monosyllables in a row, 'swart flies move.' This rhythmical image of arrested flow serves as a powerful antidote to the kind of kinetic response he has evoked.

One may seek to parallel Douglas's aesthetic with that other Modernist's, James Joyce's, at least with the principles advocated by Stephen Dedalus in *Portrait of the Artist as a Young Man*. Stephen, too, eschews the lower 'kinetic' arts, the affective strategies of didacticism and pornography; he extols the higher forms, classical tragedy most typically: suspended within an antithesis like Douglas's, between the terror and pity resulting from tragedy, Stephen enjoys 'the luminous silent stasis of aesthetic pleasure.'

Of course the parallel skews the critical context. Douglas

is simply not an artist of Joycean status. He remains a poet of topical interest, in the final appraisal, a poet of war. Yet the very qualities we identify as classical and Joycean, as departures from the main tradition of modern war poetry, may serve to place him more centrally within that tradition. Let us consider in conclusion a remark in Douglas's brief essay **'Poets in This War'** (1943). Here he seems convinced that there is nothing new in the poetry of the present war, a failure he explains thus:

> The reasons are psychological, literary, military
> and strategic, diverse. . . . They do not write
> because there is nothing new, from a soldier's
> point of view. . . . [H]ell cannot be let loose
> twice: it was let loose in the Great War and it is
> the same old hell now. The hardships, pain and
> boredom; the behaviour of the living and the ap-
> pearance of the dead, were so accurately de-
> scribed by the poets of the Great War that every-
> day on the battlefields of the western desert—
> and no doubt on the Russian battlefields as
> well—their poems are illustrated. Almost all
> that a modern poet on active service is inspired
> to write, would be tautological.

Here and throughout the essay Douglas clearly values the realism of modern war verse. But the rhetorical and polemical incentive behind that realism, as we have seen, is offensive to him. In just that disaffection, however, may lie his ambiguous hope for a place in the modern tradition. Disliking one aspect of the legacy may be a creative initiative, an impetus to remake and revitalize it. As he dispenses with oratory, as he ignores our conventional expectations of pity and defies our conditioned sensibilities, he dislocates the familiar detail of war poetry into fresh perspectives, more striking configurations. The very coolness, aplomb, diffidence with which he writes of the horror can serve to give that horror a new reality. He has renewed the modern tradition of lyric realism in war poetry; it owes an extended life to this sceptical inheritor. (pp. 300-03)

> *Vincent Sherry, "Hectic Stasis: The War Poet-
> ry of Keith Douglas," in* University of Toronto
> Quarterly, *Vol. LVIII, No. 2, Winter, 1988-
> 89, pp. 295-304.*

FURTHER READING

Banergee, A. "Keith Douglas and the Dead Soldier: An Artistic Confrontation." *The Literary Half-Yearly* XV, No. 1 (January 1974): 85-91.
> Discusses how Douglas used both poetry and visual art to try to capture the image of the dead soldier, which he ultimately rendered in "Vergissmeinnicht."

Blunden, Edmund. Introduction to *Keith Douglas: Collected Poems*, by Keith Douglas, edited by John Waller, G. S. Fraser, and J. C. Hall, pp. 17-20. New York: Chilmark Press, 1966.
> Recollects his acquaintance with Douglas, whom he tutored at Merton College, Oxford.

Durrell, Lawrence. Introduction to *Alamein to Zem Zem,* by Keith Douglas, edited by John Waller, G. S. Fraser, and J. C. Hall, pp. 11-13. London: Faber and Faber, 1966.

Eulogizes Douglas, remarking on his poetic development and wartime career.

Fuller, Roy. "The Warrior Bard: Douglas after Thirty Years." *Encounter* XLIII, No. 3 (September 1974): 75-9.

Reviews *Keith Douglas, 1920-1944: A Biography,* by Desmond Graham.

———. "The Definitive Douglas." *The Times Literary Supplement,* No. 3,968 (21 April 1978): 439.

Favorable review of *The Complete Poems of Keith Douglas,* identifying Douglas as "unarguably the finest English 'war poet' to come out of the Second World War."

Gardner, Philip. "Keith Douglas and the Western Desert." In *A Festschrift for Edgar Ronald Seary: Essays in English Language and Literature Presented by Colleagues and Former Students,* edited by A. A. Macdonald, P. A. O'Flaherty, and G. M. Story, pp. 182-200. Memorial University of Newfoundland, 1975.

Chronologically examines Douglas's development as a poet.

Gibbons, Reginald. "A Sharp Enquiring Blade." *Parnassus* 9, No. 1 (Fall/Winter 1981): 315-31.

Relates Douglas's visual perceptiveness to the images he employed in his poetry.

Graham, Desmond. *Keith Douglas, 1920-1944.* London: Oxford University Press, 1974, 295 p.

Biography of Douglas.

Hamilton, Ian. "The Forties—I." *The London Magazine* 4, No. 1 (April 1964): 81-9.

Considers war poets in the context of English poetry of the 1940s.

Hammond, Mac. "Normandy to Christ's Hospital." *Poetry* 79, No. 6 (March 1952): 356-58.

Criticizes Douglas's poetry as juvenile and bathetic in a review of *The Collected Poems of Keith Douglas.*

Matterson, Stephen. "Douglas's 'Vergissmeinnicht.'" *The Explicator* 45, No. 2 (Winter 1987): 57-9.

Explores the dichotomy between "soldier" and "lover" in Douglas's poem "Vergissmeinnicht."

Ormerod, David. "Keith Douglas and the Name of the Poem I Can't Write." *Ariel: A Review of International English Literature* 9, No. 2 (April 1978): 3-22.

Argues that Douglas's "Bête Noire" theme developed as an approach to the intellectual problem of the nature of perception.

Scannell, Vernon. "Keith Douglas." In his *Not without Glory: Poets of the Second World War,* pp. 23-51. London: The Woburn Press, 1976.

Assesses the effect of war on Douglas's poetry.

Sigler, Ernst. Review of *Alamein to Zem Zem,* by Keith Douglas. *Poetry Quarterly* 9, No. 4 (Winter 1947-48): 246-48.

Compares Douglas favorably with other English poets of the Second World War.

Stanford, Derek. "Two Poets: Aiken and Douglas." *Poetry Quarterly* 13, No. 3 (Autumn 1951): 135-39.

Favorable review of *The Collected Poems of Keith Douglas.* Stanford lauds Douglas's poetry as superior to that of most World War II poets.

Tomlinson, Charles. "Poetry Today." In *The Modern Age: Volume 7 of the Pelican Guide to English Literature,* edited by Boris Ford, pp. 458-72. Baltimore: Penguin Books, 1961.

Notes Douglas's departure from the neoromantic poetry of his time.

Waller, John. Introduction to *The Collected Poems of Keith Douglas,* by Keith Douglas, edited by John Waller and G. S. Fraser, pp. xv-xxi. London: Editions Poetry London, 1951.

Brief biographical sketch recalling Waller's friendship with Douglas during World War II.

Henry James

1843-1916

American novelist, short story writer, essayist, critic, biographer, autobiographer, and dramatist.

The following entry presents criticism of James's novel *The Portrait of a Lady* (1881). For discussion of James's complete career, see *TCLC*, Volumes 2 and 11; for discussion of the novella *The Turn of the Screw*, see *TCLC*, Volume 24.

The Portrait of a Lady is considered James's first major work and a masterpiece of American fiction. Representative of an early stage in the development of the complex style for which its author became known, the novel concerns, as James stated in the preface, "a certain young woman affronting her destiny." More generally, *The Portrait* elaborates a subject central to James's work in its meticulous illustration of disparities between American and European culture.

According to biographer Leon Edel, James predicted two years prior to its completion that *The Portrait* would be his first significant work. Having already earned recognition with such novels as *Roderick Hudson, The American,* and *The Europeans,* James began writing *The Portrait* in 1879 while traveling in Italy. He later recalled that his conception of the novel "must have consisted not at all in any conceit of a 'plot' . . . but altogether in the sense of a single character, the character and aspect of a particular engaging young woman." While many critics speculate that James based the novel's main character, Isabel Archer, on Minny Temple, a cousin whom James held in high regard and who died at a young age, others maintain that the heroines in George Eliot's *Middlemarch* (1871-72) and *Daniel Deronda* (1876) served as the models for James's protagonist. The serialization of *The Portrait* in 1880 in the English periodical *Macmillan's Magazine* and the American *Atlantic Monthly* met with immediate popular success and was followed the next year by its book publication in both English and American editions. James's extensive revision of the novel for publication in his collected works, commonly known as the New York Edition, resulted in what is today regarded as the definitive text.

The Portrait centers on Isabel Archer, a young American woman characterized as bright, idealistic, innocent, and somewhat egotistical. Invited by her expatriate Aunt Touchett to travel in Europe, Isabel is determined in her experience of life abroad to adhere to her convictions concerning the importance of personal freedom, an endeavor both facilitated and undermined by the generous financial support of the Touchett family and her eventual inheritance of £60,000 upon the death of her uncle. Isabel's financial status gains her acceptance into a diverse society of Americans and Europeans; at the same time, her newly acquired wealth prompts the marriage proposal of the manipulative and deceitful Gilbert Osmond, who intends to obtain her money as a dowry for Pansy, his illegitimate daughter. At-

tracted to Osmond's independent nature, fastidious aesthetic principles, and worldly knowledge, and believing that he will respect her autonomy, Isabel accepts his proposal of marriage and goes to live with him in Italy. Isabel's discovery of Osmond's true character leads to one of the novel's most dramatic moments. Sitting all night by the firelight in a drawing room, she contemplates the ways in which both her own naivete and the false sense of freedom afforded her by the inheritance have damaged the quality of her life. Praised as a scene which derives all of its energy and drama from James's adept portrayal of human introspection, Isabel's meditative vigil is one of the most acclaimed chapters in American fiction. Against her husband's wishes, she travels to England to visit her invalid cousin, Ralph Touchett, with whom she shares an emotional attachment, and considers leaving Osmond permanently. The implications of her decision to return to Italy and her unhappy marriage, at the novel's conclusion, continue to spark controversy.

Much of the commentary on *The Portrait* focuses on the psychological make-up of Isabel and the impetus for her decisions. Suggesting that Isabel's fear of the complexities inherent in personal relationships prompts her visit with

Ralph Touchett in opposition to her husband's wishes, Tony Tanner views Isabel's return to Osmond as a sign of facing such fears. Richard Chase, on the other hand, interprets the decision as one in a series of errors committed by Isabel in James's portrayal of a tragic heroine. Arnold Kettle has examined the restrictive nature of Isabel's marriage as a remonstration of her exaggerated desire for personal freedom. Other interpretations attribute Isabel's motives to James's espousal of realism in fiction. For example, Louis Auchincloss argues that a woman of Isabel's position in the Victorian era would be expected to preserve her marriage regardless of the deception on which it was based. Furthermore, Dorothea Krook emphasizes Isabel's role in this deception, noting her pretense, while being courted by Osmond, of dependence and malleability, characteristics that Osmond deems necessary in a proper European wife.

The preeminent "international theme" of cultural confrontation between Americans and Europeans in James's fiction has prompted many critics to evaluate Isabel's actions in terms of her American heritage. F. R. Leavis has contended that the strength of *The Portrait* lies exclusively in its detailed examination of sociocultural issues, suggesting that Isabel represents American willfulness and uncompromising morality, qualities which often foster poor judgment. Chase regards Isabel's actions as a reflection of her American perspective, citing her romantic view of the isolation she experiences in her unhappy marriage as a legacy of Emersonian Transcendentalism, while observing that the staunch adherence to moral standards exhibited in her decision to uphold her marriage vows recalls Puritanism. More recently, Auchincloss has suggested that while Isabel's idealism is stereotypically American, the "international theme" has received critical attention disproportionate to that merited by the novel's emphasis on characters as individuals rather than as representatives of their culture.

An important issue in critical analysis of *The Portrait* is James's use of language in the novel, particularly as revealed in comparisons between the original novel and its 1908 revision. While detractors of the prose style of James's mature works argue that the revisions serve to obscure authorial intention and result in "overwriting" in the New York Edition, others, most notably F. O. Matthiessen, regard the alterations as clarifying themes in the novel; Matthiessen's discussion of the tonal shifts effected by the revisions remains one of the most widely accepted examinations of James's craftsmanship. Focusing on his deletions, additions, and substitutions of specific words and phrases, Matthiessen demonstrates the subtlety with which the themes of the novel emerge in the 1908 edition, arguing that a more discriminating use of terms such as "picturesque" and "romantic," which in the later version James reserved for describing Isabel's point of view, imply that the heroine's exaggerated romantic inclinations are largely responsible for her unhappiness.

After writing *The Portrait,* James feared that his audience might find the novel incomplete due to the lack of exposition on the aftermath of Isabel's return to Osmond. Against this criticism James argued that "The *whole* of

anything is never told; you can only take what groups together. What I have done has that unity—it groups together." Finding this "inconclusiveness" an important part of the novel's endurance, Robert Emmet Long has written that "the reader is forced to put himself in Isabel's place, to see beyond what is strictly known, to take part in a drama that is critical to Isabel's life and is, indeed, inward."

(See also *Contemporary Authors,* Vol. 104; *Dictionary of Literary Biography,* Vols. 12, 71, and 74; and *Concise Dictionary of American Literary Biography, 1865-1917.*)

John Hay   (review date 1881)

[*A prominent American man of letters best remembered for his service as U. S. secretary of state, John Hay was a frequent contributor of editorials and book reviews to* The New York Tribune. *In the following excerpt, Hay praises the literary achievement of* The Portrait of a Lady.]

If there is anything in the motto of "art for art's sake," if the way of doing a thing is, as many claim, of more importance in literature than the thing done, then [*The Portrait of a Lady*] needs no justification or apology. No work printed in recent years, on either side the Atlantic or on either side the English Channel, surpasses this in seriousness of intention, in easy scope and mastery of material, in sustained and spontaneous dignity and grace of style, in wit and epigram, and, on the whole, in clear conception and accurate delineation of character. The title was a stumbling-block to many, as the story pursued its leisurely course in *The Atlantic Monthly,* and now that it is finished it is the title which affords to criticism its easiest attack. It is claimed that the heroine is of all the characters the one least clearly painted, least perfectly understood. But it would not be difficult to say that we know as much of her and of her motives as the author chooses for us to know, and the interest of the novel comes in great part from the vagueness of our acquaintance with Miss Archer; and after all, when we lay down the book, we cannot deny, if we are candid, that we know as much of the motives which induced her to refuse two gallant gentlemen and to marry a selfish and soulless scoundrel as we do of the impulses which lead our sisters and cousins to similar results. No one can complain of the clearness with which the other characters are drawn. There is hardly a sharper portrait in our literature, and certainly none more delightful, than Ralph Touchett. None who read the opening chapters of the story a year ago can forget the slight shiver of apprehension they felt when Mr. James distinctly announced that Ralph Touchett was clever, and when Lord Warburton declared that "he was never bored when he came to Gardencourt; one gets such uncommonly good talk." It shows a fine arrogance in the most hardened jouster to throw down such a challenge as that. It is said that Shakespeare killed Mercutio early in the play where he appears, for fear of being killed by him; but Mr. James evidently has no such fear of his own creations. From the first chapter to the last, Ralph is "clever, witty and charming," as Mr. James tells us in the beginning, with a charm which overcomes the tedium of hopeless illness and the repulsiveness of death. The book is full of living and breathing characters. Mr. Trollope has never drawn a better English nobleman than Lord Warburton, the splendor of whose environment is delicately suggested, never described, and whose manners are painted in a dozen subtle phrases like these: "He had a certain fortunate, brilliant, exceptional look—the air of a happy temperament fertilized by a high civilization—which would have made almost any observer envy him at a venture"; "his English address, in which a vague shyness seemed to offer itself as an element of good breeding; in which the only defect was a difficulty of achieving transitions." The portrait of Osmond is one of those wonderful pictures in which Mr. James excels, drawn entirely from the outside, but as perfect as if his acts and conversations had been supplemented by voluminous pages of soliloquy. His sister the Countess is equally good; so is the dry, practical, caustic Mrs. Touchett; so is the travelling newspaper woman, Miss Stackpole. (pp. 69-70)

Of the importance of this volume there can be no question. It will certainly remain one of the notable books of the time. It is properly to be compared, not with the light and ephemeral literature of amusement, but with the gravest and most serious works of imagination which have been devoted to the study of the social conditions of the age and the moral aspects of our civilization. The story is of the simplest possible. A young girl richly endowed in mind, person and character, but with slight knowledge of the world, unexpectedly receives a great fortune. She has previously rejected two men of entirely suitable position and qualities, not because she doubts their worth but because she has certain vague ideals. She falls into the company of a fascinating woman of forty who marries her to an old paramour of her own. There is positively no incident in the book—there is not one word of writing for writing's sake; there is not a line of meretricious ornament. It is a sober, consistent study of a single human character, with all its conditions and environments, in situations not in the least strained or exceptional. There is nothing exceptional about the book but the genius of the author, which is now, more than ever before, beyond question. This simple story is told with every imaginable accessory of wit, observation, description of nature and of life. But the reader must take his pleasure as he goes along. He can get none from the issue of the story, for no one in it really prospers. The heroine and her ideals come to a sorry market. Even the wicked are not happy. The little people who furnish the comedy of the play go out with the half comic despair of children sent to bed without the toys they had been promised. The nearest approach to content is the case of Mrs. Touchett, who, after the deaths of her husband and her only child, reflects

> that after all, such things happened to other people and not to herself. Death was disagreeable, but in this case it was her son's death, not her own; she had never flattered herself that her own would be disagreeable to anyone but Mrs. Touchett. She was better off than poor Ralph, who had left all the commodities of life behind him, and indeed all the security; for the worst of dying

was, to Mrs. Touchett's mind, that it exposed one to be taken advantage of. For herself, she was on the spot; there was nothing so good as that.

(pp. 75-6)

John Hay, in a review of "The Portrait of a Lady," in Henry James and John Hay: The Record of a Friendship *by George Monteiro, Brown University Press, 1965, pp. 69-76.*

H. E. Scudder　(essay date 1882)

[*A noted American author of short stories for children during the late nineteenth century, Scudder was the editor of the* Riverside Magazine for Young People *and founder of the Riverside Literature series, which provided editions of literary works for schools. Also known as a critic and biographer, he contributed reviews to the* Atlantic Monthly *and served as that magazine's editor during the 1890s, and authored such acclaimed studies of American writers as* James Russell Lowell: A Biography *(1901) and* American Men of Letters: Noah Webster *(1881). In the following excerpt, he offers a favorable review of* The Portrait of a Lady.]

[Henry James] gives us this advantage, that all the elaboration of his work looks distinctly to the perfection of the central figure. One can repeat almost in a single breath the incidental story of [*The Portrait of a Lady*]. That is dissolved immediately, if the incidents deposited are the critical ones of Isabel's meeting with her aunt, her rejection successively of Goodwood and Lord Warburton, her accession to wealth, her marriage with Osmond, her temporary separation, and her final return. A person hearing the narrative might be pardoned if he failed to see the making of a great novel in it, but only when one has recited it does he become aware how each step in the fatal series is a movement in the direction of destiny. By a fine concentration of attention upon the heroine, Mr. James impresses us with her importance, and the other characters, involved as they are with her life, fall back into secondary positions. It is much to have seized and held firmly so elusive a conception, and our admiration is increased when reflection shows that, individual as Isabel is in the painting, one may fairly take her as representative of womanly life today. The fine purpose of her freedom, the resolution with which she seeks to be the maker of her destiny, the subtle weakness into which all this betrays her, the apparent helplessness of her ultimate position, and the conjectured escape only through patient forbearance,—what are all these, if not attributes of womanly life expended under current conditions?

The consistency of the work is observable under another aspect. Mr. James's method is sufficiently well known, and since he has made it his own the critic may better accept it and measure it than complain of it. What renders it distinct from, say, Thackeray's method, with which it has been compared, or from George Eliot's, is the limitation of the favorite generalizations and analyses. If the reader will attend, he will see that these take place quite exclusively within the boundaries of the story and characters. That is to say, when the people in the book stop acting or speaking, it is to give to the novelist an opportunity, not to indulge in general reflections, having application to all sorts and conditions of men, of whom his *dramatis personæ* are but a part,—he has no desire to share humanity with them,—but to make acute reflections upon these particular people, and to explain more thoroughly than their words and acts can the motives which lie behind. We may, on general grounds, doubt the self-confidence or power of a novelist who feels this part of his performance to be essential, but there can be no doubt that Mr. James's method is a part of that concentration of mind which results in a singular consistency.

Yet all this carries an intimation of what is curiously noticeable in his work. It is consistent, but the consistency is with itself. Within the boundaries of the novel the logic of character and events is close and firm. We say this after due reflection upon the latest pages. There can be little doubt that the novelist suffers more in the reader's judgment from a false or ineffective scene at the close of his story than he gains from many felicitous strokes in the earlier development of plot or character. The impatient, undiscriminating objection, "It does not end well, although it may incense the writer," is an ill-formulated expression of the feeling that the creation lacks the final, triumphant touch which gives life; the sixth swan in the story got a stitch-weed shirt, like the rest, but in the hurry of the last moment it lacked a few stitches, and so in the transformation the youngest brother was forced to put up with one arm and to show a wing for the other. Isabel Archer, with her fine horoscope, is an impressive figure, and one follows her in her free flight with so much admiration for her resolution and strong pinions that when she is caught in the meshes of Osmond's net one's indignation is moved, and a noble pity takes the place of frank admiration. But pity can live only in full communion with faith, and we can understand the hesitation which a reader might feel before the somewhat ambiguous passage of Isabel's last interview with Goodwood. The passage, however, admits of a generous construction, and we prefer to take it, and to see in the scene the author's intention of giving a final touch to his delineation of Goodwood's iron but untempered will, Isabel's vanishing dream of happiness, and her acceptance of the destiny which she had unwittingly chosen. We suspect that something of the reader's dissatisfaction at this juncture comes from his dislike of Goodwood, the jack-in-the-box of the story, whose unyielding nature seems somehow outside of all the events.

To return to our point. This self-consistency is a separate thing from any consistency with the world of reality. The characters, the situations, the incidents, are all true to the law of their own being, but that law runs parallel with the law which governs life, instead of being identical with it. In Andersen's quaint story of the Emperor's New Clothes, a little child discovers the unreality of the gossamer dress, and his voice breaks in upon the illusion from the outer world. Something of the same separation from the story, of the same unconscious naturalness of feeling, prompts the criticism that, though these people walk, and sit, and talk, and behave, they are yet in an illusionary world of their own. Only when one is within the charmed circle of the story is he under its spell, and so complete is the isola-

tion of the book that the characters acquire a strange access of reality when they talk about each other. Not only so, but the introversion which now and then takes place deepens the sense of personality. In that masterly passage which occupies the forty-second section, where Isabel enters upon a disclosure of her changed life, the reader seems to be going down as in a diving-bell into the very secrets of her nature.

What is all this but saying that in the process of Mr. James's art the suggestion always seems to come from within, and to work outward? We recognize the people to whom he introduces us, not by any external signs, but by the private information which we have regarding their souls. The smiles which they wear—and one might make an ingenious collection of their variety—do not tell what is beneath the surface, but we know what they mean, because we already have an esoteric knowledge. Mr. James is at great pains to illustrate his characters by their attitudes, their movements, their by-play, yet we carry away but a slight impression of their external appearance; these are not bodily shapes, for the most part, but embodied spirits, who enjoy their materialization for a time, and contribute to a play which goes on upon a stage just a little apart from that great stage where the world's play, with men and women for actors, is carried forward. (pp. 127-28)

> *H. E. Scudder, in a review of "The Portrait of a Lady," in* The Atlantic Monthly, *Vol. XLIX, No. CCXCI, January, 1882, pp. 127-28.*

Mrs. Oliphant   (essay date 1882)

[*Oliphant was a prolific nineteenth-century Scottish novelist, biographer, critic, and historian who contributed regularly to* Blackwood's Edinburgh Magazine. *In the following excerpt, she provides a favorable estimation of the characterization and style of* The Portrait of a Lady.]

[Henry James's] work in the world seems to be a peculiar one. It is to record and set fully before us the predominance of the great American race, and the manner in which it has overrun and conquered the Old World. All, or almost all, of his social studies have their scene laid on the Continent, or in this island. It is true there are occasional interludes of America, but it is not in these that he seems most at home. The manner in which the heir of time—in the shape of the cultivated and accomplished son, or, still more, daughter of the West—dominates the old-fashioned scenery of countries which were, as old people say, great and powerful before America was ever heard of, is both amusing and impressive. Italy and France and Old England have lived their lives and had their reverses, and built their old castles and towns, and even arranged their landscapes—for him. The chief use of their old families is to furnish victims, in the shape of elder sons, for those delicate beauties who come conquering and to conquer from the fashionable circles of New York or the exotic plains of California. They inspect our antiquities as Germans criticise Hamlet, with the view of showing that we ourselves are unable to appreciate, and take comparatively little interest in, either the Tower or the Poet; and they patronise our institutions, most frequently from the high aristocratic side of the question, and object to our reforms, as the Solomons of the earth—who have tried all that man can do in that direction and found it naught—have perhaps some right to do. In short, they overshadow altogether the background against which they pose, and make London and Paris and Rome into Western settlements, with the most easy consciousness that they are lords of all. In some of M. Tourgenieff's books the same position is tacitly claimed, more or less, for the Russian; but then it is only world-playgrounds (which, if we remember rightly, is the dignified title by which some philosophers on our own side honour Switzerland) which are represented as in the possession of the Muscovite. English performances of the same kind are of a more modest description. We do indeed plant our little colonies of pleasure all about, yet we give them, when we can, some relation to the "natives," and love to show our respect for that society into which, we are humbly aware, we are but sparely admitted. But Mr. James shows us his countrymen in the attitude of conquerors, dominating, not intruding, upon the foreign world about them. Sometimes the picture is not quite favourable, as when he sets before us, with a few touches of his delicate pencil, the American colony in Paris, of which we may at once present the reader with the following sketch. Mr. James's style is so clear, so fluent, and so delicate, that one of his fine sketches may be detached to read by itself, not only without disadvantage, but almost to its benefit,—since, when we peruse a description like the following, in the course of something which is supposed to be a story, and to possess a certain amount of dramatic interest, it is scarcely possible to take time enough to get the whole good of it.

> Mrs. Luce had been living in Paris since the days of Louis Philippe: she used to say seriously that she was one of the generation of 1830—a joke of which the point was not always taken. When it failed, Mrs. Luce used always to explain, "Oh yes, I am one of the romantics:" her French had never become quite perfect. She was always at home on Sunday afternoons and, surrounded by sympathetic compatriots, usually the same. In fact she was at home at all times, and led in her well-cushioned little corner of the brilliant city as quiet and domestic a life as she might have led in her native Baltimore. The existence of Mr. Luce, her worthy husband, was somewhat more inscrutable. Superficially, indeed, there was no mystery about it; the mystery lay deeper, and resided in the wonder of his supporting existence at all. He was the most unoccupied man in Europe, for he not only had no duties, but no pleasures. Habits certainly he had, but they were few in number and had been worn threadbare by forty years of use.

(pp. 374-76)

The political opinions of this type of American occupiers of the soil are easily divined. It is not from any sympathy with republican institutions that they chose France for their headquarters; indeed they are to be found in Italy in as great luxuriance as in France, regretting everything that

has passed away—the Pope's supremacy and the French occupation, as well as that bland Tuscan Court where all was so amiable, and the days when Rome wished for nothing more than a good season, and Italy continued to be medieval for the gratification of its visitors. Here are Mr. Luce's views upon the subject in France:—

> Like many of his fellow-colonists, Mr. Luce was a high—or rather a deep—Conservative, and gave no countenance to the Government recently established in France. He had no faith in its duration, and would assure you from year to year that its end was close at hand. "They want to be kept down, sir—they want to be kept down; nothing but the strong hand, the iron hand, will do for them," he would frequently say of the French people: and his ideal of a fine government was that of the lately abolished Empire.

The young of the species is still more accurately and acutely put upon the canvas. The type in this instance is Mr. Edward Rosier, who has been brought up in Paris, and whom the reader who has had any acquaintance with Anglo-Saxon society abroad, will at once recognise. The heroine had met him at an early age, when living the strange life common to American (and, alas! sometimes to English) children in great Continental hotels, when he spoke "a queer little dialect of French-English, expressing the properest sentiments," and told his new friend that "he was 'defended' by his *bonne* to go near the lake, and that one must always obey to one's *bonne.*" (p. 376)

We linger upon these sketches of the dominant race, of which all readers have come to appreciate the importance through Mr. James's very popular works, because it is more easy to enjoy studies so fine and so keen, cut with the precision of an old gem, than to find our way, as we should like, through the maze of delicate analysis and psychological study, tempered with a number of brilliant social sketches, which makes up in three very large volumes *The Portrait of a Lady.* The one thing which the book is not, is what it calls itself. There are several portraits of subordinate ladies—of Mrs. Touchett and Miss Stackpole, for example, both of which are admirable pictures; but of the heroine, upon whom the greatest pains have been expended, and to whom endless space is afforded for the setting forth of her characteristics, we have no portrait, nor, even with the enormous amount of material supplied by Mr. James, do we find it easy to put together anything which will serve to supply the defect. We doubt much whether, in all the historical records that exist, we have as much material for the construction, let us say, of a recognisable portrait of Queen Elizabeth—no insignificant figure—as we have for that of Isabel Archer, the young lady who suddenly appears in the doorway of an old English countryhouse, inhabited like most other desirable places by American tenants—in this case her uncle and her cousin—fresh from her native country, prepared to take instant possession of her birthright as the explorer, discoverer, and conqueror of the old country,—and, in fact, reducing the gentlemen who meet her into instant subjection in the course of half an hour. How she does so, except by being very pretty, as we are told she is, we do not know; though the gentlemen in question are too experienced and clever in their own persons to be immediately subjugated by simple beauty. "Her head was erect, her eye brilliant, her flexible figure turned itself lightly this way and that, in sympathy with the alertness with which she evidently caught impressions. Her impressions were numerous, and they were all reflected in a clear, still smile," is Mr. James's description of his heroine; and it is about the clearest view we get of the young lady. For once in a way he is outside of her: but as he goes on he gets more and more within the circle of this irresistible young woman's personality; and we have to receive both herself and her immediate surroundings, not so much as they actually are, but as they are seen through her eyes. This is always confusing; for self-knowledge at its closest has many limitations, and the most impartial student of his own mind will probably get more light upon it by overhearing one sharp characterisation from outside than by weeks of self-examination. Isabel's aspect from outside is conveyed to us only in the raptures of her adorers; for all the men she encounters fall in love with her: first, her cousin Ralph Touchett, then Lord Warburton, then Osmond, whom she marries: besides a persistent Boston man, who makes nothing of crossing the Atlantic to get a glimpse of her, and turns up again and again with a sort of dogged inappropriateness at every new stage of her career.

There is but little vicissitude, however, in her career; she comes to "Europe" with something of the intention which Mr. James illustrated with, we think, a great deal more power, though less of the extremely refined and cultivated skill of which he is now master, in **The American,** the first work by which he was known in England; that is, to get everything she can out of her life and its opportunities,—all the sensation, the information, the variety of experience which it is possible it can convey. There is this difference between the young and visionary girl and the mature man, that whereas Mr. James's first hero wanted practical satisfaction for his desires, and to get possession of all that was best, including, as the most indispensable article of all, the fairest and most costly flower of womanhood which was to be found or purchased anyhow,—Isabel prefers not to have anything but the sense of having—the wealth of spiritual possession. For this reason she likes to retain a hold upon the lovers whom she will not marry. The English lord with all his fine qualities—and it cannot be said that our American author and heroine do not do full justice to these qualities with a refined sense of the admirableness of the position, and the importance which attaches to so curious and desirable a specimen of humanity—gives her the most agreeable consciousness of power, though all his advantages do not tempt her to marry him, and she is sorry for vexing him—almost as sorry as she is agreeably excited by the incident altogether. Indeed it would appear that this accompaniment of homage is natural to the young American woman, and that she would feel herself to be treated unfairly if at least one English lord, besides innumerable other candidates of different descriptions, did not attest her power. This is very different from the more vulgar development of the American young woman, who is bent on securing a title for herself. Mr. James's young ladies never do this. They are totally different from the Irene Macgillicuddys. Their curiosity about the English aristocrat is fresh and eager. They contemplate him attentively

as the greatest novelty within their reach, and like and admire him as one of the wonders of the world; but they do not care to go any further. Isabel Archer passes through this phase very serenely, liking the new interest it puts into her life. But as a matter of fact she does not care for anything much except new interests. The adventures, or rather encounters, through which we are permitted to accompany her, are in reality but a small part of her career. There are gaps in which she travels far and wide—rapidly, eagerly, arduously. "She was like a thirsty person draining cup after cup," but always coming back again to the old investigation—the earnest study of all new phenomena—the consideration of how everything affected herself. Her desire for new experiences never fails, even when she gets into the dead block in which, as is natural, her perpetually increasing circle of moral enlightenment and sensation ends. (pp. 377-79)

It was inevitable that such a heroine should end unhappily—even if it were not inevitable that all Mr. James's books should break off with a sharp cut of arbitrary conclusion, leaving all the questions they so skilfully raise unsolved. Isabel, through the means of a wonderful woman whom she meets in her aunt's house, and who is a sort of symbol of unusual experience, as the younger woman is of the craving for it, falls under the fascinations of a certain æsthetic and beauty-loving American, Gilbert Osmond by name, who lives on one of the heights which surround Florence, a poor yet elegant *dilettante* life, "picking up" rarities of all kinds, making amateur drawings, surrounded by the faded silks and crafty embellishments of a collector, with a pretty little Dresden shepherdess of a daughter, newly returned from the convent, whose perfect conventional simplicity, freshness, and submission, afford Mr. James the means of making one of his most finished and perfect sketches. We confess to being quite unable to understand how it is that Isabel falls into Osmond's toils, unless it is because so elaborate and self-conscious a personality recoils instinctively, even though full of an abstract admiration for truth, from the downright and veracious, and finds in the complications of an elaborately conventional mind something that has the air of being larger and richer than the true. The reader is never for a moment taken in by the superiority of this most carefully dressed and posed figure, whose being altogether is mysterious, and of whom, notwithstanding the author's elaborate descriptions, we never penetrate the *fin mot*. . . . It is to be supposed, therefore, that this refined and philosophical *dilettante,* secluding himself among his faded silks and æsthetic ornaments, in his villa on Bellosguardo, is like a spider in his web awaiting the arrival of the fly which it shall be worth his while to capture. But, after all, these elaborate preparations were scarcely necessary for the capture of a young lady who was only Miss Archer, with a fortune of sixty thousand pounds. Had a Grand Duchess been his aim, it would have been comprehensible. There is far too great an effort for an insufficient result; and the almost immediate failure of their after relations is confusing and unaccountable. Something of the same curious failure we remember to have found in *Daniel Deronda,* where Gwendolen and her husband, after their elaborate drawing together, fly asunder the moment they are married, with a suddenness and bitterness—brutality on the man's part, and misery on the woman's—for which we find no adequate motive, since there was neither passion between them to die out, nor motive enough beforehand to force a union which was to end so abruptly. That Isabel should discover her husband to be, as he describes himself, not only conventional, but convention itself, when she believed him to be nobly superior to the world, is one thing; but that she should discover him to hate her is quite another; and his jealousy and tyranny in the one development seem out of character with his easy gracefulness and gentlemanliness in the other.

The last volume is full of the complete and utter failure to which the heroine's hopes and high desires have come; but it cannot be said that she acquits herself with the dignity that might have been expected of her under the disappointment. Not only does she allow her wretchedness to be taken for granted by all her friends, but it would almost seem as if, in the utter collapse of the world about her, this most abstract and intellectual of heroines is driven at last to the conclusion that the only good in life is to make a snatch at happiness anyhow—to take what is offered her at last in utter relinquishment of any better hope. (pp. 379-80)

In following out the chief thread of this elaborate work, we have in reality neglected the best of it, which is to be found in the characters which are secondary. Mrs. Touchett the aunt, who introduces Isabel to all the dangers of Europe,—the little dry independent woman, whose correspondence with her family is by curt telegrams—who consults her own independent fancy in all she does, asks little, and gives little in the way of affection, yet is by no means destitute of kindness,—is a curiously individual figure, so real and so odd that she must, we suspect, come from the life—that shelter of all eccentricities. Her son Ralph Touchett is by far the most lovable character in the book. The easy spectator position which his bad health and his temperament alike made natural; the smiling renunciation of life and all individual hopes which he has made without a word, without the sympathy or support of any consoler; his shuffle of easy contemplative indolence; the mild half-pathetic fun which he gets out of every incident,—go to our heart from the first appearance he makes on the scene. His love and care for his father; his profound tenderness and half-amused watch over his cousin, changing towards the end into a melancholy sense that his own act in securing her possession of a fortune has been her ruin; his unfailing courage and sweetness of temper,—make his appearance always delightful. If he did not smile in the face of fate, and turn off his worst pangs with a jest, we know and he knows that there would be in the world no more melancholy spectacle than this gradual going down of youth and hope and intelligence into the grave, imbittered by the sense that his weakness makes him powerless to help the being he loves best, and that his death will leave her to fight alone with a thousand troubles. He is conscious of all this, yet is amused with the vagaries of existence to the last, and keeps sorrow at arm's-length—keenly though he is aware of its presence. Miss Stackpole, too, is delightful in her genial Americanisms. We feel, indeed, that this lady—the correspondent of the *Interviewer,* who comes to Europe half with the intention of watching over her friend, and more than half with the determination to fathom the inner life of England, especially in the homes of the great—is a concession on Mr. James's part to the British public,—a somewhat defiant proof that he is not afraid to take up even the conventional American of commonplace satire and make her captivate and charm the unbelieving. Her perfect boldness, combined with a modesty and purity so complete, that we are ashamed even of the thought that it is necessary to give her credit for qualities so innate and self-evident, are made delightfully comical by Henrietta's own unconsciousness of anything odd in her perfectly dauntless proceedings—her roamings about the world with Mr. Bantling in attendance—her free movements and still more free speech. Her speech, however, is free only in the way of interrogation and advice, in which her self-confidence is absolute—as is also, whenever there is any call for it, her kindness and devotion. Mr. James is not so successful with the personages who are not American. Lord Warburton is a very careful study of a fair big Englishman of rank and every heroic quality—but the author has too much the air of walking round and round the typical figure he admires so much, and pointing out his proportion—the size and nobility, the unconscious and easy grace of the aristocrat who puts his aristocracy so little forward, and is so modest and genial. And perhaps his contrast of the inanimate and submissive young ladies, who are Lord Warburton's sisters, as of the perfect little Pansy—the convent child of French and Italian breeding,—with his all-fascinating and all-intelligent American young woman, is not a very fair proceeding. This, however, we leave to his own conscience.

The book altogether is one of the most remarkable specimens of literary skill which the critic could lay his hand upon. It is far too long, infinitely ponderous, and pulled out of all proportion by the elaboration of every detail; but there is scarcely a page in it that is not worked out with the utmost skill and refinement, or which the reader will pass over without leaving something to regret—that is, if he has leisure for the kind of reading which is delightful for its own sake in complete independence of its subject. The conversation in it is an art by itself. To give an appearance of actualness and spontaneity to an artificial production so careful, refined, and elaborate, must have required a prodigious effort. We have heard it characterised very cleverly as resembling one of those games in which one of the party has to go out while the others task their ingenuity in devising how to puzzle him. When he returns with his mind on the full strain, the ingenious succession of questions and answers which are struck out by a party accustomed to the art may approach, if it is very well done, the perfection of the endless pages in which Mr. James carries on his word-fence with the most curious *vraisemblance* and air of being real. But nothing so elaborate ever could be real, and the dazzle sometimes fatigues, though the effect is one which cannot be contemplated without admiration. (pp. 381-83)

Mrs. Oliphant, in a review of "The Portrait of a Lady," in Blackwood's Edinburgh Magazine, *Vol. CXXXI, No. DCCXCVII, March, 1882, pp. 374-83.*

Henry James   (essay date 1908)

[*In the following excerpt from his preface written for the 1908 edition of* The Portrait of a Lady, *James describes the imaginative process and technique employed in his composition of the novel.*]

The house of fiction has . . . not one window, but a million—a number of possible windows not to be reckoned, rather; every one of which has been pierced, or is still pierceable, in its vast front, by the need of the individual vision and by the pressure of the individual will. These apertures, of dissimilar shape and size, hang so, all together, over the human scene that we might have expected of them a greater sameness of report than we find. They are but windows at the best, mere holes in a dead wall, disconnected, perched aloft; they are not hinged doors opening straight upon life. But they have this mark of their own that at each of them stands a figure with a pair of eyes, or at least with a field-glass, which forms, again and again, for observation, a unique instrument, insuring to the person making use of it an impression distinct from every other. He and his neighbours are watching the same show, but one seeing more where the other sees less, one seeing black where the other sees white, one seeing big where the other sees small, one seeing coarse where the other sees fine. And so on, and so on; there is fortunately no saying on what, for the particular pair of eyes, the window may *not* open; "fortunately" by reason, precisely, of this incalculability of range. The spreading field, the human scene, is the "choice of subject"; the pierced aperture, either broad or balconied or slit-like and low-browed, is the "literary form"; but they are, singly or together, as nothing without the posted presence of the watcher—without, in other words, the consciousness of the artist. Tell me what the artist is, and I will tell you of what he has *been* conscious. Thereby I shall express to you at once his boundless freedom and his "moral" reference.

All this is a long way round, however, for my word about my dim first move toward *The Portrait,* which was exactly my grasp of a single character—an acquisition I had made, moreover, after a fashion not here to be retraced. Enough that I was, as seemed to me, in complete possession of it, that I had been so for a long time, that this had made it familiar and yet had not blurred its charm, and that, all urgently, all tormentingly, I saw it in motion and, so to speak, in transit. This amounts to saying that I saw it as bent upon its fate—some fate or other; *which,* among the possibilities, being precisely the question. Thus I had my vivid individual—vivid, so strangely, in spite of being still at large, not confined by the conditions, not engaged in the tangle, to which we look for much of the impress that constitutes an identity. If the apparition was still all to be placed how came it to be vivid?—since we puzzle such quantities out, mostly, just by the business of placing them. One could answer such a question beautifully, doubtless, if one could do so subtle, if not so monstrous, a thing as to write the history of the growth of one's imagination. One would describe then what, at a given time, had extraordinarily happened to it, and one would so, for instance, be in a position to tell, with an approach to clearness, how, under favour of occasion, it had been able to take over (take over straight from life) such and such a

constituted, animated figure or form. The figure has to that extent, as you see, *been* placed—placed in the imagination that detains it, preserves, protects, enjoys it, conscious of its presence in the dusky, crowded, heterogeneous back-shop of the mind very much as a wary dealer in precious odds and ends, competent to make an "advance" on rare objects confided to him, is conscious of the rare little "piece" left in deposit by the reduced, mysterious lady of title or the speculative amateur, and which is already there to disclose its merit afresh as soon as a key shall have clicked in a cupboard door.

That may be, I recognise, a somewhat superfine analogy for the particular "value" I here speak of, the image of the young feminine nature that I had had for so considerable a time all curiously at my disposal; but it appears to fond memory quite to fit the fact—with the recall, in addition, of my pious desire but to place my treasure right. I quite remind myself thus of the dealer resigned not to "realise," resigned to keeping the precious object locked up indefinitely rather than commit it, at no matter what price, to vulgar hands. For there *are* dealers in these forms and figures and treasures capable of that refinement. The point is, however, that this single small corner-stone, the conception of a certain young woman affronting her destiny, had begun with being all my outfit for the large building of *The Portrait of a Lady.* It came to be a square and spacious house—or has at least seemed so to me in this going over it again; but, such as it is, it had to be put up round my young woman while she stood there in perfect isolation. That is to me, artistically speaking, the circumstance of interest; for I have lost myself once more, I confess, in the curiosity of analysing the structure. By what process of logical accretion was this slight "personality," the mere slim shade of an intelligent but presumptuous girl, to find itself endowed with the high attributes of a Subject?—and indeed by what thinness, at the best, would such a subject not be vitiated? Millions of presumptuous girls, intelligent or not intelligent, daily affront their destiny, and what is it open to their destiny to *be,* at the most, that we should make an ado about it? The novel is of its very nature an "ado," an ado about something, and the larger the form it takes the greater of course the ado. Therefore, consciously, that was what one was in for—for positively organising an ado about Isabel Archer.

One looked it well in the face, I seem to remember, this extravagance; and with the effect precisely of recognising the charm of the problem. Challenge any such problem with any intelligence, and you immediately see how full it is of substance; the wonder being, all the while, as we look at the world, how absolutely, how inordinately, the Isabel Archers, and even much smaller female fry, insist on mattering. George Eliot has admirably noted it—"In these frail vessels is borne onward through the ages the treasure of human affection." In *Romeo and Juliet* Juliet has to be important, just as, in *Adam Bede* and *The Mill on the Floss* and *Middlemarch* and *Daniel Deronda,* Hetty Sorrel and Maggie Tulliver and Rosamond Vincy and Gwendolen Harleth have to be; with that much of firm ground, that much of bracing air, at the disposal all the while of their feet and their lungs. They are typical, none the less, of a class difficult, in the individual case, to make a centre of interest; so difficult in fact that many an expert painter, as for instance Dickens and Walter Scott, as for instance even, in the main, so subtle a hand as that of R. L. Stevenson, has preferred to leave the task unattempted. There are in fact writers as to whom we make out that their refuge from this is to assume it to be not worth their attempting; by which pusillanimity in truth their honour is scantly saved. It is never an attestation of a value, or even of our imperfect sense of one, it is never a tribute to any truth at all, that we shall represent that value badly. It never makes up, artistically, for an artist's dim feeling about a thing that he shall "do" the thing as ill as possible. There are better ways than that, the best of all of which is to begin with less stupidity.

It may be answered meanwhile, in regard to Shakespeare's and to George Eliot's testimony, that their concession to the "importance" of their Juliets and Cleopatras and Portias (even with Portia as the very type and model of the young person intelligent and presumptuous) and to that of their Hettys and Maggies and Rosamonds and Gwendolens, suffers the abatement that these slimnesses are, when figuring as the main props of the theme, never suffered to be sole ministers of its appeal, but have their inadequacy eked out with comic relief and underplots, as the playwrights say, when not with murders and battles and the great mutations of the world. If they are shown as "mattering" as much as they could possibly pretend to, the proof of it is in a hundred other persons, made of much stouter stuff, and each involved moreover in a hundred relations which matter to *them* concomitantly with that one. Cleopatra matters, beyond bounds, to Antony, but his colleagues, his antagonists, the state of Rome and the impending battle also prodigiously matter; Portia matters to Antonio, and to Shylock, and to the Prince of Morocco, to the fifty aspiring princes, but for these gentry there are other lively concerns; for Antonio, notably, there are Shylock and Bassanio and his lost ventures and the extremity of his predicament. This extremity indeed, by the same token, matters to Portia—though its doing so becomes of interest all by the fact that Portia matters to *us*. That she does so, at any rate, and that almost everything comes round to it again, supports my contention as to this fine example of the value recognised in the mere young thing. (I say "mere" young thing because I guess that even Shakespeare, preoccupied mainly though he may have been with the passions of princes, would scarce have pretended to found the best of his appeal for her on her high social position.) It is an example exactly of the deep difficulty braved—the difficulty of making George Eliot's "frail vessel," if not the all-in-all for our attention, at least the clearest of the call.

Now to see deep difficulty braved is at any time, for the really addicted artist, to feel almost even as a pang the beautiful incentive, and to feel it verily in such sort as to wish the danger intensified. The difficulty most worth tackling can only be for him, in these conditions, the greatest the case permits of. So I remember feeling here (in presence, always, that is, of the particular uncertainty of my ground), that there would be one way better than another—oh, ever so much better than any other!—of making it fight out its battle. The frail vessel, that charged with

George Eliot's "treasure," and thereby of such importance to those who curiously approach it, has likewise possibilities of importance to itself, possibilities which permit of treatment and in fact peculiarly require it from the moment they are considered at all. There is always the escape from any close account of the weak agent of such spells by using as a bridge for evasion, for retreat and flight, the view of her relation to those surrounding her. Make it predominantly a view of *their* relation and the trick is played: you give the general sense of her effect, and you give it, so far as the raising on it of a superstructure goes, with the maximum of ease. Well, I recall perfectly how little, in my now quite established connexion, the maximum of ease appealed to me, and how I seemed to get rid of it by an honest transposition of the weights in the two scales. "Place the centre of the subject in the young woman's own consciousness," I said to myself, "and you get as interesting and as beautiful a difficulty as you could wish. Stick to *that*—for the centre; put the heaviest weight into *that* scale, which will be so largely the scale of her relation to herself. Make her only interested enough, at the same time, in the things that are not herself, and this relation needn't fear to be too limited. Place meanwhile in the other scale the lighter weight (which is usually the one that tips the balance of interest): press least hard, in short, on the consciousness of your heroine's satellites, especially the male; make it an interest contributive only to the greater one. See, at all events, what can be done in this way. What better field could there be for a due ingenuity? The girl hovers, inextinguishable, as a charming creature, and the job will be to translate her into the highest terms of that formula, and as nearly as possible moreover into *all* of them. To depend upon her and her little concerns wholly to see you through will necessitate, remember, your really 'doing' her."

So far I reasoned, and it took nothing less than that technical rigour, I now easily see, to inspire me with the right confidence for erecting on such a plot of ground the neat and careful and proportioned pile of bricks that arches over it and that was thus to form, constructionally speaking, a literary monument. Such is the aspect that to-day **The Portrait** wears for me: a structure reared with an "architectural" competence, as Turgenieff would have said, that makes it, to the author's own sense, the most proportioned of his productions after **The Ambassadors**—which was to follow it so many years later and which has, no doubt, a superior roundness. On one thing I was determined; that, though I should clearly have to pile brick upon brick for the creation of an interest, I would leave no pretext for saying that anything is out of line, scale or perspective. I would build large—in fine embossed vaults and painted arches, as who should say, and yet never let it appear that the chequered pavement, the ground under the reader's feet, fails to stretch at every point to the base of the walls. That precautionary spirit, on re-perusal of the book, is the old note that most touches me: it testifies so, for my own ear, to the anxiety of my provision for the reader's amusement. I felt, in view of the possible limitations of my subject, that no such provision could be excessive, and the development of the latter was simply the general form of that earnest quest. And I find indeed that this is the only account I can give myself of the evolution of the fable: it is all under the head thus named that I conceive the needful accretion as having taken place, the right complications as having started. It was naturally of the essence that the young woman should be herself complex; that was rudimentary—or was at any rate the light in which Isabel Archer had originally dawned. It went, however, but a certain way, and other lights, contending, conflicting lights, and of as many different colours, if possible, as the rockets, the Roman candles and Catherine-wheels of a "pyrotechnic display," would be employable to attest that she was. I had, no doubt, a groping instinct for the right complications, since I am quite unable to track the footsteps of those that constitute, as the case stands, the general situation exhibited. They are there, for what they are worth, and as numerous as might be; but my memory, I confess, is a blank as to how and whence they came.

I seem to myself to have waked up one morning in possession of them—of Ralph Touchett and his parents, of Madame Merle, of Gilbert Osmond and his daughter and his sister, of Lord Warburton, Caspar Goodwood and Miss Stackpole, the definite array of contributions to Isabel Archer's history. I recognised them, I knew them, they were the numbered pieces of my puzzle, the concrete terms of my "plot." It was as if they had simply, by an impulse of their own, floated into my ken, and all in response to my primary question: "Well, what will she *do?*" Their answer seemed to be that if I would trust them they would show me; on which, with an urgent appeal to them to make it at least as interesting as they could, I trusted them. They were like the group of attendants and entertainers who come down by train when people in the country give a party; they represented the contract for carrying the party on. That was an excellent relation with them—a possible one even with so broken a reed (from her slightness of cohesion) as Henrietta Stackpole. It is a familiar truth to the novelist, at the strenuous hour, that, as certain elements in any work are of the essence, so others are only of the form; that as this or that character, this or that disposition of the material, belongs to the subject directly, so to speak, so this or that other belongs to it but indirectly—belongs intimately to the treatment. This is a truth, however, of which he rarely gets the benefit—since it could be assured to him, really, but by criticism based upon perception, criticism which is too little of this world. He must not think of benefits, moreover, I freely recognise, for that way dishonour lies: he has, that is, but one to think of—the benefit, whatever it may be, involved in his having cast a spell upon the simpler, the very simplest, forms of attention. This is all he is entitled to; he is entitled to nothing, he is bound to admit, that can come to him, from the reader, as a result on the latter's part of any act of reflexion or discrimination. He may *enjoy* this finer tribute—that is another affair, but on condition only of taking it as a gratuity "thrown in," a mere miraculous windfall, the fruit of a tree he may not pretend to have shaken. Against reflexion, against discrimination, in his interest, all earth and air conspire; wherefore it is that, as I say, he must in many a case have schooled himself, from the first, to work but for a "living wage." The living wage is the reader's grant of the least possible quantity of attention required for consciousness of a "spell." The occasional charming "tip" is an act of his intelligence over and beyond this, a golden

apple, for the writer's lap, straight from the wind-stirred tree. The artist may of course, in wanton moods, dream of some Paradise (for art) where the direct appeal to the intelligence might be legalised; for to such extravagances as these his yearning mind can scarce hope ever completely to close itself. The most he can do is to remember they *are* extravagances.

All of which is perhaps but a gracefully devious way of saying that Henrietta Stackpole was a good example, in *The Portrait,* of the truth to which I just adverted—as good an example as I could name were it not that Maria Gostrey, in *The Ambassadors,* then in the bosom of time, may be mentioned as a better. Each of these persons is but wheels to the coach; neither belongs to the body of that vehicle, or is for a moment accommodated with a seat inside. There the subject alone is ensconced, in the form of its "hero and heroine," and of the privileged high officials, say, who ride with the king and queen. There are reasons why one would have liked this to be felt, as in general one would like almost anything to be felt, in one's work, that one has one's self contributively felt. We have seen, however, how idle is that pretension, which I should be sorry to make too much of. Maria Gostrey and Miss Stackpole then are cases, each, of the light *ficelle,* not of the true agent; they may run beside the coach "for all they are worth," they may cling to it till they are out of breath (as poor Miss Stackpole all so vividly does), but neither, all the while, so much as gets her foot on the step, neither ceases for a moment to tread the dusty road. Put it even that they are like the fishwives who helped to bring back to Paris from Versailles, on that most ominous day of the first half of the French Revolution, the carriage of the royal family. The only thing is that I may well be asked, I acknowledge, why then, in the present fiction, I have suffered Henrietta (of whom we have indubitably too much) so officiously, so strangely, so almost inexplicably, to pervade. I will presently say what I can for that anomaly—and in the most conciliatory fashion.

A point I wish still more to make is that if my relation of confidence with the actors in my drama who *were,* unlike Miss Stackpole, true agents, was an excellent one to have arrived at, there still remained my relation with the reader, which was another affair altogether and as to which I felt no one to be trusted but myself. That solicitude was to be accordingly expressed in the artful patience with which, as I have said, I piled brick upon brick. The bricks, for the whole counting-over—putting for bricks little touches and inventions and enhancements by the way—affect me in truth as well-nigh innumerable and as ever so scrupulously fitted together and packed-in. It is an effect of detail, of the minutest; though, if one were in this connexion to say all, one would express the hope that the general, the ampler air of the modest monument still survives. I do at least seem to catch the key to a part of this abundance of small anxious, ingenious illustration as I recollect putting my finger, in my young woman's interest, on the most obvious of her predicates. "What will she 'do'? Why, the first thing she'll do will be to come to Europe; which in fact will form, and all inevitably, no small part of her principal adventure. Coming to Europe is even for the 'frail vessels,' in this wonderful age, a mild adventure; but what is truer than that on one side—the side of their independence of flood and field, of the moving accident, of battle and murder and sudden death—her adventures are to be mild? Without her sense of them, her sense *for* them, as one may say, they are next to nothing at all; but isn't the beauty and the difficulty just in showing their mystic conversion by that sense, conversion into the stuff of drama or, even more delightful word still, of 'story'?" It was all as clear, my contention, as a silver bell. Two very good instances, I think, of this effect of conversion, two cases of the rare chemistry, are the pages in which Isabel, coming into the drawing-room at Gardencourt, coming in from a wet walk or whatever, that rainy afternoon, finds Madame Merle in possession of the place, Madame Merle seated, all absorbed but all serene, at the piano, and deeply recognises, in the striking of such an hour, in the presence there, among the gathering shades, of this personage, of whom a moment before she had never so much as heard, a turning-point in her life. It is dreadful to have too much, for any artistic demonstration, to dot one's i's and insist on one's intentions, and I am not eager to do it now; but the question here was that of producing the maximum of intensity with the minimum of strain.

The interest was to be raised to its pitch and yet the elements to be kept in their key; so that, should the whole thing duly impress, I might show what an "exciting" inward life may do for the person leading it even while it remains perfectly normal. And I cannot think of a more consistent application of that ideal unless it be in the long statement, just beyond the middle of the book, of my young woman's extraordinary meditative vigil on the occasion that was to become for her such a landmark. Reduced to its essence, it is but the vigil of searching criticism; but it throws the action further forward than twenty "incidents" might have done. It was designed to have all the vivacity of incident and all the economy of picture. She sits up, by her dying fire, far into the night, under the spell of recognitions on which she finds the last sharpness suddenly wait. It is a representation simply of her motionlessly *seeing,* and an attempt withal to make the mere still lucidity of her act as "interesting" as the surprise of a caravan or the identification of a pirate. It represents, for that matter, one of the identifications dear to the novelist, and even indispensable to him; but it all goes on without her being approached by another person and without her leaving her chair. It is obviously the best thing in the book, but it is only a supreme illustration of the general plan. As to Henrietta, my apology for whom I just left incomplete, she exemplifies, I fear, in her superabundance, not an element of my plan, but only an excess of my zeal. So early was to begin my tendency to *overtreat,* rather than undertreat (when there was choice or danger) my subject. (Many members of my craft, I gather, are far from agreeing with me, but I have always held overtreating the minor disservice.) "Treating" that of **The Portrait** amounted to never forgetting, by any lapse, that the thing was under a special obligation to be amusing. There was the danger of the noted "thinness"—which was to be averted, tooth and nail, by cultivation of the lively. That is at least how I see it to-day. Henrietta must have been at that time a part of my wonderful notion of the lively. And then there was another matter. I had, within the few preceding years, come

to live in London, and the "international" light lay, in those days, to my sense, thick and rich upon the scene. It was the light in which so much of the picture hung. But that *is* another matter. There is really too much to say. (pp. 46-58)

Henry James, "Preface to 'The Portrait of a Lady'," in his The Art of the Novel: Critical Prefaces, *Charles Scribner's Sons, 1960?, pp. 40-58.*

Rebecca West　(essay date 1916)

[*West was an English novelist and critic. While her early criticism reflects her commitment to feminism and her Fabian socialist concerns, West's later criticism explores the psychology of the individual, an area on which she focused her full-length study* Henry James. *In the following excerpt from that work, she contends that inconsistencies in the characterization of Isabel Archer detract from the novel.*]

The Portrait of a Lady is given a superficial unity by the beauty of its heroine; on the first reading one cannot take one's eyes off the clear gaze that Isabel Archer levels at life. As she moves forward to meet the world, holding her fortune in hand without avarice yet very carefully, lest she should buy anything gross with it, one thinks that there never was a heroine who deserved better of life.

> She spent half her time in thinking of beauty, and bravery, and magnanimity; she had a fixed determination to regard the world as a place of brightness, of free expansion, of irresistible action; she thought it would be detestable to be afraid or ashamed. She had an infinite hope that she would never do anything wrong.

One is glad to see that the girl has the most wonderful friend, a woman who is at once the most flexible *femme du monde* and the freshest and most candid soul; and among the kindnesses this friend does her is her introduction to a certain Tuscan villa that looks down on the valley of the Arno, where on a mossy stone bench tangled with wild roses there sits Gilbert Osmond, a gentleman of great dignity who has been too fine to partake in the common struggle and so lives in honest poverty, with his daughter Pansy, a little girl from whose character conventional training has removed every attribute save whiteness and sweetness, so that she lies under life like a fine cloth on a sunny bleaching-green. Here, of all places in the world, she is least likely to meet the jealousy and falseness and cruelty which were the only things she feared, and so she marries Osmond in the happy faith that henceforth nothing will be admitted to her life save nobility. But all her marriage brings the girl is evidence of increasing painfulness that her friend is a squalid adventuress who has preserved her appearance of freshness as carefully as a strolling musician his fiddle, in order that she might charm such honest fools as Isabel; that Osmond has withdrawn from the world, not because he is too fine for it, but because he is a hating creature, and hates the world as he now hates his wife; that Pansy is the illegitimate child of these two, and her need of a dowry the chief reason why Osmond has married Isabel. It is a tale which would draw tears from a reviewer, and yet the conduct invented for Isabel is so inconsistent and so suggestive of the nincompoop, and so clearly proceeding from a brain whose ethical world was but a chaos, that it is a mistake to subject the book to the white light of a second reading. When we are told that Isabel married Osmond because "there had been nothing very delicate in inheriting seventy thousand pounds, and she hoped he might use her fortune in a way that might make her think better of it and would rub off a certain grossness attaching to the good luck of an unexpected inheritance," we feel that this is mere simpering; for there could be nothing less delicate than to marry a person for any reason but the consciousness of passion. And the grand climax of her conduct, her return to Osmond after the full revelation of his guilt has come to augment her anguish at his unkindness, proves her not the very paragon of ladies but merely very ladylike. If their marriage was to be a reality it was to be a degradation of the will whose integrity the whole book is an invitation to admire; if it was to be a sham it was still a larger concession to society than should have been made by an honest woman. Yet for all the poor quality of the motives which furnish Isabel's moral stuffing, *The Portrait of a Lady* is entirely successful in giving one the sense of having met somebody far too radiantly good for this world. (pp. 67-70)

Rebecca West, in her Henry James, *Henry Holt and Company, 1916, 128 p.*

F. O. Matthiessen   (essay date 1944)

[*Matthiessen was an American educator and literary critic. As a critic, he believed that the examination of a given work of literature must also consider the social and historical context of that work. Concerning his study of American literature, Matthiessen stated: "I wanted to place our masterworks in their cultural setting, but beyond that I wanted to discern what constituted the lasting value of these books as works of art." Matthiessen's works include* American Renaissance *(1941) and* Henry James: The Major Phase. *In the following excerpt from the latter work, he offers an examination of James's 1908 revision of* The Portrait of a Lady.]

One sign of how little technical analysis James has received is the virtual neglect of his revisions. Beyond Theodora Bosanquet's sensitive remarks in 'Henry James at Work' and occasional citation to annotate the elaborations of his later manner, they have been passed by. . . . Yet James made these revisions at the plentitude of his powers, and they constituted a *re-seeing* of the problems of his craft. He knew that it would be folly to try to recast the structure of any of his works. In the first preface that he wrote, that to *Roderick Hudson,* he developed an analogy for his aims in the way his fellow-craftsman on canvas went about to freshen his surfaces, to restore faded values, to bring out 'buried secrets.' He undertook, in particular, a minute verbal reconsideration of the three early novels that he chose to republish.

My reason for singling out *The Portrait of a Lady* is that it is a much richer book than either [*Roderick Hudson* or *The American*]. *Roderick Hudson* is full of interest for James' development, since the two halves of his nature,

the creator and the critic, are in a sense projected in Roderick and Rowland. Moreover, he there first tried out his device of having his narrative interpreted by the detached observer. But the book as a whole remains apprentice work. The revision of *The American*—the most extensive of all—might tell us, among other things, how James tried to repair what he had himself come to consider the falsely romantic aspects of his denouement. But *The Portrait of a Lady* is his first unquestioned masterpiece. By considering all the issues that the revisions raise, we may see it with renewed clarity.

Larger changes are very few. A page of conversation between Ralph Touchett and Lord Warburton (at the very end of Chapter XXVII) was recast in a way that shows James' more mature sense of a dramatic scene. What had been two pages of psychological scrutiny of Osmond just before his proposal to Isabel (Chapter XXIX) were felt by James to be otiose, and were cut to ten lines—an item of interest for the conventional view that the older James always worked the other way. But, with two important exceptions later to be looked into, we are to be concerned here with the tiniest brush strokes. What must be kept constantly in mind, therefore, is the design of the canvas as a whole. If that is done, we may have the intimate profit of watching the artist at his easel and of gaining insight into his principles of composition.

The writer's equivalent for the single flake of pigment is the individual word; and two words which James felt to be in need of consistent readjustment—'picturesque' and 'romantic'—form in themselves an index to his aims. He had begun the book in Florence and had finished it in Venice. He had been at the time still strongly under the spell of Italian art, which, as he wrote William, had first taught him 'what the picturesque is.' He had consequently used the word freely as a kind of aesthetic catchall, too loosely as he came to feel, for he struck it out in almost every case. He had applied it to Gardencourt, to Isabel's grandmother's house in Albany, to Osmond's *objects d'art;* he changed it in the first case to 'pictorial,' in the others to 'romantic.' Some of its many other occurrences must have made the later James wince, especially where he had said that Madame Merle had 'a picturesque smile.' That was altered to 'amused.' It is significant that when the word was retained, it was qualified by the speaker, by Isabel, who says that she would be a little on both sides of a revolution, that she would admire the Tories since they would have 'a chance to behave so exquisitely. I mean so picturesquely.' 'So exquisitely' was added in the revision, and it is no accident that where, in the earlier version, Lord Warburton had remarked that Isabel found the British 'picturesque,' he was later made to say ' "quaint." ' That putting into quotation marks underscores Isabel's attitude, as, indeed, do several instances where James introduced 'romantic' not merely as a substitute for 'picturesque.' Isabel's first judgment of Caspar as 'not especially good looking' becomes 'he was not romantically, rather obscurely handsome'; and her initial response to Warburton as 'one of the most delectable persons she had met' is made much firmer—she judges him, 'though quite without luridity— as a hero of romance.' And when we find that she doesn't tell her sister about either his or Osmond's proposal, not simply because 'it entertained her to say nothing' but because 'it was more romantic,' and she delighted in 'drinking deep, in secret, of romance,' we have the clue to what James is building up through his greatly increased use of this adjective and noun. He is bound to sharpen the reader's impression of how incorrigibly romantic Isabel's approach to life is, an important issue when we come to judge the effect of the book's conclusion.

Another word that shows the drift of James' later concern is 'vulgar.' One of James' most limiting weaknesses, characteristic of his whole phase of American culture, was dread of vulgarity, a dread that inhibited any free approach to natural human coarseness. But here the increased intrusion of the word does no great damage. When 'the public at large' becomes 'a vulgar world,' or when Henrietta Stackpole asserts that our exaggerated American stress on brain power 'isn't a vulgar fault' (she had originally pronounced it a 'glorious' one), or when Isabel adds to her accruing reflections that Osmond had married her, 'like a vulgar adventurer,' for her money, we simply see more sharply the negative pole of James' vision.

His positive values come out in a whole cluster of words affecting the inner life of his characters, words in which we may read all the chief attributes of Jamesian sensibility. Ralph's 'delights of observation' become 'joys of contemplation.' Warburton's sisters' 'want of vivacity' is sharpened to 'want of play of mind,' just as Isabel's 'fine freedom of composition' becomes 'free play of intelligence.' On the other hand, Warburton, in Ralph's description, is toned down from 'a man of imagination' to 'a man of a good deal of charming taste,' in accordance with the high demands that James came to put upon the imagination as the discerner of truth. It is equally characteristic that Isabel's 'feelings' become her 'consciousness,' and that her 'absorbing happiness' in her first impressions of England becomes 'her fine, full consciousness.' She no longer feels that she is 'being entertained' by Osmond's conversation; rather she has 'what always gave her a very private thrill, the consciousness of a new relation.' Relations, intelligence, contemplation, consciousness—we are accumulating the words that define the Jamesian drama. No wonder that James came to feel that it had been flat to say that Isabel was fond 'of psychological problems.' As he rewrote it, she became fond, as he was, 'ever, of the question of character and quality, of sounding, as who should say, the deep personal mystery.'

To progress from single words to questions of style, we note at once the pervasive colloquialization. The younger James had used the conventional forms, 'cannot' and 'she would'; in his revised conversation these always appear as 'can't' and 'she'd.' Of more interest is his handling of the 'he said—she said' problem, upon which the older James could well take pride for his ingenuity. Isabel 'answered, smiling' becomes Isabel 'smiled in return' or Isabel 'gaily engaged.' Osmond 'hesitated a moment' becomes that Jamesian favorite, Osmond 'just hung fire.' And for one more out of a dozen other evasions of the obvious, the Countess Gemini no longer 'cried . . . with a laugh'; her sound and manner are condensed into one word, 'piped.'

James' humor has often been lost sight of in discussion of the solemnities of his mandarin style. But he didn't lose it himself. His original thumb-nail characterization of Isabel's sister was descriptive: 'Lily knew nothing about Boston; her imagination was confined within the limits of Manhattan.' A graphic twist brings that to life with a laugh: 'her imagination was all bounded on the east by Madison Avenue.'

The later James was more concrete. He had also learned what a source of life inheres in verbal movement. 'Their multifarious colloquies' is heavily abstract, whereas 'their plunge . . . into the deeps of talk' takes us right into the action. So too with the diverse ways in which James launched his characters into motion, as when Henrietta 'was very well dressed' became 'she rustled, she shimmered'; or when the Countess, instead of entering the room 'with a great deal of expression,' did it 'with a flutter through the air.' Such movement means that James was envisaging his scenes more dramatically; and, in the passage where Isabel has just been introduced to Osmond, we can see how natural it had become for the novelist to heighten any theatrical detail. Where he had formerly written that Isabel sat listening to Osmond and Madame Merle 'as an impartial auditor of their brilliant discourse,' he now substituted 'as if she had been at the play and had paid even a large sum for her place.' And as this scene advances, instead of saying that Madame Merle 'referred everything' to Isabel, James wrote that she 'appealed to her as if she had been on the stage, but she could ignore any learnt cue without spoiling the scene.'

Operating more pervasively, here as always, upon James' imagination, were analogies with pictures rather than with the stage. When he wanted to enrich his bare statement that the Countess 'delivered herself of a hundred remarks from which I offer the reader but a brief selection,' he said that she 'began to talk very much as if, seated brush in hand before an easel, she were applying a series of considered touches to a composition of figures already sketched in.' A phrase that shows us James' very process is when Isabel, instead of 'examining the idea' (of Warburton's 'being a personage'), is made to examine 'the image so conveyed.' The growth from ideas to images is what James had been fumbling for in his earlier preoccupation with the picturesque. The word might now embarrass him, but not the secret he had learned through it. He had originally opened the first of the chapters to be laid in Osmond's villa by remarking that 'a picturesque little group' was gathered there. What he meant to imply was made much more explicit in the revision: 'a small group that might have been described by a painter as composing well.'

That concern with composition grew from the conviction which he voiced in the preface to **Roderick Hudson,** that the novelist's subject, no less than the painter's, consisted ever in 'the related state, to each other, of certain figures and things.' And characters, he came to believe, could be best put into such relations when they were realized as visually, as lambently, as possible. This belief led him into one of his most recurrent types of revision, into endowing his *dramatis personae* with characterizing images. He had concluded his initial account of Ralph's ill health by remarking, 'The truth was that he had simply accepted the situation.' In place of that James was to introduce the poignancy that is Ralph's special note: 'His serenity was but the array of wild flowers niched in his ruin.' In comparable fashion, James added to his first description of Osmond, with no parallel in the original, an image that embodies the complex nature we are to find in him: 'He suggested, fine gold coin as he was, no stamp nor emblem of the common mintage that provides for general circulation; he was the elegant complicated medal struck off for a special occasion.'

Such elaborate images, more than any other aspect of James' later style, show his delight in virtuosity. Occasionally they seem to have been added purely because his eye fell on a dull patch of canvas, and he set out to brighten it up. Warburton's dim sisters don't contribute much in the original beyond 'the kindest eyes in the world.' But, in revising, James let himself go: their eyes are now 'like the balanced basins, the circles of "ornamental water," set, in parterres, among the geraniums.' In that image any functional intention may seem lost in the rococo flourish; but such was not usually the case. Take one very typical instance in the first detailed description of Caspar Goodwood—and it is significant of James' matured intentions that he introduced characterizing images of his chief figures at such important points. We are told in the first version that Caspar had undergone the usual gentleman athlete's education at Harvard, but that 'later, he had become reconciled to culture.' In the revision James conveyed much more of Caspar's energetic drive by means of a muscular image: 'later on he had learned that the finer intelligence too could vault and pull and strain.'

The full effect that James was trying for in such images might be instanced by the chapter which introduces Henrietta. Here we might follow James in the process of enlivening his sketch by a dozen fresh touches. The most interesting of these bring out Henrietta's character by the device of interrelating her appearance with her career. He did not rest content with saying that 'she was scrupulously, fastidiously neat. From top to toe she carried not an inkstain.' He changed this into: 'she was as crisp and new and comprehensive as a first issue before the folding. From top to toe she had probably no misprint.' In spite of the loudness of her voice (which caused James to alter Henrietta 'murmured' to Henrietta 'rang out'), Ralph was originally surprised to find that she was not 'an abundant talker.' But in the revision the detailed glance at her profession is sustained, and he finds her not 'in the large type, the type of horrid "headlines."' Yet she still remains fairly terrifying to Ralph, and, a few pages farther on, James emphasized that by another kind of image. To point up the fact that 'she was brave,' he added, 'she went into cages, she flourished lashes, like a spangled lion-tamer.' With that as a springboard James could rise to the final sentence of this chapter. Originally Ralph had concluded, 'Henrietta, however, is fragrant—Henrietta is decidedly fragrant!' But this became a punch line: 'Henrietta, however, does smell of the Future—it almost knocks one down!'

James remarked in his preface [see essay dated 1908] that he had given the reader 'indubitably too much' of Henrietta—a thing that could be said of most of his *ficelles;* but

in retouching he had at least done what he could to brighten every inch. In relation to her we may note another phase of his revision, his addition of epithets to characterize the world of which she is part. In Rome she is struck by the analogy between the ancient chariot ruts and 'the iron grooves which mark the course of the American horse-car.' These become more up to date: 'the overjangled iron grooves which express the intensity of American life.' Where James had written 'the nineteenth century,' he was later to call it 'the age of advertisement'; and glancing, not at America but at Europe, he named it 'an overcivilized age.' But it was Henrietta's realm he was thinking of again when, instead of having Madame Merle remark that 'it's scandalous, how little I know about the land of my birth,' he had her call it rather, in his most revelatory addition of this type: 'that splendid, dreadful, funny country—surely the greatest and drollest of them all.'

So far I have avoided the question that is usually raised first about James' revisions: Didn't he sometimes overwrite to no purpose as a mere occupational disease? Occasionally, without doubt, it is the older James talking instead of a character, as when Pansy, instead of saying, 'I have no voice—just a little thread,' is made to transform this into ' . . . just a small sound like the squeak of a slate-pencil making flourishes.' But look at another sample where at first it would appear as though James had taken twice as many words to say the same thing, where 'Marriage meant that a woman should abide with her husband' became 'Marriage meant that a woman should cleave to the man with whom, uttering tremendous vows, she had stood at the altar.' In its context we can at least see what James was after. This passage is part of Isabel's reflections, and both its fuller rhythm and density are meant to increase its *inner* relevance. The best way, therefore, to judge the final value of James' rewriting is to relate it in each case to the character involved, an obligatory proceeding in dealing with the writer who asked, in "The Art of Fiction:" 'What is a picture or a novel that is *not* of character?

The diverse types of revision demanded by the different characters may also remind us that we have in this book the most interestingly variegated group that James ever created. The center of attention is always Isabel, and the changes devoted to her may be read as a brief outline of the interpretation which James hoped we should give to his heroine. A few involve her looks. Whereas acquaintances of the Archer girls used to refer to her as 'the thin one,' James' tenderness for her was later to make this sound less invidious: 'the willowy one.' From his initial description of her in the house at Albany, he wanted to emphasize that she was less mistress of her fate than she fondly believed. He pointed this up by changing 'young girl' to 'creature of conditions.' He also, as a past master of what could be gained by the specific notation, changed the conditioning of her taste from 'a glimpse of contemporary aesthetics' to 'the music of Gounod, the poetry of Browning, the prose of George Eliot'—a change which recalls that these were also Minny Temple's tastes.

But James' chief interest in his heroine is revealed through another type of change. Warburton's belief that she is 'a thoroughly interesting woman' is made more intimate—'a really interesting little figure.' And a few lines below, when Ralph concludes that a character like hers 'is the finest thing in nature,' he says more precisely what he means by adding, in the revision, that she is 'a real little passionate force.' James devoted many of his later brush strokes to bringing her out as exactly that. Instead of passively wanting 'to be delighted,' she now wants 'to hurl herself into the fray.' It is equally symptomatic of her conduct that she refuses Warburton, not because such a marriage fails 'to correspond to any vision of happiness that she had hitherto entertained,' but because it fails 'to support any enlightened prejudice in favour of the free exploration of life.' The Isabel whom the later James saw with so much lucidity is a daughter of the transcendental afterglow, far less concerned about happiness than about enlightenment and freedom.

Another addition indicates that what is most required to make her respond is 'a bait to her imagination.' That is exactly why she is caught by Osmond. Mrs. Touchett originally said that Isabel was capable of marrying him 'for his opinions'; but she heightens this with more of the girl's romanticism in saying 'for the beauty of his opinions or for his autograph of Michael Angelo.' And that is how we see Isabel reacting to him. His 'things of a deep interest' become 'objects, subjects, contacts . . . of a rich association.' She reads into them also, in a favorite phrase of the later James, 'histories within histories.' When she defends him to Ralph, the revision makes her grounds much more explicit by adding to her question, 'What do you know against him?—'What's the matter with Mr. Osmond's type, if it be one? His being so independent, so individual, is what *I* most see in him.' And again, instead of saying 'Mr. Osmond is simply a man—he is not a proprietor,' she expands this with her feeling, 'Mr. Osmond's simply a very lonely, a very cultivated and a very honest man—he's not a prodigious proprietor.'

This is the Isabel of whom James felt it no longer adequate just to say, 'she was an excitable creature, and now she was much excited.' He transformed that into an image: 'Vibration was easy to her, was in fact too constant with her, and she found herself now humming like a smitten harp.' Such vibrations are intrinsic to the rhythm of her thought. She no longer reflects merely that 'she had loved him,' but extends that reflection with 'she had so anxiously and yet so ardently given herself.' It is not padding, therefore, when, upon discovering how wrong she has been about Osmond, she does not conclude, 'There was only one way to repair it—to accept it,' but adds ' . . . just immensely (oh, with the highest grandeur!) to accept it.'

The revisions affecting Osmond are of a very different sort. Far more of them relate to his appearance, to the polished, elegant and slightly ambiguous surface which James wants the reader to study more fully. His 'sharply-cut face' becomes 'extremely modelled and composed.' James' description of his eyes is far more careful. They are no longer 'luminous' and 'intelligent' expressing 'both softness and keenness,' but 'conscious, curious eyes . . . at once vague and penetrating, intelligent and hard.' This is quite in keeping with his smile, which is now his 'cool' smile,

and with his voice, of which it is now said that, though fine, it 'somehow wasn't sweet.' He does not speak 'with feeling' but 'beautifully'; and his laugh, instead of being 'not ill-natured,' has now 'a finer patience.' James has done an expert job of heightening Osmond's thoroughly studied effect. He underscores the fact that Osmond's taste was his only law by saying, not that he lived 'in a serene, impersonal way,' but 'in a sorted, sifted, arranged world,' where his 'superior qualities' become 'standards and touchstones other than the vulgar.'

Osmond is entirely devoted to forms, and to accent this trait, James introduces one of his most interesting later devices: he interrelates Osmond's character with his surroundings in a way that shows again how much the novelist had learned from the plastic arts. On the first occasion that Osmond entertains Isabel, James wants her to be impressed with the rare distinction of the collector's villa. Osmond's footboy is now made deliberately picturesque: instead of remaining merely 'the shabby footboy,' he becomes 'tarnished as to livery and quaint as to type,' and, with a fine added flourish, James tells us that he might 'have issued from some stray sketch of old-time manners, been "put in" by the brush of a Longhi or a Goya.' James also added in the revision that Osmond was marked for Isabel 'as by one of those signs of the highly curious that he was showing her on the underside of old plates and in the corner of sixteenth-century drawings.' As Isabel thinks over this visit afterwards, she reflects that his care for beauty 'had been the main occupation of a lifetime of which the arid places were watered with the sweet sense of a quaint, half-anxious, half-helpless fatherhood.' In the revision these thoughts rise from her impression of how she had seen him: his preoccupation with beauty made his life 'stretch beneath it in the disposed vistas and with the ranges of steps and terraces and fountains of a formal Italian garden—allowing only for arid places freshened by the natural dews,' and so on.

In building up the reasons why she took her romantic view of him, James also embarked on an extended flight:

> What continued to please this young lady was his extraordinary subtlety. There was such a fine intellectual intention in what he said, and the movement of his wit was like that of a quick-flashing blade.

What continued to please this young woman was that while he talked so for amusement he didn't talk, as she had heard people, for 'effect.' He uttered his ideas as if, odd as they often appeared, he were used to them and had lived with them; old polished knobs and heads and handles, of precious substance, that could be fitted if necessary to new walking-sticks—not switches plucked in destitution from the common tree and then too elegantly waved about.

The new passage stresses, if in oblique ways and with some needless verbiage, Osmond's utter dependence on art rather than on nature. The 'old polished knobs,' like the 'complicated medal' to which he is compared, make him indisseverable from his collector's items. It is not surprising that such a deliberately shaped work of art as he is 'mystified' Isabel. (In the first version he had merely 'puzzled' her.) It is fitting too that, as she comes under his fascination, she should feel not merely 'a good deal older than she had done a year before,' but also 'as if she were "worth more" for it,' like some curious piece in an antiquary's collection.' For, in ways that her inexperience cannot possibly fathom, that is precisely how Osmond proposes to treat her. She appeals to him, not for being 'as bright and soft as an April cloud,' but in one of James' most functional revisions, 'as smooth to his general need of her as handled ivory to the palm.'

The mystification is only Isabel's, the ambiguity is all in what Osmond concealed, not in any doubts that James entertained about him. The revision increases his 'lost' quality. His 'peculiarities' are called his 'perversities,' and where it was remarked that he consulted his taste alone, James now adds 'as a sick man consciously incurable consults at last only his lawyer.' The reader accepts entirely Ralph's judgment of Osmond as a sterile dilettante; but his quality is deepened when Ralph recognizes the futility of trying to persuade Isabel, not that the man is 'a humbug,' but rather that there is something 'sordid or sinister' in him. With that deepening even Osmond becomes poignant: his 'keen, expressive, emphatic' face becomes 'firm, refined, slightly ravaged'—a far more telling portrait.

The character in this book around whom ambiguity gathers most is Madame Merle, since she has to play a double rôle throughout. James' changes involving her are chiefly of two sorts. He decided, for one thing, that her surface should be less transparent to Isabel. And so it is when Isabel asks her if she has not suffered that her 'picturesque smile' is elaborated into 'the amused smile of a person seated at a game of guesses.' She is also called 'smooth' instead of 'plump.' When Madame Merle introduced her to Osmond, Isabel wondered about 'the nature of the tie that united them. She was inclined to imagine that Madame Merle's ties were peculiar.' As James looked over that, it seemed to strike too close to the actual liason, which he didn't want Isabel to suspect for a long time yet. So he toned it up to 'the nature of the tie binding these superior spirits. She felt that Madame Merle's ties always somehow had histories.'

But in the other type of change for Madame Merle, James felt, as he did with Osmond, that he must make her character unmistakable to the reader. So he no longer endowed her with 'a certain nobleness,' but with 'a certain courage'; not with 'geniality' but with 'grace.' Even in changing the music that Isabel overheard her playing from 'something of Beethoven's' to 'something of Schubert's,' James must have felt that he was bringing it more within Madame Merle's emotional compass. When Isabel finally comes to know her secret, the girl reflects, not just that her friend was 'false,' but 'even deeply false . . . deeply, deeply, deeply.' And Madame Merle's guilt is spoken of, not in terms 'of vivid proof,' but 'of ugly evidence . . . of grim things produced in court.'

Such details—of which there are many more—are important in allaying the usual suspicion that James' ambiguity is unintentional, the obscurantism of a man who couldn't make up his own mind. When the writing becomes denser, as it frequently does in the revision, this is owing rather to James' gradual development of one of his special gifts, the ability so to handle a conversation that he keeps in the air not merely what is said, but what isn't—the passage of thoughts without words. The situation here which challenged most this skill of the later James was when Warburton turned up again after Isabel's marriage. What she had to decide was whether, despite his honorable pretensions, he was still in love with her. Their interplay is made more subtle. To judge the value of this kind of rewriting you must follow the whole chapter, but one series of slight changes may show what James was about.

As they met again, in the first version, Isabel 'hardly knew whether she were glad or not.' Warburton, however, 'was plainly very well pleased.' In the revision his feelings are not given to us so explicitly: he 'was plainly quite sure of his own sense of the matter.' Only as the conversation advances do Isabel—and the reader—gain the evidence she is after. In a moment or two, he remarks how charming a place she has to live in. In the original he said this, 'brightly, looking about him.' But this became: 'with a look, round him, at her established home, in which she might have caught the dim ghost of his old ruefulness.' That reveals to Isabel nearly all she needs, and her impression is clinched, when, instead of turning upon her 'an eye that gradually became more serious,' he gives her, in addition, 'the deeper, the deepest consciousness of his look.' From that moment Isabel knows how unwise it would be for him to marry her stepdaughter Pansy, no matter how much Osmond wants the match. (pp. 152-70)

The two most extensive passages of rewriting are yet to be looked at. One relates to the Countess Gemini, and the other to Caspar Goodwood. Both can give us insight into how James conceived dramatic structure, and how he also felt that the climax of this book needed strengthening.

In comparing the two versions, it is notable that the sequence of chapters which James pronounced, in the preface, as being the best in the book—the sequence that extends from Isabel's glimpse of the two together, with Osmond seated while Madame Merle is standing, through the long vigil in which Isabel gradually pieces together her situation—that these three chapters (XL-XLII), with their important issues, were left substantially unchanged. So too with the fateful interview between Osmond and Isabel (Chapter XLVI) which shows how hopelessly far apart they have grown. But the scene with the Countess (Chapter LI), in which Isabel's suspicions are first given explicit names, was greatly recast. Some of the reasons for this are suggested by what James wrote in his notebook at the time when the novel had begun to appear in *The Atlantic* and he was trying to see his way clear to his conclusion: 'After Isabel's marriage there are five more instalments, and the success of the whole story greatly depends upon this portion being well conducted or not. Let me then make the most of it—let me imagine the best. There has been a want of action in the earlier part, and it may be made up here. The elements that remain are in themselves, I think, very interesting, and they are only to be strongly and happily combined. The weakness of the whole story is that it is too exclusively psychological—that it depends too little on incident; but the complete unfolding of the situation that is established by Isabel's marriage may nonetheless be quite sufficiently dramatic. The idea of the whole thing is that the poor girl, who has dreamed of freedom and nobleness, who has done, as she believes, a generous, natural, clear-sighted thing, finds herself in reality ground in the very mill of the conventional. After a year or two of marriage the antagonism between her nature and Osmond's comes out—the open opposition of a noble character and a narrow one. There is a great deal to do here in a small compass; every word, therefore, must tell—every touch must count. If the last five parts of the story appear crowded, this will be rather a good defect in consideration of the perhaps too great diffuseness of the earlier portion.'

As James went on outlining his intentions, he was still undecided whether the revelation of Pansy's parentage should come through Madame Merle herself or through the Countess: 'Better on many grounds that it should be the latter; and yet in that way I lose the "great scene" between Madame Merle and Isabel.' Twenty-five years later he was still bothered by what he had lost. In the passage of deadly quietness between Isabel and Osmond, and, subsequently, between Isabel and Madame Merle, he seems to have felt that his drama was too inward, that he needed a more emotional scene. And so he rewrote nearly all the lines in which the Countess told Isabel of the liaison.

He had already given considerable attention to making the Countess' character a more lively mixture. Ralph's first description of her was changed from 'rather wicked' to 'rather impossible'; and in her own disarming self-characterization, instead of saying, 'I am only rather light,' she pronounced herself 'only rather an idiot and a bore.' James had originally said that her expression was 'by no means disagreeable'; but here he particularized: it was made up of 'various intensities of emphasis and wonder, of horror and joy.' Also, to a quite astonishing degree, by recurring to a bird-image for her, he sustained her in a whir. For example, in her first meeting with Isabel, she delivered her remarks 'with a variety of little jerks and glances.' But the bird-motif gave these the momentum of 'little jerks and pecks, of roulades of shrillness,' with the result that James was stimulated to a further flight of his own, and added that her accent was 'as some fond recall of good English, or rather of good American, in adversity.'

This kind of a character had dramatic possibilities, and, in his revision, James exploited them to the full. He did everything he could to make her revelations to Isabel into the 'great scene' he had missed. Isabel is alone, thinking of what will happen if, in defiance of Osmond's wishes, she goes to England to see Ralph before he dies. Then, suddenly, the Countess 'stood before her.' Thus the original, but in the rewriting the Countess 'hovered before her.' And to give us an intimation that something is coming, James added that the Countess 'lived assuredly, it might be said, at the window of her spirit, but now she was leaning far out.' As Lawrence Leighton, who first drew my attention to the importance of this scene for James' structure, remarked, this is like 'an extra blast from the trumpets' to announce the herald. It occurs to Isabel for the first time that her sister-in-law might say something, not 'important,' but 'really human.'

In what follows much subtle attention was paid to the

Countess' diction. James endowed her with a more characteristic colloquial patter, with such epithets as 'poverina' and 'cara mia.' Instead of saying that Madame Merle had wanted 'to save her reputation,' she says, 'to save her skin'; and, in her view, Isabel has not merely 'such a pure mind'—she calls it 'beastly pure,' as such a woman would. Her speeches are considerably increased in length, one of them by almost a page. There is hardly any addition to her ideas, but as Mr. Leighton also observed, 'James wanted a good harangue, the sort of speech an actress could get her teeth into.' Her quality is melodramatic, but it is effectively more baleful than in the first version.

James has also built up the contrast between her and Isabel. The Countess expected—and hoped—that the girl would burst out with a denunciation of Osmond. But instead she is filled with pity for Madame Merle. She thinks even of Osmond's first wife, that 'he must have been false' to her—'and so very soon!' That last phrase is an addition that emphasizes Isabel's incurable innocence, despite all the experience through which she is passing. It glances ironically also at her own situation. When she goes on to reflect that at least Osmond has been faithful to her, the Countess says it depends on what you call faithful; 'When he married you he was no longer the lover of another woman—*such* a lover as he had been, *cara mia,* between their risks and their precautions, while the thing lasted!' Everything after the dash is added, and we can hear the Countess smacking her lips over such details, while Isabel recoils into herself. Where the first version had remarked that she 'hesitated, though there was a question in her eyes,' the utter cleavage between her and her gossipy interlocutress is now brought out: she 'hesitated as if she had not heard; as if her question—though it was sufficiently there in her eyes—were all for herself.' When, a moment or two later, Isabel wondered why Madame Merle never wanted to marry Osmond, the Countess had originally contented herself with saying that Madame Merle 'had grown more ambitious.' But to that James added: ' "besides, she has never had, about him," the Countess went on, leaving Isabel to wince for it so tragically afterwards— "she *had* never had, what you might call any illusions of *intelligence.*" ' The Countess is happy to get in a dig at her brother, but for Isabel and for the reader there is the irony that Isabel herself had been fooled by just such illusions. That gives the final twist to the knife.

After this scene there remain only four chapters. There is the brief final encounter with Madame Merle, who sees in an instant that Isabel now knows everything. Isabel then says good-bye to Pansy, but promises that she won't desert her. The rest of the book is taken up with Isabel's trip to England, with her farewell to Ralph, and with Caspar's return to her. The last chapter is largely her struggle with him, and James' significant additions are led up to by the emphases that he has given to Caspar's character earlier in the book. He has introduced many details that sharpen the impression of Caspar's indomitable energy. When Isabel first compares him with Warburton, she feels that there is 'something too forcible, something oppressive and restrictive' about him. But this was made more concrete: 'a disagreeably strong push, a kind of hardness of presence.' A revelatory image was introduced to contrast Isabel's feeling about Warburton: instead of refusing to 'lend a receptive ear' to his suit, she now 'resists conquest' at his 'large quiet hands.' But Caspar is 'a kind of fate,' now, indeed, 'a kind of grim fate.' He himself gives fuller expression to the tension between them when he has first pursued her to London. Instead of saying, 'Apparently it was disagreeable to you even to write,' he makes it 'repugnant.' And he remarks bitterly, not that his insistence on his suit 'displeases' her, but that it 'disgusts.' As the best means of characterizing him, James developed a recurrent image of armor. In his first account he had merely remarked that Caspar was 'the strongest man' Isabel had ever known; but to this he added: 'she saw the different fitted parts of him as she had seen, in museums and portraits, the different fitted parts of armoured warriors—in plates of steel handsomely inlaid with gold.' Later on, his eyes, instead of wearing 'an expression of ardent remonstrance,' seemed 'to shine through the vizard of a helmet.' And when Isabel tries to measure his possible suffering, she no longer reflects that 'he had a sound constitution,' but that 'he was naturally plated and steeled, armed essentially for aggression.'

He follows her to Italy to object strenuously to her engagement to Osmond: 'Where does he come from? Where does he belong?' That second question was added in the revision, as was also Isabel's thought, 'She had never been so little pleased with the way he said "belawng." ' But, in spite of everything, Isabel cannot escape feeling Caspar's power; and in rewriting their final scene, James made an incisive analysis of his mixed repulsion and attraction for her. She is alone under the trees at Gardencourt, when Caspar suddenly appears—just as Warburton had surprised her there once before. In what follows we are made to feel her overpowering sensation of his physical presence, from the moment that James adds that he was 'beside her on the bench and pressingly turned to her.' As he insists that her husband is 'the deadliest of fiends,' and that he, Caspar, is determined to prevent her from the 'horror' of returning to him (both 'deadliest' and 'horror' were additions), Isabel realizes that 'she had never been loved before.' To that realization the original had added: 'It wrapped her about; it lifted her off her feet.' But now James wrote: 'She had believed it, but this was different; this was the hot wind of the desert, at the approach of which the others dropped dead, like mere sweet airs of the garden. It wrapped her about; it lifted her off her feet, while the very taste of it, as of something potent, acrid, and strange, forced open her set teeth.'

That image takes her as far away from her surroundings and the gentlemanly devotion of a Warburton as it does from the decadent egotism of an Osmond. For a moment she is completely overpowered. Caspar's voice, saying, 'Be mine, as I'm yours,' comes to her, not merely 'through a confusion of sound,' but 'harsh and terrible, through a confusion of vaguer sounds.' He takes her in his arms, and, in the first version, the climax is reached with: 'His kiss was like a flash of lightning; when it was dark again she was free.' But now James felt it necessary to say far more: 'His kiss was like white lightning, a flash that spread, and spread again, and stayed; and it was extraordinary as if,

while she took it, she felt each thing in his hard manhood that had least pleased her, each aggressive fact of his face, his figure, his presence, justified of its intense identity and made one with this act of possession. So had she heard of those wrecked and under water following a train of images before they sink. But when darkness returned she was free.'

That conveys James' awareness of how Isabel, in spite of her marriage, has remained essentially virginal, and of how her resistance and her flight from Caspar are partly fear of sexual possession. But the fierce attraction she also feels in this passage would inevitably operate likewise for a girl of her temperament, in making her do what she conceived to be her duty, and sending her back to her husband.

That brings us to the ending of the book, which has seldom been rightly interpreted. The difference between the two versions is one of the few of James' revisions that is generally known. Henrietta has told Caspar that Isabel has gone back to Rome:

> 'Look here, Mr. Goodwood,' she said; 'just you wait.' On which he looked up at her.

Thus the final lines in the original. But to these James added:

> —but only to guess, from her face, with a revulsion, that she simply meant he was young. She stood shining at him with that cheap comfort, and it added, on the spot, thirty years to his life. She walked him away with her, however, as if she had given him now the key to patience.

Many critics have held this difference to mean that James had changed his mind, that in the original he had given Caspar more hope. But he seems rather to have made unmistakably explicit what he had always intended to imply. He had said in his notebook outline that Isabel was to be greatly moved by Caspar's 'passionate outbreak': 'she feels the full force of his devotion—to which she has never done justice; but she refuses. She starts again for Italy—and her departure is the climax and termination of the story.' James had also observed there that Henrietta was to have 'the last word,' to utter 'a characteristic characterization of Isabel.' But he must have felt in revising that he had been too brief, that he had failed to drive home to the reader that what was being expressed was no sure promise about Isabel, but rather Henrietta's optimism, which refuses to accept defeat.

The end of Isabel's career is not yet in sight. That fact raises a critical issue about James' way of rounding off his narratives. He was keenly aware of what his method involved. As he wrote in his notebook, upon concluding his detailed project: 'With strong handling it seems to me that it may all be very true, very powerful, very touching. The obvious criticism of course will be that it is not finished— that it has not seen the heroine to the end of her situation—that I have left her *en l'air*. This is both true and false. The *whole* of anything is never told; you can only take what groups together. What I have done has that unity—it groups together. It is complete in itself—and the rest may be taken up or not, later.'

This throws a great deal of light—perhaps more than any single passage of his published work—on how James conceived of structure. He recounted in the preface to the *Portrait* how Turgenieff had encouraged him in his belief that the important thing to start with was not an air-tight plot, but rather a character or group of characters who are so living that the main question becomes to 'invent and select' the complications that such characters 'would be most likely to produce and to feel.'

Years before the *Portrait,* William James had commented on the effect of such a method, as it struck him in **"A Most Extraordinary Case"** (1868), one of the first half dozen stories that Henry had printed. William felt that here he understood for the first time what Henry was aiming for: 'to give an impression like that we often get of people in life: Their orbits come out of space and lay themselves for a short time along of ours, and then off they whirl again into the unknown, leaving us with little more than an impression of their reality and a feeling of baffled curiosity as to the mystery of the beginning and the end of their being.' William thought such a method difficult to make succeed, but 'with a deep justification in nature.' He was to grow somewhat less sure of its efficacy, as can be read in his tone about *The Tragic Muse:* 'the final winding up is, as usual with you, rather a losing of the story in the sand, yet that is the way in which things lose themselves in real life.' Henry, on the other hand, grew steadily to have more confidence in what he was doing, until he declared, in the preface to *Roderick Hudson:* 'Really, universally, relations stop nowhere, and the exquisite problem of the artist is eternally but to draw, by a geometry of his own, the circle within which they shall happily *appear* to do so.' That gives his essential conception of the kind of wholeness that form imposes.

He had been particularly concerned in the *Portrait* with launching Isabel Archer into action, with presenting her so vividly that his narrative would compose itself around the primary question, 'Well, what will she *do?*' It has recently been assumed that James believed entirely in the rightness of his heroine's conduct, and that since our age no longer feels as he—and she—did about the strictness of the marriage vow, we can no longer respond to the book except as to a period piece. But that is to misread not merely the ending, but all of James' own 'characteristic characterization' of Isabel. He could hardly have made a more lucid summary of the weaknesses that she exposed to Europe: 'her meagre knowledge, her inflated ideals, her confidence at once innocent and dogmatic, her temper at once exacting and indulgent—that whole passage of analysis on the evening after her arrival at Gardencourt, a passage untouched in the revision, is meant to have our closest scrutiny.

As Isabel embarks on her 'free exploration' of life, Henrietta is outspoken in declaring that she is drifting rather to 'some great mistake,' that she is not enough 'in contact with reality,' with the 'toiling, striving' world. Ralph tells her that she has 'too much conscience'—a peculiarly American complication in the romantic temperament. Although all her diverse friends are united in their disapproval of Osmond, she proceeds to do the wrong thing for

the right reasons. She has a special pride in marrying him, since she feels that she is not only 'taking,' but also 'giving'; she feels too the release of transferring some of the burden of her inheritance to another's conscience—James' way of commenting on how harm was done to her by her money. But once she discerns what Osmond is really like, and how he has trapped her, she is by no means supine in his toils. She stands up to him with dignity, she even asks Pansy, 'Will you come away with me now?' Yet Isabel knows that is impossible; she knows, even as she leaves, that she will have to return to Rome for Pansy's sake.

But much more is involved than that—James' whole conception of the discipline of suffering. It is notable that his kinship here to Hawthorne becomes far more palpable in the final version. Take the instance when, at the time of Ralph's death, Isabel realizes how Mrs. Touchett has missed the essence of life by her inability to feel. It seemed to Isabel that Ralph's mother 'would find it a blessing today to be able to indulge a regret. She wondered whether Mrs. Touchett were not trying, whether she had not a desire for the recreation of grief.' James made this much fuller, particularly the latter portion. Isabel wondered if Mrs. Touchett 'were not even missing those enrichments of consciousness and privately trying—reaching out for some aftertaste of life, dregs of the banquet; the testimony of pain or the cold recreation of remorse.' The view of suffering adumbrated there, even the phrasing, recalls Hawthorne's "The Christmas Banquet," where the most miserable fate is that of the man whose inability to feel bars him out even from the common bond of woe.

The common bond of sin, so central to Hawthorne's thought, was also accentuated through James' retouching. When Madame Merle finally foresees what is ahead, she says to Osmond in the original, 'How do bad people end? You have made me bad.' But James extended this with a new italicized emphasis, 'How do bad people end?— especially as to their *common* crimes. You have made me as bad as yourself.' Isabel's link with humanity, if not through sin—unless her willful spirit counts as such—is through her acceptance of suffering. The inevitability of her lot is made more binding in the revision. Her reflection that 'she should not escape, she should last,' becomes 'she should never escape, she should last to the end.' She takes on heightened stature when James no longer says that, while she sat with Ralph, 'her spirit rose,' but that 'her ache for herself became somehow her ache for *him.*' The pathos of her situation is also intensified in proportion to her greater knowledge of what is involved. 'She reflected that things change but little, while people change so much' is far less affecting than 'she envied the security of valuable "pieces" which change by no hair's breadth, only grow in value, while their owners lose inch by inch, youth, happiness, beauty.'

In both the original and the revision Isabel lays the most scrupulous emphasis upon the sacredness of a promise. Despite all her eagerness for culture, hers is no speculative spirit. Osmond comes to despise her for having 'the moral horizon' of a Unitarian minister—'poor Isabel, who had never been able to understand Unitarianism!' But whether she understands it or not, she is a firm granddaughter of the Puritans, not in her thought but in her moral integrity. In portraying her character and her fate, James was also writing an essay on the interplay of free will and determinism. Isabel's own view is that she was 'perfectly free,' that she married Osmond of her most deliberate choice, and that, however miserable one may be, one must accept the consequences of one's acts. James knew how little she was free, other than to follow to an impulsive extreme everything she had been made by her environment and background.

Thus he leaves her to confront her future, and is satisfied if he has endowed his characters with so much 'felt life' that the reader must weigh for himself what is likely to life ahead in her relation with Osmond. It may be that, as Isabel herself conjectures, he may finally 'take her money and let her go.' It may be that once she has found a husband for Pansy, she will feel that she no longer has to remain in Rome. James believed that the arbitrary circle of art should stimulate such speculations beyond its confines, and thus create also the illusion of wider life. He had about Isabel a tragic sense, but he did not write a tragedy, as he was to do in *The Wings of the Dove,* since this earlier drama was lacking in the finality of purgation and judgment. But his view of his material was not at all ambiguous. He knew how romantic Isabel was, how little experienced she was in mature social behavior. He had shown that she was completely mistaken in believing that 'the world lay before her—she could do whatever she chose.' But James also knew the meaning and the value of renunciation. The American life of his day, in its reckless plunge to outer expansiveness and inner defeat, had taught him that as his leading spiritual theme. Through Isabel Archer he gave one of his fullest and freshest expressions of inner reliance in the face of adversity. It is no wonder that, after enumerating her weaknesses, he had concluded: 'she would be an easy victim of scientific criticism if she were not intended to awaken on the reader's part an impulse more tender . . . ' (pp. 172-86)

F. O. Matthiessen, in his Henry James: The Major Phase, *1944. Reprint by Oxford University Press, Inc., 1963, 190 p.*

Richard Chase   (essay date 1957)

[*A distinguished American literary critic, Chase is the author of* The American Novel and Its Tradition, *an influential study examining the "romance" tradition in American fiction. In this work, Chase maintained that American fiction tended to be not strictly realistic, but rather abstract, symbolic, and more concerned with action than characterization, an observation which inspired in his contemporaries a reappraisal of American literature. Although at one time associated with the New Critics, Chase wrote that he leaned "rather to the historical, moral, or naturalistic approach of such contemporary critics as Lionel Trilling and Edmund Wilson." In the following excerpt from the abovementioned work, he argues that while characterization and metaphoric language in* The Portrait of a Lady *are informed by the American literary tradition of romance, James was ultimately committed to realism in the novel.*]

Henry James's *Portrait of a Lady* was the first novel by an American that made, within the limits of its subject, full use of the novel form. By comparison, no previous American novel, even those of James, can claim to be fully "done." From James's point of view the older American romance-novelists had many faults. Some of these he singles out explicitly in his biography of Hawthorne, others . . . he directly or indirectly deals with in his prefaces and critical writings. Cooper, Hawthorne, and Melville (actually James seems to know next to nothing of the last) relied too readily on extravagant events and startling characters. They failed to render experience fully. They failed to illustrate and dramatize connections and relations. They did not see (in the words of the Preface to *Roderick Hudson*) that for the true novelist "the continuity of things is the whole matter . . . of comedy and tragedy."

To read the first page of *The Portrait of a Lady* is to step into a world unfrequented by the earlier American novelists. A handsome pictorial representation, a fine old house, beautiful lawns and gardens, a group of people being set in motion—all these may be found in Cooper's *Satanstoe* or Hawthorne's *House of the Seven Gables.* But James's procedure is different from that of the earlier writers. The effect he seeks is more organic and self-contained. At the same time, there is more detail, more careful observation, for he has "researched" his subject—something which Hawthorne, as James said, tended to leave undone. We encounter at the very beginning the author's reference to his book as a "history" and we are perhaps reminded that in his essay **"The Art of Fiction"** he was to say that the novel should give the same impression of veracity as does history itself.

On the board, sloping lawn of the mansion James calls Gardencourt we discover people taking tea, and they are finding it agreeable, not only because it tastes good but because drinking it is a mild ritual by which they show themselves to be a part of a way of life, a social order which we understand is to figure strongly in the book, as strongly as does the life of the Westchester aristocracy in *Satanstoe.* Yet the life of James's characters will be illustrated and dramatized with a far more exact and also a more poetic art than one can find in Cooper's novel.

To admit, as most readers would, that there is an element of poetry in *The Portrait of a Lady* is to admit that though it has all of the novelistic virtues, it has others too. There is a sense in which one might speak of the "poetry" of *Pride and Prejudice* or *Middlemarch*—a poetry of picture and scene, a poetry felt to belong to the organized effect of character, action, and setting. But this is, so to speak, novelistic poetry, of the kind every interesting novel has. *The Portrait* has it too, but it also has a further dimension of poetry, to understand which one must perceive that James's novel is akin to romance as the others are not.

It is an important fact about James's art that he gave up what he considered the claptrap of romance without giving up its mystery and beauty. Mr. Leavis in *The Great Tradition* is not interested in James as a romancer, but he nevertheless notes that James is a "poet-novelist" and says that he combines Jane Austen's skill of observing and dramatizing manners with Hawthorne's "profoundly moral and psychological . . . poetic art of fiction." This is very well put, and it supports the supposition of this chapter that a part of James's great program for improving the novel consisted of the reconstitution, on new grounds, of romance. Often one has difficulty in pinning down any one element of a James novel as belonging to romance because the author has so completely subdued and transmuted it to suit his exacting novelistic purposes. The element of romance becomes generally subverted and assimilated; yet in turn it imparts the glow of poetry to the realistic substance of the novel. Which is to say in a different way what Mr. Leavis says in the following:

> James's own constant and profound concern with spiritual facts expresses itself not only in what obviously demands to be called symbolism, but in the handling of character, episode, and dialogue, and in the totality of the plot, so that when he seems to offer a novel of manners, he gives us more than that and the 'poetry' is major.

The conscious assimilation of romance into the novelistic substance of *The Portrait* took place in two different ways. It was assimilated into the language of the book and produced a general enrichment of metaphor. It was also brought in in the character of Isabel Archer, the heroine, who is to a considerable extent our point of view as we read. Isabel tends to see things as a romancer does, whereas the author sees things with the firmer, more comprehensive, and more disillusioned vision of the novelist. Thus James brings the element of romance into the novel in such a way that he can both share in the romantic point of view of his heroine and separate himself from it by taking an objective view of it.

The metaphors of *The Portrait of a Lady* do not often rival the amazingly elaborate figures one encounters in James's later works, but by contrast with the usual practice of the novel at the time James wrote they are notably daring—so much so that sometimes they seem to lead a life of their own within the spacious world of the book, although in each case we are led to see the relevance of the metaphor to the course of events and to the pattern of unfolding significance. There is a paradox, says James in his Preface to *The Portrait,* in trying to write a fiction at once so complex and so ambitious [see essay dated 1908]. The paradox is that a novel so conceived must "positively . . . appear more true to its character in proportion as it strains, or tends to burst, with a latent extravagance, its mould." Metaphor offered to James a kind of repository or annex in which the latent extravagance of his imagination might take form. As has often been noticed the main figures of speech in James's novel—although the variety is rich—have to do with the house and the garden.

The metaphors are sometimes extravagant. For example we read of Isabel that "her imagination was by habit ridiculously active; when the door was not open it jumped out of the window." But that is a mere piece of fancy and reminds us less of the characteristic practice of James than of the quaint wit of Hawthorne. Ordinarily, James's metaphors, in *The Portrait* as elsewhere, are not quaint and concise. They are suggestively imaginative and they are likely to be given a tone of elevated levity which at once enjoys what is being said and takes note of its extrava-

gance. As often as not the Jamesian metaphor shows that mixture of serious poetic imagination with humor which we find in other American writers, notably Melville, Mark Twain, and Faulkner. Although one would hardly mistake the style of any one of these writers for that of any other, all of them are fond of the serious, intricately sustained joke. Here is James speaking of Ralph Touchett's pose of facetious irony, which Isabel, in her earnest sincerity, finds baffling and also reprehensible. Sensing his inner despair and sorry that he is sickly, she wants to come directly to the "real" Ralph Touchett, but he himself explains the value of his pose:

> "I keep a band of music in my ante-room. It has orders to play without stopping; it renders me two excellent services. It keeps the sounds of the world from reaching the private apartments, and it makes the world think that dancing's going on within." It was dance music indeed that you usually heard when you came within earshot of Ralph's band; the liveliest waltzes seemed to float upon the air. Isabel often found herself irritated by this perpetual fiddling; she would have liked to pass—

James finds the metaphor, once launched, too good to drop—

> through the ante-room, as her cousin called it, and enter the private apartments. It mattered little that he had assured her they were a very dismal place; she would have been glad to undertake to sweep them and set them in order. It was but half-hospitality to let her remain outside.

The idea of leaving and entering a house, the contrast of different kinds of houses, the question of whether a house is a prison or the scene of liberation and fulfillment—these are the substance of the metaphors in *The Portrait of a Lady.* Figuratively speaking, the story told in the novel is of Isabel's leaving an American house—a way of life, that is—for a European house. Ostensibly she conceives of this as an escape from frustrating and cramping confinement to a fuller, freer, more resonant and significant life. Actually, it is not hard to see that although James has much admiration and tenderness of feeling for his heroine, he gives her an element of perverse Yankee idealism of the sort that he was shortly to portray in the more exacerbated form of positively per*verted* idealism in Olive Chancellor in *The Bostonians.* So that for all her dark-haired, gray-eyed beauty, her delightful young enthusiasm, and her zest for life, there is in Isabel a fatal susceptibility to a form of imprisonment worse than that she has escaped. Figuratively, the house in which she lives as the wife of Gilbert Osmond confines her in a hopeless imprisonment she could not consciously have imagined.

Our first sight of Isabel occurs when with her abrupt charm and her disarming candor she walks across the lawn at Gardencourt, the Touchetts' English estate, and presents herself to her cousin Ralph, his father, and Lord Warburton. But then in the form of a flash-back we are speedily acquainted with the general circumstances of Isabel's childhood and girlhood. We find her in the old family house at Albany talking with Mrs. Touchett and greeting with joy Mrs. Touchett's offer to take her to Europe. "To go to Florence," says Isabel, "I'd promise almost anything!" She sees in this offer an escape from the loneliness of the life she has known in the great, empty, dismal house. Yet now that escape is in view, Isabel admits that she does not hate the house or the circumstances of her early life, even though Mrs. Touchett dismisses the place as "very bourgeois." "I like places in which things have happened," says Isabel, "—even if they're sad things. A great many people have died here; the place has been full of life." And to Mrs. Touchett's query "Is that what you call being full of life?" she replies, "I mean full of experience—of people's feelings and sorrows. And not of their sorrows only, for I've been happy here as a child."

Still, the possibility of living a full life in Albany seems remote to Isabel. And the only considerable picture of her as a young girl that James gives us suggests that she had found the Albany house not so much the scene of human sufferings and joys as the somewhat bleak abode of a life of fantasy and reading, a life isolated from reality. Isabel had been accustomed to read and daydream in a room known as "the office" that lay beyond the library.

> The place owed much of its mysterious melancholy to the fact that it was properly entered from the second door of the house, the door that had been condemned, and that it was secured by bolts which a particularly slender little girl found it impossible to slide. She knew that this silent, motionless portal opened into the street; if the sidelights had not been filled with green paper she might have looked out upon the little

James's cousin Minny Temple at age eighteen.

brown stoop and the well-worn brick pavement. But she had no wish to look out, for this would have interfered with her theory that there was a strange, unseen place on the other side—a place which became to the child's imagination, according to its different moods, a region of delight or terror.

She is sitting in this room when Mrs. Touchett comes to see her, except that being now a young woman with undefined but strong purposes she is, on this fateful afternoon, not engaging in childish fantasy but, having given her mind "marching orders," she has sent it "trudging over the sandy plains of a history of German thought."

Despite her disorganized and tenuous education and the puritanism of her native Yankee temperament, Isabel is now ostensibly ready to pursue an enriched life of the emotions and of thought. A way of life characterized by its intricate amenity, its depth of emotion, and its richness of traditionally ordered experience cannot be symbolized by the house at Albany. But it can by the Tudor mansion of the Touchetts, to which Isabel is introduced when she arrives in England.

> Her uncle's house seemed a picture made real; no refinement of the agreeable was lost on Isabel: the rich perfection of Gardencourt at once revealed a world and gratified a need. The deep embrasures and curious casements, the quiet light on dark polished panels, the deep greenness outside, that seemed always peeping in, the sense of a well-ordered privacy in the centre of a "property"—a place where sounds were felicitously accidental, where the tread was muffled by the earth itself and in the thick mild air all friction dropped out of contact and all shrillness out of talk . . .

There is no paper in the windows of this house, no need to isolate oneself from the world outside. On the contrary the "greenness outside" seems "always peeping in" and the garden, where at important points in the novel Isabel will receive and reject proposals of marriage from Lord Warburton and Caspar Goodwood, seems as much a part of the house as does its own interior. Consequently, the garden makes an inevitable part of the general metaphor which represents the enriched sensibility of the heroine.

> She was always planning out her development, desiring her perfection, observing her progress. Her nature had, in her conceit, a certain garden-like quality, a suggestion of perfume and murmuring boughs, of shady bowers and lengthening vistas, which made her feel that introspection was, after all, an exercise in the open air, and that a visit to the recesses of one's spirit was harmless when one returned from it with a lapful of roses.

In a novel which describes a fall from innocence, it is suitable that the tragic action should be metaphorically mirrored in the heroine's mind by this imaginative conjunction of the garden and the ancient house, in which the garden stands for Isabel's Eve-like innocence and the house for a civilization that has lost its innocence but has acquired—along with its corruption—wisdom, maturity, and the whole involved and valuable accretion of culture. Thus Isabel is akin not only to the heroines of George Eliot, such as Hetty Sorrel, Maggie Tulliver, Rosamond Vincy, and Gwendolen Harleth, with whom James compares her in his Preface; nor is she akin only to Shakespeare's Portia, with whom James also compares Isabel, calling Portia "the very type and model of the young person intelligent and presumptuous." Isabel also resembles the strong-minded Rosalind in *As You Like It* and the innocent and expectant Miranda in *The Tempest*. And the particular charm of these girls is that they are "real," that they make positive demands on life, but that they are at the same time figures of romance. James is also thinking of the Miltonic archetype of all feminine innocence, as is suggested by his using, as Leon Edel points out, the language of *Paradise Lost* to describe Isabel as she sets out on her adventures: "The world lay before her—she could do whatever she chose."

Chapter 42 of *The Portrait* brings to its fullest realization, though not to its last refinement, the characteristic art of James, that art which I am attempting to define as an assimilation of romance into the substance of the novel. James describes this chapter by saying that, "It is obviously the best thing in the book, but it is only a supreme illustration of the general plan." In this chapter James was able to achieve supremely the "circuit" of the real and the ideal, of action and fantasy, and thus to capture along with the realistic substance of the story the wonder and beauty of romance while at the same time rejecting the conventional devices of romance.

Isabel, now the wife of Osmond, sits one evening by the fire in the drawing room of Osmond's house, and with a combination of disillusioned insight and darkly working imagination she recognizes for the first time the true character of her husband and the true nature of her predicament. The problem, as James sees it, is how to present an episode in which nothing happens except an "extraordinary meditative vigil" but which will have all the excitement of action and high adventure. The problem is how to make the "mystic conversion" of Isabel's adventures, which have actually been "mild," into "the stuff of drama," how, as he goes on to say, to produce "the maximum of intensity with the minimum of strain." The "circuit" of the real and the fantasied, the "mystic conversion" of which James speaks, is to be established not, certainly, through a mere retelling or summing-up of Isabel's "mild adventures," but by giving us her sense of them. "Without her sense of them, her sense *for* them, as one may say, they are next to nothing at all." Although there are no overt happenings in this chapter, it nevertheless, as James says, "throws the action further forward than twenty 'incidents' might have done. It was designed to have all the vivacity of incident and all the economy of picture. Isabel sits up, by her dying fire, far into the night, under the spell of recognitions on which she finds the last sharpness suddenly wait. It is a representation simply of her motionlessly *seeing,* and an attempt withal to make the mere still lucidity of her act as 'interesting' as the surprise of a caravan or the identification of a pirate."

What occurs in Isabel's mind is the kind of disillusioned

and profoundly realistic perception of truth about oneself and one's situation that is called "tragic recognition." Yet it comes to her in images that belong as much to melodrama as to tragedy. "Her soul was haunted by terrors," says James, "which crowded to the foreground of thought as quickly as a place was made for them." One of these terrors is the new image she has formed of her husband, an image which distinctly reminds us of one of the cold, selfish villains of Hawthorne, a Rappiccini or a Chillingworth. She thinks of Osmond's "faculty for making everything wither that he touched, spoiling everything for her that he looked at. . . . It was as if he had had the evil eye; as if his presence were a blight and his favor a misfortune."

She reflects that she had set out with her husband for "the high places of happiness." She had taken "all the first steps in the purest confidence," but now "she had suddenly found the infinite vista of a multiplied life to be a dark narrow alley with a dead wall at the end." The man who had so narrowed and enclosed her life, a creature of darkness, now steps forth into the light—"she had seen only half his nature then, as one saw the disk of the moon when it was partly masked by the shadow of the earth. She saw the full moon now—she saw the whole man."

But the full force of Isabel's recognition is appropriately conveyed by the metaphor of the house and the garden. She has escaped, to be sure, the isolation and girlish ignorance she had known at Albany, but she has lost the felicitous synthesis of innocence and experience symbolized as a possibility for her by Gardencourt. Her marriage, as she now sees, had made her the inhabitant of a different house.

> She could live it over again, the incredulous terror with which she had taken the measure of her dwelling. Between these four walls she had lived ever since; they were to surround her for the rest of her life. It was the house of darkness, the house of dumbness, the house of suffocation. Osmond's beautiful mind gave it neither light nor air; Osmond's beautiful mind indeed seemed to peep down from a small high window and mock at her.

And so Isabel comes to see that

> under all his culture, his cleverness, his amenity, under his good-nature, his facility, his knowledge of life, his egotism lay hidden like a serpent in a bank of flowers.

Her youthful innocence and good-will have been foully traduced, she has been the victim of an elegantly sordid conspiracy, the possibility of a full life she had envisioned has been spoiled. And we are left to recall, with a sense of its tragic irony, her early declaration to Lord Warburton that "I can't escape my fate"—that fate which Isabel had thought would consist of some rewarding involvement in life. For although she has rather grand aspirations, an essential stipulation of her fate, as she understands it, is that she shall never be exempt "from the usual chances and dangers, from what most people know and suffer." She has found knowledge and suffering no doubt, but of the grimmest sort. In her plight there can be no such clarion awakening and engagement of her human faculties as she had supposed might be the result of knowledge and suffering. Indeed there seems nothing left for her but a life of duty and abnegation. As we leave her at the end of the book she seems veritably to belong to the sisterhood of Hester Prynne.

But we know why Hester Prynne is made to suffer; conventional morality imposes on her its punishment for a sin of passion. For better or for worse, Isabel remains scrupulously virginal. She has been guilty of no misconduct in which we find any real justification for suffering. And we do, of course, want to find some measure of justification; otherwise we shall have to convict James of palming off on us under the guise of moral complexity what is morally speaking a mere melodrama of victimized innocence, a tale of merely senseless cruelty and pathos.

Is James himself subtly vindictive in his attitude toward Isabel? He clearly admires her for her almost redemptive American probity and moral spontaneity, and yet he just as clearly thinks her guilty of presumption, and of bad manners that are only just barely made tolerable by her ingenuous charm. Nor does James approve of her upbringing or of her father, one of those somewhat disorderly, nomadic Americans for whom he always shows a dislike. Isabel has been taught to "affront her destiny," as James says in his Preface; and this, one supposes, is less correct than *con*fronting it. Even supposing, as there is some speculative ground for doing, that James has a neurotic involvement with his heroine which leads him to fear her female aggressiveness and thus to take satisfaction and to derive a feeling of security in showing her, though possessed of animal spirits, to be sexually cold, and in leading her, finally, to her cruel fate—even supposing on these or other grounds a genuine animosity on the part of James toward his heroine, the fact remains that this is surmounted by his admiration of her and his profound sympathy with her. And in any case Isabel is so completely created a character that she lives her life independently of the approval or disapproval the author may feel toward her, whether we deduce his feeling from the novel itself or from our knowledge of his life and temperament.

Sometimes moved, as one must be, by a desire for a more earthly and simple morality than James's usually is, one wishes that Isabel Archer were more like Kate Croy of *The Wings of the Dove* or even the unpleasantly named Fleda Vetch in *The Spoils of Poynton,* girls in whom the general quality of self-assertion has a sexual component. But despite her deeply repressed sexuality, Isabel remains among the most complex, the most fully realized, and the most humanly fascinating of James's characters. Consequently we cannot think her a mere case of victimized innocence. She has so many powers, imperfect though they are, of knowledge, of feeling, of imagination that her fate must surely issue in some crucial way from her being the sort of person she is. If she is disqualified for triumph, it is not in the obvious way of James's other victimized innocents, like Catherine Sloper in *Washington Square,* who is homely and timid, like Maisie in *What Maisie Knew* or little Miles and Flora in *The Turn of the Screw,* who are children, or like Milly Theale in *The Wings of the Dove,* who is dying of tuberculosis. Isabel's disqualification is that of heroines and heroes throughout tragic litera-

ture—a blindness to reality, a distortion of awareness, that puts her at the mercy of the perverse and self-destructive inner motives struggling in her for the upper hand.

Without attempting any sort of full discussion of Isabel and her troubles, one may note that she sees reality as the romancer sees it. This is obvious as a general proposition, since Isabel is patently romantic in the sense that she has highly imaginative dreams which prove to be beyond the possibility of fulfillment. A realistic young woman, or, for that matter, a conventionally romantic one, would have accepted Lord Warburton as a good catch, for he is, after all, an excellent man as well as a rich and noble lord. But Isabel has higher ideals than any she thinks can be realized by a life with Lord Warburton. Her personal romance includes strenuous abstractions that lead her to aspire to far more than the conventional romance of marrying an English nobleman. She therefore perversely and no doubt quite mistakenly decides that to marry Lord Warburton would be to "escape" her "fate." "I can't escape unhappiness," she says. "In marrying you I shall be trying to." And she continues by saying that by marrying Lord Warburton she would be "turning away," "separating" herself from life, "from the usual chances and dangers, from what most people know and suffer." Lord Warburton's answer is one that would in the main turn out to be true: "I don't offer you any exoneration from life or from any chances or dangers whatever." He is brought by Isabel's behavior to a true understanding of her, and he exclaims, "I never saw a person judge things on such theoretic grounds." Her theory is that he is merely "a collection of attributes and powers," but this is clearly a false theory. Despite his being a hereditary nobleman and so, bound to the formalities and duties of his station in life, he presents himself to her with perfect candor as a man, and not a lord, who needs and desires her. Thus Isabel's vague democratic objections to English aristocracy, which in any case she seems generally to admire, are not the real reason why she rejects Lord Warburton. Nor when she does marry does she choose a man notable for democracy. She rejects Lord Warburton at the behest of her puritan spirituality, which leads her to flee from the mere physical and social realities of life as these would be should she marry him. Perversely and mistakenly, her argument is that marriage to Lord Warburton would exempt her from life. Better a collection of attributes and powers (which in any case Lord Warburton is not) than a collection of sterile tastes and appetites, which Gilbert Osmond certainly is. But Isabel does not see Osmond for what he is until too late. (I am assuming here as elsewhere that Isabel's choice is, for all practical purposes, between Warburton and Osmond. Ralph is in love with her, but his illness disqualifies him. The persistent Caspar Goodwood presents himself at intervals, but Isabel does not see him as an actual possibility. She seems to conceive of him as worthy but as rather stodgy in his conventional Massachusetts way. She scarcely thinks of him as being momentously on the scene until at the very end of the novel when he proposes to rescue her from Osmond and, in his vehemence, frightens her with his masculine aggressiveness by giving her, so far as the reader knows, her only kiss.)

How is it that the image Osmond presents to the world so

easily commands Isabel's assent? This is a hard problem, but the answer may be suggested by observing that although Isabel's vision of things is neither that of self-interested common sense nor that of worldly romance in which poor girls marry great lords, it emphatically is that of the romance associated with the American tradition of puritanism and transcendentalism. Isabel subscribes to the American romance of the self. She believes that the self finds fulfillment either in its own isolated integrity or on a more or less transcendent ground where the contending forces of good and evil are symbolized abstractions. She sees her fate as a spiritual melodrama. Her grasp of reality, though manifold in its presumptions, is unstable, and her desire for experience is ambivalent. She rejects Lord Warburton ostensibly because she fears that marrying him will exempt her from life. But Ralph Touchett, who often speaks with the wisdom of the author, has no trouble in securing a contradictory admission from his amusing and perplexing cousin. At the end of a lengthy dialogue about her rejection of Lord Warburton, Ralph conjectures, "You want to drain the cup of experience," and gets out of Isabel this surprising answer, "No, I don't wish to touch the cup of experience. It's a poisoned drink! I only want to see for myself." To which Ralph adds a comment in the partial truth of which we may see a link between Isabel and Osmond: "You want to see, but not to feel."

Ralph has hit upon a truth about his cousin. The kind of cold, amoral aloofness, the possibly morbid passion for observing life at a distance—these are real traits of Isabel's character. True, they are no more than strong strands in her fabric. But they are strong enough so that she responds to Osmond's talk about how "one ought to make one's life a work of art," without being aware of the inhumanity and the withering aestheticism such an idea may imply. Only when it is too late does she discover the cold malignancy of her husband. Only too late does she see that, apart from his need of the money she has inherited from her uncle, she is cherished by Osmond only to the extent that he can consider her another art object in his collection. Only too late does she understand the subtle corruption that leads Osmond to try to arrange his daughter's education so as to make her life "a work of art." Listening to Osmond's plans for Pansy's schooling, Isabel seems to see at last "how far her husband's desire to be effective was capable of going—to the point of playing theoretic tricks on the delicate organism of his daughter." In this way Isabel, who is herself every bit the theorist Lord Warburton accused her of being, comes to understand the perverse puritan impulse which Hawthorne called "the Unpardonable Sin." The sin is the same whether one's cold, theoretical manipulation of others has an aesthetic motive or as with Hawthorne's Chillingworth or Ethan Brand a quasi-scientific one.

Isabel's romance of the self, as was suggested above, requires that self-fulfillment shall take place only at a high level of abstraction, where the disinterested pursuit of perfection may be carried on. And although Ralph Touchett warns his cousin that Osmond is a "sterile aesthete," she sees in him at once the high priest, the devoted custodian, and martyr of the life of perfection. She is very far from believing that the ordinary vulgar circumstances of one's

life have anything to do with one's self. She finds it inconceivable and rather degrading that anyone should suppose the self to be in any sort of dialectic with the mere things one is surrounded by. In Chapter 19 there occurs an important exchange between Madame Merle and Isabel on this point. They have been talking about the inevitable "young man with a mustache" who must figure in some way in every young woman's life. Madame Merle speculatively inquires whether Isabel's "young man with a mustache" has a "castle in the Apennines" or "an ugly brick house in Fortieth Street." And when Isabel says characteristically, "I don't care anything about his house," Madame Merle replies, "That's very crude of you." And she continues by saying,

> There's no such thing as an isolated man or woman; we're each of us made up of some cluster of appurtenances. What shall we call our "self"? Where does it begin? Where does it end? It overflows into everything that belongs to us—and then it flows back again. I know a large part of myself is in the clothes I choose to wear. I've a great respect for *things!* One's self—for other people—is one's expression of one's self; and one's house, one's furniture, one's garments, the books one reads, the company one keeps—these things are all expressive.

This bit of worldly wisdom strikes Isabel as being worldly, all too worldly, but not as being wisdom. "I don't agree with you," she says. "I think just the other way. I don't know whether I succeed in expressing myself, but I know that nothing else expresses me. Nothing that belongs to me is any measure of me; everything's on the contrary a limit, a barrier, and a perfectly arbitrary one." To find the fulfillment of self through superiority to mere things and without attention to what others may think about what one does—this is the feat Isabel supposes Osmond to have accomplished. Actually as she comes tragically to see, Osmond is above all men enslaved by things and by what he supposes others to be thinking of him. "She had thought it a grand indifference, an exquisite independence. But indifference was really the last of his qualities; she had never seen anyone who thought so much of others."

The moral world shared by Isabel and Osmond—a world in which Lord Warburton has no place—is that of the high Emersonian self-culture. In the sordid elegance of Osmond's implacably willed hedonism we discover the final possibilities of corruption in this culture, which is of course no less subject to corruption than any other moral idealism. In Isabel's unhappy career we estimate the tragic implications of an idealism that in effect directs one to seek the rewards of the fully "lived life" without descending from one's high pedestal into its actual conditions. In Isabel's sincere presentation of her essentially spiritual quest as a quest for a real involvement in "the usual chances and dangers" of life lies the tragic irony of the story. And it has, furthermore, the advantage of verisimilitude since that is how an ambitious young woman in the latter part of the nineteenth century—spiritual puritan though she might be—would conceive of her quest, knowing it to be no longer inevitably the part of woman to isolate herself from the world either because of religious conviction or in acquiescence to the conventions about woman's place.

Isabel Archer may be said to have the imagination of romance most notably in the sense that she responds to character intensely only when it conceives of itself at a high level of abstraction and when its acts are symbolic of ideal values. When this imagination is confronted by an appealingly complex human being, such as Lord Warburton, it sees only "a collection of attributes and powers." Like the romancer, Isabel refuses to impute significance to human actions unless they are conceived as being exempt from the ordinary circumstances of life, whereas the genuine novelist sees in ordinary circumstances the inescapable root condition of significant actions.

So, to carry the analogy only one step along, James in the end brings Isabel's point of view around from that of the romancer to that of the novelist. Like [Hawthorne's] *The Blithedale Romance, The Portrait of a Lady* explores the limits of romance. But whereas Hawthorne seems to admit that he cannot be the true novelist and thus surrenders the imagination of the novelist to that of the romancer, James does the opposite, affirming the primacy of the novelist's imagination. But though he rejects romance as a moral view of the world, he assimilates into the very substance of the novel, by means of metaphor and the charm of the heroine herself, the appeal of romance. Thus he is able to meet superabundantly the requirement for the novel which he calls in the Preface to *The American* satisfying "our general sense of the ways things happen" and at the same time he is able to provide the novel with the poetry of romance.

So much, and as it would seem, no more is to be done with *The Portrait of a Lady* as a romance. In James's books one catches hold of the romance only just as it is disappearing into the thicket of the novel. Thus it is a thankless task to pursue too long and arduously something that is always being assimilated into something else. James is not a romancer like Hawthorne or Melville; he is a novelist to the finger tips. (pp. 117-35)

> *Richard Chase, "The Lesson of the Master," in his* The American Novel and Its Tradition, *Doubleday & Company, Inc., 1957, pp. 117-37.*

J. A. Ward (essay date 1961)

[*Ward is an American educator and critic. In the following excerpt from his* The Imagination of Disaster: Evil in the Fiction of Henry James, *he examines attitudes toward evil in* The Portrait of a Lady *as represented by the actions and intentions of the novel's main characters.*]

Like the other American heroines in James, Isabel Archer of *The Portrait of a Lady,* an enormous self-seeker who believes that reality corresponds to her ideals, whose innocence is her strength as well as her weakness, is doomed to failure. James repeatedly dramatizes the inadequacy of romance as a guide to life. He consistently shows the impossibility of complete success for his Newmans, Euphemia Cleves, and Isabel Archers, and permits them to achieve only equivocal moral triumphs through endurance of suffering. Isabel Archer's history assumes this pattern, but in *The Portrait of a Lady* James also treats a number of more commonplace marriages. There is the marriage of the expatriates Mr. and Mrs. Touchett, two different American types whose marriage is all but a total failure. Mr. Touchett preserves the quiet and honest dignity of his American nature in his English estate, while his wife is quick to seek European values and friends. There is the adulterous tie between the other expatriates, Osmond and Mme. Merle. There is the marriage of the American Henrietta and the English Bantling, both comic figures, whose union is an ironic counterpart to Isabel's, for it gives all indications of being the only successful marriage in the book. The marriage of Edward Rosier and Pansy Osmond is thwarted by Osmond. Ralph Touchett, clearly in love with Isabel, is confined to the role of a spectator by his illness. Finally, there is the Countess Gemini, Osmond's sister, who has left America in her youth and married a third-rate Italian nobleman. Her marriage is more or less in the background of the novel, but it casts a grim shadow over the proceedings in the foreground, for the Count Gemini is an impoverished gambler and the Countess has become an adulteress.

The marriage of Henrietta and Bantling is the only successful one, and this seems to be mainly a comic contrast to the failure of the others. The marriages not prevented by circumstances or intervention end in futility or disaster. James's meaning is that though theoretically the union of America—which represents morality, innocence, and spirit—with Europe—which represents manners, experience, and form—is an ideal arrangement, in actuality it can mean only misery. James recurrently explored the possibilities of a workable union of America and Europe. Perhaps Felix Young of *The Europeans* embodies this ideal synthesis, but Young is the only character of his type in James's fiction. He is somewhat like Valentin Bellegarde of *The American,* yet Valentin is too intimately associated with the traditional values of his country to realize the freedom he desires. F. R. Leavis maintains that Ralph Touchett

> is the centre, the key-figure, of James's 'system'—the poise of harmony. . . . He is neither American nor English—or he is both: that is, he combines the advantages, while being free from the limitations. He can place everyone, and represents the ideal civilization that James found in no country.

What Leavis overlooks is that Touchett is a ruined man. His incurable illness, which associates him with those Americans who are denied experience by physical, economic, or other handicaps, symbolizes impotence. Touchett can live only vicariously; he is, in effect, outside the action of the novel. More important, as Elizabeth Stevenson points out, "his living and dying as he does is a kind of reference to reality for Isabel." Like Mercutio in *Romeo and Juliet* or Angela and the Beadsman in "The Eve of Saint Agnes," he is a kind of *memento mori.*

The failure of every marriage except Henrietta's also points to James's abiding conviction that isolation is the ultimate lot of every man. Social existence precludes love, friendship, and sympathy. The James character requires completion, and, just as *The Portrait of a Lady* illustrates the limitations of Isabel and Osmond by contrasting them, it stresses the futility of any attempt at a reconciliation of opposite qualities. At best—as in the case of Isabel and Warburton—there is no alteration in either person; at worst—as in the case of Isabel and Osmond—one person's deficiency injures the other. The morally superior person is thus driven further back into himself, forced to rely on his innate strength, forever estranged from a significant social relationship.

There is clearly a revelation of an intrinsic evil in the novel's emphasis on man's inevitable conditions of isolation and failure. But in *The Portrait* James is also concerned with the process of man's decline from innocence to depravity. Nearly all James's novels treat to some extent the theme of the Fall of Man—the single theme which dominated so much of nineteenth-century American literature—but no one work so explicitly as *The Portrait of a Lady.*

In James's version of the Fall myth America is Eden. As Felix Young says of the society of the Wentworths in *The Europeans,* "It's primitive; it's patriarchal; it's the *ton* of the golden age." The idyllic American paradise suits the moral innocence of the Americans. The innocents leave their paradise of their own will. If they are expelled from Eden, the force is their own selfhood, a pride which urges them to master experience. In spite of the language of Emersonian transcendentalism with which James's Americans consider their goals, they are clearly motivated by an unhealthy egotism. Isabel, for example,

> had an unquenchable desire to think well of herself. She had a theory that it was only under this provision life was worth living; that one should be one of the best, should be conscious of a fine organization (she couldn't help knowing her organization was fine), should move in a realm of light, of natural wisdom, of happy impulse, of inspiration gracefully chronic. . . . She spent half her time in thinking of beauty and bravery and magnanimity; she had a fixed determination to regard the world as a place of brightness, of free expansion, or irresistible action. . . .

Such pride, based on a belief in the goodness and possibility of unlimited emotional and intellectual expansion, is also an active aggressiveness that can easily become evil. What distinguishes the Americans and the Europeans in *The Portrait of a Lady* is that the Americans are ambitious to possess something or someone. In this sense, the aims of Isabel and Osmond are similar, for both wish to satisfy their own cravings. But Isabel's pride is untainted by malice; rather it stems from her "meagre knowledge, her inflated ideals, her confidence at once innocent and dogmatic." When Isabel leaves the Edenlike America, she seeks a total knowledge and freedom; disillusion comes with the awareness that the two are mutually exclusive. As Leon Edel points out, "twice in the book James uses Miltonic words to describe the extent of Isabel's freedom—as if she were Eve standing at the portals of Paradise, which are closing behind her." Though Isabel is more innocent than Eve at the beginning of her adventure, her innocence is ambiguous; it combines a false notion of personal independence with an obliviousness to evil. In this sense her

original sin is simply innocence, but an innocence coordinate with pride.

It is significant that *The Portrait of a Lady* concludes with Goodwood offering Isabel a way out of her misery:

> "It's too monstrous of you to think of sinking back into that misery, of going to open your mouth to that poisoned air. . . . Why shouldn't we be happy—when it's here before us, when it's so easy? . . . We can do absolutely as we please. . . . Were we born to rot in our misery? . . . The world's all before us—and the world's very big. I know something about that."

The point is that Goodwood knows nothing about the world, for his pleas recall the former beliefs of Isabel, who at this point has so matured through her contact with evil that she can reply, "The world's very small." Goodwood proposes an enormous temptation, as only now does Isabel realize the worth of the happiness that Goodwood offers: "She had wanted help, and here was help; it had come in a rushing torrent." Isabel's renunciation of escape from Osmond and of happiness with Goodwood is a triumph of her (and James's) idealism; it avows the supreme dignity of the human being. James does nothing to minimize the suffering with which Isabel must spend the rest of her life, but he suggests that the acquired wisdom, the expansion of consciousness, represents a development far higher not only than her life in America but higher than her life with Warburton or Goodwood would have been. When Isabel partakes of the Tree of Knowledge in the world of experience she is made forcefully aware of the presence of evil, but in a sense her earlier ambitions are fulfilled. She was perhaps correct in pursuing her ideals, in accepting nothing but the fullest experiences that life can offer.

From the beginning Isabel vaguely realizes that her restlessness for knowledge will not be satisfied until she faces evil. When she tells Ralph, " . . . I don't wish to touch the cup of experience. It's a poisoned drink! I only want to see for myself " (echoing Rowland Mallet), she speaks of impossibilities, and Ralph spots the flaw in her wish: "You want to see, but not to feel." But for the most part Isabel's quest is far from superficial; she tells Warburton after rejecting his proposal, "I can't escape unhappiness. . . . In marrying you I shall be trying to." Here Isabel knows unhappiness only abstractly, but she realizes that she must experience it to fulfill her mission. On several occasions she asks Ralph to show her the ghost of Gardencourt. Ralph's reply to her first request is significant:

> Ralph shook his head sadly. "I might show it to you, but you'd never see it. The privilege isn't given to every one; it's not enviable. It has never been seen by a young, happy, innocent person like you. You must have suffered first, have suffered greatly, have gained some miserable knowledge. In that way your eyes are opened to it. I saw it long ago," said Ralph.
>
> "I told you just now I'm very fond of knowledge," Isabel answered.
>
> "Yes, of happy knowledge—of pleasant knowledge. But you haven't suffered, and you're not

made to suffer. I hope you'll never see the
ghost."

This is light banter, but it serves to point up a serious
shortcoming in Isabel: she wants a total knowledge, including a knowledge of evil, but cannot recognize that an
association with evil will require her to compromise her
enormous goals.

Knowledge, especially a knowledge of evil, proves to be
a recompense for sorrow. The Fall of Man is basically (i.e.,
morally) fortunate because through experience Isabel
loses the characteristics of her innocence which caused her
to be ignorant and proud, to believe that she could exercise
an unlimited freedom in the world. Through experience
she is enabled to realize the finer qualities of her innocence—a sense of decency, a generosity of spirit, a capacity to give—and she has learned the great lesson that one
should neither renounce his ideals nor make life conform
to them, that the ultimate achievement in life is the preservation of the integrity of the human character. For, after
all, Isabel is the winner in the end; by accepting Goodwood's offer she would in effect be rejecting her freedom,
her belief in the value of her own decision.

In spite of the European setting, *The Portrait of a Lady*
is mainly about America. James takes a gallery of American types, removes them from the limited American environment, in which they have no opportunity to change,
and places them in Europe, where they are free to indulge
in the fine art of living and susceptible to experience that
tests their moral stability. Caspar Goodwood and Henrietta Stackpole are closed from experience by their protective
Americanism; both distrust Europe and refuse to recognize its advantages over America. Ralph Touchett and
Mr. Touchett are more sensitive; yet they neither assimilate European values nor reject them, for they are destined
to inactivity, Ralph by his illness and his father by his
business and his age. Edward Rosier, the thwarted lover
of Pansy, is of little importance in himself as his function
is mainly technical. Generally, however, his response to
Europe is limited to an appreciation of its art. The other
expatriates, except Isabel, repudiate America entirely and
fully accept European standards of conduct. Mrs. Touchett, Gilbert Osmond, Mme. Merle, and the Countess
Gemini are outstanding examples of the thoroughly Europeanized American.

Mrs. Touchett is neither good nor evil. Yet she represents
negatively the defects of Europe and its injurious effects
on the American. She is in many ways like the American
women who persecute Daisy Miller; she resembles Osmond and Mme. Merle in her total devotion to forms and
convention. But with Mrs. Touchett—and unlike Mme.
Merle and Osmond—the polished surface does not disguise an inner evil. Rather it covers a kind of emptiness,
an emotional vacuum. At the deaths of her husband and
her son, she is repellingly unfeeling. After Ralph's death
she "appeared to be absorbed in considering, without enthusiasm but with perfect lucidity, the new conveniences
of her own situation." Mrs. Touchett's cool rationality
leads Isabel to wonder if her aunt "were not even missing
those enrichments of consciousness and privately trying—
reaching out for some aftertaste of life, dregs of the ban-

quet; the testimony of pain or the cold recreation of remorse." James's Americans are most often heart characters: they readily respond to intuitions and feelings. But
in *The Portrait of a Lady* Mrs. Touchett and the other
long-time expatriates are almost completely head characters. It is as if their excessive devotion to manners has
dried up all feeling.

Also Mrs. Touchett is a rover. She is rootless and unattached, aloof from her son and husband and devoted to
travelling. She is a seeker of culture and manners who is
content to remain on the surface of life. Though her ideal
is more realistic than Isabel's—she seeks the attainable—it
is also more superficial and less valuable, for Isabel, to
misuse Henrietta Stackpole's phrase, is interested in "the
inner life," a knowledge of more than forms.

The combined characteristics of formalism, rootlessness,
and rationalism are most evident in Mme. Merle and Osmond. These two, however, are incontestably evil. Their
capacity for evil is partly explained by their nationality.
The American is capable of a greater malignity than the
European because of his freedom. Furthermore, as F. W.
Dupee observes [see Further Reading], the Americans are
all self-seekers, aggressive in their plunder of Europe. The
Europeans—characters like Richard de Mauves and Ur-
bain de Bellegarde—are conservatives who resort to evil
to preserve their old values and possessions. More often
than not, their sins are sins of exclusion; they betray not
in an effort to gain, but in a refusal to give.

The significant difference between Isabel and Osmond is
that when Isabel realizes that her demands on life are ex-
orbitant she withdraws; Isabel learns through experience
that unrestrained acquisitiveness—emotional, intellectual,
or material—is inconsistent with her high moral code, as
she learns that her duty is to give rather than to receive.
Osmond, on the other hand, employs his refined awareness of the complexities of life to further his selfseeking
ends. To put it somewhat differently, Isabel's knowledge
of the world is complemented by self-knowledge, so that
her ultimate awareness is one of moral as well as social
truth, whereas Osmond's is solely of social truth.

Osmond and Isabel also differ in their ways of knowing.
Isabel responds to experience emotionally and spontaneously, eventually replacing all her dangerous abstract beliefs about freedom, experience, and happiness by a kind
of pragmatic insight, an experiential grasp of what is real
and of what is right. "I've only one ambition," Isabel says,
"to be free to follow out a good feeling." In complete contrast, Osmond lives in a world governed by impersonal
ideas. Osmond's manner derives from his conception of
what it should be; it accords with a social rather than a
personal ideal. His conduct is from beginning to end totally calculated, from his initial project to ensnare Isabel to
his posture when he forbids Isabel to visit the dying Ralph.
Negatively Osmond's coldly intelligent manner—similar
to that of the Hawthorne villain, especially Chillingworth
and Rappacini—is revealed in the absence of love and
sympathy in his dealings with those who are most intimate
with him: with Isabel, whom he marries for money; with
his daughter, whose love for Edward Rosier he suppresses;
with his one-time mistress, Mme. Merle, whom he uses as

a piece of machinery to better his position. Positively, Osmond's narrow but keen intellect is revealed in his shrewd operations to gain Isabel's favor. There is a special horror in his calculated abuse of Isabel's feelings; Osmond knows emotions only abstractly, but he knows them well. Stephen Spender has noted that in *The American* evil is "Elizabethan in its mechanism"; and in *The Portrait of a Lady* Osmond suggests Iago. His conquest of Isabel is intrigue in its purest form. Like Iago Osmond sets a series of traps and carefully plans his approach. After Osmond and Mme. Merle prearrange the marriage behind Isabel's back, each works separately to carry out the plan. The strategy is brilliant: Mme. Merle advises Isabel that the Countess Gemini is a habitual liar, thus nullifying the Countess' own strength, for the latter knows of the previous liaison between Mme. Merle and Osmond, and Mme. Merle fears that she may tell Isabel; Osmond arranges for Isabel to visit Pansy in Florence, well knowing that his daughter's innocent charm will captivate Isabel and influence her towards him. Isabel is completely fooled. Rarely in James—Maggie Verver is possibly the only exception—is there a complete balance between the head and the heart. The good are duped by the worldly-wise, who in turn lack the instinctive charity of the good. When one combines these virtues—as does Ralph Touchett—he is compelled to remain outside the story as a kind of chorus.

Gilbert Osmond's formalism is a paradoxical kind of egotism. More than anyone else in the book he stands for the impersonal values of tradition, convention, and society. Isabel Archer, for all her self-esteem, is no match for Osmond as an egotist. In his devotion to convention he has a hostility to freedom; his byword is exclusion. He marries Isabel not just to get her money, but to bend her spirit, to possess her heart and mind. "The real offence, as she ultimately perceived, was her having a mind of her own at all. Her mind was to be his—attached to his own like a small garden-plot to a deer-park." Not only is Osmond repelled by Isabel's independence, but he wishes to subjugate her as he has subjugated himself to convention. Osmond wishes to possess art, tradition, and manners: for him they are not attributes of a meaningful and well regulated society but matters to be appropriated exclusively as his own. His interest in art is especially perverse, for, unlike Edward Rosier, also a collector, who sells his valuable possessions out of love for Pansy, Osmond collects treasures for the sake of owning them and making it impossible for others to own them. As Joseph J. Firebaugh observes, "Isabel comes to realize that he values beauty, not as a mode of knowledge of human life, but as a symbol of traditional power and inherited wealth" ["The Relativism of Henry James" in *Journal of Aesthetics and Art Criticism* (1953)]. He has made an unnatural distinction between aesthetic values and human values: "He's the incarnation of taste," Ralph Touchett observes. "He judges and measures, approves and condemns, altogether by that." Just as Osmond's conduct and speech are perfect representations of traditional manners, his physical presence is hardly distinguishable from the works of art that surround him. When he accuses Isabel of treachery as she asks his permission to visit Ralph at his deathbed, Osmond is characteristically engaged in copying an antique coin.

But for all of Osmond's veneer, he is ultimately revealed as common. The gravity of his evil is obvious from its contagious effects on Isabel and Pansy, and even on Mme. Merle and Edward Rosier. Its grossness is also apparent, however, in his brutal control of Isabel. When he drops the veil of cultivation and speaks from his nature, the superficiality of his refinement becomes clear. Towards the end of the book, when Isabel learns the full truth, she finds that beneath Osmond's sophistication is the sordidness of an adulterous connection with Mme. Merle and that Osmond's supposed superiority to normal human desires is a fiction: "She found herself confronted . . . with the conviction that the man in the world whom she had supposed to be the least sordid had married her, like a vulgar adventurer, for her money." Contrasted with the elegance of Osmond and Mme. Merle, the Countess Gemini's exposure of them gains added force, for beneath the glamorous surface we find only the coarsest of animal impulses. Osmond insults Isabel in their final meeting with particular crudity; also he ridicules Caspar Goodwood in an act of gratuitous malice. At the end there is little doubt that Osmond's celebrated superiority is meretricious.

The Countess Gemini and Mme. Merle are also mainly characters of surface. "The Countess seemed [to Isabel] to have no soul; she was like a bright rare shell, with a polished surface and a remarkably pink lip, in which something would rattle when you shook it." The Countess represents an extreme decadence, the result of a lifetime of sterile existence in a corrupt society. She is neither good nor evil; she resides in the background of the story, aware of the sins of the past but incapable of redeeming the present. She does not tell Isabel the truth about Osmond and Mme. Merle until it can only make Isabel's pain even greater.

Mme. Merle resembles the Countess in her hollowness. As with Mrs. Touchett, "Emotion . . . had become with [Mme. Merle] rather historic; she made no secret of the fact that the fount of passion, thanks to having been rather violently tapped at one period, didn't flow quite so freely as of yore." Later she makes it clear that the source of her coldness is Osmond: "You've not only dried up my tears; you've dried up my soul," she tells him. Aside from Osmond's responsibility for her corruption, other factors tend to modify her evil. For she is at least partly motivated in her deception of Isabel by a regard for her daughter, Pansy: she knows not only that Isabel's money will enable Pansy to marry well, but also that Isabel's influence will counterweight Osmond's. Mme. Merle has nothing to gain from her part in the intrigue. Most important, she is finally, like Lady Macbeth, overcome with guilt. In her final scene with Osmond, she alone accepts guilt and renounces any further implication in their mutual crime. "I don't know how we're to end. I wish I did! How do bad people end?—especially as to their *common* crimes. You have made me as bad as yourself." Mme. Merle ends by going to America to accept a kind of penance, an atonement for the evil of the past. Nonetheless, Mme. Merle is a creature of free will; no extenuating circumstances can lessen her guilt. Her perception of her own baseness indicates not that she is saved, but that she is damned—and that she knows it.

As Osmond lives for art, Mme. Merle lives for society. "She's the great round world itself !" She lives "exclusively for the world." A creature of brilliant surface, she has achieved a state of social completeness. Ralph Touchett says that Mme. Merle "pushes the search for perfection too far—that her merits are in themselves overstrained. She's too good, too kind, too clever, too learned, too accomplished, too everything. She's too complete, in a word." Isabel's analysis of her friend is also acute:

> If for Isabel she had a fault it was that she was not natural; . . . her nature had been too much overlaid by custom and her angles too much rubbed away. She had become too flexible, too useful, was too ripe and too final. She was in a word too perfectly the social animal that man and woman are supposed to have been intended to be; and she had rid herself of every remnant of that tonic wildness which we may assume to have belonged even to the most amiable persons in the ages before countryhouse life was the fashion. Isabel found it difficult to think of her in any detachment or privacy, she existed only in her relations, direct or indirect, with her fellow mortals.

Mme. Merle has the same distrust of personal resources that Osmond has; she is a slave to propriety. In a crucial passage Mme. Merle remarks to Isabel that no one is important in himself but in "the whole envelope of circumstances. There's no such thing as an isolated man or woman; we're each of us made up of some cluster of appurtenances." In Mme. Merle's belief that man is entirely a social animal, she is sharply contrasted to Isabel, who modifies but never rejects her belief in the supreme value of personal resources: "Nothing that belongs to me is any measure of me; everything's on the contrary a limit, a barrier, and a perfectly arbitrary one." Like Emerson and Thoreau before him, James holds that evil consists in adopting the world's values before one's own. For Mme. Merle's devotion to the ways of the world necessarily involves her repudiation of the moral sense, which transcends convention and external systems. The James character must find his salvation by retaining and exercising his natural moral faculty in an environment which emphasizes the unnatural social values. Obviously Mme. Merle and Gilbert Osmond have sacrificed their richest American trait in order to participate in the ambiguous glory of Europe. (pp. 44-55)

> *J. A. Ward, in his* The Imagination of Disaster: Evil in the Fiction of Henry James, *University of Nebraska Press, 1961, 185 p.*

R. P. Blackmur   (essay date 1961)

[*Blackmur was a leading American literary critic of the twentieth century. His early essays on the poetry of such contemporaries as T. S. Eliot, W. B. Yeats, Wallace Stevens, and Ezra Pound were immediately recognized for their acute and exacting attention to diction, metaphor, and symbol. Consequently, he was linked to the New Critics, who believed that a literary work constituted an independent object to be closely analyzed for its strictly formal devices and internal meanings. Blackmur distin-*

guished himself from this group of critics, however, by broadening his analyses through discussions which explored a given work's relevance to society. Inspired by the moral thought of the American autobiographer Henry Adams, Blackmur conceived the critic's role as that of a crucial intermediary between artist and reader, for the dual purpose of offering literary insight as well as social commentary on the age. His belief that criticism also represented an art form in its own right led him to an increasingly poetic, impressionistic style best demonstrated in his posthumously published lecture series Anni Mirabiles 1921-25: Reason in the Madness of Letters *(1967). In the following excerpt, he explores the ways in which financial security is both liberating and destructive for Isabel Archer.*]

[*The Portrait of a Lady*] is the first of Henry James's books to sound with the ring of greatness, and in these remarks I intend to comment on some of the elements that let it ring. But first we had better put compactly what the novel is about. Isabel Archer is given the chance to do what she can with her life, thanks to her uncle's surprising bequest of some seventy thousand pounds. Everybody tampers with Isabel, and it is hard to say whether her cousin Ralph Touchett, who had arranged the bequest, or the Prince, Gilbert Osmond, who marries her because of it, tampers the more deeply. At any rate, the whole novel shows how people tamper with one another because of motives that pass like money between them. The story of the book is the story of Isabel's increasing awareness of the meaning of the relations between herself and her husband, her husband's ex-mistress Madame Merle, and the young girl Pansy Osmond (who passes as the child of the first Mrs. Osmond but is really Gilbert's daughter by Madame Merle). The money is at the center of these relations. But, surrounding these, there are also Isabel's relations with her three rejected lovers, Caspar Goodwood, Lord Warburton, and Ralph Touchett. Ralph dies, Warburton marries elsewhere; Goodwood, the ever returning signal, she finally understands, though she still rejects him, as the signal of love itself. Minor persons—Henrietta Stackpole, the Countess Gemini, and young Rosier—illuminate but are not part of either set of relations, or of the devastations in which those relations result (and in which, while we read the novel, we seem to live).

That we do not live by novels is plain enough. Novels, rather, are sometimes ways of looking at failures and successes—mainly failures—in human relations. Novels do not supply us with morals but they show us with what morals have to do. So it is with *The Portrait of a Lady,* where we see the American Princess, Isabel Archer, brought slowly to recognize as much as she can at the age of twenty-eight of the conditions of life. Then, so far as the novel goes, she disappears into the ruins of ancient Rome, which generalize for us all, and into the particular ruins of her own marriage, which we will generalize for ourselves. What will happen to her haunts us like a memory we cannot quite re-enact. We have seen a bright-brash, conceited young girl whose chief attractive power lay in her money, change into a young woman who is luminous rather than bright, human rather than brash, and whose conceit has turned to a suicidal obstinacy. She still has her money but, if we can consent to an exchange of this order, she is now worth her money. We have seen her act with her money as an instrument of destruction, and there is now the forward edge of a vision of money as an instrument of freedom. This is the latent question about money—and about morals, too—in James's novels: will they be instruments of freedom or of destruction? As Henrietta Stackpole says to Caspar Goodwood at the very end of the book: "Just you wait!"

Miss Stackpole with her button eyes meant whatever one wants her to mean; I should like her to have meant something relating to the quality of human judgment as Isabel comes to acquire and to ignore it. I hear Lord Warburton telling her when she is quite fresh in England, "You judge only from the outside—you don't care . . . you only care to amuse yourself"—words which he spoke with a bitterness abrupt and inconsequent in his voice. But I hear more clearly still these words of Madame Merle: "I judge more than I used to," she said to Isabel, "but it seems to me one has earned the right. One can't judge till one's forty; before that we're too eager, too hard, too cruel, and in addition much too ignorant." Madame Merle has more to say, which ends in this way: "I want to see what life makes of you. One thing's certain—it can't spoil you. It may pull you about horribly, but I defy it to break you up."

Madame Merle's own life, whatever the quality of her judgment, had not done so well by her. Her condition is such that she wishes to weep, to howl like a wolf, and she feels the pressure, in the company of Osmond, of "their *common* crimes." As she tells him, "You have made me as bad as yourself." But Madame Merle was false, and Isabel is given as by and large likely to be true. Madame Merle was enslaved by passions she no longer felt; Isabel, in the novel's scheme of things, should be liberated in the passion that as the book ends she has begun to feel, but which she must flee either in acceptance or renunciation—or in some peculiar state where the one doubles for the other: a shifting state, somehow not evasion, in which the sensibilities of James's heroes and heroines so often transpire. It is as well that we shall never know how Isabel might come to join her sensibility both in judgment and action. Literature is perhaps not capable of making such answers, except in the form of promises. Rather it brings us only to the threshold of discovery.

We are brought by pedagogy, by education, by training. We see Isabel change, and we see what Isabel sees as she changes and also something of what she cannot or will not or is not yet ready to see—and especially the things she has succeeded in not knowing. That is what pedagogy, education, training are like in the novel. It is for the reader to see under these heads what the heroine experienced in different degrees of aptness and response. (If experience were learned like the alphabet or the integers there would be no novels and life would be over very quickly; we should be thankful in both cases that we are such slow students. Just the same the alphabet and the integers are first helps.) In short, the novelist is offering her heroine the education suitable for her role.

The American Princess, whether Isabel Archer or another, always comes to us as innocent as possible, as innocent as the victim who reigns—yet, precisely because of that in-nocence, predatory to the fingernails upon all who come within her reach. She has, to begin with, only what she inherits. Doubtless she has been somewhere to school but she has never received any training for her job. In this respect she is not unlike another and once better known American production, nature's nobleman. But what will do quite well for one of nature's noblemen will not do at all for an American princess. The heiress to all the ages (James's own phrase) should at least know something about the age she lives in and perhaps what it has in common with the ages she inherits. It is not surprising that James's princesses, getting their training only on the job, come to bad ends, to abdication, death, or deep frustration. Yet the books these princesses inhabit constitute essays in training for active rule. It is a training they do not quite catch up with for themselves, although they often can apply it in looking at others. In Isabel's case, it sometimes seems she ought to have applied to herself the language of her mind in looking at others. Here, for example, is Isabel looking at her rightful lover, Caspar Goodwood, when he descends on her in Italy.

> Caspar Goodwood stood there—stood and received a moment, from head to foot, the bright, dry gaze with which she rather withheld than offered a greeting. Whether his sense of maturity had kept pace with Isabel's we shall perhaps presently ascertain; let me say meanwhile that to her critical glance he showed nothing of the injury of time. Straight, strong and hard, there was nothing in his appearance that spoke positively either of youth or of age; if he had neither innocence nor weakness, so he had no practical philosophy. His jaw showed the same voluntary cast as in earlier days; but a crisis like the present had in it of course something grim. He had the air of a man who had travelled hard; he said nothing at first, as if he had been out of breath. This gave Isabel time to make a reflexion: "Poor fellow, what great things he's capable of, and what a pity he should waste so dreadfully his splendid force! What a pity too that one can't satisfy everybody!"

As it turned out, it was Caspar Goodwood alone of her lovers whom she could neither deal with nor evade, unless by flight; this she was not ready to know, at that moment or when we leave her. For the present she thought she could deal with him merely by again rejecting him on the eve of her marriage to Gilbert Osmond—a marriage and a groom none of her friends approve, except perhaps Madame Merle who had arranged it all. There are moments when the force of marriage—not love but marriage—is greater than the force of the individuals who must endure it. Isabel no doubt thought herself strengthened, when merely bent or deflected, by that force. We know rather better than Isabel and know partly because of one of her own insights into Madame Merle which she had reached at about the time she became engaged. Listening to that lady's long account of herself during their trip to Greece and Egypt, Isabel got the impression they came from different moral and social climes. "She believed then that at bottom she had a different morality. Of course the morality of civilized persons has always much in common; but our young woman had a sense in her of values gone wrong or, as they said in the shops, marked down." Madame Merle was lady-in-waiting to this princess *incognita* (James's phrase) and set up for her a court decadent beyond her understanding and full of things and motives "of which it was not advantageous to hear." We observe that at this point in her education Isabel develops a deliberate deafness, as if deafness were a special form of consciousness, nearly equivalent to what she is learning to hear. I will not say this leaves her more vulnerable, but it certainly leaves her more exposed to fresh assaults she could otherwise have avoided.

Innocence does not act, unless impaired by self-will and self-deceit; that is to say innocence proceeds as a kind of infatuation without an object until it bursts or is punctured. Then, since innocence is irrecoverable, there is, together with the devastation, a necessary accommodation to be made, either a death or a life, an abdication or an assumption—or, as we began by saying, a renunciation or an acceptance. How long Isabel's innocence lasted we do not exactly know. It is present in nearly full force at the end of Chapter XXXV—more than half the length of the novel—when on the suggestion that a little girl, her stepdaughter to be, be asked to leave the room, Isabel responds: "Let her stay, please. . . . I would rather hear nothing that Pansy may not." In the next chapter, three years later in time, the innocence is virtually gone, but its consequences remain mingled with the many-troubled marriage in which we find her. Self-will has been replaced with the effort to achieve a will, and self-deceit has become the deceit of others. The public and the private in her relations have now been reversed. Where so much of her that had been private was now forced into the public, what had been her public ease was now a matter of unremitting private concern. Where previously she had had to bring her life into existence, she had now to conceal the one that had come upon her. She had not only to face a civilized morality where her values were marked down, she had also to act by a morality whose values were not hers at all—as if there were a double morality with different degradations in each. She still expected too much for the one, and she had both the wrong illusions and the wrong disillusions for the other. Nothing was clear except that her husband "spoiled everything for her that he looked at"—an obscure form of intimacy she had certainly not been prepared for. She knew only, and this not too clearly, that without Madame Merle "these things need not have been." If Madame Merle had been the force from behind, little Pansy seemed now to be the only force to draw her on—as if where her own conceited innocence had failed her, the girl could succeed in her obedient naïveté and her naïve inner rebellion against the "base, ignoble world," which yet provided the standards and scope if not the springs of compulsive action.

Isabel's first and partial *éclaircissement* comes when after a walk with Pansy among the delicate winter flowers of the Roman Campagna, she "discovered" her husband and Madame Merle in the drawing-room. "The soundlessness of her step gave her time to take in the scene before she interrupted it. Madame Merle was there in her bonnet, and Gilbert Osmond was talking to her; for a minute they were unaware she had come in. Isabel had often seen that

before, certainly; but what she had not seen, or at least had not noticed, was that their colloquy had for the moment converted itself into a sort of familiar silence, from which she instantly perceived that her entrance would startle them. . . . The thing made an image, lasting only a moment, like a sudden flicker of light. Their relative positions, their absorbed mutual gaze, struck her as something detected. But it was all over by the time she had fairly seen it."

It was all over so far as her consciousness went, but a larger form of it had entered what Freud calls the preconscious, thence to emerge from time to time—as it did that very night when she had lingered to all hours alone in her salon. It was dark in the big room. "But even then she stopped again in the middle of the room and stood there gazing at a remembered vision—that of her husband and Madame Merle unconsciously and familiarly associated." It is not conscious knowledge, or fresh knowledge, but the knowledge one did not know that one knew, or but dimly knew, that bursts upon one, an access of strength; and it bursts from inside where it has been nurtured with every unconscious skill. So it is with Isabel as she develops her judgment of her husband into action. The nurtured knowledge comes clear throughout, as it were, on the pages of fierce and eloquent polemic, those wonderful creative summaries of his character and sensibility, that are reported as a kind of constitution for her thoughts between the apparitions of the image of relations he has with Madame Merle, and into which we the readers can pour our own possibilities of coldness and egotism and greed, of worldly dilettantism without delight, of spiritual caddishness. It is the image that gives the meditations focus, and the meditations that give the image meaning.

What more is James telling us when he puts these sentences into his report of a discussion of Pansy's affairs between Isabel and Madame Merle? "More clearly than ever before Isabel heard a cold, mocking voice proceed from she knew not where, in the dim void that surrounded her, and declare that this bright, strong, definite worldly woman, this incarnation of the practical, the personal, the immediate, was a powerful agent in her destiny." A moment or two later, the *éclaircissement* was complete, except for the history and special treachery of what was illuminated. "She moved quickly indeed, and with reason, for a strange truth was filtering into her soul. Madame Merle's interest was identical with Osmond's: that was enough." The meaning of their history together, and with her, had become plain, though the history itself remained obscure and though it had been affecting her, almost absorbing her, all along.

The discovery that Pansy was daughter to Madame Merle and Osmond joined the history to the meaning. There were all sorts of things, as Osmond's sister Countess Gemini tells her, that Isabel had succeeded in not knowing, but which, as Isabel puts it, had nevertheless *occurred* to her. Now that these things had become available to knowledge as well as to experience, she could complete her judgment of Osmond. She could disobey him, leave him in Rome, and attend her cousin Ralph's death in England; and if she returned to Rome it was with another purpose than she had left it with, and with a new energy, greater in scope and intensity than before, though still with an object not altogether clear. At least she could now play her role if she could find it, and there is no place better than Rome to find a role for a princess without a proper domain. Rome is the city of Annunciation and Incarnation as well as ruins. Some such image awaits *éclaircissement* when we last see Isabel and enter her feelings. If she had renounced, it was for the sake of a later resumption, though it might be that at any given moment she might not know it—as if knowledge, for her, could never be quite *yet!* It is in souls like Isabel's not invented by Henry James but seen by him in anguished clarity, that flight, as I said above, is the first form either of renunciation or acceptance, where the one may be taken as doubling for the other. We last see Isabel on the verge of such a flight—a flight that might have any and every meaning, whatever its subsequent history—a flight from the man whom she had at last known to be her rightful lover.

I will quote nothing of this; it belongs to the reader's own participation. I will quote instead a few fragments from the long, enlivening analogy to the story of Isabel Archer, the continuing image of Rome's ruins which sit, at any moment ready to rise, throughout that city's immediate life. The experience of cities is no longer intimate, and needs reminding. Here is Isabel, treading upon the daisies, which are like American daisies only in being endemic. "She had long before this taken old Rome into her confidence, for in a world of ruins the ruin of her happiness seemed a less unnatural catastrophe. She rested her weariness upon things that had crumbled for centuries, and yet still were upright. . . . She had become deeply, tenderly acquainted with Rome: it interfused and moderated her passion. But she had grown to think of it chiefly as the place where people had suffered." And again, from another page, one sentence about the Coliseum: "The great enclosure was half in shadow; the western sun brought out the pale red tone of the great blocks of travertine—the latent colour that is the only living element in the immense ruin." It is the latent colour of Isabel's vitality we know best as the book ends: a vitality which became, through the money her cousin had gotten for her, an instrument both of freedom and destruction. The money had indeed put wind in her sails, but whether it had made her rich enough to meet the requirements of her imagination is another matter. That there may be no such riches is perhaps what the look in the eyes of this portrait of a lady is saying. (pp. 247-55)

> *R. P. Blackmur, "The Portrait of a Lady," in* Perspectives on James's "The Portrait of a Lady:" A Collection of Critical Essays, *edited by William T. Stafford, New York University Press, 1967, pp. 247-55.*

Dorothea Krook   (essay date 1962)

[*Krook is a Latvian-born Israeli educator, critic, translator, and poet. In the following excerpt, she examines two issues previously unaddressed by critics of* The Portrait of a Lady: *Isabel Archer's fear of sexual passion and her motive for returning to Gilbert Osmond.*]

[Two critical problems arise] from the story of Isabel Archer which [are] . . . important enough to require separate treatment. The first . . . [turns] upon the question, Why does Isabel go back to Osmond?, the second upon James's treatment of the sexual theme in *The Portrait of a Lady.*

(1) WHY DOES ISABEL GO BACK TO OSMOND?

This problem has, I believe, been somewhat artificially created for modern critics by a failure in critical perspective which arises from the disposition to ignore or minimise the context, historical and dramatic, in which Isabel Archer's final decision is made. I have heard it seriously argued that Isabel 'could after all have done something else'—walked out into freedom (like Nora in *A Doll's House,* presumably), or gone in for charitable works (like Dorothea Brooke in *Middlemarch*), or even perhaps taken a degree and become a pioneer in women's education, or whatever. The short answer to these bracing proposals is that Isabel Archer could have done none of these things. Her circumstances, historical, psychological and dramatic—in particular the dramatic—absolutely proscribe any 'end' to her life other than marriage, and any duties, responsibilities or even serious interests other than those belonging to or arising out of that estate. This is part of James's *donnée* in the story; and to intrude other, extrinsic possibilities—or, rather, pseudo-possibilities—is to fall into a vicious abstractionism that is fatal to literary criticism.

This is the failure in critical perspective at its most elementary level. At a less elementary level, it springs from a preconception almost as intrusive and misleading as the other—namely, a disposition to take too emancipated a view of the marriage-bond and the 'naturalness' of divorce. Why did not Isabel divorce Osmond? is now the question; and the answer is that what we are shown of Isabel Archer's nature and of her view of marriage (as distinct from her modern critics') makes it abundantly clear that divorce would be for her the least natural form of deliverance from her predicament. Leaving aside the special motive for going back to Osmond provided by Pansy and Pansy's need of her, which is explicitly emphasised, we are expected to remember that loyalty or 'devotion' was a conspicuous element of Isabel Archer's nature. Gilbert Osmond, we remember, had recognised it from the beginning: 'I like her very much', he had said to Madame Merle, 'She's all you described her, and into the bargain capable, I feel, of great devotion'. In Isabel's midnight vigil we have this confirmed in a particularly decisive (and moving) way when, reflecting on Osmond's hatred of her 'ideas', she calls her soul to witness that 'she had no opinions . . . that she would not have been eager to sacrifice in the satisfaction of feeling herself loved for it'; and this devotion or loyalty may be seen as a function of the moral consistency that springs so naturally, it seems, from her moral seriousness.

Her view of the marriage bond as in the highest degree solemn and serious is closely linked with it. Marriage for her is a complete commitment of one person to another, and as such not to be set aside even from the gravest causes; and though there is, of course, no suggestion of a Christian-theological sanction in the strict sense, it would nevertheless be true to say that Isabel Archer takes a 'sacramental' view of marriage, as a 'sanctified' union which is to be regarded as substantially indissoluble. In the earlier parts of the story, this is implicit in the exalted view she takes of her marriage to Osmond, and her faith in all that this most intimate of bonds can yield for the exercise of virtue as well as for personal happiness; in the later parts, it is several times explicitly mentioned as a prime reason for her reluctance to leave, or even to defy, her husband. Long before the end of the story, when her cousin Ralph Touchett is lying sick in his hotel in Rome, we learn that she is filled with 'shame' and 'dread' at the thought of deliberately flouting Osmond's wishes by going to see him:

> She had not as yet undertaken to act in direct opposition to his wishes; he was her appointed and inscribed master; she gazed at moments with a sort of incredulous blankness at this fact. It weighed upon her imagination, however; constantly present to her mind were all the traditionary decencies and sanctities of marriage. The idea of violating them filled her with shame as well as with dread, for on giving herself away she had lost sight of this contingency in the perfect belief that her husband's intentions were as generous as her own. She seemed to see, none the less, the rapid approach of the day when she should have to take back something she had solemnly bestowed. Such a ceremony would be odious and monstrous; she tried to shut her eyes to it meanwhile.

She cannot indeed for long shut her eyes to it; for the crisis is precipitated soon after this when Osmond virtually forbids her to go to Ralph, now dying at Gardencourt. But though she does in the end defy him and go, she still, we learn, finds the ceremony 'odious' and 'monstrous'. She has gone to her room after the scene with Osmond:

> It seemed to her that only now she fully measured the great undertaking of matrimony. Marriage meant that in such a case as this, when one had to choose, one chose as a matter of course for one's husband. 'I'm afraid—yes, I'm afraid', she said to herself more than once, stopping short in her walk. But what she was afraid of was not her husband—his displeasure, his hatred, his revenge; it was not even her own later judgement of her conduct—a consideration which had often held her in check; it was simply the violence there would be in going when Osmond wished her to remain. A gulf of difference had opened between them, but nevertheless it was his desire that she should stay, it was a horror to him that she should go. She knew the nervous fineness with which he could feel an objection. What he thought of her she knew, what he was capable of saying to her she had felt; yet they were married, for all that, and marriage meant that a woman should cleave to the man with whom, uttering tremendous vows, she had stood at the altar.

Isabel's deepest and most decisive reason, however, for going back to Osmond is to be inferred from those passages in her midnight vigil in which she comes to her painful self-knowledge, in particular the knowledge of the de-

gree in which she herself has been responsible for Osmond's self-deception about her, and the extent therefore to which she has contributed to the failure of their marriage. ('She had made herself small, pretending there was less of her than there really was . . . '; 'Yes, she *had* been hypocritical; she had liked him so much', and so on.) What she comes to feel is that, having this degree of moral responsibility, she must accept the consequences; and this means going back to Osmond and enduring, simply *enduring,* her life with him as the only expiation open to her. She never, of course, puts it to herself so explicitly; but she comes as near as she can to seeing it (and saying it) in a brief passage in her last reflections at Gardencourt, when she recognises once again that 'certain obligations were involved in the very fact of marriage, and were quite independent of the quantity of enjoyment extracted from it'— and then acts on that insight.

The most explicit statement of this final position, however, comes from Osmond himself, in the bitter exchange between them when he forbids her to go to Ralph at Gardencourt; and it is like a last turn of the screw that she should have to take her most compelling reason for continuing in her wretched condition from the man who is its principal cause. The passage, though long, is worth quoting in full because, besides giving us the poignancy of Isabel's situation, it also throws a last vivid light on Osmond's view of it, and shows us how the strange *sincerity* that lurks in his care for appearances has, more than anything, the power to break down Isabel's resistance. Osmond is speaking:

> 'I've never liked him [Ralph] and he has never liked me. That's why you like him—because he hates me,' said Osmond with a quick, barely audible tremor in his voice. 'I've an ideal of what my wife should do and should not do. She should not travel across Europe alone, in defiance of my deepest desire, to sit at the bedside of other men. Your cousin's nothing to you; he's nothing to us. You smile most expressively when I talk about *us,* but I assure you that *we, we,* Mrs Osmond, is all I know. I take our marriage seriously; you appear to have found a way of not doing so. I'm not aware that we're divorced or separated; for me we're indissolubly united. You are nearer to me than any human creature, and I'm nearer to you. It may be a disagreeable proximity; it's one, at any rate, of our own deliberate making. You don't like to be reminded of that, I know; but I'm perfectly willing because—because—' And he paused a moment, looking as if he had something to say which would be very much to the point. 'Because I think we should accept the consequences of our actions, and what I value most in life is the honour of a thing!'

Upon this speech follows the comment:

> He spoke gravely and almost gently; the accent of sarcasm had dropped out of his tone. It had a gravity which checked his wife's quick emotion; the resolution with which she had entered the room found itself caught in a mesh of fine threads. His last words were not a command, they constituted a kind of appeal; and, though she felt that any expression of respect on his part could only be a refinement of egotism, they rep-

resented something transcendent and absolute, like the sign of the cross or the flag of one's country. He spoke in the name of something sacred and precious—the observance of a magnificent form. . . . Isabel had not changed; her old passion for justice still abode within her; and now, in the very thick of her sense of her husband's blasphemous sophistry, it began to throb to a tune which for a moment promised him the victory. It came over her that in his wish to preserve appearances he was after all sincere, and that this, as far as it went, was a merit. Ten minutes before she had felt all the joy of irreflective action—a joy to which she had for so long been a stranger; but action had been suddenly changed to slow renunciation, transformed by the blight of Osmond's touch.

Isabel does go to Ralph, and to that extent does temporarily resist the blight of Osmond's touch. But his words, she presently discovers, have struck a deeper response in her than she knew at the time. What she finds in the end is that though she repudiates his reasons as blasphemous sophistry, the fact he insists on commands her most inward assent; and it is the fact that finally compels her to go back to him in despite of the reasons.

(2) THE SEXUAL THEME

To speak of James's 'treatment' of the sexual theme in *The Portrait of a Lady* would be virtually meaningless, but for the striking episode between Isabel and Caspar Goodwood in the very last pages of the book. Apart from the hint about the 'male' quality in Caspar Goodwood that troubles Isabel from the beginning, there is, or seems to be, until this episode no reference to it either explicit or implicit; and if the sexual theme in *The Portrait of a Lady* were indeed to rest entirely on this episode it would seem hardly worth examining. This, however, is only apparently the case. The last encounter between Isabel and Caspar Goodwood is not only peculiarly significant in itself but also illuminates previous, less conspicuous, episodes bearing on the sexual theme; and by tracing these connexions one can, I believe, arrive at a reasonably complete view of James's treatment of this theme in *The Portrait of a Lady.*

The fact that in this last vivid scene Isabel should again and finally turn down Caspar Goodwood raises by itself no problem. As he kisses her, 'it was extraordinarily as if, while she took it, she felt each thing in his hard manhood that had least pleased her, each aggressive fact of his face, his figure, his presence, justified of its intense identity and made one with this act of possession'; and what this means is that Goodwood will no more 'do' now than he would have 'done' before she married Osmond. For he is still, in a word, too crude; and the fact that Osmond's refinement has turned out to be terrible delusion does not make Goodwood's lack of it any more acceptable. In this I think, we are meant to see a last proof of Isabel's ultimate integrity. Even in her misery and despair at the prospect of resuming her life with Osmond, her judgement in this vital connection remains unimpaired: she knows that she ought not to give herself to Caspar Goodwood now any more than she ought to have given herself to Gilbert Os-

mond then; and this perhaps is part of what she has learnt from her disastrous mistake with Osmond.

What does raise a problem, however, is the kind and quality of the fear that Isabel appears to experience in this climactic episode. This is powerfully evoked by the sea-image (more than sufficiently 'Freudian') which expresses it here. As Goodwood ends his passionate speech, she feels herself 'floating' upon a sea in an ecstasy of incipient surrender:

> The world . . . had never seemed so large; it seemed to open out, all round her, to take the form of a mighty sea, where she floated in fathomless waters. She had wanted help, and here was help; it had come in a rushing torrent . . . She believed just then that to let him take her in his arms would be the next best thing to her dying. This belief, for a moment, was a kind of rapture, in which she felt herself sink and sink. In the movement she seemed to beat with her feet, in order to catch herself, to feel something to rest on.

Then he speaks again, in a voice 'harsh and terrible', and her sensation now is that of sinking: 'The confusion, the noise of waters, all the rest of it were in her . . . swimming head'; and as he kisses her ('His kiss was like white lightning, a flash that spread, and spread again, and stayed') and she is seized with her final revulsion, this is succeeded by a sensation of drowning: 'So she had heard of those wrecked and under water following a train of images before they sink.' The next moment the 'darkness' returns (after the flash of white lightning), and through it she speeds to 'freedom'—away from Caspar Goodwood, back to the house, and ultimately to Rome and Gilbert Osmond.

In a way unusual in James's works, the image here is left to express the whole meaning; there is none of the help so often provided by somebody's analytical comment or interior monologue; and this is significant not because the help is in fact needed but because it suggests on James's part a deliberate intention to leave as open as possible the question of the 'rightness' or 'wrongness' of Isabel's action. She is afraid—that is clear enough; but is she *right* to be afraid? Is she right in particular in view of what she herself has just a moment before recognised, 'that she had never been loved before'? This sensation, too, is conveyed by an image as violent as the white-lightning image of the kiss. Goodwood has ended his first speech with the question, 'Why should you go back—why should you go through that ghastly form?'; to which she answers,

> 'To get away from *you!*' . . . But this expressed only a little of what she felt. The rest was that she had never been loved before. She had believed it, but this was different; this was the hot wind of the desert, at the approach of which the others dropped dead, like mere sweet airs of the garden. It wrapped her about; it lifted her off her feet, while the very taste of it, as of something potent, acrid and strange, forced open her set teeth.

So Isabel Archer knows she is being for the first time 'loved'; yet she resists it fiercely (it 'forced open her set teeth'), and finally flees from the love, the lover, indeed from the knowledge itself. What frightens and repels her is plain enough. It is the sheer violence of it—'the hot wind of the desert'; and this fear and distaste in Isabel of the element of violence in the passion of love has (we now remember) already shown itself before this. There is, for instance, a significant passage in the early scene of Lord Warburton's proposal in the garden at Gardencourt, to which we are sent back by the reference here to the 'mere sweet airs of the garden' which drop dead before the 'hot wind of the desert.' Warburton has told her he is 'a very judicious animal' and does not 'go off easily', but when he does it's for life:

> 'It's for life, Miss Archer, it's for life', Lord Warburton repeated in the kindest, tenderest, pleasantest voice Isabel had ever heard, and looking at her with eyes *charged with the light of a passion that had sifted itself clear of the baser parts of emotion—the heat, the violence, the unreason—and that burned as steadily as a lamp in a windless place.* [italics mine]

Again, in an earlier passage, when Isabel dismisses Lord Warburton with seeming coldness, we are told explicitly that 'her coldness was not the calculation of her effect. It came from a certain fear'; and when, much later, she has a strenuous encounter with Caspar Goodwood in Florence and bursts into tears 'five minutes after he had gone', the main reason for the tears is again, we may suppose, 'a certain fear'.

If from these episodes we may legitimately infer that Isabel Archer has a fear of sexual passion, particularly in its more 'violent' aspect, two questions arise: first, to what extent is this fear 'culpable' in Isabel; second, how conscious was James himself of its presence in his portrait of his engaging young woman, and if he was conscious of it, what view did he mean us to take of it?

That a young woman of Isabel Archer's sensibilities should, in that time and place in particular, feel a fear of the sexual need cause no surprise. Its mystery and terror is something that not only the young and immature experience; and only the most doctrinaire of modern theorists would want to dispute the naturalness of the fear, and to that extent also its 'rightness', in someone like Isabel. This, however, seems not to be the whole explanation. The rest has to do with what we feel in Isabel as a tendency to *withdraw*—a tendency to withold herself, to refuse to surrender herself to the relationship as a whole and *a fortiori* to its sexual demands. She herself appears to recognise this, or something like it, when she asks herself at the end of one of her agitating encounters with Lord Warburton 'if she were not a cold, hard, priggish person' to find herself so unable to accept a man of such splendid parts; and the question for us is whether this seeming coldness and hardness are due to what would nowadays be called sexual frigidity, or, if they are not due to this, what their cause in fact is.

I believe it has nothing to do with frigidity, either in intention or effect, and has everything to do with that aspect of Isabel's nature . . . which James himself saw as the centre of interest in his engaging young woman. When a young woman is so constituted as to have, besides an enquiring mind and an independent spirit, an unquenchable passion for knowledge derived from direct, first-hand experience, the most serious threat to such aspirations, especially in an earlier age than the present, is that constituted by marriage and the completeness of the surrender it involves—for someone at any rate who, like Isabel Archer, takes this absolute view of the marriage bond. With the 'right person,' as we say, there is of course no problem; and Isabel, we saw, joyfully embraced the opportunity to surrender herself to the right person when she thought she had found him in Gilbert Osmond. But the right person, never to be had for the wanting, was particularly not to be had for the wanting in the circle to which Isabel Archer's life was confined; her story amply confirms this—indeed is intended to exhibit this among other unalterable facts of her condition; and so long as there *is* a doubt that the person in question (Lord Warburton, Caspar Goodwood) is 'right', a young woman like Isabel Archer cannot be careful enough. The seeming coldness and hardness are accordingly to be seen as self-protective indeed; but the end for which the self is being protected is (James wishes us to see) in the highest degree noble and worthwhile, and as such invites not censure but compassion for the means—the 'coldness' and the 'hardness', and the fear from which they spring—to which Isabel must have recourse in order to safeguard that precious end.

This, I believe, is James's principal intention in emphasising his heroine's 'fear' at certain crucial moments in the story; and it is again characteristic of James's mastery of the psychological and dramatic verisimilitudes of these moments that Isabel herself should in each instance appear puzzled and confused about its meaning, and disposed therefore to put the least creditable interpretation on her own reactions. The problem that remains turns upon Isabel's revulsion from the 'violence' of the sexual passion itself, which is so clearly apparent in the final episode with Caspar Goodwood but (I suggested) is hinted at before. On the explanation I have proposed of Isabel's fear in general, it would presumably be justified on the ground that it is intrinsically incompatible with all that is *civilised* in the ideal that Isabel aspires to realise in her life. In that case, it would seem that the element of violence in sexual passion is being equated with the uncivilised or anti-civilised; and in the passages cited this indeed appears to be Isabel's attitude. In so far as it is only Isabel's attitude, there can of course be no quarrel with it. But in so far as it may also be James's own attitude, it is a cause if not for quarrel at least for further enquiry. For (as James himself is to show in some of the most important of his later works) the 'violent' element—the importunate, the wanting and desiring, jealous and possessive element—in sexual passion, so far from being incompatible with the perfection of civilised virtue, is in fact (as James is to show in *The Golden Bowl* in particular) the necessary condition of this, as of all, virtue; and the question is whether James when he wrote *The Portrait of a Lady* knew what he later came to know, or whether he knew at this time as little as his heroine and consequently identified himself with her on this vital matter.

The internal evidences of the text suggest that the latter

was the case—that James shared his heroine's fear of, and even revulsion from, the sexual passion in its more violent, importunate forms, and for reasons *mutatis mutandis* essentially similar to hers. He, too, at this stage of his life felt it as a threat to the two things, one 'public', the other 'private' or personal, that were most precious to him—his ideal of civilisation on the one side, his aspiration to dedicate his life to the practice of his art on the other. Both ends, it would have seemed to him, were better—that is, more safely—served by a passion that (in Isabel's phrase) 'had sifted itself clear of the baser parts of emotion—the heat, the violence, the unreason—and that burned as steadily as a lamp in a windless place'; and both (so again it would have seemed to him) were in mortal danger when exposed to 'the hot wind of the desert' which Isabel experiences in the last scene of the book.

The *prima facie* reasonableness of this view is obvious, and has in any case been argued fully and eloquently enough by James himself in the group of stories—**"The Lesson of the Master"** and the rest—dealing with the life of the artist and the insoluble problems created for him by the involvements of marriage. (The sexual theme as such, it is true, is not mentioned in these stories; but readers of the story **"John Delavoy"** will have no difficulty in discerning the reason for this.) What is interesting to the student of Henry James's development as man and artist is that he came in time to change his view. His life's experience, it seems, contrived to teach him what he appears not to have known at the time he wrote *The Portrait of a Lady*—that passion, with all its dangers, is the sacred fount of all creative endeavour, and that to deny or sacrifice it in the name of any ideal, however noble, is a delusion which succeeds only in defeating the noble end for which the denial or sacrifice was made. **"The Beast in the Jungle"** is, I believe, Henry James's most poignant testimony to this hardest, most painful lesson of his life; and having learnt it, he characteristically redeems his tragic error in the most important works of his late period—*The Sacred Fount* to begin with, followed by *The Ambassadors, The Wings of the Dove* and *The Golden Bowl*—in which the power of sexual passion to redeem (as well as destroy) is exhibited with a fullness of knowledge to be found nowhere else in the English novel. (pp. 357-69)

> *Dorothea Krook, in her* The Ordeal of Consciousness in Henry James, *Cambridge at the University Press, 1962, 422 p.*

Maxwell Geismar   (essay date 1963)

[*Geismar is one of America's most prominent historical and social critics. Though he often openly confessed that literature is more than historical documentation, Geismar's own critical method suggests that social patterns and the weight of history, more than any other phenomenon, affect the shape and content of all art. Geismar's major enterprise—a multi-volume history of the American novel from 1860 to 1940—clearly demonstrates his fascination with the impact of external forces on literature. His praise of such writers as Ernest Hemingway, John Dos Passos, and John Steinbeck, and his criticism of others, such as Henry James and the post-World War II writers, depends almost exclusively on how these artists were affected by and responded to the conditions in their particular societies. Many of Geismar's contemporaries, and many scholars today, have criticized his inability to see art as anything beyond social documentation. In the following excerpt, he finds* The Portrait of a Lady *to be melodramatic and inadequate as a literary representation of the social milieu in which it is set.*]

Rather like *The American,* the opening of [*The Portrait of a Lady*] was that of leisurely, old-fashioned social comedy; the tone was warm, genial, entertaining. Again there were the overtones of great wealth, high culture, and "old world" sensitivity in the exchange of pleasantries between Lord Warburton and the Touchetts, and when the charming young American girl first encounters the vista of the lawn, the great trees, the silvery Thames, the old house, the British dogs. In one sense the *Portrait of a Lady* was an engaging domestic drama of the international scene; on this level it summarized and capped all of the early James's romantic visions of "the dream of Europe." We first see the eccentric Mrs. Touchett, who has brought Isabel Archer to England, when she is completely dressed for dinner and embracing her son with her gloved hands.

If the mother image in *Washington Square* was that of a beautiful and dead woman, the psychological cause of her daughter's ruin, the Mrs. Touchett of the *Portrait* is also separated, by her choice of an Italian residence, from her British-American family. Isabel herself, with her innocence and cleverness, her "irregular education," her strong will and high temper; her determination to learn about life and not to be bored, is a superior evocation of the series of young American girls who are the products of wealth and the victims of Europe. Is she a limited medium of literary consciousness, a rather thin and cool and "intellectual" figure as a heroine and a woman? But this whole line of early Jamesian heroines, these young American girls who were in reality rich, spoiled, untutored products of the new American fortunes, were romanticized and idealized by a writer whose own charm of craft carried along these rather dubious vehicles. Similarly Lord Warburton is a curious type of nobleman of the newest pattern, "a reformer, a radical, a contemner of ancient ways." He has a hundred thousand (pounds) a year, and owns fifty thousand acres. He has half a dozen houses to live in, a seat in Parliament, elegant taste in literature, art, science and in charming young ladies. But "the victim of a critical age," he is James's concept of a royal revolutionist.

"I should delight in seeing a revolution," says Isabel Archer herself. But in such a case, she adds, "I think I should be a high, proud loyalist. One sympathizes more with them, and they've a chance to behave so exquisitely. I mean so picturesquely." Yes, the England of the 1870's was in the throes of a social crisis produced by the injustices of the industrial revolution. But again the early James notion of "history," very much like his heroine's, was concerned not so much with principles as with the pictorial. "If I were he," says Isabel to the nobleman's two sisters, the Misses Molyneux, "I should wish to fight to the death: I mean for the heritage of the past . . . I should hold it tight." Yet Warburton was acceptable to James as an upper-class radical, at least, or as the symbol of one rather than the fact. The only valid social criticism, or social commentary, in *The Portrait of a Lady* is in the portrait of Henrietta Stackpole, the brassy American lady journalist who snoops around the British aristocracy for the benefit of the democratic "free press." She is an amusing caricature at times; she does indeed "smell of the Future—it almost knocks one down!" as James said. But Howells, before James, and Edith Wharton after him were equally sharp on the yellow journalism of the period.

The sensitive and sick Ralph Touchett is the familiar Jamesian observer in the novel. The spiritual guardian of Isabel, and then her material benefactor, he is really the other half, the conscious half of Isabel, or of a central protagonist in the *Portrait* which is feminine in essence. (Ralph's family name is a cross between "touching," which he is, and one who hardly dares to touch; while the large share of the family fortune which he gives to Isabel as a token of his affection is in the best vein of Jamesian romance about the world of the inheritors.) James had actually divided up his own sensibilities between these two central figures, as in *Roderick Hudson;* while the arrival of Caspar Goodwood in the novel points up the emotional deficiency in Lord Warburton himself. "She liked him too much to marry him, that was the truth," Isabel reflects about the British lord, but he was indeed a *personage.* "She had never yet known a personage; there had been no personages . . . in her life; there were probably none at all in her native land."

Thus *The Portrait of a Lady* was a compendium of early James prejudices, and Caspar himself is a rude, aggressive symbol of "New World vitality." But there are other elements here—his mere arrival "made the air sultry" around Isabel, and she is terrified of him, as she admits. "There was a disagreeably strong push, a kind of hardness of presence, in his way of rising before her . . . Caspar Goodwood expressed for her an energy—and she had already felt it as a power—that was of his very nature." He is the only symbol of biological or sexual energy in the novel; this post-Civil War American industrialist is a kind of early D. H. Lawrence character. "But it was as if something large and confused, something dark and ugly, would have to call upon him: he was not after all in harmony with mere smug peace and greed and gain . . . " And Isabel, drawn to him physically, has to get rid of him. "Yes, you don't at all delight me, you don't fit in, not in any way, just now." "One would think you were going to commit some atrocity!" says Caspar in return, directly before the entrance of Mme. Merle. And he is right. This is an effective climax in the early part of the *Portrait;* even though one notices that James has divided off the qualities of love, for Isabel, between two equally impossible suitors.

Mme. Merle is the old-world magician, as her name indicates, whom Isabel has been asking to initiate her into the "mystery of life," and who leads her into her fatal entrapment. Here again James used a "false," or at least a highly melodramatic plot to carry forward the action in the last half of the novel; and yet, on such an improbable base, the last half is perhaps the best part of the novel. What is remarkable is the virtuosity of James's craft which could carry forward such a thin, pure heroine—empty of all real

knowledge or real experience—and such a limited view of life, based on such peculiar propositions, even to this point. It is Mme. Merle who sets Gilbert Osmond after Isabel's fortune for the sake of little Pansy, the child of a previous affair between these two former lovers. (These two lovers, who know each other so well, have no love left, apparently; no affection, no memories, except a cold understanding of material gain.) Yes, melodrama, plus an Italian travelogue, constitute the real medium of the second half of *The Portrait of a Lady,* which is also in a sense a completely different, or a second novel.

Osmond himself, with his old curtains and crucifixes; with his bibelots, his pictures, his medallions and tapestries, and his dependence on "beauty" as the secret of existence, is the portrait of a pure esthete; a "collector." "He had consulted his taste in everything—his taste alone, perhaps, as a sick man consciously incurable consults at last only his lawyer," James wrote, and he was projecting another facet of his own temperament. "I had no prospects, I was poor . . . I had no talents even; I was simply the most fastidious young gentleman living," Osmond tells Isabel. Yet he and Mme. Merle liven up this cold-blooded and unbelievable plot to entrap the American heiress; these two, and the "Fayaway" young Pansy, and the Countess Gemini herself. This highly compromised character, as James said, by no means a blank sheet, but one that had been written over "in a variety of hands," and who exhibited "the mere floating fragments of a wrecked renown," is another message of warning to poor blind Isabel.

What Isabel is seeking from Osmond is the life of experience; what she gets from their marriage is the cold life of cultivation. This mistress of rejection arrives only at an apex of renunciation. And now James piled twist on twist of narrative complication to sustain the climax of *The Portrait of a Lady.* Ralph is slowly dying, just living long enough, as he says, for his "curiosity" to glean the conclusion of Isabel's tragic marriage—an odd motive for survival. Lord Warburton, now the "famous radical" of the London *Times* at least, re-enters Isabel's life as a potential suitor for Pansy's hand, this foster-daughter of the foster-mother whom he still loves. How fond James is of these deliberately contrived and ambiguous human relations! Notice the ingenious "domestic" and love relationships that prevail at large in the novel. Pansy's true mother, Mme. Merle, marries off her former lover for the sake of her daughter. Isabel's own child dies shortly after her marriage, while she devotes herself to Osmond's (and Mme. Merle's) child, whom the father scorns. Warburton returns as the father-lover of Pansy, while he still desires the lost wife-mother figure of Isabel. The touching relation of Isabel and Ralph becomes that of brother and sister, but of an "adopted" brother who also confers on Isabel the fortune which is meant to bring her happiness and leads to her ruin.

Was this a curious kind of oedipal fantasy, or mere fictional ingenuity, or something else still? That is the question to be determined. It is a central issue in James's craft, in his real view of life: a causative agent as well as a literary curiosity, compounded of incest and ambiguity. Meanwhile Isabel, symbol of Puritan conscience, is determined to atone for her own errors of judgment. "It was impossible to pretend that she had not acted with her eyes open; if ever a girl was a free agent she had been. A girl in love was doubtless not a free agent; but the sole source of her mistake had been within herself. There had been no plot, no snare; she had looked and considered and chosen. When a woman had made such a mistake, there was only one way to repair it—just immensely (oh, with the highest grandeur!) to accept it . . . " But this "grandeur" of the Jamesian heroine, and this lofty, touching moral suffering and resignation, were also highly suspect—were theatrical, and based on an altogether false foundation. In fact, there *was* a plot and a snare (James's own plot and snare); and it was Isabel's pride and her vanity, and perhaps her fear of life, which prevailed over her common sense, and her capacity for experience.

The later portrait of Isabel Archer contained some of James's most effective and famous descriptions of the life of restriction, depression, failure. "It was the house of darkness, the house of dumbness, the house of suffocation." These were the emotions that James knew best; and which paralleled some of his personal passages of anxiety and renunciation in the *Notebooks.* But there also was a final paradox in his famous early heroine and his own view of life. When Isabel Archer realizes the depths of her own degradation—and the absolutely contrived situation which has led her there—why shouldn't she pick up and go? Or rather, pick up her fortune and go? It is bad enough to be trapped by life; but it is totally inexcusable—isn't it?—to remain trapped by altogether contrived circumstances in life. Isabel's relation with Pansy is never convincing, while the child herself is a dubious symbol of the European jeune fille. Isabel's power over Mme. Merle, in the end, is sufficient to send that sorceress into exile in America; the worst of all possible Jamesian fates. Just as the plot of the *Portrait* is never quite credible, except as entertainment, the resolution of the novel is strained to fit the Jamesian moral rather than the realities of the European existence he was describing. The human truth of the story is constrained, or contorted on the Procrustean frame of both the author's initial concept and his limited sense of experience—or of the lack of alternatives in human choice.

The Portrait was in this sense a Victorian "novel of complications" raised to a new height of moral or intellectual analysis. It used an early and quite orderly "stream of consciousness"; but never the true currents of the unconscious; which yet, in a curious way, James somehow suggested. He could be far more free sexually, about the disreputable Italian Countess Gemini—"with her trunks, her dresses, her chatter, her falsehoods, her frivolity, the strange, the unholy legend of the number of her lovers." Nevertheless, all of his *heroine's* relations, perhaps her marriage itself, must remain pure, lofty, exalted, and, in the end, self-sacrificial, renunciatory, chaste. There is another interesting scene where Caspar Goodwood is almost overcome by his passion for Isabel—

> Now that he was alone with her all the passion he had never stifled surged into his senses; it hummed in his eyes and made things swim round him. The bright, empty room grew dim and blurred, and through the heaving veil he felt her hover before him with gleaming eyes and parted lips.

But if Caspar's seizure is almost feminine in essence, Isabel, frightened of what she reads in his face, preserves her forced smile and her composure. " 'I suppose you wish to bid me good-bye?' she said."

There is still the embrace he forces upon her, which confirms all her distaste for him. "His kiss was like white lightning, a flash that spread, and spread again, and stayed; and it was extraordinarily as if, while she took it, she felt each thing in his hard manhood that had least pleased her, each aggressive fact of his face, his figure, his presence, justified of its intense identity and made one with this act of possession. So had she heard of those wrecked and under water following a train of images before they sank. But when darkness returned she was free." Free indeed: to continue her solitary existence of suffering, the pursuit of her own heightened sensibility at the expense of all common human pleasure, companionship, fulfillment in human relations. In this sense the ending of the novel was never ambiguous. The first major heroine of James's was a woman who teased, flirted with and then fled from all of her possible lovers; while she took the one man who would never awaken her, and who had to destroy her.

This was the meaning of *The Portrait of a Lady* in any kind of depth interpretation, and perhaps it is still the reason why, despite the inadequacy of the story's origins and conclusions—and of its professed and "conscious" moral—the novel still attracts, even while it may puzzle us. Was the early James even dimly aware of the true nature of this heroine whom he described with such charm and grace and then with such magniloquence of moral grandeur? But this was a writer, as we shall see, whose unconscious emotions continued to project a series of figures, situations, and relations which are often directly opposed to, in flat contradiction to, the conscious purposes of his craft. This great "analyst" of modern American fiction, and of modern criticism, was aware of everything except his own inner springs of creative action.

The skill of craft, apparent even as early as this novel, was designed to compensate for, even to conceal, the inadequate fictional concepts of James's—to bridge the gap between his dubious propositions and his foreshortened conclusions. On the conscious level *The Portrait of a Lady* must be viewed only as a kind of superior romance melodrama which is entertaining to read, and completely inadequate as serious literary commentary on the life of James's period, or certainly our own. That the novel has another hidden source of interest is due simply to the unacknowledged conflict between the intuitions of the artist, including his own sexual fears, inhibitions and aversions which are projected through his revealing heroine, and the "literary intention" which he consciously rendered to his readers and, yes, to himself. (pp. 40-7)

> *Maxwell Geismar, in his* Henry James and the Jacobites, *Houghton Mifflin Company, 1963, 463 p.*

Tony Tanner   (essay date 1965)

[Tanner is an English critic and editor who has written extensively on American literature. In the following excerpt, he discusses Isabel Archer's decision to marry Gilbert Osmond as an error inspired by fear.]

The feeling which Isabel Archer most consistently experiences is fear. She is frightened by Warburton's offer, of Caspar Goodwood's persistence, and Gilbert Osmond's anger; she is frightened of sexual passion, of her unexpected wealth, of her 'freedom'; but beneath all these specific apprehensions there is, she admits, a deeper, radical fear—fear of herself. Seeing that it is a self which can misread Osmond so disastrously and make such a profoundly mistaken choice then, we may say, she has good grounds for her fear. But her fear, her error, and her final resolution are, it seems to me, crucial stages on a psychic journey which forms the very heart of the novel. This journey is the journey of an uncommitted, undefined self which sets out to find the right house to live in and the right partner to live with. A house—because the undefined self needs a defining shape: a partner—because the self can only realise what it is, by seeing itself reflected in the chosen and respected eyes of another; in selecting a partner it is selecting the gaze and regard which will assure it of its own reality and value. Putting it very crudely, Isabel Archer chooses the wrong house and the wrong partner. It is the full nature of this error—and her subsequent actions—that I wish to explore. (p. 205)

Isabel Archer's character has been amply analysed by many other critics so all I want to do is stress that from the outset her approach to life is very romantic, idealistic, and theoretic. 'Isabel Archer was a young person of many theories; her imagination was remarkably active' as James tells us clearly enough. And Henrietta Stackpole is certainly correct when she says to Isabel: "The peril for you is that you live too much in the world of your own dreams". What these dreams consist of we know right from the start: 'she spent half her time in thinking of beauty and bravery and magnanimity; she had a fixed determination to regard the world as a place of brightness, of free expansion, of irresistible action . . . she was always planning out her development, desiring her perfection, observing her progress'. Thus, she views the world as a benevolent sphere which will be plastic to her theories of 'free expansion' and 'irresistible action'. She seems unprepared for any harsh encounter with all that indifferent otherness which is not the self, which is not amenable to the self, and which may well prove cruel and hostile to the self. More dangerously, it is hard to see how she intends to put her theories of self-development into practice. What will that expansion and action consist of ? As we soon realise, her most characteristic response in the real world is one of refusal and rejection. Like many another character in American fiction much of her energy goes into avoiding any commitment which might serve to define and arrest her. She is generally in favour of 'the free exploration of life' and yet she shrinks from any of the solid offers that life holds forth. Caspar Goodwood suggests oppression, coercion and constraint on the plain physical level. Lord Warburton with his complex social relations and obligations suggests immobilisation on the social level. If she rejects

the first out of a distinct disinclination to enter a firm physical embrace, she rejects the second on 'theoretic' grounds because what he offers does not tally with her vague notions of indefinite expansion. So we may say, summing up, that she rejects the physical and the social in her theoretic pursuit of freedom, knowledge, and self-realisation. Why, then, does she go on to accept Osmond? As she realises, 'The world lay before her—she could do whatever she chose'—the Miltonic echo is deliberate, it recurs again. And out of the whole world to choose Osmond! Notice that she is the only character in the book who is remotely taken in by this 'sterile dilettante' as Ralph so cogently calls him. Why? When we first see her she is reading a history of German thought; that is to say, drinking from the very source of American transcendentalism. And when, later, she imagines her future married life with Osmond, she feels assured of 'a future at a high level of consciousness of the beautiful'. This implies a sort of romantic Platonism which she might well have found in her youthful reading. She wants to exist at the heights of sheer communion with ideal beauty. As opposed, we may say, to involving herself with the lower levels of un-ideal actuality, From the start she tests things and people by whether they please her 'sublime soul'; and when she receives her fortune, the vast amount of money gives her 'to her imagination, a certain ideal beauty'. Isabel's instinct for the actual is as curtailed as her longing for the ideal is exaggerated. She rejects the sexual and social life. In marrying Osmond she thinks she is embracing the ideal. She idealises herself, her motives for marrying, her ambitions, and Osmond himself. It is all pathetically wrong. But as Mrs. Touchett shrewdly says: "there's nothing in life to prevent her marrying Mr. Osmond if only she looks at him in a certain way". Looking at him in her own way—romantically, theoretically (she 'invented a fine theory about Gilbert Osmond'), consulting her yearning for a life lived on the ideal level—Osmond seems perfectly suited to Isabel's needs.

Among other things, then, her mistake is the result of a radical failure of vision: idealising too much, she has perceived all too little. But more than that, Osmond is exactly what a large part of Isabel wants. He seems to offer release from the troubling life of turbulent passions; he seems to offer a life dedicated to the appreciation of ideal beauty. As we well know, Osmond merely regards Isabel as worthy 'to figure in his collection of choice objects'; but consider how Isabel feels about herself just before her marriage and at the height of her confidence in herself: 'she walked in no small shimmering splendour. She only felt older—ever so much, and as if she were "worth more" for it, like some curious piece in an antiquary's collection'. And she enjoys this feeling. It is hard to resist the conclusion that a part of her—the theorising, idealising part—is quite prepared to be placed in Osmond's collection. The lady is half willing to be turned into a portrait. And, given her temperament, there is much to be said for becoming a work of art. It offers a reprieve from the disturbing ordeals awaiting the self in the mire of the actual. Osmond is a student of the 'exquisite' and we discover how cruel and sterile that can be. But in her own way so is Isabel. She speaks honest words about their marriage: 'They had attempted only one thing, but that one thing was to have been exquisite'. In some ways Osmond is as much a collaborator as a deceiver.

Although there are hints of the proper villain about Osmond (James perhaps goes a little too far by revealing that Osmond's favourite author is Machiavelli), he is in fact a curiously hollow, insubstantial man: "no career, no name, no position, no fortune, no past, no future, no anything" as Madame Merle says. Perhaps this apparent lightness, this seemingly empty detachment from the world is more attractive to Isabel than the solid identity, the heavy actuality of Goodwood and Warburton. Certainly his claim that he has renounced passional life and ordinary human attachments to pursue his high-minded study, his 'taste', echoes something in Isabel. The paradox, of course, as Ralph sees, is 'that under the guise of caring only for intrinsic values Osmond lived exclusively for the world. Far from being its master as he pretended to be, he was its very humble servant, and the degree of its attention was his only measure of success'. He pretends to be a devotee of the ideal, to have renounced the base world. This is what draws Isabel. But to care so totally and uncritically for forms, taste, convention ("I'm convention itself" he revealingly admits) is to be absolutely enslaved to mere appearances, never questioning essences or the intrinsic worth of things. This, precisely, makes him a dedicated inhabitant of the world of means. He has renounced the lived life of instinct and action not, like Ralph, the better to appreciate its intrinsic values, but in order to give himself over entirely to calculated surface effects. How far he will take this is of course revealed by what he does to his daughter Pansy. It is the same thing as what he wants to do to Isabel—to turn her into a reflector of himself, utterly devoid of any spontaneous life of her own. Isabel of course, having stronger and richer stuff in her, can resist. But Pansy shows the process all but complete. All her natural vitality and spontaneity have been quietly suffocated to be replaced by a perfected puppet-like behaviour which does not *express* Pansy's own inner life, but simply *reflects* Osmond's taste. Such a total appropriation of another person's life for egotistical ends is of course the cardinal Jamesian sin. But there is something in Isabel herself which is not so remote from Osmond's disposition. At one point we read that she was 'interested' (a neutral word) to watch Osmond 'playing theoretic tricks on the delicate organism of his daughter'. She should be interested, for she has spent her whole life playing theoretic tricks on her own organism. Osmond is an egotist, but so, we are told, is Isabel: he is cold and dry, but so is she: he pays excessive attention to appearances rather than realities, and up to a point so does she (I will return to this): he prefers art to life, and so does she: he has more theories than feelings, more ideals than instincts, and so does she. He is a collector of things, and she offers herself up to him as a fine finished object. Isabel accepting Osmond's proposal of marriage is the uncertain self thinking it is embracing the very image of what it *seeks* to become. Her later shock and revulsion is the self discovering the true worthlessness of what it *might* have become. Osmond is Isabel's anti-self. This is why, I think, James made Osmond American when he might well have made him a cynical European ensnaring American gullibility. He is American because Isabel is American. She of course has qualities which differenti-

ate her sharply from Osmond. But she also has tendencies which draw her straight to him. He is an actualisation, a projection, of some of the mixed potentialities and aspirations of her questing, uncommitted self. He is part of her self writ large, and when she learns to read that writing properly (she actually refers to not having 'read him right'), she is not unnaturally appalled.

I must here say a little about the other American 'parasite' and plotter, Madame Merle. As Osmond is 'convention itself' so she is 'the great round world itself'. She is totally devoted to the world of things—she thinks of it in terms of 'spoils'—and she has subjected the unruliness of authentic nature to the surface perfection of contrived manner. Isabel is not so blind as not to be able to detect her occasional cruelty, her subtle dishonesty, the sense she gives of 'values gone wrong'. But unlike Osmond, there is something pathetic about her, and something which also offers a warning to Isabel. For clearly Madame Merle was, like Isabel, first used and then abused by Osmond, and she has not gained anything from the world even though she has devoted herself to it. She keeps herself going by 'will', forcing, always, the right mask for the right occasion. But she ends up utterly dried up, unable to cry: "you've dried up my soul" she says to Osmond (it is worth recalling here that no less a writer than Shakespeare habitually depicted evil as a state of dessication, a complete lack of the very sap and tears of life). Perhaps the saddest cry in the whole novel is Madame Merle's lament: "Have I been so vile for nothing?" It at least attests to a vestigial moral sense which she has deliberately subverted for the world's ends, only to see no gains. She has been a disciple of appearances and indeed has mastered the art, but she is rewarded by being banished to America (apparently the worst fate James could conceive of for an erring character). She is a sadder case than Osmond because she knows that she is doing bad things to Isabel. Her effects are as calculated as Osmond's but at least she winces at perpetrating them. She is an almost tragic example of the scant rewards and plentiful shames awaiting those who live only for 'the world'. And it is Madame Merle who gives perhaps the most succinct expression of living in the world of means to be found in the whole book. "I don't pretend to know what people are for" she says, "I only know what I can do with them". She exactly fits Kant's (and Rousseau's) definition of the immoral world. She sees people as instruments but has no sense of their intrinsic worth: means to her hand, not ends in themselves.

In the world of Osmond and Madame Merle, self-seeking and simulation go together. They have to calculate effects: what *is,* is neglected; what *seems* is paramount. Now Isabel herself is a partial devotee of appearances. I will quote a few references to this. She has 'an unquenchable desire to please' and 'an unquenchable desire to think well of herself': thus she is 'very liable to the sin of self-esteem'. More subtly, we read of 'her desire to *look* very well and to *be* if possible even better'. A similar crucial distinction is made later: Isabel's chief dread 'was that she should *appear* narrow-minded; what she feared next afterwards was that she should really *be* so'. (My italics in both cases.) These fine hints reveal a problem of great importance for the novitiate self: which will receive more attention—

appearance, or essence? For much of the early part of her travels Isabel falls into the subtle and understandable error of devoting herself to appearances. She wishes to emulate Madame Merle. She contrives to appear to Osmond as she thinks he wants her to appear; like a fine finished work of art which re-echoes and reflects his ideas and taste. In this sense Osmond *is* a man deceived, and Isabel is right to realise that she did mislead him by appearing to be what in fact she was not. That is why Isabel has a true instinct when she says she is afraid of her self. Realising the depths of her error with regard to Osmond is also to realise that she does not know what her self is, nor what it may do. (After all there is Madame Merle, a terrible example of how the self may mutilate the self from a sense of misplaced devotion and ambition.) And indeed this is the crucial difficulty for the self. Only by engaging itself in a situation, projecting itself into the world of things and appearances, can the self realise the self (i.e. transform latent potentialities into visible realities). But once in that situation, it may find that it has chosen a position, a role, which falsifies the self. We don't know what is in us until we commit ourselves in a certain direction: then we may find that the commitment is utterly wrong. Thus all choice may turn out to be error and in this way the self may ruin the self. Certainly Isabel exacerbates her chances of choosing wrong by coldly consulting her theories, her imaginative ideals, her book-fed romanticisms; and that wrong choice does seem to threaten years to come of waste and disappointment. Seen thus, Isabel's difficulty, her error, her fate, form a journey on which we must all, in our different ways, go. For it is only through choice and commitment that we can find out what we are. In this sense error is also discovery. Isabel has to close with Osmond in order to arrive at a deeper knowledge of her self, of her distorted values, of her egotism, and of the real pain and cruelty of life. By marrying Osmond she suffers in good earnest, but she thus earns the right to see the ghost of Gardencourt. Her consolation—and it is the supreme one in James—is truer vision.

To bring out more clearly Isabel's journey as the journey of the developing but all-too-often erring self, I now want to move from the characters she meets to the buildings and settings she moves through. And first I must quote from a crucial exchange between Isabel and Madame Merle: it comes near the end of chapter nineteen and is really central to the whole book. Talking of an earlier suitor Isabel says: "I don't care anything about his house" and Madame Merle replies: "That's very crude of you. When you've lived as long as I you'll see that every human being has his shell and that you must take the shell into account. By the shell I mean the whole envelope of circumstances. There's no such thing as an isolated man or woman; we're each of us made up of some cluster of appurtenances. What shall we call our 'self'? Where does it begin? where does it end? It overflows into everything that belongs to us—and then it flows back again. I know a large part of myself is in the clothes I choose to wear. I've a great respect for *things*. One's self—for other people—is one's expression of one's self; and one's house, one's furniture, one's garments, the books one reads, the company one keeps—these things are all expressive".

Now this idea that the self is only the self that we consciously create and play at being, the self that we visibly express and project, is still being explored by existential psychologists like Sartre (for instance in *Being and Nothingness* where he discusses the waiter 'playing at being a waiter . . . the waiter in the cafe plays with his condition in order to *realize* it'), and by such imaginative sociologists as Erving Goffman (his brilliant book *The Presentation of Self in Everyday Life* is very relevant here). So Madame Merle's attitude expresses a deep truth about our society. She has gone the whole way. She is concerned only with the agents of expression—things, clothes, appearances, appurtenances. She reconstructs a false self to show the world. She is what she dresses to be. This is extreme: it entails the death of the soul and the ultimate disappearance of the individual inner self. As Isabel says to herself, it is difficult to imagine Madame Merle 'in any detachment or privacy, she existed only in relations . . . one might wonder what commerce she could possibly hold with her own spirit'. She is rather like Lord Mellifont in "The Private Life" who disappears when he is on his own. If you care only for appearances, you exist only when there are people to look at you.

However, in this key conversation, Isabel's answer to Madame Merle is also extreme. She says: "I know that nothing else expresses me. Nothing that belongs to me is any measure of me; everything's on the contrary a limit, a barrier, and a perfectly arbitrary one. . . . My clothes may express the dressmaker, but they don't express me. To begin with it's not my own choice that I wear them; they're imposed upon me by society". To which Madame Merle wryly answers: "Should you prefer to go without them?"

This is a classic formulation of a basic American attitude. Lionel Trilling once noted that there is something in the American temperament which wishes to resist all conditioning, all actual society, and aspires to a life which will permit the spirit to make its own terms. 'Somewhere in our mental constitution is the demand for life as pure spirit'. (See his essay 'William Dean Howells' in *The Opposing Self*). Emerson's 'Self-Reliance', Thoreau by Walden Pond, Whitman celebrating the self—these, of course, are the classic types for the American imagination. They certainly did believe there was such a thing as the 'isolated' self, and welcomed the fact. And characters like Bartleby and Huck Finn and Augie March reveal the ineradicable suspicion of all conditioning forces, all actual fixed social situations. They refuse, opt out, move on. Like Isabel they see barriers and limits everywhere, and much of their energy goes into avoiding the shaping pressures (and appurtenances) of society. Isabel's retort is, thus, in a great American tradition. And up to a point she is right. Things and appurtenances are not identical with the self, as Osmond and Madame Merle make them. We are not what we wear. But to see everything in the actual world as sheer barrier, hindrance, and limit is also dangerous. For without any limits the self can never take on any contours, cannot become something real. The pure spirit of the self has to involve itself with the material world of things and society in order to work out an identity for itself, indeed in order to realise itself. To that extent the self must dress itself and must choose its clothes. In laying the responsibility for her clothes (i.e. her appearance, her situation etc.) on society and calling it an arbitrary imposition, Isabel is being dangerously irresponsible. For it is her error in thinking that life can be lived as pure spirit in contempt of things that leads her to mistake Osmond's attitude. The ironic result is that she puts herself in the power of a man who wants to treat *her* as a thing. James's insight here is profound. For there is indeed a dangerously close connection between an idealistic *rejection* of 'things' and an idealising *of* 'things'. This is why Osmond is such a telling figure. In the appearance of living for the spirit in disregard of the material, he has in fact simply spiritualised the material. And James must surely have been one of the first to see into this particularly modern malaise which other American critics have mentioned in discussing modern society; namely, the confusion of the spiritual and material realms, the spiritualising of things. James knew that things and surroundings (the shell) *were* important: there was a way of being among things which manifested the quality of the self, which enabled it to realise itself. But of course there was also a way of being among things which menaced and could destroy the self. Isabel Archer's journey is hazardous but representative: and her error no less than human.

We first see Isabel—as we last see her—in a garden. This is always an important setting in James (usually indicating a place of meditation and appreciation). Gardens are certainly important in this book. At the start of her European journey Isabel regards her inner world as a garden and indeed many of her happiest moments are spent in them. She is happiest, in particular, at Gardencourt, and the very name points to the fact that this is the locale in the book which most exudes a mood of mellow reciprocity between the civilised and the natural. But Isabel is far from appreciating it at the start of her adventures. She sees it only as romantic and picturesque. It is only much later that she appreciates that it is something more real and indeed more sacred than that. After this opening glimpse James takes us back to the house in Albany, New England, where Isabel started on her travels. The most important of many suggestive details about this house is the 'condemned door', the entrance which 'was secured by bolts which a particularly slender little girl found it impossible to slide'. It is to be Isabel's later fate again to be locked in. Also, the windows are covered, but 'she had no wish to look out, for this would have interfered with her theory that there was a strange, unseen place on the other side—a place which became to the child's imagination, according to different moods, a region of delight or terror'. This of course expresses Isabel's whole attitude to life: her theories and imagined versions of reality are generated behind closed doors and covered windows. Instead of venturing forth she sits poring over books. One more detail is particularly prophetic: she 'had the whole house to choose from, and the room she had selected was the most depressed of its scenes'. James often used the metaphor 'the house of life' and indeed, of its many rooms, Isabel is yet to choose the darkest and most imprisoning.

If you see Isabel's quest as being at least in part a search for the right house then her reactions to Warburton and Osmond become even more revealing. When she rejects Warburton after visiting his house, Lockleigh, she puts her rejection in this way: she says she is unable "to think of your home . . . as the settled seat of my existence". As though the main thing about him was the fact that he doesn't have what she regards as the right house. Osmond's house is brilliantly described. First of all, it is on a hill-top, the best place for a person who wants to put the claims of the base world behind and live a life of ideal appreciation and detached observation. Clearly Isabel is attracted to this degree of rarefied removal. But we note that in the first, perfectly plausible, topographical description, the front of the house is deceptive. 'It was the mask, not the face of the house. It had heavy lids, but no eyes; the house in reality looked another way. . . . ' This, I need hardly point out, is entirely true of its owner. Even the windows bespeak Osmond: 'their function seemed less to offer communication with the world than to defy the world to look in'. Isabel's approach to this key dwelling is laced with subtle portent, and I must quote at some length here. 'The companions drove out of the Roman Gate . . . and wound between high-walled lanes into which the wealth of blossoming orchards overdrooped and flung a fragrance, until they reached the small suburban piazza, of crooked shape, where the long brown wall of the villa occupied by Mr. Osmond formed a principle, or at least very imposing, object'. They drive into the courtyard. 'There was something grave and strong in the place; it looked somehow as if, once you were in, you would need an act of energy to get out. For Isabel, however, there was of course as yet no thought of getting out, but only of advancing'. The whole drive provides a compressed analogue for Isabel's venture into life so far. The blooming promising beginning, the flung fragrance (Touchett's unlooked-for bequest perhaps), then the crooked square, the preventing wall, and the enclosing courtyard—the whole passage subtly prepares us for what becomes explicit only much later when Isabel realises that 'she had taken all the first steps in the purest confidence, and then she had suddenly found the infinite vistas of a multiplied life to be a dark, narrow alley with a dead wall at the end'. And note the geography of the following image. 'Instead of leading to the high places of happiness, from which the world could seem to lie below one, so that one could look down with a sense of exaltation and advantage, and judge and choose and pity, it led rather downward and earthward, into the realms of restriction and depression where the sound of other lives, easier and freer, was heard as from above, and where it served to deepen the feeling of failure'. Isabel thinks Osmond lives on the heights of meditation and free appreciation, but really he dwells in the depths of calculation and constricting appropriation. Her life seemed to lead up to the world of ends; instead she was plunging down into the world of means. Osmond's palace of art turns out to be 'the house of darkness, the house of dumbness, the house of suffocation'. But it was the house she chose. James knits his imagery together in the famous description of Isabel's reaction when Osmond proposes. She feels 'a pang that suggested to her somehow the slipping of a fine bolt—backward, forward, she couldn't have said which'. Is she about to be released or immured? In her most testing moment she is unable to distinguish what presages liberation and expansion, and what threatens detainment and constriction. Her radical confusion is all there in the image.

I will not here describe the many galleries and museums and other houses and rooms Isabel passes through, but all repay careful study. For in this book all the architecture means something of specific importance to Isabel, as of course it must to the self seeking both freedom *and* form. Pansy's convent, for instance, has all the appearance of a prison to Isabel's clearer vision. On the other hand, some architecture can offer consolation. For example there is a beautiful passage describing a ride she takes in Rome— 'the place where people had suffered'—some time after her discovery of the truth about Osmond. 'She had long before taken old Rome into her confidence, for in a world of ruins the ruin of her happiness seemed a less unnatural catastrophe. She rested her weariness upon things that had crumbled for centuries and yet were still upright; she dropped her secret sadness into the silence of lonely places'. It is a most moving description of the bruised and erring spirit absorbing strengthening reminders and consoling clues from the marred but splendid debris of human habitations of the past. And one of the reasons why Isabel returns to Rome at the end, renouncing the refuge of Gardencourt which she now does appreciate as sacred, is that the self has to return to the place where it made its most defining, if mistaken, choice. That is where the work of rehabilitation and re-education must go on. It is where knowledge is earned. I think this is why, in the last scene of the book, we see Isabel running from the darkening garden of meditation back into the well-lit house of life. But before exploring that decision I want to discuss the significance of Ralph.

Ralph is of course a recurring Jamesian figure—the subtly debarred spectator who enjoys everything in imagination and nothing in action. Thus Ralph has 'the imagination of loving' but has 'forbidden himself the riot of expression'. All his happiness consists of 'the sweet-tasting property of the observed thing in itself'. To appreciate the 'thing in itself' is precisely to be an inhabitant of the world of ends. Ralph is wise, he is dying: 'restricted to mere spectatorship at the game of life', banned from participation, addicted to appreciation. A true Jamesian artist figure. Suitably, he is most often seen sitting in gardens. On one occasion in particular the contrast between 'house' and 'garden' is used to good effect. This is when Ralph tells Isabel the real truth about Osmond. She, with her theories, rejects his visions—and leaves the garden. She ends the conversation 'by turning away and walking back to the house'. But Ralph cannot follow her: it is too cold for him in the house, he is too susceptible to 'the lurking chill of the highwalled court'. It does not seem to me excessive to see Ralph as the artist-meditator, who cannot function in the house of life but who indulges his imagination and speculation in the garden. He sits; he does not act. He is content to watch and appreciate Isabel; he has no thought of dominating or manipulating her. In his own way he is also an aesthete, someone who stands back and relishes the beautiful. But where Osmond is a false aesthete, Ralph has the true artistic instincts. Osmond wants to turn Isabel into a work of art (we see her at his home 'framed in the gilded doorway' already adjusting to her status as por-

trait); Ralph appreciates her living qualities artistically. Osmond hates Ralph because he is 'an apostle of freedom'. But as Isabel comes to see, Ralph is more intelligent, more just, better. Not egotistic, as Osmond always is. This leads up to the deathbed scene. Isabel is back at Gardencourt, happy at least that she is no longer having to act and falsify. At Gardencourt she can be her self, her true self. And, dying, Ralph comforts her: "But love remains". He tells her she has been adored and her response is revealingly simple. "Oh my brother". In Osmond Isabel thought she recognised a soul mate. She was very wrong. At last, having suffered, she realises who is the true image of what her self wants to be—Ralph. "Oh my brother." Having seen through the false aesthetic approach to life, she now appreciates the true artistic attitude: a vision based on love, on generosity, on respect for things in themselves and a gift of unselfish appreciation.

In taking the measure of Osmond, Isabel has started to move towards Ralph's point of view. The great chapter, forty-two, when she takes stock, is really the beginning of her deeper knowledge and clearer vision. She is starting to read things properly, as Ralph does. And with this new access of vision, Isabel becomes less active externally and more active internally. She has started on what James later called 'the subjective adventure': the adventure of trying to understand, to sound out depths, to appreciate qualities, to transcend the importunities of the ego. By the end of the book Isabel Archer has started to become a Jamesian artist.

Just before the end we see her in the garden at Gardencourt: this time pensive and quiet, much closer to a knowledge of true values than when we saw her stride so confidently on to that lawn at the start. It is now twilight: she is sitting on a bench alone. This stance, this setting, becomes a dominant one in James's later work—not only in the last great story **"The Bench of Desolation"** but in such works as *The Ambassadors* as well as in many stories like **"Crapy Cornelia"** and **"Mora Montravers"**. In that last story, for instance, we see the self-effacing Traffle, excluded, estranged, sitting staring at the approaching evening with only one consolation. As the night comes down on him he has, for company, his Jamesian mind: 'exquisite, occult, dangerous and sacred, to which everything ministered and which nothing could take away'. Clearly James had a recurring vision of a person who has somehow failed to realise him (or her) self in the physical world, who has renounced all active participation, and who withdraws into sedentary isolation consoling himself with the fruits of a finer, if sadder, consciousness. Isabel, we feel, is drawing towards her truer role as she sits in the darkening garden. But she is interrupted by Caspar Goodwood, who comes to disturb her on her bench in the garden: she cannot yet enjoy Ralph's invalid immunity from the challenge and threat of engagement. Goodwood kisses her, and in a curious cluster of images James implies that she is both wrecked and then freed. Goodwood brings a possessive lightning, 'but when darkness returned she was free'. I am not fully certain of James's intention here, but the effect is this. For a long time she has wondered if her true fate, the true realisation of her self, should not have been with Goodwood. Now for the first time she is subjected to the full force of his sexual claims. It is a shattering experience, but it is also a release. She was not made to go that way. There is no going back to the simple level of life he represents. He tries to prevent her from returning to Rome where, as he says, she has to 'play a part' and maintain a false 'form': but it is precisely this that she must, at this stage, do. She runs back to the house: 'there were lights in the window of the house; they shone far across the lawn'. She reaches the door. 'Here only she paused. She looked all about her; she listened a little; then she put her hand on the latch. She had not known where to turn; but she knew now. There was a very straight path'. James has annoyed readers by not saying what that path is. But I think the wonderful suggestivity of this last scene tells us all we need. The last pause and lingering look surely imply that she is reluctant to leave the garden—a refuge and a place of meditation. But she cannot opt out of her fate so easily, just as even more she cannot return to American innocence and physical simplicity with Goodwood. She chose her room in the house of life and she must return to it. She must return to the chill and ruins of Rome: for the self cannot back out of a mistaken course but only push through and move beyond. But she takes back with her a new vision, a deeper understanding, a capacity for modest unegotistical contemplation which all promise a richer future—a future in which she will come to a true realisation of what her real self is. It is beside the point to ask whether she will divorce Osmond. When she has attained her new vision, he simply shrinks into insignificance, just as Madame Merle melts away to America. We do not even hear his voice for the last seventy pages or so of the book, and by the end of the book we feel that Isabel has attained the most important kind of freedom, an internal one. She is liberated from her twisted vision and her confused values. She can see through all false appearances. She returns to Italy, to the 'ruins' she herself was partly responsible for. But she will not, we feel, ever again be subordinate to the deceptions and calculations of a worldling like Osmond. Even if she does not break out of the house and kick over the traces, and even if she never again indulges in any more passions, her future will be quite other. For her way of looking has changed. Now I think one might fairly suggest that James, in fact, could not see exactly what sort of future such a person might have, how she might take up her place again in the social scene. We can admire Isabel's fine stoicism and admit at the same time that it is hard to visualise the details of her future. And this, I think, is because James is already feeling the necessary connection between the artistic observation of life *and* the renunciation of active participation in it. As Isabel becomes more the artist, in her mind, so she will withdraw from social involvement, if not physically then at least psychologically. If she never returns to sit in the garden of Gardencourt, then we may be sure she will spend many later years reposing in the garden of her mind. With James's later artist figures or observers, the attempt at any active participation is all but abandoned from the start. Hyacinth Robinson finds no satisfying role or niche for himself in society and shoots himself. Lambert Strether develops a new complex comprehensiveness of vision and appreciation, but to retain it, it is essential that he must not get 'anything for myself '—no spoils, no physical

relationships. The narrator of *The Sacred Fount* is the conscience of society, at the cost of never enjoying its actual embrace. There are other such figures, but none perhaps so humanly comprehensible as Isabel Archer, in whom we can see the erring self emerging into the incipient artist. With later characters the divorce between action and observation is almost accepted as inevitable from the start. It would seem that James, in his own way, came to share Goethe's reflection that 'the acting man is always without conscience; no one has conscience but the observing man'. If nothing else, *The Portrait of a Lady* shows us the birth of a conscience out of the spoiling of a life. (pp. 207-19)

> Tony Tanner, "The Fearful Self: Henry James's 'The Portrait of a Lady'," in Critical Quarterly, *Vol. 7, No. 3, Autumn, 1965, pp. 205-19.*

David Galloway (essay date 1967)

[*In the following excerpt, Galloway examines James's use of symbolism in* The Portrait of a Lady.]

As Isabel's consciousness is shaped and matured by the characters and the episodes which act upon it, so the reader is further made aware of her movement from naïveté to maturity by James's subtle use of symbolism. The symbols in *The Portrait of a Lady,* which aid us in tracing what James might have termed 'The Figure in the Carpet', are almost entirely organic; there are few instances in which the reader senses that an image had been brought into the text by main force in order to illuminate the situations in which the characters find themselves. Perhaps the most obtrusive are Osmond's analogy to Madame Merle as a cracked cup, to himself as a rusty key 'that has no lock to fit it', and his comment to Caspar Goodwood that he and his wife are as united 'as the candlestick and the snuffers'. It is interesting that Osmond draws all of these analogies, and their obtrusiveness is perhaps relieved by a sense of irony; in any case, the pointed artificiality of the images tells us something about Osmond himself. The latter two, with their strong sexual implications, also involve peculiar inversions—a logical inversion in the former instance ('a key without a lock to fit it') and a sexual inversion in the latter, for Osmond clearly acts as the snuffer to what James describes as Isabel's 'flame-like' spirit; this reading of the image is further strengthened by a reference to the candles 'burned down to their sockets' during the long night when Isabel reviews the course her marriage has taken. But as a general rule, symbolism in *The Portrait* operates with considerably greater subtlety; indeed, since we view so much of the novel through Isabel's naïve eyes and with significantly limited information, the real symbolic import of many of James's images becomes obvious only in retrospect, creating the sense of a sort of reverse concatenation, where a late image throws into symbolic perspective a sequence of what earlier appeared merely descriptive and even unrelated images. For example, James introduces his characters of the first scene in terms of the shadows they throw on the lawn; these at first seem entirely insignificant (the aura of warmth, geniality, and wit is so much more striking)—a simple physical detail characteristic of a piece of essentially realistic description; but even these shadows are imbued with a new significance once James has described the shadows which gather in the room while Madame Merle plays the piano at the time of her first meeting with Isabel; when we see the shadows in Osmond's villa and the shaded Cascine through which Isabel and Osmond walk during their engagement; and finally when Isabel sits in the darkened room before a dead fire and burnt-out candles, realising that her life has become 'a dark, narrow alley with a dead wall at the end'. Not only do shadows become increasingly symbolic of the cultural ambiguities and moral obscurity into which Isabel is moving, they also tell us something fundamental about Isabel herself. For Isabel has always sought the shadows: Mrs. Touchett first meets her in the dimly lighted library in Albany where Isabel had taken refuge since her childhood; later she finds similar comfort in the shadowed vastness of St. Peter's; and in the conclusion of the novel she rushes from the 'white lightning' of Caspar's embrace into the darkness of the night, and then to the artificial light that spreads from the windows of Gardencourt. In part this constant seeking of the shadows is symbolic of Isabel's fear of the world, of human commitment and physical contact; similarly, Ralph sits in the fortress-like darkness of the Winchester Square dining room because there he feels 'safe'. At their richest, James's symbols answer the requirements of Coleridge's word 'esemplastic': they are continuously being shaped into new wholes, and in the case of Isabel, they are perhaps the most significant agents in portraying her character, her growing sense of self-awareness, and the shifting quality of the light in which her portrait is hung.

Houses and gardens are frequently documented sources of Jamesian symbolism: Gardencourt with its 'fine pictorial tricks'; the claustrophobic air of the Touchett house in Winchester Square; Osmond's villa with its 'antique, solid, weather-worn, yet imposing front [which] had a somewhat incommunicative character', and its massive crossbarred windows 'placed at such a height that curiosity, even on tiptoe, expired before it reached them'; and finally the Palazzo Roccanera, 'a kind of domestic fortress, a pile which bore a stern old Roman name, which smelt of historic deeds, of crime and craft and violence . . . ': Isabel comes to think of it as 'the house of darkness, the house of dumbness, the house of suffocation'. It is the Archer house in Albany, however, which offers the most subtle symbolism. The Americanness of its occupants is attested to by the fact that the family for some reason refers to Isabel's favourite room as the 'office', and its meaningless clutter of furnishings is a direct antithesis to the studiously contrived aesthetic harmony of Osmond's villa. More importantly, it is here that Isabel seals herself off from the world, never opening the bolted door that leads to the street, or even removing the green paper which covers the sidelights. She imagines herself in this way protected from what she thinks of a 'the vulgar street', but in fact she had sealed herself off from reality (as her friends all note), and it is this failure of experience, the chronic inability to assess the world as distinct from her romantic vision of the world, which will spell her doom; only in the cloistered office or the walled garden behind the house does Isabel feel safe. She lacks the courage, the energy and the conviction to meet the demands of her imagination or to test them

against life: Isabel ventures into the world only when led forth by the hand of her practical aunt or endowed by her uncle with an 'independent' income, and she takes a husband only when the marriage has been carefully arranged for her.

It is an instance of the economy of James's narrative technique that his imagery—while often brilliantly evoking the sense of place—usually conveys, as well, a considerable figurative significance; thus James immensely admired Hawthorne's search for 'images which shall place themselves in picturesque correspondence with the spiritual facts'. Though the sources from which James draws his imagery in *The Portrait of a Lady* are extremely varied, certain 'clusters' of images in the novel come to demand our attention. Architectural references abound both in the preface and in the novel itself. Ralph thinks of Isabel in terms of a remarkable 'edifice': 'he looked in at the windows and received an impression of proportions equally fair. But he felt that he saw it only by glimpses and that he had not as yet stood under the roof. The door was fastened . . . '; and when Ralph remarks that he keeps a group of musicians in his ante-room to shut away the sounds of the world and convince passersby that dancing is going on within, Isabel reflects that 'she would have liked to pass through the ante-room, as her cousin called it, and enter the private apartments'. Indeed, we could al-

James in Italy at the turn of the century.

most trace Isabel's education by reference to the houses and rooms she occupies: from the cluttered office in Albany; to the comforting spaciousness of Gardencourt; through the 'stout grey pile' of Lockleigh (to Isabel like 'a castle in a legend'); Mrs. Touchett's Florentine palace, whose air of historic happenings makes Isabel feel as though she were holding 'to her ear all day a shell of the sea of the past'; Osmond's ancient villa with its imposing front and perpetually chilled ante-chamber; the garish hotel room in which Osmond proposes marriage; the Palazzo Roccanero, that 'dark and massive structure' which Ned Rosier comes to think of as a 'dungeon'; and finally the bare, cold apartments of the convent to which Pansy is banished by her father, and whose atmosphere reminds Isabel of 'the great penal establishments'. Each of these references to architecture is a clue to Isabel's development, and, above all other sorts of images in the novel, these perhaps come closest to the ideal which James saw embodied in the work of Ibsen: the talent 'for producing an intensity of interest by means incorruptibly quiet', by an 'almost demure preservation of the usual'.

Appropriately, the fine arts provide James with one of the most frequent sources of imagery in *The Portrait of a Lady,* and such images are closely bound up with those of architecture (and gardens as well). Out of her romantic fondness for stories of war and revolution, Isabel is drawn to historical pictures, committing 'the conscious solecism of forgiving them much bad painting for the sake of subject'; she chooses books by their frontispieces, and insists on viewing the paintings at Gardencourt even in the most unfavourable light; Ralph thinks of his remarkable cousin as 'finer than the finest work of art—than a Greek bas-relief, than a great Titian, than a Gothic cathedral' (foreshadowing James's remark in **"The Art of Fiction"** that a 'psychological reason could inspire him to Titianesque efforts'). Art galleries, museums, and 'picturesque' ruins are frequent scenes of the novel's action. Ralph envies the courtly life of an elegant gentleman in a small Lancret; Madame Merle seems to Isabel to resemble a bust of Juno or Niobe; and following the death of her uncle Isabel strikes Mrs. Touchett as looking 'as solemn . . . as a Cimabue Madonna'. Osmond's beard is 'cut in the manner of the portraits of the sixteenth century', and James compares him to 'the elegant complicated medal struck off for a special occasion'; to Isabel his features were 'as fine as one of the drawings in the long gallery above the bridge of the Uffizi'. Osmond himself believes that 'one ought to make one's life a work of art', and he repeatedly thinks of both Isabel and Pansy as *objets d'art:* as porcelain, paintings, or carved ivory; so too does Ned Rosier, who is struck by Pansy's resemblance to 'an Infanta of Velasquez'. Even the bustling, unreflective Henrietta has 'a special devotion' to a Correggio in the Uffizi. Such image-gathering would be merely gratuitous if it did not do more than highlight the cultivated milieu in which James's characters move, but such imagery is also intimately bound up with the question of 'seeing' which is central to all of James's major work; Isabel must first of all learn to recognise the multiplicity of forms which surround her, and then to evaluate the intentions which rest behind them, before she is capable of achieving one of her most

frequently asserted ambitions—that of 'judging'. (pp. 30-4)

There are many other imagistic clusters in the novel, including military, animal, flower, and religious imagery, but two other sorts demand particular attention from the careful reader: water and light. The former closely parallels the use George Eliot made of it in *Middlemarch:* first of all it suggests the possibility of adventure, of 'sailing before the breeze', in Ralph's phrase, but for Henrietta it becomes a sign of danger, as Isabel moves away from one set of values without yet having found anchor in a new one; hence, she described Isabel as 'drifting away—right out to sea', and she sees her own role as one of saving 'a precious creature from drowning'. When Ralph learns of Isabel's engagement to Osmond, he is described as drifting about the house 'like a rudderless vessel in a rocky stream'. Later, reflecting on the reasons for her marriage to Osmond, Isabel remembers her initial feeling: that he was 'like a sceptical voyager strolling on the beach, while he waited for the tide', and she determines to 'launch his boat for him'. In the conclusion of the novel, water imagery assumes a further dimension of meaning: responding to Caspar Goodwood's appeal that they run away together, she feels that 'The world, in truth, had never seemed so large; it seemed to open out, all round her, to take the form of a mighty sea, where she floated in fathomless waters. She had wanted help, and here was help; it had come in a rushing torrent.' Isabel is almost swept away by the torrent, by 'the noise of waters, all the rest of it, . . . in her own swimming head'. But when he kisses her, every disagreeable fact about his 'hard manhood' passes before her eyes: 'So had she heard of those wrecked and under water following a train of images before they sink.' It is not just the thought of losing her identity to Caspar's sense of possessiveness or even of violating the 'forms' which are so vital to her, but her own fear of her persistent suitor's sexuality which is conveyed to us by this final use of water imagery; water becomes concomitant with the surrender to passion which would destroy her own image, her elaborate self-portrait, of Isabel Archer.

Similar complexities are embodied in James's use of light—as a symbol of perception (and its opposite—when Isabel views and judges the paintings at Gardencourt even though 'The light was inadequate'); as a symbol of comfort and security—as it becomes when Isabel thinks of Ralph's visit to her in Rome as 'a lamp in the darkness', and when she rushes toward the lights of Gardencourt after Caspar has kissed her; and it is, like the water imagery in the scene with Caspar, a symbol of the sexual passion she has so forcefully repressed: following on her reflection, in Chapter 6, that 'it was perfectly possible to be happy without the society of a more or less coarse-minded person of another sex', she none the less recognises that 'Deep in her soul—it was the deepest thing there—lay a belief that if a certain light should dawn she could give herself completely; but this image, on the whole, was too formidable to be attractive. Isabel's thoughts hovered about it, but they seldom rested on it for long; after a little it ended in alarms.' Such a light finally dawns for her in the 'white lightning' of Caspar's kiss, but too late to alter the course of Isabel's life, and she flees towards the artificial, domestic lights of Gardencourt.

A review of James's revisions of the novel reveals the degree to which he worked both for a more precise and for a more richly connotative use of imagery. In the serialised version of *The Portrait* Ralph had expressed his dismay over Isabel's decision to marry Osmond with the remark that 'You seem to me to be soaring far up in the blue—to be sailing in the bright light, over the heads of men. Suddenly someone tosses up a stone . . . and down you drop to the ground.' In revising the passage for book publication, James significantly altered the image to 'Someone tosses up a faded rosebud . . . and down you drop to the ground.' Not only is the new image more suggestive of the dilettantish Osmond, but it contrasts effectively with the earlier garden imagery of the novel—with Isabel's belief that introspection was a pleasant exercise so long as 'one returned from it with a lapful of roses', with the wild roses that grow outside Osmond's villa, and the pitifully unnatural flower he has made of his own daughter. Numerous alterations of this sort were made in the original magazine text (including the change of Madame Merle's name from Geraldine to Serena), but it was in the final revisions, for the New York edition, that James most dramatically reinforced the thematic suggestiveness of the language of the novel. In the climactic scene mentioned in the preceding paragraph, for example, James had originally written that Isabel's awareness of the depths of Caspar's devotion 'wrapped her about; it lifted her off her feet'. In the revised text he expanded this to achieve a far more comprehensive symbolic effect:

> She had believed it, but this was different; this was the hot wind of the desert, at the approach of which the others dropped dead, like mere sweet airs of the garden. It wrapped her about; it lifted her off her feet, while the very taste of it, as of something potent, acrid and strange, forced open her set teeth.

Similarly, James more particularly—and with far more forceful imagery—described the effect of Caspar's kiss. At first it had been imaged as 'a flash of lightning; when it was dark she was free'. This is expanded to read:

> His kiss was like white lightning, a flash that spread, and spread again, and stayed; and it was extraordinarily as if, while she took it, she felt each thing in his hard manhood that had least pleased her, each aggressive fact of his face, his figure, his presence, justified of its intense identity and made one with this act of possession. So she had heard of those wrecked and under water following a train of images before they sink. But when darkness returned she was free.

Not only does the revised passage have greater dramatic effectiveness; it also serves to clarify important issues of motivation—to explain Isabel's original rejection of Goodwood and her decision to return to Osmond.

In the preface to *Roderick Hudson,* the first which he wrote for the collected edition, James compared his intention in revising the texts to that of a painter who sets about restoring his older canvases, in order to emphasise what

otherwise might be 'buried secrets'. There are other sorts of revisions as well—attempts to achieve a smoother style, and a notable use of colloquialisms and contractions in order to give dialogue a more natural tone; but the most important revisions in *The Portrait* (including the lines added to the conclusion) are clearly attempts to bring out 'buried secrets' and to enrich the general aesthetic tone of the 'portrait' itself. (pp. 34-7)

> *David Galloway, in his* Henry James: The Portrait of a Lady, *Edward Arnold (Publishers) Ltd., 1967, 64 p.*

Dominic J. Bazzanella   (essay date 1969)

[*In the following excerpt, Bazzanella evaluates critical assessments of James's revision of* The Portrait of a Lady *and praises the revised text as representative of James's later style.*]

In an entry in his notebook early in 1881, while *The Portrait of a Lady* was being serialized in both American and English magazines, Henry James accurately forecast the most common criticisms his novel would receive. "There has been a want of action in the earlier part," he wrote, and, "The obvious criticism of course will be that it is not finished—that I have not seen the heroine to the end of her situation—that I have left her *en l'air.*"

Certainly, critics have delighted in scholarly discussions and debates concerning the artistic merits of the open-ended nature of James's novel. Leon Edel notes that "readers today—particularly those in search of a happy ending—tend to feel that the central drama of Isabel's life remains unresolved." Most critics today, however, including Edel himself, view the ending as the logical concluding brush stroke needed to complete the portrait. Laurence Holland, for example, sees the ending as the second of two "framing scenes" in the novel: the first occurs in early spring of 1871 in Albany when Isabel is awaiting Caspar Goodwood, just before Mrs. Touchett arrives; the second occurs in late May of 1877 when Caspar suddenly appears before Isabel at Gardencourt and receives his inevitable dismissal. By this device, says Holland, "the pattern is completed." F. W. Dupee feels that Isabel's decision to return to Rome "is an austere decision but inescapable." Oscar Cargill also thinks the ending inevitable: "How else could James have closed his novel?" And R. W. Stallman calls the ending "a foregone conclusion" [see Edel, Holland, Dupee, Cargill, and Stallman entries in Further Reading].

But the general agreement expressed concerning the "inevitability" of the conclusion is more apparent than real, because critical interpretations of what the ending means vary so widely. Edel writes that Isabel's "decision to return to Rome and to Osmond is motivated: she has promised Pansy that she will come back and she keeps her word." Other explanations of Isabel's "inevitable" behavior range from Dupee's opinion that "the very suffering involved in her marriage has given it a kind of sanctity" which she is morally bound to respect to Stallman's assertion that the ending of *The Portrait* is inevitable because of the "concatenation of houses Isabel visits or inhabits."

Some critics defend the ending as inevitable even though they believe Isabel is confronted with a choice between returning to Osmond and accepting Caspar Goodwood's proposal: for Walter F. Wright, Isabel's conduct in the novel "springs, not from reasoning about moral questions, but from her concept of herself as a lady" [in his *The Madness of Art* (1962)]. Thus, although he feels that her returning to Osmond is a free choice, he points out that she is fully aware that if she chose Caspar she would be "smashing the ideal portrait of herself." Other critics who agree that the ending is inevitable deny that Isabel must finally choose between Caspar and Osmond at the conclusion of the novel: in choosing to marry Osmond, Isabel has already made her choice, Laurence Holland argues, and at the end her return to Osmond is simply an acceptance of the responsibility that the choice entails.

Obviously, the debate over the motives that determine Isabel's situation at the conclusion of the novel has produced a variety of conjectures. Whatever various explanations modern critics have attached to the conclusion of *The Portrait,* however, they have at least agreed that there is no ambiguity about Isabel's decision to return to Rome. Their agreement is due, at least in part, to the fact that they are probably relying on James's revised New York Edition of the novel. In preparing that edition of *The Portrait* James carefully removed any possible ambiguity concerning Isabel's decision to return to Rome at the end of the novel. The explanation for his revision is a revealing chapter in the publication history of the novel.

The Portrait first appeared in print in *Macmillan's Magazine* in October, 1880, where it was serialized until November, 1881. A month after its initial appearance in *Macmillan's,* the *Atlantic Monthly* commenced serialization of the novel in America (November, 1880, to December, 1881). The first book publication, issued by Macmillan's on November 8, 1881, was followed eight days later by the first American edition. A second British edition was published in 1882 and a third, in three volumes, in 1883. The New York Edition of James's *Novels and Tales,* editorially superintended by James himself, contained *The Portrait* in its third and fourth volumes and was published, with James's newly written preface, in 1908.

Sydney J. Krause notes: "Between magazine and book publication James gave the novel a careful, but limited, revision. He used this revised text for all subsequent printings of the novel up to the time of the New York Edition, for which he did an extensive job of revision" [see Further Reading]. For James, of course, it was customary to revise. Edel points out that he constantly retouched his works from serialization to book and from printing to printing. [In his essay "James and the Plastic Arts," *Kenyon Review* (1943)] F. O. Matthiessen says of James that revision "meant for him literally *re-seeing.*" James's first revision of *The Portrait,* the revision from serialization to book in 1881, "brought about no changes in the theme or in the essential structure of the novel." But the revision for the New York Edition was considerably more extensive and more important. The changes that are relevant to this inquiry occur in the final paragraphs of *The Portrait:*

Caspar Goodwood was not looking at her; his eyes were fastened on the doorstep.

"Oh, she started—" he stammered. And without finishing his phrase, or looking up, he turned away.

Henrietta had come out, closing the door behind her, and now she put out her hand and grasped his arm.

"Look here, Mr. Goodwood," she said; "just you wait!"

On which he looked up at her.

Caspar Goodwood was not looking at her; his eyes were fastened on the doorstep. "Oh, she started—?" he stammered. And without finishing his phrase or looking up he stiffly averted himself. But he couldn't otherwise move.

Henrietta had come out, closing the door behind her, and now she put out her hand and grasped his arm. "Look here, Mr. Goodwood," she said; "just you wait!"

On which he looked up at her—but only to guess, from her face, with a revulsion, that she simply meant he was young. She stood shining at him with that cheap comfort, and it added, on the spot, thirty years to his life. She walked him away with her, however, as if she had given him now the key to patience.

There are three significant alterations of the 1881 edition. The first is a seemingly unimportant one, merely the addition of a question mark in Goodwood's stammer, but it makes a meaningful change in the implication of Goodwood's brief utterance: it makes Goodwood appear genuinely surprised at the news of Isabel's departure for Rome. Without the question mark as guide, the reader might easily lower the tone of his (inner) voice, reading the phrase as though Goodwood were acknowledging an unfavorable reply which he had resignedly anticipated. The question mark supplies for the reader a tonal rise on the last syllable of "started," indicates surprise, and removes any possible ambiguity concerning Goodwood's reception of the news of Isabel's departure.

The second alteration is the replacement of "turned away" with more explicit, more precise, and more dramatic prose. Thus, we are made more keenly aware of Goodwood's now obvious surprise and bitter disappointment.

James's major revision is the addition of some two and a half sentences to the 1881 ending. Few critics have concerned themselves with this revision and only F. O. Matthiessen has attempted to explain its significance. He points out that the revision does not support the contention of some critics that James had changed his mind about the ending of the novel. The 1908 ending makes "unmistakably explicit" Isabel's departure for Rome, which James "had always intended to imply," as his notebook design demonstrates. James must have felt that he had been too brief in the 1881 edition, Matthiessen concludes; he must have felt "that he had failed to drive home to the reader that what was being expressed (in Henrietta's exhortation to Goodwood: 'just you wait!') was no sure promise about Isabel, but rather Henrietta's optimism, which refuses to accept defeat."

I agree with Matthiessen that James wished to make the ending explicit and unambiguous, but Matthiessen does not examine the reasons for this particular aspect of the revision. Why did James feel it necessary to make Isabel's return to Rome and to Osmond "unmistakably explicit"? There is evidence to suggest that his revision was prompted by the criticism of some early reviewers whose misreadings of James's intentions at the close of *The Portrait* pointed to a serious and unintentional ambiguity in the work. (pp. 55-9)

At first glance, James's revising of the conclusion seems to have been more extensive than was really necessary if the elimination of ambiguity was his sole purpose for the revision. More accurately, the removal of ambiguity was the *primary* motive for the revision; there is evidence that it was further prompted by James's stylistic concerns in 1908. Quite clearly, it is James's intent to focus the novel upon the character of Isabel Archer. This is as clear in his notebook entry of 1881 as it is in his preface of 1908: "The germ of my idea . . . consisted . . . altogether in the sense of a single character." His working out of this central idea, he explains further, simply involves letting his characters work out their own destinies. Isabel's consciousness contains the center of the subject, but to "do" her well he must also concentrate upon her relationships to those around her through the "consciousness of [her] satellites." In other words, James attempts in *The Portrait* to "withdraw," hoping to leave us solely in the consciousness of Isabel and those around her. For Laurence Holland, "James's stance" is neither "that of a direct observer . . . nor that of a narrator . . . but that of a painter." It is precisely James's mature attempt to achieve aesthetic distance for his narrator that distinguishes his 1908 revision of *The Portrait*'s conclusion.

In his notebook, in 1881, James designed the conclusion of the novel by deliberately placing his readers in Henrietta's consciousness: Henrietta "has the last word—utters the last line of the story: a characteristic characterization of Isabel." The problem in 1908 did not involve the correction of a stylistic error. True to his earlier intentions, the author had not allowed the narrator to "intrude"; we had been left in the consciousness of one of the heroine's "satellites." Reviewers had indicated, however, that the ending was ambiguous, perhaps because of their interpretation of the consciousness of that "satellite."

Early in 1881, with a great deal of *The Portrait* yet unwritten, William Dean Howells had sent James a worried letter which, in part, criticized the characterization of Henrietta as "overdrawn." By 1908 James thoroughly agreed that she was "a broken reed . . . of whom we have indubitably too much." Admitting a tendency to "overtreat" his subjects, James acknowledged her characterization as an "excess of my zeal." In light of the possible ambiguity her characterization may have prompted and in light of the feelings he expresses in his preface, then, it is not surpris-

ing that James should revise his ending by taking from Henrietta the distinction of concluding the novel in her consciousness.

The revision is a smooth one, reminding a modern reader perhaps of a cinematic technique: we focus upon Henrietta as she utters her fervent phrase, but then we pull back away from her, setting her in perspective, but not stopping in Goodwood's consciousness for long either. We are there only long enough to watch Henrietta, interpreting her words with Caspar's accuracy but not lingering to sympathize with his bitterness. We continue to pull back slowly until both Henrietta and Goodwood are in distant focus, and then we fade out quietly. The novel concludes not in either character's consciousness nor in a narrative "intrusion": "She walked him away with her, however, as if she had given him now the key to patience." This last sentence is a triumph for the author, whose preface resounds with his insistence upon the artistic merits of suppressing the narrator and allowing his characters to work out their own destinies.

Such a revision represents "the later James"—the more mature craftsman consciously attempting to move towards the stance of a "disinterested" narrator. It seems reasonable to conclude, then, that in addition to the possible ambiguity of the ending, the mature development of James's style also prompted his 1908 revision of the conclusion to *The Portrait of a Lady*. (pp. 61-3)

> *Dominic J. Bazzanella, "The Conclusion to 'The Portrait of a Lady' Re-examined," in* American Literature, *Vol. XLI, No. 1, March, 1969, pp. 55-63.*

William H. Gass   (essay date 1970)

[*Gass is an American fiction writer and critic. Widely praised for the virtuosity of his prose style, he is among the most conspicuous modern proponents of the view that literature's sole meaning lies in the aesthetic forms an author creates with language. This position is developed in two collections of critical essays,* Fiction and the Figures of Life *and* The World within the Word (1978). *As opposed to the representational theory of art, which holds that literature should be a rendering of human experience more or less in the manner of history or journalism, such essays as "The Medium of Fiction" and "Philosophy and the Form of Fiction" disclaim the injunction that fiction should, or indeed is able to, present anything to the reader except an aesthetic pattern composed of rhetorical devices and the poetic qualities of words themselves. This is exemplified by Gass's demonstration in "The Concept of Character in Fiction" that a character may be defined as a series of verbal strategies focusing on a proper noun which in turn serves as one element among many in a larger aesthetic design. While such an abstract account of Gass's work might suggest that his is a purely decorative form of literature, one exclusive of human emotion, he has in fact criticized such writers as Samuel Beckett and Jorge Luis Borges for just such a lack of feeling, and he has made it clear in many of his works that for him the rhetorical substance of literature is perfectly capable of embodying, in aesthetic form, all the passions of life. In the following excerpt,*] *he examines the ways in which James's "moral passion" informs the artistry of* The Portrait of a Lady.]

It is the particular achievement of Henry James that he was able to transform the moral color of his personal vision into the hues of his famous figure in the carpet; that he found a form for his awareness of moral issues, an awareness that was so pervasive it invaded furniture and walls and ornamental gardens and perched upon the shoulders of his people a dove for spirit, beating its wings with the violence of all Protestant history; so that of this feeling, of the moving wing itself, he could make a *style.* This endeavor was both aided and hindered by the fact that, for James, art and morality were so closely twined, and by the fact that no theory of either art or morality has footing unless, previous to it, the terrible difficulties of vision and knowledge, of personal construction and actual fact, of, in short, the relation of reality to appearance had been thoroughly overcome. James's style is a result of his effort to master, at the level of his craft, these difficulties, and his effort, quite apart from any measure of its actual success with these things, brought to the form of the novel in English an order of art never even, before him, envisioned by it.

Both Henry James and his brother were consumed by a form of The Moral Passion. Both struggled to find in the plural world of practice a vantage for spirit. But William was fatally enmeshed in the commercial. How well he speaks for the best in his age. He pursues the saint; he probes the spiritual disorders of the soul; he commiserates with the world-weary and encourages the strong; he investigates the nature of God, His relation to the world, His code; he defends the possible immortality of the soul and the right to believe: and does all so skillfully, with a nature so sensitive, temperate and generous, that it is deeply disappointing to discover, as one soon must, that the lenses of his mind are monetary, his open hand is open for the coin, and that the more he struggles to understand, appreciate, and rise, the more instead he misses, debases, and destroys. (pp. 178-79)

Henry James was certainly aware that one is always on the market, but as he grew as an artist he grew as a moralist and his use of the commercial matrix of analogy became markedly satirical or ironic and his investigation of the human trade more self-conscious and profound until in nearly all the works of his maturity his theme is the evil of human manipulation, a theme best summarized by the second formulation of Kant's categorical imperative:

> So act as to treat humanity, whether in thine own person or in that of any other, in every case as an end withal, never as a means only.

Nothing further from pragmatism can be imagined, and if we first entertain the aphorism that though William was the superior thinker, Henry had the superior thought, we may be led to consider the final effect of their rivalry, for the novels and stories of Henry James constitute the most searching criticism available of the pragmatic ideal of the proper treatment and ultimate worth of man. That this criticism was embodied in Henry James's style, William James was one of the first to recognize. "Your methods and my ideals seem the reverse, the one of the other," he wrote to Henry in a letter complaining about the "interminable elaboration" of *The Golden Bowl.* Couldn't we have, he asks, a "book with no twilight or mustiness in the plot, with great vigour and decisiveness in the action, no fencing in the dialogue, no psychological commentaries, and absolute straightness in the style?" Henry would rather have gone, he replies, to a dishonored grave.

The Portrait of a Lady is James's first fully exposed case of human manipulation; his first full-dress investigation, at the level of what Plato called "right opinion," of what it means to be a consumer of persons, and of what it means to be a person consumed. The population of James's fictional society is composed, as populations commonly are, of purchasers and their purchases, of the handlers and the handled, of the users and the used. Sometimes actual objects, like Mrs. Gareth's spoils, are involved in the transaction, but their involvement is symbolic of a buying and a being sold which is on the level of human worth (where the quality of the product is measured in terms of its responsiveness to the purchaser's "finest feelings," and its ability to sound the buyer's taste discreetly aloud), and it is for this reason that James never chooses to center his interest upon objects which can, by use, be visibly consumed. In nearly all of the later novels and stories, it is a human being, not an object—it is first Isabel Archer, then Pansy—who is the spoil, and it is by no means true that only the "villains" fall upon her and try to carry her off; nor is it easy to discover just who the villains really are.

Kant's imperative governs by its absence—as the hollow center. It is not that some characters, the "good" people, are busy being the moral legislators of mankind and that the others, the "bad" people, are committed to a crass and shallow pragmatism or a trifling estheticism; for were that the case, *The Portrait* would be just another skillful novel of manners and James would be distinctly visible, outside the work, nodding or shaking his head at the behavior of the animals in his moral fable. He would have managed no advance in the art of English fiction. James's examination of the methods of human consumption goes too deep. He is concerned with all of the ways in which men may be reduced to the status of objects, and because James pursues his subject so diligently, satisfying himself only when he has unraveled every thread, and because he is so intent on avoiding in himself what he has revealed as evil in his characters and exemplifying rather what he praises in Hawthorne, who, he says, "never intermeddled," the moral problem of *The Portrait* becomes an esthetic problem, a problem of form, the scope and course of the action, the nature of the characters, the content of dialogue, the shape and dress of setting, the points-of-view, the figures of speech, the very turn and tumble of the sentences themselves directed by the problem's looked-for solution, and there is consequently no suggestion that one should choose up sides or take to heart his criticism of a certain society nor any invitation to discuss the moral motivations of his characters *as if* they were surrogates for the real.

The moral problem, moreover, merges with the esthetic. It is possible to be an artist, James sees, in more than paint and language, and in *The Portrait,* as it is so often in his other work, Isabel Archer becomes the unworked medium through which, like benevolent Svengali, the shapers and admirers of beautifully brought out persons express their artistry and themselves. The result is very often lovely, but it is invariably sad. James has the feeling, furthermore, and it is a distinctly magical feeling, that the novelist takes possession of his subject through his words; that the artist is a puppeteer; his works are the works of a god. He constantly endeavors to shift the obligation and the blame, if there be any, to another: his reflector, his reverberator, his sensitive gong. In *The Portrait* James begins his movement toward the theory of the point-of-view. The phrase itself occurs incessantly. Its acceptance as a canon of method means the loss of a single, universally objective reality. He is committed, henceforth, to a standpoint philosophy, and it would seem, then, that the best world would be that observed from the most sensitive, catholic, yet discriminating standpoint. In this way, the esthetic problem reaches out to the metaphysical. This marvelous observer: what is it he observes? Does he see the world as it really is, palpitating with delicious signs of the internal, or does he merely fling out the self-capturing net? James struggles with this question most obviously in *The Sacred Fount* but it is always before him. So many of his characters are "perceptive." They understand the value of the unmolded clay. They feel they know, as artists, what will be best for their human medium. They will *take up* the young lady (for so it usually is). They will *bring* her *out*. They will *do for* her; *make something of* her. She will be *beautiful* and *fine*, in short, she will inspire *interest, amusement,* and *wonder*. And their pursuit of the ideally refractive medium parallels perfectly Henry James's own, except he is aware that his selected lens dare not be perfect else he will have embodied a god again, and far more obnoxious must this god seem in the body of a character than he did in the nib of the author's pen; but more than this, James knows, as his creations so often do not, that this manipulation is the essence, the ultimate germ, of the evil the whole of his work condemns, and it is nowhere more brutal than when fronted by the kindest regard and backed by a benevolent will.

The Portrait of a Lady, for one who is familiar with James, opens on rich sounds. None of his major motifs is missing. The talk at tea provides us with five, the composition of the company constitutes a sixth, and his treatment of the setting satisfies the full and holy seven. The talk moves in a desultory fashion ("desultory" is a repetitive word) and in joking tones ("That's a sort of joke" is the repetitive phrase) from health and illness, and the ambiguity of its value, to boredom, considered as a kind of sickness, and the ambiguity of its production. Wealth is suggested as a cause of boredom, then marriage is proposed as a cure. The elder Touchett warns Lord Warburton not to fall in love with his niece, a young lady recently captured by his wife to be exhibited abroad. The questions about her are: has she money? is she interesting? The jokes are: is she marriageable? is she engaged? Isabel is the fifth thing, then—the young, spirited material. Lord Warburton is English, of course, while the Touchetts are Americans. Isabel's coming will sharpen the contrast, dramatize the confrontation. Lastly, James dwells lovingly on the ancient red brick house, emphasizing its esthetic appeal, its traditions, its status as a work of art. In describing the

grounds he indicates, too, what an American man of money may do: fall in love with a history not his own and allow it, slowly, to civilize him, draw him into Europe. Lord Warburton is said to be bored. It is suggested that he is trying to fall in love. Ralph is described as cynical, without belief, a condition ascribed to his illness by his father. "He seems to feel as if he had never had a chance." But the best of the ladies will save us, the elder Touchett says, a remark made improbable by his own lack of success.

The structure of the talk of this astonishing first chapter foreshadows everything. All jests turn earnest, and in them, as in the aimless pattern of the jesters' leisure, lies plain the essential evil, for the evil cannot be blinked even though it may not be so immediately irritating to the eye as the evil of Madame Merle or Gilbert Osmond. There is in Isabel herself a certain willingness to be employed, a desire to be taken up and fancied, if only because that very enslavement, on other terms, makes her more free. She refuses Warburton, not because he seeks his own salvation in her, his cure by "interest," but rather because marriage to him would not satisfy her greed for experience, her freedom to see and feel and do. Neither Warburton nor Goodwood appeals as a person to Isabel's vanity. She is a great subject. She will make a great portrait. She knows it. Nevertheless Isabel's ambitions are at first naïve and inarticulate. It is Ralph who sees the chance, in her, for the really fine thing; who sees in her his own chance, too, the chance at life denied him. It is Ralph, finally, who empowers her flight and in doing so draws the attention of the hunters.

Ralph and Osmond represent two types of the artist. Osmond regards Isabel as an opportunity to create a work which will flatter himself and be the best testimony to his taste. Her intelligence is a silver plate he will heap with fruits to decorate his table. Her talk will be for him "a sort of served dessert." He will rap her with his knuckle. She will ring. As Osmond's wife, Isabel recognizes that she is a piece of property; her mind is attached to his like a small garden plot to a deer park. But Ralph obeys the strictures **"The Art of Fiction"** was later to lay down. He works rather with the medium itself and respects the given. His desire is to exhibit it, make it whole, refulgent, round. He wants, in short, to make an image or to see one made—a portrait. He demands of the work only that it be "interesting." He effaces himself. The "case" is his concern. *The Portrait*'s crucial scene, in this regard, is that between Ralph and his dying father. Ralph cannot love Isabel. His illness prevents him. He feels it would be wrong. Nevertheless, he takes, he says, "a great interest" in his cousin although he has no real influence over her.

> "But I should like to do something for her. . . .
> I should like to put a little wind in her sails. . . .
> I should like to put it into her power to do some
> of the things she wants. She wants to see the
> world for instance. I should like to put money
> in her purse."

The language is unmistakable. It is the language of Iago. Ralph wants her rich.

> "I call people rich when they're able to meet the

requirements of their imagination. Isabel has a great deal of imagination."

With money she will not have to marry for it. Money will make her free. It is a curious faith. Mr. Touchett says, "You speak as if it were for your mere amusement," and Ralph replies, "So it is, a good deal." Mr. Touchett's objections are serenely met. Isabel will be extravagant but she will come to her senses in time. And Ralph says,

> ". . . it would be very painful to me to think of her coming to the consciousness of a lot of wants she should be unable to satisfy. . . ."
>
> "Well, I don't know. . . . I don't think I enter into your spirit. It seems to me immoral."
>
> "Immoral, dear daddy?"
>
> "Well, I don't know that it's right to make everything so easy for a person."
>
> "It surely depends upon the person. When the person's good, your making things easy is all to the credit of virtue. To facilitate the execution of good impulses, what can be a nobler act? . . ."
>
> "Isabel's a sweet young thing; but do you think she's so good as that?"
>
> "She's as good as her best opportunities. . . ."
>
> "Doesn't it occur to you that a young lady with sixty thousand pounds may fall a victim to the fortune-hunters?"
>
> "She'll hardly fall victim to more than one."
>
> "Well, one's too many."
>
> "Decidedly. That's a risk, and it has entered into my calculation. I think it's appreciable, but I think it's small, and I'm prepared to take it. . . ."
>
> "But I don't see what good you're to get of it. . . ."
>
> "I shall get just the good I said a few moments ago I wished to put into Isabel's reach—that of having met the requirements of my imagination. . . ."

The differences between Gilbert Osmond and Ralph Touchett are vast, but they are also thin.

Isabel Archer is thus free to try her wings. She is thrown upon the world. She becomes the friend of Madame Merle, "the great round world herself ": polished, perfect, beautiful without a fault, mysterious, exciting, treacherous, repellent, and at bottom, like Isabel, identically betrayed; like Isabel again, seeking out of her own ruin to protect Pansy, the new subject, "the blank page," from that same round world that is herself. It is irony of the profoundest sort that "good" and "evil" in their paths should pass so closely. The dark ambitions of Serena Merle are lightened by a pathetic bulb, and it is only those whose eyes are fascinated and convinced by surface who can put their confident finger on the "really good." Ralph Touchett, and we are not meant to miss the appropriateness of his name, has not only failed to respect Isabel Archer as an end, he has

failed to calculate correctly the qualities of his object. Isabel is a sweet, young thing. She is not yet, at any rate, as good as her best opportunities. The sensitive eye was at the acute point blind. Ralph has unwittingly put his bird in a cage. In a later interview, Isabel tells him she has given up all desire for a general view of life. Now she prefers corners. It is a corner she's been driven to. Time after time the "better" people curse the future they wish to save with their bequests. Longdon of *The Awkward Age* and Milly Theale of *The Wings of the Dove* come immediately to mind. Time after time the better artists fail because their point-of-view is ultimately only *theirs,* and because they have brought the esthetic relation too grandly, too completely into life.

In the portrait of Fleda Vetch of *The Spoils of Poynton* James has rendered an ideally considerate soul. Fleda, a person of modest means and background, possesses nevertheless the true sense of beauty. She is drawn by her friend Mrs. Gareth into the full exercise of that sense and to an appreciation of the ripe contemplative life which otherwise might have been denied her. Yet Fleda so little awards the palm to mere cleverness or sensibility that she falls in love with the slow, confused, and indecisive Owen Gareth. Fleda furthermore separates her moral and her esthetic ideals. Not only does she refuse to manipulate others, she refuses, herself, to be manipulated. The moral lines she feels are delicate. She takes all into her hands. Everyone has absolute worth. Scruples beset and surround her and not even Mrs. Gareth's righteousness, the warmth of her remembered wrongs, can melt them through. The impatience which James generates in the reader and expresses through Mrs. Gareth is the impatience, precisely, of his brother: for Fleda to act, to break from the net of scruple and seize the chance. It would be for the good of the good. It would save the spoils, save Owen, save Mrs. Gareth, save love for herself; but Fleda Vetch understands, as few people in Henry James ever do, the high brutality of such good intentions. She cannot accept happiness on the condition of moral compromise, for that would be to betray the ground on which, ideally, happiness ought to rest. Indeed it would betray happiness itself, and love, and the people and their possessions that have precipitated the problem and suggested the attractive and fatal price.

It is not simply in the organization of character, dialogue, and action that Henry James reveals The Moral Passion, nor is it reflected further only in his treatment of surroundings but it represents itself and its ideal in the increasing scrupulosity of the style: precision of definition, respect for nuance, tone, the multiplying presence of enveloping metaphors, the winding around the tender center of ritual lines, like the approach of the devout and worshipful to the altar, these circumlocutions at once protecting the subject and slowing the advance so that the mere utility of the core is despaired of and it is valued solely in the contemplative sight. The value of life lies ultimately in the experienced quality of it, in the integrity of the given not in the usefulness of the taken. Henry James does not peer through experience to the future, through his future to the future futures, endlessly down the infinite tube. He does not find in today only what is needful for tomorrow.

His aim is rather to appreciate and to respect the things of his experience and to set them, finally, free. (pp. 180-90)

William H. Gass, "The High Brutality of Good Intentions," in his Fiction and the Figures of Life, *Alfred A. Knopf, 1970, pp. 177-90.*

Louis Auchincloss   (essay date 1975)

[*An American man of letters, Auchincloss is known primarily as the author of novels of manners, in the tradition of Edith Wharton and C. P. Snow. He is also a respected critic who has written major critical studies of such authors as Henry James, Ellen Glasgow, Henry Adams and Wharton. Of his own literary scholarship Auchincloss has written: "I find in writing criticism I write more about novelists of the past, and I never write with any other object but to induce my reader to revisit them. This is not to say that I do not read my contemporaries—I do—but I feel less division than many of them do between past and present." In the following excerpt, he finds critical readings of the "international theme" to be inappropriately applied to* The Portrait of a Lady.]

It has always seemed curious to me that one of the most discussed aspects of James's fiction should be the "international situation." I have never seen what there was to be said about his treatment of this theme after one has noted that his American characters are high-minded and naive and are taken advantage of by their more worldly European acquaintances. James's American girls abroad, his Daisy Millers and Francie Dossons, may be charming creatures, but I do not even think that he deserves the whole credit for introducing them into literature. Caroline Spalding in Anthony Trollope's *He Knew He Was Right* made her appearance long before Bessie Alden in **"An International Episode,"** and she anticipates all of the latter's principal characteristics.

It also seems to me that James is playing a private game in some of these stories. He had had his share of snubs in Victorian society (which must have cultivated arrogance to a degree almost inconceivable to us), and he enjoyed paying back the nobility by having his Yankee heroines turn down their sons and heirs. Bessie Alden rejects the heir to a dukedom, and Isabel Archer in **The Portrait of a Lady** declines the honor of becoming Lady Warburton. When **"An International Episode"** first appeared James was candidly delighted with the way British readers resented Bessie Alden's democratic assumptions. Yet he was never one to overdefy his chosen countrymen, and he sounded a cautious note in a letter to his mother: "It seems to me myself that I have been very delicate; but I shall keep off dangerous ground in future. It is an entirely new sensation for them (the people here) to be (at all delicately) *ironized* or satirized, from the American point of view . . . "

To my thinking the comparison of American with European values brought out the most superficial side of James. All his life he was to harp on the "tone of time," the great European cultural advantage, yet in most of his instances this "time" does not take one back much earlier than the eighteenth century, which had, after all, its American

counterpart. The culture in which James encased himself, literary, artistic, and even architectural, was usually not more ancient than that. Another element that he emphasized was the "thinness" of the American air as contrasted to the richness of the European. One presumes that he was referring to the cultural atmosphere—although there are instances where he appears to be actually speaking of the air he breathes—and certainly it is true that the American field of letters and arts was bleak compared to that of England and France at the time of his initial expatriation, but he clouds his distinctions by continually confusing "culture" with the picturesque ways in which the British upper class amused itself. Somehow hunting and riding and weekending and dinner partying seemed to strike James as parts of the cultural scene. The fact that he had a sharp eye for the shoddy in the English aristocracy did not keep him from losing his head over the beauty of the right kind of peer with the right kind of tradition in the right kind of castle. There are moments when his vision of England seems as bland as a travel poster.

Now, of course, in his own life (as opposed to that of his characters) he did not live exclusively in the social world. When he went to Paris and London he cultivated the literary figures of the day. In Paris, as a young man, he made the acquaintance of Zola, Daudet, Maupassant, Bourget, and Flaubert. In London he met George Eliot and Tennyson. Over a long life I estimate that he knew, with some degree of intimacy, more eminent men and women of letters, from Thackeray to Ezra Pound, than any other writer in literary history. The literary world provided a continual and necessary balance to the millionaires and the peerage. But this balance is not provided for the characters in the early international tales. As a result they seem constantly absorbed in petty activities.

The baroness in **The Europeans** is bothered by the fact that there are not more servants in the entrance halls of American hotels. She tries to make herself at home in a Boston suburb by spreading shawls over the furniture. Daisy Miller causes a scandal in Rome by a nocturnal visit to the Colosseum with an Italian escort, unchaperoned. Isabel Archer is reproved by her aunt for wanting to sit up at night in the drawing room with two gentlemen, of whom one is her own first cousin, after her hostess has retired. And when characters of different nationalities converse it is almost always about the tighter line of class distinctions drawn to the east of the Atlantic.

I do not question the accuracy of these observations about rules of conduct. I question their importance. For people in society do not live by their own social principles unless it suits them. They show little consistency. If there is a reason for liking Daisy Miller, they will pooh-pooh her walks in the Colosseum or look the other way. If there is a reason for disliking her, they will cut her dead. Proust understood this as no other novelist has ever understood it. James came in time to be vaguely aware of it, but he never liked it. He considered that manners had deteriorated, and he saw this deterioration as symptomatic of a general cultural decline. In manners and morals, he was always a tremendous conservative.

But James usually knew what was wrong with his work.

When he sensed triviality in a theme, he put his foot down hard on the moral pedal. To complicate the oversimplicity of these bright, sparkling, but superficial tales, he introduced stern ethical judgments. The American ingenue is seen as not merely more democratic and freer than the Europeans whom she encounters; she is purer and more honest. If she is headstrong, naive, abrupt, even blunt, she is also shiningly, incontrovertibly good. If she is made unhappy, or even done to death, by a cynical, dirty-minded old Europe, it is a tragedy. Good against evil, the brave New World against the wicked Old, such is the melodramatic international conflict as James conceived it. **"Madame de Mauves"** is the earliest example of this. The American heroine's only fault is that she is naively romantic; her French husband's only virtue is that he ultimately commits suicide after perversely and belatedly falling in love with her.

My trouble is that I do not believe in any of it, and I wonder if James really did. I suppose that there were Daisy Millers in Rome in his day, but I doubt that any of them died of snubs. James was soon enough to see his rich compatriots as predators, prowling about a crumbling Europe and bearing off masterpieces. He thought that the situation had changed. Maybe it was simply that his angle of vision had improved. But the redeeming thing about his overconcern with the "international situation" was that it produced *The Portrait of a Lady.* The explanation of the paradox that so deep a work of fiction should spring from so shallow a subject is that the subject provides the novel with no more than its starting point. James went on to ponder questions which had a good deal to do with his characters being American but much less to do with their being international. Isabel Archer's tragedy might almost have been acted out in New York. (pp. 56-61)

Although all the action of *The Portrait of a Lady* (except for a brief chapter in Albany) takes place in England, France, and Italy, the characters, except for Lord Warburton, are all Americans. Isabel Archer, Caspar Goodwood, and Henrietta Stackpole are Americans of origin and upbringing who are having their first adult European experience as the novel commences. Mr. and Mrs. Touchett are Americans who have lived in Europe all their adult lives but who have been reared at home and have preserved their essential American characteristics. Ralph Touchett, their son, has lived all his life in England, but has kept in touch with his native land. He is the one true cosmopolitan of the novel. Edward Rosier, Madame Merle, Gilbert Osmond, and the Countess Gemini, on the other hand, are Americans who have ceased to think of America or to take the smallest interest in their birthplace. They have been Europeanized without ever entirely belonging to Europe. What James has done by setting these characters against a backdrop of London, Florence, and Rome is to put different facets of the American character into higher relief than he could have done with an American situs. From a strictly artistic point of view I have always regretted the British nationality of Lord Warburton. Impenitently, I see him as a younger American banking partner of Mr. Touchett.

Isabel is, of course, the victim of a plot. The clever Madame Merle induces her indolent and selfish ex-lover, Gilbert Osmond, to court her so that he may obtain her fortune and endow Pansy, the bastard daughter of Osmond and Madame Merle. And Isabel's fortune, which so proves her undoing, is the result of another, if kinder plot. Ralph Touchett has induced his father to leave it to Isabel because, as a beneficent but too curious invalid, he wants to see what she will do with "a little wind in her sails." So one might say that Isabel is the victim of a double conspiracy: one, an old-fashioned mercenary scheme of the European sort and the other, a naive but perverse American form of pastime. But the person who really ties the cords of Isabel's fate is Isabel herself. And this is the essence of the novel.

She is the loveliest and most appealing of all James's heroines. She is very fine, very straight, totally honest, and candid to a fault, and she has a charm which captivates every other character as well as the reader. Isabel has a high sense that she must be prepared for her destiny—whatever that destiny may be. She has no great opinion of her own capacities, but she appreciates that she is not made of common materials. She apprehends that she may be reserved for something, if not necessarily illustrious, at least rather fine. She does not for a minute assume that it will be happy. Indeed a certain anticipation of her doom appears to hang about her from the beginning. It is this which gives her her especially American flavor.

Success crowds in on her, jostles her. Her rich aunt, Mrs. Touchett, swoops down to take her off to Europe. Caspar Goodwood, a brave young textile manufacturer, follows her with passionate proposals of marriage. Her cousin Ralph devotes all his waking thoughts to her. Lord Warburton offers to make her his viscountess. Her uncle bequeaths her a fortune. Remarkably, James makes Isabel's success quite credible; she seems to offer to each new acquaintance precisely what he or she most needs. But Isabel does not care for easy successes. They seem crude, perhaps obvious to her. She has a kind of hubris about the gifts of the gods. The smashing forcefulness of Caspar Goodwood, the high social position of Lord Warburton, the glitter of her own inherited wealth—these things make her uneasy. She cannot believe that her fate is so simple. She tells Lord Warburton that she would be trying to escape it if she marries him. "I can't escape unhappiness," she declares. She confesses to her cousin Ralph that Warburton is too perfect and that his perfection would irritate her.

She must give as well as take, then, in the strange romantic destiny that she dimly descries. Of course, it need not be a "successful" fate, by simple American or English standards. And when Madame Merle guides her to Gilbert Osmond, poor Isabel sees in his love of art and beauty, in his seeming scorn of the world, in his very idleness, the independence of a great mind which has cast aside the trappings of the workaday existence of busy American industrialists and of politically minded British peers. Osmond, surrounded by his perfect pictures and bibelots on the top of his hill beside Florence, makes even the best natured of her good-natured friends seem shallow. "He was like a sceptical voyager strolling on the beach while he waited for the tide, looking seaward yet not putting to sea. It was in all this that she had found her occasion. She would launch his boat for him; she would be his providence; it would be a good thing to love him."

I know of no finer passages in all of James than those where he uncovers the true character of Osmond and the terrible disillusionment of Isabel. The fact that he has already indicated the wrongness of her choice, not only through direct glimpses of Osmond but through the unanimous adverse opinion of all Isabel's friends, somehow does not make her horror on encountering the "mansion" of her husband's mental habitation an anticlimax: "It was the house of darkness, the house of dumbness, the house of suffocation. Osmond's beautiful mind gave it neither light nor air; Osmond's beautiful mind indeed seemed to peep down from a small high window and mock her."

And what of the vulgar world from which Osmond had seemed so carefully to remove himself, from which they were to live unspotted? This base, ignoble world, it appears, "was after all what one was to live for; one was to keep it for ever in one's eye, in order not to enlighten or convert or redeem it, but to extract from it some recognition of one's own superiority." Everything that Osmond does is pose. "His life on his hilltop at Florence had been the conscious attitude of years. His solitude, his *ennui,* his love for his daughter, his good manners, his bad manners, were so many features of a mental image constantly present to him as a model of impertinence and mystification."

Isabel's acceptance of her fate is explained in the title. She sees the deceit and the entrapment, but she also sees that she has made a choice. "When a woman has made such a mistake, there was only one way to repair it—to accept it." Her friends think that she must fear her sinister husband, but the wonderful thing about Isabel is that she is not in the least afraid of him. She is afraid only of the ugliness of a public rupture of her marriage, of demonstrating her private failure to the world. However misguided this may seem to our century—and indeed it seemed so to many readers in the last—one cannot deny that Isabel's sticking to her wretched home and to her wretched stepdaughter shows a certain high style. Nor is she in the least subservient to Osmond. She crosses his wishes whenever she deems it right to do so, as when she interferes between his daughter Pansy and Lord Warburton and when she goes to Ralph's deathbed in England. She is always perfectly direct and honest with Osmond. But she has agreed to be his wife before the world, and this she will be while she has breath in her body. For better or worse. That was to be a lady in her time.

Isabel's pathetic plight, as I have said, is American in its particular combination of romantic idealism with a willingness to suffer, even an expectation of suffering. She is a dupe, but such a lovely one and such a splendidly good sport, so square in admitting her own folly, that her being "put in a cage," as her cousin expresses it, is even more heartbreaking than if she had not made love to her destiny. But the evil that confronts her, the evil that captures her—is it European? Madame Merle wishes to convert Isabel's fortune into a dower for her daughter, and Osmond wishes to use this same money to build the lavish setting for his ultimate pose. But might such a pair not have operated in

New York? Nineteenth-century Manhattan had more than its share of such adventurers. There is, of course, a suaveness and a style about the conspirators that seems more European than Yankee, but I suggest that Madame Merle and Osmond represent integral parts of the American psyche.

The most important reason, to my mind, for setting the novel in Europe is simply that the visual background provides the same rich charge to Isabel's imagination that it did to James's own. The drama of an American girl with the world at her feet was more exciting in the 1870s if that world was the glittering Old World rather than the still raw New. Furthermore, it is difficult to see how a dilettante in New York could have captured Isabel's fancy in quite the same way as could a dilettante living in Florence. One does not immediately see Osmond in a small flat on Washington Square filled with bibelots, taking Isabel on a guided tour through the still exiguous collection at the newly founded Metropolitan Museum of Art. No, it is better to see him in his hilltop abode with a beautiful Florence, which he thoroughly understands, at his feet.

When I say that the *Portrait of a Lady* is not, properly speaking, an international novel, I mean that the contrast of manners and mores no longer has the importance that it had in the earlier stories. Isabel adapts herself to European standards with almost no trouble at all. She has one brief scene, already cited, with her aunt about sitting up in the drawing room with two gentlemen after Mrs. Touchett has retired, but unlike Daisy Miller she wisely gives in to her aunt. She knows that these small conventions make little difference. To defy them is to make too much of them. (pp. 62-7)

Louis Auchincloss, in his Reading Henry James, *University of Minnesota Press, 1975, 181 p.*

Edward Wagenknecht   (essay date 1978)

[*Wagenknecht is an American biographer and critic. His works include critical surveys of the English and American novel and studies of Charles Dickens, Mark Twain, and Henry James, among many others. His studies of Dickens and Twain employ the biographical technique of "psychography," derived from American biographer Gamaliel Bradford, who writes of this method: "Out of the perpetual flux of actions and circumstances that constitutes a man's whole life, it seeks to extract what is essential, what is permanent and so vitally characteristic." In later works Wagenknecht has focused more on the literary than biographical aspects of his subjects, though he states: "I have no theories about writing except that I think people should write about what they care for." In the following excerpt from a full-length study of James's female characters, he examines strengths and weaknesses in Isabel Archer's personality.*]

Though there is a sense in which the female protagonist of any work of fiction may be called its "heroine," the term seems quite appropriate only when applied to characters of a certain stability and integrity. *The Portrait of a Lady* was James's first "big" novel, and there can be no doubt that Isabel Archer is one of his important heroines. Yet she has grave limitations and displays a lack of judgment which brings almost fatal consequences upon her. Not only does she not achieve her full stature until nearly the end of the novel, but there is some doubt about what the ending is and whether the decision Isabel makes even then is the right one.

Isabel was the "intellectual superior" among the three Archer girls of Albany (neither the "beauty" nor the "practical one") and a great trial to her brother-in-law, who disliked "originals," found her written in a foreign language, and hoped she would not "develop" more. She loved Browning, George Eliot, and Gounod. When her aunt, Mrs. Touchett, discovered her and carried her off to England, she judged her "a clever girl" who had a strong will, a high temper, and "no idea of being bored." She was indeed "very fond of my liberty," did not consider herself a candidate for adoption, and would not promise to do everything she was told even to be taken to Europe. She took herself seriously, tried very hard to do right, and was intensely humiliated whenever she felt she had put herself in the wrong or become ridiculous. She was idealistic and for the most part ignorant of the evil she condemned or disdained. Her cousin, Ralph Touchett, thought her too conscientious and urged her to keep her conscience for great occasions ("Don't try so much to form your character—it's like trying to pull open a tight, tender young rose"). In the manner of the girls of the young American republic, Isabel had been encouraged to self-expression from her youth. She disdained timidity and conventionality as unprofitable luxuries and believed that to judge wrongly was less disgraceful than not to attempt judgment at all. Theoretically she recognized the danger of pride and struggled against it, but she accepted the unique value of her own individuality and was unwilling to be expressed by anything outside of herself. When she reached England, the whole country and its people went on trial before her. She wanted to see life, but she was very fastidious in her choice of experiences, and she did not wish to suffer for nothing. She did not like to have everything settled beforehand (sometimes she thought her idea of happiness was a swift carriage rattling through a dark night over an unseen road), but she would accept having things settled for her if they were settled as she liked.

Isabel has been plausibly related to Dorothea Brooke and less plausibly to another George Eliot heroine, Gwendolen Harleth; at one point or another, it sometimes seems, every heroine of fiction who has ever shown a modicum of spunk has been considered in connection with her. The influence of Turgenev, which James himself acknowledges in another connection in the Preface to the *Lady* in the New York Edition, is one of the more reasonable suggestions; another is Oscar Cargill's reference to George Sand's *Indiana* [see Further Reading]. One critic has called Isabel an Emersonian Becky Sharp; another, an Emersonian Saint Joan. She is neither. She is no Becky Sharp because she is neither an adventuress nor an exploiter, and she is no Saint Joan because she has no mission. One might think that having her an Emersonian Isabel Archer might be enough.

This she unquestionably is. To have found her reading Emerson's *Essays* when Mrs. Touchett comes upon her at her home in Albany would have been to give a more direct hint than James was capable of, but he suggests the same idea obliquely by having her turn over the pages of a history of German philosophy, so important for the Concord Transcendentalists. "You must be our crazy Aunt Lydia" is her greeting to Mrs. Touchett; no wonder that lady's first observation concerning her is that she is very independent. This is not the only time she gives an impression of bluntness, self-esteem, or girlish caprice, but in her position it would be difficult for any young girl, essentially ignorant of the world and untutored in its ways, to avoid this, and allowances must be made for her inexperience. Isabel's notion of freedom may be romantic and impractical, but her ideal is never merely to do as she likes. She wishes to be free so that she may devote her life to the highest conceivable values, achieving maximum development for herself at the same time that she performs maximum service to others and to the cosmos, and when the Touchett inheritance suddenly and unexpectedly makes her a rich woman, she welcomes her wealth because she believes it must increase her power to do these things. Nothing, surely, could be more Emersonian than this.

Isabel had at least one important nonliterary source in James's cousin, Mary (Minny) Temple (1845-70). Neither as a man nor as an artist did he ever forget her; many years later she was to supply him with Milly Theale in *The Wings of the Dove.* There is probably less of her in Isabel, but James himself admits that in some sense he had her in mind. Milly is allowed to die, as Minny had died, but James spares Isabel to live as his cousin's surrogate. There has been much speculation whether James ever loved Minny. In some sense of that capacious word he certainly did; in some sense, too, she loved him, and though there were never any love passages or any kind of understanding between them, the least we can say is that you can make a better case for her as "the starved romance of my life" than for any other woman. As a matter of fact, there are no other candidates.

Whether or not James loved Minny Temple, however, he certainly loved Isabel Archer, and if we allow his awareness of all her little gaucheries to blind us to his affection, we shall go utterly astray. Though it is not consistently centered in her consciousness, as James suggests, *The Portrait of a Lady* was built around her—a "frail vessel," the "mere slim shade," complex as she is, "of an intelligent and presumptuous girl." The key passages to support this reading occur early in the novel, the first in Chapter VI, where we are told of her that "she would be an easy victim of scientific criticism if she were not intended to awaken on the reader's part an impulse more tender and more purely expectant," and the second in Chapter XII, where we read that

> she was a person of great good faith, and if there was a great deal of folly in her wisdom those who judge her severely may have the satisfaction of finding that, later, she became consistently wise only at the cost of an amount of folly which will constitute almost a direct appeal to charity.

The ordeal she undergoes is carefully prepared for. She is told at the outset that she will never be able to see the Gardencourt ghost until she has suffered, to which she replies that people suffer too easily, that we were not made to suffer, and that the great point is to be as happy as possible. Mr. Touchett has no doubt that there is "room" for her in England but fears that she may have to pay too much for it. In making her a rich woman, Ralph and his father take a calculated risk, well knowing that her wealth will make her more attractive to the fortune hunters, and Henrietta Stackpole thinks it may well prove a curse in disguise. And when her marriage to Gilbert Osmond is under consideration, practically everybody, including Osmond's own sister, fears the worst for her. I do not say that all this is subtly or masterfully done; much of it seems to me anything but that. But the intent is therefore no less plain.

I have said that Isabel Archer is neither an exploiter nor a missioned spirit; one thing more should be noted. She is no artist, and she has no talent but merely a desire to make her life itself a beautiful thing. Her problem therefore, is considerably more complicated than that, say, of the actress Miriam Rooth in *The Tragic Muse,* and this greatly increases James's difficulty in portraying her. Today artistic power is the only kind that many writers trust, wherefore the only characters they are capable of portraying meaningfully must themselves be artists. But whatever moral problems may be involved in the grand old ideal of self-cultivation, the Gospel of Art has, in the long run, as great shortcomings as the Gospel of Work. That a man keeps busy may be either good or bad, the answer depending wholly upon the value of what he produces. And surely if life has any meaning, it must be an end in itself, not merely a means toward an end, even if that end be the creation of a beautiful work of art. How can it be worth while to write about a triumphant life if such a life is not worth living? And how can the portrait of a beautiful woman be of more value than the woman herself? If it be the sole function of either work or art to keep us so absorbed that we may forget how unendurable life would be without them, our case is desperate indeed. Children often come closer to reality in these matters than adults, which is the reason why when we ask them what they "did" today we are generally told only that they "just played." And the little girl who, upon being told that she must live for others, inquired who, then, the others were supposed to live for gave richer promise of developing a philosophical mind than her teachers did.

Isabel's first suitor is the American industrialist Caspar Goodwood. She has refused him in America; she refuses him again in England; in fact, she goes on refusing him to the end of the book. Though Caspar is a very good and respectworthy man, no reader has ever had any difficulty in understanding her decision. Once her aunt has opened up a suddenly enlarged way of life to Isabel, Caspar does not "fit in"; instead he represents everything she is trying to get away from. Isabel is still naive enough to believe that if he had lived a little earlier Caspar might have been a great figure in the Civil War and to allow her imagination to be stimulated by him in this hypothetical aspect, but she has no more taste for the American businessman than was possessed by her creator. Caspar, we are told, has

"a kind of hardness of presence" with "a disagreeably strong push." His jaw is "too square and set and his figure too straight and stiff."

Her rejection of Lord Warburton, an English nobleman of wealth, sound character, excellent disposition, and liberal principles, is a more complicated matter, and Ralph Touchett and his mother are not the only ones who have found it difficult to understand it. Isabel's first reaction to Warburton is very favorable; she sees him, "though quite without luridity," as a romantic hero. His person emits a "radiance of good-feeling and good fare," surrounding him "like a zone of fine June weather," and she admits frankly that she likes him very much. Nevertheless he always has much less chance with her even than Caspar, and the reasons are clear enough, though they are not all spelled out. To begin with, of course, she is not in love with him; had she been, nothing else would have counted for much. As Mr. Touchett tells her, girls are not required to give reasons for rejecting their lovers, and she herself writes Warburton that "these things cannot be reasoned about." When he first approaches her, she is not yet ready to be married, which is not an unbelievable situation for a girl in her position, and if it be objected that she changes pretty quickly when she is captivated by Osmond, it may be replied that this is not unusual with girls either.

Her essential objection to Lord Warburton is that, despite all his radicalism, he is part of a system that she does not wish to be drawn into. "She couldn't marry Lord Warburton; the idea failed to support any enlightened prejudice in favour of the free exploration of life that she had hitherto entertained or was now capable of entertaining." Much as Europe attracts her, Isabel has no idea of being swallowed up by it; she desires more to subsume than to be subsumed. She tells Mrs. Touchett that she wishes to know what girls must not do in Europe not so that she may do it but simply so as to choose; she wishes also to remain an American girl who has possessed herself of whatever Europe possesses that has meaning for her. Moreover, though she thinks it vulgar for a girl to think about marriage very much, her ideal is very high; if she takes a husband, she must surrender to him completely, and she cannot see Warburton in this light.

Later, when Osmond wins her, his lack of all nonspiritual "advantages" are all hers—to give away—and she values her acquired wealth as an extension of her love. Half mystically, half crazily, she feels that she would, in a sense, be evading life or escaping her fate by marrying Warburton, and even Ralph sees a certain validity in this. But it is more important that, even from the beginning, Isabel has sensed a certain inadequacy in Warburton; though he has no real faults, he is something of a lightweight. Later, when he is courting her stepdaughter Pansy, she feels that he is limited, as Pansy herself is limited, and also, not quite consistently, "that it was strange a man of his mettle should take an interest in a little maid." So, I think, it is, under the circumstances posited, and when this courtship too comes to naught, partly because Pansy does not respond to Warburton even as much as Isabel did, he becomes engaged to a young lady of the aristocracy whose name Mrs. Touchett does not even remember.

With Caspar it was different. In her early days in America, Isabel had admired and respected him beyond any other "splendid young man" she had ever seen, and even at the end she is still wondering whether she might not have married him if she had never come to Europe. She turns pale when his partisan, Henrietta Stackpole, mentions him, and admits that she had once encouraged him. Rejecting him again in England, in Chapter XVI, she not only refrains from closing the door absolutely but, once he has gone, falls on her knees beside the bed and buries her face. Later, in Chapter XXXII, she bursts into tears after sending him away from her in Florence, and as late as Chapter XLVII she feels that he alone holds an unsatisfied claim upon her. Even at the end she does not dismiss him until she has "listened to him as she had never listened before." She tells him frankly that she is returning to her husband to get away from him and begs him to leave her if he loves and pities her. But in her heart she knows that "to let him take her in his arms would be the next best thing to her dying," and when he kisses her passionately (it is the only passionate kiss she receives in the novel), the effect is like white lightning. No, poor Lord Warburton never had anything like this.

Isabel's marriage to Gilbert Osmond is the result of a conspiracy between that fine gentleman and his discarded mistress, Madame Merle, the mother of his illegitimate daughter, but it is engineered so that Isabel, who is ignorant of all this background, imagines herself to be choosing freely, and there can be no doubt that she is deeply in love, not indeed with Osmond, for she does not know him, but rather with what she believes him to be. She has "invented a fine theory about him," and, as Mrs. Touchett says, there is nothing to prevent her marrying him if she looks at him in a certain way. Not all readers have found her choice completely convincing, for, while nobody could seriously question that such tragic mismatings do occur in life, we do not perhaps feel the inevitability of the doom by which Isabel is drawn quite as strongly as it is satisfying to feel such things in a work of art.

James has helped us and himself to a degree by omitting most of the courtship and the beginning of their married life; improbabilities are never strengthened by elaborating their details or arguing about them. So we pass abruptly from the happy, deceived engaged girl to the tortured wife of a man who has "deliberately, almost malignantly, . . . put the lights out one by one," making everything he touches wither, spoiling everything he looks at, "as if his presence were a blight and his favour a misfortune." For *The Portrait of a Lady* is not a love story, and our whole interest in Isabel's disastrous marriage is to be centered upon how Isabel reacts to her changed situation and how her "portrait" is to be altered by it.

He married her, of course, for her money. But did this completely cover the case? Did he ever, in any sense, love her? Was he, to any degree, disappointed in her, as she was in him? Such questions hardly seem worth asking about a man whom Graham Greene [see Further Reading] has described as a "precious vulgarian, cold as a fishmonger's slab," and they might be safely dismissed if James himself had not told us that Isabel's first year of married life had

been happy, and if Ralph Touchett, who loathed Osmond and was not likely to give him unearned credit for anything, had not reminded her, during their last interchange, that "He was greatly in love with you," to which she replied, "Yes, he was in love with me. But he wouldn't have married me if I had been poor." This, then, must have been part of James's idea, though I do not think he makes the reader feel it. This much *is* true, however, that Isabel's beauty and social charm were not unappreciated by Osmond. He relished them as he relished the innocence of his daughter Pansy, whom he brought up "in the old way," and whom he sent back to her convent school at twenty, after he failed in his plan to marry her off to Lord Warburton!

Osmond has no morals whatever, and the only reason he is not a libertine is that he lacks the requisite passion; he is not even a good enough man to be dissipated. "He always had an eye to effect," as Ralph perceives, "and his effects were deeply calculated. They were produced by no vulgar means, but the motive was as vulgar as the art was great." He is incapable of regarding wife, daughter, or anybody else except in abject subservience to himself; he is a connoisseur who must possess his collection like the Duke in Browning's "My Last Duchess." What he wanted with Isabel was to "tap her imagination with his knuckle and make it ring," and even when they are hopelessly estranged, he tries to cover up by telling Caspar that they are "as united . . . as the candlestick and the snuffers." The horrible simile he has chosen is the right one for him, and it is part of his damnation that he could never understand why every sensitive reader of *The Portrait of a Lady* has shuddered over it.

What attracts Isabel to Osmond is his freedom from all the soiled attachments and involvements of this world: he does nothing; he has nothing; thus he seems to her "a specimen apart," a surpassingly beautiful, perfectly pure individual, who has achieved a completely symmetrical development of all the highest human powers without ulterior motive. On the other hand, "he knows everything, he understands everything, he has the kindest, gentlest, highest spirit." Unless we are intended to regard Isabel as a complete fool, we must therefore be intended to think of him as possessing extraordinary personal charm when he chooses to exercise it, though nobody in the book besides Isabel seems to feel it. It was a fine touch to have his sister, the Countess Gemini, who, though an immoral woman, is not without heart, warn Isabel against him. Mrs. Touchett sums him up quite fairly when she says, "There's nothing *of* him," and Caspar Goodwood is hardly more harsh than this when he calls him "the deadliest of fiends," for what is this but to be nothing in the Elizabethan sense? ("O Regan, thy sister's nought!")

In Osmond, then, James has offered as devastating a study of the emptiness of a life stripped of all save aesthetic values as Walter de la Mare achieved in his wonderful story, "The Connoisseur." Whether he ever loved Isabel or not, we may well believe that, at some point in his now hopelessly corrupted life, he did love beauty for its own sake. At some point, there may even have been an element of honest moral revulsion in his turning away from the prizes which a corrupt world can give. All this, however, was long ago, and Osmond as we know him rejects only what he knows he cannot have and wraps himself in scorn as a garment. Dread of vulgarity, as Ralph says rightly, is his special line, and no one could be so afraid of vulgarity as he is without being in bondage to it. He is "a prince who has abdicated in a fit of fastidiousness and has been in a state of disgust ever since," and Dorothy Van Ghent has noted how suitable it is that when Isabel comes to tell him of Ralph's impending death he should be engaged in *copying* (demons cannot *create*) an ancient coin [see Further Reading]. For him even art is dead, as it must always be for those for whom it is cut off from any vital relationship with life. Since there are no values left for him but aesthetic values, he can "live only by taste and by appreciation of form, form of the visual and of the social and traditional." Even his own child he must approach from this angle, feeling an "aesthetic relish" of Pansy's innocence. It has been said of Osmond that he hates his wife because he cannot dominate her as he dominates his daughter. This is true, but it is not the whole truth. Osmond fails even with Pansy, though he is too stupid to find it out. Unlike Isabel, Pansy is no heroine, but she is a strangely incorruptible phenomenon for Osmond and Madame Merle to have produced. She submits to her father's authority without complaint—and turns for comfort to the wife he loathes. Her spirit he cannot touch. In the last analysis, there is nothing left for him but form, even as a father, and he has nothing to live for save the figure he cuts in the eyes of the world he pretends to scorn and which has always ignored him.

As for Isabel, he nearly kills her. At one time, there is even danger of corruption, for, in the first agony of her disillusionment, she learns to live, like a fine lady, on the surface of life, but this does not last long. Yet at the end, having defied his wishes by going to Ralph in England when he is dying, she returns to him. Or does she? Yes, she returns, but I do not see how critics can say the book has an "open" ending and still be sure she returns to stay. If this is surely known, then the issue is closed; they cannot have it both ways. *The Portrait of a Lady* originally ended, in 1881, with Henrietta's advice to Caspar—"just you wait!"—"on which," James added, "he looked up at her." In the New York Edition, James weakened the element of hope here by adding that Caspar could see she only meant that he was young. "She stood shining at him with that cheap comfort, and it added, on the spot, thirty years to his life. She walked him away with her, however, as if she had given him the key to patience." Yet if James was merely laughing at Henrietta, he would seem to have committed an error in emphasis by giving her the last word. She has been painted in primary colors throughout, but she has been clear-sighted enough about Isabel's marriage. And Isabel herself had told Ralph, just before his death, that she did not know whether she was going back.

If Isabel were a Catholic, it would be easier to be happy with her return to Osmond, but she is not. Religion has very little to do with *The Portrait of a Lady,* in which respect it differs markedly from some of the later and greater novels. The only clergyman we ever hear of Isabel being brought in touch with is the athletic Vicar of Lockleigh, whom she likes but whom she can hardly think of as a spiritual guide. There is no positive evidence that religion motivates her actions at any point, but we are told specifically that though there was (from the Catholic point of view) no gentler nor less consistent heretic than she, "the old Protestant tradition had never faded" from her imagination. For Osmond, the Church, like everything else, is a form. He would have liked to be pope, but it is the power of the papacy which attracts him; for him the pope is a prince of this world, and one cannot imagine him experiencing any of the Christian humility which a good man must feel confronting such an office. When his daughter is brought back to him from the convent, he asks one of the sisters what they have made of her. The answer is, "A good Christian, monsieur," but this does not interest him. "Yes," he asks, "and what else?" Both he and the sister drop their eyes for a moment, but, says James, "it was probable that the movement in each case had a different spring." Nevertheless, he believes that the convent has a very important place in society: "it corresponds to an essential need. . . . It's a school of good manners; it's a school of repose." But Isabel sees it, as Osmond employs it, as "a well-appointed prison" for Pansy, requiring "the surrender of a personality." Yet she retains "all the traditional decencies and sanctions of marriage" and comes close to preserving all the inflexibility of the sacramental conception with none of its advantages.

Two different motives have been alleged for Isabel's returning to a husband who hates her. The first is that she has promised Pansy not to desert her. (Mrs. Touchett has long been aware that Isabel thinks a great deal of her promises). But this hardly seems her main motive. If Pansy is as remarkable as her warmest admirers believe, she hardly needs Isabel, and if she is not, it is difficult to see what Isabel can do for her besides making her aware of her sympathy. That, no doubt, is something. But Osmond's attitude toward Isabel being what it now is, she is about the last person he could be expected to allow to come between his daughter and himself; indeed, Pansy might well have to suffer more for Isabel's championship of her.

It is interesting that James should have allowed Osmond of all people to state the case for the continuance of the marriage:

> "I take our marriage seriously. . . . I'm not aware that we're divorced or separated; for me we're indissolubly united. You are nearer to me than any human creature, and I'm nearer to you. . . . I think we should accept the consequences of our actions, and what I value most in life is the honour of a thing!"

The devil can cite Scripture for his purpose, and all this is about as convincing as Hitler's (or any warmaker's) boasted devotion to peace. In a spiritual sense, the marriage to which Osmond boasts of his allegiance, if it ever existed, has already been destroyed, yet in a way he means exactly what he says, for the form remains, and form is the only thing that has ever meant anything to this hollow man anyway.

This does not mean, of course, that Isabel's final decision, if it is that, cannot be rationally defended. (pp. 35-51)

In the last analysis, what one believes about the ending of *The Portrait of a Lady* will be determined by what one believes about many other things. One can, however, justify James's ending without going into any of these deep moral and religious considerations. This is what Viola Hopkins Winner does [in her *Henry James and the Visual Arts*] when she declares that Isabel accepts "actuality and necessity" in what was meant to be a "tragically affirmative conclusion." Being what she was, she could not have acted in any other way. Thus it becomes true of *The Portrait of a Lady* as of every other considerable work of art that every man has the work that he deserves. (pp. 52-3)

> Edward Wagenknecht, in his Eve and Henry James: Portraits of Women and Girls in His Fiction, *University of Oklahoma Press, 1978, 217 p.*

Alden R. Turner   (essay date 1980)

[*In the following excerpt, Turner provides a detailed analysis of Isabel Archer as the novel's center of consciousness.*]

James's use of art metaphors—portrait and landscape painting, sculpture, architecture, drama, and even music—has been the subject for much of our concern with his work. The growth in our knowledge of James's perceptual modes has been sustained by the particularly fertile ground of *The Portrait of a Lady.* Certainly Matthiessen's suggestion that "The growth from ideas to images is what James has been fumbling for in his earlier preoccupation with the picturesque" [see excerpt dated 1944] indicates the relation between the development of James's aesthetic sensibility and the nature of his revisions for the New York edition of the novel. This process of the imagination's movement from ideas to images depends upon the realization of an abstract construction of meaning in terms of a concrete image by means of some created correspondence between an inner consciousness and outward perceptions. Dorothy Van Ghent explains: "The title, *The Portrait,* asks the eye to see. And the handling of this book is in terms of seeing. . . . Further, this action, moving through errors and illuminations of the inward eye, is set in a symbolic construct of things to be seen by the physical eye—paintings and sculptures, old coins and porcelain and lace and tapestries, most of all buildings: the aesthetic riches of Europe, pregnant with memory, with 'histories within histories' of skills and motivations, temptations and suffering" [see Further Reading]. Most critics approach James's art metaphors along the lines suggested by Van Ghent. Indeed, his art objects are significant to "setting and character": "They may give body to states of mind. They may dramatize discoveries, psychological tensions and conflicts" [William Gibson, *New England Quarterly* (1951)]. But we must remember that James's center of consciousness, Isabel, functions as the "eye" whereby the reader sees the process of art itself; whereby an idea becomes an image and a picture is made real. Isabel's experiences provide her with revelations about her capacity to transform ideas into meaningful realities. The fiction which results from this transformative process is, for Isa-

bel and for James, a "haunted portrait" that sustains the necessary illusion of life in art.

" 'Place the centre of the subject in the young woman's own consciousness,' I said to myself, 'and you get as interesting and as beautiful a difficulty as you could wish.' " James's comment in the 1908 Preface suggests the centrality of Isabel Archer's consciousness to the reader's understanding of *The Portrait of a Lady* [see excerpt dated 1908]. James's own sense of this consciousness rests on the representation in chapter forty-two of "her motionlessly seeing" which he calls "the best thing in the book." Here, the heroine's consciousness is trapped within "the house of darkness, the house of dumbness, the house of suffocation" where "she had suddenly found the infinite vista of a multiplied life to be a dark, narrow alley with a dead wall at the end." Isabel's internal suffering in this chapter derives its significance from the fact that her romantic consciousness begins to mature into an imagination which breaks through the "dead wall" of conventional forms to establish a more credible relation with reality. We are involved in what Isabel sees and how she sees.

The growth of Isabel's imagination mirrors James's own account of an artist's consciousness which pierces the "dead wall" of the "house of fiction" with an individual vision and will, creates a uniquely shaped point of view on life, and continually forms and re-forms one's impressions of reality:

> The house of fiction has in short not one window, but a million—a number of possible windows not to be reckoned, rather; every one of which has been pierced, or is still pierceable, in its vast front, by the need of the individual vision and by the pressure of the individual will. These apertures, of dissimilar shape and size, hang so, all together, over the human scene that we might have expected of them a greater sameness of report than we find. They are but windows at the best, mere holes in a dead wall, disconnected, perched aloft; they are not hinged doors opening straight upon life. But they have this mark of their own that at each of them stands a figure with a pair of eyes, or at least with a field-glass, which forms, again and again, for observation, a unique instrument, insuring to the person making use of it an impression distinct from every other. He and his neighbours are watching the same show, but one seeing more where the other sees less, one seeing black where the other sees white, one seeing big where the other sees small, one seeing coarse where the other sees fine.

James's theory fuses with his gradual illumination of Isabel's consciousness so that *The Portrait of a Lady* becomes a representation of the possibility for life within form: Isabel, a figuration for the artist's consciousness, is framed by the aperture of the window created by her experiences with art and with life in the "house of fiction."

During her first visit to the Touchetts' art collection, Isabel sees herself as the heroine of a romance for whom ghosts are a necessary requirement in a "romantic old house" like the Touchetts'. Her point of view is undercut by Ralph Touchett's admonition to her (and the reader) that "It's not a romantic old house. . . . It's a dismally prosaic one; there's no romance here but what you may have brought with you." Nevertheless, Isabel insists on a correspondence between her own state of mind and reality: "it seems to me I've brought it to the right place." The failure of Isabel's romantic vision to produce ghosts results from the fact that, as Ralph points out, Isabel has not "suffered": "You must have suffered first, have suffered greatly, have gained some miserable knowledge. In that way your eyes are opened to it." In other words, Isabel's childhood experience with "the London *Spectator,* the latest publications, the music of Gounod, the poetry of Browning, the prose of George Eliot" indicates that the quality of mind which sees "her uncle's house . . . [as] a picture made real" has been determined by her knowledge of romantic conventions and her avowed innocence of any broader experience of life. Ironically, Isabel's romantic expectation of seeing a ghost is fulfilled only after her romantic view of a simple correspondence between appearance and reality has been shattered.

Isabel's sustained belief in the coexistence of appearance and reality is destroyed by an image that fails to correspond with the idea of her marriage with Osmond. After returning home from the countryside with Pansy one day, Isabel is about to enter the drawing-room when she is struck by an "impression" framed by "the threshold of the drawing-room." Reality is formed into a work of art which provides her with a moment of illumination:

> Madame Merle was standing on the rug, a little way from the fire; Osmond was in a deep chair, leaning back and looking at her. Her head was erect, as usual, but her eyes were bent on his. What struck Isabel first was that he was sitting while Madame Merle stood; there was an anomaly in this that arrested her. Then she perceived that they had arrived at a desultory pause in their exchange of ideas and were musing, face to face, with the freedom of old friends who sometimes exchange ideas without uttering them. There was nothing to shock in this; they were old friends in fact. But the thing made an image, lasting only a moment, like a sudden flicker of light. Their relative positions, their absorbed mutual gaze, struck her as something detected. But it was all over by the time she had fairly seen it.

The distinctly pictorial quality of this image of Osmond and Madame Merle is suggested by the frame of the room's threshold, by the absence of any movement in the scene, through the emphasis on the arrangement of the figures in specific poses, and by the "mutual gaze" which might deceive the viewer were it not filtered through Isabel's consciousness. The figures' "relative positions" assume a value of truth communicated by the visual image of their intimacy, an image which not only overturns Isabel's romantic ideal of her experiences as "a picture made real," but suggests the ambiguous relation between art and life. Isabel's romantic notion that she can conform reality to an idea in her mind gives way to a momentary illumination of the disjunction between ideas and images.

In chapter forty-two, Isabel confronts "the strange impression she had received in the afternoon of her hus-

band's being in more direct communication with Madame Merle than she suspected." Her "extraordinary meditative vigil" exemplifies the bifurcated quality of the heroine's consciousness illuminated by the "sudden flicker of light" provided by the image of Madame Merle and Osmond. Isabel perceives her relationship with Osmond as "a gulf . . . between them over which they looked at each other with eyes that were on either side a declaration of the deception suffered. It was a strange opposition, of the like of which she had never dreamed—an opposition in which the vital principle of the one was a thing of contempt to the other." This "gulf" between Isabel and Osmond predicates a whole series of coordinate disjunctions in Isabel's consciousness. Several critics have noted the dichotomies of confinement and freedom, darkness and light, and cold and heat that James works with in the chapter. Moreover, James presents the movement of Isabel's consciousness at the time it "pierces" the "dead wall at the end" of the dark labyrinth of conventions in which she finds herself: "she broke out of the labyrinth, rubbing her eyes, and declared that her imagination surely did her little honour and that her husband's did him even less." Isabel is then able to see the contrast between her own ideal of "the aristocratic life" as "the union of great knowledge with great liberty" and Osmond's conception which is "altogether a thing of forms."

The gulf between life and artistic form is irreparably opened in Isabel's mind when she emerges from "the house of darkness, the house of dumbness, the house of suffocation":

> He had told her he loved the conventional; but there was a sense in which this seemed a noble declaration. In that sense, that of the love of harmony and order and decency and of all the stately offices of life, she went with him freely, and his warning had contained nothing ominous. But when, as the months had elapsed, she had followed him further and he had led her into the mansion of his own habitation, then, *then* she had seen where she really was.

When Isabel breaks out of the labyrinth, "this rigid system . . . draped though it was in pictured tapestries," the series of ideas and images which were initially set free by the illuminating picture of Osmond and Madame Merle effectively destroy her assumption that a consensus was ever shared between Osmond and herself. All that remains at the conclusion of Isabel's meditative vigil is the image of truth that creates an abyss in her romantic imagination. All of her previous correspondences break apart when she focuses on the picture that represents her deception: "she stopped again in the middle of the room and stood there gazing at a remembered vision—that of her husband and Madame Merle unconsciously and familiarly associated." Throughout chapter forty-two and indeed for the rest of the novel, Isabel, like James's artist at his window in "the house of fiction," continually forms and reforms this "impression" of reality.

James pictures Isabel as continually haunted by the image of Osmond and Madame Merle but gradually the image of their relationship in the drawing-room changes. The initial representation Isabel sees is Osmond and Madame

Merle "musing, face to face," their "freedom of old friends," and "their absorbed mutual gaze." At the beginning of Isabel's meditative vigil, the scene comes to represent "her husband's being in more direct communication with Madame Merle than she suspected." By the end of her meditation, the two have become "unconsciously and familiarly associated." Isabel's picture of Madame Merle and Osmond undergoes even further transformations:

> Sometimes, at night, she had strange visions; she seemed to see her husband and her friend—his friend—in dim, *indistinguishable combination.* It seemed to her that she had not done with her; this lady had something in reserve. Isabel's imagination applied itself actively to this elusive point, but every now and then it was checked by a nameless dread, so that when the charming woman was away from Rome she had almost a consciousness of respite.

Isabel's vision of the "indistinguishable combination" of Madame Merle and Osmond suggests her suspicion that the two have had an explicitly sexual relationship. Finally, Madame Merle's involvement with her husband obsesses Isabel to the point where she demands of Madame Merle: "Who are you—what are you? . . . What have you to do with my husband? . . . What have you to do with me?" Madame Merle confirms Isabel's "nameless dread" when she replies, "Everything!" That afternoon Isabel continues to be preoccupied by the image that tortures her:

> she had taken a resolution not to think of Madame Merle; but the resolution proved vain, and this lady's image hovered constantly before her. She asked herself, with an almost childlike horror of the supposition, whether to this intimate friend of several years the great historical epithet of *wicked* were to be applied. She knew the idea only by the Bible and other literary works; to the best of her belief she had no personal acquaintance with wickedness. She had desired a large acquaintance with human life, and in spite of her having flattered herself that she cultivated it with some success this elementary privilege had been denied her.

Isabel entertains the notion that the images which have tormented her imagination with the possibilities of their conceivable configurations may be interpreted as the incarnation of the word, "wicked." In other words, Isabel begins to reestablish correspondences between the things of her imagination and the things of reality in terms of her own personal experience.

The growth of Isabel's consciousness is indicated by the "little sketch" which she attributes to Osmond, but which the reader sees from her point of view. James writes: "His tone, however, was that of a man not so much offering an explanation as putting a thing into words—almost into pictures—to see, himself, how it would look. He considered a while the picture he had evoked and seemed greatly pleased with it." The attempt to represent a living thing (Pansy) as Osmond does, "as a precious work of art," is now repulsive to Isabel: "the incident struck a chill into Isabel's heart." The dilemma which confronts Isabel is the same one that faced James and which challenges any reader of the novel: if the concept of a "picture made real" does not correspond to reality (as Isabel discovers) and the corollary limitations of trying to make life into a work of art are so clearly apparent (exemplified in Osmond's treatment of Isabel and, here, Pansy), then what is the relation between art and life? After the Countess Gemini confirms the truth of Isabel's sustained but subtly changing image of Osmond and Madame Merle, James provides us with a tentative answer.

Isabel's experiences lead to her most significant revelation when she is faced with two haunted portraits which suggest a more viable correspondence between art and life. The image of Madame Merle which has tormented Isabel's mind is suddenly met with a corresponding image in reality when Isabel discovers her at the convent visiting Pansy:

> The effect was strange, for Madame Merle was already so present to her vision that her appearance in the flesh was like suddenly, and rather awfully, seeing a painted picture move. Isabel had been thinking all day of her falsity, her audacity, her ability, her probable suffering; and these dark things seemed to flash with a sudden light as she entered the room. Her being there at all had the character of ugly evidence, of handwritings, of profaned relics, of grim things produced in court.

Just as "a sudden flicker of light" is created in Isabel's mind by the drawing-room picture, her penetration beneath the surface of that initial picture brings her to a more realistic awareness of life in which appearances and reality correspond. Isabel's awareness of evil in the world, "These dark things that seem to flash with a sudden light as she entered the room," is given form and meaning by her perception of life *within* art. Similarly, Isabel's formulation for Pansy's apparent realization of the gulf between Isabel and her father is the metaphor of a haunted portrait: "Her [Pansy's] heart may have stood almost as still as it would have done had she seen two of the saints in the great picture in the convent-chapel turn their painted heads and shake them at each other." The ambiguity created by Isabel's correspondence between the picture of two saints and her own experience effectively suggests James's interest in Isabel's developing consciousness rather than in the existence of the correspondences themselves. The picture of the two saints recalls the drawing-room picture of Madame Merle and Osmond, but it could also refer to any number of confrontations between Isabel and Osmond. In essence, however, Isabel succeeds in restoring the relation between art and life through her vision of haunted portraits—works of art that live a life of their own through their capacity to suggest the continuity of the human experience:

> She rested her weariness upon things that had crumbled for centuries and yet still were upright; she dropped her secret sadness into the silence of lonely places. . . . Small it was, in the large Roman record, and her haunting sense of the continuity of the human lot easily carried her from the less to the greater. She had become deeply, tenderly acquainted with Rome; it interfused and moderated her passion. But she had grown to think of it chiefly as the place where

people had suffered. . . . There was no gentler
nor less consistent heretic than Isabel; the firm-
est of worshippers, gazing at dark altar-pictures
or clustered candles, could not have felt more intimately the suggestiveness of these objects nor
have been more liable at such moments to a spiritual visitation.

The most significant "spiritual visitations" to Isabel's developing imagination are the haunted portraits created by
the correspondence between her imagination and her experience, a correspondence which suggests the realization
of life within art as an opportunity to "see" truth.

Henry James places the subject of *The Portrait of a Lady*
in his heroine's consciousness and, insofar as Isabel comes
to understand the deeper significance of a "picture made
real," James is able to approach the problem of creating
a sense of value in art and in life when it seems apparent
that artistry resides in the mind. In **"The Art of Fiction"**
James writes: "There is one point at which the moral sense
and the artistic sense lie very near together; that is in the
light of the very obvious truth that the deepest quality of
a work of art will always be the quality of the mind of the
producer. In proportion as that intelligence is fine will the
novel, the picture, the statue partake of the substance of
beauty and truth." Similarly, Isabel is faced with a crisis
of creating a meaningful relation with reality when she is
plagued by her own capacity to achieve a radically individual relation to the world where thoughts which become visions become images, and her consciousness pierces
through the wall of the "house of fiction." On her journey
from Rome back to Gardencourt, Isabel struggles with the
problem of an apparent meaninglessness of life as suffering:

> Her thoughts followed their course through
> other countries. . . . She had plenty to think
> about; but it was neither reflexion nor conscious
> purpose that filled her mind. Disconnected vi-
> sions passed through it, and sudden gleams of
> memory, of expectation. The past and the future
> came and went at their will, but she saw them
> only in fitful images, which rose and fell by a
> logic of their own. . . . [The] truth of things,
> their mutual relations, their meaning, and for
> the most part their horror, rose before her with
> a kind of architectural vastness.

Juxtaposed against Isabel's sense of despair is her equally
strong sense that she is confined to life and to whatever she
can make of its possibilities. James writes that

> life would be her business for a long time to
> come. And at moments there was something in-
> spiring, almost enlivening, in the conviction. It
> was a proof of strength—it was a proof she
> should someday be happy again. It couldn't be
> she was to live only to suffer; she was still young,
> after all, and a great many things might happen
> to her yet. To live only to suffer—only to feel the
> injury of life repeated and enlarged—it seemed
> to her she was too valuable, too capable, for that.

Isabel's consciousness of her own suffering is represented
by James in terms of her capacity to establish correspondences between art and life. However, the pictures that

haunt her are incapable of sustaining any sense of meaning
and value beyond their representation of the evil which
has tortured her. Isabel's correspondences between reality
and her imagination depend upon the quality of her own
mind; if Isabel's suffering is to produce any meaningful results then the creative capacity of her mind's artistry must
be realized.

When Isabel Archer returns to Gardencourt she comes to
understand that the significance of the haunted portraits
does not reside in the artifacts that are the products of her
imagination, but in the process of the creative consciousness. The importance of this process is suggested by Ralph
Touchett when he says to Isabel that what endures is "the
sensation of life—the sense that we remain." He goes on
to say that "pain's not the deepest thing" and that despite
the fact that people suffer, the crucial recognition is that
"love remains." When Isabel "sees" Ralph's ghost—in
fulfillment of his prophecy that she would see a ghost if
she suffered enough—the capacity of her mind to transform Ralph's ideas into this reality figuratively sustains
our belief in the meaning and value of Ralph's redemptive
words. The ghost of Ralph Touchett haunts Isabel, but the
question of whether or not she will be able to restore life
to the sterile and empty conventional form, which characterizes her relationship with Osmond, remains unan-
swered. Ultimately, Isabel's capacity to bridge the gulf between art and life, between form and formlessness, depends upon her belief in this saving fiction that "love remains" which is preserved by her vision of Ralph's ghost.

In effect, Henry James creates a haunted portrait of Isabel
Archer herself wherein he confronts the problem of establishing some meaningful relationship between art and life.
For James, "the sensation of life" is a necessary fiction
that must be maintained in art. Through the developing
consciousness of Isabel Archer, James suggests that the
idea of a "picture made real" depends upon a meaningful
correspondence between the mind of the artist and the reality which confronts him or her. Isabel's suffering is created by her perception of the disjunction between her
imagination and the reality of the world which she enters.
The figuration of a haunted portrait reestablishes a correspondence between art and life, but fails to provide her
with any sense of meaning or value that will sustain her
life. Finally, it is not the artifact of the haunted portrait
itself which is meaningful, but rather the artistry of the individual consciousness which brings life into a procreative
relation with art. This relation is, like the ghost of Ralph
Touchett, a purely fictional creation of the mind, a necessary illusion which characterizes any representation of life
in art.

At the conclusion of *The Portrait of a Lady,* Isabel's consciousness has become so "real" to the reader that Caspar
Goodwood's sudden appearance before her, as she sits on
a garden bench remembering him, seems to be both an illusion and a reality. This indistinguishable relation produces an endless range of possibilities for Isabel in the
reader's mind. James writes: "The world, in truth, had
never seemed so large; it seemed to open out, all around
her, to take the form of a mighty sea, where she floated
in fathomless waters." Isabel's final illumination occurs

"like white lightning, a flash that spread" and she experiences life without form as a kind of death: "So had she heard of those wrecked and under water following a train of images before they sink." The necessity and value of artistic form is affirmed by James. As James E. Miller points out, " 'Hinged doors opening straight upon life,' without the framing of the window or the 'prime sensibility' of the writer, would plunge the reader into the meaningless, undifferentiated stream of life itself—a state neither possible nor desirable" ["Henry James in Reality" in *Critical Inquiry* (1976)]. James returns Isabel to the "house of fiction" where art and life are ultimately separate, but where he affirms that a continuity—a continuity denoted by the figuration of the haunted portrait—is maintained by the realization of a truly artistic consciousness which has learned the value of life within form. (pp. 228-37)

> Alden R. Turner, "The Haunted 'Portrait of a Lady'," in Studies in the Novel, *Vol. XII, No. 3, Fall, 1980, pp. 228-38.*

Leon Edel   (essay date 1986)

[*An American critic and biographer, Edel is a highly acclaimed authority on the life and work of Henry James. His five-volume biography* Henry James *(1953-73) is considered definitive and brought Edel critical praise for his research and interpretive skill. In the following excerpt, he identifies Isabel Archer's specifically American qualities.*]

Henry James's *The Portrait of a Lady* had its hundredth birthday in 1981. It starts its second century by being in print around the world—in the United States and Britain in its variant texts—and more widely translated than at any time in its existence. . . . In recent years, it has acquired a particular distinction as the first major "feminist" work of modern times, an American artistic successor to George Eliot's fictions, which dwelt most often on troubled and worldly heroines. In writing the novel, James sought to place his "portrait" in the great fictional gallery of modern ladies—among portraits of women like Anna Karenina or Emma Bovary, or the heroines of Jane Austen or the Brontës, or the young women of Thackeray or Trollope. Most of them sought, in a world that denied them equality, forms of freedom from being simply parties in marriage contracts. James's ironic intention was to lift Isabel Archer out of the marriage market by endowing her with the largest measure of freedom; he wished to demonstrate also the prohibitions and boundaries that society nevertheless imposed on her. "The idea of the whole thing," he wrote in his notebooks, "is that the poor girl, who has dreamed of freedom and nobleness, who has done, as she believes, a generous, natural, clear-sighted thing, finds herself in reality ground in the very mill of the conventional."

James seems to have had another intention as well. This was to paint Isabel within a "myth" of America. In one of his early letters to W. D. Howells about his prospective novel he remarked, "My novel is to be an *Americana*—the adventures in Europe of a female Newman, who of course equally triumphs over the insolent foreigner." This con-

ception of Isabel as an "Americana"—a female counterpart to his hero of *The American,* Christopher Newman—permits us to ask ourselves: In what way did she, in her creator's imagination, become one of his "representative" Americans? His first novel had dealt with the fate of an American sculptor in Rome; his second had been the story of an American businessman who goes to Paris in search of a wife. Christopher Newman had decidedly been enveloped in certain American myths—a teller of "tall tales," at ease with himself, and carrying his native world with him into foreign lands. Isabel Archer's personality was modified in the writing of the novel; she became, as James again told Howells, "a great swell, psychologically: a *grande nature.*" He endowed her with many American qualities and many American beliefs. In examining these, it should be possible for us to discern the American myth or myths that were in the background of her author's mind.

The direct use of recorded myths in a literary work offers no particular problem for criticism. James Joyce made no secret that his *Ulysses* was an odyssey in Dublin: and his text amply demonstrated the wanderings of Leopold Bloom. What he kept secret, but leaked to the critics, was his plan for using episodes that paralleled the adventures of Ulysses. Thomas Mann's Joseph series is drawn directly from the Old Testament story. The indirect or implied use of myth, such as we find in James's *American* and in *The Portrait of a Lady,* calls for a "dissecting out" of the mythological themes. Mircea Eliade, the eminent authority on myth, suggests this to us when he speaks of the modern novel taking the place "of the recitation of myths in traditional and popular societies." He adds that in modern fiction there has been "a literary survival of great mythological themes and characters" and these, as he says, need to be "dissected out."

Such dissection is not easy, and there are many scholars whose delight in the "literal" makes them turn away from what is implied, and from what requires psychological or thematic penetration. The method we use can only be through the study of the author's icons, the allusions and references that in the weaving of the tales create for us the memory of analogous older myths or those current at the time of the writing. As James used his intuitive psychological observations to delineate character, so he skillfully explored mythic substance. His saturation in American life and habits—on the level of the imagination and the public folklore—was deep and acute. He tells us in his memoirs of his boyhood visits to Barnum's Museum, his nights in the old Bowery theaters, his absorption of popular fiction and stories told by the continual visitors to his father's drawing room. As he matured and began to write, he had a threefold vision: he was sensitively aware of the myths that Americans—on their great new land mass—were creating about themselves. He equally discerned the myths Europeans were creating about Americans. In turn, he created and explored the myths that emerged from the encounter of the two. There was, for example, the phenomenon—or the myth of—the pursuit by American women of British titled husbands. There was also the opposite: the pursuit by titled Britons of American heiresses. As James put it, in his essay on **"The Art of Fiction,"** "for a Bostonian nymph to reject an English duke is an adventure only less stirring, I should say, than for an English duke to be rejected by a Bostonian nymph." Isabel Archer's refusal to marry a British peer in *The Portrait of a Lady* not only repeated a myth James had already written out in another form in **"An International Episode"**; James implied that the refusal had its roots in America's refusal, in the Declaration of Independence, to accept British institutions. (pp. 8-9)

[Henry James's] first thought had been to create an Americana. She was to be as unworldly and as pragmatic as Christopher Newman. But when he came to write his *Portrait of a Lady,* he abandoned his notion of a flag-waving heroine bent on outdoing the Europeans. He found himself seeking different national ingredients and exploring Isabel Archer's psychological depths. Newman embodied the rough and ready macho spirit of the American frontier and much of its humor. James sketched it in roughly from his old saturation in popular novels. He had known no businessmen; he knew even less of the frontier. As for the frontier women, they were a blank. We can see this in his caricature woman Mrs. Headway (in **"The Siege of London"**), who has had many divorces and comes to London to try to marry a fortune and a title. It was inevitable that James would switch from his early concetto of Isabel as a rough and ready female version of Newman to the kind of American girl he knew best. His choice of his lady sprang from his own rearing. He had been brought up in an unworldly way, close to domesticity and the women of the James household. He tells us in a late preface how as a writer he knew nothing of what was going on in Wall Street; but during the period when he tried to write in New York, "seated for several months at the very modest altitude of Twenty-fifth street," he felt himself "day by day alone . . . with the music masters and French pastry-cooks, the ladies and children." It was inevitable that Isabel Archer should be drawn from this environment and from the females of Cambridge and Newport—and Concord. She is Emerson's self-reliant American, a child of the transcendental movement—this is the kind of self-reliance James creates in opposition to Newman's free and easy western attributes.

However, James still clung to the idea that he had to have some kind of national counterpart to Newman in his new novel. If Isabel was not to have it, he would give it to Isabel's very American friend Henrietta Stackpole, the female journalist. Isabel herself describes Henrietta as "a kind of emanation of the great democracy—of the continent, the country, the nation. I don't say that she sums it all up, that would be too much to ask of her. But she suggests it; she vividly figures it." The word "suggests" speaks for what James wanted to suggest: he needed to keep the idea of Christopher Newman's expansive open-air Americanism. Henrietta Stackpole—her name suggests the pinnacle from which a flag flies—often talks as if there were a large Stars and Stripes waving at the top in the breeze. James could not resist, however, wrapping the more perceptive Isabel in the national flag as well. Her cousin, Ralph Touchett, accuses her of a patriotism "so heated that it scorched." He draws a cartoon of her "in which she was represented as a very pretty young woman dressed, on

the lines of the prevailing fashion, in the folds of the national banner." The allusion to the "prevailing fashion" reminds us of the then recent centenary. *The Portrait* contains an overflow of the centennial emotion which animated *The American.* It was on the whole an ideal moment—a century after 1776—to ask questions about "the American character," and to seek its evolution.

James's badinage about America, the pros and cons of democracy, is made lightheartedly in the drawing-rooms of houses, villas and palazzos, with Isabel and Henrietta as the animators. When he describes Isabel's "love of knowledge" as coexisting "in her mind with the finest capacity for ignorance," he is describing a republic of ignorance about which he is concerned. Isabel is also "a real little passionate force" and "the finest thing in nature"; here he is describing the national drive and the national passion as well. And yet, possessed of this drive, Americans seemed to him often conservative—"there were no conservatives like American conservatives." And so the picture develops—the American quest is a "pursuit of happiness" rather than a pursuit of life and living with all the difficulties and despair, as well as joy, of existence. Americans are weighed down by their conscience and afraid of making mistakes—and of having to acknowledge them. The rich do not know how to enjoy their money, as against the Europeans who are organized for activity and creativity and even productive idleness—with much less affluence. When Isabel becomes poetic about the stretch of the prairies and says to Ralph that "a strong sweet, fresh odour" seems to rise from the hinterland, Ralph points to Henrietta and says that she "does smell of the Future—it almost knocks one down." Madame Merle speaks of American as "that splendid, dreadful, funny country," but when her treachery is unmasked she suddenly announces she will return (after decades of absence) to Brooklyn. Mrs. Touchett's rejoinder to this news is: "To America? She must have done something very bad." In Mrs. Touchett's eyes the homeland is a form of punishment.

This give-and-take about the United States is James's way of dramatizing the deeper myth he is fashioning. The debits and credits of the nation speak, in one way or another, for qualities and values, the total dream of America. Madame Merle's "splendid, dreadful, funny" represents apparently a deeper sense of her country. Certainly there was no doubt of its splendor in its early years, the greatness of its extent "stretching away beyond the rivers and across the prairies," as Isabel said. There was equally no doubt that to the Europeans, or to a Europeanized American like Merle (a *merle* being a "blackbird," and doubtless migratory), some aspects of America were funny—as Europe often seems to Americans. But the word "dreadful" also has its special meaning, and this remains to be determined by seeing, in the sum total of *The Portrait of a Lady,* where the "dreadfulness" lies. Certainly not in Henrietta Stackpole, the generous, good-hearted, if abrasive and meddlesome newspaperwoman. In spite of her nagging Americanism, she ends up marrying an Englishman and living in England. Her realism is stronger than her patriotism. Isabel becomes in the end a symbol of an unresolved democracy; in the portrait of his unfinished heroine James probes the unfinished national character more deeply than he succeeded in doing in Christopher Newman. Isabel has been badly educated. She has no sense of history; no authoritative voices have given her the essential values or structure of civilization. She is occupied—that chronic occupation of Americans—in trying to better herself. At times she sounds like the modern Americans whose thirst is endless for books on "how to do" things, how to behave, act at home and in society, conduct personal hygiene and sex. "She was always planning out her development, desiring her perfection, observing her progress." James dissects her without mercy. She has many theories. They come not out of inquiry or study, but out of the limitations of her mind. Her desire for knowledge is immense. However, "her thoughts were a tangle of vague outlines which had never been corrected by the judgement of people speaking with authority. In matters of opinion she had had her own way and it had led her into a thousand ridiculous zigzags." She has an "unquenchable desire to think well of herself." James adds ironically, foreshadowing American "isolationism," that she felt she should try to be her own best friend "and to give one's self, in this manner, distinguished company." Isabel, he tells us, "had a certain nobleness of imagination which rendered her a good many services and played her a great many tricks." She wants always to do the right thing, to know "the things one shouldn't do." "So as to do them?" her aunt queries. "So as to choose," the self-assured Emersonian Isabel answers.

James uses these brush strokes to reveal to us the fundamental egotism and self-centeredness of his heroine, the narcissistic elements in the American "style." Her intentions are honest, her sincerity never in question, and she has been brought up to respect the virtues of society. "It was wrong to be mean, to be jealous, to be false, to be cruel." James adds, "she had seen very little of the evil of the world." The portrait of the young Isabel suggests how poorly she had been prepared for the more violent and primitive things of life, or the deceitful and the Machiavellian. And when James comes to summarize her character he is unabashedly "editorial":

> Altogether, with her meagre knowledge, her inflated ideals, her confidence at once innocent and dogmatic, her temper at once exacting and indulgent, her mixture of curiosity and fastidiousness, of vivacity and indifference, her desire to look very well and to be if possible even better, her determination to see, to try, to know, her combination of the delicate, desultory, flamelike spirit and the eager and personal creature of conditions: she would be an easy victim of scientific criticism if she were not intended to awaken on the reader's part an impulse more tender and more purely expectant.

If James is talking about Isabel Archer, he is also talking of the country that made her. He asks us to take his American "lady" on trust, while he shows us what she is like in her high-flying and floundering youth, within the wrappings of the American flag. She seems to have been put together out of the same bundle of negatives and positives as Christopher Newman, who has an eye "Frigid and yet friendly . . . confident yet shy, extremely intelligent and extremely good-humoured." Such an individual would seem to be committed to a life of tergiversation; but a groundwork of complacency and self-satisfaction makes for firmness and even dogma. As Constance Rourke puts it, we can see in these Jamesian Americans "narrow aggressions and an insular nobility, a careless honesty, a large and delicate purpose." Not quite, however, in the case of Newman. His purpose is too broad and too comic. In proclaiming his wealth as his pile of gold, he also proclaims that he wants to marry a lady and put her on top of the pile "like a statue or a monument."

Isabel's thoughts run to less monumental things. She is more philosophical, more preoccupied with her feminine being and with the choices open to her. "I try to judge things for myself; to judge wrong, I think, is more honourable than not to judge at all." And also: "I don't wish to be a mere sheep in the flock; I wish to choose my fate and know something of human affairs." What distinguishes Isabel, as a young American woman, is that she has many more options than her European sisters. Emma Bovary, who was also badly educated, had no grasp of reality and no American wealth to help her. The Russian Anna Karenina was trapped in an aristocratic society from which she could not—though she tried—break away. Even as Isabel believes she should be her own best friend, so she thinks she can be her own oracle. In this sense the American woman was much more an heiress of the ages than the European. In the Miltonic words, "the world is all before" Isabel, as it was before Adam and Eve when they turned from the closing gates of Paradise. There is, however, an important difference. Adam and Eve had eaten of the Tree of Knowledge and learned to distinguish between Good and Evil. Isabel has not tasted of this fruit.

In his account of the gaps in Isabel's learning, Henry James is quietly undermining the Emersonian doctrine that expressed one of the deepest myths of the frontier. The frontier perforce had to be self-reliant: it was acting out the old utopias, seeking new worlds to conquer. But in the civilized world any attempt at such reliance had to take account of rules and standards, customs, traditions, centuries of history, a vast body of knowledge. Isabel had apparently listened too well to the philosophical optimism of Concord. "Trust thyself. . . . Insist on yourself; never imitate. . . . To believe your own thought . . . that is genius" [Ralph Rusk, *The Life of Ralph Waldo Emerson*]. This was the democratization of genius, in the manner of Rousseau. What (James seems to ask) if someone possesses none of the ingredients needed to fashion thought and build self-reliance? Knowledge is not hereditary. There is a *tabula rasa,* in a creature of meagre learning and inflated ideals, that needs to be peopled before she can truly begin to think well of herself. Isabel Archer, like Christopher Newman—and like Columbus—will have a hard passage to India: and in the end India will not be reached because of faulty geographical knowledge. Hers is a journey of ignorance. There will be, for Isabel, only the complex and often devious realities of Europe, the "complex fate" of being an American.

The positive side of Isabel's endowment is the freedom she has been given as a woman—considerably more than her European sisters. She may struggle like Anna or Emma with her own nature; yet she is offered the opportunity to experience, to grow, to develop—and ultimately she is offered boundless freedom that even men did not often possess, the freedom of considerable wealth. There was also no fixed society in America laying down its rules for Isabel as Moscow and St. Petersburg ruled for Tolstoy's Anna. Anna is allowed fewer mistakes than the bourgeois Emma, for she is of a high aristocracy. They have been produced by different societies. The fate to be hurt, to be vulnerable, to grow a thicker skin, to face defeat—Isabel has no inkling of life's struggles when she crosses the Atlantic in the slow ships of the time and finds herself transplanted to England's well-kept gardens. The strange thing (as she discovers) is that her sudden wealth provides no solution to her life's progress. Wealth gives her neither the wisdom she seeks, nor the experience she is prepared to face, even as Newman's easily made wealth proves of no use to him when he must confront the societal rules of France in the Faubourg St. Germain. Suddenly the young girl from Albany finds herself saying "A large fortune means freedom, and I'm afraid of that." Isabel Archer prophesies Erich Fromm's (and modern psychology's) studies in the desire of men and women to escape from freedom—the individual who consciously wants to be liberated but unconsciously fears responsibility. The result is an act of gross self-deception. Such individuals expect all gates to be open even while making sure they are securely locked. We are told that "the acquisition of power made her [Isabel] serious; she scrutinized her power with a kind of tender ferocity." But, adds James, she was "not eager to exercise it." And so we observe her dilemma and watch her act herself out. Wanting freedom, she freely chooses a husband who will imprison her. Wanting power, and possessing it, she uses it in a way that makes her powerless. She is not ready for the selfhood she has so ardently proclaimed. She acts accordingly against herself.

Unlike some of her American sisters, she has turned down a British lord. To marry him, she feels, would make her a prisoner in Britain's social hierarchies and institutions. But she overlooks, in her spirit of self-reliance, the possibility that as a peeress she would be free to accept or reject displeasing avenues of life. And by all indications Lord Warburton is liberal and generous and likely to be a very permissive husband. Still, the reader, sensing this, allows her the anxieties of becoming trapped in an "alien system." Isabel also turns down a courting American millionaire. There is something in his masculinity that she finds too pushing, too hard, too inflexible. The libidinal content of the words used by James is clear to us today even if it may not have been to him. Isabel fears Caspar Goodwood's wooing because sex may be another form of enslavement. It is necessary to remind ourselves what the Victorian sexual freeze did to well-bred young ladies. They became excessively reckless, or excessively cautious. Goodwood seems to want to be in total possession of her. Here again Isabel, a prophet of modern feminism, chooses freedom without wanting to take her chances. And in both refusals of marriage she exercises the one form of power women in Isabel's position usually have—that of saying "no" to their suitors. James shows us Isabel, in the name of freedom, shutting doors that might have led to larger freedoms. "You judge only from the outside," says Lord Warburton, not without a touch of sharpness, "you don't

care. You only care to amuse yourself." Warburton is right. Isabel does not care. She thinks she cares, but her egotism is too great to allow her that kind of concern. She confesses this in a way: "I'm absorbed in myself," and she ruefully adds, "I look at life too much as a doctor's prescription." In reality she writes her own prescriptions, out of the imagination of her self-reliance and the power of her wealth, when she acquires it. Any one of the options James gave her could have led to another kind of novel; James's fairy tale depended on his making the fable consistent. Edith Wharton would create the other kind of novel; a muddled and reckless Isabel becomes Lily Bart in *The House of Mirth.* She also might have been her male counterpart in Wharton's *Age of Innocence.* Indeed, Newland Archer bears Isabel's name, and the "new" in "Newland" seems an easy conversion of Newman.

Isabel Archer's innocence before the treacheries of the world makes her an easy victim for the fortune-hunters, Madame Merle and her former lover, Gilbert Osmond. They do not even need to lay a trap. Isabel trusts them. She has no fear of them and no anxieties, only certain bewilderments. Judging from the outside, as Warburton told her, she is impressed by the worldliness of Madame Merle and by the seeming tenderness of Osmond's velvet gloves. Here we can observe the operation of Isabel's misgivings about her wealth, the mixture of power—and guilt—and freedom—and entrapment—that go with it. As she conceals from herself her fear of freedom, she also conceals from herself the "tender ferocity" of her love of power. She will marry Osmond under the illusion that she is conferring upon him a benefaction, that she is large and generous in spirit—"She would launch his boat for him; she would be his providence." This is quite like the distribution of American aid to an impoverished government by a Congress that expects unbounded gratitude. Osmond's stance has been one of meekness and passivity, his mask for his dictatorial and ruthless temperament. To be sure, he humorously confesses he would have liked to be the Tsar of all the Russias, or the Sultan of Turkey, or even the Pope. There is a touch of megalomania in his fantasies of power. His hypocritical rationalization is that since such exalted despotism is not available to him, he will hide his light under a bushel and live in quiet domesticity with his daughter on Bellosguardo, in a Florentine villa. His ferocity has no tenderness in it—it is rather naked—but Isabel is too innocent to read it truly. His pose of being a "nice" American, a "quiet" American, living with his artefacts, is disingenuous. She is disingenuous as well. She does not recognize that he will simply add Isabel to his collection of artefacts. In the end, Osmond emerges from his mask of quietude as a petty domestic tyrant in the palazzo Isabel buys or rents in Rome. Isabel's free choice has led her into the worst of all possible prisons. She finally faces it, "the house of darkness, the house of dumbness, the house of suffocation."

Isabel is a thoroughgoing American. She holds strongly to her American myth that democracy can do no wrong and that Americans contain within them all they need for "self-realization"—as we say today. She considers "that a morality differing from her own must be inferior to it." Endowed with a notion of her high morality and her self-reliance, supported by the power of her wealth, she has nevertheless blundered into darkness and stagnation. Her intentions have been pure; her innocence has taken account of no possible evil. Now she has to discover that there are no absolutes of autonomy and self-possession, no roads of escape from responsibility and co-existence with others, whether with her fellow-citizens or through relations with the citizens of other lands. Henrietta, in her conforming way, has told her this without fully grasping the depth of what she is saying: "you can't always please yourself; you must sometimes please other people." This is the very essence of civilization. In her self-absorption and egotism, Isabel has overlooked the reciprocities of life, the delicate balance of societies, including the cruel fact that poverty can brutalize the less fortunate to such a point that they bite the hand that feeds them. Liberty, she has to learn—that freedom she eloquently champions—is sometimes won at the expense of the freedom of others. Her sense of absoluteness and wealth made her think that she could be Osmond's providence. But "power corrupts."

In this way the novel Henry James wrote a hundred years ago weaves certain remarkable national ironies within the portrait of his particular lady—the elements of a national myth embodied in the woman he called his *Americana*— an ideal of freedom and equality hedged with historical blindness and pride; a self-interest that often assumes generous forms—and then a sense of hurt when this generosity is challenged as a wielding of power. The slogan "Yankee go home" had not yet been coined when James wrote his novel. But the mythic content of the book predicted error and disillusion, and implied even international terror, confusion, and wrath.

It takes a great artist to create dynamic characters and to show them in the act of living out not only their private destinies but the mythic destinies of their nation as well. In Isabel Archer, James was perhaps only half-consciously prophesying the destiny of the United States in its second century. America had to discover it could not be self-reliant and isolationist; like Isabel it had to learn that there exist other nations possessing their dreams and aspirations and that these are engaged also in an elusive quest for life, liberty, and the pursuit of happiness. The United States would have to face the world and seek to arrive at some liberal international domesticity. In that sense, Isabel is a symbol of her country, and the national banner in which Ralph wraps her speaks for the myth she lives out. As she had to take into account her relationships with her eager suitors abroad and at home, so the United States has had to take a larger account of its relations with its friends and its enemies among the nations of the world. There resides in the pages of James's best-known novel, as we can discern, an allegory built around a profound American myth.

The myth of wealth and the power of wealth, the mixture of historical ignorance and great responsibility, could not be resolved in Henry James's portrait of his American lady. National myths have to run their course, sometimes through many centuries, playing out variations, driven by the winds of historical change and the evolution of nationhood and national character. But the evolution of James's heroine, the development of *her* character, lay within the novelist's reach. James warned us of this when he told us to use "scientific criticism" with some caution. Isabel, the unfinished young woman from Albany, could be wrapped in the national flag so long as she was living out her youth, making her mistakes, discovering the world's deceptions and treacheries. In the middle of the story James pauses. He allows seven years to elapse. Unlike Anna Karenina, his Isabel is not driven to throw herself under the wheels of a train or to take a massive dose of arsenic in the way of Emma Bovary. Having made her choice, Isabel stays with it. She faces the music. She is very American in this— in her tenacity and in her puritan idea of lying in the bed she has made.

We watch, then, the transformation of the young lady from Albany into maturity. Her portrait is conveyed to us in the magnificent and terrible chapter in which Isabel, sitting late at night by her fire, relives her life, looks at her mistakes, recognizes that the choice of her fate has not been altogether hers. So, too, the fates of nations are determined by history, by choices made elsewhere, sometimes by other nations, by remote conditions and disasters over which they have no control. Isabel moves from the plane of her youthful and presumptuous hopes and dreams into a true engagement with life and living, and we leave her deceived but uplifted, bereaved but stoical. She recognizes herself as the protectress of her stepdaughter, and she prepares to acknowledge her mistakes and accept her responsibilities. "The whole of anything is never told," James wrote—and far from leaving us up in the air, as some readers complain, James sees that his novel has achieved what he set out to do. The portrait has been painted. We have seen Isabel in her nonage: we see her now in her maturity: she is fixed in our memory in this maturity. James has no need to go into her aging, the dimming of her brightness— and into the future of her existence, which is unpredictable. We leave Isabel in her thirties. The best portraits record only what is visible to the artist at the time they are painted. The rest is implied. She has "affronted" her destiny: and she is arrested in time. The century that has passed has brightened the colors, enlarged our vision, confirmed the prophecies—the prophecies implicit in the myth. The American myth in turn has shaped itself in history, and its story is unfinished—the continued generosities and the truculence of the elected, the wars, the attempt to be a providence, the outreach across continents and oceans, the declaring of boundaries of its own making, the creation of world-annihilating explosives, and always the disregard of history: and the sense that the course of history can be changed—as if all eventualities can be foreseen.

In that sense we can say that the analogue of the myth was completed in the character of Isabel. But her country's myth, the country in which she was nurtured, continued to form and reform itself along unpredictable paths— continued to fulfill Isabel's fantasy of riding into the unknown, but not with the speed of new travel in air and in space. The novel (and Isabel) is finite: its mythic meaning is unaltered; what it might stand for in the future depends on the evolution of the myths adumbrated in the novel. (pp. 11-17)

Leon Edel, "The Myth of America in 'The Portrait of a Lady'," in The Henry James Review, *Vol. 7, Nos. 2-3, Winter-Spring, 1986, pp. 8-17.*

William T. Stafford   (essay date 1986)

[*Stafford is an American educator and critic. In the following excerpt, he examines the character of Serena Merle.*]

For the current reader, for this current reader, at any rate, the undeniably manipulative and allegedly villainous Madame Merle is the most intricately rendered character in *The Portrait of a Lady.* She is its energizing force, its complication, and, in at least one central sense, its resolution. She propels almost all the significant action. Ostensibly a structural parallel and contrast to Henrietta Stackpole, she is more suggestively a parallel and contrast to Isabel, who works her will. Finally exposed, unloved, seemingly defeated, and returned to America, Serena Merle is still in play on the last page of the novel. For whatever the ambiguous intricacies of Isabel's complex motives in returning to Rome at the end of the novel, unabashedly central to them is a willed dedication to the care of Pansy, Serena Merle's daughter. And if one considers anxious concern—admittedly, ambivalent anxious concern—for the wellbeing of that daughter also to be the spring that motivates Madame Merle's every ploy, then the question is not simply rhetorical when, in her last scene with Osmond (and in one of the great lines of the novel), she wails, "Have I been so vile all for nothing?" It is thus perhaps a deep irony in this deeply ironic book that its most troubled villain is simultaneously its most persistent enigma.

Although Serena Merle was described by Joseph Warren Beach in 1918 as "perhaps the most perfect creation" in *The Portrait of a Lady* [see Further Reading] and although extensive attention was given to her as recently as 1975 [William Veeder, *Henry James—The Lessons of the Master*] in what is described by an even more recent commentator as "the fullest and most penetrating analysis of . . . [her] that has been made" [Wagenknecht, *Eve and Henry James: Portraits of Women and Girls in His Fiction* (1978)], this first "great bad heroine" of the James canon speaks to the contemporary reader, I believe, in unexpected ways.

The centrality of her role in the novel is apparent enough. Yet there are some touches, in her initial appearance when Isabel first meets her, that come to one only from hindsight, though James himself, in his preface, links the scene to the even more famous one of Isabel's solitary vigil before the fireplace of chapter 42, describing both as "two very good instances" of what he there calls "conversion," scenes that were to be "a turning point in . . . [Isabel's] life" that required for the writer the task of "producing the maximum of intensity with the minimum of strain."

When one re-examines this scene, two or three suggestive aspects arise that possibly would not originally have struck one. Some readers will remember that Serena Merle was born in the Brooklyn Naval Yard, a daughter of a "high officer in the United States Navy," one who "had

a post—a post of responsibility—in that establishment at the time." And perhaps most readers will have remembered that Isabel first thought her to be French and was later even more intrigued to discover her to be a compatriot ("rarer even than to be French seemed it to be an American on such interesting terms"). But some of the details of the word-play that establishes her American roots have implications that cannot fully be seen without a retrospective view of the entire novel. The pertinent passage is expressed thus:

> It would never have been supposed she had come into the world in Brooklyn—though one could doubtless not have carried through any argument that the air of distinction marking her in so eminent a degree was inconsistent with such a birth. It was true that the national banner had floated immediately over her cradle, and the breezy freedom of the stars and stripes might have shed an influence upon the attitude she there took towards life. And yet she had evidently nothing of the fluttered, flapping quality of a morsel of bunting in the wind.

That the narrator himself follows this characterization with the qualification that "her manner expressed the repose and confidence which comes from a large experience"—he had earlier described her as possessing a "world-wide smile, a thing that over-reached frontiers"—should not blind one to the curious inspiration that had James also place her "under the shadow of the national banner," as Madame Merle herself so teasingly describes the spot of her birth. The full force of her intransigent formidableness will not come to the reader until much later. And an awareness of the intricate relation of her "Americanness" to that of Isabel will possibly come even later still. Perhaps, therefore, more than inspired playfulness, more than whimsy, is at stake in James's having "rooted" Serena Merle in, of all places, the Brooklyn Naval Yard.

Other apparent "play" in this fine opening scene involves such tactics as James's having originally introduced Isabel only to Madame Merle's back—she has appeared somewhat mysteriously at Gardencourt and is seated at the piano playing something by Schubert when Isabel wanders in—a back, however, that is described as an "ample and well-dressed one." But James's more central opening tactic appears to have been one of contrasting others' views of Madame Merle (the narrator's, Mrs. Touchett's, Ralph's) to those of the clearly intrigued Isabel, to deepen *her* interest in Madame Merle, to deepen our interest in both. The narrator, for example, says explicitly, "she was . . . not pretty"; Isabel clearly thinks otherwise. Mrs. Touchett describes her as "too fond of mystery," but Isabel is said to have "not been struck with the force of Mrs. Touchett's characterisation of her visitor." And Ralph's recognized facetiousness in describing her as one who "does everything beautifully. She's complete" has as its counterpart Isabel's shrewd observation, "you don't like her."

But from the perspective of hindsight, I suppose the most suggestive detail in this opening scene is in Isabel's view of Madame Merle's classically arranged hair, "as if she were a Bust . . .—a Juno or a Niobe." The Niobe reference is especially to be noted, not only in its comic contrast to Ralph's subsequent remark to Isabel that Madame Merle "fortunately" has no children ("Fortunately for the child," he explains; "she'd be sure to spoil it"), but in Isabel's serendipitous linking of Madame Merle with a mournful, perpetually weeping mother of lost children. In her very first appearance, therefore, Serena Merle is more complexly conceived, more intricately rendered, than one might at first have supposed. She appears to fascinate her creator no less than she fascinates Isabel—or, indeed, the reader.

The enigma of Madame Merle's character is also the central force of her final appearance in the novel. After the sordid revelations by the Countess Gemini and the bitterly poignant confrontation between Isabel and Madame Merle as they converge in the convent to say good-bye to Pansy, the now-revealed daughter to one (and paralleled step-daughter to the other), Isabel is said, while traveling from Rome to England, to have had but one regret, "that Madame Merle had been so—well unimaginable. Just here," the narrator continues, "her intelligence dropped, from literal inability to say what it was that Madame Merle had been." That she can later remark to her aunt, in the last reference to Madame Merle in the novel, that when she returns to her homeland she will "make a convenience of America" detracts not at all from the literal inexplicableness that is the final judgment assigned to Isabel about Serena Merle. In some ways she is hardly more explicable to the reader.

James's comments about Madame Merle in his **Notebooks** clearly reveal his awareness of her complexity. But his problems in rendering that complexity perhaps have implications he did not at first foresee. Recognizing at once that the "whole matter of Madame Merle is . . . a very ticklish one—very delicate and difficult to handle," he nevertheless sees it as "not . . . an impossibility." It is "perfectly natural," he writes to himself, that Madame Merle's "old interest in Osmond remains in modified form; she wishes to do something for him, and she does it through another rather than through herself." But what James calls "the strangeness of her conduct" toward Pansy is, he says, "greater. . . . We must remember," he continues, "that we see only its surface—we don't see her reasoning. Isabel has money, and Mme Merle has great confidence in her benevolence, in her generosity; she has no fear that she will be a harsh stepmother, and she believes she will push the fortunes of the child she herself is unable to avow and afraid openly to patronize."

Describing Madame Merle's behavior toward Osmond as "perfectly natural" is provocative enough. But more intriguing is James's recognition of what he calls the "strangeness of her conduct" toward Pansy. And more intriguing still is his concomitant justifying rationale that we see "only its surface—we don't see her reasoning." James will later write that he "was not sure that it would not be best that the exposure of Mme Merle should never be complete." "She should not denounce herself," he says. Such behavior, he continues, "would injure very much the impression I have wished to give of her profundity, her self-control, her regard for appearances." It will be enough,

James still later explains, that Isabel *believes* the Countess Gemini. "Isabel may charge her with the Countess G.'s secret. This Madame Merle will deny—but deny in such a way that Isabel knows she lies; and *then* Isabel may depart."

The final provocative revelation of these **Notebook** entries about Serena Merle is James's stated rationale for having her reveal to Isabel her conviction that "it was Ralph who had induced her [*sic*] father to leave her the £70,000." This is done, James somewhat bizarrely explains, so that Isabel will defy Osmond, will leave him, "so that she may be away from Pansy." A few lines later James will repeat this intended motive for Madame Merle's revelations with even more explicitness—she "tells it with the view . . . of *precipitating* [my italics] her defiance of Osmond."

On reflection, some of these reflexive musings are indeed passing strange. It is said to be "natural" for Madame Merle to want to provide her ex-lover with a new wife because "her old interest in Osmond remains in modified form." Her attitude toward the unacknowledged daughter that resulted from this illicit relationship, though said to be "strange," is explained on the ground that Isabel is known to be kind and may indeed support Pansy with money—issues that can be handled if we see only the "surface" of Madame Merle, not her "reasoning." Madame Merle is nowhere to denounce herself; her "exposure . . . should never be complete." And yet, we are also told, her motive for revealing to Isabel that it was Ralph who persuaded his father to leave her a fortune is to effect a break with Osmond!

Nothing is quite unintelligible in these Jamesian ruminations about the problems of rendering Serena Merle and her complex motivations. What is finally rendered, moreover, is infinitely more important than any initial speculative intentions that a writer might have had while in the process of composition—even a writer so knowledgeably self-conscious as Henry James. Even so, we can see in these **Notebook** entries about Madame Merle certain delicate, almost hesitant musings that perhaps give one more to digest than one can comfortably chew.

I am not convinced that James himself, any more than Isabel, finally knows quite what to make of Madame Merle. She is structurally conceived to parallel and foil Henrietta Stackpole. And Sister M. Corona Sharp [see Further Reading] has demonstrated with admirable thoroughness the variety of ways these two confidantes to Isabel are indirectly juxtaposed throughout the novel. Henrietta, candid, outgoing, chauvinistic, above all, comic, "equipped with utter frankness and fearlessness" and said to see "Isabel both from the outside and the inside," nevertheless "does not succeed in altering Isabel's life." It is the secretive, devious, worldly, and perhaps tragic Serena Merle who determines Isabel's fate. And although both Henrietta and Serena Merle could literally and accurately be described as pragmatists, the kinds of pragmatism they respectively display are more notable for their differences than for their similarities. Moreover, the respective ultimate fates of this neatly conceived pair of confidantes result in what I can describe only as ineffable distinctions that reach somewhere beyond the superb comic twist of its being Henrietta who gives up her homeland, marries Mr. Bantling, and moves to Europe, and Madame Merle who returns to America. Madame Merle, we must remember, chooses to return to her homeland. "I shall go to America," she is said to have "quietly remarked" as her last words in the novel. And when Isabel later remarks to Mrs. Touchett that Madame Merle will even "make a convenience of America," she is said to have said so "smiling."

I am thus no longer quite convinced that Sister Corona Sharp's impressive summation of Serena Merle's numerous disappointments is quite as adequate as I once thought it to be. After asserting that Madame Merle's "role as villainess in a tragedy destines her for a dark future," Sharp continues:

> Her frustrations are more numerous than those of other confidantes: a loveless marriage; an episode in another man's life, from which she could emerge only as the loser; the sacrifice of her child for the sake of respectability; the failure to contract a brilliant, second marriage—all these are truly great disappointments. Ironically, pity is accorded to her only by her victim. . . . The man for whom she has worked, plotted, and suffered, makes no secret of his being tired of her. Nothing, indeed, is spared her; and one is forced to admire the pride that can hold her head erect to the very end.

Although it might occur to anyone, as it now occurs to me, that this compelling summation is hardly less appropriate as a description of Isabel's fate than it is of Madame Merle's, the parallel turns their destinies take perhaps have not been noticed.

Very early in their relationship Isabel describes the "talents, accomplishments, [and] aptitudes of Madame Merle" as those she would most like to emulate. " 'I should like awfully to be *so*!' Isabel exclaimed, more than once." I have already indicated my belief that this wish is granted—and with a vengeance. But the variety of ways Isabel does indeed become "so" is as intricate as it is extensive: their respective "loveless" relations with Osmond, for whom both have uselessly "worked, plotted, and suffered"; their "failed" relations with other men (Madame Merle's with her husband and with Osmond, Isabel's with Ralph, Warburton, and Goodwood); their mutual, if somewhat disparate, concerns for the well-being of Pansy; their imperious pride. Is, moreover, Isabel any less "manipulative" (toward Lord Warburton's suit for Pansy, say) than Madame Merle is toward Isabel herself? They are even linked, as Isabel herself recognizes, in their final misery. Just before Isabel declares that she would "like never to see her again," Madame Merle says, "You're very unhappy, I know," but she adds, "I'm more so."

Nowhere in the novel are the *initial* differences between Madame Merle and Isabel more apparent than in their early and often-cited discussion about "things." The famous passage follows an exchange of confidences about their youthful ambitions, their hopes and dreams, during the early days of their acquaintance at Gardencourt. Madame Merle has just previously confessed to Isabel her awareness that Ralph does not "like" her, her calm accep-

tance of that condition as perhaps simply "an antipathy of nature," and then she has closed the subject with the observation that Ralph is nonetheless too much the gentleman ever to say or do anything underhanded. Isabel is reminded by that confession of Ralph's earlier inexplicit but nonetheless perfectly apparent antipathy toward Madame Merle, but tactfully she does not pursue the issue further. "With all of her [Isabel's] love for knowledge," we are told, "she had a natural shrinking from raising curtains and looking into unlighted corners. The love of knowledge," the narrator obtrusively inserts, "coexisted in her mind with the finest capacity for ignorance."

It is only a few paragraphs later, following a discussion about the place young men might have played in their youthful dreams and about how what they owned or where they lived affected one's attitude toward them, that we get Madame Merle's forthright expression of the impossibility of separating one's self from one's appurtenances. "When you've lived as long as I," she pontificates,

> "you'll see that every human being has his shell and that you must take the shell into account. By the shell I mean the whole envelope of circumstances. There's no such thing as an isolated man or woman; we're each of us made up of some cluster of appurtenances. What shall we call our 'self'? Where does it begin? where does it end? It overflows into everything that belongs to us—and then it flows back again. I know a large part of myself is in the clothes I choose to wear. I've a great respect for *things!* One's self—for other people—is one's expression of one's self; and one's house, one's furniture, one's garments, the books one reads, the company one keeps—these things are all expressive."

Isabel at this stage explicitly disagrees, describes herself as thinking "just the other way," and contends that though she might not succeed in "expressing" herself, she knows that "nothing else expresses" her. "Nothing that belongs to me," she says, "is any measure of me; everything's on the contrary a limit, a barrier, and a perfectly arbitrary one. Certainly the clothes . . . I choose to wear . . . don't express me; and heaven forbid they should!"

The initial "ignorance" that "coexisted" with Isabel's "love of knowledge" is nowhere better caught in the novel than in this exchange. Equally evident, however, is the eloquent pull of her romantic and idealistic yearnings, her absolute conviction that nothing "outside" of herself is capable of expressing her true "inner" self. Conversely, the clear-sighted practicality, the psychological acuteness, and the reality-based knowledgeableness of Serena Merle are equally apparent—and equally eloquent in expression. The self, for Madame Merle, is an intricately complex entity, as irreducibly connected to those forces that flow into it as it is to those that flow from it. Madame Merle, as Leon Edel once remarked to me, "would never ride horses into an unknown darkness." True. Yet Serena Merle's decision to return to America at the end of the novel is in some sense a ride into darkness, Isabel's final claim that she will make a convenience even of America notwithstanding. And Isabel's final return to Rome must also have something in it of a then-held conviction that "things" outside one's self do indeed determine what one can do, what one can be. Hence, from even this most polarized example of the differences between Serena Merle and Isabel Archer we see developed a kind of interchanging coalescence, Isabel becoming something of a Serena Merle, Serena Merle becoming something of an Isabel Archer.

The question of who becomes more of whom leads into my final speculations about the enigma of Serena Merle. From one point of view, she is simply the designing villainess who is finally exposed and gets her predictable comeuppance. And in this vein she is undeniably effective. There is explosive dramatic force in Isabel's "I believed it was you I had to thank" when Serena Merle reveals to her Ralph's crucial part in her misadventures. But from another point of view, is it not Serena Merle who has come through the whole less scarred than Isabel herself? It is perhaps even Serena Merle, through the loss of the love of her child, who most poignantly suffers. And yet it is also Serena Merle who can also be said to have most unequivocally achieved what she finally set out to achieve—a loving and generous caretaker for her unacknowledged child, whatever the unfathomable motives that led her originally to bring Isabel and Osmond together. The truth of the matter is that no one else in this novel so movingly, if ambiguously, "wins"—certainly not Isabel, not Ralph, not Warburton, not Goodwood. Her paired confidante and sister *ficelle*, Henrietta Stackpole, is perhaps the exception. But *her* victory is through the staged comedy of a melodramatic international marriage. Madame Merle's is much more complex, more human, more demanding, more *interesting*.

The already-cited *Notebook* entries indicate clearly enough how initially intriguing, however "difficult," James found his conception of Serena Merle to be. How crucially central he retrospectively *saw* her to have been is equally apparent in his comments about her in his preface to the novel, also already cited. But none of these references is ultimately as revealing of the inspired impact Serena Merle made upon the creative imagination of this still relatively early Henry James as the re-appearance of her "type" in his later fiction. After *The Portrait of a Lady* James was never again to create a villain as one-sidedly drawn as Osmond, nor a "good" American as woodenly drawn as Caspar Goodwood. He was never again to indulge his early sense of the comic with a character as thin as Henrietta Stackpole. And although we are later to see some aspects of Isabel in characters as diverse as the rigidly idealistic Fleda Vetch (of *The Spoils of Poynton*) and the adventuresomely romantic Lambert Strether, it is more frequently Serena Merle who was to appear and reappear in major fiction after major fiction.

More than a touch of her, for example, is in the steely surface of the ambiguously drawn Mrs. Brookenham of *The Awkward Age.* Madame Merle's description of herself as having come from the "old, old world" ("I was born before the French Revolution") could have as well described Mme. de Vionnet of *The Ambassadors.* The vividly drawn Kate Croy of *The Wings of the Dove* "controls" that novel as inexorably as Serena Merle controls *The Portrait*—and

departs from it as equivocally as Serena Merle departs from hers. (Is it Densher who rejects Kate, or Kate who rejects Densher, in that magnificent final scene of *The Wings?*) And of course we see Madame Merle everywhere in the duplicitous Charlotte Stant of *The Golden Bowl,* from her impecunious American beginnings through her enigmatic return to American City as Mrs. Adam Verver. We even see a good deal of her, I think, in this last and perhaps greatest of James's novels, in Maggie Verver. For what Maggie "all tragically has to become to regain the Prince," as I have written elsewhere, "a Prince who prefers the now more devious and deceitful Maggie over the less devious and deceitful Charlotte *because* Maggie is capable of being better at the game than Charlotte, is a fully knowledgeable and corrupt woman." The "pity and dread" with which Maggie buries her head in the breast of her Prince in the last great line of that great novel clearly has in it some of the same fervent force as Madame Merle's woeful wail, "Have I been so vile . . . for nothing?" following her final meeting with Osmond.

All of which is in no way to suggest that Serena Merle is more important for what her conception becomes than for what it is in *The Portrait.* Quite the contrary. *The Portrait of a Lady* is in part a great novel because Serena Merle is what Serena Merle is *in* that novel: problematic, to be sure, fallible, certainly, but, above all, enigmatically and believably human. (pp. 117-22)

> *William T. Stafford, "The Enigma of Serena Merle," in* The Henry James Review, *Vol. 7, Nos. 2-3, Winter-Spring, 1986, pp. 117-23.*

FURTHER READING

Anderson, Quentin. "News of Life." In his *Henry James,* pp. 183-206. New Brunswick, N.J.: Rutgers University Press, 1957.

> Contends that *The Portrait of a Lady* reflects a departure from the humanistic philosophy which James espoused in his earlier books and which the critic attributes to the influence of James's father, Henry James, Sr.

Beach, Joseph Warren. "Early Prime: *The Portrait of a Lady.*" In his *The Method of Henry James,* pp. 205-11. New Haven, Conn.: Yale University Press, 1918.

> Discussion of *The Portrait of a Lady* as an example of James's early style.

Berkson, Dorothy. "Why Does She Marry Osmond? The Education of Isabel Archer." *The American Transcendental Quarterly,* No. 60 (June 1986): 53-71.

> Considers *The Portrait of a Lady* as a *bildungsroman,* in which Isabel Archer enters into adulthood through her naive and idealistic decision to marry Gilbert Osmond.

Berland, Alwyn. "The Sacred Quest: *The Portrait of a Lady.*" In his *Culture and Conduct in the Novels of Henry James,* pp. 90-135. Cambridge, England: Cambridge University Press, 1981.

Examines the decisions made by characters in the novel in order to illuminate philosophical influences on James.

Bowden, Edwin T. "The Mighty Individual." In his *The Dungeon of the Heart,* pp. 66-102. New York: The Macmillan Company, 1961.

Discusses *The Portrait of a Lady* as a distinctly American work in which Isabel "defeated the isolation of the spirit and reached out from the dungeon of the heart to a larger life that will sustain [her]."

Buitenhuis, Peter, ed. *Twentieth Century Interpretations of "The Portrait of a Lady."* Englewood Cliffs, N.J.: Prentice-Hall, 1968, 122 p.

Collects previously published criticism of *The Portrait of a Lady,* including commentary by F. W. Dupee, Leon Edel, and Pelham Edgar.

Cargill, Oscar. "The Drive to Distinction: *The Portrait of a Lady.*" In his *The Novels of Henry James,* pp. 78-119. New York: The Macmillan Company, 1961.

Discusses characterization and style with a survey of critical reaction to the novel.

Connaughton, Michael E. "American English and the International Theme in *The Portrait of a Lady.*" *The Midwest Quarterly* XXII, No. 2 (Winter 1981): 137-46.

Examines British and American dialects as expressed through word choice rather than phonetic spelling in the novel.

Dupee, F. W. "The Tree of Knowledge." In his *Henry James,* pp. 87-125. New York: William Sloane Associates, 1951.

Includes a discussion of marriage as not only a central theme in *The Portrait of a Lady* but also a "condition . . . of Isabel's existence."

Edel, Leon. Introduction to *The Portrait of a Lady,* by Henry James, pp. v-xx. Boston: Houghton Mifflin Company, 1956.

Provides an analysis of Isabel Archer, concluding that she is one of the most memorable characters in fiction.

Edgar, Pelham. "The Major Novels." In his *Henry James: Man and Author,* pp. 232-343. 1927. Reprint. New York: Russell & Russell, 1964.

Finds the characterization in *The Portrait of a Lady* to be flawed but considers the novel as the groundwork for the "subtlety and power" of James's later works.

Friend, Joseph H. "The Structure of *The Portrait of a Lady.*" *Nineteenth-Century Fiction* 20, No. 1 (June 1965): 85-95.

Chronological examination of the novel's events, focusing on the irony of Isabel's decision to marry Gilbert Osmond.

Gard, Roger, ed. *"The Portrait of a Lady."* In *Henry James: The Critical Heritage,* pp. 93-120. London: Routledge & Kegan Paul, 1968.

Compiles early critical assessments of the novel, including published reviews and commentary from the personal correspondence of such figures as William Dean Howells and Henry Adams.

Gilmore, Michael T. "The Commodity World of *The Portrait of a Lady.*" *The New England Quarterly* LIX, No. 1 (March 1986): 51-74.

Contends that James manipulates his characters and his characters manipulate each other in a way that is "at once a rejection and a corollary of a social order in which some persons are the tools or commodities of others."

Greene, Graham. Introduction to *The Portrait of a Lady,* by Henry James, pp. v-xi. London: Oxford University Press, 1947.

Discusses the novel in light of James's description of Isabel Archer as "a certain young woman affronting her destiny."

The Henry James Review, Special Issue: "The Portrait of a Lady" 7, Nos. 2-3 (Winter-Spring 1986): 1-195.

Includes articles assessing the novel's structure, motifs, characterization, and historical and critical contexts, with an extensive annotated bibliography of secondary sources.

Holland, Laurence B. "James's *Portrait.*" In his *The Expense of Vision: Essays on the Craft of Henry James,* pp. 3-54. Baltimore: The Johns Hopkins University Press, 1964.

Analyzes James's preface to *The Portrait of a Lady,* the marriage of Isabel and Osmond, and the plot and descriptive techniques of the novel.

Jones, Peter. "Pragmatism and *The Portrait of a Lady.*" *Philosophy and Literature* 5, No. 1 (Spring 1981): 49-61.

Suggests that narration and characterization in the novel are informed by the philosophic methodology of pragmatism advanced by James's brother, William James.

Kaul, A. N. *"The Portrait of a Lady:* Henry James and the Avoidance of Comedy." In his *The Action of English Comedy,* pp. 250-83. New Haven, Conn.: Yale University Press, 1970.

Explores comic effects in the novel produced by the confusion Isabel experiences in making decisions.

Krause, Sydney J. "James's Revisions of the Style of *The Portrait of a Lady.*" *American Literature* 30, No. 1 (March 1958): 67-88.

Detailed analysis of James's revisions of the novel, concluding that they "demonstrate that James was capable of a measure of flexibility in style which has too rarely been appreciated."

Laird, J. T. "Cracks in Precious Objects: Aestheticism and Humanity in *The Portrait of a Lady.*" *American Literature* 52, No. 4 (January 1981): 643-48.

Analyzes two scenes in the novel containing references to porcelain art objects in order to examine the "conflict between aestheticism and humanity."

Levine, George. "Isabel, Gwendolen, and Dorothea." *Journal of English Literary History* 30, No. 3 (September 1963): 244-57.

Disputes the common comparison between *The Portrait of a Lady* and George Eliot's *Daniel Deronda,* favoring instead a comparison with Eliot's *Middlemarch.*

Levy, Leo B. "Melodrama and the Imagination of Disaster." In his *Versions of Melodrama: A Study of the Fiction and Drama of Henry James, 1865-1897,* pp. 36-69. Berkeley and Los Angeles: University of California Press, 1957.

Discusses *The Portrait of a Lady* as "a novel of moral education, a study of the idealism that seeks the freedom of a generous life and courageously invites self-knowledge."

Long, Robert Emmet. *"The Portrait of a Lady:* The Caging

of the Beautiful Striver." In his *Henry James: The Early Novels,* pp. 101-27. Boston: Twayne Publishers, 1983.

   Analyzes imagery and characterization in *The Portrait of a Lady* and examines the novel's controversial conclusion.

McElderry, Bruce R., Jr. "The Middle Years: 1880-1890." In his *Henry James,* pp. 55-84. New York: Twayne Publishers, 1965.

   Overview of the main characters and themes in *The Portrait of a Lady.*

Mackenzie, Manfred. "Ironic Melodrama in *The Portrait of a Lady.*" *Modern Fiction Studies* XII, No. 1 (Spring 1966): 7-23.

   Argues that *"The Portrait* is constructed from the materials of melodrama, and its intensities arise from the action of James's irony upon these materials; it might best be described as an ironic melodrama."

Marcell, David W. "High Ideals and Catchpenny Realities in Henry James's *The Portrait of a Lady.*" In *Essays in Modern American Literature,* edited by Richard E. Langford, pp. 26-34. DeLand, Fla.: Stetson University Press, 1963.

   Suggests that Isabel's perception of the aristocracy as free from responsibilities, and her subsequent emulation of that ideal, restrict her involvement in relationships.

Matthiessen, F. O., and Murdock, Kenneth B., eds. *The Notebooks of Henry James.* New York: Oxford University Press, 1947, 425 p.

   Includes James's notes on characters and plot elements he planned to use in *The Portrait of a Lady* as well as annotations by Matthiessen and Murdock describing James's creative process.

Millet, Fred B. Introduction to *The Portrait of a Lady,* by Henry James, pp. v-xxvi. New York: Random House, 1951.

   Discusses the structure of the novel, James's theories of fiction as expressed in the preface, and his 1908 revision of the work.

Montgomery, Marion. "The Flaw in the Portrait: Henry James vs. Isabel Archer." *The University of Kansas City Review* XXVI, No. 3 (March 1960): 215-20.

   Criticizes James's characterization of Isabel Archer as inconsistent and unrealistic, concluding that "James's instinctive artistry, which demands sufficient freedom of form, is at odds with his dogmatic principles which demand strict form. He does not allow himself a freedom of execution worthy of his conception."

Morrow, Nancy. "Playing by the Rules: Henry James's *The American* and *The Portrait of a Lady.*" In her *Dreadful Games: The Play of Desire in the Nineteenth-Century Novel,* pp. 118-43. Kent, Ohio: The Kent State University Press, 1988.

   Traces the "metaphor of the game" in *The Portrait of a Lady* and *The American,* focusing on the ways in which "the language of games indicates how [a] cycle of betrayal and revenge is broken" in the novels.

Poirier, Richard. *"The Portrait of a Lady."* In his *The Comic Sense of Henry James: A Study of the Early Novels,* pp. 183-246. New York: Oxford University Press, 1967.

   Argues that among James's early works, *The Portrait of a Lady* "offers the fullest expression . . . of the drama and comedy of choice."

Porte, Joel, ed. *New Essays on "The Portrait of a Lady."* Cambridge, England: Cambridge University Press, 1990, 166 p.

   Collection of previously unpublished essays on *The Portrait of a Lady,* including feminist and Freudian analyses of the novel.

Powers, Lyall H. *"The Portrait of a Lady:* 'The Eternal Mystery of Things'." *Nineteenth-Century Fiction* 14, No. 2 (September 1959): 143-55.

   Suggests that Isabel's motive for returning to her husband is to "confront the evil of the world, to work at the redemption of that evil, to do in short whatever work the spiritually regenerate necessarily undertake here below."

Reid, Stephen. "Moral Passion in *The Portrait of a Lady* and *The Spoils of Poynton.*" *Modern Fiction Studies* XII, No. 1 (Spring 1966): 24-43.

   Compares Isabel Archer with Fleda Vetch of James's *The Spoils of Poynton,* proposing that the heroines' staunch moral codes belie their rationalization of "emotional needs."

Sangari, Kumkum. "Of Ladies, Gentlemen, and 'The Short-Cut'." *New Literary History* 19, No. 3 (Spring 1988): 713-37.

   Analyzes the "specific paradigm of individuality created in the novel [which] identifies 'femaleness' as a mode of higher bourgeois consciousness, deploys femaleness as a thematic for desired cultural change, and in the process draws on the individualism latent in nineteenth-century feminism even as it marginalizes the more disruptive aspects of this feminism."

Sharp, Sister M. Corona. "The Major Confidantes: *The Portrait of a Lady.*" In her *Henry James: Evolution and Moral Value of a Fictive Character,* pp. 67-96. South Bend, Ind.: University of Notre Dame Press, 1963.

   Examines the opposing functions of Madame Merle and Henrietta Stackpole as confidantes to Isabel Archer.

Snow, Lotus. "The Disconcerting Poetry of Mary Temple: A Comparison of the Imagery of *The Portrait of a Lady* and *The Wings of the Dove.*" *The New England Quarterly* XXXI, No. 3 (September 1958): 312-39.

   Addresses the theme of betrayal in *The Portrait of a Lady* and James's later novel *The Wings of the Dove.*

Stafford, William T., ed. *Perspectives on James's "The Portrait of a Lady."* New York: New York University Press, 1967, 303 p.

   Compilation of previously published essays and reviews.

———. *"The Portrait of a Lady:* The Second Hundred Years." *The Henry James Review* II, No. 2 (Winter 1981): 91-100.

   Appreciative essay occasioned by the centenary of the publication of *The Portrait of a Lady,* focusing on syntax and structure in Chapter 47.

Stallman, Robert W. "The Houses That James Built—*The Portrait of a Lady.*" In his *The Houses That James Built, and Other Literary Studies,* pp. 1-33. Athens, Ohio: Ohio University Press, 1961.

   Examines James's use of such architectural structures as churches, theaters, and houses as symbols for moral values and states of mind in *The Portrait of a Lady.*

Stein, William Bysshe. *"The Portrait of a Lady:* Vis Inertiae."

Western Humanities Review XIII, No. 2 (Spring 1959): 177-90.

> Finds Isabel's "simpering inanity" and "sexlessness" representative of a common depiction of femininity during the Victorian era.

Templeton, Wayne. "*The Portrait of a Lady:* A Question of Freedom." *English Studies in Canada* VII, No. 3 (Fall 1981): 312-28.

> Examines the social and philosophical beliefs implied in Isabel's attempt to realize the "American dream" of freedom.

Van Ghent, Dorothy. "On *The Portrait of a Lady.*" In her *The English Novel: Form and Function,* pp. 211-28. New York: Holt, Rinehart & Winston, 1953.

> Discusses the novel's major themes.

Warner, John M. "Renunciation as Enunciation in James's *The Portrait of a Lady.*" *Renascence* XXXIX, No. 2 (Winter 1987): 354-64.

> Suggests, through a comparison between *The Portrait of a Lady* and *The American,* that Isabel is engaged in a search for spiritual and cultural fulfillment which she attains, at the novel's conclusion, by returning to Rome.

Wegelin, Christof. "The American as a Young Lady." In his *The Image of Europe in Henry James,* pp. 56-85. Dallas: Southern Methodist University Press, 1958.

> Examines James's presentation of the moral values typical to Americans and Europeans, suggesting that Isabel, an American girl in Europe and the character with whom James most sympathizes, embodies the more noble values of each culture.

Westervelt, Linda A. " 'The Growing Complexity of Things': Narrative Technique in *The Portrait of a Lady.*" *The Journal of Narrative Technique* 13, No. 2 (Spring 1983): 74-85.

> Cites the narration of particular events in the text as indicative of James's innovations in novelistic technique.

Gertrud Kolmar

1894-1943

(Born Gertrud Chodziesner) German poet, short story writer, and novelist.

Kolmar is chiefly remembered as the author of lyric poetry that focuses on children, animals, and women's experiences. Regarded as highly original, her poems feature figurative language and images most often derived from nature.

Kolmar was the oldest of four children born into a prominent Jewish professional family. She spent her youth in Berlin, where she was educated in local schools. Described as an introverted child, she took little interest in social pursuits, preferring instead to read and study. The relative seclusion of her life during this early period has been compared to that of Emily Dickinson. After she had begun writing, Kolmar, like Dickinson, avoided contact with her contemporaries, a tendency cited by biographers as one factor in the development of her idiosyncratic poetic style. After completing high school in 1911, Kolmar studied English, French, and Russian, gaining a familiarity with foreign languages and literature that also contributed to the evolution of her poetry. While it is uncertain exactly when Kolmar began to write, a volume of her verse, *Gedichte,* was published in 1917. Several events at this time provided subject matter and themes for much of her poetry, including an unhappy love affair, her teaching of handicapped children, and her family's move to the picturesque surroundings of Finkenkrug, a rural suburb of Berlin.

During the 1920s and 1930s, Kolmar wrote prolifically, producing *Eine Mutter,* a novel which was published posthumously, as well as what scholars consider her most important poems. After the publication of *Gedichte,* only two more collections of Kolmar's poems appeared during her lifetime: *Preussische Wappen, (Prussian Coats of Arms),* a cycle of poems inspired by heraldic shields and addressing such elemental experiences as birth, love, and death, and *Die Frau und die Tiere,* two cycles of poems about women and animals. This last collection met with great critical success in the Jewish press. As the Nazis gained power in Germany during the 1930s, Kolmar's comfortable middle-class lifestyle underwent severe changes. Alarmed at the increasingly violent anti-Semitism condoned under Adolf Hitler's government, members of Kolmar's family fled the country. Kolmar, who voluntarily remained in Germany to care for her aged and ailing father, was able to write in relative safety throughout this ordeal, sending her last poem cycle, *Welten (Worlds),* to her sister in Switzerland. Conditions for Jews in Germany worsened, however, after *Kristallnacht,* a particularly vicious pogrom that occurred in 1938. Kolmar and her father were obliged by law to sell their estate at Finkenkrug and move to a crowded tenement in a Berlin ghetto. There, Kolmar worked long hours as a forced laborer in a factory. Despite this rigorous existence, she continued to write, corre-

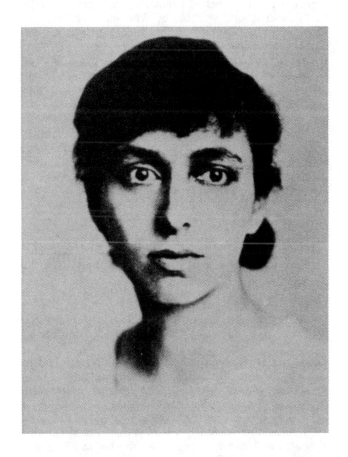

sponding with her sister and composing both the short story "Susanna," which she managed to smuggle out of the country, and poems written in Hebrew that have not survived. In 1941 her father was deported to Theresienstadt, an extermination camp. After 22 February 1943, Kolmar's communication with her sister ceased and she was never heard from again. It is believed that she perished at Auschwitz.

Each of Kolmar's poetry cycles addresses specific subjects and themes. The poems in "Weibliches Bildnis" ("Image of Woman"), for example, explore the stages in a woman's development, considering her as lover, mother, and elder. Themes of childlessness, abandonment, and unrequited love are also exhibited throughout this cycle, as woman is forced by the circumstances of life to give up all that she loves. "Tierträume" ("Animal Dreams"), a cycle of animal poems, and "Kind," poems about children, display similar themes of unfulfillment and solitude. In *Worlds,* poems about animals, nature, women, and domesticity, Kolmar laments the transitory quality of life, creating an idealized Asia to symbolize the possibility of enduring realms. Kolmar's subjects and themes are supported by figurative language and imagery derived from her precise observation of the natural world. Used as similes, metaphors, and images, flowers and animals attain symbolic significance as in "Bild der Rose" ("Rose Sonnets") and "Animal Dreams." Of particular interest, in view of her background and era, are Kolmar's frank descriptions of female sexuality. Much of Kolmar's poetry in such cycles as "Rose Sonnets," "Image of Woman," and "Animal Dreams" demonstrates strict adherence to metrics and rhyme reminiscent of the folksong form after which these poems were modelled. However, her last cycle, *Worlds,* departs from this pattern in its use of free verse and language echoing the cadences of the Old Testament. Since the posthumous publication of her works during the postwar era, Kolmar's literary stature has grown steadily, leading Richard Exner to conclude that Kolmar "will become recognized as one of the best women poets of the century."

PRINCIPAL WORKS

Gedichte (poetry) 1917

Preussische Wappen (poetry) 1934
  [*Prussian Coats of Arms,* published in *Dark Soliloquy: The Selected Poems of Gertrud Kolmar* (partial translation), 1975]

**Die Frau und die Tiere* (poetry) 1938

Welten (poetry) 1947
  [*Worlds,* published in *Dark Soliloquy: The Selected Poems of Gertrud Kolmar* (partial translation), 1975]

†*Das lyrische Werk* (poetry) 1955; also published as *Das lyrische Werk* [enlarged edition], 1960

"Susanna" (short story) 1955; published in *Das leere Haus: Prosa jüdischer Dichter*

"Das Bildnis Robespierres" (essay) 1965; published in journal *Jahrbuch der deutschen Schillergesellschaft*

Eine Mutter (novel) 1965; also published as *Eine jüdische Mutter,* 1978

Briefe an die Schwester Hilde, 1938-1943 (letters) 1970

Selected Poems of Gertrud Kolmar (poetry) 1970

Dark Soliloquy: The Selected Poems of Gertrud Kolmar (poetry) 1975

---

*This volume contains the poem cycles "Weibliches Bildnis" ("Image of Woman") and "Tierträume" ("Animal Dreams"), partially translated in *Dark Soliloquy: The Selected Poems of Gertrud Kolmar,* and the poem cycle "Kind."

†This volume contains the poem cycle "Bild der Rose" ("Rose Sonnets"), partially translated in *Dark Soliloquy: The Selected Poems of Gertrud Kolmar.*

Jacob Picard (essay date 1950)

[*In the following excerpt, Picard focuses on the technical artistry of Kolmar's poems.*]

It is difficult to convey the quality of poetry as unique as [the] later work of Gertrud Chodziesner without the reader's having before him a selection of the poems in the origi-

nal German. For they not only extend the area of experience that the lyric has dealt with, but also possess the consummate formal perfection, the organic inevitability of form, so vital to the genre. Many of the verses of this poet are crystalline in their rigor of form, and at the same time spare and pure in their intellectual and emotional quality, to a degree that we otherwise find only in the work of men, and then only seldom. There is nothing in her poetry of cheap and passing irony, and none of those modish psychological experiments in subject matter—mere prose turned mechanically into verse—which one meets with so often these days in this country.

The poems in *Welten* are composed of loose, long, flowing unrhymed lines of free verse on the order of Walt Whitman's, but there is imposed on them—even more, perhaps, in her work than in Whitman's—the inner constraint of a kind of fugal meter. Yet the old essential melos is preserved. By an act of unique intuition, the poems succeed in objectifying the writer's ultimate inner experience of plants, animals, visionary landscapes, in achieving mastery over the dark forces of the inexplicable to which the poet is peculiarly close. We might call some of the poems elegies of a unique sort, others are in essence ballads, and in many there is a demonism at work such as has never before been encountered in poetry written by a woman.

The work recently published in *Sinn und Form* may perhaps be said to be even more strikingly perfect. In these last poems, written shortly before her death, in the full consciousness of what surely awaited her, Gertrud Chodziesner completely realized herself as artist and human being. The form she uses is again the severe stanza of her first important work published ten years before [*Die Frau und die Tiere*]. All was written—it cannot be sufficiently emphasized—under the pressures of that period of dreadful expectancy, and it is moving to see how the quiet resolution displayed in the letter quoted at the beginning of these remarks is unflaggingly maintained in these poems. Not one of the events of those fearful days is used directly in journalistic fashion for the subject of a poem; but one can feel in the very rhythms of the poems the tremors of what was taking place and the great and bitter melancholy of death and decline. There is the absolute beauty and perfection of such a poem as **"Abschied" ("Parting")**, which might almost have been written by Christina Rossetti. . . . (pp. 462-63)

There have been few lyric poets able always to resist being seduced by their verbal dexterity into the making of verse that might just as well have remained unmade, verse lacking all inner life. In the work of Gertrud Chodziesner there is not a single such poem; each springs from a deep inner need to which the poet, with inexorable self-discipline, has given the one possible form. (p. 464)

> *Jacob Picard, "Gertrud Kolmar: The Woman and the Beasts," in* Commentary, *Vol. 10, No. 5, November, 1950, pp. 459-65.*

Henry A. Smith (essay date 1975)

[*In the following excerpt, Smith discusses the major themes of Kolmar's poetry cycles "Image of Woman,"*]

"Kind," and "Animal Dreams," and the collection Welten.]

If Gertrud Kolmar succeeds in establishing a permanent literary reputation, this reputation will be based largely on the three cycles "Weibliches Bildnis," "Kind" ("Child"), and "Tierträume" ("Animal Dreams"). With the exception of a few examples from the late collection **Welten,** the poems in these three cycles are her greatest. And more than any other portion of her work they serve to define her identity as a poet. Had all her other works but these been lost, our image of Gertrud Kolmar would remain essentially unchanged. She would remain the poet of "woman and animals," the title she gave to the last publication of her verse during her lifetime (**Die Frau und die Tiere,** Berlin, 1938), a collection drawn exclusively from the three cycles in question. All three share a common period of composition (from approximately 1928 to 1937) and a common, rather conservative approach to form. The majority of the poems are long (twenty lines or more) and constructed of stanzas containing four lines in common meters (four to six beats per line), usually with alternating end rhymes. Within the three cycles we also find the full range of Gertrud Kolmar's thematic concerns, nearly all of which circle incessantly around the primal image of woman.

The seventy-five poems of "Weibliches Bildnis" ("Image of Woman" or "Female Portrait") are divided into four "rooms" or "spaces," an indication of the author's will to see her work in terms of concrete, three-dimensional reality. The poems of each room have only a loose thematic interconnection, but all are specifically concerned with one subject: woman in her many ages, roles and symbolic transformations. Remarkably, every one of these poems is written in the first person, a testimony to Gertrud Kolmar's intense desire to personally identify with the many varieties of women she portrays. In the first room of the cycle we are introduced to the poet and to all her exotic worlds of metamorphosis. The poem titles, here and in the other rooms, are for the most part feminine nouns, imaginative names for the myriad reincarnations of woman: **"The Traveling Woman," "The Witch," "The Robber Girl," "The Woman Tramp," "The Mother," "The Gardener," "The Lover," "The Abducted Woman," "The Sea Spirit."** The second room is devoted primarily to the young woman, her attractiveness, and her erotic desires. The third emphasizes the mature lover . . . the sufferer, the Jew, and the woman bereaved of her child. The fourth and final room presents woman facing old age and death.

In the poems of "Weibliches Bildnis" we can already discern the five major transformations of the "lyric self" that characterize Gertrud Kolmar's poetry. In all of these transformations we see Gertrud Kolmar as a woman in love. She is a lover of the earth, of her people, of animals, of men, and of children—often tragically aware that she must lose the things she loves.

The first poetic metamorphosis reveals woman as a geographical presence, a mythical entity of gargantuan proportions:

> I will rest on my bed and cover the earth.
> Over the lands of Europe and Africa I lie,

> My left arm reaching deep into Asia,
> And the right towards America.
> My snaking hair will frighten the auk in Arctic
>   seas.
>
> ["Girl"]

In thus identifying with the enormity of earth itself (a gesture reminiscent of the expansive ego of Walt Whitman) Gertrud Kolmar does more than monumentalize woman as a kind of "earth mother," closely linked to the elements. The earth, with its many forms of terrain, its hidden treasures, its plants and animals, things seen and unseen, becomes symbolic of the immutable physical presence of woman and the infinite variety of her spiritual secrets:

> I too am a continent.
> I have unexplored mountains, bushland impene-
>   trable
>   and lost,
> Bays, stream-deltas, salt-licking tongues of
>   coast,
> Caves where giant crawling beasts gleam dusky
>   green,
> And inland seas where lemon-yellow jellyfish are
>   seen.
>
> ["Woman Undiscovered"]

But the "terrestrial woman," like all of Gertrud Kolmar's other metamorphoses of the eternal feminine, also has its negative or tragic dimension:

> I am a continent that one day soon will sink
>   without a sound into the sea.
>
> ["Woman Undiscovered"]

In another transformation Gertrud Kolmar presents woman—in each case one must almost say: herself—as an historical presence. She is the Jew, who, along with her people, endures through the ages despite unceasing persecution:

> Now I seem strange, no longer know myself,
> For I was there before great Rome and Carthage
>   were,
> Because in me the altar fires ignite
> Of Deborah and her tribe.
>
> ["The Jewish Woman"]

Gertrud Kolmar's love for the Jewish people was matched by her anguish over their persecution at the hands of the Nazis. One of her finest poems, **"Wir Juden" ("We Jews")** gives eloquent testimony to her compassion for her people, and, despite her powerlessness, her enormous desire to help:

> And when your throat is gagged, your bleeding
>   cry suppressed,
> When brutal shackles bind your trembling arms,
> Oh let me be the voice that echoes down the
>   shaft of all eternity,
> The hand stretched high to touch God's tower-
>   ing heaven.

As if the suffering of the moment were not enough, she feels the crushing weight of all the injustices the Jews have suffered throughout history:

> And we, we have proceeded through the gallows
>   and the rack.

This bursting of our hearts, this sweat of death,
    this gaze without a tear,
And the eternal windblown sigh of martyrs at
    the stake,
The withered claw, the weary fist with veins like
    vipers
Raised against the murderers from ropes and fu-
    neral pyres of ages,

The gray beard singed in hellfires, torn by devils-
    grip,
The mutilated ear, the wounded brow and flee-
    ing eye:
Oh all of you! Now, when the bitter hour strikes
    I will arise
And stand like a triumphal arch above your cav-
    alcade of anguish!

At the same time she is always aware of the imminent threat to her own existence, and, in one moving line, can prophecy her own doom:

And I can feel the fist that drags my weeping
    head toward the hill of ashes.

But despite all this she is able to transcend the current suffering to see, in the very history of their persecution, a hope for the Jewish people. "God lets them fall in ruin," she says of the towers symbolizing her heritage, "and yet they stand for ages more." In the long perspective of history, the endurance of her ancient people will prove itself again:

For one day your weary wandering shoes will
    stand upon the necks of all the mighty!

In "Weibliches Bildnis" (and most certainly in "Tier-träume") we find ample evidence of a third transformation: Gertrud Kolmar's close identification with animals. Not all the countless animals in her poems serve, of course, to receive the poet's identity. But many do, and when, in her poetry, she chooses to inhabit the form of a beast, it is usually for one of two reasons. In the first of these transformations she seeks to potentiate her female sexuality by linking it with the elemental ferocity of animals:

A bat, I hang down rigid from a rafter,
Drop free and catch your scent and follow after.
Oh, man, I dream your blood; my bite is death.
I'll claw into your hair and suck your breath.
                        ["Metamorphoses"]

Elsewhere, she identifies with animals as creatures mistreated and exterminated by man:

Alive you call us game or cattle; dead, a catch
    of meat—
You grant us not an ocean drop, no grain of
    earth to keep.
You pass away with heaven and hell; when we
    die off we're trash.
And when we die, your one regret: we can't be
    killed again.

But once I gave my images to you, to which you
    prayed,
Until you found a human god, no longer god of
    beasts,

And my descendants then were killed, my spring
    walled in with stone,
And you called Holy Writ the things dictated
    you by greed.
And you have hope and pride, and a reward for
    all your pain,
And afterlife where you can safely flee into your
    soul.
But I endure a thousandfold in feathered cloaks
    and scales.
I am the carpet, when you weep, on which your
    sorrow kneels.
                        ["The Animal"]

The most important of Gertrud Kolmar's metamorphoses are those dealing specifically with woman. Often, and especially in "Weibliches Bildnis," we encounter poems depicting woman in her fourth transformation, as lover. One of the most extraordinary aspects of Gertrud Kolmar's work is the unprecedented frankness and intensity of her portrayal of female sexuality. This is especially remarkable when one considers that Gertrud Kolmar was born in the nineteenth century and was surrounded by a taboo-ridden bourgeois moral code that barely admitted the existence of sexual needs in women. Since it is also known that she was a model of reserve and decorum in her personal life, it is all the more remarkable that she was able to inject such furious power—"elevated," to be sure, to a high plane of poetic art—into her evocations of sexual desire. These poems, with their potent concrete imagery, present severe, sometimes almost brutal views of a sexuality far from any cliché-norms of "feminine" delicacy and discretion:

Nude, I crouch on taloned toes
Sharpened red on rended meat;
In the reeds of swampy groves
I hide hunted and in heat.
Vipers wriggle through my fingers,
Snails wet my hair with slime,
And around my loins there linger
Colored toads of many kinds.

Tearing teeth crack brittle bones,
Crusted stems and hardened seeds.
Suddenly, with howling moans
Out I leap from mud and weeds,
Claws and body dragging down
A wanderer who lost his way.
Breast and flanks force to the ground . . .
Gasping, I devour my prey.
                        ["Troglodyte"]

When, at times, these expressions of erotic desire become still more intense, they reach a stage the poet Karl Krolow has called "menadic madness":

You. I want to wake you in the waters!
You. I want to melt you from the stars!
You. I want to lick you from the earth,
A bitch! And bite you out of fruit,
A savage! You. I want so much—
Dear. Dearest. Can't you give yourself to me?
And spend the blossoms, white,
Atop your flowering stem?
                        ["You"]

But such bacchantic states are short-lived, and at other

times there is a kind of remorse, or better, a tragic awareness of her helpless subjection to her own erotic nature,
accompanied by the affirmation of an inner "chastity" that
allows her soul, despite its passion, to "chant the psalms":

> All that is true. I am not sinful, am not evil,
> Do not steal the manhood of the dead or stab the
>   childlike eyes of birds,
> Or break the trusting infant's tender spine.
> I gnaw myself away in burning cries: oh set me
>   free!
>
> I am as martyrs burning at the stake, devoured
>   by snapping fangs
> A woman, mate and mother, pregnant womb.
> Above all those who now beget and are begotten
>   blazes my eternal heart.
> And yet my soul kneels down and chants the
>   psalms.
>
> > **["The Sinner"]**

And finally, among the many lovers in "Weibliches Bildnis" there is the woman forsaken by the man she loved,
as in the poem **"The Abandoned Woman,"** which has already been quoted above.

Woman's fifth and final transformation in the poems of
"Weibliches Bildnis" is as a mother: often an imaginary
one, and always a mother threatened with the loss of her
beloved child—as is strikingly illustrated in the poem
"Murder." This most important of Gertrud Kolmar's poetic identities was given its own complete cycle entitled
"Kind."

In many respects the poems of "Kind" ("Child") can be
considered an extension of "Weibliches Bildnis." Although few of the "Kind" poems use the feminine noun
titles characteristic of the other cycle, most share the same
approach to form, style, and first person perspective. And
these poems too present "female portraits," only this time
they are portraits exclusively of woman as mother. The evidence of this cycle alone would be enough to establish beyond doubt Gertrud Kolmar's obsessive concern for her
own potential motherhood. It is a tragic concern, for although some of the poems could conceivably have been
written by an actual mother about her own real children,
most betray the author's painful awareness that her only
children are offspring of the imagination:

> My words are mad. My darkness calls you to
>   me.
> For in all my days you never were.
>
> > **["A Mother"]**

These poems of unachieved motherhood are sometimes
little more than desperate cries for the fulfillment she
knows to be impossible:

> Oh come.
> My child. Oh come, oh come my child.
> Oh come.
> My hollow drumbeat deadens me no more.
>
> > **["Come"]**

Gertrud Kolmar's fantasies concerning childlessness
might easily seem pathetic or even morbid were they not
distilled into beautiful poetry:

> The night outside the door, the cradle void.

> And rocking it, a woman, pallid-faced,
> With stringy hair as black and thick as tar.
> And in her heart there gathers gray on gray.
>
> She minds a babe perhaps already dead,
> And nods toward a child she never bore;
> It was so lovely, white, carnation pink
> With silver strands within its flaxen hair.
>
> The night stands inside, and the cradle void.
> And rocking it, a woman, driven mad,
> Who loosens silken hair like ocean waves
> The somber blue of fragrant hyacinths.
>
> > **["Madness"]**

There can be little doubt that Gertrud Kolmar is one of
the world's great writers of "animal poems." We need no
further evidence of this than the forty-nine poems of the
cycle "Tierträume" ("Animal Dreams"). Certainly no
other German poet has devoted such poetic skill to the
portrayal of so many wild creatures. Even Rilke's unquestioned masterpieces from his *Neue Gedichte* ("Der Pan-
ther," "Die Gazelle," "Das Einhorn," "Papageien-Park,"
"Die Flamingos") are no match for the number and intensity of the Kolmar poems. Unlike Rilke, she does not use
animals merely as objects for metaphysical speculation.
She is profoundly interested in the animals *themselves,* and
is deeply compassionate with their suffering at the hands
of men. A striking example of this concern is her long
poem from "Tierträume" entitled **"The Day of Accusation."** Here she presents an apocalyptic vision, a day of
judgment for mankind, not at the hands of God, but by
all the animals that men have tortured, mutilated and enslaved. Out of the earth and from the waters swarm the
hordes of resurrected creatures, all bearing the marks of
their suffering: flies without wings or legs, blinded birds,
carps with bellies slashed. Out of laboratories stream dissected rats, disfigured mice; and the zoos release their multitudes of benumbed captives. All congregate in a gigantic
open space where they pass final judgment on their oppressor:

> A thousand bodies showed him all their graves,
> A hundred thousand more their torture cells,
> No dove came soaring now to rescue him.
> No lamb appeared to hold the shepherd's staff.

Man's egocentric God has failed him, and in His place:

> There came a new God, dragonlike,
> That spat his flame toward a new horizon.

This awesome dragon-god at the poem's conclusion represents another vision of the animal found in "Tierträume."The beast is not only a sufferer, he is the symbol
of the mysterious forces of nature (as in **"The Herons"** or
"Hyenas"). At times he takes the form of some indifferent
power that drives the universe, a cruel "god" whose ways
are beyond man's understanding or control. One example
of such a "beast god" is the vulture in the poem of that
name:

> As mad volcanoes spurt,
> Cold-sparkling glaciers slide,
> You clench the clods of dirt
> Where anthill cities hide.
> And when your blazing head
> Looks down upon our earth,

No single tear is shed
Into the endless dearth.

(pp. 18-28)

For the period between March 1935 . . . , and August 1937 . . . , we have no concrete indication of [Gertrud Kolmar's] creative activity. It is possible that she fell silent for a time, perhaps out of political frustration and resignation. But, more likely, she soon returned to her work on the cycles "Weibliches Bildnis," "Kind," and "Tierträume," selections of which were to be published in 1938.

Whatever the significance of the apparent caesura between 1935 and 1937, one indisputable result of this period was a radical change in Gertrud Kolmar's poetic style. The poems of the cycle **Welten** (**Worlds**), written from August to December, 1937, represent a considerable departure from her earlier approach to form. These works, her last poetry to have been preserved, impress us most of all with their expansiveness. Her usual four-to-six beat line has grown, casting off all metrical regularity, and stretching to the extreme limit of what can be recited in a single breath (often twenty words and more). Interspersed among these far-reaching lines are contrasting short ones, sometimes no more than a word long, that serve as resting points for gathering the great energy to be expended in the long lines to follow. Rhyme, too, has been abandoned—of necessity—along with regular length of line.

The language of **Welten** is changed as well. Without rhythmic regularity and rhyme the poems show none of the qualities that typified her earlier verse: the tone of folksong or the sound of chanted liturgy or whispered magic charms. The new poems have lost all the former attributes of compression and cyclic formality. For once the outward form of Gertrud Kolmar's poetry appears to match its inner "elemental" drive. The sustained power of the language in **Welten,** and its elevated, sometimes almost scriptural dignity, is almost certainly patterned after the prose of the Old Testament. This is perhaps most evident in a poem based on an explicitly Biblical theme such as **"The Animals of Nineveh":**

But Jonah went,
And the burden over Nineveh that he had seen,
    weighed on his head.
But he, in heavy brooding, strode away.—

A painted stone broke from the solid battlement
    atop the royal castle,
And there arose a howling and a shrieking in the
    storm, and then a voice cried out:
"For their sake!
For the sake of all the animals, clean and un-
    clean!"
And the prophet of the Lord was frightened and
    looked up; but all was darkness and he heard
    no sound but ceaseless rush and roar
That grasped his robe and pulled and shook his
    garment like a pleading hand, as, merciless, he
    fled.
But he did not turn back; he traveled on
And close about him gathered up his robe.

In a letter, Gertrud Kolmar herself admitted to this influence: "I have read Luther's Bible all my life, and people qualified to judge such things have said that its language has clearly influenced mine as a poet."

There are seventeen poems in Gertrud Kolmar's last cycle, and each, in truth, contains its own "world." The poems are brimming with the "things of the earth," with the concrete images of sensory experience. These worlds are imaginary places of refuge from a harsh reality. Often they reflect the actual pleasures of her life at Finkenkrug, pleasures which, with her extraordinary ability to build on simple sense experiences, became exciting and exotic refuges for her soul: the garden (**"Garten in Sommer"**), the kitchen (**"Dienen"**), or walks through the surrounding countryside with her Russian wolfhound Flora (**"Barzoi"**).

Other animals, besides the dog, are present too. Continuing her myth-making in the animal world she presents the unicorn (in **"Das Einhorn"**) as a mysterious natural force with sexual overtones. In **"The Animals of Nineveh"** a cat, a dog, and a vulture are recipients of God's compassion along with a shepherd boy and a beggar child.

In other "worlds" Gertrud Kolmar reviews memories of her love affairs—real or imaginary (**"Die Stadt," "Der Engel im Walde," "Sehnsucht"**). And once again we encounter the transformations of woman: the menadic lover (**"Sehnsucht"**), the unfulfilled mother (**"Fruchtlos"**), the old woman remembering her lost love (**"Die alte Frau"**). The awareness of death fills these poems, and just as their worlds were a temporary refuge for the living poet, they also project the image of a permanent refuge for her soul:

And now I stumble forward on the stony, stub-
    born path.
Jumbled rocks and thistles wound my groping
    hands:
A cave awaits me
That conceals inside its deepest crack the
    bronze-green, nameless raven.
I will enter
And crouch down to rest beneath the sheltering
    shadows of his giant wings,
And sleep, my brow turned eastward,
'Til the dawn.

The protective towers of the poem **"The Jewish Woman,"** symbolic of her ancient heritage, reappear to offer another possible sanctuary:

Perhaps my soul forgot me in my dream,
And sank, wings spread towards morning,
    where the tower stood to meet its wandering
    flight,
And roved through hot, enchanted, lifeless
    rooms,
In search of ancestors,
And touched the hovering strings that still
    resound . . .

The awareness of her coming death is also implicit in the poem **"Das Opfer" ("The Sacrifice")**, wherein she identifies with a woman of the Old Testament facing ritual sacrifice to a golden idol. But it is always to the East, to the expanses of Asia, that Gertrud Kolmar turns in search of a promised land to which she might escape. Again, as in her "geographical" transformation, she feels she can embrace the earth, here the Ural Mountains:

> When I seize the darkness, rough crags
> Wound my hand.

Another refuge is the **"Mergui Isles,"** a real island chain off Burma, which becomes a fantastic archipelago of dreams, a repository for all the secret visions that obsessed the poet:

> My Mergui Isles do not bathe singing in the Indian Ocean.
> They rise silently from seas of night into an ever-dayless twilight,
> Domed and shaggy green and black,
> The withers of some giant buffaloes that graze the brownish seaweed from the ocean floor.

No poem better expresses Gertrud Kolmar's longing for the life-transcending paradise of a visionary Asia than the last of the "worlds":

> Mother,
> Mine before my own had held me,
> I am coming home.
> Let me stand before you.
> Let me sit in silence at your feet, and gazing up, discover you:
> A proud, enshrouded figure rising mighty from your mythic throne
> That rests upon the pillared feet of white stone elephants,
> Its armrests jade-tongued dragons made of bronze.
> I see your solemn, sun-gold face, spun round with silken, blue-black hair,
> Your brow, the walled preserve of noble thoughts,
> Your eyes, now gleaming dark obsidian,
> Now deep and somber velvet jungle flowers.
> Oh let me touch your robes that breathe the scent of amber trees and myrrh, of sandalwood and cinnamon,
> Your flaming robes that blazed from Indian looms,
> Your robes of pale corn-yellow that a Chinese girl embroidered with a brownish twig, an almond blossom and a small, rust-colored butterfly.
> Show me your crowns: the southern one,
> Green-golden leaves of palm, bedewed with pearls and mixed with blooming tourmaline and emerald and hyacinth and sapphire,
> And the northern one that sparkles gems of ice and aquamarine droplets from Siberian seas.
> Oh brush my forehead with your hand whose palm still holds the fragrant oil of Persian fruits,
> And let the singing shawm play round my ear, as David's shepherd's pipe·once sang across the meadows at Beth-Lechem.

At the end of this poem, the last one left to us by Gertrud Kolmar, the image of the towers returns once again. More enigmatic than before, this last religious vision declares her faith in the ancient "Asian" roots from which she sprang, and anticipates reunion with the mythical East, the eternal truth toward which she feels her soul directed:

> . . . you have plunged down to the deepest center of our star, into the foaming bath of fire . . .
> Oh burn . . .
> And hide in shame . . . your inmost secret that received the flaming seed,
> And let your progeny, the vulture-demons, circle endlessly above the towers of death,
> The towers of silence . . .

(pp. 37-42)

> *Henry A. Smith, "Gertrud Kolmar's Life and Works," in* Dark Soliloquy: The Selected Poems of Gertrud Kolmar, *by Gertrud Kolmar, translated by Henry A. Smith, The Seabury Press, 1975, pp. 1-52.*

Michael Hamburger   (essay date 1976)

[*Hamburger is a German-born English poet, translator, and critic. An accomplished lyric poet in his own right, he has been widely praised for his translations of several German poets previously unfamiliar to English readers, including Friedrich Hölderlin, Georg Trakl, and Hugo von Hofmannsthal. He has also written extensively on modern German literature. In the following excerpt, Hamburger comments on the nature of Kolmar's poetry and its reception among readers and critics.*]

At some point it will become necessary to separate Gertrud Kolmar's work from the circumstances that drew attention to it in the immediate post-war decades; but that will be difficult, not because it cannot stand up to such a separation but because the circumstances of her Jewishness and of her femininity are of true relevance to her poems and imaginative prose. Nor would the separation be necessary if all poetry were not in constant danger of being read for the wrong reasons, as something other than poetry, only because it has been thrown on the market by the exploiters of this or that trend, this or that pressure group. True, the alternative, in a brutally commercialized society, is almost complete neglect. At present it is Gertrud Kolmar's femininity that is most likely to be used as a pretext for drawing attention to her work as something other than poetry. So it is as well to state that her preoccupation with being a woman was as different from that of militants now at work as her preoccupation, under the pressure of persecution, with being a Jew. Both were marked by a fervent acceptance that was fiercer and stronger than militancy, because it could not be broken or violated by anything that was done to her. "And all the grief that came over me and may come over me I shall take upon myself as atonement, and it will be just. And I shall bear it without complaining and somehow find that it belongs to me and that I was born and have grown to endure it and somehow to outlive it," she wrote in one of her last letters, when she was doing forced labour in a factory and preparing for deportation and death. If she renounced sexual fulfillment at a much earlier period, she did so without bitterness and without primness. Her poems celebrate sensuality, as they celebrate everything that is of the earth, even while renouncing or transcending it. (p. 66)

Michael Hamburger, "The Poetry of Gertrud

Kolmar," in Boston University Journal, *Vol. 24, No. 2, 1976, pp. 65-7.*

Lawrence L. Langer   (essay date 1978)

[*In the following excerpt, Langer chronicles Kolmar's spiritual and artistic development during her last years of struggle in Nazi Berlin as revealed in her letters of this period.*]

Like many other great artists, Gertrud Kolmar did not live to hear the acclaim her work would one day receive: it was the final irony in a career that resembled a tragedy of unfulfilment. She never enjoyed a steady reciprocity to the love she felt so capable of giving, never bore the child she longed for, never even suspected the reputation her art would earn for her. Yet she never surrendered hope and clung to the solace that she could still control her attitude towards her destiny, if not the events themselves. Her imagination quickened as the difficulties of her daily existence grew, and we are left with the paradox of her determination to perceive life more intensely even as the prospects for expressing her exuberance diminished. Her tragedy of unfulfilment is thus mitigated by the ripening of her inner vision.

Our access to this vision is aided by a unique volume, her *Briefe an die Schwester Hilde,* letters written to her sister between September 1938 and February 1943, when together with other Jewish forced-labourers in Berlin she was rounded up in a *Fabrikaktion* and deported to Auschwitz. She was never heard from again. Her letters comprise her spiritual autobiography during the darkest years of modern German and Jewish history, and they are all the more dramatic because she had no way of knowing for certain how very black these years were. In addition, since she was writing to her sister in Switzerland, she was forbidden by censorship to mention daily events. Thus her letters cannot contain a history of Jewish anguish during this fatal period.

But they contain equally important revelations. They record the struggle of the poet to retain her spiritual independence while history sought to quench its flame. A superficial reading might suggest that Gertrud Kolmar was totally unaware of the doom that threatened her, but she was in the difficult position of having to satisfy the censor and her own sister's need for psychological support. Hence despair was virtually banished from the letters as a theme, and she even apologises occasionally for making her sister believe that she is suffering excessively. Whatever pain she feels she turns inward, and it emerges in a series of searching analyses of the creative process and the dilemma of the artist during a time when external reality was hostile to her imaginative endeavours.

For example, for fifteen years Gertrud Kolmar had lived with her family at Finkenkrug, a suburb of Berlin, with its spacious gardens and appealing natural surroundings. She never recovered from the forced sale of this home in 1938, when after the *Kristallnacht* harsh Nazi laws against the Jews' owning of real estate were enacted. Together with her father she moved to an urban neighbourhood in Berlin, and the quality of *Fremdheit* or strangeness that infuses so many of her poems owes part of its inspiration to this unhappy experience. She reports to her sister with some dismay her failure to accustom herself to her new surroundings:

> The day before yesterday I was walking along Martin-Luther-Strasse and Neue Winterfeld-strasse, which I don't know very well. I suddenly realised with some bewilderment that contrary to my usual custom I hadn't really noticed the houses, the shops, or the people I encountered at all. "Be observant and pay attention", I commanded myself. Good. But five minutes later I stopped "seeing" again, and my gaze once more turned inward, as it were, like a day-dreaming and inattentive pupil in school. Soon we'll have been here for six months, and I simply can't establish a relationship—bearable or unbearable—with this neighbourhood. I'm as alien here as I was on the first day.

Curiously enough, in the same letter she informs her sister that she has turned her face "toward the East", acknowledging an impulse that has been in her since she was a child. "I am really a kind of 'restrained Asiatic' ", she confesses, "and would be happy if the restraint could be removed." Lurking behind this fascination with the East is a partial explanation of her failure—or refusal—to flee westward like other members of her family—a brother went as far as Australia. "My duty", she writes, "has always lain, as it were, within me; it still does, and I only seek the appropriate place to devote myself to it. And I don't know . . . I've always thought that in America I wouldn't find the appropriate place." Four months after the outbreak of the Second World War she still was prepared, like Boris Pasternak after her, to accept harassment even unto death rather than exile from the atmosphere that nourished her creative vision. The inhospitable welcome Switzerland accorded her sister, who was having great difficulty establishing a life for herself and her little daughter, must have strengthened Gertrud Kolmar's resolution to remain in her native land.

The intensification of anti-Jewish legislation and finally the war itself overwhelmed her with a sense of the rapid transformation of external reality. She retreated inward in a desperate effort to find a stable point of reference, a refuge from the uncertainties threatening her status as a human being:

> It seems to me that things are changing their face and shape today with a furious swiftness; everything is altered, whirls about, nothing remains still, and what once took years or decades to change now needs only a few days. And meanwhile I've withdrawn deeper and deeper into the lasting, the existing, that which happens eternally (this does not have to be only "religion", it can also be "nature", can also be "love").

She speaks of the kaleidoscopic shifting of temporal experience and confesses the impossibility, not to say pointlessness, of organising it into meaningful patterns. "In the street", she writes, "I often have a feeling of numbness and stupefaction, and yearn to awaken from it—but to no avail". Eventually this disorientation must have affected her poetic impulse, since she appears to have written very few poems during the final five years of her life—in any event, none have survived. In 1940 she began the study of Hebrew, almost as if she hoped to liberate or revive that impulse by turning to another language, one also close to her heritage, and she did indeed compose some verses in Hebrew which her teacher thought worthy of publication—but these too seem to have disappeared.

Nevertheless she devoted considerable space in her letters to the *idea* of art, even when she was not creating, and this helped to sustain her during these last years. She wrote much to her sister about form, about the need to germinate the seed and nurture the full flower of a poem or story in the imagination before committing it to paper. She deplored the practice of a writer-acquaintance of her father's, who was busy working on the end of a biography when the opening chapters were already in print. *Fabrikbetrieb,* factory labour, she scornfully calls such assembly-line procedure, which offends her sense of artistic integrity; her own work habits required a manuscript to lie for weeks or months before she took it up for revision. "She creates for the times", she distinguishes herself from her father's friend, "and I, probably with insufficient energy, try to create for eternity. In any event she has success, and I—well, it's not important enough to me."

What *was* important to her was her unviolated sense of herself. She was exasperated by the talk of the tenants who shared the apartment with her and her father about relatives who had emigrated; one wonders whether her displeasure betrays a secret misgiving about her own decision to stay behind. Her analogy, when writing to her sister on this subject, is illuminating:

> for me it's a little like what I observed during the last war in soldiers returning from battle: without really noticing it, they and those who had remained behind didn't understand each other any more, they spoke different languages. And a mutual good intention to draw closer together changed nothing. Perhaps a similar situation exists between the émigrés and those who remained here.

The impending Holocaust crystallised her isolation, and in an odd way helped to justify it in her own mind. Battle-scarred within by a vision that ranged from gloom to luxuriance, she spoke a different language (and imagined a different life) from those whose daily conversation hovered over the theme of escape. One suspects that she needed to control the substance of any conversation on which she expended energy, as if her imaginative time were precious and she were committed to squeezing the last drop of value from every second of it.

Her goal was a kind of autism of the imagination, that would allow undistracted free reign to the vigorous power of her inner vision. At work one day she noticed a young gypsy woman whose tired face betrayed an enviable aloofness:

> an impenetrable seclusion, a tranquillity, a distance that was now unreachable by any word or glance from the outside world . . . And I knew: this was what I always wanted to have, but still

didn't possess completely; because if I had it, nothing and no one from outside could touch me. But I'm well on the way to getting there, and that makes me happy.

No wonder the geography of space did not tempt her; the inward geography of the mind and imagination was the crucial locus of her existence.

On Christmas eve of 1941 she wrote Hilde the longest letter of the collection, and though she obviously had more time just before a holiday, the subject clearly was of vital importance to her. It is impossible to tell today how much of it is real and how much fantasy, but she presents the account of her unconsummated love affair with a twenty-one-year-old fellow factory worker (she herself was past forty-seven) with such patient detail and attention to gestures and nuances that one is encouraged to accept it as true in the reading of it. At moments like these one penetrates the essential loneliness of Gertrud Kolmar's life and realises that her poems were a version of *and* a shield against the reality that she longed for and feared. Evidently Hilde was disturbed by this exaggerated love story, because in her reply, as we discern from Gertrud's own next response, she warned her sister against disappointment and confusing illusion with reality. Gertrud was defensive and even truculent as she sought to justify the authenticity of her relationship with the young man, as if deep down she herself suspected the fragility of her expectations. Through her argument shines the essentially tragic nature of her world view, seeking happiness in conjunction with pain, perceiving that the two partake of each other. She did not fear disappointment because she recognised in advance the high price a human being had to pay for the brief radiance of love. Perhaps this explains her ability to accept her situation in Berlin with such equanimity—she had no illusions about her ultimate fate. But there is also a touch of pathos in her confession to her sister some months later: "what I experience, slight as it may be, somehow affects me more forcibly than it used to". If the uneventful life is not worth living, the invented one must take its place. Experience not only becomes the stuff of her art; in regard to her factory romance, it becomes an expression of art itself.

Perhaps the most revealing admission about the secret of Gertrud Kolmar's ability to endure her destiny as a Jew in war-time Berlin with a kind of heroic resignation occurs in a letter of July 1942. Perverse as it may sound, the hardships she faced under Nazi persecution tested the resourcefulness of her spirit as the challenges of peace-time Germany could not. She was determined to resist the Nazi attempt to erase her dignity and humanity through humiliation and contempt. In fact, she seemed to grow inwardly stronger as the external situation began to deteriorate; but accompanying this growth was an increasing isolation from her Jewish companions in the factory. There is even some evidence that she enjoyed her martyrdom, though I speak only of the "martyrdom" of forced labour in Berlin, not of the chamber of horrors in Auschwitz. "Unfortunately", she laments,

> what depresses me so is that my view or attitude, wherever I express it, almost never finds an echo.

So I express it seldom enough. I can't transfer to my fellow-sufferers any of the spiritual strength that I possess. If I enter into a deeper relationship with any of them, they can only diminish it in me, without having any benefit from it themselves. They don't understand me, perhaps consider me supercilious.

As a child, she writes, she wanted to be a Spartan woman, and later, a heroine. The circumstances of Nazi oppression provided her with an opportunity to become what she needed to become in order to express the fullness of being latent within her, and she modestly acknowledged that such simple logic deserved no special admiration. She required an antagonist commensurate with her capacity for spiritual strength and self-assertion; her resolution to meet the aggressor with a posture of firmness, betraying no vestige of the craven or submissive, confirms the heroic quality of her inner life. Only today do we savour the bitter irony of her celebration of Goethe's aphorism: "Was man in der Jugend sich wünscht, hat man im Alter der Fülle."

The letters represent not so much a growth of the poet's mind as a gradual disclosure and assertion of qualities within her that had long sought expression. Her loneliness is certainly not new, but it has been brought into sharper focus by the National Socialist policies against the Jews. Similarly, her impulse to embrace her destiny, whatever it may be, is not new, but external conditions have clarified its importance in her life; and, as she so often does, she conjures up a metaphor to define its significance, one ripe with organic form. Unlike Napoleon's soldiers, who, she says, returned home after his fall from power proclaiming that they had forgotten nothing and learned nothing, Gertrud Kolmar has forgotten nothing but learned much: "Above all, this: *amor fati*—love of fate. To be sure, the germ has always been within me, perhaps even as a green stalk; but only now have blossoms developed and burst forth from their buds." The vitality of the image contradicts the resignation implicit in the idea of *amor fati*, but such a tension is at the heart of Gertrud Kolmar's personality, and much of her art. Her statement about love of fate appears in a letter written little more than a month before her deportation, and suggests the struggle of a vital spirit to survive in an atmosphere polluted by hatred and oppression.

Probably no one who has not experienced the constant uneasiness of this period—especially for a Jew still living in Berlin in 1943—can fully understand the anguish Gertrud Kolmar must have suffered during the final weeks of her life. But anyone with the patience to trace her spiritual history through her correspondence during the crucial years 1938 to 1943 cannot fail to admire her efforts to retain her human equilibrium as her burdens increased. Near the end of 1942 she recorded a conversation with a certain Dr. H., a Spinoza scholar, about the freedom of the human will in the midst of bondage. I felt, she says,

> that I understood this very well from my own experience. Since I had not had the option to accept or reject this factory work, which I had been ordered to do, I had to acquiesce and was compelled to do it. But I was free to consent to it or refuse it *inwardly*, to approach it reluctantly or willingly. In that moment when I *consented* to it in my heart, it ceased to oppress me; I was determined to regard it as "education" and to learn as much as possible. In this way I've remained free in the midst of my bondage.

But freedom in the midst of bondage in a Berlin factory while living under what one could call comparatively comfortable conditions is one thing; forced labour in a concentration camp is quite another. We should not make the mistake of trying to translate Gertrud Kolmar's personal formula for spiritual survival in Berlin into a universal principle of resistance against all forms of oppression. From the vantage point of today her determination is both admirable and naïve, overestimating as it does the power of the will to control our response to external reality. She did not and of course could not yet recognise the more severe challenges to her physical freedom, to say nothing of the will's capacity to resist them, that lay before her eight weeks hence. Thus her philosophical exertions to master present hardships and prepare for future anguish, admirable as they may be, echo for us with a mournful irony, since nothing in her prior experience, or in Jewish experience, or in human experience could possibly prepare her for the unprecedented cynical brutality of the Nazi final solution. Camus has taught us to face the death implicit in a hostile or indifferent universe with a Sisyphean courage beyond despair; but Sisyphus had only his rock to face, not the gas chambers and ovens of Auschwitz.

So if we ever are tempted to praise Gertrud Kolmar for heroically embracing the destiny which awaited her at the end of her journey, we must tread carefully; I do not believe, nor is there any evidence, that she had the slightest conception of where the sudden factory roundup of Jews in Berlin in February 1943 would end—nor would she have embraced such a destiny if she had. The strength she derived from acknowledging and accepting the possibility of a tragic destiny was a natural fruition of her previous spiritual development, as woman, as poet and as German Jew; but it must be understood within the context of her Berlin years between 1938 and 1943, and not of her post-deportation experience, about which we know absolutely nothing. To suggest, as some have done, that she would have carried to the very gates of Auschwitz her idea about the power of inner freedom to mitigate the harshness of fate is to stain her memory and to pervert her idea of inner freedom. Like Camus, whose austere sense of human tragedy resembles her own, she would have loathed the ruthless, impersonal disregard for individual dignity which characterised the extermination of millions of her fellow Jews.

Indeed, her conviction that "seelische Kraft" or spiritual strength was sufficient to combat the physical humiliation of the Jews was one of the last illusions to be shattered by the grim details of the Holocaust, and our faith in the resourcefulness of such strength has never been the same. She speaks near the end of 1942 of meeting her fate with a fierce, almost scriptural intensity, though unlike Job she is not prepared to charge her God or the universe with injustice:

> I want to walk beneath my fate, be it tall as a

tower or dark and oppressive as a cloud. Even though I'm not aware of it yet: I've consented and adjusted to it in advance, so that I know it will not crush me or find me inadequate . . . I will bear it without complaint and somehow find that it is fitting, and that with the essence of my being I was created and have grown up to endure and somehow to surmount it.

Is it courage or wariness of the censor that prompts her to place the full burden for survival on herself and to ignore her persecutors? Her defiance is never explicit, is self-assertive without being critical, and this may defuse and deflect some of her secret apprehensions. The sufficiency of eloquent language to pacify the fears provoked by an unspecified disaster is at best questionable; what power it had against the mocking motto that greeted her at the entrance to Auschwitz—"Arbeit macht frei"—we will never know. Nevertheless, her resolution to accept and transcend suffering without cringing or lamentation is in the tradition of Jewish tragic dignity, and hers must be one of the last pre-Holocaust voices in that tradition.

The allusive style Gertrud Kolmar invented to circumvent the wary eyes of the censor cannot completely disguise her devotion to her religious heritage. "For me a part of what has been has grown so deeply into what is", she wrote a month before the end, "that I can't tear it out without gravely injuring myself." The context makes it clear that she was speaking about her Jewish identity, but if there is any doubt that her imagination was moving in this direction during the closing days of her life, one need but turn to her last letter of all, written a week before her deportation. Its opening words ironically anticipate her own doom and the fate of her people, but more important, and perhaps not so unconsciously, they celebrate an ancient Jewish tradition and link it with a modern equivalent. The final letter to her sister begins, "The sun has just set", and continues, "and I intended to read several of Martin Buber's 'Chassidic Tales' for Oneg Shabbat." But she lays Buber aside to write this letter—and presumably it is the last literary act of her existence. Was it foreboding, or some other hidden force, which led her to write instead a description of her creative process, a lucid assertion of the artist's self against the rock that was about to crush her:

> I never create from a feeling of exultation or strength, but always from a feeling of impotence. Should I allow myself to be lured to my desk following a sudden inspiration or creative impulse, I usually don't carry through to the end: the fire burns down, the well dries up, and the poem remains a fragment. When on the contrary I begin a new work in a state of impotence or despair, I'm like someone who prepares in the lowlands to climb a mountain; first the goal is still far away, the view is obstructed, but as I advance the prospect becomes broader and more beautiful. By such gradual climbing I don't grow weary, as happens to me when I give way to a swift upsurge of the imagination . . . Only after I say "I can do nothing more. My strength is exhausted. I won't accomplish anything more", is the proper hour there.

Given this philosophy, what might she not have done had

she survived! "Impotence" and "despair" clearly describe her external situation as the "proper hours" diminished in number; and although she may here be describing her creative process throughout her career, her words grow more luminous when we recall that they are uttered by a Jewish poet in war-time Berlin on the brink of deportation. Her resolution to preserve the vigour of her imaginative life was her chief weapon against the world that was closing in on her; and if it finally proved futile against such overwhelming odds, we can go on wielding it for her through the shared experience of her art. (pp. 247-53)

> *Lawrence L. Langer, "Survival through Art: The Career of Gertrud Kolmar," in* The Leo Baeck Institute of Jews from Germany Yearbook, *Vol. XXIII, 1978, pp. 247-58.*

Frederic V. Grunfeld   (essay date 1979)

[*In the following excerpt, Grunfeld discusses the reception of Kolmar's work in Germany and her distinguishing qualities as a German poet of the World War II era.*]

[Walter Benjamin's cousin Gertrud Kolmar] was two years younger than Benjamin; a slender, dark-eyed, dark-haired woman who considered herself plain-looking, though others found her beautiful even when she was in her forties and working as a forced laborer, packing cartons in a factory. Benjamin had always admired his cousin, and he conceded being "extremely impressed" by her poetry. In a short introduction which he wrote for two of her poems in *Die Literarische Welt* in 1928, he went as far as a conscientious critic could go in recommending the work of a gifted relative, saying that he wanted "to win the reader's ear for tones that have not been heard in the work of a German poetess since Annette von Droste" (the foremost lyric poetess of the early nineteenth century). He also did his best to persuade editors like Max Rychner to publish her poetry. But she was not to write her best work until he had already gone into exile, and the bulk of her poetry was not published until 1955, twelve years after her death.

One had every right to expect that this talented young woman "of good family," surrounded by literary influences and fluent in several languages, would produce something worthwhile: a slim volume or two, perhaps of more than passing interest to the historians of German literature, particularly in view of the painful circumstances in which her last poetry was written. And one would expect her verse to say the things that doomed women have a right to say about love, beauty and their autumnal longing for a world to which they know they must bid farewell. All the more astonished, then, were the postwar critics who first rediscovered her work among the ruins of German literature. Gertrud Kolmar's poetry seemed more like a slap in the face than an album of pressed flowers. *Nicht biegen kann ich. Nur zerspringen*—"I cannot bend, only explode"—she writes in one of her Robespierre poems. The critics who assessed her work agreed that Gertrud Kolmar had been one of the great German poets. Oda Schaefer described her as "an important poetess whose language is powerful in its beauty and its wealth of images like hardly another's." Friedhelm Kemp compared her not only to Annette von Droste but to Christina Rossetti and Emily Dickinson. Rolf Schroers declared that she had written "some of the most vivid and some of the purest and most profound works in the German language." She was called "the third great figure among the German-Jewish poetesses"—together with Lasker-Schüler and Nelly Sachs. Jacob Picard went one step further and wrote that she was unequivocally "the greatest Jewish poetess who ever lived"—in any country. Fortunately there was no need for a *Sängerkrieg* between the admirers of Kolmar and the supporters of Lasker-Schüler: they had belonged to different generations—Kolmar was twenty-five years younger than Lasker-Schüler—and regarded the world from two very different points of view. (pp. 257-58)

In her book of interpretive poems on Prussian coats-of-arms, **Preussische Wappen,** published in a tiny edition in 1934, [Gertrud Kolmar] had analyzed the violent forces at work in their medieval symbolism of towers, swords, eagles. These heraldic images were being revived and distributed throughout Germany as cigarette premiums: for her they were a dream-book from which to prophesy the future. In the coat of arms of Loitz an der Peene, for example, she could perceive the significance of the two massive clubs glittering in gold against a red field:

> Die goldenen Keulen werken Tag und Nacht.
> Sie geben nicht Ruhe: alles wird totgeschlagen.
> Der hört den Bumm, der einsam im Düstern
>   sitzt,
> Und hört das Rollen der ewigen Leichenwagen
> Und sieht das Schreien, das an sein Fenster
>   spritzt. . . .

> The golden clubs work day and night.
> They do not rest: everything is beaten to death.
> He who sits alone in the darkness hears the thud,
> Hears the rolling wheels of the endless wagons
>   of corpses
> And sees the cries that spurt against his window.

Like Kafka, she knew that she was living on murderer's row: *Die Mörder gehen in der Welt herum. / Die ganze Nacht, O Gott, die ganze Nacht!*—"The murderers are abroad in the world; / The whole night, oh God, the whole night!" Still, nothing frightened her. "Even as a child I always wanted to be a Spartan woman," she recalled, and she had once held her hand into the fire, like the Roman hero Mucius Scaevola, to see how brave she could be. Now, as she wrote in December 1942, "I will also step up to accept my fate, be it high as a tower, black as a cloud." She wrote her last letters and poems at midnight or at five in the morning, in the few hours that were left after an exhausting day at the factory. In the letters she wrote to her sister in Switzerland she had to be circumspect: they were subject to censorship and she chose her words with care, disguising the important events in an elaborate private code. But in her poetry she felt no such compunction: she had a defiant vision of herself as Judith bearing aloft the head of Holofernes, the enemy of her people. By the same token she wanted to stay alive and to go on writing until the last possible moment because it fell to her, the trial lawyer's daughter, to write the case for the prosecution—

the great *J'accuse* against human cruelty (*Menschheitsgrausamkeit*) whose end she foresees in an apocalyptic poem of the last judgment, **"Der Tag der grossen Klage."** Her tone is that of impeachment rather than lament: not mercy but justice is what she demands. "Oh that I could raise my voice like a flaming torch in the dark desert of the world: *Gerechtigkeit! Gerechtigkeit! Gerechtigkeit!*" (Justice! Justice! Justice!). The note of triumph was unmistakable: "I want to be the arch of triumph through which our torments pass." (pp. 260-61)

At a time when the German poets of the so-called "inner emigration" were taking refuge in veiled allusions or Kierkegaard's "silent despair," Gertrud Kolmar was the last to use the German language, in all its Baroque splendor, to call things by their real names. *Und wenn ein Knebel dir im Mund den blutenden Schrei verhält*—"and though a gag stifles the bleeding cry in your mouth"—she would raise her demonic cry for justice, "the shout that falls into the shaft of eternity." . . . (pp. 261-62)

Frederic V. Grunfeld, "Ultima Multis," in his Prophets without Honour: A Background to Freud, Kafka, Einstein, and Their World, *Holt, Rinehart and Winston, 1979, pp. 220-63.*

Michael C. Eben   (essay date 1984)

[*In the following excerpt, Eben offers an analysis of Kolmar's novel* Eine Mutter, *and the short story "Susanna."*]

Like a number of poems belonging to the 'Weibliches Bildnis' cycle, **Eine Mutter** is steeped in the text and tone of an Old Testament demand for revenge, atonement and justice. Yet it is also a documentary view of early twentieth-century Berlin, familiar from George Grosz caricatures. Without becoming tiresomely preoccupied with the theme, and manifesting no particular aptitude for clairvoyance in 1930-31, Kolmar makes significant allusion to the increasing anti-Semitism in Germany. However, the strength of the novel lies in the mythological dimension of the lonely heroine Martha Jadassohn who, with stoic single-mindedness, stalks the rapist-murderer of her child Ursula. Like Kolmar herself, Martha chooses solitude. In the case of the poet, the powers of verse grow out of a preferred isolation; in the case of Martha, loneliness fires a relentless commitment to revenge. This emotional intensity prevails throughout the work. Accentuated by the theme of a lost (murdered) child, motifs already expressed in many poems abound in the novel: sexuality, a longing for motherhood, guilt and atonement. In his appraisal of Martha Jadassohn as the archetypal woman, Henry A. Smith writes:

> Gertrud Kolmar's poetic vision [is] mythologized in all her transformations: from bacchantic lover, to mother, to animal, to historical presence. . . . Martha is monumentalized as the vampire-like lover, the she-wolf mother, the lonely elk threatened with extinction, the stone idol of an ancient goddess, or as the ageless symbol of Jewish womanhood.

From the outset of the novel, Martha is portrayed as a

woman of alarming strength and stamina. Her marriage to the gentile Friedrich Wolg is rejected by the latter's father who is prophetic about the icy and mysterious Jewess, a 'Jerusalem am Nordpol.' He has warned his son against the marriage: 'Entweder du reisst aus, order sie bricht dich in Stücke. Ohne Gnade.' Nevertheless, they marry, only to confirm the anxiety of the old father. Martha and Friedrich are completely incompatible. Their single shared experience is in the matrimonial bed; otherwise, Martha chooses to remain alone. The bewildered husband, increasingly locked out of his own marriage, can only wonder: 'Dies vielleicht, dass sie aus anderem Blut, dass sie Jüdin war.' When the child, Ursula, is born, Martha becomes a possessed she-wolf mother, ' . . . wie eine Tiermutter, die um ihr Junges zittert.' She insists that her husband is not to have any contact with their daughter. Broken and dismayed, Friedrich soon dies after an unsuccessful venture in America. Martha is of course rejected by her in-laws and becomes an animal photographer in order to support herself.

Returning from work, after having left Ursula with a neighbour, Martha learns that the child is missing. The utterly distraught mother embarks on a long and painful search only to discover her child close to death, abandoned on a junk heap, the victim of a rape. Martha is filled with self-reproach for not finding Ursula earlier and agonizes in the hopelessness of watching her daughter barely cling to life. Protective of her grief and pride, the she-wolf mother rejects all offers of sympathy and aid. Fiercely independent, she bears the pain alone and finally makes the decision to end her daughter's misery. From this moment on, the themes of guilt, revenge and expiation dominate the work. Martha Jadassohn's 'J'accuse' consumes the rest of her life. Police, lawyers and even a fortune-teller are of no help in her relentless search for the murderer. She wanders the streets of Berlin ' . . . wie eine Jägerin [. . .] auf heimlicher Pirsch, bedacht, das Wild, ihre arglose Beute, nicht aus dem Blick zu verlieren.' Her brief moment of solace occurs when she visits the zoo and commiserates with the animal kingdom which, she feels, is also humiliated and imposed upon by mankind. Here . . . the writer gives cause to remember her poem **'Der Tag der grossen Klage'** in which she warns that on this day the disfigured animals from man's laboratories and the creatures which have been imprisoned in the zoos will be released and congregate in order to consult and pass final judgement on their human oppressor.

Kolmar proceeds to place Judaism, symbolized by the synagogue to which Martha makes an unsuccessful visit, in second position to nature, whose animal and plant life offers far greater consolation to the grieving woman. Nonetheless her allegiance to her mission of revenge grants few moments of rest: 'Als hielte sie diese Rache schon und man wollte sie ihr entreissen. Wie ein wütendes Tier, in sein Schlupfloch gehetzt, gesträubten Haars sich mit Klauen und Zähnen verteidigt.'

Martha's eventual decision to take a lover is two-fold. Her seduction of Albert Renkens fulfils her sexual needs and the more important additional requirement of having a detective help her find Ursula's murderer. However, Mar-

tha's physical needs cast her in the role of a heartless vampire who is in heat and in search of a male. Renkens feels more and more trapped and eventually leaves, a result of the insensitive relationship he experiences with Martha. When she finally confesses her love for him, he is not convinced: ' . . . Es hat immer nachts zwischen mir und dir diese Kindesleiche gelegen.' Her dubious personal feelings for him have only grown out of her single ambition to gain a final measure of revenge.

Martha appears oblivious to much of the rest of society around her; however, one moment of social commentary gives Kolmar's heroine cause to ponder. Awaiting Albert in the hope of persuading him to return to her, she reads an anti-Semitic magazine. The pamphlet accuses the Jews of being parasitic plants on the German tree, of unyielding arrogance. The author, in the words of Martha Jadassohn, reveals her voice of exhortation and defiance:

> Hochmut. .? Wir sind nicht hochmütig, leider nicht; aber wir könnten es sein. Ja, wir dürften es sein. Wir haben Rom überstanden, Byzanz in Trümmern gesehen; auch dieser Feind hier wird uns nur töten, wenn wir uns selbst verderben. Wir müssen nur stark und tapfer sein, wieder zu sinken, zu tragen . . . Wir müssen nur wieder in uns hineingehn; dahin kann uns keiner verfolgen . . . 'Israel ist wie der Staub der Erde: alle treten ihn mit den Füssen; der Staub aber überlebt alle.'

The words indicate a fearlessness and resilience in the light of a tragic social and political situation, yet this brief meditation must take second place to the issue of Martha's personal plight. Confessing to Renkens that she herself was forced to take Ursula's life and that her revenge is no longer all-consuming, she only succeeds in alienating him even further. He rejects her love and leaves her.

Full of hopeless resignation, and imagining that she is carrying her beloved Ursula in her arms once again, Martha ' . . . wollte nichts rächen mehr. Sie hasste nicht mehr. Sie zürnte jetzt keinem Menschen. Sie zürnte nur ein wenig sich selber, nicht lang. Ich habe dich einmal getötet, du Freude, Gott ist gerecht: wer dich anrührt, muss sterben.' Consumed by grief, she drowns herself in the river Spree. Only then do Martha's perseverance and loneliness find final relief and peaceful reunion with her daughter.

It was almost ten years before Kolmar took up her pen to write another fictional work. In early 1939 she and her father were forced to move to a crowded tenement in Berlin. The ever-increasing number of boarders in the house and the mounting restrictions placed on all Jews in Germany gave little chance for the poetic muse to offer much creative inspiration. However, the poet's inner strength prevailed and she began the short story **'Susanna'** in December, 1939, her last prose work. The story, one of striking simplicity and concision, was drawn, in part, from the author's earlier days as a teacher-tutor of handicapped children. Once again, a world of fantasy and myth evolves as strange animals and people are introduced through the character of Susanna herself. It is in such a world of mystical experience that both Kolmar and her heroine resist and defy the intrusions from their oppressive physical environs.

In the simplest of terms, 'Susanna' is the tale of a tutor's experience as a private nurse-teacher of an unusual adolescent female. To the few people around her, Susanna is an emotionally disturbed young girl who, in order to counter her boredom with the rest of society, lives in a fantastic world inhabited by her Russian wolfhound Zoe and various other primeval creatures and images. For Susanna, the animal is a marriage of man and beast: 'Sie ist eine Hündin und ist eine Fürstin, Kaiserin von Byzanz. Aber sie lebt nicht mehr. Sie heisst Zoe und lebt in einem ganz alten Jahrhundert . . . '. The tutor, employed by the legal ward of the girl, enters into Susanna's world of vividly imagined lovers and visitors. She becomes a confidante to her charge's dreams and secret wishes to marry a 'Fischadler' or a 'Meerkönig . . . [mit] ein[em] Wuchern von Tang wie Haar und grüngraue[n] Augen.' The girl imagines herself as a Jewish princess, the daughter of King David or perhaps Saul. She is unashamed of her Jewishness whereas the tutor conceals her faith.

Reminiscent of themes from poems of earlier Kolmar cycles, Susanna's unusual interests reveal an extraordinary intimacy with small creatures and objects of nature—spiders, webs, shells, pebbles. Her love of tales and sagas fires her own imaginary journeys, all of which compel the unnerved tutor to be constantly vigilant. Soon the world of myth makes contact with the real. An unexpected witness to a night-time rendezvous between Susanna and her Sea-king lover (a young man from the village), the tutor listens to their passion, frozen by the mysterious yet innocent expression of love: ' . . . vielleicht hatte mich dies Unwirkliche gehemmt . . . '. The disconcerted woman feels, however, that it is necessary to curtail the relationship. While Susanna is confined to her bed with a cold, the result of her late night encounter, the tutor happens upon Herr Rubin, Susanna's beloved, in the town. She finds this unexpected meeting difficult, for she herself is unfamiliar with the feeling of love. To add to her uneasy state, her relationship with Zoe becomes equally problematical. The animal remains aloof from the tutor's friendly overtures and seems to caution her from entering the magical world which she and Susanna inhabit. The dog guards Susanna's mystical realm and keeps it free from harmful intruders.

Later, the tutor again meets Herr Rubin only to learn that the young man, hopelessly in love with the unstable Susanna, is leaving for Berlin. The young girl learns of this and writes a passionate plea to him. Unfortunately the letter does not reach Rubin but is read by his mother who, in a cruel and painful scene, accuses Susanna of seducing and ruining the prospects of her son. Unable to bear the recriminations and the charge that she is a prostitute, the desperate girl disappears the next day and is eventually discovered lying dead on the tracks leading to Berlin. During the search the scornful Zoe had been of no help, knowing full well that her mistress's only relief was to be found in suicide. The tutor herself now appears to show a greater insight into the reasons for Susanna's death. Her last thoughts reveal the author's resolution to preserve Susanna's final peaceful solitude:

Sie hätte vielleicht nicht mehr leben mögen, wenn sie erst ihr Verlassensein kannte; sie ahnte ja nichts, dachte: ich werde verfolgt, umlauert, solange es noch tagt. Nun war sie aus ihrem Versteck gekrochen und wanderte nachts auf dem Gleis dahin, . . . und ging zu ihrem Geliebten . . .

In the two stories, Gertrud Kolmar emphasizes the identity and independence of Martha Jadassohn and Susanna. Each resists the practice of established tenets of social behaviour and defies the external laws which are forced upon her. Their refuge is the other world, one of eternal love between reunited mother and child, Susanna and her beloved. (pp. 202-05)

> *Michael C. Eben, "Gertrud Kolmar: An Appraisal," in* German Life & Letters, *Vol. XXXVIII, No. 3, April, 1984, pp. 197-210.*

FURTHER READING

Blumenthal, Bernhardt G. "Gertrud Kolmar: Love's Service to the Earth." *The German Quarterly* XLII (September 1969): 485-88.

    A discussion of theme and imagery in Kolmar's poetry.

Boney, Elaine E. Review of *Dark Soliloquy: The Selected Poems of Gertrud Kolmar,* translated by Henry A. Smith. *The German Quarterly* L, No. 3 (May 1977): 354-55.

    Reviews Henry A. Smith's translation of Kolmar's poetry, calling it "a major contribution toward recognition of the value of [Kolmar's] literary legacy."

Domandi, Agnes Körner, ed. "Gertrud Kolmar: (1894-1943)." In *Modern German Literature: A Library of Literary Criticism, Vol. II, K-Z,* pp. 58-9. New York: Frederick Ungar Publishing Co., 1972.

    Includes five excerpts translated from German studies of Kolmar's poetry.

Exner, Richard. Review of *Das lyrische Werk,* by Gertrud Kolmar. *Books Abroad* 36, No. 1 (Winter 1962): 54.

    Review of the expanded 1960 edition of Kolmar's poetry in which Exner concludes that Kolmar "will become recognized as one of the best women poets of the century."

Kipp, David. Foreword to *Selected Poems of Gertrud Kolmar,* translated by David Kipp. pp. 7-8. London: Magpie Press, 1970.

    Introduction to the first English translation of a selection of Kolmar's poems.

Langman, Erika. "The Poetry of Gertrud Kolmar." *Seminar* XIV, No. 2 (May 1978): 117-32.

    Examines the theme of unfulfillment in Kolmar's poetry.

Moore, Harry T. "Poetry in the Time of the Nazis." In his *Twentieth-Century German Literature,* pp. 99-103. New York: Basic Books, 1967.

Brief biographical and critical introduction to Kolmar's poetry.

Ozick, Cynthia. "Out of the Flames: The Recovery of Gertrud Kolmar." In her *Art and Ardor: Essays by Cynthia Ozick,* pp. 229-32. New York: Alfred A. Knopf, 1983.

A reprint of Ozick's foreword to *Dark Soliloquy: The Selected Poems of Gertrud Kolmar* in which she rejoices that Kolmar's work did not perish during World War II.

Rosenfeld, S. Review of *Eine jüdische Mutter,* by Gertrud Kolmar. *World Literature Today* 53, No. 4 (Autumn 1979): 681.

Review of *Eine jüdische Mutter.* Rosenfeld states: "Beyond doubt, Gertrud Kolmar demands recognition . . . as a poet, one whose eminence has yet to be properly acknowledged; but this powerful story, especially its first section, which contains moments of pure creative genius, leads the reader to wonder, in reverence and melancholy, to what heights of accomplishment the author might have risen had she not perished in a Nazi death camp."

Mikhail Kuzmin

1872?-1936

(Full name Mikhail Alexeyevich Kuzmin) Russian poet, dramatist, novelist, short story writer, and essayist.

A controversial figure of early twentieth-century Russian literature, Kuzmin wrote esoteric and allusive poems, plays, and novels that are remembered as much for their frank treatment of homosexuality as for their literary merit. Writing in a period when Russian Symbolism was the dominant literary movement, Kuzmin rejected what he perceived as its false metaphysical pretensions, advocating instead an aesthetic based on concrete experience.

Born into a family of the minor nobility in the city of Ya-roslavl, Kuzmin was educated at St. Petersburg Universi-ty and initially planned a career as a composer. He began to study under Nikolay Rimsky-Korsakov at the St. Pe-tersburg Conservatory, but discontinued his musical edu-cation in 1894, completing only three years of a seven-year course. The following year, he traveled to Egypt with his mother, and he settled in Alexandria after she returned to Russia; his years in the city were to inspire his most ac-claimed collection of poetry, *Alexandryskie pesni* (*Alexan-drian Songs*). In 1897 he visited Italy, later basing much of his novel *Krilya* (*Wings*) on his experiences there. Re-turning to St. Petersburg, Kuzmin again turned to com-posing music. *Istorya rytsaria d'Alessio* was originally in-tended as the text for a musical piece he had written, but it became his first professional literary work when it was published as a drama in 1905. A year later, the literary journal *Vesy* published *Wings*. The novel's subject, a young artist's homosexual encounters in Italy, caused a scandal in St. Petersburg literary circles, and the contro-versy over Kuzmin intensified with the 1908 publication of *Seti,* a collection of poetry that contained explicitly erotic scenes. Between 1910 and 1917, Kuzmin wrote nu-merous dramas, becoming a prominent figure in St. Pe-tersburg's theater community. After the Bolshevik Revo-lution in October of 1917, Kuzmin's opportunities for publishing original work were limited, so he turned to writing reviews and translating the works of William Shakespeare and other writers. After 1929, the year in which his noted poem cycle *Forel razbyvaet lyod* (*The Trout Breaks the Ice*) appeared, government regulations dictated that Soviet literature fulfill a primarily didactic function, and Kuzmin's works were proscribed for their aestheticism as well as their controversial subject matter. Leon Trotsky deemed them "completely and entirely su-perfluous to a modern post-October man." Kuzmin died of pneumonia in 1936.

In his works, Kuzmin often depicted love and sex in a way that challenged conventional morality, insisting that the pursuit of human affection is the individual's most solemn obligation. This theme is realized in a variety of historical

and geographical settings, ranging from the ancient Rome of *Alexandrian Songs* to the eighteenth-century Venice of *Venetsianskie bezumtsy* (*Venetian Madcaps*). While his concern for an idealized past is a trait that he shares with the Russian Symbolists, critics note that in his poetry he spurned their usage of complex and personal metaphors to express primarily metaphysical concepts. Kuzmin's ec-static celebration in *Alexandrian Songs* of "Chablis on ice, a toasted bun," is often cited as an example of his intention to mine spirituality from everyday experience. This senti-ment has led critics to stereotype Kuzmin as a poet of triv-ial pleasures, but such later works as *The Trout Breaks the Ice* contain expressionistic and surreal imagery that indi-cates the versatility of his imagination. In this cycle of poems, considerably more complex than *Alexandrian Songs,* the trout is a symbol for love, which is active and unpredictable, while the ice represents the enemies of love—repression and death.

In his dramas, Kuzmin subscribed to the aesthetic beliefs of the director Vsevelod Meyerhold, who rejected the the-atrical realism then popular in Russia in favor of stylized and experimental productions, and who brought his vision of a new Russian theater to Kuzmin when they collaborated on various productions. Kuzmin's dramas featured elaborate costumes and scenery and incorporated his own songs and poems, and these aspects of production were considered as important as the acting and writing. Alexandr Blok's successful drama *The Fairground Booth* of 1906 exerted a strong influence on Kuzmin, and in works such as *Venetian Madcaps* he exhibits an ironic humor that critics have compared to Blok's. Kuzmin used fiction as the forum for presenting and elaborating his theories of human relationships. Like *Wings, Plavayushchie puteshestvuyushchie* depicts complicated entanglements and both heterosexual and homosexual partnerships, examined in detail during late-night arguments in bohemian cafés. In his novels' frequent philosophical dialogues, characters also discuss art, religion, and literature in a manner that has been described as "dilettantish," but has also been praised for its socially progressive vision.

The Soviet publication of Kuzmin's collected writings and the English translations of many of his works sparked a renewal of critical interest in the 1970s. Recent commentators have unearthed complexities in Kuzmin's themes and techniques, celebrating the diversity of his achievements and recognizing his influence on such important Russian poets as Velimir Khlebnikov and Anna Akhmatova, who once called Kuzmin "my wonderful teacher." Such critical efforts, in the words of Simon Karlinsky, "should help restore Kuzmin to his rightful place among the foremost Russian poets of this century."

PRINCIPAL WORKS

Istorya rytsaria d'Alessio (drama) [first publication] 1905

Krilya (novel) 1906
    [*Wings,* 1972]

O Alexee, cheloveke Bozhem (drama) 1907

Seti (poetry) 1908

"O prekrasnoy yastnosti" (essay) 1910

Osennie ozera (poetry) 1912

Venetsianskie bezumtsy (drama) 1912
    [*Venetian Madcaps,* 1973]

Glinyanie golubki (poetry) 1914

Plavayushchie puteshestvuyushchie (novel) 1914

Sobranie sochineny. 9 vols. (poetry, dramas, novels, short stories, and essays) 1914-18

Dvum (poetry) 1918

Zanaveshennye kartinki (poetry) 1920

Alexandryskie pesni (poetry) 1921
    [*Alexandrian Songs,* 1980]

Ekho (poetry) 1921

Nezdeshnie vechera (poetry) 1921

Paraboly (poetry) 1923

Uslovnosti (essays) 1923

Forel razbyvaet lyod (poetry) 1929
    [*The Trout Breaks the Ice,* 1980]

Sobranie stikhov. 3 vols. (poetry) 1977-78

Selected Prose and Poetry (poetry, short stories, and drama) 1980

Nikolai Gumilev   (essay date 1912)

[*Gumilev was one of the founders and major figures of the Acmeist movement in early twentieth-century Russian poetry. The Acmeists reacted against the earlier school of the Russian Symbolists, whose work they criticized as abstract, diffuse, and alienated by mysticism from the beauties and value of the physical world. Gumilev and other Acmeists, including his wife Anna Akhmatova and the poet Osip Mandelstam, briefly established a poetics that demanded concise and concrete renderings of physical reality, emphasizing a neo-Classic formalism that contrasted with what the Acmeists considered the loose transcendental verbiage of the Symbolists. In the following review of* Autumn Lakes, *Gumilev discusses the originality of Kuzmin's treatment of love.*]

The poetry of Mikhail Kuzmin is for the most part "salon" poetry—not that it is not genuine or beautiful poetry, on the contrary, "salon-ness" is given to it as some extra quality making it unlike others. It has responded to everything that for some years past has excited the drawing rooms of Petersburg. The eighteenth century from Somov's point of view, the Thirties, Russian schismatism, and everything that has occupied literary circles: ghazals, French *ballades,* acrostics and occasional verse. And one feels that all this is first-hand, that the author was not following the vogue, but took part in its creation himself.

Like **Nets,** Mikhail Kuzmin's first book, **Autumn Lakes** is almost exclusively devoted to love. But instead of the former tender wit and intimacy so characteristic of love, we find impassioned eloquence and the somewhat solemn seriousness of sensual attraction. The bonfire has flared up and, from a welcoming flicker, it has become majestic. Even if all the familiar places are mentioned—Boisson's photographic studio, Moscow's "Metropol"—it is clear to the reader that only one ancient image dominates the dreams of the poet, the mythological *Amour,* the marvelously animated "naked lad in a field of rye" shooting golden arrows. The poet divines him, and only him, both in a fashionable dinner jacket and beneath the regulation cocked hat. This even explains the repetition, rather strange in contemporary poetry, of the words "bow," "arrows," "pierce," "prick," that under other conditions would seem like intolerable rhetoric.

This very same *Amour* with a traditional quiver flies down to the poet at noon from a golden cloud and sits with him in the noisy hall of a restaurant. Both here and there—the same "familiar visage." It is madness, yes, but it has another name too—poetry.

Somewhat detached but in profound inner accordance with the whole stands the section of Eastern ghazals—**"Spring Garland"** and **"Spiritual Verses,"** together with **"Day of the Most Holy Virgin."** In the first, covered by the shadow of Hafiz [a fourteenth-century Persian lyric poet], the impassioned eloquence of sensuality of which I spoke earlier was successfully harmonized with the bright colors of Eastern nature, bazaars and festivals. Mikhail Kuzmin passed by the heroic poetry of the Bedouins and settled upon the poetry of their urban followers and successors, which is well-suited to refined rhythms, affected difficulty of locution and magnificence of vocabulary. In his Russian poems, the second face of sensuality—its solemn seriousness—became religious lucidity, simple and wise beyond any stylization. It is as though the poet himself prayed in Volga-side cloisters and lit lamps before ikons of antique design. He, who feels in everything the reflection of Another, be it God or Love, he has the right to speak these triumphal lines:

> I do not believe the sun that moves toward
>   nightfall.
> I do not believe the summer that moves toward
>   decline,
> I do not believe the cloud that darkens the vale,
> Nor a dream do I believe—death in the form of
>   a monkey.
> I do not believe the deceitful ebb of the sea,
> The flower I do not believe, that insists: "she
>   loves me not!"

Mikhail Kuzmin holds one of the first places among contemporary Russian poets. Only a few are blessed with such an amazing harmony of the whole, combined with free diversity of details. As a spokesman, however, for the views and feelings of a whole circle of people united by a common culture and by rights ascended to the crest of life, he is a poet of this earth, and finally, his fully developed technique never overshadows the image, but only inspires it. (pp. 119-20)

> *Nikolai Gumilev, in a review of "Autumn Lakes," in his* Nikolai Gumilev on Russian Poetry, *edited and translated by David Lapeza, Ardis, 1977, pp. 119-20.*

Prince D. S. Mirsky   (essay date 1926)

[*Mirsky was a Russian prince who fled his country after the Bolshevik Revolution and settled in London. While in England, he wrote two important histories of Russian literature,* Contemporary Russian Literature *(1926) and* A History of Russian Literature *(1927). In 1932, having reconciled himself to the Soviet regime, Mirsky returned to the USSR. He continued to write literary criticism, but his work eventually ran afoul of Soviet censors and he was exiled to Siberia. He disappeared in 1937. In the following excerpt, Mirsky evaluates some of Kuzmin's prominent writings.*]

[Michael Alexeevich Kuzmin, though a member of the Symbolist set,] as a writer stands apart from the Symbolist school. He is a pure æsthete. His favourite periods in the past are the Alexandrian age, the early Byzantine times, and the eighteenth century. On the other hand, he is firmly grounded in the Russian religious tradition and has a peculiar sense of sympathy for the Old Believers. There is a distinct religious strain in his work, but it is not like that of the Symbolists—it is not metaphysical, but devotional and ritual. This religious element is inseparable in him from a refined and perverse sensuality. The two make a piquant blend which is not to the taste of all. His poetry is different from that of the Symbolists in that it is more concrete and less solemn. The feeling he expresses in it is almost invariably love. His craftsmanship is very high and his verses are often exquisite. His first poetical sequence, *Songs of Alexandria* (1906), is also his best. It was in-

spired by the example of Pierre Louÿs' *Chansons de Bilitis;* but there can be no doubt that the Russian poet's reconstructions of Alexandrian love-songs are far more delicate, refined, and suggestive. These songs were followed by the whimsically exquisite "eighteenth-century" pastoral *The Seasons of Love* (1907), where his wonderful, almost acrobatic skill in handling rhyme is at its best. His later poetry consists partly of rather tedious allegorical love-poems in the style of Petrarch's *Trionfi,* partly of exquisitely frivolous evocations of "the charming trifles" of life, in which he has no equal. In prose he vindicates the ideal of "beautiful clarity," inspiring himself by the example of the late Greek romancers, the Lives of the Saints, the Italian *novella,* and the French novel of the eighteenth century. His style is affected and advisedly Frenchified. Its charm lies in its piquant and perverse flavour, for though he writes novels of pure adventure, he is curiously lacking in the power to tell a story. His stories of modern life (the longest is the novel *Gentle Joseph,* 1910) are indifferently constructed and seldom interesting. But what is admirable in them is the dialogue, which goes even farther than Tolstoy's in reproducing the actual accents and freedom of spoken language. He has also written scenarios for ballets, operettas, and plays. They are usually mischievous and frivolous, and their principal charm lies in the rhymed passages. The most exquisite of all is *The Comedy of St. Alexis,* an early work (1907), which is especially typical of his manner of treating sacred things and which contains some of his best songs. (pp. 238-39)

> *Prince D. S. Mirsky, " 'Stylizators': Kuzmin," in his* Contemporary Russian Literature: 1881-1925, *Alfred A. Knopf, 1926, pp. 238-39.*

Renato Poggioli   (essay date 1960)

[*Poggioli was an Italian-born American critic and translator. Much of his critical writing is concerned with Russian literature, including* The Poets of Russia: 1890-1930 *(1960), which is one of the most important examinations of this literary era. In the following excerpt from that work, Poggioli describes Kuzmin as the only Russian representative of the* crepuscolari *movement in European poetry.*]

Mikhail Kuzmin was born in Jaroslavl' in 1875, into a family which on his mother's side claimed a French ancestry. He considered Moscow his home town, although he divided his time between Moscow and Petersburg. It was in the latter city, which had lost its capital status and been renamed Leningrad, that he died in 1936. He spent the last twenty years of his life, if not in silence (he managed to publish a few new books of verse and prose up to 1928), at least in obscurity, solitude, and distress. In a minuscule autobiography, written in 1907, he had mockingly composed the inscription he would have liked to see engraved on his tomb, with words which seem to echo Stendhal's *scrisse, visse, amò,* and which may be read as a prophecy of the early decline of his fame and fortune: "He lived thirty years, sang and mused, loved and smiled."

Kuzmin at first thought of becoming a musician, and studied composition under Rimskij-Korsakov. Later he set to music poems by himself and others, and collaborated enthusiastically on Djagilev's Russian Ballets. His literary career, the beginning of which was greeted by the acclaim of Valerij Brjusov, started rather late, at about the time of the "little revolution" of 1905. In all the verse he wrote he proved to be a craftsman and a virtuoso, and showed great abilities also in his prose works. It is perhaps worth remembering that he gained his first success as a prose writer with the tale *Wings,* which appeared in 1906, although it was a *succès de scandale,* since what the author preached in that story was the cause of perverted love. Kuzmin's fiction is even more elegant and refined than his poetry: this is especially true of the novel *The Adventures of Aimé Lebeuf* (1907), set in eighteenth-century France, and relating the life story of an adventurer who looks very much like Casanova or Cagliostro, and *The Deeds of Alexander the Great,* a sophisticated version of the French medieval romance by the same title. The fastidious delicacy of Kuzmin's taste is no less evident in a later collection of critical essays, fittingly entitled *Conventions* (1926). Yet the best part of his literary production is to be seen in the half-dozen collections of lyrics he published up to the First World War, of which the most important are *Alexandrian Songs* (1906), *Nets* (1908), *Lakes of Autumn* (1912), and *Clay Doves* (1914). To these one may add two later collections, *Unearthly Evenings* (1921) and *Parabolas* (1923), and an earlier composition, unique in his work, *The Carillon of Love* (1906), a charming pastoral in eighteenth-century setting, for which he composed the music himself.

All those books presented to the Russian public a graceful, minor poet, who hailed with delight the concrete reality of daily experience, and who seemed to liberate Russian poetry from the daydreams and nightmares of Symbolism, as well as from its visions and wonders. Kuzmin was aware of the novelty of his task, and in one of his most significant poems he described himself as "alien to all obedient miracles and faithful to your flowers, O gay earth." With him poetry appeared once more to touch solid ground; yet, being a light balloon, Kuzmin could do so only thanks to a heavy ballast of literature.

A genuine, although a slight, artist, Kuzmin worked at his best when he could give weight to the light product of his talent with matter taken from the creation of other writers and poets. This applies not only to the structure and style, but even to the themes and the imagery of his work. In the poem mentioned above there is a stanza portraying one of those ephoebic figures which haunt all too often the effeminate fantasies of this poet. To convey the effect of meretricious charm which that face provokes, Kuzmin finds no better way than to compare it to such aesthetic impressions as those produced by the *lazzi* of a gay farce, by the capricious quill of Marivaux, and by Mozart's *Mariage de Figaro*. The very choice of these literary and artistic references reveals Kuzmin for what he is: a connoisseur who extends his connoisseurship from the field of life to that of art as well as vice versa. In the opening of the same poem, which may be considered his *ars poetica,* he asks himself where one might find the style best suited to describe all those small delights which a more pretentious poet would choose to ignore, and which Kuzmin exemplifies in a morning walk, a few slices of toasted bread, a plate of ripe cherries, a bottle of chilled Chablis wine. The mod-

esty implied in that rhetorical question is a false one, since Kuzmin knows very well that, better than any other artist or poet, he had found the ways and means to represent all the "magic trifles" or "merry levities" which brighten and enliven the days of a hedonist endowed with a refined taste and eager to enjoy all the good things of life. Kuzmin, however, is not only a hedonist, but also an aesthete, and as such he indulges all too often in artificial, as well as in natural, pleasures. He likes not only the fruits and flowers which grow spontaneously from our earth, but also those which man may nurse in his hothouses, or manufacture out of alabaster or even papier-mâché. In brief, Kuzmin is a Decadent of a new kind and perhaps of a lesser brand. As such, he is a unique figure within the Russian poetry of his time, where he acts as the single representative of a minor, and yet widespread, trend, which considerably affected the development of Western poetry during the first decade of the century. That trend is little known, perhaps because there is not yet a general term by which to identify it. Yet one could easily define and designate it by extending to other literatures the name given in Italy to the local representatives of that trend.

It was the critic G. A. Borgese who coined the label "twilight poets" (*crepuscolari*) for a group of secondary poets who flourished immediately before the First World War, and who transposed into a minor key the themes and attitudes which [Gabriele] D'Annunzio had expressed in his *Poema Paradisiaco.* In that book D'Annunzio had replaced the barbaric and panic vigor of his early inspiration with the sickly languor of a convalescent soul, morbidly enjoying the fading beauty of a neglected garden or of an abandoned villa, as well as the pale charm of old-fashioned objects and things. The *crepuscolari* translated the same vision from its still aesthetic and aristocratic background to a more prosaic and vulgar one, or more precisely, to a provincial, bourgeois, and domestic milieu. The best of them, Guido Gozzano, sang of all those "good things in bad taste" which are the strange and familiar signs of bourgeois status and bourgeois psychology. Thus Gozzano and his peers became the pathetic ironists of a petty bourgeois aestheticism, of a middle-class Decadence, both comfortable and uncomfortable in its mediocrity.

Few poets expressed more typically than Gozzano a mood which he shared with many other poets of his time, and which he had not been the first to express. That mood had already appeared in the work of two French poets whom the Italian *crepuscolari* later treated as their models and masters, Francis Jammes and Jules Rodenbach. Jammes' and Rodenbach's example, joining with the belated influence of two extravagant masters of early Symbolism, Jules Laforgue and Tristan Corbière, spread the same sensibility to other literatures, making possible the appearance in Germany of the poetry of Franz Werfel, and adding in Poland another chord to the lyre of Julian Tuwim. The mood ruled for a while even Anglo-American poetry, as shown by the early works of T. S. Eliot, whose youthful poems, especially *Prufrock,* were at once a pathetic manifestation and a detached satire of the same mood. In brief, all the poetry written in that key was but an attempt to portray the softness, emptiness, and weakness of the modern soul; to convey and to condemn at the same time that bourgeois decadence which is the spiritual disease of the modern world.

There is no doubt that Kuzmin is the only Russian poet who represented that trend, and it is equally certain that he expressed it in a manner all his own. He faced the little world of Decadent twilight without bourgeois ambiguity; he accepted its reality with a feeling of sympathy, rather than with indulgent compassion, or with mocking irony. An aesthete and Decadent in miniature, he felt at home within that mood, which he depicted in lines both subtle and firm. Thus he stands out among the poets of the Decadent twilight not only for the fluid limpidity of his style, but also for the directness with which he treated the literary materials which fed that mood. While Gozzano or Jammes submitted those materials to the acid test of parody, Kuzmin preferred to imitate and recreate his own precedents or models in a spirit of lively gaiety, of innocent fun. It is highly significant that his little, yet exquisite, masterpiece is but the pastiche of a pastiche: the free and original reworking of an amusing literary mystification of the beginning of the century. This is the cycle of poems entitled **Alexandrian Songs,** written after the pattern of Pierre Louÿs' *Chansons de Bilitis,* which purported to be translations of the newly discovered lyrics of a *hetaira* of ancient Alexandria. The persons speaking in the first person in the poems of Kuzmin's cycle are a young man or a girl, an old poet or a poor scribe, all singing the praises of pleasure and desire, of love and youth. Elegant but not precious, exquisite in rhythm and delicate in sound and speech, literary but not pedantic, these pieces reveal Kuzmin's ability to give a new moving voice to that commonplace philosophy of life which had already found classical expression in such poets as Horace, Anacreon, or Omar Khayyâm.

The French eighteenth century, as reinterpreted by the Goncourts, or as expressed in such works as *Les liaisons dangereuses* and in such figures as Manon Lescaut and the Chevalier de Faublas, is another of the cultural backdrops against which Kuzmin likes to fix his miniature view of life in the filigree patterns of his art. In his attempt to re-evoke that age and milieu, Kuzmin found his master and model in the Verlaine of *Fêtes galantes,* which conveys the sentimental futility and the frivolous elegance generally associated with eighteenth-century life in a series of scenes which look like a pastoral dumb show. Kuzmin is often fully aware that his own creations or recreations are lacking in vital power; and he confesses as much in the title piece of **Clay Doves.** The poet portrays himself first in the act of shaping, with assiduous hands, little doves of blue clay, and then in the attempt to infuse life into them with his breath. Of a sudden, says he, they rustlingly moved. But their flight was a short-lived illusion, since they were made of water and mud, not of flesh and blood. "And I felt," the poet concludes, "that my mysterious handicraft was lifeless." This may be all too true; yet it is only fair to remember that in the world of culture there is place not only for the imitation of nature and the representation of life, but also for artifice and for the imitations of art. Thus, in the gallery of modern Russian verse, there is also a place for the charming showcase of Kuzmin's poetry, with its Rococo or Biedermeier artifacts. (pp. 218-23)

Renato Poggioli, "The Neoparnassians," in his The Poets of Russia: 1890-1930, *Cambridge, Mass.: Harvard University Press, 1960, pp. 212-37.*

Andrew Field   (essay date 1963)

[*An American biographer, essayist, translator, and critic of Russian literature, Field is best known for his biographical and critical studies of Vladimir Nabokov—* Nabokov: His Life in Art *(1967) and* Nabokov: His Life in Part *(1977). In the following essay, he presents an overview of Kuzmin's prose writings, characterizing them as deceptively simple.*]

In the forest of Russian literature Mikhail Kuzmin (1875-1936?) is an unexpected and strangely beautiful ladyslipper. Delicate, alien, and yet self-assured, his art is a diminutive and stylized blossom in a twilight period of Russian history and literature:

> The sun is my predilection
> To a faded mirror's reflection,
> But I am found and fast caught,
> Like Saul, in a kingdom unsought.

The uniqueness of Kuzmin's vision is its acceptance of (or better, acquiescence to) the *jejune* bourgeois culture in which he lives. He is aristocratic and proud of his refinement and his heritance, but he does not, as the Symbolists before him did, use the past as an escape from the present. Rather, he brings the past—the eighteenth century, Rome, Alexandria—to bear upon the present. Kuzmin's art is an improbable admixture of sensitivity and triviality, naiveté and decadence, gaiety and weariness. Its very virtues are also its limitations.

The range of Kuzmin's work is broad. He wrote six volumes of poetry, a book of penetrating essays, a large number of short stories and novellas, and several dramas. In addition, Kuzmin, at one time a student of Rimsky-Korsakov, composed music for his own verse as well as for ballet and drama, most notably the music for Alexander Blok's play *The Puppet Show.* It is his prose which offers the best opportunity to understand and evaluate Kuzmin. The important Russian critic Boris Eichenbaum, one of the few to touch upon Kuzmin's prose, said of it: "Seemingly light and demanding nothing from the reader except a love of reading, his prose has however a strange, unusual, and puzzling appearance." This element of strangeness found in his prose but not in his verse offers a key to the subleties which underlie the seemingly obvious forms of Kuzmin's art.

In 1909 when the famous Symbolist journal, *The Scales,* ceased publication, the Russian literary journal which took its place was *Apollo,* the very name of which indicates its aesthetic position: neoclassical simplicity "in protest against the formless recklessness of art which has forgotten the laws of cultural continuity." The reaction against the excesses of Symbolism had many divergent aspects and involved many schools, some real and some existing in name only. The first formal declaration of the new direction was Kuzmin's essay **"On Beautiful Clarity"** which appeared in 1910 in the fourth number of *Apollo.* The article is inevitably cited as a poetic credo, but it is important to remember that its sub-title is "notes on prose."

Kuzmin states explicitly that he is primarily concerned neither with the artist's *Weltanshauung* nor with the literary point of view from which he expresses it but with the more basic problems of syntax and the proper correlation of form and content. He proposes restricting the free word position allowed by Russian and the adoption of a lexicon that will bring forth the native clarity and spirit of the language. In fact, though he does not say so, Kuzmin is advocating an imitation of the stylistic ideals characteristic of French literature from the time of Malherbe. And the novelists whom he cites as being proper models are almost all European:

> The forms for both the story and the novel starting with Apuleius and the Italian and Spanish novelists and going through L'Abbé Prévost, Lesage, Balzac, Flaubert to Anatole France and, finally, the incomparable Henri de Régnier must be sought, of course, in the Latin lands.

From these names it is evident that Kuzmin is suggesting a return of the novel to its earlier, less pretentious function of telling a story well. He would, with a few exceptions, bypass the nineteenth-century novel—a genre overburdened with psychology, social criticism, mysticism, and symbolism—and turn instead to *The Golden Ass,* the novelle of Boccaccio, the picaresque tales of the seventeenth and eighteenth centuries.

The "clarism" which Kuzmin speaks of in his article never became a formal movement for at least one very simple reason: the new artistic generation contained almost no novelists. Moreover, while the general tone of the article could and did meet with approval, its specific literary preferences were too closely tied to Kuzmin 's own unique cultural background. He read widely as a child, but he had very little contact with the mainstream of Russian literature. The names Pushkin, Gogol, Dostoevsky, Turgenev, and Tolstoy are conspicuously absent from his list of "favorite authors" which contains instead names like Ostrovsky and Leskov. By the time he was a gymnasium student Kuzmin knew French and Italian well and could read Greek and Latin. The French blood in his family and his musical interests centering on the work of Rossini and Schubert were other factors which served to orient him towards Europe. After an unsuccessful three-year attendance at the St. Petersburg Conservatory of Music (he attempted to poison himself), Kuzmin made two long trips abroad to convalesce. One of these was to Italy, where he spent an entire year. Kuzmin's personality extended far beyond the narrow limits imposed by the circumstances of the time and country of his birth. Another poet expressed it curiously, writing of him: "In 20th century St. Petersburg there was a Frenchman of the 18th century from the island of Martinque." But whether his affinity for France and Italy and the eighteenth century was inherent or cultivated, it clearly was very real and not mere affectation.

For Kuzmin the form of the picaresque novel was both appealing and ideally suited to express his understanding of how life is lived:

> Here's how well-made novels are ended—
> All's made clear, a period's appended;
> Who Arman and the widow are all can tell
> And whose daughter Elisa is as well.
>
> But the path of my tale's disposition
> Has not a trace of such composition.
> It prances along the surface in flight
> As freely, and more, as a gazelle might.

Kuzmin does not deny the existence of metaphysical "abyss," but he pays no more attention to it than most of us do in our own day-to-day lives. Thus his novels are at once both a frivolous stylization and a fitting reflection of life.

One of the most characteristic of his stylized tales is *The Adventures of Aimé Lebeuf* (1906). Jean Aimé Ulysse Bartholomé Lebeuf is an eighteen-year-old lad who, through no effort on his own part, is carried through a series of colorful adventures, first in eighteenth-century France and subsequently in Italy. Among his many adventures Aimé plays the part of a servant in order to travel with his lover, disguises himself as a girl (whereupon he is propositioned by a monk), and assumes the role of an alchemist and court advisor. Episode succeeds episode, and the narrative is never complicated. Kuzmin's loose, whimsical style is delightful and vivid:

> It was already light, and, hurrying past a large puddle, I nonetheless stopped to have a look, attempting to see my own face as though it were a stranger's. I saw a rounded face with a straight, sharp nose, light gray eyes, a large mouth, and thick golden eyebrows; the cheeks were peach-colored, slightly covered with fuzz; small ears, long legs, and a tall stature completed the exterior of the happy mortal graced with the love of Louise de Thombelle.

Even in the light fabric of this novel, there are many of the features which also figure in Kuzmin's more complex work. Kuzmin extols love as the most important human activity, and he places no moral restrictions upon it—when Aimé is posing as Ambrosius, not only Princess Amalia but also her brother fall in love with him. Abnormal love in Kuzmin is never actually described (for that would be the greatest of sins, tastelessness), it simply *is* and is never questioned by either the author or his characters. Aimé, like all of Kuzmin's protagonists, is a passive character who lets fate act upon him. The measure of Kuzmin's affection for a character may be said to be inversely proportional to the degree to which that character asserts himself. At one point Aimé is speaking with someone who will, we know, take part in the coming French revolution:

> "We shall free the world!"
>
> "Free it from what? me for instance?"
>
> "From tyrants," exclaimed the youth, reddening.
>
> "But the fact is that prejudices, accepted customs, our feelings are, in the end, more terrible tyrants than are crowned rulers."

The things people do are not as important to Kuzmin as

people themselves. This same motif is repeated in three other picaresque novellas. In *The Journey of Sir John Fairfax in Turkey and Other Remarkable Countries* (1909), the central character is also a markedly passive young man; and in *The Marvelous Life of Joseph Balzamo, the Count Cagliostro* (1916), Joseph never acts himself but is always the instrument of Lorenza's whims. While it is true that Kuzmin's version of the Alexander the Great tale, *The Exploits of the Great Aleksander* (1907), shows Alexander as a man of action, he too ends by marching on with his army when there is no longer either a foe or a goal before him.

The very anachronism of such prose being written in the twentieth century ought in itself to have been sufficient evidence of a carefully calculated artistic design. But Kuzmin was taken at his word ("The best test of talent is to write about nothing."), and his works were read as curious and meaningless trifles. Kuzmin, according to the account of one of his contemporaries, did his writing standing up and with a little band of aesthetes sitting at hand smoking Egyptian cigarettes and eating English biscuits. He would write for pages at a time without making any corrections, and he declared that anything one had written was worth printing. Without even stopping on the question of legend in the stories about Kuzmin—is it really likely that the poet Valery Briusov "taught" the young musician how to write a poem?—I would point out that such eccentricities are characteristic of all the European post-symbolist aesthetes. We have only to think, for example, of Ronald Firbank who reputedly wrote his novels on large pale-blue postcards, or of Francis Jammes who once told André Gide that he never changed a line after he had written it down. The circumstances under which a work of art is written and the personality of the author can, of course, be interesting and valuable addenda, but they are not a surrogate for critical examination of the work itself.

Nothing, at first glance, could be more simple than Kuzmin's 1906 story, **"From the Letters of the Young Girl Claire Valmont to Rosalie Toutelle Meyer."** It consists of letters written in the eighteenth century by a young girl to her old aunt. Claire falls in love with a boy named Jacques who works for her father, a shoemaker, and becomes pregnant. Jacques, who disappears, was really, it seems, Satan. The baby perishes, or is killed, in a Gothic manner, and in the final letter Claire describes how all the shoes made by Jacques, save one pair owned by an old Jew, were burned in the town square. But the simplicity of the story completely vanishes if the dates of the letters are taken into account, for then it becomes clear that Claire actually became pregnant about three months earlier than her own account would indicate when she was still writing her aunt maidenly innocent letters. Thus Kuzmin's lace fantasy turns back upon itself and takes on an entirely different aspect.

The best use of his technique of stylization is his 1913 novel, *Travellers on Land and Sea,* in which the form of the eighteenth-century novel is used to tell a contemporary story. The novel is divided into many short chapters each of which relates an episode in the lives of a group of blasé residents of St. Petersburg. The title refers to the emptiness and hopelessness of their lives, dominated by intrigues, affairs, and activity for its own sake. Kuzmin emphasizes the parallel he wishes to draw: "Polina Arkadevna continually carried the first volume of *Gil Blas* about with her, expressing surprise at how primitive in their demands our ancestors were." Each of the characters is searching in vain for that "excellent life" which is the myth of the eighteenth century and which they can never find because it does not exist. They are incapable of love, and their efforts to achieve it result only in banal affairs. The novel gives a vivid and ironic portrayal of café society in pre-revolutionary St. Petersburg:

> You're going to be here long? You must promise to come see me. I live on Podyacheskaya. There are some beautiful things at my place. I'll declaim Kuzmin's **Alexandrian Songs,** and you'll dance, or simply lie in a pose. There'll be lots of flowers. We shall become breathless from them. And our friends, only the very closest friends, will grasp how beautiful it is. Friends of mine have a leopard-skin rug, I'll get it and it will serve as my costume. Imagine—just a leopard skin and nothing else.

Homosexuality figures in the novel in the relationship between Orest Pekarsky and his young nephew Lavrik. The turning point of *Travellers on Land and Sea* is the suicide of Zoya Lilienfeld, a well-known actress and the one character who has complete control over her feelings and deeds. Her unexpected act expresses the despair of all the characters. As the novel ends, Orest and Lavrik, now travellers in fact, sail for England (the land of Wilde) convinced of the futility of attempting to order their lives.

The role of homosexuality must be a question of central importance in any critique of Kuzmin's prose. Kuzmin was himself a rather effeminate person. He used perfume and would receive guests in a Japanese kimono fanning himself. Russian literature, indeed Russia, had never known anything quite like him before. Actually, Kuzmin was only the first (and finally, the most authentic) manifestation of a wave of "European decadence" that swept through Russia after the 1905 revolution. The way had been prepared by extensive translations of European decadent literature in the preceding years and the strong decadent note in the work of the Russian Symbolists. The disillusionment and bitterness which followed the failure of the little revolution were all that was necessary to provide a receptive atmosphere for perverse and self-indulgent literature. But with the single exception of Kuzmin, none of these decadents (the most important ones were Nagrodskaya, Verbitskaya, Artsybashev, author of the infamous *Sanin,* and, to a certain degree, Andreev) produced anything which may be properly included under the classification of belles-lettres.

The use of homosexuality as a thematic device does not mar Kuzmin's work from an aesthetic point of view because of the restraint with which he handles the subject. He is never "cute" about it. His homosexual characters are either cultured men or sensitive boys, never depraved or foppish, and they are invariably presented sympathetically. Also, homosexual relations are justified by contrast with the pretense and poverty of the conventional relationships of other characters. Finally, the intimation of homosexuality is a leitmotiv which runs through nearly all of Kuzmin's prose and which often serves the very useful function of contributing dramatic tension to otherwise tenuous plots. It is interesting to compare the analogous manner in which Firbank repeatedly mentions Negroes in his novels, making of these references (and not the figure of the Negro himself) a sort of running joke.

Kuzmin's most famous novel and the one in which abnormal sexuality is most pronounced is his first, the notorious **Wings.** It was at first refused for publication by the journal to which Kuzmin had been contributing his work, but it finally appeared in *The Scales* in 1906 and was reprinted many times after that. Roughly speaking, it may be said to occupy much the same place in the history of Russian literature as does *À rebours* in French literature. Larion Strupp, an Englishman living in Russia, becomes the friend of a young lad named Vanya, and **Wings** is about how he wins his love. At first Vanya does not himself understand why he is drawn to Strupp (again, the theme of passivity), but he ends by making the conscious choice to remain with and give himself up to him. Strupp is, to a large extent, a vehicle for his author. He declares to Vanya:

> There are miracles surrounding us at every step: there exist muscles, sinews in the human body which it is impossible to view without a thrill! . . . We are Hellenists, lovers of the beautiful, the bacchants of the coming life . . . through the seas, through the mist and gloom we, the Argonauts, are coming! In completely virgin soil we shall recognize the most ancient roots, in never seen radiances we shall sense our native soil!

Conversation about art and literature comprise a diverse and extensive catalog of decadence. **Wings** is a novel *à thèse* which attempts to find a positive ethic in Eros to replace the no longer meaningful tenets of Christianity. The novel poses questions the resolution of which forms the basis of much of Kuzmin's later work:

> As one of ours put it: "How can you read Jesus' Canon after the theater? It's easier when you have killed someone." And really, one can steal and fornicate in any faith, but to understand *Faust* and use a rosary in prayer with conviction, that's inconceivable, or else, God only knows, it's teasing the devil. And if a man doesn't commit sin and fulfills the commandments without believing in their necessity and ability to save, then that is worse than not to fulfill them but to believe. How can one believe what can't be believed? How can you not know what you know, not remember what you remember?

Rome, where much of the action in **Wings** takes place, is the city of sensuality and decadence, but it is also, of course, the city of Christianity. The synthesis of Christianity and Eros was, however, to prove a precarious and finally untenable one.

In 1909 Kuzmin began to produce a series of works which deal with the problem of man's obligation to his fellow man. Given his personal religious and sexual beliefs, Kuzmin now asked himself the question, "Does a person have the right to make another person happy by force?" The problem is always posed in terms of the relationship between a weak and a strong character. In the short story **"The Dangerous Guard"** (1910) a mother attempts to take part vicariously in her daughter's romance but ends by destroying it and earning her hatred. Kuzmin rejects the path of hedonism as morally unacceptable even if, as in this story, the result is also beneficial for the person who is acted upon. In three works, *The Gentle Joseph* (1909), *The Dreamers* (1912), and *The Quiet Guard* (1915), he develops the theme of the primacy of passive execution of God's will over base self-gratification.

The Quiet Guard represents Kuzmin's final moral and aesthetic position. The protagonist, Pavel Miusov, is an hagiographic character. He has an intense and pure love for his older brother Rodion, and when Rodion becomes involved with a disreputable entrepreneur and his life is threatened, Pavel decides to sacrifice himself to save Rodion. The structure of Kuzmin's novel is an obvious parody of Dostoevsky's *Brothers Karamazov*. A striking and neat analogy exists between Kolya Zaitsev of *The Quiet Guard* and Ivan Karamazov, Father Aleksei and Father Zosima, Pavel Miusov and Alyosha Karamazov, Kuzmin's Lyuba and Vereiskaya and Dostoevsky's Liza and Grushenka, and Rodion Miusov and Dmitri Karamazov. Even the elder Miusov, although he does not appear in the novel, corresponds perfectly to old Fyodor Karamazov. The question of whether or not force is justifiable to make someone happy parallels Ivan Karamazov's question of whether paradise may be justified at the expense of one child's suffering. Kuzmin consistently "corrects" Dostoevsky. Kolya Zaitsev—his own Smerdyakov—kills Father Aleksei, thereby removing the representatives of both atheism and orthodoxy from the narrative; and the invalid Lyuba is restored to mental and physical health by her love for Pavel and will marry him. The entire novel, in contrast to its model, has an air of serenity and control. **Wings** concludes with Vanya's letter to Strupp in which he accepts Strupp's offer. *The Quiet Guard,* on the other hand, ends with Pavel's letter of farewell to Rodion. Pavel realizes that he has done as much for Rodion as he can and that he will best serve his brother now by allowing him to realize himself as an individual. *The Quiet Guard* is, like everything Kuzmin wrote, a derivative work, but it is a work which speaks with its own voice and which is original in the very method of its imitation. It is not too much to say that it is the most successful and purposeful parody in Russian literature.

Kuzmin's art is polished and elegant, and it is for the most part decadent in any fair sense of the term, but it has, for all that, a surprising depth and sophistication of meaning hidden behind the deceptive cloak which he called beautiful clarity. "Kuzmin could be called understandable," wrote his friend the poet Vyacheslav Ivanov, "if they understood him." If his prose is simple, it is a cunningly intricate simplicity, and for that reason it must be approached with great care. Kuzmin belongs to that small group of artists which includes Pierre Louys, Henri de Régnier, and, in more recent times, Vladimir Nabokov and the Argentine, Jorge Luis Borges, all of whom in their several ways raise stylization and pastiche to the level of serious creativity. (pp. 289-300)

Andrew Field, "Mikhail Kuzmin: Notes on a Decadent's Prose," in The Russian Review, *Vol. 22, No. 3, July, 1963, pp. 289-300.*

Vladimir Markov   (essay date 1972)

[*Markov is a Russian-born American critic and translator who has written extensively about Russian poetry. In the following excerpt, he places* Wings *and* Alexandrian Songs *in the context of Russian literature.*]

The novel *Wings* brought Mikhail Alekseyevich Kuzmin (1875-1936) a lasting notoriety, while the *Alexandrian Songs* cast a spell which few of the poet's contemporaries were able to resist, and some critics are still of the opinion that these poems are Kuzmin's best work.

Strictly speaking, Kuzmin had made his bow as a writer a year earlier, in 1905, when he published a rambling play and some not very distinguished sonnets in the *Green Collection of Verse and Prose:* it is curious to note that his partner in this enterprise was a future chief of the Communist secret police, Vyacheslav Menzhinski (perhaps some future researcher will reveal that Malyuta Skuratov also dabbled in literature and was the author of a number of saints' lives). *Wings* first appeared in 1906 in the Symbolist journal *The Scales* and went through several editions in book form between 1907 and 1921, since when it has not been republished. Eleven of the *Alexandrian Songs* appeared in the July, 1907 issue of *The Scales,* and the complete sequence was included in Kuzmin's first book of verse, *Nets,* the following year; it was only in 1921, however, that the *Alexandrian Songs* were issued in a separate collection.

Wings, it may be supposed, represented for Kuzmin the final stage in a process of self-liberation and self-acceptance, for the somewhat scanty information we have about Kuzmin's early life (there is mention of a suicide attempt) indicates that the transparent equilibrium in which his personality held a number of seemingly self-contradictory elements was by no means easily attained. On one hand there was the *fin-de-siècle* aesthete, the belated disciple of Walter Pater, on the other, the mystic drawn to the tradition of the Old Believers—an antinomy which is perfectly embodied in Kuzmin's chosen city of Alexandria, where a refined eroticism and a poetry of the most exquisite artificiality existed alongside the mysteries of the Gnostics. By an odd coincidence, at this very time—and, it would seem, quite independently—a native Alexandrian poet, Constantine Cavafy, was creating his own poetic myth of Alexandria, one which is often surprisingly close in conception to that of the Russian poet.

Travel was important to Kuzmin, as it is to the characters of *Wings.* Alexandria had changed his life; he spent some months in Italy—a stay reflected in the last part of *Wings*—and the literary *beau monde* of St. Petersburg was later to gossip avidly about this legendary visit. In 1907 Kuzmin began a brief autobiographical note with the words: "For thirty years he lived, sang, looked, loved and

smiled." The statement is more precise than it seems—the five verbs wonderfully suggest the subject matter and mood of most of his writings—and if it sounds a trifle banal, Kuzmin had the wisdom not to despise banality.

Wings may seem something of a period piece now, but when it appeared it shocked the reading public with its homosexual theme, and gave the journalists of the day endless occasion for discussion, parody and innuendo, all in the best tradition of cheap Russian journalism. The "serious" critics are best exemplified by G. S. Novopolin, who wrote in his inane survey *The Pornographic Element in Russian Literature* (1909): "The heart of the matter is not the fact of the perverse relationship between Stroop and the sauna attendant Fyodor, or between him and Smurov. It is said that such practices are widespread in the Caucasus, as well as among aristocratic circles in both our capitals. It had never occurred to anyone before, however, to give open publicity to this unnatural vice. No one had dared to glamorize it, and only Kuzmin's blasphemous brush did not tremble to introduce such propaganda into life [?] and belles-lettres." Elsewhere, Novopolin describes Stroop, Daniil Ivanovich as "reptiles who suck at Smurov's young soul and befoul it with their perverse lusts."

Kuzmin's depiction of homosexuality is hardly likely to shock anyone in the 1970s—not, at least, in an English translation; even at the time, his presentation of the theme as a liberation of the personality ("You know, Vanya, I think you have it in you to become a completely transformed being"; "And it's hard, Vanya, to deny the heart's longings—and sinful too, maybe") was not entirely novel; after all, André Gide's *L'immoraliste* had appeared a few years earlier, in 1902. [In a footnote, the critic adds, "Kuzmin's verse is another matter. It is the only example of first-class Russian poetry with a homosexual theme, though here too the inescapable Pushkin is a precursor with his little gem *'Otrok milyi, otrok nezhnyi'* ('Sweet lad, tender lad'); here there is no 'propaganda,' no 'problematics,' no stress on social stigma—instead Kuzmin chooses to dwell on 'love' rather than 'homosexual,' so that the object of his feelings becomes almost incidental."] Of course, the presentation of the homosexual theme in a Russian setting gives the novel considerable curiosity value for the non-Russian reader, illuminating as it does an area of life which emerged from unmentionability for a brief period at the beginning of the century; the relaxation of taboos at this time is illustrated by the almost simultaneous publication of Lydia Zinovyeva-Hannibal's *Thirty-Three Freaks,* which probably marks the first appearance of lesbians in Russian literature. Interesting too, in the light of present rediscoveries, is the book's Art Nouveau atmosphere: the characters of *Wings* are tireless name-droppers—Nietzsche, Klinger, Swinburne, Thoma, D'Annunzio, Maeterlinck, *et al.*

The contemporary reader is less likely to be carried away by the central theme of *Wings* or by the "gray eyes" of certain of its dramatis personae (here, as in the *Alexandrian Songs* and elsewhere, a favorite Kuzmin "signal"), than to be diverted by the novel's links, both predictable and unexpected, with earlier Russian narrative prose; beyond that, he will, hopefully, perceive that Kuzmin has a modest but quite distinctive contribution of his own to make to the Russian tradition. Like Tolstoy, Kuzmin not only depicts "seekers after truth" (his own brand, to be sure), but also, like the author of *Anna Karenina,* juxtaposes town and countryside, the capital and the provinces. In the manner of the Pushkin-Turgenev school, he likes to strew his pages with telling cultural detail—books read, theatrical performances attended, paintings admired. Like Dostoevski and Leskov, he does not shun drama—even melodrama—in his plots. He shares with Ostrovski and Leskov an ear for the colorful idiom of the uneducated, and with Melnikov-Pecherski (and again Leskov) he opens a door into the very special world of the Old Believers. What is peculiarly his own, however, is an oddly un-Russian lightness of texture (un-Russian, that is, if we forget Pushkin). Authentic and personal too is the St. Petersburg he sets before us: not the doomed, phantasmal city of Pushkin and Gogol, Dostoevski and Bely, but an everyday setting for everyday family scenes, and one observed with loving attention to detail, from the color of the air to the door-knobs. In fairness to Kuzmin, it should be said that in *Wings* he is still learning his craft as a writer, and that greater refinement and subtlety are to be found in his later novels and short stories—for example, some of the stories in *Grandmother's Trinket Box* and *Entr'actes in the Ravine,* or the short novels *Tender Joseph, The Dead Woman in the House* and the late short story *"The Blue Nothing."* Nevertheless, *Wings* retains its significance as an attempt to provide a credo for aestheticism in Russia.

When Vanya Smurov enters Stroop's apartment in the first part of *Wings,* he hears a man's voice singing one of Kuzmin's own *Alexandrian Songs* to piano accompaniment; although the singer is not identified, it is obviously Kuzmin himself (who before turning to poverty had studied composition at the St. Petersburg Conservatory under Rimski-Korsakov, and was well known as a performer of his own songs), who thus follows the Pushkin of *Eugene Onegin* in introducing himself as a character into his own fiction.

Mention has already been made of Kuzmin's early visit to Alexandria; it is quite possible that as a poet Kuzmin came into being there, and the Alexandrian experience continued to echo in his work after the composition of the *Alexandrian Songs*—in such works, for example, as his romance about Alexander the Great and, considerably later, in the Gnostic poems of 1917-1918. In Russia, lovers of poetry immediately took the *Alexandrian Songs* to their hearts; and if these poems are little known there today, it is only because of the officially-sponsored attempt over the past decades to dismiss much of the best Russian poetry of this century as "bourgeois-decadent." But even stern, bespectacled Marxists, who would have been hard put to unearth any redeeming social value in these lyrics, were enchanted by this blend of Pushkinesque "transparent sadness" and triumphant life-affirmation, of delicate sensuality and smiling regret for the passing of all "dear and fragile things?" The answer surely lies in that elusive quality of charm with which Kuzmin endowed everything he touched; charm has been in short supply in Russian poetry, and Kuzmin is a consummate charmer. At the heart

of this quality is perhaps the ability to see the familiar, even the cosy, in the exotic and remote, and vice versa.

Another thing about the *Alexandrian Songs* which astonished Kuzmin's contemporaries was the naturalness, the nonchalance even, with which he presented them with the first sizeable body of free verse in Russian—a form which defies metrical analysis, and one in which many a poet has foundered since Kuzmin's day. Free verse was first introduced to Russia in the eighteenth century by Alexander Sumarokov, who used it in his imitations of the Psalms; however, the form did not exert any strong attraction for Russian poets until the latter part of the nineteenth century, when Heine's poetry came into vogue and translators had somehow to cope with *Die Nordsee.* Experiments in free verse by Kuzmin's contemporaries—those of Alexander Blok come to mind—seem hesitant and isolated beside his, and it is hardly too much to say that it was Kuzmin who opened the way for free verse in Russian, although his only true follower has been Velimir Khlebnikov— Kuzmin's pupil in more senses than one (not that there has been any lack of vers-librists in Russia since Kuzmin; in the post-war generation of poets one might mention Vinokurov and Ksenia Nekrasova).

Nets, Kuzmin's first book of verse, of which the *Alexandrian Songs* form the final section, included a famous "manifesto" poem—a thrust at the cloudy portentousness of the Symbolists—in praise of "Chablis on ice, a toasted bun" and the "spirit of trifles, airy and exquisite," in consequence of which Kuzmin has been stereotyped as a poet of exquisite trifles—a description which is entirely inadequate, indeed downright misleading, when applied to his later work; for if the early Kuzmin was an integral part (as well as the *enfant terrible*) of Russian Art Nouveau, the Kuzmin of such verse collections as *Parabolas* (1923), with its intersecting planes, and the expressionistic *The Trout Breaks the Ice* (1929) belongs unmistakably to the avant-garde. (pp. viii-xiii)

> *Vladimir Markov, in a preface to* Wings: Prose and Poetry, *by Mikhail Kuzmin, edited and translated by Neil Granoien and Michael Green, Ardis, 1972, pp. viii-xiii.*

Michael Green (essay date 1973)

[*In the following excerpt, Green describes the aesthetic goals of Kuzmin's dramas.*]

"Kuzmin, Mikhail Alexeevich (1875-1936), poet, prosaist, dramatist"—so runs the lapidary description in the index to the most recent edition of [A. A.] Blok's collected works. For the sake of completeness, "composer, critic, translator" might have been added to the inventory, but one need have no quarrel with the ordering of the literary metiers practiced by Kuzmin; such an ordering, after all, would be no less suitable for Pushkin (perhaps Kuzmin's only true ancestor in Russian literature) and would not imply that Pushkin's dramatic work is negligible or lacking in interest.

For most of his life Kuzmin was closely involved with the theater, both as dramatist and composer. "Charming actors of limited talent / Who played 'Mahomet' in Russia" are among the forebears mentioned in the well known poem **"My Ancestors" ("Moi predki")** which opens his first collection of verse, *Nets* **(*Seti*)**. Perhaps Kuzmin was being unduly modest here, since one of these theatrical ancestors was Jean Aufresne-Rival, who left the Comédie Francaise in 1785 to become a member of the French troupe in St. Petersburg (his *emploi*—kings and noble fathers), and whose talent won the admiration of both Voltaire and Catherine II. There was a strong theatrical streak in Kuzmin's own nature: his delivery of his own songs at the piano, whether at Vyacheslav Ivanov's "Tower" or at the favored haunt of St. Petersburg bohemians, The Stray Dog, made him the chosen entertainer of the capital's literary and artistic set; he delighted too, at least in the early part of his career, in playing to the hilt roles which expressed certain aspects of his own contradictory nature—the decadent dandy with the made-up eyes or the bearded, long-robed Old Believer. It was an extravagantly theatrical age—an age of pose and artifice, of mask and masquerade—and Kuzmin was a child of the age.

Kuzmin began as a composer, and he approached the theater as he approached poetry—through music. For a few years (1891-1894) he was a member of Rimsky-Korsakov's composition class at the St. Petersburg Conservatory, and his first attempts at drama were intended for the musical theater. In a later essay directed against "the two enemies of art—naturalism and tradition," Kuzmin was to cite opera as the paradigmatic art form because of its peculiarly conventionalized nature. During the nineties Kuzmin worked on two unproduced and unpublished operas, *Esmeralda* and *Cleopatra*. The titles of these works indicate that he did not follow Rimsky-Korsakov and the nationalist school in drawing on Russian history and legend for his subjects. Naturally drawn to the clarity and grace of French opera, Kuzmin was later to exalt Grétry, the developer of the *opéra comique*, at the expense of the noble reformer Gluck. In the operas of Grétry Kuzmin found a "neatly carpentered text, full of life, sometimes amusing, sometimes touching," equipped with "light songs, arias, duets, choruses, comic numbers, dances and ensembles." Nothing could be more Kuzminian than this preference for small, neat, clearly defined forms in a context both gay and unpretentious; the characteristic stageworks of the poet's maturity seek to recapture this lost rococo world.

One suspects that *Esmeralda* and *Cleopatra* were more ambitious and remained uncompleted because Kuzmin's very modest gift as a composer was unable to sustain the kind of romantic opera these titles suggest. His models, perhaps, were Massenet and the "Russian Massenet"—Tchaikovsky. Kuzmin remarked that the two composers had "the same characteristic gentleness, elegiacism and femininity"; he also notes that they share a predeliction for adapting as libretti first-rate literary works which are invariably sentimentalized and diminished in their treatment—thus Tchaikovsky with *Eugene Onegin, The Queen of Spades, Mazepa* (Pushkin), *Vakula the Smith* (Gogol) and *The Maid of Orleans* (Schiller); thus Massenet with *Manon* (Prévost), *Le Cid* (Corneille), *Thais* (France),

Werther (Goethe) and *Don Quichotte* (Cervantes). In his early operas Kuzmin seems to have followed a similar course: *Esmeralda* is presumably based on Victor Hugo's *Notre Dame de Paris,* while *Cleopatra* may have been inspired by Pushkin ("Egyptian Nights") or Gautier. Massenet and Tchaikovsky, Kuzmin points out, reserved their creative sympathy for their female characters; a woman is the central figure in each of these unfinished operas. Furthermore, in his two heroines Kuzmin presents the two faces of Woman as she appeared in the iconography of the Decadence: the voluptuous, cruel, bejewelled temptress, the Salome who dances in Moreau's paintings and Beardsley's drawings, and the Ophelia-like child-woman who glides somnambulistically from the canvases of the Pre-Raphaelites into the plays of Maeterlinck. Kuzmin's affiliations with Art Nouveau, in particular with the Munich school, are made abundantly clear in his novel *Wings,* that breviary of estheticism in Russia.

Though Kuzmin's natural allegiance was to Mozart and the *opéra comique,* as a committed esthete he could hardly fail to pay tribute to the supreme magnus of the age, in Mallarmé's words, "the threatening peak of the absolute to be revealed after the disappearance of the clouds, glittering up there, naked and alone"—Richard Wagner. There is surely a paradox in the sway which Wagner's heroic creations exerted over the etiolated *fin de siècle;* one is put in mind of Max Beerbohm's caricature of Browning, pink-cheeked, plump and full of vulgar energy, surrounded by his pale and languid "esthetic" admirers—a beetroot ringed with wilting lilies. Certainly, the earnest and rather banal Wagnerian discussions in which the characters of *Wings* frequently engage are apt to strain the patience of a modern reader; they are, however, symptomatic of the period (it is interesting that in a letter of 1907, two years after the writing of *Wings,* Kuzmin includes Wagner, along with Beethoven and, oddly, Schumann in a list of his musical dislikes). Wagner it is who lurks behind Kuzmin's early ambition to create a grand *Gesamtkunstwerk* in which music, poetry, dance and the visual arts would combine to embody the credo of St. Petersburg estheticism as it was formulated by the World of Art group. Kuzmin was a dedicated "world of arter" (*miriskusnik*) whose esthetic views were formed in the ambience of Diagilev's circle.

The composer Ugo in *Wings* envisions a work encompassing the novel's themes in mythological guise—the Argonauts, Prometheus, Pasiphae, Icarus, Phaeton, Ganymede—culminating ecstatically in a scene which presents "through a palpitating mist the forty-eight positions of human coupling from the Indian *manuels érotiques,*" after which "everything begins spinning in a double orbit, each in its own sphere, in ever-widening circles, faster and faster, until all outlines merge into one and the whole whirling mass takes shape, becoming suddenly still above the glistening sea and the treeless, yellow, sun-beaten cliffs as the colossal, radiant figure of Zeus-Dionysus-Helios." While it contains nothing quite so *outré* as this, Kuzmin's first published attempt at drama—and indeed his first published work—**The History of the Knight d'Alessio (*Istoriia rytsaria d'Alessio*)**, which appeared in *Green Miscellany* (*Zelenyi sbornik*) in 1905, is hardly less grandiose in scope, ranging from early Renaissance Italy to a sultan's harem in Smyrna, a courtesan's palazzo in Venice, a crusader's tent in Palestine, the monastic community of the Thebaid and, finally, a Masonic temple. The play is subtitled "dramatic poem in eleven tableaux," but it is significant that Kuzmin's friend, the dramatist and theatrical historian Evgeny Znosko-Borovsky, refers to it as a "libretto." *The History of the Knight d'Alessio* is certainly a curious concoction; as Blok observed, the restless hero is a mixture of Faust, Don Juan and Hamlet, while other discernable influences include *Peer Gynt, Tannhäuser, Die Zauberflöte,* the "Little Tragedies" of Pushkin (in particular, *The Stone Guest*) and *The Tempest;* and no doubt other things besides.

It would be easy to dismiss this immature work out of hand: it is derivative, it is poorly constructed, the blank verse is not immune from bathos (a world away from the seemingly casual mastery of the blank verse in *The Trout Breaks the Ice,* written some twenty years later), and it might well be objected that *The History of the Knight d'Alessio* looks backward to the moribund and untheatrical poetic drama of the Romantics rather than forward to the theater of the Symbolists. Nevertheless, both as an early attempt to break loose from the constructions of the realistic theater (it deserves to be ranked alongside comparable—and hardly more successful—attempts by Bryusov, Vyacheslav Ivanov, Balmont and Bely) and as a work containing the seeds of much in the later Kuzmin, it deserves some attention.

The History of the Knight d'Alessio appears to have been written almost concurrently with Kuzmin's first novel, *Wings;* and the two works would have been published side by side in the pages of the *Green Miscellany,* had not the sexual unorthodoxy of *Wings* proved too alarming for the collection's editors. Novel and play are virtually "twins," imposing similar patterns on similar themes. Both are deeply autobiographical in a way which is alien to the impassive art of the later Kuzmin; both are flawed by too immediate an involvement on the author's part which prevents personal concerns and urgencies from being completely resolved in artistic form (there is a grain of truth in [Blok's] gibe that *Wings* was the *What Is to Be Done* of its day.) *Wings* and *The History of the Knight d'Alessio,* it is clear, reflect the wanderings, the spiritual quest of the author's own troubled—and sometimes desperate—youth. Astorre and Vanya, the somewhat passive protagonists of, respectively, *The History of the Knight d'Alessio* and *Wings,* are led through a great variety of experience and environment to eventual illumination; each of the three short parts of *Wings* is set in a different location and Vanya is subjected to all kinds of moral and cultural influences (Hellenism, Catholicism, the Old Believers, Shakespeare, Wagner, estheticism); Astorre, untrammelled by novelistic verisimilitude, is whirled by his guardian spirit from one corner of the globe to another. Episodes in the novel clearly parallel those in the play: Vanya's stay with the Old Believers corresponds to Astorre's visit to the Thebaid; the depraved Cibo, that Art Nouveau siren with her "mermaiden eyes," has a sister in Bianca, the coldly sensual Venetian courtesan who fails to seduce Astorre; Maria Dmitrievna, whose stifling embraces Vanya so unceremoniously rejects, has her counterpart in the lascivious Sultana, whose attentions all but bring about Astorre's ruin.

"Too late have I discovered that all women are shameless and frivolous, and that the best of the best, the pearl among pearls, is not worth the shoe of my sable steed"—such is the moral pointed by an old storyteller in the Islamic episode of *The History of the Knight d'Alessio,* and indeed the play's misogyny is hardly less obsessive than that of *Wings.* Kuzmin's Eros is a masculine one; for him there is no *"ewig Weibliche"* to help man transcend his brute nature. Yet, for all his delight in the senses, in delicate artifice, in the social round, Kuzmin's work is no less haunted than Blok's by the urge toward the transcendental, and just as in Blok's work the "Beautiful Lady"—the feminine principle—moves through a variety of guises, so the boy spirit (" . . . the open glance / Of greenish eyes, grave and tender, / A build something between boy and youth, / And curls more radiant than amber") who is Astorre's "servant and lord" will undergo many transformations, appearing now as the archangel-like figure of the Guide (*Vozhatyi*) in *Nets,* now as the mysterious dilletante Stroop in *Wings,* now as Antinous in the *Alexandrian Songs,* now as the remote and virginal figures who are the still center of the novel "trilogy" *The Quiet Sentinel* (*Tikhii strazh*), *Tender Joseph* (*Nezhnyi Iosif*) *The Dreamers* (*Mechtateli*) and finally as the "twin" of *The Trout Breaks the Ice,* that ravishing re-enactment of the Aristophanic myth.

The final scene of *The History of the Knight d'Alessio* is set in a Masonic temple and is strongly reminiscent of *Die Zauberflöte* (there are even "two youths with swords"). Astorre is admitted to the company of the elect: a voice asks, "Who made his soul ardent and winged, so that he thirsted after the light before he became pure?" and the chorus responds, "A boy spirit touched him with his lips and his soul became ardent and winged, and the kisses of women became cloying to him . . . " The play's homosexual idealism, expressed in this earnest ritualism, is akin to that of Stefan George, one of the few modern German writers whom Kuzmin admired. Looking at his first and last published works, one is struck by Kuzmin's faithfulness to the spiritual quest and to the idea of his beloved Plotinus that man is doomed to spiritual death unless he undertakes an eternal pilgrimage in search of Beauty, which is Truth.

If *The History of the Knight d'Alessio* cannot be considered an artistic success, it is a work which the student of Kuzmin will find interesting as a storehouse of themes and motifs developed in later work.

Between the appearance of *The History of the Knight d'Alessio* in 1905 and the publication of a number of short plays by Kuzmin in 1907 an event occurred which was to have far-reaching significance for the development of the Russian theater. The revolt against the "unneeded truth" (Bryusov's phrase) of Stanislavskian stage naturalism which had for some time been apparent in the Symbolists' call for a new, non-realistic theater, found a leader in the person of Vsevolod Meyerhold; invited by the idealistic and much-admired actress Vera Komissarzhevskaya to take over the directorship of her theater, Meyerhold at last had the opportunity to mount stylized and experimental productions. The two indisputable artistic success of the opening phase of this momentous theatrical partnership were the production of Maeterlinck's *Soeur Beatrice* (first given on November 22, 1906) and Blok's *The Fairground Booth* (Balaganchik), which received its premiere on December 30 of the same year.

Kuzmin, who would no doubt have agreed with Wilde that nature imitates art, in **Wings** compares an Italian garden at twilight to the set for the 1904 Moscow Art Theater production of Maeterlinck's *L'Intérieur.* Maeterlinck's name is scarcely incidental in the context of Kuzmin's novel; the Belgian Symbolist enjoyed a brief but intense vogue at the beginning of the century, and his plays were seen by the Russian avant-garde as prototypes of the new theater which they wished to create. Maeterlinck's plays for a few years provided the Russian theater with its greatest challenge: how was this musical, static and highly formalized drama to be staged. Clearly the carefully wrought realism of the Moscow Art Theater, up to this time the most "revolutionary" movement in the Russian theater, would not do. In his production of a trio of Maeterlinck's playlets (one of them is referred to above), Stanislavsky made a brave effort (but, it is generally agreed, unsuccessful) to find a non-naturalistic style. Stanislavsky failed, it may be surmised, because his attempt at stylization lacked conviction and consistency; the set for *Les aveugles,* for example, combined "stylized decorative monumentality in the spirit of Munich Art Nouveau with the naturalistic solidity of certain forms."

Meyerhold was of the opinion that Stanislavsky's production failed because it lacked the "vague, dim tones of impressionism" and the voices of the actors were without the "mystery and gentleness of an implied world of fantasy." In his own production of Maeterlinck's *La mort de Tintagiles,* undertaken while he was director of the short-lived experimental studio attached to the Moscow Art Theater in 1905 and never publicly performed, Meyerhold matched the play's deathward drift, its languid, hypnotic rhythms and paucity of movement with a style of sparse, deliberate gesture, with the actors often in profile, suggesting the carefully composed groups of an antique bas-relief; formalized movement was complemented by formalized speech, measured, unemphatic and drained of all expressiveness, each syllable falling, in Meyerhold's own memorable phrase, like a pebble into a deep well. Such was the genesis of the so-called "static theater" (*nepodvizhnyi teatr*) in which Meyerhold attempted to resolve the contradition of two-dimensional backdrop and three-dimensional actors by "flattening" his actors. This style was put to effective use in the production of *Soeur Beatrice,* like Kuzmin's **The Comedy of Eudoxia of Heliopolis (Komediia o Evdokii iz Geliopoliia)** a play on the favorite *fin de siècle* theme of the harlot-saint; it was said that those who participated in this production "did not act but performed a solemn ritual," and surviving photographs convey something of this rapt devotional atmosphere.

It was Blok's *The Fairground Booth,* however, which gave the anti-realists their first great victory and pointed toward the future. Blok's play, with its constantly shifting planes, its convoluted irony, its conjuring with identity, its air of enigmatic masquerade and deft manipulation of *Commedia dell'arte* masks, and, above all, its immense theatrical vitality, afforded the opportunity for just such a collaboration of the arts as the esthetes envisaged. Sapunov, an intimate of Kuzmin's, designed the sets and costumes, while Kuzmin's own music, "piquant, highly spiced, disturbing and voluptuous" to the ears of [G. Chulkov], made its own contribution to the evening's success; at the end of the performance, not only Blok and Meyerhold, but also Sapunov and Kuzmin were called on stage by that part of the audience which favored the new theater—an indication of the new position of artist and composer as partners rather than subordinates of director and dramatist (Stanislavsky made use of competent, dim artists who did as they were told, Meyerhold preferred to work with painters of brilliance and strongly developed individuality, such as Sapunov, Sudeikin and Golovin).

The Fairground Booth made a deep impression on Kuzmin: "On the subject of remuneration for the music to *The Fairground Booth,* I simply don't know what to say to you," he wrote in a letter to Meyerhold dated December 22, 1906, "I'm so fond of this work of Alexander Alexsandrovich, value your talents—his, your own and Nikolai Nikolaevich's [Sapunov's]—so highly, am so genuinely devoted to your theater. . . . " He learned, no doubt, from the irony and concision of Blok's play, and Meyerhold's use of puppet-like effects (like the hero of Stravinsky's *Petrushka,* the personages of *The Fairground Booth* are tragically arrested between doll and human being; the tragic puppet is a powerful theme of the pre-revolutionary years) must have interested him greatly. Maeterlinck himself had intended certain of his plays for performance by puppets, and Kuzmin too was attracted by the puppet theater, as well as by other such "minor" forms as the circus and, later, the American silent film comedy; he was attracted less perhaps by the possibilities for grotesque and even sinister effects (which certainly interested Meyerhold) than by the virtuosity of technique, the laconism and speed to be found in this "little world of irony, fantasy and satire." Significantly, Kuzmin's little play **Mary's Tuesday (Vtornik Meri),** published in Petrograd in 1921, is described as performable by "live or wooden dolls."

Kuzmin, unusually, is a writer whom it is illuminating to consider in the context of the visual arts. He was closely associated with three Russian painters whose work is distinguished by elegant stylization, a nostalgia for eighteenth century France, for the age of Catherine and for the 1830s, a pervasive eroticism and a deliberate theatricality—Konstantin Somov, Sergei Sudeikin and Nikolai Sapunov. The most refined of these, Somov, who painted a well known portrait of Kuzmin, inspired the *fete galante* poems in **Nets** as well as an admiring essay in **Conventions (Uslovnosti).** With both Sudeikin and Sapunov, Kuzmin was bound by ties of intimate friendship (Sapunov is the "drowned artist" who appears among the poet's ghostly visitors—old friends and lovers—in the "second prologue" to **The Trout Breaks the Ice**) as well as by professional collaboration: both painters designed sets and costumes for a number of plays and operettas by Kuzmin. One senses here an extraordinary unity of vision, so that it becomes impossible to say whether the poet is trying to give verbal expression to the painters' world, or whether they in their turn are seeking to transform his words into color and form. The following two passages describe the work of the two artists, but could not they equally well be applied to the world of Kuzmin's plays? Of Sudeikin: "Everything is festive, carefree, tender, amusing, caressing, and at the same time insubstantial, ephemeral and of an almost doll-like artificiality . . . even his fluttering ballerinas, even his bucolic sheep, his trees and china figurines seem like fragile imitations." Of Sapunov: "These people are dolls who are ridiculous in their merriment because it is not given to them to know why they live and for what reason they make merry. Deliberately, they are berouged, deliberately, they are decked out in gaudy finery. With unconscious submissiveness they allow the Director Life to pull their strings." Sudeikin painted "puppet people" and of Sapunov it was said that he viewed life as "a fairground booth of living automata." Sapunov, we are told, "wore large, extravagant neckties, dyed his whiskers and painted his lips;" Kuzmin too was known to embellish nature—not only, we may conjecture, *pour épater le bourgeois,* but also to transform life itself into a theatrical spectacle.

Much of Kuzmin's work for the theater had the nature of divertissement—as light, fragile and evanescent as the beauty which he celebrates in the *Alexandrian Songs:* pantomimes, ballets, masquerades, pastorals, children's plays. No theme, it seems, was too trivial, no occasion too insignificant;"The best test of talent is to write about nothing, as Anatole France, the greatest artist of our day, knows so well how to do," such was his *profession de foi,* and many of his theater pieces are just such airy children of nothingness; some, indeed, have dissolved back into their parent element, leaving behind them nothing but their names—what shall we ever know about *Alice Who Was Afraid of Mice (Alisa, kotoraia boialas' myshei), The Fairy, the Bassoon and the Stage-hand (Feia, fagot i mashinist), The Phenomenal American Girl (Fenomenal'naia amerikanka)* and *The Mirror of Maids (Zerkalo dev)*?

On October 29, 1916 a special evening was arranged at the cafe-cabaret The Players' Rest (*Prival Komediantov*) to celebrate the tenth anniversary of Kuzmin's literary debut. Casting a retrospective eye, with this pretext, over his work in the theater, the drama critic of *Apollo* expressed regret that while Kuzmin the poet and prosaist had received due critical appreciation, "his activity as a dramatist has been left in the shade." For all their mastery of dialogue, their skilful deployment of actors, their extreme elegance and scenic grace, Kuzmin's plays had not found the favor they deserve with the theater-going public. Kuzmin, the critic concluded, "occupies the leading place in our theater of underground classics, whose plays can be put on only in some 'Waning Moon' of a cellar or some 'Old Dovecote' of an attic." Little theaters, cabarets, domestic theatricals—these were the not inappropriate setting for Kuzmin's plays; and if all this smacks of dilettantism, "dilettante" was a word which Kuzmin would never have shied away from, using it as he did in its true sense

of "disinterested love of art, discerning amateur;" was it not, after all, a group of discerning amateurs at the Mantuan court who had by a happy accident invented opera?

The first plays to be written by Kuzmin after *The History of the Knight d'Alessio,* and the first to be distinctively Kuzminian, are to be found in a slim volume entitled *Three Plays* (1907), which contains *The Dangerous Precaution (Opasnaia predostorozhnost') Two Shepherds and a Nymph in a Hut (Dva pastukha i nimfa v khizhine)* and *The Choice of a Bride (Vybor nevesty)*. These entertainments, delicate miniatures which mingle verse with prose and songs with dancing, are described respectively as a "comedy with singing," a "pastoral for a masquerade" and a "mime ballet" and suggest nothing so much as divertissements to be presented to some rococo court. A rather dissolute court perhaps, since the most amusing of these playlets, *The Dangerous Precaution,* was found by the censorship to be so provokingly naughty that the little volume was sentenced to confiscation.

One may wonder why *Wings,* which had appeared in the previous year and was no less open in its advocacy of homosexual love, should have escaped a similar fate; perhaps because the novel was a "serious" treatment of "the problem," while the play cheerfully declines to recognize that a "problem" exists. *The Dangerous Precaution* is an adroit minuet of sexual identities which pokes fun at conventional morality. At the play's center is the androgynous figure, the boy-girl so frequently encountered in the art and writing of the *fin de siècle;* Floridal is imagined by the young Prince Rene to be a girl, Dorita, in disguise; Rene's betrothed, Klorinda, finds herself neglected for the supposed "Dorita," and begs her "rival" to find a means of returning Rene's affections to her; Floridal, disturbed to find himself attracted to Rene, convinces him that he is not a girl in a charming song:

> Are women's cheeks as red
> As mine are?
> Are women's bodies as supple
> As mine is?
> Are women's handclasps as firm
> As mine are?
> Are women's embraces as passionate
> As mine are?

Rene declares that whether Floridal is a boy or a girl his feelings are unchanged; the two exchange a prolonged kiss, Rene calls for a lively English jig ("not the rustle of skirts, but the stamping of feet"), and the play ends on a note of unbounded merriment. In the figure of the courtier-minstrel Gaetano (did Blok remember this name when he came to write *The Rose and the Cross?*) Kuzmin voices the esthete's disdain for hypocritical bourgeois conventions; rebuked for an "indecorous" song in which he praises the charms of young men as well as those of women, Gaetano boldly counters: "I am a free poet; decorum is a matter convention—*ergo:* my verses avoid what is conventional—that's one. Apart from which, they tell the truth—that's two. Apart from which, they have measure, grace and wit."

The playlets of *Three Plays* represent a conscious attempt to return to the traditions of the Russian eighteenth century theater over the head, as it were, of the nineteenth century; *Two Shepherds . . . ,* for example, recaptures with considerable art the artlessness of the Russian pastoral operetta. In *The Dangerous Precaution,* however, one is also conscious of a faint but unmistakable wafting from the world of Shakespeare's late romances: the "sea coast in Bohemia" kind of setting, the equivocal sexuality of the hero-heroine and even the names of characters such as Postumy (Posthumus in *Cymbeline*) and Floridal (Florizel in *The Winter's Tale*). In considering Kuzmin as a dramatist, it is worth remembering his deep and abiding interest in Shakespeare; *Romeo and Juliet* plays some part in Vanya's awakening in *Wings,* the Sonnets are both decor and subtext in *The Trout Breaks the Ice,* while Shakespeare, together with Apuleius and E. T. A. Hoffmann (two other Kuzmin favorites) is one of the presiding spirits of the lyrico-musical triptych *The Grove (Lesok);* in later years Kuzmin was to devote much time to translating the great Elizabethan, either alone (*King Lear*) or in collaboration (the two parts of *Henry IV*). It might be argued that, for all his fellow-feeling for the miniature and the lighthearted in art, he is saved, in his best work at least, from falling into mere preciosity by the magnetic influence which the "indelibly vital" works of supreme art—Shakespeare, Mozart, Pushkin—never ceased to exercise over him. It is Pushkin whom Kuzmin brings inevitably to mind in his ability to absorb and re-embody an extraordinary variety of cultures—an ability for which terms such as "stylization" and "pastiche" seem both insufficient and ungrateful. Like Pushkin, Kuzmin is a poet of culture, like Pushkin, his center is esthetic, like Pushkin he seeks always to "clarify his darkness," and if any Russian writer breathes the air of the blithe and crystalline zone which is Pushkin's, that writer is surely Kuzmin.

The three *Comedies (Komedii)* published in 1908 ("mysteries" is perhaps a more adequate translation than "comedies"), have been the most admired of Kuzmin's dramatic works: Blok praised the "sparkling prose" and "airy verse" of *The Comedy of Eudoxia of Heliopolis,* pronouncing it "the most perfect creation in the field of lyrical drama in Russia;" D. S. Mirsky found *The Comedy of Alexis, Man of God (Komediia o Aleksee cheloveke Bozh'em)* to be "the most exquisite of all" of Kuzmin's plays as well as "especially typical of his manner of treating sacred things" [see excerpt dated 1926]; the scholar-esthete Pavel Muratov praised the life-like quality of the same play's depiction of early Christian Rome; while the drama critic of *Apollo* previously referred to was of the opinion that "rarely does one encounter the wonderful equipoise which we observe in this lonely, tragically belated attempt to create a liturgical drama for our day. The holy naiveté of the narrator of medieval miracles is here joined with the refined mastery of a French Renaissance poet."

The equipoise of which the critic speaks is between irony and piety, and it is indeed maintained throughout these enigmatic and perfectly achieved works. More than one commentator has pointed to this irony: Blok speaks of *Eudoxia* as "infused with the most refined poisons of that irony which is so characteristic of Kuzmin's work;" Znosko-Borovsky draws attention to the "pious irony" with which Kuzmin treats his saintly ascetics. It is a sunny

irony, far removed from the bitterness of the disillusioned idealist which we find in Blok's *The Fairground Booth.* Kuzmin's master here is the most urbane of ironists, Anatole France, his favorite contemporary writer and the "great teacher" of *Wings. Eudoxia* clearly takes its theme, tone and setting from France's Alexandrian novel *Thais,* with its courtesan turned saint and sceptical yet not unsympathetic depiction of early Christian fervor; Kuzmin, however, does not venture on the final triumphant irony of *Thais,* the reversal of roles by which saint becomes sinner and sinner saint. Kuzmin's success in embodying saintliness (a notoriously difficult task) can be gauged if we compare *Eudoxia* with Maeterlinck's *Soeur Béatrice,* another play on the theme of the saintly harlot, which, unsharpened by irony, slips into the mawkishness of Catholic repository art.

It may strike us as odd that Kuzmin, the passionate advocate of sexual fulfilment in *Wings* ("Asceticism is essentially a highly unnatural phenomenon, and the supposed continence of certain animals is pure fiction") should in these plays present the achievement of grace through the mortification of the flesh: Alexis flees on his nuptial night, leaving his bride a virgin; Martinian treads hot coals underfoot lest he should surrender to the wiles of a courtesan; Eudoxia, the "rose of Heliopolis," leaves riches and lovers to achieve sainthood, converting the infatuated youth who attempts to lure her back to worldly life. The paradox, however, is more apparent than real, since the sexual relationships rejected are all heterosexual ones; in *Wings* (and *The History of the Knight d'Alessio*) heterosexual relationships are presented as an impediment to spiritual growth.

Two connected leitmotivs frequently encountered in Kuzmin's work sound repeatedly in these dramas: wise passivity (Kuzmin does not like "doers") and a joyful acceptance of the divine wisdom hidden in the workings of fate:

> Only he who does not think ahead can be joyful.
> **(Alexis)**
>
> . . . . .
>
> Howsoever we may strive, God's Will
> Guides invisibly the fates of men.
> Swift is our lot, and finds us out.
> **(Alexis)**
>
> . . . . .
>
> Fate forges the chain of events
> At the beginning the end cannot be seen [. . .]
> The Lord has hidden the end from us—
> He is unknown to us, unfathomed.
> God gives the cross, God gives the crown.
> And we accept submissively.
> **(Eudoxia)**

Self-willed activism is represented by the figure of Mastridia in *Alexis* (the dreadful Natasha of *The Three Sisters* in Roman garb):

> But what we desire shall surely be,
> To patience and will the victory!
> The wise man casts his line betimes,

The sluggard sleeps till lunchtime.

(Alexis)

Mastridia's self-will is lack of grace; she neither understands nor accepts the miracle of her husband's sainthood.

The idea of a religious drama was one close to the hearts of the more mystically inclined of the Russian Symbolists (and indeed to European Symbolism in general). Bely asked: "Does not the musical spirit, the symbolism of modern dramas indicate the aspiration of the drama to become mystery? The drama was born of the mystery. To the mystery it is destined to return." Vyacheslav Ivanov's notion of *community* (*sobornost'*) in the theater, with actors and spectators uniting as in a religious ritual, is also of some relevance here. Yet the efforts of Kuzmin and Remizov to revive the medieval mystery play as a popular form could hardly be other than foredoomed; there is more hopefulness than real conviction in Kuzmin's assertion in his review of a production of Remizov's *The Tragedy of Judas* (*Tragediia o Iude*) that "of course this is a fine popular show and not in the least an esthetic exercise or a laboratory experiment." (pp. 243-57)

"The Venice of Goldoni, Gozzi and Longhi" is the setting which Kuzmin specifies for **The Venetian Madcaps** ([Pavel Muratov, in his *Images of Italy,* 1924] incidentally, had dwelt on Longhi, "the last of Venice's painters" and his evocations of the masked revelry of the Rigotto), his own drama of jealousy, murder, fate and retribution. Although it may be said that the Venetian theme was "in the air" at the time (Blok, for example, was in 1913 contemplating a drama set in eighteenth century Venice with "cards and candles"), it would appear that there is more than a chance connection between **Madcaps** and the Meyerhold *Masquerade.* Kuzmin wrote his Venetian play in 1912, although it was not performed until two years later; now it was at this very time that he must have been intimately acquainted with Meyerhold's plans for *Masquerade,* for we are told that "all the music for *Masquerade* was composed by M. A. Kuzmin and then two years later, new music was commissioned from A. K. Glazunov." It is difficult to resist the suspicion that **Madcaps** was not only an offshoot of *Masquerade,* but also an attempt to steal some of Meyerhold's thunder.

For all that it was the product of a passing vogue, **Madcaps** is an unmistakably Kuzminian piece. The theme of a male partnership endangered by a female interloper which appears with such obsessive frequency in Kuzmin's work (**Wings, The Dangerous Precaution, Two Shepherds and a Nymph in a Hut,** "Aunt Sonya's Sofa," **The Trout Breaks the Ice,** etc.) is here, for once, brought to a tragic denouement; in the figure of Finette, the sado-masochistic seductress dear to the Symbolist imagination finds memorably icy embodiment. As for the Count, beneath his domino he is the last of the St. Petersburg dandies, uncompromising in an estheticism which recognizes no laws but those of beauty and caprice ("I, who live for dreams and beauty and care no more for truth than I do for the stone which paves the embankment"); he is doomed and knows it.

Madcaps reminds us of Kuzmin's admiration for Blok's *The Fairground Booth;* the episode in which Finette is

greeted by Narcisetto as though she were Death clearly reflects a similar moment in Blok's play, when the Mystics address Colombina in much the same terms. The eighteenth century setting gives Kuzmin ample opportunity to indulge his gift as a pasticheur, and the Abbe's little poem looks forward to the Russian version of Tredyakovsky's French poems which Kuzmin was to make in 1932. The Gondolier's song bears what is perhaps more than a chance resemblance to the verse "frontispice" (*sic*) with which Henri de Régnier (a great favorite of the Russian esthetes and an undoubted influence on Kuzmin both as poet and prosaist) prefaced his 1912 book on Venice, *Images Vénitiennes:*

> L'eau luit; le marbre s'ébrèche;
> Les rames se font écho,
> Quand on passe à l'ombre fraiche
> Du Palais Rezzonico.

The Venetian Madcaps received its first performance on February 23, 1914 at the Moscow mansion of some wealthy patrons of arts, E. P. and V. V. Nosov. Kuzmin himself composed the music and Sudeikin designed the sets and costumes. The cast included a number of celebrated beauties and *femmes fatales,* among them Genrietta Girshman, the subject of Serov's well known portrait, M. S. Morozova, the adored "Nadezhda Zarina" of Bely's poem *The First Tryst* (*Pervoe svidanie*), and Olga Glebova-Sudeikina, the artist's wife, with her "wonderful golden braids like Melisande's," the "Putanitsa Psikheia" of Akhmatova's *A Poem Without a Hero.* Though amateur, the production was both stylish and extravagant; to [Arthur Lur'e] it seemed in retrospect a "magical spectacle." Some of this magic has been preserved in the beautiful limited edition of 1915, in which some of Sudeikin's costume designs are reproduced. (pp. 261-63)

> *Michael Green, "Mikhail Kuzmin and the Theater," in* Russian Literature Triquarterly, *Vol. 7, 1973, pp. 243-66.*

Neil Granoien   (essay date 1975)

[*In the following excerpt, Granoien portrays the literary climate in which* Wings *was published.*]

Perhaps the literary world really was waiting impatiently for Valery Bryusov's latest opus, but if that was the case, it would simply have to wait a bit longer. Bryusov had been tardy in submitting his manuscript of *The Fiery Angel* to the Symbolist journal *The Scales,* and its place in the eleventh number for 1906 was taken by Mikhail Kuzmin's novel **Wings.** Whether **Wings** was printed as an example of what Bryusov called the "new art which carries within itself the best energies for spiritual life on earth," or whether it was a last-minute substitution to keep subscribers at bay is not known. Whichever the case, there must have been some uneasy feelings at *The Scales*— Kuzmin's novel had been rejected by *The Green Miscellany,* an anthology of new writers in which he had made his literary debut the previous year, and was certain to provoke a reaction with its homosexual theme. As it turned out, the appearance of **Wings** was a positive scandal. In 1907 *The Scales* published a missive from Zinaida Gippius which she signed with her critic's pen-name "Anton the Extreme." "Our literature has become completely erotic," she fumed, ". . . . or rather not erotic, but simply pornographic. Given our general lack of culture, which has reached epidemic proportions and pervades the very atmosphere, it is not surprising that our erotic nakedness has been bathed in a stream of patent hooliganism. . . . *The Scales* repudiates the hooligan in Gorkian rags—but is it so difficult to discern the hooligan in the Alexandrian toga of a new style 'ex' when he's wearing a smoking jacket?" *The Scales'* reply was printed immediately following:

> We wholeheartedly share the "faith" of Anton the Extreme "in the future of Russian culture," and we are prepared to echo him in saying, "There do exist the seeds of that culture! . . . . They must exist!" But we feel that Anton the Extreme is gravely mistaken when, castigating the enemies of that future culture, he includes among them the author of another novel "which stands beside *The Thirty-Three Abominations.*" He is, of course, referring to M. Kuzmin and his novel *Wings,* printed for the first time in *The Scales.* We are profoundly convinced that M. Kuzmin marches in the forward ranks of those who are fighting for the very same culture as Anton the Extreme. It is to the cultural activist (and not only to the talented poet in Kuzmin) that *The Scales* has opened its pages in the past and will continue to open them in the future.

By the time of the appearance in 1908 of *Nets,* Kuzmin's first volume of poetry which contained intimate erotic scenes of an apparent autobiographical nature, he had acquired a fame which, in the words of Alexander Blok, "I wouldn't wish anyone." Feelings against Kuzmin rose to the point where an official boycott of the man and his works was planned by certain of the Petersburg *literati.* "Perhaps you don't know," he wrote to his friend Vsevolod Meyerhold, "that some of those who will be participating in the *soirée* on November 5th have declared an official boycott against me. A. A. Blok, my musician friends and my artist friends will refuse in that case to take part in the *soirée* in order not to demonstrate any sympathy for the boycott by their silence."

The uproar over *Wings* continued for many years, probably due in part to the several editions Kuzmin authorized. Tediously similar expressions of moral indignation followed one after the other:

> Never before had it occurred to anyone to propagandize openly this unnatural vice, no one had dared to idealize it, but Kuzmin's blasphemous brush did not tremble at bringing this doctrine to life and to belles-lettres.

> . . . . .

> . . . . gross lack of taste. . . . Kuzmin has lost all sense of proportion and has descended to the level of boulevard-novel pornography.

Kuzmin survived this difficult period and went on to become an accomplished stylist in prose and, although widely unrecognized, one of the finest Russian poets of the twentieth century. That he emerged without scars, howev-

er, is perhaps doubtful—he was a sensitive and fragile man who seemed always to be seeking the protection of someone sturdier. The huge audiences that notoriety draws must have dismayed him; his works were intended rather for an intimate circle of sympathetic friends whose praise and assurances had more meaning for him than general acclaim.

It was among friends that *Wings* found its defenders; Blok thought it was "wonderful," but unfortunately didn't say why. Konstantin Somov, one of the younger artists among those associated with *The World of Art,* was so enraptured by the novel that he would stop people on the street to tell them about it. Admittedly, the acclaim of friends is never without bias, but there was perhaps more than mere friendship behind it. G. G. Shmakov has suggested that Blok was sympathetic to the "spiritual experiences" in the novel which illustrate "the possibility of the spiritual rebirth of a man concealed in a love of beauty and in the emotional cognition of it." Blok's life-long search for the solace of sublime ideas in a harsh and unfeeling world is well known and is perhaps the most meaningful point at which he and Kuzmin crossed paths.

Wings is largely autobiographical, describing in turn the convention-ridden bourgeois family life of Petersburg, the quaintness and piety of Old Believers in the trans-Volga region and the esthetic inspiration of Italy, all of which played a significant role in the author's own life. And the self-identity and fulfillment found by Vanya Smurov—the youthful hero of the piece—in the love of beauty and the beauty of love are the essence of Kuzmin's esthetic and moral credo. To a literary world bounded on one side by critical realism and on the other by Symbolism Kuzmin offered the alternative of estheticism in its most all-embracing form—that is, not merely as an appreciation of beauty for its own sake, but as an entire philosophy of life in which self-improvement is based on the higher notions of existence as they are found in beauty. And art with its emotion, aspiration and activity offers a fascinatingly human display of that beauty. From the ever-changing importunings of realism—and of reality itself, for that matter—estheticism offered the solace of the eternal and the inspirational. Symbolism had also tended in this direction, but its meaningless eschatological speculations, alienation and self-depreciation were a disappointment to more sensitive natures. Adherents of *fin de siecle* estheticism formed no real movement but rather shared a world of their own making founded on a general affinity in taste and ideas. Contemplation of beauty in the arts and in life provided them with a means of self-culture and an escape from despised materialism and moralism to the consolation of intellectual pursuits and the immediate pleasure of art.

An often-heard criticism is that Kuzmin had pretentiously littered the pages of *Wings* with such familiar names as Wagner, Klinger, Thomas, Segantini, Debussy, Nietzsche and France in a vain attempt to conjure an obsolete age of esthetic interests and create in his novel a superficial atmosphere of culture. But if the philosophy of *Wings* appealed to the Alexander Bloks, then perhaps this evocation of the recent cultural past was dear to the Konstantin

Somovs, for it kindled vivid memories of the first of the *avant-garde* Russian journals, *The World of Art.*

Kuzmin was at least loosely associated with *The World of Art,* although Leon Bakst's biographer pictures him hard at work in the journal's literary section; if this is true, he never received any credit for his labors. He was, however, a friend of the journal's four founders—Sergei Diaghileff, Alexandre Benois, Dmitri Filosofov and Walter Nouvel, whom he met not long after leaving the St. Petersburg Conservatory of Music—he had spent three unsuccessful years there studying composition. Kuzmin knew them formally through the "Evenings of Modern Music," a group of music lovers who met regularly to hear the latest foreign and domestic productions, and decidedly less formally through "Hafiz' Tavern," an intimate group dedicated to drinking and revelry, each of whose members was given a nickname from antiquity. Kuzmin was "Antinous." There is a description in *Wings* of the period:

> How he loved this spacious room with its translucent greens, haunted by echoes of Rameau and Debussy. . . . these arguments; these late bachelor suppers, convivial with wine and lighthearted talk; this study lined with books from floor to ceiling, where they read Marlowe and Swinburne; this bedroom with its toilet stand and its garland of terra-cotta fauns dancing on a background of bright green; this dining room with its coppery hues; these tales of Italy, Egypt, India; this ardent responsiveness to all poignantly lovely things, whatever age or clime had brought them forth; these strolls about the Islands; these discussions which at once fascinated and disturbed. . . .

When *The World of Art* began to appear, Kuzmin was drawing to the end of a fifteen-year course of self-education, during which he had studied cultural phenomena as diverse as Franciscan poetry and Nietzsche. He must have been particularly appreciative at that time of the display of famous names in the journal, many of whom eventually found their way into his prose and poetry. (pp. 393-98)

Of course it is difficult to say exactly what Kuzmin felt about the artists he mentions in *Wings,* especially as their names occur casually in conversations. One can do no more than guess what he might have liked, given the man's general views. In Thoma, it was perhaps his works on religious and classical themes done in the studied devout manner of the Nazarenes, rather than the landscapes and interiors which led Grabar to call him the most German of German painters. In Klinger, it might have been his mythological allegories of passion and his revelations of the artist's path and artistic inspiration, rather than the nightmarish visions for which he is commonly remembered. Gionvanni Segantini is the only artist who has a specific work mentioned in the novel—*L'Amore alla Fonte della Vita*—and from this one might conclude that Kuzmin felt more in tune with him than with the others. Indeed Segantini's statements of love, both in paint and print, he no doubt found enthralling. In an article on contemporary trends in European art Grabar quotes Segantini himself. "The joy of life is in knowing how to love. At the base of every good work of art lies love. Love is the source of beauty." And Grabar continues, "A love that is healthy, joyous, unhampered by any barriers, that is almost elemental, is what charms us in Segantini's art."

Attitudes vary among those at *The World of Art* toward Franz Stuck, the master of the Munich Secessionists who is mentioned perhaps more frequently in the journal than any other artist. Diaghileff remarked on his daring use of color. Grabar, once an enthusiast, felt that Stuck's appointment to the Academy and the constant adulation of the public had spoiled him and caused a marked decline from the brilliance of such earlier works as "Die Sunde," that transfixing vision of the fatal woman. It is possibly just such works as "Die Sunde" that aroused sufficient distaste in Kuzmin to make Stuck a commonplace of idle feminine gossip in *Wings.* The German artist no doubt represented for him the malady of the age, that is, the preoccupation with the lustful side of love and the infantile worship of the *femme fatale,* the most constant themes of decadent art. In an article printed in *The World of Art* the Polish playwright Stanislaw Przybyszewski described the sado-masochistic mania as it was seen most explicitly in the art of Felicien Rops: "Rops' woman is a terrible cosmic force. His woman is a woman who arouses a man's passion, shackles him to herself with perfidious caresses, breeds him to be a monogamist, sharpens his instincts, forces the element of his desires into new forms and injects him with the poison of satanic pain."

Rops' misogyny led paradoxically to his vulgar obsession with the feminine image. Out of Kuzmin's misogyny came a philosophical and artistic statement opposing the deleterious effects of man's love for woman to the edifying noble passion of Socrates. During his stay in Italy the hero of *Wings* is presented with the clinching argument. In an allegory of destructive passion a young Russian artist succumbs to the charms of an Italian *femme fatale* with green mermaiden eyes, whose wickedness is reminiscent of the women of the sixteenth century. This portrait, by the way, is remarkably like that of the Comtesse du Tremblay in Barbey D'Aurevilly's "The Story Behind a Game of Whist," from his tales of female monsters, *Les Diaboliques.* Kuzmin knew Barbey's words—he wrote an introduction to the Russian edition of *Dandyism and George Brummel*—and admired him for his exquisite prose, but this admiration could not have extended to the Frenchman's excesses. In fact, the description in *Wings* of a dissolute old Italian count bears a striking resemblance to Barbey himself.

As *The World of Art* was devoted primarily to the visual arts, little was said of music except in connection with the magic name of Wagner, whose "Art of the Future" provided exciting opportunities for the artist as well as the musician. Benois had long been an admirer of the great man and imparted his enthusiasm to his colleagues. Alexander Serov, the father of *The World of Art*'s most highly esteemed artist-associate, was called "the Russian Wagner"—he was an able conductor of his works, he had written a good deal on Wagner, and he had even sent his opera "Judith" to Bayreuth for approval.

Wagner's theoretical attempt in his "Art of the Future"

to recapture the magic of the Greek theater must surely have excited esthetic sensibilities at the time. Excerpts from Henri Lichtenberger's *Richard Wagner, poete et penseur,* printed in *The World of Art* in 1899, explain this appeal: "In the tragedy of Aeschylus and Sophocles poetry, music and the dance merged to charm the whole man, his senses, his sight and his hearing, as well as his mind. And in this merging each individual art form achieved the greatest results by virtue of this fruitful union." And of Wagner's melodies: "The musician's sphere of activity is sound—its nuances endlessly rising and falling, its timbre and intensity—all of which serve as a natural and precise outpouring of the various shades of pure emotion, of feeling itself, beyond the reasons that explain it or the circumstances that accompany it."

It is no wonder that the musician, the philosopher and the dilettante in *Wings* feel "prophetic tremors" when confronted with a spectacle like Venusberg. The merging of the arts into one sublime essence was a widely-entertained notion at the turn of the century—"All art constantly aspires to the condition of music," as Pater put it—and the gushing remarks of the characters in *Wings* were perhaps echoes of the inspired conversations among Kuzmin's friends. Such utterances occasionally made their way into print, as when a review of the latest offerings of the "Evenings of Modern Music" spoke of "the charming *Poemes des Montagnes* of Vincent D'Indy, which in their tenderness and inimitable elegance are reminiscent of the harmonious tints of Segantini's alpine landscapes." (On that same program was a work by Vladimir Rebikov who in the nineties had composed a piece for the piano inspired by Franz Stuck whose colleague Max Klinger had made a well-known series of etchings inspired by Brahms and—to complete the circle—later undertook a monument in Leipzig to Richard Wagner.)

Some of the comments on Wagner in Kuzmin's novel may go back to his student days, rather than to life among he *cognoscenti.* Wagner was reigning genius at the Conservatory, "an institution distinguished," according to Alfred Nurok, "by an architectural ugliness rare even for Petersburg."

Rimsky-Korsakov, from whom Kuzmin took lessons in composition in the early nineties, fell under Wagner's spell late in his career and admitted to a considerable influence in his own works, beginning with his opera "Mlada" in 1892. As Rimsky was such a recent convert to Wagner and as he was also the strict master of his pupils, one can easily imagine students exchanging the latest revelations with much the same enthusiasm as the budding Italian composers in *Wings* who ape Puccini "with their neckties and fat, beardless faces." Incidentally, a frequent visitor at the Conservatory in those days was surely Rimsky's young protege N. M. Shtrup, who no doubt lent his exotic surname to the principal player in Vanya Smurov's transformation.

In *Wings* Kuzmin offers two telling criticisms of the Wagnerian legends. He cannot bring himself to accept Tannhauser's eleventh-hour renunciation of the pleasures of beauty in favor of the duty and sacrifice of religious asceticism. This denial of the flesh is completely at odds with the esthete's goal of the beatific state attained by means of the senses. And the mystic link between love and death and the apotheosis of love in death—the theme of "Tristan and Isolde"—is wholly alien to Kuzmin. His metamorphosis through love can only be achieved in life. In most philosophies of estheticism there is a latent fear of death and a constant anxiety over the fragility and impermanence of worldy things. Each fleeting moment of life must be filled with images of beauty to attain that rapturous state where there is a continuous play of the senses upon the emotions. Kuzmin exhorts those who "go about like the blind, like the dead, when they might create for themselves a life burning with intensity in every moment, a life in which pleasure would be as poignant as if you had just come into the world and might die before the day were done. It is with such greed that we must fling ourselves upon life. Miracles crowd upon us at every step. . . . " And for Walter Pater, ". . . . to burn always with this hard, gemlike flame, to maintain this ecstasy, is success in life."

Diaghileff once described an esthete as one who is incorrigible in his insistence upon forgetting life and in his refusal to face it. Perhaps this rather imperious view suited the imposing person of the critic and entrepreneur for whom success in life was success itself. But the picture of the artist and the esthete as superior beings disdainful of the world would not have suited Kuzmin. He preferred to think of himself and the artist as joyous celebrants in the miraculous ritual of life, and *Wings* is a part of the liturgy. (pp. 401-404)

Neil Granoien, " 'Wings' and 'The World of Art'," in Russian Literature Triquarterly, *Vol. 11, 1975, pp. 393-405.*

Joachim T. Baer   (essay date 1976)

[*In the following essay, Baer examines prominent imagery and themes in* Alexandrian Songs.]

In 1908 Modest Gofman published an anthology entitled *Kniga o russkix poètax* that has been available as a reprint in the West since 1970. The value of Gofman's anthology to this day rests in the discriminating selection of representative Symbolist poets and their work, the compilation of brief critical assessments by various authors of each poet's original aspects, and in the short handwritten biographical sketches in which each poet says what he considers essential about himself. Here we read in the hand of Kuzmin:

> Modesty which behooves man and lack of space force me to limit myself to a sort of epitaph which might contain the following: "He lived for thirty years, he sang, he looked around, he loved and smiled." Only a little may be added by saying that my native town was Jaroslavl', by family background I belong to the nobility, my ancestors were French and my second home town has been Petersburg; that originally I was engaged in music and began to publish in 1905. Feelings of tender and grateful pride force me to mention that I received my first encouragement from V. Ja. Brjusov. Well, and that is all.

Aleksandrijskie pesni appeared first as part of Kuzmin's collection *Seti, pervaja kniga stixov* (1908). It was later republished separately by the Prometej Publishing House. After fifteen years of Symbolism in Russian poetry the opening lines to his first collection which focused on the simple joys of life and illustrated Kuzmin's concept of "beautiful clarity" were received as a new discovery: . . .

> Where are the words
> to catch a walk that tarries,
> Chablis on ice, fried buns, ripe agate-cherries:

The cycle, *Aleksandrijskie pesni,* consists of seven sections: Vstuplenie (Introduction), Ljubov' (Love), Ona (She), Mudrost' (Wisdom), Otryvki (Fragments), Kanobskie pesenki (Songs of Kanobus), and Zaključenie (Conclusion). The number of poems in each part varies, but their total is thirty-two. The first two poems in the Introduction are an invocation in free iambs to the marvelous world associated with the ancient Egyptian city, Alexandria. The poet's imagination derives sensuous and aesthetic pleasure from the recreation of a rich array of auditory, visual, and other sensory perceptions associated with this richly blessed city. Alexandria affects him first of all by its sounds: . . .

> Like a mother's lullaby
> over her baby's cradle,
> like a mountain echo
> answering the shepherd's pipe at daybreak,
> like the remote surge
> of my native sea, long unbeheld,
> thy name rings in my ears,
> thrice-blessed: Alexandria!
>
> Like the hesitant whispering,
> in the oak's deep shade, of love's confessions,
> like the mysterious murmur
> of the shadowy sacred groves,
> like the tambourine of great Cybele,
> bringing to mind far thunder and the moan of
>   doves,
> thy name rings in my ears,
> thrice-sapient: Alexandria!
>
> Like the sound of a trumpet before battle,
> the scream of eagles over the abyss,
> the rushing wings of flying Nike,
> thy name rings in my ears,
> thrice-mighty: Alexandria!

The sound of the word Alexandria affects the poet tenderly—*kak pesnja materi* (like a mother's lullaby); it affects him with emotional warmth—*kak gornoe èxo* (like a mountain echo) and *pastušij rožok* (the shepherd's pipe). It affects him like the distant surf—*kak dalekij priboj*—which is regular and soothing. The emotional tenderness of these pictures is underlined by emotionally evocative sounds which make abundant use of *l*'s and *r*'s: "kolybel' rebenka," "pastušij rožok," "rodnogo morja," "triždy blažennoe."

This tenderness of feeling is coupled with sensuousness in imagery and sound: "šopot ljubovnyx priznanij" (the whispering of love's confessions), "tainstvennyj šum tenistyx rošč svjaščennyx" (the mysterious murmur of the shadowy sacred groves), "golubej vorkovan'ju" (the moan of doves). These two emotional strata, tenderness and sensuousness, unite in an elevated mystical feeling of rapture at the sound of the word Alexandria, a mystical feeling that is linked to a recognition of the divine: "Kibely velikoj" (the great Cybele), "letjaščej Niki" (the flying Nike). The sounds and images of Alexandria represent the essence of the poet's creative imagination. Beloved by the gods, this city possesses elements of the divine and eternal: "blessed," "sapient," and "mighty."

After the theme has been established of this city with divine associations, the poet provides further development in the second poem: . . .

> When I hear the word "Alexandria,"
> I see the white walls of a house,
> a little garden with a clump of stock. . . .

Thus the auditory imagery of the first poem is enriched by visual imagery. What are his associations now? He first sees—"belye steny doma" (the white walls of a house), "nebol'šoj sad s grjadkoj levkoev" (a little garden with a clump of stock), "blednoe solnce osennego večera" (the pale sunlight of an autumn evening); and in the second stanza: "zvezdy nad stixajuščim gorodom" (stars over the quieting town), "p'janyx matrosov v temnyx kvartalax" (drunken sailors in shady hangouts), "tancovščicu, pljasuščuju 'osu' " (a dancing girl whirling in the "wasp"); and in the third stanza: "bledno-bagrovyj zakat" (a faded crimson sunset), "moxnatye migajuščie zvezdy" (fleeced and winking stars), and "svetlye glaza pod gustymi brovjami" (clear gray eyes beneath thick brows). Reality and dreams fuse repeatedly throughout the cycle. The "svetlye glaza pod gustymi brovjami" are obviously associated with a real person since the poet rather unexpectedly comments on this image in the final two lines of the third stanza: "kotorye ja vižu i togda, kogda ne govorjat mne: 'Aleksandrija' " (which I see even when I do not hear the word "Alexandria").

Alexandria and the evocation of its name are linked with the concrete impressions of the senses. Transformed into song, the imaginative flight coupled with the concrete sensuous delights of daily life are turned into an experience of beauty and charm. The imagined beauty of the past and the freshness of the present are very well communicated in the third and last poem of the Introduction: . . .

> The twilight enshrouding the warm sea at eve-
>   ning,
> the beacons that flame to the darkening heavens,
> the drift of verbena when feasting is done with,
> the freshness of dawn after nights spent unsleep-
>   ing,
> the walk along the paths of a garden in spring
>   time,
> the shouting and laughter of womenfolk bath-
>   ing,
> the peacocks of Juno that walk in her temple,
> the vendors of violets, pomegranates, and lem-
>   ons,
> the moaning of doves and the dazzle of sun-
>   light—
> Oh when shall I see thee, adorable city?

Again the poet's imagination evokes delightful pictures

and physical sensations. Imagination and experience unite when he speaks of "zapax verbeny" (the drift of verbena), "svežee utro" (the freshness of dawn), "progulka v allejax" (a walk along the paths), "kriki i smex kupajuščixsja ženščin" (the shouting and laughter of womenfolk bathing). These sensations are complemented with the experience of quiet grandeur and beauty: "večernyj sumrak nad teplym morem" (twilight enshrouding the warm sea at evening), "svjaščennye pavliny u xrama Junony" (the peacocks of Juno that walk in her temple). When the poet exclaims at the end, "kogda uvižu tebja rodimyj gorod" (Oh when shall I see thee, adorable city?), we are convinced that Alexandria is the divinely blessed land of his imagination and the inspiration for which his soul longs.

In the next three sections we follow the poet on his voyage through the pleasures Alexandria has to offer: "Ljubov'" (Love), "Ona" (The Girl), and "Mudrost'" (Wisdom). The seven poems in the section entitled "Love" develop this theme with a wealth of imagination. The greatest intensity of feeling is experienced in love which has a physical and an aesthetic side. This aesthetic aspect is exquisitely expressed in the final poem of this group where the poet speculates on what he would do if he were an army commander, or an adroit thief, or a second Antinous, a great sage, or finally his beloved's lowliest slave: . . .

> Were I your lowliest slave,
> I would sit in a dungeon
> and once a year or once in two years
> I would glimpse the golden tracery of your sandals
> when you chanced to walk by the prison house,
> and I would become happier than any man in Egypt.

This focus on the golden embroidery of the beloved's sandals transforms the experience of sensuous love into an aesthetic experience, bestowing upon the minor things in life the role of refined and precious enjoyment.

Section four is entitled "Mudrost'" (Wisdom), which means no less than the recognition of death and the passage of things. The poet, however, is not depressed by the transitoriness of this world; on the contrary, as others before him, he sees his enjoyment in life intensified by the brevity of joyous moments: . . .

> What's to be done . . .
> if the wine will be drained to the lees,
> the fragrance flee upon the air
> and even precious stuffs
> fall to dust
> as the centuries pass?
> Am I the less to love
> these dear and fragile things
> because they must decay?

The world and all precious things are redeemed from death by our appreciation and recollection of them. They live with us as long as we experience them, be it in our imagination, or in reality. Beauty exists as long as we are conscious of it and even in death we are not deprived of its experience: . . .

> . . . to return from a pleasant stroll
> to the house you no longer own,

> to eat a leisurely supper,
> and having read the tale of Apuleius
> for the hundred and first time,
> to lie in a warm, fragrant bath,
> and without hearing a single farewell
> to open your veins,
> while through the long ceiling window
> the scent of stock comes drifting in,
> the sunset glitters
> and the sound of flutes comes floating from afar.

The themes of love and death complement each other in this cycle. One is impossible without the other. We love because we recognize the brittleness of all that is precious to us. We love because what we love is marked by death; so do we not love death as well: . . .

> How I love, eternal gods,
> a lucid sadness,
> a love with no tomorrow,
> death without regret
> for this sweet life,
> which I love (by Dionysus I swear it)
> with all my beating heart
> and all my cherished flesh!

Everything essential has been said with these lines. What follows are variations on the same themes of love and death: sections entitled "Otryvki" (Fragments) and "Kanobskie pesenki" (Songs of Kanobus): . . .

> We know that the body we cherish
> must utterly perish.
> Such is our knowledge,
> such our love—
> then let us the more tightly cling
> to every fleeting, fragile thing.

Kuzmin is respected as an original poet and read with delight for his ability to express in his verse the joys of sensuous pleasures of many kinds, all seen under the aspect of their transitoriness bearing the mark of death. But finally it is not death that triumphs but beauty, physical joys experienced as beauty and transformed into poetry: . . .

> What's to be done . . .
> if my verse,
> which I value no less
> than Callimachus
> (or any other great one) his,
> wherein I lay away my love
> and all my tenderness
> and winged thoughts from the gods—
> the solace of my mornings,
> when the sky is clear
> and the scent of jasmine drifts in through the window—

Alexandria represents for the poet the greatest intensity of sensuous delights. In this sense *Aleksandrijskie pesni* is a collection of poems about love, physical love. Alexandria has passed into history as a city of great love affairs, primarily in connection with her queen, Cleopatra. But this cycle is more than a collection of verses about love and joyous life affirmation. With the theme of death and perishability so prominent, the question of the transformation of life and its experiences, above all of physical love, is raised. Transformation into aesthetic beauty is the answer and poetry is a means to it. In Kuzmin's poetics the sensuous and aesthetic experience are closely linked, indeed are indivisible:

> The body itself, the physical substance, will perish, and perhaps even the creations of art— Phidias, Mozart, Shakespeare—will perish, but the idea, the form of beauty contained in them cannot perish, and this, perhaps, is the only thing of value in the changing and transient diversity of life. And these ideas are divine and pure, no matter how rude their embodiment.

Alexandria suggests happiness and perfection, but the poet's musings about it are mingled with sorrow: . . .

> Many wonders shall I see,
> into many eyes shall I gaze my fill. . . .
> All things I shall see, save thee alone!

This expression of resignation might be the answer to the poet's earlier exclamation in the Introduction: "Kogda uvižu tebja, rodimyj gorod!" (Oh when shall I see thee, adorable city!). But it is ambiguous since the Conclusion had started with the line: "Ax, pokidaju ja Aleksandriju" (Alas, I am forsaking Alexandria). So presumably he has been there with his lyre and his poems are the fruit of his visit.

But who is the "thee" in the last line whom he will never see, and why this emphatic negative assertion? Is it his muse, is it a real woman, or maybe even a man? We don't know. The cycle closes with that intriguing ambiguity suggesting that love and beauty have been and will again come into the poet's reach, but that the object of his deepest longing, call it fulfillment or perfection, will always elude him. (pp. 22-30)

> *Joachim T. Baer, "Mikhail Kuzmin's 'Aleksandrijskie Pesni',"* in South Atlantic Bulletin, *Vol. XLI, No. 1, January, 1976, pp. 22-31.*

John E. Malmstad and Gennady Shmakov (essay date 1976)

[*In the following excerpt, Malmstad and Shmakov analyze the structure and meaning of* The Trout Breaking through the Ice.]

The cycle ***The Trout Breaking through the Ice,*** which both opens Kuzmin's final collection of verse and provides its title, was written during one week in July 1927. It is one of the poet's most mature and accomplished works and among the most difficult of all of his late writings. The framework of the cycle is a classic love triangle, a miniature *liubovnyi roman v stikhakh* with every formal element of the genre: the meeting, the awakening of love, the appearance of a third party, the gradual estrangement of the lovers, the parting, the torments of separation, the recovery of the beloved, and a radiantly "happy ever after" ending. While the cycle follows a traditional formula, the triangle is unusual in that a woman disrupts an affair between two men. Kuzmin's homosexuality is well known, and this triangle is deeply autobiographical. (Autobiographical elements, often extremely candid, nourished Kuzmin's art all his life.) It is based on a central episode

in the private life of the poet. In the early 1920's, Kuzmin's closest companion, the minor writer Iurii Iurkun, briefly left the poet to live with the young actress Olga Arbenina, a legendary Petersburg beauty who inspired many tributes in verse, from Mandelstam, for example, as well as from Kuzmin himself. There are also references in the cycle to at least two previous friends or lovers of Kuzmin, the first the famous artist and stage designer Nikolai Sapunov (the *"khudozhnik utonuvshii"* in the "Second Introduction"), the second the young officer and poet Vsevolod Kniazev, the *"gusarskii mal'chik s prostrelennym viskom"* in the "Second Introduction" and the Pierrot of Anna Akhmatova's "Poema bez geroia" ("Poem without a Hero"). As a result, the portrait of the young man in the cycle as well as the actual events behind the cycle are composite, and the portrait of the woman may be as well, having features of perhaps three women: Arbenina herself, the poetess Anna Radlova, and the famous actress and *femme fatale* Olga Glebova-Sudeikina.

Although the cycle is thematically unified by the love triangle, the poet's exposition of the affair is deliberately distorted. Even the identity and presentation of the major actors in the drama are purposefully confused or deflected by the introduction of seemingly extraneous personages or events. The strange, highly elliptical exposition is not provoked by a desire to confuse a prudish censor (that the situation is homosexual is clear, and that the work was published in Soviet Russia in 1929 is remarkable) but is dictated rather by the agent of memory itself. It is memory which confuses past and present—or rather, sees both time and nature as indivisible, a frequent occurrence in Kuzmin's poetry. It is memory which whimsically arranges and rearranges events in a series of associative chains, in which events and the participants in them are treated as motifs or links to be arranged into associative patterns seemingly at will. It is Kuzmin's mature artistic task to recreate and give meaning to his own experience— to transform that experience into a personal myth—by crystallizing these memories around a single thematic pivot, a highly concentrated metaphor: love as a trout breaking through the surface of a frozen brook.

The role of memory in the work recalls Bergson's concept of involuntary memory (the past friends or lovers who appear in the poem are called "uninvited guests"), a concept which together with the theories of psychoanalysis leads to the Surrealist concept, Breton's in particular, of "automatism," and the texture of Kuzmin's work appears at first glance so illogical that one is tempted to call it Surrealistic. But if the agent of memory is presented as itself beyond logic or total control, the resulting work of art can ultimately be discussed as a carefully plotted and very deliberate structure. The method is associative (Kuzmin called the work "my associative long poem" [*moia assotsiativnaia poema*]) but there is little if any of the seemingly uncontrolled play of unconscious, free association so common in Surrealist poetry. We say seemingly because the concept of automatic writing, despite some of the extravagant pronouncements and experiments of the Surrealists, is more an ideological and aesthetic myth. Art, as many maintain, can be called automatic only if the adjective is understood as a synonym for "spontaneous," for the act of representing the unconscious can be only a conscious act. Avant-garde irrationalism tends to conceive of thought only as a mechanical association of ideas. It insists, as does Breton for example, on arbitrariness or at its most extreme, pure chance (the aleatory). While the images or symbols in Kuzmin's cycle are extremely personal and the explanation of their association equally private, the final organization is far from arbitrary. There are rather definite associative chains in which each link is a carefully determined image or theme. The reader can always make imaginative sense of the text once the key to its organization becomes clear. The great accomplishment of Kuzmin, who was aware of both Surrealism and Dadaism, is to have created such a rigorous structure and yet to give the impression of total nonchalance, even playfulness, as though indeed principles of free and essentially irrational association governed the work. This off-hand attitude is reminiscent of the narrator's pose in *Eugene Onegin,* and Kuzmin's work intentionally makes several references to Pushkin's masterpiece.

On first reading, however, the work may seem an obscure if intriguing amalgam. The "First Thrust" simultaneously combines at least two events, one in the present and the other in the past: a spiritualist seance and the poet's meeting at a performance of Wagner's *Tristan und Isolde* with a young man with green eyes. The internal poetic cohesion of these events is complex, but the choice of the opera *Tristan* is far from arbitrary. Wagner's opera, with its mystic ideas of the rebirth of love through death (the famous *Liebestod*) and death as emblematic of transformation is inextricably connected with the poet's remembrance of past loves—some now dead, others departed, but none forgotten. For the poet, love—along with art, which is guided by love and is its supreme expression in life—is the only human entrance into an ideal world. It is a constant and universal force which guides man and which can never absolutely cease to exist. An affair may end, a lover may die, but despite such losses, love is endlessly creative and a new love must appear and triumph. The poet does not compare the opera performance to a spiritualist seance, but places an equal-sign between the two events by destroying the temporal chronology of the two and by moving with no transition from one to the other. Although no direct comparison between the two events is made (one may in fact question whether the seance is an event at all and not, rather, a totally realized and therefore submerged metaphor), they are associated in the poet's mind because the music, like a medium summoning spirits, has resurrected from the poet's memory recollections of past love: . . .

> But a slight tapping inside would not be interrupted,
> as though a fish were beating its tail against the ice.

The association of an image of a fish with both memory and love is a crucial identification.

The central image of the trout is given in the "First Introduction": an unrhymed fourteen-line description of a trout, imprisoned by winter, beating its tail against the brittle aquamarine surface of an icy brook. This central image perhaps came to Kuzmin by a simple parallelism: the nimble, darting movements of the fish, unpredictably

and sharply twisting and turning, suggested the unexpected and unpredictable changes of mood and emotion of love itself. Kuzmin may also have known that the trout when laying its eggs becomes extremely active, even aggressive, and can indeed break through the ice of a pond or brook. And so for the poet love also, if stubborn and aggressive, can reach its ultimate goal and full development (this is stated explicitly in the cycle's "Conclusion"). Or colloquial Russian itself (whose intonations and speech patterns Kuzmin so masterfully incorporated into his verse) may have somehow unconsciously prompted the image: by simple changes in the expression *bit'sia kak ryba ob led* Kuzmin reaches an opposite meaning.

The search for parallels which suggested the image to the poet is ultimately futile, however; for this is a perfect example of the modern metaphor with only one term, the self-contained image so common in Symbolist verse. Chamfort, in an attack on modern poetry, remarked that "Aristotle excellently observed in his *Rhetoric* that every metaphor founded on analogy ought to be equally appropriate even when inverted. Thus one says old age is the winter of life. Invert the metaphor and you will find it equally appropriate to say winter is the old age of the year." It is this inversion the modern metaphor so successfully resists, taking as its motto Mallarmé's statement: "I cancel the word 'like' from the dictionary." The modern image bases itself rather on a private and thus hermetic affinity or draws on myth to supply the missing analogy. Thus even more than the simple parallels we have suggested—private affinities of the poet—the fish is a complex and suggestive image in traditional symbolism. From ancient times a phallic symbol, it is also one of the earliest symbols of Christianity, where it is associated with Christ's resurrection and transfiguration. Interestingly this association was first made in Alexandria, a city to which Kuzmin was attached from the beginning of his literary career (the famous *Alexandrian Songs*) and which he had himself visited. Kuzmin, who had a thorough knowledge of Classical philosophy as well as of Gnostic and Christian beliefs, must have been aware of the usefulness of the fish image in these parallels with the themes of his cycle. The fish, along with the ice in which it is trapped, also contributed the dominant colors of the cycle, the shades of blue and green characteristic of the northern river or brook trout.

The fish, beating its tail against the ice, is thus metaphorically likened to love and its imperishability and ultimate triumph. Every thrust of the fish's tail against the surface of the ice and the resulting fracture of the surface will signify the appearance of the loved one or the memory of him in each of the poem's sections or "thrusts" (*udary*). In other words, each of the twelve thrusts into which the work is divided—by analogy with the twelve months of the year—demonstrates a new hypostasis of the lyrical hero who is physically transformed throughout the cycle, who appears in many different guises and forms, but who remains the unchanging object and ideal of love for the poet throughout the work. The use of twelve months has an obvious metaphorical meaning as well, that is, the cycle of seasons suggesting life, death, and rebirth ("this faithfulness of reality" as [Wallace] Stevens wrote in "An Ordinary Evening in New Haven"). The twelfth sign of the Zodiac is also, perhaps not coincidentally, Pisces. This possible connection of the number twelve with the Zodiac (always for Kuzmin symbolic of the well-ordered universe) is without doubt related, more specifically, to the use of the number in Classical Antiquity, where it was associated with the god of the mystery cults, the Spirit of the Year (among the many names attached to this god). Initiates of the cult identified themselves with the god and underwent twelve emblematic transformations, passing through twelve stages or hypostases before undergoing a ritual death and rebirth. The transformations thus embody a process of spiritual perfection and ascent to God. This notion was used by Apuleius, himself a Platonist and initiate of Isis (a goddess mentioned by Kuzmin in several poems), in *The Golden Ass,* subtitled "The Transformations of Lucius," in which the hero spends twelve months in the ass's skin before being "reborn." Kuzmin's translation of this Latin classic remains the standard Russian version.

The word "hypostasis" is associated with the philosophy of Plotinus, whom Kuzmin much admired and whose philosophical system he used frequently as a source of metaphor and imagery for poems of the 1920's. Plotinus saw the world as a place of ceaseless change and transition, viewing life as a process of the soul's continual drive to its source, an ascendancy to the One, with the soul constantly changing its form as it approached perfection and unity with the One. Kuzmin uses this system as a poetic model of love, substituting for the Plotinian soul the lover who moves endlessly through stages of seeming death, transformation, and resurrection. Love and the loved one ascending through different phases are seen here in the various guises of the lyrical hero himself who moves, as though on a journey, toward ultimate unity with the lover, the poet himself. Thus in Plotinus, while the essential identity of the soul is unchanging, its forms undergo continual metamorphosis, becoming body now in this, now in that manner. But the soul itself, like love, can never be destroyed or die. So too in Kuzmin's cycle love, the loved one, and the trout are seen as one—a unity—but images traditionally associated with one of these or suggested by it constantly may replace one another so long as an associative chain is preserved. Characteristically for Kuzmin's poetry of the 1920's many of the images suggested to him are from Gnosticism, early Christianity, European and Russian literature, music, and even the film. To give but one musical example, the "First Introduction" makes reference to Schubert's famous lied "Die Forelle" and the "Second Introduction," in which the dead lovers or friends appear to the poet, refers to the song by using a meter (iambic trimeter, rare in Kuzmin) which exactly parallels that of the text of the Schubert song. As a result this section of the cycle—as well as the "Seventh Thrust," in which a literal identification of the trout and the beloved young man is made—may be sung to the melody of the Schubert song.

It is natural that Kuzmin would associate his ideas with the music of Wagner and in particular with *Tristan,* an opera which has been called the most complete realization of mythic eroticism in Western art. The Tristan motif is first clearly given in the "First Thrust," January on the cycle's time scale. The color tonality of the cycle, suggested by the trout and the ice in the "First Introduction," is also first elaborated here: . . .

> A green land beyond a sky-blue mist . . .
> A rather sky-blue icy light
> Poured freely through the wide window.
> The moon shone as if from the north:
> Iceland, Greenland and Thule.

These cold northern colors, the northern referents Iceland, Greenland are obviously related both to the basic trout image and its icy prison and to *Tristan* as well. The mention of Thule recalls, of course, the real geographical location, but more importantly the Greek belief in the existence of a land most distant from all living things (Ultima Thule), a land almost synonymous with Hades itself and thus one that suggests death, something icy and cold and fixed in a distant land to which man voyages—an ancient myth. This notion of the supremely distant land also recalls Plotinus' belief that the greater the soul's distance from the One, the weaker the light, until it loses itself in darkness, emptiness, and nothingness. Many ancient myths of death and rebirth are connected with long voyages on or under the sea, and Plotinus employs these myths in his philosophy of the Soul's ascent to the One: "With this spirit it [the Soul] embarks in the skiff of the universe: the 'spindle of Necessity' then takes control and appoints the seat for the voyage, the seat of the lot in life. The Universal circuit is like a breeze, and the voyager, still or stirring, is carried forward by it." These are, of course, metaphors in Plotinus, and in the cycle the lover's association with this distant land need be understood as nothing more than his absence from the beloved, although this will be actualized in the cycle in many ways, among them journeys. This situation is connected also with the tragic triangle of Tristan, Isolde, and King Mark, and the legend's (and the opera's) dominant theme of love born and fully realized through death. The distant green land is thus a place of love—although love is pictured as destructive passion—and of death (in *Tristan und Isolde* a character exclaims, "You have drunk not love alone, but love and death together"), but as in the opera death promises the triumph of love.

The poet's meeting in the "First Thrust" with the young man with green eyes is the birth of love or its rebirth: the opera's tale of a *smertel'naia liubov'* acts on the poet's memory and evokes past loves; the young man himself at first takes the poet for someone else. It is likewise the first thrust of the fish itself and the first hypostasis of the lyrical hero. These basic images connected with the two primary associative series, that of *Tristan* and that of the trout itself, are now varied and manipulated in the remainder of the cycle. Their association and transformation complicate the reader's understanding of the cycle's chronology, which is unfolded in the following way.

In the "Second Thrust," a Gothic scene set in the Carpathians in an atmosphere redolent of works by Merimée and E. T. A. Hoffmann, the poet and the young man swear an oath of eternal love and become blood brothers: . . .

> Blood quietly drips into the glasses:

> A sign of exchange and a sign of protection . . .

The phrase "a sign of exchange" (*znak obmena*) is crucial here because it points to the central use of changing guises of the lyrical hero (and the composite nature of the portrait as well), the hypostases or the process of interchange as the young man, the lyrical hero, approaches his final perfect union with the poet. In the "Third Thrust" the poet senses the imminence of parting, but the reasons for it are unclear to him. Only a quick reference to Shakespeare's sonnets—"You had only just gone out, [the volume] of Shakespeare was open, a cigarette was [still] smoking, the Sonnets!! . . . (*Vy tol'ko-chto ushli, Shekspir / Otkryt, dymitsia papirosa / Sonety!! . . .*)— another *drame à trois*, in this case a duplicate of the cycle's triangle (a poet, a young man, and a mysterious "dark lady"), and the mention of youth's capriciousness anticipate the departure of the young man.

The "Fourth Thrust" depicts the departure of the young man. In it the poet for the first time compares himself and the loved one to identical or Siamese twins, an image which will be actualized in the future "plot" of the cycle. As first expressed, the image is of Siamese twins exhibited as freaks at a fair, and the poet states: . . .

> Express the exchange literally—
> A sideshow phenomenon will come out of it.

This striking image is then developed very differently: . . .

> We are two wings—one soul,
> We are two souls—one creator,
> We are two creators—one crown . . .

Kuzmin thereby points to Plotinus' theory of love and further to his concept of the fall and regeneration of the soul, which is seen in terms of "two souls"—one soul eternal and indestructible, the other subject to change and suffering, passing, as it approaches the first soul or moves away from it, through many forms of existence. More particularly the poet points to Aristophanes' discourse on love in Plato's *Symposium,* which sees love as a reunification of two parts of one person, that "people in love are those who are seeking for their other half," an idea actualized later in the development of the identical twins theme. Apuleius in *The Golden Ass* employs a similar method in his use of the myth of Cupid and Psyche, in which, taking hints from passages in Plato, Apuleius turns the myth into a philosophical allegory of the progress of the rational soul toward ideal love.

In the "Fifth Thrust" the poet, now separated from the young man, receives a letter in which the beloved tells him of his love for "Ellinor," a name which is certainly meant to recall Poe's mysterious ladies and the destructive passion associated with them. Not surprisingly, the letter has the postmark "Grinok" (the Scottish town Greenock), and the beloved identifies the place as a "green country" (*zelenaia strana*), a deliberate reference to the Greenland, Iceland, Thule series of the "First Thrust." Thus the young man's situation is clearly seen as a form of love which must inevitably lead to death, so long as he remains separated from the poet ("Who ever conceived the idea that peaceful landscapes cannot be an arena of catastro-

phes?"—*Kto vydumal, chto mirnye peizazhi / Ne mogut byt' arenoi katastrof?*). Characteristically the young man is seized not by love but by passion (*strast'*), which in the mature works of Kuzmin is always destructive. Compare the end of the second chapter of the poet's unpublished novel "The Golden Sky" ("Zlatoe nebo"): "Eros is a good and wise divinity. Many regard him as the most ancient separator of chaos, the father of harmony and of creative power. And, in truth, much on earth would fall to pieces without the unifying force of love . . . God is not at fault, if people turn his virtues and gifts into evil and call disorderly and destructive passions love." So here the young man is pictured as one possessed (*v bredu*) and the rose, a symbol of love's perfection, is in this distant place both a "wild rose" (*shipovnik*) and something like a madman (*bezumstvuet*).

These images are further developed in the "Sixth Thrust," a literary ballad derived from several sources: Tennyson's "Enoch Arden" (the name Annie Ray, for example), Scottish traditional ballads on the theme of the "Demon Lover," Bürger's popular "Leonore" ballad (and its Russian adaptations), and Coleridge's *Rime of the Ancient Mariner.* While outside the actual "plot," the ballad is intimately connected with the notion of a journey, with the Wagnerian motifs of the "First Thrust" and even more pointedly with Wagner's *Der Fliegende Holländer,* whose plot relies on the legend of a sailor eternally searching for salvation through love. (The reader will now recall the model Dutch boat mentioned in the "Third Thrust" with its sail like a wing, one of the most frequent symbols in Kuzmin for the soul and its movement to perfection.) In Kuzmin's ballad a sea captain, Ervin Grin (Erwin Green), long thought dead, returns to his fiancée from a northern land where "There shines to all a green light in heaven, on earth" (*Tam svetit vsem zelenyi svet na nebe, na zemle*) and where he has seen a flower emerging from the depths of the sea—symbolic of the hero's eventual return (rebirth) from the water. The sailor is a kind of double of the lyrical hero of the cycle, a further hypostasis of this central figure. The name "Green" is obvious, as are the reasons for his green eyes and the references to the green land from which he has returned. Clear, too, are the further suggestions that he is returned from the dead in a new and more perfect form, as we see the forty-year-old sailor take on the ruddy coloring of a young man before the terrified eyes of his new wife: . . .

> She glances this way and that,—
> She can't come to her senses . . .
> Where is the forty-year-old sailor
> With whom she will lead her life
> [He is now] both noble and tall,
> No wrinkles can be found . . .
> In such a form no one had seen
> The sailor even in his childhood . . .

This story of the sailor's return thus predicts and makes clear the inevitability of the beloved young man's return to the poet and restates the central theme of the resurrection, transformation, and return of love, and the ultimate reunification and triumph of the two lovers in a perfect state.

The "Seventh Thrust" also stands apart from the temporal

and physical action of the cycle. It introduces yet another hypostasis of the lyrical hero—a young man, an "unknown swimmer" (*nevedomyi kupal'shchik*) swimming alone in a pond. As the "Sixth Thrust" restated the basic Wagnerian themes in a particularly concentrated way, the "Seventh Thrust" places the new hypostasis firmly in the associative series of the trout itself. It is hardly surprising that these two thrusts are the exact structural center of the cycle, each respectively preceded and followed by five thrusts. The semantic unity, previously noted, of the conception of love, the loved one himself, and the trout, is nowhere clearer in the cycle than in the "Seventh Thrust" where the image of the swimming young man is united to and doubles that of the trout, creating a realized poetic identity: . . .

> Under the water his entire body
> Sparkles and is shot through with
> The color of green mica.
> Keep to the left
> And you will run into the shallows!
> The silver [trout] is beating
> The trout, the trout, the trout!

The "Eighth Thrust" picks up the interrupted plot line of the cycle. The young man returns very briefly and already in a different guise ("And different hands were shaking my hand"—*I ruku zhali mne drugie ruki*). Separated from the poet, he is now perishing both physically and spiritually, but is helpless to stop it: . . .

> Well, here I am. . . . I have no strength left. I
>   am perishing.
> Our angel of transformations has flown off.
> Just a little longer and I will be completely blind,
> And the rose will become a rose, the sky only the
>   sky,
> And nothing more! Then I will be dust
> And I will return to dust! My blood,
> Bile, brains, and lymph have dried up.

Characteristically the destruction of the young man is pictured as the disappearance of the "interchange phenomenon" (he exclaims, "Oh, Lord! There is neither any reinforcement nor any exchange!"—*Bozhe! I podkreplen'ia net i net obmena!*) which had characterized their former life together and the reduction of reality in the present to a primitive "one-to-one" relationship (the "rose a rose, the sky only the sky"). His passion for "Ellinor" is physical only, without the spiritual dimension, the power of transformation which love provides. The "Eighth Thrust" also restates the "Tristan" theme: . . .

> The crystal breaks the rays
> Into their component parts—and a rainbow is
>   visible,
> And merry little rays of light are alive.
> In order to be born again, one must die.

This image of the "destruction" of light in a prism, and its "rebirth" in the color spectrum, is given as a kind of final postulate, which, in the context of the cycle, duplicates the central idea. The phrase "In order to be born again, one must die" not only refers to John 12:24 ("Verily, verily, I say unto you, Except a corn of wheat fall into the ground and die, it abideth alone: but if it die, it bringeth forth much fruit") and to the "sterben und werden"

of Goethe (whom Kuzmin admired and translated), but points, again, to the great second-act duet of *Tristan und Isolde.*

These two themes are commented on and illustrated by a dialogue of the poet and the young man, a dialogue structured on an interweaving of the two associative series. The first is the Wagnerian, that of the lover-wanderer returned from a green land with attendant attributes and objects—green eyes, a green cloak—who is changing, entering a new hypostasis: . . .

> "But your green cloak?"
> "A green cloak? Which one?" "You came in it."
> "That was an apparition—there is no green
>   cloak."

The second series is connected with the metaphorical likeness between the loved one and the elusive trout itself: . . .

> I am indestructibly surrounded by glass
> And beat about, like a fish . . .
> With every passing day I am sinking deeper and
>   deeper!

The "Ninth Thrust," the poet's lyrical digression on the theme of solitude, reintroduces the themes of the green land and the possibility of the beloved's return from "Grinok," the distant land where he is perishing. If the beloved is being destroyed by this separation, the poet is gravely affected as well and for him too, reality is being reduced to but one plane; there are now no multiple meanings, there is no *"obmen,"* that is, the power to create metaphor is gone, and thus no creativity, no poetry is possible: . . .

> —Greenock? There's such a place. A little Scot-
>   tish town.
> All metaphors hung suspended [in the air] like
>   smoke,
> But they will pass away in a ring beneath the
>   ceiling,
> Sober day will dispel all chimeras.

The poet now fears that all hope for the young man's return is futile, and he is tempted to deny the existence of the ideal (and thus destroy it). But an inner voice warns him never to forget the love in a refrain which once again states the basic theme of the cycle and clearly identifies the various hypostases of the lyrical hero as one: . . .

> One can hear the noise of the green river,
> And we can not save the little skiff.
> A hand in kid gloves
> Will continue to beckon from afar,
> Until you accept in your heart
> Erwin Green, the sailor.

The "Tenth Thrust" is the culminating meeting of the poet and his friend. Almost every image in it has been generated by the thematic mosaic of the cycle. The beloved appears in a new hypostasis, but one suggested in the "Fourth Thrust": as the poet's identical twin, now accidentally discovered by the poet in the curio collection of an eccentric (who resembles the Dr. Caligari of the film classic) whom he meets in a gambling house. The poet finds the loved one displayed against a special green background. The resemblance of this twin to the personage from the green land is underlined—"Through his skin a greenness visibly glimmered" (*skvoz' kozhu zelen' iavstvenno skvozila*)—and the American coat and necktie and the "rose champagne"-colored cap, details of the hero in the "Eighth Thrust," only intensify this identity. Finally the poet places an equal-sign between the loved one and the wanderer resurrected from the dead, that is, from the green land, in his passionate outcry which concludes the section: . . .

> Open, open your green eyes!
> I don't care in what form you were sent
> Back to me by the green country!
> I am your mortal brother. You remember there,
>   in the Carpathians?
> You still have not finished reading Shakespeare,
> And like a rainbow the words dissipate.
> The final shame and complete felicity! . . .

The line of meeting and recognition which culminates in this "thrust" is continually interrupted by the second associative series of the trout, beating its tail against the ice. The semantic identity of this image, that is, of love and the loved one himself, was previously noted. Therefore the prominent appearance in this "thrust" of an aquarium covered with glass "like ice" and containing a trout is perfectly clear. The trout moves lazily in the aquarium as we first see it, but as the lovers approach recognition and unity it begins to move more and more savagely, beating its tail against the glass until the section closes with: . . .

> And the fish is beating, and beating, and beating,
>   and beating.

Given that in this "thrust" the poet and his beloved are presented as identical twins, it is interesting that for the first time in the cycle the poet too, sitting at a gambling table covered with green felt, is associated with the trout image: . . .

> It seemed to me that I was sitting under water.
> The green canvas reminded me
> Of a green land beyond a sky-blue mist . . .

The "Eleventh Thrust," a dialogue between the reunited poet and his lover, is an elaborately developed metaphorical picture of the return of the lyrical hero who is transformed in a series of couplets, gradually taking on flesh and becoming himself: . . .

> "Are you breathing? Are you alive? You are not
>   an apparition?"
> "I am the first-born of the green void."

It is a metamorphosis from something cold-blooded (and thus fishlike), foreign, even lifeless: . . .

> I hear the beat of the heart, the blood grows
>   warm . . .
> The cheeks are more ruddy, decay is
>   disappearing . . .
> A mysterious exchange is taking place . . .
> "What does your revived vision first see?"
> "The trout, I see, is breaking through the ice."

This change from something like a fish to the human being is a clear case of an incarnation to a higher level (hinting

at Christ's incarnation) and the idea of the hypostases is clear too in the young man's statement: "I am stepping onto the next rung!"—*Vskhozhu na sleduiushchuiu stupen'!* The "thrust" closes with a solemnly triumphant statement signifying the final perfect union of the two lovers: "And is our angel of transformations here again?" / "Yes, the angel of transformations is here again"—*I angel prevrashchenii snova zdes'? / Da, angel prevrashchenii snova zdes'.* The essential idea of the imperishability of love is also clearly stated: "They have not died whom love has called"—*Ne umerli, kogo zovet liubov'.*

The final "thrust," the twelfth, is a joyous New Year's Eve dinner shared by the reunited lovers, with only a clock beating the final midnight hour: . . .

> You can hear, the clock in the hall
> Is leisurely striking twelve . . .
> That is my trout resoundingly
> Breaking through the last of the ice.

The trout has appeared for the final time, now fully realized in the perfect love of the poet.

The conclusion (*Zakliuchenie*) deliberately pokes fun at the conventions of storytelling, much as Pushkin had gaily mocked the conventions of his own day in *Eugene Onegin*. The work caps its many Pushkin reminiscences in the final lines, which recall the endings of Pushkin's comic verse tales, as the poet playfully defends his cycle: . . .

> I preserved the twelve months
> And gave the approximate weather,—
> And that is not so bad. And then I believe
> That a trout can break through the ice
> When it is persevering. That's all.

The conclusion, however, more seriously points to many of the cycle's structural principles and devices, as if challenging the reader to separate the poet's actual memories, events, and people ("I was overwhelmed by a crowd of memories / The dead got mixed up with the living"—*Tolpoi nakhlynuli vospominaniia / Pokoiniki smeshalisia s zhivymi*) from the multiple literary references ("Fragments from novels I have read"—*Otryvki iz prochitannykh romanov*). Thus the conclusion teasingly and rather cryptically points to the artistic method underlying the work, a method of constant metaphorical transformation of the semantic material. With this poetic method, one often employed by Kuzmin, not only in this cycle but in many works of the 1920's, the poem becomes a kind of code in which experience is broken into component parts that are deformed and varied by means of a governing metaphor and then recombined into the work of art by means of a complex associative series. The medium for the re-expression or restructuring of experience is often another work of art or a series of artistic references. Kuzmin himself, in the "Second Introduction" to the cycle, describes his method in a near aphorism: . . .

> Memory—a housekeeper,
> Imagination—"boy" . . .

From the store-house of memory, compared to a housekeeper, storing up its precious past, the poet's imagination, like a young boy sent on errands (the "boy" is not only a comparison, but a command as in "boy, go fetch this"), selects the valuable and significant, transforms it according to the required poetic task, and combines it all into the final pattern. The poetic meaning grows out of the seemingly capricious combination of the transfigured elements, thanks to which the poet's subjective reality, which in Kuzmin is not opposed to "Reality" but is identical to it, is created and fixed. Because of the transformations and strange combinations of realia and artistic reference, the images yield to a rational decoding only with the greatest difficulty. This method offers the poet the possiblity of creating a poetic texture "many-planed" in the extreme.

Although much modern art has moved toward abstraction and so-called "pure art," an equally strong countercurrent (for example, Surrealist and Dadaist painting) delights in a mixture of genres, narrative situations, and iconographic schemes, much as does Kuzmin's cycle. The paradox, however, is that instead of leading to greater illumination, such techniques lead more commonly to greater mystification. Certainly in the love story of Kuzmin's cycle, its "plot" is the barest framework of the work—its surface alone—and it will not take the reader very far into the cycle's meaning. In fact, if one treats the work in terms of its development as a story as we have done, this method illuminates aspects of the work, but oversimplifies it as well, because one must of necessity follow only the major images or associative series. There are others—the rose or the star, for example—which complicate this scheme and are, moreover, some of the most mysterious elements in the work.

The cycle obviously depicts a movement to perfection or wholeness and harmony and it demonstrates a belief in the constant renewal of life, but the meanings of this movement are so interwoven that to talk of one level alone is virtually impossible. Certainly it is the movement of love, but it is also of the soul (the fish itself is after all one of the oldest symbols of the soul). Or does the movement describe the process of artistic creation? (One thinks of the final two stanzas of Stevens' "Study of Images II": "As if, as if, as if the disparate halves / Of things were waiting in a betrothal known / To none, awaiting espousal to the sound // Of right joining, a music of ideas, the burning / And breeding and bearing birth of harmony, / The final relation, the marriage of the rest.") Or does it describe the process of the individual's integration? The only obvious feature is that the work goes far beyond the limitations of allegory. Clear in all of this is a strong element of aesthetic dissent, that is, a conscious departure from traditions in Russian verse and a search for new means of artistic expression. (pp. 138-62)

> *John E. Malmstad and Gennady Shmakov, "Kuzmin's 'The Trout Breaking through the Ice',"* in Russian Modernism: Culture and the Avant-Garde, 1900-1930, *edited by George Gibian and H. W. Tjalsma, Cornell University Press, 1976, pp. 132-64.*

Simon Karlinsky   (essay date 1979)

[*In the following review of* Sobranie stikhov, *Karlinsky*

The last volume of poetry that Mikhail Kuzmin (1872-1936) was able to publish during his lifetime was *The Trout Breaks through the Ice (Forel' razbivaet led)*. A sequence of narrative and lyric poems, couched in the strikingly original surrealistic and visionary mode characteristic of this poet's later work, the book appeared in Leningrad in 1929. Where Kuzmin's first two major collections, *Nets (Seti)*, 1908, and *Autumnal Lakes (Osennie ozera)*, 1912, were acclaimed and eulogized by many of the leading poets and critics of the time, *The Trout Breaks through the Ice,* except for two contemptuous brief notices, was passed over in silence by the Soviet press.

Still, the book had its admirers among the more discerning members of the Soviet literary community. Among them was Lidia Chukovskaia, who confided to Anna Akhmatova in 1940 that she began to understand and to love Kuzmin only after *The Trout Breaks through the Ice.* Akhmatova, whose own early poetry betrayed Kuzmin's strong influence, and who, in 1912, had asked Kuzmin to write a foreword to her first collection of verse, *Evening,* inscribing the copy she gave to him "To my wonderful teacher," had, it turned out, not yet read her erstwhile teacher's last book. Chukovskaia lent it to her and one month later recorded Akhmatova's judgement. Apart from a few individual poems which she liked, Akhmatova thought the entire book derived from German expressionist cinema and therefore lacking in originality. She found what she called the book's "obscenity" (*nepristoinost'*) most depressing: "Kuzmin has always been homosexual in his poetry, but here he exceeds all boundaries. Before, one could not do this: Viacheslav Ivanov might wince. But in the twenties, there was no longer anyone to be wary of [*uzhe ne na kogo bylo ogliadyvat'sia*]. Perhaps Villon was able to manage this sort of thing, but as for Mikhail Alekseevich—no. It is utterly disgusting."

For a person familiar with Kuzmin's literary career and with Russian cultural history of this century in general, the statement is astounding. Male homosexual love, it is true, has always been a major (but by no means the only) theme in Kuzmin's poetry. Before he made his name as a poet, he acquired considerable notoriety for his autobiographical *roman à thèse, Wings (Kryl'ia)*. Initially published in 1906 in a special issue of *Vesy,* one of the most prestigious literary journals of the day, and later as a separate volume that became a best seller, *Wings* sought to demonstrate that for people who are homosexually inclined it is better to accept their orientation, making it a part of a productive and satisfying life, than to reject and fight it. This presupposition also underlies much of Kuzmin's poetry. In this sense, his last collection, which so shocked Akhmatova, did not "exceed" any boundaries that had not already been crossed in all his other writings, beginning with the earliest. Nor is the treatment of the homosexual theme in *The Trout Breaks through the Ice* and Kuzmin's other collections any more or less explicit than it is, for example, in the "Calamus" section of Walt Whitman's *Leaves of Grass* (a book which Akhmatova much admired in Kornei Chukovskii's translation) or in the cycles "Parallélement" and "Hombres" of Paul Verlaine (surely it was Verlaine whom Akhmatova must have compared with Kuzmin, since Villon did not write on homosexual themes). Furthermore, graphic descriptions of male homosexuality are to be found in the poetry of Kuzmin's contemporary, Nikolai Kliuev, a poet who lost his freedom and eventually his life because of a poem he wrote in defense of Akhmatova (a line from which appears as an epigraph in her *Poem without a Hero*) and of whom she has written with warmth in her memoir of Osip Mandelstam.

Could Akhmatova have really forgotten the liberalized air of that last prerevolutionary decade, when all sorts of previously unmentionable themes—social, religious, political, and sexual—had become acceptable for literary treatment? The content of Kuzmin's love lyrics did not prevent poets as diverse as Annenskii, Blok, Khlebnikov, and Tsvetaeva from regarding him as one of the greatest poets of their time. The only major poet of that period who chose to make an issue in print of Kuzmin's homosexuality was Gumilev, who in 1912, in his review of *Autumnal Lakes* (written while he was still married to Akhmatova), complimented Kuzmin on being what in the parlance of the 1970s would have been called "a spokesman for Russia's gay community" [see excerpt dated 1912].

As for Viacheslav Ivanov—whose collection *Cor Ardens,* published one year before Kuzmin's *Nets,* contained a whole section ("Eros") inspired by Ivanov's own homosexual experiences—he was surely the least likely person to have acted as Kuzmin's censor. Akhmatova may not have known Viacheslav Ivanov's journal for 1906, where Kuzmin is described as a pioneer of the future age of sexual tolerance, but she must have been aware that Kuzmin had shared a residence for a number of years with Ivanov and, until her untimely death, with Ivanov's wife Lidia Zinov'eva-Annibal, a fiction writer who specialized in the theme of lesbian love.

Akhmatova's statement on Kuzmin recorded by Chukovskaia, on which I have dwelt at such length, is important in two ways. It is a key to the genesis of Akhmatova's own much admired, but often misunderstood, poetic masterpiece *Poem without a Hero,* which is in essence her response to Kuzmin's *The Trout Breaks through the Ice* and possibly also to his earlier novel *Travelers by Land and Sea* (*Plavaiushchie-puteshestvuiushchie,* 1915). It is also indicative, in general, of the extent to which Kuzmin's role in prerevolutionary cultural life and the reception of his work by his contemporaries have been forgotten and his writings unread in postrevolutionary times.

In his essay on Kuzmin's poetry included in [*Sobranie stikhov*], Vladimir Markov makes abundantly clear that everything printed about Kuzmin in literary histories, encyclopedias, and textbooks, from the 1930s to this day, is misleading, wrong, or incomplete. Kuzmin is often listed as an Acmeist poet, which he never was. His best or most important works are usually said to be the verse cycles *Alexandrian Songs* and "Chimes of Love" ("**Kuranty liubvi**") and the essay "**On Beautiful Clarity,**" which, in terms of his overall achievement, is comparable to saying that Tolstoy's most important works are *Childhood* and "Sevastopol Stories." A wide-ranging poet whose output encompasses important historical, metaphysical, and mystical themes, as well as erotic, humorous, and light verse, Kuzmin is invariably dismissed as a frivolous hedonist who was able to write only of trivia and trifles. His three major collections of verse that were published in the 1920s constitute about one-half of his total poetic output by volume and represent some of his most serious and original work. Until now, however, they have remained unnoticed by literary scholars and historians.

Coming as it does after some four decades of critical and popular neglect of Kuzmin, the new edition of his complete poetry prepared by John E. Malmstad and Vladimir Markov produces the impression of a wide gate suddenly flung open onto a whole new country, partly forgotten and partly unexplored. A slow and careful reading of the seven major collections leaves one astounded at the scope and variety of this supposedly "graceful minor poet" (Renato Poggioli's term for Kuzmin [see excerpt dated 1960]). The unprecedented precision and intimacy with which Kuzmin's poetry of 1906-8 reflected life, its insistence on the concrete beauty of our world and the joys of here and now, which so struck his contemporaries, began alternating already in the later sections of *Nets* with mystical insights derived from Kuzmin's study of gnosticism as well as from his Old Believer heritage. This alternation continued in his later work and its persistence makes mincemeat out of all critical attempts to fit Kuzmin into either the Acmeist or the Symbolist mold. Alexander Blok was neither whimsical nor paradoxical when he saw the roots of Kuzmin's art in "the awakening of the Russian Schism, in the dark religious forebodings of fifteenth-century Russia, in the memory of the trans-Volga *startsy* who would come out of obscure marsh bogs into squat, smoke-filled peasant huts."

An aspect of Kuzmin not found in other poets of his time is his habit of organizing his lyric poetry into cycles with easily discernible plots, which results in a hybrid genre that combines the features of the traditional lyric with those of a narrative *poema*. This is the form in which much of his autobiographical poetry is couched. It culminates in the remarkable novellas in verse of *The Trout Breaks through the Ice,* which belong among the finest examples of Russian twentieth-century narrative poetry. Kuzmin is a master of a variety of larger narrative verse structures, such as the remarkably beautiful *poema* "**The Cavalier**" ("**Vsadnik**") (included in *Autumnal Lakes*), which was surely the point of departure of Marina Tsvetaeva's epic poems "On a Red Steed" and "Tsar Maiden"; the extended ode in free verse, "**The Hostile Sea**" ("**Vrazhdebnoe more**"), written in 1917, and dedicated to Vladimir Mayakovsky, which mingled Homeric themes with the mood of Russian revolution; or the visionary and surrealistic longer poems of the last two collections. (pp. 92-5)

At a ceremony in honor of Kuzmin's birthday in 1920, the speakers included, *inter alios,* Alexander Blok, Nikolai Gumilev, Boris Eikhenbaum, and Viktor Shklovskii. In his speech, Blok expressed a wish that conditions be created in the future where a literary artist as unique as Kuzmin would have the right "to remain himself." We know that things did not turn out as Blok had wished, and that, after Soviet culture took the form it did, the mere fact of Kuzmin's sexual orientation contributed to reducing an admired poet to a pariah and a nonperson, so that even a poet of Akhmatova's stature and independence was able to turn against him with puritanical vindictiveness and depict him in *Poem without a Hero* as an evil demon responsible for bringing on cultural decline. The new publication of his complete poetry, combined with the important critical contributions by John E. Malmstad and Vladimir Markov, should help restore Kuzmin to his rightful place among the foremost Russian poets of this century. (pp. 95-6)

> Simon Karlinsky, "Death and Resurrection of Mikhail Kuzmin," in Slavic Review, *Vol. 38, No. 3, September, 1979, pp. 92-6.*

FURTHER READING

Green, Michael. Introduction to *Selected Prose and Poetry,* by Mikhail Kuzmin, edited by Michael Green, pp. ix-xxviii. Ann Arbor, Mich.: Ardis, 1980.

> Introduction to Kuzmin's life and career.

Malmstad, John E. "The Mystery of Iniquity: Kuzmin's 'Temnye ulitsy rozhdaiut temnye mysli'." *Slavic Review* 34, No. 1 (March 1975): 44-64.

> Presents and explicates a poem concerning the murder of the ballet dancer Lidiia Ivanova.

Slonim, Marc. "After the Symbolists." In his *Modern Russian Literature: From Chekhov to the Present,* pp. 211-33. New York: Oxford University Press, 1953.

> Survey of Russian literature that states, "In the era of political reaction Kuzmin's 'mellowed honey' sensuality had the acrid reek of decay and perversion. This aesthete and scholar . . . could easily be regarded as a typical embodiment of a declining cultural cycle."

Trotsky, Leon. "Pre-Revolutionary Art." In his *Literature and Revolution,* translated by Rose Strunsky, pp. 19-55. New York: International Publishers, 1925.

> Includes Kuzmin in the category of writers whose works "are completely and entirely superfluous to a modern post-October man."

Malcolm Lowry

1909-1957

(Full name Clarence Malcolm Lowry) English novelist, short story writer, poet, and screenwriter.

The following entry presents criticism of Lowry's novel *Under the Volcano* (1947). For discussion of Lowry's complete career, see *TCLC,* Volume 6.

Under the Volcano is acknowledged as a classic twentieth-century novel and is the achievement on which Lowry's reputation rests. Focusing on the final day in the life of an alcoholic diplomat, the novel presents his spiritual collapse through a richly allusive and complex narrative, prompting critics to compare it to James Joyce's *Ulysses* (1922). Owing to what Ronald Binns has termed the "fertility and complexity of Lowry's narrative," the novel has inspired a multitude of interpretations. These include readings of *Under the Volcano* as political allegory, as religious manifesto, and as personal confession.

After publishing one unacclaimed novel and failing as a screenwriter in Hollywood, Lowry moved with his wife to Mexico in 1936. There he wrote a short story, "Under the Volcano," concerning three people—an alcoholic Consul, his daughter Yvonne, and her lover Hugh—and their discovery of a murdered peasant. Lowry never published the story, which eventually became the basis for chapter eight of the novel. An alcoholic himself, Lowry drank heavily throughout 1937 while working on the first draft of *Under the Volcano,* and his unruly drunkenness effectively ended his marriage. In 1939, while living in Los Angeles, Lowry met his second wife, Margerie Bonner. By this time he had completed a second draft of *Under the Volcano,* and the following year he wrote a third draft, in which the Consul and Yvonne are no longer father and daughter but husband and wife, and Hugh becomes the Consul's half-brother. Judging from the evidence of the manuscript pages, Margerie acted in a significant editorial capacity for this draft, rewriting entire pages and even determining Yvonne's fate in the novel. In January 1941, Lowry's agent notified him that the third draft had been rejected by four publishers. Between February 1941 and Christmas Eve 1944, Lowry produced the fourth and final draft. Lowry's most important influence during this last rewrite was Charles Stansfield-Jones, a spiritualist and expert in the Cabala, the mystic rabbinical philosophy of the middle ages. Stansfield-Jones owned a large library of occult texts and these provided Lowry with the background enabling him to fortify the Cabalistic framework of *Under the Volcano.*

In November 1945, the publisher Jonathan Cape accepted the manuscript of *Under the Volcano* on the condition that Lowry make a number of emendations. The reader's report sent by Cape stated that "the author has over-reached himself, and is given to eccentric word-spinning and too much stream of consciousness stuff." Instead of submitting to the demands of the publisher, which would have

meant cutting the work nearly in half, Lowry replied with what Douglas Day has called "a document absolutely unique in literary history." The "Cape letter," as it is now called, is about 20,000 words in length and defends the novel with a chapter-by-chapter justification of its apparent excesses. The letter succeeded in persuading Cape to accept the novel without significant revisions, and *Under the Volcano* was finally published in 1947. Though some reviewers complained of the complexity of the novel's structure, it was generally well received and praised by at least one reviewer as a work of genius.

Under the Volcano begins on 2 November, the Mexican Day of the Dead, 1939. Jacques Laruelle, a French film director, recollects the deaths of Geoffrey Firmin—"the Consul"—and his wife, Yvonne, which took place exactly one year earlier. The rest of the novel chronicles that day. Yvonne returns to Mexico after a long separation from her husband in order to settle their differences, but the memories of her infidelity with Laruelle and the Consul's half-brother Hugh interfere with their reconciliation. This tension is exacerbated by the Consul's perpetual drunkenness and increasingly self-destructive antics, and in the ensuing events of the day Yvonne is trampled by a horse and the

Consul is executed by the Mexican authorities after being charged with espionage. Interwoven into the narrative are lengthy flashbacks, alcoholic hallucinations, and the "eccentric word-spinning" referred to by the Cape reader. The resulting complexities have allowed critics to reach several diverse opinions regarding *Under the Volcano.* While Dale Edmonds has written, "It is on the most immediate level—the level of people, places, events, and circumstances . . . —that the novel communicates most effectively," most critics have traced patterns of allusion and symbolism that they claim are essential to an understanding of the novel. For instance, Carole Slade has stated that the most important literary source for *Under the Volcano* is Dante's *Inferno,* while others have stressed the novel's links to the Faust dramas of Christopher Marlowe and Johann Wolfgang von Goethe. Additionally, the myths of Sisyphus and Prometheus, and the poetry of Percy Bysshe Shelley are cited as primary sources. Critics have also sought to identify images within the novel that can serve as metaphors for some of its larger themes. Many view the poster of the Peter Lorre movie *Las manos de Orlac* (*The Hands of Orlac*), which is recurrently seen throughout the novel, as an emblem of the Consul's guilty conscience. Other critics have emphasized the sign posted in the Consul's garden which reads, "¿Le gusta este jardín?" ("Do you like this garden?") as a warning about the recklessness of humanity. Another sign, reading "No puede vivir sin amar" ("One cannot live without loving") has been interpreted as the single unifying message of the novel.

Because of the constant references to drinking in *Under the Volcano,* there has also been some critical debate over the significance of the Consul's alcoholism. In his preface to the French version of the novel, Lowry professed to have written "an authentic drunkard's story," and critics have expanded this claim to correlate the alcoholism of the Consul with the chaotic state of Mexico, the Western world, and the human race as a whole. Amidst all of these various aspects of the novel, critics point out, it is important to accept as the seminal work of criticism of *Under the Volcano* Lowry's own "Cape letter," which closes: "The book was so designed, counterdesigned and interwelded that it could be read an indefinite number of times and still not have yielded all its meanings or its dramas or its poetry: and it is upon this fact that I base my hope in it, and in that hope that, with all its faults . . . I have offered it to you."

(See also *Contemporary Authors,* Vol. 105, and *Dictionary of Literary Biography,* Vol. 15.)

John Woodburn   (essay date 1947)

[*In the following review, Woodburn describes the story of* Under the Volcano *and characterizes the novel's strengths.*]

When I had finished reading [**Under the Volcano**] for the first time I could not bring myself to set down what I

thought of it. I was so much within its grasp, so profoundly affected by the tides of its prose, the faltering arc of its tragic design, a design which gave me the feeling of wonder and beauty and fear, of melancholy and loneliness, the indescribable loneliness I have always felt at seeing a falling star describe its incorrigible curve of disintegration across the face of night, that I said to myself: you are this book's fool, it has stolen you and mastered you by some trickery, and you cannot appraise it tranquilly until it leaves you alone. It has not let me alone. In the street, in my room, where it has set its sorrowful music to the metronome of my clock, in the company of many or only one, it has been with me insistently. I have now read it twice, and the second time has bound me to it more tightly than before. For it added to the pleasures of anticipation and recollection the puzzle-pleasure, the story has extended itself as do the drawings of shaded cubes which first seem but four, then, miraculously, eight, and then, incredibly, sixteen. It led me to unravel the skeins of inference and nuance, and the swift *agenbite of inwit* of which Joyce was the cool master and Malcolm Lowry his apt, not aping, creative pupil. Many of these I passed over at first reading, caught as I was in the undertow of its emotion; but the second, returning time, there was still the emotion but it was not the same. I knew it would come, and when, and I could await it; so I had time to wander and watch, and it was then that the esthetics became clear, and the intricate, convoluted architecture was articulated. The first reading was the reading of impact, the war-head; the second was the reading of exploration and discovery, in which the feathering of the arrow is observed, when each of the thin laminae becomes distinct, and the myriad references and cross-references of the book fall into symmetry, and what I had sometimes skimmed as casual detail took on exquisite relevance.

The story itself is dolorous and simple; its complexities are in its radiations. It begins in 1939, in November, near sunset on the Day of the Dead, in Quauhnahuac, in Mexico. Two melancholy, tired, and sensitive men, a Frenchman about to return to France and a Mexican doctor going nowhere, talk, over their anís, of a man whom they have not seen for exactly a year: Geoffrey Firmin, once British Consul, compulsive alcoholic, wanderer within himself, an elegant, disintegrating, pitiable, and appealing symbol of self-destruction. Dr. Vigil has known the Consul for an evening; Jacques Laruelle has shared Geoffrey's boyhood and his wife. As Laruelle walks townward from the Casino in the failing light, he recalls disquietly the events of that day one year before and, inducing still more an already oppressive melancholy, remembers the shy, coltish year at Leasowe with the Consul, in England when they were boys. This chapter, which has a deep sombreness and great beauty, is of the first importance to the reader, being a sort of epilogue in prologue-place, and containing, as it does, the unobtrusive clues to the story. It is in this chapter that the small tapers are lit which illumine the subsequent narrative. This chapter at once ends itself and begins the story of that day a year before, with a magnificent sentence of elision: "Over the town, in the dark, tempestuous night, backwards revolved the luminous wheel . . . "

It is 1938, the morning of the Day of the Dead. The Consul, who has not slept, sits in a *cantina,* precisely, deliberately sustaining his alcoholic euphoria. The little foxes of remorse and failure which gnaw at his vitals are drowsy with grape. His wife, Yvonne, whom he loves helplessly and who has left and divorced him and gone to America, appears suddenly, unbelievably in the doorway. A little way down the street is the rococo house of M. Laruelle, who has been her lover, and on whose wall is inscribed, as the Consul remembers bitterly, *No se puede vivir sin amar.* And arriving that day is Hugh, the Consul's younger half-brother, a Leftist journalist, troubled at leaving Spain without sharing her agony. And from this moment, as the Consul's grasp tightens on his glass and his tenuous hold on reality relaxes—slowly, almost imperceptibly at first, the events of that day begin to arrange themselves into a pattern of doom.

Involuted and radiant, the terror and beauty and chaos of that day are not to be told, can only be awkwardly suggested. Through the fevered, credible dazzle of the Consul's conversation, above his flights of free association, there is a kind of silent agony, of a wild crying unheard, so that one feels that, behind the brittle, brilliant words which divert and assure, a man is falling, turning, tumbling, falling into space.

I tell you, I cannot stop thinking of this book; of the sweet morning ride in the light, cool air, before the heat, the mares followed by the gracile foals; of the dying man lying by the roadside, the horse, already ominous, standing beside him; the swift, symbolic tropical storm, and the odorous jungle; and the scene, like a bright nightmare, in the crowded cantina, at the book's ending, when the Consul finds that all the days of his life have led to that swarming room.

I do not mean to imply that *Under the Volcano* is immaculate of flaws. I do not quite believe in Yvonne, not that she is false, but that she is given obliquely, and Lowry seems strangely to have neglected her. Hugh, who is the Consul's *alter ego,* comes alive for me wholly only in the scene in the bull-ring. I accept the dramatic device of the behavior of the horse in the storm, while I misdoubt its natural probability. But these are so little wrong where so much is so wonderfully right.

There will, I suppose, be the expected comparisons with Jackson, Hemingway, Wolfe. With *The Lost Weekend* only because it deals with the tyranny of the grape. True, it is about alcoholism in Mexico, as a friend of mine said, but it is also true that *Ulysses* is about neuroticism in Dublin. In any comparison with *The Lost Weekend,* and I do not wish to denegate Mr. Jackson's achievement, Malcolm Lowry emerges as an artist, to say the least, and Charles Jackson, to say the most, as an able writer. As for *The Sun Also Rises,* it was good in its time, but this book would have bettered it then, and it is better, far better, now. Lowry has Wolfe's wild eloquence and bravura, but more grace and discipline and more compassion. On page 37 there is a sentence which is 32 lines long and does not falter in its music and can be read aloud without burdening the breath, and that is more than Wolfe ever did for me. Malcolm Lowry has created his own *genre,* and bent it to his will. He is Joyce's own child, there is no doubt, but he

is also his own man, an original. There are going to be a lot of new monkeys around now, I tell you, and you will recognize them. They are the ones Malcolm Lowry has made out of some of his contemporaries, the ones who have become our complacent idols, whom we have saluted as truly McCovian, and I feel sorry for them, in their tottering ivory towers or wherever they may be; because they are going to have to go back to their typewriters and start writing with their heads and their hearts and their jolly old genes, the way he does, if they wish to stand beside the author of this book. Some of them won't like this novel, and they'll say so, but they will have to admit to themselves that here is a man who can write a prose that is like wine, who can make the English language serve him like a slave. Otherwise, they had better start ignoring such positive phenomena as wind and storm and the bright veins of lightning in the sky.

I have never before used the word in a review, and I am aware of the responsibility upon me in using it, but I am of the opinion, carefully considered, that *Under the Volcano* is a work of genius.

Ladies and gentlemen: this magnificent, tragic, compassionate, and beautiful book—and my neck. (pp. 9-10)

> *John Woodburn, "Dazzling Disintegration,"
> in* The Saturday Review of Literature, *Vol.
> XXX, No. 8, February 22, 1947, pp. 9-10.*

Robert B. Heilman   (essay date 1947)

[*Heilman is an American critic who has written extensively about drama. In the following review of* Under the Volcano, *he praises the novel's evocative character and highlights some prominent images and themes.*]

Oscar Wilde once remarked that Browning used poetry as a medium for writing in prose; modern fiction often uses prose as a medium for writing poetry. In Malcolm Lowry's *Under the Volcano* the overt, external action itself is slight, but it takes on a heavy symbolic weight which must be felt in its relation to the symbolism of numerous objects, properties, occurrences, and even ideas and recollections and observations. The nexuses are imaginative rather than casual, or logical, or chronological; hiatuses compel a high attention; dextrous leaps are called for. In such a sense *Under the Volcano* may be understood as poetic—not in the sense that a mistily atavistic syntax and a half-hearted iambic hauteur, as often in the seeking theatre, pass for poetic.

The "story," as I have said, is slight: Yvonne, the wife of alcoholic Geoffrey Firmin, returns, after a year's separation, to her husband in Mexico. The events all take place on the day of her return. Geoffrey's passing desires to pull out with Yvonne are overcome by a far more urgent passion for alcohol. A French movie-producer, former lover of Yvonne, is with them for a while and incredulously lectures Geoffrey. Geoffrey's brother Hugh, ex-reporter and sailor, now about to run arms to the Spanish loyalists, in love with Yvonne, spends the day with them. The chief event is an outing by bus—Lowry's own wayward bus ("making its erratic journey"), which stops for a while near a wounded Indian left by the roadside but leaves without anybody's having done anything. Late in the day Geoffrey, who has constantly been getting separated from Hugh and Yvonne, outrageously abuses Yvonne and runs into the woods near Popocatepetl. Yvonne and Hugh pursue. Yvonne and Geoffrey lose their lives by means symbolically associated with the episode of the unattended roadside Indian.

Hugh makes his boat for Spain: this we have learned from a retrospective prologue—the contents of which are certain words and thoughts of the French movie-man a year after the day of the main story. This prologue is supposed to introduce all the main themes; but there is too much there to assimilate, especially since most of the material is not dramatized. It is a cold beginning, and then one has to keep going back to it as to an index—which is not the kind of re-reading that a concentrated book may legitimately demand. Further, on technical matters: the retrospects on which a one-day story must rely tend to be flaccid in style (Hugh's) or foggy in detail (Yvonne's); and coincidence has a fairly large hand in things. But, once into the story, one is less aware of these things than of the imaginative richness. The minds of the characters are sensitive recording instruments, tenacious alike of facts and of their suggestive value. The book is a cornucopia of images; both the psychic and the outer worlds have a tangibility which a thoughtless slice of realism could never produce; humor and horror are never alleged but are moulded into a hard and yet resilient narrative substance. But one is always driven to seek out the evocations that trail off behind the facts.

So, besides reading the story as story, we are always aware of a multitude of suggestions which, in their continual impingement upon us, remind us of the recurrent images of Shakespeare. The action takes place in November, on the Day of the Dead; Geoffrey feels his "soul dying"; a funeral takes place; burial customs, the shipping of a corpse are discussed; an earlier child of Yvonne's is dead; Geoffrey thinks he is seeing a dead man; a cantina is called La Sepultura; Geoffrey's recalls Dr. Faustus's death; a dead dog is seen in a ravine; a dying Indian is found by the roadside. Always there are vultures, pariah dogs, the noise of target practice. There are a decaying hotel, a reference to the House of Usher, the ruins of the palace of Maximilian and Carlotta. Geoffrey's soul appears to him "a town ravaged and stricken"; an imaginary "little town by the sea" burns up. Frustrations and failures are everywhere— engagements are missed, the light fails in a cinema. Always we are reminded of the barranca, or ravine, near the town—a horrendous abyss. Once it is called "Malebolge"; there are various allusions to Dante's *Inferno*; Geoffrey feels he is in hell, quotes Donne on sin, looks at Cocteau's *La Machine Infernale,* takes a ride in a Maquina Infernal; calls ironically-defiantly, "I love hell"; at the end he is in a bar "under the volcano." "It was not for nothing the ancients had placed Tartarus under Mt. Aetna. . . ." There are continual references to Marlowe's Faustus, who could not pray for grace, just as Geoffrey cannot feel a love that might break his love for alcohol, or rather, symbolize a saving attitude; as in the Faustus play, *soul* is a recurrent word. There is an Eden-Paradise theme: a public sign be-

comes a motif in itself, being repeated at the end of the story: "Do you enjoy this garden, which is yours? Keep your children from destroying it!" Geoffrey once mistranslates the second sentence: "We evict those who destroy." Geoffrey's own garden, once beautiful, has become a jungle; he hides bottles in the shrubbery; and once he sees a snake there.

Mr. Lowry does not use his rich resources merely to create moods; rather he uses the moods as clues to reality and thus fuses thought and feeling. Geoffrey's tremendous drinking can simply be considered pathological, of course; but it becomes, morally, an escape, an evasion of responsibility, a separation from life, a self-worship, a denial of love, a hatred of the living with a faith (there is an always pressing guilt-theme: Geoffrey, who was a naval officer in World War I, is a kind of sinning ancient mariner, caught by Life-in-Death, loathing his slimy creatures, born of the d. t.'s, whom he cannot expiatorily bless but must keep trying to drink away). The horror of Geoffrey's existence is always in the forefront of our consciousness, as it should be; but in the horror is involved an awareness of the dissolution of the old order, of the "drunken madly revolving world," of which Hugh says, "Good god, if our civilization were to sober up for a couple of days, it'd die of remorse on the third—" At the end, Geoffrey, unable by act of will to seize upon the disinterested aid of two old Mexicans, is the victim of local fascists: fascism preys upon a world that has already tossed away its own soul.

The episode which most successfully unifies the different levels of meaning is that of the Indian left wounded by the roadside. He is robbed by a Spanish "pelado," a symbol of "the exploitation of everybody by everybody else." Here we have echoes of the Spanish conquest and a symbol of aggression generally. Yvonne can't stand the sight of blood: it is her flaw, her way of acquiescing in the *de facto.* Geoffrey finds rules against doing anything; everyone feels that "it wasn't one's own business, but someone else's." It is modern irresponsibility and selfishness; the reader is prepared also to think of the "non-intervention" policy by the refrain which echoes throughout the book, "they are losing on the Ebro." But this is above all the story of the Good Samaritan—only there is no Samaritan. Devil take the least of these. (Geoffrey's ship, a gunboat disguised as a merchantman, had been named the "Samaritan"—a comment upon modern Samaritanism).

Hugh, held back by Geoffrey, is almost the Good Samaritan—Hugh who is going to run arms to Spain. To Geoffrey and Yvonne, he is "romantic"; doubtless he is and he has his own kind of guilt; but at least he insists on action, disinterested action. Here we come to what is apparently the basic theme of the book: man, in the words of a proverb repeated chorally, cannot live without love. Lowry flirts with the danger of the topical: the Spanish war is likely to give the novel the air of a political tract. But ultimately, I think, the author does succeed in keeping the political phenomena on the periphery of the spiritual substance, keeping them symbolic, using them for dramatic amplification of his metaphysic. It would be possible to read Geoffrey, always impersonally called the Consul, as dying capitalism, as laissez faire, or as sterile learning, like the speaker in Tennyson's *Palace of Art.* But such readings, though they are partly true, too narrowly circumscribe the total human situation with which Lowry is concerned.

The Consul's climactic acts of hate are a world's confession. Yvonne thinks of the need "of finding some faith," perhaps in "unselfish love." Whence love is to be derived, or how sanctioned and disciplined, is a question which the symbols do not fully answer. Yet it is the effect of Lowry's allusions—Dante, Faustus—to push the imagination toward a final reality that transcends all historical presents, however much each present may comment upon and modify it. Most of all this effect is secured by his constant allusion to Christian myth and history—the crucifixion, Golgotha, the last supper, original sin. Lowry is hardly writing a Christian allegory; indeed, some of the Christian echoes are decidedly ironic. But his whole complex of image and symbol is such as to direct a dissolving order, in search of a creative affirmation, toward that union of the personal and the universal which is the religious.

The two extremes which are the technical dangers of this kind of work are the tightly bound allegory, in which a system of abstract equivalents for all the concrete materials of the story constricts the imaginative experience, and a loose impressionism, in which a mass of suggestive enterprises sets off so many associations, echoes, and conjectures that the imaginative experience becomes diffuse. It is the latter risk that Mr. Lowry runs. For the present account, though a long one as reviews of fiction go, consistently oversimplifies the ingredients that it deals with, and it fails to deal with many other ingredients—for instance, the guitar motif, the cockfight motif, the theme of mystics and mysteries, the recurrent use of Indians, horses, the movie *The Hands of Orlac,* etc. Mr. Lowry has an immensely rich and vigorous imagination, and he never corks his cornucopia of evocative images and symbols. Some disciplinary rejections, some diffidence in setting afloat upon the imagination every boat that he finds upon the shore, would reduce the distractedness to which the reader is occasionally liable and would thus concentrate and shape the author's effect more clearly. But, if his synthesis is imperfect, there is great power in what Mr. Lowry has written—in his solid world of inner and outer objects in which the characters are dismayed and imprisoned as in Kafka's work; and in the implied coalescence of many levels of meaning that we find in Hermann Broch. Such a multivalued poetic fiction, with its sense of horrifying dissolution, and its submerged, uncertain vision of a hard new birth off in clouded time, is apparently the especial labor of the artistic conscience at our turn of an epoch. (pp. 488-92)

> *Robert B. Heilman, in a review of "Under the Volcano," in* The Sewanee Review, *Vol. LV, No. 3, Summer, 1947, pp. 488-92.*

Malcolm Lowry   (poem date 1947?)

[*The following poem expresses Lowry's ambivalence regarding the success of* Under the Volcano.]

"After Publication of *Under the Volcano*"

Success is like some horrible disaster
Worse than your house burning, the sounds of
    ruination
As the roof tree falls following each other faster
While you stand, the helpless witness of your
    damnation.

Fame like a drunkard consumes the house of the
    soul
Exposing that you have worked for only this—
Ah, that I had never suffered this treacherous
    kiss
And had been left in darkness forever to founder
    and fail.

> *Malcolm Lowry, "After Publication of 'Under the Volcano',"* in his *Selected Poems of Malcolm Lowry, edited by Earle Birney with Margerie Lowry, City Lights Books, 1962, p. 78.*

Malcolm Lowry   (essay date 1948)

[*In the following preface Lowry wrote for the French edition of* Under the Volcano, *he recounts his difficulties publishing the novel in its original length and form.*]

I like prefaces, I read them. Sometimes I do not read any farther, and it is possible that you may do the same. In that case, this preface will have failed in its purpose, which is to make your access to my book a little more easy. Above all, reader, do not regard these pages as an affront to your intelligence. They prove rather that the author here and there questions his own.

To begin with, his very style may assume an embarrassing resemblance to that of the German writer Schopenhauer describes, who wished to express six things at the same time instead of discussing them one after the other. "In those long, rich parenthetical periods, like boxes enclosing boxes, and crammed more full than roast geese stuffed with apples, one's memory above all is put to the task, when understanding and judgment should have been called upon to do their work."

But to take a criticism of style—as Schopenhauer conceived it—as a criticism of the mind and character of the author or even, as others would like, of the man himself, is beside the point. That at least is what I wrote in 1946, on board a bauxite ship in the middle of the waves between New Orleans and Port-au-Prince. That preface was never published. As for this one, the first reason for my drafting it was the fact that in 1945 my book received a very lukewarm welcome from an English firm (which has since done me the honour of publishing it). Although the publishers considered the work "important and honest", they suggested wide corrections which I was reluctant to make. (You would have reacted in the same way had you written a book and been so tormented by it that you rejected and rewrote it many times.) Among other things, I was advised to suppress two or three characters, to reduce the twelve chapters to six, to change the subject, which was too similar to that of *Poison;* in short, to throw my book out of the window and write another. Since I now have the honour of being translated into French, I take up once again my letter of reply to my publisher and friend in London. The enterprise was doubtless a foolish one: to give all kinds of good esoteric reasons why the work should stay just as it was in the beginning.

Those reasons I have now almost completely forgotten, and perhaps that is lucky for you. It is in fact all too true, as Sherwood Anderson has remarked, that in all concerning his work a writer assumes the most extraordinary pretensions and is ready to justify anything. It is also likely that one of the few honest remarks an author has ever made was that of Julien Green on the subject, I believe, of his masterly *Minuit:* "My intention was—and has ever since remained to me—obscure."

In writing this book, which was started when I was twenty-six (I am now about to salute my fortieth year) and finished five years ago, my intention did not at first seem to me obscure, although it became more so as the years went on. But, whether obscure or not, it still remains a fact that one of my intentions was to write a book.

And, indeed, my intention was not to write a tedious book. I do not believe a single author, even the most irascible of them all, has ever had the deliberate intention of wearying his reader, though it has been said that boredom can be used as a technique. But once this book did in fact appear boring to a reader—and a professional reader at that—I thought it necessary to reply to the observations of that professional reader [see excerpt in *TCLC,* Vol. 6, pp. 235-36], and here is the gist of what I wrote. All this may perhaps appear to you terribly vain and pompous, but how can you explain to someone who claims to have been bored by your prose that he was in the wrong for letting himself be bored?

"Dear Sir," I wrote then, "Thank you for your letter of the 29th November 1945. I received it only on New Year's Eve. Moreover, it reached me here in Mexico where, entirely by chance, I am living in the tower which served as a model for the house of one of my characters. Ten years ago I had only seen that tower from the outside, and—in chapter VI—it became the place where my hero too experienced some slight vexations as a result of delayed mail . . . "

Then I went on to say that if my work had already assumed the classic form of the printed page instead of the sad and desolate aspect which characterises an unpublished manuscript, the opinion of the reader would certainly have been entirely different because of the various critical judgments that would have assailed his ears. Since the tiresomeness or otherwise of the beginning of **Under the Volcano** appeared to me dependent on the reader's state of mind, on his readiness to seize the author's intention, I suggested—doubtless in desperation of my cause— that a brief preface might neutralise the reactions which my professional reader foresaw. I continued thus: "If you tell me that a good wine needs no label, I may perhaps reply that I am not talking about wine but about mescal, and that even more than a label—once one had crossed the threshold of the tavern—mescal calls for the accompaniment of both salt and lemon. I hope at least that such a preface may bring a little lemon and salt."

In this way I wrote a letter of round about 20,000 words,

which took me the time I might just as well have employed on starting the first draft of a new novel, even more boring than the other. And since, in the eyes of my reader, the first chapter seemed to be the novel's greatest crime, I limited myself to an analysis of that long first chapter which establishes the themes and counter-themes of the book, which sets the tone, which harmonises the symbolism.

The narrative, I explained, begins on All Souls' Day, in November, 1939, in a hotel called Casino de la Selva— selva meaning *wood.* And perhaps it would not be out of place to mention here that the book was first of all conceived rather pretentiously on the sempiternal model of Gogol's *Dead Souls,* and as the first leaf in the triptych of a kind of drunken *Divine Comedy. Purgatory* and *Paradise* were to follow, with the protagonist, like Chichikov, becoming at each stage slightly better or worse, according to one's point of view. (However, if one is to believe a recent authority, the incredible Vladimir Nabokov, the progression postulated by Gogol was rather: Crime, Punishment, Redemption; Gogol threw almost all of Punishment and Redemption into the fire.) The theme of the dark wood, introduced once again in Chapter VII when the Consul enters a lugubrious cantina called El Bosque, which also means *wood,* is resolved in Chapter IX, which relates the death of the heroine and in which the wood becomes reality and also fatality.

This first chapter is shown through the eyes of a French film producer, Jacques Laruelle. He establishes a kind of survey of the terrain, just as he expresses the slow, melancholy and tragic rhythm of Mexico itself: Mexico, the meeting place of many races, the ancient battleground of social and political conflicts where, as Waldo Frank, I believe, has shown, a colourful and talented people maintained a religion which was virtually a cult of death. It is the ideal setting for the struggle of a human being against the powers of darkness and light.

After leaving the Casino de la Selva, Jacques Laruelle finds himself looking into the barranca which plays a great part in the story, and which is also the ravine, that cursed abyss which in our age every man presents to himself, and also, more simply, if the reader prefers it, the sewer.

The chapter ends in another cantina where people are talking refuge during an unseasonal storm, while elsewhere, all over the world, people are crawling into the air-raid shelters; then the lights go out, just as, all over the world as well, they are going out. Outside, in that night created by the tempest, the luminous wheel is turning.

That wheel is the Ferris wheel erected in the middle of the square, but it is also, if you like, many other things: the wheel of the law, the wheel of Buddha. It is even eternity, the symbol of the Everlasting Return. That wheel, which demonstrates the very form of the book, can also be considered in a cinematographic manner as the wheel of Time, which is about to turn in an inverse direction, until we reach the preceding year. For the beginning of the second chapter brings us to All Souls' Day a year before, in November, 1938.

At this point I tried modestly to insinuate that my little book seemed to me denser and deeper, composed and carried out with more care than the English publisher supposed; that if its meanings had escaped the reader, or if the latter had deemed uninteresting the meanings that float on the surface of the narrative, this might have been due at least in part to a merit rather than a failing of mine. In fact, had not the more accessible aspect of the book been designed so carefully that the reader did not wish to take the trouble of pausing to go below the surface? "If that is true," I added, not without a certain vanity, "for how many books can it be said?"

In a more sentimental tone, but with only an appearance of greater modesty, I then wrote as follows: "Since I am asking for a re-reading of the **Volcano,** in the light of certain aspects which may not have occurred to you, and since I do not wish to undertake a defence of every paragraph, it may be as well for me to admit that in my view the principal failing of the book, from which all the others flow, lies in something which cannot be remedied: the mental baggage of the book is subjective rather than objective; it would better suit a poet—I do not say a good poet—than a novelist, and it is a baggage very difficult to carry as far as its destination. On the other hand, just as a tailor who knows his customer's deformity tries to hide it, I have tried as far as possible to hide the faults of my understanding. But since the conception of the work was primarily poetic, these deformities may hardly matter after all. Besides, poems often call for several readings before their meaning is revealed—is exposed in the mind as I believe Hopkins said—and it is precisely that notion which you have overlooked."

I demanded the most serious examination of the text, and I asked how, without appreciating its contents, the reader had reached his view that the book was too long, particularly since his reaction might well be different after a second reading. Did not readers, just as much as authors, take a risk of falling over themselves by going too fast? And what a boring book it must be if so hasty a reading were all that could be granted!

I went on to explain that my novel consists of twelve chapters, and the main part of the narrative is contained within a single day of twelve hours. In the same way, there are twelve months in a year and the whole book is enclosed within the limits of a year, while that deeper layer of the novel—or the poem—which derives from myth is linked at this point with the Jewish Cabbala, where the number twelve is of the greatest importance. The Cabbala is used for poetic ends because it represents Man's spiritual aspirations. The Tree of Life, its emblem, is a kind of complicated ladder whose summit is called Kether, or Light, while somewhere in its midst an abyss opens out. The spiritual domain of the Consul is probably Qliphoth, the world of husks and demons, represented by the Tree of Life turned upside down and governed by Beelzebub, the God of Flies. All this was not essential for the understanding of the book; I mentioned it in passing so as to give the feeling, as Henry James has said, "that depths exist".

In the Jewish Cabbala the abuse of magic powers is compared to drunkenness or the abuse of wine, and is expressed, if I remember rightly, by the Hebrew word *sod.* Another attribution of the word *sod* signifies garden, or

neglected garden, and the Caballa itself is sometimes considered as a garden (naturally similar to that where grew the tree of forbidden fruit which gave us the Knowledge of Good and Evil), with the Tree of Life planted in the middle. In one way or another these matters are at the base of many of our legends regarding the origins of man, and William James, if not Freud, might be in agreement with me when I affirm that the agonies of the drunkard find a very close parallel in the agonies of the mystic who has abused his powers. Here the Consul has brought everything together in a magnificently drunken fashion. In Mexico, mescal is a formidable drink but a drink which one can get in any cantina much more easily, if I may say so, than Scotch whisky in the Impasse des Deux-Anges. (Let me say in passing that I see I have done wrong to mescal and tequila, which are drinks I like very much, and for that I should perhaps present my apologies to the Mexican government.) But mescal is also a drug which is taken in the form of mescalin, and the transcendance of its effects is one of the best-known experiments among occultists. It seems as though the Consul has confused the two states, and perhaps after all he is not in the wrong.

This novel, to use a phrase of Edmund Wilson, has for its subject the forces that dwell within man and lead him to look upon himself with terror. Its subject is also the fall of man, his remorse, his incessant struggle towards the light under the weight of the past, which is his destiny. The allegory is that of the Garden of Eden, the garden representing this world from which we are now even a little more under the threat of ejection than at the moment when I wrote this book. On one level, the drunkenness of the Consul may be regarded as symbolising the universal drunkenness of war, of the period that precedes war, no matter when. Throughout the twelve chapters, the destiny of my hero can be considered in its relationship to the destiny of humanity.

"I hold to the number twelve," I then added. "It is as if I heard a clock sounding midnight for Faust, and when I think of the slow progression of the chapters, I feel that neither more nor less than twelve should satisfy me. For the rest, the book is stratified in numerous planes. My effort has been to clarify as far as possible whatever at first presented itself to me in a complicated and esoteric manner. The novel can be read simply as a story during which you may—if you wish—skip whole passages, but from which you will get far more if you skip nothing at all. It can be regarded as a kind of symphony or opera, or even as something like a cowboy film. I wanted to make of it a jam session, a poem, a song, a tragedy, a comedy, a farce. It is superficial, profound, entertaining, boring, according to one's taste. It is a prophecy, a political warning, a cryptogram, a crazy film, an absurdity, a writing on the wall. It can be thought of as a kind of machine; it works, you may be sure, for I have discovered that to my own expense. And in case you should think that I have made of it everything except a novel, I shall answer that in the last resort it is a real novel that I have intended to write, and even a damnably serious novel."

In short, I made terrific efforts to explain my own idea of this unfortunate volume; I waged a notable battle for the work as it stood, as it was finally printed, and as it today appears for my French readers. And remember, I wrote all that in Mexico, in the very place where ten years before I had started my book, and in the end I received, from the hands of the same tiny postman who brought the Consul his delayed postcard, the news that it had been accepted.

After this long preamble, my dear French reader, it would perhaps be honest of me to admit to you that the idea I cherished in my heart was to create a pioneer work in its own class, and to write at last an authentic drunkard's story. I do not know whether I have succeeded. And now, friend, I beg you continue your walk along the Seine, and please replace this book where you found it, in the second-hand bookseller's 100-franc box. (pp. 23-9)

> *Malcolm Lowry, "Preface to a Novel," in* Canadian Literature, *No. 9, Summer, 1961, pp. 23-9.*

Anthony R. Kilgallin   (essay date 1965)

[*In the following excerpt, Kilgallin discusses the Faust myth as the primary theme in* Under the Volcano.]

The best introduction to any critical study of **Under the Volcano** is Lowry's **"Preface to a Novel"** [see essay dated 1948] in which he analyzes " . . . that long first chapter which establishes the themes and counter-themes of the book, which sets the tone, which harmonizes the symbolism." The uppermost of these themes is that of Faust: "It is as if I heard a clock sounding midnight for Faust," writes Lowry in justifying his use of twelve chapters. The Consul Geoffrey Firmin, God-free and infirm, is a man fallen from Grace, in the Christian or Catholic sense, and a black magician on another plane. The entire novel is built upon the ramifications of his fall:

> This novel, to use a phrase of Edmund Wilson, has for its subject the forces that dwell within man and lead him to look upon himself with terror. Its subject is also the fall of man, his remorse, his incessant struggle towards the light under the weight of the past, which is his destiny . . . Throughout the twelve chapters, the destiny of my hero can be considered in its relationship to the destiny of humanity.

The third epigraph to the novel is a quotation from Goethe's *Faust:* "Whosoever unceasingly strives upward . . . him can we save." Goethe himself set these lines in inverted commas in his masterpiece to emphasize them as a fundamental pronouncement. In his eighty-second year he spoke vital words to Eckermann about this passage:

> In these lines the key to Faust's salvation is contained: in Faust himself there is an activity mounting ever higher and purer to the end, and from above eternal love which helps him in his need. All this is completely in harmony with our religious conceptions, according to which we enter into bliss not by our own strength alone, but by the divine grace vouchsafed to us.

In terms of the Consul these lines are to be profoundly ironic.

The narrative of **Under the Volcano** opens on a "gigantic red evening, whose reflection bled away in the deserted swimming pools scattered everywhere like so many mirages". The metaphor is reminiscent of the famous line of Marlowe's Faustus: "See, see, where Christ's blood streams in the firmament!", as Faustus pleads for one drop of blood to save his soul. Geoffrey is first identified with Faustus through a related simile:

> What had happened just a year ago today seemed already to belong in a different age. One would have thought the horrors of the present would have swallowed it up like a drop of water. It was not so. Though tragedy was in the process of becoming unreal and meaningless, it seemed one was still permitted to remember the days when an individual life held some value and was not a mere misprint in a communiqué.

Almost the last of Faustus' pleas was, "O soul, be changed into little waterdrops,/And fall into the ocean, ne'er be found!" In vain does Faustus seek an escape through anonymity. His tragedy, in fact, still serves as the best known archetype of its kind; likewise, the tragedy of the Consul's death is unforgettable.

Chapter One of the novel is presented through the consciousness of Jacques Laruelle, acquaintance since childhood of Geoffrey, and sometime movie-producer who has been considering "making in France a modern film version of the Faustus story with some such character as Trotsky for its protagonist". Unrecognized by Laruelle, Geoffrey's life has been this very story; it is purposefully ironic that ten months later Trotsky is murdered in Mexico City, an exile with a short pointed beard like the Consul who, on the night of his death, is to be called "Trotsky". To prepare for his movie, Laruelle has borrowed a volume of Elizabethan plays from Geoffrey himself, among which is Marlowe's *Doctor Faustus.* Opening the book at random he reads, "then will I headlong fly into the earth: / Earth, gape! it will not harbour me". He sits "oblivious of his surroundings, gazing at the words that seemed to have the power of carrying his own mind downward into a gulf, as in fulfilment on his own spirit of the threat Marlowe's Faustus had cast at his despair". Looking closer at the passage, he realizes he has misread the word "fly" for the actual word "run". This simple slip is intensified when, several pages later, we hear the line, "where I come from they don't run". The speaker is Weber, a witness to Geoffrey's murder, which, in Geoffrey's own way, was a literally physical attempt to enact Marlowe's quotation on his last night of life. The word "fly" calls to mind the inscription on Faustus' arm, "*Homo fuge:* whither should I fly".

Playing the game of "sortes Shakespeareanae" Laruelle turns again coincidentally to a quotation from *Doctor Faustus:*

> Cut is the branch that might have grown full straight,
> And burned is Apollo's laurel bough,
> That sometimes grew within this learned man,
> Faustus is gone; regard his hellish fall—

Geoffrey had "gone" exactly one year ago; the play's next line, "Whose fiendful fortune may exhort the wise", is a potential warning to Laruelle and to the reader to observe, and profit from, the example of Geoffrey the damned soul who supposedly had once considered writing an occult volume to be entitled "Secret Knowledge".

Inside the book of plays Laruelle finds an unsent letter of Geoffrey to Yvonne, his divorced wife, imploring her to return to him "if only for a day". That the Consul could not bring himself to send the letter, a plea for salvation, indicates partially his inability to communicate this desire. He writes, "But this is what it is to live in hell. I could not, cannot ask you. I could not, cannot send a telegram". Despite the Good Angel, Faustus is also unable to communicate his desire for deliverance. To confirm this parallel situation Lowry subtly compares another reference to Faustus' predicament with the Consul's former plight. Faustus exclaims, "How! bell, book, and candle—candle, book, and bell,— / Forward and backward, to curse Faustus to hell". Bell, book, and candle is the old ceremony of major excommunication. The bell announced this to all; the book represented authority; while the candle was believed to symbolize the possibility that the ban might be lifted by the repentance and amendment of its victim for, just as the candle was used and extinguished, so the excommunication itself might be. *Twelve* priests and a bishop all held lighted candles; the bishop recited the formula which ended:

> We separate him, together with his accomplices and abettors, from the precious body and blood of the Lord and from the society of all Christians; we exclude him from our holy mother, the Church in heaven and on earth; we declare him excommunicate and anathema; we judge him damned, with the Devil and his angels and all the reprobate, to eternal fire until he shall recover himself from the toils of the Devil and return to amendment and to penitence.

Those present answered, "So be it!" The candles were extinguished by being dashed on the ground. The ceremony ended. Laruelle's misquotation of "fly" for "run" is due to the "elusive flickering candlelight"; finishing the letter he holds it into the candle flame until it is extinguished. Then, "suddenly from outside, a bell spoke out, then ceased abruptly: *dolente. . .dolore!*" Again the ceremony has ended.

Geoffrey's affliction is drunkenness in its most compulsive and irremediable state. In the **"Preface to a Novel"** Lowry wrote, "on one level, the drunkenness of the Consul may be regarded as symbolizing the universal drunkenness of war, of the period that precedes war, no matter when." In his letter Geoffrey writes, "this is how I drink too, as if I were taking an eternal sacrament". It is essential to recall Faustus celebrating the sacrament of the Black Mass. Lowry certifies this intended analogy in the **"Preface"**: "William James . . . might be in agreement with me when I affirm that the agonies of the drunkard find a very close parallel in the agonies of the mystic who has abused his powers." Indeed, in *The Varieties of Religious Experience*, James concludes a passage on this very subject with the statement that "The drunken consciousness is one bit of the mystic consciousness. . . ." Since Lowry also conceived of the drunken Consul as a universal symbol, the

Faust theme expands to wide-ranging socio-political implications. In *The Decline of the West* Oswald Spengler characterized the spirit of modern Europe and America as Faustian, a condition which pictured man as ageing and wasted, but still hoping to comprehend and achieve everything, including the impossible. Nevertheless, western man, having become civilized, is effete, *in firm,* and defenceless, and therefore must perish. Visible then in the fall of Geoffrey is the fall of our Faustian civilization. Spengler, quoted by Hugh Firmin, Geoffrey's half-brother, is an important functional reference throughout *Under the Volcano.*

The symbolic importance of the frequent cinema advertisements for *Las Manos de Orlac* is due partially to the Faustian allusions in Maurice Renard's book, *The Hands of Orlac,* from which the film was adapted. Resine, the blonde wife of the pianist Stephen Orlac who, in an operation to save his hands, is given the hands of a supposed murderer, is haunted by a devil's head—a Mephisto—a Fantomo. Indeed, Yvonne refers to Geoffrey as a "phantom". For the Yvonne-like Rosine " . . . it was a partial and chance resemblance, inspired by the character in Faust." Stephen's studio, where he retrains his hands for the piano, becomes "the Temple of Hands. Here were installed the two electric machines, the practise keyboard, and all the physical and chemical apparatus with which he had provided himself. And there were also some special books in a pile. The place soon looked like Dr. Faust's den." Like Faustus, who "surfeits upon cursed necromancy", Stephen also becomes interested in the subject: he observes that " . . . necromants or necromaticians make it a practice to evoke the dead so as to obtain by their aid some light upon the future." Lowry's entire technique of literary allusion has particularly this same purpose. Apart from common references to Baudelaire and to secret and occult books, two motifs of *The Hands of Orlac* also run through *Under the Volcano:* " . . . from day to day he was slipping down into an abyss", and "The dead are coming back to life."

Into the third chapter Lowry introduces a pair of Faustian familiars who battle to direct Geoffrey's conscience. By definition, a familiar is a spirit supposed to attend and obey a sorcerer; also, in naming them "guardian angels" Lowry makes his allusion to Faustus' Good and Evil Angels obvious. The opening paragraph of this chapter includes a Faustus paraphrase: "Look up at that niche in the wall over there on the house where Christ is still, suffering, who would help you if you asked him: you cannot ask him". Faustus observes and does ask momentarily, "Ay, Christ, my Saviour, / Seek to save distressed Faustus' soul!" The latter lines significantly follow the last pleas of both angels in the play. Likewise, Geoffrey's familiars do not finally abandon him until an hour before his end. The Evil Angel strikes first, urging the Consul to drink rather than think of Yvonne: " . . . the voice he recognized of a pleasant and impertinent familiar, perhaps horned, prodigal of disguise, a specialist in casuistry." The Good Angel angrily retorts: "Neither do I believe in the strychnine, you'll make me cry again, you bloody fool Geoffrey Firmin, I'll kick your face in, O idiot!" The "first familiar" wins this round as Geoffrey downs half the strychnine.

The Good Angel threatens Geoffrey again, unsuccessfully. Both reappear before temporarily leaving the Consul, their battleground. The final reference to *Doctor Faustus* in this chapter comes when Geoffrey interjects, "please remind me to get back my Elizabethan plays".

Faust, as distinct from Dr. Faustus, is alluded to in this third chapter as Geoffrey thinks uneasily of "Goethe's famous church bell in pursuit of the child truant from church". Lowry has cleverly summarized Faust's soliloquy in which bells and voices in the Eastern Dawn prevent him from taking his life. Geoffrey and Faust are ironically juxtaposed; the former poisons his soul with each drink, while the latter is persuaded by a choir of angels, all Good, against self-destruction by poison. As a boy, Faust strayed in fields and forests but was always entranced by the sabbath bells. Their sounds now help prevent him from committing suicide. Geoffrey, however, is hardened against such precautions: "Goethe's church bell was looking him straight between the eyes; fortunately, he was prepared for it". Before conquering his despair Faust had cried, "I hear, but lack the faith, am dispossessed." Similarly, Geoffrey has been referred to as a "poor, lonely dispossessed trembling soul". Both men recognize the soul's life-giving source, but only Faust aspires to seek it. Both men thirst after knowledge, but Geoffrey's unquenchable alcoholic thirst takes precedence in his case. At one time he had hoped to write a book on Atlantis, the main part of which was to be "the chapters on the alchemists". On this topic he refers to "the old alchemists of Prague . . . living among the cohabitations of Faust himself".

In chapter four, Bernal Diaz, William Blackstone, Geoffrey and Faustus are all employed to illustrate precisely a viewpoint noted by Spengler in *The Decline of the West:* "Dramas like that of the emigration to America—man by man, each on his own account, driven by deep promptings to loneliness,—or the Spanish Conquest, or the Californian gold-rush, dramas of uncontrollable longings for freedom, solitude, immense independence . . . these dramas are Faustian and only Faustian." Limitless space is the prime symbol of the Faustian soul. Thus, Geoffrey's paraphrase of Diaz, the author of *The Discovery and Conquest of Mexico 1517-1521,* and his wish to escape like Blackstone are understandable. To quote Spengler again: "To fly, to free one's self from earth, to lose one's self in the expanse of the universe—is not this ambition Faustian in the highest degree?" Unfortunately, Mexico has been plagued by exploiters ever since Cortez and Diaz. Hugh remembers once hearing the potential solution: "For man, every man, Juan seemed to be telling him, even as Mexico, must ceaselessly struggle upward", a paraphrase of the novel's epigraph from *Faust.* This quotation is part of the song of the angels who bear the immortal remains of Faust to heaven. Man and the world must follow Juan's advice to achieve a final salvation similar to Faust's. Geoffrey, however, sleeps throughout the chapter, but retains his Faustian identity in the minds of Hugh and Yvonne. Hugh asks, "How much does he really know about all this alchemy and cabbala business? How much does it mean to him?", and even jokes, "Maybe he's a black magician!"

The Faustian familiars reappear in Chapter Five as Geoffrey awakens from his Indic dream with "demons gnattering in his ears". The evil one advises him to ". . . just take one drink, just the necessary, the therapeutic drink: perhaps two drinks", but before he does so another voice retorts, "Put that bottle down, Geoffrey Firmin, what are you doing to yourself ?" "The emptiness in the air after filled with whispers: alas, alas. Wings it really meant." Geoffrey's last hours are literally flying away as, at the chapter's end the good familiar cries out in desperation, "Stop it, for God's sake, you fool. Watch your step. We can't help you any more."

The role of Geoffrey as a Faustian magician is strengthened by a quotation from Shelley's *Alastor:* "Twelve o'clock, and the Consul said to the doctor: 'Ah, that the dream of the dark magician in his visioned cave, even while his hand—that's the bit I like—shakes in its last decay, were the true end of this so lovely world." Lines 681-6 of *Alastor* read as follows:

> O, that the dream
> Of dark magician in his visioned cave,
> Raking the cinders of a crucible
> For life and power, even when his feeble hand
> Shakes in its last decay, were the true law
> Of this so lovely world!

The misquotation of "end" for "law" is a noteworthy Freudian slip since Geoffrey is inadvertently comparing the magician's last stages with his own and the world's, whereas Shelley does not imply that the death of the magician causes the world's end. He puns on the word "Katabasis" but the application of the term underlines the present predicament. This *is* a descent into the nether world, into an inferno. Indeed, the attempt to insert a katabasis into the second part of *Faust,* first as a descent to the Mothers, and then as the Classical Walpurgis Night, was evidently one of the most baffling structural problems of that work, as well as being one of the most crucial sections of the play.

The familiars are mentioned by Geoffrey next in Chapter Seven: "As for the demons, they were inside him as well as outside; quiet at the moment—taking their siesta perhaps—he was none the less surrounded by them and occupied; they were in possession." In *Doctor Faustus* the evil demons appear as the Seven Deadly Sins. Faustus' line, "O, I'll leap up to my God!—Who pulls me down?" seems to be applicable to a momentarily penitent Geoffrey when "the weight of a great hand seemed to be pressing his head down." Jacques disparagingly compares Marlowe's sense of perspective to Geoffrey's: "Christopher Marlowe, your Faust man, saw the Carthaginians fighting on his big toenail. That's the kind of clear seeing you indulge in. Everything seems perfectly clear, in terms of the toe-nail." Ironically, the analogy gives great compliment to Geoffrey's powers of vision. He remarks, "It was already the longest day in his entire experience, a lifetime" when a few lines earlier the pun *Dies Faustus* had appeared. Marlowe's Faustus loved knowledge and power more than he did Christ, while Goethe's Faust would have reached the same tragic end were it not for the love of Margareta who brings him salvation. Geoffrey's fate fluctuates between these two poles. His potential saviour, Yvonne, first dreamed of

Lowry in the Lake District.

making a new start with Geoffrey in British Columbia on Lake Pineaus where he owned an island. Coincidental or not, in *Faust: Part Two* the lower Peneus is a similar lotus-land Eden.

In Chapter Ten the personal and the political are two main frames of reference. Spengler's observation on this point is helpful: "There are two sorts of Destiny, two sorts of war, two sorts of tragedy—public and private. Nothing can eliminate this duality from the world." As a private individual and as a public representative, the Consul symbolically portrays an ambivalent character; a Faust figure and an Everyman figure simultaneously. He uses one of Marlowe's most famous lines as a point of departure. Looking at Cervantes' prize-fighting cock he asks, "Was this the face that launched five hundred ships, and betrayed Christ into being in the Western Hemisphere?" In Conrad Aiken's *Blue Voyage,* an important literary source for parts of **Under the Volcano,** the main character, Demarest, had used this same line for his own comic points of departure: "Is this the face that scuttled a thousand ships?" Chapter Ten concludes with Geoffrey voicing a Faustus-like frustration. Into the oncoming storm he cries out, "I love hell. I can't wait to get back there. In fact I'm *running.* I'm almost back there already." Faustus' soul was divided between a desire for mastery and a sense of guilt. Geoffrey despairingly envisions a comparable di-

chotomy: "What is man but a little soul holding up a corpse?" Like Faustus, he is tragic because he recognizes this dilemma as real. As Faustus boasts that his soul is his own to dispose of as he will, he hears the fearful echoes thundering in his ears. Similarly, as Geoffrey proclaims his love of hell there is also a contradictory emendation, for, "the queer thing was, he wasn't quite serious." Nature forewarns Geoffrey, just as it did Faustus: "Before him the volcanoes, precipitous, seemed to have drawn nearer. They towered up over the jungle, into the lowering sky— massive interests moving up in the background."

A letter from Lowry to his American editor, Albert Erskine, July 15, 1946 shows Lowry's concern with *Faust* in Chapter Eleven. Remembering Julian Green's note in his *Diary* to end a book with the image of the heroine rising to heaven, Lowry added to this idea one contained in the opera *Faust* when Margareta rises to heaven while Faust descends to hell. Thus, the simultaneous actions of Yvonne and Geoffrey in Chapters Eleven and Twelve parallel the splitting of the path as two roads diverge into the Mexican wood to two opposing destinies.

Geoffrey's last hour commences when he sees "a clock pointing to six". The Faustian parallel of the last hour permits an ironic contrast. After the clock strikes eleven, Faustus, aware of impending damnation, exclaims, "Now hast thou but one bare hour to live. / And then thous must be damn'd perpetually!" Through an almost fatalistic determinism, Geoffrey's approaching death is similarly inevitable. He, however, apathetically accepts the end, totally lacking Faustus' frantic longing for life. Yet Geoffrey's death is fully in accord with Spengler's theory of the determinism of inevitable decline for the Faustian spirit of Western man in the twentieth century, the death of modern man, as Jung put it, in search of his soul. Asking "What is a lost soul?" Geoffrey, in answering himself, describes himself: "It is one that has turned from its true path and is groping in the darkness of remembered ways."

Time ticks on: "the ticking of his watch, his heart, his conscience, a clock somewhere." In vain Faustus ordered, "Stand still, you ever-moving spheres of heaven, / That time may cease, and midnight never come." Geoffrey makes no such plea, but only notes and recalls while his familiars make their last supplications. He hears them argue, and then "the voices ceased". They return as "daemonic orchestras" and "insolent archfiends", and lastly come to him as he lies with Maria, the prostitute, "hissing and shrieking and yammering at him: 'Now you've done it, Geoffrey Firmin!' Even we can help you no longer . . . Just the same you might as well make the most of it now, the night's still young." Young it is, but for Geoffrey it is almost over. Even Maria is part of the Faustian tradition, for in ancient Coptic manuscripts the magician and the prostitute played an equal role to that of the magician and the virgin, Yvonne in this case. Now, at six-thirty, "A bell clanged frantically in the distance" just as for Faustus the clock strikes the half-hour. Spengler wrote that, "Besides the clock, the bell itself is a Western 'symbol'." As such it is a Faustian symbol as well.

The crag of the Malebolge reminds Geoffrey of Shelley's *The Cenci,* Coleridge's *Kubla Klan,* and Calderon. The last reference is probably to Calderon de la Barca's play *The Wonder-Working Magician,* to whose Faust theme Goethe was indebted. The play opens in a wood where Cyprian and a Demon argue about the unity of God. Cyprian later sells his soul for Justina, his beloved. The two die on the scaffold and ascend to heaven. The following lines from Calderon's play depict imagery visible also in the Malebolge: "Though from that proud height you fall / Headlong down a dark abyss"; "Abyss of hell, prepare, / Yourself the region of your own despair!" and especially the following lines:

> This mountain's brow is bound
> With curling mist, like streaming hair
> Spread out below, and all the horizon round
> Is one volcanic pyre!

Geoffrey describes the sunset as "A mercurochrome agony down the west". The suggestion of a blood-red crucifixion is comparable to the description by Faustus: "See, see, where Christ's blood streams in the firmament! / One drop would save my soul, half a drop," a parallel that occurs elsewhere as I have already indicated, one year later, as a "gigantic red evening, whose reflection bled away in the deserted swimming pools". Faustus' futile plea for even half a drop is paralleled in Geoffrey's thirst: "the thirst that was not thirst, but itself heartbreak, and lust,

was death, death, and death again". He remembers once carrying a carafe of water in the hotel *El Infierno* but unable to put it to his lips he hears a voice saying "you cannot drink of it", and believes "it must have been Jesus who sent me this". The comparable line in *Doctor Faustus* is "Ah, rend not my heart for naming of my Christ!" Meanwhile we hear "the clock ticking forward" with Geoffrey abandoning "The hope of any new life together, even were it miraculously offered again".

Reflecting on "that extraordinary picture on Laruelle's wall, *Los Borrachones,*" Geoffrey applies the book's epigraph from *Faust* to himself:

> When he had striven upwards as at the beginning with Yvonne, had not the "features" of life seemed to grow more clear, more animated, friends and enemies more identifiable, special problems, scenes, and with them the sense of his own reality, more *separate* from himself? And had it not turned out that the farther down he sank, the more those features had tended to dissemble, to cloy and clutter, to become finally little better than ghastly caricatures of his dissimulating inner and outer self, or of his struggle, if struggle there were still?

In his descent, his katabasis, Geoffrey becomes a corporate and composite character, incorporating all damned souls, just as with successive masks he has been all of the literary models alluded to, a timeless Everyman. He joins the "downward flight" of souls beyond salvation, just as Yvonne has already joined the ascending flight, à la Margareta, although her death follows Geoffrey's.

Time moves on, "One, two, three, four, five, twelve, six, seven". Geoffrey's last twelve hours conclude in this twelfth chapter at seven o'clock. "The clock outside quickly chimed seven times." As the clock for Faustus strikes twelve, thunder and lightning ensue. Similarly, "Thunderclaps crashed on the mountains and then at hand," and "Lightning flashed like an inch-worm going down the sky". "A bell spoke out: *dolente . . . dolore!*" Faust and Dante are again echoed in this tolling, just as they are combined one year later for Jacques. It is Geoffrey's passing bell, his funeral bell, but it also tolls for everyman.

Even the horse who, escaping from the clutching hands of Geoffrey, gallops uncontrollably through the forest to kill Yvonne, is ironically anticipated by Faustus' line, itself a quotation from Ovid's *Amores, "O lente, lente currite, noctis equi,"* but time and the horse wait for no man. Just as Faustus cries "O, I'll leap up to my God!—Who pulls me down?" Geoffrey experiences a similar prevention of his attempt upward: "He raised his head again; no, he was where he was, there was nowhere to *fly* to. And it was as if a black dog had settled on his back, pressing him to his seat." Similarly, Faustus has nowhere to fly to. He pleads, "Mountains and hills, come, come, and fall on me, / And hide me from the heavy wrath of God!" Likewise, Geoffrey deliriously deludes himself that in the Himalayas, imaged by Popocatepetl, is a final resting place. Carrying "the Hotel Fausto's information" in his pocket, he mentally attempts to climb the volcano, as his father had climbed the Himalayas. Faustus had also hoped to be borne aloft to heaven in the volcano's breath:

> Now draw up Faustus, like a foggy mist,
> Into the entrails of yon labouring clouds,
> That, when you vomit forth into the air,
> My limbs may issue from your smoky mouths,
> So that my soul may but ascend to heaven!

Goethe presents a similar hell intended for Faust:

> out from the arching jaw
> A raging swill of fiery flood is spewed;
> See, in the seething fume of that dread maw,
> The town of flames eternally renewed.
> Up to the teeth, the molten red comes rushing,
> The damned swim wildly, hoping to be saved,
> Then, where the huge hyena's jaws are crushing,
> Renew their path with burning brimstone paved.

"Somebody threw a dead dog after him down the ravine." Bunyan and Faustus come instantaneously to mind. In the Bunyan epigraph to *Under the Volcano* the dog's soul is not doomed to perish in Hell as is man's, yet man must die like an animal. The pariah dog, a symbol of guilt, has followed Geoffrey throughout the book, and even earlier in this last chapter is still associated with his fate: "And it was as if a black dog had settled on his back, pressing him to his seat" as I have quoted above. As an outcast of society Geoffrey is a pariah.

Suggestions of a cyclical reincarnation are latent in Chapter One. Vigil talks of sunset when begin "all the dogs to shark". When Laruelle is in the cinema "Dark shapes of pariah dogs prowled in and out of the stalls". Lastly, talking to Laruelle, Sr. Bustamente, the cinema manager, refers to Geoffrey as "the *bicho,* the one with the blue eyes". Certainly, Laruelle is haunted by the spiritual ghosts of Yvonne and Geoffrey, if not also by a physical embodiment of each. Faustus wished to be reincarnated to escape damnation. Finally, in lines that Bunyan might well have known and paraphrased, Faustus cries:

> Why wert thou not a creature wanting soul?
> Or why is this immortal that thou hast?
> Ah, Pythagoras' metempsychosis, were that true,
> This soul should *fly* from me and I be chang'd
> Unto some brutish beast! all beasts are happy,
> For, when they die,
> Their souls are soon dissolv'd in elements;
> But mine must live still to be plag'd in hell.

Employing the Faust archetype, Lowry has achieved the sense of ironic dissimilarity and yet of profound human continuity between the modern protagonist and his long dead exemplars; he has also locked past and present together spatially in a timeless unity by transmuting the time-world of history into the timeless world of myth, the common content of modern literature. (pp. 43-54)

> *Anthony R. Kilgallin, "Faust and 'Under the Volcano'," in* Canadian Literature, *No. 26, Autumn, 1965, pp. 43-54.*

Dale Edmonds   (essay date 1968)

[*In the following excerpt, Edmonds presents an "immediate level," or literal, reading of* Under the Volcano.]

In August of 1945, after Malcolm Lowry's agent, Harold Matson, had written that he could not place the manuscript of *Under the Volcano* because it was "too long and full of talk," Margerie Lowry, the writer's wife, replied to Matson, "only a person whose whole existence *is* his work, who has dominated and disciplined the volcano within him, at what cost of suffering even I do not wholly understand, could have written such a book." Mrs. Lowry's statement, while an apt description of her husband's involvement with his work, and a perceptive comment on his psychological makeup, suggests an approach to *Under the Volcano* which, it seems to me, obscures the fact that the work is a novel. Lowry did live a life of legendary proportions, and he did write himself into his work—but autobiographical interpretation should not color the fact that the novel is a work of art. This temptation to confuse art with autobiography is one of the major problems facing the critic who seeks to explain and assess *Under the Volcano.*

The substance of another major problem is revealed in this statement by David Markson in his article "Myth in *Under the Volcano*": "For all that it has been taken to mean on its more immediate levels of communication, Lowry's *Under the Volcano* also happens to be one of the most complex novels ever written" [see Further Reading]. Markson offers a selective list of writers and influences he finds functioning "operatively" in *Under the Volcano:* Jung, Spengler, Freud, Frazer, Spinoza, Jessie L. Weston, Oriental metaphysics, and "the occult." Certainly, evidence of these influences—and more—can be found in the novel, but I am troubled by Markson's somewhat cavalier dismissal of the "more immediate levels of communication." I maintain that it is on the "most immediate" level—the level of people, places, events and circumstances within a fictional world that much resembles our own—that the novel communicates most effectively.

When *Under the Volcano* was reissued in the Fall of 1965, critics and reviewers lavished praise upon it, perhaps in partial recompense for the almost two decades of neglect into which it had fallen. I think that the novel deserves the praise it received, but I also think that few critics have emphasized sufficiently the fact that the novel exists powerfully as a story about people. Since, to my mind, there has been no wholly satisfactory reading of the novel on these terms, I propose . . . to offer such a reading, a detailed analysis and explication of the story of *Under the Volcano.* I do not insist that mine is the best or the only way to read the novel, but I do think that it is basic to all other approaches.

To the objection that the literal level of meaning must be obvious to anyone who reads the novel, I must answer that critical commentary to date does not support this contention. Nor do my numerous conversations with students, colleagues, and others who have read the novel indicate that a reading such as I propose to offer is either unnecessary or unimportant. (pp. 63-5)

The success of *Under the Volcano* on the immediate level derives principally from the skill and completeness with which Lowry has drawn his characters. In a review of the 1947 edition, Charles J. Rolo asserted that characterization in the novel is "virtually nonexistent" [see Further Reading]. This could be considered a valid statement if Rolo means by "characterization" old-fashioned, discursive exposition of each character's outward and inward traits. Lowry does not present his characters in this manner. Instead, he lets them emerge through their own actions, words, and thoughts, and through the actions, words, and thoughts of others—that is, his method of characterization is dramatic rather than discursive.

A glance at point of view in each of the twelve chapters reveals that Lowry gives the reader ample opportunity to observe the interplay of thought and action among the main characters. Five chapters are told from the point of view of the Consul (III, V, VII, X, and XII); three chapters from the point of view of Yvonne (II, IX, XI); three chapters from the point of view of Hugh (IV, VI VIII); and one chapter from the point of view of Jacques (I). Technically the point of view in each of these chapters is that usually called limited omniscience (or selective omniscience). However, Lowry employs many of the devices associated with twentieth-century experimental fiction, such as interior monologue and sensory impression, to amplify and enrich his treatment. In several of the chapters Lowry ranges widely and deeply into the respective pasts of the characters by means of reflections generated by their present actions, associations, and circumstances. As the paths of the characters cross, the portraits of each are compounded by the reactions and observations of the others. Thus we see each character from at least three external viewpoints, as well as from within the character's own consciousness. Consequently our understanding of the characters deepens as we progress through the novel.

Mark Schorer [in his essay "The Downward Flight of a Soul" in the *New York Herald Tribune Weekly Book Review,* February 23, 1947, p. 2] has said that the two basic themes of *Under the Volcano* are "the sense of the past, of innocence and vanished pleasure, of wasted opportunity and unrelinquished memory, of *Paradise Lost.* . . . [and] the sense of the doomed future, 'the spirit of the abyss,' death, damnation, the descent into hell. . . . " These themes appear graphically in the roles of the characters, for they are trapped, individually and collectively, by their separate and interrelated pasts, by their distressing present circumstances, by their dying hopes, and by their fears of extinguishable or meaningless futures. I cannot stress too much the fact that the four main characters of the novel, the Consul, Yvonne, Hugh and Jacques, share a bondage of guilt stretching over a period of years—the situation is far more complex than that of a "simple triangle" which a reviewer in *Time* saw. A more perceptive critic in *The Times Literary Supplement* well described the situation in the novel with the observation that Lowry plays "with almost musical fascination on the unfolding variations to be evolved out of the groupings and regroupings of a single quartet of characters" [see Further Reading].

On the Day of the Dead in 1938, the four principal charac-

ters find themselves in the city of Quauhnahuac, Mexico. Some readers see a flaw in this confluence of characters, because, in the opinions of these readers, there seems no logical reason for the presence of the characters at this time and place. These objections may be put aside by close examination of the circumstances. The Consul is in Quauhnahuac because, until a short time before the day of the novel's action, he had served as British Consul there. After his resignation from the service, the Consul remains in the city, paralyzed by alcoholism and grief over his wife's departure, and, as shall be argued later, because he may have some unspecified semi-official undercover business there.

Yvonne has returned to Quauhnahuac after almost a year's absence: she and the Consul separated in December of 1937; she then returned to the United States where she secured a divorce. Her purposes in returning are not clear in her mind. When Hugh says to her, "I'd like to know precisely what the situation is," she answers, "So would I." Then he asks if she has gone back to the Consul and she answers, "Yes, No . . . Yes. I've gone back to him all right all right." But she has no firm plans for saving the Consul, nor does she ever tell him unequivocally that she has returned to him for good, no matter what.

Hugh arrived in Quauhnahuac about a week earlier than Yvonne, on October 24 or 25, hoping, as he puts it, to "kill several birds with one stone": to see the Consul (and possibly Yvonne, for he was not aware of the separation and subsequent divorce) and to cover a story for the *London Globe,* for which he has been a correspondent. His natural desire to see the Consul (his half-brother, whom he naturally loves) and, possibly, Yvonne (whom he has loved, if he does not still), along with his desire to cover a story which appeals to his romantic imagination, make his presence in Quauhnahuac understandable.

The only seemingly implausible presence on the scene, then, is that of Jacques Laruelle. Jacques had been in Quauhnahuac since about November of 1935. As to why he came in the first place, we are never told specifically. At one point the Consul speculates, "Was it not much as though he, the Consul, from afar, had willed it [Jacques's presence in Quauhnahuac], for obscure purposes of his own?" Jacques's activities while in Quauhnahuac offer little clue: "He had made few friends. He had acquired a Mexican mistress with whom he quarrelled, and numerous beautiful Mayan idols he would be unable to take out of the country. . . . " As far as Jacques's "work," his moviemaking, is concerned, about all he has done is borrow a volume of Elizabethan plays from the Consul because, "for some time he had been carrying at the back of his mind the notion of making in France a modern film version of the Faustus story with some such character as Trotsky for its protagonist . . . " But he does not open the volume until the Day of the Dead in 1939, some eighteen months after he borrowed it. Thus there is no "logical" explanation for Jacques' presence. We know from evidence in Chapter I that he has thought about the improbability of his meeting there with the Consul: "probably it was just one of those meaningless correspondences that might be labelled: 'favourite trick of the gods'." Jacques's presence in Quauhnahuac can be explained only by virtue of coincidence, fate, mystic correspondence, or happenstance—all time-tested and time-honored fictional explanations.

Why do the Consul and Jacques remain in Quauhnahuac after Yvonne has left? Jacques says in Chapter I that the involved relationship between himself and the Consul, along with the fact that Yvonne has gone, "might have seemed a good enough reason for putting the whole earth between themselves and Quauhnahuac!" Yet neither leaves; they seem to be held by a "strange melancholy force" which is the "weight of many things, but mostly that of sorrow."

At this point, with the characters, as it were, poised on the brink of the Day of the Dead, I would like to emphasize why the events of this day reach such a peak of emotional intensity: precisely because the affairs of these characters have been curiously tangled in the past. A clear understanding of the relationships of the four main characters is necessary for full appreciation of the extent of the agony which each experiences on the Day of the Dead. The events of the day are more distressing because they bear not upon isolated individuals, but upon a closely interwoven group.

Geoffrey and Hugh had the same father; thus they are half-brothers. After Geoffrey's mother died, his father married again, with Hugh the issue of this second marriage. A year or so after Hugh's birth, the father walked into the Himalayas one day and disappeared (the family was living in Kashmir), leaving the boys in the care of Hugh's mother. Unfortunately this lady died shortly after her husband's disappearance (around 1910), when Geoffrey was about fourteen and Hugh about two. There was nothing left for the boys to do but to sail for England, where they had relatives.

Once back in England the Firmin brothers generally seem to have gone separate ways, in the care of various "collateral relatives." One such group of relatives was the family of Abraham Taskerson, an English poet. Through this family Jacques Laruelle entered the life of Geoffrey Firmin. After a chance encounter with the young French boy during the summer of 1911 at Courseulles, in Normandy, the Taskersons, with whom Geoffrey was vacationing, invited Jacques to join them for September in England. The friendship between Jacques and Geoffrey that had begun in Normandy, grew stronger at Leasowe, the Taskerson family seat of the English northwest coast. Since neither Geoffrey, a rather shy lad, nor Jacques, himself shy and sensitive, took to the Taskerson boys' routine of prodigious walks, accompanied by prodigious amounts of beer, they found themselves together much of the time. During one of their outings something happened which was to have serious repercussions upon Geoffrey's personality and upon his relationship with Jacques. Jacques and a girl he had picked up, while strolling across a golf course, inadvertently stumbled upon Geoffrey and his girl in a preliminary sexual encounter in the course's "Hell Bunker." Making the best of the situation, Geoffrey and Jacques took the girls to a pub called "The Case Is Altered," but were turned out because they were minors. Their friend-

ship, as Jacques observes in Chapter I, "did not for some reason survive these two sad, though doubtless providential, little frustrations." They did not see each other again until their encounter in Quauhnahuac in 1937, but the memory of the Hell Bunker episode remained with Geoffrey, to be compounded over the years into a sort of general sexual guilt (which may be one of the factors contributing to his alcoholism, as I suggest later).

His early encounter with Geoffrey, despite its brief duration, assumed a lasting significance for Jacques. In Chapter VII the Consul looks at Jacques as they walk down the street and muses:

> . . . it did not seem too outlandish to suggest that his [the Consul's] influence still reached him [Jacques] strongly. If not, why the English-looking tweed coat similar to the Consul's own, those expensive expressive English tennis shoes . . . the English white trousers . . . the English shirt . . . ? There was even, in spite of his slight stoutness, an English, almost an ex-consular sort of litheness about his movements. . . . So brief their friendship and yet . . . how enormous, how all-permeating, permeating Jacques' whole life, that influence had been, an influence that showed even in his choice of books, his work. . . .

Jacques does not seem to realize that it is the Consul's influence that has virtually shaped his being in the ensuing years, but the details of the book suggest that this is so.

The contacts between Geoffrey and Hugh, from their boyhood until after Geoffrey's marriage, were sporadic: "once back in England there were too many guardians, too many surrogates in Harrogate, too many establishments and schools, not to mention the war. . . ." The fact that Geoffrey was some twelve or thirteen years older than Hugh probably kept them from being very close. Also, Geoffrey's career in the Diplomatic Service kept them apart: he "was always in Rabat or Timbuctoo," and his contact with Hugh was by cable, if at all. In about 1926 Hugh, then seventeen, proposed to "run away to sea." The relatives with whom he was living objected violently, but Geoffrey cabled: *"Nonsense. Consider Hugh's proposed trip best possible thing for him. Strongly urge you give him every freedom."* This gesture, which deprived Hugh's trip "of any possible flavour of rebellion," proved to have a serious effect, for, as Hugh says, he never wholly forgave the Consul for this interposition.

In 1935, in Granada, the Consul meets and marries Yvonne Constable (in this same year Jacques arrives in Quauhnahuac). Yvonne serves the function of bringing the three male characters together in a single point of focus: her person. "The sweet beginnings" of the marriage, (in the Consul's phrase from the letter Jacques discovers in the book of Elizabethan plays) could have lasted only little more than a year, if that. For a brief time their life together had "not been without triumph. Yet for how brief a time. Far too soon it had begun to seem too much of a triumph, it had been too good, too horribly unimaginable to lose, impossible finally to bear: it was as if it had become itself its own foreboding that it could not last, a foreboding that was like a presence too, turning his steps toward the taverns again.''

This turn "toward the taverns" apparently had taken place before Hugh joined the Consul and Yvonne in Paris (probably in 1936). Hugh came from Aden, in some trouble over his *carte d'identite*. The Consul was able to straighten the matter out, although, as he admits, he and Yvonne had already been brought close to disaster because of his drinking. The relationship between Hugh and Yvonne in Paris is never presented explicitly in the novel, because neither they nor the Consul wish to recall the painful incident, and Jacques doesn't know about it. But we may infer what happened from certain passages. Hugh and Yvonne probably first conspired to help the Consul; then, as the Consul sank deeper into alcoholism, their conspiracy grew into a love affair (that at one time there was a strong attraction between Hugh and Yvonne is attested to by the stunned disbelief with which each learns that the other is in Quauhnahuac). Hugh attempted to justify their brief affair to himself on the grounds that the Consul was absorbed in a debauch; then he tried, in the Consul's phrase, "to forget in the cruel abstraction of youth." Hugh's guilt for his affair with Yvonne is revealed during their morning ride. For a moment he sees an image of his happiness with Yvonne, but this is no more than "a glimpse of what never was at all, of what never can be since brotherhood was betrayed. . . ." Yvonne refuses to think of her affair with Hugh because the memory is too painful. In the arena at Tomalín she recalls for an instant an image of Hugh and Paris, then quickly puts the image from her mind.

The Consul was aware of the adulterous betrayal, probably shortly after it happened. He reveals his feelings in subtle insinuations, as when he calls Hugh, "you old snake in the grass!" At another point he says to Hugh, "But I really think you two [Hugh and Jacques] ought to get together, you have something in common". In the *Salón Ofélia* in Chapter X, the Consul's feelings erupt into bitter words which Hugh and Yvonne cannot answer: "What an uncommon time you two must have had, paddling palms and playing bubbies and titties all day under cover of saving me. . . ." Whether Yvonne initially turned to Hugh through despair, or simply because she was attracted to him, we do not know (her subsequent affair with Jacques could be used to argue either position), but there is ample evidence that on the Day of the Dead in 1938, she has not forgotten Hugh; even in moments of distress about the Consul she is aware of Hugh's capabilities as a past lover and his possibilities as a present or future lover.

The adultery of Hugh and Yvonne affects the Consul in two ways: first, and more obvious, is the fact of adultery itself, which the Consul regards as a violation of the sanctity of marriage; second, is the fact that the agent of the betrayal is the Consul's half-brother. To the Consul it seems that Hugh not only has committed a crime against marriage, but also against blood—thus the crime, to the Consul, assumes an even darker cast. Hugh's act seems more reprehensible, also, because of the Consul's love for him and trust in him. There is another suggestion to this adultery as well: it is almost as if the Consul, through the blood tie with Hugh, has himself violated his marriage. He knows that he has failed Yvonne; thus, to affix the seal to this failure, he not only permits the adulterous act by his dissipation, but he also, in a sense, engages in the act through his closeness to Hugh.

If the Paris sequence took place some time during 1936, only a short period elapsed before the Consul and Yvonne came to Quauhnahuac in the Spring of 1937. On the Day of the Dead, 1938, the Consul recalls that he met Jacques in Quauhnahuac "eighteen months ago," which would place their meeting sometime in late April or early May of the previous year. Jacques remembers in Chapter I that the Consul had been in Quauhnahuac for six weeks before they met; thus the Consul and Yvonne probably arrived sometime in March of 1937. Since Yvonne left the Consul in early December of 1937, her affair with Jacques took place sometime during the span May-December.

As with the adultery of Hugh and Yvonne, there is little explicit detail about the adultery of Jacques and Yvonne, but once again we may infer a great deal. After the Consul met Jacques in Quauhnahuac, it was natural that he should introduce his old friend to Yvonne. As Yvonne reflects in Chapter IX, her meeting with Jacques was "such a shattering and ominous thing in her life" because they had both the Consul and Hollywood in common. Once the Consul discovered the cantinas, it was only a matter of time until Yvonne, drawn to Jacques by their mutual interest in the movies, should turn to him to share her anguish and to find solace. One of Yvonne's passing reflections in Chapter IX gives us an idea how this came about: "And once too in his [Jacques's] studio, where the Consul was so obviously not going to arrive. . . . " In Chapter VII the Consul looks around Jacques's room: "Was it here he had been betrayed? This very room, perhaps, had been filled with her cries of love."

To Yvonne, her affair with Jacques seems to have been something of the moment only. When she meets him on the Day of the Dead, she is disturbed, but not as she is with Hugh. She gets away from Jacques as quickly as possible, revealing no latent passion, as she does with Hugh. The affair with Jacques is an unpleasant memory to Yvonne, but she seems able to gloss it over in her mind, as there seems to have been little emotional involvement on her part. It is Jacques who seems shattered by the sudden reappearance of Yvonne. In Chapter I we see clearly that Jacques's love for Yvonne was deeply felt—a year after her death he has not been able to forget her. His love "had brought back to his heart, in a way he could not have explained, the first time that . . . he had seen . . . the twin spires of Chartres Cathedral. His love had brought a peace for all too short a while, that was strangely like the enchantment, the spell, of Chartres itself, long ago. . . . "

As with the adultery of Hugh and Yvonne, that of Jacques and Yvonne assumes a dual significance. We have seen that to Jacques the Consul has been much more than a friend, has been an influence over Jacques's life, an extension of himself almost. When Jacques commits adultery with Yvonne, then, it is as if another of the Consul's "brothers" has betrayed him. Also, the Consul not only acquiesces in the betrayal, through his neglect of Yvonne, but seems almost to participate in the act through the closeness of his ties with Jacques. With these circumstances in mind, a strong parallel between the two cases of adultery seems to exist.

Yvonne left the Consul in December of 1937; the Consul and Jacques remained in Quauhnahuac, reunited for a time, not through remorse but "more the desire for that illusory comfort, about as satisfying as biting on an aching tooth, to be derived from the mutual unspoken pretence that Yvonne was still . . . [there]." The period between Yvonne's departure and her return nearly a year later may be described on the Consul's part as a heartbroken, agonized plunge to the depths of alcoholism. The interval finds Jacques languishing in Quauhnahuac, his will to act enervated by a sense of guilt and loss.

The morning of the Day of the Dead in 1938, then, finds these four characters in Quauhnahuac. The explosive possibilities inherent in their collective pasts should be evident from the foregoing discussion. Some commentators have been misled by the fact that the novel's bulk (Chapters II-XII) covers a period of only twelve hours. Careful examination of the flashbacks throughout reveals that Lowry provides a richness of material from the pasts of the character to deepen the impact of the day's events.

As the other characters' lives have been intertwined with that of the Consul *prior* to the events of the Day of the Dead, this intertwining becomes more complicated on this day until the Consul is virtually enmeshed by his past, in the form of the three people to whom, perhaps, he is closest in the world. In Chapter II the Consul tells Yvonne that he "nearly passed out altogether under the stress of [Hugh's] . . . salvage operations." This could be said of the "salvage operations" of Yvonne and Jacques as well. It is almost as if the three unwittingly conspire to bring about the Consul's destruction, rather than his resurrection. First, we can cite Jacques and the dubious comfort he has rendered the Consul in the months following Yvonne's departure. On the day of her return, Jacques delays the three Tomalín travelers for a time in his house, causing untold distress to the Consul by his very proximity to Yvonne. When Hugh and Yvonne escape for a brief tour of the fiesta, Jacques's aid takes the form of watching the Consul drink several tequilas while his own nervousness and uncertainty, resulting from his encounter with Yvonne, underscore the fact that he has been her lover. His ostensibly well-meant admonitions in the *Cafe Paris* about the Consul's drinking only serve, it seems, to determine more firmly in the Consul's mind the character and direction of his ultimate plunge.

Hugh acts even more clearly as a deterrent to any attempt on Yvonne's part to extricate the Consul. In Chapter IV Hugh has been so caught up by the romantic atmosphere of his ride with Yvonne, that he envisions a "Northern Paradise" to which the Consul and Yvonne might escape: "At this moment the best and easiest and most simple thing in the world seemed to be the happiness of these two people in a new country." But while he and Yvonne are out riding, the Consul, awakened from a fitful slumber, is stumbling toward the "ambush" of a tequila bottle hidden in his garden. Later, as the three set off for Tomalín, Hugh

has seen that his usefulness is exhausted, his and Yvonne's " 'plot' subtly lamed by small circumstances, of which not the least was his own continued presence." Although he realizes his presence is unnecessary—even harmful— Hugh remains. By squiring Yvonne around the fiesta and, during the rest of the day, conspiring with her under the pretense of working for the Consul's salvation, Hugh insinuates himself once more into Yvonne's affection to the degree that their mutual passion is almost rekindled. Yvonne recognizes Hugh's expendability as the three watch the bull-throwing at Tomalín ("Hugh . . . seemed now an interloper, a stranger . . . ") but she does not ask him to leave. In Chapter XI Hugh and Yvonne set off on the trail to Parián to find the Consul, who has rushed away from the *Salón Ofélia* after vilifying them about their past adultery. Because of the obvious drunkenness and lack of control that the Consul has revealed, Hugh and Yvonne's course of action would seem clear: they should, as quickly as possible, find the Consul and in some way, by force if necessary, get him back to Quauhnahuac. Hugh and Yvonne do look for the Consul, but their conduct does not prefigure success for their never-to-be-realized future "salvage operations" (Yvonne's with the Consul and Hugh's with the Spanish Loyalist forces). They make a pardonable error of judgment in choosing the wrong path to Parián; the path they take will get them to Parián eventually, and it does take them past two other cantinas where the Consul might be found. But had Yvonne and Hugh taken the direct path to Parián, they might have arrived in time to save the Consul.

But, given their error of judgment in taking the wrong path, it seems that they should check the cantinas and then proceed with all dispatch to Parián. But what do they do? In the *El Petate* Hugh, after inquiring about the Consul, has a quick drink with the customers, while Yvonne frees a captured eagle from its cage. As they leave, Hugh takes Yvonne's arm and asks her tenderly if she remembers the armadillo they saw on their morning ride. "I haven't forgotten, *anything!*" she answers, "not knowing quite what she meant."

At the next cantina on the road, the *Hotel y Restaurant El Popo,* after looking around for the Consul, Hugh orders two beers. While they drink these they reminisce warmly about the "wooly dog and the foals that came with us and the river with those swift birds overhead—." Even as they discuss the urgency of getting to Parián, they have another drink—mescal this time. While Hugh goes off to look once more, Yvonne drains her glass, and the liquor takes immediate effect: the *El Popo* no longer seems quite so awful to her. Hugh buys a guitar; they examine a menu scrawled with the Consul's handwriting. It is 6:45; Yvonne and Hugh's actions after leaving the *Salón Ofélia* have taken about an hour and a quarter. Even though they took the indirect route to Parián, they would have arrived in time to save the Consul if they had hurried. Instead, by the time they leave the *El Popo,* the Consul's fate has been decided.

The crowning irony of the novel occurs on Yvonne and Hugh's walk through the forest toward Parián, after they leave the *El Popo.* At the exact moment they hear the pistol shots that kill the Consul ("More target practice,"

Hugh laughs), Yvonne, looking up at the treetops, has been thinking of her morning ride with Hugh, "some night essence of their shared morning thoughts, with a wild sea-yearning of youth and love and sorrow." The drinks they have had together contribute to their delay, and partially cause Yvonne's shaky climbing of the fallen log and her loss of balance. Yvonne is trampled to death by the horse freed moments before by the Consul (who has since been shot), as Hugh stumbles blindly and rather drunkenly about in the forest, singing a revolutionary song and strumming his guitar.

Thus we have seen that Hugh, Yvonne, and Jacques fail to translate thier vague desires to aid the Consul into viable plans. In fact, their indecision and selfishness actually become a part of the chain of circumstances leading to the Consul's death.

The Consul's murder at the *Farolito* in Parián is not a trick of fate, but is the outcome of a series of interrelated circumstances, depending upon the Consul's past, his role in Quauhnahuac, and conditions in Mexico during the time of the novel's action. Careful scrutiny reveals that the events of Chapters II-XII form an intricate mosaic of doom for the Consul. This mosaic is formed upon a background of the political situation in Mexico in 1938-39. Because many of the occurrences in the novel fail to make full sense without an awareness of this background, I shall summarize it briefly.

Mexico in the mid- and late 1930's was in a state of turmoil. In addition to internal difficulties, foreign communist and fascist interests sought to influence affairs in Mexico. Lázaro Cárdenas, elected president of Mexico in July of 1934, proved himself a different man from what Plutarco Elías Calles expected when he selected Cárdenas as presidential candidate (Calles had been the power behind the Mexican political scene since 1928 when he left the presidency). Under Cárdenas Calles had hoped to retain virtual control of the government, as he had during the presidencies of Emilio Portes Gil, Pascual Órtiz Rubio, and Abelardo Rodríguez. But, according to Henry Bamford Parkes, in *A History of Mexico,* Calles "discovered that he had supplied the left wing not merely with a figurehead but with a leader. Cárdenas proved himself not only a man of integrity but also a remarkably able politician." In April of 1936, to avoid possible trouble, Cárdenas deported Calles to the United States. "To American newspapermen," Parkes writes, "Calles explained that he had been banished because he was an enemy of Communism, and it was observed that he was carrying a copy of Hitler's *Mein Kampf.*"

Strong support for Cárdenas came from labor, including a federation of labor unions formed in 1936 called *Confederacion de Trabajadores de Mexico,* or C.T.M. Another source of support for Cárdenas was the small farmer. One of his most important policies was a firm and energetic program of agrarian reform—anathema to the Callistas and other reactionary elements in Mexico. According to Parkes, "By 1940 he [Cárdenas] had distributed forty-five million acres of land . . . among three quarters of a million peasant families located in nearly twelve thousand different villages." Obviously such a program antagonized

wealthy hacienda owners who watched their holdings being pared away. Under Cárdenas, Parkes writes, "the agrarian reform included not merely the distribution of plots of ground upon which peasants could grow corn, but also the organization of large cooperative farms for the production of commercial crops on a profit-sharing basis." The *ejido,* a tract of common land for a village, had been a Mexican institution since pre-Cortesian days, but the institution often was abused or ignored altogether. Cárdenas breathed new life into the *ejido* concept. The money for financing the operation of the new *ejido* concept was administered through the *National Bank of Ejido Credit,* an institution that will figure in an important way in **Under the Volcano.**

Although Cárdenas' collectivist sympathies should be apparent from the foregoing discussion, he was not a doctrinaire socialist, nor was he, as his enemies charged, a communist. Perhaps his most controversial act was his expropriation of foreign oil companies in March of 1938, following the refusal of these companies to answer government demands for increasing wages and training native Mexicans for managerial positions. The government of Great Britain protested the expropriation, with the result that diplomatic relations between the two countries ceased in the spring of 1938.

Nazi Germany had good reason for being interested in Mexico: opposition to Cárdenas was strong enough to indicate that Germany might be able to help overthrow him and thereby gain a toehold in the Western Hemisphere. As a result of Germany's interest, Parkes relates, "there was a marked growth of reactionary and fascistic groups who were encouraged by German agents and assisted by German money. These forces received further stimulus from the victory of Franco in the Spanish Civil War." Cárdenas and his government were outspokenly pro-Loyalist, another attitude that antagonized reactionary elements in Mexico. Among the extreme rightist groups that came into existence in the late 1930's was the *Union Nacional Sinarquista,* which received encouragement from the Spanish Falange and probably from Nazi Germany. The *Unión Militar* of **Under the Volcano** seems to be an arm of such an organization. One of the chief targets of the rightist organizations was Cárdenas' agrarian reform program, and the agencies and individuals by which it was administered. In **Under the Volcano,** the *National Bank of Ejido Credit* is such an agency, and the Indian who rode the horse with the number "7" branded on its rump is such an individual.

The foregoing sketch of the political situation in Mexico in the mid- and late 1930's suggests the actual background for some of the more important events in **Under the Volcano,** a background with which Lowry was familiar from his residence in Mexico. But the important point here is neither biographical nor historical: Lowry uses details from the Mexican political situation in his intricate development of the story of **Under the Volcano.**

Several critics have remarked that after finishing **Under the Volcano** one should immediately reread the first chapter; and so one should because Chapter I resolves a number of apparently puzzling questions raised in Chapters II-

XII. Jacques, Dr. Vigil, and Señor Bustamente have had a year in which to reflect on the events of the Day of the Dead in 1938, and the political situation has come into sharper focus. Particularly important in Chapter I is material about the Consul's political role in Quauhnahuac and how this role related to the events leading to his death.

Shortly after dusk on the Day of the Dead in 1939, a year after the Consul's death, Jacques and Señor Bustamente, manager of the cinema, sit in the *Cervecería XX* next door to the cinema and discuss the Consul. The immediate impetus of their discussion is the Consul's volume of Elizabethan plays which Bustamente has just returned to Jacques (Jacques left it in the cinema the day he borrowed it, some eighteen months before). This conversation between Jacques and Bustamente is extremely important for the interpretation of events it suggests, although Lowry deliberately presents this material in a tentative and speculative way, not insisting upon any one interpretation. In much of Lowry's fiction we can never be certain that we are dealing with reality (in terms of the fictional world created), with the result that any conclusions we draw must consider the enigmatic nature of the material. In the analysis which follows I do not ignore the possibility that Bustamente's suspicions may be unfounded, but I also do not ignore the possibility that Jacques's refutation of these suspicions may be unfounded.

Bustamente remembers the days of Porfirio Díaz when every small American border town harboured a Mexican "Consul"; indeed, Mexican consuls even were found in towns some distance from the border. These Consuls supposedly looked after interests of trade between Mexico and the United States, but this was merely a front, as most were spies for the Díaz regime. Bustamente hints, "without offence, and perhaps not altogether seriously," that Geoffrey Firmin had been such a Consul, a British Consul, of course, but one "who could scarcely claim to have the interests of British trade at heart in a place where there were no British interests and no Englishmen, the less so when it was considered that England had severed diplomatic relations with Mexico." Bustamente seems half-convinced that Jacques has been taken in, that the Consul really was a "spider" (as he, and other Mexicans in the book, express the English word "spy").

Then comes an important passage, actually a reflection by Jacques generated by Bustamente's expression of sympathy for the Consul: " . . . [the Consul wandered] hatless and desconsolado and beside himself around the town pursued by other spiders who, without his ever being quite certain of it, a man in dark glasses he took to be a loafer here, a man lounging on the other side of the road he thought was a peon there, a bald boy with earrings swinging madly on a creaking hammock there, guarded every street and alley entrance. . . . " Each of these possible "counter-spiders" appears at least once in the course of the narrative in Chapters II-XII; the man with dark glasses appears several times.

The impression the Consul gave Bustamente was of a man living in continual terror of his life, for reasons more tangible than alcoholic hallucination. After Jacques, by citing the Consul's war record, has pointed out that the Consul

was not a coward, Bustamente agrees, then explains the difference in Mexico between fearing for one's life and being a coward. Bustamente suggests, "might not just such a character and distinguished record as M. Laruelle claimed was his [the Consul's] have precisely qualified him for the excessively dangerous activities of a spider?" These qualities might—but then again, they might not, Jacques believes. He thinks it useless to try to explain to Bustamente that the Consul's job in Quauhnahuac was "merely a retreat . . . a position where he was least likely to prove a nuisance to the Empire. . . . " This is so of the Consul's official post—but what of his activities that were not included in the specific duties of a British Consul? From my earlier discussion of the political situation in Mexico at the time, it should be clear that ample opportunity existed for all manner of espionage activities. If German agents were so active in Mexico, British agents might have been similarly active. Of the Consul's precise duties as a British spy (if he is one) we never learn, but we may assume that they included keeping his eyes open for, and reporting upon, any suspicious individuals or activities—specifically fascist—he observed.

England's position in regard to Mexico was paradoxical: on the one hand, she resented Mexico's expropriation of her oil companies; on the other hand, she sympathized with certain of Cárdenas' aims (such as equitable land distribution) which fascist forces would have opposed. The situation might be described in this manner: the fascist agents in Mexico were anti-Cárdenas, anti-collectivist; the British agents—including, perhaps, the Consul—were not so much pro-Cárdenas as they were, simply, pro-British, concerned with anything that might in some way affect the interests of the British Empire.

The Consul's role in Quauhnahuac at the time the events of Chapters II-XII take place may be summarized as follows: he no longer is officially British Consul (after breaking off diplomatic relations with Mexico, England called her Consuls home), but remains to "look after the interests" of England, which he does, primarily, by reporting fascist activities. The events of Chapters II-XII corroborate this view. (pp. 66-81)

In addition to his embroilment in the political situation, another major factor contributing to the Consul's end is his acute alcoholism and the symptoms by which this affliction is manifested. The amount the Consul drinks on his last day renders him increasingly incapable of reasonable action and paralyzes his will and his desire to save himself. (p. 91)

But it is Lowry's ability to convey to us, not just the amount the Consul drinks, but what the intake of alcohol does to him that is so striking. We soon learn from our absorption in the Consul's drink-steeped consciousness of the diseased and disordered state of his being, of the degeneration of his soul, the lesion of inner vitality and strength that permit him to sink to the death he finds at the *Farolito*. Lowry once wrote [see excerpt dated 1948] that in *Under the Volcano* he wanted to write an "authentic drunkard's story." There is no doubt that he has done this; in fact, his depiction of Geoffrey Firmin may be the most complete portrait of the alcoholic in English fiction.

Within the large framework of the drunkard's world, Lowry powerfully portrays the workings of the drunkard's mind. While the Consul, just returned from his tequila foray in his garden in Chapter V, and Dr. Vigil are discussing the Consul's alcoholism, the effect of the tequila ebbs and the Consul remembers that he has been without a drink for nearly ten minutes. He removes his dark glasses and peers out at the garden:

> . . . it was as though bits of his eyelids had broken off and were flittering and jittering before him, turning into nervous shapes and shadows, jumping to the guilty chattering in his mind, not quite voices yet, but they were coming back, they were coming back; a picture of his soul as a town appeared once more before him, but this time a town ravaged and stricken in the black path of his excess, and shutting his burning eyes he had thought of the beautiful functioning of the system in those who were truly alive, switches connected, nerves rigid only in real danger, and in nightmareless sleep, now calm, not resting, yet poised: a peaceful village. Christ, how it heightened the torture . . . to be aware of all this, while at the same time conscious of the whole horrible distintegrating mechanism, the light now on, now off, now on too glaringly, now too dimly, with the glow of a fitful dying battery—then at last to know the whole town plunged into darkness, where communication is lost, motion mere obstruction, bombs threaten, ideas stampede—

The drunkard's distortion of reality is revealed in the Consul's interior monologues. In one passage which vividly illustrates this distortion, the Consul is standing at the door of the *Farolito*, watching the activity in the square. Suddenly he observes that on his extreme right "some unusual animals resembling geese, but large as camels, and skinless men, without heads, upon stilts, whose animated entrails jerked along the ground, were issuing out of the forest path the way he had come." He shuts his eyes, opens them again, and sees a policeman leading a horse up the path, nothing more.

In the mind of the drunkard, human identity is in a constant state of flux. No one is entirely and distinctly himself, without, that is, at some point becoming someone or something else. The face of a legless beggar changes before the Consul into that of Señora Gregorio, then into that of his mother; the face of the Chief of Rostrums hints of that of Jacques; the face of the Chief of Gardens becomes that of the Consul himself.

Lowry conveys the almost indescribable terrors of the drunkard's night in a shattering manner:

> . . . [the dreadful night with] daemonic orchestras, the snatches of fearful tumultuous sleep, interrupted by voices which were really dogs barking, or by his own name being continually repeated by imaginary parties arriving, the vicious shouting, the strumming, the slamming, the pounding, the battling with insolent archfiends, the avalanche breaking down the door, the proddings from under the bed, and always, outside, the cries, the wailing, the terrible music . . .

One of the finest sustained passages in the novel is in Chapter X, at the *Salón Ofélia*. Here Lowry presents vividly the confusion in the drunkard's mind of past, present, and future, and of reality and unreality. The Consul finds himself seated in the toilet: "he was not, at the moment apparently, having dinner with the others, though their voices came plainly enough." He muses, "Perhaps there was no time, either, in this stone retreat. Perhaps this was the eternity that he'd been making so much fuss about. . . . " As he continues to sit there, the words of Yvonne and Hugh filter into his retreat to alternate with passages he reads from a tourist folder Cervantes has brought him. In addition to the words he hears at the moment, there return to the Consul's drink-soaked consciousness snatches of half-remembered conversations that have occurred earlier. There are moments of clarity when the Consul notices the progression of Hugh and Yvonne's conversation, but there are moments in which there is no order, no separation of past, present, and future, as when into the Consul's mind suddenly come fragments of Dr. Vigil's talk: "I am very sorry you cannot come me with"; "For she is the Virgin for those who have nobody with." Then the Consul's mind becomes a montage of memory and impression, of words of others and words of his own, uttered and unuttered, punctuated by the pidgin prose of the Tlaxcalan tourist folder he finds in his hand. One of the Consul's "familiars" says to him, "You can't escape me," which triggers a memory of Yvonne's earlier, "—this is not just escaping. I mean, let's start again, really and cleanly"; a snatch of the Consul's conversation with Quincey, about William Blackstone, flies past; then, wildly, the dying end of an allusion to *War and Peace,* that "Napoleon's leg twitched"; "—might have run over you, there must be something wrong, what?" races into the Consul's mind, a fragment from the English "rescuer" who found him face down in the *Calle Nicaragua;* "They plugged 'em too. They shoot first and ask questions later"—this is a bit of Weber's ranting at the *Bella Vista* bar early that morning; "Guzman . . . Erikson 43"—this recalls the Consul's abortive attempt at Jacques' to place a telephone call; finally, "A corpse will be transported by—," takes us back to the moment at the *Bella Vista* when Yvonne first appears. The last thing the Consul perceives before leaving the toilet is a schedule from the tourist folder of railroad and bus service between Mexico City and Tlaxcala, which precipitates his bizarre attempt to organize an excursion to Tlaxcala.

It should be clear from the foregoing that Lowry's presentation of the drunkard's world is realized in a series of master strokes, and that the Consul's immersion in drink parallels his downward swirl into the maelstrom of circumstance which leads to his doom. But an important question—perhaps *the* most important question about the Consul's alcoholism—has not yet been answered: *why* does he drink?

There are several reasons from the Consul's past which, it seems to me, would be sufficient cause for anyone's alcoholism. First, there is the sorrow of his family background. The death of his mother, the mysterious disappearance of his father, the death of his stepmother, all in rapid succession, throw young Geoffrey into a world of

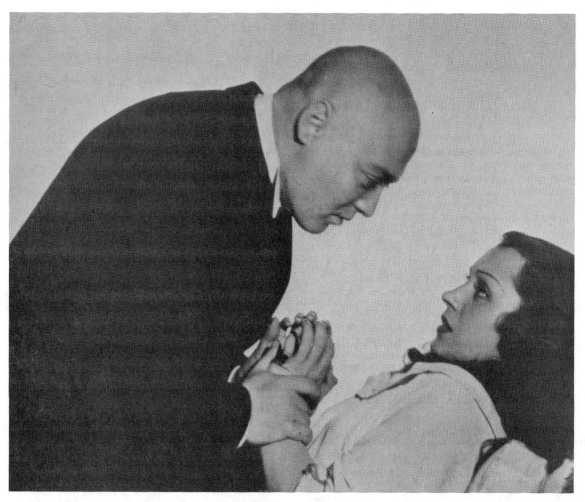

Peter Lorre in The Hands of Orlac.

strangers, a world in which he never feels at home. Another reason from his past may be his obscure sexual guilt arising from the Hell Bunker episode at Leasowe. That the Consul has not forgotten this disquieting incident is clear from a passage in Chapter VII. On the catwalk at Jacques's house the Consul peers through binoculars at the countryside, and thinks, "It was as if they were standing on a lofty golf-tee somewhere. What a beautiful hole this would make. . . . " The Consul's mind pursues the subject of golf, culminating in a reference to "The Case Is Altered," the name of the pub to which he and Jacques took their girls following the Hell Bunker incident. It seems that after this incident, the Consul inevitably associated feelings of embarrassment and guilt with sex. While he and Yvonne seemed to have enjoyed sexual happiness for a time, it is clear that the more the Consul drank, the less effective he was as a lover, with the result that Yvonne sought satisfaction elsewhere. The Consul on the Day of the Dead is incapable of sex relations with Yvonne, though he is capable of a possessionless, virtually pleasureless, act with the whore Maria. He can mentally revile Yvonne for her transgressions; he can view Jacques's penis with horror; he can scream at Hugh, in Yvonne's presence, that he is "only one of the hundred or so other nin-

eyhammers with gills like codfish and veins like racehorses—prime as goats all of them, hot as monkeys, salt as wolves in pride!" who have coupled with Yvonne—but he cannot face the fact that his incapacity may have driven her to seek satisfaction with others.

One other event from the Consul's past could be a possible reason for his drinking, his part in the *S.S. Samaritan* incident. During World War I the Consul served on the *S.S. Samaritan,* a submarine-chaser disguised as an unarmed merchantman. After capturing the crew of a German U-Boat, the *Samaritan* returned to port, but none of the German officers returned with it. It was rumored that they had been burned alive in the ship's furnaces. Although the Consul received the British Distinguished Service Cross for his part in the capture, he first was court-martialed and acquited of any blame in the disappearance of the officers. The reader never knows, even from Jacques's reflections in Chapter I, exactly what the Consul's role was. Did he stuff the officers of the captured German submarine into the *Samaritan's* furnaces, or didn't he? In his drunken colloquies with Jacques after Yvonne's departure, he proclaims his complete guilt, but, as Jacques observes, "the poor Consul had already lost almost all capacity for telling the truth and his life had become a quixotic oral fiction."

Allusions to the *Samaritan* incident in the rest of the book do not clear up the matter. In Chapter V, suspecting the existence of an elaborate plot against him, the Consul shapes imaginary monstrous headlines such as: "Old Samaritan case to be reopened, Commander Firmin believed in Mexico." But later, talking to Hugh about a picture of the *Samaritan* he cut from a German magazine, the Consul reveals no feelings of guilt. Hugh observes that the presence of the picture "must surely discount most of those old stories. . . . " The ironic name *Samaritan* is a recurring obsession of the Consul's besotted consciousness. One of his dying thoughts is that he is lying by the wayside "where no good Samaritan would halt." Finally, we are unable to assess exactly the significance of the *Samaritan* incident, or its effect on the Consul, although we can say with assurance that he never forgot it and that his role in the incident would not be likely to confirm him in a life of temperance or abstinence.

There is yet another reason, or basis, that could be offered for the Consul's alcoholism, one that relates to a significant theme in the novel. The Consul turns to alcohol to assuage not only his feelings of personal guilt and remorse, but also his strong awareness of the guilt and shame that all men share for the human condition at the mid-point of the twentieth century. Lowry uses the Consul's alcoholism as a symbol of the sickness which afflicts the whole of mankind in our century, but this general guilt is felt strongly by the Consul on the non-symbolic or literal level. He is a man of sensitivity and extraordinary mental power; thus it is reasonable to assume that he feels more deeply than many the guilt that is a part of all modern men's burden (some, of course, fail to perceive that they share this burden, or refuse to acknowledge the fact, or, if they do realize it, it is of no importance to them). Geoffrey Firmin cannot bear to think of the dismal state to which man has sunk; thus, he seeks solace and succor for his general woe in alcohol. In Chapter IV, while on the horseback ride with Yvonne, Hugh discusses the problem of the Consul's drinking and what should be done about it. He mentions his attempt to sober the Consul up by administering the strychnine mixture, but, he reflects, "What's the good? Just sobering him up for a day or two's not going to help. Good God, if our civilization were to sober up for a couple of days it'd die of remorse on the third—." Thus the Consul stays drunk to keep from acknowledging the world, a world with blood and guilt in its past, and disaster on its horizon.

Another approach to the Consul's alcoholism is to regard it as a disease. As they sit on the verandah of the Consul's house, Dr. Vigil says to him, "sickness is not only in body, but in that part used to be call: soul." "Soul?" the Consul queries. Dr. Vigil answers, "Precisamente . . . The nerves are a mesh, like, how do you say it, an eclectic systemë [he means electric system]. . . . After much tequila the eclectic systemë is perhaps un poco descompuesto [a little decomposed], comprenez, as sometimes in the cine: claro?" The relation of the physical aspects of alcoholism to the mental aspects is difficult to ascertain. Does mental disturbance lead to drinking, or does drinking lead to mental disturbance? In the Consul's case, I believe the best an-swer would be to say, simply, that he is a man with severe mental and physical ills caused by, contributing to, or associated with alcoholism.

But is there not, perhaps, a positive aspect to the Consul's drinking, or, perhaps, even *two* positive aspects? First, the Consul seems to employ alcohol as a means of mystical release, as a means of freeing what he, and others, seem to see within him as occult powers. On his morning ride with Yvonne, Hugh says, "with almost avuncular relish," that maybe the Consul is a "black magician." He may be— undeniably he is a genius, with mystical tendencies. Aside from the symbolic associations of alcohol, its power to influence the brain in a manner not entirely obfuscatory is well known. Some people drink to "free" their minds—or so they think—from worldly ties. This may be one reason why the Consul drinks. He apparently has talked to Jacques in this vein, for in Chapter VII, Jacques refers to the trouble the Consul's drinking causes, while "what is mystical in you is being released, or whatever it is you imagine is being released . . . ". Perhaps the Consul *is* a black magician, or some sort of mystic, and perhaps he drinks to "free" his powers—Lowry's presentation of this matter is tantalizingly enigmatic.

And there may be a second positive side to, or interpretation of, the Consul's alcoholism. It is true that after he sees the picture "Los Borrachones" at Jacques's house, he suddenly feels "something never felt before with such shocking certainty. It was that he was in hell himself." Immediately, however, the "ferment within him, the squalls and eddies of nervousness" are held in check by the thought of the *Farolito*, "The Lighthouse, the lighthouse that invites the storm, and lights it. . . . That prospect filled him with an almost healing love and at this moment, for it was part of the calm, the greatest longing he had ever known." We have seen that the "light" from the *Farolito* is a deceptive one—or is it? It seems to me that one reason the Consul drinks is that he *loves* to drink. The Consul's drinking subjects him to unmentionable horrors, it destroys him, but it also is the one thing about which he has, in John Barth's words from *End of The Road* "the feelings one usually has for one's absolutes." Shortly before 10:00 a.m., he grips the bottle of Johnny Walker with both hands and murmurs, "I love you." Then, as he falls asleep, he sees white clouds, racing across the sky, which say to him, "Drink all morning . . . drink all day. This is life!" The joy of this world is conveyed in the perhaps unspoken ("the Consul seemed to be saying") message he gives to Yvonne in the *Bella Vista* bar:

> . . . you misunderstand me if you think it is altogether darkness I see, and if you insist on thinking so, how can I tell you why I do it? But if you look at that sunlight there, ah, then perhaps you'll get the answer, see, look at that way it falls through the window: what beauty can compare to that of a cantina in the early morning? . . . . for not even the gates of heaven, opening wide to receive me, could fill me with such celestial complicated and hopeless joy as the iron screen that rolls up with a crash, as the unpadlocked jostling jalousies which admit those whose souls tremble with the drinks they carry unsteadily to their lips. All mystery, all

hope, all disappointment, yes, all disaster, is here, beyond those swinging doors. . . .

Nor is the Consul's fall an uncontrolled headlong plunge; he is never without a certain amount of control, a certain amount of self-humor and objectivity. Watching a drunken horseman who sprawls all over his mount, his stirrups lost, yet who manages to hold on by the reins and never once grasps the pommel to steady himself, Jacques thinks, " . . . this maniacal vision of senseless frenzy, but controlled, not quite uncontrolled, somehow almost admirable, this too, obscurely, was the Consul. . . ."

Hugh tells Yvonne that Dr. Guzman's analysis of the Consul's condition is "simply that, so far as he [Guzman] knew, there was nothing wrong with Papa [the Consul] and never had been save that he wouldn't make up his mind to stop drinking." The Consul has made up his mind to keep drinking; one could argue that his destruction is the result of an act of will. "What ever I do, it shall be deliberately. . . . The will of man is unconquerable," the Consul observes, standing on the mirador of Jacques's house, and later, to Jacques, "I shall certainly win, if I want to. . . ." But he doesn't want to win, at least if winning involves "escaping" to some haven of sobriety.

In Chapter V at the *Salón Ofélia,* he makes his choice clear: he chooses hell, because he *likes* it. Yet—an important qualification—"he wasn't quite serious," even as he runs into the forest toward the *Farolito.* The Consul isn't "quite" serious about the life (or death) he chooses, nor is Lowry ever "quite" serious about the Consul—both can see the element of absurdity in their respective creations. But this does not alter the fact that Lowry employs the Consul's alcoholism as one of the most important motifs in the novel—important for its symbolic resonances, and important for its functional contributions to the complication, development, and final resolution of the story.

Moments from death the Consul thinks, "No se puede vivir sin amar . . . which would explain everything. . . ." This phrase will explain a great deal, if not everything about *Under the Volcano,* at least on its "immediate level." This motto is inscribed in large, thick letters of gold leaf on a panel of stone set into the wall of one of the towers of Jacques's house. As the Consul, Yvonne, Hugh and Jacques pass the tower on their way into the house, the Consul does not permit himself to recall what the inscription says. A short time later, as the Consul and Jacques emerge, the Consul reads the words without comment, but does not translate them into English, for he cannot face the implications. I would render the phrase in English as "One cannot live without loving"—the relevance of this idea to the individual and collective fates of the four main characters of the novel should be evident. They all fail in love; they cease to exist, essentially, because they are incapable of loving, incapable of the selfless giving that Lowry suggests is necessary for real love.

"No se puede vivir sin amar," Jacques says to Dr. Vigil as the two drink anís on the terrace of the *Hotel Casino de la Selva* at the book's opening. In a moment Jacques offers the first part of the traditional Mexican toast, "Salud y pesetas." "Y tiempo para gastarlas," Vigil answers. Neither Jacques nor Vigil adds "Y amor" to the toast. In Chapter XI, at the *Hotel y Restaurant El Popo,* Hugh and Yvonne drink mescal while, a short distance away, the Consul courts destruction. "Salud y pesetas," Yvonne offers, as she drinks. "Salud y pesetas," Hugh answers. Then, as if to underscore the absence of "y amor" from the toast, Yvonne reiterates, "Salud y pesetas." The omission of "y amor" is of major significance. There is a considerable difference between "Good health and money, and time in which to enjoy them," and "Good health, money, and *love,* and time in which to enjoy them." One of Lowry's central concerns in the novel is what John McCormick has called, "the nature of love in a fragmented society" [see Further Reading]. Lowry's conception of the nature of love in the world of 1938-39, which may be taken as a paradigm of the twentieth-century world, is profoundly disturbing.

Jacques loves Yvonne, in his way, but the image of his regard for her can never be divorced from the scene in his studio where, in the Consul's painful conception, he approaches his design "with Tarquin's ravishing strides. . . ." Love came too late for Jacques, and in the wrong circumstances, and at the expense of his friend, the Consul.

Hugh, the "professional indoor Marxman" (as Jacques describes him) does, on the surface, seem to have a hope of "changing the world" (again in Jacques's phrase). But his attitude and conduct stem as much from a desire to gratify personal romantic whimsy as from genuine love for humanity. "Christ why can't we be simple, Christ Jesus why may we not be simple, why may we not all be brothers," Hugh thinks at one point during the bus ride to Tomalín. This is an earnest and admirable wish, but there is little evidence in the course of the novel to suggest that Hugh either is making, or will make a significant contribution toward the betterment of mankind. Although he is planning to help convoy a load of explosives to the beleaguered Spanish Loyalist forces, he realizes that the war in Spain is already lost and that his gesture will be devoid of any real meaning. Thus we must conclude that in his hopes and aspirations Hugh is on the other side of the angels, but in the process of living he is at one with fallen man.

Hugh's love clearly fails on a personal level. We have seen how his machinations with Yvonne are more detrimental than benefiical to the Consul. And, although he has a "pain in his heart" and a "faint giddiness" when he sees Yvonne, we have no real evidence for thinking that his feelings for her rest on much more than a purely physical basis. Hugh's love (or lust) for Yvonne, not condemnatory, certainly, in itself, becomes so in that it is directed toward the wife of his half-brother. In light of the love and kindness the Consul has shown for Hugh in the past, Hugh's adultery with Yvonne and his thoughtless usurpation of her on the day of the Consul's great need strike the reader as unforgivable.

Lowry's depiction of Hugh as the idealistic, ineffectual, perhaps basically destructive individual reveals only one aspect of his view of the nature of love. When we reflect upon the relationship of the Consul and Yvonne, we discover the full import of Lowry's conception of love in our time. Lowry seems to regard the failure of marriage as one of the most distinct and distinctively tragic failures of all; he sees the inability of man and woman to live together in harmony and love as indicative of the whole modern malaise. But the symbolic overtones of the failure of the marriage of Yvonne and Geoffrey are less important than the personal tragedy: "you loved yourself, you loved your misery more than I . . . you loved only yourself," Yvonne says to the Consul in the scrap of conversation Jacques overhears in the ruins of Maximilian and Carlotta's summer palace. Yvonne's charge may be true, but she fails to understand that she has been as selfish, and therefore as culpable as the Consul. The Consul's alcoholism—as any case of alcoholism—can be regarded as unqualified selfishness; but Yvonne's indulgences with other men and her inability to respond to her husband at crucial times are scarcely less selfish. It is not that love has ceased to exist in our world, Lowry implies; it is that selfish rather than selfless love is the characteristic form. During the Red Cross Ball debauch with Dr. Vigil, the Consul goes to a church in Quauhnahuac where he prays to the Virgin "For those who have nobody with": "Please let me make her [Yvonne] happy, deliver me from this dreadful tyranny of self . . . Teach me to love again, to love life." But this plea is futile, for, as one of the Consul's "familiars" says to him, "All you love is the cantinas now: the feeble survival of a love of life now turned to poison. . . ."

The Consul's unsuccessful attempt to make love to Yvonne signifies their whole failure together. When Yvonne consents, it does not seem from weariness only, but "to a solution for one shared instant beautiful as trumpets out of a clear sky. . . ." Then, as the Consul tries the "prelude, the preparatory nostalgic phrases on his wife's senses," the image of his possession fades slowly and inexorably into that of a cantina in the early morning. He returns to the present briefly, but awareness that completion of the proposed act is, at best, a remote possibility drives him back to the image of the cantina: "Ah, none but he knew how beautiful it all was. . . ." With this image suffusing him, and with the effect of alcohol only too obvious, the Consul says, "Sorry, it isn't any good, I'm afraid," and leaves the room. The pattern is established: the rest of the day holds a series of failures on the part of the Consul and Yvonne to come together with any real communication or hope between them.

On the balcony of Jacques's house the Consul apparently makes a move toward Yvonne, wanting to say something tender to her, to kiss her. Then he realizes that "without another drink, shame for this morning would prevent his looking into her eyes." The moment passes. In the bus to Tomalín the Consul takes Yvonne's hand and holds it tightly, which she remembers hopefully later at the arena. With Hugh astride the bull in the ring, and buoyed by her vision of the Northern Paradise, Yvonne asks, "Why don't we go away, now, tomorrow, today . . . what's to stop us?" The Consul leans his head against her and says wearily, "Why not? Let's for Jesus Christ's sweet sake get away . . . Away from all this." But neither makes a positive movement toward "escape" for the rest of the book.

Yvonne could not remain faithful to the Consul in the past; although he was at least partially to blame for her infidelity, he cannot forgive her. Not until almost the end does he fully realize the heartbreak he has caused her; then it is too late. Both are guilty; both fail. The marriage dies because of the inadequacy of love without understanding and compassion—or so Lowry seems to be saying. In more general terms, this theme of the novel is, in Walter Allen's phrase, "the necessity of love and the appalling difficulty of love" [see Further Reading].

In the letter which Jacques finds in the volume of Elizabethan plays in Chapter I, the Consul writes, "Love is the only thing which gives meaning to our poor ways on earth: not precisely a discovery, I am afraid." Not precisely a discovery, no, but in the process of bringing the Consul to this awareness, Lowry provides the reader with insight into the nature of the individual and collective tragedies of the characters of the novel, and makes a powerful statement concerning the plight of man and woman in the twentieth century. (pp. 94-105)

> *Dale Edmonds, " 'Under the Volcano': A Reading of the 'Immediate Level'," in TSE: Tulane Studies in English, Vol. XVI, 1968, pp. 63-105.*

Victor Doyen   (essay date 1969)

[*In the following essay, Doyen argues that* Under the Volcano *requires a "spatial reading," that is, one in which the reader must reconstruct details that are scattered throughout the novel.*]

Malcolm Lowry's principal novel **Under the Volcano** cannot be understood in depth when read for the first time: images, names, printed notices and fragments of conversations often return in an apparently haphazard way, yet with additional details in each new context; different elements are felt to be related though not explicitly linked, and deeper levels of symbolic meaning are gradually revealed. Therefore what Joseph Frank wrote about *Ulysses* also applies here: 'All the factual background—so conveniently summarized for the reader in an ordinary novel—must be reconstructed from fragments, sometimes hundreds of pages apart, scattered through the book. As a result the reader is forced to read *Ulysses* in exactly the same manner as he reads poetry—continually fitting fragments together and keeping allusions in mind until, by reflexive reference, he can link them to their complement [. . .]. A knowledge of the whole is essential to an understanding of any part'. Therefore it is useful briefly to sketch the plot before analysing some of these elements of spatial form.

On the eve of his departure from Mexico Jacques Laruelle reflects upon a tragedy which happened to his friends, exactly one year before. On that 'Day of the Dead' Yvonne returned to her husband, Geoffrey Firmin,—'the Consul'—whom she had left on account of his dipsomania. In spite of the troubles of Yvonne and his half-brother Hugh, and in spite of his own longing for Yvonne, Geoffrey cannot abstain from alcohol. His drunkenness leads both him and his wife towards death.

This is the story. The meaning of the novel however is

much more complex. On a first level *Under the Volcano* is an account of the individual's struggle for life, of man's fight against himself, against his dreams and disillusions; on a second level the relation between man and wife, the theme of love, is analysed; on still another level the novel offers a confrontation of opposite ideologies, the eternal theme of war and peace, of conquest and fight for freedom.

In their personal life, all the characters are haunted by memories of the past. Geoffrey is brooding over his lost honour. Yvonne tries to escape the nightmares of her youth and the doom of her family which was ruined by alcohol. Hugh is a romantic who draws up the inventory of the—failed—first part of his life. He is an enthusiastic communist who dreams of changing the world, but often considers himself a traitor. Even Laruelle, although a minor character, plays his role on this level of the personal conflict. The tragedy of the others has destroyed his last hope. He leaves the country depressed under a burden of personal and universal guilt.

In the novel however this personal conflict is never separated from the theme of love and the ideological debate. Yvonne's return is an unexpected factor in Geoffrey's self-imposed misery. He has to choose now between love and drinking, between disinterested extroversion and masochistic isolation. If he chooses love, he has to accept also the consequences, namely complete pardon to Yvonne—even for her affairs with Laruelle and with Hugh—and, for himself, 'admission of total defeat'. 'To drink or not to drink' is for this Hamlet-of-the bottle a question of life and death. His intoxication, combined with a frustrated sense of honour, prevents him from loving her unconditionally. To him her return appears to be a kind of interference with his own personal freedom. When she calls on Hugh's help he suspects them of conspiring against him. The ideological debate between Geoffrey and Hugh, in chapter X, is at the same time a personal drama. Geoffrey's ideological conclusion leads to his personal catastrophe. He claims the right to deteriorate if he pleases, and chooses his own ruin. Since Geoffrey refuses to love her, life becomes impossible for Yvonne too.

The theme of war and peace is always present in the background: the civil war in Spain, the inner difficulties in Mexico, Hugh's defence of the Communist system against the growing threat of the Nazi system. In an even more distant background—so remote that it becomes symbolic for all kinds of war and oppression in all ages—we meet the theme of the *conquistadores*.

This article will show how these three levels of themes are constantly deepened, broadened and interrelated by a web of symbolic references. Perhaps it should be phrased the other way round, because the meaning of this novel is an *a posteriori* in which symbols and metaphors play a constitutive role. Therefore it seems better not to point out how themes are developed on symbolic levels, but to start from elements of spatial form and see how they have a function in the whole. In the first part we follow some threads on their way through this linguistic tapestry. In the second we start from a knot of threads at a certain point and see how different themes are interlocked.

The first paragraph of the novel offers a panoramic description of the setting: Quauhnahuac, a Mexican town situated 'on the nineteenth parallel in about the same latitude as [. . .] the southernmost tip of Hawaii and [. . .] the town of Juggernaut, in India'. Two far-off places are brought together within one spatial frame and linked to the place of action. Only later shall we learn that there is indeed a relation between them: Geoffrey comes from India, Yvonne was born in Hawaii.

Quauhnahuac is dominated by two volcanoes, Popocatepetl and Ixtaccihuatl. In the first chapters they seem no more than a part of the scenery; but in chapter III Geoffrey thinks of them as 'that image of the perfect marriage'. This metaphor, however, painfully contrasts with the situation of Geoffrey and Yvonne at that moment: he has not been able to seal his wife's return by a marital union. While she is crying in the bedroom, he is lying in a chair with a bottle in his hands watching the clouds that say to him: 'Drink all morning, drink all day'. In Yvonne's mind the volcanoes play a similar symbolic role. In chapter IX when looking in her mirror she sees only Popocatepetl:

> However she moved the mirror she couldn't get poor Ixta in, who, quite eclipsed, fell away sharply into invisibility.

This description of nature has a deeper meaning. She identifies herself with Ixtaccihuatl (=sleeping Woman), whereas Popocatepetl stands for Geoffrey. But this can only be understood in chapter XI, where the old Indian legend is explained:

> Chimborazo, Popocatepetl—so ran the poem the Consul liked—had stolen his heart away! But in the tragic Indian legend Popocateptl himself was strangely the dreamer; the fires of his warrior's love [. . .] burned eternally for Ixtaccihuatl, whom he had no sooner found than lost, and whom he guarded in her endless sleep . . .

In this context one could also think of *La Despedida*, the picture of a split rock appearing, in chapter II, in a window with *wedding invitations*. For Yvonne it reflects the enigma of her own marriage:

> La Despedida, she thought. The Parting! [. . .] The violence of the fire which split the rock apart had also incited the destruction of each separate rock, cancelling the power that might have held them unities [. . .] She longed to heal the cleft rock. She was one of the rocks and she yearned to save the other, that both might be saved.

This metaphor finds an echo in Geoffrey's comment on another split rock in the last chapter:

> And the crag was still there too [. . .] the huge stack clinging to the mass of earth, as if resting on life, not afraid to fall, but darkening, just the same, where it would go if it went. It was a tremendous, an awful way down to the bottom. But it struck him he was not afraid to fall either.

In these images we recognize the tragic contrast between two different visions of life. Yvonne wants to cure Geoffrey of his dipsomania and save their marriage. Geoffrey cannot accept this. He prefers to disintegrate; he chooses his own Hell.

This leads us to another element of spatial form, the *Hell Bunker.* In Laruelle's flashback to his youth (chapter I), the name of this hazard on a golf course in Leasowe already has a symbolic connotation. After he found his friend Geoffrey there with a girl, they all went to a tavern with the queer name 'The Case is Altered'. 'It was patently the first time the Consul had ever been into a bar on his own initiative'. In the novel we meet Geoffrey as an incurable drunkard. In chapter III, when he is unable 'to perform his marital duties', and starts drinking again he notices two old golfballs in the cupboard: 'Play with me I can still carry the eighth green in three. I am tapering off'. This is a reminiscence of the Hell Bunker. But we have to go back to the first chapter to find the link. Indeed, 'in the middle of the longsloping *eighth* fairway [. . .] the abyss yawned in such a position as to engulf the *third* shot of a golfer like Geoffrey, a naturally beautiful and graceful player' (ital. mine). In the new context of physical decay and sexual impotence Geoffrey's allusion has a tragic impact. In chapter VII the image of the Hell Bunker returns. Geoffrey has agreed to join Yvonne and Hugh in a trip to Tomalin. Still he thinks of an escape to the Farolito in Parián, where he could drink mescal and forget everything. In his mind's eye the whole country turns then into a huge golf course with the *barranca* as 'the Golgotha Hole':

> Over the hills and far away, like youth, like life itself, the course plotted all over these plains, extending far beyond Tomalin, through the jungle, to the Farolito, the nineteenth hole . . . The Case is Altered.

Geoffrey's thoughts are full of dramatic irony: that evening he runs through the jungle from Tomalin to the Farolito; there he is shot down and thrown in the barranca. At the same time the symbolic meaning of the Hell Bunker is directly related to that of the Farolito, by the allusion to the tavern 'The Case is Altered'. For Geoffrey the Farolito *is* Hell—just like 'that other Farolito', a bar in Oaxaca called 'El Infierno'. A picture of doomed drunkards, *Los Borrachones,* immediately reminds him of the Farolito! Still the prospect of going there fills him with 'the greatest longing he had ever known', for it is the only place where he can find *peace.* In Tomalin (chapter X) he drinks mescal, which becomes fatal for him. His intoxicated mind turns the town of a tourist folder into a Paradise for drunkards: a white empty mescal city 'where one could drink for ever on credit', and with no one 'to interfere with the business of drinking, not even Yvonne'. In the syntax of a distorted phrase Tlaxcala and Hell are identified: 'I choose—Tlax—[. . .] Hell [. . .] Because [. . .] I like it'. Then he runs off to *his* Tlaxcala: the Farolito. In chapter XII he has arrived there. When he visits the protitute Maria, the Hell Bunker appears again, but now in a very disguised way:

> The Consul's eyes focused a calendar behind the bed. He had reached his crisis at last [. . .] In the dim blue light he even made out the names of the Saints for each December day [. . .] S. Nicolas de Bari, S. Ambrosio: thunder blew the

door open, the face of M. Laruelle faded in the door.

But Laruelle is playing tennis with Dr. Vigil at that moment! The point is in Geoffrey's free association between the next December day on the calendar—Mary's Immaculate Conception—, and that which happens to the other Maria. But neither is said. Instead we find a colon and an association with a similar situation in the Hell Bunker.

A role, similar to that of the Volcanoes and the Hell Bunker, is played by printed notices and fragments of conversation. The fact that they are seen or heard by *dramatized* narrators is very important. Their interpolation in the text is more than an objective record. It implies not only that a sign *is* there, but also that the narrator is aware of its presence and reacts to it. This however is not to deny that these elements have a deeper symbolic function which transcends the point of view of a single narrator.

In chapter V Geoffrey sees a placard on the fence that separates his own neglected garden from the new public one:

> a sign, uprooted or new, whose oblong pallid face stared through the wire at him. *Le gusta este jardin?* it asked . . .
>
> ¿LE GUSTA ESTE JARDÍN?
> ¿QUE ES SUYO?
> ¡EVITE QUE SUS HIJOS LO DESTRUYAN!
>
> The Consul stared back at the black words on the sign without moving. You like this garden? Why is it yours? We evict those who destroy!

Geoffrey knows that 'perhaps the sign didn't mean quite that', but in his inaccurate translation he considers it a warning for himself. In chapter VII when he has dismissed Laruelle's help and good advice, the sign returns: 'The man had nailed his board to the tree. ¿LE GUSTA ESTE JARDÍN?' When Hugh sees the placard in chapter VIII he translates correctly, and there is no indication that the warning should have the same ominous meaning for him as it has for the Consul. After Geoffrey's death however the text returns once more, covering the whole last page of the novel, as a kind of epilogue. Here it is an 'authorial' conclusion, referring to the Consul's subjective interpretation. Geoffrey has condemned himself by refusing Hugh and Yvonne's 'offers of a sober and non-alcoholic Paradise'. He prefers his own Eden: Tlaxcala—the Farolito—Hell. His death near the Farolito is the execution of his sentence.

The biblical symbolism of this sign '¿LE GUSTA ESTE JARDÍN? adds a new dimension to the paradigmatical axis of the novel. The Garden symbol is already present in the first chapter, when Laruelle passes Geoffrey's house and notices that 'long after Adam had left the garden the light in Adam's house burned on—and the gate was mended'. The latter part of this phrase means, on a first level, that the gate—which indeed was 'off its hinges and lying just beyond the entrance'—is repaired now. But at the same time it indicates that the Garden of Eden is closed now for Geoffrey. In chapter V his neglected garden is contrasted with his neighbour's. He offers then his own version of 'the old legend of the Garden of Eden [. . .] What if Adam wasn't really banished from the place at all? [. . .] What if his punishment really consisted [. . .] in his having to *go on living there,* alone, of course—suffering, unseen, cut off from God. . . . ' When Yvonne arrives home she is shocked by this overgrown garden: 'Geoffrey this place is a wreck!' It is a symbol of the failure of their own marriage. Even the fact that she and Hugh try to clean up the garden could be understood as a symbolic correlate of their attempts to restore her marriage. Later Yvonne dreams of a little sea-side shack where she and Geoffrey could start again and be happy together (chapter IX). This paradisiac image has a striking resemblance to Geoffrey's own vision, described in his letter in the first chapter. But there is still another parallel: the image of her burning dream (chapter XI) recalls also the burning of Geoffrey's letter. Reunited they could have built up their own Paradise. Now they are evicted. The Garden theme adds universal meaning to the tragedy of these two people.

Life is impossible without love. This idea is also expressed in another leitmotif of the novel: the text on Laruelle's house, mentioned for the first time in his conversation with Dr Vigil about the Consul:

> *'No se puede vivir sin amar',* M. Laruelle said . . . 'As that *estúpido* inscribed on my house'.

An allusion to this text appears in chapter II, where Yvonne tries to escape the impact of the words by neglecting them—'the house to their left with its inscription on the wall she didn't want to see'. The same happens when the Consul arrives at Laruelle's house in chapter VII:

> These gold letters though very thick were merged together most confusingly [. . .] they formed that phrase of Frey Luis de León's the Consul did not at this moment allow himself to recall.

But when he leaves the house he sees the text again. This time it is interpolated: '*No se puede vivir sin amar,* were the words on the house'. At his death the phrase returns when he believes he hears the voices of Laruelle and Vigil:

> [They] would set Hugh and Yvonne's minds at rest about him. '*No se puede vivir sin amar',* they would say which would explain everything, and he repeated this aloud.

A poster for a murder film, *Las Manos de Orlac,* adds to the special atmosphere of this Day of the Dead. Already in the first chapter it is a symbol of murder in general. Afterwards it appears at regular intervals along the road until Geoffrey, Hugh and Yvonne reach the place where the wounded Indian is found. Here murder is concretely realised. 'The *pelado's* smeared *conquistador's* hands' remind us again of *Las Manos de Orlac.*

Other printed notices and placards could be added. But we can as well mention some fragments of conversation or recurrent thoughts which have the same function as elements of spatial form.

There is, for instance, Weber's set of stock-phrases. When Yvonne meets Geoffrey in the Bella Vista Bar (chapter II), her first words are interrupted by an unidentified voice. In chapter IV we recognize one of these phrases in Hugh's

reminiscence of Weber, the man who flew him to Mexico—'*They shoot first and ask questions later*'. The same line returns in Geoffrey's mind during his delirium in chapter X. Later, in the Farolito, this Weber turns up again and introduces himself to the Consul, with almost literally the same words as we heard in the first chapter. In the new context we become aware of their ominous meaning for Geoffrey.

In the same way one could describe Dr Vigil's question 'Did you never go to the church for the bereavèd here?' or Hugh's recurrent references to the battle of the Ebro, or the opening line of the second chapter (the beginning of the central story): 'A corpse will be transported by express!' . . . Let us stick to the last. It takes three pages before the reader knows that it is Geoffrey who pronounced this 'singular remark'. He found it in a 'Mexican National Railways time-table' and during the whole chapter he offers variants on this leitmotif. In chapter III he proposes as an advertisement for a new job: 'will accompany corpse to any place in the east', and in chapter X the first line turns up in the context of a gravedigger and a railway guide. This theme of the corpse is part of the general theme of Death. But from the very beginning it is related to another element of spatial form, the Blackstone-theme: 'Talking of corpses [. . .] personally I'd like to be buried next to William Blackstone [. . .] the man who went to live among the Indians', says Geoffrey to Yvonne. In chapter V he explains to his neighbour that Blackstone wanted to escape from the Puritans, 'these fellows with ideas'. In chapter X the idea of 'going to live among the Indians, like William Blackstone' returns in his mind, whereas Hugh and Yvonne and all those who want to interfere in general are rejected as 'people with ideas'. Only a dog is praised—'these animals, these people without ideas'. Geoffrey promises to the cripple dog: 'Yet this day, *pichicho,* shalt thou be with me in—'. He cannot finish his phrase, but when he dies, a dog follows him into the ravine. To the police he maintained that his name was Blackstone. . . .

From the foregoing quotations we notice already that the Blackstone-theme is deepened in its turn by symbolic references to the person of Christ. In the Farolito, where a sailor speaks of 'the Old Testament of Mozart', a dead-drunk Geoffrey preaches, as a second Christ, *his* New Testament, the glad tidings for wretches—like himself—, but at the same time a gospel of non-interference:

> Only the poor, only through God, only the people you wipe your feet on, the poor in spirit [. . .] if only you'd stop interfering, stop walking in your sleep, stop sleeping with my wife, only the beggars and the accursed.

Geoffrey dies in the barranca, to which he once referred as 'The Golgotha Hole'. In this context of biblical metaphors a new light is also thrown on the relation between Geoffrey and his half-brother. In chapter IV Hugh identifies himself with Judas because he has betrayed Geoffrey through his affair with Yvonne. The Hugh-Judas parallel corresponds here to the Geoffrey-Christ parallel.

To give a good idea of the complex metaphorical structure of this novel it is necessary not only to indicate different lines of symbolic references throughout the book, but also to show how these elements are connected. Therefore we have to choose a strategic point in the novel and to see how a whole web of references begins to vibrate when one of its threads is touched.

The best place to start from would be Geoffrey's delirium in chapter X. When we read this passage for the first time, it sounds like pure gibberish. And in a certain sense it is. But it is also an experiment in spatial form. When we accept the novel as a linguistic and literary whole and detect the different contexts out of which these fragments are lifted, we gradually discern, in this mass of loose phrases, the outlines of a new construction. The underlying emotion is not described but revealed in a play of associations.

For practical reasons however we have to use a less complex example. Therefore I prefer the above-mentioned passage about the wounded Indian. Here too several lines of spatial elements converge. Besides the reference to *Las Manos de Orlac,* pointed out before, there is the horse with the branded number seven, the theme of the conquest, and what I would like to call the 'Parable of the Bad Samaritan'. Let us take the latter first.

The wounded Indian is the man who 'fell among thieves'; the occupants of the bus and the diplomatic car are the people passing by. But there is nobody to take care of the man, only a thief to rob him of his last money! When Geoffrey is shot down he remembers the incident: 'Now he was the one dying by the wayside where no good Samaritan would halt'. The biblical name is the link between that incident and another which happened long before: the mysterious death of the captured German officers on board the s.s. Samaritan (a rather cynical name for a disguised warship). Although Geoffrey had probably no personal guilt in this affair, the Samaritan-case keeps haunting his mind. We do not know whether or not he could have prevented that tragedy by interfering. But we do know that he prevents Hugh from playing the good Samaritan in chapter VIII. Later he defends his attitude: 'Why should we have done anything to save his life? Hadn't he a right to die, if he wanted to?' The fundamental contrast between Geoffrey's vision of life and Hugh's can be summarized in two lines of their discussion:

> Why can't people mind their own damned business!'

> 'Or say what they mean?'

Geoffrey advocates a policy of non-involvement on the personal as well as on the political level. In his eyes there is little difference between help and interference. A Samaritan may be a disguised conquistador.

Here we touch a second element, the conquest. The meeting of Montezuma (the last Aztec emperor) and Cortez (the conquistador) is praised on a calendar in the Bella Vista bar as a symbol of the amalgamation of two high civilisations. In fact it is a symbol of the exploitation of one race by another, as the drunken Consul explains to Laruelle in connection with the Rivera Murals. The conquest becomes a universal symbol of imposition. In chapter X the discussion starts from the personal case of the wounded Indian and the *pelado* (the thief), broadens into the opposition between Fascism and Communism, goes back to conquests and wars of independence all over the world, and ends again in a particular case, Geoffrey's choice of personal freedom.

A third element is the horse. Hugh and Yvonne met the horse-rider on their morning walk, at a *pulqueria* called *'La Sepultura'* (!), under a tree with a poster for *Las Manos de Orlac.* When Geoffrey sees that same Indian (in chapter VII) the horse reminds him of Goethe's phrase: 'Weary of liberty he suffered himself to be saddled and bridled, and was ridden to death for his pains'. From an 'authorial' point of view this line is reminiscent of another opening quotation of the novel, a line from Sophocles: '[Man] tames the horse of shaggy mane, he puts the yoke upon its neck'. When we know however that in this novel the horse will not be tamed but released, and that precisely this act is the cause of both Geoffrey's and Yvonne's death, we become aware of the striking dramatic irony of this quotation which ends in: 'only against Death shall he call for aid in vain'.

Finally we have the number seven, a symbol in itself. In the first chapter Laruelle's Day of the Dead ends shortly after seven o'clock. The action of the central story takes place between seven a.m. and seven p.m. In an allusion to the Indian belief it is revealed that a cock crowing seven times announced death: at the end of the novel, when the clock strikes seven times, the cock appears also. The number seven has the connotation of perfection. For both Yvonne and Geoffrey it is the End of Time. In the context of the other biblical allusions the seventh stroke of the bell reminds us of the opening of the seventh seal. The horse released by Geoffrey becomes an apocalyptic animal, inflicted upon mankind and bringing death to Yvonne. This is again a biblical metaphor—like the references to Adam, Christ, Golgotha, Emmaus—, a metaphor which develops even into a kind of allegory. But this is only one of the various strata of symbolism which give deeper and universal meaning to the personal conflict of one particular man. Geoffrey's struggle for life (and drink) has Faustian greatness. His dipsomania becomes a means of reaching ultimate peace. On still another symbolic level his journey on the Day of the Dead is a descent into Dante's Hell.

In this article the personal conflicts of Hugh, Yvonne and Laruelle have not been analysed; nor has the universal theme of War and Peace. A few elements only have been offered for a spatial reading of this novel which brings to light some of its many levels of symbolic meaning. Obviously this could be developed further, but even in its incompleteness the investigation shows that a spatial reading is less a reconstruction of the factual background than a descent under the volcano. (pp. 65-74)

Victor Doyen, "Elements Towards a Spatial Reading of Malcolm Lowry's 'Under the Volcano'," in English Studies, *Netherlands, Vol. 50, No. 1, February, 1969, pp. 65-74.*

Clifford Leech   (essay date 1970)

[Leech was an English critic. In the following excerpt, he discusses the sense of time in Under the Volcano.*]*

Apart from Chapter I, the events directly presented [in **Under The Volcano**] occur between an early morning and the same day's dusk. There are only three characters whose fortunes we follow throughout: the Consul (no longer a consul), his wife Yvonne, his younger brother Hugh. They move about in or near the town of Quauhnahuac, never out of sight of the twin volcanoes that dwarf the men at their feet and contain within themselves the threat and promise of destruction—twins, male and female, brother and brother, gods yet men too in their joint rooting in the earth, their joint reaching away from it, their shared element of suppressed fire. In the main line of narrative there is no movement back and forth, apart from the retrospective Chapter I. The day's action occurs in 1938, but in Chapter I it is a year later than that: Dr. Arturo Díaz Vigil and M. Jacques Laruelle remember, as they drink together, the dead Consul, the dead Yvonne, the bereft Hugh. Yet Lowry is strangely inexplicit in this opening chapter. We are never firmly told about the deaths of the husband and wife until we come to the end of the book, and many a reader has gone on to Chapter II, and far beyond, in the belief that the main narrative follows, not precedes, the conversation of the two men with which the book begins and the musings of Laruelle that form the remainder of Chapter I. What Lowry may intend here is to give a fuller sense of life to his main characters by not simply asserting in advance what happened to them on their day of disaster, while at the same time making Vigil's and Laruelle's comments ominous enough and gradually letting them appear as retrospective. Moreover, the inexplicitness make the Consul and the others seem alive when they are being referred to in Chapter I, and this is a mode of defying the operations, even the fatal operations, of time. To have lived and to be the subject of anguish in recollection is in some sense to be living still. Perhaps, however, a very perceptive reader may get the time-scheme right at once: my own experience was not that, and is borne out by that of other readers I know.

In the rest of the book there are passages of recollection, of course, as there are in any substantial novel, but attention is centred on the events of the day. Outside this centre there exists an extensive periphery. Because it is 1938, the war in Spain is going on and the Nazi threat, strong over Europe, finds sympathetic reverberations among the small bullies of Mexican officialdom. What Lowry also does is to make us aware of the cultural complexity of a human being's store of memory. A man of our time may think in terms of Dante, for example, of the Elizabethan dramatists, of (especially in 1938) German films of the 1920s, early 'westerns' from Hollywood: strangely, the trivial and the masterwork can function similarly in providing the skeleton for thought, the interpretative symbol. When Yvonne and Hugh go riding in the morning, the great ravine they cross and skirt is called the 'Malebolge', because Dante provides the suggestions of depth and corruption and miscellaneous horror: it is this ravine into which the Consul is thrown, where he dies as he descends. Repeatedly we hear of the film *Hands of Orlac* being shown at the cinema in Quauhnahuac, a poor film with Peter Lorre acting in vain, a re-make of a German silent film in which Conrad Veidt had played: that, too, was poor enough. The Lorre version is already old, poignant therefore as a reminder of lost time, but it provides also a chance link with the 1920s, a time when the characters of the book were younger and Europe was not yet wholly dark: it acts therefore as a double filter for memory. Moreover, the melodramatic idea of the film—of the musician who lost his hands in an accident and had a dead murderer's hands grafted on in their place—becomes a symbol of the duality of the human being, making yet fearful of destroying, led on to destruction by the very instruments with which he makes. It is Hugh's love for Yvonne that leads him to betray his brother's trust; Yvonne's strong wish for a stable relationship with her husband that makes her despairing and promiscuous; the Consul's power of perception that makes him destroy his marriage, refuse Yvonne on her return, and finally acquiesce in the violence offered him. Any 'present' moment, when experienced in full consciousness, is a focal point not only for a patterning of memories but for an interpretation of both personal and political life in terms of cultural experience. So much so that one can never respond simply to what the moment itself offers. In Chapter IV Hugh and Yvonne are riding: the day is not yet hot, the country is gracious, the man and woman are in sympathy with each other:

> Earlier it had promised to be too hot: but just enough sun warmed them, a soft breeze caressed their faces, the countryside on either hand smiled upon them with deceptive innocence, a drowsy hum rose up from the morning, the mares nodded, there were the foals, here was the dog, and it is all a bloody lie, he thought.

Hugh goes on to recognize an appropriateness in the fact that this is a day of solemnity for the Mexicans, a day given over to honouring the dead, who 'come to life' for the occasion—like the memories of betrayal in one's own life. Even so, this is life at its best:

> Another thought struck Hugh. And yet I do not expect, ever in my life, to be happier than I am now. No peace I shall ever find but will be poisoned as these moments are poisoned.

A little later he almost forgets:

> Christ, how marvellous this was, or rather Christ, how he wanted to be deceived about it, as must have Judas, he thought—and here it was again, damn it—if ever Judas had a horse, or borrowed, stole one more likely, after that Madrugada of all Madrugadas, regretting then that he had given the thirty pieces of silver back—what is that to us, see thou to that, the *bastardos* had said—when now he probably wanted a drink, thirty drinks (like Geoff undoubtedly would this morning), and perhaps even so he had managed a few on credit, smelling the good smells of leather and sweat, listening to the pleasant clopping of the horses' hooves and thinking, how joyous all this could be, riding on like this under the dazzling sky of Jerusalem— and forgetting for an instant, so that it really *was* joyous.

He too could forget 'for an instant, so that it really *was* joyous'. The moment just after this, when he and Yvonne come to the brewery and drink the cold dark German beer and Yvonne hankers after buying the armadillo as a pet, is the book's idyllic moment, but *we* are never allowed to forget the recurrent personal betrayal, the burden of the mind's obligation to interpret, the large-scale disaster of the Spanish war, the coming extension of international strife, the hostility of nature to man. Only at a glance was the armadillo gentle:

> Each time the armadillo ran off, as if on tiny wheels, the little girl would catch it by its long whip of a tail and turn it over. How astonishingly soft and helpless it appeared then! Now she righted the creature and set it going once more, some engine of destruction perhaps that after millions of years had come to this.

Apart from forgetting, there is the sheer mystery of the past. Yvonne's is shadowy, linked with her success as a child-star in ephemeral films; Hugh's is barely given to us, but we know of the political urge that is on him, of his former relation with Yvonne, of the rift this makes between the brothers; the Consul is neither affirmed nor denied to have been guilty of a special atrocity in the First World War; the details of the first separation of Yvonne from her husband are never explicit for us. The past always has its obscurity and its defiance of credibility: he, or she, could surely not have done that, is commonly our response to what is alleged, and is as unbelievable to the one who has actually done it (whether heroism or ignominy is involved) as it is to those who know him on terms of intimacy. The roots of the present are things we feel we must refuse to accept or must leave as a question-mark.

The human mind has a further mode of self-tormenting. It is not easy on the best of occasions to forget that—'even now, now, very now'—things are happening in the world at large that mock at a present joy. So Hugh is recurrently conscious that, as he talks and journeys through the day, the battle of the Ebro is being fought and lost. But the special plague is not merely that we are doing nothing, can do nothing, to prevent the disaster far away: it is also that we believe each act of ours contributes to a total pattern that ensures the future: because one raises or puts down a glass, the battle of the Ebro will be lost; if one had acted, even in a trifle, differently, a different future would have been ordained. This is not rational, but is part of our deep-seated sense of a total developing pattern, imposing a responsibility on us for all that is to happen. Yet there is no power along with the responsibility: only in retrospect are we convinced that, if we had not done such-and-such a thing, the future would not have been doomed: we should have broken through the straitjacket of destiny. The more aware we are of what is happening in the world outside our immediate view, the more fully this kind of self-tormenting, this sense of total responsibility with a total absence of power, will impinge on our present moments.

Yet in another way this book insists on a multiplicity of futures. There is what will happen, regardless. There is also the future we can imagine, and this is as much part of our experience as the thing that must be. The Consul and Yvonne dream recurrently of a free life by the woods and waters of British Columbia, the more idyllic because of its remoteness alike from Mexico and from the more thronged stages of the world. Lowry himself, of course, spent much of his last years in British Columbia, and he is making no claim in his novel that even the natural splendour of Canada's west coast is a guarantee of contentment. But for Yvonne and the Consul it could appear to be, and the dream was part of their last day. The most precarious of dreams, of course: as Yvonne in Chapter IX sees in her mind the house above the beach she might share with her husband, she cannot fully concentrate on the simple image:

> Why was it though, that right in the centre of her brain, there should be a figure of a woman having hysterics, jerking like a puppet and banging her fists upon the ground?

And there is, too, the future beyond one's own death, which we have seen in personal terms in Chapter I, and which in Chapter XI, near the fact of death for the Consul and Yvonne, becomes extended beyond the time when this or that person of our 'now' can be remembered. The night sky will be observed so long as man lasts, and always the basic questions concerning purpose and cause will be raised. Then even Yvonne's infidelities and the Consul's drinking, even the battle of the Ebro and the things done in our time in the name of race or for gain's sake, will be forgotten: there will be only recurrence, of delight and fragile hope, of shame and loss, of questioning and failure to answer.

Meanwhile there is the present, charged full with memory and ambivalent response. An instant is indeed of copious content: under contemplation its extent can become enormous, as the stream-of-consciousness novelists have long made us know. Lowry has reinforced this by packing the one-day's sequence of Chapters II-XII with action and movement. It might appear that the intense activity could not have been borne by the three people concerned. The Consul begins the day hung-over and still drinking, Yvonne and Hugh have travelled overnight. Yet after her first sad encounter with her husband, she is seeing how her garden has become a wilderness, and then sets out with Hugh on their ride through the morning sunlight outside the town. Later they visit Laruelle, enter into the town's festivities on this day of solemnity, and then travel to Tomalín on the bus for the bullthrowing. Even then the journey is not over: there is the twilit road to Parián to be covered, where in the end the horse waits for Yvonne and the ravine for the Consul. When one thinks how little one does on most days, when one thinks of the dust and the heat and the nervous tension and the drinking, this day in a novel is frightening. Yet there are days that most of us have known, especially those days when tension has been at an extreme, which have strangely filled themselves with activity beyond normal endurance. In the result we are not wholly incredulous that the novel's people could have managed it, but we are conscious that such days are commonly days of crisis and shadow forth the characteristic depth of the existential moment. Yvonne in Chapter IX follows a boy's gaze into the sky as he looks for an airplane he can hear: 'she made it out for herself, a droning hyphen in abysmal blue.' That is an image for the momentary in its ungraspability, fugitiveness—in relation both to what we call 'now' in its strictest sense and to the lives we live in the whole context of time. But the hyphen drones, which suggests continuity, extension. The day, the individual's life, are also brief, but they take shape, they stretch profoundly by virtue of one's store of consciousness. What gives this extension is made up of personal relations and the nexus of cultural experiences. There is a lifetime in the moment, in the day of crisis. It is this that gives peculiar power to the novel or the drama that observes the Unity of Time, but this 'Unity' in its fullest employment is not one of mere restriction: it encompasses the all that a man knows. (pp. 100-07)

> *Clifford Leech, "The Shaping of Time," in his* The Dramatist's Experience: With Other Essays in Literary Theory, *Chatto & Windus, 1970, pp. 87-107.*

Richard Hauer Costa   (essay date 1972)

[*Costa is an American critic and reviewer. In the following excerpt, he details the artistic qualities that make* Under the Volcano *a masterpiece.*]

Although **Under the Volcano** has won mention as a "contemporary classic," "the finest and profoundest work of fiction by an Englishman" during the 1940s, and "a masterpiece as rich and humorous as *Ulysses* and far more poetic," the book has been more talked about than read. Admittedly, Lowry is given to *longueurs*—the whole strategy of his book, as will be shown, is circular. He was also a combination of crammer-inner and never-ender. But, for those who will *give* themselves to the *inevitability* of the Consul's fate—an inevitability which eschews any marked line of suspense—the extraordinary *lucidity* of the book will take over. The "story" is always there. While probing to the deepest Dostoevskian level—that aspect of a man he cannot even acknowledge to himself—Lowry never allows the story line to bow to the labyrinthine. I agree with Dale Edmonds that it is on the " 'most immediate level'— the level of people, places, events and circumstances within a fictional world that much resembles our own—that *Volcano* communicates most effectively" [see excerpt dated 1968].

There is no part of this book that is not touched by the shadow of *Volcano.* The next two chapters deal almost exclusively with it. Nowhere, however, do I take up a chapter-by-chapter résumé. The best and the worst of Lowry's books resist any such linear push. This chapter pursues the novel at the "impact level." The less the initial reader thinks about symbols, levels of meaning, and literary allusions, the more he will be able to give himself fully to the impact of this book. The chapter seeks to suggest the nature of addiction—the Consul's full awareness of his condition—and the reasons why this most philosophical of men rejects all offers of human salvation and love. Chapter 4 lays open, largely through analysis of the several versions, the ten-year evolvement of the novel. With Lowry it is what Matthew Corrigan calls the "final expurgatory look" that counts. Even though *Volcano* is Lowry's single major success, few writers of greater quantitative achieve-

ment could have brought off a masterpiece under the conditions of Lowry's life in which he, in a sense, fought his genius all the way.

The beginning of **Under the Volcano**—a 42-page opening chapter—is such that the word "controversial" may not be inappropriate. Jonathan Cape's reader demanded that Lowry drop it altogether because nothing happens. The fact is, *everything* happens. The chapter has the somberness and beauty of the past recalled in tranquility. It also posts the dread markings—the clues—to the action of exactly one year earlier. If the reader is not caught up in its spirit—if, like the Cape reader, he is bothered by "long initial tedium"—he might wish to reread the first chapter after he had finished the other eleven.

Considered in terms of conventional fiction, then, the opening chapter is all wrong: an epilogue in the place of a prologue; an opening in which the fate of the two main characters is revealed (they are dead, though by means left ambiguous); a chapter which is a series of intricate flashbacks and where Mexican local color, as the Cape reader put it, is "heaped on in shovelfuls." To the objection that the opening is tedious, Lowry replied in a long and justly famous letter [see excerpt in *TCLC*, Vol. 6, pp. 235-36] He wrote that readers of like mind might be "conditioned" to

Lowry in London, 1931.

accept the slow start if a "preface or blurb" was appended. This thought led Lowry to a characteristically amusing analogy. A preface, he said, will serve for his novel as bush for the wine. He could not resist an aside: "I am not talking of good wine but mescal, and quite apart from the bush . . . mescal needs salt and lemon to get it down." Then, in another characteristic ploy, he turned for an ally to an acknowledged classic. He asked if anyone would have ventured into the drought of *The Waste Land* on his own without some "anterior knowledge and anticipation of its poetic cases."

When he got down to business, Lowry defended the opening chapter on the only grounds tenable: its vitality to the "feel" of the whole novel. He made these claims: (a) Chapter I sets the mood and tone of the book, (b) it sets the slow melancholy tragic rhythm of Mexico—its sadness, and, (c) above all, it establishes the book's "terrain," a word Lowry underlined. By "terrain," he undoubtedly means many things. It is the physical landscape of the novel. The reader is introduced to all the talismanic landmarks which Lowry, so profligately in early versions and so brilliantly in the final, posts: the twin volcanoes, the Malebolgean barranca, the ruins of the palace where Maximilian and Carlotta, earlier "empurpled lovers," declared their doomed love, the dark Dantean wood. The chapter also keys the spiritual landscape. If the reader is denied the suspense of *impending* tragedy, Lowry gives him something equally dramatic, something more consonant with the atmosphere of the book: a sense of dread at what has *already occurred,* a thing so shattering that it has left the survivors no peace during the intervening year.

Lowry's Cape letter went on to assert that the opening chapter, while appearing epilogic, actually prepares the stage for the book's concerns, which are "the forces in man which cause him to be terrified of himself . . . the guilt of man . . . his remorse . . . his ceaseless struggling toward the light under the weight of the past." The last five words cannot be overstressed, for "the weight of the past" is what really haunts the book. One sees it best in the stamp of *former-ness*—pastness—on the characters: Geoffrey Firmin, dispossessed *former* consul; his half-brother Hugh, a *former* fighter for the Republic in the Spanish Civil War; Yvonne, *former* Hollywood child film star and the *former* consul's *former* wife; a French *former* film director who is the *former* consul's closest friend and his *former* wife's *former* lover. There is no escape from the past. Lowry, like Joyce, Proust, and Virginia Woolf—writers whose major works he insists he did *not* read—makes the inescapable past hover like a pall. Lowry, it will be seen, makes a major time shift—one year backward—from Chapter I to Chapter II. After the explicit shift, time becomes a phantasmagoria, conditioned by the Consul's "mescalusions."

The novel opens in 1939, in November, near sunset on the Day of the Dead, in a town in the Mexican interior called Quauhnahuac. Two tired and sensitive men wail inwardly for a friend who died exactly a year ago. The death of this man (Geoffrey Firmin)—once a British consul in a remote Mexican outpost but more lately a compulsive alcoholic—is never made explicit, but the feeling of his death is too

pervasive in the chapter's lush melancholy ever to be doubted. Dr. Vigil, a Mexican physician whose name lacks only the "r" to form *Virgil* of the *Inferno* whose mosaic this novel unobtrusively follows, has known the Consul for an evening; Vigil's companion, Jacques Laruelle, is a French ex-film director who has shared Geoffrey's boyhood and his wife. They talk over their drinks, and every word pleads Milton's question to the living about the dead:

> Where were ye Nymphs when the remorseless
>   deep
> Closed o'er the head of your lov'd Lycidas?

Dr. Vigil finally puts the question: "Did you never go to the church for the bereavèd . . . where is the Virgin for those who have nobody with?" The question bears that compelling Hispano-English imperfection of which Lowry was master . . . and it is important as one of the chapter's closely-packed clues.

The Frenchman finds himself able to laugh over Vigil's syntax, says good-bye (for M. Laruelle is to leave Mexico the next day), and walks in the dying light of evening amid landmarks whose topography is more spiritual than physical. Lowry slowly unravels strands of the story which he will knit again in later chapters. Laruelle pauses by the railroad tracks and recalls a farewell of a year ago involving himself and Hugh Firmin, the Consul's half-brother and the third side of the novel's triangle. He looks to the twin volcanoes, "terrifying in the wild sunset." Laruelle offers still another farewell—to the Palace of Maximilian—and the chord of tragic love is struck.

> . . . he immediately regretted having come. The broken pink pillars, in the half-light, might have been waiting to fall down on him: the pool, covered with green scum, its steps torn away and hanging by one rotting clamp, to close over his head. The shattered, evil-smelling chapel, overgrown with weeds, the crumbling walls, splashed with urine, on which scorpions lurked—wrecked entablature, sad archivolt, slippery stones covered with excreta—this place, where love had once brooded, seemed part of a nightmare.

Laruelle thinks briefly of Maximilian and Carlotta, and almost imperceptibly it is "the Consul's voice, not Maximilian's, M. Laruelle could almost have heard in the Palace." It is not the ancient and historical dead but the recent, still-living dead that haunt Laruelle's memory in this epilogic prologue. He leaves the rotting palace that was haven for two sets of star-crossed lovers in exile for the Calle Nicaragua, the street that a year ago conveyed the Consul to the ravine. Laruelle approaches a bridge over a barranca. He looks down into it. For reasons the reader cannot know unless he has skipped to the last page, the ravine looms as an aftershadow in the position of a foreshadow (" . . . here was finality indeed . . . wherever you turned the abyss was waiting. . . . Dormitory for vultures and city Moloch"). The reader does not yet know the dread significance of the barranca in the Consul's tragic history, and the chronicler drops only hints.

Lowry shifts the gears of his time-eclipsing device; by association, the barranca triggers Jacques's thoughts to Hell's Bunker, the lover's knoll on the golf course where the Taskerson boys took their girls. Now with the Taskerson episode, Laruelle is monitoring an earlier past: the boyhood scenes at a Channel resort (Leasowe) when he and Geoffrey Firmin were the guests of the family of an English poet, Abraham Taskerson. From Jacques Laruelle's always shifting focus of consciousness, Lowry creates a surrealistic landscape. The astute Stephen Spender finds Lowry's technique in playing with scenes and language to resemble that of a film cutter [Spender, Stephen, "Introduction," in *Under the Volcano,* 1965]. In Chapter I, the film clips are compiled and sorted by Laruelle's memory; in later chapters, they will be filtered through the Consul's mescal-befogged lens.

Jacques remembers the "air of innocence" about the whole business of picking up girls and taking them to Hell's Bunker. He thinks back to the time when he accidentally came upon Geoff scrambling out of the bunker with a girl. Shaken by his unmasking, Geoff takes his friend to a bar and, for the first time in his life, orders a round of whiskeys, which the waiter refuses to serve to the two minors. "Alas" (the foreboding again), "their friendship did not for some reason survive these two sad, though doubtless providential, little frustrations." Lowry has forged an underground connection between events of the distant and the recent pasts.

The trail of clues to later developments is pervasive. The reader is introduced to the horse and rider. A drunken man on horseback interrupts Laruelle's reveries by hurtling up the Calle Nicaragua (a riderless horse will be seen near the body of a dying Indian in Chapter XI). A movie marquee advertises an old Peter Lorre film, *Las Manos de Orlac.* This film about a man unable to wipe the blood off his hands proves to be the same film that was playing one year earlier, during the novel's main action. A love letter from the Consul to Yvonne, never mailed, falls from the Consul's book of Elizabethan plays, borrowed by Jacques but never returned. The novel, in a sense, becomes an enactment of the dilemma poignantly described in the letter: the knowledge that in love lies the only path upward combined with the failure of desire for that upward path.

As if somehow to exorcise the ghosts of the recent past, Laruelle holds the letter from the dead to a candle whose

> flare lit up the whole cantina with a burst of brilliance in which the figures at the bar—that he now saw included besides the little children and the peasants . . . several women in mourning . . . and dark-faced men in dark suits . . .—appearing, for an instant, frozen, a mural. . . .

And, for just a moment, Lowry's prose elegy is in stasis. Then the elegiac words are tolled by a bell: *dolente . . . dolore!* The mourning is interrupted in the kaleidoscopic frenzy of a carnival ferris wheel. "Over the town, in the dark, tempestuous night," concludes the chapter, "backwards revolved the luminous wheel . . ." But there is one thing more. Like Joyce, Lowry uses the graphic arts—in this case to convey a vital time shift. Thus a single line car-

ries from the last word of Chapter I across the page to Chapter II.

Lowry's lark with time, then, is in the tradition of the finest elegiac writing, a memorializing of the past as a means of returning the dead to life. Calendar time exists as a reminder to us, if we care to acknowledge it, that a world was dying in November, 1939, even as the Mexican dead were being honored.

Lowry plays a similar game with place. Although described in painstaking details from the first word of the novel (the Cape reader's words, "heaped on in shovelfuls," are accurate though wrong-headed), the interior of Mexico really exists only in the green interior of Malcolm Lowry's imagination. In the actual world of November, 1938, British consuls like Geoffrey Firmin had lost their occupation; England had severed diplomatic relations with Mexico over President Cárdenas's expropriation of foreign oil companies in March, 1938, following the refusal of these companies to answer government demands for increasing wages and training native Mexicans for managerial positions. In the world of Lowry's imagination, the dispossessed Consul is the prisoner of a malaise whose interior geography is the main business of the book. When, in the first chapter, Lowry guides the reader on a tour of Quauhnahuac, it is in the interests of forming a correspondence between habitation and humor, between outer and inner geography. Although it was still possible until recently to visit Cuernavaca and walk the Calle Nicaragua where the drunken Consul wandered and to peer down into the barranca where he perished, the facts of place as Lowry assembles them have a different function from the old Fitzpatrick travelogues. The reality that Lowry seeks to evoke in the early pages is hidden and inexpressible until we enter what William H. Gass called Lowry's "conceptual country [where] there are no mere details, nothing is simple happenstance, everything has meaning . . ." [see excerpt in *TCLC,* Vol. 6, p. 244].

Lowry starts obliquely. He locates the scene first, not by the symbolic furniture of landscape, but by the precise directions a map maker or navigator would appreciate.

> Two mountain chains traverse the republic roughly from north to south, forming between them a number of valleys and plateaus. Overlooking one of these valleys which is dominated by two volcanoes, lies, six thousand feet above sea level, the town of Quauhnahuac. It is situated well south of the Tropic of Cancer, to be exact on the nineteenth parallel, in about the same latitude as the Revillagigedo Islands to the west in the Pacific, or very much further west, the southernmost tip of Hawaii—and as the port of Tzucox to the east on the Atlantic seaboard of Yucatan near the border of British Honduras, or very much further east, the town of Juggernaut, in India, on the Bay of Bengal.

From a navigator's map of Quauhnahuac, Lowry moves to a kind of aerial photograph.

> The walls of the town, which is built on a hill, are high, the streets and lanes tortuous and broken, the roads winding. A fine American-style highway leads in from the north but is lost in its

narrow streets and comes out a goat track. Quauhnahuac possesses eighteen churches and fifty-seven cantinas. It also boasts a golf course and no less than four hundred swimming pools, public and private, filled with water that ceaselessly pours down from the mountains, and many splendid hotels.

One paragraph later, Lowry narrows his focus still more—to the Hotel Casino de la Selva. Here, for the record, Lowry may be said to have opened his book's bottomless bag of allusions. "Selva means wood," he told Jonathan Cape, "and this strikes the opening chord of the *Inferno*." Much more important is the felt life generated in the scene:

> Palatial, a certain air of desolate splendour pervades it. For it is no longer a casino. You may not even dice for drinks in the bar. The ghosts of ruined gamblers haunt it. No one ever seems to swim in the magnificent Olympic pool. The springboards stand empty and mournful. Its jai-alai courts are grass-grown and deserted. Two tennis courts only are kept up in the season.

Like Durrell's Alexandria, Lowry's Quauhnahuac is a mind construct where, as Gass brilliantly notes, "there are no menacing volcanoes, only menacing phrases, where complex chains of concepts traverse our consciousness. . . . " The tone sought and achieved is identical to that of the opening sentences of E. M. Forster's *A Passage to India*:

> Except for the Marabar Caves . . . the city of Chandrapore presents nothing extraordinary. Edged rather than washed by the river Ganges, it trails for a couple of miles along the bank, scarcely distinguishable from the rubbish it deposits so freely. There are no bathing-steps on the river front, as the Ganges happens not to be holy here. . . . The streets are mean, the temples ineffective, and though a few fine houses exist they are hidden away in gardens or down alleys whose filth deters all but the invited guest. . . . Houses do fall, people are drowned and left rotting, but the general outline of the town persists, swelling there, shrinking here, like some low but indestructible form of life.

The tone of both is of unproud decadence, of ruin, of the unburied dead. For E. M. Forster, only the Marabar Caves ("the extraordinary caves") interrupt "the endless expanse." For Lowry, the two volcanoes, "clear and magnificent," alone can temper the lush bleakness. Laruelle's hand trembles as it grasps a bottle of anis "from whose label a florid demon brandished a pitchfork at him." The king of this realm is alcohol and its crown prince is the Consul. "I meant to persuade him to go away and get dealcoholisé." The words are Dr. Vigil's, and the reader, hardly aware of it, has entered the recollected world at whose center is the Consul.

> Sickness is not only in body, but in that part used to be call: soul. Poor your friend, he spend his money on earth in such continuous tragedies.

Dr. Vigil has touched the elegiac chord, but it is Laruelle who will orchestrate it.

What had happened just a year ago to-day seemed already to belong in a different age. One would have thought the horrors of the present would have swallowed it up like a drop of water. It was not so.

In the Lowry canon, it can never be so. The past always haunts the present. And it is to time past—to time exactly one year past as well as to time in earlier pasts—that Lowry will now turn.

After the long overture-elegy of Chapter I, Lowry gives over the second chapter to Yvonne, the Consul's estranged wife. His choice is logical—he had made a crucial departure from early versions in making Geoffrey and Yvonne husband-wife instead of father-daughter—and, more important, wise fictionally. Yvonne, unbelievably, has returned to Quauhnahuac and to the Consul after almost a year's absence: she and Geoffrey separated in December of 1937; she then returned to the United States where she obtained a divorce. Her reasons for leaving him are painfully clear within a few pages; the reasons for her return are less clear. In fact, her return would not have "worked" at all without the Consul's anguished plea—the epistolary voice in Chapter I of one dead lover to another—which Laruelle finds, unposted and slipped between the pages of the Consul's book of Elizabethan plays.

We meet the Consul, then, through Yvonne's eyes. Theirs is not treated as a conventional reunion of lovers. Lowry's diffusion of emotion saves the scene. Of course, the overt problem from which Yvonne fled a year ago confronts her as she enters the bar.

> Then he looked up abruptly and saw her, peering short-sightedly about him before recognizing her, standing there, a little blurred probably because the sunlight was behind her, with one hand thrust through the handle of her scarlet bag resting on her hip, standing there as she knew he must see her, half jaunty, a little diffident.
>
> Still holding the timetable the Consul built himself to his feet as she came forward: "—*Good God*."

But *another* consciousness, operating on the fringes of Yvonne's, draws on the objective world to relieve the subjective. The same group of *borrachos* whose dialogue had earlier intersected Yvonne's chat with a Mexican cabbie now crowd in on the intimacy between her and the Consul. The scene is cinematic. Lowry's technique is exactly the same as that, for example, used by David Lean, the director of a British film version (1947) of a Noel Coward story, "Brief Encounter." As the lovers, played by Celia Johnson and Trevor Howard, say a final good-bye in a seedy railway station (she will remain with her husband; he will embark permanently for a medical post in Africa) their precious last moments together are interrupted by the nonstop chatter of a woman acquaintance of the heroine. In the blatant face of the outrage, the lovers can only commune mutely. The horror of the scene lies in the invasion of privacy, the unknowing destruction of an intimacy the unfulfilled lovers would always have had in the tranquility of recollection.

Lowry's avoidance of explicit anguish in the reunion is pervasive. Although his aspirations, pleaded in the unmailed letter, seem possible of fulfillment with her return, Geoffrey can only make feeble jokes about his cuckoldry, his case of the shakes, his dismissal from his consular post. When he offers a drink to the woman who has left him because of his drinking, the poignancy of the moment is suggested by her unspoken words: a dash enclosed in quotation marks.

The rest of the chapter can best be described as contrapuntal. Yvonne's inner dialogue—her memories of the events leading to their parting a year ago—plays against the Consul's efforts to be casual (an echo of Laruelle's recollection of the boyhood hikes and pubs: "The drunker they became, the more sober they should appear"). Other counterpoint to the dolor of the lovers is provided by the words of a boxing advertisement and the names of shops in the square where they walk. Lowry is always aware of the effective incongruity of English words that have never been assimilated into the Spanish.

The chapter's second important disclosure, in fact, appears between a boxing ad and the marquee words of the talismanic film, *Las Manos de Orlac*. It comes as the Consul, using his walking stick like a blind man, staggers up the Calle Nicaragua while Yvonne reviews a tableau that is all too familiar. Geoffrey is not too intoxicated to point to the villa of the Frenchman Laruelle ("And he's still there too. . . . hasn't budged an inch either"), chidingly remind Yvonne that he has not forgotten that she cuckolded him with Jacques, and finally drops news of incalculable significance to her and to the novel:

> "Something else, I repeat, very important, that perhaps I ought to tell you."
>
> "Yes. What is it?"
>
> "About Hugh."
>
> Yvonne said at last:
>
> "You've heard from Hugh. How is he?"
>
> "He's staying with me."
>
> —BOX! ARENA TOMALIN. FRENTE. AL JARDIN XICOTAN CATL. *Domingo 8 de Noviembre de 1938. 4 Emocionantes Peleas.* EL BALON *vs.* EL REDONDILLO.
>
> *Las Manos de Orlac. Con Peter Lorre.*
>
> "*What!*" Yvonne stopped dead.

Chapter II thus establishes the physical presence of the four protagonists in Quauhnahuac, Mexico, on the Day of the Dead in 1938. Dale Edmonds [see excerpt dated 1968], writing of the novel "on the immediate level," goes to great lengths to shorten the arm of coincidence. He demonstrates that Lowry has rendered this "confluence of characters" plausible, but he is much more cogent when he notes that "the affairs of these characters have been curiously tangled in the past. . . . [and the] events of the day are more distressing because they bear not upon isolated individuals but upon a closely interwoven group." What interweaves them is that galvanic negative capability which caused Melville's Bartleby *to choose not to* and Camus's Meursault to remain impassive at his mother's funeral. Not since Hemingway brought Jake Barnes and his entourage to the good fishing and bull fights at Pamplona has a group of fictional characters so moved us by their very inability to move.

The Consul is Promethean, he is fallen, and his estrangement from life, as Anthony Burgess wrote in a recent reassessment of the novel, "etches the desired opposite . . . where inability to love defines what love is" [see Further Reading]. *No se puede vivir sin amar* were among the first serious words spoken between Jacques Laruelle and Geoffrey Firman's medical friend, the Mexican Dr. Vigil, in the opening chapter. Moments from death, the Consul will repeat them, adding his own significance: "*No se puede vivir sin amar . . .* which would explain everything." The phrase can be rendered as *one cannot live without love* or, better, *one cannot live without loving*. The book, at the "impact" level, will dramatize this forfeiture of love as being due to various forms of hubris. Certainly the four principals have all tried to live without loving. Their sickness is not only physical, as when the Consul suffers from the d.t.'s, but, in the words of Dr. Vigil, "in that part used to be call: soul." Lowry poses the tortured relationship of the Consul and Yvonne, and, within that greater agony, lesser ones in the abortive liaisons between Yvonne and Jacques and between Yvonne and the Consul's doppelgänger, his half-brother Hugh: all symbolic of the modern malaise. As Dale Edmonds notes, it is not that love has ceased to exist in our world; it is that selfish rather than selfless love is the characteristic form. "Ah," sighs the Consul—it is one of his last coherent reflections—"who knows why man, however beset his chance by lies, has been offered love?"

But hope keeps seeping through: always, for Lowry, the necessary condition, the coexistence, emphasized at the end of his rope by F. Scott Fitzgerald, of aspiration amidst futility. The Consul, reunited with the one person he believed a year before could save him, now attempts to build himself up to meet this threat to oblivion. He is partially successful. Yvonne smiles, "full of thoughts that had already swept her a thousand miles in frantic retreat from all this." She hears the Consul hum; it braces her against her guilt.

> Yvonne felt her heart melting. A sense of a shared, a mountain peace seemed to fall between them; it was false, it was a lie, but for a moment it was almost as though they were returning home from marketing in days past. She took his arm, laughing, they fell into step. And now here were the walls again, and their drive sloping down into the street where no one had allayed the dust . . . and now here was their gate, off its hinges and lying just beyond the entrance, as for that matter it always had lain, defiantly, half hidden under the bank of bougainvillea.
> "There now, Yvonne. Come along, darling . . . We're almost home!"
>
> "Yes."
>
> "Strange—" the Consul said.
>
> A hideous pariah dog followed them in.

Under the Volcano, in a sense, begins where a book like *The Sun Also Rises* ends. Jake Barnes's war wound is a phantom which will affirm the irony of his last words to Brett who has just asserted her belief in their chances together: "Isn't it pretty to think so?" The Consul's phantom is better explained by psychic than by physical wounds. It is an attendant spirit, a familiar, which will endlessly pace counter to Yvonne's consoling but unwanted shadow. Never to be exorcized by drink and never to respond to Dr. Vigil's appropriately fractured entreaty, "Throw away your mind," Geoffrey Firmin's phantom will live a life of its own on the edge of his tortured consciousness.

But there is another Malcolm Lowry which may key best of all with the times: the comedian wearing a tragic mask. Conrad Aiken has said that while Lowry wrote his book in the grip of an unappeasable vision—that while he knew life was an infernal machine tearing him apart—the tragic was only one of Lowry's disguises. To have turned himself into the maker of sad myths was, for Aiken, a deception perhaps without parallel: "It was a great joke: his whole life was a joke: never was there a gayer Shakespearean jester. A fact that I think we must remember when everyone is saying What Gloom, What Despair, What Riddles! Nonsense. He was the merriest of men."

Under the Volcano is also a very funny book. Lowry's humor arises naturally out of a scrupulous observation of life. The comedy is of the Joycean—the domestic—kind: glimpses of human frustration which are both devastatingly true and devoutly compassionate. Lowry's "consular" humor is Pickwickian rather than Black, not *sick* but *wise* laughter arising above the impending tragedy.

> In his finely cut tweeds . . . and blue and white striped Chagfordian tie . . . his thick fair hair neatly slicked back, his freshly trimmed brownish greying beard, his stick, his dark glasses, who would say that he was not, unmistakably, a figure of complete respectability?

And who would know, since the Consul never whined, that his situation was hopeless; that with one side of his mind he sought the volcano's summit while with the other—the dominant, the daemonic, side—he would know surcease only in the barranca?

So, to the tragedy of an addictive Faust, elegized in Chapter I and proclaimed in Chapter II, are added the domestic pitfalls of a Falstaff in Chapters III and V. After a long unpunctuated inner debate between two sides of himself at the start of Chapter III ("But can't you see you cabrón that she is thinking that the first thing you think of after she has arrived home like this is a drink," the Consul's guilt-imperative loses out to the drink-imperative. He needs alcohol to support his fragile balance. He runs from the house while Yvonne finishes her bath.

> But suddenly the Calle Nicaragua rose up to meet him. The Consul lay face downward on the deserted street.

The Consul's alcoholic haze—a certain Mr. Magoo quality—has taken over. The bibulous inertia of the dipso had

probably never been rendered in imaginative literature until Lowry and this novel. The Consul lies face down until given assistance by someone who in his state of diffused attention he imagines to be Hugh.

> —Hugh, is that you old chap lending the old boy a hand? Thank you so much. For it is perhaps indeed your turn these days to lend a hand. Not that I haven't always been delighted to help you! I was even delighted in Paris that time you arrived from Aden in a fix over your carte d'identité and the passport you so often seem to prefer travelling without and whose number I remember to this day is 213112. It perhaps gave me all the more pleasure in that it served a while to take my mind from my own tangled affairs. . . . Are you listening, Hugh—do I make myself clear?

A three-page apostrophe to Hugh follows, but Hugh has not heard a word of it. The Consul's rescuer turns out to be a Colonel Blimp type whose possession of a bottle of Irish whiskey is more important to the Consul than his identity. There follows one of the novel's best set pieces, and it provides the first broad humor of the book:

> "But damn it all I say you were lying right down in the road there, might have run over you, there must be something wrong, what? No?" The Englishman switched his engine off. "I say, haven't I seen you before or something."
>
> "—"
>
> "—"
>
> "Trinity." The Consul found his own voice becoming involuntarily a little more "English." "Unless—"
>
> "Caius."
>
> "But you're wearing a Trinity tie—" the Consul remarked with a polite note of triumph.
>
> "Trinity?" . . . Yes. It's my cousin's, as a matter of fact." The Englishman peered down his chin at the tie, his red face become a shade redder . . . "Wonderful country this. Pity about all this oil business, isn't it? Bad show.—Are you sure there're no bones broken or anything, old man?"

We can only assume that the combination of the Irish and an in-person reminder of his obligation to the Union Jack has perked up the Consul. Lowry shifts place. The Consul, back at the house ("innocently as a man who has committed a murder while a dummy at bridge"), enters Yvonne's room. His intention is finally to effect a physical reconciliation with his former wife. Drink oozing from every gland, he proves impotent; and, while Yvonne cries in the bedroom, he retires to the veranda, where he drinks himself into insensibility. The booze inflates him, and in his best W. E. Henley style he pontificates: "The will of man is unconquerable. Even God cannot conquer it." That authorial consciousness on the borders of Geoffrey's—the one which observed the hideous pariah dog at the end of Chapter II—now perceives "vultures waiting . . . like burnt papers floating from a fire which suddenly are seen to be blowing swiftly upward, rocking." The Consul passes out as the chair under him collapses. Mr. Magoo has given way to Chaplin. As such, the scene is broadly humorous—the would-be lover failing in love, unable even to remain upright. Like a Chaplin film, it contains a spiritual dimension, too; the Consul's impotence is only the outward and visible sign of a much larger spiritual impotence.

Our next direct encounter with Geoffrey comes in Chapter V, the Garden chapter, the most Falstaffian of the book. On the overt level, the Consul is awake again and wandering about in the lushly deteriorating garden behind the house in search of a bottle of tequila he had hidden there days before. He stumbles about and fuzzily ponders a crude sign he notices on the edge of his property. (¿LE GUSTA ESTE JARDIN? / ¿QUE ES SUYO? / ¡EVITE QUE SUS HIJOS LO DESTRUYAN!). It is enough to note that the Consul both misreads and mistranslates. ("Do you like this garden? It is yours. We evict those who destroy!") But the misrendering is the talisman, the key, to the novel's Eden-and-eviction theme. The Consul is a forlorn Adam; his own garden, once beautiful, has become a jungle where he hides liquor bottles; once he even sees a snake there.

It is instructive of Lowry's growth as a novelist to see that, although he evidently had allegorical intentions from the start, he was unable to assimilate the Adamic myth into the dramatic flow. In the earliest version of *Volcano,* he bludgeons the reader with an Adamic conceit and ends with a series of lofty rhetorical questions:

> Yes, it was a regular sarpint, as an old bosun he had known used to say, and calling, perhaps, into being some reflection of an eternal dilemma. In what, precisely, now did the *temptation* inhere? Through what medium had the sibilant invitation to partake of the fruit of the tree of knowledge been already accepted, and, in the course of time, passed on to him? And what, if any, was the form of this knowledge?

Here Lowry over-explicitly affirms the Consul's link to Adam. But he might just as well have taken on Milton's task of justifying the ways of God to man for all he accomplishes. The scene bristles with the evidence of contrivance.

In the published version, however, the "ruined" garden appears to the Consul, his senses both heightened and jaded by drink, as lending "an added charm. He liked the exuberance of the unclipped growth at hand." When the familiar keep-off-grass sign rears up, the Consul greets it, not with an implausible cosmic despair and the series of unanswerable questions, but with a sense of his precise domestic dilemma.

> Words which, perhaps a final judgment on one, were nevertheless unproductive of any emotion whatsoever, unless a kind of colourless cold, a white agony, an agony chill as that iced mescal drunk in the Hotel Canada on the morning of Yvonne's departure.

The garden—the world—has all the attributes of an Eden, but, as Lowry told Jonathan Cape, "if you don't want to bother about the symbolism, you needn't." Lowry draws back from conventional symbol-watching no less than he does from conventional tragedy-marking. The Consul, although endowed with some of the qualities of heroes in Greek and Christian mythology, is above all a man in his own right, a product of our own period, and his dilemma, while undoubtedly allegorical, is also immediate.

After pondering the sign, he drinks the tequila and moves on—lurches on—to pleasantries with his neighbor, an American conveniently named Quincey (lacking only the "De" to stand in ironic alignment with one of English literature's most illustrious addicts). Quincey mocks him for his drunkenness. The Consul has hiccups. It is difficult for him to answer his neighbor's surly questions. Instead, we get one of the book's first—perhaps its major—Adamic references—one skillfully and plausibly tailored to the ears of an American tourist like Quincey.

> "Perhaps Adam was the first property owner and God, the first agrarian, a kind of Cárdenas, in fact—tee hee!—kicked him out. Eh? Yes," the Consul chuckled, aware, moreover, that all this was possibly not so amusing under the existing historical circumstances, "for it's obvious to everyone these days—don't you think so, Quincey?—that the original sin was to be an owner of property."

But Geoffrey's attempts to regain some semblance of sobriety and dignity do not work; for one thing, his fly is still unbuttoned from his abortive sexual advances on Yvonne. When he whistles at Quincey's cat, and the creature's ears twirl in pleased response, he says that "she thinks I'm a tree with a bird in it." "I shouldn't wonder," retorts Quincey.

The kinship of this chapter to Joyce, both in terms of the complex time shifts and the brilliance of the Lowry-*cum*-Aiken puns, has been noted in the first chapter. Quincey's cat, introduced as a foil for the Consul's wordplay, slinks off to allow the intrusion on Geoffrey's blighted consciousness of Yvonne and Hugh. Lowry never breaks narrative stride. He gives us the simultaneity of the Consul's world: a complex that can include a cat playing with a trapped insect as well as paranoid impulses that his wife and brother are talking only about him.

> In this preposterous fashion, the Consul stooping, the cat dancing just out of reach, the insect still flying furiously in the cat's mouth, he approached his porch. Finally the cat extended a preparate paw for the kill, opening her mouth, and the insect, whose wings had never ceased to beat, suddenly and marvelously flew out, as might indeed the human soul from the jaws of death, flew up, up, up, soaring over the trees: and that moment he saw them. They were standing on the porch; Yvonne's arms were full of bougainvillea, which she was arranging in a cobalt ceramic vase. "—but suppose he's absolutely adamant. Suppose he simply won't go . . . careful, Hugh, it's got spikes on it, and you have to look at everything carefully to be sure there're no spiders." "Hi there, Suchiquetal!" the Consul shouted gaily, waving his hand, as the cat with a frigid look over her shoulder that said plainly, "I didn't want it anyway; I meant to let it go,"

> galloped away, humiliated, into the bushes. "Hi
> there, Hugh, you old snake in the grass."

The imagery of the liberated insect, soaring to freedom,
is a foreshadowing perhaps of how the soul of the Consul
will ascend to the top of Popo on the last page of the book.

While he takes liberties with time and place in Chapter V,
Lowry never leaves the reader marooned. The long single
line which connected the two Days of the Dead between
Chapters I and II is now repeated, though shortened. Perhaps an hour has elapsed. The Consul has had a blackout.
Defoliated, he is back in his bathroom half deliriously trying to sort out what he remembers of the missing interval.

> Why then should he be sitting in the bathroom?
> Was he asleep? Dead? Passed out? Was he in the
> bathroom now or half an hour ago? Was it
> night? Where were the others. . . . Yet for a
> moment he could have sworn the house had
> been full of people; why, it was still this morning,
> or barely afternoon, only 12:15 in fact by his
> watch. At eleven he'd been talking to Mr.
> Quincey. . . .

What he remembers is couched in those intersecting dialogues Lowry learned from *Blue Voyage,* but, as is not always the case in Aiken's work, they carry the story along.
Will they go that afternoon to Guanajuato, a city of life
for which Dr. Vigil opts, or to the bull-throwing at Tomalín, which involves Parián (death) and the Farolito (the
cantina which Vigil says half-jokingly "es un infierno")?

Dr. Vigil, a character based on a close Mexican friend who
shared with Lowry the infernal 1936-38 period, is the one
character who can recognize that the Consul, despite his
wife's return, is truly one of "those who have nobody them
with." Vigil, in fact, almost under his breath issues an
exact forecast of the Consul's doom: "But I think if you
are very serious about your *progresión a ratos* you may
take a longer journey even than this proposed one." The
journey to Tomalín will be indeed the longest one of Geoffrey Firmin's life: not in linear time—it will be only a few
hours' travel to the Farolito and the barranca—but in the
sense of the long day's journey of the soul which has denied love.

For a time the Consul's deliberate alliance with Marlowe's
Faustus flying headlong into the gaping earth (see epigraph to novel) is offset by a series of parodies of Prometheus enacted by Leopold Bloom. Chapter V ends with
Geoffrey standing in the shower, waiting for the sobering
shock of cold water that never came and still clad in his
tuxedo trousers. The Consul's push towards self-
destruction is never more tragicomically portrayed than
in the loop-the-loop scene (Chapter VII) when he becomes
trapped, upside down, at the top of the carnival machine
as all his possessions fall from his pockets into the hands
of the children waiting below. For Geoffrey, the experience with the loop-the-loop is far from funny: he is horrified and sees himself as Ixion, caught forever on a wheel
turning in hell (the machine, not so strangely, as Douglas
Day reminds us, is named *La Maquina Infernal*—the infernal machine of Cocteau's play, that cruelly and inexorably unwinds, slowly destroying the human lives caught
up in it). Yet even in the grips of his own unappeasable

passion for self-obliteration, the Consul's obsession is diffused by residual fragments of his Britishness ("This was
scarcely a dignified position for an ex-representative of His
Majesty's government to find himself in.") Although mor-
tally wounded by Mexican Fascists in the book's last
scene, he can still manage to tell himself: "This is a dingy
way to die."

Under the Volcano is the dramatic enactment of something Dostoevsky's Underground Man referred to as the
"one most advantageous advantage . . . for which, if necessary, a man is ready to act in opposition to all laws . . .
in opposition to reason, honor, peace, prosperity. . . ."
This advantage beyond advantage, one which induces the
Underground Man to speak with savage irony of the Man
of Action—is, of course, one's own free unfettered choice,
one's own fancy even when worked up to the point of madness. The Consul, with Bartleby, with the Underground
Man, with Meursault, simply chooses *not* to—not to act,
not to alter his course for love, not to save himself. The
Consul's opportunities to requite Yvonne's love raise
questions of utmost significance to his existence as a free
agent, and it is only by willing his own destruction that
he can assert his freedom of choice. "To this end," writes
Stanley Jedynak, "it is necessary for the Consul to reject
all offers of human salvation . . . they are spurious offers
because not in touch with the supreme reality of death and
with that sense of chaos . . . at the bottom of everything."
Human options pale beside the Consul's battle for the survival of consciousness, which is another way of saying his
imperative for preserving his own identity, however harmful to himself are the means.

Lowry's triumph in *Under the Volcano* lies in his making
forceful the attempts of the other three principals to save
the Consul while making inevitable the Consul's rejection
of those attempts. One believes that Yvonne cannot live
without loving but that her loving is mainly of herself.
Hugh's "indoor Marxmanship" often has the sound of
conviction, but it is badly blunted by the Consul, intoxicated as he is, in their bitter dialectical joust at the end of
Chapter X. As the Consul observes, Hugh protests too
much; his rhetoric has "nothing constructive at bottom,
only acceptance really, a piddling contemptible acceptance of the state of affairs that flatters one into feeling
thus noble or useful." Jacques Laruelle, the man of many
faces, is a purveyor of the *appearance* of reality, a flawed
film-maker. It is he, Professor Jedynak reminds us,

> who takes on to himself the motto "no se puede
> vivir sin amar" and makes a mockery of it. It is
> also he who rightfully accuses the Consul of un-
> necessary suffering, who denies the greatness of
> the Consul's battle against death, but who is
> afraid of the nightmare of life and attempts to
> hide his fear behind that ironically spurious [for
> him] inscription at the entrance to his home.

Some readers may believe that Lowry allows the Consul's
addiction to mescal to take over. The quality of diffused
attention, admittedly, is intensified by drink, but it is also
in his drunkest moments that the Consul sees most clearly.
His last remembered words to Hugh and Yvonne (Chapter X) before his fatal flight from them are about his verdict for death against life:

> "For all you know it's only the knowledge that it most certainly is too late that keeps me alive at all . . . You're all the same, all of you, Yvonne, Jacques, you, Hugh, trying to interfere with other people's lives . . .
>
> "True, I've been tempted to talk peace. I've been beguiled by your offers of a sober and non-alcoholic Paradise. At least I suppose that's what you've been working around towards all day. But now I've made up my melodramatic little mind. . . . "

Actions in the man of sensibility are conditioned by the fateful knowledge of good and evil. The Consul knows the world, and he opts out of it. Beyond that knowledge comes the realm of the deed. It is only here that man's real worth can be assessed. Moralistic knowledge (Hugh's) does not imply strength. Recognition of the need for love is forfeited by romanticizing (Yvonne's). Man is cursed by a constant dilemma: to know and not to be able to act appropriately. Hugh's and Yvonne's indecision in the human matter of the dying Indian (Chapter VIII . . .) become rationalizations for following the ritual of a bad law, to allow a man to die. The Consul, of course, is no more decisive, drunkenly longing for the bus to stop at the next cantina, but at least he does not assume vain postures.

The Consul, aware that the attempt to act must be made, knows that he cannot make it in a way that is appropriate to his equivalent of the Underground Man's most advantageous advantage: his unconquerable will to assert his own identity. He hovers between the "either" and the "or"—between the illusion of Paradise and the reality of the barranca—but he never really doubts when the test comes what the result will be. He chooses addiction, death, and destruction. He takes the path to Parián; he will meet the ultimate reality. Reality, as Professor Jedynak cogently put it,

> is the Farolito, the *barranca* beneath it, Popocatepetl towering above. Man lives under the volcano; he is cleft, like . . . the glacial rock, always crumbling, yet clinging to life like a parasite. He is surrounded by false, unknown authorities who interfere with his probing into the intensity of life, who attempt to foil his choice of death.

The Consul is destroyed, to be sure, but his soul survives, ascending to the volcano's summit, even as his body is hurled into the pit, to lie with offal and dead dogs. (pp. 61-83)

> *Richard Hauer Costa, in his* Malcolm Lowry, *Twayne Publishers, Inc., 1972, 208 p.*

Chet Taylor   (essay date 1973)

[*In the following excerpt, Taylor contends that the underlying philosophy of* Under the Volcano *is essentially nihilistic.*]

Much is made of Lowry's extensive, intricate use of myth but, in spite of Lowry's interest in James Joyce and T. S. Eliot, his use of myth is more old-fashioned; it parallels and illuminates the tragic situation of [*Under the Volcano*] but never becomes the object of central attention. There is an obvious grab-bag of mythology—the lost Atlantis, the descent to hell, Faust, the determinism of astrology and numbers, the Renaissance concept of the Wheel of Fate, the local mythology such as the Day of the Dead and the volcanoes, a corrupted Garden of Eden, Jewish Kabbala patterns; common to all of this heterogeneous mixture is a consistency of tone, one of foreboding doom.

This tone is reinforced by the motifs and symbols that recur: wars, pariah dogs, the child's coffin, the dead Indian, the looming volcano, the deep barranca, the corpse on the express train, the vultures, the sound of gunfire from Parian, the old woman in the back of the cantina playing dominoes, the rejection of civilization by Blackstone and the Consul's father, the fascism of Mexico. Advertising for the seemingly never-ending movie, *Las Manos de Orlac*, mocks the Consul. The movie has an obvious thematic significance; its plot concerns the cliché horror situation of a pianist whose grafted hands are those of a murderer, hands which go on killing against the pianist's conscious will. The consciousness of the artist infers that of the Consul's who comes to a full awareness of the uncrossable gap between intention and action, between will and effect. The Consul too is like Peter Lorre, the film's star, who is considered a good actor in a bad part. Also recurrent is the expression *no se puede vivir sin amar* (it is not possible to live without love). The consul accepts this truth, making his final, total awareness of the impossibility of love lead to an inevitable conclusion: death.

A common misreading of **Under the Volcano** is the result of an undue emphasis placed on the Consul's drinking problem. The Consul's alcoholism must be seen not as the central conflict of the novel but as a vehicle which gives expression to both his alienation and his awareness. The Consul comes increasingly to realize that alienation is a basic truth of the human condition, a truth that cannot be transcended, making his own death basically self-willed. Lowry's theme is not optimistic, and a rebellion from a full recognition of this often occurs in readers. Too used to seeing existential man as eventually triumphant (the final maturity in Durrell's "Alexandria Quartet", the acceptance in Bellow's *Henderson The Rain King* and *Herzog*, the triumph of the protagonist-prisoner's own resources in Camus's *The Stranger* and Malamud's *The Fixer*, even the enduring stoicism of the Hemingway code hero), it is difficult to admit that a self-awareness of "man as victim" does not automatically include some sort of affirmation; but, rather, Lowry seems to be saying: to be aware of the true human condition is only to lose the comfort of illusions. To be sure the Consul does break through to a frontier of consciousness ("a triumph of consciousness" as Spender observes in his introduction to the Signet edition [see *TCLC*, Vol. 6, pp 238-39]; however, these are "victories" of a different order. To Lowry, consciousness means awareness of the inextricable tangle of guilt, pain, suffering, and helpless involvement. This explains the Consul's intense identification with the pelado on the bus. The pelado, drunk and impoverished, had stolen the dead Indian's money; "pelado" means "peeled one", one who is both victim and victimizer. It is as the Consul says: "What's the use of escaping. . . . from ourselves?"

Once locked in an insufferable awareness, it is impossible to authentically "reach" another. All real communication is stifled in the novel. Addresses are not known and letters are lost or delayed for years by vagaries of the world postal system. By law the main characters are barred from aiding the dying Indian by the roadside. Most critical is the inability of the Consul and Yvonne to even say the words of love, face to face; after her return they are at home together for the first time and "for a time they confronted each other like two mute unspeaking forts". Neither are they able to join sexually.

Hugh, the Consul's half brother, and Yvonne are both romantics and, as such, serve structurally as necessary counterpoints to the Consul. Hugh thinks that the world can be affected by external actions—and he thinks that effective actions are possible through acts of the will. He is perpetually trying to force external reality into an order, into a meaning. He leaps into the bullring; he wants to climb the volcano, Popo; he plans an heroic running of the Fascist blackade to rescue his comrades in the Spanish Civil War. His hero is the Christ-figure Juan Cerillo, who eludes bandits while delivering money to the poor rural peasants. When Hugh first appears he preens in his new cowboy outfit, having just come across the border on a free-lance journalistic escapade from a Texas cow ranch. His attitudes can be seen in his perspective of the novel's setting:

> There was something in the wild strength of this landscape, once a battlefield, that seemed to be shouting at him, a presence born of that strength whose cry his whole being recognized as familiar, caught and threw back into the wind, some youthful password of courage and pride—the passionate, yet so nearly always hypocritical, affirmation of one's soul perhaps, he thought, of the desire to be, to do, good, what was right. It was as though he were gazing now beyond this expanse of plains and beyond the volcanoes out to the wide rolling blue ocean itself, feeling it in his heart still, the boundless impatience, the immeasurable longing.

Hugh is the incurable romantic: "So now, as I approached the second half of my life, unheralded, unsung, and without a guitar, I am going back to sea again: perhaps these days of waiting are more like that droll descent, to be survived in order to repeat the climb".

It is Hugh who daydreams:

> The time has come for to join your comrades, to aid the workers, he told Christ, who agreed. It had been His idea all the while, only until Hugh had rescued Him these hypocrites had kept Him shut up inside the burning church where He couldn't breathe. Hugh made a speech. Stalin gave him a medal and listened sympathetically while he explained what was on his mind. "True. . . . I wasn't in time to save the Ebro, but I did strike my blow". He went off, the star of Lenin on his lapel; in his pocket a certificate: Hero of the Soviet Republic, and the True Church, pride and love in his heart.

The Consul dismisses Hugh's romanticism as tilting with windmills.

Hugh thinks it is possible to engage reality; Yvonne feels it is possible to escape. Both positions are romantic and for the Consul, illusory. The episode in which Hugh and Yvonne go horseback riding provides an ineffectual thematic and dramatic counterpoint to the Consul's nihilism. After a lyrical description of the "new lane, peaceful, quite shady" and "pools, beautifully reflecting the sky":

> Now it was as though they were a company, a caravan, carrying for their greater security, a little world of love with them as they rode along. Earlier it had promised to be too hot; but just enough sun warmed them, a soft breeze caressed their faces, the countryside on either hand smiled upon them with deceptive innocence, a drowsy hum rose up from the morning, the mares nodded.

Yvonne, a former Hollywood child star, is obsessed with the notion that somehow the tragedy impending could be avoided, could be escaped, by merely changing geographical location; she clings to her false hopes, false dreams of an utopia in the uncorrupted innocent green forests of Canada:

> But their house was in her mind now as she walked; their home was real; Yvonne saw it at sunrise, in the long afternoons of southwest winds, and at nightful she saw it in the starlight and moonlight, covered with snow; she saw it from the forest, with the chimney and the roof below her, and the foreshortened pier; she saw it from the beach rising above her, and she saw it, tiny in the distance, a haven and a beacon against the trees, from the sea.

Just as the Consul rejects, but recognizes, the romanticism of Hugh and Yvonne, so does he understand the psychological motivations that have created Yvonne's supposed "love" for him. The Consul is, after all, an alcoholic, a weak man by conventional standards, and considerably older than Yvonne: all casting him in the psychological image, to her, of her dead father, about whom she feels a deep guilt. Her "love" for the Consul is inauthentic, one more aspect of man as naturalistic object rather than aware, free-functioning agent. The Consul is thus, against his conscious will, her victimizer.

The minor characters exist on the periphery of conflict. M. Laurelle, the narrator of the elegaic section, is a former director of serious films. He seems a passive, impotent, ineffectual romantic in his future film plans and in his love for Yvonne. The novel is "about" many things but central is the failure of love, and it is highly relevant that all three men—the Consul, Hugh, and Laurelle—love Yvonne, though all are unsuccessful.

Dr. Vigil may be viewed as a positive counterpoint to the Consul. . . . [It] was Lowry's intention to include *Under the Volcano* in a much larger body of work which would take man from hell to redemption. His early death—a direct result of his own drinking problem—ruined this master plan and *Under the Volcano* must stand alone. The figure of Vigil can be seen as an ironic comment on the redemption Lowry never attained. The name itself characterizes the man, so much like the Consul in his awareness and his alcoholism; the two feel a deep kinship. Dr. Vigil

Calle de Humboldt, Cuernavaca, on which Lowry modeled the Calle Nicaragua in Under the Volcano.

is a humanist who, unlike the Consul, can turn his attention to his fellow human beings, watching over and caring for them as he attempts to do with the Consul. Little emphasis is given Vigil by Lowry though, and the underdeveloped Vigil does not, personally or thematically, deserve dominant attention.

It is the Consul's awesome awareness of the desperate absurdity of human existence that dominates the novel:

> this is how I sometimes think of myself, as a great explorer who has discovered some extraordinary land from which he can never return to give his knowledge to the world: but the name of this land is hell.

> It is not Mexico of course but in the heart . . . I think I knew a good deal about physical suffering. But this is the worst of all, to feel your soul dying.

The Consul feels himself being shattered by the very forces of the universe. Central to his core of consciousness is the realization that the world is indeed absurd in the sense that though man must have a meaning to live, there is no meaningful potential existent: "it seems to me that almost everywhere in the world these days there has long since ceased to be anything fundamental to man at issue at all".

The Consul says, "It is this silence that frightens me—this silence—".

Unlike many other contemporary existential heroes (or "anti-heroes") who fall back on the strength of the individual spirit and resolution, the Consul can only come to the conclusion that all is futile. This interpretation is critical to an understanding of Lowry's use of the Garden of Eden myth. The repetition of the mocking *Le Gusta Este Jardin?* (Do you like this garden?) refers symbolically to the corrupt, absurd, abused earth—as tangled as the Consul's overgrown private backyard garden—that man is bound to, and in which the Consul suspects man, rather than being expelled, has been condemned to "go on living there, alone, of course—suffering, unseen, cut off from God". As the Consul tells Laurelle, his struggle is "against death. . . . My battle for the survival of the human consciousness". It is a battle he loses:

> with what blind faith, could one find one's way back, fight one's way back, now, through the tumultous horrors of five thousand shattering awakenings, each more frightful than the last, from a place where even love could not penetrate.

In his symbolic garden the Consul considers "the final frontier of consciousness" as his "genius", then adds ironically that "genius will look after itself". Genius is the "gift" of uncommon perception, and it is this perception that leads the Consul to the only possible peace in such a world: suicide, or, at least, a search for destruction—the only solution in a cosmos in which the alternative is to take the responsibility for devastating wars, *companeros* dying uncomforted, prisoners murdered, a woman he loves suffering in her inability to engage him.

No se puede vivir sin amar. That the Consul needs love to reach beyond the alienated, agonized self is obvious in his early, unsent letter to Yvonne found by Laurelle in the first chapter: "I have been deliberately struggling against my love for you. I dared not submit to it. . . . I can deceive myself no longer. If I am to survive I need your help. Otherwise, sooner or later, I shall fall". But love simply is not possible: "You cannot know the sadness of my life. Endlessly haunted waking and sleeping by the thought that you may need my help, which I cannot give, as I need yours, which you cannot". If it is not possible to live without love and is not possible, the conclusion is obvious: self-destruction of the consciousness. The Consul says in the same letter: "Sometimes I am possessed by a most powerful feeling, a despairing bewildered jealousy which, when deepened by drink, turns into a desire to destroy myself by my own imagination—not at least to be the prey of—ghosts". (Note that drink only "deepened" the death wish; it did not create it). (pp. 138-46)

Arguments stressing a more optimistic interpretation are often attempted. Douglas Day feels that some sort of transcendence occurs which redeems the Consul's soul. This interpretation does not bear up after an examination of the exact text of the closing section in which the Consul's actual death occurs:

> ah, he was being rescued at last. He was in an ambulance shrieking through the jungle itself, racing uphill past the timberline toward the peak—and this was certainly one way to get there!—while these were friendly voices around him, Jacques' and Vigil's, they would make allowances, would set Hugh's and Yvonne's minds at rest about him. "No se puede vivir sin amar," they would say, which would explain everything and he repeated this aloud. How could he have thought so evil of the world when succour was at hand all the time? And now he had reached the summit. Ah, Yvonne, sweetheart, forgive me! Strong hands lifted him. Opening his eyes, he looked down, expecting to see, below him, the magnificent jungle, the heights, Pico de Orizaba, Malinche, Cofre de Perete, like these peaks of his life conquered one after another before this greatest ascent of all had been successfully, if unconventionally, completed. But there was nothing there: no peaks, no life, no climb. Nor was this summit a summit exactly: it had no substance, no firm base. It was crumbling too, whatever it was, collapsing, while he was falling, falling in to the volcano, he must have climbed it after all, though now there was this noise of foisting lava in his ears, horribly, it was in eruption, yet no, it wasn't the volcano, the world itself was bursting, bursting into black sprouts of villages catapulted into space, with himself fall-

ing through it all, through the inconceivable pandemonium of a million tanks, through the blazing of ten million burning bodies, falling, into a forest, falling—Suddenly he screamed and it was as though this scream were being tossed from one tree to another, as its echoes returned, then, as though the trees themselves were crowding nearer, huddled together, closing over him, pitying . . .
> Somebody threw a dead dog after him down the ravine.

This powerful image, formulated through the dissolving narrative consciousness of the Consul, creates an unmistakable motif of personal nihilism, the only truth surviving after the devastation of romantic illusions in an insane world. An anonymous reviewer for *The Times Literary Supplement* summarized succinctly: "There is no hint of possible salvation, religious or political, by faith or by works" [see Further Reading].

Under the Volcano is often referred to as a tragedy. But when all the old gods have died, and external reality is apprehended as inherently absurd, then the only concept of "true tragedy" left is ironic. Camus has said that the only real philosophical problem for the fully conscious individual is the problem of suicide. This is the frontier of awareness to which ***Under the Volcano*** has pushed. (pp. 148-50)

> Chet Taylor, "The Other Edge of Existential Awareness: Reading of Malcolm Lowry's 'Under the Volcano'," in The Literary Half-Yearly, Vol. XIV, No. 1, January, 1973, pp. 138-50.

Barry Wood   (essay date 1978)

[*Wood is a Canadian-born critic. Regarding influences on his critical writings he has stated, "The strongest personal influences have come from Northrop Frye, at the University of Toronto, and Alan Watts, author of numerous books and a general interpreter of Zen Buddhism in the West. From about 1964 Watts was the major shaper of my thought and style. My personal contact with Frye dates back to 1963, and his approach to religious literature has influenced me ever since. Frye's archetypal and mythic approaches to literary criticism which continue to appear in published form have asserted themselves in my own thinking and writing since 1975 and will continue to hold an important place in my development as a literary critic." In the following excerpt, Wood examines autobiographical and metafictional elements in* Under the Volcano.]

Innumerable events of Lowry's life eventually found their way into ***Under the Volcano,*** though apparently not with the inevitability that we might initially assume. In June 1933, Lowry met a glamorous young American girl called Jan Gabrial, whom he married on January 6, 1934. From the start this marriage was a rocky affair. By late 1936, after a series of moves, separations, and returns including the sojourn at Bellevue Hospital in New York, the ill-fated couple had found their way to Los Angeles. Unable to find work (scriptwriting) and short of money, they decided to move to Mexico where expenses would be lower. Arriving in Acapulco on November 1 or 2, they were, by Christmas, living in a three-room bungalow at Number 15, Calle de Humboldt, in Cuernavaca, within sight of the volcanoes Popocatepetl and Ixtaccihuatl. The house had a garden and a swimming pool, and bordered on one of the town's several *barrancas*. Here, almost immediately, Lowry wrote the short story **"Under the Volcano"**; moreover, as soon as it was done he apparently began to expand it into a novel. By May 1937, he had written a complete version of some 40,000 words—though the manuscript was later lost. Over the next several months, according to those who visited the Lowrys—Conrad Aiken, Arthur Calder-Marshall—Lowry not only drank a great deal but experienced severe marital problems as a result of Jan's infidelities. Then, after a flamboyant affair with a neighbor, Jan abandoned Lowry in December 1937. Immediately following this estrangement Lowry took a trip alone to Oaxaca some 300 miles south of Cuernavaca—a kind of descent deeper into Mexico to what Lowry later termed "a city of dreadful night." According to letters written to John Davenport, Conrad Aiken, and James Stern, the next few weeks were a dark night of the soul, full of hallucinations, suspicions, horrible dangers, "an absolutely fantastic tragedy" of isolation. He may have imagined being pursued and watched by the police but he was, at least once, thrown into jail. During this period, apparently, he established one remarkable friendship with an adventurous Zapotecan called Juan Fernando Márquez, with whom Lowry fenced and drank and, on at least one occasion, traveled into the hill country—until, just before the end of 1937, Márquez was transferred to Cuicuitlan. Alone again, Lowry wrote to Aiken early in January 1938: "Have now reached condition of amnesia, breakdown, heartbreak, consumption, cholera, alcoholic poisoning, and God will not like to know what else, if he has to, which is damned doubtful. . . . I have been imprisoned as a spy in a dungeon. . . . I spent Christmas—New Year's—Wedding Day there. . . . Don't think I can go on. Where I am it is dark. Lost". Somehow Lowry managed to salvage himself from this labyrinthine nightmare, finding his way back to Mexico City by June and out of Mexico by July—though not without some complications when his visa expired.

Lowry's twenty months in Mexico eventually formed the foundation and ground plan of **Under the Volcano**, which was completed in a second draft of 360 pages about a year later in Los Angeles. The terrain of the story consisted of an artistically rearranged Cuernavaca (renamed Quauhnahuac), complete with the three-room bungalow, pool, garden, towering volcanoes, and plunging *barranca*. The central figure, the British Consul, is a doomed alcoholic plummeting ever deeper into the misery of a failed marriage and incapable of being rescued by his daughter, Yvonne, who arrives on the last day of his life. The framework, drawing on Lowry's own disastrous marriage with Jan and the subsequent terrors of Oaxaca, is largely autobiographical, with one difference: Lowry escaped the fate that his Consul could not.

As time went on the autobiographical elements in the novel accumulated. In Hollywood, in June 1939, Lowry met Margerie Bonner, a striking woman who had behind her a successful career as a horsewoman in western movies dating to the era before the talkies. Margerie followed Lowry to Vancouver, Canada, where they were married some time after settling in the idyllic Burrard Inlet community of Dollarton. There, with Margerie's help, Lowry wrote the third draft of **Volcano**, completed in the spring of 1940, and subsequently rejected by twelve publishers. In the course of the fourth draft, written between 1941 and 1944, the Consul's daughter Yvonne was altered to become his wife with a background strikingly like Margerie's—a brief career in Hollywood Westerns and an impressive knowledge of astronomy. All of this was superimposed on the original story drawn from Lowry's earlier marriage to Jan. Added too, was the distant northern wilderness which is so much a part of Yvonne's desire and dream through Chapter 9 of the published book—a paradise drawn from the tiny squatters' community at Dollarton where the Lowrys were living.

This kind of summation might lead one to imagine **Under the Volcano** to be rather thinly disguised autobiography, whereas the autobiographical basis is not discoverable from the novel alone. The finished book has such a powerful layering of meaning and symbolism that it reads initially as a remarkable work of imagination—as indeed it is. Few readers can imagine a real life as densely hopeless as the Consul's giving birth to a book of such cosmic proportions.

Since Lowry had successfully turned life into art of immediately acknowledged greatness, the question naturally arises as to why he chose another direction in subsequent works. Why did he not simply take up other experiences and invest them with the same kind of symbolic layering which made **Volcano** a remarkable success? Admittedly, he was well on the way in the unfinished **October Ferry to Gabriola;** but almost all of the other materials left at his death veered into metafiction. The explanation for this shift lies in a perhaps unexpected place.

The crucial factor in the emergence of Lowry's metafiction after 1947 is the ten-year-long process of writing **Under the Volcano,** including the multiple drafts and publishers' rejections. One of the book's earliest admirers, Robert B. Heilman, has placed Lowry, along with Dostoevsky, Melville, and Lawrence, in the tradition of Plato's Ion as a possessed artist [see Further Reading]. Heilman's evidence is textual:

> The sense of a largeness that somehow bursts out of the evident constriction [the enclosing illness of the protagonist], the fertility that borders on the excessive and the frenzied, the intensity that is not a surrogate for magnanimity, and finally an apprehension of reality so vivid that it seems to slide over into madness—these are symptoms of the work of the "possessed" artist. . . . The materials appear to use him as an instrument, finding in him, as it were, a channel to the objective existence of art, sacrificing a minimum of their autonomy to his hand, which partly directs and shapes rather than wholly controls. This is how it is with Lowry.

Putting it perhaps more succinctly, with the emphasis on the artist rather than the art, Margerie herself wrote to

Harold Matson, Lowry's literary agent: "I tell you this: that only a person whose whole existence *is* his work, who has dominated and disciplined the volcano within him, at what a cost of suffering even I do not wholly understand, could have written such a book."

Even without such testimony, however, the successive manuscripts tell a story of their own. Together they add up to more than 400,000 words, exclusive of the 1100 pages of "working notes" that led up to the final, fourth draft. The Herculean labor of all this, especially the writing of the fourth draft after twelve rejections, speaks eloquently of Lowry's determination to complete this novel; and the exegesis found in his 18,000-word letter to Jonathan Cape—"a document absolutely unique in literary history," as Douglas Day describes it—reveals his intention from the beginning to write a truly monumental novel.

It was Lowry's particular genius that he recognized his own obsession with the novel, ferreted it out, explored it, and eventually wrote it into the life of the Consul. Lowry's realization that a writer obsessed with greatness is a man entangled in his own work provided the paradigm which was then transformed and projected as the web of doom in which Geoffrey Firmin is caught. Like Lowry, the Consul is both a writer and an alcoholic; but Lowry's situation—an obsession with writing, and alcoholism as a minor complication—is reversed in the Consul, whose alcoholism becomes the metaphorical expression of his overwhelming obsession with self. So completely does his alcoholism dominate that the Consul's unrealized desire to write slips far into the background, a minor example of his paralysis of will, almost entirely overshadowed by his other demons. Lowry discovered that an obsessed life is a kind of living death, for it destroys everything else in its path: friendships, marriage, trust, desire, will, reason— even sanity. In *Volcano* he dramatized this discovery by presenting a life that was itself a living death, layering it with motifs from the *Inferno, Doctor Faustus, The Waste Land,* and *La machine infernale* to secure the vision. What appears in the novel to be an overworked foreshadowing is really the Consul's obsession with the very doom which his obsession brings about. It is precisely this circular web—an obsession with death which guarantees it, a confounding of cause and effect—that reveals the origin of Lowry's metafiction. The writer obsessed with his own writing can possess only one story, and thus must write himself into his own fiction.

The implications of this dilemma are significant. Clearly the artist who is totally obsessed with his art must find himself in an unreal—which is to say, fictional—situation. Metafiction, at least in Lowry's case, is not simply a disguised account of a real life. Lowry writes from the other side of the metaphor, attempting to capture the sense that his life as an artist feels fictional: that much of the time his writing, with everything that the process entails, induces a sense of unreality.

Lowry's novel works at what Dale Edmonds calls "the immediate level" [see excerpt dated 1968] because Lowry created in the Consul's dipsomania an objective correlative for his own obsessions. But the novel works at numer-

ous levels of symbolic meaning, too, and one of the most important—from the standpoint of the later metafiction— is to be found in the cabbalistic system running through the story. According to Margerie Lowry, Malcolm "jolted up" from his work on the book one day in the spring of 1942 and declared to her that his Consul was a black magician, or a white magician who had lost control and so was doomed by his own powers, which had turned against him. This twist of fate subsequently added a whole new range of symbolic layering to the book. Already conversant with such esoteric writers as Ouspensky, Swedenborg, Blake, Boehme, and Yeats, Lowry immediately plunged into *The Cabbala;* shortly after this he met a real Cabbalist, Charles Stansfeld Jones, better known in the Chicago group he formed as Frater Achad. Without attempting to follow the results of this influence through *Volcano,* it is sufficient to note that Lowry apparently believed in the power and efficacy of an invisible reality symbolized in *The Cabbala;* and he made the same kind of belief, though vastly disrupted, an integral part of the Consul's inescapable doom. In later works, too, suggestions of powerful magical forces continue to appear: the suggestion of poltergeists in **"Ghostkeeper,"** the witchcraft of Cosnahan's mother in **"Elephant and Colosseum,"** and Ethan Llewelyn's cabbalism in **October Ferry to Gabriola.**

By the time Lowry had completed **Under the Volcano** late in 1944 the very writing of the book had created a stage upon which he would move for some time. In a certain sense this was simply an exaggerated version of the framework every author creates for himself with his works, beginning with their writing and continuing through the reading of galleys, page proofs, book reviews, and the inevitable contacts with new people that writing brings. In Lowry's case it was time to visit Mexico again, not only to look up Juan Fernando Márquez, his Oaxacan friend, but also to take Margerie to the landscape of volcanoes, *barrancas,* and cantinas that had occupied their imaginations so long. At this point, on a stage set by **Volcano,** Lowry suddenly felt his life turning into a fictional drama. During the final stages in its writing Lowry had felt the achievement of the book might be undercut by the appearance of Charles Jackson's bestseller, *The Lost Weekend;* en route to Mexico, dining one night in Los Angeles with Margerie's family, he found himself seated beside a photographer who had helped to film the movie version of Jackson's book. This was the first of what Lowry regarded as ominous events. Arriving in Cuernavaca and seeking accomodations, they found themselves directed to Number 24 on the Calle de Humboldt, the house which had served as the model for Jacques Laruelle's house in **Under the Volcano.** Immediately, as Lowry noted in his journals, he began to wonder if his fiction was consuming his life: if perhaps the death that he had evaded in 1938 was not about to consume him. The possibility that he had described his own death in the final chapter of his novel terrified Lowry. Perhaps *he* was enmeshed in a magical web; perhaps his obsession with death would lead to his own. When Jonathan Cape publishers suggested, then, that **Under the Volcano** (which they had kept for some six months) might not be publishable as it stood, Lowry was overwhelmed. One night, in the midst of writing his long reply to Cape, he made a halfhearted attempt to slash his wrists. Five days later (January 16, 1946), having mailed the letter to Cape, Lowry set off with his wife for a visit to his "city of dreadful night," Oaxaca, only to discover that the friend for whom they were searching, Juan Fernando Márquez, had been dead since 1939. Like Geoffrey Firmin, he had got completely drunk in a cantina, and, after getting into an argument with another drunk, had been shot to death. Thus, while Lowry had escaped the death invented for the Consul, his best friend had somehow been caught in the fiction.

Early in March, at the instigation of Margerie, they traveled to Acapulco, the scene of Lowry's visa problems in 1938. On the second morning after their arrival they were apprehended by representatives from the Immigration Office, ostensibly for an unpaid fine from 1938—a situation calling for the payment of *la mordida,* the extorted bribe familiar to tourists in Mexico. With little money and their passports back in Cuernavaca, they found themselves entangled in a monthlong struggle which confirmed Lowry's long-held belief that Mexico was his private hell. Identifying with his Consul, he found himself moving in a world he had invented: "It was as if *he* were the character, being moved about for the purposes of some other novelist and by him, in an unimaginable novel, not of this world, that did not, indeed, exist." (pp. 7-14)

> Barry Wood, "Malcolm Lowry's Metafiction: The Biography of a Genre," in Contemporary Literature, *Vol. XIX, No. 1, Winter, 1978, pp. 1-25.*

Stephen Tifft   (essay date 1978)

[*In the following excerpt, Tifft interprets* Under the Volcano *as a tragedy in which the main character continually reflects on his own tragic condition, thereby making the novel a self-reflexive "meditation on itself."*]

Under the Volcano moves toward catastrophe with classical directness. Yet a baroque system of analogies continuously modifies and complicates the novel's tragic design; moreover, Firmin's awareness of his self-determined role further belies the apparent simplicity of the tragedy. If Lowry has managed to coordinate all the analogical substructures, however, we ought to find their unifying principle at the core of this novel's particular definition of tragedy. Many have pointed to the basic tragic shape of **Under the Volcano,** but few have attended to the reasons for the fall or the way it comes about; but only by doing so can we discern the novel's essential tragic principle.

According to two common but fallacious interpretations, the crux of the Consul's tragedy is either alcoholism, or the inability to love. These theories are easily dispensed with. The first maintains that Firmin's "tragic" purpose is merely to have another drink—that the idea of tragedy is itself a rationalization projected by the Consul. But Lowry takes pains to attribute only a relatively small proportion of the Consul's suffering, whether on the political, the domestic, or any other level of the tragedy, directly to alcoholism. The Consul's consciousness of his broad catastrophic pattern is sufficient to raise him above the pathos

of mere alcoholism, and he even draws a certain qualified grandeur from his tragic heritage. The second and more interesting interpretation defines the Consul's *hamartia* by reference to the recurrent theme, *"no se puede vivir sin amar"* (one cannot live without loving). The maxim certainly carries symbolic weight, but it serves little purpose as a formulation of Firmin's tragic flaw. Only by resorting to shifting definitions of "loving" can one convert the theme from one level of tragic analogy to another; and making excessive claims for the theme of *"no se puede . . . "* too often leads one to ascribe to Lowry a saccharine argument for Good Samaritanism, surely beyond what the text warrants. Lowry's ironic handling of the Good Samaritan theme, and especially of its manifestation in Hugh as a foil to the Consul, bespeaks an ambivalence that can hardly be ignored.

So much for the false *hamartia.* Tragedy turns on a purpose held or an action undertaken by the protagonist, whether such purpose or action be an error or not. The crux of tragedy is the intimate relation between this purpose or action and the catastrophe which issues from it inevitably. Although the inevitability results from special conditions in the given world of each tragedy, the tragic action originates solely with the protagonist. Firmin's manifold tragedy comprises two independent downfalls, the rupture of his reconciliation with Yvonne and his murder by the fascists. Furthermore, he endures throughout a postlapsarian state of continuous suffering, like that of Prometheus. A single tragic purpose propels the Consul's multiple tragedy.

That purpose, the essence of the tragic definition of **Under the Volcano,** is as follows: the Consul dedicates himself to the tragic destiny which—he is convinced—is his.

It will be immediately evident that this tragic purpose is purely reflexive—tragedy proceeds from the conviction that it must proceed. This is an elegant refinement of the tragic mode: tragedy as a meditation on itself. The Consul's purpose may sound tautological, but it is not. Firmin's fidelity to his doom does not amount to the same thing as the catastrophe itself; only within the given world of the novel is his tragic purpose lethal. Seen as a *hamartia* within that world, the Consul's reflexive preoccupation with tragedy is characterized by a curiously inverted form of hubris: his powerful, obsessed mind does not soar, but plummets; it sets him apart from normal society nonetheless.

If the tragic purpose I have suggested is correct, it will give access to the working out of the Consul's tragedy within each of the major analogical substructures. Arguing for a *"Gestalt* reading" of **Under the Volcano,** Douglas Day suggests five levels on which such a reading might proceed: chthonic, human, political, magical, and religious [see *TCLC,* Vol. 6, pp. 247-49]. Adapting the scheme to levels of tragedy, we can organize the analogical substructures into the following categories: interpersonal, religious, occult, mythical/literary, and political. In this way we can account for not only the two major *mythoi* (in Frye's sense of narrative patterns)—namely the Yvonne-Geoffrey catastrophe and the political plot that culminates at El Farolito—but also three main sorts of tragic motif.

Though these levels of the Consul's tragedy present slightly different landscapes, they have in common his one paradigmatic tragic purpose: to remain faithful to his tragic destiny.

We are left with an important question: What does Lowry mean by creating a character who reads his own tragedy concurrently with the reader? Lowry conceived of the Consul's tragic reflexiveness as far more than cement for the artifice. The idea of reflexiveness and the way reflexive perception can affect reality permeate Lowry's presentation of character, his theory of art, his mimesis of reality—even perhaps his own experience of reality. The Consul's reflexiveness not only unifies the structural elements of the novel, but is also its main subject. *Under the Volcano* is not merely an artifice that counterfeits reality: by describing tragedy as a meditation on tragedy, by blurring the boundaries between fictive interpretation and concrete experience, the novel continually inverts fiction and reality.

Although Lowry never fully reveals the origins of the Consul's tragic fatalism, they are suggested in the way Firmin's reflexiveness affects the crucial events of the domestic tragedy. His tragic conviction that all is lost frustrates each attempt at reconciliation with Yvonne and creates a vicious circle in which his actions can only lead to impasses which reinforce prior assumptions. The Consul recognizes something like this cycle of frustration at the heart of his drinking problem:

> ". . . the whole trouble being as we see it that Yvonne's long-dreamed-of coming alas but put away the anguish my boy there's nothing in it," the voice gabbled on, "has in itself created the most important situation in your life save one namely the far more important situation it in turn creates of your having to have five hundred drinks in order to deal with it. . . . "

Indeed, this vicious circle—perhaps a spiral would be a more apt figure—serves as a paradigm of the tragic action in general. Propelled by his fatalism, the Consul cycles through repeated rounds of guilt-resentment-withdrawal-guilt as he approaches catastrophe.

The reasons for Firmin's guilt over his treatment of Yvonne are obvious. What is less evident, but crucial, is the way a free-floating sense of guilt—a pure guilt, prior to any culpability—cripples his actions before he can take them. In its clearest manifestations, this abstract guilt is secreted whenever an impending performance overwhelms the Consul with a premature sense of failure. During his abortive attempt to make love with his wife, for example, Firmin's guilty longing for escape, which cannot be attributed solely to alcoholic craving, precedes his impotence with Yvonne. Evidently his dread of failure has ensured it (he later succeeds with María when considerably more drunk; the stakes are lower then). Lowry alludes to Firmin's dread of performance, which leads to guilt in advance of its earning, at most of the pivotal moments in the domestic plot. The motif most frequently employed is the "Hell Bunker", where, in Firmin's youth, another abortive sexual performance was discovered (this event is neatly tied by its location to Geoffrey's obsessed, successful performance as a boy golfer).

Like his sexual endeavours, the Consul's drinking, or rather his attempt to carry it off, is one life-long performance, a point Lowry likes to convey by refering to the Consul's erect bearing in almost all conditions. Thus Geoffrey's humiliation in the Hell Bunker is compounded when subsequently, with all eyes upon him, he is refused drinks at a pub significantly named "The Case Is Altered". He spends the rest of his life making good the failure. Turning to the crucial rejection of Yvonne's white flag in Chapter VII, we find Lowry employing this double motif of performance anxiety to its greatest possible effect at the moment when the Consul knows reconciliation to be incumbent upon him. Whether Lowry means to attribute the Consul's performance anxiety to sexual guilt, or to guilt at failing to live up to the standards set by his surrogate family, the Taskersons, he expresses it in fatalistic terms, as a kind of speculation in guilt which yields devastating dividends.

The Consul requires a lover who will demonstrate absolute acceptance of him whatever he does, one "who, upon that last and final green, though I hole out in four, accepts my ten and three score. . . . Though I have more". Despite Yvonne's commitment to Geoffrey, she has blundered badly by betraying him with Hugh and then with Laruelle. She certainly had good reason to do so, but she seems unaware of the ways in which her infidelity has reinforced some of the Consul's overwhelming insecurities, and so has increased his fatalism. Her efforts to retrieve the marriage always waver at the crucial moments, through her own fatalism, and she too effectively blocks reconciliation with her faulty and untested assumptions—a point that is frequently overlooked. The following passage, for example, is often cited as the best expression of the attractions that induce the Consul to choose alcohol over his wife.

> . . . for not even the gates of heaven, opening wide to receive me, could fill me with such celestial complicated and hopeless joy as the iron screen that rolls up with a crash, as the unpadlocked jostling jalousies which admit those whose souls tremble with the drinks they carry unsteadily to their lips.

In fact, these are Yvonne's thoughts. Within minutes of her arrival in Quauhnahuac, she has already assumed that Geoffrey is rejecting her appeal, and imagines this as his explanation for the denial. For all her hope, Yvonne starts the day with fatalistic assumptions that will fulfill themselves by nightfall.

Lowry is careful to link Firmin's feeling of betrayal, and with it his fatalistic sense of his own perdition as a tragic figure, to psychological configurations established deep in his past. As a child Geoffrey had suffered from the death of his mother and abandonment by his father; from these traumata his tragic world-view began to evolve. The Consul frequently follows up thoughts of Yvonne's betrayal of him with allusions to this early abandonment. He cannot forgive those who were supposed to take care of him and did not: his father, or in a loftier sense, God; and his stepmother, or Yvonne. At the pivotal moment in Chapter VII, when he is alone with Yvonne at Jacques' house, and on the brink of reconciliation, the Consul reveals again the subconscious link between betrayal and childhood abandonment:

> "I do love you. Only—" "I can never forgive you deeply enough": was that what was in his mind to add?
>
> —And yet, he was thinking all over again, and all over as for the first time, how he had suffered, suffered, suffered without her; indeed such desolation, such a desperate sense of abandonment, bereavement, as during this last year without Yvonne, he had never known in his life, unless it was when his mother died.

From his childhood the Consul has had a fatalistic distrust of the possibility of anyone's understanding devotion to him, which allows him to see perfect logic in Yvonne's infidelity. Nonetheless, he has consistently craved such devotion, and his reaction when he does not receive it is profound, unforgiving resentment. When "abandoned", that is, not accepted without question, he takes umbrage at the wrong-doing of the beloved; his guilt leads to his resentment, Yvonne's infidelity being a useful bridge. The process is intensified by her campaign to save him, which he resents because it forces him to admit his culpability—thus aggravating his guilt—and because of the implication that Yvonne is less at fault than he would like her to be. Resentment immediately precedes each of the major breakdowns of the reconciliation.

Withdrawal follows resentment. The Consul thinks of withdrawal as a form of self-reliance, a thumbing of the nose at the loved ones on whom he had so dangerously depended. Actually it is an expedient closer to escape. His chief avenue of escape is drinking, which escalates with each successive crisis. Yet the Consul manages to turn his hallucinatory voyages into Dionysian celebrations of dissolution which supercede the pathos of mere escape. As he sublimates the impulse to withdraw, in the form of a grand Dionysian gesture, the Consul attains to the impersonality that he needs as a tragic protagonist: he withdraws not simply from Yvonne, but from the world. But the Dionysian cannot avoid extremity. The apotheosis of impersonality is the absolute dissolution of self; withdrawal from the world must finally be physical as well as mental. Although the Consul moves toward the abyss in logical fulfillment of a mythic withdrawal, he has started merely by withdrawing from Yvonne, and the larger tragedy may be more than he bargains for. As a compromise he reiterates the eremitic motif of William Blackstone, renouncer of civilization, but Sr. Chief of Rostrums, Zuzugoitea rejects the compromise and ushers the Consul to the ultimate withdrawal.

Although the Consul wavers between an innocuous eremitism and a visionary self-destructiveness, in either case his last withdrawal from Yvonne is decisive. He breaks with her when he flees the Salón Ofélia and completes the interpersonal catastrophe at El Farolito by sullying himself with the whore María. A fatalistic resentment seems to master him, yet he rejects the waning possibility of reconciliation deliberately:

> . . . some reckless murderous power was drawing him on, forcing him, while he yet remained passionately aware of the all too possible consequences and somehow as innocently unconscious, to do without precaution or conscience what he would never be able to undo or gainsay . . .
>
> So this was it, the final stupid unprophylactic rejection. He could prevent it even now. He would not prevent it.

Just beneath the surface of the Consul's conviction of the finality of his act, a hint of guilt appears in the suggestion of venereal disease. The reader may feel that objectively Firmin is wrong about Yvonne's unforgiveness, but the Consul's guilt tends always to lead him to ensure the accuracy of his misgivings, transforming the subjective into the objective. If his fornication with María makes him feel so guilty that the thought of reconciliation is intolerable, then the act *is* final: "But now too at least this much was clear. He couldn't go back to Yvonne if he wanted to".

This sort of self-fulfilling prophecy could generally be corrected if the Consul and Yvonne were simply to confide in one another. But as Lowry presents it human interaction is constantly beset by crossed signals and blockages of communication, whose pervasiveness he stresses by making them a part of his narrative technique. Each chapter imprisons us within a particular mind, underscoring each character's difficulty in trying to understand the others. To escape one's subjectivity and make contact with another requires an enormous leap of faith, but a conviction of doom blocks such a leap. This crippling fatalism hampers even Yvonne's optimism, and is insuperable in the Consul's case. The hopeless round of guilt, resentment, and withdrawal is woven into the fabric of the Consul's being, as he knows. He does not recognize so clearly that his inbred fatalism infects the future as well. Even when all was going well, he could not shake off a sense of doom which compelled him to see catastrophe in the fact of happiness:

> Far too soon their life together had begun to seem too much of a triumph, it had been too good, too horribly unimaginable to lose, impossible finally to bear: it was as if it had become itself its own foreboding that it could not last, a foreboding that was like a presence too, turning his steps towards the taverns again.

The mixture of fatalism and guilty resentment that poisons the Consul's last chance for a reconciliation with Yvonne also compels him to reject help from other quarters, especially from figures of authority. Lowry deepens the significance of this spiritual ailment by extending the principle to the level of religious analogy, in the motif of the Consul's fall from God's grace. The epigraph that Lowry selects from the work of John Bunyan underscores the religious analogy as a paradigm for all aspects of Firmin's tragedy:

> . . . animals had no soul to perish under the everlasting weight of Hell or Sin, as mine was like to do . . . yet that which was added to my sorrow was, that I could not find with all my soul that I did desire deliverance.

Bunyan was heavily influenced by Calvin, and the Calvinist doctrine of predestination provides another apt context for the fatalism and the unanchored sense of guilt discussed in the last section. Like Bunyan in the first half of his autobiography, *Grace Abounding to the Chief of Sinners,* the Consul feels that he is a predestined reprobate, and the conviction throttles repentance; his constant preoccupation with the possible signs of his sinful state mires him deeper in hopelessness.

Sin is the stigma of a reprobate, but Lowry handles the concept of sin obliquely. Numerous allusions identify the Consul as an avatar of Adam; having no such clearly defined sin as that of Adam, the Consul assumes for Adam a surrogate sin—the ingratitude of hating the Garden:

> And of course the real *reason* for that punishment . . . might well have been that the poor fellow, who knows, secretly loathed the place! Simply hated it, and had done so all along. *And that the Old Man found this out. . . .*

The Consul, in the guise of Adam, expresses his sense of sin by rejecting the salvation God offers, just as he had rejected Yvonne and her help. Again the Consul's consciousness of his own ingratitude makes him feel guilty. Guilt in general is the Consul's Pavlovian response to any thought of God. Firmin mentions repeatedly the sunflower which "Stares, Fiercely. All day. Like God!" God's stare is not innocuous: "I know [the sunflower] watches me and I know it hates me". The garden is the prime locale for the Consul's guilty certainty of God's surveillance. But like his guilt toward Yvonne, the Consul's guilt before God is general—disproportionate to and often quite detached from any of his actions. In this respect guilt is like original sin, a fact of the Consul's being independent of his actual behaviour. Where there is no cause for guilt, he will invent one—like the *Samaritan* incident.

Bunyan's guilt made him so ashamed that he could not bear to pray to God. Shame may also help to explain the Consul's inhibition: "Christ . . . would help you if you asked him: you cannot ask him". But there is a further explanation: fatalism convinces both men that prayer is useless. Bunyan despairs, "now to pray, seeing God has cast you off, is the next way to anger and offend him more than you ever did before;" the Consul echoes, "God has little patience with remorse!" The Consul would prefer to flee all contact—hence his vicarious loathing of Paradise. Thus the fatalism of guilt can be seen as the cause, as well as the result, of Firmin/Adam's ingratitude.

The Consul's unorthodox meditations on Adam's expulsion are touched off by his drunken misreading of the sign, *"¿Le gusta este jardin que es suyo? ¡Evite que sus hijos lo destruyan!,"* as "You like this garden? Why is it yours? We evict those who destroy!" Drawing on Thomas Burnet's description of the earth as a Paradise damaged by sin, Lowry links the motif of the ruined garden to the Consul's ungrateful loathing for his Paradise, and presents the ruined garden as a subjective and individual phenomenon: Mr. Quincey's garden, unlike the Consul's, is neatly kept. In his exposition of the Paradise myth to Mr. Quincey, the Consul interprets eviction as loosely as destruction. The eviction is not physical but spiritual: "his punishment really consisted . . . in his having to *go on living there,*

alone, of course—suffering, unseen, cut off from God". Thus the sin and the punishment are virtually the same— hating the Garden that God provided. By construing this hatred as punishment, the Consul manages to find in it fresh evidence of his guilt, thereby perpetuating and intensifying the whole cycle.

Lowry has arranged his religious motifs as a closed circuit which illustrates perfectly the Consul's compulsion to fuel his own reflexive tragedy: the Consul ruins his garden by the "sin" of hating it; he hates it because his guilt makes him perceive it as ruined. By this subjective, fatalistic vicious circle we return to the Calvinist doctrine of predestination. The Consul believes that he is one of the reprobate, rather than one of the elect. He will therefore do nothing to save himself, but will occupy himself only in looking for indications of his reprobation. His pride will not permit him to endure the shame of a confrontation with God, so convinced is he of the outcome of such a confrontation; he prefers, like the lost souls of Canto II of Dante's *Inferno,* to rush eagerly toward Hell. His sin, like that of Marlowe's Faustus, is the sin against the Holy Ghost—"pride and despair, inextricably linked". (pp. 46-55)

Acceptance of the tragic lot ushers in catastrophe on the level of political analogy as surely as on any other. The causal connexion between tragic reflexiveness and the political tragedy presents itself most clearly in the way the Consul's murder comes about. Lowry provides unmistakable evidence at numerous points that the Consul knows well what iron fist rules Parián—the fascist *Union Militar,* led locally by Sanabria and Zuzugoitea. Despite this, and despite the fact that "the Consul was more afraid of the police than death", he goes deliberately "into that glorious Parián wilderness . . . towards ineluctable personal disaster"—a disaster he actively seeks after the fiasco at the Salón Ofélia. Zuzugoitea's finding Hugh's anarchist card on the Consul may seem merely fortuitous, though crucial; but the card is the last piece of a great deal of evidence gathered by the fascists. The Consul is a marked man, a consul in a country where consuls are thought to be spies, and one who has remained after his country has broken diplomatic relations with Mexico. (The Consul's decision to stay in Mexico, which he himself recognizes as a surrender to tragic fate, is the first step in the political tragedy.) The fascists have kept up on him to the extent of knowing that he is a cuckold, and seem to have been waiting for a convenient excuse to lock him up. In defiance of his parlous state, the Consul remains in the bar, entranced by his doom, providing such excuses until his assumption that "it's too late" proves correct. Then he exchanges imprisonment for death by attacking the police and freeing the horse.

These are the mechanics of the Consul's catastrophe on the political level. But Lowry also uses that personal tragedy as a metaphor for a tragedy engulfing not only Mexico but the world at large.

We have seen the operation of the eremitic instinct on the interpersonal and the religious levels of the Consul's tragedy: when faced with his sins and shortcomings, and with the responsibility for their correction, the Consul tends to withdraw from the challenge, feeling unequal to it. This applies equally to political responsibility. He sees little hope for the world, and his solution is to try to be left alone. His incognito is William Blackstone, a colonial settler who escaped society to seek asylum among the Indians, and then withdrew from them to total solitude. The Consul characterizes all of the influences from which he is escaping under the title, "fellows with ideas", i.e. those who would try to correct him, help him, or otherwise remind him of his responsibilities; or more generally, those who, unlike him, do not believe that their cause is lost. The modern wilderness to which he escapes is hidden within himself: " '*Now*, little cat,' the Consul tapped his chest indicatively . . . 'the Indians are in here' ". The Consul's problem is that an internal wilderness does not provide enough shelter. He takes the fascists for Indians, but "The only trouble was one was very much afraid these particular Indians might turn out to be people with ideas too".

Hugh, in contrast to the Consul, helps to demonstrate the absurdity and peril of his brother's fatalistic isolationism. We have seen that Hugh evinces a Goethean striving for political amelioration; the dramatization of this worthy quality is his attempt to help the Indian dying on the wayside. We must be careful with Hugh's idealism, however, for Lowry qualifies and even mocks it on several fronts. Of Hugh's brush with the vigilantes, the Consul remarks drily, "Never mind, old boy, it would have been worse than the windmills". Beyond his Quixotic impracticality, Hugh can be criticized for his failure to live up to his principles, as he himself knows too well. His guilt over his failure to *act* recurs through the motif, "They are losing the Battle of the Ebro." He associates revolutionary songs with men of principled action like Juan Cerillo, but while he is drunkenly singing these songs in the woods, both Yvonne and the Consul are dying.

Nonetheless, the mere desire to achieve good is preferable to the Consul's fatalistic, *laissez-faire* determinism:

> Why should anybody interfere with anybody? . . .
>
> . . . Can't you see there's a sort of determinism about the fate of nations? They all seem to get what they deserve in the long run.
>
> . . . Read history. Go back a thousand years. What is the use of interfering with its worthless stupid course?

Such fatalism will have tragic consequences—for Mexico as well as for the Consul. In the wayside incident Mexican law hamstrings the Mexican people—no one is allowed to help the Indian because such aid would make one an accessory after the fact. And ironically, the police and even the taxicab drivers are of no help to those they should serve, because they are all on strike. Here the Consul's theory of non-intervention, modified slightly as the peasant women's ethic of prudence, runs aground:

> And yet, in these old women it was as if, through the various tragedies of Mexican history, pity, the impulse to approach, and terror, the impulse to escape (as one had learned at college), having replaced it, had finally been reconciled by pru-

dence, the conviction it is better to stay where you are . . .

> And the truth was, it was perhaps one of those occasions when nothing *would* have done any good. Which only made it worse than ever.

Lowry explicitly formulates the historical issue according to his tragic paradigm. Similarly, he applies to Mexico the related theme of the Consul's self-victimization. The Indian is a payroll rider for the National Bank of Ejido Credit, which was part of President Cárdenas' policy of agrarian reform in the late thirties, providing funds for collective farming. This was a prime target for fascist groups, who hindered the programme by hiring vigilantes of the kind who, we assume, murdered the Indian. The self-victimization of the Mexican people, then, is carried out by these vigilantes and also in the person of the *pelado*, the low individual who steals the money of the dying Indian, thus fulfilling the image of Mexico preying upon herself— an image duplicated in references to the traitorous Tlaxcalans. The prudence of the peasant women will not help prevent this kind of abuse. Nor can the Consul's principles of withdrawal and of resignation to fate; he realizes this suddenly as he dies, a victim of the fascists like the Ejido rider. He sees himself simultaneously as the bloody-handed *pelado*, a predator upon himself.

As Lowry has applied the Consul's destructive fatalism to Mexico, he extends the theme to global relevance through the Mexican fascists, whose connexion with Nazi Germany is made clear at numerous points. As the fascists are a more menacing version of the *pelado*, the analogue to the prudent old women and the non-interfering Consul is Neville Chamberlain; hence the two diplomatic cars which cruise serenely past the trouble at the wayside, shortly after Hugh has thought of the Munich agreement. The Consul serves as a link between the personal and the global: Hugh refers to his snore as "the muted voice of England long asleep".

If the Consul's snoring is English, his drunkenness is universal, a metaphor for the world's crazed self-destructiveness on the eve of World War II. Hugh suggests that the world, like the Consul, is chiefly concerned with evading its sense of guilt: "Good God, if our civilization were to sober up for a couple of days, it'd die of remorse on the third". The persistent symbol of world-guilt is the film *Las Manos de Orlac*, recurring throughout the novel by means of a poster showing the murderer's bloody hands, which Laruelle sees as "the hieroglyphic of the times. For really it was Germany itself". Hitler presides over the world's drunken nightmare like a Faust or a black magician—and in some ways, like the Consul.

Hugh finds Hitler less dangerous than the paralysis which seizes the world at his approach:

> . . . this world . . . was now pretending to be horrified at the very thing by which it proposed to be engulfed the first moment it could be perfectly certain the engulfing process would last long enough.

This passive complicity is identical to that of the Consul before his fate, and to that of the prudent bystanders at the wayside. Lowry suggests an interpretation of passive complicity which helps to explain both the helplessness of Hugh's idealism and the Consul's fatalism, and which touches again on the theme of a reflexive sense of tragedy:

> [the Indian] is, obviously, mankind himself, mankind dying—then, in the Battle of the Ebro, or now, in Europe, while we do nothing, or if we would, have put ourselves in a position where we *can* do nothing, but talk, while he goes on dying. . . .

We have put *ourselves* in this position—for Lowry, this is the equivalent of the destruction of the Garden of Eden, and warrants ejection. The warning recurs at the end of the novel on the sign, "Do you like this garden, which is yours? See to it that your children do not destroy it!" But on the brink of war, mankind has already delivered the Garden over to the hands of Orlac: the *"Jefe de Jardineros"* ("Chief of Gardeners") is Fructuoso Sanabria, a Spanish fascist invited by traitorous elements in Mexico to exert his dark control over a fallen paradise. Sanabria reminds the Consul of his own former tenure of the unfallen garden at Granada; but now, sickened like Hamlet at the prospect of the unweeded garden, the Consul has lost the will to act. He can only accede to his catastrophe, and as he falls into the abyss,

> the world itself was bursting, bursting into black spouts of villages catapulted into space, with himself falling through it all, through the inconceivable pandemonium of a million tanks, through the blazing of ten million burning bodies, falling. . . .

The Consul cannot organize his tragedy neatly into levels of analogy; for him the analogies penetrate one another constantly. At every turn he confronts an image of his tragic plight, and he scarcely has a chance to react to one form of his perdition before it metamorphoses, with frightening fluidity, into another equally formidable. The same mental process which makes his back yard into a fallen Eden transforms it as quickly into Elsinore, or Munich. Since he always projects himself onto the world, he encounters his reflected image everywhere, variously distorted but consistently foreboding. This pernicious interconnectedness is an outgrowth of the Consul's reflexiveness; but his reflexiveness verges on an aesthetic impulse which imbues his experience with the beauty of formal coherence.

The Consul is engaged in a dizzying interchange: as his world mirrors the image of himself, so he in turn mimics that reflected image in his subsequent actions. "Mirror," "projection," "image"—such tropes suggest delusion, and indeed, the Consul's confreres find his obsessions phantasmal and unnecessary. Yet Lowry asserts an idealism by whose standards the exasperated common sense of Yvonne and Hugh is revealed as naïve and irrelevant. The Consul's hallucinations substantiate such idealism; they are frighteningly, palpably real. Lowry follows a favourite philosopher, Ortega, who writes that "Appearance is an objective quality of the real"; and he echoes Nietzsche in attributing to subjectivism a creative agency—we *make* what we perceive. By extending this function in time one arrives at Ortega's metaphor, which Lowry so admired, of man as the novelist of himself.

But although man creates himself constantly, he lacks complete artistic freedom. He can image himself only within the parameters of his experience; for as Ortega also suggests, "man is 'what has happened to him.' " This tension between his disquieting freedom to create himself anew at every moment, and his subjugation to the dictates of his past, baffles the Consul's sense of moral responsibility. When events ratify his tragic apprehensions, he is incapable of determining whether those events are self-fulfilling prophecies or confirmations of a transcendent necessity—in other words, whether he is governed by internal or external necessity.

Granted that the Consul's subjective interpretation of the world is real, in Ortega's sense, we may go a step further and conclude that his habit of interpreting and projecting fictions is in no way aberrant. Indeed, Lowry is careful to expose this habit in all the major characters; in each case their preoccupation with their fictions stands in the way of realizing them. Even what one may describe as harsh "realities" are inextricable from fiction-making: the action that objectifies the Consul's tragic projections—his murder by the fascists—results from the fiction that he is an anarchist spy.

Nevertheless, one can at least vary and privilege one's fictions. The Consul's subjectivism involves interpretation as well as projection, and in the former act his reflexiveness confers a blessing: it provides him with a critique of himself. For he is not only an obsessive reader of himself and his world; he is also a keen one, capable of seeing loopholes and interpreting himself quite dispassionately from the outside, as we might read him. At times the Consul is so critically aware of his fictions that he will puncture his own tragic rhetoric with a comic self-irony that is quite charming and humanizing. For while the Consul is an *alazon,* "an imposter in the sense that he is self-deceived or made dizzy by hubris" [Northrop Frye, *Anatomy of Criticism*], he is also an ironist who occasionally reveals unexpected levels of self-knowledge and judgment. Yet the irony is not merely reductive; it works in both directions, finding some truth in both his postures and his self-mockery.

The Consul's problem is that this perspectivism holds him in suspension. Knowing his tragic identity to be at once authentic and delusory, he is paralysed—and through his paralysis the tragedy becomes authentic by default. Lowry himself cannot make up his mind about the dilemma. While he encourages the reader to sympathize with the Consul's internal constraints, he also seems to levy a judgment on his paralysis, particularly in the political context. Yet it is significant that the only model of selfless and fruitful striving, Juan Cerillo, is absent from the ruined garden. No character in the novel succeeds in pulling himself out of the subjective mire. Even when the Consul judges himself, facing death (the final critique of his paralysis), Lowry backs away from the judgment through the paradox of death as a "real abstraction":

> . . . he had become . . . the pilferer of meaningless muddled ideas out of which his rejection

of life had grown, who had worn his two or three little bowler hats, his disguises, over these abstractions: now the realist of them all was close.

Yet out of this relativistic chaos, one incontrovertible truth emerges: that all the fictions are human fictions, with palpable effects on human joy and suffering. The Consul has steadily been driven by his past to pursue his future; his situation derives a mesmerizing unreality from the intense vertigo of defining himself in flux. When his fictions issue in praxis, when his spiritual tragedy becomes bodily, the Consul is taken by surprise: "Now he realized he had been shot. . . . 'Christ,' he remarked, puzzled, 'this is a dingy way to die.' "

Here the determining past at last collides with the projected future, and image and fact become one—the Consul is what he has become, and his reflexiveness falls away. This is his anagnorisis, "the recognition of the determined shape of the life he has created for himself . . . [and of] the uncreated life he has forsaken" [Frye, *Anatomy of Criticism*]. The Consul finally rejoins humanity, from which he has long alienated himself, in a community of suffering: " . . . someone had called him 'compañero' " . . . It made him happy". His suffering also releases the Consul from the burden of moral judgment:

> Not that the truth is "bad" or "good": it simply *is,* is incomprehensible . . . being perpetually protean. Hence a final need probably for an acceptance of one's limitations, and of the absurd in oneself.

> ["Ghostkeeper"]

Here is the afterglow of catharsis, a balm which Lowry felt compelled to provide. In most tragedies, a sense of inexorable movement toward a goal helps to relieve the suffering. The Consul's reflexiveness threatens that movement: instead of progress, we confront the dreadful possibility of an endless, meaningless shuttling between image and action. The Consul's death provides a momentary discharge of the tension into an event, a transitory pattern; yet the relief scarcely mitigates the claustrophobic terror of his reflexiveness. (pp. 62-9)

> *Stephen Tifft, "Tragedy as a Meditation on Itself: Reflexiveness in 'Under the Volcano','" in* The Art of Malcolm Lowry, *edited by Anne Smith, 1978. Reprint by Barnes & Noble Books, 1978, pp. 46-71.*

Ronald G. Walker   (essay date 1978)

[*Walker is an American critic. In the following excerpt, he evaluates the literal and figurative depiction of landscape in* Under the Volcano.]

The consideration of setting in imaginative writing involves an inescapable paradox. On the one hand the writer is at pains to create an environment in time and space which will provide the fictional action with a necessary dimensionality and which will convince the reader that he is confronting a world that is, in some sense, real and meaningful. Yet at the same time, even if there is an overt identification of the setting with an actual place such as

London or Hannibal or Tabasco, the writer will probably not wish to depend so heavily or exclusively on a literal verisimilitude that the reader expects to find—at the "correct" address—a municipal garden with all the streaks of the tulips therein numbered accurately. Instead the writer generally seeks a means by which he may exercise his prerogative to heighten reality where necessary in order to accommodate his imaginative vision while also satisfying in some manner the reader's instinctive desire for an intelligible orientation to the fictive world. Thus we find William Faulkner creating his own mythical kingdom complete with map and dates and social groupings; or D. H. Lawrence pitting the prosaic activities of the Mexico City drawing-room society against the ceremonials of the visionary company of Quetzalcoatl; or Graham Greene reconstructing the terrain and the boundaries of his "godless state" in southern Mexico, and synecdochizing the quality of life there by frequent references to various kinds of scavengers.

The paradoxical elements of place in fiction may be seen in perhaps their most extreme form in Malcolm Lowry's **Under the Volcano** (1947). In the justly celebrated letter to his English publisher Jonathan Cape [see excerpt in *TCLC,* Vol. 6, pp. 235-6] Lowry described his choice of setting for the novel as follows.

> The scene is Mexico, the meeting place, according to some, of mankind itself, pyre of Bierce and springboard of Hart Crane, the age-old arena of racial and political conflicts of every nature, and where a colorful native people of genius have a religion that we can roughly describe as one of death, so that it is a good place, at least as good as Lancashire, or Yorkshire, to set our drama of a man's struggle between the powers of darkness and light. Its geographical remoteness from us, as well as the closeness of its problems to our own, will assist the tragedy each in its own way. We can see it as the world itself, or the Garden of Eden, or both at once. Or we can see it as a kind of timeless symbol of the world on which we can place the Garden of Eden, the Tower of Babel and indeed anything else we please. It is paradisal: it is unquestionably infernal. It is, in fact, Mexico. . . .

Lowry's Mexico, then, is intended to be both the Mexico of history, where one can still find cantinas and cockroaches and the religion of death, and a land that lends itself with relative ease to the symbol-making eye of the imaginative observer. In choosing to view Mexico as both paradisal and infernal, Lowry lays claim to the same mythopoetical construct as Lawrence and Greene had before him. And his readiness to emphasize "unquestionably" the primacy of the infernal divulges which side of the duality has the greater hold on his imagination.

Critics have been sharply divided, however, over the degree of Lowry's success in **Under the Volcano** in rendering a locale that "is, in fact, Mexico." George Woodcock has asserted that the novel is "influenced and even dominated by the peculiar nature of Mexican existence." But the novelist William Gass goes to the opposite extreme in his observation that Lowry is "constructing a place, not describing one; he is making a Mexico for the mind where, strictly speaking, there are no menacing volcanoes, only menacing phrases. . . ." [see excerpt in *TCLC* Vol. 6, p. 244.] Lowry's biographer Douglas Day lends support to Gass's views when he contends that the Mexican setting of *Under the Volcano* is only an "accident of geography," that Lowry's fictional world is dominated by a landscape which is strictly within. Day believes that "like most visionary artists" Lowry

> was acutely egocentric: his gaze was almost always inward, so much so that he was very nearly blind to the world outside—except in so far as it reflected his own thoughts and feelings. From time to time he would try mightily to focus on something outside himself—the world situation, friends, wives, the sound of a voice, the color of a sky—and hope that alcohol would help him get through such adventures. But, of course, it only helped him back inside himself, where an elusive inner Malcolm Lowry alternately laughed at and sorrowed with his brilliant, incompetent outer self. Such a man could write only about himself, which is precisely what Lowry did. It would be a cliché to say that he wrote "thinly veiled autobiographies"; but it would be the truth.

Certainly there is much validity in Day's observations. Lowry was obviously a solipsistic writer given, with increasing frequency in later years, to observing himself in the act of observing himself. However, so far as *Under the Volcano* is concerned, it is a serious misjudgment to dismiss the choice of the Mexican setting as a mere accident of geography. For one thing, the visionary in Lowry found in the landscape and culture of Mexico a willing accomplice for his imaginative designs—something which he did not find in Canada, his other major fictional setting. As the Mexican novelist Carlos Fuentes has pointed out, "the physical nature of Mexico—a cruel, devouring, sunbaked landscape—is filled with portents of magical distraction. Every force of nature seems to have a mythical equivalent in Mexico. No nation is quite so totemic. . . ." Furthermore, the euhemeristic myth of Mexico's past fostered by the Revolution—with its emphasis on the integrity of indigenous cultures, the deracination of those cultures by the conquering Europeans, and the re-conquest of the homeland by modern Revolutionists—inspired Lowry to scrutinize Mexican history in search of events, figures, and patterns which would enrich his own "drama of a man's struggle between the powers of darkness and light."

That Lowry sought out those aspects of the Mexican scene which, as Day says, "reflected his own thoughts and feelings," there can be little doubt. For that matter, the same thing could be said of Lawrence, Huxley and Greene. None of the Mexican novels by these four English writers is really *about* Mexico, in the way that B. Traven's "jungle novels" clearly are. Rather, all four treat the ways in which their protagonists undergo a violent experience of self-revelation in a land which dramatizes and embodies their deepest anxieties and hopes in stark and elemental terms. In Mexico one encounters great extremes of various kinds existing side by side, openly, even blatantly. As Terence Wright has said, "Colourful, grotesque, savage, Mexico is a land outside the normal world, a land in which life

is 'tightened up a screw,' a land in which anything can happen" [see Further Reading]. In the case of *Under the Volcano* the particular role played by the Mexican setting is both large and varied, and it is well worth close attention.

Lowry's novel takes place for the most part in a town called Quauhnahuac (according to Lowry a Nahuatl word meaning "where eagle stops," from which the Spanish name Cuernavaca derives), located in the mountains about fifty miles south of Mexico City. In the extended description which opens the *Volcano* Lowry tells us that Quauhnahuac is a resort town of faded grandeur, with eighteen churches, fifty-seven cantinas, 400 swimming pools and many splendid hotels. Despite such accoutrements which have attracted a considerable population of foreigners, the town maintains beneath its surface something of the dark and threatening force of indigenous Mexico, a force which, as the following passage suggests, is inimical to modern civilization: "The walls of the town, which is built on a hill, are high, the streets and lanes tortuous and broken, the roads winding. A fine American-style highway leads in from the north but is lost in its narrow streets and comes out a goat track." In general, one might say that Lowry's Mexico has a similar blighting effect upon the four principal characters who incessantly wander its broken and winding paths.

Indeed, before the end of the novel two of these four people meet violent deaths, so it is not without significance that the action occurs on that peculiar Mexican holiday known as the Day of the Dead. More accurately, the story encompasses one full year beginning and ending on the Day of the Dead. Chapter I is set on November 2, 1939, exactly twelve months *after* the events recounted in the other eleven chapters have occurred. The Day of the Dead is the Mexican version of All Soul's Day. During this fiesta in Mexico one is likely to encounter such sights as Indian women in shawls peddling *flores para los muertos,* ragged children playing gaily with paper skeletons suspended on a string and gorging themselves on little pieces of bread or candy shaped into human skulls, ironic verses called *calaveras* (literally, skulls) printed in the newspapers "eulogizing" living persons as though they were dead, processions of mourners making their way to local cemeteries to honor their departed friends and relatives—and, if one is fortunate enough to be included in a native family's festivities, one may find that the favorite meal of deceased loved ones has been prepared and an extra place set at the table. As this description suggests, for Mexicans the fiesta of *los muertos* is an occasion for both sadness and gaiety. Perhaps it is this combination, along with the macabre trappings it has inspired, which frequently bewilders and intimidates so many foreign visitors who behold the spectacle.

The fiesta has its origins in the more harrowing death-rituals of the pre-Cortesian inhabitants of Mexico. While it is doubtful that many modern Mexicans bother to deliberate upon the more serious implications of their festival, the unabashed manner and the great popularity of the celebration do suggest that something of the ancient attitude toward death—that is, that death is a natural and positive part of the life process and is therefore to be neither ignored nor dreaded as the end of being—remains in the collective Mexican psyche. In his chapter on the Day of the Dead in *The Labyrinth of Solitude,* the poet Octavio Paz offers a provocative interpretation of the Mexican attitude toward death in relation to that quality of the national personality which Paz feels constricts daily life: solitude, masked by stoicism and *machismo.* In the century of "health, hygiene and contraceptives, miracle drugs and synthetic foods," the Mexican still maintains an intimate relation to death. He "jokes about it, caresses it, sleeps with it, celebrates it; it is one of his favorite toys and his most steadfast love. True, there is perhaps as much fear in his attitude as in that of others, but at least death is not hidden away: he looks at it face to face, with impatience, disdain or irony. . . ." Collectively, the Mexicans "are seduced by death. The fascination it exerts over us is the result, perhaps, of our hermit-like solitude and the fury with which we break out of it. The pressure of our vitality, which can only express itself in forms that betray it, explains the deadly nature, aggressive or suicidal, of our explosions. . . ."

In his only explicit commentary on these matters, Lowry's interpretation, if somewhat more affirmative, has much in common with that of Octavio Paz. Musing on the Zapotecan ruins at Monte Albán, Lowry writes:

> The sense of this past, of sorrow, of death: these are factors intrinsic in Mexico. Yet the [modern] Mexicans are the gayest of people, who turn every possible occasion, including the Day of the Dead, into a fiesta. The Mexicans laugh at death; that does not mean they don't take it seriously. It is perhaps only by the possession of a tragic sense of life such as theirs that joy and mirth find their place: it is an attitude that testifies to the dignity of man. Death . . . is tragic and comic at once.

This ambivalent attitude informs Lowry's treatment of the theme of death in *Under the Volcano,* though the tragic element is clearly dominant. The novel carries an enormous load of death and dying—and even, as we shall see, love of death. The first words in the novel spoken by the protagonist, Geoffrey Firmin, are these: " 'A corpse will be transported by express!' " In fact, these five iambs become a major refrain in the book. Not quite so poetic, almost the last thing Geoffrey says at the end is " 'Christ . . . this is a dingy way to die.' " In between these two lines there are (to mention but a few examples) a child's funeral, a hallucination of a man lying dead in a garden, references to the death and damnation of Marlowe's Doctor Faustus and to the House of Usher, a cantina called La Sepultura, scorpions who sting themselves to death, vultures "who wait only for the ratification of death," a dead dog lying at the bottom of a *barranca,* a wounded Indian found dying by the roadside, frequent allusions to the doomed Loyalist cause in Spain ("they are losing the battle of Ebro") and visions of the worse holocaust to come. The second of November is indeed a day of the dead in Quauhnahuac—a day which fairly crepitates with dying itself in 1938 and again with the painful memory of the dead a year later. "It should not be forgot-

ten," Lowry wrote to Jonathan Cape, "that on that day in Mexico the dead are supposed to commune with the living." As George Woodcock has aptly observed,

> the exaggerated Websterian violence in real life—which actually existed in Mexico until comparatively recently—provides the setting and the symbolism through which Lowry's characters and their disaster are raised out of the personal frame of their author's life and into an autonomous world where their adventures, sordid and pathetic in themselves, are realized on the level of genuine tragedy.

There is more to Lowry's Mexico, however, than death and tragedy alone. True, these are the primary strains, but the pattern as a whole is considerably more complicated. Chapter I, in which Lowry attempts above all to establish the emblematic terrain of his apocalyptic drama, contains some magnificent and suggestive descriptions of the mountainous landscape around Quauhnahuac—descriptions which, due as much to the suppleness of the style as to the kinesis perceived in the landscape, cannot rightly be called set-pieces.

> How continually, how startlingly, the landscape changed! Now the fields were full of stones: there was a row of dead trees. An abandoned plough, silhouetted against the sky, raised its arms to heaven in mute supplication; another planet, [Jacques Laruelle] reflected again, a strange planet where, if you looked a little further, beyond the Tres Marias, you would find every sort of landscape at once, the Cotswolds, Windermere, New Hampshire, the meadows of the Eure-et-Loire, even the grey dunes of Cheshire, even the Sahara, a planet upon which, in the twinkling of an eye, you could change climates, and, if you cared to think so, in the crossing of a highway, three civilizations; but beautiful, there was no denying its beauty, fatal or cleansing as it happened to be, the beauty of the Earthly Paradise itself.

With its snow-capped twin volcanoes, its lush gardens, and its thick and sprawling forests, the Mexican landscape beguiles with beauty. It seems indeed to be paradisal. But for this very reason, in *Under the Volcano,* the landscape ultimately emerges as a conspirator in Geoffrey Firmin's damnation. For the twisting path which carries one amidst all the apparently Edenic splendor invariably brings one to the brink of that ominous feature of the Mexican terrain which has been there all along at one's feet, waiting:

> [Laruelle] passed the model farm on his right, the buildings, the fields, the hills shadowy now in the swiftly gathering gloom. The Ferris wheel came into view again . . . then the trees rose up over it. The road, which was terrible and full of potholes, went steeply downhill here; he was approaching the little bridge over the barranca, the deep ravine. Halfway across the bridge he stopped . . . and leaned over the parapet, looking down. It was too dark to see the bottom, but: here was finality indeed, and cleavage! Quauhnahuac was like the times in this respect, wherever you turned the abyss was waiting for you

round the corner. Dormitory for vultures and city Moloch!

The pattern suggested by the two passages above—the redemptive ideal dissolving into infernal reality, the lost paradise, the reversal of beatific longing or expectation—is central to the novel. Douglas Day has offered a very useful commentary on this pattern in terms of what he calls the *chthonic* or earthbound level of meaning, "composed of natural elements either on or beneath the earth." Day points out that though Lowry's characters frequently dream of climbing the volcanic "magic mountains," they are sooner or later confronted with what lies *under* the volcano: the reeking, cloacal abyss. There is much talk of seeking water, the sea, fresh streams, a clear lake, but "the only water of significance in the novel is conspicuous by its absence: the cleansing, revivifying fountain [of life]. . . . Instead of water, we have alcohol. . . ." The many gardens which exist in the novel are mostly untended, ruined, overgrown. The forest which surrounds Quauhnahuac and the village of Parián where the last two chapters take place is equated with Dante's dark wood, and the winding path running through it leads only to colossal danger. Thus the various clusters of *chthonic* images gradually mesh into a web of doom which entraps the characters, not despite but precisely because they aspire to impossible transcendent ideals. The imagery, says Day, is

> archetypally demonic in nature: that is, it employs the traditional affirmative apocalyptic images of the Mount of Perfection, the fertile valley, the cleansing stream or fountain, and the blossoming garden, but employs them in an inverted, ironic form. What had indicated fruition, now indicates sterility; what had represented cleansing, now represents corruption, and what had symbolized the soul's striving upward toward salvation, now symbolizes the descent into damnation. It is of a world turned upside down that Lowry writes. . . .

It is difficult to think of another setting that could have suited Lowry's purposes in **Under the Volcano** as perfectly as did Mexico. (pp. 237-46)

> Ronald G. Walker, "The 'Barranca' of History: Mexico as Nexus of Doom in 'Under the Volcano', in his *Infernal Paradise: Mexico and the Modern English Novel, University of California Press, 1978, pp. 237-80.*

George Rhys Garnett　(essay date 1980)

[*In the following excerpt, Garnett discusses the Consul as a mythic figure who conforms to C. J. Jung's definition of the "hero" as an individual who extends human consciousness.*]

In chapter seven of **Under the Volcano,** Laruelle challenges the basic validity of the Consul's quest. The Consul first defends himself by stating that:

> 'You are interfering with my great battle . . . Against death . . . My battle for the survival of the human consciousness.'

"[I]t never occurred to me," wrote Lowry, in a letter published several years after **Under the Volcano,** "that consciousness itself could be of any aid, quite the contrary, and let alone a goal. . . ."

For a moment, the Consul is able to see this goal—the integration of unconscious contents into consciousness. Yet Laruelle, although essentially advising abandonment of this struggle, nevertheless points to what is lacking in the Consul's method of conducting his "great battle." It is, argues Laruelle, "precisely your inability to see . . . the things so important to us despised sober people, on which the balance of any human situation depends . . . that turns them into instruments of the disaster you have created yourself."

The Consul has indeed lost—or failed to find—"balance," and puts fatally at risk consciousness of any sort. The case Laruelle puts is for *normalcy,* a condition that is the equivalent of defeat for the Consul (as demonstrated by Laruelle himself, living in a state of permanent exile from his creative-destructive self). "But had they ever led a normal happy life," the Consul has asked himself, has it "ever been possible for them?" Laruelle's argument is not likely to convince one who in the darkness of the shadow has glimpsed a "brightness" infinitely more alluring than the pusillanimous compromise of Laruelle's normalcy.

> 'And you forget' [Laruelle adds] 'what you exclude from this, shall we say, feeling of omniscience. And at night, I imagine, or between drink and drink, which is a sort of night, what you have excluded, as if it resented that exclusion, returns—' 'I'll say it returns', the Consul said, listening at this point. . . .

What you have excluded, as if it resented that exclusion, returns—but what Laruelle fails to understand is that he is suggesting only an alternative and inferior form of exclusion. What the Consul would have to exclude from an attempt at "normal" life with Yvonne would *also* "as if it resented that exclusion" return. Laruelle's escape-route from conflict is inferior because it holds out no hope for growth—growth towards individuation—of the personality, merely the sealing off (in a dubiously secure persona) of what are for the Consul the sources of potential growth. The fascination and terror of the Farolito is that it may offer not only death but also rebirth for "the human consciousness."

" 'Facilis est descensus Averno,' " argues Laruelle, " 'it's too easy.' " " 'You deny the greatness of my battle? Even if I win. And I shall certainly win if I want to,' the Consul added. . . ." A real danger to the Consul is revealed here in this too glib and vainglorious assertion. The danger—described by Jung as "inflation"—is the Consul's presumptuous if intermittent belief that he can at any point control *by an act of will* those fundamental sources of human motivation and behaviour of which he has obtained such confused and uncertain yet vital knowledge. The danger is emphasized by a quotation that springs into his mind as he makes this statement:

> *Je crois que le vautour est doux à Prométhée et que les Ixion se plaisent en Enfers.*

" 'I love hell,' " he declares later, " 'I can't wait to get back there. . . .' " But between Prometheus and Ixion there appears to be a crucial distinction in achievement.

Prometheus stole fire from the gods and gave it to man; Ixion attempted to seduce the goddess Hera, Jove's wife, but was outwitted by Jove who "shaped a cloud into a false Hera with whom Ixion, being too far gone in drink to notice the deception, duly took his pleasure." He was scourged and bound "to a fiery wheel which rolled without cease through the sky." Both were punished for their presumptuousness, but whereas Prometheus' terrible punishment did not discredit that symbolic advance in *consciousness* for man that he achieved, Ixion's was a consequence both of presumptuousness and incapacity. He presumed to *know* the anima in her highest form, yet lacked the wisdom and alertness not to be deceived by the false anima that Jove created for him.

The Consul claims, in effect, to have Promethean ambitions ("My battle for the survival of human consciousness"). C. G. Jung provides his interpretation of the significance of the Prometheus myth—of the achievement of this "hero" and of his punishment:

> every step towards greater consciousness is a kind of Promethean guilt: through knowledge, the gods are as it were robbed of their fire, that is, something that was the property of the unconscious powers is torn out of its natural context and subordinated to the whims of the conscious mind. The man who has usurped the new knowledge suffers, however, a transformation or enlargement of consciousness, which no longer resembles that of his fellow men . . . but in doing so has alienated himself from humanity. The pain of this loneliness is the vengeance of the gods, for never again can he return to mankind. He is, as the myth says, chained to the lonely cliffs of the Caucasus, forsaken of God and man.

Elsewhere, he adds: "The crucifixion evidently betokens a state of agonizing bondage and suspension, fit punishment for one foolhardy enough to venture like a Prometheus into the orbit of the opposing principle."

Here, clearly enough, the punishment fits the crime; and both crime and punishment are undoubtedly heroic in stature. The Consul may, by implication, claim such heroic stature for *his* "battle." But is this claim entirely convincing? In some respects, he is perhaps closer to Ixion:

> The Consul was gazing upward dreamily at the Ferris wheel . . . tonight it would be lit up . . . the *wheel of the law rolling*. . . .

He, like Ixion, is drunkenly *un*-heroic when he penetrates *his* "false" anima, the Maria/Yvonne of the Farolito; and he too, like Ixion, is—albeit briefly—whirled helplessly round on the giant wheel of the "Infernal Machine" at the Quauhnahuac Carnival.

In a curious passage, he appears to become aware of this possibility—that his "battle" may be both presumptuous and futile (the passage is curious, because it is unclear whether it is spoken by Laruelle, by the Consul, or is a combination of both, merging within the Consul's mind):

To say nothing of what you lose, lose, lose, are losing, man. You fool, you stupid fool . . . You've even been insulated from the responsibility of genuine suffering . . . Even the suffering you do endure is largely un-necessary. Actually spurious. It lacks the very basis you require of it for its tragic nature. You deceive yourself. . . .

He then sees a sign being nailed to a tree: "*Le gusta este jardin.* . . ." It is a sign which recurrently reproaches his neglect of the garden of the self, and sounds an ominous warning of his final incapacity to wrest the knowledge that he confusedly seeks from "the gods" who, whether he succeeds or fails, will exact their vengeance for the attempt. But how should he respond to this suggestion that his "suffering" is both self-indulgent and self-destructive? That the Consul's quest may well be presumptuous is a warning he ought to heed; and that it is being undertaken with unbalanced and flawed equipment he must—for survival's sake—recognize. Yet these signs and suggestions may be acting as do those voices and illusions which attempt to convince the Grail-seeking knight of his unworthiness or of the futility of his quest. And if he is, still, potentially *either* Ixion or Prometheus, only one consequence is at this stage certain—he has invited and will suffer the vengeance of the "gods."

Prometheus, although "crucified" in punishment, first returned with the gift of fire for mankind. But what of a would-be thief of fire who is consumed by the prize that he seeks? Is his whole endeavour thereby rendered worthless, shown to be both "spurious" and futile? If so, it would be difficult to explain why, and how, such myths still persist and still fascinate. "Man started from an unconscious state," wrote Jung, "and has ever strived for greater consciousness. The development of consciousness is the burden, the suffering, and the blessing of mankind," and: "Every advance in culture is, psychologically, an extension of consciousness," and the role of the individual, the "hero," is to cut "a new path through hitherto untrodden territory. . . ." Additionally, he states that: "The goal is important only as an idea: the essential thing is the *opus* which leads to the goal: *that* is the goal of a lifetime."

It is arguable, therefore, that the question of whether or not the Consul's heroic-tragic pretensions are justifiable need not be answered only in terms of his success or failure in achieving a "goal" that he is, indeed, never able to identify (yet which is imposed most vividly in his dream-vision of "the mighty mountain Himavat"). It can be answered also in terms of the *nature* and *quality* of his "opus." In these respects, perhaps, he can be shown to be triumphant—not in his "fall," but in the nature and persistence of his quest, in the "extension of consciousness" *towards* enabling "Modern man . . . to know how he is to reconcile himself with his own nature—how he is to love the enemy in his own heart and call the wolf his brother."

"The myth of the hero," wrote Jung, " . . . is first and foremost a self-representation of the longing of the unconscious, of its unquenched and unquenchable desire for the light of consciousness." *Under the Volcano* embodies such a myth, and the Consul is such a hero. (pp. 31-4)

The value of **Under the Volcano** does not depend on the success of its hero in carrying the myth through its full cycle, but in *revitalizing* the myth in its crucial central stage. I quoted Jung as stating that "Every advance in culture, is psychologically an extension of consciousness," the role of the individual being to cut "a new path through hitherto untrodden territory." Paradoxically, this "new" path may be a very old path; the path pursued by the Consul has, in a sense, been trodden before—by those medieval alchemists whose parables and formulae Jung demonstrates to be, at best, profound explorations of the process of individuation; and by writers such as Melville, Poe, Baudelaire, Goethe, to whom Lowry pays more than occasional tribute; and, in innumerable myths and legends, by "the hero with a thousand faces."

The important achievement, Jung argues, is "not to *know* the truth, but to experience it." In this instance, "knowledge" appears to mean intellectual understanding, and "experience" to be equivalent to the *combination* of intellectual understanding with emotional—with the "feeling value" of the experience . . .[To] read **Under the Volcano** and to absorb its imaginative revitalization of the aspects of the myth with which it is centrally concerned, this is to move very much further towards "experience." And the value of this experience depends, crucially, upon the imaginative vitality and profundity with which the myth is explored. A playing with myth, as a kind of decorative embellishment to art, or as a more or less pretentious assertion of the universality and (therefore!) profundity of the theme that is treated, is likely to have the effect not of revitalizing the myth and its symbols, but of trivializing and thereby devaluing them (a process that is frequently at work in the "consciousness" of Dana Hilliot, and which can arguably be seen to operate, for example, in the drama of Jean Anouilh, and the fiction of John Fowles or John Barth).

Jung states:

> Eternal truth needs a human language that alters with the spirit of the times. The primordial images undergo ceaseless transformation and yet remain ever the same, but only in a new form can they be understood anew.

This statement contains the key to Lowry's achievement in **Under the Volcano.** "Not for a moment," declares Jung, "dare we succumb to the illusion that an archetype can be finally explained and disposed of. Even the best attempts at explanation are only more or less successful translations into another metaphorical language. (Indeed, language itself, is only an image.) *The most we can do is to dream the myth onwards* and give it a modern dress." In **Under the Volcano** Lowry attempted not to explain the myth ("knowledge") but both to explore and to reformulate it, and by doing so to enable the reader to *experience* it—indeed, to enable *himself* to experience it. This attempt to "dream the myth onwards and give it a modern dress" is triumphantly successful.

In this sense, Lowry is the hero who wrests meaning from the chaos of his life. In **Under the Volcano** he brings back into "common-day life" a complex yet integrated symbol of the powers of consciousness to penetrate and discover vital meanings within the ever-threatening darkness of the unconscious. That this achievement gave meaning to a life otherwise characterized by a most painful and pathetic *inability* to come to terms with a (therefore) most hostile and destructive libido, is all too evident in his biography. That the achievement simultaneously exhausted his potential for any further sustained struggle towards conscious-unconscious integration, is similarly demonstrated both in the life and the work of his last ten years.

What Lowry confronts us with in **Under the Volcano,** if we seriously attempt to enter its world and to "dream the myth onwards," is what Jung regards as a crucial moral problem:

> The shadow is a moral problem that challenges the whole ego-personality, for no-one can become conscious of the shadow without considerable moral effort. To become conscious of it involves recognizing the dark aspects of the personality as *present* and *real.* This act is the essential condition for any kind of self-knowledge.
> [My italics.]

"Knowledge" of this problem is of strictly limited value; "experience" is essential if the problem is to be regarded as "real" rather than (merely) theoretical or suppositional. In so far as such experience can be provided by art—specifically, by literature—it must be discovered for us, and by us, through the symbol—not, as Jung emphasizes, a symbol reduced to sign and "finally explained and disposed of," but a symbol which finds "a human language" that has altered "with the spirit of the times," a "new form" in which it can be "understood anew." "Wholeness," writes Jung, "is realized for a moment only—the moment that Faust was seeking all his life." The Consul fails to resolve the moral problem of the shadow, yet Lowry convinces us that his striving for "greater consciousness," both in spite of and because of its all too human confusion and limitation, is potentially the "blessing," as well as actually the "burden, the suffering . . . of mankind"; and he does so by finding a "human language" that is able to symbolize not only "the dark aspects of the personality as present and real," but also to realize convincingly and "for a moment only" in the Consul's psyche such a moment as "Faust was seeking all his life," the glimpse of the beauty and intensity of "Wholeness" so briefly and poignantly achieved in the Consul's dream-vision of "the mighty mountain Himavat."

Jung writes that "One does not become enlightened by imagining figures of light, but by making the darkness conscious." In an essay "On the Relation of Analytical Psychology to Poetry," he explains how he believes the writer can contribute to this Promethean task:

> The creative process, so far as we are able to follow it at all, consists in the unconscious activation of an archetypal image, and in elaborating and shaping this image into the finished work. By giving it shape, the artist translates it into the language of the present, and so makes it possible for us to find our way back to the deepest springs of life. Therein lies the social significance of art: it is constantly at work educating the spirit of the age, conjuring up the forms in which the age is

most lacking. The unsatisfied yearning of the artist reaches back to the primordial image in the unconscious which is best fitted to compensate the inadequacy and one-sidedness of the present. The artist seizes on this image, and in raising it from deepest unconscious he bring it into relation with conscious values, thereby transforming it until it can be accepted by the minds of his contemporaries according to their powers.

That Lowry is such an artist as Jung describes here could be established by the identification of archetypal images that become activated in his key works and, by a detailed examination of the elaboration and shaping of these images, their translation into "the language of the present." Such an examination would show *how* this artist, having seized upon these images—or, rather, having found these images thrust upon him—brings them "into relation with conscious values," how through language, the medium of his art, he makes visible to us the inner vitality of those forces that live in "darkness" and their "unquenched and unquenchable desire for the light of consciousness." (pp. 37-9)

> *George Rhys Garnett, "The Myth of the Hero," in* Canadian Literature, *No. 84, Spring, 1980, pp. 31-40.*

Ronald Binns   (essay date 1984)

[*In the following excerpt, Binns discusses* Under the Volcano *as a work whose encyclopedic structure precludes fixed meanings.*]

'A civilization,' Yeats wrote, 'is a struggle to keep self-control, and in this it is like some great tragic person.' In **Lunar Caustic** Lowry had portrayed four characters whose derangement was intended as an expression of the malaise of civilization; **Under the Volcano** repeats this formula, switching the action from New York in 1936 to a fictional town in Mexico in the autumn of 1938. Lowry's novel is set on a single day, and in this it bears some resemblance to Joyce's *Ulysses* (1922) and Virginia Woolf's *Mrs Dalloway* (1925).

Sartre proclaimed the importance of Joyce's example to post-war writers, arguing that faced by the urgent imperatives of modern history the great technical problem was 'to find an orchestration of consciousness which may permit [the writer] to render the multi-dimensionality of the event.' Twentieth-century history actually plays little part in *Ulysses*. Joyce (who wrote his novel between 1914 and 1921) was intent on memorializing Edwardian Dublin on 16 June 1904, and neither the outbreak of war in 1914 nor the 1916 Easter Rising (which resulted in the destruction of Dublin's city centre) deflected him from that task. Despite its experimentalism *Ulysses* now seems like the last Victorian novel, an exhaustive portrait of a provincial backwater expressing little sense of evil or violence. (pp. 42-3)

In *Mrs Dalloway* and **Under the Volcano** we witness the forces of modern history beginning to rupture the liberal-humanist values which Joyce chose to celebrate. Woolf's

novel, which is set on a June day in 1923, takes us to the heart of British society at a specific historical moment and shows us the moral disintegration of its ruling class. Clarissa Dalloway's Westminster society is one where people 'solidify young' and become dull, reactionary, mired in convention. (Woolf originally conceived that Mrs Dalloway's response to this bloodless high Tory society should be suicide.) It is a class which has lost the will to govern. The signs of its passing are indicated on the margins: the spectre of Labour rule, rebellion in India. The strokes of Big Ben which sound through the novel seem to be tolling its doom.

As social prophecy *Mrs Dalloway* proved to be wide of the mark. One year after its publication the outcome of the General Strike showed that the Richard Dalloways were still very much in control. Stasis, stagnation, insularity remained the order of the day. A dozen years later, George Orwell, returning from the Spanish civil war, grumbled that England was still a place where it was difficult

> to believe that anything is really happening anywhere. Earthquakes in Japan, famines in China, revolutions in Mexico? Don't worry, the milk will be on the doorstep tomorrow morning, the *New Statesman* will come out on Friday. [. . .] it was still the England I had known in my childhood [. . .] the men in bowler hats, the pigeons in Trafalgar Square, the red buses, the blue policemen—all sleeping the deep, deep sleep of England, from which I sometimes fear that we shall never wake till we are jerked out of it by the roar of bombs.

Lowry possibly had this passage in mind in the scene where Hugh hears the Consul's snores 'wafted to his ears: the muted voice of England long asleep.' The Consul *is,* to an extent, England, and the contemporary historical context forms an inescapable part of his decline.

Lowry situates the main action of the novel on 2 November 1938, shortly after the Munich agreement was signed. The Spanish civil war was then in its closing stages and provides a constant reference point in the novel. There are references to Hitler, Stalin, Chamberlain, Gandhi, Nehru, the Italian invasion of Abyssinia. More pressingly, there is the domestic crisis of Mexican politics. In 1938 Mexico was torn by political divisions. President Cárdenas, a populist socialist, supported the democratic side in the Spanish civil war, expropriated the holdings of foreign oil companies, gave Trotsky exile, closed down the Casinos, and embarked on a radical programme of land redistribution. In parts of the country law and order had broken down and various fascists and paramilitary groups plotted against the socialist government, including the fanatical Catholic *sinarquistas* and the Union Militar of General Almazán. All these aspects of the political crisis enter into **Under the Volcano.** The Consul's world-weary liberal humanism might not have been out of place in Clarissa Dalloway's drawing room, but in Mexico it is absurdly, even dangerously inappropriate.

Lowry's provincial town in Mexico is (rather like Conrad's Africa but unlike Joyce's Dublin) a reflector of the condition of western civilization, packed with symptoms of decay and impending catastrophe. The opening page of the novel establishes Quauhnahuac's global centrality. In the first paragraph the perspective is an aerial one, reminiscent of the zooming-in-on-a-map technique which featured in the opening sequences of many 1940s movies (a stereotype recently parodied at the start of David Hare's *Saigon—Year of the Cat* (1983). The second paragraph develops the clichéd cheerfulness of tourist brochures and advertising (the reference to *fifty-seven* cantinas sounds suspiciously like an echo of the famous Heinz advertising slogan). The irony of this is quickly made apparent. These opening pages establish a pervasive mood of entropy and decay. Words like *desolate, ruined, empty, mournful, deserted, melancholy* make the first of their numerous appearances in the text. In a manner which resembles the opening pages of *Nostromo* and *A Passage to India* Lowry establishes the symbolic nature of the terrain.

Quauhnahuac is a waste land, littered with wreckage. Its universality is again stressed: it is a place where you encounter 'every sort of landscape at once'—English, French, American, African. It resembles Eden but it is a paradise where the Day of Wrath has arrived. The 'dark swift horses surging up the sky' signify the arrival of the four horsemen of the apocalypse; the 'immense archangel, black as thunder' seems to have flown straight out of the Book of Revelation.

It is against this landscape that Geoffrey Firmin's tragedy

Margerie Lowry.

is enacted. Significantly, the four main characters are nationals of major world powers. Laruelle is French, Yvonne American, Hugh and the Consul English (Anglo-Indians, representatives of the British Empire, to be precise). The Consul is an ex-public school, ex-Cambridge man, a member of the governing class. As a former Consul he has directly represented the Crown. His attitude to the dying Indian is one of cautious non-involvement. Like the British government of Neville Chamberlain in the face of aggression by Hitler, Mussolini and Franco he shies away from *doing* anything. Ultimately this attitude rebounds upon him and he finds himself in the same situation as the Indian (or democratic Spain), attacked by fascists, dying alone and friendless.

The political theme is first introduced in chapter 1, from Laruelle's retrospective viewpoint. The Frenchman recalls Señor Bustamente's suggestion that the Consul was actually not really a diplomat at all but a spy—something Laruelle breezily dismisses. But Laruelle reveals himself to be an astonishingly complacent and egocentric individual. His attitude to the outbreak of the Second World War is bland in the extreme: 'He had few emotions about the war, save that it was bad. One side or the other would win. And in either case life would be hard. Though if the Allies lost it would be harder. And in either case one's own battle would go on.' This demonstrates something more solidly established later in the book: that where anything is concerned Laruelle thinks first of all of himself. He regards the fascist Unión Militar merely as 'tiresome'. He considers making a version of the Faustus story with someone like Trotsky for its protagonist, which as [Roger] Bromley points out is 'a false cultural-political synthesis [. . .] Laruelle's intention would transform Trotsky into a cultural fiction and downgrade his real significance' ["The Boundaries of Commitment: God, Lover, Comrade—Malcolm Lowry's *Under the Volcano* as a Reading of the 1930's," in Francis Barker, ed., *The Sociology of Literature,* Vol. 1]. (There is also the irony that the downfall of the Consul—who at one point is jeeringly identified as Trotsky because of his beard—can be seen as precisely the sort of Faustian tragedy Laruelle envisages, though the Frenchman seems blind to this.) When Laruelle reveals that Sr Bustamente seemed half-convinced that he had been taken in about the Consul's identity it is clear that Sr Bustamente may well be right. Later in the book there is plenty of evidence that the Consul may well be under surveillance, and if he gave the impression 'of a man living in continual terror of his life' we can only recall (as Laruelle does not) that he was indeed murdered by the political police. (There is also the question of the Consul's relationship with Señora Gregorio, who, we are cryptically told, 'had had some difficult explanations to make.')

The Consul actually seems remarkably well-informed about local politics. At Laruelle's house the names of his murderer's accomplices jump out of the telephone directory at him, a coincidence which is nowhere explained. He points out one of the local 'fascist joints' to Hugh, and tries to tell him (Hugh is deep in conversation with Yvonne and doesn't hear) that the Farolito is a local Nazi headquarters. Later, Hugh explains to Yvonne that the dying Indian may have been a messenger for the socialist government's Ejidal bank, but concludes (wrongly) that the fascists 'don't [. . .] have any hold here to speak of.'

The murder of Geoffrey Firmin is ambiguous and open to a variety of interpretations. The Consul sees the deputies as 'phantoms of himself,' an explanation accepted by many critics. There are other constructions which we can put upon the episode, however. The political sub-plot which runs through the novel prepares us for the possibility that the Consul is indeed a spy, working for the British government against the pro-Axis Unión Militar. The Chief of Rostrums may have a concrete political motive for disposing of him. Or it may be that the fascists have confused Geoffrey's identity with that of his anarchist-card-carrying brother. Or it may simply be that the vigilantes are responding in a typically Mexican fashion to the verbal and physical assaults of the drunken, belligerent Consul.

Mexico still has one of the highest murder rates in the world. Graham Greene, who was in Mexico in 1938, noted how 'Several people had been shot by a police chief in a quarrel—that was the regular feature of a Mexican paper; no day passed without somebody's being assassinated somewhere.'

Under the Volcano counterpoises two basic political positions: to change the world (through socialism or art) or to accept it. Laruelle dreams of making great films and effecting a cultural transformation, but the novel places him as a failure, past his prime.

> Yet in the Earthly Paradise, what had he done?
> He had made few friends. He had acquired a
> Mexican mistress with whom he quarrelled, and
> numerous beautiful Mayan idols he would be
> unable to take out of the country, and he had—
> M. Laruelle wondered if it was going to rain.

As Laruelle himself dimly perceives, the sum of his achievements simply doesn't bear thinking about. His life is dead; he is merely a consumer, one who acquires objects, both animate and inanimate.

Hugh seems a more commanding figure, troubled by his conscience, haunted by the Spanish civil war, determined to be involved. But he, too, is revealed as inadequate, 'a professional indoor Marxman' who for all his talk of fight and engagement takes on nothing more strenuous than the procession of wooden ducks which he shoots at at the fairground. Significantly, he is the Consul's *half*-brother, symbolically incomplete, someone who is to be found 'stretching himself to his full mental height of six foot two (he was five feet eleven).' The ideal of revolutionary socialism is represented more convincingly by Hugh's friend, Juan Cerillo. Cerillo is a native Mexican who has fought for Republican Spain and who is working (like the murdered Indian) for the Ejidal bank. Cerillo does not put in an appearance in the novel but remains off-stage, a remote, fleetingly presented ideal in Hugh's mind. He is, importantly, the only character of significance who is not subjected to irony.

The episode involving the dying Indian brings Hugh's concerns to the fore. As a messenger for the Ejidal the Indian provides a concrete example of a man victimized by the forces of fascism and repression. He also represents the condition of contemporary Spain. The Indian's dying word *compañero* ('comrade') was the word of greeting used by the Spanish republicans. The two-hatted *pelado* with the crucifix who steals the Indian's money represents the combined force of Catholic-Francoist reaction, and the two diplomatic cars which speed past are obviously intended to symbolize France and Britain.

Set against Hugh's passionate, intoxicated desire for social transformation is the blithe indifference of Yvonne and the weary cynicism of the Consul. Yvonne is wealthy and rootless, the daughter of an American Consul who later became a failed capitalist. Her background makes her kin with the forces of imperialism and exploitation. She has been brought up by a wealthy uncle with financial interests in South America. Hugh apostrophizes her as the archetypal product of 'centuries of oppression.' Yvonne is only dimly aware of the shattering changes which Cárdenas is instituting in Mexico:

> 'Isn't it an adorable farm,' Yvonne said. 'I believe it's some government experiment. I'd love to have a farm like that. . . .

Her blindness to the real state of things is pinpointed by her failure either to notice the bloodstained coins in the *pelado*'s hands or to realize their significance. As [Robert Heilman] noted in 1947 [see excerpt above], 'Yvonne can't stand the sight of blood: it is her flaw, her way of acquiescing in the *de facto*.' (In fact Yvonne turns away not at the sight of blood but at the *suspicion* of it.)

Yvonne's indifference to political reality is symptomatic of her narcissism. She is a worldling, nothing more. (Laruelle's translated Shakespeare points up the ironic difference between 'merry wives' and 'Joyeuses Bourgeoises'.) The Consul's self-absorption is compounded of more complex matter. Despite his fascination with occultism and the realms of the transcendental the Consul has some distinctly earthbound interests which put him, too, among the exploiters of mankind. He has been sued for back wages by one or more of his servants; he owns property; he evidently plays the stock exchange; he refers mysteriously to his 'habit of making money.' As Stephen Tifft points out, the Consul is not entirely an exemplary figure: 'While [Lowry] encourages the reader to sympathize with the Consul's internal constraints, he also seems to levy a judgement on his paralysis, particularly in the political context' [see excerpt dated 1978].

The shadow which the Spanish civil war casts over the novel underlines the urgency of the case which Hugh is making, however ineptly, for social change. When the Consul pictures his soul as 'a town ravaged and stricken in the black path of his excess [. . .] the whole town plunged into darkness, where communication is lost, motion mere obstruction, bombs threaten, ideas stampede—' Lowry probably intends to evoke the bombing of Guernica. The novel looks ahead to the horrors of the Second World War; Hugh has a monstrous vision of 'children piled up, many hundreds,' an image echoed at the end by the dying Consul's prophetic glimpse of 'ten million burning bodies.' The imperatives of the Spanish after-text are solemnly exclamatory, as if time is running out.

Roger Bromley has argued that Lowry is

> a writer who probably offers the most searching interrogation of the violence exercised by the symbolic forms of power in Western society since Lawrence. [. . .] At one point in *The Fate of the Earth,* Jonathan Schell says, 'We deny the truth that is all around us. Indifferent to the future of our kind, we grow indifferent to one another. We drift apart. We grow cold. We drowse our way toward the end of the world. . . .' It is not too pretentious, or fanciful I hope, to suggest that this is at the heart of **Under the Volcano,** the failure of Western society to reproduce itself in forms other than those of tyranny, fissure, and destruction.

This is a salutary contemporary reading which makes **Under the Volcano** relevant to our own time. But I am reminded of Tariq Ali's strictures on *Midnight's Children* (1981). Salman Rushdie has asserted that the multitudinous teeming form of his novel 'is the optimistic counterweight to Saleem's personal tragedy. I do not think that a book written in such a manner can really be called a despairing work. But, Ali argues, this defence is not totally convincing; there is a streak of pessimism and nihilism in *Midnight's Children* which is inescapable and, of course, understandable as a modern vision. **Under the Volcano** likewise possesses a strong undercurrent of nihilism. The Consul scornfully spurns his brother's socialism:

> Can't you see there's a sort of determinism about the fate of nations? They all seem to get what they deserve in the long run. [. . .] Not so long ago it was poor little defenceless Ethiopia. Before that, poor little defenceless Flanders. To say nothing of course of the poor little defenceless Belgian Congo. And tomorrow it will be poor little defenceless Latvia. Or Finland. Or Piddledeedee. Or even Russia. Read history. Go back a thousand years. What is the use of interfering with its worthless stupid course?

There is much in **Under the Volcano** that lends support to the Consul's despairing *Weltanschauung.* Lowry portrays Hugh's grasp of Mexican politics as pathetically obtuse; ironically it is the Consul who seems to know exactly what the local fascists are up to. On the bus it is, revealingly, not Hugh but the Consul who spots the *pelado* is a thief. In their drunken argument at the restaurant the dice are loaded in the Consul's favour. The angry outburst quoted above is historically prescient. In the year after the Consul's murder Latvia was occupied by the Soviet army. Finland was invaded by the USSR on 30 November 1939. In June 1941 Russia was in turn invaded, by Germany. The Consul, apparently only a self-deluding drunk, actually possesses a clairvoyant insight into the future.

The course of Mexican history, as represented by Lowry, seems to justify the Consul's despair. In the sixteenth century Cortés conquered Mexico with the assistance of his Indian mistress and the treacherous Tlaxcalans. In 1846 the USA declared war and seized half of Mexico. In the 1860s Napoleon III encouraged his ambitious young son the Archduke Maximilian of Austria to accept the crown of Mexico, then betrayed him by withdrawing the troops on which his power rested. Maximilian surrendered to the rebel forces and was shot on the orders of Juarez. His wife, Carlotta, went mad. In 1876 Porfirio Diaz launched a revolution but betrayed his country by handing over the land to foreign owners. (Hugh's reverie about Juan Cerillo in chapter 4 describes this phase of Mexican history; significantly Cerillo's father fought with Huerta but then turned traitor.) By the twentieth century Mexico purported to have a socialist regime but it was one in name only. In 1934 Calles appointed Cardenas as the next puppet president. Cardenas promptly established a power base, expelled Calles from the country and set about putting some of the platitudes of the revolution into practice. The 1938 oil crisis and the conflict between socialists, Communists, fascists and Nazis brings the long history of Mexico's betrayals up to the present time of the novel. **Under the Volcano** seems to suggest that history is merely a perpetual process of betrayal and exploitation, of conquerors and victims.

Hugh, Laruelle and Yvonne are themselves part of this pattern. They have each betrayed the Consul. But the Consul is equally burdened with sexual guilt (the Hell Bunker, Lee Maitland). At the same time as Hugh and Yvonne are becoming drawn into a compromising situation in the woods, the Consul is lured, not unwillingly, into the prostitute's room. In addition all four are citizens and representatives of imperialist nations which have preyed on Mexico, and the Consul is perhaps more involved in exploitation than any of them (his mysterious phone call from Tom implies murky share dealings). Like the *pelado* the Consul is both exploited and exploiting. The last two words spoken to him after he has been shot are *pelado* and *compañero,* signifying the polar extremes of self-absorption and comradeship.

Self-absorption, however, is the very condition of the text itself. **Under the Volcano** is curiously self-regarding, both physically, as a book, and as a fiction. Lowry was acutely conscious of the physical appearance of the printed page, advising (for example) in chapter 10, 'some experiment [. . .] with the typesetting such as the occasional use of black letter for the headings juxtaposed with anything from cursive down to diamond type for the rest.' Each page is a visual feast for the eye. The typography forms an integral part of the meaning of the book. It is often used to indicate distortions or displacements of consciousness. Characteristic devices are paragraphs which end with ellipses, and apostrophes which simply enclose (instead of the expected dialogue) other syntactical figures—a hyphen or a hyphen and a question-mark. These sets of three dots and hyphens point to areas of discourse which are being suppressed (perhaps because they are too painful to be communicated). Spanish syntax is introduced to defamiliarize Lowry's fictional world, the upside-down exclamation marks and questionmarks buttressing the reader's impression of a topsy-turvy Alice-in-Wonderland reality. Italic type (significantly a *sloping* type) indicates the irruption of foreign words into the customary discourse of the novel. The general effect is of a breaking-down and blurring of any single homogenous stable reality.

The narrative has a cyclical structure, in which (like the Quauhnahuac cinema) 'the same features come back over and over again.' Lowry may have learned something from *Finnegans Wake* (1939), published while he was working on *Under the Volcano.* Like Joyce he sought to create a kind of timeless narrative continuum; at the end of the book the reader is expected to turn back to the first page and begin again. The structural image of the wheel recurs in numerous forms in *Under the Volcano* (the Ferris wheel, the 'infernal' looping-the-loop machine, the madman with an old bicycle tyre, the wheeling planets, the constellations), signifying eternity. Time is imprisoning and inescapable. Lowry stresses the fictionality of his characters. They are figures locked into a larger structure, illusory phantoms endlessly repeating situations over which they have no control. Lowry was fond of 'the Bergsonian idea that the sense of time is merely an inhibition to prevent everything happening at once—brooding upon which it is pretty difficult to avoid some notion of eternal recurrence.' He used a wide range of hermetic literature (astrology, the Tarot, the Cabbala, and the writings of pop metaphysicians like J. W. Dunne, Charles Fort and P. D. Ouspensky) in establishing the cosmology of his fictional universe.

There are three major spiritual symbols in the novel—the ruined garden, the hellish abyss, and the faraway celestial mountain. The Consul is at the centre of this triangle of possibilities, gazing back at the garden he has made into a Waste Land. As his name (an anagram of 'infirm') implies, he is the modern Fisher King. His sacrifice is necessary in order that the arid land can be made fertile once again. The Consul also possesses some of the attributes of the Magician, the Fool and the Hanged Man in the Tarot pack. He is trapped in a demonic universe in which satanic agents—dogs, scorpions, a malevolent sunflower—are tangibly and terrifyingly present. Lowry's use of numerology reinforces this sense of a meshed, imprisoning world. Quauhnahuac is situated on the nineteenth parallel and the Consul is doomed to die at nineteen hundred hours. When the Consul tries, unsuccessfully, to make a telephone call, the number that jumps out at him is 666, the number of the horned beast in the book of Revelation.

What Lowry called the 'borrowings, echoes, design-governing postures' derived from other texts and bodies of knowledge are present in abundance in *Under the Volcano.* The narrative draws upon material as diverse as astronomy, Indian mythology, Mexican history, global geography, music, painting, geomorphology, drama, metaphysics, politics, poetry and other novels. *Under the Volcano* aspires (as other encyclopedic novels do) to be a book of books. It represents itself as a compendium of world literature, recreating the fictions of the past.

A major literary analogue is Dante's *Divine Comedy.* The infernal aspect of Lowry's Mexico is comically signalled by the demon brandishing a pitchfork on the label of Laruelle's bottle of beer. Lowry twice refers to the famous opening lines of the *Inferno:*

> Nel mezzo del cammin di nostra vita
> Mi ritrovai per una selva oscura
>
> (In the middle of our journey of life
> I woke to find myself in a dark wood)

On the first page of the novel we encounter the Hotel Casino de la Selva; later, Hugh half-quotes these lines at the start of chapter 6. There are a number of other allusions to woods, leading up to the real dark wood of chapter 11. Moreover at the close of chapter 1 a bell rings out *'dolente . . . dolore!',* echoing the words inscribed above the gates of Dante's hell:

> Per me si va nella città dolente,
> Per me si va nell' etterno dolore
>
> (Through me the way to the city of desolation,
> Through me the way to eternal sorrow)

At the end of the book the Consul is thrown into the abyss, which Hugh, alluding to the Eighth Circle of the *Inferno,* identifies as 'the Malebolge'. The point of these allusions is to indicate the tormented condition of Lowry's characters as they descend (the first line of chapter 8 is simply: 'Downhill . . . ') deeper into their private infernos, towards judgement. Lowry's characters are guilty of many of the failings of Dante's sinners—lust, deception, hypocrisy, theft, hoarding, the sowing of discord. Whereas Dante is guided through hell by the poet Virgil, embodying wisdom and morality, the fallen nature of modern man is signified by the vocation of the Consul's guide, Dr Vigil, a specialist in sexual diseases.

Lowry echoes a great number of other texts, including the Bible, the *Mahabharata,* Marlowe's *Dr Faustus,* Goethe's *Faust,* and Kafka's *The Castle* and *The Trial* in his evocation of the condition of mankind in 1938. Perhaps Lowry's most ambitious 're-telling' was of that other twentieth-century book-of-books, Joyce's *Ulysses.* The relationship between the Consul, Hugh and Yvonne presents many parallels to that of Bloom, Stephen Dedalus and Molly. The Consul's 'Greek e's' mirror Bloom's epistolary efforts ('Remember write Greek ees'). Like Bloom he talks to a cat, calculates what a sum of money would equal in terms of drinks, quotes *Hamlet,* is pursued by a stray dog, is featured sitting on the toilet and has his identity mistaken by phantasmagoric figures of authority. The list of books in Bloom's library and his budget for the day are both directly imitated in *Under the Volcano.* There are dozens of other allusions and echoes, of which the most audacious is Lowry's ironic echo of Molly's famous reply to Bloom's proposal. Hugh urges Yvonne out of the El Popo back into the dark wood, a suggestion which is partly sexual in motivation: 'Yvonne said yes.' But whereas Molly Bloom's last words ('I said yes I will Yes') signify fertility, affirmation, life, Yvonne's 'yes' is almost literally her last word, before her death.

In his decline the Consul relives some of the major myths of western civilization. He is Adam, about to be expelled from Paradise; Christ, the sacrificial scapegoat for man's sins; Dante, journeying through an inferno of the damned; Hamlet, disgusted by human sexuality, paralysed by the knowledge of betrayal; Faustus, due to be cast into hell for abusing his powers. (Although *Under the Volcano* sets out to be a book-of-books it is nevertheless very partial in its sources. Lowry completely passes over the tradition of Richardson, Fielding, Defoe, Jane Austen, Scott, Thackeray, George Eliot; his literary affiliations were fundamentally romantic and modernist. Lowry's sensibility was the opposite of Joyce's. [According to Richard Ellman] Joyce preferred his mythic voyagers to be 'men of substance and family' as opposed to 'Prometheus, Lucifer and Faust, those bachelors, disobedient sons and brilliant failures.')

There are hints that the Consul is a black magician, an identification with profound implications for the meaning of the novel:

> Yet who would have ever believed that some obscure man, sitting at the centre of the world in a bathroom, say, thinking solitary miserable thoughts, was authoring their doom.

The answer is that the reader is persuaded to believe it. It is important to understand the ways in which Lowry seeks to convince us that the Consul is somehow right to reject the alternatives proposed by the other three, that it is *his* vision of life which is the deepest, the most profound.

In chapter 7 Laruelle bitterly criticizes the Consul for his deviation from normal standards of good behaviour; in chapter 9 Yvonne tries to lure the Consul back to married life; in chapter 10 Hugh puts forward his belief in the brotherhood of man. The Consul spurns each of them and retires once more within himself. When critics consider these moments in the novel they invariably side with the Consul against the other characters. T. Bareham's description of the Consul as 'infinitely the most sensitive and intelligent person in the book' is a fairly typical one [see Further Reading].

Partly this is a matter of point-of-view. As Nabokov tartly remarks of a character in *Transparent Things* (1972), 'This Henry Emery Person, our Person's father, might be described as a well-meaning, earnest, dear little man, or as a wretched fraud, depending on the angle of light and position of the observer. From the intimacy of the Consul's mind the angle of light does not favour the other characters, and almost half the novel is seen through his eyes. But, more crucially, there is an underlying complicity between the narrative and the Consul. Lowry's fictional universe endorses the Consul's intuition of mysterious occult connections at the heart of things. Mexico emerges as a sinister, magical world of uncanny symmetries. The role of the pariah dogs as Faustian familiars or demons is underlined by puns: 'the pariah dog [. . .] appeared familiarly at heel'; 'It was a pariah dog and disturbingly familiar.' There are all kinds of odd reverberations in the novel. Dr Vigil's phrase 'progresión a ratos' ['journey from time to time'] is echoed by Zuzugoitea's semi-obscene 'Progression al culo' ['journey to the bottom']. The postman's grunt, 'Ei ei ei ei ei ei' is echoed by Laruelle's 'Ei ei ei ei'. Hugh's whinny, *'Wh-wh-wh-wh-wh-wh-wh-wh-wheeee-u,'* is echoed by Dr Vigil's 'Wheee'.

Lowry's fictional universe is one which perpetually duplicates and reduplicates itself. Connections are established, but they are sometimes absurd or irrational, more the fabric of a dream world than a naturalistic reality. Lowry explained that his intention was 'to make a noise like music' rather than to achieve a consistent realism. The narrative proceeds analogically and the real, historical world of 1938 often seems to crumble away into a dream world.

It is as if the whole novel is actually taking place inside the Consul's mind. The language and values of Hugh, Yvonne and Laruelle tend to express, surreptitiously, the Consul's. Hugh, for example, characterizes Yvonne as the archetypal American female:

> Women of medium height, slenderly built, mostly divorced, passionate but envious of the male—angel to him as he is bright or dark, yet unconscious destructive succubus of his ambitions—American women, with that rather graceful swift way of walking, with the clean scrubbed tanned faces of children, the skin finely textured with a satin sheen, their hair clean and shining as though just washed, and looking like that, but carelessly done, the slim brown hands that do not rock the cradle, the slender feet—how many centuries of oppression have produced them?

This is an extraordinary passage which goes to the heart of the narrative's contradictory presentation of Yvonne. Though Lowry tacks on a political motive for Hugh's spasm of revulsion (Yvonne doesn't care who will win the Spanish civil war), it is clear that what really repels him is her ruthless sexuality. Yvonne is both whore and angel, a mixture of experience (passionate, divorced) and childlike innocence, as beautiful and smartly dressed as a model but with revealingly brown skin. She is a threatening figure with (it is hinted) an indiscriminate sexual appetite. She spurns the claims of the nuclear family, since her hands will never 'rock the cradle'. She is also 'envious' of men, though why this should be so is not made clear, especially since the ways in which she destroys their ambitions are 'unconscious,' and the nature of those ambitions remains unspecified. It is as if Lowry wanted his heroine to seem like Nicole in Scott Fitzgerald's *Tender is the Night,* the destroyer of a man's promising career.

These thoughts are doubly curious coming from Hugh, who, unlike the furious and disgusted Consul, knows nothing of Yvonne's affair with Laruelle. Odd, too, is Hugh's particularly virulent branding of Yvonne as a 'destructive succubus'. This again highlights the sexual nature of his hostility (a succubus is a female demon supposed to have sexual intercourse with sleeping men). The term is a strange one for Hugh to use and belongs much more with the Consul's occult vocabulary.

Yvonne is the source of three other violent outbursts of sexual disgust in the novel, and each comes from the Consul: his reaction to the sight of Laruelle nude, his description of Yvonne's first husband's lovemaking, and his Shakespearean jeers at the other two in the restaurant. The passage in fact seems quite inconsistent with Hugh's character. He is unaware of Laruelle's role in Yvonne's life and seems quite free of sexual neuroses. There seems to be no reason, in the light of his progressive left-wing views, why he should be at all concerned about Yvonne's indifference to the bourgeois goal of settling down and raising a family. Lowry seems to have indulged in ventriloquism at this point in the novel, making Hugh express an attitude which more properly belongs to the Consul.

The Consul's jealousy of Laruelle colours the entire novel. The Frenchman's penis ('that hideously elongated cucumiform bundle of *blue* nerves and gills' (my italics)) is symbolically anticipated by his '*blue* polka-dotted scarf' (my italics), an 'extraordinary scarf that suggested M. Laruelle had once won a half-blue.' Freud suggested that 'In men's dreams a necktie often appears as a symbol for the penis [. . .] because neckties are long, dependent objects and peculiar to men'. The sexual link between Yvonne and Laruelle is signified by her smart *slate-blue* travelling suit, which the Consul associates with her latest lover, perhaps the mysterious Louis (hence that 'despondent American tune, the St Louis Blues'). Hugh has formerly been in a group compared to Venuti's Blue Four and the sexual link between the three men and Yvonne makes them, metaphorically, another 'blue four'. We also learn that Cliff Wright's '*rating as an eligible bachelor was absolutely blue ribbon.*' But Yvonne's first husband turns out to be unfaithful to her, not 'Mr Right' at all. Significantly the *pelado,* who has 'huge, capable and rapacious' hands, who is 'gathering strength for more debauchery' and who holds himself *erect,* also happens to be wearing a *blue* suit. Finally, at the end of the novel, the Consul takes his revenge on Yvonne with the prostitute, whose room is lit by 'a single blue electric bulb.'

Under the Volcano is packed with this kind of dream logic, where meaning multiplies in a blur of associations. Colours, numbers, even letters of the alphabet express buried symmetries and hidden meanings which the reader can locate and reassemble according to choice. Critics tend to talk about levels of meaning in *Under the Volcano,* but the metaphor is misleading. The novel's structure is not made up of distinct, discrete elements which can be neatly distinguished like the storeys of a building. There is, rather, an interpenetration and overlapping of the magical and the social-historical, the metafictional and the realistic, the world of the book and the world of the reader. Identity is always in doubt in *Under the Volcano.* The novel is, to use a word which frequently crops up in the narrative, a very *suggestive* book. The Q-ship, for example, is a ship in disguise, its reality the reverse of its appearance, and the dream-logic of Qs continues in the 'real' exterior world of the novel. The identity of Quauhnahuac is imprecise in the sense that the novel supplies the reader with two translations, one positive (to do with an eagle, signifying transcendence), the other negative (to do with the dark wood of error in Dante's *Inferno*). Mr Quincey is the bourgeois comic antithesis of his great romantic addict namesake. Mr Quattras (a *bookmaker,* and hence a kind of mock-Faustian surrogate writer) is a black man who has lost his racial identity through being brought up by whites. Meaning blurs or reverses itself; the narrative aspires to the promise on the coal company advertisement: '*It's a black business but we use you white.*' (pp. 43-60)

The narrative [of *Under the Volcano*] adamantly resists the extraction of a single coherent 'reading' which can account for the book as a totality. Ambiguity is rooted in the very grammar of the narrative. Numerous sentences and paragraphs are snapped off at the ends with a hyphen or a trail of dots, left unfinished, never to be completed. Words like 'seemed,' 'obscure,' 'perhaps,' 'apparently' constantly appear, underlining the baffling nature of relationships, of what connects A to B. Uncertainty, hesitation, ignorance and doubt are the basic conditions of

Lowry's fictional universe. The reader is perpetually faced by absolute opacity or, conversely, a baffling plurality of possible meanings. In the words of Gabriel Josipovici (speaking of the fiction of Robbe-Grillet), 'the reader is forced to move again and again over the material that is presented, trying to force it into a single vision, a final truth, but is always foiled by the resistant artefact.' *Under the Volcano* is full of problematic episodes like this:

> Once the swing door opened, someone glanced round quickly to satisfy himself, went out: was that Hugh, Jacques? Whoever it was had seemed to possess the features of both, alternately. Somebody else entered and, though the next instant the Consul felt this was not the case, went right through into the back room, peering round furtively.

The technique is reminiscent of Beckett's; authoritative statements are juxtaposed with cancellations of that authority. The two mysterious figures may be real, but equally they may be phantoms of the Consul's mind. Their quick, furtive glances echo Firmin's own guilt-ridden actions. Any sense of an objective reality collapses. The reader's interpretation of this episode will depend on the way he or she chooses to see the Consul—as the cuckolded husband being kept under observation by his wife's lovers, as the anti-fascist being spied upon by his political enemies, or as the hallucinating visionary, projecting his anxieties on to the contingent world. It is the narrative technique Roland Barthes calls '*jamming,* acknowledgement of the insolubility of the enigma,' and the metaphor is apt, since reading *Under the Volcano* is rather like listening to a radio programme which is subject to constant distortion and interference.

Under the Volcano is an encyclopedic novel, like the three twentieth-century novels with which it probably has most in common technically—namely *Ulysses,* Nabokov's *Ada* (1969) and Pynchon's *Gravity's Rainbow* (1973). To talk about levels of meaning in *Under the Volcano* is to imply hierarchies of meaning. But encyclopedism is a narrative mode which notoriously resists the privileging of meaning. All perspective tends to get lost, often dissolving into comedy. In the Cyclops section of *Ulysses,* Joyce pokes fun at the Irish heroes and heroines of antiquity by making an inventory of eighty-seven names. The list begins heroically enough ('Cuchulin, Conn of hundred battles, Niall of nine hostages') but soon collapses into absurdity with the introduction of some unexpected and inappropriate names: 'the Last of the Mohicans, the Rose of Castille, the Man for Galway, the Man That Broke the Bank at Monte Carlo, the Man in the Gap, the Woman Who Didn't, Benjamin Franklin, Napoleon Bonaparte.' In a like manner though the Consul may resemble Adam, Christ, Dante, Faustus, Hamlet, Hercules, Prometheus and Odysseus he is also identified with other cultural prototypes which critics usually judiciously ignore—Humpty Dumpty, Peter Rabbit, the Nose with the Luminous Dong. The problem with these analogues is that in total they cancel each other out, and that in isolation they provide only a partial accounting of the novel's dense complexity. The 'meaning' of *Under the Volcano* is no sooner tentatively established than it tends to slip away and reappear in a contradictory form.

The novel may be tragic, sombre and mythic, but it is also . . . very funny, full of exuberant comedy and parodies. Even at moments of great extremity and suffering the Consul engagingly regards himself as 'an Englishman, and still sporting' and an 'old rascal'. Although he cries out that he loves hell and can't wait to get back there is a crucial and rarely quoted qualification: 'the queer thing was, he wasn't quite serious.'

Under the Volcano presents the reader with a sequence of episodes which do not add up. Lowry's fictional universe is one of shifting, elusive connotations and unbridgeable contradictions between which lie only hiatuses, voids. But, simultaneously, there is a surplus of signifiers which invite the reader to fill in these voids with all-embracing explanations which yoke together disparate and irreconcilable realities, thereby asserting continuity, meaning. The dying Consul imagines he hears Laruelle and Dr Vigil comforting Hugh and Yvonne: ' "No se puede vivir sin amar," they would say, which would explain everything.' But the whole thrust of the book is to deny answers as simple as this. The teeming contradictions and confusions of life, Lowry seems to suggest, do not permit such easy consolations. (pp. 62-4)

> *Ronald Binns, in his* Malcolm Lowry, *Methuen, 1984, 96 p.*

Thomas B. Gilmore (essay date 1987)

[*Gilmore is an American critic. In the following excerpt, he examines the function of alcoholic hallucinations in* Under the Volcano.]

Most critics of *Under the Volcano* have concentrated on its density of symbolic meaning and its relationship to other modern literary masterpieces. These focuses are necessary, but they may have led critics to overlook one of the most salient and distinctive features of the novel: the fact that the hero is a drunkard, one with such monumental thirsts that other drunkards of literature (one might think of Don Birnam in *The Lost Weekend,* because Lowry feared that its nearly contemporaneous success would undermine his own) seem pale and timid by comparison. No one has fully appreciated Lowry's almost breathtaking audacity in forging a modern Everyman or Dantesque figure from a man with a uniquely gargantuan craving for alcohol. Nor has anyone sufficiently noticed the importance in the novel of a result of such excesses, a result that is well enough known to observers of alcoholism but that, to other readers, may be one of the strangest characteristics of the story: its hero's numerous and vivid alcoholic hallucinations.

The frequency with which Lowry employs hallucinations of varied types and for varied purposes distinguishes his novel even from other stories about alcoholics. For example, instead of being repeatedly subjected to hallucinations, as Lowry's Consul is, Birnam, of *The Lost Weekend,* several times escapes from his alcoholic miseries into nostalgic memories of childhood. His one genuine and fully developed hallucination, that a bat is attacking and devouring a mouse, is vivid and horrible but also brief and sharply set off from the rest of the novel.

Lowry was interested in conveying the awe and wonder, the pity and terror that alcoholism could arouse if its victim was a person otherwise intelligent and noble. The hallucination became one of his chief vehicles for reaching these effects as well as a major expression of his imagination. Appreciation of Lowry's imagination is enhanced by contrast with Jack Kerouac's *Big Sur* (1962), in which the protagonist's hallucinations are confined to less than twenty pages near the end of the novel and are scarcely enough to compensate for over two hundred pages of apparently structureless, slice-of-life observations. The continual mingling and blurring of hallucination with reality, their frequent overlapping or indeterminacy, are one source of the great richness of texture in *Under the Volcano,* a fecundity like the riotous jungle growth that Yvonne and Hugh press through on their way to Parián. This mingling and indeterminacy aid in the depiction of a more compelling and complex protagonist than Don Birnam or the hero of *Big Sur.* If the Consul is as certainly fated as Birnam by his alcoholism, the considerable suspense generated by his story lies not in our ignorance of what will happen but in the ingeniously imagined, increasingly hallucinatory ways in which it will be brought about.

Another source of suspense or tension in *Under the Volcano* is our sense that the Consul is engaged in a struggle of almost epic significance against dark, demonic, terrifying forces that are in large part represented or bodied forth by hallucinations. More heroic still, the Consul struggles not so much to avoid succumbing to the hallucinations as to make sense of them. Birnam's intelligence, though acute, is applied to less titanic aims: mainly to finding the means, financial and physical, to go on drinking. It is not surprising then that Lowry, in his extremely long and important letter to his eventual publisher, Jonathan Cape [see excerpt in *TCLC,* Vol. 6, pp. 235-36], the letter that persuaded Cape to accept *Under the Volcano* without change, expressed resentment and exasperation at the comparisons that Cape's editorial reader had repeatedly made between his novel and Charles Jackson's. For all his self-doubts and insecurities, Lowry thought his book incomparably better. He was right, largely because of its hallucinatory power.

That Lowry himself recognized the importance of hallucinations in *Under the Volcano* is demonstrated in his letter to Cape. He was pleased that Cape's editorial reader found "the mescal-inspired phantasmagoria," the Consul's "delirious consciousness," impressive, objecting only to the reader's complaint that these effects are "too long, wayward and elaborate." Lowry added that, when he undertook to revise the novel, it became "a spiritual thing." This apparent connection of the squalor of alcoholic hallucinations with spiritual matters suggests one characteristic quality of Lowry's mind: its tendency to blur distinctions or to combine ideas or categories usually kept discrete. On various occasions, for example, the Consul hears voices that he hears his "familiars." At one level these are auditory hallucinations, which some scientists regard as more common among alcoholics than the visual kind. These voices, however, are sometimes also Lowry's versions of good and bad angels; consider the novel's epigraphs from Bunyan and from Goethe's *Faust,* and several allusions within the novel to Marlowe's *Faustus*, in some respects an even closer analogue to the Consul. If, as Douglas Day maintains, *Under the Volcano* is "The greatest religious novel of this century," [Day, Douglas, *Malcolm Lowry: A Biography*, 1973] the authority of its vision derives to a great degree from the soil of the alcoholic hallucinations. In this juxtaposition of the sordid or debased with the exalted, similar to that which Yeats explored in "Crazy Jane Talks with the Bishop," Lowry was adept at perceiving correspondences.

Though mostly in sources not familiar to the student of literature, records of actual hallucinations are abundant. There are, to be sure, many different species of hallucinations. For example, there seems to be wide agreement that alcoholic hallucinations differ from drug-induced hallucinations, which (at least in the early stages of drug use) often consist of recurrent geometric patterns or designs and vivid colors with either a neutral or a pleasing emotional effect. In contrast, the typical alcoholic hallucination can perhaps best be described as paranoiac, involving schemes or plots of persecution, threats of violence, or the perpetration of violence, sometimes leading to the death of the hallucinator-victim. Some rather specific variants of these recurring delusions are also common: for example, according to a survey of 382 hallucinating alcoholics, no less than 48 believed that hostile gangs or the police were pursuing them.

We have no way to determine, of course, exactly how much of *Under the Volcano* portrays alcoholic hallucination actually experienced by Lowry. It can scarcely be mere coincidence that an important element of the novel—the recurrent motif that the Consul is being spied on, which turns into full-blown police persecution in the last section—bears so striking a resemblance to a common type of alcoholic hallucination. Moreover, although Lowry almost certainly spent some time in jail in Oaxaca, Mexico, in late 1937 or early 1938, several of his letters explaining his incarceration and the events leading up to it—the details in some instances found their way into the novel—sound so overwrought that they can only be regarded as largely the product of hallucinations. Lowry's major biographer, Douglas Day, acknowledges that the police must have been aware of Lowry because of his flagrant drunkenness, surely a more likely reason for his jailing than the claim in his correspondence (later partly incorporated in the novel in the police confusion of Hugh with the Consul) that he was mistaken for a Communist friend. Day rejects this claim as "pure romance" and regards Lowry's stories of ruthless, mysteriously malevolent police persecution as "almost certainly exaggerated." This is an excellent assessment. The paranoiac exaggeration probably took the form of hallucinations. If we realize that these were later transferred *mutatis mutandis* to the novel, we may better understand why several explanations of the Consul's fate, especially in the final section, are not quite convincing. Hallucinations remain ultimately intractable; they cannot be reduced to rational intelligibility.

That Lowry transfers to the novel some of his own hallucinations is not in itself remarkable. It is the uses to which he puts hallucinations—some probably experienced, others perhaps wholly invented, still others perhaps a combination of experience and imagination—that call for further comment and evoke admiration, for they are one of the most striking manifestations of Lowry's genius.

Most hallucinations recorded in medical or scientific works are evidently the fruit of mediocre minds: in spite of the lurid or sensational circumstances giving rise to them, they make rather dull reading. Not so the Consul's hallucinations. In the closing section of the novel he sits in the Farolito tavern, sinking into despair. He is faced with the prospect of hallucinating, whether or not he continues to drink; nevertheless, he seems incapable of anything less than an arresting vividness. The following passage seems to be almost a synoptic reprise of hallucinations he has frequently suffered:

> his room shaking with daemonic orchestras, the snatches of fearful tumultuous sleep, interrupted by voices which were really dogs barking, or by his own name being continually repeated by imaginary parties arriving, the vicious shouting, the strumming, the slamming, the pounding, the battling with insolent archfiends, the avalanche breaking down the door, the proddings from under the bed, and always, outside, the cries, the wailing, the terrible music, the dark's spinets.

Even this passage, as close to being abstractly typical of alcoholic hallucinations as any to be found in the novel, possesses a couple of distinctive touches. Though the "daemonic orchestras" and "insolent archfiends" may be strictly metaphorical or slightly humorous (or both), they may also be fleeting signs of what almost every other hallucinatory passage in the novel confirms: that even the most seemingly simple hallucination is endowed with moral or spiritual overtones. Just after his arrival at the Farolito, the Consul has what seem to be a couple of auditory hallucinations. Unlike the common run of these, which are merely persecutory, the Consul's are packed with moral meanings or hints: "the place was not silent. It was filled by that ticking: the ticking of his watch, his heart, his conscience, a clock somewhere. There was a remote sound too, from far below, of rushing water, of subterranean collapse". The Consul and the reader know why he should have a bad conscience; he has run off from his brother and his former wife after some particularly vicious words to them. And the rushing noise may be from the nearby barranca, the ubiquitous ravine symbolizing a kind of cloacal hell into which the Consul's body is finally hurled. The phrase "subterranean collapse" thus hints physically or literally at the barranca and metaphysically or morally at the Consul's spiritual condition. The use of hallucinations to convey moral meaning or significance will receive more extended treatment later, as will another of their qualities also evident in this passage: they usually have contact with or basis in reality. That is, there may actually be a clock ticking somewhere in the bar, and there certainly is a barranca, though whether it is the source of the rushing sound in this passage is left problematical.

The hallucinations, then, are ordinarily placed in some non-hallucinatory matrix, seen as connected with or emerging from reality. This is one means that Lowry discovered for naturalizing the device, for making it believable. To gain the same end he had other means as well. One function of the first section of the novel is to establish Mexico as a land whose scenes are objectively surreal or hallucinatory, a land in which even the Consul's friend Jacques Laruelle perceives the birds as "something like monstrous insects" and in which, he reflects, "you would find every sort of landscape at once, the Cotswolds, Windermere, New Hampshire, the meadows of the Eure-et-Loire, even the grey dunes of Cheshire, even the Sahara, a planet upon which, in the twinkling of an eye, you could change climates, and, if you cared to think so, in the crossing of a highway, three civilizations." In such a setting the Consul's hallucinations will seem less bizarre than they might otherwise. (pp. 18-23)

In general, the further along we are in the novel, the more complex and problematical is the relationship between hallucination and reality. Section X begins with a new and foreboding development: the Consul is for the first time drinking mescal, which he has already associated with his doom. Almost immediately following this disclosure is the first really long passage whose character remains irresolvably ambiguous. It involves a memory (perhaps a remembered hallucination) of a time when, after drinking all night, the Consul was supposed to meet a woman, Lee Maitland, at a train station. There are suspiciously improbable circumstances. The woman never appeared; even her reality is somewhat doubtful ("Who was she?" asks the Consul in retrospect). The trains that pass through are described as "terrible . . . shimmering . . . in mirage." The clickety-clack noise they make is repeatedly emphasized, as it might be in an auditory hallucination. Finally, at evening, "the next moment" (as though an alcoholic blackout had filled the intervening time), the Consul recalls himself "in the station tavern with a man who'd just tried to sell him three loose teeth." On the other hand, there are entirely plausible naturalistic details in the recollection: as the Consul waited in the early morning, "the dehydrated onion factory by the sidings awoke, then the coal companies. . . . A delicious smell of onion soup in sidestreets of Vavin impregnated the early morning. Grimed sweeps at hand trundled barrows, or were screening coal." Are we dealing with remembered hallucination, remembered reality, or some inextricable combination of both?

Such complicated interweaving of hallucination and actuality, with an increased uncertainty about the identity and time of the latter, recurs in the same section. The Consul, dining with Hugh and Yvonne in a Tomalín tavern, suddenly (that is, after an apparent blackout) finds himself seated on a toilet, from which vantage point he alternately reads from a tourist brochure about Tlaxcala and listens to the continuing conversation of Hugh and Yvonne, to which he makes an occasional contribution. Or so it seems at first; but if the preceding is an accurate description of reality, it soon appears that the overheard bits of conversation are not merely from Hugh and Yvonne but from various times and people; and then it appears that we are dealing not only with remembered reality but with remembered and current auditory hallucinations, these shifts and confusions all developing in the space of a few minutes. Perhaps it is no coincidence that the tavernkeeper of this

section is named Cervantes; *Under the Volcano* is as adept as *Don Quixote* at mingling hallucination or fantasy with reality, and the two stories, by means of their ambiguities, raise perplexing and not always answerable questions about the validity of conventional distinctions between sanity and insanity, reason and imagination, fantasy or hallucination and reality. (pp. 28-9)

> *Thomas B. Gilmore, "The Place of Hallucinations in 'Under the Volcano'," in his* Equivocal Spirits: Alcoholism and Drinking in Twentieth-Century Literature, *University of North Carolina Press, 1987, pp. 18-35.*

FURTHER READING

Ackerley, C. J. "*Barbarous Mexico* and *Under the Volcano.*" *Notes and Queries* n.s. 31, No. 1 (March 1984): 81-3.
　　Cites John Kenneth Turner's *Barbarous Mexico* as a chief source for *Under the Volcano.*

Allen, Walter. "The Masterpiece of the Forties." In *On Contemporary Literature,* rev. ed., edited by Richard Kostelanetz, pp. 419-21. New York: Avon Books, 1969.
　　Judges *Under the Volcano* the finest English novel of the the 1940s.

Arac, Jonathan. "The Form of Carnival in *Under the Volcano.*" *PMLA* 92, No. 3 (May 1977): 481-89.
　　Notes the intermingling of comic and serious elements in the novel.

Bareham, Tony. "Paradigms of Hell: Symbolic Patterning in *Under the Volcano.*" In *On the Novel: A Present for Walter Allen on his 60th Birthday from his Friends and Colleagues,* edited by B. S. Benedikz, pp. 113-27. London: J. M. Dent and Sons, 1971.
　　Explains that Lowry used symbols to "give an artistic coherence" to "his always nearly-factual fiction."

———. "*Under the Volcano.*" In his *Malcolm Lowry,* pp. 41-77. London: Macmillan, 1989.
　　Catalogue of recurrent symbols and dominant motifs in the novel.

Barnes, Jim. "The Myth of Sisyphus in *Under the Volcano.*" *Prairie Schooner* XLII, No. 4 (Winter 1968/69): 341-48.
　　Claims that the myth of Sisyphus is a recurrent theme in *Under the Volcano,* and that the Consul's guilty conscience is expressed through the use of the myth.

Baxter, Charles. "The Escape from Irony: *Under the Volcano* and the Aesthetics of Arson." *Novel* 10, No. 2 (Winter 1977): 114-26.
　　Identifies several instances in the novel where books or letters burn. Baxter writes, "The image of a man setting fire to words suggests the simultaneously reverent and murderous attitude held toward language, particularly the language of art, in Lowry's novel; it represents the ambivalence of the Consul, who genuinely fears what he regards as his only means of salvation."

Binns, Ronald. "*Under the Volcano:* Modernism and the

Self." In his *Malcolm Lowry,* pp. 30-41. London and New York: Methuen, 1984.

    Labels *Under the Volcano* a Modernist work due to its use of irony and its staying within the limited perspectives of its characters.

Birkerts, Sven. "Malcolm Lowry." In his *An Artificial Wilderness: Essays on 20th-Century Literature,* pp. 193-203. 1987. Reprint. Boston: Nonpareil Books, 1990.

    Praises the "seemingly infinite resonance" of *Under the Volcano.*

Bradbrook, M. C. "Lowry's Tartarus (*Under the Volcano,* 1946)." In her *Malcolm Lowry: His Art & Early Life,* pp. 54-68. London and New York: Cambridge University Press, 1974.

    General summary of the story and symbols of the novel.

Brooke-Rose, Christine. "Mescalusions." *London Magazine* 7, No. 1 (April 1967): 100-05.

    Disparages *Under the Volcano* as a "pseudo-masterpiece" whose "inflated language . . . is its [own] villain."

Burgess, Anthony. "Europe's Day of the Dead." *The Spectator* 218, No. 7,230 (20 January 1967): 74.

    Praises *Under the Volcano* for its formal brilliance.

Costa, Richard Hauer. "*Pietà, Pelado,* and 'The Ratification of Death': The Ten-Year Evolvement of Malcolm Lowry's *Volcano.*" *Journal of Modern Literature* 2, No. 1 (September 1971): 3-18.

    Traces the unusually long process of writing and revising the novel.

Cripps, Michael. "*Under the Volcano:* The Politics of the Imperial Self." *Canadian Literature,* No. 95 (Winter 1982): 85-101.

    Discussion of politics and political theory in *Under the Volcano.*

————. "Lost in the Wilderness: The Puritan Theme in *Under the Volcano.*" *English Studies in Canada,* X, No. 4 (December 1984): 457-75.

    Exploration of Puritanism in the novel as revealed by frequent references to William Blackstone, an early settler in Massachusetts.

Cross, Richard K. "*Under the Volcano:* A Book of the Dead." In his *Malcolm Lowry: A Preface to His Fiction,* pp. 26-64. Chicago: The University of Chicago Press, 1980.

    Summary of each chapter in the novel, with an emphasis on character development.

Dodson, Daniel B. *Malcolm Lowry.* New York and London: Columbia University Press, 1970, 48 p.

    Includes a summary of the plot of *Under the Volcano* and a discussion of the novel's three epigraphs.

Dorosz, Kristofer. *Malcolm Lowry's Infernal Paradise.* Uppsala, Sweden: Acta Universitatis Upsaliensis, n.d., 166 p.

    Prescribes a way of reading *Under the Volcano* that focuses on language instead of story or character.

Edmonds, Dale. "Mescallusions or the Drinking Man's *Under the Volcano.*" *Journal of Modern Literature* 6, No. 2 (April 1977): 277-88.

    Calls *Under the Volcano* "a drinker's paradise" and illuminates the Consul's alcoholic excesses with pertinent historic, scientific, and anecdotal information. The essay features three appendices: Appendix A records every instance of the Consul's intake of alcoholic beverages during the twelve-hour course of the novel, arriving at a "Grand Total" of 61 ounces; Appendix B lists the 74 alcoholic beverages mentioned by name in the novel; Appendix C gives six definitions of *mescal* from various sources, supporting Edmonds's proposal that Lowry— and therefore the Consul—overestimates the potency of "perhaps the most important drink on the list in terms of *Under the Volcano.*"

Epstein, Perle S. *The Private Labyrinth of Malcolm Lowry: "Under the Volcano" and the Cabbala.* New York, Chicago, and San Francisco: Holt, Rinehart and Winston, 1969, 241 p.

    Explores Cabbalistic symbolism in the novel and views the Consul as a black magician.

Falk, David. "Self and Shadow: The Brothers Firmin in *Under the Volcano.*" *Texas Studies in Literature and Language* 27, No. 2 (Summer 1985): 209-23.

    Identifies the image of the dead Indian as the Consul's psychological "shadow." Falk proposes that the "struggle between self and shadow permeates every level of the book, supplies its unifying vision, and creates the laws by which the characters interact."

————. "The Descent into Hell of Jacques Laruelle: Chapter I of *Under the Volcano.*" *Canadian Literature,* No. 112 (Spring 1987): 72-83.

    Analysis of the ways in which Chapter I of *Under the Volcano* establishes themes that are developed over the course of the novel.

Flint, R. W. "Weltschmerz Refurbished." *Kenyon Review* IX, No. 3 (Summer 1947): 474-77.

    Praises aspects of *Under the Volcano* but concludes that it lacks moral and political depth.

Grace, Sherrill E. "*Under the Volcano:* Narrative Mode and Technique." *Journal of Canadian Fiction* II, No. 2 (Spring 1973): 57-61.

    Analysis of narrative technique in the novel.

Hardwick, Elizabeth. Review of *Under the Volcano,* by Malcolm Lowry. *Partisan Review* XIV, No. 2 (March-April 1947): 196-200.

    Concludes that "the most interesting thing about *Under the Volcano* is that in it one returns to the flavor and color of the bohemian Twenties."

Harrison, Keith. "Allusions in *Under the Volcano:* Function and Pattern." *Studies in Canadian Literature* 9, No. 2 (1984): 224-32.

    Identifies historical, mythical, and literary allusions in *Under the Volcano.*

Hays, H. R. "Drunken Nightmare of the Damned." *The New York Times Book Review* (23 February 1947): 5.

    Early review of *Under the Volcano* which observes that "the really moving aspect of the Consul's damnation is the contrast between his great gifts and the devilish and poetic ingenuity with which he evades moral responsibility and poisons not only his own life, but the lives of those closest to him."

————. "The Possessed Artist and the Ailing Soul." *Canadian Literature,* No. 8 (Spring 1961): 7-16.

    Praises *Under the Volcano* for its "sense of largeness."

Hill, Art. "The Alcoholic on Alcoholism." *Canadian Literature,* No. 62 (Autumn 1974): 33-48.
    Asserts that Lowry wrote so accurately about the Consul's alcoholism because he himself was an alcoholic.

Hochschild, Adam. "The Private Volcano of Malcolm Lowry." *Ramparts* 12, No. 8 (March 1974): 45-8.
    Profile of Lowry focusing on the publication of *Under the Volcano.*

Kazin, Alfred. "A Dream of Order: Hemingway." In his *Bright Book of Life,* pp. 1-20. Boston: Little, Brown and Co., 1971.
    Praises *Under the Volcano* as a novel "that constantly asserts itself as the most expressive form of conjunction between man's inner and outer worlds."

Longo, Joseph A. "*Under the Volcano:* Geoffrey Firmin's Tragic Epiphany." *Notre Dame English Journal* XII, No. 1 (October 1979): 15-25.
    Denies that the Consul is redeemed at the conclusion of the novel.

Lytle, Andrew. "The Hero with the Private Parts." In his *The Hero with the Private Parts,* pp. 42-59. Baton Rouge: Louisiana State University Press, 1966.
    Discusses Lowry's conception of hell in *Under the Volcano.*

Markson, David. *Malcolm Lowry's "Volcano": Myth, Symbol, Meaning.* New York: Times Books, 1978, 308 p.
    Chapter-by-chapter explication of themes, symbols, allusions, and organizing structures of *Under the Volcano.*

McCormick, John. "Death, Manners, and Ideas." In his *Catastrophe and Imagination: An Interpretation of the Recent English and American Novel,* pp. 67-98. London: Longmans, Green and Co., 1957.
    States that Lowry's primary concerns in *Under the Volcano* are "the necessity of love and the virtual impossibility of realizing it," and "the relationship between action and contemplation, between life and death; action means death, contemplation life."

Middlebro', Tom. "The Political Strand in Malcolm Lowry's *Under the Volcano.*" *Studies in Canadian Literature* 7, No. 1 (1982): 122-26.
    Examination of the political discourse in the novel, as compared to that of Thomas Mann's *Doktor Faustus.*

Moon, Ken. "Lowry's *Under the Volcano.*" *The Explicator* 46, No. 3 (Spring 1988): 37-9.
    Focuses on the image of the poster of *Los Manos de Orlac* as it appears in *Under the Volcano.*

O'Kill, Brian. "Aspects of Language in *Under the Volcano.*" In *The Art of Malcolm Lowry,* edited by Anne Smith, pp. 72-92. New York: Barnes and Noble, 1978.
    Exploration of rhetoric and syntax in the novel.

Paz, Octavio. "Landscape and the Novel in Mexico." In his *Alternating Current,* pp. 14-16. New York: The Viking Press, 1973.
    Praises Lowry's treatment of Mexican landscape in *Under the Volcano.*

Pottinger, Andrew J. "The Consul's 'Murder.'" *Canadian Literature,* No. 67 (Winter 1967): 53-63.
    Explores the moral ambiguity of *Under the Volcano.*

Prescott, Orville. "Outstanding Novels." *The Yale Review* XXXVI, No. 4 (June 1947): 765-68.
    Praises the "verbal power" of *Under the Volcano* but objects to its obscurities and complexities.

Raab, Lawrence. "The Two Consuls: *Under the Volcano.*" *Thoth* 12, No. 3 (Spring/Summer 1972): 20-9.
    Assesses the Consul as a character who both elicits the reader's sympathy and provokes the reader's exasperation.

Rolo, Charles J. "The New Novel." *Tomorrow* 7, No. 9 (May 1948): 53-5.
    Praises *Under the Volcano* as one of the best novels of the 1940s.

Savage, D. S. Review of *Under the Volcano,* by Malcolm Lowry. *Spectator* 179, No. 6,224 (10 October 1947): 474, 476.
    Criticizes the novel's imprecision and prolixity, but states, "In spite of its many defects . . . , I must testify that *Under the Volcano . . .* is certainly the most interesting, the most perceptive and the most promising novel . . . so far this year."

Slade, Carole. "'Under the Volcano' and Dante's 'Inferno' I." *The University of Windsor Review* 10, No. 2 (Spring-Summer 1975): 44-52.
    Elaborates on parallels between the two works.

———. "The Character of Yvonne in *Under the Volcano.*" *Canadian Literature,* No. 84 (Spring 1980): 137-44.
    Character study of Yvonne.

Tiessen, Paul G. "Malcolm Lowry and the Cinema." *Canadian Literature,* No. 44 (Spring 1970): 38-49.
    Examines cinematic techniques and allusions in *Under the Volcano.*

"Mortal Distractions." *The Times Literary Supplement,* No. 2,381 (20 September 1947): 477.
    Applauds Lowry for creating the Consul, "a character in whose individual struggle is reflected something of the larger agony of the human spirit."

"The Fate of the Consul." *The Times Literary Supplement,* No. 3061 (28 October 1960): 693.
    Calls *Under the Volcano* "a dinosaur of a book, with the ominous power of *Moby Dick,* the verbal intricacy of *Ulysses* and the sheer horror of the works of William Burroughs."

"A Prose Waste Land." *The Times Literary Supplement,* No. 3,141 (11 May 1962): 338.
    Interprets *Under the Volcano* as "a closed circuit, whose introduction is also its epilogue, thus leading round and round on its own axis."

Vice, Sue. "The Mystique of Mezcal." *Canadian Literature,* No. 112 (Spring 1987): 197-202.
    Challenges Thomas Gilmore's theory (see excerpt dated 1987 in entry above) that the Consul suffers from alcoholic hallucinations. Vice contends that his behavior reflects the use of mescaline, the drug, and not mescal, the drink.

Weeks, Edward. "Mexico and Moscow." *The Atlantic* 179, No. 5 (May 1947): 144, 146.
    Praises Lowry's "gift of balancing the spoken word and the hidden thought."

Widmer, Eleanor. "The Drunken Wheel: Malcolm Lowry and *Under the Volcano.*" In *The Forties: Fiction, Poetry, Drama,* edited by Warren French, 217-26. Deland, Florida: Everett/Edwards, 1969.
    Views *Under the Volcano* against the background of Lowry's life.

Wood, Barry, ed. *Malcolm Lowry: The Writer and His Critics.* Ottawa, Canada: The Tecumseh Press, 1980, 278 p.
    Reprints important reviews and critical essays on Lowry's novels, short stories, and poetry, as well as Lowry's letter to Jonathan Cape.

Wright, Terence. "*Under the Volcano:* The Static Art of Malcolm Lowry." *Ariel* 1, No. 4 (October 1970): 67-76.
    Sees *Under the Volcano* as concerned with presenting a static "contemplation" of the Consul's fallen state rather than the changing "process" of his fall into death and disintegration.

Young, Vernon A. "The Southwest: Truth and Poetry." *Arizona Quarterly* 3, No. 3 (Autumn 1947): 276-83.
    Considers *Under the Volcano* a failure due to its "involution, 'literary' effects, erudite associationalism, intellectual puns . . . , reverie in long unpunctuated sentences, thematic symbolism: all inherited from Joyce, one risks, and not as intriguing as when Joyce first forged 'the uncreated conscience of [his] race'."

Paul Nizan

1905-1940

(Full name Paul-Yves Nizan) French novelist, essayist, journalist, and critic.

A politically active Communist during the interwar period, Nizan was the author of novels that express Marxist ideals in a manner considered both artistically successful and polemically effective. In his works, Nizan advocated selfless commitment to collective political action and disparaged what he perceived as the characteristics of bourgeois life: shallow relationships, unrealized hopes, and a lack of satisfaction in one's work. Unlike many works of politically "engaged" literature that are little more than ideological propaganda, Nizan's novels are praised for realistic character portrayal, complex themes, and consideration of issues beyond the political realm.

Nizan was born in Tours to a working-class family and attended schools in Tours and in Paris, where he became friends with Jean-Paul Sartre. While his early interests were focused more on literature than politics, Nizan demonstrated political awareness at a young age. During 1926 and 1927, he spent a year as a tutor for a wealthy family in Aden, a seaport on the Arabian peninsula under British dominion at the time. This experience prompted the essay *Aden, Arabie,* a condemnation of capitalist imperialism and the French higher educational system. Nizan joined the French Communist party in 1927 while continuing studies necessary for a teaching degree. His position as a teacher of philosophy in a Paris lycée during 1931 and 1932 influenced his second essay, *Les chiens de garde* (*The Watchdogs*), which decries as meaningless any philosophy lacking practical applications and denounces the leaders of the intellectual establishment as tools of the bourgeoisie. Subsequently, Nizan wrote and worked for various Communist periodicals, taught courses for the French Communist party, and traveled throughout Europe to advance the communist cause.

Nizan's first novel, *Antoine Bloyé,* was published in 1933 and received consideration for the Prix Goncourt. In 1934, during a yearlong stay in the Soviet Union, Nizan attended the First Congress of the Union of Soviet Writers, at which the doctrine of socialist realism was instituted by the government censor, Andrey Zhdanov, who enjoined authors to create a literature "optimistic in essence, because it is the literature of the rising class of the proletariat." Nizan's second novel, *Le cheval de Troie* (*The Trojan Horse*), was not well received, but was followed in 1938 by the novel *La conspiration* (*The Conspiracy*), which won the Prix Interallié. The next year, Nizan left the party when it failed to oppose the Hitler-Stalin Pact of 1939, which established mutual nonaggression between fascist Germany and the communist Soviet Union. The French Communists, in turn, declared him a traitor to their cause. During the Second World War, Nizan became involved in

the military efforts against the Axis powers and was killed at Dunkirk at the age of thirty-five.

Observing the relationship between social conditions and individual destiny, Nizan's novels are considered rare examples of successful fictional works inspired by communist ideology. *Antoine Bloyé* was based on the life of Nizan's father, whose unhappy personal life is depicted in the novel as a direct result of the moral compromises he made in his rise from lower-class laborer to comfortable bourgeois. In addition to the political ideas underlying *Antoine Bloyé*, critics admire Nizan's portrait of the aging main character: his diminishing physical powers, lost opportunities, and fear of a meaningless death. Richard Elman states that *Antoine Bloyé* "is one of the few truly great Marxist novels, . . . a work that treats of the alienation of ordinary men from their fellows and their work yet does so without once becoming scolding, combative, or sneering." In *The Trojan Horse,* Nizan depicted individuals who find fulfillment through collective political action. However, he also acknowledged that individual choices must be made and that communism offers little solace to the individual confronted with death. Because Nizan avoided exaggerated villains and heroes and simplistic moral codes, critics find that the novel rises above the typical works of socialist realism. In *The Conspiracy,* which is considered his best novel, Nizan provided a mocking yet sometimes sympathetic portrayal of young intellectuals who are unable to constructively channel their rebellion against family and society. Nizan articulated the need to oppose the status quo, although he was only guardedly optimistic about the outcome. This call for positive change through political action regardless of the risk is at the heart of all Nizan's writings. Walter Redfern explains: "Politics in a work of literature, said Stendhal, is an intrusion of loudness, and yet a thing to which it is not possible to refuse one's attention. Nizan's whole effort is exactly this: to force readers to look when they would prefer to turn away."

(See also *Dictionary of Literary Biography,* Vol. 72.)

PRINCIPAL WORKS

Aden, Arabie (essay) 1931
  [*Aden, Arabie,* 1968]
Les chiens de garde (essay) 1932
  [*The Watchdogs,* 1971]
Antoine Bloyé (novel) 1933
  [*Antoine Bloyé,* 1973]
Le cheval de Troie (novel) 1935
  [*The Trojan Horse,* 1937]
La conspiration (novel) 1938
  [*The Conspiracy,* 1988]
Chronique de septembre (essay) 1939

Jean-Paul Sartre (essay date 1938)

[*A French philosopher, novelist, dramatist, and critic, Sartre was one of the chief contributors to the philosophical movement of Existentialism. Along with Martin Heidegger and Albert Camus, Sartre is the most prominent representative of the atheist branch of this movement, as distinguished from the Christian Existentialism of such writers as Karl Barth and Gabriel Marcel. Both groups, however, share the common assumptions that the individual is free to choose a course of action according to his or her will and is under a moral imperative to acknowledge a responsibility to society and act in accordance with this responsibility. In addition, Sartre's doctrine of Existentialism posits a universe with neither a God nor an absolute meaning. For Sartre, the human condition is best characterized as a state of anxiety in which individuals are "condemned to be free" to create what they will of their lives. Sartre's numerous literary and philosophical essays appear in the ten volumes of his* Situations *(1947-76). The literary essays chronicle the development of Sartre's critical theories and are considered by many critics as outlines for his studies of Charles Baudelaire, Jean Genet, and Gustave Flaubert. These studies examine their subjects in light of the social conditions under which they wrote and the changes they un-* derwent as a result of historical events. This method is described in part in* Qu'est-ce que la littérature? *(1964;* What Is Literature?*). In this work, Sartre denies the importance of stylistic analysis in literary criticism, favoring instead an examination of the social and political issues that make up the substance of a given work of literature. According to Sartre, the "function of the writer is to act in such a way that nobody can be ignorant of the world and that nobody may say that he is innocent of what it's all about." The following essay was first published in 1938 as a review of* The Conspiracy.]

[In *The Conspiracy*] Nizan speaks about youth. But a Marxist has too much historical sense to describe an age of life—such as Youth or Maturity—in general, just as it marches past in Strasburg Cathedral when the clock strikes midday. His young men are dated and attached to their class: like Nizan himself, they were twenty in 1929— the heyday of 'prosperity' in the middle of the postwar period that has just ended. They are bourgeois, sons for the most part of that grande bourgeoisie which entertains 'anxious doubts about its future', of those 'rich tradespeople who brought up their children admirably, but who had ended up respecting only the Spirit, without thinking that this ludicrous veneration for the most disinterested activities of life ruined everything, and that it was merely the mark of their commercial decadence and of a bourgeois bad conscience of which as yet they had no suspicion.' Wayward sons, led by a deviation 'out of the paths of commerce' towards the careers of the 'creators of alibis'. But in Marx there is a phenomenology of economic essences: I am thinking, above all, of his admirable analyses of commodity fetishism. In this sense, a phenomenology can be found in Nizan: in other words, a fixing and description, on the basis of social and historical data, of that essence in motion which is 'youth', a sham age, a fetish. This complex mixture of history and analysis constitutes the great value of his book.

Nizan lived his own youth to the dregs. When he was immersed in it and it barred his horizon on every side, he wrote in **Aden, Arabie:** 'I was twenty, I won't let anyone say those are the best years of your life.' He felt then that youth was a *natural* age, like childhood, although far more unhappy, and that responsibility for its miseries should be laid at the door of capitalist society. Today he looks back on it and judges it without indulgence. It is an artificial age, which has been made and which makes itself, and whose very structure and existence depend upon society: the age of inauthenticity, *par excellence.* Workers at twenty, however, are protected from it by misfortunes, by worries, by the contact they must make in order to survive: they 'already have mistresses or wives, children, a profession . . . in short a life'; once they leave adolescence, they become young men, without ever having been 'young people'. But Laforgue and Rosenthal, sons of bourgeois families, students, live that great abstract ennui to the full. Their fatal lightmindedness and their aggressive futility are due to the fact that they have no duties and are by nature irresponsible. They 'improvise' and nothing can engage them, not even their membership of extremist parties: '. . . these diversions . . . had no great consequences for the sons of bankers and industrialists, who could always return to the embrace of their class. . . . ' Very wise perhaps, if these improvisations sprang from a brief contact with reality. But they remain in the air and their authors forget them at once. Their actions are puffs of smoke, they know this and it is what gives them the courage to undertake things—though they pretend not to be aware of it. What are we to call them, these undertakings so serious yet so frivolous, if not 'conspiracies'? But Laforgue and Rosenthal are not Camelots du Roi: young bourgeois can come and make their plots at the other end of the political spectrum, even in the parties of grown men. We can see what that fine word 'conspiring' hints at in the way of whisperings, little mysteries, hollow consequence and invented dangers. Tenuous intrigues: a game. A game—that great 'Dostoievskyan' plot hatched by Rosenthal, the only traces of which will be two incomplete and in any case totally uninteresting files at the back of a drawer. A feverish, angry game, an abortive conspiracy, that manufactured love which Rosenthal entertains for his sister-in-law. From calling it a game, moreover, it is but one short step to calling it play-acting: they lie to themselves because they know they are running no risk; they strive in vain to frighten themselves, in vain—or almost—to deceive themselves. I can just imagine the great, dumb sincerity of labour and physical suffering and hunger that Nizan would counterpose to their endless talk. Bernard Rosenthal—who from anger and sloth has performed the irreparable actions of suicide—will in fact know no other reality than the agony of death. The agony of death alone will show him—but too late—that 'he had missed love . . . that . . . he no longer even loved Catherine and he was going to die cheated'. Yet those young people have the semblance of good intentions: they want to live, to love, to rebuild a world that is tottering. But it is at the very heart of these good intentions that the abstract, self-assured frivolity lies which cuts them off from the world and from themselves: 'their politics is still based only upon metaphors and shouts'. For youth is the age of resentment. Not of the great anger of men who suffer: these young people define themselves in relation to their families; they 'tended to confuse capitalism with important people'; they expect to find 'a world destined for great metamorphoses', but what they want above all is to give their parents a bit of trouble. The young man is a product of the bourgeois family, his economic situation and his world-view are shaped exclusively by the family.

These young people are not all bad men. But Nizan shows very clearly how only through revolution can one leave this age, which Comte called 'metaphysical'. Youth does not bear its solution within it: it must collapse and be rent apart. Either it is the young man who dies, like Rosenthal, or he is fated by his family inferiority complex like Pluvinage to drag out a perpetual, wretched adolescence. There is a breakdown of youth for Nizan as there is a breakdown of childhood for Freud: the pages in which he shows us Laforgue's painful initiation to man's estate are among the finest in the book.

I do not think Nizan wanted to write a novel. His young people are not novelish: they do not do much, they are not very sharply distinguished from one another; at times they seem only an expression, among many others, of their families and their class; at other times, they are the tenuous thread connecting a number of events. But this is intentional: for Nizan, they do not deserve more; later, he will make them into men. Can a communist write a novel? I am not convinced of it: he does not have the right to make himself the accomplice of his characters. But in order to find this book strong and fine, it is enough that on each page you find the obsessive evocation of that unhappy, guilty time of life; it is enough that the book constitutes a hard, true testimony at a time when 'the Young' are forming groups and congratulating themselves, when the young man thinks he has *rights* because he is young, like the taxpayer because he pays his taxes or the father because he has children. It is a pleasure to find, behind these derisory heroes, the bitter and sombre personality of Nizan—the man who does not forgive his youth—and his fine style, taut and casual: his long Cartesian sentences, which sink in the middle as though no longer able to sustain themselves, but all at once spring up again to finish high in the air; and those rhetorical transports which suddenly come to a halt, giving way to a terse and icy verdict. Not a novelist's style, sly and hidden: a style for combat, a weapon. (pp. 243-46)

> *Jean-Paul Sartre, in an afterword to* The Conspiracy *by Paul Nizan, translated by Quintin Hoare, Verso, 1988, pp. 243-46.*

Jean-Paul Sartre   (essay date 1960)

[*In the following excerpt from a foreword to* Aden, Arabie *that originally appeared in French in 1960, Sartre presents his view of the psychological basis of Nizan's writings and of Nizan's relationship to the Communist party.*]

Nizan was a kill-joy. He issued a call to arms, to hatred. Class against class. With a patient and mortal enemy there can be no compromise: kill or be killed, there is nothing in between. And never sleep. All his life he had repeated, with his graceful insolence, looking down at his fingernails, "Don't believe in Santa Claus." He was dead, the war had just ended. By every French chimney shoes and boots had been set out, and Santa Claus was filling them with American canned goods. I am sure that at that time, those who started to leaf through [*Aden, Arabie*] or *Antoine Bloyé* quickly laid the book aside with condescending pity: "Pre-war literature—simplistic and decidedly dated." What need had we of a Cassandra? We thought that if Nizan had lived he would have shared our new subtlety—that is, our compromises. What had preserved his violent purity? A stray bullet, that's all, nothing to brag about. This wretched dead man was quietly laughing his head off. He had written in his books that a French bourgeois past forty is nothing but a carcass. And then he had slipped away. At thirty-five. Now we, his classmates and comrades, puffed up with this flatulence we called our souls, reconciled with our enemies, were running about the public squares embracing everybody we met. And we were forty. Protecting the innocent, that was our business. We were the Just and we dispensed Justice. We left *Aden* in the hands of the Communists because we detested anyone who questioned our worth. (pp. 11-12)

[Nizan] spoke little about the human condition, a great deal about social matters and our alienations. He knew terror and rage rather than the sweetness of despair. In the young bourgeois with whom he associated he saw his own reflection and hated it—whether they were despairing or not, he despaired of them. His books were kept for the lean years, and rightly so. (pp. 13-14)

The error that I want my readers to avoid is one that I made myself. And I made it during Nizan's lifetime, notwithstanding the fact that we were such close friends that people used to mistake us for each other. One day in June of '39, Léon Brunschvicg ran into us at the offices of Gallimard and congratulated me on having written *Les chiens de garde,* " . . . although," as he said without bitterness, "you were pretty hard on me." I smiled at him in silence; Nizan stood smiling beside me. The great idealist left without realizing his mistake. This confusion between us had been going on for eighteen years—it had become our status in society, and we had come to accept it. Particularly between 1920 and 1930, when we were students together at the lycée and then the École Normale, we were indistinguishable. Nevertheless, I did not see him as he really was. (p. 18)

[The] Party came between us. I was in sympathy with the Party, but I was not a member. I remained his boyhood friend, a petty bourgeois he was still fond of. Why didn't I understand him? There was no lack of signs. Why did I refuse to see them? I think it was out of jealousy. I denied feelings I could not share. I sensed at once that he had incommunicable passions, a destiny that would separate us. I was afraid and I closed my eyes. At fifteen this son of a pious woman wanted to enter into Orders. I didn't know about it until a long time afterward. But I still remember how shocked and bewildered I was when he said to me one day as we strolled around the schoolyard at the lycée, "I had lunch at the minister's." He saw my stupefaction and explained with a detached air, "I might become converted to Protestantism." "You?," said I indignantly, "but . . . you don't believe in God." "No," he replied, "but their morality appeals to me." Madame Nizan threatened to cut off his allowance and the project was abandoned. But in that instant I had glimpsed behind this "piece of childishness" the impatience of a sick man who turns over and over in bed to escape his pain. I didn't want him to have this inaccessible pain—we had superficial melancholy in common and that was enough. For the rest, I tried to impose my optimism on him. I kept telling him that we were free. He would not answer, but the thin smile at the corner of his lips spoke volumes. At other times, he called himself a materialist—we were scarcely seventeen—and it was I who smiled disdainfully. Materialist, determinist: he felt the physical weight of his chains; I did not want to feel the weight of mine. I hated him to be involved in politics because I didn't feel the need of it myself. Communist, then royalist, then communist again, it was easy to mock him, and I did not deny myself the pleasure. In reality, his wide swings were the mark of his obstinacy. Nothing is more excusable at the age of eighteen than to hesitate between two opposite extremes. What never varied was his extremism. In any case, he was sure of one thing: the established order must be destroyed. For my part, I was pleased that

this order existed so I could take pot shots at it with words. Nizan had a real need to unite with other men, so that together they might lift the stones that suffocated them. (pp. 21-2)

[When] the individuality of his body is reflected in the individuality of the work he has undertaken, a young man integrates his death with his life and sees it as just one more risk along with all the others that threaten his work and his family. For those few men who are lucky enough to love what they do, the final shipwreck, which grows less terrifying the nearer it comes, is converted into the small change of day-to-day concerns.

I have described the fate common to us all. That is nothing. But when the terror of death outlasts adolescence, when it becomes the profound secret of the adult and the mainspring of his decisions, the sick man understands his affliction: his terror of soon ceasing to live simply reflects his horror at still having to live. Death is the irrevocable sentence. It condemns the wretched, for all eternity, to have been only that: shameful calamities. Nizan dreaded that fate. He was a monster crawling blindly among all the other monsters, afraid that one day he would explode and there would be nothing left of him. When he put the following words in the mouth of one of his characters, he had known for a long time that death was the definitive illumination of life: "If I think about my death, it's for good reason. My life is hollow and death is all it deserves." In the same book, Bloyé comes to fear "the uniform visage of his life . . . and [this fear] rises from a yet deeper region of the body than the bleeding places where the warning signs of disease are formed." (pp. 25-6)

[Nizan] was the child of an old couple, two adversaries who had begotten him during a truce and, when he was born, resumed their quarrel. His father, who had been first a railroad worker then an engineer, set him the example of a way of thinking that was technical, unbelieving and adult, and revealed in his conversation a sad loyalty to the class he had left. From earliest childhood, Nizan internalized this mute conflict between an old and childish woman of the bourgeoisie and a renegade member of the working class. It became the foundation for his future personality. No matter how young he is, the child of a charwoman participates in his family's future: the father makes plans. But the Nizans had no future. Monsieur Nizan was general foreman of a railroad yard, almost at the height of his career. What had he to look forward to? A promotion due him, a few honors, retirement and death. (p. 29)

[It] is impossible to understand Nizan's anguish unless one recalls what I said earlier: he interpreted the present, which for him was laborious, disenchanted, broken only by brief periods of exaltation, in the sinister light of a future that was really his father's past. "I was afraid. My departure was the child of fear." Fear of what? He says it in [*Aden, Arabie*]: "Mutilations . . . awaited us. After all, we knew how our parents lived." He has developed this sentence in a long and beautiful novel, *Antoine Bloyé.* In it he recounts the life and death of his father. And although Nizan hardly appears in the book, he continually speaks of himself. First, he is the witness of his father's decay. Second, since his father confided in no one, we know that all the thoughts and feelings attributed to him have been torn from the author's heart and projected onto the distraught old man. This constant dual presence is a sign of what the analysts call identification with the father.

I have said that in his early years Nizan admired his father. He envied his strength, which was sterile but visible, his silences, his hands that had toiled. Monsieur Nizan used to talk about his former comrades, and fascinated by these men who knew the truth about life and who apparently loved each other, the little boy saw his father as a worker and wanted to be like him in everything. He would have his father's earthly patience. It would take nothing less than the obscure inner density of things, of matter, to save the future monk from his mother, from *Monsieur le Curé,* and from his own idle chatter. "Antoine," he said admiringly, "was a corporal man. His mind was not so pure that it took no interest in the body which nourished it and which for so many years had provided it with an admirable proof of existence."

But the admirable man staggered. All of a sudden the child saw him start to disintegrate. Nizan had given himself to his father without reservation: "I will be like him." Now he had to watch the interminable decomposition of his own future: "That will be me." His mother's prattle triumphed. He saw Matter sink beneath the waves, while the Soul remained afloat like foam after a shipwreck. What happened? Nizan tells the story in **Antoine Bloyé.** For reasons which I do not know—because while he stayed fairly close to the truth in his book, he doubtless changed the circumstances—the man on whom he modeled Antoine tried to draw up a balance sheet when he was only forty. Everything had begun with that false victory he had won—the crossing of a line—at a time when the bourgeoisie was promising everyone "the great future of equal opportunity," a time when "every workingman's son carried in his school bag . . . a bourgeois' diploma with the name left blank." By the time he was fifteen his life was already like the express trains he would later run, trains that were "borne along by a force full of certainty and suffocation." And then, in 1883, he was graduated from the École des Arts et Métiers, eighteenth out of a class of seventy-seven. Shortly thereafter, at the age of twenty-seven, he married Anne Guyader, the daughter of his general foreman. From that time on, "everything was settled, established. There was no appeal." He sensed this at the very moment when the curé united them, and then he forgot his misgivings. The years passed, the couple went from one city to another, constantly moving in and moving out, never settling anywhere. Time wore on, and life remained provisional. Every day, in its abstraction, was like every other day. Antoine dreamed, without too much conviction, that "something would happen." Nothing happened. He consoled himself with the thought that he would show what stuff he was made of when real battles came along. But while he waited for great circumstances, the little ones rubbed against him and imperceptibly wore him down. "True courage consists of overcoming small enemies." Nevertheless he advanced irresistibly. At first, listening to the bourgeois sirens, he experienced "the most insidious peace." By fulfilling the false duties set before him—duties toward the Company, toward Society, *even*

toward his former comrades—he achieved what might be called a vital minimum of good conscience. But "the years piled up," the desires, hopes, and memories of youth sank into that shadowy realm of condemned thoughts where human forces founder. The Company devoured its agents. For fifteen years there was no more selfless man than Antoine Bloyé, driven by "the demands, the ideas, the judgments of his work." He hardly ran his eye over the newspapers: "the events they recounted were taking place on another planet and did not concern him." But he was fascinated by "descriptions of machines" in technical journals. He lived, or rather his body imitated the attitudes of life. But in reality the mainspring of his life, the motives for his acts, did not lie within him. "Complicated powers prevented him from planting his feet firmly on the earth." One could apply to him, with hardly a change of words, what Nizan writes about a rich Englishman in Aden: "Each of us is divided among the men he might be, and Mr. C. has allowed to triumph within him that man for whom life consists of making the price of . . . Abyssinian leather go up or down. . . . Fighting abstract entities such as firms, unions, merchants' guilds—are you going to call that action?" Of course Bloyé did not have so much power as the Englishman, but what of that? Was not everything in his job abstract: plans, estimates, red tape? Was not everything already decided somewhere else, very far away, by other men? The man had become an extension of his company, and his total immersion in his work still left a vital part of him unused. He slept little, never spared himself, carried sacks and beams on his back, and was always the last to leave his office, but as Nizan says, "all his work concealed the fact that he was essentially idle." I know. I spent ten years of my life under the thumb of a graduate of the École Polytechnique. He killed himself on the job—or rather, somewhere, in Paris no doubt, the job had decided that it would kill him. He was the most insignificant of men. On Sunday he would withdraw into himself, find a desert there, and lose himself in it. He held on, though, saved by his sluggishness or his rages of wounded vanity. Fortunately, it was war time when they retired him. He read the papers, clipped articles and pasted them into a notebook. At least he made no pretense: his flesh was abstract. But for Bloyé's young son, there was the shock of an unbearable contradiction. Antoine had a real body that was tough and capable and had once been avid, and that body imitated life. And yet, set in motion by distant abstractions, he had scuttled his rich passions and voluntarily transformed himself into an abstraction.

> Antoine was a man who had a profession and a temperament, that was all. That is all a man is, in the world in which Antoine Bloyé lived. There are nervous merchants, full-blooded engineers, bilious workers, choleric notaries. People say those things and think they have made an effort to define a man. They also say a black dog, a striped cat. A doctor . . . had told him, "You, you're the nervous, full-blooded type." There. That said everything. Everyone could handle him, like a coin whose value is known. He circulated among other coins.

The boy worshipped his father, and I do not know if he would have noticed this inner poverty by himself. Nizan's misfortune lay in the fact that his father was better than the next man. After having ignored many danger signs, Monsieur Nizan finally realized what he was, too late, and came to have a horror of his life. He saw his death and loathed it. For nearly half a century he had practiced self-deception, trying to believe that he could still "become a new man, a different man who would be truly himself." Suddenly he realized that it was impossible for him to change. This impossibility was death at the heart of life. Death draws a line and adds up the sum, but for Nizan's father the line was already drawn and the sum added. This schematic creature, who was as much a generalization as an individual, shared the bed of a woman who was no more a particular person than was he, but rather a broadcasting station for the dissemination of pious thoughts manufactured in Rome, and who, like himself, had doubtless repressed simple and voracious needs. He proclaimed their double failure to his frightened son. He would get up at night,

> throw his clothes over his arm, and dress at the foot of the stairs. . . . He would go out. . . . "I'm a fifth wheel," he would say to himself, "I am superfluous, I serve no purpose, I have already ceased to exist, if I let myself fall into the water no one would notice it, there would just be the announcements edged in black. I'm a failure, I'm finished. . . ." He would turn back toward the house . . . shivering, pass his hand over his face and feel that his beard had grown during the night. Near the house his awakened wife and son would be looking for him, calling him. He would hear their shrill voices from afar but would not answer, leaving them in anxiety until the last minute, as if to punish them. They were afraid he might have killed himself. . . . When he came up to them, he would say with stifled anger, "So I can't do as I please any more . . . ?" And he would go back up to his room without paying any further attention to them.

These nocturnal flights are not an invention of the novelist. Nizan used to talk to me about his father, and I know that it is all true. Meditation on death drives a man toward suicide—it makes him dizzy and impatient. I ask you to imagine the feelings of an adolescent whose mother wakes him up at night saying, "Your father is not in his room. This time I'm sure he's going to kill himself." Death enters into him, death takes up its stand at the crossroads of all his routes; it is the end and the beginning. [Nizan's] father was already dead and wanted to go before he was summoned. That is the meaning and the conclusion of a stolen life. But his father's life occupied Nizan like a foreign power. His father infected him with the death which was to come. (pp. 31-5)

From the time we were sixteen I thought we were united by the same desire to write. I was mistaken. A clumsy hunter, I was dazzled by words because I always missed them. Nizan was more precocious and his gamebag was full. He discovered words everywhere, in dictionaries, in books, and even at large, on people's lips. I admired his vocabulary, and the ease with which he worked newly acquired words into his rough drafts—words like "bimetal-

ism" and "percolator." But he was far from being totally committed to literature. I was in it up to my ears, the discovery of an adjective enchanted me. As for him, he wrote better than I did and watched himself write—with the mournful eyes of his father. Words burst apart or withered into dead leaves: can one justify oneself by words? In the face of death, literature became a parlor game, a variation on canasta. It is only natural for a professor to write, he is encouraged to do so. The same traps serve for the writer as for the engineer: flattery, temptations. At the age of forty all these lackeys will be carcasses. Honors hid Valéry. He lived off princes, queens, and powerful industrialists. He dined at their table because he worked for them. The glorification of the Word is of direct profit to the high and mighty: it teaches men to take the word for the thing, and that is cheaper. Nizan understood that. He was afraid of wasting his life collecting the breath of voices. (pp. 36-7)

As early as his second year at the École Normale he had been drawn to the Communists. In short, he had come to a conclusion. But decisions are made in the dark, and without realizing it, we struggle for a long time against our own will. He had to knock on every door, try everything, experiment with solutions he had long since rejected. I think he wanted to experience the good things of this world before he took the vow of poverty. (pp. 41-2)

Did he finally find what he was looking for? What could the Party give to this man who had been skinned alive, who suffered to the very marrow of his bones from the sickness of death? We must be scrupulous about asking this question. I am telling the story of an exemplary life, which is just the opposite of an edifying life. Nizan shed his skin, and yet the old man, the old young man, remained. From 1929 to 1939 I saw less of him, but our meetings were all the more lively for being brief, and they taught me much about him. Nowadays, I understand, one chooses the family as opposed to politics. Nizan, however, had chosen both. Aeneas had grown weary of carrying gloomy old Anchises for so long, and with one shrug of the shoulders had sent him sprawling. Nizan had rushed into marriage and fatherhood in order to kill his father. But becoming a father is not in itself a sufficient cure for childhood. On the contrary, the authority vested in the new head of a family condemns him to repeat the age-old pieces of childishness handed down to us from Adam through our parents. It was an old story to my friend. He wanted to finish off once and for all the father who in each generation was murdered by his son only to be reborn again in him. He would become a *different* man, and would keep himself from capricious behavior in the family by public discipline. Let us see if he succeeded.

The doctrine satisfied him completely. He detested conciliations and conciliators, and most especially their Great Master, Leibnitz. When he was required to study the *Discourse on Metaphysics* in school, he took his revenge by making a talented drawing of the philosopher in full flight, wearing a Tyrolean hat, with the imprint of Spinoza's boot on his right buttock. To pass from the *Ethics* to *Das Kapital,* however, was easy. Marxism became his second nature or, if you prefer, his Reason. His eyes were Marxist, and his ears. And his head. At last he understood his incomprehensible wretchedness, his wants, his terror. He saw the world and saw himself in it. But above all, at the same time that Marxism made his hatreds legitimate, it reconciled in him the opposing discourse of his parents. The rigor of technique, the exactitude of science, the patience of reason, all that was retained. But the doctrine also went beyond the pettiness of positivism, with its absurd refusal to "know through causes." The dreary world of means, and of the means of means, was left to the engineers. To the troubled young man who wanted to save his soul, Marxism offered absolute ends: play midwife to history, bring forth the revolution, prepare Man and the Reign of Man. The doctrine did not concern itself with salvation or personal immortality, but it gave him the chance to live on, anonymously or gloriously, in the midst of a common enterprise that would end only with the species. He put everything into Marxism: physics and metaphysics, his passion for action and his passion for retrieving his acts, his cynicism and his eschatological dreams. Man was his future. But now was the time to slash. It would be up to other men to sew the pieces together again. His was the pleasure of cheerfully ripping everything to shreds for the good of humanity.

Everything suddenly took on weight, even words. He distrusted words because they served bad masters, but everything changed when he was able to turn them against the enemy. He used their ambiguity to confuse, their vague charm to beguile. In the service of the Party, literature could even become idle chitchat. The writer, like the ancient sage, could turn a triple somersault if he wanted to. All the words belonged to the enemies of man; the Revolution gave permission to steal them, that was all. That was enough. For ten years Nizan had been plundering, and all of a sudden he brought forth the sum total of his thefts: vocabulary. He understood his role as a communist writer, and he understood that it was the same thing for him to discredit the enemies of man and to discredit their language. No holds barred—the law of the jungle. The Word of the masters is a lie. Not only will we pick their sophisms apart, but we will invent sophisms to use against them, we will lie to them. We will even indulge in farce, to prove by our speech that the speech of the Master is a farce. (pp. 43-5)

The mission of the intellectual was to muddle the words and tangle the threads of bourgeois ideology. Snipers were setting fire to the brush and whole linguistic sectors were being reduced to ashes. Nizan rarely played the clown and did not go in much for sleight of hand. He lied, as we all did in that golden age, when he was very sure that no one would believe him. Calumny had just been born. It was nimble and gay and had a touch of poetry about it. But these practices reassured him. We know that he wanted to write—against death—and that death had changed the words into dead leaves under his pen. He had been afraid of being duped, afraid of wasting his life playing with wind. Now he was told that he had not been mistaken, that literature was a weapon in the hands of our masters. He was given a new mission: in a negative period, a book can be an act, if the revolutionary writer makes it his business to change the conditions of language. He could do anything he wanted, even create his own style. For the wick-

ed, it would be the sugarcoating on the bitter pill; for the good, a call to vigilance—when the sea sings, don't leap into it. Nizan studied negative form. His hatred was a pearl diver. Nizan took the pearls and threw them to us, rejoicing that it was his lot to serve the common ends by so personal a work. Without changing its immediate objective, his private struggle against the particular dangers that threaten a young bourgeois became his public function. He talked about hate and impotent fury, he wrote about the Revolution.

Thus it was the Party that made the writer. But the man? Did he have his "field" at last? His fulfillment? Was he happy? I do not think so. The same things that deprive us of happiness render us forever incapable of enjoying it. And then, the doctrine was clear and confirmed his personal experience. His alienations were bound up with the present structures of society and would disappear with the bourgeois class. But he did not believe that he would live to see socialism or, even if he did catch a glimpse of it during the last days of his life, that there would be time for the world metamorphosis to transform the old habits of a dying man. Nevertheless, he had changed. Never again did he experience the old sense of desolation, never again was he afraid he was wasting his life. He experienced tonic rages, and joys. He was very willing to be only the *negative man,* the writer who demoralizes, who exposes the hoax. Was that enough to satisfy the grave child he had never ceased to be? In a sense, yes. Before joining the Party, he clung to his refusals. Since he could not be real, he would be empty, he would derive his sole value from his dissatisfaction, from his frustrated desires. But a feeling of numbness began to come over him, and he was terrified that one day he might let go and sink into consent. As a Communist he consolidated his resistances. Up until then he had always been afraid of social man as of a devouring canker. The Party socialized him painlessly. Its collective being was none other than his individual person. He had only to *consecrate* the swirling eddies within him. He thought he was a monstrous freak. They hoisted him onto the stage and he displayed his deformities saying, "This is what the bourgeois have done to their own children." Before, he had turned his violence against himself; now he made it into bombs and hurled them against the palaces of industry. The masonry was not damaged, but Nizan was liberated. He gave free rein to his sacred rage, but was no more conscious of it than a strong singer is of the sound of his own voice. The rebellious young man became a holy terror.

He did not liberate himself so easily from death, or rather from the shadow it cast across his life. But when he became an adult, the adolescent who had been consumed by another man's anguish earned the right to die on his own. Marxism revealed to him his father's secret: Antoine Bloyé's solitude came from his betrayal. This worker-turned-bourgeois was always thinking about "the companions he had had in the workshops along the Loire and in the booking-rooms at the railroad depots, companions who were on the side of the servants, on the side of life without hope. He used to say—and it was a remark which he later tried to forget but which disappeared only to reappear in the days of his decline, on the eve of his own death—'So I am a traitor.' And he was." He had crossed the line and betrayed his class only to find himself a mere molecule in the molecular world of the petty bourgeois. He regretted his desertion a hundred times over, and especially one day during a strike, when he stood watching the demonstrators march. "These men of no importance were carrying far away from him the strength, the friendship, the hope from which he was cut off. That evening Antoine reflected that he was a man of solitude. A man without communion. The truth of life was on the side of those who had never 'succeeded.' Those men are not alone, he thought. They know where they are going."

The turncoat had disintegrated, and now he was swirling in the bourgeois cloud of dust. He came to know the alienation and unhappiness of the rich because he had become the accomplice of those who exploited the poor. That communion with the "men of no importance" would have been a weapon against death. With them, he would have known the fullness of misery and friendship. Without them, he remained exposed: he was already defunct, a single sweep of the scythe had severed his human ties and his life.

Was Monsieur Nizan really this sorrowful deserter? I do not know. In any case, that is the way his son saw him. Nizan discovered, or thought he discovered, the reason why he opposed his father in a thousand little ways: he loved the man in him and hated the betrayal. I invite the well-meaning Marxists who have studied my friend's case and explained it by an obsession to betray, to reread his works with their eyes open, if they still can, and not to hold out against the obvious truth. It is true that this son of a traitor often speaks of betrayal. In *Aden* he writes: "I might have been a traitor, I might have suffocated." And in *Les chiens de garde:* "If we betray the bourgeoisie for mankind, let us not be ashamed to admit that we are traitors." Antoine Bloyé is a traitor to mankind. Another traitor appears in *La conspiration,* the unfortunate Pluvinage, son of a cop and a cop himself. And so what does it mean, this oft-repeated word? That Nizan sold out to Daladier? When they start talking about other people, the members of the Left Establishment in France are shamefully ready to be shocked. I know of nothing dirtier and more puerile, unless it is "decent" women gossiping about a free woman. Nizan wanted to write and he wanted to live. What need had he of thirty miserable pieces of silver drawn on secret funds? But as the son of a worker who had become a bourgeois, he wondered what he really was: a bourgeois or a worker? There is no doubt that his chief preoccupation was this civil war inside him. A traitor to the proletariat, Monsieur Nizan had made his son into a traitor to the bourgeoisie: the bourgeois-in-spite-of-himself would cross the line in the other direction. But that is not so easy. When communist intellectuals feel like joking, they call themselves proletarians: "We do manual labor at home." Lacemakers, so to speak. Nizan was more lucid and more demanding. He saw in them and in himself petty bourgeois who had sided with the working class. There is a gaping gulf between a Marxist novelist and a skilled laborer. They smile prettily at each other across it, but if the author takes a single step he falls into the abyss. That's all very well for a bourgeois, the son of a bourgeois and the grandson of a

bourgeois—having your heart in the right place can't change the facts of birth. But Nizan was a blood relative of his new allies. He remembered his grandfather who had remained "on the side of the servants, on the side of life without hope," Nizan had grown up like the children of railroad workers, in landscapes of iron and smoke. But an engineering diploma had sufficed to plunge his childhood into solitude, to impose on his entire family an irreversible metamorphosis. Never did he cross the line again. He betrayed the bourgeoisie without going over to the enemy camp. . . . Till the very end he was the friend of "those who had never 'succeeded,' " but he never managed to become their brother. No one was to blame except the bourgeois who had made his father into a bourgeois. This discreet void always bothered him. He had heard the bourgeois sirens, and because he was conscientious he was always worried. Since he could not participate in the "communion of servants, of those who live without hope," he never thought he was sufficiently protected against temptation, against death. He shared in the camaraderie of the Party members but he never escaped from the solitude that was the heritage of a betrayal. (pp. 45-9)

I considered him the perfect Communist. It was convenient: in my eyes he became the spokesman for the Party's Political Bureau. I took his moments of ill temper, his illusions, frivolities, and passions for attitudes agreed upon in high places. In July of '39, in Marseille, where I met him by chance and for the last time, he was gay. He was about to sail for Corsica. I read in his eyes the gayety of the Party. He talked about the war, thought that we would escape it. I instantly made a mental translation: "The Political Bureau is very optimistic, its spokesman declares that the negotiations with the USSR are going to be successful. By fall, he says, the Nazis will be on their knees."

September taught me not to confuse the opinions of my friend with the decisions of Stalin. I was surprised. Annoyed. I was apolitical and reluctant to make any commitment, but my heart was on the Left, of course, like everyone else's. Nizan's rapid rise had flattered me and given me a sort of revolutionary importance in my own eyes. (pp. 50-1)

He wrote the foreign policy pieces for *Ce soir.* One theme only: unite with the USSR against Germany. He had developed it so often that he had become convinced of it. While Molotov and Ribbentrop were putting the finishing touches on their Pact, Nizan was shouting himself hoarse demanding, with threats, a rapprochement between France and the USSR. During the summer of '39, in Corsica, he saw some of the leaders. They were friendly to him and congratulated him on his articles. But at night, after he had retired, they held long secret confabulations. Did they know what was in store for us? Nothing is less certain. The Party, still in the middle of vacation, was thunderstruck by the revelation of September. In Paris frightened journalists blindly assumed the gravest responsibilities. In any case, Nizan never doubted for a moment that he had been lied to. It was not his vanity that suffered, or even his pride—he had been wounded much more deeply: in his humility. He had never crossed the frontier between the classes and he knew it. Not trusting himself, he saw the silence of the leaders as evidence that the people did not trust him. Ten years of obedience had not allayed their suspicions. They would never forgive this doubtful ally for his father's betrayal. (p. 53)

He had joined the Party in order to save his life, and the Party robbed him of life; he was fighting for the Party in order to stave off death, and death came to him through the Party. I think he was mistaken. The massacre was brought forth from the womb of Earth and it sprang to life everywhere. But I am talking about what he thought: Hitler, his hands freed, was going to throw himself upon us. Nizan imagined that our army of workers and peasants was going to be exterminated with the consent of the USSR, and he was stupefied at the thought. To his wife he spoke of another fear: the war would be interminable, and when he came back it would be too late, he would be worn out. He would survive only to brood over his regrets and his bitterness, haunted by the counterfeit coin of memories. In the face of these reawakened threats, the only thing left was revolt, the old, anarchic, desperate revolt. Since everything betrayed mankind, he would preserve what little humanity was left by saying "no" to everything. (p. 54)

> *Jean-Paul Sartre, in a foreword to* Aden, Arabie *by Paul Nizan, translated by Joan Pinkham, MR Press, 1968, pp. 9-56.*

A portrait of Nizan in 1936.

David L. Schalk   (essay date 1973)

[*Schalk is an American educator and critic. In the following excerpt, he discusses the relationship between the intellectual and politics as presented in Nizan's* The Watchdogs.]

La trahison des clercs (1927) [is] Julien Benda's famous polemic against the intelligentsia of his day. Benda's intransigent idealist position was attacked from many quarters, perhaps most perceptively and tellingly by the young French Communist, Paul Nizan, in his bitter denunciation of those whom he termed *Les chiens de garde.* There can be no doubt that Benda was one of Nizan's primary targets, and in many ways the two books provide natural foils for each other. . . . I intend to present, as accurately and objectively as possible, Nizan's arguments against the professorial guardians of the *status quo,* and test the validity of his message for the contemporary intellectual. (p. 79)

Nizan's primary focus in *Les chiens de garde* is on teachers of philosophy, but it is clear that his arguments apply to all other disciplines. We shall examine these arguments in some detail. André Gide, though he recommended *Les chiens de garde* to his skeptical friend Roger Martin du Gard, in defending his own evolution toward greater political involvement, found the book badly put together and full of repetitions. "One has understood three times over what he wants to say, and he still continues to speak. But, such as it is, the book is a sign of the times. The *game* is no longer permissible, even if it is that of the intelligence" [André Gide, *Journal, 1889-1939* (1951)]. Gide's own flirtation with communism has been extensively documented, both by biographers and in his own *Journal,* his famous *Retour de l'URSS,* the *Retouches à mon retour de l'URSS,* and in the collection entitled *Littérature engagée.* All agree that Gide had little understanding or sympathy for the doctrinal and theoretical aspects of Marxism, and Gide himself often admitted that he struggled valiantly with Marx but could never read him. It seems probable that Gide did not fully grasp what Nizan was saying; the anger and the vitriolic denunciations appealed to him, but he did not see that Nizan was obliged to detail his documentation because he was trying to describe a very sophisticated system of maintaining social stability, backed up with elaborate intellectual constructs. Only Sartre and the existentialists, after World War II, began to develop and elaborate upon his analyses, and much of Nizan sounds as modern as Herbert Marcuse.

The question Nizan begins with in *Les chiens de garde* is: Can one continue to study philosophy without any sense of the meaning and direction of his research? He wants to debate this question openly, since many young people are engaged in philosophical studies—often motivated merely by the vague notion that philosophy involves "good intentions" toward men, and that through the pursuit of philosophy peace will spread among men of good will. It is not quite so simple, Nizan argues, reminding his readers that a number of men have paid with their lives or their freedom for the practice of philosophy.

Nizan's first premise is that some philosophies are beneficial to men, and that others are fatal. There is no generally utilitarian philosophy. . . . If there is no single philosophy *en soi,* there are instead a whole series of philosophies, just as there are Arabs, Frenchmen, etc. A philosophy is, after all, an effort to unify and structure different elements; it is not and never was *"univoque,"* but is always *"équivoque."* About all philosophies have in common is an "entity of discourse," and one could add that they have a "formal unity of aim," in that they claim to be able to formulate "dispositions and directions for human life."

Thus Nizan has proven to his satisfaction that philosophy remains equivocal. One enterprise for critical thought would be to define the *current* equivocations surrounding the word "philosophy." It can be assumed that there will be variations in each generation. If, despite the argument Nizan has presented, one still holds the view that philosophy is univocal, and if one finds the doctrines of Bergson or someone else repugnant, one is forced to say that this is merely a "temporary deviation," an accidental sickness in *"la Philosophie éternelle."* For Nizan the explanation is much more simple: Bergson, Boutroux, and the other professionals belong to a family of philosophers whom he regards as the enemy. How and why he will explain in a later part of his book—definitely not because he has a different vision of the eternal destination of philosophy. "I have no confidence in Destiny."

Nizan takes the anti-positivist position, rather widely accepted today but quite unique in his time, that intelligence *per se* can be used for or against man. Intelligence is after all only a servant. As he puts it, on the one side there are the idealist philosophers who emit Truths on Man, and on the other "the map of the incidence of tuberculosis in Paris which says how men die. . . ." He gives other examples of the professionals' emphasis on elegance of argument, technical subtlety, a high (*hautaine*) manner of philosophizing, and urges students not to wander off onto the "polished paths" and "frozen corridors" of a spiritualist philosophy.

As far as the relationship of these philosophers to history is concerned, they profess to live apart from other social groups, are free from passing time and the chains of *emplacement.* They are a "head without a body." They abstain from reality, live in a state of "scandalous absence," are "lighter than angels" with their abstract definitions of liberty. Nizan has already tried to show that all philosophy possesses a temporal and human significance, despite the protestations of the academic philosophers, their attacks on thinkers like Marx who want to change, not interpret the world. "The decision simply to look passively at the world is as much an earthly decision made by philosophy as the decision to change the world." Nizan later stresses that if men resign from active life, they are making *"décisions de partisan."* "Abstention is a choice," and even the uneducated person is aware of this truth. The so-called purity of the philosopher is imaginary; every one of them, and Nizan surely meant to include even Julien Benda, "participates in the impure actuality of his time." (pp. 85-7)

After arguing that philosophy is equivocal and that philosophers cannot escape the actuality of their time, Nizan turns to a third major point, which is an attempt to explain the philosophers' emphasis on timelessness and abstrac-

tions in Marxist terms. Very simply it is an element of "bourgeois thought." Men like Bergson and Brunschvicg live very comfortably, accept and love "the present order." They shun any philosophical conclusions potentially detrimental to that order. Always they strive to remain within the strict terms of their philosophical systems, and claim to be responsible only to their colleagues, "present and to come." Nizan says no to all this and demands a real philosophical democracy.

One way Nizan illustrates his hypotheses concerning what really motivates the intellectual leaders of his day is to point up the tremendous contradictions between what these "pure spirits" promise, between their high ideals, and what they produce. He takes as an example their reactions to the First World War; they have not really considered the war, have not tried to measure this terrible event. During the actual years of conflict, they did what the generals said; if they were too old to be mobilized they "followed with docility the ignorant popular movements and exorted those who were mobilisable to die. . . ." Each of their dead students was a "witness (*témoignage*) for their philosophy." Bergson saw the victory of France as his victory; the Marne seemed to Brunschvicg a "striking verification of his philosophy." In other words, when they did get involved, they labored on behalf of the established order. Nizan feels that it is time to get these men into a corner and force some straight answers from them: What are their thoughts on war, colonialism, factories, love, unemployment, suicide, abortion? They are not really deceiving anyone any more; if they refuse to take sides, it is apparent that the particular kind of partisan decision they have made is to support the *status quo.* They live well within society as now constituted, they have opted "for their spiritual comfort, and for the temporal guarantees of that comfort. . . ."

Already in 1932, before intellectuals became widely involved in anti-fascist leagues, and two years before the Popular Front movement began to gather momentum, Nizan found that unusual pressures were mounting against the *clercs.* Concrete problems from the outside world were imposing more and more upon the consciousness of the *clercs,* seriously disturbing them. The equivocations of a man like Julien Benda provide a striking illustration of the development Nizan is portraying. Gide, of course, reacted by moving toward nearly full *engagement,* and even Roger Martin du Gard, often portrayed as totally withdrawn from the actuality of his day, moved toward greater political involvement in the 1930's.

Most of these intellectuals, Nizan continues, will try to drive these problems out of their minds by spending all their time learning a method, never attacking a particular situation, never approving or condemning, never engaging themselves. They would remain, he thought, "docile clerks" of the bourgeoisie. . . . The question of what constitutes viable involvement for the intellectual was a frequent theme in Nizan's writings. His essential point is that he believes it almost impossible for intellectuals to carry the revulsion they may feel upon learning of some incident—perhaps a colonialist atrocity—to any sort of conclusion. They are content with mere "outlines of indignation, or revolt." They cannot go as far as a "radical refusal," which might mean a refusal of their comfort, security, order, even their lives. "To renounce themselves. To wish for the annihilation of their own nature." They cannot admit the real aims and essence of their own class; so they throw up clouds of reasoning like a smoke screen, and end by searching for validating reasons for bourgeois domination, for stock dividends and all the rest. Of course Nizan himself has a solution, the classical Marxist one. The intellectual must finally opt for the party of the oppressed and for revolution. We remember that this solution worked for him only until 1939.

Nizan would be pleased if as a first step the academic philosophers could admit that "Any philosophy is an act. M. Parodi himself [an influential academic administrator and idealist philosopher] knows that every thought is an action." The time has come, Nizan feels, to mount an offensive against these academics, a really revolutionary action of demolishing. It must be stated openly that college teachers, in fact the whole university system, which is of course a public institution, the professors being paid functionaries of the State, operate for exactly the same purposes as do politicians, generals, and the like. The professors are involved in a more subtle means of domination; they try to win over by persuasion. The University has taken over the role of the Church in the *Ancien Régime*—the University is "the spiritual lever of the State." The eminent professors are the new bishops and cardinals; they are not innocent old men, but *identical* to police at a demonstration, only with less naked power. The philosophers and other professors try to persuade young men and women to ignore social, political, and economic realities. One of their sources of power is their service as government inspectors who determine the careers of young teachers within the system. (Many would find this arrangement similar to the American system, with the senior professors at the professional conventions, surrounded by their coteries of graduate students searching for employment.) The French intellectual leaders of 1932, Nizan adds, have an elaborate quasi-official doctrine, one of obedience, a lay positivism, a dedication to the *status quo*.

Nizan was convinced that the period of upheaval the Western world was traversing in the early 1930's would not prove to be a temporary deviation, but rather that the epoch of bourgeois domination was ending. Still the intellectuals have not, for the most part, made a move away from their silence and their abstractions. When they do feel these new pressures too strongly, Nizan predicted that reactionary philosophies would take up the slack in a last ditch stand—some form of fascist doctrine would be adopted. (One could cite Nizan's own classmate Robert Brasillach or Drieu La Rochelle as examples validating his prediction. He also thought that Social Catholic groups like the Personalists would find themselves forced into the fascist camp, both by events and by the inherent contradictions of their doctrines.) On the other side, Nizan believed, Communism would stand.

In his conclusion, Nizan makes his rebuttal to Julien Benda's *La trahison des clercs* even more explicit, by asserting very forcefully that to remain faithful to abstract

clerical ideals is a *trahison* ["treason," "betrayal"], a pretended fidelity which, by offering spiritual salvation to men who receive physical blows, hides a "supreme desertion." This infidelity to men is the "true *trahison des clercs.*" What Nizan calls for is another form of betrayal—that of one's own class. The cultivation of intelligence is a weapon, and in the universities young men are learning to use it, to turn against their fathers, to hasten the death of the old world. They will be useful and not just apostles, they will become revolutionaries of the type described by Lenin, and the creation of values will come after the Revolution. For the moment the intellectual must cooperate completely with the working-class movement, in practical, day-to-day tasks. The philosopher should become a new variety of specialist, an expert in the indignation of exploited men, skilled in the denunciation of illusions and false perceptions—in reality a variety of propagandist.

> In a world brutally divided into masters and servants, we must at last frankly admit a hidden alliance with the masters, or proclaim our allegiance to the party of the servants. No place is left for the impartiality of the *clerc*. Nothing remains but the combats of partisans.

One is either with the bourgeoisie or the proletariat. The time of ruse is over; one cannot hide under veils of Eternity, Reason, Justice. If philosophers today blush in admitting that they have betrayed men for the bourgeoisie, if we betray the bourgeoisie for men, "let us not blush in admitting that we are traitors."

It is easy to see how Nizan laid himself open to the official PCF [Parti Communiste Français ("French Communist Party")] attack on him; Henry Lefebvre did not have much difficulty in finding treachery in all his work. The theme of betrayal is always present in his writing, and is especially strong in *Antoine Bloyé* (the story of a man who betrays the working class for the bourgeoisie), and in *La conspiration* (which involves a complex series of betrayals on several levels, besides the obvious example of the character Pluvinage, who becomes a police informer and discloses the whereabouts of the Communist leader Carré to the authorities). Betrayal is, as we have seen, the key to *Les chiens de garde.*

It is equally obvious that Nizan was a traitor only in the sense of breaking with the Party over a crucial matter of policy. He always claimed that he was a Communist. (pp. 87-92)

Les chiens de garde, and the entire *corpus* of Nizan's work, are major documents in intellectual history, for at least two reasons. First, they present with unusual clarity and persuasiveness—and very early, probably for the first time—the argument that the result of the intellectual's rational reflection on his environment must lead to *engagement.* (Or, at least, the awareness that *engagement* is an ethical imperative, and that any other course of action must involve betrayal.) Because the particular direction that was appropriate for Nizan is no longer a viable one, the *engagement* of the intellectual, in the West at least, involves far more complications and uncertainties. Perhaps in some ways this is a better situation, even if it tends to render the intellectual impotent, eternally unable to choose.

Nizan has also made a significant contribution to that branch of intellectual history which is almost identical to historical sociology, the study of the behavior of intellectuals as a class. As has been shown, many of the theories—especially about educational systems—of that loose and tenuous coalition, which can for convenience be termed the "New Left," have their origins in Nizan's thought and in his personal example. Thanks to Nizan and to Sartre, whose ideas on *engagement* and on the nature of literature owe so much to **Les chiens de garde** and the living example of his friend, the particular kind of watchdog behavior perpetrated by so many of today's "Establishment Intellectuals" is widely understood to be an ignoble form of *trahison,* a deception and perversion of the intelligence, of reason and understanding. The revolutionary implications of a true culture, real education, real learning, are as apparent to many today as they were to Nizan in 1932, when he extracted them from the mass of academic discourses showered by the *chiens de garde* upon their victims, the students. Many would find the situation today indentical to that which Nizan so bitterly castigated—a situation where a place in the academic hierarchy was the promised reward for ignoring the real world, for continuing to betray in the right fashion, the fashion needed for the continuance of the peculiar mix of freedom and repression which was the Third Republic.

In these senses Nizan's immediacy is obvious and striking. (pp. 95-6)

> David L. Schalk, "Professors as Watchdogs: Paul Nizan's Theory of the Intellectual and Politics," in Journal of the History of Ideas, Vol. XXXIV, No. 1, January-March, 1973, pp. 79-96.

James Atlas   (essay date 1973)

[*Atlas is an American critic and biographer. In the following excerpt, he distinguishes Nizan's* Antoine Bloyé *from the works of his French contemporaries who were also influenced by socialism.*]

The long debates over Socialist Realism that have been a characteristic feature of literary history in the Communist countries since the 1930s have produced little in the way of literature. There is no longer much question about the negative effects this doctrine had and continues to have. Instituted at the 1934 Soviet Writers' Congress, when Andrei Zhdanov put forward the demand that literature "depict reality in its revolutionary development," it provided the rationale for a program that was to dissipate the creative impulses of Russian writers until there was nothing left of the energy that had been marshaled during the initial stages of the Revolution. Zamyatin, Mayakovsky, Aleksandr Blok and Anatol Lunacharsky, to name only those who come most readily to mind, had all participated in the cultural enterprise of Bolshevism, and their resourcefulness in establishing a rational transition between two epochs owed a good deal to their having belonged to the old intelligentsia. Like Trotsky, who believed in leaving writ-

ers to their own devices, these were men willing to honor what could be salvaged of the past. But once Stalin had assumed control of every aspect of Soviet life, including literary themes and purposes, the entrenched party line began to wreak the kind of damage that is documented in Nadezhda Mandelstam's *Hope against Hope*—and has been doing so ever since.

Of course, it was not only in Russia that the implications of the Writers' Congress were felt. Just as the Communist Parties of Europe looked to Moscow to determine their political line, so Communist writers felt obligated—and were obliged—to uphold the doctrine of Socialist Realism. In France, Gide and Malraux attended the 1934 Congress (though Gide's address, urging a policy of "Communist individualism," was enough to discredit him) and, if neither ever joined the party, still their fascination with Russia reflected the temper of French literature during that epoch. Many other French writers, including at one time or another virtually all the Surrealists, became card-carrying members. But what texts exist that we can accept as being examples of Socialist Realism and genuine works of literature at the same time? Surely not Aragon's novels, or Eluard's few poems to Stalin. Sartre, Malraux, even Gide wrote works that seized on and exploited revolutionary situations, but these are more readily assimilable to the tradition that Lukács has called "Critical Realism," differing from the definition of Socialist Realism in that the works in question observe life in society "from the outside." Now, what distinguishes Paul Nizan's **Antoine Bloyé** from the work of his fellow writers in France is the manner in which it illustrates the character of dialectical materialism "from the inside"—without sacrificing the aesthetic possibilities of realism. (pp. 407-08)

Antoine Bloyé is a brilliant example of modern European literature [that] . . . can serve to refine our awareness of the life and work of a significant literary figure.

Nizan belonged to that generation of overwrought, talented intellectuals who graduated from the Ecole Normale Supérieure together, to find themselves plunged into the atmosphere of the radical 1920s, when the French Communist Party had just been founded and the possibilities awakened by the 1917 Revolution were in the air. Nizan participated in several publishing ventures, all devoted to theoretical issues in keeping with Lenin's axiom, "No revolutionary movement without a revolutionary theory." From the start, Nizan's anger was genuine, even if its object needed to be identified more precisely. In this respect, he differs from Sartre, Simone de Beauvoir and Henri Lefebvre, all of whom were later to portray him in, respectively, *The Words, The Prime of Life* and *Existentialism*. These memoirs vacillate between suspicion and sympathy; what their authors have most in common is the opportunity to look back on the past and write about a man who died at Dunkirk when he was 35. W. D. Redfern notes in his recent study of Nizan, *Committed Literature in a Conspiratorial World,* that those who survived him had "a set way of seeing Nizan exclusively as a negator"; his rage against the bourgeoisie seemed to them unfocused, his invective uncontrolled. But Nizan's impulse was toward the concrete, the practical realities of capitalism in France;

Sartre's claim that the proletariat was "the incarnation and vehicle of an idea" exemplified the sort of thinking he was anxious to correct. No work of Nizan's more effectively challenges that view of history than *Antoine Bloyé.*

Nizan's father had been a railroad engineer at Tours, so that Nizan knew first hand the world depicted in the novel, "a little moving world which changed its position in conformity with its own laws, along its own trajectory, with its own customs, language and virtues." And it was a world Nizan came to detest, not because it oppressed him but because he had watched it destroy his father. His own experience of the oppressive workings of capitalism is to be found in *Aden, Arabie,* but in his novel the chosen subject was a man, Antoine Bloyé, whose own father had been a mere ticket inspector and who had risen through the ranks from locomotive engineer to supervisor, depot master and eventually manager, overseer of a thousand workers. In the space of 250 pages, Nizan examined his father's entire life, from his birth in 1864 to the moment of his death in 1927. It was a life not without events, not without a coherent order; but it was not *lived.* Set against the backdrop of 19th-century France in the closing years of the Second Empire, "the turbulent era of Guizot, Lamartine and the Prince President," through World War I and its aftermath, Nizan's novel registers the rapid industrial expansion that transformed the land—"capital seeking investments"—while "the shops of the School of Arts and Trades [ran] with the motion of well-oiled machines, turning out their human products."

This was the essence of Nizan's bitterness, the rise of alienated labor. The epigraph to *Antoine Bloyé* is a passage from *The German Ideology* of Marx and Engels calling for the abolition of "labor," or rather of that species of labor that "has lost all semblance of self-activity." Elsewhere in the chapter Nizan cites, its authors speak of "abstract individuals," and that is what Antoine Bloyé had become, a man whose work allied him to a vast productive force, but whose own being had been absorbed by the machines he served.

What makes Nizan's chronicle of a wasted life so vivid is the author's awareness of Bloyé's human possibilities. Writing from within the mind of an "ordinary" man, he was able to depict the circumstances, emotions and desires the consciousness of which is necessarily diminished in those whom labor has robbed of the ability to reflect. School, sexual adventures, marriage into a bourgeois family, the death in early childhood of a daughter, the birth of a son, promotions, vacations: these are mere events, and their qualities as lived experience lie buried beneath obligation and blind will. Nizan tells us that Antoine Bloyé wasn't "meditative," that "events rolled past without his taking notice." But the texture of Nizan's prose, viscous and laden with sensation, imitates the world through which Bloyé moves. While his own life is crushed, "caught like an insect in this quivering web of railway lines," the richness of the natural world surrounds him like a penumbra of unrealized hope. And that is what is most remarkable about Nizan's achievement. Despite Antoine Bloyé's docility, he sees, through the lens of Nizan's sensibility, the world's possibilities: the heaviness and indolence of

Sunday, summer evenings on the waterfront, the memories of childhood whose atmosphere settled over the dinner table on visits to his parents' home.

This realm of the inward, lived moment does not appear in isolation. Nizan follows the transformation of the landscape during his father's life, "the spectacular arrival of the turbulence of the twentieth century." Just as Balzac provided exact information about law, medicine, finance or journalism, so Nizan included statistics, salaries, elaborate dissertations in the Naturalist mode about the mechanics of diesel engines. Such were the realities of that epoch, and Bloyé's failure to transcend them, or even to comprehend their nature, can be traced to his alienation from the very objects that dominated his life. Nizan's own training in Marxism and philosophy allowed him to interpret what Antoine Bloyé, who "lived in a world where the word philosophy meant laziness and cowardice," could only sense: the relation between social conditions and individual destiny.

There is a quality of unconcealed rage in this portrait, rage against the squandering of human lives, against the manipulation of men, against all those oppressive forces latent in capitalism. When Antoine Bloyé, whose career has advanced to the limits imposed on his class, is compelled to retire during World War I, having been held responsible for an error in the manufacture of munitions, he suffers a nervous breakdown. "He had nothing more to look forward to. No human struggle, no pastimes, no resources. He found nothing in his past life to help him." Nizan's was less the conventional hostility of the son toward the father than a refusal to capitulate to "the influx of nothingness" that threatened them both. He would have accepted Merleau-Ponty's evaluation [see Further Reading] of his work: that it located "a general principle of alienation" within our own dread of spiritual emptiness. (pp. 408-09)

> James Atlas, *"Just to Pass the Time Away . . . ,"* in The Nation, *New York, Vol. 217, No. 13, October 22, 1973, pp. 407-09.*

Karl Miller   (essay date 1973)

[*Miller is an English educator and critic. In the following excerpt, he questions the value of* Antoine Bloyé *as social criticism.*]

Antoine Bloyé opens with the hero's death (it seems right to refer to him as a hero, though his story is proclaimed as that of a wasted life), and his burial according to the rites of the French bourgeoisie. Their interments are a slow and circumstantial business, and it is soon obvious that Nizan goes in for literal statement, some of it very effective, and for matters of fact. Despite the emblems and ceremonies with which it is saluted, Bloyé's death changes him into a "silent object" which will no longer issue orders or heed them, and the text of the death notice in the newspapers is supplied verbatim. Later, we are given the details of his growing salary and the slips of paper on which the company formally acquaints him with his promotions. [Richard] Elman refers to him [see Further Reading] as a "nobody" in whom Nizan has enabled us to take an interest: Nizan's literal statements appear to be telling the reader that he is also an anybody—anybody, that is, who fails to fight the class war on the right side.

Nizan then reverts to the start of this wasted life. Bloyé (b. 1864) is of peasant stock. His father has come off the land to work as a railway porter and, in time, the family moves to St. Nazaire, where Antoine gets the education which equips him to attend one of the country's technical schools: these have become important, and self-important, institutions. He joins the railways at a higher level than his father, and is destined for the middle ranks of management. Early in his career he yields to an impulse to take part in a strike, which proves abortive. This lapse is forgiven him by his masters; by the writer, it is seen as of a piece with his rejection of the woman with whom he has been happily sleeping—in favor of the empty daughter of his immediate superior in the railways.

Meanwhile the railways themselves, in the era of their expansion or explosion, have laid claim to a leading role in the novel. The tracks are forcing their way, inch by inch, across the plains and water meadows of *la belle France*. A huge organization exists to serve them, divided into rival categories (passenger, maintenance, and so on), each equally devoted to the cause, and each equally at the mercy of a ruling group of stockholders and financiers: an organization which accepts that there will be accidents, loss of life, and that the lost lives will not be those of the stockholders and financiers. Issuing from their blackened roundhouses, locomotives become relentlessly fiercer and faster.

A girl is born to the Bloyés, but her health is poor, and before long she dies. A boy takes her place, and father and son go on country walks together, with the wife, Anne, occasionally joining them, on sufferance. By now, Bloyé is Depot Superintendent at Tours, and an accredited though uneasy member of the local bourgeoisie, who dream without rancor of the vices of the upper class and indulge their resentment of the workers—whom Bloyé covertly thinks he has betrayed. (p. 26)

It is worth looking at two passages in the novel in which the notions of Bloyé as a class traitor, and of his life as nothingness, are expressed. Midway through his career, one of his men is killed in an accident, and he has to let the family know. There's a striking account of the introduction of the corpse into the house, with its dazed child, the beds still warm from the women's bodies, the reproaches which the widow directs at the company. On such occasions, Nizan has pointed out, "the bosses sometimes experience the uncomfortable feeling of guilt." And Bloyé is no exception. "What terrible weight a dead man is"—Bloyé has to lay out the driver's body on a bed, and take it in his arms. "A wounded man still knows how to make himself light. . . ." Bloyé duly experiences a boss's uncomfortable feeling of guilt: "He wanted to ask for forgiveness as though he had killed him with his own hands." Nizan then states:

> When you did not die before retiring, you received a bronze or silver medal, a medal stamped with a locomotive, hung on a tricolor ribbon, like a life-saving medal. You received a letter: "In return for your good and faithful services."

Live and die for a medal, for nothing.

> But he, Antoine Bloyé, who commanded others, who transmitted orders from above like an adjutant—and soldiers can also be killed in peacetime, in target practice or on the march, by a stray bullet, or by sunstroke—but he, who was not the enemy of these men, was he then their enemies' accomplice? In vain did he try to defend himself, telling himself that it was the fault of the track maintenance division, summoning to his aid the thoughts of the functionary. He knew full well that he had passed to the side of the bosses, that he was their accomplice. All his efforts, all his memories, altered not one jot of his complicity. He thought of his father, who was one of those who took orders, of his comrades in the shipyards of the Loire and in the railway depots who were also on the side of those who serve, on the side of life without hope. And returning home in the icy Auvergne dawn, he repeated to himself a phrase that held good for the whole of his life, a phrase that he forced himself to forget, that only disappeared in order to reappear in the time of his adversity, on the eve of his own death: "So, I am a traitor."

And he was.

Someone in Bloyé's situation at that time might well feel—and he might feel it at other times too—that he was a traitor. But it can hardly be the case that these railway men lived and died "for a medal." Since Nizan is prone to making assertions, let me state that, from what I know of such men now, when their craft is a comparatively mundane one, their predecessors probably did this job because they needed the money and because they liked it. Many railway men have been proud of their work, and excited by it, even when they were aware of the restrictions and humiliations which it imposed. In Bloyé's day, the team of men who worked on the railways had something of the character of a guild or an elite military force. They established an elegance for themselves—in the midst of the restrictions and the risks, and the noise and the dirt—which is not entirely, even now, a thing of the past.

Nizan persuades the reader, though he does not himself admit, that Bloyé's was an interesting job. He alludes to Bloyé's memories here, his memories of the work he has done—but only to suggest that these memories lack validity, that they can't compete with the grand fact of his complicity. The work done by "any" superintendent is dirty work. It resembles the "filthy works" condemned by Calvinist theologians, who were clear that dutifulness could not compete with the grace of God. Superintendents cannot be saved. Certainly the capacity to make a fetish, or a supreme virtue, of their work cannot save them. And the fact that, in an important sense, he was always a worker as well as a commander, that he bore his share of toil and risk, and that he cared about, and behaved well toward, the men under his command, cannot alter the fact that Bloyé is damned. Nizan is unfair to bosses, and it is not necessary to believe that the French railways should never have been nationalized in order to conclude that he is even unfair to financiers: they are damned too, and rather dimly apprehended, as no more than a set of predators.

As for the "nothingness" of Bloyé's life, I realize that this is a technical term in Existentialism. Sartre, incidentally, was a school friend of Nizan's—they both shone at the Ecole Normale in Paris—and has written admiringly about him [see excerpt dated 1960]. This is a term to which more than one generation, in more than one country, has been gravely attentive. But Nizan doesn't mean anything very deep or difficult by it here: it has the aspect of a libel on the politically unacceptable. Toward the end of the book he invokes "the influx of nothingness." Bloyé

> was beyond all help. When nothingness appears, all else is destroyed. Worries, amusements, people, treatments, and pleasures afford men little protection from the pang of nonexistence. It takes a great deal of force and creation to escape from nothingness. Antoine had created nothing. He had let his forces go to waste. He had invented nothing. He had not dealt with men.

It is true that he was a man who lived his adult life without close friends. But this is also true of many. . . . It is not true that he did not deal with men: he did, and he was worried that he had let them down. Nizan, of course, is intent on showing that if Bloyé is a nobody, it is the system's fault—the system which commanded him to work and obey and command, and to make a good marriage to a silly woman. Nizan is intent on showing that while he is defeated, and treacherous, he is neither a cipher nor a fiend. Bloyé is allowed to retain a measure of dignity, despite his betrayal of his class. Traitors, however, are traitors, and it takes "a great deal of force and creation" to show convincingly the dignity that may be retained by someone whom it would be reasonable to call a traitor. Nizan does not expend that force. Bloyé does not look like a traitor to me.

What would Bloyé have needed to do to be saved—to avoid vilification (and it is something not very different from that which we have to do with at times) as a traitor? He would have had to throw in his lot with the railway workers when they went on strike, and perhaps become a militant leftist. Nizan wrote his novel during one of those periods when capitalism, according to hostile diagnosticians, is in its death throes, and during this period the French Communist Party was doing well, and expanding. Here was a huge organization, divided into rival categories, each equally devoted to the cause, and each equally at the mercy of a ruling group. In other words, and in some lights, membership in the Party might have looked very like a job on the French railways in the heyday of their exploitation by financiers.

It may be supposed indecent to say so at a time when the Communist Party does not have much appeal even for the revolutionary young, but it is unpleasant to be told, in effect, that you are likely to prove a traitor if you accept responsibility within an industrial concern, and if you refuse to accept the type of discipline that has been exercised within the Communist parties of the West. Nizan broke with the Party over the Hitler-Stalin pact, and he was vilified by them thereafter. But at the time when his novel was published he would, I think, have been willing to have it read as enjoining a response compatible with a fair degree of trust in organized Communism.

Nizan's subject is a fascinating one, and no defensive feelings on the part of readers (and reviewers) who are inured to gainful employment should be permitted to obscure this. He is writing about a man who does not have the inner resources to live his life, outside the sphere of work. The book has a genuine appreciation of the human material from which Bloyé has been constructed (Nizan's own father, it seems, was drawn upon), and a vivid sympathy with his predicament which will often be seen as tempering, or as justifying, the firm resolve to interpret that predicament in terms of promotion and complicity. I am not sure that it does either of these things, but Bloyé is as far from being a nobody as he is from being a traitor.

Nizan appears to be saying—communist though he was, and constrained though he was in saying so by the requirements of militancy—that an effort must be made to stop people working like this. Let the people play. Here I think he is right. We have had enough work. (pp. 26-8)

All the same, the most striking feature of the novel is one which the novelist's scheme seeks to deny: and that is the picture which it gives, despite itself, of the satisfaction and excitement associated with the furtherance of the railways, of men breaking their backs and molding their lives to make the trains run on time, and faster. The image that lingers in the mind is that of the raising of a locomotive from a river bed. Nizan was excited by these matters himself, but he allows them to be washed away by the influx of nothingness, and we are meant to suppose that all they got for raising the locomotive was a medal.

Nizan was killed, at thirty-five, during the retreat to Dunkirk at the beginning of the Second World War. Had he lived, he might have developed a greater respect for types of work which are very different from those of metropolitan writers and polemicists, and a more indulgent attitude toward old age. For this is the book of a young man, a young man who was ready to command an audience and who helped to devise what was to become the favorite rhetoric of an élite. As he employs it, this rhetoric has its moments of utter abdication and inanity. There were certain old men, he writes, including Bloyé, who were "already bored with the boredom of the dead." He cannot be blamed for what was done by the bosses of the French Communist Party, any more than Bloyé can be blamed, though Nizan blames him, for what was done by the financial interests which controlled the French railways. To be contentious about it, he was no more of an accomplice than Bloyé. To be fair about it, he was less of an accomplice, in that he seems to have stood out against the apparatchiks, and to have paid for it. So he may have been a virtuous communist, one with a human face. But he was also the kind of human being who states that those who do not behave as he wishes are nothing. (p. 28)

Karl Miller, "Episodes in the Class War," in
The New York Review of Books, Vol. XX, No.
18, November 15, 1973, pp. 26-9.

Richard Wasson   (essay date 1977)

[*In the following essay, Wasson uses* Antoine Bloyé *to demonstrate the value of synthesizing Marxist criticism with the strain of postmodernist criticism which is concerned with history and social processes.*]

Postmodernist criticism, of whatever variety, assumes it is different from the past. Archetypalism and formalism recede; historicism, particularly of the positivist and liberal variety, proves an uncomfortable critical grandfather. The new "new-criticism" claims blindness is insight, true reading is insightful misreading; criticism becomes de-creation of the text. In other sectors the task of the critic is defined as the defense of the castle of Western culture, or to give comfort so that despair at its fall is less than catastrophic. A few celebrate the death of culture and literature, urging pornography as new literary form.

As is usual in cultural matters, the new criticism turns out to be not so new after all, for in most cases "reality" is defined as subjective, as linguistic, as a hidden structure. Though Freud and Jung, Kierkegaard and Sartre often stand repudiated, psychoanalytical and existential concerns inform and shape postmodernist criticism much as they informed and shaped modernism. Faith in the irrational, concern with the self, and alienation from social reality, from language, still guide most postmodernist critical perceptions.

Yet within postmodernism a drive exists toward the world, toward history, toward involvement with social processes. The idea of an identifiable postmodernist period implies at least the possibility of distinguishing between one historical time and another. Of particular importance is the Heideggerian strain in this criticism which sees the work in the context of a number of "situations." As one commentator has summed up the thrust of Heideggerian aesthetics:

> In an encounter with a work of art we do not go into a foreign universe, stepping outside time and history; we do not separate ourselves from ourselves. Rather we become more fully present; our whole self understanding is risked. . . . The work is putting a question to us, the question that called it into being. [Richard Palmer, *Hermeneutics: Interpretation Theory in Schleiermacher, Dilthey, Heidegger, and Gadamer* (1969)]

This drive into the world, into history, this concern with origins is the most fruitful direction in postmodernist criticism, for it contains within it the seeds of a genuine departure from varieties of formalism, of positivist historicism, or of irrationalism. It is to this trend that a Marxist criticism can most fruitfully speak, because Marxism is above all concerned with the question of traceable origins within social and historical contexts. Marxism centers on the historical and social processes in which the self acts and relates to others and the world. At the core of all relationships for Marxism is the organization of the labor process.

Of course, the mere mention of Marxism, of the labor process, instantly produces in most critics an anxiety, the defense against which is the pose of boredom. Often critics erect a stereotype of Marxism as a monolithic system ready to stuff reality into a dogmatic world view. Like all stereotypes, this one contains its measure of truth. Yet, one need only look at the variety of critical practice represented in the four recent Marxist anthologies, at the newly

translated work of Benjamin, Adorno, Lukács, and Brecht (to say nothing of the Sino-Soviet split and the complexities of Marxist theory and practice in Portugal, Angola, Spain, Italy, and the United States) to see that Marxism is anything but monolithic at this point in history. Then too, many critics who are not repelled by the conversion into jargon of psychoanalysis (repression, unconscious, sublimation) or of existentialism (angst, throwness-into-freedom, alienation) balk at even legitimate uses of Marxist categories (social relations of production, use-value, socially necessary labor time). Worse still, they take their version of Marxism not from Marx, or Engels, or Lenin, but from enemies or revisers of Marx.

Yet, the misuse of Marxist language and concepts cannot really explain the critical resistance to Marxism. Roland Barthes was nearer the truth in *Mythologies*. The use of Marxist language, particularly the language of class, is ruled out of court in the cultural realm because it is genuinely threatening to the established order. The capitalist class claims to be the spokesman for universal human values, the establisher of a social and economic order that is the culmination of history. Like all ruling classes, they claim to provide universal values in politics, in economics, in ethics, in culture, in personal relationships. Marxism, of course, challenges that claim, arguing that while the capitalist class did indeed expand the scope of human freedom, culture, productivity, and relationships, the bourgeois class has now become the force restraining human development. While the bourgeoisie is forced to use the words "capital" and "labor" in economics, it is less likely to do so in the political realm (at least no party claims to be the Capitalist or Bourgeois Party, while several compete for the word "labor" or "worker"). In the cultural realm, Barthes says, the matter is more complex, for the very attribution of values to classes threatens the bourgeois claim to universality. Once that claim is placed in doubt, the ideological underpinnings of the ruling class begin to crumble.

The task, then, for both Marxist and postmodernist criticism is to overcome the cultural taboos of bourgeois culture in order to engage in serious discussion. Paul Nizan's ***Antoine Bloyé*** can only serve to further that encounter. Nizan, a brilliant student of philosophy at the Ecolé Normal, a man of letters fully conversant with the modernist movement during the twenties and thirties, was a Marxist, a member of the French Communist Party, an organizer of the unemployed, and a candidate for elective office. He was an acquaintance of Jean-Paul Sartre from the time he entered the *lycée,* sharing a study with him in college. For Sartre, Nizan was the model Communist upon whom he based not only much of his notion of the Party, but most of the Communist characters in his novels and plays. More importantly, Sartre saw Nizan as not only the upholder of the Party line, but as a Marxist of the eyes and ears as well as of the intellect. ***Antoine Bloyé*** thus is the work of a Marxist intellectual of keen sensuous perception who was also an activist in the twenties and thirties.

An explication of the themes and techniques of the novel, of Nizan's exploration and presentation of the relationships between personal feeling and the labor process, speaks directly to the problematics of postmodernist criticism. As art work it embodies the most serious aspects of modernism and provides an aesthetic critique of those attitudes. Key concepts of the irrational self, derived from both psychoanalytical and existential models—in particular the notions of dissociation and alienation—are subjected to criticism. Nizan aesthetically shows how class shapes the individual identity at each stage of life and conditions the individual death. An analysis of the novel can only demonstrate the richness of Marxist insights, of Marxist language, in relation to the tasks postmodernism is articulating for itself.

Put rather generally, Nizan structures the novel to show the shaping effects of the labor process, or in more Marxist language, the social relations of production, on the feelings and attitudes of an individual. As the son of peasants turned urban workers, Antoine knows from very early in his life that he must sell his ability and power to labor for a wage in order to survive and have children. To Nizan this central fact of most human existence becomes also a category of thought through which to criticize psychoanalytical and existential descriptions of human experience. His art is dedicated to showing how the particulars of an individual life—the sense of self, the experience of love, of work, of time and memory—are contoured by one's relation to the process of production. Of course, as both Marxist and artist Nizan knew that though such experiences are structurally similar, they can only occur to individuals in particular ways.

Moreover, as both modernist and Marxist, Nizan knew he faced difficult technical problems. First, the character's experience must be rendered in its own terms. Like so many characters in modernist fiction from Dostoyevski's Underground Man through Leopold Bloom to Willy Loman, Antoine possesses neither the intellect nor the perception to fully understand his own experience. In particular, he is out of touch with both his own emotion and the process of history within which he lives. Nizan carefully chooses a set of narrative techniques that enables him to render Antoine's experience in typically modernist ways yet leaves him in a position to fully analyze the character's experience; his use of narrative voice, then, is different from both modernism's limited and traditional literature's omniscient author. However, Nizan's use of narrative voice can only be understood in relation to the central theme: the effect of the social relations of production on Antoine's life.

One of Nizan's most dramatic presentations of the effects of class occurs not in a scene of overt exploitation or victimization of Antoine; nor does it occur in a factory or at a political event. Rather, one of the key moments in Antoine's consciousness of class occurs at his graduation from secondary school. Hard working and intelligent, he finds himself on stage to receive the academic prizes he has won:

> A man standing behind a table handed him a bundle of books. He turned around; he saw the little ripple of heads and hats surge forward and break gently on the backs of the musicians. Horse chestnuts fell in the morning silence

which the crowd did not disturb. An outgoing ocean liner tooted. All of a sudden several people started clapping. In the first row, a well dressed lady in a purple dress fringed with slightly yellowed lace clapped. Her white hands fluttered like a pair of fleshy wings above the hair of the trombone player. They were detached like ariel beings. Further back, Antoine made out his mother in her tight black skirt, neat bodice, and her loose-fitting provincial bonnet. She stared at the platform and applauded. Her round cheeks were rosy with pleasure. Through the black mesh of her net, Antoine saw the white strands of his mother's hair—turned white at thirty. A schoolmate, who in turn had received his share of the prizes, gave him a shove. He stepped down and walked across in front of the musicians. The lady in the front row leaned over to her neighbor and started laughing. Undoubtedly she was laughing at him, she followed him with her eyes. He fancied he heard her say "the little peasant."

In a typical modernist style (reminiscent of the imagists) Nizan renders Antoine's feelings of dissociation by describing his perception of sights and sounds—the fall of chestnuts, the liner's whistle—rather than his feelings. In an almost surreal image the lady's hands become the disembodied wings of a corporeal angel, the hint of corruption contrasting with his mother's rosy cheeks. Unable to incorporate these sensations, and too confused to act, Antoine has to be pushed from the stage by the following prize winner.

Such experiences of dissociation are not uncommon to characters in modern or, for that matter, postmodern fiction. But Nizan gives neither a psychoanalytic nor an existential interpretation to Antoine's feelings. In *Hidden Injuries of Class,* Sennet and Cobb, contemplating the relationship between the feelings expressed by the workers they interviewed and Sartrean existentialism, point out that for working class people the existential wound shows up as a sense of class shame. Subject most of their lives to teachers and bosses, put into competition with each other for meager rewards, workers are always measuring themselves against others in the social hierarchy. Over a period of time the standards of such measurement are internalized and workers shame themselves.

In the graduation scene, Nizan shows the process at work. Because of his hard work and intelligence, Antoine is rewarded. Yet he is simultaneously reminded that his achievements cannot alter his class origins. More importantly, the lady need not make the slurring remark nor need Antoine hear it. Having internalized the standards of the social hierarchy, Antoine not only knows that the lady has the power to make such a comment but that he has no defense against her power. By the time Antoine is conscious of the power of class slurs to harm him, he is subjectively defenseless against them. He can only feel shame and embarrassment over his class identity. The myths and realities of class, like those of race, mutilate the sense of self.

Antoine's awareness of his vulnerability to the contradictions of the class system sharpens quickly. The night of his graduation he sits on the stoop of his father's house contemplating the relation of his education to his future and past. He realizes not only his position before the lady and others of her ilk and class, but his position in relation to his parents. While his mother cannot read or write and relies on sorcery and peasant proverbs to interpret the world, he has been educated. Where his father is condemned to a life of manual labor, his education opens the way to a rise in class. He begins

> to feel that the world toward which his studies are impelling him is considerably removed from the world where his parents have lived since their youth. He feels the beginnings of estrangement. He is no longer of their kith and station. He is already unhappy as though after a farewell, an irrevocable breach of faith. . . .

Vulnerable to those from the class to which he aspires, Antoine is cut off from those with whom he was raised. He can only experience his new identity as different, as other than his real self. Thus alienation, estrangement, and shame are rooted not in some metaphysical feeling of homelessness nor in some neurosis nor even in conditions of the job; rather they are rooted in the class nature of society as it affects Antoine's educational experience. Class then comes to contour Antoine's sense of self, of isolation, of vulnerability in the concrete situation of his graduation from secondary school.

Of course, Nizan's presentation of the shaping power of class does not rest on one scene. Rather, he shows that Antoine's feelings and attitudes are the result of interplay among a number of social forces. For example, Nizan, like Lawrence and most modernists, is aware of the power of machinery to change the human psyche and bodily rhythm. The young Antoine is captivated by the movement of machines, "the walking beams of the steam engines, the belts of the railways, the blast furnaces and the factories." The movement of machines awakens

> Antoine from the earthy rut where he had germinated, and whence he had been shaken prematurely. . . . The country indifference and passivity, which he had absorbed through all his pores beneath the trees at the foot of the ancient hills of Finistère, passed from him with every engine throb, with every ship that sailed, with every incoming train.

But Nizan goes beyond such Lawrentian perceptions. It is not merely the rhythms of machines but the very movement of trade, of industry, of economic expansion that shapes Antoine's feelings. During his youth St. Nazaire undergoes a phenomenal boom. The Second Empire's "men of big trade" decided, looking at a map, that a huge port facility built in Antoine's city would cut "three days from the Atlantic crossing," thus saving them "so many days pay at sea, so many tons of coal. . . ." An "orgy of construction," which powerfully shapes Antoine's imagination follows. "How could a boy of fifteen resist the industrial fervor that seized the grownups?" By his midteens Antoine "is incapable of picturing his life anywhere save in the shadow of scaffolding amid the clang of steel plate, of rivets and hammers, where steam sirens shatter the sky and tall skeletons of shipyards loom." By the time he is sixteen Antoine "is capable of conceiving human ac-

tion only under the industrial forms that dominate the dangerous days of his youth."

The boom shapes Antoine's feelings in both positive and negative ways. As a working class youth, he finds that the industrial work site quickly becomes the arena for action, the place in which he plans to expend his life energies. Where most modernists see technology and industry only as destructive to the human psyche, to sexual and spiritual values, Nizan presents it concretely as the arena in which working people spend most of their lives. Antoine is fascinated by the productive power of machines and quickly learns that "the man who counts most is the man closest to production." Experiencing a typical working class perception, Antoine determines that his future will be as a participant in that production. Like the workers in Zola's *Germinal,* who, during the hard-fought strike, refuse to destroy machines because they respect their productive power, and like those in Sembene's *God's Bits of Wood,* who understand that in a proper relationship with machines they can increase their power, knowledge, and freedom, Antoine understands that machines could increase his creative power. Nizan understands a relationship between working men and women and machines to which postmodernists might well pay attention.

Of course there is a negative aspect to Antoine's participation in the economic boom and the industrial work place. Obviously, in as much as Antoine can only imagine

Nizan at the lycée Louis-le-Grand, 1923.

human action within the industrial arena, he is limited, mutilated once again. And as he discovers later in life that the economies of managers render machines unsafe for workers (causing needless injury), his faith in the sheer productive power of machines is altered. Then too, Antoine loses a valuable relationship with nature.

But the most destructive aspect of Antoine's involvement with the industrial boom is the effect it has on his ambition. Antoine notices that the splendid buildings and the magnificent movement of trade do little to help his parents and neighbors. Contrasting the energy of the boom with the life of workers in his section of the city, he becomes

> conscious of his poverty; he early experienced the painful ambition of workers' sons, who would see the doors of a new life open part way before them. How could they refuse to leave the joyless world where their fathers had never had their fill of air and nourishment, their fill of leisure, love, and security?

To overcome the negative aspects of working class life, Antoine "childishly pictured himself in the post of manager." His imagination is, of course, fed with promises of "a great future and equal opportunity, the dawn of democracy." The net effect of the boom on Antoine, then, is to make him think that the negativities of working class life can be overcome by a rise in class.

Thus, Antoine makes crucial choices in response to a complex set of relationships—to parents, to machines, to boom times, to the dual signals of the educational and social hierarchy. If he is "thrown-into-freedom," he is also thrown into a place, a particular moment of history, of economic and technological development, a family, an educational system. His town and the boom, his family and the school are hardly abstractions; his situation is social and concrete, not metaphysical. He responds as an individual to specific conditions and sensations and chooses a rise in class—and thus experiences continued alienation.

But class affects Antoine's emotional life even more directly. As the son of peasants, he absorbs their ideas. To them, the social system and one's place within it are fixed by some inhuman force—God, the stars, fate, chance—outside of human control. The chief guide to behavior, his parents think, is acceptance of one's personal lot within the system and obedience to higher social authority. Not only do they inculcate those values in Antoine, beating him for minor transgressions, but they fail to comprehend the significance of other forms of action and of historical events. When the Paris Commune occurs, they see only the actions of atheists and "reds"; consequently, Antoine learns nothing of events that are "capable of casting in a definite mold, the feelings, the wrath, the simple aspirations of a child of his class."

Deprived of knowledge of this historical struggle of his class, Antoine can give his "wrath," his class anger, no direction; rather, he is disciplined to repress it. For example, while at the *Polytechnique* learning to become a railway engineer, Antoine notices both the contempt the teachers have for his fellow students and the harsh working conditions of the job he must have to pay for his education. One

day he spontaneously leaps to a lumber pile and urges his fellow workers to strike. His action is, of course, out of place, since there is no organized union, and the workers pass him by. For his efforts Antoine is lectured by the company manager and by his father on the necessity of obedience if he is to rise in class. From that moment on Antoine knows that the price of promotion is the repression of anger.

Antoine learns he must repress and discipline his other feelings as well. If he is to rise in class, he must change his manners, his mode of dress, and, as all of us who teach freshman rhetoric know, his language. For example, he gives up his erotic attachment to a working class woman to marry the daughter of a station master. His wife, Ann, teaches the half-willing Antoine the rules of middle class marriage and social behavior. Though their relationship is a personal and individual one, it is nevertheless governed by a set of regulations which direct Antoine's major energies into the work place, while Ann devotes herself to the home. As a conforming woman, Ann teaches Antoine how to behave socially and, in particular, how to control his working class speech and anger. If Madame Bovary represents the romantic and class aspirations of a middle class woman, then Ann represents that woman totally defined by acceptable social roles. Her central task is to see to manners and decorum in the domestic and political spheres.

Of course, such behavior carries with it the promise of real love and intimacy, but it ends only in repression, only in the enforcement of conventional roles. Eros withers: "Barely do they interpret the moods born of the body." The "icy ceremonies—meals, walks, anniversaries, children's lessons, weekly accounts—take the place of real feeling." Antoine, committed to the rhythms of work, to the acceptable social forms of marriage, has little knowledge of the sexual needs of his wife or insight into the power of real eros. If machines and the economic expansion wrench Antoine's bodily rhythms from peasant earthiness, the form of his marriage stifles his and Ann's sexuality. His body becomes primarily, if not exclusively, an instrument of labor for others.

Where most modernists dealing with the problem of sexuality would emphasize the struggle to release repressed energy, Nizan emphasizes the repressive power of the manners and mores of the petit bourgeois class. He accomplishes this end to some extent by describing Ann's injunctions on Antoine's behavior; but his most effective device is to ironically use the narrative voice to repeat the catch phrases of that class. As an epic narrator would use his narrative powers to speak of the heroic values of a people, Nizan uses those powers to satirize the emotional impoverishment of a whole class: " 'You don't treat your wife like your mistress,' they say with proverbial wisdom. 'You must respect the person you love and respect yourself too; we are not animals.' " Through such oft repeated "proverbial" phrases, the men and women of Antoine's newfound class enforce sexual discipline on each other. For Nizan, then, repression of sexuality is neither the result of some childhood conflict, some continuing battle between id, ego, and superego, nor is it something that takes a police state to enforce; rather, it is the result of well-defined social roles that stem from the division of labor. In short, repression is rooted in the social relations and ideology of everyday life.

Antoine's experiences, his ambition, his sense of shame, his alienation from his family and friends, the repression of his feelings, particularly of anger and love, put him in a curious relationship with time. He comes to live in a "continuous present" in which the days and "years went by like unmoored boats." Time is measured in the alternation of work and domestic duty, by yearly vacations, by promotions and transfers. Clock time and calendar time, however, give no sense of genuine movement, and the repetitions of daily life give no sense of change. Of course, such experiences as Antoine's are hardly unusual in modernist fiction. Yet most modernist authors—Stein, Joyce, Lawrence, Woolf, Kafka—tend to see such perceptions first as requiring new literary forms and new metaphysical explanations. In short, they seek aesthetic and idealist explanations and solutions to the problem. Nizan, however, roots his explanations in the labor process. For example, Antoine in his youth forms his conception of his own future in relationship to an industrial boom and to the industrial work place. As the rhythms of his body are altered, he comes to measure time not in the seasonal cycles of agricultural production but in terms of the needs of industrial production. To win his place as manager, he must study and work hard to get through the *Polytechnique.* Consequently, "fortune denies him any time to waste. In those years when young people learn to know themselves— years which are hard for the mature man to make up for— Antoine does not have the spare time for vacations." Nor does he have "the spare time to meditate on the fact that he is endowed with strength and with vast desires he will never be able to satisfy." Caught up both imaginatively and physically in the industrial boom, Antoine finds himself "propelled along a turnless road, with no room for bodily or spiritual relaxation, where there are no crossroads, no interludes of idleness, but only brief halts." His "life is already like the express trains he will drive tomorrow, impelled by an overwhelming force."

Seeking to escape the negativities of working class life, Antoine ironically finds that a rise in class brings no leisure. Time becomes not money, but work. The industrial expansion in France requires that the cycles of production, of transportation, of selling, of circulation of capital, be increasingly shortened. Of course, to make this rotation even more swift, machines, processes, and institutions are introduced which require Antoine and others to work faster:

> There are thousands of ravenous machines that thus involve men in their rotation: the banks, the mines, the big stores, the ships, the railways. Scarcely has anyone time to catch his breath. It requires too much attention to work as swiftly as their cogs work, to avoid their driving belts, their motors.

For Nizan, then, the relentless effort of capital to reduce the time it takes to transform raw materials into goods, to transport and sell those goods, to circulate capital, becomes a central factor in Antoine's temporal disorienta-

tion. The time scheme of industrial capitalism, unlike that of agricultural production, which concentrates labor at planting and harvest, requires the constant and intense expenditure of human energy and labor. Antoine, obsessed with industrial time, spends eighteen hours a day keeping the trains running on time. "Even at home he lived haunted by time, always in a hurry, racing with the clock." Caught in this process, Antoine finds no time to develop the potentialities of self, to release and fulfill repressed emotion.

Thus the negativities of working class life appear in slightly different forms in petit bourgeois life; his rise in class has not brought him love, leisure, joy. Even worse, Antoine's new life requires the renunciation of his peasant and working class identity. The process of alienation and estrangement that began the night of his graduation continues as his promotions and transfers require that he set himself apart from, and finally against his own past. Both at home and on the job Antoine finds himself pitted against workers and the working class part of himself. At home he must listen to Ann and his neighbors justify, like Robinson Crusoe's father, their own "middle state." Protecting their image of themselves, they characterize workers as childlike, disorderly, dirty, promiscuous, brutish, irrational, and finally violent. Listening to such attitudes, Antoine's sense of anger and shame is intensified. For him the past is better forgotten and his anger kept from view.

But more important estrangements from the past occur at work. For Antoine closeness to the productive process was a source of joy and pleasure. But a rise in rank, in class, removes him from such labor. As manager, Antoine sometimes stops "behind a worker pondering the fact that he had reached the point where he watched the hands of others work. His job consisted exclusively in giving orders and making plans." Thus, he can measure his life neither in relation to things produced nor in experiencing the pleasure of having produced. Rather, his life is increasingly absorbed in record keeping, the "etiquette," as Antoine calls it, of capitalism. His fascination with production, his pleasure in it, is ultimately frustrated and another dream of his youth dies.

But a more decisive split with his past occurs when the workers go out on strike. As manager, Antoine is forced to spend his days with the soldiers and police who occupy the plant, to listen to their derogatory comments about workers, to dissuade them from attacking the strikers. He realizes that he is at war not only with members of his own class but with his own past and, hence, with himself. " 'I am my own enemy,' he would say to himself. His division against himself, the splitting of his life, the chasm that divided youth from maturity, were unhappily brought home to him during these conferences with police." Antoine is estranged from family, from class, from his childhood, and from self; the cause is not metaphysical, but rooted in the division of labor, the opposing interests of workers and capitalists.

The strike marks the intrusion of historical events into Antoine's life. Living in a continuous present, ignoring historical developments, Antoine is little prepared for this act of anger and strength on the part of the workers. Yet it is their action in history that brings Antoine to his keenest awareness of his psychic divisions. A second historical event contributes even more to his disintegration. Though he and his neighbors cling to the illusion that peace is unbreakable, World War I occurs. The railway repair yard is converted into a munitions factory supervised by military engineers. Antoine's inexperience, or rather his over-specialization in repairing locomotive engines, and the carelessness of military inspectors result in a shipment to the front of improperly balanced shells. The military investigation finds Antoine responsible; he is consequently demoted and sent off to manage a small supply station. Removed from the last tenuous contacts with productive labor, the process of personal disintegration begins to move more rapidly.

Historical events, then, have personal consequences; petit bourgeois illusions of peace, of the unimportance of historical developments, and, for that matter, modernist and postmodernist attempts to diminish the importance of history through theories of myth or contingency, only leave the individual more vulnerable. The strike and the war separate Antoine from his own past, from a sense of the self's continuity within time. So severe are the consequences on him that he literally loses his memory.

For Nizan, as for so many modernists, memory constitutes "the true possession of time." But for him the experience of that possession is anything but a private or transcendental experience. It is not made possible by the uncovering of some mythic pattern, as in Joyce or Eliot; nor does it depend on the suffering and death of others, as in *Mrs. Dalloway;* nor is it spurred by associational patterns based on sensations, as in Proust; neither is it won through some opening, some discovery in language. Rather, for Nizan memory, the true possession of time, is dependent upon the actualization of social bonds and relationships within history.

As Antoine grows older, he seeks confirmation of the realities of his childhood and of his past life through his relationships with others. For a time Antoine finds in conversation with his father confirmation of his own life. But when his father dies, "the loss of his first existence" is completed. "His father no longer answered him as he had during those three or four days a year at the time of his vacation when Antoine renewed his store of youth, reestablished contact between the extreme limits of his years." After his father's death, Antoine turns for solace to the men with whom he has worked. To be sure, these men have memories, but because they are professionals—engineers, calculators, time table keepers—who, like Antoine, have poured their life's energy into work, their memories consist almost entirely of events on the job. These memories are only "fragments detached from their lives" and "differ as much from the true possession of time as blueprints covered with figures and white lines differ from an engine in the fullness of its strength." Ultimately, their deeds did

> not belong to them. They were isolated acts imposed on them by an external and inhuman force as cold as that which directs the workers, acts that were not a genuine part of human life, that had no real consequences. Acts that were merely registered and bound in dusty ledgers, that merely helped ensure the profits of factories and companies and the submissiveness of workers. They recalled no real achievements or genuine human relationships, their workers and their superiors were to them enemies. They were solitary actors, actors devoid of any dignity. They pretended to be proud of their memories, but in their secret hearts they did not cherish them.

From these men Antoine can receive no confirmation of his childhood, of the working class part of himself, or of his feelings and emotions. As he grows old and faces death, he can only experience silence and "the influx of nothingness." But unlike so many modernists and postmodernists who use these existential slogans, Nizan does not present the experience of silence and negativity as an inherently necessary or mysterious aspect of human experience. Rather, it is rooted in the fundamental social experience of shame: "Men who are stranded on their lonely little islands call this silence shame." Early in life Antoine felt that shame in the presence of the rich lady at graduation. Society gave her the authority—which Antoine internalized—to reduce his achievements and identity to his "inferior" class position. But Antoine, shaped by the industrial boom, his parents, the educational system, all the manifestations of division of labor along class lines, sought to take on a new class identity. However, achievement of that identity required the sale of his power to work and create, and repression of his feelings; yet, though petit bourgeois life has had its rewards, he has not won the leisure, the job, or the love which were so obviously absent in working class life. His shame results from his failure to claim for himself—and for his class—the right to the products of his labor in the economic, political, and psychological senses. His self, his memory, was sold to others for little price.

Nizan's narrative technique is shaped by his own sense of the social nature of memory, of "the true possession of time." Where Antoine lived in a-historical, day-to-day time whose meaning is in wages, promotions, retirement, Nizan knows that he himself is living at a particular moment in history. Nizan began the book shortly after his father died. As Sartre has pointed out, the book begins with the question "What kind of man was my father?" and moves to the question "What can I learn from the mutilations he suffered?" While writing the book Nizan, as we saw earlier, was a member of the French Communist Party actively organizing the unemployed, running for office, and writing reviews focusing on Fascist themes in literature. He seeks, then, to find in the memory of his father a meaning for his own moment in history.

Sartre correctly describes two of those meanings [see excerpt dated 1960]. First, Nizan, a Ph.D. in philosophy, studies the mutilations his father suffered in order to protect himself from the temptations of a bourgeois academic life, the lure of a career lived largely with words acceptable to the same bosses who mutilated his father. Secondly, Nizan releases into the book the anger he feels at his father's oppression. Thus Sartre recommends the book primarily to the angry young of the late fifties and sixties. But

Sartre's criticism fails to comprehend the full effect of the novel because, existentialist to the end, he does not fully comprehend Nizan's historical materialist use of memory. In his "Theses on the Philosophy of History," reprinted in *Illuminations,* Walter Benjamin comments that the true articulation of the past "means to seize hold of a memory as it flashes up at a moment of danger." Those who write from the perspective of historical materialism, Benjamin argues, wish "to retain the image of the past which unexpectedly appears to a man singled out by history at a moment of danger." More importantly, the memory of "enslaved ancestors" provides historical materialists with images which nourish in the working class both the "hatred and . . . the spirit of sacrifice" necessary to create a class revolution. These memories must be rescued, Benjamin claims, because as long as the present rulers remain victorious, the tradition of the oppressed is likely to be lost:

> Even the dead are not safe from the enemy. . . .
> In every era the attempt must be made anew to wrest the tradition away from the conformism about to overpower it. In rescuing that tradition we learn that the "state of emergency" in which we live is not the exception but the rule. We must attain a conception of history in keeping with this insight. Then we shall realize that it is our task to bring about a real state of emergency.

In writing *Antoine Bloyé,* Nizan has rescued his father's life from that oblivion; as narrator of the novel, writing from his personal and historical situation, Nizan reclaims his father's life from the ruling class and claims it for the class struggle. As narrator, then, he restores to that life its meaning in both past and present. As narrator, Nizan employs neither the limited narrative voice characteristic of both modernism and postmodernism, nor the omniscient voice of more traditional literature. Rather, as narrator, Nizan takes a stand in history, a stand that requires us as readers to analyze and react to our own moment of danger. He accomplishes that end both by supplying historical facts and analysis that are beyond his character and by responding with anger to the forces and powers that oppress and mutilate Antoine. For example, in describing the forces that created the *Polytechniques,* Nizan writes:

> He [Antoine] did not know that along with many other adolescents of his age he was one of the pawns of the huge game that the supreme masters of the French bourgeoise were beginning to play. He had simply been told he could escape the poverty and precariousness of a worker's life and these promises accorded far too well with the temptations his city offered him. Far from him, even before he was born, in offices, at shareholder's meetings, in the parliament, in learned bodies, factory owners had for thirty years past been voicing their demands. Industry required new human material. It felt a growing need for men able to read a blueprint, to supervise the making of a part. . . . It was not love of man that on March 15, 1858, had prompted the parliament to adopt the draft of a law on professional education.

In this passage Nizan, conscious of history, explains the historical processes of which Antoine is ignorant and

vents his sarcastic anger at the exploitive educational policies of the bourgeoisie. That knowledge and that anger confront the book's readers, requiring that they become more fully present, that they risk their self-understanding. The work puts its questions to us, challenges us. Nizan's memory, his anger, and his sense of living in historical time become part of the reader's moment in history. The tradition of the oppressed is rescued and brought to bear on the present. Nizan's memory has become a bridge between his father's situation and his own, and between their situation and ours.

For Sartre, Nizan ultimately became only a petit bourgeois freak showing the wounds of his childhood to workers. Had he lived (Nizan, killed by a ricocheting bullet at Dunkirk, had joined the French army at the outbreak of World War II in defiance of the Party's line that the war was inspired by French and English war mongers and that Party members therefore should refuse to support it), he could have become oppressed by the Party in the same way Antoine was oppressed by the bosses, Sartre argues. But Nizan is more than a lucky, dead freak. His memory of his father's oppression enabled him first to join the Party, and second, when in his judgment he found the Party no longer defending the oppressed, to react against it. He was free, as Sartre never was, both to join the Party and to resist it. In short, Nizan's active memory of the past, of his father's oppression, enabled him to react to a state of emergency. His book and his life speak not just to the angry young, but to all those who experience the alienation of their labor, the fragmentation of self, and the repression of life energies, potentialities, emotions. He enables us to recognize that the state of emergency in which we live is not the exception but the rule; perhaps his work can bring us closer to recognizing that our task is to create a real state of emergency and win the true possession of time. (pp. 395-410)

> *Richard Wasson, " 'The True Possession of Time': Paul Nizan, Marxism, and Modernism," in* boundary 2, *Vol. V, No. 2, Winter, 1977, pp. 395-410.*

Susan Rubin Suleiman   (essay date 1983)

> [*Suleiman is a Hungarian-born American educator and critic who has written extensively on contemporary political and intellectual movements. In the following excerpt from* Authoritarian Fictions: The Ideological Novel as a Literary Genre, *she discusses* The Trojan Horse *as an example of a* roman à thèse *("thesis novel") whose structure is based on a confrontation between good and evil.*]

[The type of story I call "confrontational" or "antagonistic"] is always, in the last resort, that of a "struggle between heaven and hell." The *roman à thèse* assumes this Manichean view and prides itself on it, like the revolutionary character in Malraux's *L'espoir* who affirms that "Every revolutionary is a born Manichean—as is every political man." (p. 101)

[Nizan's *Le cheval de Troie*] presents a particularly

"pure" version of the structure of confrontation in the *roman à thèse*. . . . (p. 103)

Le cheval de Troie tells a story set in a small city in the center of France in the summer of 1934. The central event is a street battle between the working-class population led by the Communists, and a group of fascist demonstrators who "invade" the city for a mass meeting. The fascists disband rather quickly and are replaced by the police and the armed and helmeted national guard. A Communist is killed; the workers are driven back to their own neighborhood and dispersed. But the Communists, who organized and led the battle, regroup in private and vow to continue the fight for human freedom and dignity. The war they are waging is a long one, but worth fighting and dying in: they are helping a new world to be born.

Of course this summary, like all summaries, is reductive and designed to make a point. But anyone who has read the novel will, I think, agree that I have not distorted its "message." The elements I have left out (notably the episodes involving Lange, and the death of Catherine) can be shown to reinforce the message rather than contradict it. If one may invoke the old comparison between a novel and a symphony, then this one has a very clear melodic line and virtually no discords in its harmonies. (p. 105)

The pertinent characteristics of the hero in a *roman à thèse* that realizes the structure of confrontation in its "pure" form are the following: he espouses, from the beginning, the values defined as good, and is ready to expound on them; he represents, or is part of, a group that fights for the triumph of those values; and as far as his adherence to those values is concerned—that is, in terms of his most fundamental outlook on life—he does not change in the course of the battle. The antagonistic hero—and I use the term "hero" in its strong sense, since the protagonist in a story of confrontation is always positively valorized—is barely an individual, if by an individual one means a character whose destiny is important because it is the destiny of that *particular character* and not of someone else. In the case of the antagonistic hero, individual destiny tends to merge with a collective one: it is as the representative and spokesman of a group that the hero elicits our interest.

I should note that the hero thus defined (as the representative of a group) is not identical to the "typical" hero envisaged by Lukács and some other Marxist critics. According to Lukács, the "typical" hero found in Balzac or Tolstoy, for example (and generally in great realistic fiction), is an individual who sums up, most often without knowing it, the aspirations and the contradictions of a social group (or more exactly of a social class) at a given historical moment. The antagonistic hero is not "typical" in this sense; rather, he is the conscious representative of a group whose values he expresses and with which he identifies himself. It is his identification with the group that allows the hero to be only minimally individualized. Even if he bears a proper name that sets him apart, the antagonistic hero tends to merge into the anonymity (and unanimity) of the heroic group.

This becomes quite clear if one looks at the Communist characters of *Le cheval de Troie.* Although they are named and are endowed with different physical traits and different personal histories, the overall effect when one watches their actions or hears them speak or "overhears" their thoughts through the narrator's commentaries is that they are interchangeable. Toward the beginning of the novel, for example, when the group begins to discuss the possibility of organizing a confrontation with the fascists, one of the characters says: "If we organize a counter-demonstration, they'll call in the National Guard, and with those creeps . . . " to which another replies: "It would really be too bad to die before the revolution." Then the narrator comments: "Everything seemed to them to be just beginning . . . France, where workers were not often killed in the streets, was becoming a country like the others, where it was possible to die other than through illness, or an accident or a crime—to be simply killed. That was the thought they had." Not only do the characters merge into a single "thought," but the narrator himself espouses that thought in reporting it. Individual differences in interpretation and judgment, whether among the characters or between the characters and the narrator, are eliminated in favor of unanimity. The members of the group merge into a single collective hero. And since the omniscient narrator shows himself from the beginning to be someone who shares their fears and their aspirations, his commentaries underline the unanimous (in a hostile perspective one would say totalitarian) character of the group whose story he is telling.

The intellectual in the group, Pierre Bloyé, might appear to constitute an exception, since we see more of him and know more about his inner world than about the others. Bloyé is a *lycée* professor, a graduate of the Ecole Normale Supérieure, who has renounced his bourgeois background (he is in fact the son of Antoine Bloyé)—in other words, he has gone through a positive exemplary apprenticeship. But by the time the story begins, Bloyé's apprenticeship is far behind him; it is part of his past history, and is merely evoked retrospectively by the narrator: "It had taken him years to rid himself of the manners and customs of that world of screens and dodges from which he had started out; he had had to reverse the direction of his thought, but now it was done; his comrades thought of him as one of them." Bloyé's "reversal of thought" (a notion that, from a post-Stalinist perspective, appears somewhat sinister—but Nizan was writing in less disenchanted days) has made him into a "comrade" like the others. The whole point of this retrospective evocation is to reinforce Bloyé's nonindividuality, his merger with the heroic group. (pp. 105-08)

The group's object is the triumph of certain values or the realization of an ideal, defined from the start as "good." The receiver of the object is the community at large, and by extension humanity in general. The category of helper is occupied by those who provide material or moral support to the hero and share the latter's values; the category of opponent, by those who affirm values contrary to the hero's. But the opponent should in fact be split into two separate categories: that of anti-subject, who leads the fight against the hero (in the name of the "wrong" values); and that of anti-helper, who aids the enemy materially and/or morally. This division has the advantage of making the . . . categories more symmetrical; it also shows that the enemy is a negative "double" of the hero—having similar characteristics, but in reverse (endowed with negative value in the context of the work). (pp. 113-14)

[In *Le cheval de Troie*, the] heroes' object is a double one. In the short term, it is simply the triumph of antifascist values, the latter being defined indirectly in the course of a long scene that shows a dinner party at the home of the *Préfet* a few days before the demonstration (chapter 5). The discussion between Lange and the other guests suggests that fascism is in its essence a philosophy of solitude and death. The struggle against fascism is thus a struggle for solidarity and life. This struggle is overshadowed, however, by yet another one: the long-term struggle for the coming into being of a new world, which "we [the Communists] must help to be born." In this new world, "there will no longer be any deaths for which men alone are responsible . . . death in an accident because the machines were faulty, or because the contractor had saved money on his scaffoldings; death because one has lost all hope of getting work, death because of tuberculosis, death because of torture." The long-term object of the hero is thus a world of equality and justice for all, defined as a world from which the *avoidable* death of men—and women—will have been eliminated.

We can see here how one of the major themes of the interwar and the immediate postwar period in French literature, the existential theme of death, is orchestrated by a Communist writer. Nizan, a graduate of the Ecole Normale and an *agrégé de philosophie* like his friend Sartre, had found in Communism the solution to the question posed by so many works of the 1930s and 1940s, and that was posed, perhaps most urgently, in Sartre's short story "Le mur": how can one find life meaningful, knowing that death exists and that after death there is nothing? In *Le cheval de Troie*, Pierre Bloyé, the Communist intellectual who resembles Nizan like a brother, formulates the answer: "We can begin by destroying all the unjust ways of dying, and then, when we'll be left only with the kind of death for which no one is responsible, we'll have to try and make it meaningful (*lui donner un sens*) as well. It's not dying in battle that's difficult, but dying alone, under torture, or in your bed. We must die uncompromising deaths; confront illness like an enemy, so that dying should be a final honor, a final victory of consciousness." This is "Marxist humanism" with a vengeance—or, some might say, the Marxism of a philosopher immersed up to his ears in bourgeois culture. Those are not necessarily negative traits, however; if one had to choose among Marxisms, one could do worse than choose the humanistic kind. (pp. 115-16)

> *Susan Rubin Suleiman, "The Structure of Confrontation," in her* Authoritarian Fictions: The Ideological Novel as a Literary Genre, *Columbia University Press, 1983, pp. 101-48.*

Walter Redfern (essay date 1983)

[*Redfern is an English educator and critic who special-*

izes in modern French literature. In the following essay, he examines the importance of death to the political ideology presented in Nizan's works.]

I start with an apology (a false one). My approach, my preferences, my professional formation (and deformation) are mainly literary. But I want to argue that literature, and in this instance one haunted by death, can still contribute something of value to political reflection. To dwell on death is no doubt to begin with the end. Yet some centuries ago Pascal found that this was an efficient intellectual and rhetorical strategy. In our own time, writers of the broadly 'Existentialist' persuasion—Malraux, Sartre, Camus—have given a lay extension to Pascal's theological terrorism. Instead of the fear of God, they have sought to instil in us the dread of the unlived life. Nizan belongs with this tradition.

In the late 1920s, Nizan bolted from Paris and the Ecole dite Normale et prétendue Supérieure to Aden. He was suffering from intimations of asphyxia. As a *Normalien,* he experienced the very special world of that select establishment as a hothouse severed from and insulated against reality, a buffer-state against the facts of life. Like most well educated (indeed over educated) young Frenchmen, until the recently erupting counter-culture began to devalue literature and to promote optical effects, rhythms and noise, Nizan was a very literary youth. (The question of bookishness is almost always crucial in any consideration of French writers, who could nearly all say, like Camus's Clamence: 'au-je lu cela ou l'ai-je pensé?' Did I read that somewhere, or was it my own idea? This is why *Madame Bovary* is so central a text in the French tradition). Nizan exploited this bookishness against the ruling class that he had begun to hate. His essay, *Aden, Arabie,* focuses on the twin targets of the *Université* and colonialism: the parochial and the universal. (Though some Frenchmen are notoriously given to mistaking their *alma mater,* or Paris, for the whole world. This has been called umbilicism.) The connection between the two targets is that the spurious values inculcated by the first agent (the *Université*)—the cult of impersonal reason, which leads to a-historical stances and to political absentionism (i.e. conservatism)—permit and indeed encourage the practice of the second: colonial exploitation. Aden itself lies in the centre of an extinct volcano, like a huge shell-crater, and ecologically it is largely sterile. It must be an apocalyptic landscape, and Nizan's figurative description of it as 'the mouth of hell' hardly an exaggeration. Spotting fishbones exposed on the beach led him to see Aden as a skeletal image of Europe. The sign-language of capitalism, its obsession with ciphers on paper, create an abstract drama with two-dimensional supernumeraries. Yet these phantoms, these superior submen, exercise real powers of life and death over their employees. Seeking to do the dirty on his class of origin as a small blow of solidarity for the oppressed workers, Nizan, in line with Lenin's instruction to steal back and to use against the bourgeoisie what it had stolen from others, exploits capitalist imagery and expropriates a lordly register, in order to indict the bosses on behalf of the bossed. But his critique is not all turned outwards. Having seen Western man resumed in an Eastern context, he felt he was receiving a terrible warning of his own imminent collapse into death-in-life. *Aden, Arabie* is the account of a near-miss. Nizan treats sardonically his own foolish need to travel abroad in order to discover some home truths. His cerebral vertigo would begin to abate only when he could find a precise direction for his hatred and his energy. He was always pregnable. His work is built on the tensions of the narrow escape, last-ditch salvage, precarious survival. The movement of *Aden, Arabie* goes not so much from dilemma to solution (Nizan was caustic, a long time before Sartre's *Les mots,* towards the whole concept of the writer-as-saviour: no man can be a St. Bernard dog), as from a nameless fear to an identifiable opponent.

His first novel, *Antoine Bloyé,* brooded more comprehensively on the question of death-in-life. It starts and ends with the death of its hero. In between, his life-curve is pictured as a treadmill. He is a brighter than average lad of peasant stock, directed by his 'betters' to a technical education designed to provide the middle management for the railway-boom of the late-nineteenth century. He moves steadily through the stages of driver, engineer, depot manager, in the course of a life which is outwardly successful but inwardly frustrated. At intervals, this inarticulate good worker senses that much of his being lies fallow, but he does nothing to get himself off the rails of his seemingly preordained life. He never integrates his spasmodic anger into political action. Though written by a Communist, this novel deals with a pre-Communist man. This is Marxism with a strong emphasis on personal responsibility as well as on economic determinism. Antoine, besides, is caught not only in the spider's web of capitalist industrialism, but also in the 'saccharine slavery' of a respectable bourgeois marriage. Nizan makes full room for psychology, for the role of dreams, for the private self. Indeed, the most impressive section of this powerful novel describes the aging of Antoine: his impotent sex-furies, his naked terror of dying before he has truly lived. He has been living what Céline would later call *la mort à crédit,*—death on the instalment plan.

This novel accommodates not only Marx and Freud, but also Pascal. Bloyé's life is one long *divertissement* ['diversion']. In a rare moment of awareness, Antoine telescopes a lifespan of seventy years into one day. The idea of dying 'at midnight' instead of in some vague 'thirty years from now' has a real Pascalian flavour and punch. Shortly before his actual death, Antoine sees a 'defeated image of himself, that headless being that walked in the ashes of time with hurrying steps, aimlessly'. Disciples of F. R. Leavis might well judge this novel's death-motif life-denying, but I myself find here not gratuitous morbidity but a generous concern for what men do, or sadly fail to do, to counteract their imposed fates. Besides, as well as the convincing account of alienated labour, this novel includes, by way of counter-balance, an equally persuasive picture of fulfilling and exciting work (in Antoine's youth). Nizan's first novel clearly accentuates the negative, but as a way of building an honest foundation for the positive. Its protagonist, or rather agonist, submits to the 'call of the tame', but his son's growing anger foretells different options for the next generation. *Antoine Bloyé* says, in effect: here are the facts. Now, what are we to do with what is done to us?

Nizan's second novel, *Le cheval de Troie,* switches from the helpless solitary to the militant group: Communist workers and intellectuals in the French provinces. It is the time (the early 1930s) of the physical confrontation between Fascist and anti-Fascist groups. In a climactic street-battle, the latter are eventually routed by the riot police after putting the Fascists to flight. Their losses mean that any sense of victory is reduced and tempered, but at least they have learnt in their bones the value of solidarity in action. Any propagandist element in this novel is likewise muted, or diversified, by Nizan's awareness that political commitment does little to abolish private anguish. While the workers are winning their dubious battle on the streets, the wife of one of them dies agonisingly and alone after an abortion. In Nizan's non-miraculous world, everything has to be paid for. Real death, then, confronts combatants and non-combatants alike. A more metaphysical, cerebral variety obsesses an intellectual, Lange, who ends up siding with the Fascists, when his speculations, spinning around in a void of scepticism and indeed nihilism, propel him to grab a gun and to fire on the crowd of workers. Abstract, unattached thought, for Nizan (and he probably had in mind figures like Drieu la Rochelle) can easily veer into lethal options. *Le cheval de Troie* can no more be summed up as 'edifying' than *Antoine Bloyé* could be as 'negative'. Nizan's true domain is the problematical, and this is quintessentially that of the genuine writer.

While writing his novels and essays, Nizan was also functioning as a party hack, or at least journeyman, penning foreign affairs commentaries, book reviews and polemical cultural articles for a wide range of Communist or fellow-travelling journals. Within the Communist Party, his position was one of animation, but perhaps of the suspended variety. I think Pascal Ory is right to stress how much Nizan refused to say or to think in such circumstances. As a boxer can pull his punches, so Nizan increasingly 'pulled' his initial sectarianism. Although on his ritual tour of Soviet Russia Nizan was sincerely impressed by some of the improving metamorphoses he witnessed, he never forgot to ask the sixty-four dollar question: does Communism help you to face death with any more equanimity?

In *La conspiration,* he provided the most achieved and balanced of his three novels. In it, he states: 'a young man is the only one with guts enough to demand all-or-nothing, and to feel robbed if he does not get it'. But simultaneously he was offering the counter-proposition: 'I will not allow anyone to tell me that youth is the best years of our lives'. It is this coexistence of passion and cold-eyed judgment that gives Nizan's prose its characteristic tone.

The young men in question are university students in Paris in the mid–1920s. But beyond this particularised area, it is general French intellectual life in one of its habitual postures that is being scrutinised here: the readiness to believe that a thought is an action, that the mere fact of verbalisation actually influences situations. Nizan's young rebels indict their society which they persist in seeing mainly in terms of their families. The periodical that they launch is directed much more against the idealist philosophy of the

Sorbonne than towards concrete militant action. The first issues provoke that response intolerable to rebels: impunity (or, in a later term, 'repressive tolerance'); they find they can say, if not do, what they feel like. For all his cloak-and-dagger intellectual bravado, the peer group's leader, Rosenthal, frets over what Nizan calls 'the family poisons which his liver and kidneys would never be able to evacuate'. When he embarks on an adulterous love affair, he keeps it within the family: his sister-in-law. Summoned before a family tribunal after the affair has been discovered, and having already lost interest in his would be seditious plans for military and industrial espionage on behalf of Soviet Russia, Rosenthal concludes precociously that the only irrevocable option left open to him is the will to die, and he commits suicide. After taking poison, he at last sees clearly that he is the victim of a robbery, though not clearly enough that he himself connived at the robbery by not asserting his independence forcefully. I think it is a measure of Nizan's imaginative powers that he can persuade us both that Rosenthal is a fake, a *poseur,* and that his premature death is a waste of someone who could have made of his life something more useful to others and hence to himself. He is something of a luxury victim, but luxuries are important in the general economy of Nizan's world view.

Another young man, Laforgue, altogether more serious than Rosenthal, borrows from his readings in anthropology the notion of the puberty rites of primitive tribes. Whereas young tribesmen accept physical testing and educative punishment, Western youths are left to wallow in their psychic malaise. When Laforgue falls gravely ill, his illness acts as his initiator, his 'medicine-man'. For the first time, he is obliged to immerse himself totally in an experience. When the coma eventually relents, he is bowled over by the sheer and simple joy of survival. His second go at life begins, but the price he pays is the knowledge that, after twenty years of marking time, he is now living towards death. And the lucid, but not paralysing, consciousness of death is essential to Nizan's conception of how to live authentically. Although the idealistic Rosenthal kills himself; and another young man, the absolutist turncoat Pluvinage, ends up in moral suicide, *La conspiration* finishes with Laforgue's symbolic death and rebirth, his change of life in an initiation rite. Nizan always insisted on the painfulness of all transitions.

This novel features two Communist Party members: the veteran Carré, sure of his choice and its meaningfulness, and young Pluvinage, a misfit. Anticipating the Sartrean motif of *le regard* ['the look'], Nizan stresses that it was the condemning gaze of his family that first induced in the as yet guiltless adolescent a sense of guilt. Indeed, so full of empathy is Nizan's motivation of Pluvinage, this novel's chief betrayer (he eventually consents to becoming a police informer), that when Nizan left the Party at the time of the Hiter-Stalin Pact in 1939, his erstwhile comrades claimed hysterically that he was a twenty-four carat traitor and that his understanding of Pluvinage proved it. This is rather like saying that Walt Disney must have been a rodent to conceive Mickey Mouse. To me, all that Nizan's close attention to the young man's act of betrayal proves is that Nizan knew his duty as a novelist (and in-

deed as a student of politics): know your enemy, think his thoughts.

The father of Pluvinage was the director of the Paris registry of deaths. The boy was conditioned by the mortuary world from early childhood, to the extent that his juvenile collection was of catalogue pictures of coffins and tombstones. Nizan gives him all the trappings of the Dostoevskyan morbid intellectual, a marginal being terrified of becoming totally superfluous. He has an early intuition of the complex structure of social organisation, and is much preoccupied with the contrast of underworlds and overworlds. He is clearly already ripe both for joining the Communist Party and then later deserting it for the secret police. Just as Rosenthal takes his own life, Pluvinage hands over his: two forms of self-destruction after two abortive existences. (If you think that, in his treatment of Pluvinage's death-haunted environment and his hapless life, Nizan is piling it on thick, then you are dead right. But medical opinion accepts the condition known as accident proneness. Should we not also allow for the state of misery-proneness, a natural or induced affinity with the lugubrious?) Through Pluvinage, Nizan warns that Communism may be the salvation only of those who devote themselves to its aims generously, and that it cannot afford to be a foster home for the neglected children of the bourgeoisie who refuse to grow up. *La conspiration* finishes, not with Pluvinage's end-stopped position, but with Laforgue's as yet shapeless and incipient transformation (which was due to be developed in a later novel, lost when Nizan was killed in 1940). Some of the elements of Nietzsche's recipe for rebels in an unrebellious age are already present and active within Laforgue: 'objection, joyous distrust and love of irony are signs of health: everything absolute belongs to pathology'.

I want to stress that Nizan's own sense of humour, of fun, was as deep rooted, as visceral, as his nightmares and his frequent gloom. His photos make him look disconcertingly like Harold Lloyd, one of his culture heroes. Like Harold Lloyd, Nizan was as obsessed with the death-defying (what Malraux would more pompously call *'l'anti-destin'* ['anti-destiny']) as he was with death itself. Acrobatically, Nizan survived being a member of the Communist Party all those years, a *funambule* ['acrobat'] to Louis Aragon's *fumiste* ['practical joker']. He never went in for what linguisticians call 'the mucker-pose' (i.e. the affectation of sub-standard speech), and indeed was always something of a dandy, like another of his heroes, the poet Jules Laforgue, who also died young and who also sported a mask of insolent nonchalance over deep-seated anxieties. Nizan's fixation on death never made him limp or fatalistic. It always seemed to act as a spur, because it was teamed with anger. Like Dylan Thomas, he could urge: 'do not go gentle into that good night'.

Nizan was murdered, posthumously, by the hatchet-men of the French C.P. It has of recent years become possible for a few party intellectuals to admit, and to regret, this attempted liquidation. But Nizan has been since his death, as his loyal friend Sartre put it, 'a vigorous corpse'. . . . Nizan's splendidly vital widow, Henriette, commented recently that Nizan, in each of his novels, tries on different forms of death, as a means of exorcising his own fixation on dying. Perhaps *memento mori* has always been a more usable motto than *dulce et decorum est pro patria mori* ['it is sweet and fitting to die for one's country']. I think Nizan himself put it best, in **Le cheval de Troie:** 'on ne change rien qu'au risque de la mort, on ne transforme rien qu'en pensant à la mort' ['one changes nothing except at the risk of death, one transforms nothing except by thinking about death']. He uses death to measure life, to ask all the awkward questions: who does our thinking for us, and why do we allow it? Why do we let ourselves live so badly? No doubt the reader will add his own awkward questions. (pp. 57-63)

> *Walter Redfern, "Nizan: A Matter of Death and Life," in* Socialism in France: From Jaurès to Mitterrand, *edited by Stuart Williams, St. Martin's Press, 1983, pp. 57-63.*

W. S. Di Piero   (essay date 1985)

[*In the following excerpt from an essay originally published in* Tri Quarterly *in 1985, Di Piero maintains that Antoine Bloyé exemplifies the paradoxical nature of the Marxist conception of labor.*]

Paul Nizan was a son of the railroad. His father rose through the ranks during the great expansion of the French railway system at the end of the nineteenth century, advancing from the "low" position of engineer to the more prestigious levels of lower management. Nizan came of age between the big wars, and his intellectual companions were writers like Sartre and Camus. Like them, he became a political writer of all trades—novelist, essayist, polemicist. *Antoine Bloyé,* published in 1933, is the novel that established his small but controversial reputation. It expresses with angry clarity the structures of habit and how one destiny is determined, and ill fortuned, by the conjunction of habit and a certain kind of economy. The structures of habit are really overlayerings of desire, palimpsest chronicles of the unhappiness which in turn replenishes habit and gives it even stricter control over life. Habit, while it seems to publicize convenience and necessity, in fact hides and seals away from us the anarchy of desire; it wrestles anarchy into daily repetitions, actions without recognitions, ritualized offerings to necessity.

Nizan introduces the story of Antoine Bloyé, another son of the railroad, with an epigraph from *The German Ideology:* "If communism is to put an end both to the 'cares' of the bourgeois and the needs of the proletarian, it is self-evident that it cannot do this without putting an end to the cause of both, 'labor.' " Marx scholars note the contradiction between this remark and another that comes a few pages earlier: "Men begin to distinguish themselves from animals when they begin to produce their means of subsistence." Man is distinguished from animals because he labors, but the laboring process which is man's essential activity also binds him to larger natural cycles. Labor affects "the metabolism between man and nature." It is "an eternal necessity imposed by nature." In *The Human Condition,* Hannah Arendt describes the equivocation: "The fact remains that in all stages of his work [Marx] defines

man as an *animal laborans* and then leads him into a society in which this greatest and most human power is no longer necessary." Presumably Marx intended the emancipation from labor to be the emancipation from necessity, and that is the most disarming utopian strain in his work. In the early *Economic and Philosophic Manuscripts,* he emphasized that labor is the expression of a human being's "sensuous nature" and in a communist society that nature could be expressed freely, not urged and constrained by necessity. In the course of his life, Antoine Bloyé advances beyond the menial labor his father performed and becomes a manager, a boss. In his passage he surrenders more of the opportunity to engage his sensuous nature in work, he becomes thus a stranger to his own nature, though no less enslaved to necessity.

As a teenager, studying at the School of Arts and Trades and working seasonally in the shipyards, Antoine is vital, expressive, answering the press of necessity without being reduced by his own answer. He is "endowed with strengths and with vast desires he will never be able to satisfy." He studies hard, works summers to pay tuition and gladly steeps himself in his work. Once he leaves school, however, he becomes a regular wage-earner. The difference between a worker and a wage-earner is that one ideally is defined by his activity, the other by the object or consequence of the activity. Antoine soon begins to live for the future in a present muffled by habit and expectations. He wants to win with his labor the prize of normalized relations in every sector of his life—wife, home, children, things. The necessity he feels now is defined not by natural "metabolisms" but by economic and social forces, which are the devitalized codifications of those metabolisms. Obedient to what he thinks are the "new" necessities, he suffers terrible reverses: he becomes a strikebreaker, betraying the class of workers which produced him; he loses his position finally because of poor "quality control" of war material; he backslides into a modest, miserable retirement punished by regret, reviewing unexpressed desires formalized into habits.

The ambiguity of our relation to habit—it sustains and reduces us, so do we celebrate or condemn it?—is caught in Nizan's description of Antoine's daily routine at the office:

> Each morning he went to his office; he hung up his umbrella or his overcoat. Winter came and then summer; first the season of derby hats, then the season of straw hats, of panamas. He sat down, lit a cigarette, and went and opened the door of the neighboring office as soon as he heard the sounds of a man, coughing, footsteps, a slight whistle, snatches of humming, the heavy sound of a body depositing its weight in an armchair. This meant the engineer had arrived.

The dull march of parallel phrases enacts what Nizan calls the "cotton wool" of habit in which workers wrap their lives. It protects, it softens the shock of the world, but it also packs us into a self-justifying indifference toward all that looms outside the laminations of habit. It is the most available vaccine against the contagion of political activism. Upon morning repetitions are laid the ritual organizations of the workday, in turn covered over by the habitual return, the evening meal, and the preparations for the next morning's round. The pattern is not limited to regular wage-earners. Rilke learned from Rodin the lesson of ritual application to the task at hand. For Nizan, the layerings of habit form an emblem of mental habits, of insulation against change. It is the habit of thinking about reality in a familiar way and living, unquestioningly, by those steady lights. When Halley's Comet passes, Antoine's neighbors try to joke about the perturbation in the familiar sky, but they are obviously troubled by what they cannot control:

> They believed themselves wise, they believed themselves stable, they believed themselves happy. They were capable of the greatest anger, the most reckless courage to defend the wisdom, the stability, the happiness of their small exacting lives against all change, all forces. They thought with deepest hatred of revolutions, of the workers who would make them. They were the kind of people who loved the gendarmes. And Antoine lived among them, he was one of them. Month after month, he sank deeper into this soothing languor of habits.

Habit is also a way of domesticating necessity so that we do not feel so entirely subject to its demands. In Marx's communist society, once the need to labor is dissolved, so too will be its fixed regularities. In *The German Ideology*, he says that in a new society people will be able to "do this today and that tomorrow, who hunt in the morning, go fishing in the afternoon, raise cattle in the evening, are critics after dinner, as they see fit, without ever becoming hunters, fishermen, shepherds or critics." But if we surrender the usually painless capitulations of habit, we also give up the illusion of controlling our circumstances and being less tyrannized by necessity.

Nizan's sympathies are stretched thin in *Antoine Bloyé*. He looks for a Marxist formulation of class problems, but he demonstrates an artist's loyalty to the sufferings of an individual who is not so much the casualty of a social system as he is a powerful sensuous nature incapable of articulating his desires to himself. Although he does not know what happiness is, Antoine knows that he wants it. As a young man he hates the poverty he sees around him. He does not think to change it, nor to understand it; he wants only to escape it. He knows from his father's experience that in a capitalist economy one gets trapped in a job of everlasting repetitions. (Arendt's critique of Marx turns on her belief in labor as an almost celebrative participation in nature's processes, in its repetitions.) His father, a porter, tells Antoine what it is like to be "anchored to a certain lot in the world, a lot ordained for the rest of his life, a lot which he surveys as a tethered goat measures the circumference of its rope, a lot which, like every lot in life, was willed by chance, by riches, by the rulers." The Marxist element absent here is nature's rule of necessity. The sour irony of the story is that in order to escape the submissiveness described by his father, Antoine enters the middle class, where he is even more trapped than his father because more circumscribed by compound responsibilities and more implicated in an economic structure whose power he cannot share. He is even more ineffectual

than his father. He may have his own garden behind his own house, but he is a tethered goat there. (pp. 242-46)

> *W. S. Di Piero, "Work," in his* Memory and Enthusiasm: Essays, 1975-1985, *Princeton University Press, 1989, pp. 239-57.*

Patrick McCarthy   (essay date 1985)

[*McCarthy is an English educator and critic. In the following excerpt, he describes Nizan's conception of politically committed writing and the influence it had upon Jean-Paul Sartre.*]

Paul Nizan haunted Sartre from the day he entered the classroom in Henri IV until the last years of Sartre's life. He and Nizan were comrades in arms both at Henri IV and at the Ecole Normale but then, says Sartre, "the party came between us" [see excerpt dated 1960]. A study of the Sartre-Nizan relationship teaches us, however, to sift through Sartre's statements about his life and thought and we may decide that Nizan's communism, which indeed separated him from his friend, also fascinated Sartre and that in general Sartre's retrospective view of his pre-1939 years can be misleading. The fascination Sartre felt was strengthened by Nizan's death in 1940, even if the Sartre of the Liberation and the Cold War still did not know what to make of his friend. Not until 1960 did he offer a convincing portrait of Nizan in the preface to *Aden, Arabie.* Even then he returned to him in the *Nouvel Observateur* interviews of 1975 which are perhaps Sartre's most dispassionate review of his youth. The study of Nizan's role in Sartre's life is, then, a study of the various answers which Sartre found to the problem of political commitment.

Meanwhile Nizan had left five major books: two pamphlets, *Aden, Arabie* and *Les chiens de garde,* and three novels, *Antoine Bloyé, Le cheval de Troie* and *La conspiration.* Although all spring from his decision to embrace Marxism and join the PCF (the French Communist Party), these are complex and varied works. Are they satisfactorily interpreted by Sartre? Probably not and indeed Nizan's admirers are severe in their judgments of Sartre's efforts. "Sartre n'a jamais vraiment compris Nizan . . . il s'est simplement rapproché de lui" ("Sartre never really understood Nizan . . . he merely became closer to him."), writes one of them [Annie Cohen-Solal, *Paul Nizan, Communiste impossible* (1980)]. Even if one must modify this statement it is a good starting-point from which to analyse the presence of Nizan in Sartre's thought.

Certainly Sartre's preface is an attempt less to understand Nizan than to reconstruct a mythical figure, a Sartrian character who could be an ally in the political battles of the 1960s. The preface should be read in conjunction with *La critique de la raison dialectique* and the essays on the Algerian War. Similarly Sartre's earlier and less successful attempts to grapple with Nizan in his 1938 article on *La conspiration* [excerpted above] and in *Qu'est-ce que la littérature?* (1948) as well as through the character of Vicarios-Schneider in *Les chemins de la liberté* reflect his interest in phenomenology and his conflicting post-Liberation view of the PCF. But Sartre was not simply drawing closer to Nizan. To state only the most obvious difference between the two men—even at the moment when he was most favorable to the PC and wrote *Les communistes et la paix,* Sartre never joined the party, whereas Nizan's decisions to join and then in 1939 to leave the PC were the crucial decisions of his adult life. Nizan was to Sartre brother, rival and opposite; he was a guide towards political commitment but Sartre followed him by different paths. Moreover Sartre's writings do elucidate certain aspects of Nizan's achievement. If he hesitates over *La conspiration,* he casts a powerful beam of light on the pamphlets and *Antoine Bloyé.* And it was the preface which triggered the revival of interest in Nizan which took place in the 1960s. (pp. 191-92)

In 1975 Sartre admitted that his year in Germany awakened him to the evils of Fascism and that he was already an antifascist. He attributes this to Nizan's example: "I adopted a position close to that of Nizan." So Nizan was steering Sartre towards political commitment, even as he was also throwing up a barrier—"I felt that Marxism was challenging me because it was the thinking of a friend and it was cutting across our friendship." Impressed by Nizan, Sartre received this double and contradictory influence. Moreover it tended to falsify his view of his friend. Whether he admired or resented Nizan's membership in the PC, Sartre considered him the perfect communist, briefed in the diplomatic secrets guarded so jealously by the International, and always in agreement with the party's policies. The unorthodoxies of Nizan's writing and his opinions eluded Sartre, which explains the hesitations of his article on *La conspiration.*

Before turning to this article one must consider Nizan's work which is one of the best examples of committed writing in the France of the 1930s. His books are based on a fundamental decision which also involves a series of further choices. As Sartre puts it, "ses yeux furent marxistes; et ses oreilles; Et sa tête." ("His eyes were Marxist, and his ears, as well as his head.") But Nizan's books were anything but propaganda for the PC and, as his biographers have pointed out, the party complained that there was insufficient economic analysis of colonialism in *Aden, Arabie* and that in *Antoine Bloyé* the critique of capitalism was not accompanied by an apology for the new Marxist culture. Yet Nizan's work is Marxist in that political commitment gives structure to his anger and makes literary discourse possible. Then he experiments with several forms of discourse from the fury of the pamphlets to the nuanced irony of *La conspiration.*

The cry of condemnation hurled at capitalist society is well suited to the pamphleteers who need such intolerance because it permits them to divide the world into good and evil. Marxism, says Carré, the communist leader of *La conspiration,* is the least pluralist of all doctrines. Such wilful simplicity suits the genre of the pamphlet and enables Nizan to renew a tradition of pamphleteering that runs from the late nineteenth century on and includes both right-wingers like Drumont and, albeit less frequently, left-wingers like Vallès. From this tradition Nizan borrows his rhetoric, his *ad hominem* attacks and his deliberate contempt for subtlety. When he first read *Aden, Arabie*

Sartre considered it "un tourbillon de paroles légères" ("a whirlwind of airy words") which prompts him later to yet more self-criticism. But if he had omitted the adjective, his observation would have been correct because Nizan's pamphlets are literary exercises inspired by the insight into the social order which Marxism has given him.

In *Les chiens de garde* he does not refute what he calls the idealist philosophers; instead he accuses them; "Nous vivons dans un temps où les philosophes s'abstiennent. Ils vivent dans un état de scandaleux écart, une scandaleuse distance entre ce qu'énonce la Philosophie et ce qui arrive aux hommes." ("We are living in a time when the philosophers are abstaining. They are living in a scandalous state of absenteeism. There is a scandalous divergence, a scandalous gap between what Philosophy propounds and what happens to men.") If the tone of this passage, which is characteristic of *Les chiens de garde,* reminds us of certain passages in Sartre, then this is a sign that there is in Sartre too a pamphleteer who emerges precisely in the preface. Nizan anticipated Sartre in the discourse of anger.

Each of his novels offers a different although equally Marxist voice. *Antoine Bloyé* has the trappings of nineteenth-century realism: a regular procession through time, lists of objects, description of the environment. But instead of the remote, clinically objective narrator, there is present in the book a critical consciousness which interprets Bloyé to the reader. In the preface Sartre writes that, although this novel is ostensibly about Nizan's father, Nizan himself is present. This is another way of saying that there is a Marxist narrator who links Bloyé's career to the growth of French capitalism. The analysis of the railway system—the epitome of nineteenth-century capitalism—has as counterpoint Bloyé's imprisonment by it "Antoine était pris comme un insecte dans cette toile vibrante des voies ferrées." ("Antoine was caught like an insect in this quivering web of railway lines.")

After this critique of the old order Nizan depicts the birth of the new culture in *Le cheval de Troie.* Although partly written in the Soviet Union and in the aftermath of the 1934 Moscow Congress, which saw the triumph of socialist realism, and although seeming to answer *L'humanite*'s rebuke by portraying a group of communists, *Le cheval de Troie* does not depict the inevitable triumph of the revolution. Nizan uses the technique of the film shot to depict each of the communists in action and out of their actions there emerges a greater but partial understanding of history. The PC militants have no infallible party secretary to guide them and they are inventing the revolution as they go along. As one of Nizan's critics puts it, this is "an open-ended book" [William Redfern, see Further Reading entry dated 1972], it is Marxist in its depiction of men in rebellion against the capitalist order but it is unstalinist in its lack of dogmatism.

This is the link with Nizan's last novel, *La conspiration,* where the Marxist awareness is most obviously present as irony. The narrator, a mature communist, looks back on the group of young bourgeois conspirators and in a sentence that was to become all too famous Nizan writes: "Rosenthal publia dans la *Guerre civile* des pages qui n'avaient pas de chances sérieuses d'ébranler le capitalisme." ("In the *Guerre civile,* Rosenthal published views which could not seriously shake the foundations of capitalism.") Yet, contrary to what Sartre affirms, the book is not entirely written by a narrator who smiles sarcastically as his characters struggle. *La conspiration* shifts from one discourse to another—from the authoritative but brief pronouncements of Carré to the flat despair of Régnier's diary. The sarcasm that marks the early depiction of Rosenthal gives way to sympathy and even complicity as he struggles against his family. *La conspiration* is a polyphonic novel where Nizan uses the diverse possibilities which Marxism offers a writer.

Although *Le cheval de Troie* seems the most Sartrian of these novels, Sartre's first attempt to grapple with Nizan was his article on *La conspiration.* Chiefly interesting as a guide to Sartre's concept of the novel and as a preface to his article on Mauriac, this review does not show great understanding of Nizan and illustrates the differences rather than the parallels between the two friends. After making a half-hearted attempt to annex Nizan to phenomenology, Sartre criticizes the characters of *La conspiration* and draws the conclusion: "Un communiste peut-il écrire un roman? Je n'en suis pas persuadé: il n'a pas le droit de se faire le complice de ses personnages." ("Can a communist write a novel? I am skeptical: he does not have the right to become his characters' accomplice.")

The conception of the *"complice"* ["accomplice"] will be clarified in the essay on Mauriac published three months later. According to Sartre, Mauriac indulges in a "va-et-vient" ["back and forth"] between himself and his heroine: now Thérèse speaks for herself, now Mauriac speaks through her with the insight of an omniscient narrator. This destroys her liberty and prevents the appeal to the reader's liberty which Sartre considers the crux of the author-reader relationship.

Although Sartre admits there can be Christian novelists and cites Dostoevsky as an example, he seems to think that communists are bound to interfere with the freedom of their creations. Because of their claim to understand the workings of history, they crush their characters and prevent them from engaging the reader. This criticism, which might possess a certain validity if directed at *Antoine Bloyé,* where the narrator does impose one view of Bloyé's experience, can only apply to *La conspiration* if one accepts the notion that Nizan toys with his young conspirators from the heights of some communist Olympus. If one considers the shifts of point of view they may discover the *"complice"* concept which Sartre extols. But Sartre, disturbed by Nizan's Marxism, insists on defining Nizan as the perfect communist, indeed as a Stalinist communist.

When he returns to Nizan in *Qu'est-ce que la littérature?,* his view of his friend has partially changed because his own concept of liberty has changed. The dialogue between author and reader is now situated within history; the committed writer will encourage the reader to treat the other members of society as an end and not, as the capitalist ethos dictates, as a means of production; the reader will be stirred to exercise his freedom by political and social action. The political element in Sartre's thought, which was potential and hesitant before 1939, is now crystallized

and he draws closer to Nizan. *Le cheval de Troie* and *La conspiration* are cited as examples of works which liberate their readers, and Nizan is implictly contrasted with nineteenth-century novelists who denounced existing society without provoking the reader to imagine new forms of freedom. (pp. 196-200)

Sartre's interpretation of Nizan is of course arbitrary. His attempt to analyse Nizan's life through his novels has drawn a cry of pain from at least one of Nizan's critics. Nor does he tackle all of Nizan's books, concentrating instead on the pamphlets and *Antoine Bloyé.* This is less a literary study than a political portrait, while the preface as a whole is best read as a political pamphlet. (p. 203)

>   *Patrick McCarthy, "Sartre, Nizan and the Di-*
>   *lemmas of Political Commitment," in* Yale
>   French Studies, *No. 68, 1985, pp. 191-205.*

Michael Scriven   (essay date 1988)

[*Scriven is an English educator and critic. In the following excerpt, he discusses* The Trojan Horse *as the most conspicuous example of an ideological dualism in Nizan's fiction, which advances both communist politics and Existentialist philosophy.*]

Nizan was convinced that the novel in the contemporary period was as significant a genre as tragedy had been in the classical period. For Nizan an authentic modern writer was, of necessity, primarily a novelist. Nizan himself was actively engaged in writing novels from 1931 to 1932, when he began the production of *Antoine Bloyé,* until his death in 1940, when he was involved in the drafting of *La soirée à Somosierra.* His novels, unlike other aspects of his literary production, span the full period of his adult writing career and constitute a global critical mirror in which are reflected, distorted, concealed and exaggerated the social, political and metaphysical problems of this particular historical period.

The novels are also the privileged site in Nizan's work where politics and metaphysics collide, where an uneasy balance is maintained between metaphysical *angst* and political construction. Unlike his exclusively militant writings in which the principal concern is to foreground the political and the social (the sectarian polemics of *Les chiens de garde* at one extreme, the discreet implications of *Chronique de septembre* at the other), his novels accomplish a disturbing fusion between metaphysical disorientation and political action. It is precisely this fusion which constitutes the originality of Paul Nizan.

The novel is in many ways a problematical form for the communist writer. Synonymous for the most part with the hegemonic culture of the bourgeoisie, the novel is not a form easily adapted to the demands of a revolutionary communist ideology explicitly contesting the assumptions of the class by which the form itself was fashioned. Nizan is not unaware of the problem, but chooses to minimise its significance, stressing instead the critical, revelatory and educative aspects of the novel form. He is resolutely determined to counter the allegation that communism and the novel are incompatible, maintaining that the structural integrity of the novel is in no sense impaired by the introduction of ideology:

> My status as a communist and my status as a novelist are not irreconcilable. . . . Communism, like all profound experiences, serves the novelist precisely because the novel is a means of raising consciousness and communism is an experiential method of consciousness-raising.

Nizan makes no apologies for the presence of communism in the novel. Communism is not simply compatible with the novel. In Nizan's theory of the revolutionary novel it is elevated to the status of necessary pre-condition of authentic writing practices. There can be little doubt that Nizan was ideologically committed to the view that a writer's allegiance to communism enabled him/her to grasp the true significance of political developments *from the inside,* that is to say, from the perspective of the proletariat. By contrast, a writer whose allegiances ultimately lie with the bourgeoisie would necessarily understand political developments *from the outside,* that is to say from the perspective of an oppressive class.

For Nizan the moral strength afforded the writer by revolutionary ideology eliminates the need for self-justification within the ethos of his work, eliminates the need to apologise for failing to conform not only to the conventions of bourgeois political structures, but also to the conventions of bourgeois literary structures. The moral righteousness of communist ideology, in short, transforms apologetic social reformism into legitimate revolutionary demands, injects passion into writing and redesignates the novel as the site of political and moral regeneration.

Technical disturbances arising from the interaction between communism and the novel form are consequently in Nizan's eyes merely the logical outcome of the communist writer's refusal to acquiesce to what are perceived as the oppressive structures of bourgeois politics, ethics and culture. To confront and openly subvert the privileged literary form of an oppressive class is to voice the legitimate grievances of the proletariat within the cultural homeland of the bourgeoisie. The formal disruption is itself the visible manifestation of the political demand.

It is precisely this formal disturbance in the texture of Nizan's fiction that constitutes the very essence of his project as a communist novelist. Lodged at the heart of Nizan's fictional enterprise are two competing discourses struggling in narrative combat. In his novels Nizan speaks with a forked tongue; he uses two different languages, two different voices within each narrative site, one political and historical, the other literary and metaphysical:

> Language 1: Communist discourse—Historical authority—LENIN

> Language 2: Existential discourse—Metaphysical *angst*—DOSTOIEVSKY

At one level Nizan's novels proclaim certainty, truth, authority. This is the voice of communism relaying to the reader unfaltering ideological orthodoxy, pushing the reader constantly towards greater political, social and historical awareness. It is the voice of Nizan speaking the language of Lenin.

At another level, Nizan's novels betray uncertainty, disorientation, doubt. This is the voice of existentialism transmitting to the reader a sense of metaphysical alienation and despair arising from the contemplation of death. It is the voice of Nizan speaking the language of Dostoievsky.

From a strictly communist perspective, the secondary existential discourse could be dismissed as 'petty bourgeois' and 'alienated' since it overflows the boundaries of orthodox communist ideology and points to an alternative vision. However, to classify this secondary discourse in a pejorative sense is to remain blind to the dynamic configuration of Nizan's narrative technique.

The object of the following analysis is not to carry out a Stalinist witch-hunt of the text in order to pillory a deviant, existential, petty-bourgeois discourse ensconced illegitimately at the centre of Nizan's literary production. The object is rather to demonstrate that the success of Nizan's writing technique is ultimately dependent on the interaction of two different but, in the final analysis, mutually dependent discourses.

These two discourses are at times indistinguishably fused, at times distinctly separate. Separate or fused, they contradict and complement each other simultaneously. The precise disposition, organisation and arrangement of these two discourses constitutes the basic fabric of Nizan's fictional technique. Irrespective of the content of each novel, whether it is a tale of apprenticeship (*Antoine Bloyé* and *La conspiration*), or of confrontation (*Le cheval de Troie*), the formal articulation of the content is achieved by means of two competing discourses. Nizan's global project as a novelist can therefore be defined above all else as the evolution of two interactive discourses.

What needs to be stressed at this point is that this evolution is rooted in a very specific historical moment of production. The formal and technical development of Nizan's novels reflects in a mediated form the changing historical circumstances in which each text was produced. In each novel the specific configuration of the two discourses, authoritative communist on the one hand, disorientating existential on the other, is the product of two overriding influences: first, the economic, political, ideological and cultural forces that together produced each particular text; secondly, and this is but a superstructural reflection of the first point, Nizan's divided ambitions as a novelist, attempting at one level to exploit bourgeois culture in order to disseminate communist ideology effectively (the communist project), and at another level to create a cultural product of value beyond its immediate moment of production (the bourgeois project). (pp. 113-16)

The socialist realist pedigree of Nizan's second novel, *Le cheval de Troie,* has done little to enhance its reputation. Perceptions of this novel not only as a 'classic example of Zhdanovite socialist realism' [A. Cohen-Solal and H. Nizan, *Paul Nizan, Communiste impossible* (1980)], but also as a 'particularly "pure" version of the structure of confrontation in the *roman à thèse*' [see Suleiman excerpt dated 1983], are doubtless reassuring to critics seeking to restrict the novel within established ideological and technical boundaries, but are ultimately an impoverishment of the problematical textual specificity of the novel itself.

This lack-lustre critical performance is compounded by the significant omission of *Le cheval de Troie* from Sartre's otherwise globally positive assessments of Nizan's work. Sartre is, in fact, curiously tight-lipped regarding this particular novel. His eloquence when speaking of other aspects of Nizan's literary production stands in marked contrast to a decided unwillingness even to mention *Le cheval de Troie,* an unwillingness that can only be interpreted as tacit criticism. Such reticence could be explained in political or technical terms, given Sartre's opposition to socialist realist literature. More likely, however, is a purely personal explanation. Despite Nizan's protestations to the contrary, Sartre remained convinced that the character of Lange, an abstract, solitary individual obsessed by thoughts of death and ultimately aligning himself with fascism, was based on himself. The discretion with which Sartre treats *Le cheval de Troie* is consequently more probably motivated by personal than by ideological or literary reasons.

Ultimately, however, hostile, condescending and even discreetly critical value-judgements merely function as an ideological screen, an obstacle impeding understanding. In order to assess the legitimacy of categorising *Le cheval de Troie* as an unproblematical exemplification of Zhdanovite socialist realism, it is necessary to probe the specific ideological and formal structure of this novel by focusing on the relationship between its historical moment of production and the configuration of its two dominant discourses.

Le cheval de Troie was published in 1935. It was written partly in the Soviet Union in 1934 in the aftermath of the Soviet Writers' Congress, and partly in France in 1935 amidst growing popular front optimism engendered initially by the events of February 1934. Its moment of production therefore coincides with a highly significant transition phase politically, ideologically and culturally. *Le cheval de Troie* is in this sense a unique text since it reflects in mediated form Nizan's attempts not merely to formulate a technical response to the exigencies of socialist realist doctrine as articulated in the 1934 Congress, but also to formulate a political and ideological response to the transformed historical climate that was to culminate in the governments of the Popular Front.

It is important to stress the transitional nature of this moment of production. Since the ideological objective of the novel is to pinpoint the year 1934 as a historical watershed, a moment when political consciousness was transformed, there are of necessity two perspectives encoded in the narrative: a past perspective of communist party isolationism and working-class docility and defeatism prior to the events of 1934, and a future perspective of popular front cooperation and working-class social awareness and militancy subsequent to the events of 1934. Although the novel is divided into two distinct parts corresponding in terms of the narration of events with a past perspective of despair and a future perspective of hope, the text overall testifies to a sustained tension between a sectarian and a popular front ideological stance, a tension reflecting this

transitional moment between two phases in the political development of the French communist party.

Despite a residual sectarianism manifesting itself in this narrative ideological tension, *Le cheval de Troie* unquestionably constitutes a radical departure from Nizan's previous writing practice, and graphically illustrates his conviction that 'Nobody in 1935 is capable of writing the sequel to the books of 1933'. There are major differences politically, historically and technically between *Antoine Bloyé* published in 1933, and *Le cheval de Troie* published in 1935.

The political development could not be more visibly apparent. The lessons of the negative exemplary narrative, *Antoine Bloyé,* recording the story of a father alienated in the deathly existence of the petty bourgeoisie, have been learnt and put into practice by his son, Pierre Bloyé, a militant communist party member who is elevated to the status of narrator in *Le cheval de Troie.* The centre of gravity has consequently shifted decisively from the analysis of petty-bourgeois alienation to the description of communist party militancy. A negative tale of apprenticeship within an oppressive class has been transformed into a positive tale of confrontation with the same oppressive class.

It is the change in historical perspective, however, which is the most profound development and which has the most far-reaching consequences for the tone, structure and content of the novel itself. Unlike *Antoine Bloyé,* a 'balance-sheet' novel aimed at drawing up an account of a closed historical period, *Le cheval de Troie* is manifestly 'problem-centred'; that is to say, set in the confusing flux of contemporary events at a moment when the full implications of the events themselves are far from clear. The fact that Nizan was attempting to disclose the significance of the events of February 1934 *in their immediate aftermath* cannot be overemphasised. He was, in other words, writing history as it was being made. The risks for the political novelist are self-evident.

The epic tone of the narrative, clearly signalled in the title of the novel itself, a title eventually preferred to the more immediately evocative but less morally uplifting *Le jour de la colère,* is consequently not the product of casual imitation of Soviet socialist realist models. It is a narrative tone that coincides precisely with the sense of moral and political regeneration that the events of February had appeared to have sparked off, and which seemed to be sweeping the country before it in a Popular Front crusade.

The fundamental shift in historical perspective accomplished in *Le cheval de Troie* has implications beyond mere narrative tone, however. The focusing of attention on the contemporary struggle in its unfolding produces a marked attenuation of the voice of omniscient historical narration legislating a definitive Marxist interpretation of events, the legislating voice itself becoming part of the process of History in the making. This is an important point since it highlights the significance of the material presence of the communist party in this particular novel. Unlike *Antoine Bloyé,* where the depoliticised consciousness of the central character, and the material absence of the communist party itself, created an ideological space in the novel which was ceaselessly filled by the voice of an omniscient communist narrator, a disembodied discourse at a distance from the concrete social relations depicted in the text, the ideological presence of communism in *Le cheval de Troie* is guaranteed by the physical presence of communist militants. The thoughts, emotions, words and deeds of the party activists become the natural expression of communist ideology organically linked to the theme and structure of the narrative. The ideological content of the novel is therefore predominantly communicated to the reader by the social actors themselves.

The transformed historical perspective in *Le cheval de Troie* also produces a movement away from the examination of individual characters as exemplifications of the lifestyle of a particular class, towards the description of class conflict at a moment of political and social realignment. Specifically, whereas **Antoine Bloyé** was centred on the situation of one individual progressively ensnared in the serial relations of the petty bourgeoisie, **Le cheval de Troie** seeks to capture the defining characteristics of a communist group at a moment of intense political activity. In *Antoine Bloyé* the focus was the *analysis* of a given life, in *Le cheval de Troie* the focus becomes the *description* of a conflictual political event.

This development is reflected in the epigraphs that Nizan selects for the two novels. For **Antoine Bloyé** an extract from Marx's *German Ideology,* locating the root cause of bourgeois alienation and proletarian oppression in the work process itself, gives pre-eminence to a Marxist discourse aimed at disclosing the underlying causes of class conflict. For **Le cheval de Troie,** by contrast, an extract from a worker's letter addressed to the editorial committee of *Iskra,* Lenin's revolutionary newspaper, requesting assistance in the search to understand the processes of living and dying within the class struggle, gives pre-eminence to a communist discourse aimed at describing the problems and actions of men and women directly implicated in class conflict.

The centre of the novel is consequently no longer the distant voice of history dispassionately recording the alienation and death lodged at the heart of an oppressive class. It becomes the ideologically charged description of the social, moral and emotional predicament of the members of two opposed classes at a moment of political confrontation. The challenge issued by one class to another constitutes an act of social and moral regeneration. The challenge itself is the narrative centre of **Le cheval de Troie.**

The events recorded in *Le cheval de Troie* take place in June 1934 in the town of Villefranche. The novel begins one Sunday afternoon amidst the relaxed and peaceful atmosphere of a country setting just outside the town, and ends the following Sunday afternoon amidst an atmosphere of violence and polarised class conflict inside the town itself. The stark contrast between the opening scene depicting docile workers slumbering in the bosom of nature, and the concluding scenes depicting militant workers struggling in the heart of the city is pointedly symbolic. The journey in text, time and space, from initial to final chapter, from one Sunday to the next, from country to town, is a journey of deepening political and social awareness.

The division of the novel into two distinct parts, the first recording the gradual build-up of events during an entire week beginning in the peace and calm of an initial Sunday afternoon, the second recording the explosive streetfighting of the subsequent Sunday afternoon, is a structural reflection of this progressive conscientisation of the working class. In the first part, the various social actors are presented to the reader within their own specific living and working environments. Each distinctly separate group of social actors is situated within a global economic, political and cultural hierarchy which regulates the town. In the second part, the stultifyingly predictable social existence of the town is shattered. The town's principal actors are involved in a dramatic and dynamic performance of class conflict set in the public square, suitably and ironically named 'La place du théâtre'. Years of pent-up resentment and anger explode violently in the June sunlight. In a festival of confrontation, the injustice and oppression of the town's political and social hierarchies are publicly denounced.

The extent to which this fictionalised movement from social and political stasis described in part 1 to dynamic fusion and growing working-class consciousness described in part 2 reflects an ideological movement from sectarianism to popular frontism can be gauged by an assessment of the evolution of the communist discourse within the narrative itself.

A sectarian discourse is clearly visible in the opening pages of the novel. The initial scene of relaxation in the countryside serves several purposes. Not only does it function as a peaceful counterpoint to the subsequent violence. It also acts as an effective means of presenting the communist group to the reader. In this introductory ceremony the communist militants are described at a moment of respite when they are briefly withdrawn from the front-line of an endless political battle. The image of the group projected in this opening sequence is that of an isolated sect, surrounded on all sides by powerful political enemies, and locked in a desperate life and death struggle against the forces of Darkness:

> They were men and women who lived all their lives in a world of anxiety and struggle. They were familiar with factories, workshops, the police. They lived in a world which was divided and torn apart, a world resembling the background of those pictures by painters of the Middle Ages, separated into celestial and infernal divisions, a conflict between heaven and hell. They were at war with their town, with their own lives, in a struggle which had not yet been lit up by heroic explosions and where there had been only isolated deaths; but it was a battle in which they had little protection, in which the blows aimed against them usually found their mark. For them, hunger, homelessness, prison, the destruction of love, incurable diseases, were not monstrous fables but merely misfortunes which they had escaped for the time being. The future appeared to them as an awesome and pitiless snare.

What is striking in this passage is not only the extent to which this fundamentally manichean image of the communist group as besieged and isolated coincides with the reality of a sectarian French communist party during the late 1920s, but also the extent to which it plays down the possibility of epic events at this juncture in the narrative. On this initial Sunday afternoon in June 1934 there is as yet no premonition of the imminent political explosion that is about to detonate Villefranche. The communist group is described simply as committed to pursuing its bitter struggle, with little hope of major success in the foreseeable future.

It is significant, in fact, that the concluding pages of the opening chapter focus on the setbacks and failures of the past as recollected by individual members of the communist group. The conversations between the militants, centred as they are on the development of the labour movement since the outbreak of the First World War, enable historical assessments to emerge organically from the fictional situation itself. Although buoyed by distant memories of anarchist rebellion in 1910 and 1911, there is no attempt at self-delusion. It is recognised that after 1920 the working class entered a historical phase of division and disenchantment. The only beacon of hope on the horizon was the possibility that the political consciousness of the labour movement might be reactivated by the growing world economic crisis.

The tragic communist discourse in which the voice of sectarianism takes stock of the oppressed and isolated existence of the working class in general and the communist group in particular is, nonetheless, progressively abandoned in the course of the narrative and replaced by a more optimistic, occasionally euphoric discourse climaxing in the concluding explosive confrontation.

A significant moment of transition occurs at the point at which the threat of fascism is introduced. Mid-way through the first half of the novel the enemy is clearly signalled. Posters announcing a fascist meeting to be held the following Sunday inject into the text the catalyst of working-class solidarity. The communist narrator reacts immediately, shifting the emphasis from division and defeatism to the imminent struggle against fascism.

> Things were beginning to stir in France. On Sundays, in town squares which had known centuries of tranquillity, squares which had occasionally not even observed the passing shadows of revolutions, of wars and of invasions, where the inhabitants had for generations not experienced a quickening of their heart-beat, hostile groups were confronting one another. The French had for a long time lived in their own isolated little world; Europe was seething around this rock of France, and all the while the French continued to look upon Germany, Italy, Spain, all their neighbours, with the detached gaze of spectators. . . . Then suddenly, on these same squares, stones were being hurled, horses were galloping, truncheons were crashing down on heads, and guns were being fired. In every town secret meetings were being held, hatred and anger were growing more intense. People were getting to know hunger and privation at first hand. Despair was assuming an explosive potency. It was a period which called to mind the beginning of the religious wars, when the barns of Protestants went up in flames and men took to the highways to fight.

The epic tone of this passage in which the forthcoming conflict is likened to a religious war, stands in marked contrast to the tone of the opening pages of the novel where emphasis was placed on a more mundane struggle for existence. Nonetheless, despite a clear recognition that the advent of fascism has fundamentally transformed the political and social situation, attention at this stage is focused primarily on the brutal emergence of conflict and violence in the political sphere, rather than on popular front opposition to fascism itself. It is significant, in fact, that there is no global coordination of political strategy in the first half of the novel. Each political party acts independently, holding separate meetings to devise individual responses to the fascist threat. Although a popular front strategy is doubtless implied, it comes into existence only at the moment of the counter-demonstration itself when communists, socialists, radicals, trade-unionists, the unemployed, unite spontaneously to form a coherent and unified group facing a common enemy.

The sense of burgeoning political consciousness conveyed in the novel occasionally borders on the apocalyptic. Segments of the narrative which project a violent and courageous political stance based on heroism in the face of death are doubtless the product of a residual anarchism in Nizan's personality, so clearly visible in the early and violently iconoclastic text, ***Aden, Arabie.***

The presence of such violent epic discourse within ***Le cheval de Troie*** can also be explained organically, however, as an expression of the anarchist tendencies of the working-class characters portrayed in the novel. So deep-rooted, in fact, are the anarchist traditions in this region that the workers of Villefranche are described as bearing a resemblance on occasions to 'sectarian, orthodox Protestants', capable of experiencing fervently religious emotions at the thought of a general strike. In this sense, the

Nizan delivering a speech at a collective farm in central Asia, 1934.

violently ethical discourse which functions primarily as a direct appeal to the reader to support the anti-fascist struggle, does nonetheless arise naturally from the fictional situation itself.

Although the appeal to support the anti-fascist struggle is clearly located at the political centre of the novel, the emergence of the fascist threat is paradoxically presented not only as a moment of impending catastrophe, but also as a moment of political opportunity. Above all, the communist discourse presents fascism as the catalysing agent which unmasks the democratic pretensions of bourgeois society, forces the working class into political self-consciousness, and in the process rejuvenates a previously isolated communist party.

The presentation of fascism within the narrative is, in other words, ideologically motivated. *Le cheval de Troie* is not a democratic, anti-fascist text. It is a strategic narrative which aims at analysing the fascist phenomenom from a Marxist perspective in order to re-situate the French communist party at the centre of the political arena.

The strategic nature of the presentation of fascism is clearly visible in the bourgeois dinner party sequence located towards the end of the first half of the novel. Leaving aside the highly idiosyncratic contribution of Lange, the dialogue between these representatives of bourgeois law and order is a narrative pretext designed primarily to disclose the underlying economic contradictions of fascism threatening the continued stability of bourgeois democracy. The industrialist, Provost-Livet, informs both the dinner party guests and the reader in an implacably cynical voice that despite his personal ideological attraction to fascism, economically it is a dangerous and misguided ideology. Once the demagogic economic promises of fascism have proved to be illusory, he asserts, the consequent social disorder unleashed will become uncontrollable and the only remaining solution will be war.

This dialogue illuminates the fact that fascism simultaneously threatens the social stability of the bourgeoisie and activates the political rebellion of the working class. It is consequently not fascism as such which is the subject of this novel. It is rather the twin effects that fascism itself produces: on the one hand, the disruption of the bourgeois state, on the other, the politicisation of the proletariat. The second half of the novel, although centred on an anti-fascist counter-demonstration, is in reality a festival of liberation in which a fascist meeting is exploited as a means of exploding the law and order of the bourgeoisie and of celebrating the political activism of the working class.

It is quite clear at the end of the novel that the significance of the events themselves is not primarily the struggle against fascism but the rebirth of working-class political consciousness:

> The political significance of the day was perhaps simply that thousands of men had at long last given vent to their anger. Resistance and militancy, fundamental values of the working class, had once again entered into their lives with a certainty and clarity which exalted them.

Fascism is opposed in the novel. But the overriding teleol-

ogy of the novel is to designate the working class as politically active after a long period of docility. Significantly, fascism disappears from the conclusion of the novel which is dominated by images of the political re-awakening of the labour movement.

The transitional moment of production of the novel is consequently reflected in the progressive development of the communist discourse in the narrative. Throughout, there is a sustained tension between a sectarian and a popular front strategy. Initially sectarian and defensive, the narrative adopts a progressively more combative stance with the emergence of fascism, climaxing in the popular front fusion of the anti-fascist counter-demonstration. However, fascism recedes into the distance in the conclusion where attention is focused on the rebirth of working-class political consciousness and militancy. At the same time the entire narrative is bathed in a persistent anarchist tone, echoing Nizan's early iconoclasm, the political culture of the workers portrayed, and the anti-authoritarian, undisciplined quality of the counter-demonstration itself.

From a purely political and historical perspective, therefore, *Le cheval de Troie* resists classification as an archetypal exemplification of Zhdanovite socialist realism. A secondary, existential discourse adds a further dimension to such resistance.

Death is an inescapable presence in *Le cheval de Troie.* Death is not an external, supernatural phenomenom that descends upon the world unexpectedly. Death is a deadly poison which enters into the pores of life at birth, relentlessly corrodes the body fabric of the living, and is secreted only at the moment of dying. This ceaseless flow of death in life's bloodstream is the metaphysical centre of *Le cheval de Troie.*

Death refuses to recognise class boundaries. The revolution does not banish the fears that death instils in the minds of men and women. Nizan's bitter realisation that even the Soviet revolutionary state ultimately did not protect its citizens from an anguished confrontation with death is never far from the surface of the narrative of *Le cheval de Troie.* Unlike *Antoine Bloyé,* where death was for the most part presented as the defining characteristic of the existence of an oppressive class, in this second novel men and women on both sides of the class divide are equally tormented by death, although in different ways.

The clear-cut distinction between a deathly bourgeois existence and a dynamic communist existence is nonetheless retained in *Le cheval de Troie.* An explicit comparison is made between the burgeoning, life-giving existence of the communist militants on the one hand, and the dead, oppressive life-style of the bourgeois teaching profession on the other. Bloyé's professional colleagues are described as frightened, ghostly figures, desperately seeking ways of masking the emptiness of their lives and the inevitability of their death. Their existence is dismissed as a cowardly pretence, a life sentence in which genuine human relations have been abandoned in a sadistic teaching environment dominated by mindless, self-deluding petty-bourgeois careerism.

The links between death and the bourgeoisie, the central

theme of *Antoine Bloyé,* are analysed in a more deeply metaphysical vein, however, in *Le cheval de Troie.* The character of Lange, exploited in the narrative to symbolise the deathly void at the heart of bourgeois existence, graphically exemplifies the intricate interweaving between the metaphysical and the political in the novel.

Lange is presented as an extreme example of petty-bourgeois alienation, a man who inhabits a ghostly, shadowy world, and whose thoughts centre morbidly on death and the production of a book describing the desolation of a solitary individual exploring the death-filled landscape of an urban environment. There is a haunting intensity in the description of Lange's nocturnal prowling in the town which reaches beyond the limitations of stereotypical socialist realist literature. Lange, Roquentin and Sartre become merged in the deathly twilight existence of Villefranche.

The highly metaphysical presence of Lange is, however, not gratuitous to the political message. As well as offering a hallucinating example of the aberrations of petty-bourgeois alienation in an extreme form, the character of Lange also functions as an integral part of the global ideological thesis that emerges from the novel. In the dinner party sequence Lange's metaphysical anguish appears naïve compared to the cynical economic views of the industrialist Provost-Livet. Yet the strategic objective of the dialogue itself is to highlight the imminent bankruptcy of the bourgeoisie not only politically and economically (Provost-Livet), but also spiritually and ethically (Lange). The alienated voice of Lange communicates to the reader the desolate conclusion that the only surviving values in bourgeois society are the values of death. Lange projects the deathly spiritual void at the heart of bourgeois society and in the process completes a picture of total bourgeois degeneration.

The figure of Lange consequently poses the more general problem of the regeneration of spiritual and ethical values in a society defined by death. Lange's final response, aligning himself with fascism at the moment of the street confrontation, is not merely aimed at highlighting the need to progress beyond sterile intellectual masturbation and engage in political action. It is also pointedly symbolic of the need articulated generally in the novel to search for a response to a wider ethical problem. Although the narrative of *Le cheval de Troie* makes it abundantly clear that Lange's response is misguided, and that the solution is to be found on the other side of the class divide in the ranks of the communist militants, none the less the importance of this character resides primarily in his expression of the death, decay and disintegration of the entire value-system of bourgeois society. Metaphysics in this instance lends effective support to politics.

It is symbolic that whereas the descriptions of the bourgeoisie evoke images of death that are linked primarily to the sterile and anesthetised process of *living,* the descriptions of the working class evoke images of death that are centred primarily on the heroic and painful moment of *dying.* Beyond the general exploitation of the death theme to symbolise the oppressive living and working environment of the communist militants, the process and the act

of dying are together exploited to project a specific ideological message.

Two deaths in the narrative are effectively orchestrated to serve the ideological objectives of the novel itself: the deaths of Catherine and Paul. Catherine dies totally alone, bleeding to death after an abortion. Paul dies in the company of communist comrades, hit by a stray bullet during the street fighting. The reader is given little insight into the personality of either of these characters. The strained marital relationship between Albert and Catherine is briefly sketched but the overriding objective is to explain the tensions and emotional problems of private life as the inevitable product of a society which makes back-street abortions necessary. Paul remains a totally anonymous figure, an unknown militant who comes to symbolise the essential qualities of the political struggle itself.

Catherine dies almost without a struggle, at the precise moment when the militant cries of working-class protest are ringing through the streets of Villefranche. She dies of a haemorrhage, her life blood streaming from her as she secretes her own death. This harrowing episode, which interrupts the narrative flow of the street-fighting, is strategically placed. The reader, confronted by the sickening description of a young woman dying in a pool of blood, unaided, helpless, too weak to resist, is forced to reflect not only on the injustice of one particular death, but also on the inescapable presence of death in life. For a brief moment, the narrative subsumes the dominant political thesis beneath broader metaphysical concerns, before pointing a finger of accusation at the society of unequal chances which makes such a death possible.

This process of fusion between the political and the metaphysical is prominent in the narrative exploitation of the death of Paul. Compared to the meticulous description of the moment of Catherine's death, Paul's moment of dying is but briefly described. Yet this death in the heat of the street battle prompts the articulation of the global political/metaphysical message of the novel.

Dying alone and at a distance from the struggle, Catherine dies a pointless, insignificant death. Her death merely highlights the waste of an entire existence. Hers can only be a negative exemplary tale. Dying for the party in the midst of the struggle, by contrast, Paul dies a heroic, exemplary death. His death comes to symbolise a victory not only over political enemies but also over death itself: 'Either lead a fearful life of anguish, or risk death in order to conquer life itself ', notes Bloyé towards the end of the novel, highlighting a fundamental choice to be made between defensive, *angst*-ridden acquiescence and militant, risk-taking combat. Such a conclusion not only foregrounds the twin struggle against death and the bourgeoisie, it also signals a synthesis between two discourses, existential and communist, within the narrative itself.

The existential discourse encoded in the narrative, although enmeshed inextricably in communist ideology, does nonetheless occasionally strike a different chord. Segments of the narrative drift tantalisingly close to metaphysical speculation devoid of ideological ballast. Certain passages depicting Lange's metaphysical *angst,* certain aspects of the description of Catherine's death cannot be entirely subsumed within the communist framework. Likewise, the concluding pages of the novel contain elements which attach an importance to the metaphysical oppression of death which transcends orthodox communist ideology:

> For years at a time we do not think about death. We simply have sudden brief intimations of its existence in the midst of our lives, although there are people who think of it more often than most: they are born like that. Death passes nearby, a cloud poisoning the earth upon which its shadow falls, and our spirit is caught by fear. Then we recover, and begin again to live as though we were immortal; we continue to play the game of cheating death, we take medicines and follow diets or indulge in passionate pursuits. But still it appears again. However much we try, we cannot forget the army of men who die each second, the vast cavalcade of funerals proceeding towards all the cemeteries of the earth. We need only see the mangled body of a cat lying on the shiny surface of a road to realise that death may come and that our hearts may stop.

The principal foe here is death, not political oppression. The paradox of *Le cheval de Troie* is revealed in these lines. This text, which is the most visibly politicised of Nizan's novels, is at the same time the most deeply metaphysical. Politics and metaphysics collide in a kaleidoscopic confrontation.

The formal structure of *Le cheval de Troie* reflects the global political, metaphysical and cultural position that Nizan had reached during 1934 and 1935. His political perception had been transformed by the events of February 1934. His cultural views had been influenced by the Soviet Writers' Congress of the same year. His sense of metaphysical alienation had been heightened not only by his realisation that death remained a formidable presence even in the revolutionary Soviet state, but doubtless also by his close contact with André Malraux in the Soviet Union. *Le cheval de Troie* is consequently a formal synthesis of a global ideological development which represents a clear development from *Antoine Bloyé.*

The ideological view that emerges from *Le cheval de Troie* is inherently more problematical than the view that is presented in *Antoine Bloyé.* Whereas in *Antoine Bloyé* the implication of the narrative was that avoidance of a deathly existence could be achieved by breaking with an oppressive bourgeois class and entering the dynamic, living existence of the working class, in *Le cheval de Troie* it is apparent that death is a metaphysical presence which even encroaches upon the lives of the communist party militants. The consequences of this all-pervading presence of death in *Le cheval de Troie* is a fusion between the collective effort of all the communist militants to struggle against the oppression of a deathly class enemy, and the individual effort of each communist militant to struggle against the oppressive presence of death itself. This revised ideological view inevitably has implications for the formal structure of the novel itself.

Most strikingly, the material presence of the party in *Le cheval de Troie* facilitates the organic emergence of communist ideology from within the text. The uneasy presence of abstract segments of narrative in *Antoine Bloyé,* where an omniscient communist narrator legislates the significance of historical developments, is replaced by the voices of the communist militants themselves expressing their own political convictions in the context of their living environment.

Occasionally, such dialogue sequences are not entirely convincing. Specific utterances do not ring true, sounding more like the unmediated slogans of the party than the ideas of the individuals voicing them. Yet for the most part, this technical device is skilfully handled and enables the effective integration of communist ideology into the narrative.

The structural division of the narrative is also ideologically significant. The first half of the text, a series of separate tableaux depicting the hierarchical divisions and class distinctions in the town, constitutes an analytical phase in which the social actors are introduced, and the reader is allowed time to reflect upon the established economic and political order. The second half of the text, by contrast, depicting the violent confrontation and fusion of the various social groups in conflict, conjures up vivid images of political struggle, and propels the reader relentlessly to the concluding synthesis of the narrative. The individual characters soon fade from the reader's mind. What remains is the memory of a powerfully evoked scene of political confrontation which reinforces through its emotional intensity the comparisons previously made between two classes, two life-styles, two social and political orders. This enduring memory of class division, class conflict and class consciousness is the ultimate proof of the ideological potency of this novel.

This ideological potency is also greatly enhanced by a more effective use of images evoking natural settings and the passage of time. Unlike *Antoine Bloyé* where the naturalising effect of such images tends to subvert the potency of the historical dimension of the novel, images of time and nature in *Le cheval de Troie* work to the ideological advantage of the text.

The time-scale is limited to one week. The reader's thoughts are consequently focused on immediate practical action, not the irretrievable passage of time as in *Antoine Bloyé.* The reader's attention, in other words, is not diverted from the passage of *historical* time by a sad lament on the passage of time *in general.* Images of nature are also exploited in a more effective, contrastive fashion. Whereas in *Antoine Bloyé* images of natural settings tend to mask the realities of urban existence, in *Le cheval de Troie* nature is presented as the image of a counter-culture in opposition to the town, a refuge from oppression, a place to breathe freely. This contrastive technique ultimately reinforces the ideological message of the novel aimed at disclosing the oppressiveness of working-class living conditions in the town.

Ultimately, however, the most important aspect of the narrative technique is the merging of the communist and existential discourses within the text itself, a merging which reflects the intimate relationship that Nizan perceived at this stage in his ideological development between the political struggle against the oppression of a hated class and the metaphysical struggle against the oppression of death itself. It is precisely the extra dimension given to this text by the existential discourse woven into the fabric of the narrative that enables the effective insinuation of ideology into the reader's mind.

This strategic merging of communist and existential discourses not only releases *Le cheval de Troie* from the authoritarian grip of Zhdanovite socialist realism. It is also the crucial factor explaining Nizan's success in achieving a fine balance between artistic means and ideological ends. More than fifty years after its moment of production, *Le cheval de Troie* remains a powerfully evocative and mobilising image of a group in fusion, a vivid illustration of the leap from acquiescence and seriality to rebellion and authenticity. (pp. 132-48)

> *Michael Scriven, in his* Paul Nizan: Communist Novelist, *Macmillan Press, 1988, 200 p.*

Robert Thornberry   (essay date 1989)

[*In the following excerpt, Thornberry maintains that while Nizan was radical in his social and political ideology, he was conservative in his approach to literature.*]

Though less well known than many of his contemporaries, the French novelist, *pamphlétaire* ["pamphleteer"] and essayist Paul Nizan was a highly representative author of the inter-war years. In fact, the case of Nizan illuminates the hypothesis that the most pressing preoccupations of a particular historical period are sometimes most forcefully crystallized in the works of a writer of secondary importance, and this is one of the principal reasons for taking him seriously.

In France, the "entre-deux-guerres" ["interwar era"] was a period of great upheaval, in literature and in art, as well as in politics, and one of the most coherent responses to this upheaval was delineated by Nizan. In two polemical yet little-known essays (*Aden, Arabie* and *Les chiens de garde*), as well as in hundreds of articles published in left-wing newspapers and magazines throughout the thirties, Nizan formulated an aesthetics that stressed the social and political responsibilities of the individual writer. In so doing, he became an official spokesman, and the most articulate apologist, for the French Communist party at a time when the literary canon, relatively stable for almost a century, was undergoing serious challenge from many different quarters. (p. 87)

Nizan's novels have elicited much critical commentary. . . . (p. 88)

However, one dimension of Nizan's aesthetics has been largely overlooked by his critics and biographers. Though a self-proclaimed revolutionist, Nizan was usually quite circumspect and often downright hostile in his discussions of literary works that, directly or indirectly, proposed an alternative to, or even challenged, the orthodox Marxism of the 1930s. From a primarily literary point of view, in

spite of his dedication to revolutionary violence, he was anything but a revolutionary, as I shall attempt to show. In fact Nizan was adamantly opposed to the application (and attenuation) of the word "revolution" to designate changes that were occurring in industry, the arts and other areas of human endeavour. In 1932, he asserted that: ". . . révolution n'a au vrai que deux sens rigoureux, l'un géométrique et mécanique, l'autre politique" ("revolution has really only two defined meanings, the one geometrical and mechanical, the other political"), and proceeded to define Revolution in the following manner:

> Nous prendrons la Révolution pour ce qu'elle est: le renversement violent d'un ordre social par un autre, la rupture d'une économie et d'une culture. Une seule Révolution mérite ce nom: c'est la Révolution prolétarienne, le renversement du régime capitaliste, l'établissement d'un État par le prolétariat.

> ("We shall take Revolution for what it is: the violent overthrow of one social order by another, the breaking of an economy and a culture. Only one Revolution deserves this name: the proletarian Revolution, the overthrow of the capitalist regime, the establishing of a State by the proletariat.")

And then, in a striking repudiation of the populism of Henri Poulaille, he proceeded to define proletarian literature not by its subject matter, but by its point of view:

> Elle [La littérature révolutionnaire] doit décrire n'importe quel objet, mais du point de vue du prolétariat, du point de vue du prolétariat révolutionnaire; [. . .] la tâche de la littérature révolutionnaire paraît être d'élever la conscience révolutionnaire du prolétariat [. . .] Elle est composée de tous les écrits exaltant, préparant la révolution prolétarienne, puisant en elle tous ses thèmes et ses inspirations. Cette littérature veut évidemment rompre avec les traditions spirituelles et formelles de la littérature bourgeoise.

> ("It [revolutionary literature] must describe any object, but from the point of view of the proletariat, from the point of view of the revolutionary proletariat; [. . .] the task of revolutionary literature seems to be to raise the revolutionary consciousness of the proletariat [. . .] It is made up of all those writings which exalt, which prepare the proletarian revolution, drawing from that revolution all its themes and inspirations. This literature clearly seeks to break with the spiritual and formal traditions of bourgeois literature.")

Nizan was only 27 when he wrote these words, and though his political allegiance is not as unproblematic as it is usually made out to be, he remained faithful to this conception of proletarian literature and the Revolution, until the signing of the nonaggression pact between Nazi Germany and the USSR on August 13, 1939, at which time he severed all ties with the French Communist party. Prior to that shattering betrayal, as a militant within the ranks of the Communist party, he had sought to implement his beliefs in many different ways: by standing as the Communist candidate in Bourg-en-Bresse in the legislative elections of 1932, by lecturing to workers' groups on art and literature, by making a pilgrimage to and residing in Moscow, the new Mecca; and, in his triple capacity as editor of Marxist periodicals, correspondent for *L'humanité* and *Ce soir* and literary critic for various other communist publications, he defined and defended a concept of literature that we would probably identify nowadays as socialist realism. Sanctioned by Stalin, promulgated at the Kharkov Congress in November 1930 and elevated to the status of official literary doctrine of the Third International, socialist realism is, however, a term that is rarely used by Nizan in his numerous essays and book reviews. For example, even in his favourable 1935 assessment of Aragon's manifesto *Pour un réalisme socialiste,* in which he espouses the theses advanced by his contemporary, he usually employs the terms *realism* and *reality* without qualifying them in any way. Apart from this reluctance to accept the official terminology of the Communist International, Nizan's aesthetics are clearly predicated upon the notion of representation.

In the hundreds of articles he contributed on a weekly basis to the communist newspapers already mentioned and to weekly or monthly reviews such as *Commune, Regards, Russie d'aujourd'hui*—only a small selection of which has been included in **Pour une nouvelle culture**— the Marxist Nizan subjects both his contemporaries and the previous generation of writers to a consistently withering attack upon their "bourgeois values". In spite of the variety of material covered—no writer wrote so provocatively about so many of his fellow writers—it is possible to distil from the different reviews a fairly coherent line of reasoning predicated upon his essentially manichean view of the world. For Nizan, the bourgeois writer and artist is identified above all by his fundamental idealism, a panoply of vacuous abstractions that conceal rather than reveal the flagrant social and economic injustices of a Europe bedevilled by the twin menaces of capitalism—"la plus vaste entreprise d'écrasement et d'humiliation que l'humanité ait jamais vue" ("the greatest undertaking of crushing oppression and humiliation that humanity has ever seen")—and totalitarianism. Bourgeois writing is concerned with the world of appearances, it is divorced from a true understanding of the concrete realities of the moment and its proponents seek refuge in ethereal generalizations about universal man and universal humanism. Nizan is probably at his best in his general indictment of the numerous subterfuges to which bourgeois intellectuals resort in order to deny their sense of responsibility, and he is specially acerbic in his criticisms of *la vie intérieure,* interiority, spiritualism, mysticism, *personnalisme,* phenomenology and, above all, that umbrella-word, "Esprit":

> Ils parlent. Ils parlent assez mal. Leur discours est merveilleusement éloigné de la véritable misère du monde. Éloigné comme un jeu. Il y a l'Esprit, le Saint-Esprit, qu'ils désignent avec pudeur par périphrase, il y a l'Etre, les Notions Spirituelles, l'Ame, la Possession de toute la Vie, la Contemplation, l'Intelligence-Épée: une flotte d'idées s'avance, toutes voiles dehors, une flotte de majuscules.

> ("They speak. They speak quite badly. Their dis-

course is wonderfully distant from the real wretchedness of the world. As distant as in a game. There is the Spirit, the Holy Spirit, to which they refer discreetly with a circumlocution, there is the Being, Spiritual Notions, the Soul, the Possession of all Life, Contemplation, the Sword of Intelligence; a flotilla of ideas advances, under full sail, a flotilla of capitals.")

This amalgamation of political adversaries such as Drieu la Rochelle and Henri Massis with the Surrealist André Breton, the anarchist Céline and "bourgeois" writers like Mauriac, Maurois, Alain, Morand and Julien Green demonstrates an approach to literature that was often disarmingly simplistic as well as uncompromisingly utilitarian.

In arguing the priority of the political interpretation of texts, Nizan exemplified an approach to literature that, in the words of Fredric Jameson in *The Political Unconscious,* conceived of "the political perspective not as some supplementary method, not as an optional auxiliary to other interpretive methods [. . .] but rather as the absolute horizon of all reading and all interpretation". There is no mention of Nizan in Jameson's masterful study—his name is conspicuously absent from the writings of another great Marxist critic, Lukács, too—and the American philosopher argues his case much more persuasively and with greater subtlety than the French novelist. Nevertheless, the underlying principle is fundamentally the same: it is an ideological fallacy to distinguish between texts that are social or political and those that are not. Nizan subscribed to this and what sets him apart from other Marxist critics of his time is not so much his dogmatism and the peremptory tone with which he judges other writers, but his lucid, unapologetic and impassioned espousal of literature as propaganda:

> Toute littérature est une propagande. La propagande bourgeoise est idéaliste [. . .] la propagande révolutionnaire sait qu'elle est propagande, elle publie ses fins avec une franchise complète. L'art est pour nous ce qui rend la propagande efficace, ce qui est capable d'émouvoir les hommes dans le sens même que nous souhaitons.

> ("All literature is propaganda. Bourgeois propaganda is idealistic [. . .] revolutionary propaganda knows that it is propaganda, it publishes its ends with utter frankness. Art, for us, is that which makes propaganda efficient, that which is capable of moving men in that particular direction we desire.")

This assertion may appear iconoclastic, even outrageous but, as several contemporary *poéticiens* have pointed out, Nizan's pragmatic definition of rhetoric differs very little from Aristotle's dictum on rhetoric as the art of persuasion. Todorov in particular has observed, in 1977:

> La rhétorique a pour objet l'éloquence; or, l'éloquence se définit comme une parole efficace, qui permet d'agir sur autrui. La rhétorique ne saisit pas le langage comme forme—elle ne se préoccupe pas de l'énoncé en tant que tel—mais le langage comme action [. . .].

> ("The subject of rhetoric is eloquence; eloquence

can be defined as efficient speech, which allows an effect on someone. Rhetoric does not take language as form—its interest is not in an utterance for its own sake—but language as action [. . .]".)

Nizan was possessed by a sense of duty, he was haunted by a seering awareness of the responsibility of the writer, he was an apostle of *engagement* fifteen years before Sartre. Nizan was convinced that we never read innocently, that the words passing before our eyes convey not universal truths, but images of particular, time-bound and alterable realities, and that it was the writer's role to reveal these realities. Literary criticism too is not an elitist pursuit, a sterile academic exercise, it is always an affirmation of one's *vision du monde.* Like Walter Benjamin, in *Theses on the Philosophy of History,* Nizan was tormented by the knowledge that: "There has never been a document of culture which was not at one and the same time a document of barbarism". Both literature and literary criticism are not ways of transcending immediate, concrete situations but, in the words of Marx, ways of transforming them, slowly, individually—the efforts of the individual cannot be entirely discounted—or, better, collectively, and thus contributing to revolutionary upheaval. Nizan was fond of quoting, approvingly, Marx's famous dictum, enunciated in the thesis on Feuerbach, on the need to change the world rather than merely interpret it.

In this respect, Nizan was largely a product of his time, the thirties. In referring constantly to the division of labour and the class struggle, even when dealing with literary matters, and in constantly upholding the Soviet model as an ideal, he was a somewhat orthodox, even dogmatic Marxist, until he resigned from the Communist party in 1939. By the same token, his rejection of complexity, his insistence upon the need to create exemplary characters and myths, his stern moralizing and his distrust of the potentially subversive nature of avant-garde literary movements that stress the autonomy of language and the ludic, are further indications of his essentially anti-revolutionary or cautious conservative reaction to the innovations and experiments of his time. Many of these were naturally overshadowed in the struggle against Nazism and Fascism, and let us not forget that Nizan died in that same struggle, at Dunkirk in 1940. Since it would be an injustice to view Nizan exclusively through the prism of socialist realism, it might be appropriate to outline what his intellectual contribution to the world of ideas actually was. It was not obviously as an original thinker. It is undoubtedly apparent that many of the previously quoted passages constitute a gloss on the writings of Marx, a protracted commentary in French of seminal Marxian concepts: praxis, human nature as a social construct. If the dead-weight of history resides chiefly in his unrelenting didacticism, in his unquestioning adherence to a political philosophy that has been utterly discredited, in his suspicion of modernism, in his realism and his trust in referentiality, these negative factors are counterbalanced by other insights and procedures.

Irrespective of the irrelevancy, to a present day audience, of the alternatives proposed, Nizan provided:

1) a coherent and revolutionary critique of the ideology of bourgeois capitalism, and the structures whereby it conceals its manipulation of power beneath the rhetoric of universalism;

2) a demystification of what we would now term liberal humanism, an ideology (perhaps the only one) that claims to be above ideology;

3) a systematic debunking of the fallacy of disinterested research, disinterested scholarship, disinterested literature, disinterested professors and intellectuals, the "watch-dogs" of the existing order, as he once dismissed them in a cruel yet memorable formula;

4) an indictment of a *vision du monde* in which the political and the ideological are mere secondary or public adjuncts to the content of a real private life;

5) a sustained yet essentially negative diagnosis of contemporary culture in which escapist literature predominates: all those detective stories, sentimental tales, novels of adventure, sports and fashion magazines that constitute the opium of the masses; and, above all, in so doing—and I think this is ultimately where his greatest originality as a writer resides—he revealed himself as one of France's most devastating ironists, a dimension of his works that has gone unheeded and which may rescue him from the status of secondary writer that I somewhat arbitrarily assigned to him earlier in this brief study.

Compared to Flaubert, Malraux, T. E. Lawrence, for example, . . . Paul Nizan may seem a less stimulating figure. However, as a critic, Nizan displayed an almost instinctual drive to get not just to the heart of the matter, be it a particular, political problem or the *Weltanschauung* of a specific author, to strip it down to the bones, to reduce it to its bare essentials, to display its stark skeletal reality. This undervalued characteristic may have been his peculiar genius.

We should therefore cease to situate Nizan in the traditions of naturalism and socialist realism and place him in a much wider context, that of the *moraliste,* albeit a *moraliste* with the malevolent wit, mordant irony and polemical gifts of Voltaire. Somewhat paradoxically, since Nizan decried the *esprit de négation* that marked his era, we should see him as a *moraliste* whose subversiveness resides not in his affirmation of a new socioeconomic order, but in the destruction or undermining of the accretions of falsehood, conventions and *idées reçues* that, at any time, pass for truth. In this way, we can rescue him from an antiquarian approach to literary history, we can de-fossilize him by discounting his outmoded message, we can appropriate his iconoclasm, without betraying him. Nizan has already endured too many betrayals. In this way we can perhaps, as readers, accomplish a revolution in our perspectives of him. (pp. 88-94)

Robert Thornberry, "Paul Nizan: Revolutionary in Politics, Conservative in Aesthetics," in Literature and Revolution, *edited by David Bevan, Rodopi, 1989, pp. 87-95.*

FURTHER READING

Beauvoir, Simone de. *The Prime of Life,* pp. 42ff. Cleveland: World Publishing Co., 1962.
> Refers frequently to Sartre's and de Beauvoir's friendship with Nizan.

Connolly, Cyril. "The Nizan Case." In his *Ideas and Places,* pp. 153-58. New York: Harper and Brothers, 1953.
> Presents published arguments of those defending the political reputation of Paul Nizan and the retorts which they elicited.

Cranston, Maurice. "Only Salvation Matters." *The Washington Post Book World* VI, No. 17 (23 April 1972): 9.
> Reviews *The Watchdogs,* focusing on Nizan's attack on the established schools of Western philosophy.

Elman, Richard. "About *Antoine Bloyé.*" *The Columbia Forum* 1, No. 4 (Fall 1972): 40-2.
> Praises *Antoine Bloyé* as one of the few convincing Marxist portraits of the social and political alienation of the common person.

Kadish, Doris Y. "Narrative Voice and Vision in Paul Nizan's *Antoine Bloyé.*" *The International Fiction Review* 14, No. 1 (Winter 1987): 3-7.
> Examines how the portrayal of characters in *Antoine Bloyé* advances the novel's concern with "unthinking bourgeois life."

Merleau-Ponty, Maurice. Introduction to *Signs,* by Maurice Merleau-Ponty, pp. 3-35. Evanston, Ill.: Northwestern University Press, 1964.
> Questions Sartre's personal and literary assessment of Nizan.

Porter, Catherine. "Nizan's *Cheval de Troie* and the Problem of the *roman à thèse.*" *Romanic Review* LXIII, No. 2 (March 1982): 233-48.
> Defends Nizan's integration of art and ideology in *The Trojan Horse.*

Redfern, Walter. *Paul Nizan: Committed Literature in a Conspiratorial World.* Princeton, N.J.: Princeton University Press, 1972, 233 p.
> Examines the relationship between the circumstances of Nizan's life and his literary style and themes.

———. "Critic of France: On Paul Nizan." *Encounter* LXXII, No. 2 (February 1989): 49-52.
> Generally favorable review of Michael Scriven's *Paul Nizan: Communist Novelist.*

Stoekl, Allan. "Nizan, Drieu, and the Question of Death." *Representations,* No. 21 (Winter 1988): 117-45.
> Discusses *The Trojan Horse* as an example of a *roman à thèse* that is ideologically amorphous.

Todd, Olivier. "Paul Nizan: An Appraisal." *Time and Tide* 42, No. 13 (30 March 1961): 524.
> Presents a brief overview of Nizan's career.

Mrs. J. H. Riddell

1832-1906

(Born Charlotte Elizabeth Lawson Cowan; also wrote under the pseudonyms F. G. Trafford, Rainey Hawthorne, and R. V. Sparling) Anglo-Irish novelist and short story writer.

Riddell is regarded as one of the most skilled Victorian authors of supernatural fiction. While best known for her ghost stories, which comprise about one-third of her fiction, Riddell was also a prolific author of novels dealing with London business and professional life. Conventional in format, as well as characteristically Victorian in their decorous prose style and moralistic tone, Riddell's works are distinguished by her skillful use of detail to create a realistic depiction of the milieu she portrayed.

Riddell was born in Carrickfergus, a small town near Belfast. Her father was High Sheriff for the county in which they resided, and her family lived comfortably in an Italianate villa on extensive grounds. However, her father's illness and subsequent death in 1852 left Riddell and her mother in poverty, forcing them to resettle in a small village in County Down. Three years later the two moved to London, where Riddell pursued a literary career as a means to support herself and take care of her ailing mother. In 1856 Riddell published her first novel, *Zuriel's Grandchild. The Moors and the Fens,* Riddell's second effort, was published two years later, some months after her marriage to Joseph Hadley Riddell, a civil engineer. Her husband's poor handling of their finances forced Mrs. Riddell into "many years of hard toil liquidating his debts," according to E. F. Bleiler, who speculates that she was thus "driven into schedules and a type of writing that prevented her from doing her best work." Riddell wrote prolifically, publishing nearly fifty novels and collections of stories, anonymous publication of much of her work preventing a more accurate summation. Following her husband's death in 1880, Riddell continued to work earnestly to pay off his debts, but was eventually compelled to accept financial help from the Society of Authors during her last years. She died in 1906.

Riddell was the first author to write successfully on business life in England, romanticizing a subject that was generally avoided by her contemporaries. *George Geith of Fen Court* established Riddell's reputation in this genre, and remained the book for which she was best known throughout her lifetime. Describing the experiences of Riddell's eponymous hero, whose fascination with accounting draws him to the city, *George Geith* was succeeded by works such as *Austin Friars* and *Mortomley's Estate,* which deal with financial ruin and bankruptcy; *Alaric Spenceley; or, A High Ideal* and *The Race for Wealth,* which examine corruption and unscrupulous business practices; and *Home, Sweet Home* and *The Mystery in Palace Gardens,* which concern the implications of differences in social rank. Bleiler summarizes the prominent

themes in Riddell's fiction as being "the social geography of London, the ethnology of business, [and] the dynamics of social mobility in a period of change." In her supernatural fiction, these themes are treated as part of an adeptly depicted background of daily life against which the paranormal is evoked. James Campbell notes that "the supernatural in Riddell's stories and novellas acts to reinforce the natural world—ghosts, banshees, and hell itself work to right wrongs, punish evil doers, unravel mysteries, recover lost property, and reform human behavior when it goes wrong." *Weird Stories,* a six-story collection considered Riddell's best in this genre, includes ghost stories that combine standard elements of mystery, detection, and romantic love in a haunted-house setting, Riddell's most frequently used design. In one of her most popular novels, *The Uninhabited House,* Riddell presents a story involving a wealthy financier's supposed suicide which, through the investigative efforts of a young London clerk, is revealed to be murder. The ambitious protagonist's courage in maintaining an overnight vigil at the deceased's haunted mansion is inspired by the offer of a generous remuneration, and is further rewarded when his courtship of the victim's daughter culminates in marriage. In discussing this work, Bleiler highlights "an interesting touch" in which Riddell's "characters work as law clerks, pensioners, real estate speculators with detailed plans, and developers," effecting a "note of exactness that conveys conviction." Besides providing further evidence of Riddell's exceptional competence in depicting business and domestic life, *The Uninhabited House* exemplifies the skills which led Campbell to call her, "next to Le Fanu, . . . the best writer of supernatural tales in the Victorian era."

PRINCIPAL WORKS

Zuriel's Grandchild (novel) 1856; also published as *Joy After Sorrow,* 1874
The Moors and the Fens (novel) 1858
The Rich Husband (novel) 1858
Too Much Alone (novel) 1860
City and Suburb (novel) 1861
George Geith of Fen Court (novel) 1864
Maxwell Drewitt (novel) 1865
The Race for Wealth (novel) 1866
"The Miseries of Christmas" (short story) 1867; published in journal *Routledge's Christmas Annual*
Austin Friars (novel) 1870
A Life's Assize (novel) 1871
Fairy Water (novel) 1873; published in journal *Routledge's Christmas Annual*
Home, Sweet Home (novel) 1873
Frank Sinclair's Wife, and Other Stories (novellas and short stories) 1874
Mortomley's Estate (novel) 1874
Above Suspicion (novel) 1876
The Disappearance of Mr. Jeremiah Redworth (novella) 1878; published in journal *Routledge's Christmas Annual*
The Mystery in Palace Gardens (novel) 1880
Alaric Spenceley; or, A High Ideal (novel) 1881
The Senior Partner (novel) 1881
The Prince of Wales's Garden Party, and Other Stories (short stories) 1882
A Struggle for Fame (novel) 1883
The Uninhabited House and The Haunted River (novels) 1883
Berna Boyle (novel) 1884
Susan Drummond (novel) 1884
Mitre Court (novel) 1885
Weird Stories (short stories) 1885
Idle Tales (short stories) 1888
The Nun's Curse (novel) 1888
A Mad Tour; or, A Journey Undertaken in an Insane Moment through Central Europe on Foot (nonfiction) 1891
The Head of the Firm (novel) 1892
The Banshee's Warning, and Other Tales (short stories) 1894
The Ruling Passion (novel) 1896
A Rich Man's Daughter (novel) 1897
Handsome Phil, and Other Stories (short stories) 1899
The Footfall of Fate (novel) 1900
Poor Fellow (novel) 1902

The Spectator (essay date 1866)

[*In the following essay, the critic presents a negative review of* The Race for Wealth, *denouncing the work as lecturing and morally unsound.*]

It is difficult sometimes to look at a picture plausibly clever, attracting attention almost magnetically by force of its deep-toned colouring, yet false in its tendency, and calmly criticize alone the faults of drawing. Some one has well said no artist can put more into a head than he has in his own, and so, in looking at some picture, we may perceive instinctively that the thought which conceived is more untrue than the hand which executed it.

We think it is so in [*The Race for Wealth*]. With the plausible cleverness which can at least caricature, if it fails in sketching; full of the bitterness which is not strength, but to many minds perhaps its sufficient counterfeit; of the cynicism which jars like a false note through all the chords of life, it is life looked at through the smoke of fires of whose origin we know nothing, but which makes the eyes smart, and the pen give, however honestly, a false report of the scenes on which those eyes are looking. It is at all times difficult to trace the exact province of fiction, and we are by no means inclined to look with special tolerance on the books whose heroes and heroines are mere exponents of the novelist's pet theories. Clearly one part at least of his business is to hold up a glass to human nature, and we have no right to complain if he chooses that fools and villains shall see themselves therein, nor perhaps any right to be annoyed, if his puppets seem to us grotesque, overdrawn, or unnatural. The drama may revolt us, and be none the less truly dramatic, but if the dramatist steps before the curtain to lecture the audience and challenge the value of their most deeply rooted convictions, he surely has no right to grumble if the gauntlet he thus flings down be taken up. Now, in this last novel of Mrs. Riddell's, this is the attitude the authoress assumes. At every second or third page she drops her story to lecture her audience, and in our judgment to make statements we believe utterly hollow, yet mischievous in their plausibility. The outline of the story is soon sketched. Lawrence Barbour, son of a proud but ruined country gentleman, sick of the perpetual combination of pride and poverty which meets him in his own home, disinclined for the gentlemanly poverty implied in an ensigncy or the worse struggles of clerical life, chooses wealth as the goal of his ambition, and the business of a distant connection in East London as the shortest road to it. The business thus entered is supposed to be that of a manufacturing chemist, really that of a manufacturing grocer. "Nutmegs that had never seen a foreign shore, coffee-berries that had never grown on a tree, arrowroot extracted from potatoes, rhubarb useless as a medicine, peppercorns made out of molasses and pea flour,—these were a few of the articles manufactured in Distaff Yard, and distributed thence through the length and breadth of England." The heads of this most reputable business are well drawn. Mr. Perkins, the man with a clear brain, kindly nature, and some conscience where business was not actually concerned, with his vulgar wife and still more vulgar children always dragging him down, is recognizable, even if slightly caricatured. Mr. Sondes, the other partner, living two distinct lives—one for his business, the other for his little niece, Olivine, the good heroine of the story—is even better described; but before Lawrence Barbour makes their acquaintance, Mallingford End, his father's place in the country, has been let to a Mr. Alwyn, a clever speculator, and one of the *nouveaux riches.* His daughter, Etta, is "ill-tempered, hypocritical, unfeeling, cruel, but at the same time beautiful and fascinating exceedingly." In defiance of all laws of physiognomy, the specially wicked creations of most modern novelists show that they are orthodox at least in their belief that Satan is never so like himself as when he transforms himself into an angel of light. This girl is the evil genius of the story. Lawrence, though vowing to devote himself to East London, and bitterly scorning the possessors of the wealth he envies, yet determines to scan them from some vantage-post in Hyde Park. The Alwyns are in town, Miss Alwyn, whom Lawrence has seen at Mallingford, and "despises in his heart," is riding in the Row and is thrown. Lawrence saves her, sustaining injuries in the attempt which ruin his own health for ever; and at this point we are met by one of the authoress's bitter invectives against society and the world, whatever those much abused words may happen to mean. "It is a hard thing," she says, "for a wealthy man to be struck down suddenly from strength to weakness, and when my lord gets his fingers blown off his hand, or loses the sight of one of his eyes, or is thrown in hunting, and crippled to the extent of never being able to waltz again, the world is lavish enough of its sympathy and commiseration. Society speaks of the man softly and in whispers, and throws a certain romance over him, and compassionates the accident which has injured his health, or impaired his good looks, or prevents his killing partridges, or bearing away the brush, with much kindness and persistency. Poor Lord Adonis, and poor Sir Charles Stalwart, and poor Mr. Millionaire, and that dear deformed boy, the Earl of Mammon's son! Are these people not pitied?" &c. "But the world is not tender to its workers; fortunately, perchance, for them; because no man ever works so well as he who, thrusting his fist in the face of the world, denouncing its shams, cursing its hypocrisies, despising its soft words. . . . strips himself for the conflict, trusting in nothing save the assistance of his Maker and the strength of his own right arm," &c., through another page and a half; and then, "Behold the application—carriages, sympathy, earnest inquiries for the young lady who was not hurt—for the young lady who, had she been hurt, was daughter to so rich a father that every luxury would have been at her command; while, for the worker, a lift to the nearest hospital." Well, of course, all that is very bitter, very cynical, very plausible, but is it true? It is just because we believe it to be a piece of the false sentimentality which is more and more serving to lengthen the winter of our discontent, and more and more paralyzing the living sympathies which are at the very root of all true work, that we think it worth while to notice it at all. What is this omnipotent "world," with its condolence, this "society," so exalted on its pedestal, so lavish of its kind inquiries, but the small surroundings of each man's life, which revolve round him?—and the friend of the hour who helps Lawrence Barbour—"worker"—to the hospital is probably as true in his sympathy as Sir Somebody Somebody who helps the heiress to a carriage. The skill which cures him

is as great as the other case could have had, and the friends who cluster round the injured man's hospital bed, the Perkinses, and Joneses, and Smiths, of East London, are as truly anxious in their care, as much his relatives, his society, his world, as if they crowded in from Belgravia. It is an evil thing to suffer without sympathy, but it is not on the world's workers that that evil falls; they are too closely bound to their fellows. It is rather they "who can lie in bed or sit at home in easy chairs, with cushions to their backs, with eau-de-Cologne to their heads," who get the pity which is not sympathy, and suffer from the bitter mental loneliness such a lot almost inevitably brings. There are problems enough yet unsolved in the world, evils enough yet uncured, without arraigning Providence for imaginary ones, the shallow sophisms of a diseased mind. This is the colouring of the whole picture. Here is another morsel of bitter irony:—"Of course there is no such thing as prospective jealousy in the world; it is human nature, is it not, to smile on the man or woman who is to fill up your place in the world when you are grown old, and weary, and obsolete; it is human nature to like those who come after you, whose feet will travel the road to success, when your limbs are tottering and feeble, whose ears will listen to the throbbings of other men's hearts when yours are deep and treacherous?" &c. "Is this human nature? Ah! reader, is not this rather artificial nature, conventional nature—the nature men put on when they summon up all their courage?" &c. "Do people like being hung? No. Well, there is a time of youth, and popularity, and sunshine for most of God's creatures, and after that, the eternity of temporal nonentity, and age, and winter gloom." Again we ask, is all this true? These are not words put into the mouth of some hypochondriacal grandsire, maundering by a cold fireside; they are distinct assertions, thrown at us for our reception. We analyze them, and they crumble to pieces. Why is winter more eternal than summer, cold than sunshine, or how can "a temporal nonentity" be an eternity? Is the love of parents for their children, who, we imagine, are the people who generally come after them, conventional? Is growing old always equivalent to being hung? Our author's notions of the possibility of happiness, however, are decidedly limited, for though she has just told us there is a time of youth, and popularity, and sunshine for most of God's creatures, we find the last two gifts are never bestowed on clever people till they reach old age, or rather, the eternity of temporal nonentity; for a little while before she writes, " 'Sweet youth! innocent youth! guileless youth! trusting youth! ingenuous youth!' exclaim our poets, and rhapsodize accordingly, but it never enters into the head of even the most practical of writers to say there is anything charming about youth if it be clever." And apparently the youth "pressing onward to distinction" must be content to pursue his way in solitude, "thinking the world perhaps as hard and cold as the world thinks him disagreeable and conceited." Rather hard upon him, considering the kind of eternity which lies before him when youth is past. But our authoress is above the weakness of consistency. If "Belles and ladies of fashion" are recommended in one page to "fall back upon the graces of simplicity or the beauties of perfect naturalness," they are asked in another, "Shall we babble about nature unadorned? Shall we say a pretty woman is equally pretty in any attire? Bah! There are times and places when dress is everything. Given a man who has not seen much of female society, and see which divinity he falls down and worships—the pure and simple or the gorgeous and sensuous, bare-footed virtue or vice resplendent with diamonds," &c.

But if we return to the story, there are yet graver errors in the sketching. Lawrence falls in love with Etta Alwyn, with "the girl who in his inmost heart he despised himself for loving," but she refuses him through fear of poverty, and marries, for his wealth, a man she dislikes. Lawrence marries Olivine, who worships him, but continues to love Etta, and on her becoming a widow forsakes his wife for the woman who "netted him with the hair he was wont to laugh at, with the eyes which had in them neither a pure nor a holy light, with the hands which were so white and treacherous, with the smile which was so sweetly cruel, with the rich attire which became her so royally,"—for the woman who had no compunction for her own sin, no pity for the forsaken wife, and who treats Lawrence's offer of marriage when his wife would have given him a divorce with "contemptuous scorn,"—a hard, coarse, mercenary nature, which the hero understands and despises, yet for whom he has a mad passion, against which he strives—well, at all events, unavailingly. And because the wife who has trusted him utterly, and towards whom his whole life has been a lie, is roused from her ordinary gentleness to a fit of very timid indignation, we are told, "She was very sweet, she was very pure, she was very innocent, she was what a man might desire the mother of his children to be in every thought, and word, and deed, but she never could be to him what many a worse woman can prove to one she loves in the hour of his blackest despair, of his deepest need." We are heartily sick of the affectation which is perpetually claiming the kind of sympathy for the sinner which means, in plainer English, the palliation of the sin; and we enter our protest the more strongly, because the authoress of *George Geith* has done so much better things than the *Race for Wealth.* If she would cease to pander to an already diseased appetite, get a clearer idea of the value of the landmarks she is at present helping to remove, and consider that the man who "denounces shams and curses hypocrisies" (manufacturing coffee-berries the while) is a negative character, in comparison with him who recognizes the eternal principles of right and wrong, justice and purity, we may yet have from her pen a story infinitely worthier than any she has yet given us. (pp. 1257-58)

A review of "The Race for Wealth," in The Spectator, *Vol. 39, No. 2002, November 10, 1866, pp. 1257-58.*

The Spectator   (essay date 1883)

[*In the following essay, the critic offers a positive assessment of* A Struggle for Fame.]

Mrs. Riddell's books have always had one merit that perhaps even the most *blasé* novel-readers can scarcely appreciate as keenly as reviewers must; they do not all turn upon the same subject and run in the same groove as every

other novel that has been published within the last twenty years. After perusing we dare not say how many hundreds of three-volume, or (far too seldom), one and two-volume works of fiction, all dedicated exclusively to what one of the characters in the *Struggle for Fame* rather profanely terms "the love-and-twaddle business," or what another speaker in the same book expresses more elegantly as "love and beauty and children, and dress and jewels, and parties and pleasure, and everything coming right at the end," the relief has been great at finding a novel in which the characters do not devote their whole energies to making love, or having it made to them; in which men and women can be heartily in love, and yet go about their daily work like rational beings, and we may add, like real people. Still greater, perhaps, has been the boon Mrs. Riddell has conferred upon novel-readers by not obliging all her important characters to be "in society," and so delivering us from that dismal condition of fiction in which everybody drinks five-o'clock tea, dines at eight, plays lawn-tennis (or croquet, ten years ago), shops at Marshall and Snelgrove's, and goes out of town at the end of the season. Novelists, especially of the feminine gender, content themselves far too much with depicting this kind of life over and over again, weaving in a thin plot of love or crime, and then they call it representing human life at the present day, unable to perceive that they really only scratch the surface of this nineteenth-century life with their pens, and give about as deep a view of human nature as a looking-glass does. Probably the cause may be found in the fact that people write when they should be reading or observing, and that every one is in too great a hurry to look beneath the surface, but Mrs. Riddell's kind of novel may be best described in the words that she herself applies to her heroine's successful work:—

> She gathered all her parts together, wove into the narrative the trials, the sorrows, the self-denials, the successes of trade—explained processes of manufacture unknown utterly to the reading public—took the outside world due East in London, and asked it to walk into dreadful little manufactories, and listen to "shop" talk, and take an interest in the doings and sayings of men who had probably never been to a dinner-party in their lives, and knew nothing of Sir Bernard Burke, and were not acquainted with lords or baronets; but who were yet some of them gentlemen, and some of them cads, following the nature of their kind.

In the book now before us, our author has not given us much of the City life which she so excelled in depicting; and we regret it, for there is a great charm in studying a kind of existence so entirely unlike our own, and in learning how the great heart of London works its apparatus; but she is always unconventional (which does not mean objectionable), and many of her sketches of character are delightful. Are Mr. Vassett's views, we wonder, still held by publishers in general, and are they—worse still!—likely to be true?

> No one knew better than he did that the works he published were not likely to live, but in their generation they were good, useful, amusing. That they were not likely to go down through

the ages did not much trouble the gentleman who had assisted at their birth. He felt they would live long enough; they had served their purpose, and could die when they pleased. He felt no such frantic desire for posthumous fame as rendered him unhappy because he could not compass it. If Shakespeare had come back to earth, Mr. Vassett would not have risked anything he considered very valuable, say, for instance, the lease of his house in Craven Street, for the honour of standing godfather even to a second Shylock. The world's applause he did not consider worth the loss of one night's sleep; further, he had a notion, not uncommon among those who prefer to seek their mental food among the past of literature, rather than browse on the light productions of the present, that no more great books would ever be written. Mr. Vassett was no optimist concerning the books of the future. Looking around, he saw what he considered almost a dead-level of mediocrity. Whether the few who struggled out of the mass and achieved distinction, who were run after by readers and run down by the critics, would be thought much of in succeeding generations, was a question he professed himself glad he had not to decide. He admitted they had many merits; but when asked if they would stand the test of time, he returned the safe answer that he did not know.

Mr. Vassett may be old-fashioned and wanting in enterprise, but he is always a courteous gentleman, and an agreeable contrast, therefore, to the newer type of publisher whom Mrs. Riddell depicts further on, as the head of the brilliantly successful firm of Felton and Laplash:—

> "Hillo!" cried the great publisher, as he beheld his St. Mary Overy acquaintance, "what wind has blown *you* here?"—"Your letter," answered Barney.—"I never wrote you any letter, though I should have written to you long ago, if I had known your address."—"Well, somebody, at any rate, sent a letter. Here it is.". . . .—"But this is to Mr. Kelly, the author of 'Street Sketches.'"—"I am Mr. Kelly."—"God bless me! why, I thought he was some great swell."—"Did you?" said Barney. He could not have prevented the blood rushing into his face at this unexpected slap, if he had died for it.—"Oh, I didn't mean any offence," exclaimed Mr. Felton, quickly. "What I meant was a tip-topper, regular out-and-outer, aw-awing sort of fellow. You understand, don't you? . . . . The street you live in, though, I daresay may have given rise to the notion. You lodge there, I suppose?"—"Yes, I'm only a lodger," answered Barney. . . . "Now, we'd better get to business," suggested Mr. Felton; "what have you to offer us, Kelly?"—Barney winced a little; he had not been prepared for such an amount of familiarity, but nevertheless answered the question with tolerable composure.—"Nothing except what has appeared before?" said Mr. Felton; "that's bad, Zack, eh?"—Zack replying to this interrogatory with a grunt of acquiescence, Barney ventured to observe Mr. Vassett had never found that the fact of previous publication in a magazine interfered with the sale of a volume.—"Oh, Vassett!" ex-

claimed Mr. Felton, with lofty scorn, "don't talk to us of Vassett; what he does, or finds, or says, or thinks is no rule for us;" at which utterance Mr. Laplash laughed a dog's laugh. . . . "No, no!" went on Mr. Felton, encouraged by this sign of approval, almost imperceptible though it was, "we don't want any Vassetts held up here for our example. We've shown that good gentleman a thing or two already, and before we've done with him, we'll show him and others a thing or two more. But now to settle with you; how much do you want for the lot? . . . . Will that do?"—"Yes, that is something nearer the mark," replied Barney.—"Very well, then, we will send you on the agreement."—"Thank you."—"And 'rush' one book, at all events, as soon as possible."—"Will not that be somewhat imprudent, considering how recently a work of mine has been brought out?"—"Exploded nonsense," commented Mr. Felton, "there are some authors I only wish I could get a book from every week in the year."—"The wisdom of the ages, then, seems foolishness to you?"—"I should think so, indeed. I am my own wisdom, and my own age, and my own everything; and if you can show me any other man who could have done as much as I have done out of the same material, I'll give you leave to call me what you like.". . . .—"I only imagined I might venture to make a suggestion concerning the time of publication of my own work."—"Then you were mistaken," retorted the genial publisher. "No, Sir, I allow no interference here. I bring out my books when I think I will, and I don't bring them out when I think I won't. If I once allowed that sort of thing," he added, viciously, "I might soon give up command of the ship."

Even Mr. Felton shines in contrast with his partner, who, when he becomes head of the firm, and is publishing Mrs. Lacere's successful novels, sits with his hat on to receive her, greets her by asking her if her husband has got any work yet, and goes on, "I can't speak to you to-day. Look in to-morrow;" or, "You're a nice sort of young woman. Where's the rest of that manuscript?" or, "I had your note, but it's no use asking me for any money, we ain't got none here;" or, "That last reprint of yours was a bad business for me; I wish it had been at the — before I ever was such a fool as to take it;" and all the time, while he was insulting her position, and depreciating her work, and grinding her down to the last penny, he was, as she found out afterwards, making a good income from her books, and finding her, as Mr. Butterby truly said, "the best steed in his stable." It is a satisfaction to know that this "great" publishing firm failed at last, and we may hope that nothing like it has ever arisen since; but it is a pity that we cannot quote any brighter pictures of human nature to set against these dark ones,—not that there are none such through *A Struggle for Fame,* but they must be read, not quoted. The charming Bohemianism, for instance, of the eminently life-like Dawton menage,—though, by the way, Will Dawton must have known London better than to think that an Atlas omnibus would take him to Paddington!—is sprinkled through nearly the whole of one volume, and so is the pathetic heroism of Mr. Lacere's married life. We could hardly expect a book from Mrs. Riddell in which the principal married couple did not somehow, with the best intentions, fail to make each other happy; why they fail in this story it is not quite easy to see, unless we accept the disparity of age and the unpleasant relations as sufficient cause; but even then it is difficult to believe that a woman like Glenarva Westley could have lived so long with her husband, and remained blind to all his real greatness. She does at length perceive that "everything in her books the world thought great and true and useful, was due to the husband who had never been able to make his mark. Without him she could have done nothing—nothing—and in return she had not half loved him as she ought;" not, perhaps, an isolated experience; but, of course, in her case it comes almost too late. Mrs. Riddell certainly does not favour the "married and lived happy ever after" style of human life; her married people are generally melancholy during the greater part of their lives, and only achieve happiness through much suffering or sin, or both; indeed even while they are enjoying brief intervals of sunshine, she has a way, which we consider rather tiresome, of stopping the story to inform us that if they had known all that was going to come upon them before long, they would never have felt as cheerful and happy as they did then,—a sort of "if you know'd who was near, I rather think you'd change your note, as the hawk remarked to himself with a cheerful laugh, when he heard the robin red-breast singing round the corner." But her characters are always human, there is much humour as well as pathos in her books, and considering that every one who has not published something is apparently dying to do so, this straightforward, unvarnished history of what *A Struggle for Fame* really means; who those are who succeed, and those who fail, ought to be read with keen interest by a very large and varied number of educated people. (pp. 1285-86)

A review of "A Struggle for Fame," in The Spectator, Vol. 56, October 6, 1883, pp. 1285-86.

The Spectator (essay date 1886)

[*In the following review of* Mitre Court, *the critic examines Riddell's skill in depicting character.*]

Had **Mitre Court** been the work of a writer of less established reputation than Mrs. Riddell, we should have been inclined to speak of it with almost unqualified admiration. The interest is well sustained throughout, and the characters are in many cases admirably drawn. Of these last we may select two as examples, both for their intrinsic excellence of portraiture and for the sharp antagonism between them. On one side we have Mr. Jeffley, a character of the blunt, honest, Anglo-Saxon type in which some classes of novelists revel. Mr. Jeffley comes of an old family of yeomen, who "could trace a pedigree calculated to put to shame many a mushroom lord,"—no great boast perhaps; he is not a man of many ideas, but those he does possess are in the highest degree praiseworthy. Absolute honesty, unwearying industry, and unquestioning obedience and submission to his employers are qualities rare enough in these days to invest a personage, not perhaps with a halo of romance, but at any rate with that estimable atmo-

sphere of irreproachable respectability which is suitable to the beneficent character who occupies a secondary position in the story, but is quite capable of playing the *deus ex machinâ* on occasion,—especially when the hero is uninteresting. In strong contrast to this plain, blunt Englishman is the wily and scheming German, Mr. Katzen. Mr. Jeffley distrusted foreigners, and it seems to us that Mrs. Riddell sympathises with him. Not that we mean for a moment to suggest that it is her deliberate intention to set Mr. Katzen before us as a type of even the foreign speculator in the City. But we object to the constant use of that convenient process, known in logic as dichotomy, by which the human race in general is divided into English and not-English, or foreigners. The former class is, indeed, admitted to comprise many different species, but in the latter it appears that there are no such distinctions, even of nationality. Does Mr. Katzen assume an attitude of studied carelessness in the middle of a conversation,—"Foreigners," says Mrs. Riddell, "sometimes overdo the thing;" and Mr. Katzen's interlocutor naturally shares the opinion, and is inclined to interrupt the intended communication. Does he smile a secret smile to himself at his insight into other people's minds,—it is remarked that "it is really most curious to consider how exhaustively foreigners comprehend the weaknesses of all human beings except themselves." But in spite of this curious tendency to mass all that portion of the human race who have not the happiness to be her Majesty's subjects indiscriminately into one class, Mrs. Riddell has perhaps never achieved a more subtle delineation of character than that of the German swindler. Karl Katzen is introduced to us with bad antecedents; he has already figured with little credit in Germany and in America. He is absolutely devoid of principle, and has no serious thoughts of anything but his own interest; but in private life, where he has nothing to gain or lose, he appears in no unamiable light. A sneer may be allowed at times, a malicious fancy for amusement at other people's expense be indulged, but nothing is more intensely characteristic than the good-humour, the kindly impulses even, which animate the unscrupulous schemer, when they are not in the way of his profit,—arising partly from the dislike of anything painful or unpleasant (a more fertile source of kindness than is sometimes supposed), and partly from the natural good-nature of a man who is getting on well himself, and has no objections to others doing well too, only not quite so well. The account of this worthy gentleman and his exploits is, in our opinion, the best part of the book, whether it deals with his whimsical courtship of the heroine, or his enterprises in the City. The story of the New Andalusian loan, organised by him as Consul for that State, and the reception of the idea by the New Andalusians, is delightfully told:—

New Andalusia expressed herself as well satisfied with her Consul. No country perhaps was ever so much surprised as that favoured land when first the suggestion of a loan reached her shores. In wildest dreams such a notion had not entered the minds of her rulers. They were so much astonished indeed, that their acceptance of Mr. Katzen's scheme seemed almost cold. They had no objection, they stated, to a loan. "I should think not," commented their Consul, "they would be simpletons indeed if they had."

We could have wished that Mr. Katzen's great fraud had been perpetrated by some more ingenious method than that of merely pocketing the money subscribed for his loan. We should have expected from him some bolder and more original conception. There is an inspector of police in one of Dickens's later novels who draws a distinction between robbery and murder,—robbery, he says, requires 'prenticing, but as for murder, we are all up to that. It seems to us that we ourselves, with little knowledge of the wicked ways of swindling, could have done what Mr. Katzen did. But we do not wish to detract; perhaps this may be considered as one of those great designs which are all the greater for their simplicity.

The other characters are scarcely so interesting. The extremely independent young lady who does duty as the heroine is often amusing; but it is surely unnecessary to get up the little mystery about her birth, which finally ends by her turning out to be the daughter of some lady of high degree, of whom we do not hear till the third volume, and whose total absence from the book we should have borne with patience and resignation. This is all the more superfluous as we have already got a very transparent mystery touching the identity of the uninteresting hero, who, to do him justice, is at least the son of a character with whom the reader is already acquainted. Mrs. Jeffley, the bustling, active, selfish landlady, is well drawn; and there is considerable humour in the character of Mrs. Childs, the charwoman. But why cannot Mrs. Riddell be satisfied with giving us an interesting and well-written novel, without cramming down our throats a number of absolutely irrelevant antiquarian disquisitions, and abuse alike of the fiends who pull down, and the demons who restore old buildings? Even granting that Mr. Katzen, in the course of a business conversation with a disreputable compatriot, would go out of his way to speak of "the churchyard where lies Shaughsware," in order to give Mrs. Riddell an opportunity of informing us, in a footnote, who Shaughsware was, and how he was buried, there is certainly no excuse for the interpolation in the early part of the book of a whole chapter of invective against the Metropolitan Board of Works, or whatever other person or persons are responsible for the changes in the City. These barbarous destroyers have not even spared the scenes of Mrs. Riddell's former novels. "If George Geith strayed tomorrow into 'Fen Court,' " we are told, "he would not recognise the changed face of the once retired nook where he and Beryl were so happy." This is very sad, no doubt, but the casual reader may remonstrate that it is not his fault; that not to him should be addressed such very strong expressions as, "Out upon you! Anathema Maranatha!" that the accusations should be levelled against the real offenders; and that the fervent language of the "plaint" could have been more usefully employed, for instance, to prevent the return to Parliament of the Chairman of the aforesaid Board, or for some other purpose alike refreshing to the antiquarian mind and beneficial to the Liberal Party. Setting aside, however, the lamentations over the City, and the constant moralising in which the author indulges, *Mitre Court* is a really good, readable novel, decidedly above the average level of serial stories. (pp. 117-18)

A review of "Mitre Court," in The Spectator, *Vol. 59, January 23, 1886, pp. 117-18.*

E. F. Bleiler (essay date 1977)

[*In the following excerpt, Bleiler surveys Riddell's non-supernatural fiction.*]

Mrs. Riddell's earliest work is best forgiven, apart from an occasional felicity of place description, which she always handled well. Her first work of modern interest is *George Geith of Fen Court* (1864), which novel made her fame and fortune, such as they were. Although it is ultimately rooted in a neo-Gothic alienation plot, it describes City life and personalities so aptly that it is still enjoyable reading. *Maxwell Drewitt* (1865), set in Ireland, has moments of melodrama, but well-drawn minor characters and a fine, long description of a riotous Parliamentary election.

Home, Sweet Home (1873) is, in my opinion, Mrs. Riddell's best non-supernatural novel. It is the first-person narrative of a vapid country girl of lowly birth who has remarkable musical ability. Her childhood among unsympathetic relatives, her dilemma at being caught between two sets of standards, her experiences in the family of a German voice-coach and musician, and her problems on the concert circuit are all set forth in a wealth of realistic detail that outweighs a very weak ending. [*Mortomley's Estate* (1874)] . . . analyzes a situation in business law, plus social repercussions, quite well.

The Mystery in Palace Gardens (1880) should be mentioned in passing, not because it is remarkably successful, but because its title has misled many into thinking it is a detective story. It is not. It is a story of social-climbing and adultery. Similarly, the reader should be warned about *A Life's Assize* (1871), which has been misleadingly described as a murder mystery. It is about a clergyman who accidentally kills a man in self-defense, stands trial with a verdict of Not Proven, and languishes under an assumed identity for the remainder of his life. Mrs. Riddell is better at realism.

Miss Gascoyne (1887) quite possibly dips into Mrs. Riddell's life for motivations. An older woman falls desperately in love with a very young man, and tries to buy his love. This novel was written at the time that Mrs. Riddell was associated with A. H. Norway, the young man with whom she made the foot tour of the Black Forest described in her travel book, *A Mad Tour.*

The Nun's Curse (1888) ranks second among Mrs. Riddell's realistic novels. There are supernatural implications in the background, it is true, but it is questionable how these are to be interpreted. During Reformation times a nun who had been hunted like an animal placed a curse on the Connors: No Connor son shall ever succeed his father to the estate, and there shall be perpetual war between father and son. The curse has always been fulfilled, even to the present middle nineteenth-century situation. But Mrs. Riddell also makes the point that all the Connors have been highly irresponsible, and that this was the real curse. Her portrayal of the present Connor, who is a fool; his fiancée, who is a selfish, cold snob; and a host of very fine minor characters make this novel well worth reading.

The Head of the Firm (1892) is based on two themes, the downfall of an amiable, intelligent attorney who turns embezzler, and the sudden acquisition of a fortune by a young female greengrocer. The greengrocer, like Eliza Doolittle, must undergo instruction in speech and deportment to make her fit for her new life. Her situation is created in excellent detail.

Three themes permeate Mrs. Riddell's non-supernatural fiction: London, business or commerce, and social rank. These were probably areas of great importance for her readership.

London is a living force in her work to an extent unmatched by any other novelist of her day. No one else has so savored the old courts and odd passages, and charted the walks and rides of his or her characters with such precision, enthusiasm, and almost compulsion. Often after describing astonishing medieval or renaissance survivals she will make the melancholy comment, "Or, so it was some twenty years ago, where the railroad now is situated." She knew the suburbs well, too, the roads leading to them, the pre-railroad transportation, their social evolution from outlying village to developed suburb to semislum, the classes that inhabited each, the small businesses and farms.

The largest overt theme in her work is business or commerce, and in her lifetime she was known as the Novelist of the City. Through her husband she knew many businessmen, and she seems to have been the first to recognize that business life had a dynamics and glamor of its own. Many of her business novels follow out a topic: *George Geith of Fen Court* is concerned with a man of family who simply finds accounting fascinating; *Austin Friars* is devoted to a financial swindler; *Mortomley's Estate* involves bankruptcy; and *The Race for Wealth* and *Alaric Spenceley* cover business opportunism, greed, and unscrupulousness. Some of Mrs. Riddell's characters are consulting engineers who perform actual tasks; others are inventors and manufacturers; others are lawyers, accountants, or simply speculators. Mrs. Riddell may offer technical information lightly about dyeing in *Mortomley's Estate,* the adulteration industry in *The Race for Wealth,* loan sharking in *The Nun's Curse,* and scientific farming in *Maxwell Drewitt.* In *The Head of the Firm* we learn how a fruiterer obtains supplies from a jobber, who loads the cart, and how much money is likely to be made. This concreteness lends her work a peculiar substantiality that goes some distance toward removing the limitations of circumscribed plots.

Difference of rank, too, is one of Mrs. Riddell's concerns. If the reigning county family betrays its social duty toward a family of the yeoman class, as in *Home, Sweet Home,* what will happen? What is to be the fate of the exceptional person; should she try to escape from the strict social structuring of the countryside, or should she remain in her birth-lot? What is the domestic result of a mesalliance

when a young man of family runs off with a handsome farm girl, as in *The Mystery in Palace Gardens?* Will the marriage be stable? How does a City merchant of position, wealth and education, as in *City and Suburb,* relate to an impoverished member of the older landed aristocracy?

These three themes—the social geography of London, the ethnology of business, the dynamics of social mobility in a period of change—were treated seriously by Mrs. Riddell, even though she apparently made concessions in other areas of writing. They interest us today, and they obviously interested the female readership of the better periodicals. Such readers were comfortable urbanites interested in their husband's livelihood and sensitive about their own spirit-position on the British totempole. Mrs. Riddell's concept of limited democracy probably pleased them.

Sensationalism, of course, was the call of the day in fiction, and Mrs. Riddell made half-hearted attempts to be sensational, but this area was not her forte, and sensational elements usually give the appearance of being afterthoughts to her leisurely, detailed, realistic development. One can guess that husbands who meet their prostituted wives, as in *Daisies and Buttercups;* or bigamistic ladies who consort with murderers, as in *The Moors and the Fens;* or adultresses who suppress correspondence from their supposedly dead husbands, to maintain their position, as in *The Mystery in Palace Gardens;* or squires who substitute corpses for their own children, in order to gain control of an inheritance, as in *The Ruling Passion,* were sops to the prevailing trends.

Despite her role as a popular novelist feeding the periodical mind, Mrs. Riddell was in a certain sense a tragic moralist, not in the cosmic sense of Hardy, whose writing career nearly paralleled hers in time, but in a realistic, psychological sense. Many of her leading characters are posited as beings with character flaws; stories develop out of their reactions in certain situations, and they come to bad ends. Engineer Ruthven in *City and Suburb,* for example, is possessed of a ridiculously aggressive family pride, which will not permit him to associate with lesser mortals. When a strike emerges at his plant Ruthven's hauteur restrains him from even speaking to his workers. The brilliant young doctor in *A Rich Man's Daughter* is money-mad, ambitious to make guineas, as he says, instead of shillings. He marries a girl for her money, then discovers that he cannot tap it. The goodhearted lawyer, Edward Desbourne, in *The Head of the Firm,* is estimable in most ways, but he cannot say no, to his wife, to his friends, to supplicants, and his fall is pitiable. Weakness, bad heredity, crookedness, temper, greed, overweening ambition all drag their possessors down, simply as a law of human inevitability. Fate, for Mrs. Riddell, always lurks behind the weed or the rose.

If one considers Mrs. Riddell's non-supernatural fiction as a body, one characteristic is outstanding: its unevenness, both from one work to another, and even within the single work. One can find pages of nicely written concise prose, and one can find pages of inflated gush riddled with stylistic affectations. One can read through several hundred pages of fine development and characterization, to come upon a sentimental ending that almost spoils everything that went before. The reason for these flaws, probably, was her writing circumstance: she wrote out of desperation most of the time and bent to the editor. Hardy, it will be remembered, found his earliest work rejected because it was not sensational enough, and also tried to oblige.

Because of the flaws in her work, Mrs. Riddell is not to be numbered among the giants of general Victorian literature. But this does not mean that she is to be discarded. At her best she had a touch which permits her to enter the company of the great. She need yield to few in evocation of landscape or setting, and she is excellent in situations that call for the invention of consistent life detail. Her second strength lies in the creation of minor characters, many of whom can stand comparison with the work of her greatest contemporaries. They remain with the reader long after the plots and the major characters are forgotten. On the other hand, she had more difficulty with major personalities, perhaps because these had perforce to act in sentimental or melodramatic situations.

All in all, once one has read a large quantity of Mrs. Riddell's non-supernatural work, one emerges with the recognition that she was not a negligible writer, even though many of her novels fall below standard and she seldom realized her potential. Even in her weakest work there is always an interesting personal element. (pp. xii-xvi)

> *E. F. Bleiler, in an introduction to* The Collected Ghost Stories of Mrs. J. H. Riddell, *edited by E. F. Bleiler, Dover Publications, Inc., 1977, pp. v-xxvi.*

FURTHER READING

Black, Helen C. "Mrs. Riddell." In her *Notable Women Authors of the Day,* pp. 10-25. Glasgow: David Bryce and Son, 1893.
    Biographical essay based on an interview with Riddell, who provides anecdotes on her literary career.

Bleiler, E. F. Introduction to *Five Victorian Ghost Novels,* edited by E. F. Bleiler, pp. v-xiv. New York: Dover Publications, 1971.
    Includes a sketch of Riddell's literary career. Bleiler asserts that Riddell was "in many ways the Victorian ghost writer par excellence."

———. Introduction to *Three Supernatural Novels of the Victorian Period,* edited by E. F. Bleiler, pp. vii-xiii. New York: Dover Publications, 1975.
    Brief discussion of Riddell's life and works.

Campbell, James L., Sr. "Mrs. J. H. Riddell." In *Supernatural Fiction Writers: Fantasy and Horror,* Vol. 1, edited by E. F. Bleiler, pp. 269-77. New York: Charles Scribner's Sons, 1985.
    Summarizes Riddell's literary achievement, praising her supernatural fiction for its realism in depicting character and setting.

Ellis, S. M. "Mrs. J. H. Riddell: The Novelist of the City and of Middlesex." In his *Wilkie Collins, Le Fanu, and Others,* pp. 266-335. 1931. Reprint. Freeport, N.Y.: Books for Libraries Press, 1968.
    Important biographical outline of Riddell's literary career, including a sampling of her personal correspondence and recollections.

"Recent Novels." *The Nation,* London 38, No. 979 (3 April 1884): 300-03.
    Negative review of *Susan Drummond.* The critic asserts that "the plot is absolutely unconsidered, and there is no evidence that the author ever heard of a theory of artistic and satisfying construction."

Stewart, J. I. M. "Fits of the Horrors." *The Times Literary Supplement* No. 3,952 (23 December 1977): 1493.
    Review of E. F. Bleiler's edition of *The Collected Ghost Stories of Mrs. J. H. Riddell.* Stewart commends Riddell's realism but finds her stories to be "a little dull."

Wolff, Robert Lee. Introduction to *The Nun's Curse,* by Mrs. J. H. Riddell, pp. v-ix. New York: Garland Publishing, 1979.
    Sketch of Riddell's life and works, focusing on her Irish novels.

George Santayana

1863-1952

(Born Jorge Augustín Nicholas Ruiz de Santayana y Borráis) Spanish-born American philosopher, critic, poet, novelist, autobiographer, essayist, and dramatist.

Santayana was one of the most prominent American philosophers of the first half of the twentieth century. During his twenty-three years on the faculty of Harvard University, he was an often vociferous critic of his colleagues. In a climate of Protestant values and religious beliefs, Santayana was an atheist who at the same time declared his adherence to the moral and social traditions of the Catholic Church. Similarly, he opposed modern academic philosophers absorbed with narrow technical matters of theory, following instead an older school of speculative thought devoted to understanding all aspects of existence and coming to terms with the largest questions posed by human life and death. As Michael Weinstein explains, "Santayana overturned the table of values set up by the American puritan philosophers and replaced it with another one in which the supreme principle was that 'the acme of life is to understand life.' "

Santayana was born in Madrid in 1863. When his parents separated in 1866, he stayed with his father for three years before being taken to Boston to live with his mother and her three children from a previous marriage. He attended the prestigious Brimmer School and Boston Latin school before entering Harvard University in the fall of 1882. As an undergraduate, he studied under such noted philosophers as Josiah Royce and William James. In his autobiography, *Persons and Places,* he reported that as a Catholic he did not feel at ease in Harvard's largely Protestant milieu. He did, however, participate in the university's intellectual circles, contributing to the *Harvard Monthly* and the *Harvard Crimson* as well as drawing cartoons for the *Harvard Lampoon* and acting in Hasty Pudding theatricals. He spent two years in Berlin earning his doctorate before returning to Harvard in 1889 as a member of the faculty. Santayana taught courses in philosophy and literature, counting among his pupils T. S. Eliot, Van Wyck Brooks, and Robert Frost, and most of his published works were written during his years at Harvard. After the publication in 1894 of *Sonnets and Other Verses,* he continued to write poetry but concentrated on philosophy, the five-volume *Life of Reason* earning him a reputation as an original thinker with a highly poetic prose style. He also published extensive, often scathing commentary on the subject of American life; "The Genteel Tradition in American Philosophy," an account of what Santayana perceived as the repressed and weak-willed legacy of American thought, created a controversy upon its publication in 1911. Santayana's distaste for the United States in general and Harvard in particular never waned, and when his mother died in 1912, leaving him a large enough inheritance to make teaching unnecessary, he retired to Europe. Thereafter, Santayana spent most of his time in Rome,

continuing to publish books on a wide variety of subjects. Writings of this period include his only novel, *The Last Puritan,* and the four-volume *Realms of Being,* in which he propounded his system of philosophy. In 1941, he moved to the Blue Nuns clinic in Rome, where he received numerous visitors including Tennessee Williams, Gore Vidal, and Robert Lowell. Santayana died of liver cancer at the age of eighty-eight.

While philosophy was his prime interest, Santayana wrote accomplished works in numerous genres. His poetry consists mainly of love sonnets written during his early years at Harvard. Although critics find his poems excessively abstract, they agree that Santayana was a skillful technician. Santayana's novel, *The Last Puritan,* which is based on his experiences in Boston, tells the story of Oliver Alden, Harvard student and football player, and has been compared to Joseph Conrad's *Lord Jim* for its concern with the moral development of an individual. Nominated for the Pulitzer Prize in fiction, the novel was a best-seller in 1936, a fact which Santayana's biographers report greatly pleased him. Santayana's two works of literary criticism are concerned with texts of established importance rather than contemporary writings. *Interpretations of Poetry and Religion* includes essays on Shakespeare, Robert Browning, and Homer, among others. It is in this work that he introduces his theory that poetry and religion serve essentially the same function. In *Three Philosophical Poets,* Santayana evaluated the ideas of Lucretius, Dante, and Johann Wolfgang von Goethe.

Santayana's philosophic works begin with the aesthetic treatise *The Sense of Beauty* and ultimately address major aspects of life and thought, including human nature in *Scepticism and Animal Faith* and politics in *Dominations and Powers. The Life of Reason* remains the best-known of his philosophic writings. Studying the human mind's evolution toward rationality, the five volumes of *The Life of Reason* examine, in order, common sense, society, religion, art, and science. For Santayana, the basis of all philosophic discourse should be materialism, depending on concrete observations of the natural world. In a letter about *The Life of Reason,* William James wrote: "His naturalism, materialism, Platonism, and atheism form a combination of which the centre of gravity is, I think, very deep." *Realms of Being,* Santayana's other major work of philosophy, articulates his conception of human existence, devoting one volume each to what he defines as its four components: essence, matter, truth, and spirit. His detailed analysis of the origins and purposes of each realm revised and strengthened his overall system, which Bertrand Russell described as "urbane, historical, free from fanaticism, and the expression of an exceptionally sensitive intellectual perception."

While praise for Santayana's intellect and writing style is virtually unanimous, there has been some debate over particulars of his thought. For example, some critics have noted an apparent inconsistency in an atheist who also considered himself a Roman Catholic, causing one commentator to quip that for Santayana, "there is no God and Mary is His mother." Others have criticized Santayana's writings, particularly *Persons and Places* and his letters, for elitism. Lois Hughson's biographically-based criticism has sought to explain his personal and philosophical "detachment" in terms of his family history. Because Santayana's works entered into so many disciplines, and because he tended to voice unpopular beliefs, critical response continues to be voluminous and wide-ranging.

(See also *Contemporary Authors,* Vol. 115, and *Dictionary of Literary Biography,* Vols. 54 and 71.)

PRINCIPAL WORKS

Lucifer: A Theological Tragedy (verse drama) [first publication] 1894; also published as *Lucifer; or, The Heavenly Truce: A Theological Tragedy* [revised edition], 1924

Sonnets and Other Verses (poetry) 1894; also published as *Sonnets and Other Verses* [revised edition], 1896

The Sense of Beauty: Being the Outlines of Aesthetic Theory (treatise) 1896

Interpretations of Poetry and Religion (essays) 1900

A Hermit of Carmel, and Other Poems (poetry) 1901

The Life of Reason; or, The Phases of Human Progress. 5 vols. (treatises) 1905-1906

Three Philosophical Poets: Lucretius, Dante, and Goethe (essays) 1910

*Winds of Doctrine: Studies in Contemporary Opinion (essays) 1913

Egotism in German Philosophy (essays) 1915; also published as *The German Mind: A Philosophical Diagnosis,* 1968

Character and Opinion in the United States: With Reminiscences of William James and Josiah Royce and Academic Life in America (lectures) 1920

Soliloquies in England, and Later Soliloquies (essays) 1922

Scepticism and Animal Faith: Introduction to a System of Philosophy (treatise) 1923

Dialogues in Limbo (philosophical dialogues) 1926; also published as *Dialogues in Limbo* [enlarged edition], 1984

Platonism and the Spiritual Life (essay) 1927

Realms of Being. 4 vols. (treatises) 1927-1940

The Genteel Tradition at Bay (treatise) 1931

Some Turns of Thought in Modern Philosophy (essays) 1933

The Last Puritan: A Memoir in the Form of a Novel (novel) 1936

Obiter Scripta (lectures, essays, and criticism) 1936

Persons and Places. 3 vols. (autobiography) 1944-53

The Idea of Christ in the Gospels; or, God in Man (essay) 1946

The Poet's Testament (poetry and dramas) 1953

Letters of George Santayana (letters) 1955

Dominations and Powers: Reflections on Liberty, Society, and Government (essays) 1956

Essays in Literary Criticism (essays) 1956

The Idler and His Works (essays) 1957

Animal Faith and Spiritual Life (essays) 1967

The Genteel Tradition: Nine Essays by George Santayana (essays) 1967

George Santayana's America: Essays in Literature and Culture (essays) 1967

The Birth of Reason, and Other Essays (essays) 1968

Santayana on America (essays) 1968

Physical Order and Moral Liberty: Previously Unpublished Essays of George Santayana (essays) 1969

Lotze's System of Philosophy (treatise) 1971

The Complete Poems of George Santayana (poems) 1979

*This collection contains the essay "The Genteel Tradition in American Philosophy."

Paul E. More   (essay date 1900)

[*More was an American critic who, along with Irving Babbitt, formulated the doctrines of New Humanism in early twentieth-century American thought. The New Humanists were strict moralists who adhered to traditional conservative values in reaction to an age of scien-*

tific innovation and artistic experimentalism. In regard to literature, they believed a work's support for the classic ethical norms to be of as much importance as its aesthetic qualities. More was particularly opposed to Naturalism, which he believed accentuated the animal nature of humans, and to any literature, such as Romanticism, that broke with established classical tradition. His importance as a critic derives from the rigid coherence of his ideology, which polarized American critics into hostile opponents (Van Wyck Brooks, Edmund Wilson, H. L. Mencken) or devoted supporters (Norman Foerster, Stuart Sherman, and, to a lesser degree, T. S. Eliot). He is especially esteemed for the philosophical and literary erudition of his multivolume Shelburne Essays *(1904-21). In the following essay, More appraises* Interpretations of Poetry and Religion.]

A good deal of courage was required of Prof. Santayana, we fancy, to publish his ***Interpretations of Poetry and Religion,*** for he must have known that the outspoken Catholic tone of the volume would offend many of his readers, and that his criticism of Shakespeare and Browning and Emerson would arouse righteous indignation among the worshipers of these literary idols. Further than that, his setting of measure and repose and inner significance above stress and passion must seem perilously near effeminacy to many believers in Anglo-Saxon force. Let us make haste to say that to one reader at least this book of essays has seemed the wisest and most fascinating work in constructive criticism that has appeared in English for several years; and this judgment we would maintain, although the determining thought of the whole cannot be acceptable to us.

Every paragraph in the closing chapter, where the author sums up his interpretation of poetry and religion, is the product of long and subtle reflection. To follow him in the ascending climax, as he shows how "poetry rises from its elementary and detached expressions in rhythm, euphuism, characterization, and story-telling, and comes to the consciousness of its highest function, that of portraying the ideals of experience and destiny," to read his acute and often profound observations on the nature and office of each of these elements, is to acquire a new faculty for the understanding and enjoyment of the poets. Such criticism is constructive in the true sense of the word; and withal the language employed is so clear and sensuous, and the emotional interest of the author in his ideas is so manifest and contagious, that the expression would seem to need only the addition of rhythm to be itself poetry. Yet at the last, when he comes to his final generalization, we are brought face to face with a note of unreality which runs as an undercurrent through the whole book, and does much, as it appears to us, to conceal the true wisdom of most of his critical work. "This higher plane," he says in conclusion, "is the sphere of significant imagination, of relevant fiction, of idealism become the interpretation of the reality it leaves behind. Poetry raised to its highest power is then identical with religion grasped in its inmost truth; at their point of union both reach their utmost purity and beneficence, for then poetry loses its frivolity and ceases to demoralize, while religion surrenders its illusions and ceases to deceive."

To understand these "illusions" which religion surrenders we must turn to the first chapter, where the author unfolds the philosophic theory lying at the base of his criticisms. Now we shall not presume to argue with Prof. Santayana on the philosophic question at issue, being but indifferent metaphysicians ourselves. We are concerned with his views only as they bear upon the conduct of life, and consequently upon the validity of literature; we are concerned to find why, in the critical slang of the day, his essays, despite the beauty of their language and the subtlety of their thought, fail to "convince." His philosophy is based on that peculiar phase of mind when active faith, as the world commonly understands the word, has disappeared, and in its stead is left a sort of aesthetic faith such as may be found in many of the earlier Romantic writers. Beyond perception and reason stands the imagination building up its own beautiful or monstrous world out of material afforded by the lower faculties. "The imagination, therefore, must furnish to religion and to metaphysics those large ideas tinctured with passion, those supersensible forms shrouded in awe, in which alone a mind of great sweep and vitality can find its congenial objects." Nor is this realm of the imagination an indifferent one; though it have nothing to do with reality in the ordinary sense of the word, yet it has everything to do with the values of life. When considered apart from the conduct of life this ideal world is the sphere of poetry, when related to conduct it is religion. A beautiful theory no doubt and one that deserves to be decked out in all the flowers of rhetoric; it may be true in metaphysics; but to the unmetaphysical reader there is in the end something hollow and unsatisfying about it. No great religion was ever founded unless the prophet believed that the visions he proclaimed were as real, and existed outside his own imagination as absolutely, as does a stock or a stone to popular perception. And in so far as poetry is related to religion, no great poem was ever composed whose author did not have equal faith in the reality of the ideal world. And the greatest of philosophers has been a living force in the world largely for the very reason that ideas existed for him objectively and with a reality which the world of phenomena does not possess. When religion "surrenders its illusions," when faith ceases to be "the substance of things unseen," they cease equally to be vital and to be the source of true art.

Prof. Santayana's attitude toward that other world which is the home of faith is shown most clearly in his treatment of mysticism. If there is a faculty by which man may grasp or at least approach a region beyond the reason, then mysticism may be a positive activity; if there exists no such faculty, then mysticism is, as our author maintains, a mere progressive negation of the categories of thought. In the end the mystic reaches, as Prof. Santayana affirms, a state of Nirvana, or complete negation. Now we cannot refrain from pointing out here that Nirvana was never admitted by Buddha to be a state of nihilism, nor can we conceive that any great religion should have arisen which made such a negation its ultimate goal. The point is important enough to be insisted upon. There is in one of the Buddhist books a curious discussion between the disciple Vaccha and the Master, wherein the disciple seeks for an elucidation of the doctrine of Nirvana. After repeated answers to the disciple's questions Gotama at last cries out: "Enough,

O Vaccha! Be not at a loss what to think in this matter, and be not greatly confused. Profound, O Vaccha, is this doctrine, recondite, and difficult of comprehension, good, excellent, and not to be reached by mere reason, subtile, and intelligible only to the wise. . . . The saint, O Vaccha, who has been released from what is styled form, is deep, immeasurable, unfathomable, like the mighty ocean. To say that he is reborn would not fit the case. To say that he is not reborn would not fit the case. To say that he is both reborn and not reborn would not fit the case. To say that he is neither reborn nor not reborn would not fit the case." Now we do not pretend to be one of the wise to whom this doctrine is intelligible, nor do we think it will be intelligible to many persons to-day in the western world; but we do maintain that it conveys something very different from a complete negation, and is in fact a positive statement of transcendental faith. And we do maintain that when faith ceases to be or to seem to be the apprehension of an objective reality and becomes a work of the imagination dealing with the values of life, immediately religion becomes poetry in quite a different sense from that which is upheld in the present volume, while poetry itself is cut off from its vital source.

We have dwelt so long on this essential question that little space is left to comment on the chapters of individual criticism wherein, as we think, Prof. Santayana has displayed a judgment no less bold than it is discriminating and profound. At first reading it may seem somewhat audacious to criticise so severely the lack of specific religious doctrine in Shakespeare, yet after being sickened by the indiscriminate laudation commonly bestowed on the great Elizabethan, it may be wholesome now and then to dwell for a moment on the defects of his work. Certainly the present essay does much to explain a curious mental phenomenon we have ourselves often observed. While reading Shakespeare we are always carried away by the intensity of his passion and the manifold wonders of his genius, but for some reason his plays do not dwell in the mind and arouse reflection on the great problems of life as do the tragedies of ancient Greece or the great epics of literature. It is wholesome at times to have our minds withdrawn from the admiration of exuberant force and wilful fancy to dwell on the orderly development of a more organic view of life.

To this same desire to set orderly thought and spiritual significance above force and license may be ascribed the criticism of Walt Whitman and Browning, the coupling of whose names together will, we opine, seem to many Browningites little less than presumptuous blasphemy. Yet so keen and consummately wise an estimate of Browning's work we do not remember ever to have read. Only in the chapter on Emerson, it seems to us that the note of disparagement is somewhat too strongly emphasized. "The source of his [Emerson's] power," we read, "lay not in his doctrine, but in his temperament, and the rare quality of his wisdom was due less to his wisdom than to his imagination." And farther on: "But his mind was endowed with unusual plasticity, with unusual spontaneity and liberty of movement—it was a fairyland of thoughts and fancies." We suspect that Emerson's power was due not so much to his imagination as to that principle of faith

which, in effect at least, is quite a different faculty. (pp. 19-23)

Paul E. More, "Santayana's 'Poetry and Religion'," in The Harvard Graduate's Magazine, *Vol. 9, 1900-01, pp. 19-23.*

William Archer   (essay date 1901)

[*A Scottish dramatist and critic, Archer is best known as one of the earliest and most important translators of Henrik Ibsen's plays and as a drama critic of the London stage during the late nineteenth and early twentieth centuries. Archer valued drama as an intellectual product and not as simple entertainment. For that reason he did a great deal to promote the "new drama" of the 1890s, including the work of Ibsen and Bernard Shaw. Throughout his career he protested critical overvaluation of ancient drama, claiming that modern works were in many ways equal to or better than Elizabethan or Restoration drama. Similar in prescience to his dramatic criticism is his* Poets of the Younger Generation *(1902), one of the first critical studies of many important modern English poets, including A. E. Housman, Arthur Symons, and W. B. Yeats. In the following essay, Archer praises the craftsmanship of Santayana's poetry, paying special attention to the sonnets.*]

His name, and two lines in his **"Ode to the Mediterranean"**:

> For I was born where first the rills of Tagus
> Turn to the westward—

lead one to conclude that Mr. George Santayana is of Spanish parentage. There is nothing in his pure, supple, sedulously refined English to suggest that he is not writing in his native tongue. Yet perhaps the fact that he is not bound by ancestral ties to the land of his sojourn—which I take to be America—may in part account for the extremely abstract quality of his verse. The world has scarcely any objective existence for him. Though in weaving his similitudes he uses the traditional apparatus of flowers and stars, mountains, rivers and the sea, these things are pure ideas to him, divested of all material attributes. There is scarcely a line of description in his work. A single piece of half a dozen stanzas, entitled **"Cape Cod,"** is the exception that proves the rule; and even here the landscape does not merely mirror, but symbolises a mood. The pageantry of life means little or nothing to him. He has no vision for external nature, but only for the summaries, essences, abstracts of phenomena, recorded in the concave of his soul. He comes near to some such confession in the lines:

> There may be chaos still around the world,
> The little world that in my thinking lies;
>
> . . . . .
>
> Within my nature's shell I slumber curled,
> Unmindful of the changing outer skies.

It is true that the "shell" he has here in mind is moral rather than intellectual; but it is none the less true that the "little world" of his thinking pursues its orbit in disdainful aloofness from the chaos of sense-impressions. One might almost conceive the poet to have been born blind, and to treat of the visible universe merely from hearsay.

Theoretically, this characteristic ought to imply a serious defect in Mr. Santayana's work; practically, I find it no defect at all, but rather a source of distinction. It is a relief, for once in a way, to escape from the importunate details of the visible world into a sphere of pure thought and pure melody. For Mr. Santayana is a very remarkable and extremely accomplished poet. The bulk of his work is so slight—it consists, so far as I know, of some sixty sonnets and fifty pages of other verse—that large epithets seem disproportionate. Yet it is difficult, without using terms of a certain emphasis, to express one's sense of the well-nourished suavity of his style, the flawless beauty of his metrical form, the aptness of his imagery, the elevation of his thought. He is a master of the sonnet, of that there can be no doubt. . . . [There] is nothing specious or superficial about Mr. Santayana's workmanship. Take this as an example:

> **"On The Death Of A Metaphysician"**
> Unhappy dreamer, who outwinged in flight
> The pleasant region of the things I love,
> And soared beyond the sunshine, and above
> The golden cornfields and the dear and bright
> Warmth of the hearth—blasphemer of delight,
> Was your proud bosom not at peace with Jove,
> That you sought, thankless for his guarded grove,
> The empty horror of abysmal night?
> Ah, the thin air is cold above the moon!
> I stood and saw you fall, befooled in death,
> As, in your numbèd spirit's fatal swoon,
> You cried you were a god, or were to be;
> I heard with feeble moan your boastful breath
> Bubble from depths of the Icarian sea.

With what admirable skill is the metrical scheme of this sonnet employed to emphasise its dramatic phrasing! The seventh line is perhaps a little cumbrous, and "numbèd" in the eleventh line seems to me a nerveless epithet. Otherwise it is hard to find a flaw in the poem, and harder still to find adequate praise for the splendid intensity of the close.

The main body of Mr. Santayana's sonnets falls into two sections: the first purely philosophical, the second consecrated to a spiritual love. The opening sonnet of all tells how the poet worshipped in youth at

> the piteous height
> Where God vouchsafed the death of man to share,

but afterwards descended in search of

> a garden of delight,
> Or island altar to the Sea and Air,
> Where gentle music were accounted prayer,
> And reason, veiled, performed the happy rite.

Then the next poem opens thus:

> Slow and reluctant was the long descent,
> With many farewell pious looks behind,
> And dumb misgivings where the path might wind,
> And questionings of nature, as I went.

> The greener branches that above me bent,
> The broadening valleys, quieted my mind,
> To the fair reasons of the Spring inclined
> And to the Summer's tender argument.

If there be not in such writing as this a very peculiar delicacy and suavity, I am the more deceived. It would be a fascinating task to follow the process of Mr. Santayana's thought from sonnet to sonnet; but it must not be attempted here. "Process," perhaps, is scarcely the right word; I doubt whether any logical development is traceable in either sonnet-sequence. Rather it would seem that, singly or in groups of two or three, the sonnets express disconnected phases of thought. At all events, as I have not space to follow out a continuous thread of reasoning, I need not go about to search for it. Each poem has certainly an individual beauty and significance of its own, quite apart from its possible relation to an ordered whole.

My last quotation was the octave of the second sonnet; here now is the sestett of **"Sonnet VII.,"** which begins "I would I might forget that I am I," and deals with the burden of personality:

> Happy the dumb beast, hungering for food,
> But calling not his suffering his own;
> Blessèd the angel, gazing on all good,
> But knowing not he sits upon a throne;
> Wretched the mortal, pondering his mood,
> And doomed to know his aching heart alone.

There is a sort of cruelty, however, in dismembering a sonnet, even when one portion of it, like these six lines, forms an independent epigram. Why present the stem without the flower or the flower without the stem? I feel I must renounce the attempt to pick out brief passages of more than ordinary beauty, and let one complete sonnet represent the sequence. After much hesitation, I choose the following—the ninth. It is a noble piece of work; yet it would be unjust to Mr. Santayana to claim for it any singular pre-eminence.

> Have patience; it is fit that in this wise
> The spirit purge away its proper dross.
> No endless fever doth thy watches toss,
> For by excess of evil, evil dies.
> Soon shall the faint world melt before thine eyes,
> And, all life's losses cancelled by life's loss,
> Thou shalt lay down all burdens on thy cross,
> And be that day with God in Paradise.
> Have patience; for a long eternity
> No summons woke thee from thy happy sleep;
> For love of God one vigil thou canst keep
> And add thy drop of sorrow to the sea.
> Having known grief, all will be well with thee,
> Ay, and thy second slumber will be deep.

The first series consists of twenty sonnets, the second of thirty; and the second is the finer as well as the longer of the two, in something like the same proportion. As one reads it, one is more and more haunted by a sense of familiarity, not in the ideas or the images, but in the mellow music of the verse. Original, Mr. Santayana is, beyond a doubt; yet the smooth, firm texture of his lines is not new to us, his honeyed cadences bring with them some far-off association. "That strain again!" we say, "It had a dying fall"—and the enigma is solved. Though writing always in the strict Petrarcan form, Mr. Santayana has evidently steeped his mind in the melody of Shakespeare's quatorzains. So thoroughly has he done this that a captious criticism might borrow the epithet employed by Francis Meres and complain that Mr. Santayana's sonnets were over "sug'red." They have not the complex, billowy movement of Rossetti's sonnets, but aim rather (and that consciously, one cannot but suppose) at Shakespearean definiteness of crystallisation. The reader may not unnaturally cry out upon this comparison as extravagant, and to prove it, not only just, but inevitable, I should have to reprint the whole sequence. It is a cumulative effect that I am seeking to indicate, not one that can be adequately exemplified in a single sonnet, or in two, or three. Yet some hint of it may surely be conveyed by such a sonnet as this—the sequel to one in which the poet has besought a painter to record in line and hue his lady's beauty: "the sweet eyes tender and the broad brow cold."

> Yet why, of one who loved thee not, command
> Thy counterfeit, for other men to see,
> When God himself did on my heart for me
> Thy face, like Christ's upon the napkin, brand?
> O how much subtler than a painter's hand
> Is love to render back the truth of thee!
> My soul should be thy glass in time to be,
> And in my thought thine effigy should stand.
> Yet, lest the churlish critics of that age
> Should flout my praise, and deem a lover's rage
> Could gild a virtue and a grace exceed,
> I bid thine image here confront my page,
> That men may look upon thee as they read,
> And cry: Such eyes a better poet need.

This sonnet exemplifies the one besetting fault of form which can be laid to Mr. Santayana's charge. The final couplet, essential to the Shakespearean sonnet, seems to me to detract notably from the beauty of the Petrarcan rhyme scheme. It is true that Mr. Santayana scarcely ever leaves the final couplet isolated, but is careful to attach it to a previous line, usually (as in this case) the eleventh. Nevertheless, the chiming close is always thin and wiry in its effect, like the twang of a final chord on the banjo, contrasted with the gradual evanishing of a cadence on the violin.

It is not for us to speculate how much of reality and how much of fantasy there may be in the situation adumbrated in this second sequence. The fact that several of the sonnets seem mutually irreconcilable in their presentment of the relation between the poet and the lady, appears to point to a large admixture, at any rate, of pure fancy. In one poem, for instance, there seems to be a perfect understanding between them:

> Be mine, be mine in God and in the grave,
> Since naught but chance and the insensate wave
> Divides us, and the wagging tongue of men.

A little farther on, again, the lady is represented as absolutely unconscious of the poet's worship:

> For, when God tells you, you will not despise
> The love I bore you. It is better so.

But why should we be concerned to analyse the soil of fact from which sprang such a flower of poetry as this:

> As when the sceptre dangles from the hand
> Of some king doting, faction runneth wild,
> Thieves shake their chains and traitors, long exiled,
> Hover about the confines of the land,
> Till the young Prince, anointed, takes command,
> Full of high purpose, simple, trustful, mild,
> And, smitten by his radiance undefiled,
> The ruffians are abashed, the cowards stand:—
> So in my kingdom riot and despair
> Lived by thy lack, and called for thy control,
> But at thy coming all the world grew fair;
> Away before thy face the villains stole,
> And panoplied I rose to do and bear,
> When love his clarion sounded in my soul.

Is not this noble? Is not this classical? Note the perfect simplicity and purity of Mr. Santayana's diction, his resolute avoidance of verbal ostentation or metrical eccentricity. Here is English undefiled indeed, unvulgarised even by obtrusive ornament, importunate, self-conscious beauty. There is as little to surprise and startle as there is to offend us in such work as this. It is only exquisite; it is only right. And if, in the foregoing sonnet, the form is ideal, in this which follows ideal form is wedded to tragic loftiness of thought:

> We needs must be divided in the tomb,
> For I would die among the hills of Spain,
> And o'er the treeless melancholy plain
> Await the coming of the final gloom.
> But thou—O pitiful!—wilt find scant room
> Among thy kindred by the northern main,
> And fade into the drifting mist again,
> The hemlocks' shadow, or the pines' perfume.
> Let gallants lie beside their ladies' dust
> In one cold grave, with mortal love inurned;
> Let the sea part our ashes, if it must.
> The souls fled thence which love immortal burned,
> For they were wedded without bond of lust,
> And nothing of our heart to earth returned.

If there is a flaw in this sonnet it is the twelfth line, which is perhaps not absolutely clear, not perfectly luminous. But how trivial a blemish in how lovely a piece of work! (pp. 373-80)

Mr. Santayana's other verses, though full of accomplishment, are less remarkable than his sonnets. Among them are five odes, written in Sapphic and Adonic stanzas, and a very striking dramatic fragment named *Lucifer*. It consists of a dialogue between Hermes and Lucifer, partly in irregular choric measures, partly in rhymed pentameters. Lucifer, according to his own story, has been banished to the desolate, inclement region where Hermes visits him, for disturbing the complacency of heaven by tactless questions, such as—

> Tell, O Lord, the cause
> Why sluggish nature doth with Thee contend
> And Thy designs, observant of the laws,
> By tortuous paths must struggle to their end.

There is something a little comic in this conception of inopportune curiosity as the sin by which the angels fell; but the dialogue is admirably written, none the less. Lucifer in the end makes ready to return the visit of Hermes, and thus addresses his henchman, Lyal:

> We must away; this night shall have its dreams.
> Thou shalt behold a green land, watered well,
> Where large white swans swim in the lucent
>   streams;
> And bosky thickets where the harpy screams;
> And centaurs scouring fields of asphodel,
> While young fauns pluck their beards, and start
>   away
> At great Pan's feast to pipe an interlude.
> There mermaids with the painted dolphins play,
> Splashing blue waves for rainbows in the spray;
> And friendly poets, straying through the wood,
> Lay finger to the mouth, to watch askance
> How in wild ring the nymphs and satyrs dance.

Does such a passage as this seem to contradict my opening remarks as to the lack of objectivity in Mr Santayana's work? Surely not. We have here a picture, it is true, and a beautiful one; but its elements are entirely conventional. When Mr. Santayana wants to paint a glade in Arcady, or by the Sicilian shore, he does not dream of transferring to it a single touch studied from the woods or seaboard of Massachusetts. He goes straight to literature for his material; or rather he conjures up the required picture from an imagination impregnated with the choicest literary essences. He lives, in short, in a Palace of Art, with little or no outlook upon the material world. But it is a palace of all that is exquisite in art, and, shut in though it be, there is nothing sickly or stifling in its atmosphere. If there are no windows in the frescoed walls, at least there are sky-lights in the dome, through which the stars shine large and clear. (pp. 380-82)

> *William Archer, "George Santayana," in his* Poets of the Younger Generation, *1902. Reprint by Scholarly Press, 1969?, pp. 373-84.*

Lewis Mumford   (essay date 1923)

[*Mumford is an American sociologist, historian, philosopher, and author whose primary interest is the relationship between the modern individual and his or her environment. Influenced by the works of Patrick Geddes, a Scottish sociologist and pioneer in the field of city planning, Mumford has worked extensively in the area of city and regional planning, and has contributed several important studies of cities, including* The Culture of Cities *(1938),* City Development *(1945), and* The City in History *(1961). All of these works examine the interrelationship between cities and civilization over the centuries. Also indicative of much of his work is Mumford's concern with firm moral values to assure the growth of civilization. Writing in the* Saturday Evening Post, *Mumford noted that "the test of maturity, for nations as well as for individuals is not the increase of power, but the increase of self-understanding, self-control, self-direction, and self-transcendence. For in a mature society, man himself, not his machines or his organizations, is the chief work of art." In the following excerpt, Mumford praises* The Life of Reason *for its originality and relevance.*]

The Life of Reason . . . is an inquiry into the facts of existence and the values of human life. In this monumental work of five volumes, philosophy, after a long historic pilgrimage through natural science, apologetics, theology, and epistemology, becoming ever weaker and wanner as its rags were appropriated by the filial sciences, returns again to its Socratic beginnings, as wisdom. Those who would make philosophy study residual problems not embraced by the particular sciences; those who would fashion out of philosophy a vacuous Absolute which would both embrace and sanctify all existence; and finally those who would discipline philosophy in the scientific method; all these schools and systems are set aside, or rather put in their place, in **The Life of Reason.**

The Life of Reason sees two worlds, the world of nature and the world of mind; and each of these worlds calls for a different means of comprehension; the first mode being embodied in physics, the generic name for the natural sciences, and the second in dialectic, the usual designation for mathematics, logic, and certain aspects of ethics. In the continual traffic that an organism must maintain with its environment, the mind makes a record and keeps account, and any gains outside of a buoyant animality which may accrue in this intercourse are gains in the mind. What is rational or good or beautiful is an essence, as it were, that the mind squeezes out of the pulp of existence, and, having squeezed, independently feeds upon. These essences are ideal, in the sense that a mathematical figure, a religious symbol, or an artist's form is ideal; that is, they are not "given" in existence but are added thereto by man—they are a "new dimension to experience." It is difficult to compress statements which Mr. Santayana has worked out with graceful amplitude; but the gist of the philosophy is that nature and mind, although intimately related, have separate existences and separate validities, and that while science is true to its own mode when it follows the curves and undulations of nature, as a topographic map follows the contours of the country it describes, man has proper to himself certain ideal purposes which, were he strong enough, he would embody in society.

Those who think of Mr. Santayana's philosophy as something cold, formidable and remote, have no notion of either his style or the sort of facts upon which he dwells. **The Life of Reason** opens with an examination of the data of common sense, inquires into the life of man in society, and then contemplates religion, art, and science as elements that lay the foundation for a meeting-ground where, having risen above marriage, friendship and disinterested sympathy, and the conditions proper to a natural and a free society, "ideal interests themselves take possession of the mind." So far from departing from a world peopled by men and women, filled with egotisms and irrational urgencies as well as with a "pathetic capacity . . . to live nobly," Mr. Santayana's philosophy faces that world manfully; and the glistening torrent of his argument pours through it like a river through the Augean stables. The anthropologist will not perhaps care for Mr. Santayana's method of treating marriage; nor will the politician like his discussion of patriotism and armies; nor yet will the formalist find himself in sympathy with Mr. Santayana's distaste for a sterile æstheticism in art; but the peculiar virtue of Mr. Santayana's thought, as of all true philosophy, is that it is free from the professional's obsessions. It is able to compass all existence because, in wisdom if not in science, all existence can be united in a generous personality.

Like the genuine classic that it is, *The Life of Reason* has the air of having been written but yesterday; and its thought is fresher and newer than our accepted novelties. Much of what we have learned in psychology from Freud and Trotter during the last ten years is already adumbrated in Mr. Santayana's pages. In a paragraph he says almost as much about the instincts of the herd as Mr. Trotter succeeded in doing in a book; while his sense of life as beginning in the chaos of a dream, and never quite shaking itself out of this medium, gives perhaps a better general interpretation of the part of dreams in normal existence than the pathologist, with his vast medley of case records, can furnish us. It is not that the general statement of philosophy takes the place of the particulars of science, but that it shrewdly points to them. Is it not a tribute to the catholicity of Mr. Santayana's work to observe that it contained in its matrix the nuggets of other men's thoughts, sometimes indeed before those nuggets had been brought to light? Thus, in the volume on *Reason in Society,* Mr. Santayana anticipated William James in pointing out the need for a moral equivalent of war, since war itself, whilst irrational, nevertheless expresses a deep instinctive need for conflict which can not be denied; and in suggesting sport as a substitute. One expects to find Plato and Aristotle in Mr. Santayana's pages; but it is a mark of his philosophic genius that one also finds Mr. John Dewey, whose doctrines of morality in "Human Nature and Conduct" are summed up, it seems to me, in this excellent passage in *Reason in Art*:

> We in Christendom are so accustomed to artificial ideals and to artificial institutions, kept up to express them, that we hardly conceive how anomalous our situation is, sorely as we may suffer from it. We found academies and museums, as we found missions, to fan up a flame that constantly threatens to die out for lack of natural fuel. Our overt ideals are parasites in the body politic, while the ideals native to the body politic, those involved in our natural structure and situation, are either stifled by that alien incubus, leaving civic life barbarous, or else force their way up, unremarked or not justly honoured as ideals. Industry and science and social amenities, with all the congruous comforts and appurtenances of contemporary life, march on their way, as if they had nothing to say to the spirit, which remains tangled in a cobweb of dead traditions. An idle pottering of the fancy over obsolete forms—theological, dramatic, or plastic— makes that by-play to the sober business of life which men call their art or their religion; and the more functionless and gratuitous this by-play is the more those who indulge it think they are idealists. They feel they are champions of what is most precious in the world, as a sentimental lady might fancy herself a lover of flowers when she pressed them in a book instead of planting their seeds in a garden.

The only modern philosopher who can be compared with Mr. Santayana in comprehensiveness is, perhaps, Benedet-

to Croce; but Mr. Santayana is as free from Signor Croce's ponderousness as he is from his paradoxes. William James, who disliked the very texture of Mr. Santayana's thought, said of *The Life of Reason* that "it will probably be reckoned great by posterity" and that "its centre of gravity, is, I think, very deep" [see Further Reading]; and this tribute from an intellectual adversary may well take precedence over any minor criticism or judgment. Our final salute to Mr. Santayana might, however, best be paraphrased in the words that he himself applied to Emerson: "He remains a 'friend and aider of those who would live in the spirit.' If not yet a fixed star in the firmament of philosophy, he is certainly a star of the first magnitude. Alone as yet among American philosophers, he may be said to have won a place there, if not by the originality of his thought, at least by the originality and beauty of the expression he gave to thoughts that are old and imperishable." (pp. 259-60)

> Lewis Mumford, "Mr. Santayana's Philosophy," in The Freeman, *New York, Vol. VII, No. 167, May 23, 1923, pp. 258-60.*

J. B. Priestley   (essay date 1924)

[*A highly prolific English man of letters, Priestley was the author of numerous popular novels that depict the world of everyday, middle-class England. In this respect, Priestley has often been likened to Charles Dickens. His most notable critical work is* Literature and Western Man *(1960), a survey of Western literature from the invention of movable type through the mid twentieth century. In the following essay, Priestley examines Santayana's characteristic ideas and his abilities as a prose stylist.*]

About the time that America discovered in W. H. Hudson "one of the greatest masters of English Prose" and so on and so forth, she lost and we gained for a season a prose stylist who is at least Hudson's equal if not his superior— Mr. George Santayana. Mr. Santayana is a unique figure in modern letters. In the first place, he is a genuine cosmopolitan; born some sixty years ago where there runs one of the narrowest and deepest traditions of nationality, in Spain, he went at an early age where nationality is only in the making, to the United States; the rest may be related in his own words, in one of those complimentary passages of his *Soliloquies in England* in which he repays, with astonishing munificence, like some fairy godmother, any debt of gratitude to those who have made him welcome here:

> It was with a premonition of things noble and tender, and yet conventional, that after a term at the University of Berlin I went to spend my first holidays in England. Those were the great free days of my youth. I had lived familiarly in Spain and in the United States; I had had a glimpse of France and of Germany, and French literature had been my daily bread; it had taught me how to think, but had not given me much to think about. I was not mistaken in surmising that in England I should find a *tertium quid,* something soberer and juster than anything I yet knew, and at the same time greener and richer.

I felt at once that here was a distinctive society, a way of living fundamentally foreign to me, but deeply attractive. At first all gates seemed shut and bristling with incommunication; but soon in some embowered corner I found the stile I might climb over, and the ancient right of way. Those peaceful parks, and those minds no less retired, seemed positively to welcome me; and though I was still divided from them by inevitable partitions, these were in places so thin and yielding, that the separation seemed hardly greater than is requisite for union and sympathy between autonomous minds. Indeed, I was soon satisfied that no climate, no manners, no comrades on earth (where nothing is perfect) could be more congenial to my complexion.

Here, then, is one who spent his childhood in Madrid, who has since learnt and taught at Harvard, gaped for a season at Berlin, lectured at the Sorbonne, and meditated at Oxford; who has babbled in Spanish, chopped logic in German, read in French, and written in English; a philosophical and literary League of Nations. The advantages of such a position as citizen of the world are perhaps more easily realized than the disadvantages. But it must not be forgotten that philosophers, like other creatures born of women, arrive in this world at a certain time in a certain place; they imbibe preferences and prejudices with their mother's milk, and tradition, the tradition of their time and place, plays its part one way or the other, inclining them either to a joyful acceptance or a bitter rebellion. The cosmopolitan, who has sat in all the Opera Houses and eaten all the entrées from Paris to Pekin, brings with him a fine air of freedom and knowledge, and appears to stride unfettered by any national prejudices and vices of mind; but more often than not he is only a tourist instead of a citizen, and has been called upon to face only the trivial problems of the tourist in place of the graver problems of the citizen; he has lightly avoided the poisonous berries of national life, but so too he has never been sustained by its ancient and life-giving roots. The settled life of a nation, that which it presents to the eye of a traveller, is not really a show hastily though hopefully put together for the benefit of gaping strangers; it is the result of a long and arduous battle with circumstance, in which human nature has probably been tried to the full extent of its powers and has taken on strange shapes; there was more in Ithaca than was ever imagined by the traveller who passed an hour or so with the elderly dozing Ulysses and his Penelope. A certain air of detachment and condescension in Mr. Santayana, the air of one who watches a revolution in a little alien state, is the result of this cosmopolitanism of his, which is also partly responsible, I imagine, for his curious eclecticism, his trick of making the best of half a dozen different philosophical worlds.

In the second place, though Mr. Santayana is a philosopher who has spent half his life teaching the subject, he differs from all contemporary philosophers of any importance in three particulars, the breadth of his interests, the manner of his approach to his subject, and his actual style, three particulars that cannot really be separated. He is read and enjoyed by persons who shudder at the sight of the ugly machinery set up by most contemporary philoso-

phers to grind out their speculations on the ultimate nature of reality. Unless we are prepared for it, we are at once surprised and delighted when we take up a volume of contemporary philosophy, a certain *Scepticism and Animal Faith,* let us say, by a Mr. Santayana, and discover passages of this kind almost on every page:

> We may have such determinate minds that the suggestions of experience always issue there in the same dogmas; and these orthodox dogmas, perpetually revived by the stimulus of things, may become our dominant or even our sole apprehension of them. We shall really have moved to another level of mental discourse; we shall be living on ideas. In the gardens of Seville I once heard, coming through the tangle of palms and orange trees, the treble voice of a pupil in the theological seminary, crying to his playmate: "You booby! of course angels have a more perfect nature than men." With his black and red cassock that child had put on dialectic; he was playing the game of dogma and dreaming in words, and was insensible to the scent of violets that filled the air. . . .

or find the author, pushing his way forward to an ultimate scepticism, denying the past and future to the sceptic, in this fashion:

> The world present to the sceptic may continue to fade into these opposite abysses, the past and the future; but having renounced all prejudice and checked all customary faith, he will regard both as painted abysses only, like the opposite exits to the country and to the city on the ancient stage. He will see the masked actors (and he will invent a reason) rushing frantically out on one side and in at the other; but he knows that the moment they are out of sight the play is over for them; those outlying regions and those reported events which the messengers narrate so impressively are pure fancy; and there is nothing for him but to sit in his seat and lend his mind to the tragic illusion. . . .

There is here some hint of the poet, and if we read on and go from book to book, staying longest with the *Soliloquies in England,* we shall find more of him, this poet who can make the quiet style, so often deceptively quiet, flow everywhere into appropriate, persuasive, enchanting imagery, who can seemingly think in imagery and not merely rouge and perfume his prosaic thought, who can press forward to his conclusions by way of his images, so that they appear to us the living flesh on the bones of his logical structure and not, as often, mere brocaded cloths flung over a lay figure. We open the *Later Soliloquies* and discover such a passage as this:

> There is an obscure rumour that after the fall of Troy Helen never returned to Sparta, but was spirited away to Egypt, whilst a mere phantasm resembling her accompanied her dull husband back to his dull fastness by the pebbly Eurotas. This turn given to the fable hints darkly at an unearthly truth. Helen was a phantom always and everywhere; so long as men fought for her, taking her image, as it were, for their banner, she presided over a most veritable and bloody battle;

but when the battle ceased of itself, and all those heroes that had seen and idolized her were dead, the cerulean colours of that banner faded from it; the shreds of it rotted indistinguishly in the mire, and the hues that had lent it for a moment its terrible magic fled back into the ether, where wind and mist, meteors and sunbeams, never cease to weave them. The passing of Helen was the death of Greece, but Helen herself is its immortality. . . .

or, earlier, come upon him contrasting two faiths most effectively, though not with complete justice, simply by contrasting two vivid little pictures:

Protestant faith does not vanish into the sunlight as Catholic faith does, but leaves a shadowy ghost haunting the night of the soul. Faith, in the two cases, was not faith in the same sense; for the Catholic it was belief in a report or an argument; for the Protestant it was confidence in an allegiance. When Catholics leave the church they do so by the south door, into the glare of the market-place, where their eye is at once attracted by the wares displayed in the booths, by the flower-stalls with their bright awnings, by the fountain with its baroque Tritons blowing the spray into the air, and the children laughing and playing round it, by the concourse of townspeople and strangers, and by the soldiers, perhaps, marching past; and if they cast a look back at the church at all, it is only to admire its antique architecture, that crumbling filigree of stone so poetically surviving in its incongruous setting. It is astonishing sometimes with what contempt, with what a complete absence of understanding, unbelievers in Catholic countries look back on their religion. For one cultivated mind that sees in that religion a monument to his racial genius, a heritage of poetry and art almost as precious as the classical heritage, which indeed it incorporated in a hybrid form, there are twenty ignorant radicals who pass it by apologetically, as they might the broken toys or dusty schoolbooks of childhood. . . .

Protestants, on the contrary, leave the church by the north door, into the damp solitude of a green churchyard, amid yews and weeping willows and overgrown mounds and fallen illegible gravestones. They feel a terrible chill; the few weedy flowers that may struggle through the long grass do not console them; it was far brighter and warmer and more decent inside. The church—boring as the platitudes and insincerities were which you listened to there for hours—was an edifice, something protective, social and human; whereas here, in this vague unhomely wilderness, nothing seems to await you but discouragement and melancholy. Better the church than the madhouse. . . .

We have a right to transfer the creator of these fabrics of rich and meditative prose from the narrow field of philosophy proper to the wider field of letters.

If Philosophy, a school-marm for ever trying to live down her past indiscretions, has looked somewhat coldly upon Mr. Santayana, Literature, who holds out her arms to her

children no matter from what queer place they start up, will give him all the warmer welcome. Philosophy, however, has some excuse for her attitude. An American historian of modern speculative thought begins his notice of our author by remarking that—

George Santayana's lack of influence in proportion to the weight of his contribution to philosophical sanity and clarity, perhaps due in part to the academic distrust of literary gifts, is also not unconnected with a tone of condescension which he is apt to adopt toward competing views, as calling for indulgence rather than for serious argument. In consequence his work is more impressive as an imaginative picture of a certain outlook on the spiritual life of man, than for its explicit dialectical groundling.

In an able notice of Mr. Santayana in the *Times Literary Supplement,* an anonymous philosophical critic, after commenting adversely on his author's methods and conclusions, remarked—

To look through the **Life of Reason** again after seventeen years is to feel even more strongly than at the original reading how sterile that system must be from which the insight, the sympathy, the imaginative sweep, the richly furnished memory of Mr. Santayana can elicit no better answers to radical questions. In book after book since that treatise was first published Mr. Santayana has gone on adding to our best treasures of literary and social criticism; but if, as he allows us on the whole to presume, he still retains his old standpoint in philosophy, how little he has to offer in that field!

In an essay in the **Soliloquies, "On My Friendly Critics,"** he discusses, half-playfully, half-earnestly, the various criticisms that have been passed both upon him and his work:

As to my person, my critics are very gentle, and I am sensible of the kindness, or the diffidence, with which they treat me. I do not mind being occasionally denounced for atheism, conceit or detachment. One has to be oneself; and so long as the facts are not misrepresented—and I have little to complain of on that score—any judgment based upon them is a two-edged sword: people simply condemn what condemns them. I can always say to myself that my atheism, like that of Spinoza, is true piety towards the universe and denies only gods fashioned by men in their own image, to be servants of their human interests; and that even in this denial I am no rude iconoclast, but full of secret sympathy with the impulses of idolaters. My detachment from things and persons is also affectionate, and simply what the ancients called philosophy: I consent that a flowing river should flow; I renounce that which betrays, and cling to that which satisfies, and I relish the irony of truth; but my security in my own happiness is not indifference to that of others; I rejoice that every one should have his tastes and his pleasures. That I am conceited, it would be folly to deny: what artist, what thinker, what parent does not overestimate his own offspring? Can I suppress an irresistible sense of seeing things clearly, and a keen delight in so seeing them?

There is, of course, a good deal that could be said about the above by those friendly critics, who might ask, for example, how much affection goes with detachment and how far something more than indifference to the happiness of others makes for the security of one's own happiness. He then passes on to discuss his impersonal opinions, and though the remainder of the essay is much too long to quote in full, it is worth noticing because it gives us, I think, a better clue to his real position than his more formal statements elsewhere. It is all curiously shifting. He defends his extreme naturalism:

> Any existing persons, and any gods exercising power, will evidently be parts of nature. . . . Every assertion about existence is hazarded, it rests on animal faith, not on logical proof; and every argument to support naturalism, or to rebut it, implies naturalism. To deny that there are any facts (if scepticism can be carried so far) is still to dogmatize, no less than it would be to point to some fact in particular; in either case we descend into the arena of existence, which may betray our confidence. Any fact is an existence which discourse plays about and regards, but does not create. . . .

The basis of this naturalism is really science:

> I have no metaphysics, and in that sense I am no philosopher, but a poor ignoramus trusting to what he hears from the men of science. I rely on them to discover gradually exactly which elements in their description of nature may be literally true, and which merely symbolical: even if they were all symbolical, they would be true enough for me. . . .

But on this thoroughgoing naturalism is magically erected a kind of picturesque Platonism that is a dream without even a dreamer; values flower out of nothing; if, as Mr. Santayana declares:

> I am quite happy in this human ignorance mitigated by pictures, for it yields practical security and poetic beauty: what more can a sane man want? In this respect I think sometimes I am the only philosopher living: I am resigned to being a mind . . .

he seems like a mind in mid-air. Later, he remarks that "men of the world, when they dip into my books, find them consistent, almost oppressively consistent, and to the ladies everything is crystal-clear"; it is only the philosophers who misunderstand. This is probably true, but what the men of the world and the ladies find consistent and crystal-clear is the writer's temperament and his manner of expressing that temperament; the philosophers are in search of convictions and discover that Mr. Santayana's are for ever eluding their grasp. After further discussing a tendency of his to take up various philosophical positions that were, however, nothing more to him than "theoretic poses or possibilities; vistas for the imagination, never convictions," merely waking dreams to be entered into even yet at will; he comes to a point that is of particular interest:

> In moral philosophy (which is my chosen subject) I find my unsophisticated readers, as I found my pupils formerly, delightfully appreciative, warmly sympathetic, and altogether friends of mine in the spirit. It is a joy, like that of true conversation, to look and laugh and cry at the world so unfeignedly together. But the other philosophers, and those whose religion is of the anxious and intolerant sort, are not at all pleased. They think my morality very loose: I am a friend of publicans and sinners, not (as they are) in zeal to reform them, but because I like them as they are; and indeed I am a pagan and a moral sceptic in my naturalism. On the other hand (and this seems a contradiction to them), my moral philosophy looks strangely negative and narrow; a philosophy of abstention and distaste for life. What a horrible combination, they say to themselves, of moral licence with moral poverty! They do not see that it is because I love life that I wish to keep it sweet, so as to be able to love it altogether: and all that I wish for others, or dare to recommend to them, is that they should keep their lives sweet also, not after my fashion, but each man in his own way. . . . Now I am sometimes blamed for not labouring more earnestly to bring down the good of which I prate into the lives of other men. My critics suppose, apparently, that I mean by the good some particular way of life or some type of character which is alone virtuous, and which ought to be propagated. Alas, their propagandas! How they have filled this world with hatred, darkness, and blood! How they are still the eternal obstacle, in every home and in every heart, to a simple happiness! I have no wish to propagate any particular character, least of all my own; my conceit does not take that form. I wish individuals, and races, and nations to be themselves, and to multiply the forms of perfection and happiness, as nature prompts them. The only thing which I think might be propagated without injustice to the types thereby suppressed is harmony; enough harmony to prevent the interference of one type with another, and to allow the perfect development of each type. The good, as I conceive it, is happiness for each man after his own heart, and for each hour according to its inspiration. . . .

This is well said, though it is, of course, an overstatement; the first part of it would suggest that he was depriving himself of any licence to criticize, and actually a good deal of his work, and that not the least valuable, consists of social criticism that is at once very acute and very decided; whereas the little clause about "harmony" so quietly insinuated into the last part would suggest that he is also depriving himself of any license to enjoy, for what, we may ask, constitutes "harmony" when every type tends to interfere with every other, and what types are to be suppressed, and on what grounds. The sternest and narrowest moralist would ask for little more than this, if he were allowed to interpret "harmony" as he pleased. Nevertheless the statement will serve as a last link in the little chain of evidence that began with Mr. Santayana's cosmopolitanism and detachment; and we can see now where he is.

His attitude is really an æsthetic one. Had he attended to

nothing but his emotions and allowed them to well up into passionate rhythmical expression, he might have been a poet (he has written poetry), like Wordsworth; had he passed his time observing the private life of men and women in society, he might have written novels, like Meredith; had he chosen to brood perpetually over literature and art, he might have been a critic (as he is, of course, to some extent), like Pater; but he has chosen the myths and allegories, the ideas and dreams of men as his subject, and them he weaves into many-coloured meditations and epics of gorgeous illusion that loom and glow and pass and fade like sunset clouds. With him, we feel that the details of expression, the crisp epigram that contrasts so felicitously two faiths or the magnificent piece of imagery that describes the mind under the sway of some philosophical idea, are not the means, of which the assertion of some underlying conviction is the end, but are rather the end themselves, and that the thesis, though by no means contemptible, is really only an excuse for their existence. The temperaments of most philosophers are writ large over their systems; unconsciously they indulge their leading characteristics and shape a universe in which they themselves can move freely. Even Mr. Bertrand Russell, who breathed for so long the rarefied air of pure mathematics and only descended from the heights of inviolate being to give us his "logical atomism" and to express his horror of humanistic systems, clearly takes pleasure in the cold starlit universe he fashions and enjoys to the full his stoic counsels of brave despair. Mr. Santayana has only indulged his temperament a little more frankly. Artist that he is, he is a spectator content to lounge for ever in the playhouse of the moon-coloured myths, the shifting allegories and systems, the dance of ideas and dreams, bringing to the show a delicate imagination and an easy sympathy that is without a speck of passion, only occasionally rising from his seat to hiss off some outrageous mystic or rigid pompous idealist who has occupied the stage too long. There are books, he once told us, "in which the footnotes, or the comments scrawled by some reader's hand in the margin, are more interesting than the text. The world is one of these books." But in this instance, we gather, the book is "real," while the footnotes and comments are only part of a shifting dream. Only the Indian philosophers, meditating for decades in their savage and vivid jungles that were nothing more to them than idle mist and smoke, have travelled further along the path that leads to the hollow land of illusion beyond illusion. In one place, Mr. Santayana very characteristically exclaims:

> It is this sorry self of mine sitting here in the dark, one in this serried pack of open-mouthed fools, hungry for illusion, that is responsible for the spectacle; for if a foolish instinct had not brought me to the playhouse, and if avid eyes and an idealizing understanding had not watched the performance, no part of it would have abused me: and if no one came to the theatre, the actors would soon flit away like ghosts, the poets would starve, the scenery would topple over and become rubbish, and the very walls would disappear. Every part of experience is illusion; and the source of this illusion is my animal nature, blindly labouring in a blind world. . . .

Once more the spectacle and the playhouse, Prospero before his ghostly revels.

There can be discovered in nearly all philosophical systems some hint as to what their ingenious creators consider to be the chief end of man, to which all the monstrous activities of Nature have so far pointed the way; and time and again the philosophers show their hands in this fashion; one will offer us a Prussian civil servant, another a reformer on the Town Council, another a professor and examiner, and so forth; and Mr. Santayana, himself a half-wistful, half-cynical spectator at the show of life, has with more than usual frankness produced a system that is at heart nothing but an elaborate defence or even glorification of the spectator's attitude. Behind his Life of Reason there stands, most plain to see, a company of comfortable, cultured, fairly sensitive, much-travelled and knowledgeable gentlemen with fine prose styles. The Life of Reason, which is not only the title of his most ambitious performance, but is really the subject of everything he has written, is perhaps the best philosophical defence there has been of the æsthetic attitude. It demands some explanation. (Though it is high time I pointed out that to me, who am no philosopher, not even a thoroughgoing student of philosophy, but only a kind of literary critic with spasmodic and uncertain philosophical interests, all this is very dangerous ground.) What Mr. Santayana calls Reason, then, has two functions. In the name of Science, it investigates and reports upon that world of matter in which we, as animals, have our place; everything that exists has its source in the world of matter, this physical universe; which is not a creation of our own minds (though every interpretation of it is), which does not necessarily accommodate itself to our needs (though they will probably find satisfaction in what, after all, created them), and from which there is no appeal. The human consciousness is, of course, but one other product of matter, and we are, so to speak, kept going in such a world just as all its other creatures are kept going, by what Mr. Santayana has lately called our "animal faith." But Reason has another and greater task than to report this "real" world (greater because knowledge itself is, after all, a value), and that is to bring harmony into the ideal realm of values, which has a significance for us not possessed by the "real" world, if only because it is shaped by the special needs and preferences of our own particular nature. The two worlds are bridged by Mr. Santayana's system of "essences" which are what is perceived by consciousness and understood to be what has been called the "nature" of things, the first cousins of "substance" or the Platonic "idea." Out of such "essences," of course, the Life of Reason builds up its ideal realm in which we discover the ends of all those things that have their root in our animal life. Here, for example, is Mr. Santayana's account of love:

> In popular feeling, where sentiment and observation must both make themselves felt somehow or other, the tendency is to imagine that love is an absolute, non-natural energy which, for some unknown reason, or for none at all, lights upon particular persons, and rests there eternally, as on its ultimate goal. In other words, it makes the origin of love divine and its object natural: which is the exact opposite of the truth. If it were once

seen, however, that every ideal expresses some natural function, and that no natural function is incapable in its free exercise, of evolving some ideal and finding justification, not in some collateral animal, but in an inherent operation like life or thought, which being transmissible in its form is also eternal, then the philosophy of love should not prove permanently barren. For love is a brilliant illustration of a principle everywhere discoverable: namely, that human reason lives by turning the friction of material forces into the light of ideal goods. There can be no philosophic interest in disguising the animal basis of love, or in denying its spiritual sublimations, since all life is animal in its origin and all spiritual in its possible fruits.

There never was a better system for the purely contemplative mind, and even from this inadequate account it can be seen how he has magnificently indulged his temperament and, passing quickly over the quagmires of metaphysics, has given himself permission to wander at will over the hills and through the jungles of human thought and dream:

> The life of Reason, as I conceive it, is simply the dreaming mind becoming coherent, devising symbols and methods, such as languages, by which it may fitly survey its own career, and the forces of nature on which that career depends. Reason thereby raises our vegetative dream into a poetic revelation and transcript of the truth. . . .

And if, scuttling from Philosophy back to Literature, we regard him as a kind of artist in philosophic reverie, we can see now that many characteristics that so far have seemed to stand to his disadvantage really give him a great advantage over other persons in the same field, and make him what he undoubtedly is, a unique figure. Thus his cosmopolitan detachment enables him to survey the centuries and the nations without passion, and yet, not being a visitor from another planet, but simply a man who owes his ancestry and childhood to one race, his education to another, something of his culture, perhaps, to a third, and so on, he can claim some sort of kinship with many men and things and is able to brood over them with a sympathy that owes something to such kinship. Indeed, although he may appear to be all of a piece, those who read him closely may observe even yet certain warring elements that suggest that he has not yet completely harmonized the influences of two continents and two cultures; thus, as one critic has pointed out, a tendency towards a certain prim and bloodless intellectuality competes in his mind with the artist's joyous acceptance of whatever is original and engrossing; and we may say that in him the Spanish-American War is still languishing. But most readers, however, are more likely to complain of his consistency, the closeness and apparent sameness of his murmurous undulating text, than of his inconsistency, his failure to blend together indistinguishably the Spaniard and the American, the Catholic poet and the naturalistic philosopher, the professor and the artist.

His literary approach to his subject, his power as a stylist, however it may affect the schools, is all sheer gain to us,

not merely because his style makes him so much more pleasant to read, but because his meditations and reveries are partly those of a poet, no matter what their subject-matter may be, for they describe states of mind and these can be more scrupulously pictured with the aid of bright images and cunning rhythms. His style runs back to an older kind of prose, the prose of men who, like him, loved the contemplative life, leisurely thought and vivid and quaint imagery, the prose of our seventeenth century. There is an echo of that old prose, perhaps not more than that; the differences are too great, and if they were any less Mr. Santayana would not be a writer with a fine personal style, but an archaic trifler, a philosopher at a literary fancy-dress ball. But we have only to remember that our ornate seventeenth-century prose took as its basis the paragraph and not the sentence, and substitute lighter stops for the modern writer's periods, and the likeness is plain. There is nothing deliberately archaic in the two following passages, and yet they make light of the intervening centuries:

> To be born is painful, and the profit of it so uncertain that we need not wonder if sometimes the mind as well as the body seems to hold back. The winds of February are not colder to a featherless chick than are the surprises which nature and truth bring to our dreaming egotism . . .

or again:

> There is an uncovenanted society of spirits, like that of the morning stars singing together, or of all the larks at once in the sky; it is a happy accident of freedom and a conspiracy of solitudes. When people talk together, they are at once entangled in a mesh of instrumentalities, irrelevance, misunderstanding, vanity, and propaganda; and all to no purpose, for why should creatures become alike who are different? But when minds, being naturally akin and each alone in its own heaven, soliloquize in harmony, saying compatible things only because their hearts are similar, then society is a friendship in the spirit; and the unison of many thoughts twinkles happily in the night across the void of separation. . . .

Both these passages are from the *Soliloquies in England*, in which volume our author's style, reaching out to all manner of subjects, is probably at its best. His more ambitious work, the five volumes that compose the *Life of Reason* and survey religion, philosophy, art, and society, he has called "a presumptive biography of the human intellect, which instead of the Life of Reason might have been called the Romance of Wisdom." But in truth, all that he has written might very well carry both titles, for everything he touches is so much coloured stuff for the loom on which the Life of Reason is woven, and it is all a soliloquy, a mind that the reader overhears recounting all men's fables and old dreams. A philosopher, as he has told us himself, is not necessarily every "logician or psychologist who, in his official and studious moments, may weigh argument against argument or may devise expedients for solving theoretical puzzles"; philosophy is a way of life, the contemplative attitude of mind; and of philosophers in this sense, as distinct from the horde of official reasoners and speculators, the professors, and examiners, we have all too few; such men have the poet's wonder, but it takes a different direction and overflows into wise reverie.

The reader who is himself something of a philosopher in this sense and who has been driven out of the well-trodden groves by the raving prophets, the shouting propagandists, the ceaseless noise of axes at the grindstone, will discover in this remoter grove, where the birds can still be heard singing in the trees, heaped treasures of thought. And he may take this body of work in one of two ways, or in both. He may regard it as so many essays on all manner of subjects, from Skylarks to the Irony of Liberalism, from Queen Mab to the British Hegelians, just as Mr. Logan Pearsall Smith has done in his admirable anthology of *Little Essays* selected from the works of Mr. Santayana; or he may choose to follow Mr. Santayana's epic sweep and go wherever the Life of Reason bids him follow, and this will be the wiser choice, because then the epic note, the fullness of the vision, is not lost, and because some of Mr. Santayana's more gorgeous and elaborate traceries, such as the description of the ancient world, the rise of Catholicism and the advent of Protestantism in that great little history, *Reason in Religion* (*The Life of Reason*), must be read in full and in their place to be appreciated. But whatever the approach, the riches, imaginative, critical, historical, are there; and in this endless reverie, woven so closely, with its slow undulating rhythm, there is almost everything that prose can offer, from gorgeous passages of description, image upon image, vista beyond vista, to witty epigrams as thick as October blackberries. Flashes of wit light up every page; we have only to dip into the volumes to bring out wise and witty sentences by the handful:

> Popular poets are the parish priests of the Muse, retailing her ancient divinations to a long since converted public. . . .

> Dickens entered the theatre of this world by the stage-door. . . .

> Nothing is more pitiable than the attempts people make, who think they have an exquisite sensibility, to live in a house all of one period. The connoisseur, like an uncritical philosopher, boasts to have patched his dwelling perfectly together, but he has forgotten himself, its egregious inhabitant. . . .

> Nietzsche was far from ungenerous or unsympathetic towards the people. He wished them (somewhat contemptuously) to be happy, whilst he and his superman remained poetically wretched. . . .

> I do not profess to know what matter is in itself, and feel no confidence in the divination of those *esprits forts* who, leading a life of vice, thought the universe must be composed of nothing but dice and billiard-balls. . . .

> The critic, feeling that something in the artist has escaped him, may labour to put himself in the artist's place. If he succeeded, the result would only be to make him a biographer; he would be describing in words the very intuitions which the artist had rendered in some other medium. To understand how the artist felt, howev-

er, is not criticism; criticism is an investigation of what the work is good for. . . .

Often the richest philosophies are the most sceptical; the mind is not then tethered in its home paddock, but ranges at will over the wilderness of being. The Indians, who deny the existence of the world, have a keen sense for its infinity and its variegated colours; they play with the monstrous and miraculous in the grand manner, as in the *Arabian Nights*. No critic has had a sharper eye for the outline of ideas than Hume, who found it impossible to believe that they revealed anything. . . .

The extent to which æsthetic values are allowed to colour the resultant or highest good is a point of great theoretic importance, not only for art, but for general philosophy. If art is excluded altogether or given only a trivial rôle, perhaps as a necessary relaxation, we feel at once that a philosophy so judging human arts is ascetic or postrational. It pretends to guide life from above and from without; it has discredited human nature and mortal interests, and has thereby undermined itself, since it is at best but a partial expression of that humanity which it strives to transcend. If, on the contrary, art is prized as something supreme and irresponsible, if the poetic and mystic glow which it may bring seems its own complete justification, then philosophy is evidently still prerational, or, rather, nonexistent; for the beasts that listened to Orpheus belong to this school. To be bewitched is not to be saved, though all the magicians and æsthetes in the world should pronounce it to be so. Intoxication is a sad business, at least for a philosopher; for you must either drown yourself altogether, or else when sober again you will feel somewhat fooled by yesterday's joys and somewhat lost in to-day's vacancy. The man who would emancipate art from discipline and reason is trying to elude rationality, not merely in art, but in all existence. He is vexed at conditions of excellence that make him conscious of his own incompetence and failure. Rather than consider his function, he proclaims his self-sufficiency. A way foolishness has of revenging itself is to excommunicate the world. . . .

We all know that enthusiastic, excellent but occasionally irritating friend who keeps us from our gossip while he reads out passage after passage from the book he has last read and admired. There are limits beyond which even the critic, with his licence to quote, should not go, and unfortunately I have already passed those limits, although Mr. Santayana's volumes on the table still bristle with slips that mark quotations illustrating half a dozen different characteristics. There is perhaps no better proof of a writer's ability to wed together clear-pointed thought and sharply etched expression than this desire to quote on and on, brushing aside any suggestions of paraphrase or mere comment. In an age that turns aside from contemplation and wise reverie, an age that delights in bludgeoning the nearest passer-by with the first idea it comes upon, Mr. Santayana, even without his wit and style, would still be a notable figure by reason of his wide knowledge, rich imagination, and contemplative attitude, telling over the innumerable signs and symbols of the world. Fortunately, the wit and the style are there, too, and he is more than notable, he is a unique figure:

> Voyaging through strange seas of Thought,
> alone . . .

and returning to heap the treasure at our feet. (pp. 165-87)

> *J. B. Priestley, "Mr. George Santayana," in his*
> Figures in Modern Literature, *1924. Reprint*
> *by Books for Libraries Press, 1970, pp. 165-87.*

Archibald MacLeish   (essay date 1925)

[*A Pulitzer Prize–winning American poet and dramatist, MacLeish also served as a lawyer, university professor, Librarian of Congress, and assistant secretary of state. His philosophy of art rejects isolationism in favor of activism; he argues: "To declare, as the American aesthetic seems to do, that the effort to act upon the external world in the making of a work of art is a betrayal of the work of art is a misconception of the nature of art. The nature of art is action, and there is no part of human experience, public or private, on which it cannot act or should not." In the following essay, MacLeish praises Santayana's poetry.*]

George Santayana, the poet, disappeared from the world of polite letters a great many years ago, leaving as the principal reminder of his existence a thin volume of sonnets. It was not understood at the time that his disappearance

A 1936 version of a sonnet first drafted by Santayana in 1911.

was to be permanent and the usual appreciations were omitted. There is a certain danger in appreciating poets who may return to outsell the appraiser. But the passage of time and certain intimations from what the *Times* would call "reliable sources" make the matter reasonably clear. Santayana is not to reappear. And it is a fair inference from the evidence that he was never expected to reappear; that his heir and executor, the philosopher, had dealt with him privily but effectively and acquired a very certain hold upon the inheritance. Not banishment from the Republic as became a poet but death and determination were adjudged upon him. "Youth and aspiration", wrote the philosopher, "indulge in poetry; a mature and masterful mind will often despise it and prefer to express itself laconically in prose." And so that drug wherewith philosophers have a poisonous familiarity was administered, and the poet dreamed the forbidden dream and died.

It would be interesting to consider the motives of the deed in all their considerations of reason and intent. But failing an actual knowledge of the facts, presumptions are a necessity, and the fairest of presumptions puts the crime upon a generous ground, a basis of principle. George Santayana was removed because he was not a proper poet within the meaning of the philosophies. He had not, it would appear, grasped the poetic function. He did not understand that it was his, retaining an "innocence of the eye" to "repair to the material of experience, seizing hold of the reality of sensation and fancy beneath the surface of conventional ideas", quarrying from the sensuous world pictures and emotions wherewith the philosopher should construct the temple of divinity. On the contrary he desired not only to hew stone but to build towers. He was no poet royal to the philosophical household, but his own king and philosopher. He did not propose to serve the religious sense by gesturing in inarticulate images toward the Almighty, but rather to find God out in his dark and difficult universe and close with his divinity. And if he had eyes they were not the eyes of innocence. He saw nature with no embarrassed and Wordsworthian surprise but mirrored at two or three reflections from herself in the unbreathed metal of his mind. He was not to be startled by daffodils but

> To the fair reason of the Spring inclined
> And to the Summer's tender argument.

And when he did capture in immediate words the taste and smell and feel of the natural world it was never for remembrance' sake but to throw open windows of sense upon the brain's far faint discoveries—

> Out of the dust the queen of roses springs;
> The brackish depths of the blown water bear
> Blossoms of foam: the common mist and air
> Weave Vesper's holy, pity-laden wings.

We may say that if this is not within the philosopher's conception of poetry then the worse for philosophy. But we may not doubt that within the *Interpretations of Poetry and Religion* George Santayana was an altogether improper poet.

There are, however, various conceptions of the poetic method and the poetic function. There have been philosophies in rhyme since the "De Rerum" and there had been poems of religious experience before the **Sonnets** of Santayana. And it is not the least of Santayana's triumphs that he was later justified out of the mouth of his traducer in the **Three Philosophical Poets.** Of the imagined most high poet the philosopher says:

> He should live in the continual presence of all experience and respect it; he should at the same time understand nature, the ground of that experience; and he should also have a delicate sense for the ideal echoes of his own passions, and for all the colors of his possible happiness.

And it is given him for task "to reconstitute the shattered picture of the world". He is permitted the kingdom of the brain at last and every avenue of realization is thrown open to him.

George Santayana was very clearly not the most high poet nor was he within measurable reach of such greatness. But the air he inhabited was the air the expected genius must climb and his defects were the defects of supreme qualities. He stood upon experience but his experience was æsthetic altogether. He painted the colors of a possible happiness but indirectly and in fitful relief against a dark and brooding present. He relimned fragments and glimpses of the shattered picture of the world but it was a world in which he lived alone. There is nothing universal, nothing drawn from common experience, in his verse. He stands altogether aside from that great tradition of English poetry which has laid hold upon earth and the flavor and saltiness of earth, imaging man as a figure in the pageant of the world who may rebel against the blind mischance of life but who will never challenge its reality nor deny his blood kinship to beasts and trees and all things that die upon the grass. Santayana is too perfect an artist to reach perfection in poetry. His sense is too delicate to give him apprehension of the deep tones and slow vibrations of the seasonal earth; it is only the overtone of human passion that he hears, and faintly and silverly and far away.

And yet the joy of his verse is not so much its delicacy as its brilliance and the temper of its strength. His manner is the manner of swordsmanship, and the blade, though daintily raised, bites in. He is an exquisite in thrust and parry and a master of the subtle feints of fence, but there is more than swordplay in his skill. There is sometimes a desperate courage in the stab of a phrase as though he drove against a shadowy antagonist always at point to strike and overwhelm. Against the mockery of nothingness he turns the deftness of that line which has for hope

> To trust the soul's invincible surmise—

and against an inexplicable fate the words:

> So in this great disaster of our birth
> We can be happy and forget our doom.

It is disaster that is sure and hope that is adventurous.

> Wait for the Spring, brave heart, there is no knowing.

And man's victory over earth is at once the realization and the destruction of the brain's hope for an eternal victory:

> Sing softly, choristers; yet sing
> Not faith alone, but doubt and dread.
> Ring wildly, Easter bells; ye ring
> For Christ arisen, and hope dead.

But for all its intensity the poetry of George Santayana never fails of a fine restraint and an unobtrusive mastery of form. His glimpses of reality are labored into closely articulated epigrams, and his phrases of wonder or of doubt or grief are inevitable unities, perfect to the uses of his will. His use of rhyme and rhythm is beyond praise. Under his hand the reiterated iambic insistence of the line is so softened that the stubborn sonnet becomes at once flexible and a thing of change. And even the rigors of the strict Italian form never drive him to forced, or flat, or uncertain rhymes. Whatever may be the relative merits of prose or verse as a vehicle for the philosophies, this much is sure— Santayana's was an art in poetry that should not have heaped the sacrifice to any god. (pp. 187-89)

> *Archibald MacLeish, "Santayana, The Poet,"*
> *in* The Bookman, *New York, Vol. LXII, No.*
> *2, October, 1925, pp. 187-89.*

Daniel MacGhie Cory   (essay date 1927)

[*Cory was an American editor and essayist who served as Santayana's literary secretary for many years. In the following essay, he analyzes the ideas advanced in* Scepticism and Animal Faith. *According to a footnote from the editor of the journal from which this essay was taken, Santayana read the study and praised it as "an excellent and accurate exposition of his philosophy."*]

This paper is intended to be an interpretation of what I shall venture to call—the *deliberate* philosophy of Santayana, as outlined in his recent and most penetrating book: **Scepticism and Animal Faith.** I refrain from employing the battered term metaphysics, because this candid "lover of wisdom" has reminded us that his system is not metaphysical, "except in the mocking literary sense of the word." What the vulgar (among which I count myself), however, understand by the term, he is guilty of offering in this mature work. It is my desire to try and see his philosophy under the searchlight of contemporary discussion; and I shall introduce some remarks of my own on what I consider significant Realistic issues of the day. My philosophy, however, on *nearly* all conditions, *has been formed by, and is in concord with,* the system here expounded.

THE STATUS OF ESSENCE

As Rene Descartes in the seventeenth century endeavoured to free his mind of all cant and bias, by faithfully undergoing a long session of suspended judgment and critical destruction of belief, so Santayana in these muddled, later years has begun his philosophy by diligently sweeping as clear as possible from prejudice the delightful and rich coloured chambers of his own mind. He has moved all the old furniture and treasures, compelling with their long emotional association, out of the mansion of mentality; had them redraped and polished, perhaps, and then carefully and definitely placed back among the freshly painted but familiar walls. And his spiritual house-cleaning has been even more drastic, more searching than Descartes; for he has left no neglected *cogito, ergo sum* hidden in the dust of the attic, behind some shadowy rafter. Santayana, in the first eleven chapters of this book, has shaken the sieve of scepticism free of every particle of belief, and he has discovered what he believes to be the indubitable, the eternal country where the doubt-weary mind may rest—the Realm of Essences. His discipline has been a match for Carneades at his best.

"But," gasps the bewildered reader, "what are essences? What are these poor forlorn flowers that the scythe of criticism has left us?"

When the immediate and indubitable datum is simply and impartially regarded as being merely what it is in itself—a subsisting logical entity; when all the heat of emergency and faith has been dissolved in this innocent attitude of the mind—then, and not until then, have we discovered what essences are in their own haven of being—the only possible home for the honest solipsist. But we must abrogate every form of belief, even the most intimate and compelling: belief in self-consciousness; in the reality of transition; in the validity of personal memory. For not until our temperaments have submitted to this ultimate catharsis, and every invidious proclivity to posit has been trapped, will the wide prairie of essences open before us in all its infinite innocence. This is the ultimatum of all logical solipsism; the last mountain peak of the exhausted Pyrrhonist; the final, triumphant effort of the mind to free itself from the clutches of convention.

Essences are universals; for they *exist* nowhere and are defiant of space and time. There is infinite and minute discrimination among them, each essence being a positive and eternal peculiarity in itself. As Mr. Santayana says:—

> . . . although essences have the texture and ontological status of Platonic ideas, they can lay claim to none of the cosmological, metaphysical, or moral prerogatives attributed to those ideas. They are infinite in number and neutral in value.

Try and think of them as merely what the sceptic is left with, when, as I have said, every inclination to posit has been suspended: simply the indubitable data that are continually being given and continually retreating into that Sheol of all possible discourse—the domain of essences.

That the subjective idealists have already suspected and dodged elusively this inevitable conclusion of their own logic, is only too apparent. Berkeley with his 'silly' God and miraculous "notion" of fellow-minds is the salient example. But there is no limp in Santayana's reasoning; it has run its course courageously and breasted the final tape of doubt.

There is a feeling of security impregnated in this conception of essences, which becomes enhanced and moralized when understood in the light of Santayana's interpretation of Truth. I shall discuss this later. But the sense of permanence is here, which no contemporary verdict on the attenuated and fleeting nature of matter is quite able to remove. Perhaps I am yielding to a mystical—a poetical impulse:—

> Nothing has changed; with the same hollow thunder
> The waves die in their everlasting snow.

I have suspected this subtle refinement of speculation in regard to essences, and wondered if merely because a specific gradation of crimson is identical on the leaf of a rose or the lips of a lady, and may be revived later in a less æsthetic object or situation, we have any legitimate right to call it *eternal*. Perhaps the impatience of so clear and sound a philosopher as John Dewey was justified, I thought:—

> . . . individually qualified things have some qualities which are pervasive, common, stable. They are out of time in the sense that a particular temporal quality is irrelevant to them. If anybody feels relieved by calling them eternal, let them be called eternal. But let not 'eternal' be then conceived as *a kind of absolute perduring existence or Being.* It denotes just what it denotes: irrelevance to existence in its temporal quality [my italics].

But the important aspect of this argument to remember is that *when essences are revived they are identical.* You must grant them this *intrinsic loyalty,* or chuck in the sponge and towel at once; for when memory is knocked out, nothing remains but to raise the right hand of solipsism and go home—the fight is over. Language is impotent to convey my feelings in this matter; but the fact that essences *continue as possibilities for future survey* is a *morally* sufficient reason for calling them eternal. They subsist in an ideal or ontological fashion as *useful entities* for later discourse. Perhaps this last will satisfy Mr. Dewey—it has a pragmatic smell about it.

ESSENCE AND MATTER

Mr. Whitehead shares Santayana's attitude in regard to the *eternity* of these ideal elements. He says in very persuasive words:—

> Every scheme for the analysis of nature has to face these two facts, *change* and *endurance.* There is yet a third fact to be placed by it, *eternality* I will call it. The mountain endures. But when after ages it has been worn away, it has gone. If a replica arises, it is yet a new mountain. A colour is eternal. It haunts time like a spirit. It comes and it goes. But where it comes, it is the same colour. It neither survives nor does it live. It appears when it is wanted. The mountain has to time and space a different relation from that which colour has.

The significant distinction between these two dissectors on the point narrows down to the manner in which they *connect* these elusive universal terms to the vibrating configurations of events in nature. So far as I can discover, there is an absolute severance in Santayana's system between the realm of essences and "the facts or events *believed* to occur in nature" (my italics). At no most sanguine and irresistible moment in perception do we unveil the flowing robes of nature and behold her in all her naked and transient existence. The primary qualities themselves are merely regarded as being habitual symbols—"those essences which custom or science continue to use in their description of things." The only possible relation that I gather from this system is a purely *formal* one: like that of a sheet of musical notes (the groups of events in the body) to the golden melody (the essences lit by the flickering candle of intuition) that charms the auditorium. And it is precisely this ultimate "bifurcation of nature" that Whitehead and the Neo-Realists consider so metaphysically repugnant. (Their frenzied desire for unity is very apparent; it has almost a mystic heat of certainty.)

For Mr. Whitehead feels that what he calls "eternal objects" are much more vitally and authentically *allied* with the structures of occurrences in nature: they are *the ideal elements that compose the texture of these structures.* In fact, with the fundamental underlying activity, "whereby the actual world has its character of temporal passage to novelty," and the vague (for me) entity called God, these *formative elements* are *all* that constitute his inclusive universe. The difference of his attitude as compared with that of Santayana is illustrated by his definition of nature as "what we are aware of in perception." For by "nature" he here seems to understand *not only essences* but *existence* or *activity* as well—and only *essences* are ever *accessible to awareness.*

I do not think that I have over-emphasized the severe discrimination made by Santayana between essences and the physical system of events. The latter remains always, from a *theoretical* standpoint, a *compelling assumption* made by an animal in the heat of adaptation; and Santayana, realizing that, besides being a philosopher, he is also a normal human being, functioning in a transient and exacting environment, *believes* firmly in its existence. Nevertheless, he is convinced that nothing *given* in awareness *exists as such:*—

> The realm of matter can never be disclosed either to hypothesis or to sensation in its presumable inmost structure and ultimate extent: the garment of appearance must always fit it loosely and drape it in alien folds, because *appearance is essentially an adaptation of facts to the scale and faculty of the observer* [my italics].

Here, I believe, a clean-cut bifurcation is apparent.

His essences, as I have said, are helpless and impartial; and there is no *teleological significance* to be derived from observing that certain *enduring patterns of æsthetic value* have been woven among them by the habits of matter.

The Aristotelian God that has lately been adopted (minus a few cosmological prerogatives) by Mr. Whitehead to crown his metaphysics, is understood to be "an actual but non-temporal entity" that *determines* the *ideal fabrics* of events by the *imposition* of His all-wise and complete nature. The Ecstatic Contemplator of Aristotle has once more thrown his *awful* shadow across philosophy. Without such divine control, Mr. Whitehead feels that sheer, unlimited activity, taken with the inexhaustless world of ideal forms, would be helpless to *achieve* anything. The religious culmination of Mr. Whitehead's patient and profound reasoning is manifested in the faith of the following beautiful paragraph:—

> The order of the world is no accident. There is

nothing actual which could be actual without some measure of order. The religious insight is the grasp of this truth: That the order of the world, the depth of reality of the world, the value of the world in its whole and in its parts, the beauty of the world, the zest of life, the peace of life, and the mastery of evil, are all bound together—not accidentally, but by reason of this truth: that the universe exhibits a creativity with infinite freedom, and a realm of forms with infinite possibilities; *but that this creativity and these forms are together impotent to achieve actuality apart from the completed ideal harmony, which is God* [my italics].

Now Santayana has also considered this beautiful reading of nature—considered it only to reject it ultimately as being too poetical—too incredible. But he has felt the lure of the conception:—

> If the cosmos were a single animal, as the ancients supposed, and *had an aim and a life* which, like human life, could be fulfilled in the contemplation of certain essences, then a life like that of Aristotle's God would be involved in the perfection of nature, if this perfection was ever attained.

. . . . .

> . . . the cosmic intellect in act would not be the *whole* of the realm of essence, *nor any part* of it. *It would be the intuition of so much of essence as that cosmos had for its goal* [my italics].

And this last sentence would seem to be in concord with Whitehead's *exclusion of evil* from the nature of God.

The word God is burdened with personal and ancient emotion. I cannot see or hear the term without recalling wild panoramic images, sombre and reverberating naves, or remote, leaf-cool shrines. It is apt to be misleading, even when introduced with the caution and intellectual chastity exercised by Aristotle and Whitehead. I think Santayana has been prudent in avoiding it. His interpretation of nature is humble and less pretentious. He does not make *demands* upon her, but accepts the innocent conditions under which she operates as the only legitimate answer to the eternal Why of existence. The "order of the world" is not arbitrary *to its substance,* but it *might* have fallen into other rhythms quite as well. The blunt, bald fact that nature has staged one specific drama instead of another, and that thereby a vast umbra of Truth has trembled over the field of Essence, is not due to any divine purpose inherent in or luring onwards from above, the innocent flow of events. I cannot help feeling that the following outburst by Lloyd Morgan is metaphysically dangerous:—

> For better or worse, I acknowledge God as the Nisus through whose Activity emergents emerge, and the whole course of emergent evolution is directed.

. . . . .

> Without denying a felt push from the lower levels of one's being—to me it feels like a drawing upwards through Activity existent at a higher level than that to which I have attained.

Santayana's system is wary of these *teleological compensations*. There are no broad, hurried generalizations—no heated embracing of conclusions immediately suggested by a temperamental reading of evolution, or a partial understanding of the beautiful marriage of space and time. He would never say, for instance, with Samuel Alexander, that time was "the mind of space." Why be so honorific to one of these Great Lovers of the universe? *Space and time are both abstractions from a physical system yielding more or less settled dispositions of expression in the world of forms.* An electron, as we know it, is such a settled disposition; a human organism is a group of such dispositions. And there is no *logical or moral necessity* that I can discover for calling a rather propitious disposition of nature the handiwork of God. A Floridian Tornado is as natural and innocent in her eyes as a bird-song thrilling the hush of dawn.

Nor does Santayana give his faith to acrobatic or logical dexterity in the arena of essences: the cool and moderate *climate* of his philosophy is neither infected with the germs of a presumptuous dialectic or with teleological odours. While admitting with Mr. Whitehead the unlimited comedies and tragedies that *might* be written in essences, the fact that one mammoth drama has been created does not logically necessitate the hypothesis of a God; but, on the contrary, shows to an unbiassed mind the *principle of contingency* in existence. May I quote his own words [from *Soliloquies in England*]:—

> Existence is indeed distinguishable from the platonic essences that are embodied in it precisely by being a conjunction of things mutually irrelevant, a chapter of accidents, a medley improvised here and now for no reason, to the exclusion of the myriad other farces which, *so far as their ideal structure is concerned,* might have been performed just as well. This world is contingency and absurdity incarnate, the oddest of possibilities masquerading momentarily as a fact.

This is a rather amusing contrast for two great thinkers to arrive at! To roam so far afield together, only to snarl over the same bone in the end! The vulgar will chortle at this, and cry to both of them in derision—"quo vadis?" But I dismiss the unmitiated—the unsympathetic as irrelevant. Probably in the end it merely is a *matter of taste* between these thinkers—of *juggling* with the terms God or Nature. So in a rather embarrassing situation like this, let us hark to the wise and practical words of John Dewey:—

> . . . to call existence arbitrary or by any moral name, whether disparaging or honorific, is to patronize nature.

Santayana, in one fundamental respect, is in sympathy with a strong philosophical movement in America known as "Critical Realism." The cardinal tenet of this school is that *certain aspects* in the data of sense-perception are *not necessarily constituents of a common world.* As Mr. Drake, one of its foremost exponents, states:—

> Sensuous qualities are merely a simplification for intent of the unimaginable complexities of existence; they are existence blurred, fused for han-

dling. Thus they are not brand-new creations; there is merely omission or consciousness of multitudinous detail.

And it is precisely this realization of the masks that nature wears in perception that appeals to Santayana from the standpoint of epistemology. But Santayana, as we have seen, is more drastic in his severance of the two realms of existence and essence; for him they are *identical at no point,* while Mr. Drake (and most of the other critical realists) affirms that they often *overlap,* especially in regard to certain spatial configurations given in perception.

Alas! as Mr. Joad has said:—

> The theory . . . is not an easy one to follow, nor is the task of the student made lighter by important differences that lie concealed beneath the statements of their views made by the various essayists.

One thing, however, I believe may be said with assurance. The intrinsic or distinctive texture of essences is not due, for Santayana, to any *cognitive peculiarities* of the perceiver. The ideal items which are given in perception are positive and self-subsistent entities; they acquire a *moral* value when they are bathed in the innocent but saving light of intuition. There are no Kantian prerogatives implicit in Santayana's conception of cognition: *Intuition discloses, but never modifies an essence.*

Of course, such a theory as that delineated by Santayana will immediately be contrasted with the prevailing mode of Realism so ably expounded in this country by men like Bertrand Russell, and in America by Perry and Holt. These thinkers generally assume that the objective world itself is composed of elements similar to those realized in perception, and that the distinction between mental and physical is essentially one of degree—of complexity and arrangement of a common—a *neutral* stuff. As Russell declares:—

> I believe that the realization of the complexity of a material unit, and its analysis, into constituents analogous to sensations, is of the utmost importance to philosophy, and vital for any understanding of the relations between mind and matter, between our perceptions and the world which they perceive.

But for Santayana this is an honorific and absurd compliment paid to essences—you cannot juggle in this fashion with the nonexistent. The trouble arises through a confusion of the realms of matter and essence: there must always be the quivering strings to free the music—the cold and unknown face behind the mask. He does not profess to know what matter *is in itself,* and his humility in addressing nature is admirable and persuasive in these days of metaphysical bravado. If a physical object is to him almost as mysterious as the Kantian Ding an Sich, is it, frankly, any more unsatisfactory than regarding *an object as a fardel of loose sensations somehow strung together by the laws of motion?* I think not.

And we must not forget that so eminent an authority as Lloyd Morgan has also made an absolute bifurcation between his worlds of "inference" and "reference," the former never being directly accessible to "enjoyment."

THE READING OF SPIRIT

The interpretation of intuition, or awareness, given by Santayana is rather unusual in these days, and to me, at least, most beautiful and sacred. He considers the capricious *light* of awareness as nontemporal and discrete in being from the complex of events in the organism that are its basis. The latter he has termed the Psyche, by which we are to understand not electrical particles or events taken in isolation, nor yet a Monad; but "a complex of more minute habits of matter, or a mastering rhythm imposed upon them by the habit of the species" [*Soliloquies in England*]. The last half of this definition would appear to agree with the "organic" view of Nature so beautifully expounded by Whitehead. Compare it with the following sentence of his:—

> . . . an electron within a living body is different
> from an electron outside it, by reason of the plan
> of the body.

But, of course, to Santayana a *plan* merely means a *more or less stable disposition* that matter has fallen into. If people would read him a little more patiently, and dry minds attempt to tolerate the poetry of his words, they would discover that his *natural philosophy* (although dressed in familiar technicalities, which have been resifted by his fertile mind—such as "substance"—"matter"—"Psyche") is not *unaware* of current gestures in physics and biology. If he differs in his opinions, it is because at times he feels he cannot accept the latest and somewhat hurried conclusions of science.

But the point to emphasize in regard to his reading of intuition is the ineffectual character of this faculty, from a *casual* consideration. *The function of spirit is merely to disclose, never to control.* The group of occurrences in the cortex, or (perhaps Santayana would prefer) the complex of habits that compose the organism, are the *indispensable conditions* for its birth, duration and survey. Such a conception may possibly be accused, by some people, of being a "hangover" from the nineteenth-century notion of the mind as analogous to an aureole about the head of a saint, or the faint phosphorescence diffused by decaying bodies. Be that as it may, I believe that his reading of awareness is justified by *experimental* psychology, and that we shall all return to it yet again some unborn day.

Now this understanding of the nature of spirit may seem recondite and superfluous to many minds, especially those bent on absorbing all matter and consciousness into mere sensation. I mean the Neutral Monists. But several factors have combined to convince Santayana of its veracity. Let me attempt to explain them briefly.

An analysis of essences in their own native isolation, and a comprehension of discourse or thinking, reveals the utter necessity of our believing in the *identity* of essences in various frames divorced by time. If we do not grant this initial assumption, *all dialectic is at once paralysed,* for we can affirm nothing with confidence. Memory becomes at once a hollow and most heartrending mockery. This is the first reasonable step out of the darkness of solipsism into the light of faith. And remember, no essence has any peculiar or moral prerogative to be manifested to spirit—

> not shared by every Cinderella-like essence that
> lies eternally neglected in that limbo to which all
> things intrinsically belong—the limbo of un-
> heard melodies and uncreated worlds [*Solilo-
> quies in England*].

A realization of this neutrality of status, together with their identity of texture in different settings and instances, seems to imply, that as long as there actually is a *partiality of survey* in discourse, this partiality must be due to another factor entering the situation—namely: the evanescent moonlight of intuition playing upon the cold and infinite sea of essences. This is the second rational assumption of animal faith, and it is *logically prior* to any belief in matter or physical events.

It appears to me that we must admit the existence of this faculty, if we are honest and unbiassed in our analysis. Mr. Bertrand Russell is the most drastic philosophical barber now shaving among us—I mean he has used Occam's famous razor more savagely and pitilessly than any of his contemporaries. But some of us have tender skins, and object to a very close shave, and when Mr. Russell obliterates all distinction between intuition and the datum, cutting away any "act of thought," and reducing mind entirely to "mnemic phenomena," I for one feel he has ceased to shave whiskers, and is cutting into raw flesh. He states:—

> To say that one occurrence is 'conscious' of an-
> other is, to my mind, to assert an external and
> rather remote relation between them.
>
>   . . . . .
>
> The . . . criticism I have to make is that the *act*
> seems unnecessary and fictitious. The occur-
> rence of the content of a thought constitutes the
> occurrence of the thought. Empirically, I cannot
> discover anything corresponding to the sup-
> posed act; and theoretically I cannot see that it
> is indispensable.

Let me consider the above remarks for a moment. Santayana would agree that *one occurrence is never conscious of another:* the reacting nervous system yields awareness of some *essence* which is *not an occurrence.* The latter is some collateral event in the cortex—the complicated existential *backing* of the essence *not given in detail* to intuition. Now the organism is undoubtedly adjusting itself to some external factor then influencing it, and in so doing the simplified and specious essence is posited or *falsely felt to dress* that factor out there in space. *This is, I am convinced, the only valid analysis of the epistemological situation.* It is simple and comprehensive when correctly understood, and solves at once the ancient and exhausting problem of how simple qualities are related to actual events in the brain, and yet felt to describe objects in *public* regions of space. All we have to remember is the nature of motor adjustments in the organism, and realize candidly that *intuition can never enjoy actual events in the same immediate and fresh way that it possesses an essence.* But to return again to Mr. Russell as exemplifying what I consider to be a false Realistic attitude in this matter. In the second part of the above quotation he speaks of "the occurrence of the content of a thought" as constituting "the occurrence of the thought." This is very bad reasoning. *He would italicize or strain phenomena, as it were, until the poor things shrieked and yielded awareness in their own texture—an absurd impossibility!* Mr. Whitehead has realized the foolishness of trying to knit together a world entirely out of sensations and images, and has admitted the discrete reality of cognition in his last book. What Russell's statement *really* implies is a universal spirit that serves as a medium for—and observes—the occurrence and its relations. This would be a remote and antique smell of transcendentalism. For how could "mnemic phenomena" acquire the sudden and magical *ability* attributed to them by Mr. Russell, merely by being arranged and exercised in certain habitual, nervous structures of reaction? In their *intrinsic character* images are *not* different from sensations—why worship them? Nor does Mr. Strong convince me that a mere "accumulation of (sentient) energy" in the reacting nervous tissues of the cortex can account for *the strange and dissecting light of attention,* which is, as Santayana says—

> A spiritual counterpart of attitude and action.

A second consideration that appears to justify the uniqueness of spirit is the non-temporal character of intuition. I for one feel certain that spirit is not in time, but transcends it. As Professor Warren of Princeton University states:—

> The 'now' of perception is not the same as the physicist's conception of the 'present.' It is not a thin knife-edge separating the past from the future, but a fair-sized interval of time.

> "According to careful experimental investigation the *perceptual present* (sometimes called the 'specious present') is a duration of about six seconds (Titchener). All impressions within this period of time are present to us *at once.* This makes it possible for us to perceive changes and events as well as stationary objects.

To say that spirit may *really* be in time, although in consciousness it *seems* above or *tangential* to it, is merely to put an empirical lie in your own mouth.

I have no patience with those mathematicians who insist on reading their little "point-instants" into the pure nature of intuition. I feel about them as the musical critic of *The Times* seems to feel about the modern "jazz" composers who are revising and distorting the classics of music. I say this with all respect for the indispensable machinery of mathematics; and on the æsthetic side, especially in geometry, I believe I can appreciate the cold and impersonal beauty of its virgin structures. As a modern singer, Miss Millay, has said in regard to the original discoveries of Euclid:—

> Oh, blinding hour—oh, holy terrible day—
> When first the shaft into his vision shone
> Of light anatomized! Euclid alone
> Has looked on Beauty bare; fortunate they
> Who though once only, and then but far away,
> Have heard her massive sandal set on stone.

But to get back to business. We are likely to make the same error in regard to this reality of spirit that so many of the Neo-Realists are committing to-day in their analysis of the simple qualities of perception. I mean when they reduce the sensation of red to a certain measurement—a specific degree of rhythm in the light-waves, they may be *approximately* correct in regard to the actual occurrences: *the confusion and error arises when they attempt to absorb the obvious frugality of detail of the given datum into the infinite complexity of those inferred events.* The distinction between essences and events, I believe, is *ultimate.* They must recognize, if they are sincere to the everyday facts of their own eyes, and not to some ulterior metaphysical yearning, that the existential complexity *behind* any essence is not there as a *conscious phenomenon.* Those minute rhythmic properties ascribed by the physicist to sensations are not to be found in ordinary perception; and I sincerely doubt if the most delicate and penetrating microscope of the future will ever *expose* the naked, ultimate *physical texture* of the universe. I do not presume to know its intrinsic characters, but I *believe firmly* in its existence. Matter will always remain, however, the unquestioned assurance of animal faith, although philosophers may dance around the epistemological May-pole until the crack of doom.

It is precisely in regard to the ancient problem that, to my mind, the Critical Realists have scored to-day. Their analysis has been honest and exhaustive, and they have reported candidly the facts of their own eyes. I do not understand how so able a New Realist as Mr. Holt, for instance, can be guilty of the following remark:—

> A quality may seem as unitary as possible, and may nevertheless *be,* still merely as a conscious phenomenon, complex.

But is it not, *prima facie,* perfectly obvious that *as a given or "enjoyed" datum it is not complex?* How can we evade the blunt facts of our own eyes with such bald untruths? The Critical Realists are not denying that *something does exist* in all cases of perception; they are merely refusing to admit a simplified or incoherent essence as an *actual occurrence* in the natural world. If their epistemological position could only be grasped and allowed, there would be no trouble in explaining such things as bent oars, a false oasis imagined on the desert horizon, reflections in mirrors, and lavender elephants seen in dreams. All these things are simply *essences:* what *exists* is a neutral pattern of events in the brain. In reacting upon an external object these specious essences are *felt* to exist out there in the region of the stimulus. I have spoken in this essay of events in the brain as *sine quibus non* of the waking of given essences. This seems to be the attitude of Drake and Strong, but Santayana is not so sanguine on the point. He realizes our remote understanding of cerebral metabolism, and I imagine he would prefer *to consider the specific locality of the existential support of given essences as undecided.* If we speak of *organic habits in nature* as the basis of essences and spirit, we are more modest and nearer to Santayana in our interpretation.

I would like to ask these energetic New Realists, and all others of kindred disposition in this matter, to stroll quietly out into their several gardens, and gaze candidly at a crimson or yellow tulip glittering in the sunlight; and then think over soberly what I have been led to say and believe about essences by the persuasive discourse of Mr. Santayana, and the honest efforts of the American Critical Realists. Perhaps, also, Critical and New Realists and Neutral Monists alike might suspect once more the reality of the strange light of awareness, that Mr. Santayana has suggested, like Aristotle of yore, into our circle of discussion. I imagine he means by it a sort of *glowing* of kinetic energy in the heat of adaptation. Something of a *spiritual unity or seizure* I am convinced is the key of awareness—although it is difficult to ensnare my meaning in weak words.

THE MORAL OF TRUTH

Santayana's conception of the realm of Truth is a little difficult to grasp at first, but when realized it is a beautiful and majestic masterpiece of interpretation. It has a certain tragic solemnity—a hint of purple robes and low chanting—that to an imaginative person is both compelling and terrible with significance. It is impossible in a paper of this brevity to play with details of exposition (especially if one is a poet and inclined to wander), but I will try and suggest a few of the implications contained in this understanding of Truth.

A recognition of an independent world of existence is, first of all, essential; we must have truth about something, otherwise it is mere war of opinion in the arena of essences. This may be a disagreeable dose for the radical empiricist to swallow, not to mention digest, but it is logically inevitable if we comprehend the helpless nature of essences, and remember the lonely destiny of the radical solipsist.

As spirit can never *dissect* the latent and ultimate composition of matter, but can merely *describe* it in symbols appropriate to human discourse; so truth does not *lasso* existence, but *is simply the ideal settings in the realm of essences that physical events have introduced and painted by their passage in time.* As Santayana says in his matchless language:—

> The truth, however nobly it may loom before the scientific intellect, is ontologically something secondary. Its eternity is but the wake of the ship of time, a furrow which matter must plough upon the face of essence.

Now this ideal reality of Truth—this vast eternal landscape painted in the medium of essences by the hand of Nature—can be either faithfully or falsely *visualized in part* whenever we remember, anticipate or affirm something. As Mr. Russell has said in words charged with solemn beauty—words worthy of a great poet:—

> This is the reason why the Past has such magical power. The beauty of its motionless and silent pictures is like the enchanted purity of late autumn, when the leaves, though one breath would make them fall, still glow against the sky in golden glory. The Past does not change or strive; like Duncan, after life's fitful fever it sleeps well; what was eager and grasping, what was petty and transitory, has faded away, the things that were beautiful and eternal shine out of it like stars in the night. Its beauty, to a soul not worthy of it, is unendurable; but to a soul which has

conquered Fate it *is the key of religion* [my italics].

No opinion can report *all* the Truth, for it is infinitely extended: it has been painted in essences by millions and millions of events since the first restless heave of existence. Santayana called it "the standard comprehensive description of any fact in all its relations." Obviously, no mortal mind could start from a given point and travel and describe that immutable wilderness in its entirety. Whitehead's idea of a "relational essence" belonging to every "eternal object" appears to have been adumbrated in part by Santayana—the unconscious coincidence of their logic is interesting. I have no time in this article to touch upon the disputed question concerning the reality of "internal relations." Let it suffice that such eminent logicians as Russell and Whitehead are in violent opposition on this point.

The moral and æsthetic opulence of this understanding of truth should now begin to dawn upon the reader. What has been can never perish: its *ideal immortality* is recorded for ever. The weird and desperate clutches of existence are baffled and blinded by the radiant immutable face of Truth. The God of Flux bows before this impartial Recorder of events. To a noble and candid soul this interpretation offers a legitimate—a *sufficient* immortality. Any other conception seems mean and selfish in comparison with this Hellenic attitude, which is austere and becoming to a disciplined spirit.

I can now realize with a quiet satisfaction that if I have read Santayana aright—if the wings of my spirit have been allowed by nature to hover lovingly over the true and beautiful and eternal system of essences that is his philosophy—I have *lived* with him in the Kingdom of Heaven.

Yes, we may rest assured that Shelley's lark is warbling for ever in the heaven of essences, and that Socrates is happy arguing there. While the *truly* religious heart may find a deep and authentic peace in realizing that the sanctity of our Lady of Mercies, the sublime words of her Son, and His agony upon Golgotha, are never lost to a sympathetic spirit that is destined to survey those *imperishable* essences. (pp. 349-64)

Daniel MacGhie Cory, "A Study of Santayana with Some Remarks on Critical Realism," in Journal of Philosophical Studies, *Vol. 11, No. 7, July, 1927, pp. 349-64.*

Harold A. Larrabee   (essay date 1931)

[*Larrabee is an American philosopher, translator, educator, and poet. In the following excerpt, he discusses Santayana's philosophy with respect to its "American" characteristics.*]

If George Santayana is to be reckoned an American philosopher (and his inclusion in the recently published volumes of *Contemporary American Philosophy* would point in that direction), then one of our foremost living thinkers has been absent from the country since January 1912. That the author of what has even been called "the only modern book of philosophy worthy of the name" should have passed this tacit judgment upon us, after having spent from his ninth to his forty-ninth year in our midst, is a matter which calls for no ordinary searching of the national spirit. It need not be approached in the manner of a Senate investigating committee delving into some alien scandal, or of a Chamber of Commerce secretary swelling with injured local pride, but it does call for something like an explanation, no matter how humiliating to some of our intellectual super-patriots the results of the accounting may turn out to be.

The task of writing with understanding about the life of the Spanish-born poet who became professor of philosophy at Harvard, only to betake himself to more congenial solitudes and a measure of literary fame in Oxford, Paris, and Rome, is made difficult by his extreme candor about his opinions, combined with an equal reticence about himself. Most of his many literary compositions are, in substance if not in form, soliloquies; and we are privileged (as in the case of few philosophers) to follow in detail the inner debates which have marked his transitions from one insight to the next. But until recently Santayana's personal history has been virtually a closed book, and even the most meagre information concerning the private background of his philosophy has had to be supplied by hearsay and inference. Within the past few months, however, Santayana himself has published among the "personal statements" contained in the two volumes of *Contemporary American Philosophy* a **"Brief History of My Opinions"** [see excerpt dated 1940 for a revised version of this essay], so that we are now in a much better position to judge the comparative extent of the foreign and the American influences upon his thought. While we may respect the modesty which shrinks from the glare of modern publicity, and while we may agree that the facts of a philosopher's life stand apart from the truth or falsity of his conclusions, in the case of one who is also a poet and a critic of our culture, such biographical data can hardly be other than enlightening. If, in presenting them, quotations from his own statements are numerous, it is only because, in the words of Professor T. V. Smith, "Santayana is one of the few philosophers whom no living man may hope to improve by paraphrase." (pp. 209-10)

Is Santayana an American philosopher? [And] if so, in what sense? Plainly he does not consider himself an American "except by long association". But he is hardly a Spanish philosopher, and he has shown no signs of becoming an Englishman. His primal roots are clearly Hispanic, and one judges that the vehicle of his ardent spirit will one day come to rest where he predicted in one of his sonnets in 1894—"For I would lie among the hills of Spain." As late as 1922 he referred to the Spanish as "my countrymen". Yet it is not recorded that he took any active part in the Spanish-American War, which broke out when he was thirty-five and an instructor at Harvard. It would be interesting to learn something of his conflicting emotions during that period. Presumably he escaped the humiliation of internment camps, which had not then been brought to their recent state of perfection. During the World War he lived in England, where his profoundly pro-Ally sentiments found frequent expression.

In America he found himself by dint of circumstance a sort of involuntary guest, and not in any sense an emigrant. "None of us," he says proudly, "ever changed his country, his class, or his religion." Outwardly, that is. But his temporarily-adopted country did bring about certain inward changes in all of these respects. First of all, it gave him a new medium, the English language in a state of reasonable purity, in which he early developed a rich and rhythmical style, studded with aphorisms, ornate with imagery, and subtle in its undulating charm. Born a nineteenth-century Spaniard and educated in what was soon to be twentieth-century America, Santayana belongs among the seventeenth-century English prose masters with all their leisurely magnificence. His verses, too, in which he miraculously achieves a Latin sonority by the use of short English words, are works of genuine literary distinction.

What he has to say, however, is another matter. "It is as if," he playfully assures us, "I had set out to say plausibly in English as many un-English things as possible." The statement needs qualification, for as it stands it misrepresents his almost passionate admiration for England and English manners. His native affections are for the Hellenic and the Catholic, but his second love is for Oxford. What he has said in English are as many un-American things as possible. It is as if, depressed by the cultural emptiness of America, Santayana had set out singlehanded to fill up the gap. America lacked a tradition rich in beauty, tragedy, irony? Very well, he would do his best to supply one. But not in new forms or from indigenous materials. An exiled European, a wanderer through the centuries, strayed perhaps from pre-Socratic Greece, he turned inevitably toward the great traditions of the classic era. There man had achieved harmonies that might at least be imaginatively recoverable in the present, and infinitely to be preferred to the chaos or the vacuum of modernity. Santayana's admiration for many of these things remote in time and space has about it some of the enthusiasm of the expatriate. It is hard to imagine a life-long resident of Europe becoming quite so lyrical about classicism, and for this America must be held responsible.

On the other hand, Santayana is no mere wholesale importer of worn-out European traditions. Still less does he resemble such pathetic figures as Isadora Duncan and George Cram Cook, admirers of an exotic culture in which they had no real roots. If he is wanting in sympathy for the new and the original, it is because his affections are wholly absorbed by what seems to him to be the eternal. A critic with standards derived from sources more remote in time than in space, he is intent upon judging the present by the past rather than upon transplanting the latter into the former. His philosophy is nothing if not mature, it is a *sagesse* born of centuries of experience; its skepticism is wholly European, in the gentlemanly tradition of Descartes and Hume.

But at least one trait of his personality as a thinker is thoroughly American, the fruit of association with such men as William James. That is his almost pragmatic confidence in his own commonsense investigations of the universe, unshaken by all the terrifying discoveries of the epistemologists. Of the latter he is fully aware, and has even entered into some of their debates himself. But when he comes to philosophize, he does so with a disregard for Teutonic cautions that is hardly surpassed by John Dewey himself. Socrates had no greater faith in his own reason than that set forth in the declaration that "to decipher the Life of Reason nothing is needed but an analytic spirit and a judicious love of man, a love quick to distinguish success from failure in his great and confused experiment of living". Thus to brush aside shelves of modern philosophy, and to evaluate all the realms of being, as it were right out of one's head, displays a daring that is Greek or Elizabethan or American, certainly not modern European.

There is another characteristic which Santayana has gracefully imbibed in some measure while here, and that is good humor or praised in Americans, and which one would like to think that be goodwill. Called by some "an incorrigible mocker", his irony is unfailingly genial, even when his distaste for the subject in hand can hardly be concealed. He has shown that one can be "detached from the world without being hostile to it", and while his goodwill is anything but promiscuous, he has a hospitable way of dealing with whatever experience turns up. "The American," he once wrote, "is always kindly"; and on this score, if his compliment is deserved, he is one of us.

It is futile to try to imagine what Santayana might have become in Spain or in France or in England. Certainly America, while it forced him temporarily to become a professor of philosophy, and drove him back imaginatively upon his racial traditions, cannot be indicted as the one country inhospitable to such rare spirits. Not alone against Americans are barbed the stinging lines of his ode:

> My heart rebels against my generation,
> That talks of freedom and is slave to riches,
> And, toiling 'neath each day's ignoble burden,
>   Boasts of the morrow.
> No space for noonday rest or midnight watches,
> No purest joy of breathing under heaven!
> Wretched themselves, they heap, to make them
>   happy,
>   Many possessions.

The philosopher, like the artist, has been made to feel completely at home in no country under heaven. He may speak with the voice of one land or another, but as he strives, as he must, after universal insight, he becomes both cosmopolitan and *depaysé*, a stranger everywhere, and yet instantly at home among his peers. Land of feverish enterprise and compulsory gregariousness, America accentuated Santayana's cosmic aloofness, loneliness, and rebellion. Tragically it failed to enlist him in the immediate task of building the new culture that is some day to fill our aching void. If it cannot justly be said that in Santayana America produced a modern philosopher of the first magnitude, at least we have entertained one not wholly unawares. (pp. 218-21)

As a systematic thinker, his first task is to clear the ground by a sceptical inquiry that outdoubts Descartes, for it suspends all "the conventional categories as well as the conventional beliefs" of man. It culminates in the denial of the *existence* of everything: "nothing given exists". This most

devastating of all doubts comes to rest with the stripping of a given image "of all adventitious significance, when it is taken neither for the manifestation of a substance nor for an idea nor for an event in the world, but simply if a colour for that colour and if music for that music, and if a face for that face". When it becomes, in other words, the bare intuition of an essence.

Total scepticism, Anatole France assures us, implies absolute silence. If we were disembodied spirits, we might be privileged to believe nothing and to live immersed in this unassertive intuition of essences. But it seems plain to Santayana that "the spirit that actually breathes in man is an animal spirit", subject to rude shocks from the encircling ring of material events called nature. Animals cannot be complete sceptics; "the hungry dog *must* believe that the bone before him is a substance, not an essence". The human ego confronting brute facts is likewise compelled by the exigencies of action to take its intuitions of essences as signs for the surrounding environment. This belief, "in its very soul," says Santayana, "is belief about nature; it is animal faith." The potential doubter of everything finds himself driven to the assumption, swiftly verified in practice, of a realm of matter, including his physical body, which inexorably conditions all his activities. Santayana thus stands almost alone among his contemporaries (he boldly describes himself as "a materialist—apparently the only one living") in refusing to belittle the "commonsense reality of our animal being" and its setting in a physical world. Undismayed by all the analyses of abstractionist physics and psychology, he undertakes to find out what he actually believes about the world "in his active moments, as a living animal, when he is really believing something" and not just reading books. "A philosopher," he says, "cannot wish to be deceived . . . I stand in philosophy exactly where I stand in daily life; I should not be honest otherwise."

This is Santayana's basic materialism, wrenched from his initial ultra-scepticism by natural compulsions to animal faith. But while we are forced to posit material substance, we do not know what it is. From the essences, "the infinite multitude of distinguishable ideal terms" presented to our powers of intuition and imagination, we may fashion pictures of it: myths, theologies, or scientific theories. But all data are symbolic. Knowing is a form of imagination; both science and religion are metaphorical. Nature has made us all poets unexpectedly. Our knowledge of existences "has no need, no propensity, and no fitness to be literal". Some of our symbols serve well the purposes of action for survival, and all that science can tell us is, for such purposes, and for the ensuing liberation of life on its higher levels, none too much. But behind the "dark engine of nature" is that Sphinx who, as Robert Bridges wisely remarks, "lurks in all systems" whether or not her presence is acknowledged; and we shall gain nothing by insisting upon intimacy with her. Such an ultimate agnosticism need not prevent our recognizing many of the characteristics and "habits" of this believed-in stuff of the world. Matter, to Santayana, is for instance far from dead, it is fecund and dynamic. Witness his graphic picture of its irrational whirl of changing essences: "Matter is the invisible wind which, sweeping for no reason over the field of essences, raises some of them into a cloud of dust; and that whirlwind we call existence."

Now it has often been pointed out that while Santayana is thus a firm and unappalled believer in matter, he is temperamentally no lover of it. Forced as he believes by honesty in the face of experience to accept a material version of the universe as fundamental for human life, he takes no particular delight in it, save as a spectacle, and certainly he has no wish to exalt its importance by devoting himself to manipulating physical things. "I myself have no passionate attachment to existence," he confesses, "and value this world for the intuitions it can suggest, rather than for the wilderness of facts that compose it." It is almost as if he hastens to embrace matter in order the more speedily to be rid of it. Philosophical idealists, he never tires of reminding us, have imagined that to admit the real existence of matter would be to deal a fatal blow to the cosmic standing of ideal values. They have stoutly denied the existence of dunghills, lest such an admission impugn the loveliness of roses. By so doing they have only succeeded in detaching ideals from their natural bases, in making ends visionary and action vain. Santayana will demonstrate their folly: we do exist in a material world, dung-hills originally underlie all life's roses; but it may turn out that only the roses possess importance.

For, once we have accepted the mysterious but to-be-believed-in physical world, we are then free to use it as the vehicle of the Life of Reason, or even of the Spiritual Life. These alternative modes of living are what Santayana is really interested in,—everything else in his philosophy is by way of prologue. The Life of Reason—"that part of experience which perceives and pursues ideals—all conduct so controlled and all sense so interpreted as to perfect natural happiness"—is the earlier conception, elaborated in the five volumes bearing that title. Out of a half-hostile, half-friendly material universe there arise, their author tells us, vital processes and ideal interests. Reason at last makes clear the possibility of an unification of our impulses in the light of ideal considerations,—"a harmony of material functions spiritually realized". The Life of Reason is a life of discipline and self-control, but not of abstinence. It is that "large, rich, and various life" of which President Eliot used to speak, a full life, in which nothing natural is either denied an opportunity to demonstrate its ideal possibilities, or valued until it does so. The best hints concerning the final good that life affords are to be found in art. Nature teaches man by beauty, by what Bridges calls "the irresistible predominant attraction" which is the prime mover of all human excellence. Here the voice of the poet and the philosopher are one; and well may Professor George Herbert Palmer declare of his former colleague, Santayana, that "æsthetics was his centre", paraphrasing Tennyson's Prologue to "The Palace of Art" in order to describe him thus:

> A glorious being both in heart and brain,
> That did love Beauty only (Beauty seen
> In all varieties of mold and mind),
> And Knowledge for its beauty; or if Good,
> Good only for its beauty.

This is no narrow æstheticism, it is art in its widest sense,

art in the whole range of living, in civilizing the natural "wilderness of facts" wherever that is possible.

But while the ideal ends are, as it were, latent in all natural process, they must never, according to Santayana, be mistaken for efficient causes. They are envisaged goals, broad vistas of the "inward landscape" of the imagination, which in no sense act as forces in their own realization. That they have been churned up here and there in the vast flux of existence is in itself no pledge of their cosmic importance. To insist upon the literal hypostatizing of ideals, to make dogmas out of myths, instead of treating them in their true poetic character, has been the inveterate vice of religions (and lately of sciences as well), and the most prolific source of the world's supply of superstitions. Religion has not erred in cultivating poetry, its mistake has been in demanding faith in its splendid legends as literal records of fact; whence all the follies of supernaturalism with its "fabulous projections of human morality" into the cosmos at large. It has also been falsely supposed that in the absence of such guarantees that "the cosmic dice are loaded", men would promptly cease to be virtuous. But reason in the natural man is fully capable of attaining the perfection appropriate to his native possibilities without the support of any such metaphysical fanaticism.

The Spiritual Life, as we find it portrayed in Santayana's reply to Dean Inge [*Platonism and the Spiritual Life* (1927)], is on another level entirely. It is not, like the Life of Reason, "a worship of values . . . it is the exact opposite; it is *disintoxication* from their influence". It is sheer intuition of the timeless essences, an Aristotelian divine contemplation, utterly detached from preoccupation with existence. Some human beings have achieved it, and have found a peace that the world of striving is powerless to give. But Santayana himself more or less reluctantly confesses his preference for the Life of Reason: "As for me, I frankly cleave to the Greeks and not to the Indians, and I aspire to be a rational animal rather than a pure spirit."

The several Realms of Being distinguished by Santayana in his matured philosophy may thus be assigned to three levels. There is first of all the "natural basis", the animal level of material existence, the realms of matter and of pragmatic truth, to whose inexorable conditions commonsense and science may enable us to adjust our bodily necessities. This level, the spring and scene of all our living, is entitled to our respect, as rational beings, only because of what patterns of essences it may happen to display, and what ideals it may generate and nourish. At the opposite pole lies the spiritual level, the realm of essence in all its infinite purity and profusion. Few mortals attain this Nirvana where shine the timeless Platonic forms in all their radiant nonexistence, for such disinterested contemplation is only to be achieved by the severest self-discipline.

Man finds himself situated, then, between a too-low level to which his body is chained by mortal destiny, but from which he must endeavor to rise if he is to hope for anything like happiness; and a too-high level to which he owes respect, perhaps envy, but not, apparently, allegiance. The good life for him cannot be wholly composed either of terrestrial travail or of celestial contemplation. He must seek a middle way, on what might be called the rational level, material in its conditions and spiritual in its guiding ideals. There the aspirant to the Life of Reason may construct his home, refusing to immerse himself wholly in the daily round of physical concerns, or in the mystical envisaging of the essences. By an appropriation of the traditions of the past and their transformation into a living culture, he may hope to rear a habitation for his spirit. Neither the past alone nor the present alone is enough to give a significant pattern to life. The Life of Reason is both a heritage and a promise.

With these philosophical premises in mind, one is perhaps in a better position to understand some of the counts in Santayana's indictment in **Character and Opinion in the United States** (1920) and to ascertain his position relative to the late New Humanist controversy with the aid of his most recent book **The Genteel Tradition at Bay** (1931). In the former volume, the author gives but little space to the conventional European laments about American nosiness and vulgarity. Instead the keynote sounded is: "Consider now the great emptiness of America . . . where no one, almost, lives where he was born or believes what he has been taught." Not that we are not filled with good will and good works. All, indeed, is activity and love of achievement; but all is also stark and pragmatic and deficient in grace. What ails America is (as we have heard before) the lack of a liberal cultural tradition.

Now polite, intellectual, "feminine" America, which "carried its household gods from Puritan England in a spirit of consecration", as contrasted with the crude, vital, "masculine" America, which either grew up in the wilderness or emigrated with scant cultural baggage, has had a tradition of a sort. But today it is worthy only of that shabby adjective "genteel". Doubly rooted in the agonized conscience and earnest doing-good-to-others of the decadent Puritans on the one hand, and in the aërial subjectivism and self-trusting romanticism of the Transcendentalists on the other, the genteel tradition has been kept alive only by a blithe academic disregard for most of the facts of American life. Small wonder that, cut off by the drying up of its sources, it has lacked fresh sap; that most American thought, until recently, has seemed like one long baccalaureate sermon, utterly irrelevant to the world outside the chapel door.

But if this be the moribund genteel tradition, how can it possibly be "at bay"? In his new book Santayana recognizes the unexpected character of recent developments: "Twenty years ago the genteel tradition seemed ready to melt gracefully into the active mind of the country"; but now, a turned worm, it is "darting murderous glances at its enemies", and "instead of expiring of fatigue, or evaporating into a faint odour of learning and sentiment hanging about Big Business", it seems to be courting "a death more noble and glorious than some of us had looked for". It proposes, that is, to perish at the literary barricades under the banner of humanism. But Santayana is too well aware of the marked contrast between all this and the humanism of the Renaissance to allow himself to be deceived. "The discontent of the American humanists would be unintelligible if they were humanists in the old sense." The latter appear to us today as paganizers of the Left,

smilingly hospitable to all cultures, who would find it hard to be dissatisfied even with such tawdry ingredients of happiness as our modern times supply. Whereas if the New Humanist program of fixed standards means anything, it calls for "nothing less than to brush away the four R's [identified by the critic as "Renaissance, Reformation, Revolution, and Romanticism"] from the education and sentiment of the modern world, and to reinstate a settled belief in a supernatural human soul and in a precise divine revelation". Professors More and Babbitt, being moral absolutists, are theocrats at heart, and, when they come to understand their own position, will join Newman or Mr. T. S. Eliot. For supernaturalists who are intransigeant and unabashed, Santayana has great respect, but hardly for those of our contemporaries who invoke supernatural sanctions in order to justify little more than a cautious but universal allegiance to the pensive culture of Matthew Arnold. "Can it be," he sardonically inquires, "that all Latins and Slavs, all Arabs, Chinamen, and Indians, if they were not benighted in mind and degenerate in body, would be model Anglo-Americans?"

If, on the other hand, we "discount as fabulous" all such standards of human morality projected into the supernatural, "need we thereby relapse into moral anarchy?" To this crucial question Santayana's answer has already been seen to be an emphatic negative. The alternative to a dictated absolutism is not chaos, as authoritarians would always have us believe, but an internally ordered relativism. Frankly to admit the charge of paganism, as Professor Guérard has recently reminded us, need not bring down the heavens upon our heads, or throw society into anarchy. Human values can be supported without being read into and then out of the universe. The latter can "sanction in man the virtues proper to man without needing to imitate them on its own immeasurable scale". Morality has a simple natural ground in the limited elasticities of the human organism. Virtue, as Socrates taught, is "self-knowledge taken to heart and applied prudently". Reason can produce a harmony of the passions, in which the latter come to move "with mutual deference and a total grace". Such integration yields a moral integrity far more genuine than that which issues from arbitrary and drastic suppressions. Neither the elements of the harmony nor the degree of their unison can be prescribed in advance. Perfection is multiform; and it is not compulsory. The reason can simply reveal to the imperfect man the perfection possible in his particular case. It may check, but only in order to liberate,—"that all currents, mingling in that moment's pause, may take a united course".

A position which has such abundant commerce with ideals, discipline, and tradition, and yet which eschews the supernatural and immaterialism and all the other conventional props for spirituality, is bound to draw the fire of the orthodox. To hold that such a grubby creature, as the naturalist is supposed to be, may nevertheless be capable of the highest spiritual insights accessible to the certified supernaturalist, is doubly maddening to the latter, since it renders his elaborately constructed stage-illusions superfluous. There must, it seems to him, be cheating somewhere. Unbelievers really have no right even to use the language of ideals, since in their mouths strong words standing for immense commitments in the way of belief seem to the faithful to become tenuous, ambiguous, and even evasive. But shall no man be permitted to love poetry without staunchly believing that it is more than poetry? Professor Paul Shorey in a letter to *The Saturday Review of Literature* complains of Santayana that "he wishes to eat the cake of idealism and have it too". Why anyone should deplore such an ambition, or should apparently be apprehensive lest someone should demonstrate that the finest fruits of the spirit can be cultivated in the soil of earth instead of being let down from the open heavens, is difficult to understand. Can it be a case of attempting to maintain a vested monopoly in things spiritual? At any rate the resentment remains, and seems to take form of suspicions that so unearnest and yet so seemingly adequate an æsthetic discipline must have hidden somewhere in its depths a secret longing for voluptuous indulgence. Being themselves tense in their moral convictions, the absolutists denounce those who refuse to be tense (even in opposition) as necessarily frivolous, without stopping to consider the possibility that the latter's grip on reality may be far more profound than their own. After all, to hold anything, one does not have to scowl and clench. One thinks of Chekhov's advice to a friend: "Don't look at life so much as a problem—it is, most likely, far simpler". In any case the failure to announce one's intentions of doing good by an out-thrust jaw is hardly conclusive proof that one is devoid of such carefree virtues as fearlessness, honesty, generosity, serenity, and a devout attachment to "what is eternal", any one of which may be quite as important as super-seriousness.

But in America? Who has any use for such an attitude of spectatorial aloofness and "natural piety" in what is conceded to be the land of evangelical enthusiasm, incurable optimism, social meddling, and indiscriminate enterprise *par excellence?* Americans are notoriously uninterested in detachment until they are forcibly detached from active life by some disablement that is automatically regarded as a catastrophe. Most of the furious actors in our national pageant will go right on overacting their parts, little or great, as the case may be, with scant regard for the charms of the Life of Reason, let alone those of the Spiritual Life. But among those few whose capacity and inclination to be thoughtful make their attitudes worth considering, the case may be different.

Among such intellectuals we find an uncertainty so universal that it has even given rise to a cult, the cult of chaos. The old absolutisms are plainly done for, but the new relativism has not yet taken shape, even in outline. In any such period of confusion there are always those who tell us that the disorder is merely in ourselves, and that we foolishly attribute it to the universe at large. Almost invariably they add that the remedy is a return to some previous order, now obsolete, which logical minds have more or less successfully imposed upon the cosmos at an earlier epoch. One recalls the angry advice of the Theocrats a century or more ago, with their proposals to liquidate the anarchical aftermath of the French Revolution by a return to Rome. Although it is true, as Henri de Saint-Simon observed, that "mankind was not meant to live among ruins", it is also true that efforts to reconstruct past ages

are a sorry waste of time. The command is forward, not simply to a new order that shall resemble the old, but perhaps to an entirely new type of order, yet to be imagined, invented, and believed in. If our cultural problem were simply that of groping about for a new absolutism to restore the old sense of unity of life (provided the Middle Ages ever had such a sense, which Mr. Spingarn doubts) then we might hope for a relatively speedy solution. But to change the entire nature of our demands upon thought, to learn to rest intellectually upon relativism, symbols, hypotheses, statistical trends, to ask new questions and not to expect answers to a lot of old ones—these things are infinitely more difficult.

If this approximates a fair portrayal of our predicament, have we anything to learn from the teachings of Santayana? That he has keenly diagnosed our deficiencies, has done much to make us aware of them, and has shown that we must not forget tradition in attempting to remedy them,—these contributions are obvious. It might also be claimed that he has demonstrated in his own person and works how a freedom rich in values may be achieved, even in the cities of the modern world. But he has not done so in America since 1912, nor has he ever written in an idiom characteristic of American life. As Mr. Lewis Mumford has aptly expressed it in a medical metaphor: "Though he could easily rise above it, he had not temperamentally sufficient experience of the disease to produce, from his own physiological reaction, the necessary anti-body that should combat it. He had . . . a high degree of immunity in his own right; but only one who had succumbed in some degree himself could produce an immunizing culture against it." To flee to Europe and (in most instances) to become merely one more Latin Quarter American may seem the sole way out for certain sensitive spirits, but it is a remedy only in individual cases, and hardly likely to touch the national epidemic itself. Santayana, of course, may be right in holding that there are, after all, only individual cases; but to persons accustomed to thinking in terms of cultures and institutions his philosophy will always seem weakest on its social side.

There is also a certain danger that his counsel of aloofness in the midst of so much barbarism and unreason will be embraced exclusively by the faint-hearted, as a convenient rationalization of their own impotence. The modern individual finds himself facing a world not only as motley as that described in Santayana's puzzled exclamations:— "What strange religions, what ferocious moralities, what slavish fashions, what sham interests!"—but also one that is dominated by vast social forces which seem utterly beyond his power to change or control. Influencing his fellows has become one of the major mass-industries, crowded with special-pleaders masquerading as honest men. If he is to take his part in the struggle-to-be-civilized, must he make what Mr. Mumford calls "the pragmatic acquiescence", and then strive to keep from becoming a barbarian himself? Suppose he refuses to acquiesce, what then? Must his withdrawal be interpreted as defeatism pure and simple? It depends somewhat on whether the Ivory Tower is regarded as an observation post or as a place of refuge for the easily discouraged. To the man in the thick of some perhaps-quite-meaningless fight, the detached spectator will always seem the "otiose observer" of John Dewey's phrase, and consequently somewhat cowardly and base. Yet without the glories which have flowered from years of just such apparently idle contemplation, human society would be a poor thing indeed. To locate the point where individual fastidiousness passes over into anti-social snobbery is not as easy as it looks. Surely a nation as thoroughly committed as ours to the strenuous life need hardly be alarmed by the inroads of pensive idleness, especially at a time when it has more "compulsory leisure" on its hands than it yet knows how to use.

If America is to become the New World in something more than name only, there must be a long and laborious process of cultural inter-fusion preceding rapid growth, in which many minds will have to participate by actual coöperation in social experiment as well as by isolated reflection. The immediate results, like a day-old child, may be far from prepossessing. It would be an injustice to Santayana to give the impression that he does not realize this. On the first page of his latest book stands the express statement: "But the gestation of a native culture is necessarily long, and the new birth may seem ugly to an eye accustomed to some other form of excellence." Himself a sort of belated descendant of Democritus, the laughing philosopher of the Greeks, he is often accused of bearing a grudge against the present age for having been born in it. He assures us that such is not the case, but he leaves us in doubt about his willingness to share its travails. "For my part, though a lover of antiquity, I should certainly congratulate myself on living among the moderns, if the moderns were only modern enough, and dared to face nature with an unprejudiced mind and a clear purpose. What if the prospect, when the spirit explores it, seems rather a quagmire, as it were the Marshes of Glynn, rich only in weak reeds and rank grasses? Has not the spirit always loved the wilderness?" These are words of consolation, not of encouragement. But what if the American quagmire could be made into a garden? Might not the spirit love that even more? And in that case, are we merely wilful in demanding something more than Socratic criticism, Platonic wisdom, and Olympian consolation from George Santayana? (pp. 327-39)

> *Harold A. Larrabee, "George Santayana: American Philosopher?" and "George Santayana: Philosopher for America?" in The Sewanee Review, Vol. XXXIX, Nos. 2 and 3, April-June and July-September, 1931, pp. 209-21; 325-39.*

Albert Guérard, Jr. (essay date 1936)

[*Guérard is an American novelist and critic whose writing reflects his preference for novels that, "like (Joseph) Conrad's, (combine) free imagining with tight rhetorical control of the reader." In the following review of* The Last Puritan, *he favorably compares Santayana's novelistic skills to those of Henry James and Thomas Mann.*]

George Santayana has not visited this country in a quarter of a century, yet *The Last Puritan* falls distinctly into the one essential and characterizing tradition of American literature. It is the analysis of a moral problem, and this

problem is viewed in the light of the same involuntary asceticism which sent Arthur Dimmesdale to his death, brought Lambert Strether back to Woollett, and blighted the lives of Mattie Silver and Ethan Frome. In this harsh, clear light, the ennobling effect of frustration and suffering is considered, and, whether or not the author so desired, ably defended. The Puritanism of Oliver Alden is older than the New England colonies, yet it has found its most profound expression in the works of Hawthorne, James, Edith Wharton, and, with this extraordinary novel, in George Santayana.

For the Puritanism of this "last Puritan," Oliver Alden, stems only partly from New England; it is, essentially, an innate asceticism which recurs in any age, irrespective of external freedom or discipline. The term "Puritanism" has many connotations, and two of these, at least, must be distinguished. There is, first, the traditional Puritanism of New England: right and wrong must never be confused, and morality, perforce an ascetic morality, is strictly codified and universally understood. There is, as well, a second type of Puritanism: a psychological, rather than a cultural, Puritanism. It too leads to the life of discipline, but it is, as in Oliver Alden, something innate and instinctive. It is as much at home in ancient Greece as in Colonial New England. Irving Babbitt has provided the most careful analysis of this unconscious asceticism, and has conveniently identified its psychological root in man as the *frein vital*. *The Last Puritan,* as much as *The Ambassadors,* is a dramatic textbook for this psychological thesis, and as such it assumes an immediate and permanent importance.

Dramatic? Yes, though Santayana is concerned with "poetic truth," not literal truth; though his characters bear only slight relation to the inarticulate human beings with whom we are acquainted. The dramatic character of *The Last Puritan* is of a more intense kind than that, for instance, of *Anthony Adverse*: it vivifies intellectual abstractions, and echoes the clash of ideas, not the blunt clash of "dusty, damn'd experience." It objectifies a series of moral and intellectual crises which, taken as a whole, summarize both a particular culture and an eternal psychological phenomenon. Thus it is a study of both the types of Puritanism which I have mentioned: in the tragedy of Oliver Alden, the two types combine to effect his destruction.

This destruction, Oliver's unfitness for life, is closely related to the history of New England Puritanism. Nathaniel Alden, Oliver's half-uncle, is definitely the product of a certain man-imposed moral climate: his is conventional self-righteous Puritanism; he is cold and miserly, and he accepts the ascetic discipline without question. His greatest pleasure is derived from the infliction of deserved punishment upon his moral inferiors. What he would have been, born in a different country or a different age, is problematical. He is, nevertheless, the product of a definite culture, and his tragedy is simply the tragedy of that blighted culture. Peter Alden, Oliver's father, is temperamentally a naturalist, but he is forced to observe the hated traditions in which his half-brother delighted. He is the fool of a Puritan fate, and he passes through life and suicide in a dreamy and futile effort to escape. The circumstances of Oliver's boyhood are less severe; yet he misses his chance, for his own innate asceticism, added to the formal remnants of his half-uncle's Puritanism, prevent him from satisfying his nostalgia for a fuller, more normal life. The nostalgia itself is the key to the tragedy, for it creates an unnecessary emotional struggle which determines his early death. Throughout his brief, tortured life he strives to be himself, only rarely realizing that this *self* is the self of his childhood.

What are Santayana's implicit conclusions concerning this innate asceticism? Is the *frein vital* a better master than the easy impulsiveness of Jim and Mario? If *The Last Puritan* is a defense of the animalism of Jim, or the hedonism of Mario, as the Prologue might imply, it is a half-hearted defense indeed. The reader is forced, in making a decision, to refer to Santayana's later philosophical writings, and there we find a kind of elevated naturalism, in which the highest kind of satisfaction, the most real kind of action, is to be found in contemplation; in the removal to a higher reality of "essences" and intuitions. Oliver, like his father, is defeated, yet he achieves an emotional experience, through that defeat, quite beyond the grasp of Jim or Mario. He is the spectator of his own tragedy, and by his awareness achieves, in fleeting moments, certain intuitions which his more "happy" friends could never enjoy. The tragedy is not that he failed in "life," but that he did not realize this failure to be unimportant.

Both Santayana and Henry James appear to have suffered from the doubts which seduced Oliver. On the title page of *The Last Puritan* is a quotation from Alain: "On dit bien que l'expérience parle par la bouche des hommes d'âge: mais la meilleure expérience qu'ils puissent noous apporter est celle de leur jeunesse sauvée" ["One could well say that experience speaks through the mouths of men of age: but the best experience they can bring us is that of their salvaged youth"]. Could there be a closer restatement of the yearning of Lambert Strether in *The Ambassadors*? There are further affinities with Henry James. Both Santayana and James achieve intricate analyses by means of central characters who are detached observers of life; both are interested in the "special case"; both conceive of fiction as a fine art, and proceed with infinite care for detail. Santayana, like James, seems to feel a distaste for physical love, and elevates the loves of his leading actors to a hopelessly ideal sphere. Neither James nor Santayana, then, present living characters (in the sense that the characters of Sinclair Lewis are distastefully alive), yet both achieve a higher reality by using their philosophizing puppets as symbols of basic forces in human character. The greatest affinity, of course, lies in the innate asceticism obviously common to both: Santayana and James, like Oliver, have tried to escape, not from Puritanism in the usual sense, but from the *frein vital,* and the spiritual isolation which it bred. In the end Santayana wholly, and James in part, realized the value of this isolation. It was an isolation which enabled them to produce moral commentaries of enduring value. It determined their stature as American novelists of the very first rank.

I speak of Santayana as a novelist, and as a novelist of the very first rank. And why not? Reading *The Last Puritan* is not an intellectual task, to be undertaken for much bene-

fit and little pleasure. It is profound tragedy, attaining, in scattered pages, effects as fine as any to be found in American fiction. And the characters *are* real, though they all speak, like Imlac, with the golden lucidity of their creator. From the rather unimportant consideration of truth to life alone, are there "types" more real than the sentimental Irma, who is always seeking "deeper" emotional experiences, or than Peter's mother, the butt of an irony which falls on nearly all the women in the book? This irony, grave and urbane, recalls Thomas Mann even more than Henry James. Is not Irma another Toni Buddenbrook; Peter, another Christian? Does not Oliver himself recall little Hanno, the last male Buddenbrook, who is early destroyed by the inward fire of his emotional struggles?

It is unnecessary to speak at length of the technical excellence of *The Last Puritan.* There are, in this too short novel of six hundred pages, the skillful metaphors, the trenchant epigrams, and the graceful, liquid prose which have long since established its author as the greatest living stylist in the language. (pp. 278-82)

> *Albert Guérard, Jr., "The Pattern of Puritanism," in* The Virginia Quarterly Review, *Vol. 12, No. 2, Spring, 1936, pp. 278-82.*

John Crowe Ransom   (essay date 1937)

[*An American critic, poet, and editor, Ransom is considered one of the most influential literary theorists of the twentieth century. He is best known as a prominent spokesperson for the Fugitive, Agrarian, and New Criticism movements in American literature. A pioneering New Critic, Ransom had many peers and successors in the movement, notably Robert Penn Warren, Allen Tate, R. P. Blackmur, and Cleanth Brooks, who applied the criteria of New Criticism to prose literature as well as poetry. Although the various New Critics did not subscribe to a single set of principles, all believed that a work of literature had to be examined as an object in itself through a process of close analysis of symbol, image, and metaphor. For the New Critics, a literary work was not a manifestation of ethics, sociology, or psychology, and could not be evaluated in the general terms of any nonliterary discipline. In* The New Criticism, *Ransom outlined a system of critical thought that dominated the American academic scene for nearly three decades. In the following essay, first published in 1937, Ransom discusses Santayana's changing conception of art.*]

Among philosophical personalities the most urbane and humanistic since Socrates may well be Mr. Santayana. I imagine he is what Emerson might have been if Emerson had had a philosophical instead of a theological background; in other words, if his Harvard had been the Harvard of today or yesterday. As an Emerson disturbs the theologians, a Santayana disturbs the philosophers—an admirable function. Each speaks luminously, and that dismays his professional colleagues and drives them to speak primly; and each pours out an incessant gnomic wisdom, so that the colleagues look a little innocent or empty. The likeness goes further: each possesses the technical accomplishment of verse. But here the report is not so favorable. Emerson was too much the theologian to be quite released by poetry, and Mr. Santayana is imprisoned with all his graces in the net of his intellectualism. They do not command the freedom of poets.

And here the parallel stops, for Emerson did not undertake to compete with Hawthorne in another art, but Mr. Santayana has written a big novel, at the moment when his wisdom is ripest. Unfortunately the wisdom, the great shining blocks of it, is a little adventitious for the special purpose of fiction, which on its side happened at the same moment to have reached a stage of enormously subtle proficiency. *The Last Puritan* has distinguished merits, but this is not the novel which will cause the author's secular competitors to cancel their projects and rush off to Academies and Stoas in order to acquire technical philosophy before they write again. It is still they who determine for us what fiction is to be. The flexibility of Mr. Santayana's mind, which is extreme when judged by the standards of philosophical writing, is hardly sufficient for verse and fiction. The philosopher consumes the artist; a very old story. And just as his practice does not quite indicate an understanding of the art-work, neither, I think, does his published theory.

The published theory is scarcely to be found in any one locus, for Mr. Santayana's writings are lavish and various. A good single volume for a quick look at the later and

Title page of Santayana's first poetry collection.

characteristic doctrines is the choice collection of essays, *Obiter Scripta*—an indispensable book for all amateur or general readers with the slightest pretension to knowledge. But I think we had better go farther back, to the time when the characteristic doctrines were not yet established, in order to see how and why the Santayana æsthetic had to take its form. As a Harvard professor Mr. Santayana admired Greek philosophers and abhorred German idealists. If one should offer the opinion that the five volumes published in 1905 under the general title, *The Life of Reason,* are excellent, without effecting much displacement in the existing body of theory, it would be a misinformation unless one added: But they have an extraordinary literary finish, and the vitality of a discourse that is fertilized by metaphor.

We come to Volume IV of this series, *Reason in Art*; and what is the view taken of the meaning of the arts? It is quite commonplace: they are actions which are useful and expressive at the same time. These two requirements are commented on and illustrated, and we are given to understand that they govern both industrial art, which must not be merely useful, and fine art, which must not be merely expressive. Many a pretty application of this formula can be made by a literary philosopher.

But expressiveness and utility: if the phrase sounds determinate to the uncritical, nevertheless it must be one of the best examples of the worst tradition of philosophical rigmarole. The currency of formulations like it is a disgrace to philosophy, and in particular has doomed æsthetic to remain its most undeveloped branch. This can be said without especially disparaging Mr. Santayana, who has long since thrown the foolish formula away.

Utility may stand, for at least it says something. The utility of a work is objective, and measurable in terms of the satisfactions which man as a biological species exacts of a resistant environment. Economics has appropriated this term perhaps, but the goods with which economics deals are no other than those perfectly arbitrary ones defined by the peculiar human organism. Utility will even stand, I think, with Mr. Santayana's qualifications, as one of the requirements of fine art. We are in the habit of saying that a piece of art must be important, or must have an interest, but the import and the interest are biological too. Mr. Santayana has conceded that it need not be a direct or possessive interest; Kant enforced this point, and we repeat it when we say that the interest is felt in an imaginary rather than an actual situation. The fine arts are all symbolic, and rest on a conscious fiction, or illusion; it is the illusion of reality; "true to life" as we say, or "a preparation for living" as Mr. Santayana says. Schopenhauer showed that even music must symbolize life, and otherwise could not move us as it does; Mr. Santayana shows it too, and is more explicit than Schopenhauer.

Expressiveness, on the contrary, is a term exquisitely calculated to conceal thought, if there is really thinking on these premises; or, what is more likely, to evade thought. Of what is art expressive? Mr. Santayana is thoroughly uncomfortable with the term, and in using it seems as often as not to be a species of demonologist, and to think that art expresses certain impish, irrational, and unproductive impulses, too trifling for him to track down and name, not ruled by common sense nor aiming at the worth-while biological values, insisting democratically on their right to expression, and humored without doing much harm in anomalous exercises called works of art. It is as if he said, Art is a kind of scientific performance enacted with a great deal of foolishness; but, not telling us what foolishness is, permitted us to believe the worst. By this strategy he runs the risk of instructing his readers to make a savage comment on his own pretty prose and melodious sonnets, as follows:

> We admire the utility of Mr. S.'s philosophical discourses, but it is obstructed and indignified by his weakness for rhetoric, and we think we shall return after all to those philosophers who attend strictly to business. As for his verse, which seems to have niched for itself a secure if modest corner in the monument of literature, we have looked that up and found the place where he tells us about a too-aspiring metaphysician:
>
> Ah, the thin air is cold above the moon!
> I stood and saw you fall, befooled in death,
> As, in your numbéd spirit's fatal swoon,
> You cried you were a god, or were to be;
> I hear with feeble moan your boastful breath
> Bubble from depths of the Icarian sea.
>
> This metaphysician is certainly in a plight, but it is absurd to say he has flown higher than the moon and fallen into the sea, and what is ever gained by absurdities, or by false accents and musical accompaniments? If this represents a side of Mr. S.'s nature which had to be expressed, he should have had the goodness to be ashamed of it and to express it in private; most grown men are, and do.

For by the doctrine of expressiveness, in the hands of persons not its enthusiasts, art is disreputable.

But suppose the doctrinaire says that art is expressive not of a contemptible residue of little impulses, disloyal to the practical successes of the organism, but of personality itself, which is imposing, which in fact is the whole organism? The position of art is not much improved. What an odd collocation of terms! Art as utility is dealing with perfectly objective ends, and at the same time as expression is trying to please a perfectly subjective personality. And what is personality? It can only mean: whatever in the organism is responsible for whatever in the work of art is not utility. Personality is mentioned because the doctrinaire is not analytical enough to make out the form that expression takes but can remark sagely that something, probably something big, with about five syllables, is expressing itself. If the utilitarians can point out the objective utility of art, which is indistinguishable from that of science, the personalists might try to point out the objective differentiation which removes art from science. The utility and the residue are equally in the objective record, which is the art-work itself.

Objectively, the works of art make a great show in the detritus of the civilizations; they all but rival the aggregate exhibit of the sciences. The testimony which they furnish is certainly adequate. Yet so little have philosophers done

to distinguish the art from the science that intelligent teachers of literature are still addressing astonished pupils in this manner:

> Our poem brings to us, then, young gentlemen, a nugget of wisdom, a principle that makes for righteousness and the welfare of humankind. See that you cherish it. But it is only by an abstraction that I have paraphrased it in prose and taken it out of context. The prose statement is the practical or scientific meaning. But the object really before us is the work of art, whole and untranslatable. It is richer than its scientific abstract. In what way richer we cannot exactly say, but if we are spiritually sensitive we can feel it. At best we may say that the artist has fused the bare meaning in his genius and in his personality, and made it glowing and expressive, till it has suffered this sea-change. Such is the magic and the mystery of art.

In the meantime the sceptical scientific population, perpetually on the increase, is rudely remarking that it does not believe in magic, and asking of the apologists of poetry to show what the poet has added to the scientific record except irrelevance and disorder. The apologists presently are obliged in honesty to confess that the scientific or prose value of the poem is often trite and therefore slight, as if in satisfaction of a merely formal requirement, and that the unique or characteristic value of all the poetry everywhere, a sum heroic in magnitude, must depend on other but to them invisible considerations. With which confession in their pockets, it may be predicted that the sceptics with renewed confidence and in even greater numbers will be asking whether there is demonstrably anything in the whole world of human actions except scientific ones, dictated by the animal needs of the organism; and whether any distinction can ever be made between actions except in the respect that they may have different degrees of rigor, or consistency, and therefore may be the more or the less perfect; the so-called sciences more, and the unhappy arts a great deal less.

Mr. Santayana evolved and grew, like a good biological organism, and produced doctrines which are original, within the limits which must confine originality at a late stage of philosophy. I shall refer to them so far as they seem to have consequences for æsthetic theory.

He cannot have been happy with his word expressive, and the like words, for the kind of commentary which I have improvised is too easy to have escaped him. He had an objective problem and was falling back upon a vague subjective solution: a bad business for any philosopher, and worse for one who had made it his specialty to point to the healthy metaphysical state of Greeks and to deride subjectivism. In 1923 appeared *Scepticism and Animal Faith,* a body blow at the idealists. Animal faith is the new and ingenious weapon. William James had talked about pragmatic truth and the will to believe, so that one might say to an idealist who believed in mind more than in matter that these things were perfectly optional. But Mr. Santayana says no, that belief is compulsive, in mind and in matter alike, being part of the animal function which has to act upon environment. Scepticism is not the mark of the living animal; and unbelief in matter, if it could be genuine, would be far on the road to inaction and death. Idealism, that perverse attitude, could have suggested itself hardly anywhere else than among the romantics of the Northern races. (Idealism as if by the principle of equal and opposite reactions has produced behaviorism, its latest and most precise counterpart, which believes in matter but not in mind; a punishment visited upon the world for the crimes of the Nordic idealists.)

I suppose the new doctrine has no application to æsthetic unless indirectly: it dramatizes more sharply the question whether art is really distinct from science. Is art only another work of animal faith? The form and purpose of its animality are not disclosed. And the truth is that the lover of art, who will "feel" a good deal that he cannot know explicitly, would expect to find its residuary properties quite different from those which interest animals. The Christians need not be brought into the argument, but the Greeks, including even Aristotle, held that man is in part an animal but also in part a god. If in his sciences he has insight into objective nature so far as it is serviceable to an animal, perhaps in his arts he may have a more innocent and indeed a divine insight into nature as it is. But waiving theology entirely, I am sure that many art-lovers have a secret notion which goes like this: Art distinguishes man from the other animals in kind, since they have none of it, while science distinguishes him only in power or efficiency, which means degree. Mr. Santayana had almost behaved too handsomely by animality.

He atoned for it handsomely in the two-volume *Realms of Being,* his chief philosophical work, of which *The Realm of Essence* appeared in 1927 and *The Realm of Matter* in 1930. Very properly for this Platonist, essences engaged him first; they are his version of the Platonic ideas.

A refined and even attenuated version, for Plato's have some animal odor on them as compared with the Santayana essences, upon which no animal would think of trying to support life. Yet Plato's ideas, like all the varieties of essence to which his sons have ever become attached, fall short of having the fullness of natural or material existences. Plato punished his animality through being fastidious, in a manner not necessarily aristocratic and indeed rather mean for a Greek: the manner of an animal who has become painfully self-conscious, and who has conceived a powerful preference for his rational or "higher" activities and a distaste for the fortuitous pleasures of sense. This is the ascetic or Puritan pattern of fastidiousness. It is not the only one, for Plato might have decided to embrace what he could not cure and to cultivate even the diffusive senses under the standard which is called taste. Its acquisition is laborious enough to have satisfied the schoolmaster in him. (In England the Cavaliers did not go to school less than the Roundheads but more.) But it would not have produced any Platonic ideas. The world of sense, like real property, may be "improved" in a number of ways, but taste would like to bring it under arts, fashions, rites, and manners, which emphasize those residuary splendors that are of no animal importance. Not electing this sort of discipline, Plato went in for ideas, and

created them after the likeness of his preferences: as natural substances dried out, purified, and made fit for disaffected but very rational animals. They claim to be the archetypal forms of all created things, but we know nothing about that; and they claim "really" to constitute the present natural world, but that only means that they might have done so if contingency and confusion had not got into nature. So Plato qualified them as only "real" or "essential" constituents of the world, and we need not waste time objecting; it is a locution against which it would be a great deal of trouble to legislate. But I think I know the briefest and best description of the Platonic ideas: they are *ideals*; moral and religious ones. They have a degree of practicability. They are effective in so far as they can persuade men actually to occupy their minds with rational essences rather than with the whole of the contingent world; and is there not an incorrigible and irreducible Platonic faction in every civilized Western population? It is easy to work with nature as animals must, and then to pretend that we are working with essences, which are so neat and clean.

Mr. Santayana's kind of essence abandons even the rational core of body; yet abandoning so much it is a more honest ghost than the Platonic idea. A body is a locus of properties numerically infinite, while the properties of an essence are numerically finite. But we might arrange essences in a series as including more or fewer properties, and Mr. Santayana's would stand at the end; the poorest excuse for body imaginable, but possibly for that very reason, in their void of animal utility, the noblest essences. They make no pretense to existence, and are not in the least norms or ideals. They are nothing but the pure qualities, each one unique and incomparable. Their realm comprises all the qualities in the world, but it is a grammatical or paper realm. They are the atoms of nature in a quaint qualitative sense, for they are single, when it is well understood that nature, even in its smallest and most empty-looking piece, must offer itself as a vast collocation of qualities. And how have they acquired a realm? I suppose it is very simple. Whenever one comes upon a new quality one takes a picture of it and puts it into a drawer. Perhaps one may return one day and look at the pictures. It would be a harmless pastime, though probably a dull one, not like animal pleasure, not like moral pleasure; and not, one would think, like æsthetic pleasure.

But if the realm of essence is quaint, like a child's collection of colored blocks, it is not so with the realm of matter. Essences are just harmless adjectives, but the forms of matter, the things, are nouns, and in action they are frightful things for an animal to have to deal with, because their activities are unpredictable, and evil more often than good; and they are sadly or comically unsuitable for a scientist, because they cannot be held to strict accountability like the nouns in dictionaries but are possessed of an obscene and malignant fertility for spawning fresh adjectives as long as he has the courage to observe them. Mr. Santayana's account of this realm is a great literary achievement, and should be recommended equally to soft-hearted sentimentalists and hard-headed positivists. The account is more exciting than Milton's picture of Chaos, because nothing should have been expected of Chaos except the chaotic, but in nature we hope to find perfect animal fulfilments and rational processes; for, though we may often have been cheated, we have animal faith.

The animal lives in the realm of matter, which is the natural world, and occupies himself with wresting and worrying his living out of it; and if Mr. Santayana's realm of essence were called to his attention he would find it rather beneath his notice or, as its author might say, above it; but actually he will hardly know nor care if there is such a realm. I come back to the original question, and now it will be in the new terms which Mr. Santayana has furnished: With which is the specific vision of the artist concerned, with essence or with matter?

Mr. Santayana has dallied with essences as if they were to be the fruits of his well-spent life. His long road has led him to this sharp categorical division as if precisely in order that he may justify artists at last; for I cannot find any other occasion for it. But at this stage his admirer, though hoping that he will place the feet of the artists on very firm ground, must feel many ignoble apprehensions lest they suffer the fate of his ambitious metaphysician if it should turn out that he has only essences to give them.

He has only essences. That appears from the papers relating to art which are dated from 1925 on, so far as I can judge from those in the *Obiter Scripta,* which are several. In 1925 he is emphasizing " . . . the fact that beauty, as I feel it, transports us altogether into the realm of essence, and that no pleasure, interest, or admiration becomes a sense of beauty unless it does so. Every image, however, if animal faith is suspended in its presence, is an essence seen under the form of eternity."

I may as well remark at once crudely, for it will be already clear that I do not subscribe to this view, that it seems to require us, if we would be artists or follow them, to get out of the world where essences inhere in the living substances, and into the drawer where the little flat images are kept. It does little good to say that in this drawer is a treasure which neither moths can corrupt nor thieves break through and steal, inasmuch as everything here is under the form of eternity. Essences are eternal enough; a similar way of thinking has led Mr. Whitehead to name them eternal objects. To eternize an object is to save it by withdrawing it from circulation; from circulation in the battering and incessant transaction of nature, which is life; but it is a peculiar method of salvation, amounting to death. Mr. Santayana has had a peculiar history as a philosopher. He has censured the idealists for not believing their own natural images, but that is exactly the policy he now recommends to them if they would have æsthetic experience; they are to fly to a realm too thin to pretend to support belief. If we should hold him to his verbal commitments, which might be too harsh a procedure, we should have to say that this is one of the most profound of scepticisms, and that Mr. Santayana himself is a Puritan, and in the last extremity.

A remark about essence as the scientists construe it; for we should keep all these essences straight. Of course they never permit it to receive the modest indefinite article, and this implies that they are under the bondage of animal faith when they handle it. To be scientific is to pursue an exclusive interest effectively, and so the scientists abstract from natural forms what they take to be a nucleus or core of properties, and set this aside as "the essence" of a whole series of forms. They do not put it into an attic drawer but rather into the office files. For these essences are Platonic ideas somewhat vulgarized; that is, more shrewdly selective, and believed in not as broad ideals but as sure things, or specific working formulas. Yet the sum of the scientific interests covers the whole range of animality, and if we should define the world in terms of scientific ideality it might easily wear the look of a perfect Christmas party, where all the drinks and sweets were delicious without painful consequences and all the toys obedient to the mechanics' pleasure; so much it might lack of the austerity of the Platonic vision. At any rate, scientists define "the essential" pattern of an object that interests them, and "the essential" conditions for its production. Both the scientific essences and the Santayana ones are obtained by abstraction, but theirs are for hard animal use, and his are for innocent contemplation; non-animal contemplation, I think we must say.

In 1929, Mr. Santayana reports a windfall. Proust, fullest and richest if most laborious of all the novelists, has published an æsthetic doctrine scarcely distinguishable from his. It occurs in the last volume of Proust's great work, the one in which he most broods, I think, upon his preoccupation with the past and the meaning of æsthetic joy. Mr. Santayana writes briefly upon it. I quote from his footnote and with his omissions a passage taken out of Blossom's translation:

> The being that was called to life again in me by uniting the present impression with something in the past draws its sustenance only from the essence of things, in that alone does it find its nourishment and delight. . . . Let a sound already heard or an odor caught in bygone years be sensed anew, simultaneously in the present and the past, real without being of the present moment, ideal but not abstract, and immediately the permanent essence of things, usually concealed, is set free and our true self . . . awakes, takes on fresh life as it receives the celestial nourishment brought to it. . . . This contemplation, though part of eternity, was transitory. And yet I felt that the pleasure it had bestowed on me at rare intervals of my life was the only one that was fecund and real. Is not the indication of the unreliability of the others sufficiently evident either in their inability to satisfy us . . . or in the despondency that follows whatever satisfactions they may give? . . . And so I was decided to concentrate myself to this study of the essence of things, to establish its true nature. . . . And if I recapitulated the disappointments in my life, so far as it had been lived, which led me to believe that its real essence must lie somewhere else than in action . . . I came to realize clearly that disappointment in a journey and disappointment in a love affair were not different in themselves but merely the different aspects they assumed in varying situations by our inability to find our real selves in physical enjoyment or material activity.

Commenting on this passage, Mr. Santayana thinks it

shows an awkwardness in grasping the essences, which does not affect the value of its testimony:

> No wonder that a sensibility so exquisite and so voluminous as that of Proust, filled with endless images and their distant reverberations, could be rescued from distraction only by finding certain repetitions or rhymes in this experience. He was a tireless husbandman of memory, gathering perhaps more poppies than corn; and the very fragility and worthlessness of the weeds collected may have led him to appreciate their presence only when lost, and their harsh scent only when recovered. Thus he required two phenomena to reveal to him one essence, as if essences needed to appear a second time in order to appear at all. A mind less volatile and less retentive, but more concentrated and loyal, might easily have discerned the eternal essence in any single momentary fact. It might also have felt the scale of values imposed on things by human nature, and might have been carried towards some by an innate love and away from others by a quick repulsion: something which in Proust is remarkably rare. Yet this very inhumanity and innocent openness, this inclination to be led on by endlessly rambling perception, makes his testimony to the reality of essences all the more remarkable. We could not have asked for a more competent or a more unexpected witness to the fact that life as it flows is so much time wasted, and that nothing can ever be recovered or truly possessed save under the form of eternity which is also, as he tells us, the form of art.

From the last sentence of Mr. Santayana's passage we receive the sense of a philosopher seizing on the treasure which is not a treasure, because it comes to him under the hollow form of eternity. And from the last sentence of Proust's passage we receive what? The sense that the artist finds his characteristic pleasure, though it is invidious to say that he finds his "real self," not in animal activity but somewhere else. That is one part of Proust's testimony. The other part is more difficult to translate into intelligible terms: the part which has to do with the special importance of memory in Proust's æsthetic practice. Memory is so unrelated to the doctrine of essence that it is not strange that Proust hardly knows what to do with it, nor that Mr. Santayana in effect has to cancel what he does. I do not know who is so adventurous as to dispute Proust's transcript of actual experience, but it is not to be expected that Proust will have the gift for theorizing it; and if Mr. Santayana has the gift it is hardly to be expected that he will theorize it either, being committed already to fixed theories.

Proust has a repertory of simple images which he employs to invoke the past, and with their assistance he lives and finds his delight in the past. His fiction is about the things past, and it is autobiographical. A psychologist should study these key-images to see of what sort they are; it might lead to an understanding of nostalgia, which is the clear emotional overtone of, I think, more than half of lyric poetry, and perhaps of an even larger fraction of music. Proust mentions here a sound and an odor. A sound is heard which transports him into the past, and he testifies that it is by the help of the past that he fixes upon

this sound as an essence and enjoys it. But that seems meaningless; and more important to an understanding of the experience might be the fact, which I think could be established, that it was no such sound as, say, the dinner bell; it was not a sound which might lead the animal in him into an act of retrospective imagination in order to lick its chops. (It might have been such a sound, but not in the kind of experience to which Proust refers.) An odor is caught, but it is that of a flower perhaps, not that of animal sweat, or food. Nearly any distinct and "unimportant" sound or odor would do; these senses are especially innocent, in that their images are generally not attended to in the fury of the animal processes. And once these images start the thing, other images come pouring out of the past, the past takes form again. The past which they invoke would seem to be, pending the psychologist's report, *precisely that past which the man as animal did not attend to.* Memory retained it while he was not attending to it, and memory is available. The automatic memory seems disposed to preserve an innumerable troop of meek and homeless items that the animal consciousness has rejected; but are they not just the items that are waiting to be attended to? It is in art, or in the informal indulgence of memory, that we come back and attend to them. For Proust or for us there are always images accompanying present experience which are just as innocent as those were, but it is as hard to attend to them now as it was then, since we are still, presumably, good animals.

The consequence is that what must seem like a disproportionate fraction of art is a fairly literal reading of the memory, and autobiographical; the artist already has a record of the world more complete than he can transcribe, and need not take the trouble to invent a fiction. For that matter, the fiction when it is invented has to be pieced out of the odd scraps furnished by the memory. It is by employing the device of systematic memory, which recovers a past relieved of its animal urgency, or the device of fiction, which is too hypothetical to engage the inhibitory animal, that the civilized races, who are the mechanized and the highly scienced, obtain their most solid æsthetic experience. Art serves them better than nature. And if we often seem to detect in the makeshift aspect of art the trace of something sly, roundabout, and for theoretical admiration unfortunate, when we have come from watching the bold front, the almost cynical directness, with which the confident animal moves upon his objectives, that is only another way of saying that art in action is artificial, or indirect. It has to be. It has learned its technique in a hard school.

But I cannot think it credible that Proust's joy should consist, as he and Mr. Santayana believed, in obtaining the simple sound, or odor, and then collapsing into eternity, which is trance, emptied of further consciousness, beside it. The state does not seem likely enough to be even pathological. Freudians have wonderful imaginations, and use them ingeniously to account for a strange phenomenon: the fascination and terror which an apparently simple image may exercise over the morbid; and their answer is that through the mechanism of memory it sets in motion a vast, secret, and terrifying train of imagery, so that the total agent is not simple at all. But for Proust we are told that the image is really simple, and unaccompanied; that this is its whole virtue. If it then can be the cause of so profound an experience as art, we are out of the range of the human economy so far as we have had any understanding of that.

If Mr. Santayana as a free personality in a dull professional world reminds us of Emerson, in the light of his systematic philosophy he is a diffused modern version of Schopenhauer. Both are very well aware of the customary unmannerly ferocity of man as an animal, with Schopenhauer of course grieving more than tolerant Mr. Santayana about that; the animal directing and corrupting the most remote-looking and publicly esteemed pursuits, like tribal morality, which passes for disinterested action, or science, which passes for the pursuit of pure knowledge; yet kennelled, or put to sleep, or transcended, in at least one free and charming activity, which is æsthetic experience. In art, according to Schopenhauer, we at last have knowledge without desire. It remains only to determine just what this knowledge is about, and there again the two philosophers pronounce similarly. Knowledge of the Platonic ideas, said Schopenhauer, but explained them very mistily; and knowledge of the pure essences, says Mr. Santayana, but they look inadequate.

It cannot be impertinent to refer Mr. Santayana, and those who may have followed or preceded him into the ethereal climate of essences, to that remarkable work of metaphysical description, **The Realm of Matter.** The images of art are too crowded, contingent, and energetic to be of much use to scientific animals. But the reason is that they belong to the realm of matter as scientific abstracts do not, and not to the realm of essence as scientific abstracts do. In them the scientific or useful essence finds itself accompanied by an infinite residue, and for scientists this residue is exactly what they have charged: irrelevance and foolishness, which cannot suit the limited aims of animals. But all wealth of circumstance and event is within the realm of matter; Mr. Santayana has precisely distinguished the realms and then has not looked at the right one. From it countless works of art have been equipped with their substance, yet it is undiminished and ready for fresh works. What these works intend is, simply, the widest and most unprejudiced knowledge of nature that is possible. There may not be gods to whom knowledge of this sort is the constant form of their activity, for who knows? But there is man, who is not merely animal, and whose animal preoccupations ought never to have become so binding as to exclude a constant exercise of this free knowledge. Now, in his inevitable decadence, he has fallen apart, and the pursuit of it has become one of the specialized and technical functions of his divided mind. (pp. 304-26)

> *John Crowe Ransom, "Art and Mr. Santayana," in his* The World's Body, *Louisiana State University, 1968, pp. 304-26.*

George Santayana   (essay date 1940)

[*In the following excerpt from an essay comprising earlier autobiographical statements, Santayana describes the background and evolution of his opinions.*]

When I began the formal study of philosophy as an under-graduate at Harvard, I was already alive to the fundamental questions, and even had a certain dialectical nimbleness, due to familiarity with the fine points of theology: the arguments for and against free will and the proofs of the existence of God were warm and clear in my mind. I accordingly heard James and Royce with more wonder than serious agreement: my scholastic logic would have wished to reduce James at once to a materialist and Royce to a solipsist, and it seemed strangely irrational in them to resist such simplification. I had heard many Unitarian sermons (being taken to hear them lest I should become too Catholic), and had been interested in them so far as they were rationalistic and informative, or even amusingly irreligious, as I often thought them to be: but neither in those discourses nor in Harvard philosophy was it easy for me to understand the Protestant combination of earnestness with waywardness. I was used to see water flowing from fountains, architectural and above ground: it puzzled me to see it drawn painfully in bucketfuls from the subjective well, muddied, and half spilt over.

There was one lesson, however, which I was readier to learn, not only at Harvard from Professor Palmer and afterwards at Berlin from Paulsen, but from the general temper of that age well represented for me by the *Revue Des Deux Mondes* (which I habitually read from cover to cover) and by the works of Taine and of Matthew Arnold—I refer to the historical spirit of the nineteenth century, and to that splendid panorama of nations and religions, literatures and arts, which it unrolled before the imagination. These picturesque vistas into the past came to fill in circumstantially that geographical and moral vastness to which my imagination was already accustomed. Professor Palmer was especially skilful in bending the mind to a suave and sympathetic participation in the views of all philosophers in turn: were they not all great men, and must not the aspects of things which seemed persuasive to them be really persuasive? Yet even this form of romanticism, amiable as it is, could not altogether put to sleep my scholastic dogmatism. The historian of philosophy may be as sympathetic and as self-effacing as he likes: the philosopher in him must still ask whether any of those successive views were true, or whether the later ones were necessarily truer than the earlier: he cannot, unless he is a shameless sophist, rest content with a truth *pro tem.* In reality the sympathetic reconstruction of history is a literary art, and it depends for its plausibility as well as for its materials on a conventional belief in the natural world. Without this belief no history and no science would be anything but a poetic fiction, like a classification of the angelic choirs. The necessity of naturalism as a foundation for all further serious opinions was clear to me from the beginning. Naturalism might indeed be criticized—and I was myself intellectually and emotionally predisposed to criticize it, and to oscillate between supernaturalism and solipsism—but if naturalism was condemned, supernaturalism itself could have no point of application in the world of fact; and the whole edifice of human knowledge would crumble, since no perception would then be a report and no judgment would have a transcendent object. Hence historical reconstruction seemed to me more honestly and solidly practised by Taine, who was a professed naturalist, than by Hegel and his school, whose naturalism, though presupposed at every stage, was disguised and distorted by a dialectic imposed on it by the historian and useful at best only in simplifying his dramatic perspectives and lending them a false absoluteness and moralistic veneer.

The influence of Royce over me, though less important in the end than that of James, was at first much more active. Royce was the better dialectician, and traversed subjects in which I was naturally more interested. The point that particularly exercised me was Royce's Theodicy or justification for the existence of evil. It would be hard to exaggerate the ire which his arguments on this subject aroused in my youthful breast. Why that emotion? Romantic sentiment that could find happiness only in tears and virtue only in heroic agonies was something familiar to me and not unsympathetic: a poetic play of mine, called *Lucifer,* conceived in those days, is a clear proof of it. I knew Leopardi and Musset largely by heart; Schopenhauer was soon to become, for a brief period, one of my favourite authors. I carried Lucretius in my pocket: and although the spirit of the poet in that case was not romantic, the picture of human existence which he drew glorified the same vanity. Spinoza, too, whom I was reading under Royce himself, filled me with joy and enthusiasm: I gathered at once from him a doctrine which has remained axiomatic with me ever since, namely that good and evil are relative to the natures of animals, irreversible in that relation, but indifferent to the march of cosmic events, since the force of the universe infinitely exceeds the force of any one of its parts. Had I found, then, in Royce only a romantic view of life, or only pessimism, or only stoical courage and pantheistic piety, I should have taken no offence, but readily recognized the poetic truth or the moral legitimacy of those positions. Conformity with fate, as I afterwards came to see, belongs to post-rational morality, which is a normal though optional development of human sentiment: Spinoza's "intellectual love of God" was a shining instance of it.

But in Royce these attitudes, in themselves so honest and noble, seemed to be somehow embroiled and rendered sophistical: nor was he alone in this, for the same moral equivocation seemed to pervade Hegel, Browning, and Nietzsche. That which repelled me in all these men was the survival of a sort of forced optimism and pulpit unction, by which a cruel and nasty world, painted by them in the most lurid colours, was nevertheless set up as the model and standard of what ought to be. The duty of an honest moralist would have been rather to distinguish, in this bad or mixed reality, the part, however small, that could be loved and chosen from the remainder, however large, which was to be rejected and renounced. Certainly the universe was in flux and dynamically single: but this fatal flux could very well take care of itself; and it was not so fluid that no islands of a relative permanence and beauty might not be formed in it. Ascetic conformity was itself one of these islands: a scarcely inhabitable peak from which almost all human passions and activities were excluded. And the Greeks, whose deliberate ethics was rational, never denied the vague early Gods and the environing chaos, which perhaps would return in the end: but meantime they built their cities bravely on the hill-tops, as we

all carry on pleasantly our temporal affairs, although we know that to-morrow we die. Life itself exists only by a modicum of organization, achieved and transmitted through a world of change: the momentum of such organization first creates a difference between good and evil, or gives them a meaning at all. Thus the core of life is always hereditary, steadfast, and classical; the margin of barbarism and blind adventure round it may be as wide as you will, and in some wild hearts the love of this fluid margin may be keen, as might be any other loose passion. But to *preach* barbarism as the only good, in ignorance or hatred of the possible perfection of every natural thing, was a scandal: a belated Calvinism that remained fanatical after ceasing to be Christian. And there was a further circumstance which made this attitude particularly odious to me. This romantic love of evil was not thoroughgoing: wilfulness and disorder were to reign only in spiritual matters; in government and industry, even in natural science, all was to be order and mechanical progress. Thus the absence of a positive religion and of a legislation, like that of the ancients, intended to be rational and final, was very far from liberating the spirit for higher flights: on the contrary, it opened the door to the pervasive tyranny of the world over the soul. And no wonder: a soul rebellious to its moral heritage is too weak to reach any firm definition of its inner life. It will feel lost and empty unless it summons the random labours of the contemporary world to fill and to enslave it. It must let mechanical and civic achievements reconcile it to its own moral confusion and triviality.

It was in this state of mind that I went to Germany to continue the study of philosophy—interested in all religious or metaphysical systems, but sceptical about them and scornful of any romantic worship or idealization of the real world. The life of a wandering student, like those of the Middle Ages, had an immense natural attraction for me—so great, that I have never willingly led any other. When I had to choose a profession, the prospect of a quiet academic existence seemed the least of evils. I was fond of reading and observation, and I liked young men; but I have never been a diligent student either of science or art, nor at all ambitious to be learned. I have been willing to let cosmological problems and technical questions solve themselves as they would or as the authorities agreed for the moment that they should be solved. My pleasure was rather in expression, in reflection, in irony: my spirit was content to intervene, in whatever world it might seem to find itself, in order to disentangle the intimate moral and intellectual echoes audible to it in that world. My naturalism or materialism is no academic opinion: it is not a survival of the alleged materialism of the nineteenth century, when all the professors of philosophy were idealists: it is an everyday conviction which came to me, as it came to my father, from experience and observation of the world at large, and especially of my own feelings and passions. It seems to me that those who are not materialists cannot be good observers of themselves: they may hear themselves thinking, but they cannot have watched themselves acting and feeling; for feeling and action are evidently accidents of matter. If a Democritus or Lucretius or Spinoza or Darwin works within the lines of nature, and clarifies some part of that familiar object, that fact is the ground of my attachment to them: they have the savour of truth; but what the savour of truth is, I know very well without their help. Consequently there is no opposition in my mind between materialism and a Platonic or even Indian discipline of the spirit. The recognition of the material world and of the conditions of existence in it merely enlightens the spirit concerning the source of its troubles and the means to its happiness or deliverance: and it was happiness or deliverance, the supervening supreme expression of human will and imagination, that alone really concerned me. This alone was genuine philosophy: this alone was the life of reason.

Had the life of reason ever been cultivated in the world by people with a sane imagination? Yes, once, by the Greeks. Of the Greeks, however, I knew very little: the philosophical and political departments at Harvard had not yet discovered Plato and Aristotle. It was with the greater pleasure that I heard Paulsen in Berlin expounding Greek ethics with a sweet reasonableness altogether worthy of the subject: here at last was a vindication of order and beauty in the institutions of men and in their ideas. Here, through the pleasant medium of transparent myths or of summary scientific images, like the water of Thales, nature was essentially understood and honestly described; and here, for that very reason, the free mind could disentangle its true good, and could express it in art, in manners, and even in the most refined or the most austere spiritual discipline. Yet, although I knew henceforth that in the Greeks I should find the natural support and point of attachment for my own philosophy, I was not then collected or mature enough to pursue the matter; not until ten years later, in 1896-1897, did I take the opportunity of a year's leave of absence to go to England and begin a systematic reading of Plato and Aristotle under Dr. Henry Jackson of Trinity College, Cambridge. I am not conscious of any change of opinion supervening, nor of any having occurred earlier; but by that study and change of scene my mind was greatly enriched; and the composition of *The Life of Reason* was the consequence.

This book was intended to be a summary history of the human imagination, expressly distinguishing those phases of it which showed what Herbert Spencer called an adjustment of inner to outer relations; in other words, an adaptation of fancy and habit to material facts and opportunities. On the one hand, then, my subject being the imagination, I was never called on to step beyond the subjective sphere. I set out to describe, not nature or God, but the ideas of God or nature bred in the human mind. On the other hand, I was not concerned with these ideas for their own sake, as in a work of pure poetry or erudition, but I meant to consider them in their natural genesis and significance; for I assumed throughout that the whole life of reason was generated and controlled by the animal life of man in the bosom of nature. Human ideas had, accordingly, a symptomatic, expressive, and symbolic value: they were the inner notes sounded by man's passions and by his arts: and they became rational partly by their vital and inward harmony—for reason is a harmony of the passions—and partly by their adjustment to external facts and possibilities— for reason is a harmony of the inner life with truth and with fate. I was accordingly concerned to discover what

wisdom is possible to an animal whose mind, from beginning to end, is poetical: and I found that this could not lie in discarding poetry in favour of a science supposed to be clairvoyant and literally true. Wisdom lay rather in taking everything good-humouredly, with a grain of salt. In science there was an element of poetry, pervasive, inevitable, and variable: it was strictly scientific and true only in so far as it involved a close and prosperous adjustment to the surrounding world, at first by its origin in observation and at last by its application in action. Science was the mental accompaniment of art.

Here was a sort of pragmatism: the same which I have again expressed, I hope more clearly, in one of the *Dialogues in Limbo* entitled **"Normal Madness."** The human mind is a faculty of dreaming awake, and its dreams are kept relevant to its environment and to its fate only by the external control exercised over them by Punishment, when the accompanying conduct brings ruin, or by Agreement, when it brings prosperity. In the latter case it is possible to establish correspondences between one part of a dream and another, or between the dreams of separate minds, and so create the world of literature, or the life of reason. I am not sure whether this notion, that thought is a controlled and consistent madness, appears among the thirteen pragmatisms which have been distinguished, but I have reason to think that I came to it under the influence of William James; nevertheless, when his book on *Pragmatism* appeared, about the same time as my *Life of Reason,* it gave me a rude shock. I could not stomach that way of speaking about truth; and the continual substitution of human psychology—normal madness, in my view—for the universe, in which man is but one distracted and befuddled animal, seemed to me a confused remnant of idealism, and not serious.

The William James who had been my master was not this William James of the later years, whose pragmatism and pure empiricism and romantic metaphysics have made such a stir in the world. It was rather the puzzled but brilliant doctor, impatient of metaphysics, whom I had known in my undergraduate days, one of whose maxims was that to study the abnormal was the best way of understanding the normal; or it was the genial author of *The Principles of Psychology,* chapters of which he read from the manuscript and discussed with a small class of us in 1889. Even then what I learned from him was perhaps chiefly things which explicitly he never taught, but which I imbibed from the spirit and background of his teaching. Chief of these, I should say, was a sense for the immediate: for the unadulterated, unexplained, instant fact of experience. Actual experience, for William James, however varied or rich its assault might be, was always and altogether of the nature of a sensation: it possessed a vital, leaping, globular unity which made the only fact, the flying fact, of our being. Whatever continuities of quality might be traced in it, its existence was always momentary and self-warranted. A man's life or soul borrowed its reality and imputed wholeness from the intrinsic actuality of its successive parts; existence was a perpetual rebirth, a travelling light to which the past was lost and the future uncertain. The element of indetermination which James felt so strongly in this flood of existence was precisely the pulse of fresh unpredictable sensation, summoning attention hither and thither to unexpected facts. Apprehension in him being impressionistic—that was the age of impressionism in painting too—and marvellously free from intellectual assumptions or presumptions, he felt intensely the fact of contingency, or the contingency of fact. This seemed to me not merely a peculiarity of temperament in him, but a profound insight into existence, in its inmost irrational essence. Existence, I learned to see, is intrinsically dispersed, seated in its distributed moments, and arbitrary not only as a whole, but in the character and place of each of its parts. Change the bits, and you change the mosaic: nor can we count or limit the elements, as in a little closed kaleidoscope, which may be shaken together into the next picture. Many of them, such as pleasure and pain, or the total picture itself, cannot possibly have pre-existed.

But, said I to myself, were these novelties for that reason unconditioned? Was not sensation, by continually surprising us, a continual warning to us of fatal conjunctions occurring outside? And would not the same conjunctions, but for memory and habit, always produce the same surprises? Experience of indetermination was no proof of indeterminism; and when James proceeded to turn immediate experience into ultimate physics, his thought seemed to me to lose itself in words or in confused superstitions. Free will, a deep moral power contrary to a romantic indetermination in being, he endeavoured to pack into the bias of attention—the most temperamental of accidents. He insisted passionately on the efficacy of consciousness, and invoked Darwinian arguments for its utility—arguments which assumed that consciousness was a material engine absorbing and transmitting energy: so that it was no wonder that presently he doubted whether consciousness existed at all. He suggested a new physics or metaphysics in which the essences given in immediate experience should be deployed and hypostatized into the constituents of nature: but this pictorial cosmology had the disadvantage of abolishing the human imagination, with all the pathos and poetry of its animal status. James thus renounced that gift for literary psychology, that romantic insight, in which alone he excelled; and indeed his followers are without it. I pride myself on remaining a disciple of his earlier unsophisticated self, when he was an agnostic about the universe, but in his diagnosis of the heart an impulsive poet: a master in the art of recording or divining the lyric quality of experience as it actually came to him or to me.

Lyric experience and literary psychology, as I have learned to conceive them, are chapters in the life of one race of animals, in one corner of the natural world. But before relegating them to that modest station (which takes nothing away from their spiritual prerogatives) I was compelled to face the terrible problem which arises when, as in modern philosophy, literary psychology and lyric experience are made the fulcrum or the stuff of the universe. Has this experience any external conditions? If it has, are they knowable? And if it has not, on what principle are its qualities generated or its episodes distributed? Nay, how can literary psychology or universal experience have any seat save the present fancy of the psychologist or the historian? Although James had been bothered and con-

fused by these questions, and Royce had enthroned his philosophy upon them, neither of these my principal teachers seemed to have come to clearness on the subject: it was only afterwards, when I read Fichte and Schopenhauer, that I began to see my way to a solution. We must oscillate between a radical transcendentalism, frankly reduced to a solipsism of the living moment, and a materialism posited as a presupposition of conventional sanity. There was no contradiction in joining together a scepticism which was not a dogmatic negation of anything and an animal faith which avowedly was a mere assumption in action and description. Yet such oscillation, if it was to be justified and rendered coherent, still demanded some understanding of two further points: what, starting from immediate experience, was the *causa cognoscendi* of the natural world; and what, starting from the natural world, was the *causa fiendi* of immediate experience?

On this second point (in spite of the speculations of my friend Strong) I have not seen much new light. I am constrained merely to register as a brute fact the emergence of consciousness in animal bodies. A psyche, or nucleus of hereditary organization, gathers and governs these bodies, and at the same time breeds within them a dreaming, suffering, and watching mind. Such investigations as those of Fraser and of Freud have shown how rich and how mad a thing the mind is fundamentally, how pervasively it plays about animal life, and how remote its first and deepest intuitions are from any understanding of their true occasions. An interesting and consistent complement to these discoveries is furnished by behaviourism, which I heartily accept on its positive biological side: the hereditary life of the body, modified by accident or training, forms a closed cycle of habits and actions. Of this the mind is a concomitant spiritual expression, invisible, imponderable, and epiphenomenal, or, as I prefer to say, hypostatic: for in it the moving unities and tensions of animal life are synthesized on quite another plane of being, into actual intuitions and feelings. This spiritual fertility in living bodies is the most natural of things. It is unintelligible only as all existence, change, or genesis is unintelligible; but it might be better understood, that is, better assimilated to other natural miracles, if we understood better the life of matter everywhere, and that of its different aggregates.

On the other points raised by my naturalism, namely on the grounds of faith in the natural world, I have reached more positive conclusions. Criticism, I think, must first be invited to do its worst: nothing is more dangerous here than timidity or convention. A pure and radical transcendentalism will disclaim all knowledge of fact. Nature, history, the self become ghostly presences, mere notions of such things; and the being of these images becomes purely internal to them; they exist in no environing space or time; they possess no substance or hidden parts, but are all surface, all appearance. Such a being, or quality of being, I call an essence; and to the consideration of essences, composing of themselves an eternal and infinite realm, I have lately devoted much attention. To that sphere I transpose the familiar pictures painted by the senses, or by traditional science and religion. Taken as essences, all ideas are compatible and supplementary to one another, like the various arts of expression; it is possible to perceive, up to a certain point, the symbolic burden of each of them, and to profit by the spiritual criticism of experience which it may embody. In particular, I recognize this spiritual truth in the Neo-Platonic and Indian systems, without admitting their fabulous side: after all, it is an old maxim with me that many ideas may be convergent as poetry which would be divergent as dogmas. This applies, in quite another quarter, to that revolution in physics which is now loudly announced, sometimes as the bankruptcy of science, sometimes as the breakdown of materialism. This revolution becomes, in my view, simply a change in notation. Matter may be called gravity or an electric charge or a tension in an ether; mathematics may readjust its equations to more accurate observations; any fresh description of nature which may result will still be a product of human wit, like the Ptolemaic and the Newtonian systems, and nothing but an intellectual symbol for man's contacts with matter, in so far as they have gone or as he has become distinctly sensitive to them. The real matter, within him and without, will meantime continue to rejoice in its ancient ways, or to adopt new ones, and incidentally to create these successive notions of it in his head.

When all the data of immediate experience and all the constructions of thought have thus been purified and reduced to what they are intrinsically, that is, to eternal essences, by a sort of counterblast the sense of existence, of action, of ambushed reality everywhere about us, becomes all the clearer and more imperious. This assurance of the not-given is involved in action, in expectation, in fear, hope, or want: I call it animal faith. The object of this faith is the substantial energetic thing encountered in action, whatever this thing may be in itself; by moving, devouring, or transforming this thing I assure myself of its existence; and at the same time my respect for it becomes enlightened and proportionate to its definite powers. But throughout, for the description of it in fancy, I have only the essences which my senses or thought may evoke in its presence; these are my inevitable signs and names for that object. Thus the whole sensuous and intellectual furniture of the mind becomes a store whence I may fetch terms for the description of nature, and may compose the silly home-poetry in which I talk to myself about everything. All is a tale told, if not by an idiot, at least by a dreamer; but it is far from signifying nothing. Sensations are rapid dreams: perceptions are dreams sustained and developed at will; sciences are dreams abstracted, controlled, measured, and rendered scrupulously proportional to their occasions. Knowledge accordingly always remains a part of imagination in its terms and in its seat; yet by virtue of its origin and intent it becomes a memorial and a guide to the fortunes of man in nature.

In the foregoing I have said nothing about my sentiments concerning æsthetics or the fine arts; yet I have devoted two volumes to those subjects, and I believe that to some people my whole philosophy seems to be little but rhetoric or prose poetry. I must frankly confess that I have written some verses; and at one time I had thoughts of becoming an architect or even a painter. The decorative and poetic aspects of art and nature have always fascinated me and held my attention above everything else. But in philosophy I recognize no separable thing called æsthetics; and

what has gone by the name of the philosophy of art, like the so-called philosophy of history, seems to me sheer verbiage. There is in art nothing but manual knack and professional tradition on the practical side, and on the contemplative side pure intuition of essence, with the inevitable intellectual or luxurious pleasure which pure intuition involves. I can draw no distinction—save for academic programmes—between moral and æsthetic values: beauty, being a good, is a moral good; and the practice and enjoyment of art, like all practice and all enjoyment, fall within the sphere of morals—at least if by morals we understand moral economy and not moral superstition. On the other hand, the good, when actually realized and not merely pursued from afar, is a joy in the immediate; it is possessed with wonder and is in that sense æsthetic. Such pure joy when blind is called pleasure, when centred in some sensible image is called beauty, and when diffused over the thought of ulterior propitious things is called happiness, love, or religious rapture. But where all is manifest, as it is in intuition, classifications are pedantic. Harmony, which might be called an æsthetic principle, is also the principle of health, of justice, and of happiness. Every impulse, not the æsthetic mood alone, is innocent and irresponsible in its origin and precious in its own eyes; but every impulse or indulgence, including the æsthetic, is evil in its effect, when it renders harmony impossible in the general tenor of life, or produces in the soul division and ruin. There is no lack of folly in the arts; they are full of inertia and affectation and of what must seem ugliness to a cultivated taste; yet there is no need of bringing the catapult of criticism against it: indifference is enough. A society will breed the art which it is capable of, and which it deserves; but even in its own eyes this art will hardly be important or beautiful unless it engages deeply the resources of the soul. The arts may die of triviality, as they were born of enthusiasm. On the other hand, there will always be beauty, or a transport akin to the sense of beauty, in any high contemplative moment. And it is only in contemplative moments that life is truly vital, when routine gives place to intuition, and experience is synthesized and brought before the spirit in its sweep and truth. The intention of my philosophy has certainly been to attain, if possible, such wide intuitions, and to celebrate the emotions with which they fill the mind. If this object be æsthetic and merely poetical, well and good: but it is a poetry or æstheticism which shines by disillusion and is simply intent on the unvarnished truth.

The liberal age in which I was born and the liberal circles in which I was educated flowed contentedly towards intellectual dissolution and anarchy. No atmosphere could have been more unfavourable to that solidity and singleness of conviction to which by nature I was addressed. I suffered from a slack education, conflicting traditions, deadening social pressure, academic lumber, and partisan heat about false problems. The pure philosophy to which, in spirit, I was wedded from the beginning, the orthodox human philosophy in which I ought to have been brought up, has never had time to break through and show all its native force, pathos, and simplicity. I ought to have begun where I have ended.

Would it be possible to indicate, in a page or two, what

I conceive orthodox human philosophy to be? Perhaps: because the thing is not unknown. The ancients came innocently upon it in various fields. Yet not even Aristotle, much less the moderns, ever conceived it in its entirety, with a just balance of its parts. I seem to recognise three orthodox schools of philosophy, each humanly right in its own sphere, but wrong in ignoring or denying the equal human rightness of the other two.

The Indians are orthodox in transcendental reflection. They take systematically the point of view of the spirit. For there is an invisible and inevitable moral witness to everything, not a physical or psychological self, but a higher centre of observation to which this world, or any world, or any God, is an imposed and questionable accident. Being morally inspired, being the voice of a living soul, this spirit has dramatic relations with the world which it encounters. The encounter may occasionally turn into a passionate embrace in which the spirit and all things seem merged in utterable unity. But that is a dramatic episode like any other: the tragic spirit revives and recovers its solitude. It would not be an actual spirit at all if it were not a personal moral being subject to fortune and needing to be saved. Spiritual philosophy would therefore not be orthodox if it were not ascetic and detached from the world.

The Greeks before Socrates reached orthodoxy in natural philosophy, which was re-established later in Spinoza and in modern science. Natural philosophers quarrel among themselves just because they are engaged in a common task with the issue undetermined. Yet they are all conspiring to trace and conceive the structure and history of this natural world in which everyone finds himself living.

The Greeks after Socrates founded orthodoxy in morals. I have endeavoured to retrace this theme in *The Life of Reason* and in my entire criticism of literature and religion. The principles of orthodoxy here were most clearly laid down by Plato in the *Philebus* and in the First Book of the *Republic*; but unfortunately, contrary to the modesty of Socrates himself, these principles were turned instinctively into a new mythology, in the effort to lend power and cosmic ascendency to the good: a good which is *good* only because, at each point, life and aspiration are spontaneously directed upon it. Ethics, as Aristotle said, is a part of politics, the foundation of this art being human nature, and its criterion harmony in living. But how should harmony be achieved in living if the inward spirit is distracted and the outer conditions of existence are unknown? Soundness in natural and in spiritual philosophy therefore seems requisite to soundness in politics.

That is all my message: that morality and religion are expressions of human nature; that human nature is a biological growth; and finally that spirit, fascinated and tortured, is involved in the process, and asks to be saved. What is salvation? Some organic harmony in forms and movements is requisite for life; but physical life is blind and groping and runs up continually against hostile forces, disease and death. It is therefore in the interests of life to become more intelligent and to establish a harmony also with the environment and the future. But life enlightened is spirit: the voice of life, and therefore aspiring to all the

perfections to which life aspires, and loving all the beauties that life loves; yet at the same time spirit is the voice of truth and of destiny, bidding life renounce beauty and perfection and life itself, whenever and wherever these are impossible.

In *Winds of Doctrine* and my subsequent books, a reader of my earlier writings may notice a certain change of climate. There were natural causes for this change. I was weathering the age of fifty. My nearer relations were dead or dispersed. I had resigned my professorship at Harvard, and no longer crossed and re-crossed the Atlantic. . . . My *Soliloquies in England* contain clear indications that, in spite of the war then raging, fancy in me had taken a new lease of life. I felt myself nearer than ever before to rural nature and to the perennial animal roots of human society. It was not my technical philosophy that was principally affected, but rather the meaning and status of philosophy for my inner man. The humanism characteristic of the *Sense of Beauty* and *Life of Reason* remained standing; but foundations were now supplied for that humanism by a more explicit and vigorous natural philosophy; a natural philosophy which, without being otherwise changed than as the growth of natural science might suggest, was itself destined to be enveloped later by the ontology contained in *Realms of Being*. These additions are buttresses and supports: the ontology justifies materialism, and the materialism justifies rational ethics and an æsthetic view of the mind.

Certainly materialism cannot justify moral ideals *morally*. Morally a sentiment can be confirmed only by another sentiment, for whatever that may be worth. But materialism justifies the life of reason martially, as a fighting organisation, and explains its possible strength and dominance. What from the moral point of view we call the instruments of reason are primarily the ground and cause of reason: and reason can control matter only because reason is matter organised, and assuming a form at once distinctive, plastic, and opportune. Unity of direction is thus imposed on our impulses; the impulses remain and continue to work and to take themselves most seriously; things tempt and hurt us as much as ever. Yet this very synthesis imposed upon the passions has brought steadiness and scope into the mind. The passions seem less absolute than before: we see them in a more tragic or comic light; and we see that even our noble and civilised life of reason is bought at a price. As there were wild animal joys that it has banished, so there may be divine insights that it cannot heed.

I had begun philosophising quite normally, by bleating like any young lamb: agitated by religion, passionately laying down the law for art and politics, and even bubbling over into conventional verses, which I felt to be oracular and irresistible. But my vocation was clear: my earliest speculation was at once intimate and universal, and philosophically religious, as it has always remained; yet not exclusively on the lines of that complete Christian system which first offered itself to my imagination. I was always aware of alternatives; nor did these alternatives seem utterly hostile and terrible. My enthusiasm was largely dramatic; I recited my Lucretius with as much gusto as my

Saint Augustine; and gradually Lucretius sank deeper and became more satisfying. What I demanded unconditionally was dramatic wholeness. I wanted to articulate each possible system, to make it consistent, radical, and all-embracing. Hesitation and heresy were odious to me in any quarter; and I cared more for the internal religious force of each faith than for such external reasons as might be urged to prove that faith or to disprove it. What indeed could such external reasons be but corollaries to some different system, itself needing to be believed?

A judicial comparison of various systems of life and morals was therefore not possible for me until I had found a sure foothold for criticism, other than the histrionic convictions between which my youthful sentiment could so easily oscillate. This foothold was supplied to me by human nature, as each man after due Socratic self-questioning might find it in himself, and as Plato and Aristotle express it for mankind at large in their rational ethics. There is nothing unalterably fixed in this moral physiognomy of man, any more than in his bodily structure; but both are sufficiently recognisable and constant for the purposes of medicine and politics. The point of chief speculative interest is that morality, like health, is determined by the existing constitution of our animal nature, and the opportunities or denials that materially confront us; so that we are much deeper and more deeply bound to physical reality than our wayward thoughts and wishes might suggest. The potential, in an organic being developing through time, is necessarily richer and more important than the actual. The actual is superficial, occasional, ephemeral; present will and present consciousness are never the true self. They are phenomena elicited by circumstances from a psyche that remains largely unexpressed. Yet this psyche, this inherited nature or seed, flowers in those manifestations, filling them as they pass with beauty and passion: and nothing will be moral or personal in ideas except what they borrow by a secret circulation from the enduring heart. There, and not in any superstitious precepts, lies the root of duty and the criterion of perfection.

In saying this I am far from wishing to attribute a metaphysical fixity or unity to the psyche, or to claim for my own person an absolute singleness and consistency. Some passive drifting and some fundamental vagueness there must be in every animal mind; and the best-knit psyche still participates in the indefinite flux of matter, is self-forgetful in part, and is mortal. But this only proves that no man can be wholly a philosopher or an artist, or wholly himself. We are moral individuals, we exist as persons, only imperfectly, by grace of certain essences kindly imputed to us by our own thoughts or by the thoughts of others. There is always a moral chaos, though it be a dynamic mathematical order, beneath our rationalised memory or criticism: a chaos which is an indispensable support and continual peril to the spirit, as the sea is to a ship. Yet in our nautical housekeeping we may disregard the background. The deluge keeps our rational ark afloat, and our thoughts follow our treasures.

Yet not necessarily all our thoughts. The need of keeping a look-out may generate a disinterested interest in the winds and tides, and we may end by smiling at the moral reasons which we first assigned for the deluge. In my later writings I speak of something called the spiritual life; of a certain *disintoxication* clarifying those passions which the life of reason endeavours to harmonise. Is spirit then hostile to reason? Is reason hostile to spirit? Neither: but within the life of reason there is incidental rivalry in the types of organisation attempted, in their range, and in the direction in which the inevitable sacrifices are accepted. Spirit and reason, as I use the words, spring from the same root in organic life, namely, from the power of active adaptation possessed by animals, so that the external world and the future are regarded in their action. Being regarded in action, absent things are then regarded in thought; and this is intelligence. But intelligence and reason are often merely potential, as in habit, memory, institutions, and books: they become spirit only when they flower into actual consciousness. Spirit is essentially simpler, less troubled, more lyrical than reason: it is not specifically human. It may exist in animals, perhaps in plants, as it certainly exists in children; and in its outlook, far from being absorbed in tasks and cares, like reason, it is initially universal and addressed to anything and everything that there may happen to be.

Between the spiritual life and the life of reason there is accordingly no contradiction: they are concomitant: yet there is a difference of temper and level, as there is between agriculture and music. The ploughman may sing, and the fiddler at times may dig potatoes; but the vocations pull in different ways. Being ready for everything, and a product of vital harmony, spirit finds an initial delight in art and contrivance, in adventure and discovery, for these are forms of order and enlarged harmony: yet in the midst of business, spirit suspends business, and begins to wonder, to laugh, or to pray. A family quarrel may easily arise between these mental faculties; a philosopher sympathises naturally with speculation; but the ethics of this conflict are the same as in other conflicts: to know oneself, and to impose on oneself or on others only the sacrifices requisite to bring one's chosen life to perfection.

I have always disliked mystics who were not definite in their logic and orthodox in their religion. Spirit is not a power: it comes to fulfil, not to destroy. By understanding the world we may in a certain ideal sense transcend it; but we do not transcend it by misunderstanding it: on the contrary, we remain in that case dupes of our own flesh and our own egotism. Every temperament and every vocation, even the highest, engages us in a special course that imposes sweeping renunciations in other directions. But these renunciations would not be true sacrifices if the things sacrificed were not admittedly good. Marriage and wealth, sport and adventure, dominion and war are not condemned by the spiritual man in being renounced. They are left benevolently or sadly for the natural man, who is generously and inevitably engaged in them. The passions are the elements of life; nevertheless they are deceptive and tragic. They fade from the mind of the old man who can survey their full course; unless indeed he makes himself a shrill and emasculated echo of them, forgetting the dignity of years. Sometimes these passions shock and repel a young soul even at their first assault: and then we have the saint or seer by nature, who can transcend common experience without having tasted it; but this is a rare faculty, abnormal and not to be expected or even desired. Thus there is a certain option and practical incompatibility between spirituality and humanism, between poetry and business, between sheer logic and sound sense; but the conflict is only marginal, the things are concentric, and spirit merely heightens and universalises the synthesis which reason makes partially, as occasion requires, in the service of natural interests. To make this synthesis is itself a natural interest, as the child loves to look and to explore: and spirit, the conscience of nature that sees the truth of nature, is the most natural of things.

My later philosophy, then, on the moral side, merely develops certain ultimate themes of the inner life which had run in my head from the beginning: they had dominated my verse, and had reappeared in my early accounts of poetry and religion, of Platonic love, and post-rational morality. The developments in no way disturb the biological basis assigned to all life; they do not make my naturalistic ethics dogmatic. They are proposed merely as optional. They are confessions of the sentiment with which the spectacle of things and the discipline of experience can fill a reflective mind.

Within the same naturalistic frame my later philosophy has also elaborated the analysis of perception, of belief, and of "ideas" in general; and in this direction I have come to discriminate something which seems strangely to irritate my critics: I mean, what I call essence and the realm of essence. These words, and my whole presentation of this subject, were perhaps unfortunate. I have advanced an emancipating doctrine in traditional terms; the terms excite immediate scorn in modern radical quarters, while the emancipating doctrine horrifies those conservatives to whom the terms might not give offense. I am sorry: but this accident after all is of little consequence, especially as the same doctrine—loaded, no doubt, with other accidental lumber—is being propagated by various influential writers in uglier and more timely terms. The point is to reduce evidence to the actually evident, and to relegate all the rest to hypothesis, presumption, and animal faith. What I call essence is not something alleged to exist or subsist in some higher sphere: it is the last residuum of scepticism and analysis. Whatsoever existing fact we may think we encounter, there will be obvious features distinguishing that alleged fact from any dissimilar fact and from nothing. All such features, discernible in sense, thought, or fancy, are essences; and the realm of essence which they compose is simply the catalogue, infinitely extensible, of all characters logically distinct and ideally possible. Apart from the events they may figure in, these essences have no existence; and since the realm of essence, by definition, is infinitely comprehensive and without bias, it can exercise no control over the existing world, nor determine what features shall occur in events, or in what order.

Indeed, it might seem idle to have mentioned these pure essences at all, which living thought traverses unwittingly, as speech does the words of one's native language; yet the study of grammar is enlightening, and there is a clarifying

and satiric force in the discrimination of essences. For the irony of fate will have it that these ghosts are the only realities we ever actually can find: and it is rather the thought-castles of science and the dramatic vistas of history that, for instant experience, are ghostly and merely imagined. What should mind be, if it were not a poetic cry? Mind does not come to repeat the world but to celebrate it. The essences evoked in sensation and thought are naturally original, graphic, and morally coloured. Consciousness was created by the muses; but meantime industrious nature, in our bodily organisation, takes good care to keep our actions moderately sane, in spite of our poetic genius.

Thus as in my younger days in respect to religions, so now in respect to all experience and all science, critical reflection has emancipated me from the horrid claim of ideas to literal truth. And just as religion, when seen to be poetry, ceases to be deceptive and therefore odious, and becomes humanly more significant than it seemed before; so experience and science, when seen to be woven out of essences and wholly symbolic, gain in moral colour and spirituality what they lose in dead weight. The dead weight falls back from sensuous images and intellectual myths to the material fatality that breeds and sustains them.

This fatality itself, in proving wholly arbitrary, seems to oppress us less; it inspires courage and good humour, rather than supplications and fears. Perhaps what the realm of essence, in its mute eternity, chiefly adds to our notion of nature is the proof that nature is contingent. An infinite canvas is spread before us on which any world might have been painted. The actuality of things is sharpened and the possibilities of things are enlarged. We cease to be surprised or distressed at finding existence unstable and transitory. Why should it have been otherwise? Not only must our own lives be insecure, as earthly seasons change, but perhaps all existence is in flux, even down to its first principles. *Dum vivimus vivamus.* Everything, so long as it recognisably endures, is free to deploy its accidental nature; and we may lead the life of reason with a good grace, harmonising as well as possible our various impulses and opportunities, and exploring the realm of essence as our genius may prompt.

The exposition of my philosophy is still incomplete, and in many directions, as for instance in mathematical physics, the development of it is beyond my powers. Yet virtually the whole system was latent in me from the beginning. When in adolescence I oscillated between solipsism and the Catholic faith, that was an accidental dramatic way of doing honour both to rigour and to abundance. But the oscillation was frivolous and the two alternate positions were self-indulgent. A self-indulgent faith sets up its casual myths and rashly clings to them as to literal truths; while a self-indulgent scepticism pretends to escape all dogma, forgetting its own presuppositions. With time it was natural that oscillation should give place to equilibrium; not, let us hope, to a compromise, which of all things is the most unstable and unphilosophical; but to a radical criticism putting each thing where it belongs. Without forgetting or disowning anything, myth might then be corrected by disillusion, and scepticism by sincerity. So transformed, my earliest affections can survive in my latest. (pp. 8-30)

George Santayana, "A General Confession," in The Philosophy of George Santayana, *edited by Paul Arthur Schilpp, second edition, The Library of Living Philosophers, Vol. II, Tudor Publishing Company, 1951, pp. 3-30.*

Bertrand Russell   (essay date 1940)

[*A respected and prolific author, Russell was an English philosopher and mathematician known for his support for humanistic concerns. Two of his early works,* Principles of Mathematics (*1903) and* Principia Mathematica (*1910-1913), written with Alfred North Whitehead, are considered classics of mathematical logic. His philosophical approach to all his endeavors discounts idealism or emotionalism and asserts a progressive application of his "logical atomism," a process whereby individual facts are logically analyzed. Russell's humanistic beliefs often centered around support of unorthodox social concerns, including free love, undisciplined education, and the eradication of nuclear weapons. His staunch pacifism during World War I led to a six-month imprisonment and began a history of political and social activism which culminated when, at the age of eighty-nine, he was again jailed for his active participation in an unruly demonstration advocating unilateral nuclear disarmament. After the incident Russell stated: "What I want is some assurance before I die that the human race will be allowed to continue." Regarding Russell, biographer Alan Wood states: "He started by asking questions about mathematics and religion and philosophy, and went on to question accepted ideas about war and politics and sex and education, setting the minds of men on the march, so that the world could never be quite the same as if he had not lived." In recognition of his achievements in a number of literary genres, Russell was awarded the Nobel Prize in literature in 1950. In the following excerpt, Russell examines Santayana's central philosophic concepts.*]

In attempting to characterize philosophers, no uniform method should be adopted. The method, in each case, should be such as to exhibit what the philosopher himself thinks important, and what, in the opinion of the critic, makes him worthy of study. There are some—of whom Leibniz is the most important example—who stand or fall by the correctness of their reasoning and logical analysis; the treatment of such philosophers demands minute dissection and the search for fallacies. There are others—e.g. Democritus and Descartes—who invent imaginative hypotheses of a sweeping kind, which act as a spur to detailed scientific investigation; these men owe their importance, not to the adequacy of their own grounds for their hypotheses, but to their subsequent fruitfulness. Another large group of philosophers—of whom the German idealists are the classic examples—derive their merit or demerit, according to the opinion of the critic, from an attempt to humanize the universe; these men are important if their metaphysics are correct, and unimportant if not.

Apart from the attempt to understand the world, philosophy has other functions to fulfill. It can enlarge the imagination by the construction of a cosmic epic, or it can suggest a way of life less wayward and accidental than that of the unreflective. A philosopher who attempts either of these tasks must be judged by a standard of values, aesthetic or ethical, rather than by intellectual correctness. Lucretius and Spinoza may be taken as illustrative of these two types; each has a metaphysic, but neither loses his importance when his metaphysic is discredited.

Santayana, like Spinoza, is to be read, not so much on account of his theoretical doctrines, as on account of his view as to what constitutes the good life, and of his standard of values in art and morals. I do not mean to suggest that either his opinions or his values resemble Spinoza's. Spinoza, he says, failed to reconstitute the life of reason, because "everything impassioned seemed to him insane, everything human necessarily petty. Man was to be a pious tame animal, with the stars shining above his head." The likeness to Spinoza consists in concern for the life of reason, not in the theory as to what it consists of.

When a philosophy is in this sense fundamentally ethical, the question whether, as a whole, it is to be accepted or rejected is not amenable to argument, and reduces, when honestly considered, to the question: "Do I like or dislike it?" This, however, is not the only issue for the critic. There is also the question of internal consistency: has the system in question been so deeply felt and thought as to possess a comprehensive subjective harmony? And there is another matter, less definite, namely what we may call the *importance* of the point of view. A lunatic's judgments, even if they achieve consistency, remain unimportant; Spinoza's, though not wholly consistent, are important.

As regards these three problems, I will, to begin with, briefly state my own view of Santayana's system. To a certain extent, though not wholly, I am in agreement with it; it is exceptionally self-consistent; and I have no doubt that it is important.

To understand Santayana, it is necessary to bear in mind some general features of his circumstances and temperament. While his environment has been mainly American, his tastes and preferences have remained predominantly Spanish. This clash, it would seem, produced a rare explicitness and self-knowledge as regards values. Those who have always lived in sympathetic surroundings have had no occasion to become aware of the impersonal part of their springs of action, since no one has questioned it. Unsympathetic surroundings, on the contrary, generate, in a reflective mind, an intellectual defensive system. In a world of pragmatism, democracy, mechanism, and Protestant modernism, Santayana remained a Platonizing scholastic, a theoretical believer in aristocracy, unmoved by the triumphs of scientific technique, aesthetically and politically, though not theologically, a Catholic. Perhaps his negative reaction to the modern non-Mediterranean world contains more of passion than appears in his writings, which have a possibly deceptive stylistic calm. His literary taste is incompatible with controversy, and his most incisive criticisms are aphoristic rather than argumentative. Take, for example, his judgment on Kant's ethics: "The 'categorical imperative' was a shadow of the ten commandments; the postulates of practical reason were the minimal tenets of the most abstract Protestantism. These fossils, found unaccountably imbedded in the old man's mind, he regarded as evidences of an inward but supernatural revelation." Most professorial philosophers would develop this sentiment into a volume, but Santayana is content with a polished expression of contemptuous distaste. It may well be doubted whether greater length would have added anything of value.

But it is time to leave these generalities and consider Santayana's system in more detail.

His views on metaphysics and theory of knowledge are most explicitly set forth in *Realms of Being*. Essences, matter, and truth are the three realms. (A fourth, *The Realm of Spirit*, has just been published, since the writing of this essay.) The realm of essence is "the infinite multitude of distinguishable ideal terms." An essence does not exist as such, but may be exemplified in what exists; absolute truth is "merely that segment of the realm of essence which happens to be illustrated in existence." "Sometimes," he says,

> sensation and language, instead of being passed over like the ticking of the telegraph, may become objects in themselves, in all their absolute musical insignificance; and then animals become idealists. The terms in which they describe things, unlike the things they are meant to describe, are purely specious, arbitrary, and ideal; whether visual, tactile, auditory, or conceptual these terms are essentially *words*. They possess intrinsically, on their own ontological plane, only logical or aesthetic being; and this contains no indication whatever of the material act of speaking, touching, or looking which causes them to appear. All possible terms in mental discourse are essences existing nowhere; visionary equally, whether the faculty that discovers them be sense or thought or the most fantastic fancy.

Thus essences are not mental; they are objects which may be apprehended by minds, but which are in no way affected by being apprehended, and have the kind of being appropriate to them even if they never become objects to any minds. They constitute a world of Platonic ideas, but purified from all such contact with the world of existence as sullied their purity in Plato's system.

The substance of what actually exists Santayana calls "matter." It would be verbally correct, though very misleading, to call him a materialist; it would be misleading, both because he uses the word "matter" in a somewhat peculiar sense, and because he is less interested in the material world than in the realm of essence. Essence, he says, "is a sort of invitation to the dance." "However monistic physics may choose to be, the realm of essence is the home of eternal and irreducible plurality." "Essences are definite and thinkable: existence is indefinite and only endured." This is a sentiment with which, in feeling, I find myself completely in sympathy, though it is of the South rather than of the misty North. If the world is to be conceived in terms of substance and attribute, then everything, or almost everything, that Santayana says about essence commands my assent. Whether the world should be so conceived has been often questioned, but in *The Realm*

of Essence there is no controversial defence of this fundamental assumption. Whatever may be the correct view, any adequate discussion of this question must be very technical and must be influenced by modern logic. It is, however, a fixed practice with Santayana to avoid everything that cannot be discussed in literary form. This imposes certain limitations upon his writing, and also, I think, upon his thought. He has, for instance, a chapter on "Pure Being," which would have been different if he had taken account of logical technique. Perhaps, however, the difference would not have been as to anything that he thinks important. When a previously philosophical question becomes technical, he might say, it is shown to have been not genuinely philosophical; philosophy conceived as a means to the Life of Reason must be capable of being set forth in literary as opposed to technical language.

The question as to what can and what cannot be expressed in philosophy without the use of a crabbed and difficult vocabulary and syntax is an important one, which has more influence than might be thought upon the actual content of a writer's opinions. Broadly speaking, old conceptions have acquired pleasant literary clothes, whereas new ones still appear uncouth. An aesthetic bias in favour of good literary form is therefore likely to be associated with conservatism. This does not always happen; Hume is an instance to the contrary. But Hume's innovations were only in opinion, not in the concepts applied to the understanding of the world. No one has ever surpassed Plato in the literary expression of new ideas, but even he felt compelled to abandon charm of style as he grew older. As a result of many centuries of Platonism, the language of educated men can now express even the most difficult of Plato's ideas without crabbedness; but this was not the case in his own day. The scholastics were notorious for their barbarous jargon, which caused the renaissance to despise them; yet whatever had value in their systems can be expressed by Santayana in the most smooth and exquisite English. The mathematical concepts of the seventeenth century— function, differential, integral, etc.—though immeasurably useful in understanding the world, have no means of literary expression, with the result that philosophers still think of causation in the discrete form "A causes B," and finance ministers introducing a graduated income tax cannot say "the tax shall be proportional to the three-halfth power of the income." In such ways those who insist upon elegant literary form are compelled to lag behind—often far behind—the best thought of their time. Per contra, conservatives have a great aesthetic advantage over innovators, for ideas, unlike animals, grow more beautiful as they grow older.

Every philosopher has limitations, and Santayana frequently acknowledges his own. What he has to say about the Realm of Matter is less interesting than what he has to say about the Realms of Essence and Truth. His volume on *Reason in Science*, though full of valuable material, contains very little about science, and almost nothing to console the man who has "doubts" about scientific method, in the sense in which Victorians had "doubts" about religion. This is one instance of the bearing of difficult technical discussions upon questions of value. If scientific knowledge is possible, the pursuit of it is part of the Life of Reason; if not, not. Confronted with this issue, Santayana appeals to "animal faith." I think it highly probable that there is nothing better to be done. Santayana sighs as a lover (of knowledge), and obeys as a son (of nature). But a more passionate lover of knowledge will not obey until he has explored every avenue of escape, and some of these lead into the tangled forests of probability and induction; he may even prefer to perish philosophically in the attempt to blaze a trail through these pathless wilds, rather than acquiesce in a renunciation which saps the springs of hope. To attempt the impossible is, no doubt, contrary to reason; but to attempt the possible which *looks* impossible is the summit of wisdom. Only the issue can decide whether a man is wise or a fanatical madman, and fanatics of certain kinds should therefore be treated with hypothetical respect. All this will be found admitted in various passages of Santayana's books, but it is the admission of an onlooker, not an actor. "We live in this human scene as in a theatre," he says. But it is not so that the actors and the dramatist live.

There is in Santayana's system a very complete dualism between "essence" and "matter." The category of substance—which, unlike most recent philosophers, he sees no reason to reject—applies, in his view, only to "matter," which includes "the gods." (Does it include God? And is there a God? I am not sure what his answer would be.) All natural knowledge, he says, rests on the assumption that there are things and events prior to the discovery of them and independent of this discovery; these things are "substance." All causal efficacy is ascribed to matter; the causes of mental changes are material. Substance which is not material is only grammatical. He makes fun of Leibniz and Berkeley as "muscular idealists;" in their systems, "God was comfortably pledged never to act otherwise than as if matter were acting for him." Their religiosity was "purely official; their idealism was, and was intended to be, perfectly mundane." Spirits thought of as powers "are simply mythological names for certain operations of matter, poetically apprehended, and turned into dramatic units with reference to the observer's interests or emotions." As criticism, what is said against idealism is admirable, but considered as ground for materialism it suffers from the assumption that there is no third possibility.

The divorce of essence from existence, in which I formerly believed as completely as Santayana does, has come to seem to me questionable. I re-read recently his criticism of me in *Winds of Doctrine* (1913), and found myself, broadly speaking, in agreement with him whenever he thought me in the wrong, but not when he thought me in the right. My views have changed so much that I could read what he said with almost as much detachment as if it applied to some one else. The only element that has remained constant is a certain method, notably Occam's razor, of which he disapproves as "the weapon of a monstrous self-mutilation with which British philosophy, if consistent, would soon have committed suicide." This, however, is by the way; the problem with which we are concerned at the moment is the relation of essence to existence. In his discussion of me he says:

> Nothing can ever exist in nature or for consciousness which has not a prior and indepen-

dent locus in the realm of essence. When a man lights upon a thought or is interested in tracing a relation, he does not introduce those objects into the realm of essence, but merely selects them from the plenitude of what lies there eternally.

Let us consider a particular application of this theory. Suppose—what would be quite possible—that in every spectrum a certain small finite region is dark, and that nowhere in nature is any colour to be found which has its place within this region. Are we to say that the shades of colour which would occupy this region if they existed have a timeless being in the realm of essence? I see no reason why we should say so. Words of which the meaning is universal are used in describing what exists, and if a word cannot serve this purpose I do not see in what sense it has meaning. This question, however, is too vast to be pursued further in the present connection.

The realm of Truth, as Santayana conceives it, involves both matter and essence; it depends upon the essences that happen to be exemplified in the actual world. All truth is contingent, since it describes existence. The view that truth consists in coherence is rejected as arrogant, and as yet involving impotence, since it abandons the hope that truth may really tell us something about the world. In regard to truth, "animal faith" is again very convenient so long as we can trust it, but there seems no good reason, except of a practical kind, in favour of doing so. "The only belief that I myself entertain," we are told, "because I find it irresistible, is the belief in a realm of matter, the expectation of persistence and order in a natural world; and this is a belief which I am confident the reader shares." I have not anything better to offer; I am, however, less contented with this solution than Santayana appears to be. For, after all, "animal faith" is only a name for a certain kind of blind impulse. Why, then, should we trust it?

The pragmatic answer is foreign to Santayana's whole outlook, which demands a more or less ascetic submission to a truth supposed independent of our desires and volitions. In *Scepticism and Animal Faith,* all *rational* arguments for any kind of belief are dismissed. "Belief in the existence of anything, including myself, is something radically incapable of proof, and resting, like all belief, on some irrational persuasion or prompting of life." "For all an ultimate scepticism can see, there may be no facts at all, and perhaps nothing has ever existed."

> There are certain motives . . . which render ultimate scepticism precious to a spiritual mind, as a sanctuary from grosser illusions. For the wayward sceptic, who regards it as no truer than any other view, it also has some utility: it accustoms him to discard the dogma which an introspective critic might be tempted to think self-evident, namely, that he himself lives and thinks. That he does so is true; but to establish that truth he must appeal to animal faith. If he is too proud for that, and simply stares at the datum, the last thing he will see is himself.

It is not quite clear what is intended by these passages. That belief in existence, speaking generally, is incapable of *proof,* is obvious to all who do not accept the ontological argument, since a conclusion cannot assert existence unless there is an assertion of existence among the premisses. But to call an unproved premiss "irrational" is hardly warranted. All unproved beliefs are, to begin with, mere expressions of animal faith, but the problem of theory of knowledge is to find some way of selecting some of these as more worthy of credence than others. This cannot be done by ultimate scepticism, which rejects them all, nor by animal faith, which accepts them all. If we are going to accept some and reject others, which is what every philosopher does, we need some principle intermediate between animal faith and complete scepticism. Perhaps this principle may be merely the power of resistance to scepticism, which is greater in some cases than in others; but if so, the above argument against Descartes' *cogito* loses its force. However that may be, there is, I think, a problem in regard to the rejection of scepticism which cannot be solved by an appeal to animal faith alone.

I come now to Santayana's judgments of value, as set forth in *The Life of Reason.* Although, having begun with his last comprehensive work, I am going backwards chronologically, this fact has little importance, as he is a remarkably consistent thinker, and has travelled, in his books, from the outworks of his system to the citadel. His judgments as to what parts of human life can be considered rational, which are set forth in *The Life of Reason,* are based upon a metaphysic which, in that book, is implicit, but becomes explicit in *Realms of Being.* That is why, in exposition, it has seemed best to reverse the chronological order.

Reason is considered by Santayana in five different spheres, Common Sense, Society, Religion, Art, and Science. *"The Life of Reason,"* we are told, "will then be a name for that part of experience which perceives and pursues ideals—all conduct so controlled and all sense so interpreted as to perfect natural happiness." His ideals, like those of all ages and classes before the industrial revolution, are contemplative rather than active.

> This world of free expression, this drift of sensations, passions, and ideas, perpetually kindled and fading in the light of consciousness, I call the *Realm of Spirit.* It is only for the sake of this free life that material competence and knowledge of fact are worth attaining. Facts for a living creature are only instruments; his play-life is his true life.

This is the kind of ideal which is nowadays called "aristocratic," because it values things which, hitherto, have only been open to aristocrats. For my part, I am in agreement with Santayana on this matter, as against the critics whom I can imagine pointing out the class origin of such an ethic. As a matter of fact, the Marxist ideal of honest toil is one taken over by intellectuals from employers. The genuine proletarian ideal is obviously one of idleness, as expressed in the swan-song of the dying washerwoman:

> I'm going where anthems for ever are ringing,
> But as I've no voice I get out of the singing.

Christianity has been called a religion for slaves, and its heaven is one of contemplation rather than action. It is in hell—according to *Paradise Lost*—that industrial activity

is practiced. Those who are, or imagine themselves, in power have a motive for trying to cause others to accept honest toil as an ideal, but those who have always had a plethora of work will consider rest an essential part of the good life. All this, however, is strictly irrelevant. There is no reason to suppose that the social systems which have prevailed hitherto have permitted what is best to be enjoyed by the many, nor, conversely, to condemn as not really good whatever, hitherto, has been the privilege of the few. It may be the temporary duty of the fortunate to renounce their privileges pending the creation of a better social system, but that is a question of morals, not of ultimate ideals; it is analogous to rationing during a siege.

Santayana distinguishes three stages in the development of ideals: prerational morality, rational ethics, and post-rational morality. The first precedes philosophy, the second has existed only in Greece, the third is that of the great religions of India and Christendom. The difference between rational and post-rational morality is, roughly speaking, the same as the difference between the artist and the ascetic.

> The Life of Reason is the happy marriage of two elements—impulse and ideation—which if wholly divorced would reduce man to a brute or to a maniac. The rational animal is generated by the union of these two monsters. He is constituted by ideas which have ceased to be visionary and actions which have ceased to be vain. Thus the Life of Reason is another name for what, in the widest sense of the word, might be called Art.

I think—though in this I am no longer verbally following Santayana—that the difference between the rational and the post-rational may be regarded as a difference as regards matter. To the artist, matter is raw material for the embodiment of his ideals; to the ascetic, it is the alien power by which his spiritual life is enslaved. The man who is enjoying a good dinner or carving a statue out of marble is not thinking of matter as his enemy, but as his opportunity. The ascetic, on the contrary—who, if he is logical, is a Manichaean—condemns all pleasures that depend on matter, and regards them as due to the material part of himself, from which he strives to be liberated. This condemnation applies not only to the pleasures commonly called sensual, but to the whole realm of art, since art is bound up with sense. Such a morality is an outcome of despair, and arises only when the primitive zest for life is extinct.

Reason, Santayana says, expresses impulses reduced to harmony, and its sanction is happiness. Nevertheless, he continues, democratic hedonism is mistaken, because we should not value silly pleasures. I do not quite understand how he arrives at this conclusion. Impulses are easier to harmonize if they are few and simple than if they are many and complex; therefore reason, by his own definition, should favour paucity of impulses. A man, he says

> need not limit his efforts to spreading needless comforts and silly pleasures among the million; he need not accept for a goal a child's caprices multiplied by infinity. . . . A conscience is a living function, expressing a particular nature; it is

not a passive medium where heterogeneous values can find their balance by virtue of their dead weight and number.

This seems to imply that the harmony of impulses which the rational man will seek is purely personal; he need only take account of his own impulses, and may condemn those of children or of the million as silly. Perhaps he would say that they are silly only because they cannot lead to satisfaction. "Ideals," he says, "are legitimate, and each initially envisages a genuine and innocent good; but they are not realizable together, nor even singly when they have no deep roots in the world." This seems to me a groundless dogma. The pleasure of seeing a football match or a cinema can be provided at less cost per head than that involved in a good performance of Hamlet or the C minor symphony, and I rather think that the pleasure of an uncultivated person at a cinema is greater than that of a cultivated person critically observing a production of Hamlet. Culture, I should say, subtracts more pleasures than it adds; moreover those that it adds are more expensive and less intense than those that it subtracts. If this is the case, no form of hedonism can justify the pursuit of culture.

It is natural to look for the solution of this problem in the volume on **Reason in Society.** But here we find culture frankly accepted as an ideal, regardless of the definition of Reason as a harmonizing of impulses. Thus: "Culture is on the horns of this dilemma: if profound and noble it must remain rare, if common it must become mean. These alternatives can never be eluded until some purified and high-bred race succeeds the promiscuous bipeds that now blacken the planet." "Civilization has hitherto consisted in diffusion and dilution of habits arising in privileged centers. . . . To abolish aristocracy, in the sense of social privilege and sanctified authority, would be to cut off the source from which all culture has hitherto flowed." All these statements, as history, appear to me undeniable; but if taken as ethics, they imply that culture is to be sought even at the cost of a vast accumulation of human suffering. This view is compatible with one of Santayana's definitions of the Life of Reason, as "practice guided by science and directed toward spiritual goods," provided it is understood that goods are "spiritual" when such as are enjoyed by men of culture; but it is not compatible with the definition of Reason as harmonizing impulses, nor with the statement that its sanction is happiness. (pp. 453-65)

Both **The Life of Reason** and **Realms of Being** are important books—more important than they appear on a cursory reading. The extraordinary excellence of the style has a soothing effect, which makes it easy to read on without fully apprehending the purport of what is said. The delightful aphorisms which occur from time to time temporarily dispel the reader's seriousness, and make him happy instead of earnest. But when these pleasant obstacles have been overcome, it appears that a comprehensive view of life and the world has been presented, which is all the more valuable because it is very different from any of those that are prevalent in the present age. It is urbane, historical, free from fanaticism, and the expression of an exceptionally sensitive intellectual perception.

These merits, however, inevitably entail certain limita-

Santayana at the Clinic of the Blue Nuns.

tions. They could hardly exist in a man with any originality of technique. Like almost everything aesthetically delightful, they depend upon a degree of continuity with the past which is not likely to be found in a man who makes important innovations. The temptation to hate in the present the same sort of thing that we value in the past, and to respect men in proportion to their antiquity, is one which Santayana perhaps does not always resist. He remarks, for instance, that Heraclitus was a "freer and wiser" man than Hegel. This may be true, and for my part I find Heraclitus delightful and Hegel disgusting. But how would it be if we possessed as little of the works of Hegel as those of Heraclitus? Or, conversely, what should we think if, like Plato in the *Theaetetus,* we were irritated beyond endurance by glib young men assuring us that all modern minded people agreed with Heraclitus? Heraclitus favored aristocracy against democracy in the politics of Ephesus, but this is an ancient issue, and we can allow ourselves to enjoy his invective without sharing his opinions. But Hegel's glorification of the Prussian State made him an ally of the modern governments which are attempting to enslave intelligence, and we, who are participants, can hardly view this struggle with historic detachment. I think that, if we were as remote from present-day politics as from those of ancient Greece, and knew as little of Hegel as of Heraclitus, we might see nothing to choose between the two men. I often think with envy how full of ripe wisdom I should seem if I had lived two thousand years ago, written in a dead language, and remained known only through a few of my more ponderous aphorisms. But these advantages, alas, can only be enjoyed by my "essence."

Santayana is fond of myths, and I offer him one to embody what I have been saying. Dr. Johnson said the devil was the first Whig; I suggest that he was the first Tory. When the Lord decided to create Man, He acted as a revolutionary; to Satan, when he got wind of the project, it seemed a wild and foolish innovation, since the angelic universe was well ordered, had an ancient mellow ritual, and was long since purged of all the crudities that had marred its earlier aeons. The only solution that occurred to him was to bring death into our world; he did not foresee that death would come too slowly to prevent our first parents from leaving progeny who would perpetuate the legacy of confusion. In all this dislike of rash and chaotic novelty, I feel sure that Santayana would have agreed with Satan; I should have agreed myself if I could have foreseen what Man would make of his planet. Nevertheless, it is *possible* that we should have been in the wrong.

Santayana's discussions of philosophy in America [in *Character and Opinion in the United States*] illustrate his attitude towards vigorous contemporary innovation. He speaks of himself as "not an American except by long association," but the association was so long and so intimate that his knowledge is to be trusted, though his feelings about what he knows remain those of a European. He is struck, as every foreigner in America must be, by the gulf between academic values and those of daily life. I have felt it myself to be typified by the preference of universities for Gothic architecture, and have sometimes thought that professors would be more respected if their work were carried on in skyscrapers, and I find that Santayana has expressed a similar idea. Universities in Europe were an important part of the State from the early Middle Ages to the end of the nineteenth century. Now this has ceased to be the case in Germany and Russia, and, at least temporarily, in France. In America they have never had the same governmental significance, because, in culture though not in science, they were endeavouring to keep alive an ancient tradition of which most people felt no sincere need. This tradition, in philosophy as in religion, was based upon the emotional realization of human impotence in face of natural forces. Men gave thanks to God for their daily bread; now, when not dominated by convention, they give thanks to the government or to a new fertilizer. Other men, not Nature or God, must be propitiated or restrained in order to secure prosperity. For economic reasons, this modern outlook is especially developed in America, although it is kept from explicitness by inherited piety. In philosophy, it shows itself as a revolt against what Santayana calls the "genteel tradition"—a revolt which, as he rightly recognizes, was led by William James.

Santayana's essay on William James is as sympathetic as he can make it, and filled with scrupulous fairness. But at moments his feelings are too strong for him. James, he says, tried to help his students to live a good life.

> But what is a good life? Had William James, had the people about him, had modern philosophers anywhere, any notion of that? I cannot think so. They had much experience of personal goodness, and love of it; they had standards of character and right conduct; but as to what might render human existence good, excellent, beautiful, happy, and worth having as a whole, their notions were utterly thin and barbarous. They had forgotten the Greeks, or never known them.

I think the idea that the Greeks knew how to live the good life has very little to support it. Would Harvard have been better than it was if Boston had been engaged in a long and disastrous war with New York, if William James had been executed on a charge of atheism, and his disciples had established an abominable tyranny? For my part, I am persuaded that no Athenian, not even Plato, understood the good life as well as William James did. I admit that Plato could have defined the good life with more eloquence and precision; but that is another matter. I admit also that I, as a European, feel at home with the culture inherited from the Greeks as I do not with the nascent pragmatic culture of America. Nevertheless it seems to me probable that, from a historical standpoint, and ignoring the question of relative truth or falsehood, we are seeing the beginnings of a new and vigorous philosophy, which, in the market place as well as in the schools, will replace Hellenism and Christianity, and may, two thousand years hence, have acquired all the beauties of age that now make us reverence those other equally erroneous orthodoxies which have been its predecessors. The world has changed too much to be content with the philosophies of the past, and even those who cannot adapt themselves to what is new must admit that, in time, it may become as delightful as what it is superseding—at any rate to those who will be accustomed to it. (pp. 470-73)

Santayana's general outlook is one which is not likely to be widely influential in America, because it is aristocratic, not only politically, but philosophically. He is himself a sceptic, but believes that mankind in general has need of myths. His social values are thus different from his intellectual values; the latter are for the esoteric few, the former for the multitude. For my part, I prefer this view to that which rejects the best on the ground that only a minority can appreciate it, but I shrink—perhaps irrationally—from the admission that, not only here and now, but always and everywhere, what is best worth having can only be enjoyed by a cultural aristocracy. Those who take this view have the advantage of avoiding conflict with the mob, but I would rather rouse its hostility in attempting to serve it than secure its tolerance by concealing a contemptuous aloofness. From a personal point of view, aloofness may be wiser philosophically and practically, but the opposite attitude is a heritage of Christianity, and one which is essential to the survival of intelligence as a social force. (p. 474)

Bertrand Russell, "The Philosophy of Santayana," in The Philosophy of George Santayana, *edited by Paul Arthur Schilpp, second edi-*

tion, The Library of Living Philosophers, Vol. II, Tudor Publishing Company, 1951, pp. 453-74.

W. H. Auden   (essay date 1953)

[*Often considered the poetic successor of W. B. Yeats and T. S. Eliot, Auden is also highly regarded for his literary criticism. As a member of a generation of British writers strongly influenced by the ideas of Karl Marx and Sigmund Freud, Auden considered social and psychological commentary important functions of literary criticism. As a committed follower of Christianity, he considered it necessary to view art in the context of moral and theological absolutes. Thus, he regarded art as a "secondary world" which should serve a definite purpose within the "primary world" of human history. This purpose is the creation of aesthetic beauty and moral order, qualities that exist only in imperfect form in the primary world but are intrinsic to the secondary world of art. While he has been criticized for significant inconsistencies in his thought throughout his career, Auden is generally regarded as a fair and perceptive critic. In the following review of* My Host the World, *Auden objects to Santayana's moral tenets.*]

The Middle Span ended in 1912 with Santayana shaking the dust of Harvard from his feet to engage thenceforth in "a voluntary study, a satirical survey, a free reconsideration" as "a spirit, the spirit in a stray individual." **My Host the World** leaves off in 1942 with its author come finally to rest in Rome. In the meantime, he has visited the Near East, he has resided in both Oxford and Cambridge, he has found temporary lodgments in Paris, Madrid, and Cortina, and, of course, he has written a number of books. It would be unfair to expect the last third of a philosopher's memoirs to be as fascinating as the first two. Elderly men have been known to be transformed in character by an illness, or to undergo a religious conversion, or suddenly to commit some appalling folly, but they are the exceptions. Normally, what is interesting about a grown-up writer is not his life but his books, and the most significant fact about Santayana during the years covered here is that in them he wrote his best work, **The Last Puritan.**

Nevertheless, **My Host the World** is less interesting than it need have been. A stranger to our planet, though he would find the two world wars mentioned by name, could never guess that the Russian Revolution, Mussolini, Hitler, and the Spanish civil war had taken place or that the private lives of human beings during the last fifty years had been in any way different from what they were in, say, the nineties. It is not that one expects or even wants long political disquisitions upon a scene with which we are all too familiar and about which we have read more than enough, and, in any case, if we want to know Santayana's political theory, we can read **Dominations and Powers.** Nor is one really curious to know upon which side, if any, his immediate sympathies, intellectual or animal, lay.

> Neither tribal nor commercial morality inspired me with particular horror. I knew that the first was brutal and the second vulgar; but they both were intelligible phases in human civilization,

just as Catholicism was; and it was an accident of temperament or circumstances how far my sympathies were enlisted on one or the other side.

Such a detachment could have told as much. What, for instance, would be more fascinating and illuminating than a history of these years as seen through the eyes of a precocious child, a maître d'hôtel, or a high-class courtesan? But that a man who was in an especially fortunate position to hear and see what was happening in Europe, not in chancelleries but to the daily lives of old ladies, tradesmen, doctors and lawyers, even philosophers, should not have found a single anecdote of such nature worth recording in his memoirs is, surely, rather strange, particularly when one cannot say that such abstention is due to an overwhelming wealth of other material.

Santayana was not a "visual type" or one who responded immediately and originally to the unfamiliar. He needed time to react; consequently, he had no natural gift for travel writing. The whole chapter on the "origin" countries—Egypt, Palestine, and Greece—might well have been omitted, for its only real contribution is the self-revealing comment:

> Of all periods in history the Hellenistic, between Alexander and Caesar, corresponds best to my feeling. . . . With Alexander a great part of the East, in fact, and the whole world in prospect, were introduced into the sphere of the West, into the narrow military life of the ancient city: yet the gods of the city were not abandoned; but exalted into gods of the open rational philosophic mind, they were retained to preside over a universal empire.

Again, he fails to make us see the architecture of Venice and Rome, perhaps because he likes them too wholeheartedly, for he is at his best when his feelings are mixed and admiration is crossed with malice, as in his description of King's College Chapel:

> Here concentration is perfect, the whole court drawn up in order, waiting; only the monarch is late. Meantime the arrangements continue to suggest his presence, and we may study them the more freely while we postpone our acts of homage.

For this reason, by far the most interesting chapter is the one on Earl Stanley Russell, that wonderful monster who so beguiled us when we first met him in the earlier volumes, almost as perfect a gift to a writer of memoirs as Sir George Sitwell. The reader has no doubt that Santayana was devoted to him, but his account of the Earl's love life is uproarious. Few novelists would dare invent a character who, when turned down by a lady to whom he had proposed while still married to another and having promised to marry a third when free, could write:

> It was very painful . . . and yet the relief was immense. . . . Veronica saved the situation by cutting the knot—what I regret is that fear and pique were the cause of the step. I wish I could attribute it to unselfish consideration of Martha's interests.

The friendship between Santayana and Russell had begun in youth. On Santayana's side, at least, it was genuine, and their final estrangement—not through a quarrel but through a withering of Russell's interest to the point where he kept calling Santayana Sargeaunt, the name of a Latin master at Westminster "who no doubt had been a friend of Russell's at school or in Oxford. . . . They had nothing now in common save that old sense of familiarity"—is sad.

With most of the other characters mentioned, Santayana became acquainted only later in life, and we are more conscious of his malice than of his admiration. The former is entertaining enough so long as it is directed at little foibles like Robert Bridges' detestation of hot water:

> His hands . . . were not dirty: but they hadn't the nursery-maid's pink cleanliness produced by soap and hot water. The nails were gray and thick, like talons. Admirable, no doubt, for certain purposes; but in ages when hot water is available for the toilet, delving is no longer done with the claws.

But his inability to praise anyone wholeheartedly without some derogatory comment, deserved though it often may be, leaves an unpleasant taste in the mouth. If one has claimed for oneself a praiseworthy broadmindedness by saying, "I had always been on pleasant terms with the Babe, liked him, and didn't despise him for not being intellectual or for letting Howard adopt and support him," one cannot add, two sentences later, "The Babe was certainly a minor personage and feeble." One cannot call Lytton Strachey obscene, cite as proof his leaving a pornographic book in Lady Otteline's drawing room, and then continue:

> Naturally I read on in it, for I like obscenity well enough in its place, which is behind the scenes, or bursting out on occasion in a comic, rollicking, enormously hearty mood as in Aristophanes . . . but he might have put it in his pocket, and not left it lying in the drawing room.

Hoity-toity, Professor.

The continual reiteration of his intellectual independence, of his lack of any desire to have disciples, of his resistance to "human contagion, except provisionally, on the surface, and in matters indifferent to me" becomes suspicious. As in the case of Henry Adams, whom in many ways he resembles, one begins to wonder if all these protests are not a coverup for disappointed ambition, for a feeling that his real superiority has not been properly recognized by his equals. King's College was disappointing ("the birds were not worthy of their cage"); Corpus would never do because of two faculty members, Warren and Schiller, "individuals that a novelist might like to study, interesting cases; but to be sandwiched between them as if intellectually I were such another tramp (as externally indeed I was) would have been a perpetual mortification;" after a lecture in the Natural History Museum "several dusky youths brought me books to be autographed. Did they feel that I was one of them at heart? We might have been in Singapore;" the atmosphere of the Riviera was disagreeable—too many Americans.

I like to be a stranger myself, it was my destiny; but I wish to be the only stranger. For this reason I have been happiest among people of all nationalities who were not of my own age, class, or family circle; for then I was a single exceptional personage in their world, and they a complete harmonious milieu for me to drop into and live with for a season.

This publican confession is engaging and the conscience of many of us must second it; what repels is the pharisaic excuse "It was my destiny," though it has comic possibilities. Two Free Spirits who have arrived separately but simultaneously in an Italian village are sitting at neighboring tables in the only café, glaring at each other. Presently the wine takes effect.

1ST F.S.: What the devil are you doing here?

2ND F.S.: Pardon me, Prof. I was just about to ask you the same question.

1ST F.S.: How dare you! This milieu is my destiny this season. I, sir, am The Wanderer (*hands his card*).

2ND F.S.: Wanderer schwanderer. That's me (*hands his card*).

1ST F.S.: This is an outrage. I must ask you to retire immediately to the Oxford Common Room, where you belong.

2ND F.S.: Look who's talking. Go home yourself, Princeton.

Similarly, none of us has a right to frown on Santayana for being episodic in his affections for persons and places, but one has a right to object to the platonic window dressing:

> I saw only the gifts and virtues of which, perhaps for the first time, they gave me a clear idea. They become to that extent my local shrines or the saints for that day in my calendar; but never did the places or the persons turn into idols for my irrational worship. . . . I gladly recognize the good and the beautiful in unexpected quarters; and I am not in the least daunted in my cult of those divine essences when I find that they have disappeared from a place or a person that had once seemed to possess them.

The natural human, or at least masculine, tendency, both in love and in friendship, is to be attracted by qualities rather than persons. We like people not for what they are in themselves but because they are beautiful or rich or amusing, so if they lose their looks or their money or their wit, we lose our interest. We could probably never learn to correct this tendency and love persons for themselves if life did not impose on us relationships with parents, brothers and sisters, wives, children, colleagues at work, and so on, from which, whatever our emotions, we cannot escape.

Plato, if I understand him rightly, took our romantic interest in qualities as his starting point and sought to show, by analysis, that on the temporal level it was self-defeating; if qualities, not persons, are what we want, then the proper place to look for them is in Heaven, among the

Universals. Moreover, he was concerned with the education of the political élite, whose duties in this world demanded an otherworldly detachment from personal and family ties; the governed were to be content with the unromantic pattern of family and social relations prescribed for them. If one substitutes materialist presuppositions for the idealist presuppositions of Plato, then I cannot see that the cult of divine essences becomes anything more than a genteel description of feelings that are natural and common enough but not particularly laudable: Gather ye divine essences while ye may. . . . Ah me, that delicious divine essence I met in Shanghai in 1906. . . . This divine essence isn't fun any more. I guess I better beat it.

"To possess [things or persons] physically or legally," writes Santayana, "is a burden and a snare." Quite so, but it is equally true that it is only through such possessions that most men can learn loyalty and responsibility. The danger is equally an opportunity, and to refuse to risk the one is to miss the other. Santayana's besetting sin, both in his life and in his thinking, seems to be a refusal to take risks, an abnormal horror of being "had." Hence his theory of religion as "valid poetry." Having recognized that nearly all theological statements are metaphorical, not literal, he would regard them as interchangeable. They are interchangeable—in poetry—because the world of poetry is a mirror world outside which we stand as spectators. The myth of the Apple of Discord is as valid in Homer as the myth of Adam and Eve is in Milton. Both are possible worlds. But I cannot be a spectator to my own life, and, as presuppositions concerning the cause of evil as I experience it in actual existence, they cannot be equally valid, for they impose on me completely different conclusions as to how I am to behave. To vary an analogy of Kierkegaard's, religious dogmas are to the good life as the laws of grammar are to a language. A master does not need to think about them and may sometimes shock the orthodox by his daring, but the beginner must bear them in mind. An ungrammatical, misspelled letter may have inspired life in it and a formally faultless editorial be quite dead, but the grammatical facts are not affected thereby.

Santayana tries to warn us off beliefs by pointing to the spectre of fanaticism, as if the belief that you had seen the light and were convinced that those who had not yet seen it were in darkness was in itself "Subjective Egoism." But the reason I may not torture my neighbor into believing anything, even if it is true, is that it will be I, not the truth, that is doing the torturing, and therefore, if he submits, it will be to *my* truth, not *the* truth. The fanatic is the one who secretly believes that the truth or falsehood of a belief is affected by the number of people who believe it; his is the skepticism of the minority. The fanatics of our age would never have succeeded as they have but for the skepticism of the majority, which suspects that one gospel is as good as another, a characteristic well understood by the fanatic, who knows that he is not secure unless he can keep his people in total ignorance of all gospels but his.

"Skepticism is the chastity of the intellect" is one of Santayana's most admirable epigrams. But chastity is meaningless except in relation to passion, and his own brand seems to me little more than intellectual old-maidishness fitting-

ly expressed in that genteel—and soporific—style for which he is famous. No wonder he was averse to the novels of Stendhal and to my favorite landscape, the North of England. You know, I don't think I really like him. (pp. 120-28)

> W. H. Auden, "Through the Collarbone of a Hare," in *The New Yorker, Vol. XXIX, No. 11, May 2, 1953, pp. 120-28.*

Irving Singer   (essay date 1956)

[*Singer is an American philosopher and translator. In the following introduction to a collection of Santayana's literary criticism, Singer illuminates the major themes of Santayana's critical writings.*]

Philosophers are not generally noted for their literary criticism, just as literary critics have rarely distinguished themselves as philosophers. For all its integrity, the philosophic mind always runs the danger of becoming tendentious: it knows too much, and cannot become as a little child. On the other hand, the literary mind all too often resembles the ghost of Hamlet's father: 'tis here, 'tis there, a perturbed and insubstantial spirit that flits about in mysterious darkness. It is a rare genius who can combine good philosophy with good literary criticism. George Santayana was a genius of this sort. One is even tempted to say that his genius was pre-eminently of this sort, and that in the special province of philosophical literary criticism his contribution was more unique and more permanently outstanding than in any other field. In the last two hundred years there have been better philosophers and better essayists, and certainly better poets and novelists, but hardly any critics who have blended philosophical and literary insights with as free and authentic a hand as Santayana. Even among the greatest literary critics there have been few who could do Santayana's "job of work."

Just what kind of work was it? The practice is almost lost among American writers. In the last fifty years our philosophers and critics alike have become technical, minute, and pedagogical in a way that Santayana never was. Ours is an age of instruments: we are devoted to examining the telescope, as Santayana would say, instead of looking through it. Santayana wanted to look. He was an intellectual astronomer with good eyesight and a refined sense of distance. Unlike recent critics, he was not particularly interested in the principles of rhetoric. For better or for worse, his criticism generally avoids both exegesis and linguistic analysis. He shows how the Homeric Hymns, for instance, exemplify the imaginative function of religion, but he largely ignores the poetic devices they employ. He defines religion in terms of myth and metaphor, but he never attempts a thorough analysis of either myth or metaphor. Except for a few remarks about euphony and euphuism, he has little to say about the rudiments of poetry. What excites the muse in him, and what makes his criticism so exciting, is rather an awareness of the human significance of literature—the way in which it can be used to communicate a sense of what is real and important. Santayana wished to treat literary works of art as expressions of an attitude towards the world which could be examined and criticized, not merely accepted or rejected. In this attempt he tried to make his astronomical reports as comprehensive as possible. He filled them with philosophical commentary reinforced by psychological insights, historical and biographical observations, and the expressions of his own moral and aesthetic taste. All of this contributes to a ricochet of ideas, a cross-fire that is brilliant, even dazzling—so much so that the prose occasionally explodes in a burst of elegance and one has difficulty separating the literary criticism from partisan manœuvering, on the one hand, and stylistic fire-works on the other.

Comparison with Hegel is inevitable, and in the Preface to *The Life of Reason* Santayana reports that the first suggestion for that work came to him after reading the *Phaenomenologie des Geistes.* At the same time, however, Santayana claims that Hegel approached their common subject, the history of human ideas, with sophistry and romantic madness. A similar complaint could not be made against Santayana, whatever his critical or philosophical faults may have been. He never thought that his astronomy disclosed a universe governed by Germanic (or other) orderliness, and he never allowed his own perspective to cripple and cramp everything else in the name of Universal Will. There were marches *in* history, but no march *of* history. If anything, history was a series of aimless dances. One had to catch their individual rhythms, one had to use what Keats called "negative capability" instead of forcing everything into the Hegelian three-step. All the same, there is one respect in which Santayana resembled Hegel: he had a definite point of view. Like Hegel, Santayana wrote within the framework of a personal philosophy that made up his telescope more than he may sometimes have admitted. In giving his "excuse" for writing about the three philosophical poets, Santayana says that "they have revealed to me certain aspects of nature and of philosophy which I am prompted by mere sincerity to express." But as we read on, we find that these "aspects of nature and of philosophy" turn out to be aspects within Santayana's own nature and philosophy. The philosophical poets have not been chosen at random; they serve a definite philosophical purpose, however little they may be forced to *sub-serve* it. Santayana's intention, clearly, was to choose in accordance with his personal and doctrinal needs, but then, having chosen, to report accurately and honestly what he saw. His criticism would then be a projection of himself without being a distortion of his subject-matter.

In reading Santayana's criticism as a projection of his own philosophy, we must always remember that the climate of his opinions altered as he grew older. In some ways it became warmer, more tolerant and less demanding; in other ways, colder, more remote and detached from ordinary human interests. For instance, compare **"The Poetry of Barbarism"** (1900) with **"Penitent Art"** (1922). In both essays Santayana is describing what he considers to be significant but inferior art, the work of strangely misguided genius. But where the earlier essay almost sounds like a charge of the light brigade against the dark and irrational forces of Whitman's sensualism and Browning's activism, the later essay is a melancholy sigh, a gentle shaking of the deploring head, as if Santayana had come to see that it was only fitting for the tragic twentieth century to express it-

self in an abstract, incomplete, and self-caricaturing manner. Similarly, in **"The Absence of Religion in Shakespeare"** (1896) Santayana is shocked to find that Shakespeare has little of the "cosmic consciousness," whereas in **"Tragic Philosophy"** (1936) he is more tolerant of a poet who spoke to an age that "needed no mastering living religion." It is not clear whether the later Santayana finds Shakespeare's secularism adequate for the needs of great poetry; but as against the criticism of T. S. Eliot, he defends Shakespeare for having "stuck fast in the facts of life" and he pits him against Dante in a way that one could hardly have anticipated from the early essay.

Throughout this changing climate, there perseveres a way of looking at things, an attitude or general perspective, that might be called the desire to harmonize. In book after book, Santayana defined the life of reason as the harmonization between opposing interests. In his aesthetics and literary criticism he works out patterns of harmonization between a great many divergent principles, most of which can be approached in terms of the following themes: Platonism vs. naturalism, classicism vs. romanticism, "idealisation" vs. realism, and poetry vs. prose. Each conflict poses separate problems, but the problems overlap and much of what we say about one will also apply to the others.

The struggle between naturalism and Platonism is the most striking of the four themes. Throughout all of Santayana's work there is an ambivalence of sentiment, a yearning towards the extremes of naturalism with its emphasis upon the brute materiality of existent things and Platonism with its reliance upon the value of formal characteristics. Santayana wanted to harness both, the black horse of the body and the white horse of the soul, and he wanted them to run in neatly parallel lines. In order to effect this harmonization, he used each extreme to chasten the other. They were the two masks of his drama, and his prose bristles with their dialogue. Speaking in the person of naturalism, he finds Platonism superstitious and absurdly optimistic. Because there are human values in the world, Platonism assumes that ideal entities, or purposive divinities as Christianity made them into, must provide the ultimate explanation for the existence of everything. Nothing could be farther from the materialistic truth. But speaking in the person of Platonism, Santayana finds traditional naturalism barren of hope and ignorant of spiritual goods. Devoted as it is to facts, naturalism ignores the fact of human aspiration and the quest for purified ideals. In *The Last Puritan,* where the spirituality of Oliver Alden is pitted against the naturalism of Mario Van de Weyer, the contrast between the two sides of Santayana's nature shows through time and again, sometimes with astonishing stridency. In one scene Oliver is completing an essay on Plato's *Symposium.* As his hand writes the word "philosophy" he is interrupted by Mario, who describes an unhappy carnal encounter from which he has just come and then boards a train on his way to see his dying mother. Oliver returns to his room and finds that he had not finished writing the word "philosophy." The last five letters had yet to be put down. Thus, as "philosophy" is split into its two halves, of love and wisdom, and Mario pursues the former while Oliver is characteristically arrested in his attempt to reach the latter, so too is man composed of two disparate, warring elements—matter and spirit. Santayana's thinking always has its feet on the ground and its head in the clouds. Whether there is, or ought to be, anything in-between remains a matter of controversy.

The character of Santayana's naturalism is best reflected in the essays on Lucretius and Dickens. In explaining the sense in which Lucretius is a "poet of matter," Santayana distinguishes between five different kinds of "naturalists" in poetry. Lucretius is a philosophical or cosmological naturalist—for him nature means "the principle of birth or genesis, the universal mother, the great cause, or system of causes." As a philosophical naturalist, Lucretius is contrasted with: the descriptive poet who paints a word picture of the scenery of nature, the symbolist poet who breaks up nature into elements that he re-shuffles by means of random association, the idealist poet who uses these elements of nature to construct a utopian dream-world, and the humanistic poet who depicts the moral effects that can be derived from living "in" nature. These are all naturalists, but of an inferior sort. The descriptive poet ignores Lessing's scruples about representing spatial objects in a temporal medium; the Symbolists "play with things luxuriously, making them symbols for their thoughts, instead of mending their thoughts intelligently, to render them symbols for things"; the idealistic poet is blind to the dynamism in things; the humanistic poet, such as Wordsworth, limits himself to a tiny part of the cosmic process—"adventitious human matters." Only a poet like Lucretius has his finger on the pulse of nature—its character as a force, a power, a generating and destroying agency. Only Lucretius, we may add, concerns himself with what Santayana later called "The Realm of Matter." It is interesting to note that Santayana praises Lucretius for writing "the poetry of things themselves" and in his **"Apologia Pro Mente Sua"** (1940) he calls himself a "true poet" inasmuch as his own poetry is "not a poetry of words or concepts, but a poetry of things." And yet, is this sufficient basis for elevating Lucretius above Wordsworth and the Symbolists? That a kinship of interest should make Lucretius dearer to Santayana is not at all surprising; but Santayana does not *seem* to be expressing a mere preference. He seems to be evaluating poetry on the basis of objective standards of criticism. This kind of problem recurs continually.

Since philosophical naturalism investigates the principles of genesis and decay, it is fitting that the essay on Lucretius hovers about the dualism of life and death, creation and destruction, love and strife, peace and warfare—as symbolized in *De Rerum Natura* by Venus and Mars. This awareness of the "double colouring" of things characterizes all of Santayana's writing. In his essay **"A Long Way Round to Nirvana,"** Santayana defends the Freudian notion that a universal death instinct counterbalances the drive for self-preservation. Like all philosophy, the concept of a death instinct had to be taken as a metaphoric suggestion, and not as scientific truth, but if one did take it as such one discovered something that Santayana considered a fair report of "the general movement and the pertinent issue of material facts." In emphasizing death as one of the facts of life, Santayana's philosophy wears the same tragic cast as existentialism. He wished to construct his system on the basis of a radical disillusionment. Once man *realized* that he was dust, that there was no other world, and that someday he would be dead 100%, he could freely and honestly search for the good. Santayana felt that it would be cheating for man to be bribed into virtue by hopes of a future life or by optimistic assurances that the good would win out eventually. There was no pre-arranged harmony, no ultimate dialectic, no *élan vital* that guaranteed anything. Death and evil were as indigenous to nature as life and goodness. They were to be observed and analyzed, not wished out of existence.

This naturalistic analysis takes up much of the essay on Lucretius and reappears in the succeeding ones on Dante and Goethe. The Paolo-Francesca scene, for instance, is treated as a continuation of Lucretius' theme about Venus and Mars. Paolo and Francesca are in hell because their union is unnatural, as intimacy must always be when it makes separateness and individuality impossible. An eternity of possession in a void, of inescapable love and no exit into anything or anyone else, causes the destruction of Mars in a way that prevents Venus from savoring her conquest. "Only an inspired poet could be so subtle a moralist," Santayana concludes. "Only a sound moralist could be so tragic a poet." Similarly, Mephistopheles is compared to the Mars of Lucretius, and Santayana delights in Goethe's ability to express the nothingness of things by means of him. Santayana denies that Mephistopheles can be fitted into a Hegelian dialectic, as the nay-saying that makes a higher yea-saying possible and thus unintentionally contributes to the good. On the one hand, Santayana sees the sense in which Mephistopheles is consciously, not unintentionally, benevolent: for Mephistopheles destruction is better than creation and it is destruction that he knowingly and gladly chooses. On the other hand, Santayana refuses to bleach the blackness of Mephistopheles. Creation is one thing; destruction is another. Sentimentality or barbaric romanticism results from confusing the two, from making the colors run so that neither has a determinate quality of its own.

It is a comparable desire to keep the black and the white distinct that Santayana admires most in Dickens. He finds in Dickens the same love of common people that Walt Whitman had, except that Dickens is free of all impressionistic wishy-washiness. Whereas Whitman interpreted everything else in terms of himself, Dickens saw the differences in things. Unlike Whitman, Dickens saw life as "a concourse of very distinct, individual bodies, natural and social, each with its definite interests and story." This naturalistic clarity enabled him to sympathize with the aspirations of others, to "love the love in everything" as Santayana says in **"Ultimate Religion,"** without forgetting that vice is really vice and must be annihilated for the greater good of mankind.

In seeing Dickens as an outstanding example of uncontaminated naturalism, Santayana also takes him as the prototype of all comedy. Comedy sees things externally, as brute occurrences in nature which have no necessary reason for being. The existence of anything is, as the existentialists would say, "absurd"—we can never prove deductively that anything must or must not be. Comedy cuts beneath convention in order to show the absurdity of everything, in order to reduce every existent to its fundamental materiality. Comedy requires courage, and is usually cruel. Dickens had the courage, but not the cruelty. Santayana praises him for combining naturalistic insight with a universal kindness which tempers his savage strokes and allows the reader to enjoy the comic spectacle in which he is himself a participant.

If Santayana's naturalistic mask is comic, his Platonic one is tragic. As a naturalist, Santayana joins with Sancho Panza in laughing at misadventures that result from neglecting the facts of daily life; as a Platonist, he feels the compelling pathos of a Don Quixote whose madness flows directly from his "sense of what is good." In the Preface to **The Last Puritan** Santayana complains that the critics have misunderstood the tragedy of his hero. That Oliver died young or was killed in an accident did not make him tragic, but rather "that he stopped himself, not trusting his inspiration." And in **"Tragic Philosophy"** he says that tragedy is the "conflict between inspiration and truth." Tragedy shows us human beings from their own inward point of view—as they are motivated by desires and aspirations that are serious to them, not at all absurd, though doomed to more or less failure. The life of man is tragic because it is always striving towards the accomplishment of ideals which, in the nature of the case, can never be attained. For the Platonist the actual world is inevitably the scene of tragedy.

Santayana's Platonism is most fully expressed in the essays on **"Platonic Love in Some Italian Poets," "Dante,"** and **"Shelley."** Each deals with Platonism in a different setting; and each displays the critic in a slightly different posture. In the first essay, Santayana recites the story of Beatrice and Dante, and then shrewdly reminds us that despite his life-long devotion Dante took a wife just as Beatrice had taken a husband. Did Dante's marriage fulfill his naturalistic needs and thereby release him for the more essential love of an ideal? Or did it force him into a "species of infidelity" towards Beatrice as well as his wife? Santayana never gives us a straight reply. He documents the achievement of the Platonizing Italian poets, and he praises their intense contemplation, which "disentangles the idea from the idol of sense." At the same time, he also realizes that Platonic love is based upon pervasive frustration: for the Platonist "all beauties attract by suggesting the ideal and then fail to satisfy by not fulfilling it." Platonism fascinates him by the purity of its transcendence, but he is too this-worldly to drop his naturalism completely.

In the essay on **"Dante"** as the second of the philosophical poets, Santayana is both sharper in his criticism and more enthusiastic in his praise. Like Christianity itself, Dante offends by having turned Platonism into a historical drama, thus making it the kind of *super*naturalism that Santayana could not accept. Dante evinces all the imperfections of Christian superstition and anthropocentrism, such as the belief in original sin and retributive justice. Finally, Santayana suggests that Dante was dedicated to a kind of love that is neither normal nor healthy nor natural nor manly; and he adds that "the poet who wishes to pass convincingly from love to philosophy (and that seems a

natural progress for a poet) should accordingly be a hearty and complete lover—a lover like Goethe and his Faust—rather than like Plato and Dante." Still, these naturalistic complaints are only one side of the coin; the reverse is pure eulogy. The merits of Dante's world-view redeem all his defects, for they are the merits of the Platonizing imagination writ large, of the sense of good and evil operating on a cosmic scale. The essay ends with Santayana putting Dante forth as "a successful example of the *highest species* of poetry."

The essay on Shelley is more serene than the other two: one feels that Santayana's philosophical position had developed to the point where he was more confident of reconciling the best of Platonism with the best of naturalism. And it is clear that in Shelley he sees the best of Platonism. He speaks of Shelley as a pure, winged spirit whose love of the ideal was sincere and spontaneous. Shelley was not limited by Christian beliefs and his Platonism emanated from sympathy with the misery of everything in nature, rather than personal disappointment. Although he was ignorant of the dynamic workings of matter, Shelley knew what was good and bad in things. If his poetry destroyed the everyday world, it was only to reconstruct it in a playful, selfless way "nearer to the heart's desire." Shelley's idealism is the same as the idealistic naturalism that Santayana had previously compared to Lucretius' philosophical naturalism. As a kind of naturalism, he there considered it inferior to what Lucretius gave us. But as a type of idealism, he now finds it supreme poetry. Dickens and Shelley, between them, seem to make up Santayana's vision, just as Lucretius and Dante do. Dickens rollicks through the natural world, above which the skylark Shelley soars in search of universal freedom; Lucretius hears the voice of things themselves, while Dante documents the uses to which the spirit can put them.

In moving to our second theme, we are confronted by questions of interpretation that did not arise in the first. Although it is obvious that Santayana wishes to stereoscope the partial views of naturalism and Platonism, it is not immediately evident that he wants to do the same with classicism and romanticism. Santayana is known as the defender of the one and the critic of the other; and much could be cited in favor of this interpretation. Nevertheless, it is, I think, a superficial interpretation which has to be much subtilized before it can be accepted. For one thing, we ought not to confuse "barbarism," as Santayana uses that term, with romanticism as a whole. Barbarism is only one kind of romanticism: it is romanticism which refuses to be harmonized. The barbarian is "the man who does not know his derivations nor perceive his tendencies, but who merely feels and acts, valuing in his life its force and its filling, but being careless of its purpose and its form." The romanticist values the experiential flow of his life; he becomes a barbarian when he values nothing else, when he *merely* feels and acts. Thus, it is barbarism, and not necessarily romanticism, which is incompatible with the classical sense of purpose and form that Santayana wants to advocate.

Santayana's attack upon nineteenth-century barbarism is guided by the same kind of historical or sociological analysis that T. S. Eliot took as a premise of his own literary criticism. Examining barbaric poetry "in relation to the general moral crisis and imaginative disintegration of which it gives a verbal echo," Santayana finds that the imagination of western man bears a duality of inspiration. It derives in part from classic literature, in part from Christianity. The confusion of barbaric poetry reflects the modern inability to serve both masters, or either one, or any other. Whitman and Browning are "poets of barbarism" because they reject both traditions without fully understanding them and without having anything to put in their place. They express sensations and emotions without fitting them into a rational system of any sort. To Santayana's ear and eye they are like the players Hamlet describes as created by nature's journeymen: "neither having the accent of Christians nor the gait of Christian, pagan, nor man." Even when it studies the past, as historicism did, barbarism examines a corpse instead of communicating with a vital tradition. If history preoccupies modern poets, Santayana reminds his readers at the turn of the century, it is because they are so greatly conscious of a separation from the past.

That Santayana's caustic remarks about barbarism are not intended to cover all romantic poetry is apparent from his treatment of Goethe, whom he ranks with Dante and Lucretius rather than with Whitman and Browning. The saving grace of Goethe, as Santayana sees him, is his real and honest attempt to fit romanticism into a framework of classicism. *Faust* is a return to Lucretius, though with a difference. The difference is the emphasis on life itself, on "experience in its immediacy, variety, and apparent groundlessness." This is what all romanticism emphasizes, but in Goethe it is accompanied by moments of sad and classic wisdom. One of these occurs when Faust calls forth the Earth-Spirit, the symbol of unlimited and indiscriminate experience. The ugly spectacle of unformed and unorganized life in all its infinite variations horrifies Faust. He learns, as Eliot was to say, that "human kind cannot bear very much reality," that the life of *mere* experience is not worth living. To be happy one must recognize the limits of one's nature, one must temper the fervor of youth with the discipline of age, one must make oneself by means of calculated choice. This is the classical point of view, and it is the morality Santayana expounded throughout his life.

If this classical side of Goethe redeems him in the eyes of Santayana, it is nevertheless too meager to raise him as high as Lucretius and Dante. In drawing his conclusions, Santayana arranges the three philosophical poets hierarchically: at the top, Dante, the poet of salvation; next, Lucretius, the poet of nature; and at the bottom, Goethe, the poet of life. The basis of this arrangement is not entirely clear. On the one hand, Santayana specifically denies that he is trying to indicate which of the poets is best. "Each is the best in his own way, and none is the best in every way. To express a preference is not so much a criticism as a personal confession." Just two pages later, however, Santayana sounds as if his hierarchy was based on something more objective than personal taste. ". . . taken formally, and in respect to their type of philosophy and imagination, Dante is on a higher plane than Lucretius, and

Lucretius on a higher plane than Goethe." Without pausing to examine the difficulties in Santayana's statement, we should here notice that his hierarchy places the representative of Platonism first, and the representative of romanticism last. Santayana wishes to harmonize Platonism with naturalism and classicism with romanticism; but he insists upon a specific *kind* of harmonization: one in which naturalism is subordinated to Platonism, and romanticism to classicism. It is this implicit standard which leads Santayana, in the early essays at least, to place Shakespeare below the level of Homer, Virgil, and Dante. Like Goethe, Shakespeare is a romantic poet without being a poet of barbarism. Although he was "not unacquainted with speculation," Shakespeare generally restricts himself to the poetry of ordinary experience: he chooses positivism rather than religion, and society rather than the cosmos. Even in the case of *Hamlet*—"here is no necessary human tragedy, no universal destiny or divine law." And yet, Santayana has also noted that Hamlet "lays bare the heart of a whole race, or, perhaps we should rather say, expresses a conflict to which every soul is more or less liable." But if this is so, why not admit the supremely philosophical achievement of Shakespeare? Granted that Shakespeare is not philosophical in the same sense in which Lucretius and Dante are, why not recognize and admit his equally profound understanding of everything there is to understand?

The answer to these questions turns on Santayana's imperfect appreciation of romanticism. In subordinating romanticism to classicism, he dissolves, or at least ignores, the problems that troubled the romantics. In lamenting the absence of religion in Shakespeare, he overlooks the fact that Shakespeare's philosophic interest was of a different sort. Shakespeare, like Goethe, like Whitman and Browning, and like a great many other modern writers, saw the world in terms of moral problems. Religion did not concern him since it was unable to settle the ethical doubts that structured his world-outlook. Hamlet, like all of Shakespeare's major characters, is tormented by problems of action that Shakespeare analyzes to a remarkable degree of precision. Likewise, one could interpret the trial of Faust in terms of the need to *do* something: Mephistopheles is to win his wager if he can debase Faust's libido to the point where he will do virtually anything; Faust drops dead when he passively acquiesces in the passing moment; his soul is saved because, until the moment of his death, he was unflagging in his active aspiration. The root dilemma of all romanticism was formulated by Schopenhauer when he defined the human lot as the miserable alternation between boredom and dissatisfaction. The bored man has nothing for which to act; the unsatisfied man is forced to act in any way that will relieve his discomfiture. How then can man be free? How can he act with intelligence and spontaneous good-will? Santayana ignores these problems. They did not trouble him in the way that religious problems did. It may be fortunate that he pursued his own interests. But the fact remains that these interests prevented him from penetrating to the deepest stratum of the romantic soul.

The next theme takes us into the critical theory that underlies most of Santayana's practice. His preference for classicism over romanticism, as well as his preference for

Platonism over naturalism, derives from his conception of "idealisation," an aesthetic principle that runs through all his criticism but receives full treatment only in *The Sense of Beauty.*

To explain what Santayana means by idealisation, we must first put it in the context of his general aesthetics. At the very outset Santayana defines aesthetic experience in terms of "objectified pleasure," i.e. pleasure that is taken to be an attribute of an object more or less in the way that its color is. According to Santayana, the difference between "this painting pleases me" and "this painting is beautiful" consists in the fact that the first statement describes an effect that the painting has upon the speaker whereas the second statement speaks of the painting as *itself* embodying the pleasure it causes. To the literal, scientific mind it makes no sense to speak of an object embodying pleasures; but the aesthetic experience is neither literal nor scientific. Santayana takes it to be a hangover from the primitive, animistic tendency to read into objects all of the effects that they have upon human observers. The sense of beauty causes us to project our feelings without realizing what we are doing; and this, I think, is the sense in which Santayana would say that all art is "illusion."

There is, however, a further sense of illusion which is more relevant to the underlying notion of idealisation. For after defining beauty as objectified pleasure, Santayana goes on to discuss three different kinds of beauty: the beauty of materials, of form, and of expression. Of these three the greatest is form, and in the aesthetics of form the most significant factor is the creation of types—the class concepts or general ideas by reference to which we identify particular objects. Types are especially important to the artist because they enable him to remain true to experience without *copying,* without duplicating something that has existed and therefore possesses an indefinite number of properties which are aesthetically irrelevant. In discussing the origin of types, Santayana rejects the Platonic theory which considers them independent of ordinary sense-experience. Santayana insists that a type—the general idea of man, tree, whale, or what not—is merely a lowest common denominator, a residue of particular sense-experiences on particular occasions. When Santayana later developed the doctrine of essences, he moved closer to Platonism inasmuch as he denied that the naturalistic origin of types prevented them from being independent of experience in other, and more important, respects. What remained constant in both the earlier and the later theories was the belief that typical form is the most important kind of aesthetic form.

Now we are in a position to see how Santayana conceives of idealisation, and how he reconciles it with aesthetic truth. Having defined beauty in terms of pleasure, and typical form in terms of observable recurrences, Santayana then says that typical form can have its greatest effect only if it is modified "in the direction of the observer's pleasure" and thereby turned into an "idealisation." This means that the artist must not content himself with a merely realistic portrayal of a type, any more than a realistic representation of a particular object. The former would be an unaesthetic copy as much as the latter, although a copy of "the average of things" rather than specific characteristics of particular things. Since the sense of beauty is the experience of pleasure in the object, the sense of formal beauty must be the experience of a type which has been modified for the sake of giving greater pleasure. "The mind is thus peopled by general ideas in which beauty is the chief quality; and these ideas are at the same time the types of things."

In this manner, Santayana hopes to combine the sense of reality with the sense of beauty. A mere sense of reality would disclose typical forms that might very well be harsh, shocking, brutal. A mere sense of beauty would provide indiscriminate pleasure. But when the forms themselves have been modified in the direction of pleasure, they embody human ideals as well as depicting human realities. Santayana insists that these ideals would be "true to" reality since they would be refinements of actual forms rather than fanciful ones invented by a raving artist. At the same time, they would be much more significant than the photographs of nature that so-called "realists" provide.

Thus, despite his emphasis on idealisation, Santayana does not wish to ignore the aesthetic relevance of truth. When he discusses the nature of expression in literature, he reminds us that great works often employ accurate and honest representation. But having said this, he quickly adds that "such instruction does not of itself constitute an aesthetic pleasure: the other conditions of beauty remain to be fulfilled." These other conditions are fulfilled only when the vehicle, the art object itself, provides pleasure in its direct effect, which is to say that the expression of truth cannot be aesthetic except in its subordination to the beauty of form and materials. And since the beauty of form is at its highest when it employs idealisation, the supreme aesthetic production will have to subordinate realistic representation to the creation of ideal types. In a similar vein, Santayana denies that the expression of evil can itself be aesthetic. He goes to great lengths to show that tragedies are aesthetic only in spite of the evil they represent, never because of it. Since the expression of evil is unpleasant and therefore unaesthetic, the tragedian must always cushion it by means of pleasing idealisations. With this theory in mind, it is not surprising that Santayana should prefer Platonism and classicism to naturalism and romanticism.

In applying the conception of ideal types to the specific problems of characterization, Santayana enriches it by saying that the great characters of literature are always individuals as well as idealisations. Universal characters, such as Hamlet, Don Quixote, and Achilles, are not just particular men candidly observed. Nor are they averages or realistic types. They are idealised types which have been given uniqueness or individuality. Goethe's Gretchen had no original, but is herself "the original to which we may occasionally think we see some likeness in real maidens. It is the fiction here that is the standard of naturalness." And Santayana concludes that "on this, as on so many occasions, we may repeat the saying that poetry is truer than history."

Santayana's conception of idealisation also underlies his celebrated identification of religion with poetry. As he sees it, religion is primarily poetic idealisation extended to the cosmic scene. "Poetry is called religion when it intervenes in life, and religion, when it merely supervenes upon life, is seen to be nothing but poetry." Santayana realizes that religious people have not usually *thought* that their religion was a kind of elevated poetry. They have generally taken it to be a superior science. This side of religion Santayana considers sheer superstition. In identifying religion with poetry, he is trying to release those imaginative values which can remain to the enlightened and sensitive intellect after all pseudo-scientific claims have been discounted. This residue he relates to idealisation because he thinks that a religion can fulfil its function only by symbolizing desired perfections. The religion of Apollo, for example, he considers a true religion because "the mythology which created the god rested on a deep, observant sense for moral values, and drew a vivid, if partial, picture of the ideal, attaching it significantly to its natural ground." He points out that the Christ men have loved is "an ideal of their own hearts"; and he asserts that "no poet has ever equalled the perfection or significance of these religious creations."

The trouble with Santayana's theory of idealisation is that it seems to minimize the importance of truth. Idealisations do not tell us how things are, but how they ought to be, or how the "heart's desire" would like them to be. If aesthetic excellence is primarily determined by idealisation, art is treated as wish fulfillment more than anything else. As long as we concern ourselves with the artist's idealisation, we are not especially interested in what he tells us about the world: what matters most is his dream of perfection, his prophetic blueprint. If realism ignores ideals, it will have to be subordinated; if tragedy expresses sad and bitter truths, it will have to do so in a way that is ultimately pleasurable and uplifting. Dante idealises to the fullest. He is therefore considered "the type of a supreme poet." Lucretius, Goethe, and Shakespeare idealise proportionately less, and they are fitted into the hierarchy of value accordingly. Santayana never faces up to the possibility that *a priori* there is no reason to favor idealisation over realism; and he fails to see how this preferred kind of harmonization distorts much of what is generally considered to be essential in both poetry and religion.

Related difficulties attend Santayana's way of reconciling poetry with prose. Santayana begins with the assumption that poetry and prose are two distinct modes of discourse: the former devoted to the sound and texture of words, and to the immediate experiences they can evoke or symbolize; the latter designed for practical adaptation to the material environment. Poetry *gives* us the world; prose *tells* us about it discursively. Poetry portrays life in its full immediacy; prose, as in science or philosophy, does the very opposite: it theorizes and tries to understand. How then are the two to be joined? Santayana is convinced that neither poetry nor prose can achieve its aesthetic mission without the other. He criticizes the shallow aestheticism which decrees that art and reason are incompatible and that poetry must ignore the problems of the real world. "Clarification of ideas and disentanglement of values are as essential to aesthetic activity as to intelligence. A failure of reason is a failure of art and taste." The "rational poet" whom San-

tayana deifies throughout his early writing unites intelligence with imagination: "A rational poet's vision would have the same moral functions which myth was asked to fulfil, and fulfilled so treacherously. . . . His poetry, without ceasing to be a fiction in its method and ideality, would be an ultimate truth in its practical scope. It would present in graphic images the total efficacy of real things." Such poetry succeeds by digesting prose, by putting it to aesthetic employment rather than spewing it forth.

But just how is the harmonization between poetry and prose to be effected? Santayana returns to the problem in the Introduction to *Three Philosophical Poets.* He wonders whether poetry is capable of supporting the analytical reasoning of philosophy. He replies that it cannot and that it should not, and yet that philosophical poetry is poetry at its best. He concludes that philosophy itself is poetic to the extent that it terminates in "a steady contemplation of all things in their order and worth." It was to the study of contemplation in this sense that Santayana dedicated much of his later philosophy. By "contemplation" he means the intuition of essences. By "essence" he means, as he says in the note on Proust, "the recognizable character of any object or feeling, all of it that can actually be possessed in sensation or recovered in memory, or transcribed in art, or conveyed to another mind." To discover essences one had to limit oneself to experience as it came, experience devoid of interpretation and the discursive processes of reason. In conveying a complex essence of things in their order and worth, philosophical poetry remained non-discursive, and therefore distinctively poetical, at the same time as it incorporated the over-arching visions of philosophy. Poetry was the language of intuition; in being harmonized with prose, it became the language of significant, and possibly truthful, intuitions.

Although the doctrine of essences was not fully developed until late in Santayana's life, it enters into most of his early writing. . . . I also believe that it renders most of them philosophically unacceptable. Here I can only suggest that Santayana's reliance upon intuition subordinates the ordinary processes of thought to a kind of quasi-mystical trance which no one has ever succeeded in describing with any clarity. And even if it made sense to speak of contemplation in the way that Santayana does, one still wonders how any of this is relevant to art or the definition of great poetry. That philosophical poetry depends upon general insights about the world one may well admit; but that these insights are intuitions of a special and inherently nondiscursive sort one cannot believe without a considerable amount of faith.

The nature of Santayana's faith is indicated by the extent to which the doctrine of essences led him to revise his earlier aesthetics. At some points, the revisions were minor; at others, extensive. In changing his definition of beauty, he said that he still adhered to its major import and was mainly altering the language. He no longer felt the necessity of talking about the objectification of pleasure, since on the doctrine of essences pleasure "does not need to be objectified in order to be fused into an image felt to be beautiful: if felt at all, pleasure is already an object of intuition." The idea of a special aesthetic attitude, at once intuitive and pleasurable, had always been present in Santayana's thinking; the doctrine of essences merely gave him a new, and more original, way of formulating his conception.

On the question of aesthetic excellence and the importance of philosophical poetry, however, Santayana's later views differed sharply from his earlier ones. His change of heart sounds almost like a recantation. It runs as follows:

> So anxious was I, when younger, to find some rational justification for poetry and religion, and to show that their magic was significant of true facts, that I insisted too much, as I now think, on the need of relevance to fact even in poetry. Not only did I distinguish good religion from bad by its expression of practical wisdom and of the moral discipline that makes for happiness in this world, but I maintained that the noblest poetry also must express the moral burden of life and must be rich in wisdom. Age has made me less exacting, and I can now find quite sufficient perfection in poetry, like that of the Chinese and Arabians, without much philosophic scope, in mere grace and feeling and music and cloud-castles and frolic. . . . When living substance is restored beneath the surface of experience, there is no longer any reason for assuming that the first song of a bird may not be infinitely rich and as deep as heaven, if it utters the vital impulses of that moment with enough completeness. The analogies of this utterance with other events, or its outlying suggestions, whilst they may render it more intelligible to a third person, would not add much to its inward force and intrinsic beauty. Its lyric adequacy, though of course not independent of nature, would be independent of wisdom. If besides being an adequate expression of the soul, the song expressed the lessons of a broad experience, which that soul had gathered and digested, this fact certainly would lend a great tragic sublimity to that song; but to be poetical or religious intrinsically, the mystic cry is enough.

This statement appeared in 1922, eleven years after **Three Philosophical Poets.** Since almost all of Santayana's literary criticism was written before the 'twenties, the later standard had virtually no effect upon it. Although essays such as **"Penitent Art," "Tragic Philosophy,"** and **"Literary Psychology"** reflect the change of doctrine, Santayana never attempted to reconstruct his earlier criticism. It is, therefore, extremely difficult to say just how much of his great writings on literature the older Santayana would readily have acknowledged. And what would his essays have been like if he had employed the later rather than the earlier standard? The question is intriguing, as such questions always are, but perhaps we do best to leave it as a question, since all speculation in this matter is sure to be utterly fruitless. (pp. ix-xxviii)

> *Irving Singer, in an introduction to* Essays in Literary Criticism of George Santayana, *edited by Irving Singer, Charles Scribner's Sons, 1956, pp. ix-xxviii.*

Alfred Kazin   (essay date 1956)

[*A highly respected American literary critic, Kazin is best known for his essay collections* The Inmost Leaf *(1955) and* Contemporaries *(1962), and particularly for* On Native Grounds *(1942), a study of American prose writing since the era of William Dean Howells. Having studied the works of "the critics who were the best writers—from Sainte-Beuve and Matthew Arnold to Edmund Wilson and Van Wyck Brooks" as an aid to his own critical understanding, Kazin has found that "criticism focussed many—if by no means all—of my own urges as a writer: to show literature as a deed in human history, and to find in each writer the uniqueness of the gift, of the essential vision, through which I hoped to penetrate into the mystery and sacredness of the individual soul." In the following review of Irving Singer's edition of* Essays in Literary Criticism, *Kazin discusses Santayana's literary criticism.*]

The late George Santayana had not only the characteristic over-all intelligence of the great philosopher, but a literary gift so pronounced that he could judge other writers with the instinctive fellow-feeling of the true critic. He had at his finger-tips, he enjoyed simultaneously, advantages which few critics possess: artistic competence, first-rate intelligence, comprehensive learning, a systematic and fully considered point of view. Many of the essays in [*Essays in Literary Criticism*], taken from well-known works like *Three Philosophical Poets, Interpretations Of Poetry and Religion,* and even *The Last Puritan,* are classical articulations of his austere point of view. The best essays in the book—on Dickens, on Lucretius, on "the absence of religion" in Shakespeare, on Proust's love of "essences"—are such because something in each of these writers corresponds to that point of view.

Whenever one turns back to Santayana, one is astonished all over again by the continuous brilliance, the epigrammatic thrust, the impressively direct, realistic and unrhetorical quality of his mind. Yet in the end a book of his has something tomb-like about it, impressive and alien in its tragic lonely utterance of human fate. Just as Santayana's criticism has been admired for over sixty years without really influencing anything, without for one moment entering into the stream of modern literature, so even Santayana's dazzlingly authoritative dismissal of Whitman and Browning as "barbaric," his condescension to Emerson, his abstract praise of Shelley, leave us outside the works of these writers. Only when Santayana is really in sympathy with a writer, as with the gloom of Leopardi, do we get a sense of urgent loyalty to art itself, of a direct feeling for the artist himself.

In his expert and very honest commentary on this criticism [see excerpt dated 1956], Mr. Singer notes Santayana's constant "awareness of the human significance in literature—the way in which it can be used to communicate a sense of what is real and important." Of course Santayana had this awareness; so does every good critic as a matter of course. Even the so-called new critics constantly show what an illusion "pure" criticism is, for they constantly impose their neo-orthodox ideology on all works within their reach. No critical analysis can ever fully enter into the technical complexity of the simplest work; the critic cannot duplicate technique, he cannot even fully disclose it; what makes him a critic is what he gets out of a work of art—and this material is essentially discursive and even philosophical. But in the good critics one feels that they yield to something in the work of art that cannot be translated into any terms but the artist's own; they teach us respect for a given work.

What Santayana really asks in each essay is—how far does the subject come up to my philosophy? Since Santayana's philosophy itself represents a highly literary effort to reconcile scientific materialism, like the icing on a cake, this made it possible for him to adopt conflicting positions at the expense of everyone but himself. In fact, Santayana was able to eat his cake and yet not eat it at the same time. Sometimes he was the shrewd materialist attacking the romantics for their illusions; sometimes he was the weary old Mediterranean classicist, attacking all moderns as "young." This double play is always exasperating and one can see with how little force he united his positions when one reads his brilliant yet somehow unconvinced essay on Dante.

Fortunately, he had the ability to identify sides of his philosophy in writers so different as Dickens and Proust, Shakespeare and Lucretius—and there he is very good indeed, and entirely consistent with himself. His admiration for Proust is based on their common feeling for "essences"; for Shakespeare, on their lack of religion; for Lucretius, on their naturalism. The essay on Dickens is superb, and one can see that it becomes so because Dickens is a comic realist. Fundamentally, Santayana is always a realist—with a window on those ideals into which Proust can fit.

As one goes through the essays, one notices that Dante has his homage, but Lucretius his love; and just as he cannot take Emerson seriously, so he cannot admire in Goethe that side of him which is romantic. All this tells us a good deal about the strength of writers who please Santayana and the weakness of those who don't. But it also tells us that Santayana lacked that final quality—is it humility, the surrender to a work of art in its inexplicable integrity?—that is found in critics with not a hint of his greater powers.

> *Alfred Kazin, "A Sense of the Real and Important," in* The New York Times Book Review, *November 25, 1956, p. 5.*

Lois Hughson   (essay date 1971)

[*In the following excerpt, Hughson suggests that Santayana's childhood experience of loss resulted in the sense of detachment that pervades his writings, specifically his sonnets.*]

The poetry and criticism George Santayana wrote in the 1880s and 1890s are representative of the changing concepts of art and experience which marked the transition from Victorian intellectual life to modern. His capacity to transform and transmit the tradition he inherited was deeply involved in his need to express, master and redeem the loss and deprivation at the core of his sense of life. His

poetry is properly seen as the first phase of his long and fruitful effort, on one level, to conceive a world of values to succeed the disintegrating 19th century intellectual order, and on another, to project a realm in which he would enjoy compensation for the gratification which experience denied him. The sonnet sequences, especially, reveal the constituent elements of his creative life: his naturalism, his rejection of traditional religion, his recognition of the aesthetic basis of value and his sublimation of instinctual drives in ways dictated by his traumatic childhood. The naturalism and the replacement of religious by aesthetic values were, of course, to be found in his intellectual milieu. His allegiance to them rather than to other elements in 19th century life, the private meaning they had for him, and the part they play in his work were shaped in large part by that process of sublimation. They are an intellectual aspect of his effort to deal with his feelings toward his mother whose emotional withdrawal from him was climaxed by a three-year separation from him which began when he was five, and with his experience in those three years when he lived in Spain with his father.

Santayana wrote the first sonnet sequence over a decade beginning in 1882, publishing it finally in 1894. Although it begins with a reminiscence of his childhood religion, it is not about the loss of faith; it presupposes that loss and is concerned rather with the state of mind of the poet, intensely self-conscious, isolated, full of his loss, slowly becoming aware of the sources of comfort and adequacy available to him. At bottom it is the first enactment of a reconciliation of spirit to its impotence in the life of action and its consequent liberation.

The early stage of his disillusionment with religion is marked by the confusion of meaning at the heart of **"Sonnet V"** where the lack of distinction between sight and vision, dream and truth, waking and sleeping is a source of anguish. He cannot dispel the confusion of reality and dream either here or with finality anywhere in his later work, but the energies involved in the effort to do so will be taken up increasingly by the development of a conception of truth as a combination of an independent reality and the inner world of the human imagination that was to dominate his criticism. For the time being, however, this inability to separate reality from dream led him in the succeeding poems of the sequence to an overwhelming sense of the vanity of action and a consequent emotional detachment from it.

In this detachment Santayana discovered one-half of the master strategy of his life and gave it intellectual assent. It was a natural outgrowth of his early emotional life and social experience.

His father had been a colonial civil servant; his mother, the daughter of one, who had never given his child a permanent home. She married an American in the Philippines who left her a widow with three children whom she promised to educate as Americans. Her second husband was Santayana's father and until Santayana was three, they all lived together in Spain. At that time his older half-brother, Robert Sturgis, was sent to school in America, and two years later his mother followed with her two Sturgis daughters; he remained behind with his father. (It is clear from the autobiography that part of the reason for this extraordinary decision lay in the superiority in social status of the Sturgis family in Boston over that of the Santayana family in Spain. It is also apparent that only Robert was able to benefit in any way from it.)

So it happened that when George Santayana was five, he effectively lost his mother. This physical desertion, however, must have been essentially the confirmation of an abandonment already experienced. Santayana creates in [*Persons and Places: the Background of My Life*] an image of his mother as a woman profoundly indifferent to the world, cold, reserved, regarding all things calmly from a distance, "preserving her dignity and also her leisure." This truth of her personality was so clear to Santayana and seemed to him so central to her life that he explains it in terms of a crisis produced by the only great sorrow in her life, the death of her first son as a child not yet two. "It made a radical revolution in her heart," he wrote of it. "It established there a reign of silent despair, permanent, devastating, ruffled perhaps by fresh events on the surface, but always dark and heavy beneath, like the depths of the sea." Although Santayana was reunited with his mother before he was nine, there was never any intimacy between them. He speaks of his sister, Susanna, twelve years his senior, as inspiring all the love and closeness usually reserved for one's mother. He tells us finally, that the crisis over the death of his mother's first child was a "veritable conversion," in which she surrendered earthly demands and attachments; in which "she retained her judgments and her standards, but without hope." He is confident that these must have been her feelings, he assures us, because "at about the same age," that is, when he was thirty, he had a similar conversion which "rendered external things comparatively indifferent."

This essentially mythic explanation for his mother's behavior leads us to the emotional center of his creative life. That the portrait of his mother is a dramatic creation composed of both his direct experiences with her and suppositions about the significance of her behavior which he had no way of confirming, seems clear. It is an attempt to explain her otherwise monstrous abandonment of him and her later willingness to separate herself and her young son from his father. For when Santayana was not yet nine, his father brought him to Boston, stayed one cold winter and returned alone to Spain.

The account of his mother's experience is itself a variation on the theme that runs through all his creative effort: the loss of love, reacted to first with despair, then with renunciation and finally with detachment. The personages of his fable are a mother and her son, the very actors in his real experience. The ultimate comfort of the fable lies in the fact that in it, death itself, that final fact of human life, is the cause of his abandonment. Loss of his mother's love need not be ascribed to her will or his unworthiness; it rests finally, beyond them both, on the nature of things: it was nobody's *fault* that his infant half-brother died. In the way he connects it with his own change of heart, as he calls it, that occurred when he was thirty, is further indication of the effort behind it to make it natural. In his own case, he writes, "there were no outer events to occasion it, except the sheer passage of time, the end of youth and friendship, the sense of being harnessed for life like a beast of burden."

This is how he describes his own experience in the chapter of his autobiography devoted to his mother. The end of youth and friendship and the sense of being harnessed seemed to him to be the consequences of the passage of time. Nothing *happened*; it was life itself, unavoidable, that did this to a man; again, loss is a part of the process of living. He has felt it himself. There is nothing monstrous or unnatural about his mother. He can be indifferent to her but filial. He need not hate her. But out of what an abyss of despair does a man of thirty see the sheer passage of time as bringing naturally enough the loss of friendship and the sense of being a beast of burden! The price of denying his own rage involved the denial of the vast range of possiblities life offers a man of thirty. He cannot see mature sexual relationships or professional fulfillment or any other satisfactions of adult life before him; he sees only loss and frustration. However, his metanoia, as he also called his change of heart, involving though it did extensive denials in his emotional life also marked a great freeing of energies in his poetry and his criticism. It was as much an affirmation of the kind of intellectual life he was capable of, as a renunciation of the interpersonal and social fulfillment he recognized was beyond him.

There is another section of the autobiography which indicates both the pain of the separation from his mother, which he is usually careful to deny, and the direction in which it turned his thinking and colored his conception of the world. The chapter called "Early Memories" begins by commenting on the dreamlike quality of his earliest recollections and the possibility of their greater pertinence for being dreams rather than true memories because "they would show how my young mind grew, what objects impressed it, and on what themes it played its first variations." It ends with the reflection that what he learned at Avila through his Spanish Catechism in the three years he was separated from his mother was the conception of the "omnificent power and eternal truth" which he "reasserted," as he puts it, in his philosophy in the notions of the two realms of being, truth and matter, in which man is powerless. What the child must have been learning in devastating measure was his own helplessness.

The reminiscences lying between these observations are of repeated separations. The memory he thinks may have been his first is of his mother showing him a star as she puts him to bed, telling him that Pepin, her dead firstborn, is behind that star. It is followed by the departure of Robert for America, the subsequent departure of his mother and half-sisters, the death of a cousin after the birth of a stillborn child, the loss of attention from the aunt who had cared for him but who now felt driven to devote herself to her bereaved son-in-law and his young daughters from a previous marriage (an interesting echo of his mother's compulsion), and finally the mental deterioration of his uncle. Before he left with his father to rejoin his mother in America, the household he had been entrusted to was completely destroyed.

He was profoundly aware of the significance of these

events to him, but his treatment of it is intellectual only. He saw how they determined his sense of what life was: "confused, hideous, and useless," but he maintains that life is "really" that way and denies any suffering on their account. As in his picture of his mother, he makes the tragedy of his family the tragedy of life itself, unavoidable and without recourse. This inevitability makes it easier to deny the pain of the sensitive young boy actually at the mercy of almost pathologically poor judgment in the inadequate adults on whom he depended. But to see the events of that distorted household as the type of all experience as he did, goes a long way toward explaining the emotional sources of Santayana's unwillingness to affirm experience for its own sake as well as his desire to throw all his energies into activities meant to isolate and affirm what is of value in experience only. To surrender oneself to experience, especially to feeling, was to be overwhelmed by it. If one confined himself to those aspects which could be understood, he was safe, both from loss of love and from the rage and fear that must attend that loss.

The climax of the chapter is an account of the birth of his cousin's stillborn child. He sees the dead child and finds it "most beautiful . . . something too beautiful to be alive." Like all his other childhood experiences, it supposedly caused him no pain. Instead, it suggested to him a theory about the formation of living things in which there is no safe place to grow into what one is meant to be. In this theory, experience is conceived of as mutilation. Antonita's child was exceptionally beautiful and, he imagines without explanation, would have been exceptionally brave and intelligent because he had stayed longer with his mother; but this delay in birth, seen as an advantage to the child, is paid for by his death and that of his mother. So we return again to the inevitability of the separation between Santayana and his mother, the danger of closeness and the naturalness of these events, this time in Darwinian terms of selection and adaptation in a threatening environment. The pain and desolation which cannot be admitted to in the heart of the young Santayana, or the mature one, can be clearly regarded in the world about him.

We are again here at the prime source of the despair which caused Santayana in his adolescence to see life as "ashes in the mouth," to regard the works of the human imagination alone as good, and to see the age of thirty—maturity—as the time of loss of all those things in life he valued, few as they were. We are at the source of the despair which kept him, like Henry James, who was also obsessed with the effort to convert loss into gain, from being able to make that affirmation of life which marriage signified. Against the dangers of union and attachment he employed the tactics of detachment, of perpetual exile, of emotional non-commitment, those very features he discerns in his mother's emotional life. Intellectually, against the terrors of experience, he was to invoke the safety of knowledge and art.

It is against this background that we should consider the major spiritual experience he refers to in his discussion of his mother's life and describes at length in the chapter of his autobiography called "A Change of Heart." He speaks of it as a metanoia, thereby giving cohesion and impact to

Three Philosophers, *by Winifred Rieber: Harvard professors Josiah Royce, George Palmer, and William James.*

an experience which was actually spread over a period of time even in its most crucial events: the death of a young friend, Warwick Potter, the death of his father and the marriage of his sister. These events, clustering about his thirtieth year, resulted in a reawakening for him of the old experience of abandonment and are dealt with by a striving toward spiritual liberation as he sees it in the esoteric aspects of Christianity and in Beatrice's advice to Dante: "Drop (false hopes) the seed of tears, and listen"; ascribing to it the meaning he attaches to his own second sonnet sequence: "Listen to reason. If the joys of youth and the vision of perfect love have faded from your world, will you allow any baser thing to fetter you there? Let your heart rather follow its true object where that object is gone, into eternity."

Similarly, the fourth stream which fed his metanoia is not connected with a specific event in his late twenties but is an attitude which he traces variously to a trip to Germany after his graduation from Harvard, or to a trip in his twentieth year, and ultimately to something native and congenital. For although it was an attitude that received expression in *Interpretations of Poetry and Religion* in 1900, it was so rooted in his earliest experiences that he felt it as inborn. It was an attitude which enabled him to find something to keep in a world where possession seemed impossible and loving was dangerous. If he had to give up having things, he could never be deprived of knowing them, of having ideas of them: "The whole world belongs to me implicitly when I have given it all up, and am wedded to nothing particular in it; but for the same reason no part of it properly belongs to me as a possession, but all only an idea. Materially I might be the most insignificant of worms; spiritually I should be the spectator of all time and all existence."

The thread of this "vital philosophy," as he called it, leads back from his emotional life to his poetry. The other thread connecting the two is his concept of his mother's decision to live without giving up standards and judgments but, as he puts it, "without hope." The poet who is convinced that there is some way to possess the world once he has given up all hope of getting anything out of it for himself can accept his dependency on a natural order that is indifferent to him. When he has renounced all claims, he is able to see the one value that nature cannot withhold from him: the experience of beauty. But natural beauty is subtle and evasive; he conceives of it as haunting the earth. It is enveloped in the poems in an atmosphere of elegy whose source is the implicit recognition that the possession of beauty is paid for by the necessary surrender of power in the world of action. Furthermore it is a reflection of the surrender of hope for the direct fulfillment of instinctual drives. Nevertheless, once expectation is removed Santayana is able to see his life in a new perspective in which his concept of the realm of art and spirit receive their first embodiment. In **"Sonnet XIX"** he resolves the questionings with which he began the first sonnet sequence and shows us the realm in which the whole world can belong to him in idea:

> Above the battlements of heaven rise
> The glittering domes of the gods' golden dwell-
>   ing,
> Whence, like a constellation, passion-quelling,
> The truth of all things feeds immortal eyes.
> There all forgotten dreams of paradise
> From the deep caves of memory upwelling,
> All tender joys beyond our dim foretelling
> Are ever bright beneath the flooded skies.
> There we live o'er, amid angelic powers,
> Our lives without remorse, as if not ours,
> And others' lives with love, as if our own;
> For we behold, from those eternal towers,
> The deathless beauty of all wingèd hours,
> And have our being in their truth alone.

The imagination, earlier in the sonnet sequence rendered passive and impotent by its inability to distinguish truth from dream, has aroused itself to constructive activity. It has re-ordered life. No longer caught in an impossible task of separating its inner life from the outer processes that surround and sustain it, as it had tried to do at first, it affirms the truth of its new perspective, which is the perspective not only of spirit but of art.

Since its subject is this perspective, the poem's suitable organizing images are those of sight. Since the poem is also about the conversion of loss into gain, and death into life, it progresses with the help of pairs of opposites which exchange identities through the change of perspective in the poet. The importance of the point of view of the observer for the meaning and value of what is observed is a favored structural device in the sonnets.

The realm is initially presented as a kind of Olympus from which truth, in its brightness, distance and detachment, like the stars, "passion-quelling," feeds immortal eyes. This is the first statement of the connection between truth

and eternity in terms of its relation with seeing. On an even more profound level, the visual, what is taken in by the eyes, is of preeminent value in Santayana's emotional life. On the intellectual and metaphoric level more or less under the poet's direct control, the perspective of eternity compensates for loss; the line, "The truth of all things feeds immortal eyes," reveals the role seeing plays as an emotional equivalent for primary oral gratification. Behind this metaphor in which truth becomes a food, playing its enormously fertile role in Santayana's conception of the realm of art, lies his pressing need for closeness to his mother and gratification from her which was early frustrated. By the symbolic ingestion of sight he could internalize what he was forever separated from, be fed, and control what was actually beyond his control, all by the same act. Then finally that ancient childhood rage over his abandonment and separation would be stilled. Therefore, "the truth of all things," like a constellation, is "passion-quelling."

In the second quatrain, all goods that are hidden by the past or the future, "dreams of paradise" from our memories or "joys beyond our dim foretelling,"—hopes, desires, the dark of the caves and the dim of the future are to be "ever bright." In the bright light of eternity where temporal sequence gives way to simultanity, benefit comes from detachment from the self, from dispossession. There we lose our individual lives with their memory, desire and remorse, but we share in the immortal aspect of mortality—its truth, with all the symbolic emotional gratification it embodies.

We cannot speak of the disposition of Santayana's creative energies without considering the second sonnet sequence written the year after the metanoia, in 1895, and constituting, according to Santayana, a direct expression of it. He describes his metanoia, as we have seen, as revealing to him that the root of suffering was desire. The danger of relationship was, of course, the painful lesson of his childhood. He understands that his metanoia involves denying instinctual drives and that it demands his identification with that part of him which shrinks from them, which, as he writes, "do not ask to be saved from themselves: they ask only to run on at full tilt. It is the spirit that asks to be saved from that insane predicament." In return for that salvation, the self must satisfy its needs symbolically only. He must possess only in idea.

His awareness of the process of sublimation is also revealed in his choice of platonic love poetry as the vehicle for this experience. Why, after all, did he feel an appropriateness not altogether justifiable? Platonic love sonnets traditionally celebrated the love of one good and beautiful lady so great that it opened the heart of the lover to the love of all beauty and goodness and finally led him to love of the perfect beauty and goodness of God. The emphasis was equally on the beauty of the lady and on her inaccessibility so that the lover's usual reward was the contemplation of her beauty and his own spiritual education and nothing more. There are aspects of the tradition that are not in Santayana's mind when he writes of it. What he thinks of when he thinks of Platonic love poetry is the frustration of physical love and the consequent spiritual education of the lover. He writes of Plato's notion of love as an account of the mastering of experience and the turning of it to spiritual use. This is not the whole meaning of the poetic tradition which includes Guido Cavalcante as well as Dante, but it is the significance of his metanoia. And that is why he believed the Platonic love sonnet was an adequate vehicle for his spiritual experience. They coincided at a very important point—their source of energy: instinctual drives, not simply sexual, but all the primary drives to possess, devour, dominate and transform which, when fulfilled, are our most profound gratifications.

He is aware then of what is at stake when the spirit is freed. He will write throughout the next decade about the ways sexuality affects man's other responses to life. In retrospect as an old man writing about the sonnets and the experience they render, he is concerned with understanding what happens to the energies that are denied. "The passion of love, sublimated, does not become bloodless, or free from bodily trepidation, as charity and philanthropy are. It is essentially the spiritual flame of a carnal fire that has turned all its fuel into light. The psyche is not thereby atrophied; on the contrary, the range of its reactions has been enlarged."

The key image here is the flame of carnal fire that has turned all its fuel into light. The psyche has not atrophied in the sense that it continues to be active in another way, but it does give up a certain kind of activity natural to it. It gives up the sphere of doing for the sphere of knowing. Again, in the essay on the Italian love poets, he tells us, "Nothing is more characteristic of the Platonic mind than a complete indifference to the continuance of experience and an exclusive interest in its comprehension."

It becomes clearer still, then, how Santayana could conceive of his sonnets as an adequate vehicle for his metanoia since they shared this crucial feature of sublimation. Therefore he sees no contradiction in the fact that, as he explains in answer to inquiries about the identity of the lady, there was no lady: ". . . they were a perfectly sincere *conviction,* but they were not an actual experience. . . . The lady of the sonnets . . . is a myth, a symbol: certainly she stands for Somebody, not always the same Somebody, and generally for a hint or suggestion drawn from reality rather than for any specific passion; but the enthusiasm is speculative, not erotic. . . ." Similarly, he was amused at George Howgate's effort to interpret the poems biographically, positing the existence of two ladies, the one he loves successfully but with some fulfillment escaping him, and the one who frustrated him. The true origin of these phantom mistresses seems to have been literary. Guido's poems address another lady when Giovanna is out of the neighborhood and Dante attempts to console himself with another love after Beatrice dies in *The New Life.* Furthermore, Beatrice herself appears in two guises: the unresponsive because largely unknowing object of Dante's love, and the spiritual Beatrice beyond his sexual reach.

Is the absence of an actual lady in the sonnets a result of the fact that the poems were inspired by a homosexual love? Michelangelo, one of the poets Santayana considers in his essay on Platonic love poetry, also mentions no specific lady, and was reputedly homosexual. Santayana him-self dismisses the "attempts . . . to attribute . . . [Michaelangelo's poems] to discreditable passions," and concludes: "It suffices that life wore this aspect to him; that the great demands of his spirit so expressed themselves in the presence of his world."

At the same time, Santayana remarked to Daniel Cory, the intimate companion of his last years, that it was obvious from Housman's poems that Housman was homosexual, and that he must have been that way himself in his Harvard years "although . . . unconscious of it." He thought it accounted for the feeling he had, incomprehensible at the time, that people thought him odd. He had found it very difficult to bear and had almost brought himself to ask William James about it. It had contributed to his desire to leave Harvard.

This seems at first like a very considerable confession but the phrase "unconscious of it" makes it more difficult to evaluate the behavior or state of being he is trying to characterize. If he had what is ordinarily thought of as a homosexual experience he would have known it. Nor would he have been dependent on social ostracism to indicate that it was socially unacceptable in his milieu. What seems more likely is not that Santayana was saying he was a homosexual in this sense, but that he was simply trying to characterize an emotional life in which he was cut off from intimate relations with women and relied for affection and closeness on his men friends.

In the sense that it tells us about his feelings of incapacity in respect to women, it is illuminating for the sonnets and leads us back to the more central consideration mentioned earlier. Again in his old age, and to Daniel Cory, he wrote in answer to the continuing questions about the lady of the sonnets: ". . . you have an intuitive mind, that easily conceives possibilities that may be latent and may never have come to the surface. There is my sister, for instance, certainly the most important influence in my life, psychologically my mother, and one might almost say, my wife. Not that an incestuous idea ever entered my mind or hers; but Freud might have discovered things unsuspected by ourselves."

We are led back then, by these considerations to the core emotions of separation and loss for which he enjoyed brief consolation in the love of his sister only to have the original feelings reawakened after her marriage. He was then only partly right when he spoke of speculative rather than erotic enthusiasm generating the poetry and was closer to the truth when he spoke of the carnal flame whose fuel was turned to light.

Therefore the key line, "A perfect love is nourished by despair," has implications beyond the ones he pointed out himself. First, the most interesting poems of the second sequence are embodiments of the despair, whether bitter or resigned, rather than the love. Furthermore, the experience of sexual love does not itself seem to yield the despair, because of its fleetingness, its fickleness or its likelihood of frustration. The experience is approached rather not only with that fear but with that expectation and even that desire. It is in this sense that they are "an evasion" of experience. The movement of many of the sonnets is toward death as a symbol of the denial of instinctual needs, and of the retreat from the natural sphere of actions, where change is a radical feature, to contemplation, where it has no place.

"Sonnet XXIII," for example, culminates in a vision of the carnal flame transformed:

> But is this love, that in my hollow breast
> Gnaws like a silent poison, till I faint?
> Is this the vision that the haggard saint
> Fed with his vigil till he found his rest?
> Is this the hope that piloted thy quest,
> Knight of the Grail, and kept thy heart from
>   taint?
> Is this the heaven, poets, that ye paint?
> Oh, then, how like damnation to be blest!
> This is not love: it is that worser thing—
> Hunger for love, while love is yet to learn.
> Thy peace is gone, my soul; thou long must
>   yearn.
> Long is thy winter's pilgrimage, till spring
> And late home-coming; long ere thou return
> To where the seraphs covet not, and burn.

The poem begins with that tendency to swooning away that was a feature of the Italian love poems. But no lady appears to be importuned or celebrated. The source of the poet's emotion is that spiritual love which he conceives of as the only real love, characterizing the yearnings that he feels as mere hunger for love. When spring comes in this poem it will not be in a country where the young are in one another's arms. The pilgrimage culminates in one of the finest lines of the sequence, reminding us of Yeats' Byzantium where the sages stand "in God's holy fire / As in the gold mosaic of a wall." Like Yeats, Santayana wishes to be gathered into the "artifice of eternity."

When in another sonnet, **"Sleep Hath Composed the Anguish of My Brain,"** Santayana comforts his despairing consciousness with an image of how the "April buds are growing / In the chill core of twigs all leafless now" and writes of how "Each buried seed lacks light as much as thou. / Wait for the spring, brave heart; there is no knowing," it is not an expression of trust in nature. The image of birth in his mind, as we have seen, was darkened by the early stillbirth he had seen. There was no spring that could bring to birth a perfectly shaped and beautiful humanity. Humanity was "sad, mortal and unhallowed." Because it was born it would die. Because he could hold it in his arms it would desert him. The stillborn child was perfect and beautiful and it was dead. So it is that he begs his mistress to surrender to his passion in **"XXX"** in these equivocal terms:

> Let my lips touch thy lips, and my desire
> Contagious fever be, to set a-glow
> The blood beneath thy whiter breast than
>   snow—
> Wonderful snow, that so can kindle fire!
> Abandon to what gods in us conspire
> Thy little wisdom, sweetest; for they know.
> Is it not something that I love thee so?
> Take that from life, ere death thine all require.
> But no! Then would a mortal warmth disperse
> That beauteous snow to water-drops, which,
>   turned

> To marble, had escaped the primal curse.
> Be still a goddess, till my heart have burned
> Its sacrifice before thee, and my verse
> Told this late world the love that I have learned.

Yielding to passion is yielding to death. It becomes not a consolation for mortality but an affirmation of it. The images of blood and snow, flesh and marble, love and art are transformations of the basic pair of life and eternity. For it is neither life nor death which bring fulfillment; one is vanity, the other despair—the two sides of the natural process. But marble and verse transcend that process. They are the "artifice of eternity." The desire of the first line is the fever which consumes the heart in the sacrificial fire of the last lines, yielding an ideal love and an art to embody it.

The vision of ideal love not only helps Santayana to transcend his mortality, it returns him to it with a fresh perspective. "A perfect love is nourished by despair" unites the ideal world with the real. In the octave the poet affirms again the ultimate gift of love, the ideal form of it that lives in his heart and brain without sensuous qualities. But the sestet returns love to the senses transformed into the beauties of the natural world, not of the mistress herself but all nature. In this way, that despair which threatens to separate man from life, forces him to those ideal creations of art which ultimately restore him to it. What is at work here finally is the vision of the carnal flame transformed which is at bottom the vision of the emergence of value from its natural source, a vision which constitutes the great strength and originality of Santayana's intellectual career.

Whether Santayana invokes transcendence or transformation in these early poems, it is his despair over gratification in the life of action that leads him to renounce it in favor of the life of art. Only there will possession preclude loss, and the self be restored to freedom and potency. For the sense of freedom and potency for Santayana at this period were great indeed: he was teaching and traveling as well as writing his lyric poetry, the verse drama, *Lucifer, The Sense of Beauty,* and *Interpretations of Poetry and Religion,* all in the 1890s. The surrender of a wide range of possibilities in life, dramatized in his poetry, was accompanied by a rising awareness of intellectual power and creative energy. The spiritual crisis was truly what St. Paul meant by a metanoia, a dying into life, the culmination of a process of sublimation begun many years before and a dramatic symbol for the conscious results of that process. And beyond that it epitomizes the intellectual movement of which it was a part, by which a whole segment of the culture, in painful awareness of the disappearance of its members' control over the events of life, transferred its energies to the world of art. This transference was viewed in its origins as a decadence, yet from it emerged the extraordinarily fruitful movement of the early 20th century that we call modern. (pp. 725-37)

Lois Hughson, "The Uses of Despair: The Sources of Creative Energy in George Santayana," in American Quarterly, *Vol. XXIII, No. 5, December, 1971, pp. 725-37.*

Gary R. Stolz　(essay date 1976)

[In the following essay, Stolz surveys the response to The Life of Reason *among American philosophers and examines the influence of this work on American philosophy.]*

The multi-volumed *Life of Reason; or, The Phases of Human Progress* constitutes George Santayana's most influential philosophical work. Initially published in London and New York during 1905-1906, this work was the product of a sustained intellectual effort. Developing his perception that reason was intimately related to nature, Santayana had traced the fortunes of reason in five full volumes dealing with such diverse topics as common sense, society, religion, art, and science. He suggested that men could not live a reasonable existence until they admitted the natural origins of their opinions, recognized the limitations imposed by their environment, and sought to understand themselves before formulating ideal goals.

"I have read practically no reviews of my book," wrote Santayana (in 1905), "so that I don't know if any one has felt in it something which, I am sure, is there: I mean the tears." Santayana's tears were not for the departed gods of Greece or for "the stained-glass of cathedrals broken to let in the sunlight and the air." They were shed precisely for the pitifully small amount of sunlight and fresh air which men and women of the modern world could feel and breathe. Much of Santayana's self-confessed "irritation" was the result of "seeing the only things that are beautiful treated as if they were of no account."

Had he read the reviews of *The Life of Reason,* Santayana would have found a mixed but, generally, favorable reaction. John Dewey, writing in *Science,* praised Santayana's first two volumes as affording "the potency, of the most significant contribution, made in this generation, to philosophic revision." Dewey correctly identified Santayana's point of view as that of "naturalistic idealism"; by this he was referring to Santayana's adroit linking of the ideal organizing principle of reason with its underlying natural conditions. Dewey saw clearly the ligaments of Santayana's thought:

> Nature shows itself in a life of sentiency and of impulse. But some sentient moments mean more, satisfy more, and are at a deeper level, than others. The significance of such moments, persistently entertained, constitutes reason. For so entertained, they afford standards of estimation, of criticism, of construction: they become the starting-points of sustained effort to bring all experiences into harmony with themselves.

This was at once an old view (formerly held by the Greeks) and, for the world of the early twentieth century (still divided among materialists and idealists), an important one. "With whatever of criticism and qualification," wrote Dewey, "those who think, as does the present writer, that the really vital problem of present philosophy is the union of naturalism and idealism, must gratefully acknowledge the extraordinary force and simplicity with which Dr. Santayana has grasped this problem. . . ."

Another reviewer of *The Life of Reason*—G. E. Moore—was taken aback by what he thought was a lack of clarity in Santayana's approach. He was also disturbed by Santayana's unorthodox treatment of religion. Nevertheless, Moore could see that "the chief general conclusions which Mr. Santayana seems anxious to enforce are that a great deal of real good is attainable and has been attained in human life, and that real good can thus be attained not in one way only but in a great many different ways." Moore, unfortunately, failed to acknowledge the key role played by reason in determining how the good was to be pursued, and he entirely overlooked the ground of sentience from which, in Santayana's view, our ideals must arise.

Ernest Albee, writing in *The Philosophical Review,* was more charitable than Moore. He put the rhetorical question, "Where and by whom is the constructive work [in philosophy] being done?" and he congratulated "serious writers on philosophy" who stated their "views . . . in more systematic fashion." Although Albee's review of *The Life of Reason* was, for the most part, an apology for his own good sense of balance, he acknowledged that Santayana "is always sufficiently independent without being in the least eccentric, and has much to say that is highly suggestive. . . ."

F. C. S. Schiller, a pragmatist "of idealistic antecedents," found it impossible to part company with a teleological explanation of the universe. This point of view, however, neither prevented him from praising the literary excellence of Santayana's style nor from admitting that "our primary need at present [1906] is to recall philosophy to the consideration of actual human experience. . . ." "Santayana's voice," wrote Schiller, "is of so clear and penetrating a quality that it cannot but add materially to this very necessary outcry."

Finally, one of the most interesting reactions to Santayana's *Life of Reason* came from William James. James's temperament was strikingly different from Santayana's, and it is not surprising that his view of Santayana's work should have been colored by emotion. While James was outgoing, irritable on occasion, but usually friendly in a profuse fashion, Santayana was coolly reserved, aloof in manner, and penetrating in his thought. A fairly wide gulf existed between these two men whose powerful minds ran in different channels; and yet, they did have at least one thing in common—a hatred for "the desiccating and pedantifying process" which could be observed at Harvard. This bond, as well as a mutual admiration for one another as teachers and thinkers, enabled them to engage in a trenchant and clearly epic round of criticism.

James believed that Santayana's *Life of Reason* was a great book, "if the inclusion of opposites is a measure of greatness." He thought the work would "probably be reckoned great by posterity" but noted, correctly, that it had "no *rational* foundation . . ." [see Further Reading]. Rationality, of course, was at the very pinnacle of Santayana's *Life of Reason*; its "centre of gravity," as James observed, lay elsewhere.

James thought he knew where the center of gravity in Santayana's philosophy lay. As early as 1900—in a letter to George Herbert Palmer—James had belabored Santayana as a representative of "moribund Latinity" whose "anti-realistic" views administered "reproof to us barbarians in the hour of our triumph." Santayana was antirealistic, according to James, because he viewed ideas as being independent of existence:

> Nevertheless, how fantastic a philosophy!—as if "the world of values" were independent of existence. It is only as being, that one thing is better than another. The idea of darkness is as good as that of light, as ideas. There is more value in light's *being*. And the exquisite consolation, when you have ascertained the badness of all fact, in knowing that badness is inferior to goodness, to the end—it only rubs the pessimism in.

James rejected the implications of this view. "When you come down to the facts," he wrote, "what do your harmonious and integral ideal systems prove to be? in the concrete? Always burst by the growing content of experience." James preferred the worlds of Walt Whitman and Robert Browning "ten times over." "The barbarians," he averred, "are in the line of mental growth, and those who do insist that the ideal and the real are dynamically continuous are those by whom the world is to be saved." This almost messianic fervor, on James's part, to see ideals equated with fluid experience accounts, in part, for his antagonism towards Santayana's more static and contemplative outlook.

Upon reading James's letter to Palmer, Santayana suggested that, "apart from temperament, I am nearer to you [to James] than you now believe." "What you say, for instance," continued Santayana, "about the value of the good lying in its *existence,* and about the continuity of the world of values with that of fact, is not different from what I should admit. Ideals would be irrelevant if they were not natural entelechies, if they were not called for by something that exists and if consequently their realization would not be a present and actual good." Admitting his Catholic sympathies, Santayana appealed to Plato and Aristotle in his defense of what he believed to be "the highest traditions of the human mind," and he wisely made the point that as Greece was moribund "when it transmitted to the rest of the world the seeds of its own rationalism," so too Latinity had to be laid to rest before its seeds could be transplanted and grown in new soil. There was a need, Santayana felt, for "propagating straight thinking among the peoples who hope to be masters of the world in the immediate future. Otherwise they will be its physical masters only, and the Muses will fly over them to alight among some future race that may understand the Gods better. . . ."

This exchange of letters between James and Santayana reveals that the two men were rivals; each of them possessed a highly distinctive temperament not readily given to compromise; each of them chose to champion a different intellectual and cultural perspective. In a general sense, Santayana spoke for the Latin South and James for the Anglo-Saxon North. While James applauded the views of such "barbarians" as Whitman and Browning, Santayana relied upon the opinions of such traditional thinkers as Plato and Aristotle. James enjoyed the prospect of a dynamic universe wherein the ideal and the real were continuous.

Santayana agreed with James that the worlds of value and of fact coincided, but, for the sake of logical analysis, he wished to retain the intellectual's privilege of treating them separately. These differences in perspective—although staunchly maintained by both thinkers for the remainder of their lives—were not without a broad area of common ground. Both men, for instance, recognized the validity and significance of Darwin's evolutionary findings. Both men grasped the unity of ideation and existence. In this last respect, both James and Santayana spoke for reason.

In 1905, the old lines separating Santayana and James were still visible; in fact, they seem to have grown stronger. James, in his criticism of *The Life of Reason,* acknowledged that Santayana's "naturalism, materialism, Platonism, and atheism form a combination of which the centre of gravity is, I think, very deep." But he characteristically found "something profoundly alienating" in Santayana's tone which, in conjunction with James's own radical empiricism, prevented him from entering sympathetically into Santayana's world.

Santayana himself thought that James's criticisms of *The Life of Reason* were "very generous," but he complained to James that these criticisms only touched the "periphery" of his thought. "You don't yet see my philosophy, nor my temper from the inside," he wrote; "your praise, like your blame, touches only the periphery, accidental aspects presented to this or that preconceived and disparate interest." "I am a Latin," continued Santayana, "and nothing seems serious to me except politics, except the sort of men that your [James's] ideas will involve and the sort of happiness they will be capable of."

It is now recognized that Santayana lived and wrote during the "classical period" in American philosophy—a period "corresponding to the Greek classical period from Democritus through Aristotle. . . ." Our classical period included six philosophers, Santayana himself, Charles Sanders Peirce, William James, Josiah Royce, John Dewey, and Alfred North Whitehead. These men and their ideas were all quite distinct, and yet there was an area of shared experience and a fund of mutually acknowledged assumptions. Royce and James had been Santayana's teachers; later, they became his colleagues. From Royce, Santayana gained much of his knowledge of idealism; and from James, he received his introduction to pragmatism. Santayana took little notice of Peirce but was genuinely concerned with Dewey's thought, which was so close to his own form of naturalism. Dewey was, in turn, influenced by Santayana's ideas. As Max H. Fisch has remarked, "Dewey has found more [than some other philosophers] to admire in and to learn from Santayana's works, and many contemporary philosophers owe them equal debts." Whitehead has acknowledged his agreement in many particulars with Santayana and Dewey. Many other philosophers, including Frederick J. E. Woodbridge and Morris R. Cohen, have profited considerably from a reading of their works.

Santayana's chief interest was in a life of contemplation; his major contribution to American philosophy was an integrated system of naturalism which incorporated both instinct and ideation within its confines. In the first volume of *The Life of Reason, Reason in Common Sense,* Santayana succinctly described the relationship between a life of sentience and that of reason:

> The relation of mind to body, of reason to nature, seems to be actually this: when bodies have reached a certain complexity and vital equilibrium, a sense begins to inhabit them which is focused upon the preservation of that body and on its reproduction. This sense, as it becomes reflective and expressive of physical welfare, points more and more to its own persistence and harmony, and generates the Life of Reason.

Arising whenever instinct managed to become reflective, the life of reason included two important aspects—awareness of self and knowledge of the world; sufficient comprehension in both of these areas would facilitate the formulation of ideal goals and tend to bring life's various impulses into harmony with one another. The ultimate justification for living the life of reason was the attainment of happiness.

Santayana's naturalism was at once anti-dualistic and anti-reductionist in character: nature was viewed as an all-inclusive reality; mind and matter—sometimes regarded as self-sufficient entities by nineteenth-century idealists and materialists—were treated as integral (though logically distinct) parts of nature. This philosophy looked to nature as a whole for its ultimate explanations and carefully avoided reducing mind to matter or matter to mind. As such, it appealed to many individuals who were dissatisfied with top-heavy idealisms and baser forms of materialism current in turn-of-the-century thought.

Dewey, Cohen, Woodbridge, and Santayana were the "founding fathers" of American naturalism; as teachers, they spoke to a generation of American naturalists. Referring to Dewey, Cohen, and Santayana, Joseph L. Blau remarks, "Though their differences led them to debate, . . . a survey of their major themes indicates that on these their attitudes were very similar. The poetic naturalism of Santayana, the rationalistic naturalism of Cohen, and the experimental naturalism of Dewey, different though they may be in detail, and different though their authors are in temperament, together form a solid basis for the further speculations of their students and disciples." One has only to include Woodbridge and his "humanistic naturalism" to make the story complete.

Dewey and Santayana were the chief figures during the classical period in American philosophy to espouse naturalism. Dewey was more deeply influenced by pragmatism than Santayana; for example, he regarded thought as being instrumental, that is, taking "place within nature as experience, starting from the 'actually problematic' and confused situation and ending in the satisfactory resolution of the problem or confusion." Santayana expressly denied that thought was "instrumental or servile," preferring to regard it as "an experience realized" rather than as "a force to be used"; he was willing to admit, however, that thought was "essentially practical in the sense that but for thought no motion would be an action, no change a progress. . . ."

Dewey had read *The Life of Reason* and understood its message. "No modern thinker," he suggested, "has pointed out so persuasively as Santayana that 'every phase of the ideal world emanates from the natural', that 'sense, art, religion, society express nature exhuberantly'."

The book in which this acknowledgement appeared, Dewey's *Experience and Nature* (1925), drew Santayana's interest and criticism. "It would be hard to find a philosopher," observed Santayana, "in whom naturalism . . . was more inveterate than in Dewey." At the same time, Santayana feared what he described as the "pervasive quasi-Hegelian tendency to dissolve the individual into his social functions, as well as everything substantial or actual into something relative or transitional." He accused Dewey's basically naturalistic philosophy of being dominated by the shifting foreground of material activity in America. "The pragmatist becomes, or seems to become," wrote Santayana, "a naturalist only by accident, when as in the present age and in America the dominant foreground is monopolized by material activity. . . ." This was so because from time immemorial "material activity" had involved "naturalistic assumptions." Excessive reliance upon such a foreground, in Santayana's opinion, was productive of relativistic thinking. Dewey's naturalism was "accordingly an assumption imposed by the character of the prevalent arts" and, consequently, "half-hearted and short-winded."

Dewey replied to Santayana's accusations with some heat. "To me," wrote Dewey, "Santayana's naturalism appears as broken-backed as mine to him seems short-winded." Dewey argued that Santayana's thought put a "gulf" between nature and man "reminiscent of supernatural beliefs," and he maintained that the "foreground of nature" or "experience" did merit our attention precisely because it "conducts our thought to the background." My dependence upon the social or conventional medium may be too great," Dewey pleaded, "but my faith in it does not extend to believing that the last word on matter and mind has been said by it." Dewey clung tenaciously to the foreground of human experience (whether intelligent or emotional in character), and argued that Santayana's naturalism was reducible to "a vague gesture of adoring faith in some all-comprehensive unknowable" in which "human life" was "specious and illusory." Aside from this important disagreement as to the value of immediate experience, Dewey admitted that both he and Santayana were in agreement on very many matters.

By 1939, Dewey had grown a little closer to Santayana's point of view. He continued to deny that experience was "specious," but he also denied that he held the idea that "only the immediate is real." Dewey went so far as to stress the almost virtual identity of his and Santayana's views of experience. Both views, he maintained, were, at bottom, physiological. Both views were in agreement concerning the interaction of consciousness with environment. Dewey also admitted the identity of his view and Santayana's concerning the development of ideals from nature. All things considered, the two leading American naturalists had more in common than their public differences would seem to suggest.

Frederick J. E. Woodbridge became a teacher of philosophy at Columbia University in 1902. His activities as a founder and editor of *The Journal of Philosophy* and as dean of the Columbia University Graduate School guaranteed him a place of leadership and respect in American philosophic circles. Woodbridge's reading of Santayana's *Life of Reason* was an important event in his life: he felt that he "had found in it a matchless commentary on our human thinking." Woodbridge was particularly impressed with Santayana's Aristotelian conviction that "everything ideal has a natural basis and everything natural an ideal fulfillment." He saw in this "one of the major tasks of philosophy [which Santayana had undertaken in *The Life of Reason*]: to exhibit the passage from the natural to the ideal; from common sense to reason; from animal love to ideal love; from gregarious association to free society; from practice and invention to liberal art; from mythology to enlightened religion; and from crude cosmologies to that impersonal objectivity found in science." Woodbridge also found in Santayana's naturalism "an acceptable standard of criticism"; it seemed to him that "ideals are significant as they round out and complete some natural function, and that the natural, when cut off from the ideal, must not be looked upon as affording by itself any standard of conduct or reason for its existence; it is brutally impersonal." Finally, Woodbridge believed that by clarifying the difference between "knowing a world" and "having a world to know" Santayana had "conclusively" exposed "the vanities of epistemology."

Woodbridge's reading of *The Life of Reason* allowed him a "greater freedom and clarity" in "handling" his own ideas and enabled him to better express his own naturalistic convictions. His study of Aristotle, Spinoza, and Locke crystallized into a meaningful synthesis: "Aristotle's thoroughgoing naturalism and his conception of productivity, Spinoza's rigid insistence on structure, and Locke's doctrine of the acquisition of ideas through experience, seemed to afford, when taken together, a means of backing up the philosophical enterprise with a metaphysics which would be analytical instead of controversial."

Another stimulating teacher who benefited considerably from a reading of Santayana's *Life of Reason* was Morris R. Cohen. As an inquisitive graduate student at Columbia University, Cohen had studied Aristotle with Professor Woodbridge. He had gone on to obtain a doctoral degree in philosophy from Harvard University in 1906. In 1920, when he was teaching as a professor of philosophy at New York's City College, Cohen wrote an article for *The New Republic* in which he came to terms with Santayana [see Further Reading]. For many years (since 1912) Cohen had made use of Santayana's *Life of Reason* in his courses on the nature of civilization and related topics. Now he sought to express to a wider public his reasons for appreciating Santayana and his *Life of Reason.* "If a European critic like Taine were to ask for an American book of philosophy containing a distinct and comprehensive view of human life, its aims and diverse manifestations," observed Cohen, "we could not mention anything more appropriate than Santayana's *Life of Reason.*" Santayana, according to Cohen, had "cultivated the ancient virtue of calm detachment." His "zeal, if any," was that of "the artist."

Cohen perceived the key which distinguished Santayana "from all other philosophers." It was the way in which he combined "thoroughgoing naturalism with profound appreciation of the wisdom commonly called idealism or other-worldliness." "Like Dewey, perhaps more than Dewey," affirmed Cohen, "Santayana is a throroughgoing naturalist, believing that mind is the natural effect of bodily growth and organization." Cohen was himself convinced that naturalism was "the only intelligible philosophy," and he believed that the "true life of reason" was "not to be found in willful idealistic dreams, but in the logical activity which is docile to fact and illumines the actual world. . . ."

Following a closely reasoned analytic account of the salient points contained in *The Life of Reason,* Cohen went on to explain perceptively why this work (by 1920) had appealed to only a handful of individuals:

> American philosophy has attracted two types of mind—those to whom philosophy is religion rationalized, and those (a smaller but perhaps growing number) to whom philosophy is a scientific method of dealing with certain general ideas. To the former a combination of atheistic catholicism and anti-puritan, non-democratic, aesthetic morality, lacking withal in missionary enthusiasm, typifies almost all that is abhorrent. To the scientific group Santayana is just a speculative poet who may value science very highly but does so as a well-groomed gentleman who knows it at a polite distance, afraid to soil his hands with its grimy details.

"These judgements," wrote Cohen, "illustrate the great tragedy of modern philosophy." Santayana, he thought, was "genuinely devoted" to philosophy's great task "of drawing a picture or unified plan of the world in which we live. . . ." Weak interest "in a unified world" along with philosophy's narrow concern with "logical argumentation and scientific pretensions" had combined to limit philosophy's scope. These factors also accounted for Santayana's "essential loneliness."

Cohen's appreciation of Santayana's unified vision of the world was by no means limited to one article or to the classroom. He openly acknowledged his indebtedness to Santayana in his "Preface" to his book on *Reason and Nature* (1931), and he went on to illustrate Santayana's ideas in detail in his fine study of *American Thought* (1954) Cohen's popularization of many of Santayana's leading ideas constitutes an invaluable contribution to American naturalism.

Santayana's influence may have been relatively limited prior to World War I, but during the post-war period it became more extensive as many American philosophers became interested in his ideas. Professor J. Loewenberg of the University of California at Berkeley praised Santayana's works for their depth, sanity, and wisdom. "Mr. Santayana," declared Loewenberg, "has richly variegated the only theme that really matters in all philosophy: the relation between substantive reality and the translations of it in the polyglot terms of human reason and imagination." In a similar manner, Professor William Pepperell Montague of Columbia University—who had taken Santayana's courses at Harvard—admitted that "it was a relief to hear Santayana . . . talk delightfully and quietly about the various substances of which the world might conceivably be composed." Montague also credited Santayana with having helped him to discover that "an atheistic nature red with tooth and claw could in no sense absolve man from his obligation to actualize ideals of beauty and goodness; nor could it deprive him of the consolation of knowing that those ideals were always and eternally there, be the world what it might."

Younger philosophers such as Horace M. Kallen and Harold A. Larrabee were also impressed by Santayana's account of *The Life of Reason.* Kallen was well aware of the great variety in modern thought, and he treated Santayana's ideas with a certain amount of detachment. He saw clearly that "all the potencies and virtues which Bergson ascribes to God, Santayana assigns to Matter. . . ." "The more Matter and God are denuded of the defining attitudes which distinguish them," observed Kallen, "the more certainly they coalesce. . . ." Kallen counted Santayana (along with Eddington, Bergson, Dewey, Freud, Henry Adams, Marx, Spengler, Veblen, and Whitehead) as one of "the major figures who captivated the post-War heart and stirred the post-War mind." Larrabee was likewise concerned with Santayana's place in the post-war heart and mind [see excerpt dated 1931]; he was, in fact, worried by what he interpreted as America's apparent failure "to enlist him [Santayana] in the immediate task of building the new culture that is some day to fill our aching void." To remedy this situation, Larrabee wrote two lengthy articles for the *Sewanee Review*: in the first, he traced Santayana's life in America and his intellectual development; in the second, he dealt with Santayana's roles as philosopher and critic. Although Larrabee was disappointed by Santayana's permanent departure from America in 1912 and made uncomfortable by the philosopher's Olympian gaze, he nevertheless found many things to admire in Santayana's thought and character. One of the things which caught his attention was Santayana's relationship (when he was a student) to "such commanding figures" as George Herbert Palmer, Josiah Royce, and William James. "He [Santayana] was not only ready to cross swords with them as something like an equal," noted Larrabee, "he could also maintain an inner life beside which theirs could only seem forced and bare." Santayana's fusion of naturalism and "aesthetic idealism" was also pleasing to Larrabee, who found that Santayana's philosophy "takes its departure from the midst of the Bergsonian flux, and yet . . . explores the uttermost reaches of the Platonic ideas."

Another highly perceptive inter-war critic and admirer of Santayana's was Sterling P. Lamprecht [see Further Reading]. Lamprecht saw more clearly than most philosophers the nature and implications of Santayana's thought and character. He correctly observed that the life of reason constituted "the transformation of human as well as of inanimate nature, the building up from crude impulse and wild imagination of an ordered and harmonious life." He saw that it was "a temporal career" (as opposed to a "spiritual life"), and that in it "imagination is guided by the needs of animal life, and impulse is disciplined by the

foresight of ideal possibilities. . . ." Lamprecht saw (or thought he saw) something about Santayana which has the ring of truth. "Santayana," he wrote, "takes even his contemporaries and ours, even ourselves who are his admirers and critics, as but occasions on which his vision turns to appreciation of perennial forms. He looks through us and beyond; he sees *what* we are as well as *that* we are, and he pays no more attention to the fact *that* we are than courtesy demands. He sees *what* we are, and he smiles; and in the contemplation of our essence, he has caught up all that is of worth in us for him."

In conformity with this estimate of Santayana, Lamprecht admitted that the mood "repeated readings" of Santayana produced in him was one of "exasperated delight." The delight stemmed from a consideration of Santayana's "precision of phrase" and "complete intellectual grasp" of a given topic. It was also produced by Santayana's ability—as in *The Life of Reason*—to pursue "a great theme" with such persistence. The exasperation felt by Lamprecht was, at least in part, a result of the same matter which had irritated John Dewey. Santayana, thought Lamprecht, "is naturalistic in his major persuasions and agnostic in his exclusion of the data of experience from a status in the real or 'external' world." Because—in Lamprecht's eyes—Santayana did not bring these two "traditions" into "peace" with each other, the result was "constant equivocations."

Another admirer and popularizer of Santayana's philosophy was Irwin Edman. Edman, who was a professor of philosophy at Columbia University, edited (at Santayana's request) a selection of Santayana's writings which appeared in 1936. In his "Introductory Essay" to this work [see Further Reading], Edman presented a balanced appreciation of Santayana and his thought. Although Edman placed emphasis upon Santayana's gifts as a poet and moral philosopher, he did not overlook Santayana's basic naturalism or his concern for ideal life. Edman knew that by a "rational life" Santayana meant "a harmonious realization of ideals" which was itself a reflection of animal impulse. The affinity of Edman's thought to Santayana's may be illustrated by a passage from one of Edman's most interesting works, *Adam, The Baby, and the Man from Mars* (1929). "To know the material origins of our flights," wrote Edman, "is not to deny their being or their value. To recognize the horrors and evils in the texture of existence is not to blind us to all the loveliness and liveliness there is to enjoy and to commemorate under the sun." This passage of Edman's expresses simply and beautifully the essence of Santayana's philosophy.

Santayana's influence upon the inter-war American philosophers was extensive; it was only during and after World War II, however, that the significance of his contribution to American thought was recognized. As John Herman Randall, Jr. has suggested, "the identification of 'naturalism' with the double protest, against nineteenth-century materialism as well as against supernaturalism and transcendental idealism—and in that sense the christening, if not the begetting, of the 'new' or 'contemporary' naturalism—was primarily the responsibility of that cosmopolitan spirit whose influence has been exerted almost wholly on American philosophizing, Santayana." Santayana's naturalism constituted a new way of looking at the world which in conjunction with other naturalistic views (particularly Dewey's) has appealed to a majority of the new post-World War II philosophers in America.

"Today," as Andrew J. Reck has remarked [in his *New American Philosophers*], "the naturalists are legion. . . ." Among them, three—all professors at Columbia University—may be singled out: Ernest Nagel, John Herman Randall, Jr., and Justus Buchler. "Each in his own way," in Reck's judgement, "has advanced the cause of naturalism: Nagel by heightening its scientific character; Randall by adding an historical dimension; and Buchler by deepening and reforming its metaphysics." Each of these thinkers has benefited in some degree from an acquaintance with Santayana's ideas. Nagel, for instance, recalls that his reading of *The Life of Reason,* in Cohen's course on the philosophy of civilization, was "a significant event" in his education; Santayana's book provided him with "a set of critical principles" that helped him to formulate his own "perspective on the relations of man and nature." Randall, who was "decisively influenced" by Dewey and Woodbridge, was strongly impressed by the combination of idealistic and naturalistic elements in Santayana's philosophy. His "latest thought on religion" has been "molded," at least in part, by the "early influence of Santayana." Buchler's thought owes much to Charles S. Peirce and John Dewey; his early interest in Santayana is attested to by the fact that in 1936 he and Benjamin Schwartz edited a collection of Santayana's works, *Obiter Scripta.* "In Buchler's naturalism," observes Reck, "query and method are recognized to be of equal importance. In effect, Dewey's methodological discipline is combined with Santayana's speculative imagination to mark a new phase in the development of naturalism." Santayana's influence upon the minds of many of America's most original philosophic thinkers is undeniable; through that influence, Santayana has contributed substantially to the naturalistic temper of contemporary American philosophy.

Santayana's *Life of Reason,* then, constitutes an extremely important contribution to American philosophy. Its chief message—the unity of the ideal and natural worlds—has inspired a cross section of some of America's greatest thinkers and educators. William James, confronted with Santayana's naturalism, rejected its Latin overtones but was forced to acknowledge its depth of perception. John Dewey, Morris R. Cohen, and Frederick J. E. Woodbridge all understood Santayana's message and have acknowledged their indebtedness to his *Life of Reason*; through their efforts American naturalism now flows in the mainstream of American thought. Such inter-war philosophers as J. Loewenberg, William P. Montague, Horace M. Kallen, Harold A. Larrabee, Sterling P. Lamprecht, and Irwin Edman were all favorably impressed with Santayana's ideas; their recognition of the value of Santayana's naturalism helped to popularize a little-known philosophy. Such post-World War II naturalists as Ernest Nagel, John Herman Randall, Jr., and Justus Buchler have all found much of value in Santayana's thought; in their works, the new naturalism of Santayana,

Dewey, Woodbridge, and Cohen is being brought to fruition.

Santayana's inclusion of imaginative data within the naturalistic perspective has, at once, softened a hard-edged materialism and brought an impossible idealism back down to earth. By uniting, as he did in *The Life of Reason,* the life of instinct with the life of ideation, Santayana showed how our practical concerns are related to our ideal interests. Reason is an outgrowth of material life; it is also an enlightened guide for activity. To separate mind from matter—as nineteenth-century materialists and idealists sometimes did—was to cut reason from its natural roots and to make of man either an angel or an ape. Only through a fully integrated life of reason, combining animal impulse and clear thought, could man regain a true knowledge of himself and a true mastery of the world in which he lived. Santayana's life of reason, with its reliance upon common sense and faith in the human imagination, was directed towards this end. (pp. 323-35)

> Gary R. Stolz, "The Reception of Santayana's 'Life of Reason' among American Philosophers," in Journal of the History of Philosophy, Vol. XIV, No. 3, July, 1976, pp. 323-35.

Nathan A. Scott, Jr. (essay date 1985)

[*Scott is an American critic. In the following excerpt, he synthesizes the principal elements of Santayana's thought.*]

Santayana . . . , in his ripe maturity, wanted very emphatically to insist that the real ground of his thought is to be found nowhere else than in his materialism. "My philosophy," he said, "is not an academic opinion adopted because academic tendencies seemed . . . to favour it. I care very little whether, at any moment, academic tendencies favour one unnecessary opinion or another. I ask myself only what are the fundamental presuppositions that I cannot live without making. And I find that they are summed up in the word materialism." Yet Santayana's materialism hardly proposes any sort of systematic cosmology, and nothing could be more alien to its true import than so quintessentially materialistic a dictum as that which Hobbes lays down in chapter 46 of the *Leviathan,* when he says: "The universe, that is, the whole mass of all things that are, is corporeal, that is to say, body, and hath the dimensions of magnitude, namely length, breadth, and depth . . . and that which is not body is no part of the universe: and because the universe is all, that which is no part of it is nothing, and consequently nowhere." Indeed, wherever one turns amongst the key statements of his career, whether to *The Life of Reason* or to *Scepticism and Animal Faith* or to *Realms of Being,* Santayana's profession of materialism, far from being inspired by scientific precept and far from claiming that matter and reality are coextensive, would appear to be saying nothing other than that the supporting matrix of the human enterprise formed by all the coherences and continuities of the natural order represents an absolutely recalcitrant kind of otherness which can in no way be thought to be called into being by any creative act of the human spirit itself. He conceives the controlling principle of matter or existence to be the principle of "substance," since substance is that which "actualizes and limits the manifestation of every essence that figures in nature or appears before the mind." And the account in **Realms of Being** of the "presumable properties" of substance makes a nice example of his dialectical powers at full stretch, but the doctrine of substance does, at bottom, want to assert nothing more than the primacy of that aboriginal world which primitive experience and common sense confront "as the condition of mind" and as that which makes us know that "mind . . . [is not] the condition of nature." Man does not dwell, in other words, as Santayana wants to say, in his own brain-pan but, rather, in the presence of a world which, in respect to the human agent, is *wholly other;* he is its witness, not its creator; it is to nothing more than this that his materialism comes down in the end, and to conceive it otherwise is to misconceive it.

Santayana's account of the human situation goes on, however, to insist on the dark inscrutability of that order of things *out there* with which we have our daily commerce. His German contemporary Edmund Husserl, to be sure, was launching his whole project of phenomenology with the contention that things are nothing other than what they are as "things of experience" and that the inexperienceable is beyond the domain of both thought and discourse. But to the great innovator at Freiburg Santayana would have been inclined to say: "When I rub my eyes and look at things candidly, it seems evident to me that they stubbornly refuse to be sucked into the immediacies of actual experience." And it was in this conviction that a cardinal premise of his thought was deeply rooted.

That there is a natural world by which we are surrounded and which is peopled with myriad things and creatures—this Santayana took to be a necessary postulate of that "animal faith" which the venture of living requires of us all. And he considered it to be the task of philosophy not so much to justify this assumption as to advertise its presumptiveness, and thus to keep steadily before us the essentially fideistic basis on which all our transactions with the world are conducted. But, though animal faith must take it for granted *that* the circumambient world has a genuinely real status in the realm of being, *what* the various things and creatures of our experience are, in the absolute specificity of their actual existence—this, as Santayana insists, remains forever hidden. The only "givens" that human intelligence has at hand are its apprehensions of this and that, what he calls "essences." Yet these data which are immediately present to consciousness are powerless to authenticate their own factuality, and thus Santayana finds himself driven to his sceptical conclusion, that "nothing given exists."

Santayana's "essence" is not, of course, as he frequently found it necessary to insist, merely another version of the Platonic Idea, for Platonism, as he reminds us, materializes the Idea into a supernatural power capable of acting causatively upon the natural order. In his own vision of things, however, an essence, since it does not "exist," lacks any sort of material efficacy. It is simply the indelible impression that a particular fact, that a particular chunk of

reality, scores upon the mind. Indeed, Santayana's doctrine of essence is not unlike Gerard Manley Hopkins's doctrine of "inscape." Hopkins considered all things to be "upheld by instress," and by "instress" he meant that power and drive of Being which keeps each created thing from scattering and dissolving, that ontological energy wherewith a bird or a flower or a cloud in the sky is *assembled* into the given *Gestalt* which it constitutes and made to be what it is—rather than another thing. Whereas a thing's "inscape" is just the pattern or form which its instress rivets upon the alert witness. And Santayana's essence is, basically, Hopkins's inscape: it is just that elementary *haecceitas,* that radical particularity, which is felt in *this* "red wheelbarrow glazed with rain water," in *this* girl's face when it is touched by the slanting rays of the afternoon sun, in *this* limestone landscape with its "murmur / Of underground streams"—when any one of these things manages so to penetrate (in Coleridge's phrase) "the film of familiarity and selfish solicitude" as to command upon itself a heedful gaze of the mind. "Whatsoever existing fact we may think we encounter, there will be obvious features distinguishing that alleged fact from any dissimilar fact and from nothing. All such features, discernible in sense, thought, or fancy, are essences; and the realm of essence which they compose is simply the catalogue, infinitely extensible, of all characters logically distinct and ideally possible."

The essence, however, in Santayana's conception, is not what traditional empiricism speaks of as sense-datum, for, though his materialism requires him to regard it as indeed an awareness of *something* and as thus bringing us tidings of the real, it is not so much an affair of mere unorganized sensory impression as it is a kind of symbolic form which intuition *posits* and which henceforth serves as something like a sign or portent of a certain feature of reality. So, since it is not actually intermingled with that which it exemplifies but stands rather only in a sort of parallel relation to it, he insists that an essence may not be considered to "exist": it is an expression of nothing more than that capacity of the human spirit to reach intentively beyond itself toward its environing world, that capacity which (in his transcendentalist idiom) Santayana speaks of as "spirit."

Yet, however "theoretic" the realm of essence may be, its periphery defines the limit beyond which, in Santayana's sense of things, there is no possibility of extending our cognizance of the world. Which is to say that the realm of the essences offers us our one mode of fathoming that generative order of reality which he calls "the realm of matter." So, to all intents and purposes, we dwell actually in "the realm of spirit"—which is not, as he conceives it, any sort of ghostly heterocosm but simply that region of endeavor in which we seek to organize and integrate our experience by way of religion and science and philosophy and literature and the arts. And, of course, the life of spirit reaches out, eagerly and yearningly, toward that most elusive of all the Realms of Being—namely, "the realm of truth." But essences are the only earnest of reality we can ever win, and, since they do not "exist" and tell therefore no tales about what is *actually* the case, Santayana's account of truth, perhaps expectably, is as elusive as the thing itself. For all the abhorrence he felt for the fundamental worldview of American pragmatism, he was, to be sure, occasionally inclined toward a kind of pragmatic view of our situation as one in which, by way of our dealings with essences, we dream awake and our "dreams are kept relevant to . . . [their] environment . . . only by the external control exercised over them by Punishment, when the accompanying conduct brings ruin, or by Agreement, when it brings prosperity." On other occasions, however, he seems to have been inclined to think of truth as constituted of those essences that find real embodiment in existence— though, since we have immediate contact only with the essence itself and are never therefore able strictly to verify its relation to actuality, he, in accord with his basic premises, considered *knowledge* to be assumptive, a matter of "animal faith" that the data present to the mind are indeed indicative of existing states of affairs. Yet one feels that, finally, the doctrine of truth that Santayana's scepticism found most congenial is nowhere more suggestively and poignantly adumbrated than in the concluding sentence of the Epilogue of his novel *The Last Puritan* which says: "After life is over and the world has gone up in smoke, what realities might the spirit in us still call its own without illusion save the form of those very illusions which have made up our story?"

Nor did he want even in the slightest degree to exempt his own philosophy from the kind of unillusioned stringency expressed in this concluding sentence of *The Last Puritan.* At a certain point he imagines himself being interrogated about the truth-claims he would make in behalf of his own reflections. He says:

> A rationalistic reader might . . . ask: "Is there no truth within your realm of essence? Are not unity and distinctness present in all essences, and is it not true to say so? And all that you yourself have written, here and elsewhere, about essence, is it not true?" No, I reply, it is not true, nor meant to be true. It is a grammatical or possibly a poetical construction having, like mathematics or theology, a certain internal vitality and interest; but in the direction of truth-finding, such constructions are merely instrumental like any language or any telescope. A man may fall into an error in grammar or in calculation. This is a fault in the practice of his art, at bottom a moral defect, a defect in attention, diligence, and capacity: and in my dialectic I have doubtless often clouded my terms with useless or disturbing allusions. But when consistently and conscientiously worked out and stripped to their fighting weight, my propositions will be logically necessary, being deducible from the definitions or intuitions of the chosen terms, and especially of this chosen term "essence" itself. But logic is only logic: and the systems of relation discoverable amongst essences do not constitute truths, but only other more comprehensive essences, within which the related essences figure as parts.

We are compassed about, then, by the four realms of matter, essence, spirit, and truth. And though, in the order of experience, it is the realm of essence which claims primacy, in the ontological order it is the realm of matter which is the truly aboriginal and generative dimension of reality.

But in relation to this region of things we see through a glass darkly and face, for all its pomp and circumstance, unfathomable mystery. "The light of the spirit which shines in the darkness cannot see the primeval darkness which begat it and which it dispels." Indeed, Santayana's vision of the human situation is more than a little touched by a sense of what Martin Heidegger called *Geworfenheit,* by a sense of our having been "thrown" into a world which is not of our own making and which in its sheer givenness, in its sheer thereness, confronts us with a contingency so absolute that we find ourselves staring at "dark abysses before which intelligence must be silent, for fear of going mad " [**"Ultimate Religion"** in **Obiter Scripta**]. The world in its various concrete aspects is, to be sure, easily perceptible: yet "what is most plain to sense is most puzzling to reason . . . and what is intelligible to reason at one level . . . may become arbitrary and obscure to a reason that . . . asks deeper questions." "The aim of intelligence is to know things as they are." But it finds the universe with which it undertakes to treat to be "a conjunction of things mutually irrelevant, a chapter of accidents, a medley improvised here and now for no reason, to the exclusion of myriad other forces which, so far as their ideal structure is concerned, might have been performed just as well." Ours, in short, is a world that simply cannot be brought to heel and that evokes a great *o altitudo!* of astonishment, as we find ourselves (in a metaphor of Pascal that Santayana could easily have appropriated) "in a vast sphere, ever drifting in uncertainty," where "to attach ourselves to any point and to fasten to it" is to find it wavering and slipping past us and vanishing forever. "This," says the *Pensées,* "is our natural condition, and yet most contrary to our inclination; we burn with desire to find solid ground and an ultimate sure foundation whereon to build a tower reaching to the Infinite. But our whole groundwork cracks, and the earth opens to abysses"— abysses, says Santayana, "before which intelligence must be silent."

Yet, absurd as the world appears to be in the inexplicableness of its sheer factuality, we are nevertheless in thousands of ways dependent upon it for health and sustenance. We need air to breathe and space in which to abide and the nourishment of food and drink and the countless other bounties with which nature ministers to our frailty and makes our sojourning on the earth supportable. And thus, for all the recalcitrancy of the material universe, it would be, as Santayana wants to urge, a foolish mistake for us to permit ourselves any great aversion from the realm of matter, for, were we to hold it in contempt, "it would not be merely ashes or dust that we should be despising, but all natural existence in its abysmal past and in its indefinite fertility; and it would be, not some philosopher's sorry notion of matter that we should be denying, but the reality of our animal being." Indeed, as he insists, if reverence is to be offered anything at all, it ought to be directed not toward "ideal objects" but toward "the realm of matter only," since, opaque and mysterious though it may be, it is that which chastens and corrects us, which preserves and protects us, and which with its far horizons grants us a place in which to dwell.

Now the form in which Santayana conceives this *pietas* to

find its proper expression he frequently speaks of as "pure intuition"—which may not be the happiest locution, since it can suggest what is really contrary to the final drift of his basic meaning: namely, that it is a kind of angelism, the delights of something like a Platonic heaven, at which "spirit" aims. But in ***Scepticism and Animal Faith*** he speaks of "discernment of spirit" as an affair of "attention" and "wakefulness"—which is no doubt a language more apt, for this is indeed the kind of response that, in his sense of things, a true piety will make toward the world which is at hand: "we may say that for the mind there is a single avenue to essence, namely attention." But even when he speaks in this connection of "intuition," he does not mean any sort of "divination, or a miraculous way of discovering that which sense and intellect cannot disclose. On the contrary," as he is careful to say, "by intuition I mean direct and obvious possession of the apparent." Or, as it might be somewhat differently put, by intuition or wakefulness of attention he means nothing other than a heedful openness toward all the things of earth as, in their concrete particularity, they take on the dimension of *presence:* he means the kind of openness that wants, in Richard Hovey's phrase, to "have business with the grass."

Spirit—"the light which lighteth every man that cometh into the world"—is, of course, for Santayana the name and nature of *humanitas,* of what (had he ever produced an anthropology) he would have declared to be the distinctively human thing itself. And it is simply that capacity for self-transcendence which enables the human creature to hail or salute its world and to be so awake to the furniture of existence as to discern the "inscapes" of its various items. Indeed, "the exercise of sight as distinguished from blindness," the act whereby we "greet" and pay heed to the things of earth, is precisely that which Santayana considers to be the central act of the human spirit, for it constitutes the agency by means of which "essences are transposed into appearances and things into objects of belief" and both "are raised to a strange actuality in thought." But intuition or wakefulness of attention is not merely an affair of simple awareness, for it is laden with what he (rather obscurely) calls "intent." And by intent he means that leap of animal faith whereby "spirit," though dealing always with essences which do not "exist," nevertheless *posits* a relation between the "given" (essence) and that which is not given (the existing thing)—and not only posits such a relation but holds it to be "true," in the manner of a symbolic form. What intent achieves, in other words, is a grasp of things which is "not true literally, as the fond spirit imagines when it takes some given picture, summary, synthetic, and poetical, for the essence of the world; but true as language may be true, symbolically, pragmatically, and for the range of human experience in that habitat and at that stage in its history."

It is in such terms that Santayana renders the life of spirit, and thus his whole system of reflection represents the truly human mode of being as one involving a very strict kind of receptivity and alertness to the stars of heaven and the winds of earth, to the fowls of the air and the beasts of the field, to mountains and plains, to nights and days, to the high and exalted and the low and downtrodden—indeed, to all the myriad forms of the world that presses in upon us. And, as he suggests, it is only by way of such vigilance and wakefulness of attention that we may escape the grosser forms of egotism and win through to that capaciousness and clarity of vision belonging to "the life of reason."

Nor should it go unremarked that it is just in this connection that Santayana wants to record what it is that he finds irresistibly appealing in the figure of Christ. For spirit "claims nothing, posits nothing, and is nothing in its own eyes, but empties itself completely" into that which it contemplates, and it is precisely this readiness for *kenosis,* this *disponibilité,* that he considers to be "one of the [chief] beauties in the idea of Christ." "In spite of his absolute holiness, or because of it, he shows a spontaneous sympathy, shocking to the Pharisee, with many non-religious sides of life, with little children, with birds and flowers, with common people, with beggars, with sinners, with sufferers of all sorts, even with devils. This is one of the proofs that natural spirit, not indoctrinated or canalised, was speaking in him." And it is, indeed, in the breadth of his sympathies and his quick responsiveness to every slightest bid for his attention that comes from the world about him that Santayana finds also a sort of proof of the fullness of Christ's humanity.

The kind of punctiliousness of attention that marks the life of spirit in its purest modes is, however, a moral achievement by no means easily realized, and, in a manner strikingly reminiscent of Pascal's anatomy of the various forms of *divertissement,* Santayana discriminates the several types of "distraction." "By distraction," he says, "I understand the alien force that drags the spirit away from the spontaneous exercise of its liberty, and holds it down to the rack of care, doubt, pain, hatred, and vice. And I will distinguish the chief agencies in this distraction, after the picturesque manner of Christian wisdom, as the Flesh, the World, and the Devil."

In regard to the carnal passions, it is not, of course, any kind of sour asceticism that Santayana wants to espouse, for he knows that the flesh, forming as it does "the raw material of human nature," cannot be simply discarded and that, indeed, the fleshly impulses, if merely gagged and repressed, will take their revenge, often in cruel and devastating ways. Yet he does want to lay down the necessity of taming and transmuting them in such a fashion that they will warm rather than anarchize the affections, so that spirit may not be distracted from its true vocation.

Nor does he want to preach any fanatical doctrine of contempt for the world, since he takes it for granted that the charms and delights of the world—comfort and security and favorable repute—are well enough, taken simply in and of themselves: "spirit does not come from or demand another world, or reject any form of life as unworthy. It is ready to participate in any undertaking and to rejoice in every achievement." And for him the principle of worldliness stands not for a sober accommodation to the material requirements of earthly life but rather for the kind of entanglement in the cares and trivialities of the quotidian realm that hobbles and restricts the full range of sympathy that spirit might otherwise have for the whole panorama of existence. Which is to say that the worldling's self-preoccupation leads to a certain tragic desuetude of attention: he smokes "his excellent cigar with a calm sense that there is nothing in the world better than what he does," and the tax that is levied against him for his philistinism is a very great poverty, the poverty of insentience and dullness and ennui.

And, as for the devil, Santayana says that he takes this personage to stand for "an enemy of spirit that is internal to spirit [itself]"—which makes bedevilment the subtlest and most insidious of all the snares we face. Its tempting power arises out of the strange situation in which spirit finds itself, of being committed to the intuition of essences that have no status in existence other than that which animal faith posits and of being, therefore, peculiarly susceptible to a kind of monarchism, to the dream of omniscience. It seems that "either we can know nothing, because confined to our passing dream, or we can know nothing because there is nothing but our passing dream to be known"— and, when the dream of omniscience has taken hold, it is the second alternative that will be embraced, spirit then imagining itself to be absolutely free and absolutely creative. But when spirit in this way denies its dependence on the ancestral order of nature, it is at the point of closing itself in upon itself, of forfeiting precisely that attentive openness toward the circumambient world which is its distinctive genius: its pride in its own creativeness is by way of leading it to assert its essential infinity—and this way madness lies, the kind of madness that Lucifer prepares.

The flesh, the world, and the devil, then—these three—are the great agents of "distraction." But, in so far as the spirit can be preserved from its threefold enemy, it will then proceed to do the work which it is man's special vocation to do, of building up that "ideal," symbolic universe (of science, poetry, art, religion, and metaphysics) which results from the play of the mind on the vast domain of quiddities which is called "the realm of essence." The human situation, as Santayana conceives it, is one of our being placed in a universe which is neither spirit nor spirit's vision of it: so he calls it "the realm of matter." And the vocation of spirit, after keeping for itself a proper piety in recognizing its dependence on this universe, is to *comment* upon it. But the world on which this commentary is made remains forever dark and hidden: "its powers germinate underground, and only its foliage and flowers emerge into clear light." Indeed, its very existence is no more than a postulate of animal faith, for the only terms available to any exploration of it are the essences which belong to an ontological realm wholly other than that generative order of nature which they characterize. Matter, in other words, is absolutely transcendent, for it "is always more and other than the essence which it exemplifies at any point. . . . We may enjoy it, we may enact it, but we cannot conceive it; not because our intellect by accident is inadequate, but because existence . . . is intrinsically absurd." Yet, though we find ourselves enveloped by darkness, we, since we are creatures of spirit, have it as our destiny to try to illumine the darkness—by giving the most careful heed to all the various impressions (or essences) that are scored upon the mind by, as we trust, the world *out there* and by using this material as the basis for a sym-

bolic transformation of the dazzling darkness into those fabrics of meaning that are posited by science, poetry, religion, and art.

Santayana was, of course, reluctant to advance any claim about the veridical capacities of these fabrics of meaning, since they are all wrought out of nothing more than our experience of essences. True, he was prepared occasionally to suggest that the terms of the natural sciences—as compared, say, with those of mythology—are comprised of essences which "are the fruit of a better focussed, more chastened, and more prolonged attention turned upon what actually occurs" and that, therefore, however much faith may be entailed in living by science, "not to live by it is folly." But though, at the level of practice, experience gives a certain urgency to the essences with which physics and biochemistry deal, he was not inclined, finally, to concede that they give us any real "information" about existence: they and all other sciences represent "only a claim . . . put forth, a part of that unfathomable compulsion by force of which we live and hold our painted world together." And it was with a similar agnosticism that Santayana was disposed to respond to any depositions regarding the cognitive import of poetry and the arts and religion, for, in his estimate of things, none of these has any "standing ground in fact": like science, they represent

Portrait of Santayana by Denman W. Ross.

only spirit's attempt at lighting a candle in the dark. Yet, if he ever paid any attention to a brash little manifesto called *Language, Truth and Logic* issued in 1936 by a bright young Englishman named A. J. Ayer, he must surely have felt it to express a particularly repellent kind of coarseness in its relegation of poetic and religious discourse to the province of "nonsense." For Santayana conceived the poetic and the religious imagination to be deeply a part of "the life of reason." Religion and poetry, to be sure, provide us with no information about things (about the realm of "matter")—though (as Santayana would have wanted to say to Mr. Ayer) in this respect, strictly speaking, they are no more impotent than science; but, as he felt, they do hold up "those large ideas tinctured with passion, those supersensible forms shrouded in awe, in which alone a mind of great sweep and vitality can find its congenial objects." Both, as he proposed in his famous formula, "are identical in essence and differ merely in the way in which they are attached to practical affairs. Poetry is called religion when it intervenes in life, and religion, when it merely supervenes upon life, is seen to be nothing but poetry."

For Santayana a very troublesome kind of mischief begins to be made, however, when (as Matthew Arnold put it) religion materializes itself in the fact, in the supposed fact, when it attaches its emotion to the fact—and the same mischief will be made by science and by poetry, whenever they in their way forget the virtuality of their perspectives and seek to impute to spirit the authority of matter by claiming to enunciate something like "absolute truth." What the scientist and the artist need to remember no less than the expositor of sacred mysteries is that "in so far as spirit takes the form of intelligence and of the love of truth . . . it must assume the presence of an alien universe and must humbly explore its ways, bowing to the strong wind of mutation, the better to endure and to profit by that prevailing stress." Indeed, spirit is by way of being betrayed when its devotees forget that all their fashionings are but imaginative projections and then seek to materialize them "in the supposed fact." To try thus to convert spirit into matter is merely to compound illusion with illusion. "Mind was not created for the sake of discovering the absolute truth. The absolute truth has its own intangible reality, and scorns to be known. The function of mind is rather to increase the wealth of the universe in the spiritual dimension, by adding appearance to substance . . . and by creating all those . . . perspectives, and those emotions of wonder, adventure, curiosity, and laughter which omniscience would exclude."

"The light of the spirit which shines in the darkness cannot see the primeval darkness which begat it," but, by the deepest necessities of its own nature, spirit is driven to form by processes of *poiesis* such structures of vision and belief as will permit it to dwell amidst the environing darkness in sanity and peace. These structures—what we call science, religion, poetry, and art—are, of course, grounded in essences which are "the native grammar of the mind," and thus they are not so much "maps" of reality as they are ventures of the imagination at a systematic deciphering of a world which everywhere outruns all our systems of figuration and which asks us therefore not to

insist that things are just as we represent them but to say rather of our various schematisms that *something* of the sort may be the case.

So, then, the late Henry Aiken [in his *Reason and Conduct*] was surely right in suggesting that Santayana "is best understood as a . . . philosopher of symbolic forms," for this is certainly the field of his most fundamental interest, and thus he deserves to be regarded as one of the great forerunners of what may well turn out to be the decisive enterprise in the intellectual life of our period. But though his idioms made an easily negotiable currency of exchange for the generation of Whitehead and Cassirer, they are no doubt not so readily usable in the age of Roland Barthes and Algirdas Greimas and Gérard Genette. And if one wants summarily to account for what it is in our present situation that makes Santayana's system seem now unnegotiable, one must say that the New Men are bent on hypostatizing "spirit," in a way that would to him have appeared to represent a very strange sort of astigmatism indeed. (pp. 93-104)

Nathan A. Scott, Jr., "Santayana's Poetics of Belief," in his The Poetics of Belief: Studies in Coleridge, Arnold, Pater, Santayana, Stevens, and Heidegger, *The University of North Carolina Press, 1985, pp. 90-114.*

Joseph Epstein (essay date 1987)

[*Epstein is an American critic and editor of* The American Scholar. *In the following excerpt, he provides a retrospective of Santayana's career as a philosopher.*]

In his thirtieth year, in a letter to Norman Hapgood, Santayana wrote: "It becomes clearer to me every day that both in teaching and living our need is simplification, measure and docility to the facts." Of course his own needs were immensely simplified by his early understanding that he was among those with "no other purpose but that of living to observe life," which is to say, that he was a writer. Whatever his other deficiencies, he had, *in excelsis,* "the faculty of intellectual delight," which he never lost. On a travelling fellowship in Germany he wrote to his teacher William James that "philosophy seems to me to be its own reward, and its justification lies in the delight and dignity of the art itself"; and he later confessed to James that what initially drew him to philosophy was "curiosity and a natural taste for ingenious thinking." All this makes him sound very much the cool aesthete, for whom philosophy is above all a superior game. And so it might have been but for his talent for facing unpleasant facts, the least pleasant of which he knew by the time he was twenty-three, and perhaps much earlier—that "the world isn't run in our interest or with any reference to our needs." He calls this brute fact the "ultimate lesson of experience and philosophy," and by "our" he doesn't mean dreamy young men at Harvard but all human beings.

That the world was not organized in the interest of human beings, nor had any special reference to their needs, was the last thing Santayana was likely to have learned at Harvard, where a Protestant spirit of uplift prevailed. This spirit, it does not seem too strong to say, Santayana detested. It was akin to the spirit he found in the Unitarian churches of Boston, where people flocked "to hear a sermon like the leading article in some superior newspaper calculated to confirm the conviction already in them that their bourgeois virtues were quite sufficient and that perhaps in time poor backward races and nations might be led to acquire them." He considered the great New England god Emerson "a sort of Puritan Goethe," who had "slipped into transcendentalism and moralism and complacency in mediocrity, in order to flatter his countrymen and indirectly flatter himself." One of Santayana's many complaints against Harvard's President Charles W. Eliot (who brought the system of elective courses to the university) was that he, Eliot, thought that if a thing was moral it must also be true.

Santayana detected and ultimately condemned this spirit in the philosophy department at Harvard—a department that included William James, Josiah Royce, and, between the years 1889 and 1912, Santayana himself. "Protestant philosophy," as he called philosophy in America in *Character and Opinion in the United States* (1920), "was too conscientious to misrepresent what it found," but also too moral-minded not to undermine its findings. At Harvard, philosophers felt themselves bound "by two different responsibilities, that of describing things as they are, and that of finding them propitious to certain preconceived human desires." Josiah Royce, who loved logic, labored with a powerful contradiction at the heart of his work, adducing the existence of evil to prove the existence of good, and then feeling he ought to strive to eliminate evil. Not even William James, according to Santayana, could shake off the heavy hand of Protestant moralizing: "He was worried about what *ought* to be believed and the awful deprivation of disbelieving."

Santayana has the distinction of being one of the few people to speak ill of William James with a pretty fair consistency. The feeling was not reciprocated, even though James is famously known, in a letter to George H. Palmer, his colleague in the Harvard philosophy department, to have referred to Santayana's "perfection of rottenness in a philosophy" and to his "moribund Latinity." As Professor McCormick shows, these phrases were embedded in a letter of otherwise exuberant praise for Santayana's book *Interpretations of Poetry and Religion* (1900), about which James wrote: "Although I absolutely reject the platonism of it, I have literally squealed with delight at the imperturbable perfection with which the position is laid down on page after page; and grunted with delight at the thickening up of our Harvard atmosphere . . . " [see Further Reading].

It is reasonably certain that Santayana never either squealed or grunted with delight at anything William James wrote. James was in no serious sense Santayana's mentor, but he was, within the Harvard philosophy department, his protector, helping to arrange a job for him, solidifying a permanent position, aiding in his promotion. Santayana may not have known this. Yet even had he known it, my guess is that he could not quite have let his disappointment in James be. In a letter to a Harvard colleague, after reporting that John Stuart Mill's psycholo-

gism repels him, he goes on to say, "Mill is a sort of ponderous and sober James." To the same man he earlier writes, "I love W. James as a man. But what a singularly bad thinker he is!" Yet if he claimed to love him in a letter of 1904, when he came to write about him decades later in *Persons and Places* he noted:

> I was uncomfortable in his presence. He was so extremely natural that there was no knowing what his nature was, or what to expect next; so that one was driven to behave and talk conventionally, as in the most artificial society. I found no foothold, I was soon fatigued, and it was a relief to be out again in the open, and alone.

In *Character and Opinion in the United States,* Santayana really lowered the boom on James—a velvet-covered boom, to be sure, but one that could nonetheless knock off a man's head. There Santayana writes that James was a spirited but not a spiritual man; that *The Varieties of Religious Experience* is a book that altogether overlooks the religious experience of the great mass of mankind, which "consists in simple faith in the truth and benefit of their religious traditions"; that James was chary of coming to philosophical conclusions, or, as Santayana put it, "liked to take things one by one, rather than to put two and two together"; and that, finally, "there is a sense in which James was not a philosopher at all."

Heavy praise was not part of the regular regimen of Santayana's intellectual exercise—the only thinkers who unwaveringly find favor with him are the Greeks, Lucretius, and, after a jump of seventeen centuries, Spinoza—but was there an air of spite in his treatment of William James? My own sense is that he was disappointed in James, whom he knew to be a superior man but not unfortunately superior enough to rise above what to Santayana was the stultifying atmosphere of *fin de siècle* Harvard. When James once accused Santayana of impertinence and of putting on airs, Santayana shot back: "I wonder if you realize the years of suppressed irritation which I have passed in the midst of an unintelligible sanctimonious and often disingenuous Protestantism, which is thoroughly alien to and repulsive to me, and the need I have of joining hands with something far away from it and far above it." In a later letter he charged James with not seeing "my philosophy, nor my temper from the inside." Part of this could be put down to sheer clash of temperament; yet perhaps a greater part is owing to William James's impatience with the type of the artist, which Santayana most assuredly was. Odd that a man such as William James, who had so much sympathy, should in this regard have had so little imagination. One remembers here his inevitably disappointing letters to his brother Henry about Henry's books, with his, William's, invocations to Henry to try harder to write for the multitude, to which Henry on one occasion responded: " . . . I'm always sorry when I hear of your reading anything of mine, and always hope you won't—you seem to me so constitutionally unable to 'enjoy' it, and so condemned to look at it from a point of view remotely alien to mine in writing it. . . . " As for Santayana, when he met Henry James, for the first and only time, toward the end of James's life, he seems to have understood him immediately and completely:

Those were his last years and I never saw him again. Nevertheless in that one interview he made me feel more at home, and better understood, than his brother William ever had done in the long years of our acquaintance. Henry was calm, he liked to see things as they are, and be free afterwards to imagine how they might have been. We talked about different countries as places of residence. He was of course subtle and bland, appreciative of all points of view, and amused at their limitations.

Was it the artist in Santayana who discouraged the teacher in him? He never set out to become a teacher. Had he not been offered a half-time instructorship at Harvard, Professor McCormick informs us [see *George Santayana: A Biography* in Further Reading], he would have studied architecture at the Massachusetts Institute of Technology. Santayana preferred not to be thought a professor. A poet, yes; a philosopher, certainly; a continuing student, inevitably; but a professor, "I would rather beg than be one essentially." From the day he began teaching he began saving for the day he could cease teaching. He claimed that no close friend of his was ever a professor. Lee Simonson, the stage designer who was a student of Santayana's, recalls him when lecturing "gazing over our heads as if looking for the sail that was to bear him home"—though where, exactly, home was could not have been all that clear even to Santayana, except away from Harvard.

"So you are trying to teach philosophy at Harvard," Henry Adams said to Santayana on the one occasion when they met. "I once tried to teach history there, but it can't be done. It isn't really possible to teach anything." Santayana, had he been older, would have disagreed; it could be done, all right; for him the question was always whether it was worth doing. In a beautiful but cool passage in *Character and Opinion in the United States,* Santayana neatly described teaching with an accuracy that only those who have *tried* to give their best to teaching will readily recognize:

> Teaching is a delightful paternal art, and especially teaching intelligent and warm-hearted youngsters, as most American collegians are; but it is an art like acting, where the performance, often rehearsed, must be adapted to an audience hearing it only once. The speaker must make concessions to their impatience, their taste, their capacity, their prejudices, their ultimate good; he must neither bore nor perplex nor demoralise them. His thoughts must be such as can flow daily, and be set down in notes; they must come when the bell rings and stop appropriately when the bell rings a second time. The best that is in him, as Mephistopheles says in *Faust,* he dare not tell them; and as the substance of this possession is spiritual, to withhold is often to lose it. For it is not merely a matter of fearing not to be understood, or giving offence; in the presence of a hundred upturned faces a man cannot, without diffidence, speak in his own person, of his own thoughts; he needs support, in order to exert influence with a good conscience; unless he feels that he is the vehicle of a massive tradition, he will become bitter, or flippant, or aggressive; if he is to teach with good grace and modes-

ty and authority, it must not be he that speaks, but science or humanity that is speaking in him.

Complain about teaching though Santayana did, he had a most impressive roster of students attend his classes and lectures at Harvard. Among them, as Professor McCormick reminds us, were Conrad Aiken, Robert Frost, Gilbert Seldes, Max Eastman, Harry Austryn Wolfson, Samuel Eliot Morison, Felix Frankfurter, T. S. Eliot, and Van Wyck Brooks. Wallace Stevens never took a course from Santayana, but was very much aware of his presence, and later wrote a splendid poem about him, "To an Old Philosopher in Rome" [see Further Reading]. Walter Lippmann while a graduate student was his assistant. Most of these figures came away greatly impressed by Santayana's teaching. Only T. S. Eliot would later describe his lectures as "soporific"; and Van Wyck Brooks, in his autobiography, claimed to find Santayana's "assumption of superiority" repellent and his "feline aestheticism" (Brooks was, avowedly, a canine man) no less so. Brooks was also put off by Santayana's distaste for things American, "though I could not deny that, wandering alone, a stranger and exile everywhere, Santayana lived the true life of the sage."

Did Santayana actually hate America? I think he came near to doing so, without quite hating Americans. Around the time of his preparing to depart the United States for good, he wrote to his sister that "I am far from wishing never to see my American friends again. It is only *their country* that I am longing to lose sight of." He felt America to be a country where people were interested in what might or should be, whereas his sympathies were all for preserving the already formed. In America, ideas and traditions were not refuted but simply forgotten. The serenity for which he longed was not available in America, not even in religion: "Be Christians," he claimed once to have heard a president of Yale tell his students, "be Christians and you will be successful." Returning from a trip to California and Canada, he wrote to his sister in Avila: "They are intellectually emptier than the Sahara, where I understand the Arabs have some idea of God or of Fate." In the same letter he remarks that at Harvard, "in the midst of the dull round, a sort of instinct of courtesy makes me take it [America] for granted, and I become almost unconscious of how much I hate it all; otherwise I couldn't have stood it for *forty years!*"

In 1911, Santayana worked out an arrangement whereby he would teach a single term at Harvard, leaving him otherwise free to live abroad, there to indulge his "*native* affinities to European things." But when his mother died, in 1912, he wrote, from Paris, a letter of resignation to President Abbott Lawrence Lowell of Harvard saying that his mother's death marked "the moment when I should carry out the plan I have always had of giving up teaching, returning to live in Europe, and devoting myself to literary work. Each of these things is an object in itself sufficient to determine me, and the three conspire together." He was almost fifty, and free at last.

Henceforth Santayana would guard that freedom with the most sedulous care. Financially independent—one of his Sturgis relations had invested his money for him wisely—

he had no social ambitions, required no regular circle of friends, no fixed abode, no round of engagements. He was not in any way reclusive, and rather enjoyed such people who came his way—the stray poet or philosopher, the handsome and agreeable woman—but, as he put it in *Persons and Places:* "For constant company I had enough, and too much, with myself." Besides, he "liked solitude in crowds, meals in restaurants, walks in public parks, architectural rambles in noble cities." Boundless and boundary-less, he roamed free, all of Europe his demesne, like a Henry James character from the late period with all the Jamesian sensibility, but without any interior conflict requiring resolution.

Santayana's cousin Howard Sturgis, who was a friend of Henry James's and who lived in England, accused Santayana of being abominably selfish. Santayana allowed that he was merely "profoundly selfish," the distinction residing in the sense that, while he took pleasure in the life around him, he determined never to enter into relationships that would cause him to surrender his independence. (In fact, as Professor McCormick recounts, once his books began to sell well, Santayana was most generous in providing financial help to family and friends.) He then goes on to make the distinction that his selfishness is not of a competitive kind. "I don't want to snatch money or position or pleasures from other people, nor do I attempt to dominate them, as an unselfish man would say, for their own good." Master of irony that Santayana is, in owning up to his own selfishness he makes us recognize that it is the unselfish man of that subordinate clause who is the real menace.

The power of making distinctions, which can result in parching dryness in a pedantic philosopher, is in Santayana always a pleasure to behold. The smaller the distinction, often, the more charm it has. Thus in *Persons and Places* one finds people who are argumentative but not critical, others who are cordial but not amiable; then others who have warmth but no passion. One man—specifically, Spinoza—is "virtuous but not normal"; and another—specifically, Frank Russell—is "polygamous without being inconstant." A writer able to wield a linguistic cleaver with such skill makes one feel one's own prose has been cut, most coarsely, on a large buzz saw. Santayana also had the power, which Aristotle said cannot be taught, of constructing dazzling metaphors and similes. Thus (again) in *Persons and Places* one comes upon buildings whose surfaces are stark and unyielding, thin and sharp, "like impoverished old maids"; frail elms, "like tall young women in consumption"; an aunt said to be "living out of the fifth act of the tragedy of her life"; the speech of William Lyon Phelps, "his every word . . . a cocktail, or at least a temperance drink." It was Santayana who once referred to those philosophers whose writing gave no aesthetic pleasure—among them Epicurus, St. Thomas Aquinas, Immanuel Kant—as "leafless forests"; to retain that botanical metaphor a moment longer, his own prose is a field of orchids on a mountain slope.

But, then, it occurs to me, Santayana might have been repelled by the metaphor. A field of orchids perhaps plays too strongly into the stereotype of Santayana's reputation as the most dandiacal among modern philosophers. Orchids are all very beautiful, but one cannot after all derive sustenance from them; and might not the same be said of Santayana's philosophy? Santayana is perhaps best known for his book on aesthetics, *The Sense of Beauty,* but in fact it is not a book he greatly esteemed (he also had strong reservations about his other well-known work, *The Life of Reason*); and Professor McCormick informs us that the book secured promotion for Santayana to an assistant professorship at Harvard. Yet, powerful literary critic though he could be, and thoroughly literary though his sensibility was—*The Complete Poems of George Santayana* (1979) runs to more than five hundred pages, and his single excursion into fiction, *The Last Puritan* (1935), had a popular success—Santayana thought of himself as a philosopher, and a philosopher primarily.

He was, however, a philosopher of a particular kind—and the kind can best be distinguished by his method and his temperament. He was not a logician and he did not come to philosophy through science, for he had no scientific training of any serious sort. He never claimed originality for himself, and once remarked that all he cared for "is to sift the *truth* from traditional *imagination,* without impoverishing the latter." As early as 1887, when he was twenty-four years old, he wrote to William James to say that he had no interest in the philosophy that sets out to solve problems, and that philosophy, for him, was "rather an attempt to express a half-discovered reality, just as art is, and that two different renderings, if they are expressive, far from cancelling each other add to each other's values. . . . " Nearly thirty years later he wrote to a younger man just beginning a career in philosophy that, while he could not take the teaching of philosophy seriously, he did think philosophy "might be a life or a means of artistic expression."

For Santayana, of course, philosophy was both a life and an art: he lived his philosophy and he lavished attention on the production of it of the kind that the superior artist does upon his art. As a philosopher, he was no system builder, and attempts at elaborate argument in his technical philosophy are often difficult to follow. He was himself well aware of this, and when Logan Pearsall Smith proposed an anthology of his work that eventually appeared under the title *Little Essays, Drawn from the Writings of George Santayana* (1920), Santayana, in remarking on Smith's initial selection, wrote: "my impression is that what I have to say is better conveyed in these occasional epigrams than in any of my attempts at argument or system." There was the additional difficulty that Santayana used certain key philosophical terms—"moral," "science," "genius," "substance," "intuition," and "spirit," among others—with special, sometimes quite slippery, meanings. This, too, he knew: "Philosophy seems to be richer in theories than in words to express them in; and much confusion results from the necessity of using old terms in new meanings." Owing to this, Santayana's philosophy, like certain poems, does not paraphrase easily, if at all.

Like many another artist, Santayana was a brilliant critic of practitioners of his art. Although he claimed to despise an atmosphere of contention and controversy, he could handle the stiletto with the best of them. Frequently he chose to do so in the privacy of letters, as when, in one such letter, he describes G. E. Moore's *Principia Ethica* as a book that "seems to contain a grain of accuracy in a bushel of inexperience." Such is Bertrand Russell's intelligence and clarity, that "the more wrong he is the clearer he makes the wrongness of his position; and what more can you expect a philosopher to prove except that the views he has adopted are radically and eternally impossible? If every philosopher had done that in the past, we should now be almost out of the wood." To witness Santayana at work in his job as critic of philosophers one cannot do better than to read the brief book entitled *Egotism in German Philosophy* (1916), in which, with great economy, he works up—and over—the German philosophical system builders. When he is done the landscape of German philosophy resembles nothing so much as Berlin in early 1946: scarcely any buildings are left standing, only a few shabby figures shuffle past, the smell of smoke is in the air. Toward the close of his life, he wrote: "If I were not too old and could venture to write in French, I should compose a short history of *Les Faux Pas de la Philosophie.*"

At the heart of Santayana's philosophy is a desire to be unillusioned about the world and yet, unlike (say) Nietzsche, neither in despair nor in great anguish about it. "I was never afraid of disillusion," Santayana wrote in the opening essay of *The Philosophy of George Santayana,* the volume devoted to his work in the Library of Living Philosophers series, "and I chose it." Perhaps it is just as accurate to say that disillusion chose him, given his upbringing in a house crowded with Spanish relatives, where, as a small boy, he witnessed women giving birth and, not much older, he shared a room with a half-brother of adolescent years and normal appetites. His father was an atheist, who found the idea of the existence of God ridiculous; his mother was a pantheist, who believed God existed but was everywhere and hence was quite impersonal. Being born without much of it, he early knew that money was not an illusion. He never for a moment seems to have felt that the world was "a myth, to be clarified by a little literary criticism." Yet everything in his background conduced against his overestimating the importance of human beings in the universe. As he announced in a lecture on Herbert Spencer entitled **"The Unknowable,"** life is not "an entertainment, a feast of ordered sensations . . . life is no such thing; it is a predicament. We are caught in it; it is something compulsory, urgent, dangerous, and tempting. We are surrounded by enormous, mysterious, half-friendly forces." And yet this only makes it all the more fascinating.

To feel the vanity of life—that everything changes and everything simultaneously remains the same—was for Santayana "the beginning of seriousness." To trot out the "isms," he claimed allegiance to materialism, the family of doctrines that give a primary place to matter, and to naturalism, which in *Three Philosophical Poets* (1910) he described as an "intellectual philosophy" that "divines substance behind appearance, continuity behind change, law behind fortune." But more to the point, Santayana believed that "man was not made to understand the world,

but to live in it. Yet nature, in some of us, lets out her secret; it spoils the game, but it associates us with her own impartiality." That secret, as mentioned earlier, is that the world is not organized for man, that "morally," as he put it in **Persons and Places,** "all things are neutral in themselves. It is we that bathe them in whatever emotion may be passing through us." A qualified pessimism, an almost happy pessimism, is at the center of Santayana's philosophy:

> I have never seen much evidence of happiness in human life; but personally I cannot complain of my lot. It has been tolerable enough to allow me to be disinterested in speculation and therefore happy in it, as musicians can be happy in music or mathematicians in mathematics. But as men we are all sad failures. The world is a blind power, is too much for us, even for a Napoleon or a Goethe. But the same world, as an object of thought, is a wonderful theme; to understand it, virtually and mythically, as a man may, is the supreme triumph of life over life, the complete catharsis. Nonetheless, from the point of view of the animal in man, the truth remains tragic. An animal can be confident and brave only if he does not know the truth.

This ought to be depressing in the extreme, and yet, somehow, it isn't—as it isn't in the company of two other American laughing pessimists, Justice Holmes and H. L. Mencken. There is something grand about someone who can think the worst—in this instance positing an existence in an uncaring universe whose end can only be oblivion—and yet play bravely on through. "Survival is something impossible," Santayana wrote, "but it is possible to have lived well and died well."

Santayana was in the odd category of being a nonbelieving (or free-thinking) Catholic—a believer, in effect, in the doctrine that there was no God and Mary is his mother. Although he grew up in the Church, he early lost his faith, yet never quite lost his appreciation for the Church as an ancient institution of civilization, despite his belief that "the loss of illusions is an unmixed blessing." He tolerated what he once characterized as the "absurdity and fiction in religion" because he felt that men, having "no adequate knowledge and no trained courage in respect to their destiny," have "to believe something or other, and that is their necessary religion." He himself favored a belief in something beyond man, and, it is not going too far to say, detested those who believed in nothing greater than man. Yet he was gentler in his views of paganism than he was of other modern religions. "To be a Protestant is to be cross-eyed," he once wrote. And on the Jews he was much harder.

Professor McCormick's admiration for Santayana does not blind him to the fact that Santayana had what is euphemistically known as a "Jewish problem." It can scarcely be ignored. One will be reading along, swept away by Santayana's penetration or powers of formulation or elegant wit, and, bang!, up will pop the devil. Thus, lulled by the pleasant chat of a letter written from Madrid, one comes upon the complaint that Santayana found Florence in December beastly, because "the expatriated anaemic aesthetes and the Jews surprised to find that success is not happiness made a moral atmosphere not wholesome to breathe. . . ." Such remarks do not qualify as gratuitous; they are more in the nature of compulsive. How explain this? Some of it may have been owing to Brahmanic Boston, whose anti-Semitic spirit Santayana might have caught. But even more, one suspects, may be owing to Santayana's disgust at what, in a letter written when he was not yet thirty, he termed the Jews' "incredible conceit of believing that they had made a covenant with nature, by which the mastery of the earth and all the good things thereof were secured to them in return for fidelity to a certain social and religious organization." In Santayana's philosophy, nature (or, if one prefers, God) favors no one. Yet to allow such disgust to lead into such dismal slurs is a blot of prejudice, as Professor McCormick writes, "unworthy of a man of his fineness in other matters, and scarcely comprehensible in the man who wrote *The Life of Reason* and *Realms of Being*."

It is also a blot on Santayana's disinterestedness, for, apart from his mania on the subject of the Jews, Santayana, when it came to disinterestedness, could make the calmer gods of Olympus seem as grubby as the asphalt-contractors lobby in the Texas legislature. Here was a man unassimilable by choice, who thought it an indignity "to have a soul controlled by geography" (that is, by patriotism), who wished to be associated with the impartiality of nature, and for whom it was axiomatic that "in the end every philosopher has to walk alone." When Santayana remarked that he was concerned about losing the "cruelty" of his philosophy if he remained in England, what he meant was that he was concerned about his thought losing its edge through his adopting the attachments and passions of ordinary men. However beautiful his manners or convivial his tone, there was a deep impersonality about Santayana. It was the impersonality of the classical artist devoted, in his case, to the art of philosophy.

> Time might transmute, without erasing, my first opinions and affections; I might wish to change my surroundings and way of living; I never undertook to change myself. I regard my occupations and interests somewhat as an actor regards his various parts or a painter his subjects. That a man has preferences and can understand and do one thing better than another, follows from his inevitable limitations and definite gifts; but that which marks progress in his life is the purity of his art; I mean the degree to which his art has become his life, so that the rest of his nature does not impede or corrupt his art, but only feeds it.

How did Santayana's impartiality square with his politics? Santayana was always interested in politics, but could he be said to have had politics? During World War I, he found himself siding with England, where he was living at the time. But he lived through World War II, now quite an old man, in fascist Italy, without any qualms, above it all and, by then, choosing to be quite out of it. He was conservative by temper, and in his autobiography wrote that he loved Tory England and honored conservative Spain, though not "with any dogmatic or democratic passion," adding: "If any community can become and wishes to become communistic or democratic or anarchical I wish it

joy from the bottom of my heart. I have only two qualms in this case: whether such ideals are realisable, and whether those who pursue them fancy them to be exclusively and universally right: an illusion pregnant with injustice, oppression, and war." Yet in 1977 Sidney Hook, who when a young man much admired Santayana's *The Life of Reason*, published in *The American Scholar* a series of letters that Santayana had written to him, in one of which (dated June 8, 1934) Santayana wrote:

> But I love order in the sense of organized, harmonious, consecrated living; and for this reason I sympathize with the Soviets and the Fascists and the Catholics, but not at all with the liberals. I should sympathize with the Nazis too, if their system were, even in theory, founded on reality; but it is Nietzschean, founded on will; and therefore a sort of romanticism gone mad, rather than a serious organization of material forces—which would be the only way, I think, of securing moral coherence.

Others accused Santayana of being sympathetic to fascism. Professor McCormick does not justify Santayana's late-life politics, but he does attempt to explain them, citing other factors that need to be taken into account: "He was never politically active; his attitudes were aristocratic, illiberal by any modern definition of the word, at base philosophical." I myself prefer to think it one of those embarrassing moments for a great philosopher, and an example of the danger of coming at the complexities of the contemporary world from too high, too lofty, yes, even too philosophical a position. The dogs may bark, yet sometimes the caravan is carrying parts for gas chambers and needs to be stopped.

When World War II began in 1939, Santayana was seventy-six years old and permanently settled in Rome. Two years later he moved into the Clinica della Piccola Compagna di Maria, or Hospital of the Blue Nuns, an Irish order so named because of the color of their habit. The fees for his stay were paid through another center the order maintained in Chicago, for his money, held in America, could not be sent to Italy during the war. There, isolated from the war, easily able to deflect all efforts by the nuns to convert him ("He has too much brains," he reported Mother Superior saying of him, in justification of their failure), he worked away at his final books. Unlike so many of his American contemporaries interested in artistic and intellectual life, unlike Oliver Alden, the hero of *The Last Puritan*, Santayana up to the very end showed no signs, in his own phrase, of "petering out."

When after the war Edmund Wilson, writing pieces for *The New Yorker* about Europe in the wake of World War II that would eventually be published as *Europe without Baedeker* [see Further Reading], visited Santayana in his austere room at the Hospital of the Blue Nuns, he, Wilson, was immensely impressed. It seemed to Wilson that Santayana was "perhaps the most international—or, better, the most supra-national—personality I had ever met." The fire of intellect, Wilson found, still burned in the all but worn-out furnace that was Santayana's aged body. Wilson's meeting with Santayana appears to have been rather like Santayana's with Henry James. The least sentimental of men, Wilson on this occasion was greatly moved, and closes his essay by writing that "the intelligence that has persisted in him has been that of the civilized human race—so how can he be lonely or old? He still loves to share in its thoughts, to try on its points of view. He has made it his business to extend himself into every kind of human consciousness with which he can establish contact, and he reposes on his shabby chaise longue like a monad in the universal mind." This is, of course, the way that every serious writer should like to end.

Wilson wrote that he did not imagine Santayana was troubled by the thought of his impending death, and he seems to have been right. It was cancer that reached his liver that finally brought about his death. When he knew he was going to die, he instructed his amanuensis Daniel Cory not to believe, should he not be present, any stories about his deathbed conversion to the one Church that had ever mattered to him. Two days before his death, when Daniel Cory asked if he were suffering, Santayana is said to have answered, "Yes, my friend. But my anguish is entirely physical; there are no moral difficulties whatsoever." Philosophy had been for him, as for Boethius, a consolation, but finally also life itself. In the end he died as a philosopher should, his thoughts in order, at peace. (pp. 19-27)

> *Joseph Epstein, "George Santayana and the Consolations of Philosophy," in* The New Criterion, *Vol. V, No. 10, June, 1987, pp. 15-27.*

FURTHER READING

Aaron, Daniel. "A Postscript to *The Last Puritan.*" *The New England Quarterly* IX (December 1936): 683-86.
    Exploration of the moral and social context of *The Last Puritan* as revealed in its portrayal of the characters Mario and Oliver.

Aiken, Conrad. "Santayana, George (1936)." In his *Collected Criticism,* pp. 352-54. New York: Oxford University Press, 1968.
    Reprinted review of *The Last Puritan.* Regarding the protagonist, Aiken concludes: "[Santayana's] Oliver Alden, born tired, child of a loveless and joyless marriage, austere, self-controlled, beautifully schooled and regimented, was doomed to remain a mere spectator in life, incapable of contact or immersion, incapable of animal faith."

Ames, Van Meter. *Proust and Santayana: The Aesthetic Way of Life.* New York: Russell & Russell, 1964, 176 p.
    Asserts that "[Marcel] Proust and Santayana belong, with [Arthur] Schopenhauer, to the great tradition that puts contemplation above action."

Armstrong, T. D. "An Old Philosopher in Rome: George Santayana and His Visitors." *Journal of American Studies* 19, No. 3 (December 1985): 349-68.
    Chronicles Santayana's years in Rome after World War II, when he entertained such guests as Tennessee Williams, Edmund Wilson, and Gore Vidal.

Arnett, Willard E. *George Santayana.* New York: Washington Square Press, 1968, 184 p.
    Introduction to Santayana's philosophy.

———. *Santayana and the Sense of Beauty.* Gloucester, Mass.: Peter Smith, 1969, 252 p.
    Inquiry into Santayana's aesthetic concepts.

Ashmore, Jerome. *Santayana, Art, and Aesthetics.* Cleveland: The Press of Western Reserve University, 1966, 139 p.
    Detects a "unity of views" in Santayana's aesthetics over the course of his philosophic career.

Ballowe, James. "The Intellectual Traveller: An Essay on George Santayana." *Dalhousie Review* 50, No. 2 (Summer 1970): 157-69.
    Discusses Santayana's literary criticism.

Blau, Joseph L. "Poetic Naturalism: George Santayana." In his *Men and Movements in American Philosophy,* pp. 323-34. Englewood Cliffs, N. J.: Prentice-Hall, Inc., 1952.
    Argues that despite Santayana's seemingly inconsistent philosophy, he was always a follower of naturalism.

Brantingham, Philip. "The Last Esthete: George Santayana and His Sense of Beauty." *Modern Age* 27, No. 2 (Spring 1983): 146-52.
    Biographical sketch emphasizing Santayana's preeminent status among philosophers.

Bridges, Robert S. "George Santayana." In his *Collected Essays,* pp. 143-65. London: Oxford University Press, 1934.
    Praises the humorous tone of *Little Essays.*

Buchler, Justus. Review of *The Last Puritan,* by George Santayana. *The New England Quarterly* IX (June 1936): 281-85.
    Commends *The Last Puritan* for skillfully satirizing New England and for harmoniously integrating philosophy and narrative.

Buck, Philo M., Jr. "The Search for Beauty: George Santayana." In his *Directions in Contemporary Literature,* pp. 15-35. New York: Oxford University Press, 1942.
    Focuses on Santayana's poetry and novel as manifestations of his philosophy.

Butler, Richard. *The Mind of Santayana.* Chicago: Henry Regnery Company, 1955, 234 p.
    Explication and interpretation of Santayana's philosophic system. The book is the result of Butler's consultations with Santayana during the last two years of Santayana's life.

Canby, Henry Seidel. "The American Santayana." *The Saturday Review of Literature* XV, No. 25 (17 April 1937): 3-4, 14.
    Contends that Santayana's philosophic outlook and literary style were distinctly "American."

Caws, Peter, ed. *Two Centuries of Philosophy in America.* London: Basil Blackwell, 1980, 381 p.
    Contains three essays on Santayana: "Reality Revisited: The Controlled Ambiguity of Santayana's Realms," by Morris Grossman; "Some Remarks on Santayana's Scepticism," by Herman J. Saatkamp, Jr.; and "Santayana's Unnatural Naturalism," by John J. Stuhr.

Cohen, Morris R. "On American Philosophy." *The New Republic* XXIII, No. 293 (14 July 1920): 221-23.
    Discussion of Santayana. Cohen concludes: "That

which distinguishes Santayana from all other modern philosophers is the way he combines thoroughgoing naturalism with profound appreciation of the wisdom commonly called idealism or other-worldliness."

Cory, Daniel "The Later Philosophy of Mr. Santayana." *The Criterion* XV, No. LX (April 1936): 379-92.
Evaluation of Santayana's writings after *The Life of Reason.*

————. *Santayana: The Later Years, a Portrait with Letters.* New York: George Braziller, 1963, 330 p.
Memoir by Santayana's friend and literary secretary.

————. "The Place and Relevance of George Santayana." *The Southern Review* VIII, No. 1 (January 1972): 60-88.
Asserts that Santayana deserves recognition for his achievements as a poet, a philosopher, a novelist, and a social critic.

Cowley, Malcolm. "Santayana in Society." *The New Republic* 112, No. 18 (30 April 1945): 591-92.
Accuses Santayana of being a social climber. Cowley claims that Santayana "valued kind hearts, and valued them all the more if they beat under coronets."

Danko, Arthur C. Introduction to *The Sense of Beauty: Being the Outlines of Æsthetic Theory,* by George Santayana, edited by William G. Holzberger and Herman J. Saatkamp, Jr., pp. xv-xxviii. Cambridge, Mass.: The MIT Press, 1988.
States that in the field of aesthetics, Santayana's "interests were immediate and creative, rather than theoretical and at a distance."

Davis, Joe Lee. "Santayana as a Critic of Transcendentalism." In *Transcendentalism and Its Legacy,* edited by Myron Simon and Thornton H. Parsons, pp. 150-84. Ann Arbor: University of Michigan Press, 1966.
Describes Santayana's changing attitude towards the Transcendentalists, specifically Ralph Waldo Emerson.

Dickinson, G. Lowes. "The Newest Philosophy." *The Independent Review* VI, No. 23 (August 1905): 177-90.
Says of *The Life of Reason,* "An exposition more reasonable and lucid would be difficult to find, or one more free from technical obscurities."

Edman, Irwin. "Introductory Essay." In *The Philosophy of Santayana,* by George Santayana, edited by Irwin Edman, pp. xvii-lxii. New York: Charles Scribner's Sons, 1953.
Contains brief commentary on the selections in the anthology.

Gilbert, Katherine. "Santayana's Doctrine of Æsthetic Expression." *The Philosophical Review* XXXV, No. 3 (May 1926): 221-35.
Calls Santayana's aesthetic philosophy incoherent due to its insistence on separating the functions of art.

Greenlee, Douglas. "Santayana and the Ideal of Reason." In *History, Religion, and Spiritual Democracy: Essays in Honor of Joseph L. Blau,* edited by Maurice Wohlgelernter, pp. 76-91. New York: Columbia University Press, 1980.
Defines "naturalism" as it is used in Santayana's philosophy.

Harap, Louis. "A Note on Moralities in the Philosophy of George Santayana." *The Philosophical Review* 44, No. 6 (November 1935): 577-81.

Inquiry into the changing nature of Santayana's moral philosophy.

Hecht, Anthony. "Upon the Death of George Santayana." *The Kenyon Review* XVI, No. 1 (Winter 1954): 75-6.
Poem in tribute of Santayana, calling the philosopher, "An elderly man for whom the Sisters prayed" and telling of his journey to Limbo to visit Democritus, Plato, and Socrates.

Henfrey, Norman. Introduction to *Selected Critical Writings of George Santayana,* by George Santayana, edited by Norman Henfrey, pp. 1-37. Cambridge: University Press, 1968.
Characterizes Santayana as skeptical and impressively intelligent.

Holzberger, William G. Introduction to *The Complete Poems of George Santayana: A Critical Edition,* by George Santayana, edited by William G. Holzberger, pp. 23-82. Lewisburg, Pa.: Bucknell University Press, 1979.
Chronicles Santayana's poetry from his teenage efforts at the Boston Latin school through his unfinished translation from the Italian of Lorenzo de' Medici's *Ombron and Ambra,* begun in his final years.

Howgate, George W. *George Santayana.* Philadelphia: University of Pennsylvania Press, 1938, 362 p.
Biography structured "to integrate opinion about Santayana, as well as his own varied work, on the supposition that, although many persons know a few things about Santayana, not many persons know many things about him."

Hughson, Lois. *Thresholds of Reality: George Santayana and Modernist Poetics.* Port Washington, N. Y.: Kennikat Press, 1977, 180 p.
Contends that Santayana's aesthetics influenced such Modernist poets as T. S. Eliot, Wallace Stevens, Ezra Pound, and W. B. Yeats.

James, William. Letter to George H. Palmer and Letter to Dickinson S. Miller. In *The Letters of William James,* Volume 2, edited by Henry James, 120-24, 233-35. Boston: The Atlantic Monthly Press, 1920.
Letters regarding *Interpretations of Poetry and Religion* and *The Life of Reason.*

Kallen, H. M. "America and the Life of Reason." *The Journal of Philosophy* XVIII, No. 20 (29 September 1921): 533-51.
States that, according to Santayana, "America is a young country with old memories. The duplexity is due to the conflict between this—somewhat magical—joining of crude youthful passions and polite, ancient thoughts and shibboleths in one body-politic."

Kinney, Sister M. Cyril Edwin. *A Critique of the Philosophy of George Santayana in the Light of Thomistic Principles.* Washington D.C.: Catholic University of America Press, 1942, 131 p.
Study based on the contention that "in spite of the prolific pen which Santayana wields and the charm of his literary style he has not contributed anything positive in the way of his philosophy."

Kirkwood, M. M. *Santayana: Saint of the Imagination.* Toronto: University of Toronto Press, 1961, 240 p.
Biography of Santayana, with explications of *The Life of Reason* and *Realms of Being.*

Lamprecht, Sterling. "Santayana, Then and Now." *The Journal of Philosophy* XXV, No. 20 (27 September 1928): 533-50.
Explores Santayana's contrasting ideals of reason and spirit.

———. "Naturalism and Agnosticism in Santayana." *The Journal of Philosophy* XXX, No. 21 (12 October 1933): 561-74.
Claims that "Santayana remains essentially a moralist."

Lane, James W. "The Dichotomy of George Santayana." *The Catholic World* CXL (October 1934): 20-8.
Focuses on Santayana's self-contradictory philosophy. The critic compares Santayana's "theory of two-fold truth" to a thirteenth-century theological movement called Latin Averroism, which held that "what may be true in philosophy may be false in theology, and vice versa."

Leavis, F. R. "Tragedy and the 'Medium'." In his *The Common Pursuit,* pp. 121-35. Middlesex, England: Penguin Books, 1963.
Accuses Santayana of not understanding "the poetic—and the essentially dramatic—use of language that Shakespeare's verse supremely exemplifies."

Leavis, Q. D. "The Critical Writings of George Santayana." *Scrutiny* IV (December 1935): 278-95.
Praises the impersonal character of Santayana's literary criticism.

Le Boutillier, Cornelia Geer. "Spiritual Life: Santayana's Approach to Essence." *Philosophy* XI, No. 44 (October 1936): 433-44.
Breaks down Santayana's conception of essence into three basic components: knowledge, logic, and value.

Levinson, Henry Samuel. "Santayana's Contribution to American Philosophy." *Journal of the American Academy of Religion* LII, No. 1 (March 1984): 47-69.
Affirms the significance of Santayana's aesthetic and spiritual philosophies.

———. "Meditations at the Margins: Santayana's *Scepticism and Animal Faith*." *The Journal of Religion* 67, No. 3 (July 1987): 289-303.
Characterizes Santayana as a spiritual philosopher and places him in the context of the American philosophical tradition.

Lynn, Kenneth. "Santayana and the Genteel Tradition." *Commentary* 73, No. 5 (May 1982): 81-4.
Chronicles Santayana's criticism of the American philosophical climate of the 1890s.

Lyon, Richard C. Introduction to *Persons and Places: Fragments of Autobiography,* by George Santayana, edited by William G. Holzberger and Herman J. Saatkamp, Jr., pp. xv-xl. Cambridge: The MIT Press, 1986.
Draws attention to the autobiography's two general themes: "the metaphor of the traveler" and "Santayana's difficult extrication of his spirit from the meshes of circumstance in which he found himself."

Marotta, Gary. "Pragmatism, Patriotism, and Imperialism: The Issues between William James and George Santayana." *The Markham Review* 9 (Spring 1980): 41-4.
Chronicles the philosophical and political disputes between Santayana and James, who was first his teacher and then his colleague at Harvard.

McClay, Wilfred. "Two Versions of the Genteel Tradition: Santayana and Brooks." *The New England Quarterly* LV, No. 3 (September 1982): 368-91.
Contrasts the personalities and literary styles of Santayana and Van Wyck Brooks.

McCormick, John. "George Santayana and Ezra Pound." *American Literature* 54, No. 3 (October 1982): 413-33.
Presents correspondence between Santayana and Pound and speculates on their "unlikely" friendship.

———. *George Santayana: A Biography.* New York: Alfred A. Knopf, 1987, 612 p.
Examines Santayana's life and opinions.

Munson, Thomas N. *The Essential Wisdom of George Santayana.* New York: Columbia University Press, 1962, 224 p.
Explanation of Santayana's major ideas. Munson writes: "Santayana's greatest contribution to philosophy, in my opinion, is a reaffirmation of the presence of subjective elements in a realist view of the world."

Olafson, Fredrick A. "George Santayana and the Idea of Philosophy." In *American Philosophy: From Edwards to Quine,* edited by Robert W. Shahan and Kenneth R. Merrill, pp. 148-75. Norman: University of Oklahoma Press, 1977.
Evaluates Santayana's conception of the ideal philosopher: one who is detached from social and religious motivations.

Putnam, Michael C. J. "*Three Philosophical Poets* by George Santayana." *Daedalus* 103, No. 1 (Winter 1974): 131-40.
States that Santayana's writings on Lucretius, Dante, and Goethe seem limited to the modern reader because "Santayana typified an already dying generation of scholar-aesthetes who professed to find beauty and integrity as primary concerns in life and art. We on the other hand, are obsessed by ugliness, paradox and ambiguity."

Shaughnessy, Edward L. "Santayana on Athletics." *Journal of American Studies* 10, No. 2 (August 1976): 173-83.
Describes Santayana's love for sports as evidenced by his "Athletic Ode" and the character of Oliver Alden in *The Last Puritan,* who plays football.

Singer, Beth J. *The Rational Society: A Critical Study of Santayana's Social Thought.* Cleveland: The Press of Case Western Reserve University, 1970, 139 p.
Exploration of Santayana's politics, focusing on *Reason in Society* and *Dominations and Powers.*

Singer, Irving. *Santayana's Aesthetics: A Critical Introduction.* Cambridge: Harvard University Press, 1957, 235 p.
Presents Santayana's philosophy of art, relating it to his distinction between essence and existence.

Sprigge, Timothy L. S. *Santayana: An Examination of His Philosophy.* Boston: Routledge & Kegan Paul, 1974, 247 p.
In-depth analysis of several aspects of Santayana's thought.

Stallknecht, Newton P. "George Santayana." In *Seven American Stylists from Poe to Mailer: An Introduction,* edited by George T. Wright, pp. 50-89. Minneapolis: University of Minnesota Press, 1961.

Evaluates Santayana as a philosopher, critic, novelist, and poet.

———. "George Santayana and the Uses of Literature." *Yearbook of Contemporary and General Literature* No. 15 (1966): 5-18.

Favorably assesses Santayana as a literary critic.

———. *George Santayana.* Minneapolis: University of Minnesota Press, 1971, 48 p.

Proposes that the "contrast between animal faith and spiritual contemplation constitutes the central theme of Santayana's later philosophy."

Stevens, Wallace. "To an Old Philosopher in Rome." In his *The Collected Poems of Wallace Stevens,* pp. 508-10. New York: Alfred A. Knopf, 1955.

Poem dedicated to Santayana.

Stolz, Gary R. "Santayana in America." *The New England Quarterly* L, No. 1 (March 1977): 53-67.

Chronicles Santayana's experiences in Boston between 1872 and 1912.

Trilling, Lionel. "The Smile of Parmenides." *Encounter* VII, No. 6 (December 1956): 30-8.

Admits to an ambivalence towards Santayana upon reading his letters, finding his philosophy compelling but his personality antagonistic.

Walsh, William. "Don Quixote Sane: The Writings of George Santayana." In his *A Human Idiom: Literature and Humanity,* pp. 74-105. New York: Barnes and Noble, 1964.

Attempts to rehabilitate Santayana as an important figure in American philosophy.

Weinstein, Michael A. "George Santayana." In his *The Wilderness and the City: American Classical Philosophy as a Moral Quest,* pp. 109-27. Amherst: The University of Massachusetts Press, 1982.

Explains the difference in temperament between Santayana and other American philosophers of his era.

Wenkart, Henry. "Santayana on Beauty." In *The Philosophical Reflection of Man in Literature,* edited by Anna-Teresa Tymieniecka, pp. 321-26. Boston: D. Reidel, 1982.

Summarizes Santayana's aesthetic philosophy.

Wickham, Harvey. "A Tilt with Windmills." In his *The Unrealists,* pp. 94-128. New York: The Dial Press, 1930.

Satirical rendering of Santayana's philosophy.

Williams, Donald C. "Of Essence and Existence and Santayana." *The Journal of Philosophy* 51, No. 2 (21 January 1954): 31-42.

Discusses "the primordial contrast of essence and existence," declaring, "Santayana revived the categories with a sunny caustic sophistication and stripped them to their fighting weight."

Wilson, Douglas L. Introduction to *The Genteel Tradition: Nine Essays* by George Santayana, edited by Douglas L. Wilson, pp. 1-25. Cambridge: Harvard University Press, 1967.

Discusses the repercussions of "The Genteel Tradition in American Philosophy."

Wilson, Edmund. "Roman Diary: Arrival—Visit to Santayana" In his *Europe without Baedeker,* pp. 43-63. New York: Doubleday, 1947.

Recounts a meeting with Santayana in Rome during Santayana's final years.

Woodward, A. G. "George Santayana (1863-1952)." *English Studies in Africa* 12, No. 2 (September 1969): 107-31.

Contends that "mind and feeling were at one in Santayana, and bred a coherent philosophical vision of religion, politics, civilizations and art, originating in despair and issuing in detachment."

Woodward, Anthony. "The Solitude of Santayana." *South Atlantic Quarterly* 86, No. 2 (Spring 1987): 110-22.

Biographical sketch of Santayana in his final years.

———. *Living in the Eternal: A Study of George Santayana.* Nashville, Tenn.: Vanderbilt University Press, 1988, 171 p.

Characterizes Santayana's thought, distinguishes between his early and late philosophical writings, and discusses *The Last Puritan.*

Ida Tarbell

1857-1944

(Full name Ida Minerva Tarbell) American historian, journalist, and biographer.

Tarbell is best remembered as the author of *The History of the Standard Oil Company,* an important work of the muckraking movement in early twentieth-century American journalism. Detailing the corrupt business practices of the Standard Oil Company and its director John D. Rockefeller, *The History of the Standard Oil Company* led the Supreme Court to decree the breakup of the company in 1911. Tarbell also wrote a series of popular and influential books on Abraham Lincoln, as well as works on American business and the role of women in society.

Tarbell was born in Erie County, Pennsylvania, two years before oil was discovered in nearby Titusville. Her father, Franklin Sumner Tarbell, achieved a measure of success by manufacturing wooden storage tanks before Standard Oil forced him out of business, according to Tarbell's autobiography, *All in the Day's Work.* When Tarbell entered Allegheny College in 1876 to study biology, she was one of only five female students at the institution. Upon graduation she spent two years teaching at the Poland Union Seminary in Poland, Ohio, after which she joined the staff of the *Chautauquan,* a monthly magazine published by the Methodist Church in Chautauqua, New York. Tarbell traveled to Paris in 1891 to study historiography at the Sorbonne and the Collège de France and to begin research on the life of the French revolutionary Madame Roland. During this time she reported on her experiences abroad in various American periodicals, including *Scribner's.*

Her journalistic work came to the attention of Samuel S. McClure, who was about to begin publishing a new magazine called *McClure's,* and he enlisted her services for a serialized biography of Napoleon Bonaparte. The articles, which ran in *McClure's* from November 1894 to April 1895, were credited with boosting the magazine's circulation, and the success of their publication in book form enabled Tarbell to publish her study of Madame Roland. Her next assignment for *McClure's* was a series on the early life of Abraham Lincoln. These articles were also well received, and Tarbell became profoundly interested in Lincoln. She wrote and edited several volumes concerning Lincoln's life and career, including biographies, compilations of reminiscences by those who knew him, and books for children. In 1900 McClure asked Tarbell to research the history of the Standard Oil Company, initially intending a series that would be a flattering portrait of a beneficent trust, but after several years of research, Tarbell published a work of exposé journalism exemplifying the muckraking movement in its zeal to uncover corruption. When an anonymous review in the *Nation* condemned *The History of the Standard Oil Company* as sensationalistic and biased, Standard Oil printed and circulated 500,000 copies of the article in pamphlet form to combat the nega-

tive publicity Tarbell had generated. The book's impact remained great enough, however, to prompt the Supreme Court to dissolve the trust. Tarbell continued to write for *McClure's* and later for the *American* magazine, focusing mainly on big business in America. She died of pneumonia in 1944 at the age of eighty-six.

Critics view the publication of *The History of the Standard Oil Company* as a turning point in Tarbell's career. Previous to that work she had developed her skills as a biographer, utilizing historical documents to create psychological portraits of her subjects. Her biographies of Napoleon and Lincoln were considered among the most accessible, well-crafted, and thoroughly documented of their time. With *The History of the Standard Oil Company,* Tarbell's attention shifted to depicting the practices of American big business. Critics observe, however, that in contrast to the muckrakers, with whom she is usually grouped, her politics were basically conservative. She often defended the businesses she described, championing the American capitalist system. Another aspect of Tarbell's conservatism was her criticism, toward the end of her life, of the women's suffrage movement and of women's involvement in politics and business. In such works as *The Business of*

Being a Woman, she urged women to remain at home and raise children, arguing, to the disappointment of many of her admirers, that women could be more influential as mothers than as career professionals.

Though Tarbell explored a wide range of topics in her writings, her career is unified by what Mary E. Tomkins has termed "her version of the perennially elusive American Dream." Tarbell's outlook is praised for valuing fairness above all else and for applying the same standard of judgment to all of her subjects, from Lincoln to Rockefeller. While some critics have faulted Tarbell for her conservative politics and have found a contradiction between the personal example she set for women and her limited conception of their role in society, most agree with Tomkins's assessment that Tarbell was "a great journalist who initiated a tradition of responsible journalism which has continued to serve the nation well during succeeding times of national crisis."

(See also *Contemporary Authors,* Vol. 122, and *Dictionary of Literary Biography,* Vol. 47.)

PRINCIPAL WORKS

A Short Life of Napoleon Bonaparte (biography) 1895
The Early Life of Abraham Lincoln (biography) 1896
Madame Roland (biography) 1896
The Life of Abraham Lincoln. 2 vols. (biography) 1900
The History of the Standard Oil Company. 2 vols. (history) 1904
He Knew Lincoln (biography) 1907
The Tariff in Our Times (nonfiction) 1911
The Business of Being a Woman (nonfiction) 1912
The Ways of Woman (nonfiction) 1915
New Ideals in Business: An Account of Their Practice and Their Effects upon Men and Profits (nonfiction) 1916
The Rising of the Tide: The Story of Sabinsport (novel) 1919
Boy Scouts' Life of Lincoln (biography) 1921
In the Footsteps of the Lincolns (biography) 1924
The Life of Elbert H. Gary: The Story of Steel (biography) 1925
Owen D. Young: A New Type of Industrial Leader (biography) 1932
The Nationalizing of Business, 1878-1898 (history) 1936
All in the Day's Work (autobiography) 1939

Ida M. Tarbell (essay date 1904)

[*In the following preface to her* History of the Standard Oil Company, *Tarbell describes her methods in compiling the history.*]

[*The History of the Standard Oil Company*] is the outgrowth of an effort on the part of the editors of *McClure's Magazine* to deal concretely in their pages with the trust question. In order that their readers might have a clear and succinct notion of the processes by which a particular industry passes from the control of the many to that of the few, they decided a few years ago to publish a detailed narrative of the history of the growth of a particular trust. The Standard Oil Trust was chosen for obvious reasons. It was the first in the field, and it has furnished the methods, the charter, and the traditions for its followers. It is the most perfectly developed trust in existence; that is, it satisfies most nearly the trust ideal of entire control of the commodity in which it deals. Its vast profits have led its officers into various allied interests, such as railroads, shipping, gas, copper, iron, steel, as well as into banks and trust companies, and to the acquiring and solidifying of these interests it has applied the methods used in building up the Oil Trust. It has led in the struggle against legislation directed against combinations. Its power in state and Federal government, in the press, in the college, in the pulpit, is generally recognised. The perfection of the organisation of the Standard, the ability and daring with which it has carried out its projects, make it the preeminent trust of the world—the one whose story is best fitted to illuminate the subject of combinations of capital.

Another important consideration with the editors in deciding that the Standard Oil Trust was the best adapted to illustrate their meaning, was the fact that it is one of the very few business organisations of the country whose growth could be traced in trustworthy documents. . . . This has come about largely from the fact that almost constantly since its organisation in 1870 the Standard Oil Company has been under investigation by the Congress of the United States and by the Legislatures of various states in which it has operated, on the suspicion that it was receiving rebates from the railroads and was practising methods in restraint of free trade. In 1872 and again in 1876 it was before Congressional committees, in 1879 it was before examiners of the Commonwealth of Pennsylvania and before committees appointed by the Legislatures of New York and of Ohio for investigating railroads. Its operations figured constantly in the debate which led up to the creation of the Interstate Commerce Commission in 1887, and again and again since that time the Commission has been called upon to examine directly or indirectly into its relation with the railroads.

In 1888, in the Investigation of Trusts conducted by Congress and by the state of New York, the Standard Oil Company was the chief subject for examination. In the state of Ohio, between 1882 and 1892, a constant warfare was waged against the Standard in the courts and Legislature, resulting in several volumes of testimony. The Legislatures of many other states concerned themselves with it. This hostile legislation compelled the trust to separate into its component parts in 1892, but investigation did not cease; indeed, in the last great industrial inquiry, conducted by the Commission appointed by President McKinley, the Standard Oil Company was constantly under discussion, and hundreds of pages of testimony on it appear in the nineteen volumes of reports which the Commission has submitted.

This mass of testimony, all of it submitted under oath it should be remembered, contains the different charters and agreements under which the Standard Oil Trust has operated, many contracts and agreements with railroads, with refineries, with pipelines, and it contains the experiences in business from 1872 up to 1900 of multitudes of individuals. These experiences have exactly the quality of the personal reminiscences of actors in great events, with the additional value that they were given on the witness stand, and it is fair, therefore, to suppose that they are more cautious and exact in statements than many writers of memoirs are. These investigations, covering as they do all of the important steps in the development of the trust, include full accounts of the point of view of its officers in regard to that development, as well as their explanations of many of the operations over which controversy has arisen. Hundreds of pages of sworn testimony are found in these volumes from John D. Rockefeller, William Rockefeller, Henry M. Flagler, H. H. Rogers, John D. Archbold, Daniel O'Day and other members of the concern.

Aside from the great mass of sworn testimony accessible to the student there is a large pamphlet literature dealing with different phases of the subject, and there are files of the numerous daily newspapers and monthly reviews, supported by the Oil Regions, in the columns of which are to be found not only statistics but full reports of all controversies between oil men. . . .

But the documentary sources of this work are by no means all printed. The Standard Oil Trust and its constituent companies have figured in many civil suits, the testimony of which is still in manuscript in the files of the courts where the suits were tried. These manuscripts have been examined on the ground, and in numerous instances full copies of affidavits and of important testimony have been made for permanent reference and study. I have also had access to many files of private correspondence and papers, the most important being that of the officers and counsel of the Petroleum Producers' Union from 1878 to 1880, that covering the organisation from 1887 to 1895 of the various independent companies which resulted in the Pure Oil Company, and that containing the material prepared by Roger Sherman for the suit brought in 1897 by the United States Pipe Line against certain of the Standard companies under the Sherman anti-trust law.

As many of the persons who have been active in the development of the oil industry are still living, their help has been freely sought. Scores of persons in each of the great oil centres have been interviewed, and the comprehension and interpretation of the documents on which the work is based have been materially aided by the explanations which the actors in the events under consideration were able to give.

When the work was first announced in the fall of 1901, the Standard Oil Company, or perhaps I should say officers of the company, courteously offered to give me all the assistance in their power, an offer of which I have freely taken advantage. In accepting assistance from Standard men as from independents I distinctly stated that I wanted facts, and that I reserved the right to use them according to my own judgment of their meaning, that my object was to learn more perfectly what was actually done—not to learn what my informants thought of what had been done.

It is perhaps not too much to say that there is not a single important episode in the history of the Standard Oil Company, so far as I know it, or a notable step in its growth, which I have not discussed more or less fully with officers of the company.

It is needless to add that the conclusions expressed in this work are my own. (pp. xxiii-xxv)

> *Ida M. Tarbell, in a preface to* The History of the Standard Oil Company, *edited by David M. Chalmers, Harper Torchbooks; 1966, pp. xxiii-xxv.*

George W. Alger   (essay date 1904)

[*In the following excerpt, Alger examines* The History of the Standard Oil Company *as a study of America's transportation problem.*]

Prince Metternich once said to George Ticknor: "You Americans must first suffer from an evil before you can apply the remedy; you have no preventive legislation." Miss Tarbell, as she tells us the story of the birth, growth, and present power of the oil monopoly [in ***The History of the Standard Oil Company***], is really giving the history of such an evil—one from which we are still suffering, and for which we are yet groping for a remedy. It is impossible for us to read this story and miss its meaning. It is not merely a study of, perhaps, the blackest page in the history of American commerce; it is not simply a study of what men of immense business capacity can do when actuated by an unscrupulous and almost incredible selfishness. The enormous evil which finds graphic illustration in her book is the power which the transportation companies have been given over the accumulation and distribution of wealth in this country, and how that power has been abused. (p. 217)

Miss Tarbell's book is a great contribution to the study of the transportation problem, very largely because it was obviously written with no such purpose in view. It is a statement of the facts in the history of the Standard Oil Company—facts marshaled with extraordinary logic and clearness, showing a remarkable grasp and insight into the important subject which she discusses. She has undertaken to write a history, not a treatise on economics, and if the transportation problem is in every page of her book it is because the Standard Oil Company and the transportation problem are inseparable; for, if there had been no traffic problem, there would have been no oil monopoly. The work she has done undoubtedly has been a very difficult one. The Oil Trust has had a multitude of prosecutors and a few apologists—has been the subject of excoriatory eloquence and of cynical defense; and its answer to them both has been silence—and dividends. Its history is one which it is difficult to consider calmly and dispassionately. There are too many features of its career which tend so to stir the blood as to make the impartial temper of the historian hard to maintain. The power of this book comes largely because this temper has been maintained; because there is in it an obvious desire to be exact in statement and to give all the facts, so that the reader may judge for himself whether the conclusions are justified. The researches required to gather together from such a multitude of obscure sources the material for so complete and extended a work on so complex a subject must have been enormous. Nothing seems to have escaped. The facts are there—and such facts! It is scarcely a book which a man of normal sensitiveness would care to hand down to his children and grandchildren as the story of his business career, however much he might feel that career to have been extenuated by financial success and its asperities softened in their eyes by the divisible millions of his estate. For, in the concluding chapters of the book, Miss Tarbell has something to say about the Standard Oil Trust in its influence on the great business world of which the oil industry is but a part, if a great part, on the moral tone of that world and its ideals of success. The book which she has written is not merely a contribution to a transportation problem, not simply a story of the facts of the Standard Oil Trust: it is a study of business morals.

In the athletic world there are accepted rules, in accordance with which contests in sport must be won. In law and medicine there are more or less definite codes governing conduct and distinguishing that which is professional from that which is not. In the same way, in the business world, there is a line between real success and that which is only apparent—between honest and dishonest competition, between business which is business and business which is something quite different, though masquerading under its name—a line which, in the scramble to get rich and the intensity of commercial rivalries, seems sometimes obliterated or forgotten. It is what Miss Tarbell's book will do towards making that line more distinct and better recognized, which lifts it above the dignity of a literary achievement and makes it a distinct public service.

> George W. Alger, "Miss Tarbell's 'History of the Standard Oil Company': How the Railroad Makes the Trust," in McClure's Magazine, Vol. XXIV, No. 2, Christmas, 1904, pp. 217-23.

The Nation, New York   (essay date 1905)

[*In the following review of* The History of the Standard Oil Company, *the critic accuses Tarbell of drastically misrepresenting the Standard Oil Company and John D. Rockefeller as a result of her ignorance about business practices.*]

Few luxuries are greater than to give way to righteous indignation, and the prosperity of the wicked has from the days of Job afforded the chief opportunity for this indulgence. We are all secretly conscious that our merits are not fully appreciated, nor our deserts properly rewarded, and we are only too ready to believe that great success is attained by evil means. The man who has to support a family on a dollar a day thinks it unjust that his employer should have ten dollars, and his employer is quite sure that no one can honestly earn a hundred. When it comes to incomes of a thousand dollars a day, the condemnation becomes general, and the richest man in the country is the object of universal execration. (p. 15)

[*The History of the Standard Oil Company*] seems to have

been written for the purpose of intensifying the popular hatred. The writer has either a vague conception of the nature of proof, or she is willing to blacken the character of Mr. John D. Rockefeller by insinuation and detraction. She undoubtedly knows her public, and it is unfortunate, from the dramatic point of view, that Mr. Rockefeller has been caught in no worse crimes than underselling his competitors and getting rebates from railroads. When we come to look into the matter, we find that the directors of the Standard Oil Company did not, as is commonly believed, conspire to blow up a rival oil refinery in Buffalo. But this does not discourage our author. A still did explode, or come near it, and there was a trial on a charge of conspiracy. A whole chapter is devoted to this episode, on the ground that it illustrates the evil results of "the Standard policy of making it hard for a rival to do business," and shows the judgment to be expected from a hostile public. The public "read into the Buffalo case deliberate arson." It refused to admit that there was no evidence of the guilt of the Standard Oil directors, "but demanded that they be convicted on presumption." The inference to be drawn from this chapter by the ordinary reader is that, while Mr. Rockefeller perhaps did not personally blow up the still—it is not clear that any one tried to—he would probably not have grieved had the attempt been successful if it had been made; and that he is at all events no better than he should be.

His depravity appears again in a transaction with a widow whose husband had left her a refinery in Cleveland. This property the widow had offered for sale to another party at a price considerably less than Mr. Rockefeller paid for it two years later, which price Mr. Rockefeller avers was 50 per cent. more than the property was worth. He states, indeed, that the works for which he paid $60,000 could have been replaced for $20,000. He avers further that when the widow told him that she was afraid of the future, and especially that she could not get cars enough to transport her oil, he offered to lend her his cars, or do anything else in reason to assist her. As she still wished to sell, Mr. Rockefeller's agents attended to the transaction. It is asserted by the seller that Mr. Rockefeller had told her that she might retain some of the stock in the company, a promise repudiated by his agents. The widow wrote to him at once in complaint, and the day after he received the letter Mr. Rockefeller replied, to the effect that he had understood her to prefer to receive the whole price in money, but that if she wished stock she could have it, or that he would, if she chose, return the property. When this offer was received, the seller declares that she had made such arrangements that she could not conveniently accept it, and indignantly threw the letter containing it into the fire. This transaction is represented by Miss Tarbell as taking a deep hold on the public sympathy, and as contributing to make the superstitious fear of resistance to Mr. Rockefeller almost insuperable. It is undoubtedly true, Miss Tarbell concedes, that this widow was not obliged to sell out; nevertheless, "she gave up her business to avoid ruin."

It is a matter of public notoriety that Mr. Rockefeller is offensively reticent. The most enterprising reporters cannot induce him to talk, and his perversity is so well known that the most unscrupulous do not dare to invent "interviews." Miss Tarbell complains of this exasperating taciturnity, although she tells us that the officers of the Standard Oil Company have offered her every assistance and discussed every episode in its history with her; but she has hit upon a simple and ingenious method of defeating its odious purpose. It is only necessary to attribute certain cruel and hateful intentions and sentiments to Mr. Rockefeller, and then to express them between quotation marks. This imparts crispness to style, and the ordinary reader may be trusted to be careless enough, or prejudiced enough, to carry away the impression that he has heard the monster's *ipsissima verba.* But a careful study of the records made by any one who is able to distinguish assertion from fact, does not make it clear that Mr. Rockefeller ruined all his competitors. He seems to have usually bought them out, representing that they were in danger of being beaten in the race, and to have advised them to become partners in his concern. The Standard Oil Company, like the railroad companies, has exercised a kind of eminent domain. In order to systematize a business conducted with frightful waste, property was condemned; but the owners received compensation.

Another rhetorical device is personification. In impassioned, if turgid, language, a desperate struggle is described between the powers of evil incarnate in the Standard Oil Company and the powers of goodness appearing in a metaphysical entity called the "Oil Region." This being, it appears, loved virtue for its own sake; it believed in independence and fair play; it hated rebates and secret rates; it hated, but it also feared, its adversary. Very eloquent appeals for our sympathy with this generous being are made; but when we descend to the concrete our feeling cools. The "Oil Region" means a number of men engaged in the wildest kind of speculation, many of whom proved themselves willing to engage in every kind of wickedness of which the Standard Oil Company was accused. They conspired with one another and with the adversary. They accepted secret rates and rebates when they could get them; they sold out; they limited production, they put up prices by combination, they destroyed the property of their rivals, they violated their agreements; and all these sins are attributed to them by Miss Tarbell herself. She tells us of a man who confessed that he had been stealing oil for two years from the Standard Company, and who was found innocent by a jury, the verdict being approved by the Oil Region. The blame for this apparent lapse from virtue is laid upon the victim of the theft. The hideous mien of the monster had been seen too oft; the iniquity of the Standard Oil Company was contagious; and the Oil Region might say, like the French deputy to his constituents, "So intense was the corruption that even I did not altogether escape."

Men who can remember the discovery of petroleum will smile at the suggestion that the early producers and refiners were of different stuff from what is to be found now in a mining camp. Miss Tarbell tells us that they counted on profits of 100 per cent., and had no conception of economical production. They spent their profits as fast as they got them, and when the price of oil fell they denounced every one but themselves. The managers of the Standard Company seldom made such profits; they certainly did not

spend them. They paid moderate dividends, and put their surplus earnings into their property. They displayed very great skill in carrying on their business, and it is by no means incredible that their good management resulted in economies that were equivalent to a large profit. One of the best chapters in the book is that on the legitimate greatness of the Company; and, although the particulars are inadequately given, enough is told to show that ordinary competitors could not possibly have succeeded even if their great rival had been indifferent. Yet it is true that there are and always have been independent refineries and pipe-lines. Miss Tarbell accuses the Standard Oil Company of many odious practices in the way of underselling and espionage. That such practices are odious is true; but competition is necessarily odious. Competition means that A will try to sell to B's customers, and B to A's, and the only escape from conflict is in combination. It is absurd to represent "Standard Oil methods" as peculiar.

In one sense this book is a history. It tells us profusely what was said, what was believed, what was suspected, what was charged. It repeats to a tedious extent and adopts slurs, insinuations, slanders—possibly, sometimes perjuries. But as to what was done, the record is imperfect. The great matter involved was the transportation of oil. The managers of the great railroads, in the seventies, were engaged in desperate competition. They apparently lied to one another and to their customers. They broke their agreements and granted all sorts of rebates in order to get business and to keep it from being diverted from them. Deplorable as it was, the managers of the Standard Oil Company were compelled to fight the devil with fire. If they had not obtained special rates, they would have seen their business pass into the hands of rivals who were less scrupulous. A vast mine of wealth was suddenly disclosed, great fortunes were to be made, and it was a question who should make them. Had the men who made the Standard Company never existed, other men would have done what they did, with perhaps equal gain to themselves and perhaps less gain to the consumers. It was a condition and not a theory that confronted the oil refiners, and they met the condition as best they could.

The theory of rates on which Miss Tarbell bases her denunciation is altogether untenable. She labors under the impression that rates are equal, just, and fair, only when the charge for carrying a barrel of oil is the same proportionately as that for a carload or a trainload. She tells us that in 1872 Mr. Rockefeller shipped daily from Cleveland to New York sixty carloads of oil. By moving these cars in solid trains, the time for a round trip was reduced from thirty days to ten days, the number of cars needed was reduced from 1,800 to 600, and the investment in cars from $900,000 to $300,000. To charge the same price for transportation which costs less is not to maintain equal rates; it is to discriminate in favor of small shipments, to furnish a service which costs more at the same price as one that costs less. Until this truth can be beaten into the heads of the public, the various nostrums which are presented to Congress will continue to embarrass the country, and to arouse expectations that will surely be disappointed. To determine the actual cost of carrying any commodity is literally impossible; to define precisely what rates are "equal" is beyond human capacity; and to fix rates from Chicago to New York and Philadelphia that will be accepted as fair by both cities and the rest of the country, can be done neither by the Interstate Commission nor by all the courts that now exist or can be hereafter constituted.

We have dealt with this book at length, not because it is to be taken as serious history, or because Mr. Rockefeller and his associates are in want of sympathy, but because it is desirable to protest against attempts to treat grave problems sensationally. To stir up envy, to arouse prejudice, to inflame passion, to appeal to ignorance, to magnify evils, to charge corruption—these seem to be the methods in favor with too many of the writers who profess a desire to reform society. They will not accomplish reform in this way, but they may conceivably bring on revolution. They are doing their best to stir up hatred and to excite bitter feeling. They propose to educate the people by unfitting them for calm judgment and rational inquiry. We need reforms badly enough, but we shall not get them until we have an electorate able to control its passions, to reserve its condemnation, to deliberate before it acts. When that time comes, a railing accusation will not be accepted as history. (pp. 15-16)

> *"The Standard Oil Company," in* The Nation, *New York, Vol. 80, No. 2062, January 5, 1905, pp. 15-16.*

M. Irwin MacDonald   (essay date 1908)

[*In the following excerpt, MacDonald summarizes Tarbell's career and lauds her moral vision.*]

The publication, about five years ago, of Ida M. Tarbell's *History of the Standard Oil Company* gave to the people a narrative of the discovery, development and final monopolization of petroleum in this country. As a narrative, it was confined strictly to the petroleum industry and the growth of the Standard Oil Company under the leadership of John D. Rockefeller, but as an analysis of our present commercial conditions it covered every feature of the trust situation as it exists today. Thousands of people read this history as it appeared serially in a popular magazine that goes to every part of the country, and with each succeeding chapter the interest of the public grew greater,—and so did that of the Standard Oil Company. The story of the turmoil which followed is familiar to everyone,—the shock of amazed indignation and alarm that roused the people and set the press to humming with more or less sensational "muck-rake literature," the efforts made by the money powers to discredit the writer and nullify the effects of the story, since it could not be suppressed, the fever of investigation and reform legislation which apparently has not even yet reached its height, the dragging into the light of day of supposedly inaccessible secrets of corporation methods and management. In these days it is all a twice-told tale.

Yet even now it is doubtful if people realize the full significance of this analytic history of the parent of all the trusts, or appreciate the quality which will give it a permanent place in the archives of the nation. It is the very embodi-

ment of the course which society must take to free herself from the domination of an insidious and corrupting commercial creed,—it is the truth told without fear or favor, and it is analysis, ruthless and unflinching, of hidden methods and of fair-seeming conditions. It is as exhaustively accurate as a carefully prepared legal document, as impersonal as Fate, and as full of big human interest and vital dramatic action as the most thrilling tale of discovery, war and conquest. The carefully restrained utterance of the historian whose viewpoint must be clear of all prejudice and whose judgment must be absolutely fair, keeps it so free from personal bias that there is hardly an expression of opinion from beginning to end,—only facts, facts, facts, and the revelation of their bearing upon the situation as a whole. Yet through it all rings an appeal which grips the heart,—a passionate appeal for fair play. It is never actually uttered, but it glows like an inner light through every page. It is the sort of appeal to which there is no answer in words, it demands the response of deeds.

In the rush of events which followed the publication of Miss Tarbell's narrative, the question has often been asked: What manner of woman is she and why did she do it? As she is a woman absorbed in her work and averse to personal publicity, the question has several times been answered more dramatically than accurately by writers in the sensational press,—who are somewhat noted for telling a thing as they think it ought to be, rather than as it is. In the effort to find a motive sufficiently powerful to account for the patient research and hard work that must have been involved in the writing of such a history, some have made Miss Tarbell a private secretary in the employ of Mr. Rockefeller, where she is supposed to have gained her intimate knowledge of the inner workings of the Standard Oil Company, as well as of the personal characteristics of its founder and head. Others have insisted that she is the daughter of a man who was ruined under especially harrowing circumstances by the methods employed by the Standard Oil Company to stifle competition, and that she has devoted her whole life to preparing for the magnificent revenge which she has roused the whole nation to accomplish.

As a matter of fact, Miss Tarbell never met Mr. Rockefeller but once in her life, and then exchanged only a few words with him, as any stranger would. She was born in the oil region,—at Titusville, Pa.,—and was the daughter of an oil producer, but her father suffered no more than thousands of others from the methods of Mr. Rockefeller and his associates, and the whole family took it all as a part of the inscrutable dealings of Fate, which allowed Mr. Rockefeller to monopolize the whole oil industry through his control of the means of transportation, and somehow defeated every effort made by the producers as well as the smaller refiners to obtain fair play. The feeling throughout the whole region was naturally very bitter, as was shown by the persistent and desperate fight made to preserve the independence of the industry, and the young girl was brought up in the atmosphere of general hostility and suspicion, but she went away to college when she was only eighteen, and never returned to the oil region to live.

The impress of the struggle was deep in her mind, however, and she resolved some day to write a novel which should be founded upon it and show some of its dramatic phases. But her work was to take a different course. She had a natural aptitude for historical research, and made a special study of history, going to France after the completion of her college course, and spending some years there in exhaustive study of the French Revolution and the causes which led to it. Her purpose at first was to make a study of the famous women of eighteenth-century France, showing the part they took in shaping the thought, and hence the events, of their times, but this soon developed into the larger interest of the period as a whole, and her book *Madame Roland* was really a history of the whole revolution and an analysis of the social conditions of the time, centering around one strong and typical personality. Unconsciously, Miss Tarbell was even then preparing for her most important life-work, for her analytical and logical mind went back of events to the causes which led to them, and she came out with a thorough understanding of the workings of that law of human nature by which the powerful few gain and abuse special privileges, and by which revolution comes when the people find it out.

Miss Tarbell returned to her native land a good deal of a reactionary. She had not the temperament of the extremist, but she had wide knowledge of the significance of certain social, industrial and political conditions which she found in America. Looking at the situation from the viewpoint almost of a foreigner, it seemed to her that in the whole system of American commercialism there was a moral obliquity which made it possible for monopolies to evade or break the law with impunity in the obtaining of special privileges which would give them an unfair advantage over competitors. In private life such practices would not have been tolerated, but the separation between personal honor and the code of ethics which allowed expediency to take the place of business honor, was so complete that to get the better of a rival by underhand means was regarded merely as an evidence of superior shrewdness and enterprise. It seemed to her that from having been a nation that in simpler and more rugged times was above all things honest, manly, self-reliant, our swift growth and phenomenal prosperity had made us a nation of tricksters, conducting all business transactions on the principle that the end justifies the means, and seeking always for some inside track, some special dispensation that would enable the man who was lucky enough to get it to put all his competitors at a disadvantage. Everywhere it seemed to be a question, not of fighting fair, but of being smart enough to take an unfair advantage. The whole business system apparently put a premium on rascality. The creed of John D. Rockefeller had penetrated to all parts of the commercial and industrial world, and, looked at from the viewpoint of one who had but recently made a special study of exclusive privileges and their results, conditions were not very promising for the future peace and prosperity of the country.

Yet the *History of the Standard Oil Company* was still several years in the future. The task of preparation was to be completed, and, although it was not even thought of at that time, the first important work that Miss Tarbell undertook finished her equipment for dealing "ruthlessly and unflinchingly" with men like Mr. Rockefeller and his associates. She was at that time a member of the editorial staff of *McClure's Magazine,* and, owing to her experience in historical research, she was selected to collect and edit all the material that could be found relating to the early life of Lincoln. In doing this, she traveled much among the places where he had lived and sought out the people who had known him personally, as well as all documents relating to him. She learned at first hand what had been the life of Lincoln's times and environment,—what had been the stern training of the man who is now the noblest and best-beloved figure in the history of this country. As she grew into closer sympathy with the man himself and came to a fuller understanding of the rugged, primitive conditions which had developed him, she realized that her work of collecting and editing the records which related to him must broaden into a definite biography based upon those records and her own understanding of his character, or it could not be done. So the *Life of Abraham Lincoln* was written, and stands today not only as an historical record amazing in its scope and accuracy, but the living presentation of the man in his splendid simplicity, profound wisdom, rugged honesty, quaint humor, and, above all, the brooding tenderness which took in all the world. She never tells you this, but you grow to love him as his friends and neighbors loved him, to respect him as his opponents respected him, and to realize as never before that, as she herself says, "he is the best man that America has ever produced."

Fresh from this work, and with her mind full of the evidences of what had once been the ideals and standards of this country, as contrasted with those of the present day of "progress," the next task given to Miss Tarbell in connection with her work on *McClure's* was to write a series of articles dealing with the trust question and its bearing upon our national development. Her early familiarity with the methods of the Standard Oil Company and her personal knowledge of conditions in the oil regions at the time the industry was absorbed by Rockefeller gave a definite basis upon which to begin, and from that the *History of the Standard Oil Company* grew to its present form. Collecting the records was a long and difficult task, for they must be accurate and complete. No hearsay information, no conclusions based upon a matter of opinion, could be used in an attack so serious, an exposure so complete, as this would have to be if the doing of it were to be justified in the eyes of the nation. So long months were spent in searching all available records, and many more that were by no means easily available. Only a thorough training in historical research could have fitted anyone to accomplish such a task, and that Miss Tarbell had spent years of hard work to acquire. Nothing escaped her. She went wherever there was the chance of such a record existing, examined legal documents, business agreements, Congressional reports, files of old newspapers,—everything that could furnish a thread for the firm web of evidence she was weaving around the first and greatest of the trusts, and then told the story as it is now known. In its pitiless accuracy and rigid impartiality, it is a terrific arraignment of the whole commercial theory that has produced the trusts and that, incidentally, is shaping the business side of our national character upon the lines laid down and typified by Mr. Rockefeller. It is this bigger issue, this greater menace, that gleams between every line of the simply told narrative. It is the old story of the specially privileged few and the duped and plundered many, and the reader is left to infer the possible consequences when the many grow desperate. It is the sharply-drawn contrast between the America of Lincoln's times and the America of today.

And through it all, like some unseen, malevolent power, is felt, rather than perceived, the influence of John D. Rockefeller. To Miss Tarbell he is the exact antithesis of Lincoln, and as truly typifies his times. Yet her attitude toward him throughout is just, and even kind. This is shown even more clearly in the character study of the man that was published some months after the completion of the history of his trust. His great power, as well as that of the organization he built, is fully acknowledged, and the utter pathos of his attempts to rehabilitate himself in the eyes of the world and to free himself of a little of the crushing burden of its hate by means of his immense charities and his irreproachable private life. He is a business man who keeps his accounts straight to the last cent, and he is paying his debt to civilization in his own way. But there is always the conviction that the moral debt he owes to the nation can never be paid, that the harm has been done and is irrevocable until such time as the moral sense of the people purifies itself sufficiently to once more produce a type of man like Abraham Lincoln,—sane, unselfish, devoted, and too innately honest to take unfair advantage of any man or to accept special privileges in the effort to achieve success.

That we, as a nation, are at last awakening to the necessity of this is due to the courage of those who have dared to give us "analysis, ruthless and unflinching," of conditions as they exist, and to point out whither they are leading us. The number of these analysts is increasing every day and the battle of strong powers for good and for evil is on in earnest, but when the result is recorded in the history of the future, first among the names of those who led the fight for national honor and fair play will be that of the woman who was wise enough to see the truth, and strong enough to make the people stop and listen while she told them what she saw. (pp. 5-10)

> *M. Irwin MacDonald, "Ida M. Tarbell: The Woman Who Has Made People Comprehend the Meaning of the Trusts," in* The Craftsman, *Vol. XIV, No. 1, April, 1908, pp. 3-10.*

The Dial, Chicago   (essay date 1919)

[*In the following review of* The Rising of the Tide, *the critic disparages the novel's stock characterizations.*]

Anyone who read the magazines of a dozen years ago remembers the muckrakers, that gallant lot of crusaders who acted on the assumption that America was Holy Land and Big Business the infidel in possession thereof, but who today seem as far off and abortive as the Jacquerie. Among that courageous but rather priggish set, Ida M. Tarbell was one of the foremost exposers of iniquities. It is interesting to discover, therefore, that she has experi-enced a change of heart. Ralph Gardner, the young editor of [*The Rising of the Tide*], is a muckrake wielder who might well have been one of her companions of other days; Reuben Cowder is a representative of secret and iniquitous forces. Yet almost the whole volume is devoted to proving Ralph wrong and the wealthy malefactor right. The acid test by which Cowder is shown to be the better man is that of patriotism; not that Ralph Gardner turns Bolshevik, but rather that his opponent—by manufacturing munitions—aids the Allies even before we enter the war.

The purpose of the novel is ostensibly to show the reactions of a small American community to the war spirit. What it really proves is that Miss Tarbell, during her years of literary composition, has not neglected her reading. Indeed, all her characters have come out of the current periodicals. The Reverend Dick Ingraham, her hero, who stalks from page to page preaching the good in all bad people—especially if they are prosperous munition makers—does not so much mouth platitudes as live them; he is the embodiment of an editorial in the *Times*. Otto Littman, villain, is a cartoon in *Life;* Miss Patsy McCullon, the heroine of a *Ladies' Home Journal* story; Nancy Cowder, the picture of a fine lady out of *Harper's Bazaar*. And when at last she discovers her love for the Reverend Dick, when after an hour they come out of the house "with a look of glory on their faces," one strains a little to sniff the printer's ink which is their life blood, and to catch the faint rustle of paper.

> *A review of "The Rising of the Tide," in* The Dial, *Chicago, Vol. LXVII, August 9, 1919, p. 122.*

Henry David   (essay date 1936)

[*David was an educator and historian who specialized in labor issues. In the following review of* The Nationalizing of Business, 1878-1898, *he calls attention to the inadequacies of the work.*]

The twenty-year period with which Miss Tarbell deals [in **The Nationalizing of Business, 1878-1898**] is peculiarly significant in American history. These two decades, interestingly enough, begin with recovery from the depression inaugurated in 1873 and end with the close of the depression announced by the panic of 1893. Of special importance are the years 1879-93, for they constitute, despite several lean years in the middle eighties, a major period of economic expansion.

The great advance in land occupation, the twenty-five-million increase in population, the growth of the domestic market, the striking technological advances, the tremendous exploitation of natural resources, the utilization of new sources of fuel and power, the changes in transportation and communication, the development of new business forms, the modifications in the system of distribution, and the developments in banking and finance which occurred in these years wrought profound transformations in the American scene. By 1898 an industrial capitalist order was firmly established. A once rural and agricultural land had become essentially urban and industrial.

This period was also an age of protest and revolt in which industrial laborers, farmers, and a handful of intellectuals participated. It witnessed the rapid rise and collapse of the Knights of Labor and the birth of the American Federation of Labor. It produced the pulsating labor movement of the middle eighties and bitter industrial conflicts, among which Homestead and Pullman loom large. Agrarian protest, expressing itself in turn in greenbackism, free silver, and the farmers' alliances, finally culminated in the Populist crusade. From the extreme left there came an energetic attack upon the existing order by Anarchists and Socialists, while a distinctly native radicalism appeared in the philosophy of Henry George.

All this and more falls within the scope of *The Nationalizing of Business,* and it is unfortunate that the volume contributes little to an adequate picture of these developments or to an understanding of their significance and consequences. It has no real value as a study in social history, and suffers from distressing shallowness as a work in economic history. An uncritical attitude leads Miss Tarbell to repeat many half-truths and myths, most of which have been long exploded, and to create some new ones. A complete catalogue of the sins of commission and omission with which Miss Tarbell may be fairly charged cannot be undertaken here. But some of her offenses must be indicated.

She depends to an unusual degree, in a work of this kind, upon secondary sources. Recent studies not in agreement with her views are ignored. An obvious instance is her use of the material in McElroy's *Grover Cleveland* for the Pullman strike rather than the account in Allan Nevins's biography of Cleveland. She frequently suppresses essential evidence. In her version of the Homestead strike, for example, there is no mention of Carnegie's decision to make Homestead nonunion, or of his complete support of Frick's actions. Her regard for the life of personal achievement leads to adulation of the "strong men" of the period—witness the saintly portraits of Carnegie and many of his contemporaries. She partially justifies the huge profits made by the "leaders" of industry in terms of the "benefits" the country "derived" from their activities. She says nothing about the development of banking and finance, and barely touches upon the house of Morgan. Her treatment of railroad and trust legislation and Populism are especially inadequate and superficial. She believes that "the conditions of the wage-earners had . . . greatly improved in the twenty years," but she offers no evidence. "On the whole," she writes, "labor issued from [the industrial] conflicts [of the period] more successfully than capital, primarily because what it sought was so often just."

But enough. The volume is smoothly written. Beyond that it has no major virtue, and it is no distinction for the *A History of American Life* series to have Miss Tarbell's work in it. (pp. 666, 668)

Henry David, "The Nationalization of Business," in The Nation, *New York, Vol. 143, No. 23, December 5, 1936, pp. 666, 668.*

Louis Filler   (essay date 1939)

[*Filler is an American historian whose works examine "the contours of our civilization, our education, our history and culture." In the following excerpt, he praises Tarbell's research methods and explains the impact of her* History of the Standard Oil Company.]

In about 1897 the subject of trusts, and particularly of Standard Oil, had begun to assume proportions. The State of New Jersey had opened the door wide to companies interested in getting around the law, and its easy payment plans were making a laughing stock of the Sherman Anti-Trust Act. The reading public wanted to know the meaning of the strange legal activities which made everything right, and yet not right. [Editor Samuel S.] McClure's policy, however, had not been to answer his readers' questions about such matters; he aimed only to cater to their interest in business as such. Now, however, he hit upon the idea of abandoning the general trust and business articles. He assigned Ida Tarbell to study the Standard Oil Company exhaustively, to write its story in full, showing its history, effects, tendencies. He believed that in such a long, concrete illustration the reader would learn more about big business than he could from discussions and sketches of a hundred firms.

Had McClure combed the literary circles of the nation he could have found no better writer for his purposes than his own associate editor. This tall, matter-of-fact woman, who looked much more a schoolmistress than an editor, had every attribute he might have asked. To begin with, she had been born and bred in the oil regions, in Erie County, Pennsylvania. Her birth date, 1857, approximated the date of the discovery of oil there. Her father had been one of the oil men whom Rockefeller and the oil refiners had found in the path of their monopoly. She had graduated from Titusville High School, and later yet from Allegheny College. At twenty-six she had become associate editor of *The Chautauquan,* holding that position until 1889. Because she had wanted to be a writer of biographies, and because American biography was still primitive, in 1891 she had sailed for Paris and there entered the Sorbonne and the Collège de France, where she took courses and practiced writing. It was here that McClure had discovered her.

The oil regions had apparently left no deep impression in her life. She had diligently pursued a career which led definitely away from them—toward Napoleon and Madame Roland. But the point of view of Rockefeller's enemies, the oil producers, was, as she has said, instinctive with her, and she had by no means forgotten that point of view when she sat down to write for McClure. If she harbored so much as a grain of resentment against the interests that had taken over the oil fields from their original owners, however, it did not appear on the surface. Ida Tarbell was objectivity itself.

Tarbell had two great qualities for her work: patience and the ability to simplify artlessly. Both were imperative for anyone who planned to write a history of the Standard Oil Company. For well over thirty years it had been engaged in business and litigation in a hundred parts of this country and beyond. Literally thousands of people had been intimately involved in its rise. But Rockefeller and his associates, having no eye on posterity when they undertook to consolidate the oil industry, made no effort to lighten the task of the future historian; on the contrary, they were extremely careful to hide the evidence of their business dealings from public inspection. Their record was a maze of contradictions and denials. To get to the heart of their countless activities and then to present it so that it could be understood, was a job to test the resources of any writer.

Tarbell set out to master the subject. She traveled extensively, read long and detailed records, examined libraries of information—including part of that which Henry Demarest Lloyd had collected for his own work [*Wealth against Commonwealth* (1894)]—and interviewed individuals who had been concerned in separate controversies. When H. H. Rogers, one of the leading figures of Standard Oil, heard what she was about, he sent word through his friend Mark Twain that he would be glad to help her in any phase of her work. Tarbell accepted his offer with alacrity: she would be delighted to get every point of view; she wanted her story to be impartial, complete, definitive. Such were the standards she set for herself that it was five years before her study was complete, and by that time she had become the outstanding authority on the subject.

The story, as it began to shape up, presented an aspect somewhat different from that which McClure had originally expected. Standard Oil was to have emerged as the very symbol of efficiency and organization. It did. But it was so heavily laden with questionable business maneuvers, so bound up with bribery, fraud, coercion, double-dealing and outright violence, that the fact of efficiency and organization inevitably gave place to the question of whether such a concern had the right to exist. Tarbell did not invent the serious charges. They were a matter of record: she merely gave the evidence as it appeared.

Was she secretly content to let the record speak for itself? McClure, at any rate, was deeply satisfied with the material his writer was evolving. It was just and complete in its proportions. Tarbell took the evidence of the anti-Standard men and submitted it to Standard officials for comment; she took Standard's explanations to Standard's enemies. She approached the enigmatic character of Rockefeller himself with an open-minded willingness to get at the facts.

Tarbell's style was herself: calm, analytical, factual. It is well to remember this, for after her book began to appear in serial form, the notion was quickly established that drama and excitement were its major characteristics. That notion, unfortunately, it was impossible to eradicate. *The History of the Standard Oil Company* was not really the work of an agitated investigator. Nor was it so "monumental" a study as reputation had it, for its two volumes, as they appeared in 1904, totaled only some 550 pages, with several hundred more of appendix. The agitation existed in the minds of the readers who were compelled to face the truth that Standard Oil was tangible, corrupt and inescapable; the monumental nature of the exposure lay in the fact that Tarbell had telescoped into a relatively few pages a history which had involved the nation as a whole

and still involved it at the time of reading. No wonder the series was news; no wonder the history of a business house was followed month after month as though it had been a romance!

Tarbell was already famous when her series began to run in *McClure's;* her Lincoln books had established her among the most popular writers of non-fiction. *The History of Standard Oil* skyrocketed her to a place among the most eminent people in the land. Discussion of trusts was going on everywhere, and that meant that discussion of Tarbell could not be avoided. In the West, where *McClure's*—and all the other popular magazines—sold best, her name became a household word, a slogan against the trusts. Standard Oil, which had always carefully avoided engaging in public debate with its enemies, was compelled to exert itself against the influence of her work; not directly, of course, but through loyal journalists and agreeable newspapers.

A bitter review of Tarbell's history appeared in *The Nation* [see excerpt dated 1905], which indicted her on the grounds of sensationalism, misrepresentation, and ignorance: Tarbell was an outsider, and naturally could not know as much about Standard Oil as its officials. All the muckrakers in turn were accused of being writers and not business people. *The Nation* reviewer (anonymous) declared that it was only because Miss Tarbell's so-called history was an outstanding example of a type of current writing that so much space had been allotted it in *The Nation.* Interestingly enough, this review was reprinted "by permission" of *The Nation* and scattered by the hundreds of thousands throughout the country. Other pamphlets defending Standard Oil were distributed widely. As late as 1910 Elbert Hubbard wrote a brochure of praise for the Company which was, in the main, a studied attack on Tarbell's scholarship and presentation.

No denigration or abuse could veil the fact that Tarbell's story was not sensational, but a sensation. And it is worth discovering why it should have been a sensation at all. She had not attempted to discredit Standard; she had rather taken pains to explain its "real greatness." She had noted with approval the method and devotion of its founder to his company, his long, regular work, his religious point of view, his perfect family life. She showed in great detail the savings that had accrued from the elimination of competition, the minimum of waste that consolidation had entailed, the sending of Standard products throughout the world. She described the very beginnings of the oil industry, from the first wild days when gushers had sprung up in the Pennsylvania fields and fortunes had been made and lost in minutes. Since then the pipeline system had been put into operation which had done away with the rough and ready methods of transportation. Problems presented by the crude oil had since been mastered; inventions had made it possible to use every bit of it; products of important use to the country had been evolved.

Standard had achieved its position only through illegal contracts with the railroad carriers, contracts which had meant the ruin of competitors. Tarbell told about these contracts because they were a part of the history. There was no muckraking tone to her story. If compared with that which Henry Demarest Lloyd had written, the story seemed actually complimentary to Standard. For Lloyd had made no effort to be impartial. He had written with a brilliant and burning pen. With his conviction that the trusts had captured government and were doing as they pleased, he had as much as called the public to revolt. He had frightened away the reader with the inexorable logic of his indictment, as Populism had finally frightened away the voters.

Tarbell called her readers to no action whatsoever; she simply stated what had happened. The reader was put into a position in which he had to furnish his own answers. Having admired and appreciated the business genius of Rockefeller, his regular working hours, his complete concentration on work, the reader was compelled to ask what manner of man this was who had nothing in his life but money, who had already corralled a good proportion of all that was in sight. Rockefeller's religious convictions only angered or annoyed him the more. The poor took him to be a hypocrite; the more sophisticated summed him up as a simpleton and a fool. And having understood and respected the perfection of the Standard system, the reader was compelled to face the fact that it was one of the major rulers of the country; he had to ask what the end would be when Standard had completed its quest for power and had allied itself with other industrial titans to keep the ordinary worker and small business man in its power.

Tarbell's plain facts and the thoughts they inspired, generated revolt faster than Lloyd could ever have done. No wonder Standard Oil feared Tarbell's book as it never had feared Lloyd's, and read into it a cunning and purpose which did not exist. Rogers of Standard would have done well to leave Tarbell to her own devices during her research. His advice and collaboration, with her obvious honesty and willingness to learn from everyone, made him party to the final version of the history, and so impressed the reading public with Tarbell's painstaking efforts to tell the whole truth and damned Standard Oil as no other account of its iniquities had done.

The country was overrun with trusts, and all the important ones were exposed to the public eye before the muckraking era was over. Yet no other trust ever caught the imagination of the public like Standard. This was Tarbell's consummate achievement. It was because she gave a careful, detailed account of its rise, because she described minutely the manner in which it actually functioned, because she portrayed its leaders, its departments, its daily routine, and its products, that she succeeded above all other competing writers. . . . [It] was ultimately her point of view which determined the value of her work. Her clear, dispassionate manner enabled her to produce what became a source book of information, a book that could be consulted no matter what mood the reader was in. She had focused steadily upon description; no other writing element was allowed to take precedence over it. No expression of bias interfered with the public's chance to understand a trust as a separate entity with a separate significance independent of individuals and motives. (pp. 102-07)

The History of the Standard Oil Company marked an epoch. Once it had appeared, there could never be any fur-

ther question about the existence or significance of trusts. Even the books which Tarbell wrote after muckraking had ended—books which were, for the most part, focused conservatively—were unable to modify the knowledge she had given to the public. Through newspapers and magazines the intrinsic message of her masterpiece filtered down into the very consciousness of the average American citizen.

With what result? Some Americans, even a number who had entertained radical notions, scrutinized the trust and decided that the future was inevitably with it. They abjured their radicalism and jumped upon the *laissez-faire* bandwagon: evolution would take care of everything. The majority of people stood neutral, repeating the old clichés about law enforcement, undecided but yet undefeated.

A little vanguard, however, decided to do battle with the trust and stepped boldly out to demand its dissolution. More or less openly, more or less radically, they took up arms and fought, as lawyers, as reformer business men, as politicians, or as developers of the work Tarbell had begun—that is, as muckrakers. (p. 109)

> Louis Filler, "The Mother of Trusts," in his *Crusaders for American Liberalism*, Harcourt Brace Jovanovich, 1939, pp. 102-09.

Benjamin P. Thomas   (essay date 1947)

[*In the following excerpt, Thomas favorably assesses Tarbell as a biographer of Abraham Lincoln.*]

From the middle nineties to the nineteen-twenties was a period of transition [in Lincoln scholarship], with Ida Tarbell its prophet and exemplar.

A realist, in that she welcomed truth when it was demonstrated, she tried to keep her feet on the ground. But sometimes only her tip-toes touched, as she reached to grasp a star.

Taps for the Lincoln generation was her reveille. For in the memories of these oldsters must be stories yet untold; and in attics, basements, letter files, and desk drawers surely there were treasures unexhumed.

This idea suggested itself to Samuel Sidney McClure and his partner, John S. Phillips, as they took thought for the morrow of their magazine [*McClure's*]. McClure had long esteemed and studied Lincoln, and he now conceived the idea of setting up a sort of Lincoln bureau in his editorial rooms. Through this he would conduct an organized search for reminiscences, relics, pictures, and documents bearing on the Lincoln theme with a view to popularizing Lincoln in the magazine. And in Ida Tarbell he saw an ideal person for this work. (p. 178)

Gracious, eager, apt, and dexterous with a pen, she had been a fortunate find. Already she had made her literary mark with biographies of Napoleon and Madame Roland. But why waste her talents on the figures of France, thought McClure, when a home-grown character like Lincoln needed explaining?

As the first assignment in her Lincoln work, McClure sent

her to interview the Lincoln veteran, John G. Nicolay. But to her surprise, he was cool. He could offer her nothing. The collected works of Lincoln, that he and [Logan] Hay had edited, were complete; and their ten-volume *Life* contained everything worth telling. He tried to dissuade her from her project, and when she persisted, and her articles began to appear, he called one evening to complain. "You are invading my field," he protested. "You write a popular Life of Lincoln and you do just so much to decrease the value of my property." She argued that her work would stimulate interest in all good Lincoln books; but he was unconvinced; and she thought he never forgave her.

Miss Tarbell was introduced to Robert T. Lincoln, now president of the Pullman Company, by Miss Emily Lyons, a mutual friend. In presenting her, Miss Lyons urged, "Now, Robert, I want you to give her something worthwhile." Good-naturedly, Robert agreed to oblige, although he doubted that he could be of any help. He intimated that [William H.] Herndon had stolen all the papers from his father's office, and explained that the letters of the presidential period were packed away in Washington and had already been thoroughly explored by Nicolay and Hay. But he did give her an excellent daguerreotype, supposedly the first picture of his father ever taken, and one which had never been published. McClure used it as the frontispiece for her first article.

Thereafter, Robert was always kind and friendly, but would never grant access to his father's papers. "Impossible," he said.

> They are in the safety vault of my bank. I won't allow anybody to see them. There is nothing of my father's there, that is of value—Nicolay and Hay have published everything; but there are many letters *to* him which if published now would pain, possibly discredit able and useful men still living. Bitter things are written when men are trying to guide a country through a war, particularly a Civil War. I fear misuse of those papers so much that I am thinking of destroying them. Besides, somebody is always worrying me about them, just as you are, and I must be ungenerous. I think I will burn them.

Miss Tarbell would have liked to ask Robert his opinion of many things pertaining to his father, but she feared it would be indecorous.

Miss Tarbell also sought advice and help from Jesse Weik. If he caught her "tripping," she would regard it as a "great kindness" to be shown wherein she erred. More obliging than Nicolay and Robert Lincoln, Weik supplied her with pictures and offered suggestions. Never blessed with abundance of worldly goods, he was glad to get the checks she sent in payment. He hoped to break into the series with articles of his own, but she explained that this would not be possible, although *McClure's* might be able to use them at a later date. Whenever she needed amplifying material, Weik was usually able to furnish it from Herndon's manuscripts. She planned to visit Weik in Greencastle, admitting that she hoped to "be able to get something out of you which will be valuable in my work. You don't know what a dreadful sponge I have become."

But Weik did know; and so did others. In her zeal Miss Tarbell sometimes pumped out of others things they had planned to use themselves; and without realizing that she might be harming them—wittingly she would never hurt anyone—she slipped their findings into print before the unwilling donors realized what had happened. Fond of her personally, other writers did not always welcome her visits; and at her approach they figuratively secreted their Lincoln treasures in mattresses or cubbyholes. When Katherine Helm was working on her life of Mrs. Lincoln, she was appalled to learn that Miss Tarbell planned to visit Lexington. She tried to discourage her from coming. "But," she wrote to William E. Barton, "here she is combing the town and the old newspaper files—Do you wonder that I feel like the poor little scared rabbit? Of course there is only one way she could get my *original stuff* and that would be by reading my M.S. and that . . . I will take good care she will not do."

The public response to McClure's published appeal for Lincoln material was staggeringly gratifying, and Miss Tarbell wrote hundreds of letters to track down the clues that came to light. But the material was too fragmentary and disconnected for publication; so, in lieu of the original idea, it was decided that Miss Tarbell should write a series of articles covering Lincoln's life to 1858. These were published during 1895 and 1896; and so enthusiastic was their welcome that the printers were unable to turn out copies fast enough. Within ten days *McClure's* gained ten thou-

Tarbell in the offices of McClure's, *1898.*

sand new subscribers and within three months one hundred thousand new readers were on their list. Popularly written and profusely illustrated with pictures of Lincoln and associated people and places, the articles stirred interest country-wide.

Miss Tarbell's discoveries were important and substantial. J. McCan Davis, a young Springfield attorney, searched the Springfield newspapers for her and came up with Lincoln's first speech as well as important letters bearing on his early law practice and political activities. Through interviews and search of public records he disclosed new facts on Lincoln's life in New Salem and his early years in Springfield—the record of his first vote, several maps and surveys made by him, his marriage certificate.

When the public showed no signs of weariness, McClure brought out a new series, dealing with the presidential period, which ran from November, 1898 to September, 1899.

Out of these articles grew Miss Tarbell's *The Early Life of Abraham Lincoln,* published in 1896 to meet a demand the magazine could not supply, and her two-volume *The Life of Abraham Lincoln,* published in 1900, and containing an appendix of some two hundred pages of new documents. Then came a respite while she wrote her *History of the Standard Oil Company,* during which time Weik asked her if she was through with Lincoln. "Of course, I have not dropped Lincoln," she replied; "I intend to keep hold of him as long as I live." And her interest did continue through her life. Her books ran to many printings and editions and from time to time new books and articles came from her prolific pen. She was adept at writing children's books and her *Boy Scouts' Life of Lincoln* has long been popular with boys. She was especially interested in the physical setting of events, and her work is replete with photographs, many of which she took with her own camera on trips through the Lincoln country. She was ghost writer for "Recollections of the Civil War," by Charles A. Dana, Stanton's assistant in the War Department and later editor of the New York *Sun,* which were published in *McClure's* in 1897 and 1898; and she worked with Carl Schurz as an "editorial representative" while he wrote his reminiscences. In 1924 appeared *In the Footsteps of the Lincolns,* which some consider her best book.

"I wanted to go over the story again," she explained regarding this book, "and find out whether on closer examination, with all the new material which had come out since my first study, I would feel as strongly about his work as I did before. Not only did this going over the story reenforce my judgment but it kindled a satisfaction in the man greater than I had ever had."

Aside from the new material she unearthed, Miss Tarbell's most significant contribution to the Lincoln story was her appreciation of the stimulus of frontier life, which had been regarded hitherto as immoderately squalid and unhappy. Previous biographers had tried to glorify Lincoln by magnifying the unattractive aspects of his early life, picturing it as hard, dull, enervating, practically devoid of inspiration. In their view this background contributed little or nothing to the making of the later Lincoln. He be-

came what he did in spite of it. His surmounting such a handicap was proof in itself of innate greatness.

But Miss Tarbell begged to differ. Yes, frontier life was raw and rude; but it was also buoyant and adventurous. "I have never had any sympathy with the half-pitying, half-contemptuous attitude towards Abraham Lincoln's early life or the habit that biographers had fallen into of caricaturing him," she declared. "It seemed to me high time that somebody put emphasis on the other side." To her, Thomas Lincoln—the whole family, in fact—seemed to have been purposely written down to make Lincoln greater by contrast. She saw Lincoln as a typical pioneer child of typical pioneer parents. His family and his surroundings were no better and no worse than those of thousands of pioneer boys. There was poverty, to be sure, but it was offset by the endless "delights and interests the country offers a child." The journey from Kentucky to Indiana "must have been a long delight and wonder." And while life in Indiana was rough and hard, it did not lack amusement, fun, and frolics. The nearby Ohio River and the majestic Mississippi were the American "Appian Way," teeming with lusty life, swelling with the surge of a mighty civilization. Such a background was inspiring and uplifting.

Here Lincoln "saw labor as the foundation of all that might come after it," came to know the emotions and ambitions that moved men's minds. His very speech took flavor from this elemental life. "The horse, the dog, the ox, the chin fly, the plow, the hog, these companions of his youth became interpreters of his meaning, solvers of his problems in his great necessity, of making men understand and follow him."

Thus she flung her challenge at Lamon's "dung-hill" thesis and Herndon's assertion of Lincoln's having risen from "a stagnant, putrid pool"; and if she did not succeed entirely in dispelling these misconceptions, others, following her lead, would do so later.

Miss Tarbell felt the puissance of American rural life. To Chic Sale, who enjoyed depicting her **"Man Who Knew Lincoln"** in one of his vaudeville skits, she wrote:

> I know of no one on our stage that interprets with so much sympathy, humor, and understanding the honest-to-God American of our country towns and corners. You catch his shrewdness, independence of spirit, his love of fun and its practice. I always laugh at your characters and love them because they are so entirely themselves.

And she might have added that every characteristic she enumerated was typified in Lincoln.

From Miss Tarbell's books came new appreciation of the power of the American West and what it could do in the way of fashioning a man. American historians, working in a broader field, were submitting the thesis that the influence of the frontier was a major determining factor of American national life; and Miss Tarbell, studying one man, was deducing a similar thesis about him.

Few persons realize Miss Tarbell's influence upon Carl Sandburg. She was his prime mover. Sending her page proof for his *Prairie Years,* Sandburg wrote: "Yourself and Oliver R. Barrett [the Lincoln collector] are the only persons receiving advance sheets, as you are the two who have helped me most." In his preface Sandburg credited her with putting fresh color into what had heretofore been pictured as "drab and miserable beyond the fact"; and her influence is manifest when he wrote:

> In the short and simple annals of the poor, it seems there are people who breathe with the earth and take into their lungs and blood some of the hard and dark strength of its mystery. During six and seven months each year in the twelve fiercest formative years of his life, Abraham Lincoln had the pads of his foot-soles bare against clay of the earth. It may be the earth told him in her own tough gypsy slang one or two knacks of living worth keeping.

As a college student Miss Tarbell aspired to be a microscopist; later she studied some phases of Lincoln's life as with a microscope. She questioned Herndon's account of Lincoln's reaction to the slave auction at New Orleans, where he was supposed to have vowed, "If I ever get a chance to hit that thing, I'll hit it hard." Herndon gave John Hanks as authority for this statement; and Miss Tarbell pointed out that according to Lincoln's own assertion Hanks did not accompany the party to New Orleans but left it at St. Louis. But she questioned only the details of the story, never doubting that Lincoln was impressed by what he saw.

She also showed that William Cullen Bryant was wrong in supposing that Lincoln was the "raw youth" of "quaint and pleasant mien" whom he saw in command of a company of volunteers when traveling in the West during the Black Hawk War; because Lincoln's captaincy ended in May, and Bryant arrived in June, and he never got within fifty miles of where Lincoln was.

Miss Tarbell did not doubt that liquor was sold at the Lincoln-Berry store in New Salem—a point which had been argued since the time Douglas alluded to it in one of the great debates. It was sold at every frontier store, she explained; and when Lincoln and Berry obtained a tavern license, they were permitted to sell it by the drink, on the premises, whereas, without a license, they could sell it only in bulk for consumption off the premises.

On March 6, 1896, she warned Weik that she was going to try to "explode" Herndon's story of the wedding at which Lincoln failed to appear. Possibly Weik would be inclined to "explode" her in retaliation. If so, well and good. All she wanted was the truth, "and if we can bring out any new authority, why so much the better for both of us." She did bring out new authority averse to Herndon's statements; and while her hoped-for explosion merely fizzled, later investigators proved her suspicions to be correct by finishing the job of demolition.

Thus she was instrumental in clarifying doubtful points; although, on the other hand, her ardor sometimes led her astray as in the case of Whitney and Lincoln's "Lost Speech." Fervently devoted to Lincoln, when the scales were nearly balanced, she would let her hand rest—ever so lightly, and probably unconsciously—on the side that favored him. (pp. 179-89)

The biographers before Miss Tarbell were a stubborn lot. It was a new departure to have a Lincoln author with an open mind. For Miss Tarbell had no false pride and no illusions of infallibility. Always and sincerely she expressed thanks when anyone exposed an error in her work. When Paul Angle, who was winning scholarly recognition as secretary of the Abraham Lincoln Association, informed her that he was about to publish evidence which would discredit [Henry Clay] Whitney's alleged restoration of Lincoln's "Lost Speech," she told him to go ahead. "I think you are rendering the Lincoln public a real service in this case as you have in so many others," she asserted. "It is a consolation to have a watch dog, like yourself, at the door in Springfield." As her wisdom ripened with age, she knew she was too uncritically laudatory by modern standards. "I am afraid I am over-lenient towards mistakes, having made so many myself," she admitted. When her conclusions were attacked, she could say with all sincerity, "It is a deep satisfaction to me that the work has become gradually so thorough and so scientific." "As one of the old guard, about the oldest, I think, I am never very sure of my standing with the younger Lincoln students, but I am thankful for them," she asserted at the age of eighty-four. "They are constantly unearthing things that I never found and enabling me to correct what are supposed to be facts."

She welcomed newcomers to the Lincoln field, anticipating that their point of view might be refreshing. When it was arranged that she should be a sort of counsellor to the German biographer Emil Ludwig while he wrote his *Life of Lincoln,* she immediately sent him encouragement. "I know you are going to give us something provocative and stimulating," she assured him;

> and we need something of that kind over here on Lincoln. You see, we are so close that we are not yet able to appraise. We have been dealing in the raw materials, getting him into shape for future estimates, squabbling over controverted facts— all necessary, I suppose, but it is good to get an outside view, and I am eager to see yours.

She was suspicious of Herndon; yet she appreciated what he had done. "Where we would be without him I don't know," she wrote to Weik. "Though I have in certain cases disagreed with his interpretation of documents, I held in highest regard—and never failed to express it—not only his remarkable contribution of personal recollections but his equally remarkable collection of the recollections of others." There were rumors that Herndon's collection contained many things that even he had not seen fit to reveal; and Miss Tarbell's zeal for truth is attested by her appeal to Weik to annotate and publish the Herndon manuscripts. Weik never chose to follow her advice; but years later after Weik's death, Emanuel Hertz brought out a collection of Herndon letters, some of which seemed indiscreet. But Miss Tarbell was not one to protest. "I am glad you published these papers," she wrote to Hertz.

> There has been a mystery about what was in them for so long, there have been so many hints

that there were dark and sinister revelations in them concerning Lincoln's private life and his ancestry that every serious student of Lincoln's life will be grateful to you for publishing the material showing the worst. Certainly nothing is there that impairs Lincoln for intelligent people, but I am afraid, dear Mr. Hertz, that there is considerable that impairs Herndon as a careful student, an honest and patient searcher for facts.

Nobody is more grateful to Herndon than I am for the tremendous amount of vital, human material he gathered on Lincoln, . . . but his early theory explaining Lincoln's melancholy so obsessed him that he was not willing to give the careful research the ancestry required nor was he willing to give up his notions about Tom Lincoln and Nancy Lincoln. That it was an obsession these letters and documents seem to me to prove and the tragedy of it is that it cost him the rewards that he ought to have had in his life time for a tremendous amount of valuable work.

Herndon sponsored one questionable story which Miss Tarbell was reluctant to give up. She hoped the romance of Lincoln and Ann Rutledge would never be proved untrue. "I have always been a believer in this romance," she wrote after it had come under skeptical scrutiny, "have believed it was the only time romance touched Abraham Lincoln. It seems to me that the definite proofs outside of tradition, which is of course a strong support, are sufficient to establish the fact of the love between them."

Denied romance herself—at least so far as we know—it seemed to her that a man whose life was so full of sadness and tragedy should be allowed this moment of happiness. "Frankly, I am probably influenced by my desire that the man should have had such an affair in his early life," she confessed.

How could you expect that a young man of a strong emotional nature such as Lincoln's, and his was strong if unusually well controlled, should live side by side with a girl whom everybody reported charming and not fall in love. It was a natural thing to do. I sometimes think people who dispute early romances have lived so long that they have forgotten their youth.

Miss Tarbell had idealistic tendencies; but she must be classed as a realist. She was no idolater. Her Lincoln was "altogether a man." "It is a mistake to think of him as a hero—a demigod," she declared. "It is a fine thing that he shows what a man can do with himself in spite of all handicaps, all the temptations of human beings—none of which I take it he escaped. It is the way he came through at the end that is so fine."

A young lady, an American, who was lecturing at the University of Manchester in England, once asked Miss Tarbell to explain Lincoln's ever-increasing popular appeal. To survivors of the Civil War, she replied, Lincoln was a warrior's hero, and somewhat mythical. But the contemporary feeling of admiration and respect was more soundly based. It was not due to Republican oratory, as her correspondent suggested, although the party had overlooked no opportunity to exploit him. Republican oratory of recent years was far removed from Lincoln's ideas and spirit. "They have denied him at every point," she asserted.

The problems of the World War had undoubtedly turned the country's thoughts to the man who had guided it through its last great military struggle. "His ideas of what democracy means, of the necessity of going through even a civil war to protect a great experiment in popular government, his arguments and his decisions—all these have been a subject of new study through this period," she admitted. And they went far to explain the growing Lincoln cult in England. But in America the roots were deeper.

Here, she believed, Lincoln's appeal came from the fact that he epitomized American characteristics. "Our people are much devoted to what they consider the American type," she explained, "with its characteristics of common sense, directness, humor, and a bull-dog grip—and Lincoln had all of these things." Then, too, Americans had always been attracted to the diamond-in-the-rough; so many of them, especially in the West, were diamonds-in-the-rough themselves.

This young lady correspondent wondered if Lincoln had not become too much the superman, and if his true greatness might be lost in over-adulation. But Miss Tarbell did not think so. "The people, on the whole, have him about right," she thought.

His place with us depends upon the conviction of the people that he was a man, and not that he was a superman. It is likeness to themselves, the fact that they understand the words he uses and the arguments—they understand, too, the struggle that he went through, it is so like their own. This is what binds the mass of the people to Lincoln.

Miss Tarbell had a rare appreciation of Lincoln. To a member of a discussion club who inquired whether Lincoln was interested in the "finer traits," such as art, music, color, or flowers, she explained that during the greater part of his life he lived in a community where music and art were not readily available. Yet, no man who was as passionately found of the best in literature and so eager to acquaint himself with everything that had contributed to man's cultural advancement could have been insensible to art and music when they came his way. He was a student of the drama in that he never missed an opportunity to see anything that was presented on the stage, even such poor repertory as was available on his circuit travels; and after he went to Washington he not only attended the theater regularly; he could also discuss Shakespeare intelligently with some of the best actors of his day. Few men were more familiar with Shakespeare, Burns, or the Bible.

As a woodsman, he must have known trees, and perhaps flowers; but this was not the place to look for his interest in "finer things." "It is in his devotion to high literature and his own power of expression," Miss Tarbell pointed out. "You must not forget Abraham Lincoln wrote more than one piece of prose which is universally held to be as perfect as anything that has been produced in English." That alone should be proof of his interest in "finer things."

To a superficial observer he may have seemed smirched by

a touch of grossness, she admitted. Perhaps his stories, for example, were not always in good taste. But they often helped elucidate a point and sometimes he used them for protection. "He had to push people away, and he often offended deeply by the habit."

With publication of Miss Tarbell's *History of the Standard Oil Company* in 1904, she came to be identified with the group comprising Lincoln Steffens, Charles Edward Russell, Gustavus Myers, and Upton Sinclair, who were called "muckrakers" by Theodore Roosevelt. The more sympathetic estimate of Vernon Louis Parrington depicted them as a part of the "host of heavy armed troops which moved forward on the strongholds of the new plutocracy" that had emerged in America as a result of the industrial revolution, and which, in alliance with venal politicians, was using the political machinery of democracy "to drive toward an objective which was the negation of democracy."

One is tempted to try to establish a connection between Miss Tarbell's alignment with these embattled democratic journalists and her interest in Lincoln; and to ascribe her trust-busting activities to the inspiration derived from study of the great exemplar of democracy. And while such a conclusion might be difficult to prove, the compatibility of her literary interests may not have been altogether fortuitous.

Miss Tarbell enjoyed her Lincoln studies. "I am working away at my story of the migrations of the Lincolns," she wrote in 1923, referring to *In the Footsteps of the Lincolns,* ". . . I don't know that I shall add much to the knowledge of the specialists, but I am trying to put a little flesh on the bones of Samuel and Mordecai and the rest of them. Whether the results of my work please others or not, I have gotten a great deal of interest and satisfaction out of it." Her story was built around a pilgrimage along the Lincoln route; and she was just as enthusiastic as when she traversed the same ground a quarter of a century before. At an old cemetery near Harrisonburg, Virginia, she climbed an iron picket fence to study the inscriptions on some Lincoln tombstones; and it gave her no small satisfaction that when William E. Barton, another Lincoln student, visited the same cemetery two years later, he stood outside the fence and took notes while the inscriptions were read to him. And he was only sixty-five, while she was sixty-seven!

Miss Tarbell stuck to the resolution she had expressed in her early years to Weik. At the age of eighty-four she wrote:

> Anyone who really takes up seriously the study of . . . [Lincoln's] life is never willing to lay it down. He is companionable as no public mind that I've ever known anything about, you feel at home with him, he never high hats you and he never bores you which is more than I can say of any public man living or dead with whom I have tried to get well acquainted . . . An impressive part of this acquaintance with him as a man is watching him grow, expand. Nothing was ever finished for Lincoln.

People were continually asking Miss Tarbell what Lincoln would do about problems of the present day; but she always advised that speculation of this sort was futile. This was not to say that Lincoln could offer nothing to the modern world. It could profit immeasurably by studying and following his methods. "While others talked Lincoln listened—weighed. He came slowly to his decisions. But when he arrived at them, he defended them sturdily, though never so obstinately he was not ready to consider new facts." He was "steady in storms," uncowed by criticism, unwavering when sure that he was right. He was impersonal in handling public matters, knowing neither vanity nor malice. In pressing for his goal, he took no thought for himself; and in dealing with men, he asked no more than they could give. His appeal was to the intellect; but he could stir the moral forces, too.

> It is not his opinion on a particular subject, not his wit and wisdom as expressed in his letters and speeches which are his great contribution, . . . it is from the temper with which he approached his problems, the methods by which he handled them that we can learn most. His life was a call to self-training—of training of the mind until it can form sound—workmanlike, trustworthy conclusions, training of the moral nature to justice and rightness—training of the will until it can be counted on to back up the conclusions of the mind and heart. It is a call to openness of mind, willingness to learn.
>
> His method is a constant lesson in liberality towards others, to a recognition that there may be something to be said of the other man's point of view as well as of yours, that you no more see all the truth than he does, and that if what each of you see can be fused, a larger amount of truth will result. Above all, his method is a revelation of what a man can make out of himself if he will. Indeed, I am sometimes inclined to feel that the greatest service Lincoln has done this country was to demonstrate what could be made of a mind by passionate, persistent effort. What moral heights the nature would rise to if dealt with in perfect candor.
>
> Taking him all in all, it is doubtful if this country or any country has produced a man so worthy of studying and following as is Abraham Lincoln.

This was her conception of our Lincoln heritage; and comprehension of Lincoln was her own most precious literary legacy. Small wonder that on January 7, 1944, the day after Miss Tarbell's death, the New York *Times* predicted that "her work in the field will be on any small shelf of Lincoln books for countless years to come. She was as honest, as kindly, as thoroughly American in the loftiest sense as he was. He would have loved and understood her as she did him."

Primarily Miss Tarbell was a popularizer, and with the passing years her books have been outmoded. But if she is not read as much as she once was, she should continue to be appreciated. She was the pioneer scientific investigator whose work foretold the revelation of Lincoln as he really was. "I cannot say enough for the wonderful contribution you have made in the field of Lincolniana," a Wisconsin educator told her. "In fact, you blazed the way for research work in this field." Carl Sandburg wrote to tell her how he and Oliver Barrett "talked long this evening about how much less of *fresh glint* there would be on the Lincoln legend without your work"; and when his *War Years* was published, he sent her a copy "not merely with my compliments, but with respect and affection—and something like reverence for a wisdom and integrity that have lasted so well across the years." (pp. 193-202)

> Benjamin P. Thomas, "An Idealistic Realist,"
> in his Portrait for Posterity: Lincoln and His
> Biographers, *Rutgers University Press, 1947,*
> pp. 178-202.

David Mark Chalmers   (essay date 1964)

[*Chalmers is an American historian who specializes in U.S. history of the twentieth century. In the following excerpt, he observes that the primary value espoused by Tarbell in her* History of the Standard Oil Company *is the principle of fair competition.*]

Of the muckrakers who believed in the working of a competitive mechanism, only Ida Tarbell described what the United States would look like under such a system. . . . For [her] it was the early days of the oil region. The picture she drew was one of exuberant individualism developing a vast natural wealth, and creating a forward-looking society. The value of the oil fields of western Pennsylvania, Ida Tarbell believed, had to be measured not only by the new economic product, but also by the life of the people who produced the new wealth. They were happy and earnest; in their own individualistic way they were meeting their problems and giving a meaning to their lives that was not to be found in the financial ledger. Each entrepreneur had a fierce pride in his work and independence. His business was his life. When the growth of the oil monopoly forced him out of business it was not merely an economic reverse but a personal tragedy.

The two underlying assumptions of *The History of the Standard Oil Company* were that the monopoly had destroyed healthy individualism, and that it had done so by methods that were tragically illegal and immoral. The first assumption seemed inevitably to imply the second. If competition were a vital and dynamic state, then it could not have been overwhelmed by open and legal means.

In order to show this, Ida Tarbell carefully rejected the arguments which favored the existence of Standard Oil. John D. Rockefeller had not acted in self-defense, for he had been making a profit and was in no danger. The brains and capital necessary for the industry's development would have been available without his intercession. Indeed, she maintained, the most important technological advances in the industry had been introduced as a result of independent competition, over the opposition of Standard Oil. Nor had Standard provided cheap oil. Monopoly meant that prices were kept artificially high. The Standard Oil Company, after having made generous allowances for depreciation, paid annual profits of fifty percent of its initial capitalization. The price of oil was deliberately kept high, and economies effected through size and efficiency

were given to the public only under pressure. The statistics showed that consumers had always paid more than they would have paid under a competitive price system. This, Ida Tarbell explained, was the motive for combination.

Quite clearly then, the oil trust must have risen through guile and chicanery rather than from any natural benefits accruing from size. It is not surprising, therefore, that *The History of the Standard Oil Company* was primarily a tale of illegal behavior. It was the story of the "big hand" which had reached out to steal the conquests of the men of the oil fields. In her autobiography, Ida Tarbell was to claim that she never opposed bigness *per se,* but this was certainly not the message of her *History.* "Human experience," she wrote, "long ago taught us that if we allowed a man or a group of men autocratic power . . . they used that power to oppose or defraud the public." Such was her case against Standard Oil.

Standard produced one-third and controlled all but ten percent of the supply of petroleum. It had the strength to undersell its rivals, cut off their supplies and make it impossible for them to do business. However, the key to the power of the trust lay in its influence over transportation. Standard's annual profit was too large a sum to be consumed. Most of it was invested in the railroads which were the transporters as well as the users of Standard's products. Every year the Standard Oil Company widened this investment, "wiping up the property most essential to preserving and broadening its power." Already Rockefeller men were directors of almost all of the great railroads, as well as sharing power in such enterprises as Amalgamated Copper, the Steel Trust, and the National City Bank of New York. In addition, Standard controlled potential freight in oil, timber, acids, iron and many other products. Furthermore, through its own wealth and influence in the market, it would manipulate the price of railroad stock or make it impossible for the carriers to obtain any investment funds at all.

The story of the rise of the oil trust had been one of illegal favoritism granted it by the railroads. The smaller oil producers and refiners had not been able to compete against this advantage. If the others in the industry also sought rebates—a consideration on which Ida Tarbell did not dwell—then Standard Oil had organized the practice on a scale beyond precedent. Drawbacks, the practice of getting rebates on other people's shipments, were a unique Rockefeller creation. Rockefeller had used his power over the railroads in order to build up his monopoly in oil. This control was the key to dealing with the trusts. So long as Standard Oil controlled transportation it would remain master of the industry. Investigations, laws against underselling, and anti-trust legislation such as the Sherman Act were not important.

The solution had to be both political and ethical. Public opinion was to be the motivating force. The electorate needed to exercise its sovereign rights and pass laws for Federal supervision of transportation. But regulation was not enough to turn a "bad" corporation into a "good" one. The end of discrimination in transportation would stop the unfair advantages which the oil trust enjoyed, and in time would mean its decline and eventual destruction. In achieving the suppression of monopolies, articulate public opinion was to act as the determining force. Ida Tarbell's *History* was directed as much as anything else at stimulating popular distaste for trust methods. This was the ethical side of the struggle. The greatest cost of Standard Oil was to be measured in moral rather than economic terms. America was a commercial nation which gloried in economic productivity. Business achievement justified any means by which it was attained. To get ahead in any way possible had become the highest moral goal. According to this criterion John D. Rockefeller was "the most successful man in the world."

Ida Tarbell felt that this new set of values which she strongly attacked had been in large part the contribution of John D. Rockefeller. In building his great organization, he had spread his own code of business morality among the people. It featured hypocrisy and cynicism through the use of force, bribery, and chicanery. Even his donations to education and religion had helped extend the harm by depriving those forces of their independence and giving an added cloak of respectability to his own activities. The gifts carried with them, she wrote, the Rockefeller message that might made right, which threatened to saturate American life with "commercial Machiavellism."

The dream which lay behind *The History of the Standard Oil Company* was the restoration of competition. In such a world, an ethical and moral regeneration would take place. There would be an increasing scorn of unfair play and a disdainful ostracism of those who used unfair means or sought special privileges. The new creed would take away the automatic mantle of justification from weath and in its place leave the realization that "success won by unfair means is not worth winning."

Although Ida Tarbell wrote about the fight against the street railway magnates in Chicago, lauded Governor Charles Evans Hughes of New York, and expressed an interest in tenement reform, her principal efforts were focused on two subjects: the Standard Oil Company and the tariff. The latter series was not as successful as *The History of the Standard Oil Company,* for she had had no personal knowledge of the subject and wrote what she herself later described as a second-hand study. In detailing the history of tariff legislation in the United States, she was primarily interested in showing that high rates were the result of a coalition between the manufacturers and the politicians. As in the case of Standard Oil, the most important measurement of the tariff was in the individuals it made. The results in both cases were the same: men deficient in self-respect, indifferent to the dignity of Congress, willing to bribe, barter, and juggle the truth. Ethical considerations had been cast out from the world of business, and with their departure had come shoddy goods, the destruction of the instinct of workmanship, and a weakening of the spirit of self-reliance. The tariff was, she feared, destroying the spiritual basis of democracy.

In both of her major works Ida Tarbell evidenced a somewhat limited conception as to what constituted problems of business ethics. Low wages, bad working and living conditions, the exploitation of woman and child labor, poverty, and high prices were evils that ought to be changed. They were not, however, basic problems of morality. That issue, in her view, was concerned with business privilege, poor workmanship, corruption, and the destruction of intellectual and business independence and individual initiative. To the muckrakers further to the left, the economic exploitation of underprivileged groups and classes was essentially a moral problem. It led them to seek substantial and often drastic changes in the organization of society. In separating exploitation and ethics, Ida Tarbell was implicitly limiting the amount and degree of reform that was necessary. The assumption seemed to be that the evils of an inequalitarian society would be corrected by a competitive business world which would restore self-reliance and commercial honesty.

All of the muckraker proponents of competition believed that in the final analysis everything depended on public opinion. In this reliance they did not depart substantially from the views of the other journalists of exposure. Where they did differ was in their conception of the use to which popular sentiment should be put. While the more radical journalists sought to focus it as a force for definite legislative ends and unselfish service devoted to the communal good, the believers in competition had a different understanding. Public opinion was but the total of all of the individual beliefs. Alfred Henry Lewis, Will Irwin, Burton Hendrick, and Ida Tarbell asked only that the people uphold the laws by giving up their subservience to wealth. They believed that the system was sound and that, with various amounts of tinkering, it would continue to work well. (pp. 46-51)

> *David Mark Chalmers, "Competition II: Burton Jesse Hendrick and Ida M. Tarbell," in* The Social and Political Ideas of the Muckrakers, *The Citadel Press, 1964, pp. 42-51.*

Mary E. Tomkins   (essay date 1974)

[*Tomkins is an American educator and critic whose writings reflect her interest in women's studies. In the following conclusion to her critical biography of Tarbell, she discusses the impact of Tarbell's works and evaluates her merits as a propagandist.*]

The annual publication *Paperbound Books in Print* provides an accurate indication of writers' current influence, for only works which appeal to general readers or to teachers, as textbooks for courses, survive the rigorous selection process of public taste. Of Ida Tarbell's many works, two survive in paperback editions: an abridged version of *The History of the Standard Oil Company* and its corollary volume *The Nationalizing of Business, 1878-1898.* Her gentility has become as legendary as the buccaneering activities of the Standard Oil leaders she so successfully assailed. A recent article in *American Heritage,* entitled "The Gentlewoman and the Robber Baron" [see Further Reading], triangulates the situation with a historian's precision. In the article, the author, Virginia V. Hamilton, focuses on Tarbell's interviews with H. H. Rogers of the Standard Oil Company that were conducted while she was gathering material for her history of the company. Tarbell proved to be a formidable antagonist, and her cooptation by the baronial Rogers which cynics had predicted failed to occur. Instead, Hamilton affirms, Tarbell "presented a remarkably truthful picture of the rise of Standard Oil."

The historic encounter between Ida Tarbell and the forces represented by the Standard Oil Company lives on in the public's memory; but all the other productions of her variegated career are forgotten—biographies which once were best sellers, studies of twentieth-century industry and industrial leaders, explorations of the role of women in industrial society, many uncollected articles, and her autobiography. The reason is that only the issues she raised in *The History of the Standard Oil Company* have continued to be of vital ongoing concern for the nation. The rest is history.

Tarbell generated one enduring American myth and ratified two others. The first is the myth of Lincoln's frontier greatness; the second, that of the business leader selflessly dedicated to public service; the third, that of his female counterpart, the housewife, devoting herself to the rearing of young democratic America. It is not surprising that the turbulent 1890's gave rise to two complementary hypotheses concerning the role of the frontier in the shaping of American society—that of Frederick Jackson Turner, who postulated that frontier experience had impressed itself on the American character and formed American democracy; and that of Ida Tarbell, that Lincoln's frontier background was the cause of his greatness and the salvation of American democracy. While both hypotheses have been modified by later researchers, neither has been discarded.

Serious commentators on American society usually have an inner vision of it which gives direction to their work. Tarbell had such a vision, and it was gradually articulated in the assignments she received as a writer for *McClure's* and for *The American*—seemingly random assignments which she wove together into her version of the perennially elusive American Dream. Before starting work on her biography of Lincoln, Tarbell had purged herself of lingering notions about the efficacy of revolution and feminism as vehicles of social progress. She had begun her research into the activities of Madame Roland with the expectation that she would find that Madame Roland had played a moderating, pacific part during the Revolution. Instead, the Frenchwoman, driven by the demons of "a politician with a Providence complex," had been an early instigator of the violence which eventually led to her own execution. A heavier blow had been Tarbell's disillusionment with revolution itself, for she discovered that revolution, far from being a "divine weapon" for rooting out evil and replacing it with justice, was a cyclonic destroyer which had left in its wake "the same relative proportion of good and evil as it had started with." This generalization, which resulted from her study of the French Revolution and its consequences, was verified by her personal observation of revolutionary activities from the windows of her Paris apartment in the early 1890's. The skirmishes she observed between the revolutionary activists and the military forces which quelled them seemed like stylized memorials of 1789. Likewise, her study of Napoleon convinced her

that the European political system had tragically misled him into seeking power for himself rather than social reforms for the people.

In Lincoln she found the touchstone for democracy. Then, in her next assignment for *McClure's,* she discovered in Napoleonic John D. Rockefeller a foil for Lincoln, for the magnate's revolutionary business methods represented a threat to the American way of life established by Abraham Lincoln. Rockefeller, she felt, presented an anomaly in the normal evolution of the United States, one caused by unbridled greed and justified by a hypocrisy which spread corruption throughout the nation. To counter the threat, she proposed government regulation rather than the radical solution of Socialism, then very commonly advocated by utopian and Marxist Socialists.

Tarbell's series about the tariff written for *The American Magazine* continued her attack on big businessmen and their political henchmen. *The Tariff in Our Times* was soon followed by the Supreme Court decision dissolving the Standard Oil Company. Never after that did Tarbell attack business; instead, she began to report its positive contributions to the welfare of society. She seized upon use of the Taylor efficiency techniques in industrial concerns as evidence of a cooperative spirit becoming manifest among businessmen that had converted them from "robber barons" to "industrial statesmen." Despite labor's insistence that the Taylor efficiency methods were in reality a subterfuge for production speed-ups and were therefore exploitative of factory workers, Tarbell remained convinced that the Taylor methods, if applied in the spirit of the Golden Rule by both management and labor, could lead to a democratic capitalism in the Lincolnian tradition.

In her biography of Elbert H. Gary she divined in the leader of the United States Steel Corporation an evolutionary force in the progress of business toward social responsibility. And in her biography of Owen D. Young she had found him to be the ideal business leader who not only built a great industry but also devoted many years to distinguished public service. As a writer and reformer, Tarbell had been signally influential in bringing about fundamental reforms in the relationship of business and government. This tremendous achievement quite naturally remained for her a high water mark in the fight for social justice. Nor is it remarkable that her faith in the sanction of government regulation of business should be reinforced by increased awareness among businessmen of their responsibility to the public.

David M. Chalmers notes [in *Notable American Women, 1607-1950*] concerning Tarbell's changed attitude toward business in her later works that "common to all these works was the belief that a sense of social responsibility was spontaneously developing within the American business community." In the midst of the Depression in the 1930's, she continued to rely on the good faith of industrialists as the surest guarantee of justice for their workers. Dismayed by the rise of powerful and militant labor organizations like the Congress of Industrial Organizations, she maintained, concerning Owen D. Young: "I still believe that if we could have had him active in these past years so disheartening for peaceful industrial relations, the years which have set back so far the hope of genuine understanding cooperation within industry, we should have been saved the peck of trouble we are now in."

Tarbell exerted great influence upon American women through communications media, including the radio; for she had long been regarded by the press and public relations people as a sort of semiofficial spokeswoman for her sex. She was highly regarded by other women writers and artists and was for over thirty years president of the Pen and Brush Club, organized by her and other professionals in those fields. But she sincerely believed that most women are the intellectual and emotional inferiors of men. She advised women to remain at home, noting wryly that women's suffrage had not changed politics perceptibly. The average woman would be better off, she thought, learning how to run her household with factory efficiency, leaving conduct of other than local affairs to men. Despite public distrust of politicians, the refusal of organized labor to take seriously her recipe for peaceful industrial relations, and the rejection of her conservative stand on women's rights by militant feminists, there is little doubt that a Gallup poll would confirm that public attitudes concerning the role of Abraham Lincoln in shaping the course of American democracy, those regarding the benevolence of business, or attitudes toward the status of women, remain substantially the same as Ida Tarbell's. A quick survey of Lincoln's Birthday speeches, of corporate publicity, of advertisements aimed at the female consumer will convince most persons of that possibility.

As her reverence for Lincoln deepened, Tarbell seemed to forget the implications of the conversation between him and his younger colleague Ralph Emerson which took place when both were lawyers in Illinois. Lincoln had replied to Emerson's blunt query about the compatibility of the practice of law and of the Golden Rule with a long pause followed by a change of subject. Satisfied that he had an answer, Emerson had quit practice; Lincoln had not done so; and he had soon after returned to the morally ambiguous arena of politics. Few persons can cope with the burdens of darkness, despair, and guilt under which Lincoln often staggered. Tarbell shunned uncertainty and avoided spiritual and emotional depths in her writing; she also disliked introspection, as she admitted in the short-lived journal she started to write after her father died. The Golden Rule seemed to exert upon her an almost tropic attraction; it dazzled her with its apparent attainability. To Lincoln, on the other hand, the ancient axiom must often have seemed as unattainable as a star seen from the bottom of a well.

Yet her temperament aided Tarbell to become a reform-minded journalist; she lived close to the surface of events and thus was encouraged to espouse persuasive, facile solutions for their dislocations: new laws would reform business; a Christian outlook would reform businessmen; labor would best be served by trusting management; women, by trusting everyone—but themselves. The paternalistic society she envisioned under the benevolent alliance of government and business did not allow for competing interest groups. Tarbell's pursuit of harmony led to some debatable conclusions and she seemed at times to confuse paternalism and democracy.

The economist John Kenneth Galbraith recently updated Thorstein Veblen's dictum in *The Theory of the Leisure Class:* " 'According to the ideal scheme of the pecuniary culture, the lady of the house is the head menial of the household'." According to Galbraith, Veblen's observation, made in 1899, applies as well to American society almost three-quarters of a century later. Tarbell sentimentally maintained that women's love for their families removed any aura of meniality from their lives, but her easy dismissal of them to an endless round of small tasks and small talk amounts to much the same thing, an acceptance of the idea of women as servants. While Galbraith retains the objectivity proper for an economist, it is clear in his article that he does not accept that idea; he maintains that the economy of the United States is dependent on the exploitation of women's labor in their homes, and he argues that passage of the Equal Rights Amendment is a necessary first step toward their "emancipation." He views marriage in its present state as "a comprehensive trap" for wives. He concedes that "a tolerant society should not think ill of a woman who finds contentment in sexual intercourse, child-bearing, child-rearing, personal adornment, and administration of consumption." He insists, on the other hand, that a tolerant society also "should certainly think ill of a society that offers no alternative—and which ascribes virtue to what is really the convenience of the producers of goods."

Galbraith foresees, not disruption, but a more humane society resulting from a wider choice of life-styles for women. He denies the convention, which was upheld by Tarbell, of frowning on outlets for women that might conflict with "good household management" and observes that a married woman "may serve on a local library board or on a committee to consider delinquency among the young. She may not, without reproach, have full-time employment or a demanding avocation. To do so is to have it said she is neglecting her home and family, that is, her *real* work." Tarbell would have subscribed to Galbraith's statement of the situation but have considered his ironic tone frivolous. In her estimation, motherhood was the great emancipator of women. Tarbell's espousal of a democracy based upon the household drudgery of half the population seems closely analagous to the ancient Greeks' acceptance of an Athenian democracy based on slave labor.

It could appear that Tarbell's underlying aim during the height of her influence as a journalist was to promote the interests of her own group, the white, Anglo-Saxon, Protestant middle class that was fearful of a feudal take-over by the new industrialists on one hand and of ethnic obliteration by immigrant hordes on the other. But such a view of Tarbell's intent is an oversimplification. Instead, her essentially Chautauquan vision was of an industrialized America that retained, while renewing, the institutions of the pre–Civil War era into which she had been born. Never did she advocate the imposition of these institutions or the values which helped create them, for it never seriously occurred to her to question that they were the culmination of Western civilization—Eastern civilization had only colonial status in those days, and an African one was thought to be nonexistent. The vision implicit in Tarbell's work was compounded of nostalgia for the past and a plan for a future that was to be organically evolved from it; and the vision revealed her belief in a human nature sufficiently perfectible to base actions as well as prayers on the Golden Rule. Thus would come into being a social order that would be assuredly the product of much sweat, but of no blood and few tears.

It is not difficult to understand the appeal for her and thousands like her of Mussolini's Italy of the 1920's, for he too beckoned the future from the past. In Tarbell's words, he found in Fascism

> the genius of a race reborn, the Latin tradition always at work . . . the return of the Roman idea of the State and to the faith of Christ. It is the union of the great past to a luminous future. Fascism is the cult of spiritual values as opposed to the cult of the belly, which is the only god which Socialists, Anarchists, and Communists recognize. Fascism is the liberty of the Italian people, replacing the frightful license of individuals, groups, parties; it is the triumph of work, order, discipline.

Similarly, Tarbell yearned for a future formed from the democratic past. That her projected paradise would inevitably be ethnocentric and elitist she would sincerely have denied because of her zeal for this best of all possible worlds. Such zeal, however, easily becomes subject to abstraction, loses sight of individuals, and manipulates groups into positions which please the planner, and thus becomes fatally solipsistic. Tarbell's ideal society, however real it seemed to her, is reminiscent of the toylike model communities erected by architects and urban planners. The multicultural pressures of the ethnically pluralistic American society which have become evident in recent times were at work even as she formulated her vision which was tidily contained behind a white picket fence straight out of early nineteenth-century New England.

Like all great propagandists, Tarbell prepared the ground in *The History of the Standard Oil Company* before planting seeds which could flower into reform legislation; for she was aware that there has to be some correlation between law and custom. Perhaps her great miscalculation at the height of her career was her too optimistic assumption that such a correlation was present between the Golden Rule and custom. Later, when she no longer echoed as a journalist the desires and aspirations of middle America and when she had become in the 1930's a reminder of the American past, her philosophy had become less sentimental, more stoic, more austerely pragmatic: "The time, the place, the need, the relation are what determine the value of an act." To embody nobly and without bitterness such a creed was Ida Tarbell's final achievement. But her earlier optimism, tempered in a disordered world she had never anticipated, sustained to the end her faith in the ultimate rationality of mankind as a source of order and her conviction that "work . . . backed up by such a faith makes life endurable."

Few journalists or historians have made history; journalists report daily events and historians interpret them. But Tarbell joins the select company of propagandists like Thomas Paine and Harriet Beecher Stowe whose works were like bugle calls to battle. Paine's *Common Sense* and the American Revolution are inseparable; Abraham Lincoln referred to Stowe only half-facetiously as the little lady whose book, *Uncle Tom's Cabin,* caused the Civil War; Tarbell is remembered as the journalist who bested the robber barons in a fair fight and scotched the reptilian principle of special privilege that they had attempted to substitute for the historic American principle of equal opportunity. All three writers unlocked the reservoirs of moral energy needed in times of grave national crisis when national identity was at stake and with it, seemingly, survival.

Tarbell cannot be termed a great writer, for too little of her work has endured. Her equipment as a writer was modest, but she used it well. She often achieved the sort of lucidity in her prose which paradoxically conceals beneath its very transparency the intelligence and the workmanship that make it possible. She had no aptitude for fiction, as her one novel, *The Rising of the Tide,* clearly demonstrates. She possessed a flair for illumination of character through anecdotes which enlivened her works. She also possessed steadiness, integrity, and moral courage, and it was these qualities rather than technical brilliance which lent distinction to her writing. Only in *The History of the Standard Oil Company* did intense moral outrage succeed in lifting her style from pedestrian competence to inspired lightning-bolt paragraphs and cliff-hanger chapter endings. Her main contributions as a writer were those of a pioneer, for she carried out the pioneer spirit of her ancestors in all her undertakings. She was among the first of the emancipated New Women to attend college, and she subsequently became among the foremost of the new journalists who are remembered as Muckrakers. In addition, she was a seminal pioneer in the writing of business history and in Lincoln studies. The body of her work stands as a memorial to a great journalist who initiated a tradition of responsible journalism which has continued to serve the nation well during succeeding times of national crisis.

The History of the Standard Oil Company is a particularly relevant cautionary tale at the present time, when the relationship of business and government seems once again to many observers to be working against the public interest. The morality which underlies Tarbell's historic work seems today somewhat old-fashioned in its expression and naïve in its expectations. But perhaps it is not overoptimistic to state that the same moral idealism is operational in the United States of the 1970's; were this not so, Tarbell's great work would be forgotten entirely. Instead, since her death in 1944, she has remained in the national awareness as a subliminal conscience warning Americans against their cardinal sin of materialism. Her one great work, *The History of the Standard Oil Company,* remains a timeless philippic that denounces the American Sin. She posed in it a question not yet resolved: Can democracy and corporate capitalism coexist? (pp. 151-59)

> *Mary E. Tomkins, in her* Ida M. Tarbell,
> *Twayne Publishers, Inc., 1974, 182 p.*

Robert Stinson   (essay date 1977)

[*Stinson is an American historian who specializes in American history after 1865, as well as in the history of American journalism and historical writing. In the following excerpt, he investigates Tarbell's antifeminist leanings.*]

It was more than a matter of passing curiosity . . . when, just a few years after the triumphant publication of her attack on Standard Oil—a symbol of her success in a kind of journalism well beyond the "woman's page" assignments reserved for her sex—Ida Tarbell began to emerge as a forceful defender of the nineteenth-century image of women and their social role. [Though she never married] she did tell other women to retire into marriage and spent a large part of her working time from about 1909 onward writing articles, books, and even a briefly popular novel urging women to recover their "female nature," refrain from direct participation in political affairs, and embrace their true role as wives, mothers, and homemakers.

Some people were glad for her seeming conversion, like Edward Bok, who offered her $250 for an article he wanted to place in the *Ladies Home Journal*'s antifeminist campaign to be titled **"If I Were a Man: How I Would View the Modern Feminine Tendencies."** She was the only woman he knew, he assured her, who could give the "straight-from-the-shoulder, direct talk that a man likes." But others were surprised at Tarbell's apparent defection. Suffragists were upset to see her name cited in antisuffrage literature and were dismayed when she, a successful, emancipated woman, accepted speaking engagements with local antisuffrage societies. Even John S. Phillips, the quiet-spoken editor of the *American Magazine,* which she and other former staff members of *McClure's* took over when they left S. S. McClure in 1906, was so disappointed at the illiberalism and apparent inconsistency of her views that he asked for a detailed justification and defense of them. Helen Keller reportedly said Tarbell was getting old.

Tarbell's "conversion" is still puzzling. Why did she change her mind? Or did she? Perhaps the answers can be found in two separate approaches, both of which involve larger biographical problems. One has to do with a resentment Tarbell may have felt in mid-life at having been pushed earlier into a professional career which had made domestic life impossible. The other approach is to understand the conflict between her own life of personal independence and her preaching of domesticity for others as a latent manifestation of an old ambiguity in her mind regarding women's social role—an ambiguity which can be traced far back into her childhood. Both approaches require examination, but neither is comprehensible without a preliminary analysis of the seemingly new antifeminist stance which shocked the feminists of her time.

Her antifeminist views emerged first in a series of articles Tarbell wrote for the *American Magazine* starting in 1909, but their fullest expression came in a second series begun in 1912 and later published in book form under the title *The Business of Being a Woman.* A sense of smug self-righteousness pervaded the second series, but the articles were far from polemical. What she intended was a gentle corrective to current feminist rhetoric on the equality of the sexes and especially to what she saw as a mood of unhealthy self-discussion among women about their role in society. To use her own phrase, she was directing her counsel to "The Uneasy Woman." Tarbell's corrective was the more urgent, she thought, because the "ferment of mind" she observed in individual women could spread to the families which depended on them for security, and from there it could infect the society itself. But uneasy women could regain their calm if they realized the truth of two propositions: first, that men and women possessed wholly different natures which fit them for separate social roles and made them unfit for sharing each other's work; and second, that the societal implications of women's natural work in the home were far broader than most women who were dissatisfied with that role might see. The business of being a woman was women's business alone and was satisfying only to the extent that women understood its transcendent importance.

The female nature revealed itself early in two tendencies parents everywhere observed in little girls: a craving for pretty dresses and for dolls. No one could teach a child to embrace these interests—or, for that matter, not to—because they were natural impulses and appeared or not depending only upon whether the child were a girl or a boy. They were, in a sense, teachers themselves, for, as Tarbell put it, when a girl finds herself playing with dresses and dolls, "Nature is telling her what her work in the world is to be." Correctly interpreted, then, the childhood interest in dresses was the first sign that the mature woman must take an intensely personal view of the world, manifested first in self-ornamentation but characterized later by a tendency to discuss all subjects in personal terms and a corresponding inability to understand society's affairs from a broader, more objective point of view. Interest in dolls, of course, indicated a mothering instinct. "The central fact of the woman's life—Nature's reason for her—," wrote Tarbell, "is the child, his bearing and rearing." Women's nature continued to reveal itself through the maturing process so that by the time a woman came of age she had added two new traits: a natural conservatism, useful in her adult role as guarantor of social continuity, and reliance upon intuition as opposed to reasoning.

Any woman's attempt to change these patterns would be at best futile and at worst a dangerous and unsettling violation of her nature. When Susan B. Anthony, for example, added dress reform to her campaign for woman suffrage in the 1870s and began wearing the functional dress designed by Amelia Bloomer, she met unexpectedly sharp ridicule and finally abandoned the Bloomer dress. Tarbell recounted the incident but observed with a smile that public reaction was less important in Anthony's return to prettier dresses than something more fundamental: "she met her woman's soul, and did not know it!"

More serious and more dangerous than the matter of dress was the fact that militant feminists were actively encouraging women to abandon what they claimed were the too narrow confines of the home and to seek equality in business, politics, and public affairs. Here were violations of the female nature which could not but bring unhappiness to the woman who followed the feminists' advice and disruption to the society which allowed it. Tarbell admitted that between the husband and the wife society always allowed the man "wider sweep, more interests outside of their immediate alliance," but she saw nothing arbitrary in this arrangement. If men led in business and politics it was in their nature to do so. Their more rational cast of mind, their objectivity, were masculine traits which, unavailable to women, enabled men to be more at ease in the exercise of public power. That was why there were many good women in business and the professions but never any great ones. Whether it be merchandising, manufacturing, or even Tarbell's own profession, editing, there were no women daring enough, adventurous enough, free enough from personal prejudice to succeed as well as a man. Competition in these fields came easy for men and was conducted with an intensity welcomed by the male nature, but women could compete with men in a man's world only by arming themselves with unnatural hardness, losing their affective qualities, and finally crippling their natures. A few good women survived in business and public affairs, but they were at once successful and repellent. Surely the most tragic figure of all, thought Tarbell, was the militant feminist herself: the once-attractive and now crippled woman whose nature has been destroyed by her very fight—in public—for equality.

Women would never have thought of crossing the line into the masculine world, Tarbell thought, if the feminists had not pushed them to the edge. The modern crisis of the "uneasy women" really began decades earlier in 1848 when about 300 men and women gathered at Seneca Falls, New York, under the leadership of Elizabeth Cady Stanton and Lucretia Mott for what they announced as the first Woman's Rights Convention. There on July 19, 1848, the feminists adopted by unanimous vote a "Declaration of Sentiments and Resolutions" which they modeled in language and philosophy after Thomas Jefferson's Declaration of Independence. Arguing that the "laws of nature and Nature's God" entitled women to "inalienable rights" which men had long withheld, the Seneca Falls convention did not distinguish between a male and female nature but argued for equality on the basis of women's humanity and a universal nature.

Tarbell claimed that that was where the problem lay. She countered that the relationship of men and women was not one of a superior to an inferior which, because it was created by men could be adjusted by women, but rather was a relationship between different, complementary, and unchanging natures. What the Seneca Falls "Declaration" really proposed, she said, was the imitation of men in all things—an impossible project. "If a woman's temperamental and intellectual operations were identical with a man's," she wrote, "then there would be hope of success, but they are not." The continuing assumption that they were identical was one of the things spreading unease through American society.

Another thing was women's failure to realize the full societal implications of their natural homemaking role. Women looked fretfully outward from their families only because they failed to see the richness of their work and the subtle influence it had upon the rest of society. They must certainly respect the limitations of their nature, but they must understand its broad possibilities as well. The fundamental point was that a woman was not just the manager of a household; she was nothing less than the had of a "social laboratory." She had in her care the preparation of the ideas and tools for shaping society itself. Because a woman handled the financial expenditures of her family she could, as a consumer, determine and reform what went on in the marketplace. Because she was the educator of her sons as to the value and meaning of democracy, she could influence national politics in ways more fundamental than mere voting and officeholding.

In the years following the 1912 publication of *The Business of Being a Woman* Tarbell may have gone through a period of working out in her own life some of the ideas she had put together. She would never abandon her increasingly public position in journalism, of course, and in that sense never practiced what she preached, but she did seem to exercise a personal restraint which may have indicated a desire to draw limitations and definitions for her career. She revealed this attitude by her response to two invitations President Woodrow Wilson offered her to enter government service. In 1916 he asked her to take a place on his new Tariff Commission, partly because as a champion of low tariffs he was impressed by the advocacy of downward revision in her book *The Tariff in Our Times* (1911), and also because Wilson was a moderate backer of woman suffrage and wanted to boost a woman to a prominent position in government as a way of demonstrating the abilities of women generally. But she refused to accept, and though Jane Addams pleaded with her to change her mind, Tarbell feared that her ineffective service would embarrass Wilson and disprove his point.

A few months later, just after Congress declared war on Germany, Wilson telegraphed an invitation to her to serve on the Woman's Committee of the Council of National Defense, and this time she accepted. Her work on the Committee was congenial and fitted Tarbell's ideas on the place of women in the home. It encouraged women to avoid wastage of food as their special contribution to the war effort by counseling them on canning and drying vegetables—the Committee giving over a whole morning, for example, to "reminiscences of helping grandmother string apples for drying, of the way mother dried corn and berries"—but it also did what it could to protect women in their temporary and unaccustomed role as war industry workers, and even designed and distributed a black velvet arm band for Gold Star Mothers.

Another wartime project defined her attitudes toward women further. In the spring of 1919 she published a novel, *The Rising of the Tide,* in which she attempted to characterize the effect of the war on the American homefront. Reviewers liked it only because of its message of firm support for the war effort itself, but its plot was a crudely constructed bundle of clichés. Yet her women characters are interesting. Some are long-suffering mothers who sustain with nobility the loss of sons in France; others are young girls who drive prostitutes from the community by providing a homelike canteen for lonely soldiers encamped nearby. One reviewer noted that the lead characters all seemed borrowed from the pages of popular magazines [see excerpt dated 1919]. Patsy McCullen and Nancy Cowder, the two young heroines, were much like the wholesome, strong girls who inhabited stories in the *Ladies Home Journal* and *Harper's Bazaar.* What is most interesting about Patsy and Nancy, however, is that each undergoes a character transformation. They begin the story as independent, daring country girls (Nancy is "a big strapping girl with a stride like a man's"), and it is through their work as relief workers in wartime Belgium and the Balkans that their community back home comes to understand the meaning of the Allied cause. But in the final pages each gives up her strenuous public life in preference to the quiet certainties of marriage and the family. Tarbell the novelist was underscoring what Tarbell the journalist had already set out as the proper sphere for women.

In the 1920s Tarbell's disinclination to broaden her concept of women's role in society softened only a little. Her thoughts about the woman suffrage amendment and its immediate results were an example. She had never believed that women, with the vote, would be any more capable of improving the world than men and had made a restrained opposition to the Nineteenth Amendment. For her, the question had to be framed not in terms of the emancipation of women, but on the basis of what social or political result would come of women voting. In the 1920s, perhaps because she had defined the issue so narrowly, Tarbell became ambivalent. An article in 1924 posed the question **"Is Woman's Suffrage a Failure?",** and she said it was a failure in the sense that the revolution in public affairs predicted by many suffragists had not happened, for women voters seemed as conservative and regular as men. But it was a success in that having to vote made women more conscious than they could have been before of public issues like labor conditions, the crime wave, or Teapot Dome. Elsewhere, she even challenged women to use their education and their votes to "save civilization," without, however, explaining how. Then, by 1930, she was stressing the failures again and seemed not to have changed her views at all.

All of this, from her first articles in 1909 through *The Business of Being a Woman* to her observations on woman suffrage, seemed a departure from her earlier thoughts and career. She was spending almost as much time writing on the woman question after 1909 as she was on business, and this shift is what surprised friends and feminists alike. Why did she change? David Chalmers has suggested [in *Notable American Women, 1607-1950*] that in middle life Tarbell began to regret her decision years before not to marry and raise a family. Frances Willard and other feminist leaders were occasional visitors in her home in the 1870s, and the young Ida listened to a great deal of talk about women's rights. Education and self-sufficiency seemed more important to her than marriage, but by the time she reached the age of fifty she may have begun to regret her decision and perhaps even resent the feminist influence which once made it seem wise. In some ways *The Business of Being a Woman,* with its praise of motherhood and the home and its sharp critique of feminism, is a poignantly personal book. She seemed, for example, to be re-

calling a personal experience when, in the midst of a general discussion of the women's rights movement, she wrote: "There were girls in the early days of the movement, as there no doubt are today, who prayed on their knees that they might escape the frightful isolation of marriage, might be free to 'live' and to 'work,' to 'know' and to 'do.' What it was really all about they never knew until it was too late." It was not "girls" she was thinking of here so much as it was one girl: herself at the age of fourteen, kneeling, as she would describe it later in her autobiography, to beg for the same deliverance, but sensing now, while writing **The Business of Being a Woman,** that it was, indeed, too late.

By taking, for the first time in her life, a *public* stand on this issue, Tarbell may have been seeking a way to manage a dilemma which plagued many of her contemporaries in various ways. People at all times feel the tension generated by the conflict between innovation and tradition. The Progressive Era was no exception. David Noble has shown [in *The Paradox of Progressive Thought*] that many Progressive theorists could not wholly reject the past, with the result that their works reflected a tension—a "paradox"—between the old and new. Reform novelists, too, like Frank Norris, Theodore Dreiser, and Winston Churchill betrayed similar unease as they discovered their inability to free themselves from traditional social attitudes, and even Tarbell's friend and fellow muckraker, Ray Stannard Baker, suffered a split in his private and public personality as he wrote journalism which faced critically and realistically the growing pains of urban-industrial America and, at the same time, published fiction which longed for an idyllic rural past.

Some women intellectuals found themselves caught in a special tension of their own. Many of them had grown up in middle-class families and learned reverence for the home setting as a primary lesson of their upbringing. At the same time, women like Margaret Sanger, Jane Addams, Charlotte Perkins Gilman, and Inez Haynes Gilmore grew restless at the thought of accepting the traditional role assigned to their sex and began to reach out for an independent personal fulfillment in the outside world. Then, having created a place for themselves as professionals, they were beset with feelings of alienation—a sense of severance from the old role and a sense of incomplete acceptance in the new. The journalist Inez Haynes Gilmore expressed the tension of many other women intellectuals when she wrote a "confession" for *Harper's Bazaar* in 1912:

> It seems to me that sociologically, so to speak, I hang in the void midway between two spheres—the man's sphere and the woman's sphere. A professional career . . . puts me beyond the reach of the average woman's duties and pleasures. The conventional limitations of the female lot put me beyond the reach of the average man's duties and pleasures.

Many of the women who felt this conflict tried to resolve it by moving further in the direction of feminism. Tarbell, experiencing a similar conflict and facing an aggressive public renaissance of the women's rights movement, may have tried to cope with it by maintaining her independent professional life while rejecting the feminist ideas which had led her to become a professional in the first place. She used her skill and popularity as a writer to extol the virtues of a life she thought she might have liked and from which she had become personally divorced. (pp. 218-28)

[She] began to speak out against feminism in a way that repelled many people who thought they knew her and made **The Business of Being a Woman** seem to be a denial of her own new career. What had really happened was not that she had embraced a new set of principles but rather that, with her career on one side and thoughts of family life on the other, she was just living out a new phase of an old ambiguity, a familiar tension. She had experienced doubt concerning women's role in society before, and what was new was not Tarbell's conversion to the nineteenth-century idea of women and the home but a fresh articulation, a *public* statement of those views with which she had lived in uneasy tension for thirty-five years. One can perhaps speculate that her life and her writing after 1909 represented only the hardening of a dichotomy: she would urge the uneasy woman to be faithful to her female nature while she personally followed other instincts toward liberation. . . .

Tarbell, living in the world of complex reality, was caught in a conflict between independence and marriage. She could manage the conflict, perhaps, but she could not resolve it. (p. 239)

> *Robert Stinson, "Ida M. Tarbell and the Ambiguities of Feminism," in* The Pennsylvania Magazine of History and Biography, *Vol. CI, No. 1, January, 1977, pp. 217-39.*

FURTHER READING

Bourne, Randolph S. Review of *New Ideals in Business,* by Ida M. Tarbell. *The Dial* LXII, No. 733 (11 January 1917): 133-34.
> Derides *New Ideals in Business* and labels Tarbell "an intellectual darkener of counsel rather than a bringer of light."

Brady, Kathleen. *Ida Tarbell: Portrait of a Muckraker.* New York: Seaview/Putnam, 1984, 286 p.
> Biography of Tarbell that relates "how [she] handled the human dilemma of daring great things, despite galling limitations, and succeeded admirably."

Downs, Robert B. "Birth of an Octopus: Ida M. Tarbell's *The History of the Standard Oil Company,* 1904." In his *Famous American Books,* pp. 227-33. New York: McGraw-Hill Book Co., 1971.
> Describes the content and influence of *The History of the Standard Oil Company.*

Hamilton, Virginia Van Der Veer. "The Gentlewoman and the Robber Baron." *American Heritage* XXI, No. 3 (April 1970): 78-86.
> Focuses on an encounter between Tarbell and John D. Rockefeller.

Kelly, Florence Finch. "A Group of American Biographies." *The Bookman* XLVI, No. 3 (November 1917): 325-30.
> Reviews *The Life of Abraham Lincoln,* praising Tarbell for relating Lincoln's life "to the essential principles of our national scheme."

Keyes, Helen Johnson. "Historian-Interpreter of Life and Lives." In *Careers in the Making: Readings in Recent Biography with Studies in Vocational Guidance,* edited by Iona M. R. Logie, pp. 3-14. New York: Harper and Brothers, 1935.
> Recounts an interview in which Tarbell discussed her career and philosophy.

McClure, S. S. *My Autobiography.* New York: Frederick A. Stokes Co., 1914, 266 p.
> Praises Tarbell for her work on *The History of the Standard Oil Company.* McClure writes, "When she wrote this *History of the Standard Oil Company* she was probably the greatest living expert on that subject."

Miller, Ernest C. "Ida Tarbell's Second Look at Standard Oil." *The Western Pennsylvania Historical Magazine* 39, No. 4 (Winter 1956): 223-41.
> Biographical sketch of Tarbell focusing on her interest in the oil industry.

Montague, Gilbert Holland. "The Legend of the Standard Oil Company." *The North American Review* CLXXXI, No. 3 (September 1905): 352-68.
> Questions Tarbell's data and conclusions about the Standard Oil Company.

Review of *The Life of Abraham Lincoln,* by Ida M. Tarbell. *The Nation* 70, No. 1809 (1 March 1900): 164.
> Praises Tarbell for her skillful presentation of Lincoln's life.

Newins, Allan. "Rockefeller vs. Public Opinion." In his *John D. Rockefeller: The Heroic Age of American Enterprise,* Vol. II, pp. 499-533. New York: Charles Scribner's Sons, 1941.
> Contains references to Tarbell and *The History of the Standard Oil Company.* Newins writes, "Rockefeller had overthrown the men of the Oil Regions; but in Ida M. Tarbell the Regions found a literary champion who gave them an enduring revenge."

Robinson, L. E. "Lincoln in Biography and Letters." *The Dial* LXIV (14 February 1918): 148-51.
> Praises *The Life of Abraham Lincoln* for its scholarship and comprehensiveness.

Twentieth-Century
Literary Criticism

Cumulative Indexes
Volumes 1-40

This Index Includes References to Entries in These Gale Series

Contemporary Literary Criticism presents excerpts of criticism on the works of novelists, poets, dramatists, short story writers, scriptwriters, and other creative writers who are now living or who have died since 1960. Cumulative indexes to authors and nationalities are included, as well as an index to titles discussed in the individual volume.

Twentieth-Century Literary Criticism contains critical excerpts by the most significant commentators on poets, novelists, short story writers, dramatists, and philosophers who died between 1900 and 1960. Indexes to authors, nationalities, and titles discussed are included in each new volume.

Nineteenth-Century Literature Criticism offers significant passages from criticism on authors who died between 1800 and 1899. Indexes to authors, nationalities, and titles discussed are included in each new volume.

Literature Criticism from 1400 to 1800 compiles significant passages from the most noteworthy criticism on authors of the fifteenth through the eighteenth centuries. Cumulative indexes to authors, nationalities, and titles discussed are included in each new volume.

Classical and Medieval Literature Criticism offers excerpts of criticism on the works of world authors from classical antiquity through the fourteenth century. Cumulative indexes to authors, titles and critics are included in each volume.

Short Story Criticism combines excerpts of criticism on short fiction by writers of all eras and nationalities. Cumulative indexes to authors, nationalities, and titles discussed are included in each new volume.

Poetry Criticism presents excerpts of criticism on the works of poets from all eras, movements, and nationalities.

Children's Literature Review includes excerpts from reviews, criticism, and commentary on works of authors and illustrators who create books for children. Cumulative indexes to authors, nationalities, and titles discussed are included in each new volume.

Contemporary Authors Series encompasses five related series. *Contemporary Authors* provides biographical and bibliographical information on more than 92,000 writers of fiction, nonfiction, poetry, journalism, drama, film, and other related fields. Each new volume contains sketches on authors not previously covered in the series. *Contemporary Authors New Revision Series* provides completely updated information on active authors covered in previously published volumes of *CA*. Only entries requiring significant change are revised for *CA New Revision Series*. *Contemporary Authors Permanent Series* consists of updated listings for deceased and inactive authors removed from the original volumes 9-36 when those volumes were revised. *Contemporary Authors Autobiography Series* presents specially commissioned autobiographies by leading contemporary writers. *Contemporary Authors Bibliographical Series* contains primary and secondary bibliographies as well as analytical bibliographical essays by authorities on major modern authors.

Dictionary of Literary Biography encompasses three related series. *Dictionary of Literary Biography* furnishes illustrated overviews of authors' lives and works and places them in the larger perspective of literary history. *Dictionary of Literary Biography Documentary Series* illuminates the careers of major figures through a selection of literary documents, including letters, notebook and diary entries, interviews, book reviews, and photographs. *Dictionary of Literary Biography Yearbook* summarizes the past year's literary activity with articles on genres, major prizes, conferences, and other timely subjects and includes updated and new entries on individual authors. A cumulative index to authors and articles is included in each new volume. *Concise Dictionary of Literary Biography,* a six-volume series, collects revised and updated sketches on major American authors that were originally presented in *Dictionary of Literary Biography.*

Something about the Author Series encompasses three related series. *Something about the Author* contains heavily illustrated biographical sketches on authors and illustrators of juvenile and young adult literature from all eras. *Something about the Author Autobiography Series* presents specially commissioned autobiographies by prominent authors and illustrators of books for children and young adults. *Authors and Artists for Young Adults* provides high school and junior high school students with profiles of their favorite creative artists in the media of print, film, television, drama, song lyrics, and cartoons.

Yesterday's Authors of Books for Children contains heavily illustrated entries on children's writers who died before 1961. Complete in two volumes.

Literary Criticism Series
Cumulative Author Index

This index lists all author entries in the Gale Literary Criticism Series and includes cross-references to other Gale sources. References in the index are identified as follows:

AAYA: *Authors & Artists for Young Adults,* Volumes 1-3
CAAS: *Contemporary Authors Autobiography Series,* Volumes 1-11
CA: *Contemporary Authors* (original series), Volumes 1-131
CABS: *Contemporary Authors Bibliographical Series,* Volumes 1-3
CANR: *Contemporary Authors New Revision Series,* Volumes 1-31
CAP: *Contemporary Authors Permanent Series,* Volumes 1-2
CA-R: *Contemporary Authors* (revised editions), Volumes 1-44
CDALB: *Concise Dictionary of American Literary Biography,* Volumes 1-6
CLC: *Contemporary Literary Criticism,* Volumes 1-1-63
CLR: *Children's Literature Review,* Volumes 1-23
CMLC: *Classical and Medieval Literature Criticism,* Volumes 1-6
DC: *Drama Criticism,* Volume 1
DLB: *Dictionary of Literary Biography,* Volumes 1-101
DLB-DS: *Dictionary of Literary Biography Documentary Series,* Volumes 1-7
DLB-Y: *Dictionary of Literary Biography Yearbook,* Volumes 1980-1988
LC: *Literature Criticism from 1400 to 1800,* Volumes 1-15
NCLC: *Nineteenth-Century Literature Criticism,* Volumes 1-30
PC: *Poetry Criticism,* Volume 1
SAAS: *Something about the Author Autobiography Series,* Volumes 1-11
SATA: *Something about the Author,* Volumes 1-62
SSC: *Short Story Criticism,* Volumes 1-7
TCLC: *Twentieth-Century Literary Criticism,* Volumes 1-40
YABC: *Yesterday's Authors of Books for Children,* Volumes 1-2

Bell, Madison Smartt   1957-........ **CLC 41**
See also CA 111

Bell, Marvin (Hartley)   1937-..... **CLC 8, 31**
See also CA 21-24R; DLB 5

Bellamy, Edward   1850-1898 ...... **NCLC 4**
See also DLB 12

Belloc, (Joseph) Hilaire (Pierre Sebastien
    Rene Swanton)
    1870-1953 .... **TCLC 7, 18**
See also YABC 1; CA 106; DLB 19

Bellow, Saul
    1915- ..... **CLC 1, 2, 3, 6, 8, 10, 13, 15,
                        25, 33, 34, 63**
See also CA 5-8R; CABS 1; DLB 2, 28;
    DLB-Y 82; DLB-DS 3;
    CDALB 1941-1968

Belser, Reimond Karel Maria de   1929-
See Ruyslinck, Ward

Bely, Andrey   1880-1934.......... **TCLC 7**
See also CA 104

Benary-Isbert, Margot   1889-1979... **CLC 12**
See also CLR 12; CANR 4; CA 5-8R;
    obituary CA 89-92; SATA 2;
    obituary SATA 21

Benavente (y Martinez), Jacinto
    1866-1954 .... **TCLC 3**
See also CA 106

Benchley, Peter (Bradford)
    1940- .... **CLC 4, 8**
See also CANR 12; CA 17-20R; SATA 3

Benchley, Robert   1889-1945 .... **TCLC 1**
See also CA 105; DLB 11

Benedikt, Michael   1935- .... **CLC 4, 14**
See also CANR 7; CA 13-16R; DLB 5

Benet, Juan   1927-................ **CLC 28**

Benet, Stephen Vincent
    1898-1943 .... **TCLC 7**
See also YABC 1; CA 104; DLB 4, 48

Benet, William Rose   1886-1950 ... **TCLC 28**
See also CA 118; DLB 45

Benford, Gregory (Albert)   1941-.... **CLC 52**
See also CANR 12, 24; CA 69-72;
    DLB-Y 82

Benjamin, Walter   1892-1940 ...... **TCLC 39**

Benn, Gottfried   1886-1956........ **TCLC 3**
See also CA 106; DLB 56

Bennett, Alan   1934-............. **CLC 45**
See also CA 103

Bennett, (Enoch) Arnold
    1867-1931 .... **TCLC 5, 20**
See also CA 106; DLB 10, 34

Bennett, George Harold   1930-
See Bennett, Hal
See also CA 97-100

Bennett, Hal   1930-............... **CLC 5**
See also Bennett, George Harold
See also DLB 33

Bennett, Jay   1912-............... **CLC 35**
See also CANR 11; CA 69-72; SAAS 4;
    SATA 27, 41

Bennett, Louise (Simone)   1919-..... **CLC 28**
See also Bennett-Coverly, Louise Simone

Bennett-Coverly, Louise Simone   1919-
See Bennett, Louise (Simone)
See also CA 97-100

Benson, E(dward) F(rederic)
    1867-1940 .... **TCLC 27**
See also CA 114

Benson, Jackson J.   1930-........ **CLC 34**
See also CA 25-28R

Benson, Sally   1900-1972 .... **CLC 17**
See also CAP 1; CA 19-20;
    obituary CA 37-40R; SATA 1, 35;
    obituary SATA 27

Benson, Stella   1892-1933........ **TCLC 17**
See also CA 117; DLB 36

Bentley, E(dmund) C(lerihew)
    1875-1956 .... **TCLC 12**
See also CA 108; DLB 70

Bentley, Eric (Russell)   1916-....... **CLC 24**
See also CANR 6; CA 5-8R

Berger, John (Peter)   1926- ..... **CLC 2, 19**
See also CA 81-84; DLB 14

Berger, Melvin (H.)   1927-........ **CLC 12**
See also CANR 4; CA 5-8R; SAAS 2;
    SATA 5

Berger, Thomas (Louis)
    1924- .... **CLC 3, 5, 8, 11, 18, 38**
See also CANR 5; CA 1-4R; DLB 2;
    DLB-Y 80

Bergman, (Ernst) Ingmar   1918-..... **CLC 16**
See also CA 81-84

Bergson, Henri   1859-1941........ **TCLC 32**

Bergstein, Eleanor   1938- .... **CLC 4**
See also CANR 5; CA 53-56

Berkoff, Steven   1937-............. **CLC 56**
See also CA 104

Bermant, Chaim   1929-............. **CLC 40**
See also CANR 6; CA 57-60

Bernanos, (Paul Louis) Georges
    1888-1948 .... **TCLC 3**
See also CA 104; DLB 72

Bernard, April   19??-.............. **CLC 59**

Bernhard, Thomas
    1931-1989 .... **CLC 3, 32, 61**
See also CA 85-88,; obituary CA 127;
    DLB 85

Berriault, Gina   1926-............. **CLC 54**
See also CA 116

Berrigan, Daniel J.   1921-......... **CLC 4**
See also CAAS 1; CANR 11; CA 33-36R;
    DLB 5

Berrigan, Edmund Joseph Michael, Jr.
    1934-1983
See Berrigan, Ted
See also CANR 14; CA 61-64;
    obituary CA 110

Berrigan, Ted   1934-1983 .... **CLC 37**
See also Berrigan, Edmund Joseph Michael,
    Jr.
See also DLB 5

Berry, Chuck   1926- .... **CLC 17**

Berry, Wendell (Erdman)
    1934- .... **CLC 4, 6, 8, 27, 46**
See also CA 73-76; DLB 5, 6

Berryman, John
    1914-1972 ..... **CLC 1, 2, 3, 4, 6, 8, 10,
                        13, 25, 62**
See also CAP 1; CA 15-16;
    obituary CA 33-36R; CABS 2; DLB 48;
    CDALB 1941-1968

Bertolucci, Bernardo   1940- .... **CLC 16**
See also CA 106

Bertran de Born   c. 1140-1215 ..... **CMLC 5**

Besant, Annie (Wood)   1847-1933 ... **TCLC 9**
See also CA 105

Bessie, Alvah   1904-1985........... **CLC 23**
See also CANR 2; CA 5-8R;
    obituary CA 116; DLB 26

Beti, Mongo   1932-............... **CLC 27**
See also Beyidi, Alexandre

Betjeman, (Sir) John
    1906-1984 .... **CLC 2, 6, 10, 34, 43**
See also CA 9-12R; obituary CA 112;
    DLB 20; DLB-Y 84

Betti, Ugo   1892-1953............. **TCLC 5**
See also CA 104

Betts, Doris (Waugh)   1932-.... **CLC 3, 6, 28**
See also CANR 9; CA 13-16R; DLB-Y 82

Bialik, Chaim Nachman
    1873-1934 .... **TCLC 25**

Bidart, Frank   19??-.............. **CLC 33**

Bienek, Horst   1930-............ **CLC 7, 11**
See also CA 73-76; DLB 75

Bierce, Ambrose (Gwinett)
    1842-1914?.............. **TCLC 1, 7**
See also CA 104; DLB 11, 12, 23, 71, 74;
    CDALB 1865-1917

Billington, Rachel   1942-........... **CLC 43**
See also CA 33-36R

Binyon, T(imothy) J(ohn)   1936- .... **CLC 34**
See also CA 111

Bioy Casares, Adolfo   1914-.... **CLC 4, 8, 13**
See also CANR 19; CA 29-32R

Bird, Robert Montgomery
    1806-1854 .... **NCLC 1**

Birdwell, Cleo   1936-
See DeLillo, Don

Birney (Alfred) Earle
    1904- .... **CLC 1, 4, 6, 11**
See also CANR 5, 20; CA 1-4R

Bishop, Elizabeth
    1911-1979 ..... **CLC 1, 4, 9, 13, 15, 32**
See also CANR 26; CA 5-8R;
    obituary CA 89-92; CABS 2;
    obituary SATA 24; DLB 5

Bishop, John   1935-............... **CLC 10**
See also CA 105

Bissett, Bill   1939-............... **CLC 18**
See also CANR 15; CA 69-72; DLB 53

Bitov, Andrei (Georgievich)   1937-... **CLC 57**

Biyidi, Alexandre   1932-
See Beti, Mongo
See also CA 114, 124

Bjornson, Bjornstjerne (Martinius)
    1832-1910 .... **TCLC 7, 37**
See also CA 104

Blackburn, Paul 1926-1971 ...... **CLC 9, 43**
See also CA 81-84; obituary CA 33-36R;
DLB 16; DLB-Y 81

Black Elk 1863-1950 .... **TCLC 33**

Blackmore, R(ichard) D(oddridge)
1825-1900 .... **TCLC 27**
See also CA 120; DLB 18

Blackmur, R(ichard) P(almer)
1904-1965 .... **CLC 2, 24**
See also CAP 1; CA 11-12;
obituary CA 25-28R; DLB 63

Blackwood, Algernon (Henry)
1869-1951 .... **TCLC 5**
See also CA 105

Blackwood, Caroline 1931- .... **CLC 6, 9**
See also CA 85-88; DLB 14

Blair, Eric Arthur 1903-1950
See Orwell, George
See also CA 104; SATA 29

Blais, Marie-Claire
1939- .... **CLC 2, 4, 6, 13, 22**
See also CAAS 4; CA 21-24R; DLB 53

Blaise, Clark 1940- .... **CLC 29**
See also CAAS 3; CANR 5; CA 53-56R;
DLB 53

Blake, Nicholas 1904-1972
See Day Lewis, C(ecil)

Blake, William 1757-1827 .... **NCLC 13**
See also SATA 30

Blasco Ibanez, Vicente
1867-1928 .... **TCLC 12**
See also CA 110

Blatty, William Peter 1928-........ **CLC 2**
See also CANR 9; CA 5-8R

Blessing, Lee 1949-.............. **CLC 54**

Blish, James (Benjamin)
1921-1975 .... **CLC 14**
See also CANR 3; CA 1-4R;
obituary CA 57-60; DLB 8

Blixen, Karen (Christentze Dinesen)
1885-1962
See Dinesen, Isak
See also CAP 2; CA 25-28; SATA 44

Bloch, Robert (Albert) 1917-....... **CLC 33**
See also CANR 5; CA 5-8R; SATA 12;
DLB 44

Blok, Aleksandr (Aleksandrovich)
1880-1921 .... **TCLC 5**
See also CA 104

Bloom, Harold 1930- .... **CLC 24**
See also CA 13-16R; DLB 67

Blount, Roy (Alton), Jr. 1941- ..... **CLC 38**
See also CANR 10; CA 53-56

Bloy, Leon 1846-1917............ **TCLC 22**
See also CA 121

Blume, Judy (Sussman Kitchens)
1938-................... **CLC 12, 30**
See also CLR 2, 15; CANR 13; CA 29-32R;
SATA 2, 31; DLB 52

Blunden, Edmund (Charles)
1896-1974 .... **CLC 2, 56**
See also CAP 2; CA 17-18;
obituary CA 45-48; DLB 20

Bly, Robert (Elwood)
1926- .... **CLC 1, 2, 5, 10, 15, 38**
See also CA 5-8R; DLB 5

Bochco, Steven 1944?-............ **CLC 35**

Bodker, Cecil 1927- .... **CLC 21**
See also CLR 23; CANR 13; CA 73-76;
SATA 14

Boell, Heinrich (Theodor) 1917-1985
See Boll, Heinrich
See also CANR 24; CA 21-24R;
obituary CA 116

Bogan, Louise 1897-1970..... **CLC 4, 39, 46**
See also CA 73-76; obituary CA 25-28R;
DLB 45

Bogarde, Dirk 1921-.............. **CLC 19**
See also Van Den Bogarde, Derek (Jules
Gaspard Ulric) Niven
See also DLB 14

Bogosian, Eric 1953- .... **CLC 45**

Bograd, Larry 1953-.............. **CLC 35**
See also CA 93-96; SATA 33

Bohl de Faber, Cecilia 1796-1877
See Caballero, Fernan

Boiardo, Matteo Maria 1441-1494 .... **LC 6**

Boileau-Despreaux, Nicolas
1636-1711 .... **LC 3**

Boland, Eavan (Aisling) 1944-...... **CLC 40**
See also DLB 40

Boll, Heinrich (Theodor)
1917-1985 ... **CLC 2, 3, 6, 9, 11, 15, 27,
39**
See also Boell, Heinrich (Theodor)
See also DLB 69; DLB-Y 85

Bolt, Robert (Oxton) 1924-........ **CLC 14**
See also CA 17-20R; DLB 13

Bond, Edward 1934-....... **CLC 4, 6, 13, 23**
See also CA 25-28R; DLB 13

Bonham, Frank 1914-............ **CLC 12**
See also CANR 4; CA 9-12R; SAAS 3;
SATA 1, 49

Bonnefoy, Yves 1923-........ **CLC 9, 15, 58**
See also CA 85-88

Bontemps, Arna (Wendell)
1902-1973 .... **CLC 1, 18**
See also CLR 6; CANR 4; CA 1-4R;
obituary CA 41-44R; SATA 2, 44;
obituary SATA 24; DLB 48, 51

Booth, Martin 1944-.............. **CLC 13**
See also CAAS 2; CA 93-96

Booth, Philip 1925-.............. **CLC 23**
See also CANR 5; CA 5-8R; DLB-Y 82

Booth, Wayne C(layson) 1921- ..... **CLC 24**
See also CAAS 5; CANR 3; CA 1-4R;
DLB 67

Borchert, Wolfgang 1921-1947 ..... **TCLC 5**
See also CA 104; DLB 69

Borges, Jorge Luis
1899-1986 ... **CLC 1, 2, 3, 4, 6, 8, 9, 10,
13, 19, 44, 48; SSC 4**
See also CANR 19; CA 21-24R; DLB-Y 86

Borowski, Tadeusz 1922-1951 ...... **TCLC 9**
See also CA 106

Borrow, George (Henry)
1803-1881 .... **NCLC 9**
See also DLB 21, 55

Bosschere, Jean de 1878-1953..... **TCLC 19**
See also CA 115

Boswell, James 1740-1795.......... **LC 4**

Bottoms, David 1949-............. **CLC 53**
See also CANR 22; CA 105; DLB-Y 83

Boucolon, Maryse 1937-
See Conde, Maryse
See also CA 110

Bourget, Paul (Charles Joseph)
1852-1935 .... **TCLC 12**
See also CA 107

Bourjaily, Vance (Nye) 1922- .... **CLC 8, 62**
See also CAAS 1; CANR 2; CA 1-4R;
DLB 2

Bourne, Randolph S(illiman)
1886-1918 .... **TCLC 16**
See also CA 117; DLB 63

Bova, Ben(jamin William) 1932-.... **CLC 45**
See also CLR 3; CANR 11; CA 5-8R;
SATA 6; DLB-Y 81

Bowen, Elizabeth (Dorothea Cole)
1899-1973 ..... **CLC 1, 3, 6, 11, 15, 22;
SSC 3**
See also CAP 2; CA 17-18;
obituary CA 41-44R; DLB 15

Bowering, George 1935-........ **CLC 15, 47**
See also CANR 10; CA 21-24R; DLB 53

Bowering, Marilyn R(uthe) 1949-... **CLC 32**
See also CA 101

Bowers, Edgar 1924- .... **CLC 9**
See also CANR 24; CA 5-8R; DLB 5

Bowie, David 1947- .... **CLC 17**
See also Jones, David Robert

Bowles, Jane (Sydney) 1917-1973.... **CLC 3**
See also CAP 2; CA 19-20;
obituary CA 41-44R

Bowles, Paul (Frederick)
1910- .... **CLC 1, 2, 19, 53; SSC 3**
See also CAAS 1; CANR 1, 19; CA 1-4R;
DLB 5, 6

Box, Edgar 1925-
See Vidal, Gore

Boyd, William 1952-........... **CLC 28, 53**
See also CA 114, 120

Boyle, Kay 1903- .. **CLC 1, 5, 19, 58; SSC 5**
See also CAAS 1; CA 13-16R; DLB 4, 9, 48

Boyle, Patrick 19??-.............. **CLC 19**

Boyle, Thomas Coraghessan
1948- .... **CLC 36, 55**
See also CA 120; DLB-Y 86

Brackenridge, Hugh Henry
1748-1816 .... **NCLC 7**
See also DLB 11, 37

Bradbury, Edward P. 1939-
See Moorcock, Michael

Bradbury, Malcolm (Stanley)
1932- .... **CLC 32, 61**
See also CANR 1; CA 1-4R; DLB 14

Bradbury, Ray(mond Douglas)
1920- .... **CLC 1, 3, 10, 15, 42**
See also CANR 2; CA 1-4R; SATA 11;
DLB 2, 8

Bradford, Gamaliel 1863-1932..... **TCLC 36**
See also DLB 17

Bradley, David (Henry), Jr. 1950- .. **CLC 23**
See also CANR 26; CA 104; DLB 33

Bradley, John Ed 1959- .... **CLC 55**

Bradley, Marion Zimmer 1930-..... **CLC 30**
See also CANR 7; CA 57-60; DLB 8

Bradstreet, Anne 1612-1672......... **LC 4**
See also DLB 24; CDALB 1640-1865

Bragg, Melvyn 1939- .... **CLC 10**
See also CANR 10; CA 57-60; DLB 14

Braine, John (Gerard)
1922-1986 .... **CLC 1, 3, 41**
See also CANR 1; CA 1-4R;
obituary CA 120; DLB 15; DLB-Y 86

Brammer, Billy Lee 1930?-1978
See Brammer, William

Brammer, William 1930?-1978 ..... **CLC 31**
See also obituary CA 77-80

Brancati, Vitaliano 1907-1954..... **TCLC 12**
See also CA 109

Brancato, Robin F(idler) 1936-..... **CLC 35**
See also CANR 11; CA 69-72; SATA 23

Brand, Millen 1906-1980.......... **CLC 7**
See also CA 21-24R; obituary CA 97-100

Branden, Barbara 19??- .... **CLC 44**

Brandes, Georg (Morris Cohen)
1842-1927 .... **TCLC 10**
See also CA 105

Brandys, Kazimierz 1916- .... **CLC 62**

Branley, Franklyn M(ansfield)
1915- .... **CLC 21**
See also CLR 13; CANR 14; CA 33-36R;
SATA 4

Brathwaite, Edward 1930-........ **CLC 11**
See also CANR 11; CA 25-28R; DLB 53

Brautigan, Richard (Gary)
1935-1984 .... **CLC 1, 3, 5, 9, 12, 34, 42**
See also CA 53-56; obituary CA 113;
DLB 2, 5; DLB-Y 80, 84

Brecht, (Eugen) Bertolt (Friedrich)
1898-1956 .... **TCLC 1, 6, 13, 35**
See also CA 104; DLB 56

Bremer, Fredrika 1801-1865 ..... **NCLC 11**

Brennan, Christopher John
1870-1932 .... **TCLC 17**
See also CA 117

Brennan, Maeve 1917-............ **CLC 5**
See also CA 81-84

Brentano, Clemens (Maria)
1778-1842 .... **NCLC 1**

Brenton, Howard 1942- .... **CLC 31**
See also CA 69-72; DLB 13

Breslin, James 1930-
See Breslin, Jimmy
See also CA 73-76

Breslin, Jimmy 1930-.......... **CLC 4, 43**
See also Breslin, James

Bresson, Robert 1907- .... **CLC 16**
See also CA 110

Breton, Andre 1896-1966... **CLC 2, 9, 15, 54**
See also CAP 2; CA 19-20;
obituary CA 25-28R; DLB 65

Breytenbach, Breyten 1939-..... **CLC 23, 37**
See also CA 113

Bridgers, Sue Ellen 1942- .... **CLC 26**
See also CANR 11; CA 65-68; SAAS 1;
SATA 22; DLB 52

Bridges, Robert 1844-1930........ **TCLC 1**
See also CA 104; DLB 19

Bridie, James 1888-1951 .... **TCLC 3**
See also Mavor, Osborne Henry
See also DLB 10

Brin, David 1950-................ **CLC 34**
See also CANR 24; CA 102

Brink, Andre (Philippus)
1935- .... **CLC 18, 36**
See also CA 104

Brinsmead, H(esba) F(ay) 1922- .... **CLC 21**
See also CANR 10; CA 21-24R; SAAS 5;
SATA 18

Brittain, Vera (Mary) 1893?-1970... **CLC 23**
See also CAP 1; CA 15-16;
obituary CA 25-28R

Broch, Hermann 1886-1951....... **TCLC 20**
See also CA 117

Brock, Rose 1923-
See Hansen, Joseph

Brodkey, Harold 1930-............ **CLC 56**
See also CA 111

Brodsky, Iosif Alexandrovich 1940-
See Brodsky, Joseph (Alexandrovich)
See also CA 41-44R

Brodsky, Joseph (Alexandrovich)
1940- .... **CLC 4, 6, 13, 36, 50**
See also Brodsky, Iosif Alexandrovich

Brodsky, Michael (Mark) 1948- .... **CLC 19**
See also CANR 18; CA 102

Bromell, Henry 1947-............. **CLC 5**
See also CANR 9; CA 53-56

Bromfield, Louis (Brucker)
1896-1956 .... **TCLC 11**
See also CA 107; DLB 4, 9

Broner, E(sther) M(asserman)
1930- .... **CLC 19**
See also CANR 8, 25; CA 17-20R; DLB 28

Bronk, William 1918-............. **CLC 10**
See also CANR 23; CA 89-92

Bronte, Anne 1820-1849......... **NCLC 4**
See also DLB 21

Bronte, Charlotte 1816-1855 .... **NCLC 3, 8**
See also DLB 21

Bronte, (Jane) Emily 1818-1848 .. **NCLC 16**
See also DLB 21, 32

Brooke, Frances 1724-1789 .... **LC 6**
See also DLB 39

Brooke, Henry 1703?-1783 .... **LC 1**
See also DLB 39

Brooke, Rupert (Chawner)
1887-1915 .... **TCLC 2, 7**
See also CA 104; DLB 19

Brooke-Rose, Christine 1926-...... **CLC 40**
See also CA 13-16R; DLB 14

Brookner, Anita 1928-...... **CLC 32, 34, 51**
See also CA 114, 120; DLB-Y 87

Brooks, Cleanth 1906-............. **CLC 24**
See also CA 17-20R; DLB 63

Brooks, Gwendolyn
1917- .... **CLC 1, 2, 4, 5, 15, 49**
See also CANR 1; CA 1-4R; SATA 6;
DLB 5, 76; CDALB 1941-1968

Brooks, Mel 1926- .... **CLC 12**
See also Kaminsky, Melvin
See also CA 65-68; DLB 26

Brooks, Peter 1938-.............. **CLC 34**
See also CANR 1; CA 45-48

Brooks, Van Wyck 1886-1963...... **CLC 29**
See also CANR 6; CA 1-4R; DLB 45, 63

Brophy, Brigid (Antonia)
1929- .... **CLC 6, 11, 29**
See also CAAS 4; CANR 25; CA 5-8R;
DLB 14

Brosman, Catharine Savage 1934-.... **CLC 9**
See also CANR 21; CA 61-64

Broughton, T(homas) Alan 1936- ... **CLC 19**
See also CANR 2, 23; CA 45-48

Broumas, Olga 1949-............. **CLC 10**
See also CANR 20; CA 85-88

Brown, Charles Brockden
1771-1810 .... **NCLC 22**
See also DLB 37, 59, 73;
CDALB 1640-1865

Brown, Christy 1932-1981......... **CLC 63**
See also CA 105; obituary CA 104

Brown, Claude 1937-............. **CLC 30**
See also CA 73-76

Brown, Dee (Alexander) 1908- .. **CLC 18, 47**
See also CAAS 6; CANR 11; CA 13-16R;
SATA 5; DLB-Y 80

Brown, George Douglas 1869-1902
See Douglas, George

Brown, George Mackay 1921-.... **CLC 5, 28**
See also CAAS 6; CANR 12; CA 21-24R;
SATA 35; DLB 14, 27

Brown, Rita Mae 1944-........ **CLC 18, 43**
See also CANR 2, 11; CA 45-48

Brown, Rosellen 1939-............ **CLC 32**
See also CANR 14; CA 77-80

Brown, Sterling A(llen)
1901-1989 .... **CLC 1, 23, 59**
See also CANR 26; CA 85-88;
obituary CA 27; DLB 48, 51, 63

Brown, William Wells
1816?-1884.................. **NCLC 2**
See also DLB 3, 50

Browne, Jackson 1950- .... **CLC 21**
See also CA 120

Browning, Elizabeth Barrett
1806-1861 .... **NCLC 1, 16**
See also DLB 32

Browning, Robert
1812-1889 .... **NCLC 19; PC 2**
See also YABC 1; DLB 32

Browning, Tod 1882-1962 .... **CLC 16**
See also obituary CA 117

Bruccoli, Matthew J(oseph) 1931- .. CLC 34
See also CANR 7; CA 9-12R

Bruce, Lenny 1925-1966 .... CLC 21
See also Schneider, Leonard Alfred

Brunner, John (Kilian Houston)
1934- .... CLC 8, 10
See also CANR 2; CA 1-4R

Brutus, Dennis 1924- .... CLC 43
See also CANR 2; CA 49-52

Bryan, C(ourtlandt) D(ixon) B(arnes)
1936- .... CLC 29
See also CANR 13; CA 73-76

Bryant, William Cullen
1794-1878 .... NCLC 6
See also DLB 3, 43, 59; CDALB 1640-1865

Bryusov, Valery (Yakovlevich)
1873-1924 .... TCLC 10
See also CA 107

Buchanan, George 1506-1582 .... LC 4

Buchheim, Lothar-Gunther 1918- .... CLC 6
See also CA 85-88

Buchner, (Karl) Georg
1813-1837 .... NCLC 26

Buchwald, Art(hur) 1925-.......... CLC 33
See also CANR 21; CA 5-8R; SATA 10

Buck, Pearl S(ydenstricker)
1892-1973 .... CLC 7, 11, 18
See also CANR 1; CA 1-4R;
obituary CA 41-44R; SATA 1, 25; DLB 9

Buckler, Ernest 1908-1984......... CLC 13
See also CAP 1; CA 11-12;
obituary CA 114; SATA 47

Buckley, Vincent (Thomas)
1925-1988 .... CLC 57
See also CA 101

Buckley, William F(rank), Jr.
1925- .... CLC 7, 18, 37
See also CANR 1, 24; CA 1-4R; DLB-Y 80

Buechner, (Carl) Frederick
1926- .... CLC 2, 4, 6, 9
See also CANR 11; CA 13-16R; DLB-Y 80

Buell, John (Edward) 1927-........ CLC 10
See also CA 1-4R; DLB 53

Buero Vallejo, Antonio 1916- ... CLC 15, 46
See also CANR 24; CA 106

Bukowski, Charles 1920-.... CLC 2, 5, 9, 41
See also CA 17-20R; DLB 5

Bulgakov, Mikhail (Afanas'evich)
1891-1940 .... TCLC 2, 16
See also CA 105

Bullins, Ed 1935- .... CLC 1, 5, 7
See also CANR 24; CA 49-52; DLB 7, 38

Bulwer-Lytton, (Lord) Edward (George Earle
Lytton) 1803-1873 .... NCLC 1
See also Lytton, Edward Bulwer
See also DLB 21

Bunin, Ivan (Alexeyevich)
1870-1953 .... TCLC 6; SSC 5
See also CA 104

Bunting, Basil 1900-1985.... CLC 10, 39, 47
See also CANR 7; CA 53-56;
obituary CA 115; DLB 20

Bunuel, Luis 1900-1983 .... CLC 16
See also CA 101; obituary CA 110

Bunyan, John 1628-1688 .... LC 4
See also DLB 39

Burgess (Wilson, John) Anthony
1917- ..... CLC 1, 2, 4, 5, 8, 10, 13, 15,
22, 40, 62
See also Wilson, John (Anthony) Burgess
See also DLB 14

Burke, Edmund 1729-1797.......... LC 7

Burke, Kenneth (Duva) 1897- .... CLC 2, 24
See also CA 5-8R; DLB 45, 63

Burney, Fanny 1752-1840 .... NCLC 12
See also DLB 39

Burns, Robert 1759-1796............ LC 3

Burns, Tex 1908?-
See L'Amour, Louis (Dearborn)

Burnshaw, Stanley 1906-..... CLC 3, 13, 44
See also CA 9-12R; DLB 48

Burr, Anne 1937- .... CLC 6
See also CA 25-28R

Burroughs, Edgar Rice
1875-1950 .... TCLC 2, 32
See also CA 104; SATA 41; DLB 8

Burroughs, William S(eward)
1914- .... CLC 1, 2, 5, 15, 22, 42
See also CANR 20; CA 9-12R; DLB 2, 8,
16; DLB-Y 81

Busch, Frederick 1941- ... CLC 7, 10, 18, 47
See also CAAS 1; CA 33-36R; DLB 6

Bush, Ronald 19??-................ CLC 34

Butler, Octavia E(stelle) 1947- ..... CLC 38
See also CANR 12, 24; CA 73-76; DLB 33

Butler, Samuel 1835-1902 ...... TCLC 1, 33
See also CA 104; DLB 18, 57

Butor, Michel (Marie Francois)
1926- .... CLC 1, 3, 8, 11, 15
See also CA 9-12R

Buzo, Alexander 1944-............ CLC 61
See also CANR 17; CA 97-100

Buzzati, Dino 1906-1972 .... CLC 36
See also obituary CA 33-36R

Byars, Betsy 1928-................ CLC 35
See also CLR 1, 16; CANR 18; CA 33-36R;
SAAS 1; SATA 4, 46; DLB 52

Byatt, A(ntonia) S(usan Drabble)
1936- .... CLC 19
See also CANR 13; CA 13-16R; DLB 14

Byrne, David 1953?-.............. CLC 26

Byrne, John Keyes 1926-
See Leonard, Hugh
See also CA 102

Byron, George Gordon (Noel), Lord Byron
1788-1824 .... NCLC 2, 12

Caballero, Fernan 1796-1877..... NCLC 10

Cabell, James Branch 1879-1958 ... TCLC 6
See also CA 105; DLB 9

Cable, George Washington
1844-1925 .... TCLC 4; SSC 4
See also CA 104; DLB 12, 74

Cabrera Infante, G(uillermo)
1929- .... CLC 5, 25, 45
See also CA 85-88

Cage, John (Milton, Jr.) 1912- ..... CLC 41
See also CANR 9; CA 13-16R

Cain, G. 1929-
See Cabrera Infante, G(uillermo)

Cain, James M(allahan)
1892-1977 .... CLC 3, 11, 28
See also CANR 8; CA 17-20R;
obituary CA 73-76

Caldwell, Erskine (Preston)
1903-1987 .... CLC 1, 8, 14, 50, 60
See also CAAS 1; CANR 2; CA 1-4R;
obituary CA 121; DLB 9

Caldwell, (Janet Miriam) Taylor (Holland)
1900-1985 .... CLC 2, 28, 39
See also CANR 5; CA 5-8R;
obituary CA 116

Calhoun, John Caldwell
1782-1850 .... NCLC 15
See also DLB 3

Calisher, Hortense 1911-.... CLC 2, 4, 8, 38
See also CANR 1, 22; CA 1-4R; DLB 2

Callaghan, Morley (Edward)
1903- .... CLC 3, 14, 41
See also CA 9-12R; DLB 68

Calvino, Italo
1923-1985 .... CLC 5, 8, 11, 22, 33, 39;
SSC 3
See also CANR 23; CA 85-88;
obituary CA 116

Cameron, Carey 1952-............ CLC 59

Cameron, Peter 1959-............. CLC 44
See also CA 125

Campana, Dino 1885-1932....... TCLC 20
See also CA 117

Campbell, John W(ood), Jr.
1910-1971 .... CLC 32
See also CAP 2; CA 21-22;
obituary CA 29-32R; DLB 8

Campbell, (John) Ramsey 1946-.... CLC 42
See also CANR 7; CA 57-60

Campbell, (Ignatius) Roy (Dunnachie)
1901-1957 .... TCLC 5
See also CA 104; DLB 20

Campbell, Thomas 1777-1844 .... NCLC 19

Campbell, (William) Wilfred
1861-1918 .... TCLC 9
See also CA 106

Camus, Albert
1913-1960 ... CLC 1, 2, 4, 9, 11, 14, 32,
63
See also CA 89-92; DLB 72

Canby, Vincent 1924-............. CLC 13
See also CA 81-84

Canetti, Elias 1905- .... CLC 3, 14, 25
See also CANR 23; CA 21-24R

Canin, Ethan 1960-.............. CLC 55

Cape, Judith 1916-
See Page, P(atricia) K(athleen)

Capek, Karel 1890-1938........ TCLC 6, 37
See also CA 104

Capote, Truman
1924-1984 ..... CLC 1, 3, 8, 13, 19, 34,
38, 58; SSC 2
See also CANR 18; CA 5-8R;
obituary CA 113; DLB 2; DLB-Y 80, 84;
CDALB 1941-1968

Crumb, Robert 1943- . . . . **CLC 17**
See also CA 106

Cryer, Gretchen 1936?- . . . . **CLC 21**
See also CA 114, 123

Csath, Geza 1887-1919 . . . . **TCLC 13**
See also CA 111

Cudlip, David 1933- . . . . **CLC 34**

Cullen, Countee 1903-1946 . . . . . **TCLC 4, 37**
See also CA 108, 124; SATA 18; DLB 4,
48, 51; CDALB 1917-1929

Cummings, E(dward) E(stlin)
1894-1962 . . . . **CLC 1, 3, 8, 12, 15**
See also CA 73-76; DLB 4, 48

Cunha, Euclides (Rodrigues) da
1866-1909 . . . . **TCLC 24**
See also CA 123

Cunningham, J(ames) V(incent)
1911-1985 . . . . **CLC 3, 31**
See also CANR 1; CA 1-4R;
obituary CA 115; DLB 5

Cunningham, Julia (Woolfolk)
1916- . . . . **CLC 12**
See also CANR 4, 19; CA 9-12R; SAAS 2;
SATA 1, 26

Cunningham, Michael 1952- . . . . **CLC 34**

Currie, Ellen 19??- . . . . **CLC 44**

Dabrowska, Maria (Szumska)
1889-1965 . . . . **CLC 15**
See also CA 106

Dabydeen, David 1956?- . . . . **CLC 34**
See also CA 106

Dacey, Philip 1939- . . . . **CLC 51**
See also CANR 14; CA 37-40R

Dagerman, Stig (Halvard)
1923-1954 . . . . **TCLC 17**
See also CA 117

Dahl, Roald 1916- . . . . **CLC 1, 6, 18**
See also CLR 1, 7; CANR 6; CA 1-4R;
SATA 1, 26

Dahlberg, Edward 1900-1977 . . . **CLC 1, 7, 14**
See also CA 9-12R; obituary CA 69-72;
DLB 48

Daly, Elizabeth 1878-1967 . . . . **CLC 52**
See also CAP 2; CA 23-24;
obituary CA 25-28R

Daly, Maureen 1921- . . . . **CLC 17**
See also McGivern, Maureen Daly
See also SAAS 1; SATA 2

Daniken, Erich von 1935-
See Von Daniken, Erich

Dannay, Frederic 1905-1982
See Queen, Ellery
See also CANR 1; CA 1-4R;
obituary CA 107

D'Annunzio, Gabriele
1863-1938 . . . . **TCLC 6, 40**
See also CA 104

Dante (Alighieri)
See Alighieri, Dante

Danziger, Paula 1944- . . . . **CLC 21**
See also CLR 20; CA 112, 115; SATA 30,
36

Dario, Ruben 1867-1916 . . . . **TCLC 4**
See also Sarmiento, Felix Ruben Garcia
See also CA 104

Darley, George 1795-1846 . . . . **NCLC 2**

Daryush, Elizabeth 1887-1977 . . . . **CLC 6, 19**
See also CANR 3; CA 49-52; DLB 20

Daudet, (Louis Marie) Alphonse
1840-1897 . . . . **NCLC 1**

Daumal, Rene 1908-1944 . . . . **TCLC 14**
See also CA 114

Davenport, Guy (Mattison, Jr.)
1927- . . . . **CLC 6, 14, 38**
See also CANR 23; CA 33-36R

Davidson, Donald (Grady)
1893-1968 . . . . **CLC 2, 13, 19**
See also CANR 4; CA 5-8R;
obituary CA 25-28R; DLB 45

Davidson, John 1857-1909 . . . . **TCLC 24**
See also CA 118; DLB 19

Davidson, Sara 1943- . . . . **CLC 9**
See also CA 81-84

Davie, Donald (Alfred)
1922- . . . . **CLC 5, 8, 10, 31**
See also CAAS 3; CANR 1; CA 1-4R;
DLB 27

Davies, Ray(mond Douglas) 1944- . . **CLC 21**
See also CA 116

Davies, Rhys 1903-1978 . . . . **CLC 23**
See also CANR 4; CA 9-12R;
obituary CA 81-84

Davies, (William) Robertson
1913- . . . . **CLC 2, 7, 13, 25, 42**
See also CANR 17; CA 33-36R; DLB 68

Davies, W(illiam) H(enry)
1871-1940 . . . . **TCLC 5**
See also CA 104; DLB 19

Davis, H(arold) L(enoir)
1896-1960 . . . . **CLC 49**
See also obituary CA 89-92; DLB 9

Davis, Rebecca (Blaine) Harding
1831-1910 . . . . **TCLC 6**
See also CA 104; DLB 74

Davis, Richard Harding
1864-1916 . . . . **TCLC 24**
See also CA 114; DLB 12, 23

Davison, Frank Dalby 1893-1970 . . . **CLC 15**
See also obituary CA 116

Davison, Peter 1928- . . . . **CLC 28**
See also CAAS 4; CANR 3; CA 9-12R;
DLB 5

Davys, Mary 1674-1732 . . . . **LC 1**
See also DLB 39

Dawson, Fielding 1930- . . . . **CLC 6**
See also CA 85-88

Day, Clarence (Shepard, Jr.)
1874-1935 . . . . **TCLC 25**
See also CA 108; DLB 11

Day, Thomas 1748-1789 . . . . **LC 1**
See also YABC 1; DLB 39

Day Lewis, C(ecil)
1904-1972 . . . . **CLC 1, 6, 10**
See also CAP 1; CA 15-16;
obituary CA 33-36R; DLB 15, 20

Dazai Osamu 1909-1948 . . . . **TCLC 11**
See also Tsushima Shuji

De Crayencour, Marguerite 1903-1987
See Yourcenar, Marguerite

Deer, Sandra 1940- . . . . **CLC 45**

Defoe, Daniel 1660?-1731 . . . . **LC 1**
See also SATA 22; DLB 39

De Hartog, Jan 1914- . . . . **CLC 19**
See also CANR 1; CA 1-4R

Deighton, Len 1929- . . . . **CLC 4, 7, 22, 46**
See also Deighton, Leonard Cyril

Deighton, Leonard Cyril 1929-
See Deighton, Len
See also CANR 19; CA 9-12R

De la Mare, Walter (John)
1873-1956 . . . . **TCLC 4**
See also CLR 23; CA 110; SATA 16;
DLB 19

Delaney, Shelagh 1939- . . . . **CLC 29**
See also CA 17-20R; DLB 13

Delany, Mary (Granville Pendarves)
1700-1788 . . . . **LC 12**

Delany, Samuel R(ay, Jr.)
1942- . . . . **CLC 8, 14, 38**
See also CA 81-84; DLB 8, 33

De la Roche, Mazo 1885-1961 . . . . . **CLC 14**
See also CA 85-88; DLB 68

Delbanco, Nicholas (Franklin)
1942- . . . . **CLC 6, 13**
See also CAAS 2; CA 17-20R; DLB 6

del Castillo, Michel 1933- . . . . **CLC 38**
See also CA 109

Deledda, Grazia 1871-1936 . . . . **TCLC 23**
See also CA 123

Delibes (Setien), Miguel 1920- . . . **CLC 8, 18**
See also CANR 1; CA 45-48

DeLillo, Don
1936- . . . . **CLC 8, 10, 13, 27, 39, 54**
See also CANR 21; CA 81-84; DLB 6

De Lisser, H(erbert) G(eorge)
1878-1944 . . . . **TCLC 12**
See also CA 109

Deloria, Vine (Victor), Jr. 1933- . . . . **CLC 21**
See also CANR 5, 20; CA 53-56; SATA 21

Del Vecchio, John M(ichael)
1947- . . . . **CLC 29**
See also CA 110

de Man, Paul 1919-1983 . . . . **CLC 55**
See also obituary CA 111; DLB 67

De Marinis, Rick 1934- . . . . **CLC 54**
See also CANR 9, 25; CA 57-60

Demby, William 1922- . . . . **CLC 53**
See also CA 81-84; DLB 33

Denby, Edwin (Orr) 1903-1983 . . . . . **CLC 48**
See also obituary CA 110

Dennis, John 1657-1734 . . . . **LC 11**

Dennis, Nigel (Forbes) 1912- . . . . **CLC 8**
See also CA 25-28R; DLB 13, 15

De Palma, Brian 1940- . . . . **CLC 20**
See also CA 109

De Quincey, Thomas 1785-1859 . . . **NCLC 4**

Deren, Eleanora 1908-1961
See Deren, Maya
See also obituary CA 111

Deren, Maya 1908-1961.......... **CLC 16**
See also Deren, Eleanora

Derleth, August (William)
1909-1971 .... **CLC 31**
See also CANR 4; CA 1-4R;
obituary CA 29-32R; SATA 5; DLB 9

Derrida, Jacques 1930-........... **CLC 24**
See also CA 124

Desai, Anita 1937- .... **CLC 19, 37**
See also CA 81-84

De Saint-Luc, Jean 1909-1981
See Glassco, John

De Sica, Vittorio 1902-1974 .... **CLC 20**
See also obituary CA 117

Desnos, Robert 1900-1945....... **TCLC 22**
See also CA 121

Destouches, Louis-Ferdinand-Auguste
1894-1961
See Celine, Louis-Ferdinand
See also CA 85-88

Deutsch, Babette 1895-1982 .... **CLC 18**
See also CANR 4; CA 1-4R;
obituary CA 108; SATA 1;
obituary SATA 33; DLB 45

Devenant, William 1606-1649 .... **LC 13**

Devkota, Laxmiprasad
1909-1959 .... **TCLC 23**
See also CA 123

DeVoto, Bernard (Augustine)
1897-1955 .... **TCLC 29**
See also CA 113; DLB 9

De Vries, Peter
1910- .... **CLC 1, 2, 3, 7, 10, 28, 46**
See also CA 17-20R; DLB 6; DLB-Y 82

Dexter, Pete 1943-........... **CLC 34, 55**
See also CA 127

Diamond, Neil (Leslie) 1941-....... **CLC 30**
See also CA 108

Dick, Philip K(indred)
1928-1982 .... **CLC 10, 30**
See also CANR 2, 16; CA 49-52;
obituary CA 106; DLB 8

Dickens, Charles
1812-1870 .... **NCLC 3, 8, 18, 26**
See also SATA 15; DLB 21, 55, 70

Dickey, James (Lafayette)
1923- .... **CLC 1, 2, 4, 7, 10, 15, 47**
See also CANR 10; CA 9-12R; CABS 2;
DLB 5; DLB-Y 82

Dickey, William 1928-......... **CLC 3, 28**
See also CANR 24; CA 9-12R; DLB 5

Dickinson, Charles 1952-......... **CLC 49**

Dickinson, Emily (Elizabeth)
1830-1886 .... **NCLC 21; PC 1**
See also SATA 29; DLB 1;
CDALB 1865-1917

Dickinson, Peter (Malcolm de Brissac)
1927- .... **CLC 12, 35**
See also CA 41-44R; SATA 5

Didion, Joan 1934-..... **CLC 1, 3, 8, 14, 32**
See also CANR 14; CA 5-8R; DLB 2;
DLB-Y 81, 86

Dillard, Annie 1945-........... **CLC 9, 60**
See also CANR 3; CA 49-52; SATA 10;
DLB-Y 80

Dillard, R(ichard) H(enry) W(ilde)
1937- .... **CLC 5**
See also CAAS 7; CANR 10; CA 21-24R;
DLB 5

Dillon, Eilis 1920-................ **CLC 17**
See also CAAS 3; CANR 4; CA 9-12R;
SATA 2

Dinesen, Isak
1885-1962 .... **CLC 10, 29; SSC 7**
See also Blixen, Karen (Christentze
Dinesen)
See also CANR 22

Disch, Thomas M(ichael) 1940-... **CLC 7, 36**
See also CAAS 4; CANR 17; CA 21-24R;
DLB 8

Disraeli, Benjamin 1804-1881 ..... **NCLC 2**
See also DLB 21, 55

Dixon, Paige 1911-
See Corcoran, Barbara

Dixon, Stephen 1936-........... **CLC 52**
See also CANR 17; CA 89-92

Doblin, Alfred 1878-1957........ **TCLC 13**
See also Doeblin, Alfred

Dobrolyubov, Nikolai Alexandrovich
1836-1861 .... **NCLC 5**

Dobyns, Stephen 1941-........... **CLC 37**
See also CANR 2, 18; CA 45-48

Doctorow, E(dgar) L(aurence)
1931- .... **CLC 6, 11, 15, 18, 37, 44**
See also CANR 2; CA 45-48; DLB 2, 28;
DLB-Y 80

Dodgson, Charles Lutwidge 1832-1898
See Carroll, Lewis
See also YABC 2

Doeblin, Alfred 1878-1957....... **TCLC 13**
See also CA 110; DLB 66

Doerr, Harriet 1910- .... **CLC 34**
See also CA 117, 122

Donaldson, Stephen R. 1947-....... **CLC 46**
See also CANR 13; CA 89-92

Donleavy, J(ames) P(atrick)
1926- .... **CLC 1, 4, 6, 10, 45**
See also CANR 24; CA 9-12R; DLB 6

Donnadieu, Marguerite 1914-
See Duras, Marguerite

Donne, John 1572?-1631 ...... **LC 10; PC 1**

Donnell, David 1939?- .... **CLC 34**

Donoso, Jose 1924-....... **CLC 4, 8, 11, 32**
See also CA 81-84

Donovan, John 1928- .... **CLC 35**
See also CLR 3; CA 97-100; SATA 29

Doolittle, Hilda 1886-1961
See H(ilda) D(oolittle)
See also CA 97-100; DLB 4, 45

Dorfman, Ariel 1942-............. **CLC 48**
See also CA 124

Dorn, Ed(ward Merton) 1929-... **CLC 10, 18**
See also CA 93-96; DLB 5

Dos Passos, John (Roderigo)
1896-1970 ... **CLC 1, 4, 8, 11, 15, 25, 34**
See also CANR 3; CA 1-4R;
obituary CA 29-32R; DLB 4, 9;
DLB-DS 1

Dostoevski, Fedor Mikhailovich
1821-1881 .... **NCLC 2, 7, 21; SSC 2**

Doughty, Charles (Montagu)
1843-1926 .... **TCLC 27**
See also CA 115; DLB 19, 57

Douglas, George 1869-1902....... **TCLC 28**

Douglas, Keith 1920-1944 .... **TCLC 40**
See also DLB 27

Douglass, Frederick 1817-1895.... **NCLC 7**
See also SATA 29; DLB 1, 43, 50;
CDALB 1640-1865

Dourado, (Waldomiro Freitas) Autran
1926- .... **CLC 23, 60**
See also CA 25-28R

Dove, Rita 1952-................. **CLC 50**
See also CA 109

Dowson, Ernest (Christopher)
1867-1900 .... **TCLC 4**
See also CA 105; DLB 19

Doyle, (Sir) Arthur Conan
1859-1930 .... **TCLC 7, 26**
See also CA 104, 122; SATA 24; DLB 18,
70

Dr. A 1933-
See Silverstein, Alvin and Virginia B(arbara
Opshelor) Silverstein

Drabble, Margaret
1939- ...... **CLC 2, 3, 5, 8, 10, 22, 53**
See also CANR 18; CA 13-16R; SATA 48;
DLB 14

Drayton, Michael 1563-1631........ **LC 8**

Dreiser, Theodore (Herman Albert)
1871-1945 .... **TCLC 10, 18, 35**
See also CA 106; SATA 48; DLB 9, 12;
DLB-DS 1; CDALB 1865-1917

Drexler, Rosalyn 1926- .... **CLC 2, 6**
See also CA 81-84

Dreyer, Carl Theodor 1889-1968.... **CLC 16**
See also obituary CA 116

Drieu La Rochelle, Pierre
1893-1945 .... **TCLC 21**
See also CA 117; DLB 72

Droste-Hulshoff, Annette Freiin von
1797-1848 .... **NCLC 3**

Drummond, William Henry
1854-1907 .... **TCLC 25**

Drummond de Andrade, Carlos 1902-1987
See Andrade, Carlos Drummond de

Drury, Allen (Stuart) 1918-........ **CLC 37**
See also CANR 18; CA 57-60

Dryden, John 1631-1700 .... **LC 3**

Duberman, Martin 1930-........... **CLC 8**
See also CANR 2; CA 1-4R

Dubie, Norman (Evans, Jr.) 1945- .. **CLC 36**
See also CANR 12; CA 69-72

Du Bois, W(illiam) E(dward) B(urghardt)
1868-1963 .... **CLC 1, 2, 13**
See also CA 85-88; SATA 42; DLB 47, 50;
CDALB 1865-1917

Elliott, Sumner Locke 1917- .... CLC 38
    See also CANR 2, 21; CA 5-8R

Ellis, A. E. 19??- .... CLC 7

Ellis, Alice Thomas 19??- .... CLC 40

Ellis, Bret Easton 1964- .... CLC 39
    See also CA 118, 123

Ellis, (Henry) Havelock
    1859-1939 .... TCLC 14
    See also CA 109

Ellis, Trey 1964- .... CLC 55

Ellison, Harlan (Jay) 1934-... CLC 1, 13, 42
    See also CANR 5; CA 5-8R; DLB 8

Ellison, Ralph (Waldo)
    1914- .... CLC 1, 3, 11, 54
    See also CANR 24; CA 9-12R; DLB 2;
    CDALB 1941-1968

Ellmann, Lucy 1956- .... CLC 61
    See also CA 128

Ellmann, Richard (David)
    1918-1987 .... CLC 50
    See also CANR 2; CA 1-4R;
    obituary CA 122; DLB-Y 87

Elman, Richard 1934- .... CLC 19
    See also CAAS 3; CA 17-20R

Eluard, Paul 1895-1952 .... TCLC 7
    See also Grindel, Eugene

Elyot, (Sir) Thomas 1490?-1546 ..... LC 11

Elytis, Odysseus 1911- .... CLC 15, 49
    See also CA 102

Emecheta, (Florence Onye) Buchi
    1944- .... CLC 14, 48
    See also CA 81-84

Emerson, Ralph Waldo
    1803-1882 .... NCLC 1
    See also DLB 1, 59, 73; CDALB 1640-1865

Empson, William
    1906-1984 .... CLC 3, 8, 19, 33, 34
    See also CA 17-20R; obituary CA 112;
    DLB 20

Enchi, Fumiko (Veda) 1905-1986 ... CLC 31
    See also obituary CA 121

Ende, Michael 1930- .... CLC 31
    See also CLR 14; CA 118, 124; SATA 42;
    DLB 75

Endo, Shusaku 1923- ..... CLC 7, 14, 19, 54
    See also CANR 21; CA 29-32R

Engel, Marian 1933-1985 .... CLC 36
    See also CANR 12; CA 25-28R; DLB 53

Engelhardt, Frederick 1911-1986
    See Hubbard, L(afayette) Ron(ald)

Enright, D(ennis) J(oseph)
    1920- .... CLC 4, 8, 31
    See also CANR 1; CA 1-4R; SATA 25;
    DLB 27

Enzensberger, Hans Magnus
    1929- .... CLC 43
    See also CA 116, 119

Ephron, Nora 1941- .... CLC 17, 31
    See also CANR 12; CA 65-68

Epstein, Daniel Mark 1948- .... CLC 7
    See also CANR 2; CA 49-52

Epstein, Jacob 1956- .... CLC 19
    See also CA 114

Epstein, Joseph 1937- .... CLC 39
    See also CA 112, 119

Epstein, Leslie 1938- .... CLC 27
    See also CANR 23; CA 73-76

Erdman, Paul E(mil) 1932- .... CLC 25
    See also CANR 13; CA 61-64

Erdrich, Louise 1954- .... CLC 39, 54
    See also CA 114

Erenburg, Ilya (Grigoryevich) 1891-1967
    See Ehrenburg, Ilya (Grigoryevich)

Eseki, Bruno 1919-
    See Mphahlele, Ezekiel

Esenin, Sergei (Aleksandrovich)
    1895-1925 .... TCLC 4
    See also CA 104

Eshleman, Clayton 1935- .... CLC 7
    See also CAAS 6; CA 33-36R; DLB 5

Espriu, Salvador 1913-1985 .... CLC 9
    See also obituary CA 115

Estleman, Loren D. 1952- .... CLC 48
    See also CA 85-88

Evans, Marian 1819-1880
    See Eliot, George

Evans, Mary Ann 1819-1880
    See Eliot, George

Evarts, Esther 1900-1972
    See Benson, Sally

Everett, Percival L. 1957?- .... CLC 57
    See also CA 129

Everson, Ronald G(ilmour) 1903-... CLC 27
    See also CA 17-20R

Everson, William (Oliver)
    1912- .... CLC 1, 5, 14
    See also CANR 20; CA 9-12R; DLB 5, 16

Evtushenko, Evgenii (Aleksandrovich) 1933-
    See Yevtushenko, Yevgeny

Ewart, Gavin (Buchanan)
    1916- .... CLC 13, 46
    See also CANR 17; CA 89-92; DLB 40

Ewers, Hanns Heinz 1871-1943 ... TCLC 12
    See also CA 109

Ewing, Frederick R. 1918-
    See Sturgeon, Theodore (Hamilton)

Exley, Frederick (Earl) 1929-.... CLC 6, 11
    See also CA 81-84; DLB-Y 81

Ezekiel, Nissim 1924- .... CLC 61
    See also CA 61-64

Ezekiel, Tish O'Dowd 1943- .... CLC 34

Fagen, Donald 1948- .... CLC 26

Fair, Ronald L. 1932- .... CLC 18
    See also CANR 25; CA 69-72; DLB 33

Fairbairns, Zoe (Ann) 1948- .... CLC 32
    See also CANR 21; CA 103

Fairfield, Cicily Isabel 1892-1983
    See West, Rebecca

Fallaci, Oriana 1930- .... CLC 11
    See also CANR 15; CA 77-80

Faludy, George 1913- .... CLC 42
    See also CA 21-24R

Fante, John 1909-1983 .... CLC 60
    See also CANR 23; CA 69-72;
    obituary CA 109; DLB-Y 83

Farah, Nuruddin 1945- .... CLC 53
    See also CA 106

Fargue, Leon-Paul 1876-1947 ..... TCLC 11
    See also CA 109

Farigoule, Louis 1885-1972
    See Romains, Jules

Farina, Richard 1937?-1966........ CLC 9
    See also CA 81-84; obituary CA 25-28R

Farley, Walter 1920- .... CLC 17
    See also CANR 8; CA 17-20R; SATA 2, 43;
    DLB 22

Farmer, Philip Jose 1918- ...... CLC 1, 19
    See also CANR 4; CA 1-4R; DLB 8

Farrell, J(ames) G(ordon)
    1935-1979 .... CLC 6
    See also CA 73-76; obituary CA 89-92;
    DLB 14

Farrell, James T(homas)
    1904-1979 .... CLC 1, 4, 8, 11
    See also CANR 9; CA 5-8R;
    obituary CA 89-92; DLB 4, 9; DLB-DS 2

Farrell, M. J. 1904-
    See Keane, Molly

Fassbinder, Rainer Werner
    1946-1982 .... CLC 20
    See also CA 93-96; obituary CA 106

Fast, Howard (Melvin) 1914- ...... CLC 23
    See also CANR 1; CA 1-4R; SATA 7;
    DLB 9

Faulkner, William (Cuthbert)
    1897-1962 .... CLC 1, 3, 6, 8, 9, 11, 14,
                            18, 28, 52; SSC 1
    See also CA 81-84; DLB 9, 11, 44;
    DLB-Y 86; DLB-DS 2

Fauset, Jessie Redmon
    1884?-1961................ CLC 19, 54
    See also CA 109; DLB 51

Faust, Irvin 1924- .... CLC 8
    See also CA 33-36R; DLB 2, 28; DLB-Y 80

Fearing, Kenneth (Flexner)
    1902-1961 .... CLC 51
    See also CA 93-96; DLB 9

Federman, Raymond 1928- ...... CLC 6, 47
    See also CANR 10; CA 17-20R; DLB-Y 80

Federspiel, J(urg) F. 1931- .... CLC 42

Feiffer, Jules 1929- .... CLC 2, 8
    See also CA 17-20R; SATA 8; DLB 7, 44

Feinberg, David B. 1956- .... CLC 59

Feinstein, Elaine 1930- .... CLC 36
    See also CAAS 1; CA 69-72; DLB 14, 40

Feldman, Irving (Mordecai) 1928-.... CLC 7
    See also CANR 1; CA 1-4R

Fellini, Federico 1920- .... CLC 16
    See also CA 65-68

Felsen, Gregor 1916-
    See Felsen, Henry Gregor

Felsen, Henry Gregor 1916- .... CLC 17
    See also CANR 1; CA 1-4R; SAAS 2;
    SATA 1

Fenton, James (Martin) 1949-...... CLC 32
    See also CA 102; DLB 40

Ferber, Edna 1887-1968........... CLC 18
    See also CA 5-8R; obituary CA 25-28R;
    SATA 7; DLB 9, 28

Freeling, Nicolas 1927- .... **CLC 38**
See also CANR 1, 17; CA 49-52

Freeman, Douglas Southall
1886-1953 .... **TCLC 11**
See also CA 109; DLB 17

Freeman, Judith 1946- .... **CLC 55**

Freeman, Mary (Eleanor) Wilkins
1852-1930 .... **TCLC 9; SSC 1**
See also CA 106; DLB 12

Freeman, R(ichard) Austin
1862-1943 .... **TCLC 21**
See also CA 113; DLB 70

French, Marilyn 1929- ...... **CLC 10, 18, 60**
See also CANR 3; CA 69-72

Freneau, Philip Morin 1752-1832 .. **NCLC 1**
See also DLB 37, 43

Friedman, B(ernard) H(arper)
1926- .... **CLC 7**
See also CANR 3; CA 1-4R

Friedman, Bruce Jay 1930- .... **CLC 3, 5, 56**
See also CANR 25; CA 9-12R; DLB 2, 28

Friel, Brian 1929- .... **CLC 5, 42, 59**
See also CA 21-24R; DLB 13

Friis-Baastad, Babbis (Ellinor)
1921-1970 .... **CLC 12**
See also CA 17-20R; SATA 7

Frisch, Max (Rudolf)
1911- ...... **CLC 3, 9, 14, 18, 32, 44**
See also CA 85-88; DLB 69

Fromentin, Eugene (Samuel Auguste)
1820-1876 .... **NCLC 10**

Frost, Robert (Lee)
1874-1963 ... **CLC 1, 3, 4, 9, 10, 13, 15,**
26, 34, 44; PC 1
See also CA 89-92; SATA 14; DLB 54;
DLB-DS 7; CDALB 1917-1929

Fry, Christopher 1907- .... **CLC 2, 10, 14**
See also CANR 9; CA 17-20R; DLB 13

Frye, (Herman) Northrop 1912- .... **CLC 24**
See also CANR 8; CA 5-8R

Fuchs, Daniel 1909- .... **CLC 8, 22**
See also CAAS 5; CA 81-84; DLB 9, 26, 28

Fuchs, Daniel 1934- .... **CLC 34**
See also CANR 14; CA 37-40R

Fuentes, Carlos
1928- ...... **CLC 3, 8, 10, 13, 22, 41, 60**
See also CANR 10; CA 69-72

Fugard, Athol 1932- ... **CLC 5, 9, 14, 25, 40**
See also CA 85-88

Fugard, Sheila 1932- .... **CLC 48**
See also CA 125

Fuller, Charles (H., Jr.) 1939- ...... **CLC 25**
See also CA 108, 112; DLB 38

Fuller, John (Leopold) 1937- .... **CLC 62**
See also CANR 9; CA 21-22R; DLB 40

Fuller, (Sarah) Margaret
1810-1850 .... **NCLC 5**
See also Ossoli, Sarah Margaret (Fuller
marchesa d')
See also DLB 1, 59, 73; CDALB 1640-1865

Fuller, Roy (Broadbent) 1912- .... **CLC 4, 28**
See also CA 5-8R; DLB 15, 20

Fulton, Alice 1952- .... **CLC 52**
See also CA 116

Furphy, Joseph 1843-1912 .... **TCLC 25**

Futrelle, Jacques 1875-1912 ..... **TCLC 19**
See also CA 113

Gaboriau, Emile 1835-1873 ...... **NCLC 14**

Gadda, Carlo Emilio 1893-1973 .... **CLC 11**
See also CA 89-92

Gaddis, William
1922- .... **CLC 1, 3, 6, 8, 10, 19, 43**
See also CAAS 4; CANR 21; CA 17-20R;
DLB 2

Gaines, Ernest J. 1933- ...... **CLC 3, 11, 18**
See also CANR 6, 24; CA 9-12R; DLB 2,
33; DLB-Y 80

Gale, Zona 1874-1938 .... **TCLC 7**
See also CA 105; DLB 9

Gallagher, Tess 1943- .... **CLC 18, 63**
See also CA 106

Gallant, Mavis
1922- .... **CLC 7, 18, 38; SSC 5**
See also CA 69-72; DLB 53

Gallant, Roy A(rthur) 1924- .... **CLC 17**
See also CANR 4; CA 5-8R; SATA 4

Gallico, Paul (William) 1897-1976 ... **CLC 2**
See also CA 5-8R; obituary CA 69-72;
SATA 13; DLB 9

Galsworthy, John 1867-1933 .... **TCLC 1**
See also CA 104; DLB 10, 34

Galt, John 1779-1839 .... **NCLC 1**

Galvin, James 1951- .... **CLC 38**
See also CANR 26; CA 108

Gamboa, Frederico 1864-1939 ..... **TCLC 36**

Gann, Ernest K(ellogg) 1910- ...... **CLC 23**
See also CANR 1; CA 1-4R

Garcia Lorca, Federico
1899-1936 .... **TCLC 1, 7**
See also CA 104

Garcia Marquez, Gabriel (Jose)
1928- .... **CLC 2, 3, 8, 10, 15, 27, 47, 55**
See also CANR 10; CA 33-36R

Gardam, Jane 1928- .... **CLC 43**
See also CLR 12; CANR 2, 18; CA 49-52;
SATA 28, 39; DLB 14

Gardner, Herb 1934- .... **CLC 44**

Gardner, John (Champlin, Jr.)
1933-1982 .... **CLC 2, 3, 5, 7, 8, 10, 18,**
28, 34; SSC 7
See also CA 65-68; obituary CA 107;
obituary SATA 31, 40; DLB 2; DLB-Y 82

Gardner, John (Edmund) 1926- ..... **CLC 30**
See also CANR 15; CA 103

Garfield, Leon 1921- .... **CLC 12**
See also CA 17-20R; SATA 1, 32

Garland, (Hannibal) Hamlin
1860-1940 .... **TCLC 3**
See also CA 104; DLB 12, 71

Garneau, Hector (de) Saint Denys
1912-1943 .... **TCLC 13**
See also CA 111

Garner, Alan 1935- .... **CLC 17**
See also CLR 20; CANR 15; CA 73-76;
SATA 18

Garner, Hugh 1913-1979 .... **CLC 13**
See also CA 69-72; DLB 68

Garnett, David 1892-1981 .... **CLC 3**
See also CANR 17; CA 5-8R;
obituary CA 103; DLB 34

Garrett, George (Palmer, Jr.)
1929- .... **CLC 3, 11, 51**
See also CAAS 5; CANR 1; CA 1-4R;
DLB 2, 5; DLB-Y 83

Garrick, David 1717-1779 .... **LC 15**
See also DLB 84

Garrigue, Jean 1914-1972 .... **CLC 2, 8**
See also CANR 20; CA 5-8R;
obituary CA 37-40R

Gary, Romain 1914-1980 .... **CLC 25**
See also Kacew, Romain

Gascar, Pierre 1916- .... **CLC 11**
See also Fournier, Pierre

Gascoyne, David (Emery) 1916- .... **CLC 45**
See also CANR 10; CA 65-68; DLB 20

Gaskell, Elizabeth Cleghorn
1810-1865 .... **NCLC 5**
See also DLB 21

Gass, William H(oward)
1924- .... **CLC 1, 2, 8, 11, 15, 39**
See also CA 17-20R; DLB 2

Gautier, Theophile 1811-1872 ..... **NCLC 1**

Gaye, Marvin (Pentz) 1939-1984 ... **CLC 26**
See also obituary CA 112

Gebler, Carlo (Ernest) 1954- .... **CLC 39**
See also CA 119

Gee, Maggie 19??- .... **CLC 57**

Gee, Maurice (Gough) 1931- .... **CLC 29**
See also CA 97-100; SATA 46

Gelbart, Larry 1923?- .... **CLC 21, 61**
See also CA 73-76

Gelber, Jack 1932- .... **CLC 1, 6, 14, 60**
See also CANR 2; CA 1-4R; DLB 7

Gellhorn, Martha (Ellis) 1908- .. **CLC 14, 60**
See also CA 77-80; DLB-Y 82

Genet, Jean
1910-1986 ... **CLC 1, 2, 5, 10, 14, 44, 46**
See also CANR 18; CA 13-16R; DLB 72;
DLB-Y 86

Gent, Peter 1942- .... **CLC 29**
See also CA 89-92; DLB 72; DLB-Y 82

George, Jean Craighead 1919- ...... **CLC 35**
See also CLR 1; CA 5-8R; SATA 2;
DLB 52

George, Stefan (Anton)
1868-1933 .... **TCLC 2, 14**
See also CA 104

Gerhardi, William (Alexander) 1895-1977
See Gerhardie, William (Alexander)

Gerhardie, William (Alexander)
1895-1977 .... **CLC 5**
See also CANR 18; CA 25-28R;
obituary CA 73-76; DLB 36

Gertler, T(rudy) 1946?- .... **CLC 34**
See also CA 116

Gessner, Friedrike Victoria 1910-1980
See Adamson, Joy(-Friederike Victoria)

Ghelderode, Michel de
1898-1962 .... **CLC 6, 11**
See also CA 85-88

Haavikko, Paavo (Juhani)
    1931-.................... CLC 18, 34
    See also CA 106

Hacker, Marilyn 1942- .... CLC 5, 9, 23
    See also CA 77-80

Haggard, (Sir) H(enry) Rider
    1856-1925 .... TCLC 11
    See also CA 108; SATA 16; DLB 70

Haig-Brown, Roderick L(angmere)
    1908-1976
    .... CLC 21
    See also CANR 4; CA 5-8R;
        obituary CA 69-72; SATA 12

Hailey, Arthur 1920- .... CLC 5
    See also CANR 2; CA 1-4R; DLB-Y 82

Hailey, Elizabeth Forsythe 1938-... CLC 40
    See also CAAS 1; CANR 15; CA 93-96

Haines, John 1924-.............. CLC 58
    See also CANR 13; CA 19-20R; DLB 5

Haldeman, Joe 1943-............. CLC 61
    See also CA 53-56; DLB 8

Haley, Alex (Palmer) 1921-...... CLC 8, 12
    See also CA 77-80; DLB 38

Haliburton, Thomas Chandler
    1796-1865 .... NCLC 15
    See also DLB 11

Hall, Donald (Andrew, Jr.)
    1928-.............. CLC 1, 13, 37, 59
    See also CAAS 7; CANR 2; CA 5-8R;
        SATA 23; DLB 5

Hall, James Norman 1887-1951 ... TCLC 23
    See also CA 123; SATA 21

Hall, (Marguerite) Radclyffe
    1886-1943 .... TCLC 12
    See also CA 110

Hall, Rodney 1935- .... CLC 51
    See also CA 109

Halpern, Daniel 1945- .... CLC 14
    See also CA 33-36R

Hamburger, Michael (Peter Leopold)
    1924-.................... CLC 5, 14
    See also CAAS 4; CANR 2; CA 5-8R;
        DLB 27

Hamill, Pete 1935-.............. CLC 10
    See also CANR 18; CA 25-28R

Hamilton, Edmond 1904-1977....... CLC 1
    See also CANR 3; CA 1-4R; DLB 8

Hamilton, Gail 1911-
    See Corcoran, Barbara

Hamilton, Ian 1938-.............. CLC 55
    See also CA 106; DLB 40

Hamilton, Mollie 1909?-
    See Kaye, M(ary) M(argaret)

Hamilton, (Anthony Walter) Patrick
    1904-1962 .... CLC 51
    See also obituary CA 113; DLB 10

Hamilton, Virginia (Esther) 1936-... CLC 26
    See also CLR 1, 11; CANR 20; CA 25-28R;
        SATA 4; DLB 33, 52

Hammett, (Samuel) Dashiell
    1894-1961 .... CLC 3, 5, 10, 19, 47
    See also CA 81-84

Hammon, Jupiter 1711?-1800? .... NCLC 5
    See also DLB 31, 50

Hamner, Earl (Henry), Jr. 1923- ... CLC 12
    See also CA 73-76; DLB 6

Hampton, Christopher (James)
    1946-....................... CLC 4
    See also CA 25-28R; DLB 13

Hamsun, Knut 1859-1952...... TCLC 2, 14
    See also Pedersen, Knut

Handke, Peter 1942- .. CLC 5, 8, 10, 15, 38
    See also CA 77-80

Hanley, James 1901-1985 ... CLC 3, 5, 8, 13
    See also CA 73-76; obituary CA 117

Hannah, Barry 1942-........ CLC 23, 38
    See also CA 108, 110; DLB 6

Hansberry, Lorraine (Vivian)
    1930-1965 .... CLC 17, 62
    See also CA 109; obituary CA 25-28R;
        CABS 3; DLB 7, 38; CDALB 1941-1968

Hansen, Joseph 1923-............ CLC 38
    See also CANR 16; CA 29-32R

Hansen, Martin 1909-1955 .... TCLC 32

Hanson, Kenneth O(stlin) 1922- .... CLC 13
    See also CANR 7; CA 53-56

Hardenberg, Friedrich (Leopold Freiherr) von
    1772-1801
    See Novalis

Hardwick, Elizabeth 1916- .... CLC 13
    See also CANR 3; CA 5-8R; DLB 6

Hardy, Thomas
    1840-1928 ... TCLC 4, 10, 18, 32; SSC 2
    See also CA 104, 123; SATA 25; DLB 18,
        19

Hare, David 1947- .... CLC 29, 58
    See also CA 97-100; DLB 13

Harlan, Louis R(udolph) 1922-..... CLC 34
    See also CANR 25; CA 21-24R

Harling, Robert 1951?-............ CLC 53

Harmon, William (Ruth) 1938-..... CLC 38
    See also CANR 14; CA 33-36R

Harper, Frances Ellen Watkins
    1825-1911 .... TCLC 14
    See also CA 111, 125; DLB 50

Harper, Michael S(teven) 1938- .. CLC 7, 22
    See also CANR 24; CA 33-36R; DLB 41

Harris, Christie (Lucy Irwin)
    1907-....................... CLC 12
    See also CANR 6; CA 5-8R; SATA 6

Harris, Frank 1856-1931 .... TCLC 24
    See also CAAS 1; CA 109

Harris, George Washington
    1814-1869 .... NCLC 23
    See also DLB 3, 11

Harris, Joel Chandler 1848-1908 ... TCLC 2
    See also YABC 1; CA 104; DLB 11, 23, 42

Harris, John (Wyndham Parkes Lucas)
    Beynon 1903-1969
    See Wyndham, John
    See also CA 102; obituary CA 89-92

Harris, MacDonald 1921-......... CLC 9
    See also Heiney, Donald (William)

Harris, Mark 1922- .... CLC 19
    See also CAAS 3; CANR 2; CA 5-8R;
        DLB 2; DLB-Y 80

Harris, (Theodore) Wilson 1921-.... CLC 25
    See also CANR 11; CA 65-68

Harrison, Harry (Max) 1925-...... CLC 42
    See also CANR 5, 21; CA 1-4R; SATA 4;
        DLB 8

Harrison, James (Thomas) 1937-
    See Harrison, Jim
    See also CANR 8; CA 13-16R

Harrison, Jim 1937-.......... CLC 6, 14, 33
    See also Harrison, James (Thomas)
    See also DLB-Y 82

Harrison, Tony 1937-............. CLC 43
    See also CA 65-68; DLB 40

Harriss, Will(ard Irvin) 1922-...... CLC 34
    See also CA 111

Harte, (Francis) Bret(t)
    1836?-1902................. TCLC 1, 25
    See also CA 104; SATA 26; DLB 12, 64,
        74; CDALB 1865-1917

Hartley, L(eslie) P(oles)
    1895-1972 .... CLC 2, 22
    See also CA 45-48; obituary CA 37-40R;
        DLB 15

Hartman, Geoffrey H. 1929-....... CLC 27
    See also CA 117, 125; DLB 67

Haruf, Kent 19??-.............. CLC 34

Harwood, Ronald 1934-........... CLC 32
    See also CANR 4; CA 1-4R; DLB 13

Hasek, Jaroslav (Matej Frantisek)
    1883-1923 .... TCLC 4
    See also CA 104

Hass, Robert 1941-........... CLC 18, 39
    See also CA 111

Hastings, Selina 19??- .... CLC 44

Hauptmann, Gerhart (Johann Robert)
    1862-1946 .... TCLC 4
    See also CA 104; DLB 66

Havel, Vaclav 1936-........... CLC 25, 58
    See also CA 104

Haviaras, Stratis 1935- .... CLC 33
    See also CA 105

Hawkes, John (Clendennin Burne, Jr.)
    1925-...... CLC 1, 2, 3, 4, 7, 9, 14, 15,
        27, 49
    See also CANR 2; CA 1-4R; DLB 2, 7;
        DLB-Y 80

Hawking, Stephen (William)
    1948-....................... CLC 63
    See also CA 126, 129

Hawthorne, Julian 1846-1934 ..... TCLC 25

Hawthorne, Nathaniel
    1804-1864 ... NCLC 2, 10, 17, 23; SSC 3
    See also YABC 2; DLB 1, 74;
        CDALB 1640-1865

Hayashi Fumiko 1904-1951....... TCLC 27

Haycraft, Anna 19??-
    See Ellis, Alice Thomas

Hayden, Robert (Earl)
    1913-1980 .... CLC 5, 9, 14, 37
    See also CANR 24; CA 69-72;
        obituary CA 97-100; CABS 2; SATA 19;
        obituary SATA 26; DLB 5, 76;
        CDALB 1941-1968

Hayman, Ronald 1932-........... CLC 44
    See also CANR 18; CA 25-28R

Kaufman, Bob (Garnell)
1925-1986 .... **CLC 49**
See also CANR 22; CA 41-44R;
obituary CA 118; DLB 16, 41

Kaufman, George S(imon)
1889-1961 .... **CLC 38**
See also CA 108; obituary CA 93-96; DLB 7

Kaufman, Sue 1926-1977 .... **CLC 3, 8**
See also Barondess, Sue K(aufman)

Kavan, Anna 1904-1968 .... **CLC 5, 13**
See also Edmonds, Helen (Woods)
See also CANR 6; CA 5-8R

Kavanagh, Patrick (Joseph Gregory)
1905-1967 .... **CLC 22**
See also CA 123; obituary CA 25-28R;
DLB 15, 20

Kawabata, Yasunari
1899-1972 .... **CLC 2, 5, 9, 18**
See also CA 93-96; obituary CA 33-36R

Kaye, M(ary) M(argaret) 1909?-.... **CLC 28**
See also CANR 24; CA 89-92

Kaye, Mollie 1909?-
See Kaye, M(ary) M(argaret)

Kaye-Smith, Sheila 1887-1956..... **TCLC 20**
See also CA 118; DLB 36

Kazan, Elia 1909- .... **CLC 6, 16, 63**
See also CA 21-24R

Kazantzakis, Nikos
1885?-1957.............. **TCLC 2, 5, 33**
See also CA 105

Kazin, Alfred 1915- .... **CLC 34, 38**
See also CAAS 7; CANR 1; CA 1-4R

Keane, Mary Nesta (Skrine) 1904-
See Keane, Molly
See also CA 108, 114

Keane, Molly 1904- .... **CLC 31**
See also Keane, Mary Nesta (Skrine)

Keates, Jonathan 19??-............ **CLC 34**

Keaton, Buster 1895-1966 .... **CLC 20**

Keaton, Joseph Francis 1895-1966
See Keaton, Buster

Keats, John 1795-1821...... **NCLC 8; PC 1**

Keene, Donald 1922- .... **CLC 34**
See also CANR 5; CA 1-4R

Keillor, Garrison 1942- .... **CLC 40**
See also Keillor, Gary (Edward)
See also CA 111; DLB 87

Keillor, Gary (Edward)
See Keillor, Garrison
See also CA 111, 117

Kell, Joseph 1917-
See Burgess (Wilson, John) Anthony

Keller, Gottfried 1819-1890....... **NCLC 2**

Kellerman, Jonathan (S.) 1949-..... **CLC 44**
See also CA 106

Kelley, William Melvin 1937-...... **CLC 22**
See also CA 77-80; DLB 33

Kellogg, Marjorie 1922-............. **CLC 2**
See also CA 81-84

Kelly, M. T. 1947-................ **CLC 55**
See also CANR 19; CA 97-100

Kelman, James 1946-............. **CLC 58**

Kemal, Yashar 1922- .... **CLC 14, 29**
See also CA 89-92

Kemble, Fanny 1809-1893 .... **NCLC 18**
See also DLB 32

Kemelman, Harry 1908-............. **CLC 2**
See also CANR 6; CA 9-12R; DLB 28

Kempe, Margery 1373?-1440?........ **LC 6**

Kempis, Thomas á 1380-1471 ...... **LC 11**

Kendall, Henry 1839-1882....... **NCLC 12**

Keneally, Thomas (Michael)
1935- ...... **CLC 5, 8, 10, 14, 19, 27, 43**
See also CANR 10; CA 85-88

Kennedy, John Pendleton
1795-1870 .... **NCLC 2**
See also DLB 3

Kennedy, Joseph Charles 1929-...... **CLC 8**
See also Kennedy, X. J.
See also CANR 4; CA 1-4R; SATA 14

Kennedy, William (Joseph)
1928-............... **CLC 6, 28, 34, 53**
See also CANR 14; CA 85-88; DLB-Y 85;
AAYA 1

Kennedy, X. J. 1929- .... **CLC 8, 42**
See also Kennedy, Joseph Charles
See also DLB 5

Kerouac, Jack
1922-1969 .... **CLC 1, 2, 3, 5, 14, 29, 61**
See also Kerouac, Jean-Louis Lebris de
See also DLB 2, 16; DLB-DS 3;
CDALB 1941-1968

Kerouac, Jean-Louis Lebris de 1922-1969
See Kerouac, Jack
See also CA 5-8R; obituary CA 25-28R;
CDALB 1941-1968

Kerr, Jean 1923-................. **CLC 22**
See also CANR 7; CA 5-8R

Kerr, M. E. 1927-............. **CLC 12, 35**
See also Meaker, Marijane
See also SAAS 1

Kerr, Robert 1970?- .... **CLC 55, 59**

Kerrigan, (Thomas) Anthony
1918- .... **CLC 4, 6**
See also CANR 4; CA 49-52

Kesey, Ken (Elton)
1935- .... **CLC 1, 3, 6, 11, 46**
See also CANR 22; CA 1-4R; DLB 2, 16

Kesselring, Joseph (Otto)
1902-1967 .... **CLC 45**

Kessler, Jascha (Frederick) 1929-.... **CLC 4**
See also CANR 8; CA 17-20R

Kettelkamp, Larry 1933-.......... **CLC 12**
See also CANR 16; CA 29-32R; SAAS 3;
SATA 2

Kherdian, David 1931-........... **CLC 6, 9**
See also CAAS 2; CA 21-24R; SATA 16

Khlebnikov, Velimir (Vladimirovich)
1885-1922 .... **TCLC 20**
See also CA 117

Khodasevich, Vladislav (Felitsianovich)
1886-1939 .... **TCLC 15**
See also CA 115

Kielland, Alexander (Lange)
1849-1906 .... **TCLC 5**
See also CA 104

Kiely, Benedict 1919-.......... **CLC 23, 43**
See also CANR 2; CA 1-4R; DLB 15

Kienzle, William X(avier) 1928-.... **CLC 25**
See also CAAS 1; CANR 9; CA 93-96

Killens, John Oliver 1916-......... **CLC 10**
See also CAAS 2; CANR 26; CA 77-80,
123; DLB 33

Killigrew, Anne 1660-1685........... **LC 4**

Kincaid, Jamaica 1949?- .... **CLC 43**
See also CA 125

King, Francis (Henry) 1923- ..... **CLC 8, 53**
See also CANR 1; CA 1-4R; DLB 15

King, Stephen (Edwin)
1947- .... **CLC 12, 26, 37, 61**
See also CANR 1; CA 61-64; SATA 9, 55;
DLB-Y 80

Kingman, (Mary) Lee 1919-....... **CLC 17**
See also Natti, (Mary) Lee
See also CA 5-8R; SAAS 3; SATA 1

Kingsley, Sidney 1906-............ **CLC 44**
See also CA 85-88; DLB 7

Kingsolver, Barbara 1955-......... **CLC 55**

Kingston, Maxine Hong
1940- .... **CLC 12, 19, 58**
See also CANR 13; CA 69-72; SATA 53;
DLB-Y 80

Kinnell, Galway
1927- .... **CLC 1, 2, 3, 5, 13, 29**
See also CANR 10; CA 9-12R; DLB 5;
DLB-Y 87

Kinsella, Thomas 1928- ...... **CLC 4, 19, 43**
See also CANR 15; CA 17-20R; DLB 27

Kinsella, W(illiam) P(atrick)
1935- .... **CLC 27, 43**
See also CAAS 7; CANR 21; CA 97-100

Kipling, (Joseph) Rudyard
1865-1936 .... **TCLC 8, 17; SSC 5**
See also YABC 2; CA 105, 120; DLB 19, 34

Kirkup, James 1918- .... **CLC 1**
See also CAAS 4; CANR 2; CA 1-4R;
SATA 12; DLB 27

Kirkwood, James 1930-1989 .... **CLC 9**
See also CANR 6; CA 1-4R

Kis, Danilo 1935-1989 .... **CLC 57**
See also CA 118, 129; brief entry CA 109

Kivi, Aleksis 1834-1872 .... **NCLC 30**

Kizer, Carolyn (Ashley) 1925-... **CLC 15, 39**
See also CAAS 5; CANR 24; CA 65-68;
DLB 5

Klappert, Peter 1942-............. **CLC 57**
See also CA 33-36R; DLB 5

Klausner, Amos 1939-
See Oz, Amos

Klein, A(braham) M(oses)
1909-1972 .... **CLC 19**
See also CA 101; obituary CA 37-40R;
DLB 68

Klein, Norma 1938-1989 .... **CLC 30**
See also CLR 2; CANR 15; CA 41-44R;
SAAS 1; SATA 7

Klein, T.E.D. 19??-............... **CLC 34**
See also CA 119

Kleist, Heinrich von 1777-1811.... **NCLC 2**

Mandelstam, Osip (Emilievich)
1891?-1938?.............. TCLC **2, 6**
See also CA 104

Mander, Jane 1877-1949 .... TCLC **31**

Mandiargues, Andre Pieyre de
1909- .... CLC **41**
See also CA 103

Mangan, James Clarence
1803-1849 .... NCLC **27**

Manley, (Mary) Delariviere
1672?-1724.................... LC **1**
See also DLB 39

Mann, (Luiz) Heinrich 1871-1950... TCLC **9**
See also CA 106; DLB 66

Mann, Thomas
1875-1955 ...... TCLC **2, 8, 14, 21, 35;**
SSC **5**
See also CA 104, 128; DLB 66

Manning, Frederic 1882-1935 ..... TCLC **25**

Manning, Olivia 1915-1980 ..... CLC **5, 19**
See also CA 5-8R; obituary CA 101

Mano, D. Keith 1942- .... CLC **2, 10**
See also CAAS 6; CANR 26; CA 25-28R;
DLB 6

Mansfield, Katherine
1888-1923 .... TCLC **2, 8, 39**
See also CA 104

Manso, Peter 1940- .... CLC **39**
See also CA 29-32R

Manzoni, Alessandro 1785-1873 .. NCLC **29**

Mapu, Abraham (ben Jekutiel)
1808-1867 .... NCLC **18**

Marat, Jean Paul 1743-1793....... LC **10**

Marcel, Gabriel (Honore)
1889-1973 .... CLC **15**
See also CA 102; obituary CA 45-48

Marchbanks, Samuel 1913-
See Davies, (William) Robertson

Marie de l'Incarnation 1599-1672.... LC **10**

Marinetti, F(ilippo) T(ommaso)
1876-1944 .... TCLC **10**
See also CA 107

Marivaux, Pierre Carlet de Chamblain de
(1688-1763) .... LC **4**

Markandaya, Kamala 1924-...... CLC **8, 38**
See also Taylor, Kamala (Purnaiya)

Markfield, Wallace (Arthur) 1926-... CLC **8**
See also CAAS 3; CA 69-72; DLB 2, 28

Markham, Robert 1922-
See Amis, Kingsley (William)

Marks, J. 1942-
See Highwater, Jamake

Marley, Bob 1945-1981 .... CLC **17**
See also Marley, Robert Nesta

Marley, Robert Nesta 1945-1981
See Marley, Bob
See also CA 107; obituary CA 103

Marmontel, Jean-Francois
1723-1799 .... LC **2**

Marquand, John P(hillips)
1893-1960 .... CLC **2, 10**
See also CA 85-88; DLB 9

Marquez, Gabriel Garcia 1928-
See Garcia Marquez, Gabriel

Marquis, Don(ald Robert Perry)
1878-1937 .... TCLC **7**
See also CA 104; DLB 11, 25

Marryat, Frederick 1792-1848 .... NCLC **3**
See also DLB 21

Marsh, (Dame Edith) Ngaio
1899-1982 .... CLC **7, 53**
See also CANR 6; CA 9-12R; DLB 77

Marshall, Garry 1935?- .... CLC **17**
See also CA 111

Marshall, Paule 1929- ..... CLC **27;** SSC **3**
See also CANR 25; CA 77-80; DLB 33

Marsten, Richard 1926-
See Hunter, Evan

Martin, Steve 1945?- .... CLC **30**
See also CA 97-100

Martin du Gard, Roger
1881-1958 .... TCLC **24**
See also CA 118

Martineau, Harriet 1802-1876.... NCLC **26**
See also YABC 2; DLB 21, 55

Martinez Ruiz, Jose 1874-1967
See Azorin
See also CA 93-96

Martinez Sierra, Gregorio
1881-1947 .... TCLC **6**
See also CA 104, 115

Martinez Sierra, Maria (de la O'LeJarraga)
1880?-1974.................. TCLC **6**
See also obituary CA 115

Martinson, Harry (Edmund)
1904-1978 .... CLC **14**
See also CA 77-80

Marvell, Andrew 1621-1678......... LC **4**

Marx, Karl (Heinrich)
1818-1883 .... NCLC **17**

Masaoka Shiki 1867-1902 .... TCLC **18**

Masefield, John (Edward)
1878-1967 .... CLC **11, 47**
See also CAP 2; CA 19-20;
obituary CA 25-28R; SATA 19; DLB 10,
19

Maso, Carole 19??-............... CLC **44**

Mason, Bobbie Ann
1940- .... CLC **28, 43;** SSC **4**
See also CANR 11; CA 53-56; SAAS 1;
DLB-Y 87

Mason, Nick 1945-............... CLC **35**
See also Pink Floyd

Mason, Tally 1909-1971
See Derleth, August (William)

Masters, Edgar Lee
1868?-1950......... TCLC **2, 25;** PC **1**
See also CA 104; DLB 54;
CDALB 1865-1917

Masters, Hilary 1928- .... CLC **48**
See also CANR 13; CA 25-28R

Mastrosimone, William 19??- ...... CLC **36**

Matheson, Richard (Burton)
1926- .... CLC **37**
See also CA 97-100; DLB 8, 44

Mathews, Harry 1930-.......... CLC **6, 52**
See also CAAS 6; CANR 18; CA 21-24R

Mathias, Roland (Glyn) 1915-..... CLC **45**
See also CANR 19; CA 97-100; DLB 27

Matthews, Greg 1949- .... CLC **45**

Matthews, William 1942-......... CLC **40**
See also CANR 12; CA 29-32R; DLB 5

Matthias, John (Edward) 1941-...... CLC **9**
See also CA 33-36R

Matthiessen, Peter 1927-... CLC **5, 7, 11, 32**
See also CANR 21; CA 9-12R; SATA 27;
DLB 6

Maturin, Charles Robert
1780?-1824................. NCLC **6**

Matute, Ana Maria 1925-......... CLC **11**
See also CA 89-92

Maugham, W(illiam) Somerset
1874-1965 .... CLC **1, 11, 15**
See also CA 5-8R; obituary CA 25-28R;
DLB 10, 36

Maupassant, (Henri Rene Albert) Guy de
1850-1893 .... NCLC **1;** SSC **1**

Mauriac, Claude 1914-............ CLC **9**
See also CA 89-92

Mauriac, Francois (Charles)
1885-1970 .... CLC **4, 9, 56**
See also CAP 2; CA 25-28; DLB 65

Mavor, Osborne Henry 1888-1951
See Bridie, James
See also CA 104

Maxwell, William (Keepers, Jr.)
1908- .... CLC **19**
See also CA 93-96; DLB-Y 80

May, Elaine 1932- .... CLC **16**
See also CA 124; DLB 44

Mayakovsky, Vladimir (Vladimirovich)
1893-1930 .... TCLC **4, 18**
See also CA 104

Maynard, Joyce 1953-............ CLC **23**
See also CA 111

Mayne, William (James Carter)
1928- .... CLC **12**
See also CA 9-12R; SATA 6

Mayo, Jim 1908?-
See L'Amour, Louis (Dearborn)

Maysles, Albert 1926- and Maysles, David
1926- .... CLC **16**

Maysles, Albert 1926-
See Maysles, Albert and Maysles, David
See also CA 29-32R

Maysles, David 1932-
See Maysles, Albert and Maysles, David

Mazer, Norma Fox 1931- .... CLC **26**
See also CLR 23; CANR 12; CA 69-72;
SAAS 1; SATA 24

McAuley, James (Phillip)
1917-1976 .... CLC **45**
See also CA 97-100

McBain, Ed 1926-
See Hunter, Evan

McBrien, William 1930- .... CLC **44**
See also CA 107

McCaffrey, Anne 1926- .... **CLC 17**
See also CANR 15; CA 25-28R; SATA 8;
DLB 8

McCarthy, Cormac 1933-....... **CLC 4, 57**
See also CANR 10; CA 13-16R; DLB 6

McCarthy, Mary (Therese)
1912-1989-... **CLC 1, 3, 5, 14, 24, 39, 59**
See also CANR 16; CA 5-8R; DLB 2;
DLB-Y 81

McCartney, (James) Paul
1942- .... **CLC 12, 35**

McCauley, Stephen 19??-......... **CLC 50**

McClure, Michael 1932- .... **CLC 6, 10**
See also CANR 17; CA 21-24R; DLB 16

McCorkle, Jill (Collins) 1958-..... **CLC 51**
See also CA 121; DLB-Y 87

McCourt, James 1941-............ **CLC 5**
See also CA 57-60

McCoy, Horace 1897-1955 .... **TCLC 28**
See also CA 108; DLB 9

McCrae, John 1872-1918........ **TCLC 12**
See also CA 109

McCullers, (Lula) Carson (Smith)
1917-1967 .... **CLC 1, 4, 10, 12, 48**
See also CANR 18; CA 5-8R;
obituary CA 25-28R; CABS 1; SATA 27;
DLB 2, 7; CDALB 1941-1968

McCullough, Colleen 1938?-....... **CLC 27**
See also CANR 17; CA 81-84

McElroy, Joseph (Prince)
1930- .... **CLC 5, 47**
See also CA 17-20R

McEwan, Ian (Russell) 1948- ..... **CLC 13**
See also CANR 14; CA 61-64; DLB 14

McFadden, David 1940-.......... **CLC 48**
See also CA 104; DLB 60

McGahern, John 1934-....... **CLC 5, 9, 48**
See also CA 17-20R; DLB 14

McGinley, Patrick 1937-.......... **CLC 41**
See also CA 120

McGinley, Phyllis 1905-1978 ...... **CLC 14**
See also CANR 19; CA 9-12R;
obituary CA 77-80; SATA 2, 44;
obituary SATA 24; DLB 11, 48

McGinniss, Joe 1942-............. **CLC 32**
See also CA 25-28R

McGivern, Maureen Daly 1921-
See Daly, Maureen
See also CA 9-12R

McGrath, Patrick 1950-.......... **CLC 55**

McGrath, Thomas 1916- .... **CLC 28, 59**
See also CANR 6; CA 9-12R, 130;
SATA 41

McGuane, Thomas (Francis III)
1939- .... **CLC 3, 7, 18**
See also CANR 5; CA 49-52; DLB 2;
DLB-Y 80

McGuckian, Medbh 1950-........ **CLC 48**
See also DLB 40

McHale, Tom 1941-1982........ **CLC 3, 5**
See also CA 77-80; obituary CA 106

McIlvanney, William 1936-....... **CLC 42**
See also CA 25-28R; DLB 14

McIlwraith, Maureen Mollie Hunter 1922-
See Hunter, Mollie
See also CA 29-32R; SATA 2

McInerney, Jay 1955- .... **CLC 34**
See also CA 116, 123

McIntyre, Vonda N(eel) 1948- ..... **CLC 18**
See also CANR 17; CA 81-84

McKay, Claude 1889-1948... **TCLC 7; PC 2**
See also CA 104, 124; DLB 4, 45, 51

McKuen, Rod 1933-............ **CLC 1, 3**
See also CA 41-44R

McLuhan, (Herbert) Marshall
1911-1980 .... **CLC 37**
See also CANR 12; CA 9-12R;
obituary CA 102

McManus, Declan Patrick 1955-
See Costello, Elvis

McMillan, Terry 1951- .... **CLC 50, 61**

McMurtry, Larry (Jeff)
1936- .... **CLC 2, 3, 7, 11, 27, 44**
See also CANR 19; CA 5-8R; DLB 2;
DLB-Y 80, 87

McNally, Terrence 1939-...... **CLC 4, 7, 41**
See also CANR 2; CA 45-48; DLB 7

McPhee, John 1931-............. **CLC 36**
See also CANR 20; CA 65-68

McPherson, James Alan 1943-..... **CLC 19**
See also CANR 24; CA 25-28R; DLB 38

McPherson, William 1939- .... **CLC 34**
See also CA 57-60

McSweeney, Kerry 19??-......... **CLC 34**

Mead, Margaret 1901-1978....... **CLC 37**
See also CANR 4; CA 1-4R;
obituary CA 81-84; SATA 20

Meaker, M. J. 1927-
See Kerr, M. E.; Meaker, Marijane

Meaker, Marijane 1927-
See Kerr, M. E.
See also CA 107; SATA 20

Medoff, Mark (Howard) 1940-... **CLC 6, 23**
See also CANR 5; CA 53-56; DLB 7

Megged, Aharon 1920-............ **CLC 9**
See also CANR 1; CA 49-52

Mehta, Ved (Parkash) 1934-...... **CLC 37**
See also CANR 2, 23; CA 1-4R

Mellor, John 1953?-
See The Clash

Meltzer, Milton 1915-......... **CLC 26 13**
See also CA 13-16R; SAAS 1; SATA 1, 50;
DLB 61

Melville, Herman
1819-1891 ...... **NCLC 3, 12, 29; SSC 1**
See also SATA 59; DLB 3, 74;
CDALB 1640-1865

Membreno, Alejandro 1972- .... **CLC 59**

Mencken, H(enry) L(ouis)
1880-1956 .... **TCLC 13**
See also CA 105; DLB 11, 29, 63

Mercer, David 1928-1980.......... **CLC 5**
See also CA 9-12R; obituary CA 102;
DLB 13

Meredith, George 1828-1909...... **TCLC 17**
See also CA 117; DLB 18, 35, 57

Meredith, William (Morris)
1919- .... **CLC 4, 13, 22, 55**
See also CANR 6; CA 9-12R; DLB 5

Merezhkovsky, Dmitri
1865-1941 .... **TCLC 29**

Merimee, Prosper
1803-1870 .... **NCLC 6; SSC 7**

Merkin, Daphne 1954-........... **CLC 44**
See also CANR 123

Merrill, James (Ingram)
1926- .... **CLC 2, 3, 6, 8, 13, 18, 34**
See also CANR 10; CA 13-16R; DLB 5;
DLB-Y 85

Merton, Thomas (James)
1915-1968 .... **CLC 1, 3, 11, 34**
See also CANR 22; CA 5-8R;
obituary CA 25-28R; DLB 48; DLB-Y 81

Merwin, W(illiam) S(tanley)
1927- ... **CLC 1, 2, 3, 5, 8, 13, 18, 45**
See also CANR 15; CA 13-16R; DLB 5

Metcalf, John 1938-.............. **CLC 37**
See also CA 113; DLB 60

Mew, Charlotte (Mary)
1870-1928 .... **TCLC 8**
See also CA 105; DLB 19

Mewshaw, Michael 1943-.......... **CLC 9**
See also CANR 7; CA 53-56; DLB-Y 80

Meyer-Meyrink, Gustav 1868-1932
See Meyrink, Gustav
See also CA 117

Meyers, Jeffrey 1939-........... **CLC 39**
See also CA 73-76

Meynell, Alice (Christiana Gertrude
Thompson) 1847-1922 .... **TCLC 6**
See also CA 104; DLB 19

Meyrink, Gustav 1868-1932...... **TCLC 21**
See also Meyer-Meyrink, Gustav

Michaels, Leonard 1933-........ **CLC 6, 25**
See also CANR 21; CA 61-64

Michaux, Henri 1899-1984 ...... **CLC 8, 19**
See also CA 85-88; obituary CA 114

Michelangelo 1475-1564........... **LC 12**

Michener, James A(lbert)
1907- .... **CLC 1, 5, 11, 29, 60**
See also CANR 21; CA 5-8R; DLB 6

Mickiewicz, Adam 1798-1855 ..... **NCLC 3**

Middleton, Christopher 1926-...... **CLC 13**
See also CA 13-16R; DLB 40

Middleton, Stanley 1919-........ **CLC 7, 38**
See also CANR 21; CA 25-28R; DLB 14

Migueis, Jose Rodrigues 1901-..... **CLC 10**

Mikszath, Kalman 1847-1910 ..... **TCLC 31**

Miles, Josephine (Louise)
1911-1985 .... **CLC 1, 2, 14, 34, 39**
See also CANR 2; CA 1-4R;
obituary CA 116; DLB 48

Mill, John Stuart 1806-1873..... **NCLC 11**

Millar, Kenneth 1915-1983 .... **CLC 14**
See also Macdonald, Ross
See also CANR 16; CA 9-12R;
obituary CA 110; DLB 2; DLB-Y 83

Millay, Edna St. Vincent
1892-1950 .... **TCLC 4**
See also CA 104; DLB 45

Miller, Arthur
  1915- ...... **CLC 1, 2, 6, 10, 15, 26, 47**
  See also CANR 2; CA 1-4R; DLB 7;
  CDALB 1941-1968

Miller, Henry (Valentine)
  1891-1980 ...... **CLC 1, 2, 4, 9, 14, 43**
  See also CA 9-12R; obituary CA 97-100;
  DLB 4, 9; DLB-Y 80

Miller, Jason 1939?- .... **CLC 2**
  See also CA 73-76; DLB 7

Miller, Sue 19??- .... **CLC 44**

Miller, Walter M(ichael), Jr.
  1923- .... **CLC 4, 30**
  See also CA 85-88; DLB 8

Millhauser, Steven 1943- ...... **CLC 21, 54**
  See also CA 108, 110, 111; DLB 2

Millin, Sarah Gertrude 1889-1968 .. **CLC 49**
  See also CA 102; obituary CA 93-96

Milne, A(lan) A(lexander)
  1882-1956 .... **TCLC 6**
  See also CLR 1; YABC 1; CA 104; DLB 10

Milner, Ron(ald) 1938- .... **CLC 56**
  See also CANR 24; CA 73-76; DLB 38

Milosz Czeslaw
  1911- ...... **CLC 5, 11, 22, 31, 56**
  See also CANR 23; CA 81-84

Milton, John 1608-1674 .... **LC 9**

Miner, Valerie (Jane) 1947- .... **CLC 40**
  See also CA 97-100

Minot, Susan 1956- .... **CLC 44**

Minus, Ed 1938- .... **CLC 39**

Miro (Ferrer), Gabriel (Francisco Victor)
  1879-1930 .... **TCLC 5**
  See also CA 104

Mishima, Yukio
  1925-1970 .... **CLC 2, 4, 6, 9, 27; SSC 4**
  See also Hiraoka, Kimitake

Mistral, Gabriela 1889-1957 .... **TCLC 2**
  See also CA 104

Mitchell, James Leslie 1901-1935
  See Gibbon, Lewis Grassic
  See also CA 104; DLB 15

Mitchell, Joni 1943- .... **CLC 12**
  See also CA 112

Mitchell (Marsh), Margaret (Munnerlyn)
  1900-1949 .... **TCLC 11**
  See also CA 109; DLB 9

Mitchell, S. Weir 1829-1914 ...... **TCLC 36**

Mitchell, W(illiam) O(rmond)
  1914- .... **CLC 25**
  See also CANR 15; CA 77-80

Mitford, Mary Russell 1787-1855 .. **NCLC 4**

Mitford, Nancy 1904-1973 .... **CLC 44**
  See also CA 9-12R

Miyamoto Yuriko 1899-1951 ...... **TCLC 37**

Mo, Timothy 1950- .... **CLC 46**
  See also CA 117

Modarressi, Taghi 1931- .... **CLC 44**
  See also CA 121

Modiano, Patrick (Jean) 1945- ..... **CLC 18**
  See also CANR 17; CA 85-88

Mofolo, Thomas (Mokopu)
  1876-1948 .... **TCLC 22**
  See also CA 121

Mohr, Nicholasa 1935- .... **CLC 12**
  See also CLR 22; CANR 1; CA 49-52;
  SATA 8

Mojtabai, A(nn) G(race)
  1938- .... **CLC 5, 9, 15, 29**
  See also CA 85-88

Moliere 1622-1673 .... **LC 10**

Molnar, Ferenc 1878-1952 .... **TCLC 20**
  See also CA 109

Momaday, N(avarre) Scott
  1934- .... **CLC 2, 19**
  See also CANR 14; CA 25-28R; SATA 30,
  48

Monroe, Harriet 1860-1936 .... **TCLC 12**
  See also CA 109; DLB 54

Montagu, Elizabeth 1720-1800 .... **NCLC 7**

Montagu, Lady Mary (Pierrepont) Wortley
  1689-1762 .... **LC 9**

Montague, John (Patrick)
  1929- .... **CLC 13, 46**
  See also CANR 9; CA 9-12R; DLB 40

Montaigne, Michel (Eyquem) de
  1533-1592 .... **LC 8**

Montale, Eugenio 1896-1981 ... **CLC 7, 9, 18**
  See also CA 17-20R; obituary CA 104

Montgomery, Marion (H., Jr.)
  1925- .... **CLC 7**
  See also CANR 3; CA 1-4R; DLB 6

Montgomery, Robert Bruce 1921-1978
  See Crispin, Edmund
  See also CA 104

Montherlant, Henri (Milon) de
  1896-1972 .... **CLC 8, 19**
  See also CA 85-88; obituary CA 37-40R;
  DLB 72

Montisquieu, Charles-Louis de Secondat
  1689-1755 .... **LC 7**

Monty Python .... **CLC 21**

Moodie, Susanna (Strickland)
  1803-1885 .... **NCLC 14**

Mooney, Ted 1951- .... **CLC 25**

Moorcock, Michael (John)
  1939- .... **CLC 5, 27, 58**
  See also CAAS 5; CANR 2, 17; CA 45-48;
  DLB 14

Moore, Brian
  1921- .... **CLC 1, 3, 5, 7, 8, 19, 32**
  See also CANR 1; CA 1-4R

Moore, George (Augustus)
  1852-1933 .... **TCLC 7**
  See also CA 104; DLB 10, 18, 57

Moore, Lorrie 1957- .... **CLC 39, 45**
  See also Moore, Marie Lorena

Moore, Marianne (Craig)
  1887-1972 ... **CLC 1, 2, 4, 8, 10, 13, 19,
                                    47**
  See also CANR 3; CA 1-4R;
  obituary CA 33-36R; SATA 20; DLB 45

Moore, Marie Lorena 1957-
  See Moore, Lorrie
  See also CA 116

Moore, Thomas 1779-1852 .... **NCLC 6**

Morand, Paul 1888-1976 .... **CLC 41**
  See also obituary CA 69-72; DLB 65

Morante, Elsa 1918-1985 .... **CLC 8, 47**
  See also CA 85-88; obituary CA 117

Moravia, Alberto
  1907- .... **CLC 2, 7, 11, 18, 27, 46**
  See also Pincherle, Alberto

More, Hannah 1745-1833 .... **NCLC 27**

More, Henry 1614-1687 .... **LC 9**

More, (Sir) Thomas 1478-1535 ..... **LC 10**

Moreas, Jean 1856-1910 .... **TCLC 18**

Morgan, Berry 1919- .... **CLC 6**
  See also CA 49-52; DLB 6

Morgan, Edwin (George) 1920- ..... **CLC 31**
  See also CANR 3; CA 7-8R; DLB 27

Morgan, (George) Frederick
  1922- .... **CLC 23**
  See also CANR 21; CA 17-20R

Morgan, Janet 1945- .... **CLC 39**
  See also CA 65-68

Morgan, Lady 1776?-1859 .... **NCLC 29**

Morgan, Robin 1941- .... **CLC 2**
  See also CA 69-72

Morgenstern, Christian (Otto Josef Wolfgang)
  1871-1914 .... **TCLC 8**
  See also CA 105

Moricz, Zsigmond 1879-1942 ..... **TCLC 33**

Morike, Eduard (Friedrich)
  1804-1875 .... **NCLC 10**

Mori Ogai 1862-1922 .... **TCLC 14**
  See also Mori Rintaro

Mori Rintaro 1862-1922
  See Mori Ogai
  See also CA 110

Moritz, Karl Philipp 1756-1793 ...... **LC 2**

Morris, Julian 1916-
  See West, Morris L.

Morris, Steveland Judkins 1950-
  See Wonder, Stevie
  See also CA 111

Morris, William 1834-1896 .... **NCLC 4**
  See also DLB 18, 35, 57

Morris, Wright (Marion)
  1910- .... **CLC 1, 3, 7, 18, 37**
  See also CA 9-12R; DLB 2; DLB-Y 81

Morrison, James Douglas 1943-1971
  See Morrison, Jim
  See also CA 73-76

Morrison, Jim 1943-1971 .... **CLC 17**
  See also Morrison, James Douglas

Morrison, Toni 1931- ..... **CLC 4, 10, 22, 55**
  See also CA 29-32R; DLB 6, 33; DLB-Y 81;
  AAYA 1

Morrison, Van 1945- .... **CLC 21**
  See also CA 116

Mortimer, John (Clifford)
  1923- .... **CLC 28, 43**
  See also CANR 21; CA 13-16R; DLB 13

Mortimer, Penelope (Ruth) 1918- .... **CLC 5**
  See also CA 57-60

Mosher, Howard Frank 19??- ...... **CLC 62**

Nissenson, Hugh 1933- . . . . **CLC 4, 9**
See also CA 17-20R; DLB 28

Niven, Larry 1938- . . . . **CLC 8**
See also Niven, Laurence Van Cott
See also DLB 8

Niven, Laurence Van Cott 1938-
See Niven, Larry
See also CANR 14; CA 21-24R

Nixon, Agnes Eckhardt 1927- . . . . . . **CLC 21**
See also CA 110

Nizan, Paul 1905-1940 . . . . **TCLC 40**
See also DLB 72

Nkosi, Lewis 1936- . . . . **CLC 45**
See also CA 65-68

Nodier, (Jean) Charles (Emmanuel)
1780-1844 . . . . **NCLC 19**

Nolan, Christopher 1965- . . . . **CLC 58**
See also CA 111

Nordhoff, Charles 1887-1947 . . . . . **TCLC 23**
See also CA 108; SATA 23; DLB 9

Norman, Marsha 1947- . . . . **CLC 28**
See also CA 105; DLB-Y 84

Norris, (Benjamin) Frank(lin)
1870-1902 . . . . **TCLC 24**
See also CA 110; DLB 12, 71;
CDALB 1865-1917

Norris, Leslie 1921- . . . . **CLC 14**
See also CANR 14; CAP 1; CA 11-12;
DLB 27

North, Andrew 1912-
See Norton, Andre

North, Christopher 1785-1854
See Wilson, John

Norton, Alice Mary 1912-
See Norton, Andre
See also CANR 2; CA 1-4R; SATA 1, 43

Norton, Andre 1912- . . . . **CLC 12**
See also Norton, Mary Alice
See also DLB 8, 52

Norway, Nevil Shute 1899-1960
See Shute (Norway), Nevil
See also CA 102; obituary CA 93-96

Norwid, Cyprian Kamil
1821-1883 . . . . **NCLC 17**

Nossack, Hans Erich 1901-1978 . . . . . **CLC 6**
See also CA 93-96; obituary CA 85-88;
DLB 69

Nova, Craig 1945- . . . . **CLC 7, 31**
See also CANR 2; CA 45-48

Novak, Joseph 1933-
See Kosinski, Jerzy (Nikodem)

Novalis 1772-1801 . . . . **NCLC 13**

Nowlan, Alden (Albert) 1933- . . . . . . **CLC 15**
See also CANR 5; CA 9-12R; DLB 53

Noyes, Alfred 1880-1958 . . . . **TCLC 7**
See also CA 104; DLB 20

Nunn, Kem 19??- . . . . **CLC 34**

Nye, Robert 1939- . . . . **CLC 13, 42**
See also CA 33-36R; SATA 6; DLB 14

Nyro, Laura 1947- . . . . **CLC 17**

Oates, Joyce Carol
1938- . . . . . **CLC 1, 2, 3, 6, 9, 11, 15, 19,
33, 52; SSC 6**
See also CANR 25; CA 5-8R; DLB 2, 5;
DLB-Y 81; CDALB 1968-1987

O'Brien, Darcy 1939- . . . . **CLC 11**
See also CANR 8; CA 21-24R

O'Brien, Edna 1932- . . . . **CLC 3, 5, 8, 13, 36**
See also CANR 6; CA 1-4R; DLB 14

O'Brien, Fitz-James 1828?-1862 . . **NCLC 21**
See also DLB 74

O'Brien, Flann
1911-1966 . . . . . . **CLC 1, 4, 5, 7, 10, 47**
See also O Nuallain, Brian

O'Brien, Richard 19??- . . . . **CLC 17**
See also CA 124

O'Brien, (William) Tim(othy)
1946- . . . . **CLC 7, 19, 40**
See also CA 85-88; DLB-Y 80

Obstfelder, Sigbjorn 1866-1900 . . . . **TCLC 23**
See also CA 123

O'Casey, Sean
1880-1964 . . . . **CLC 1, 5, 9, 11, 15**
See also CA 89-92; DLB 10

Ochs, Phil 1940-1976 . . . . **CLC 17**
See also obituary CA 65-68

O'Connor, Edwin (Greene)
1918-1968 . . . . **CLC 14**
See also CA 93-96; obituary CA 25-28R

O'Connor, (Mary) Flannery
1925-1964 . . . **CLC 1, 2, 3, 6, 10, 13, 15,
21; SSC 1**
See also CANR 3; CA 1-4R; DLB 2;
DLB-Y 80; CDALB 1941-1968

O'Connor, Frank
1903-1966 . . . . **CLC 14, 23; SSC 5**
See also O'Donovan, Michael (John)
See also CA 93-96

O'Dell, Scott 1903- . . . . **CLC 30**
See also CLR 1, 16; CANR 12; CA 61-64;
SATA 12; DLB 52

Odets, Clifford 1906-1963 . . . . **CLC 2, 28**
See also CA 85-88; DLB 7, 26

O'Donovan, Michael (John) 1903-1966
See O'Connor, Frank
See also CA 93-96

Oe, Kenzaburo 1935- . . . . **CLC 10, 36**
See also CA 97-100

O'Faolain, Julia 1932- . . . . **CLC 6, 19, 47**
See also CAAS 2; CANR 12; CA 81-84;
DLB 14

O'Faolain, Sean 1900- . . . . . **CLC 1, 7, 14, 32**
See also CANR 12; CA 61-64; DLB 15

O'Flaherty, Liam
1896-1984 . . . . **CLC 5, 34; SSC 6**
See also CA 101; obituary CA 113; DLB 36;
DLB-Y 84

O'Grady, Standish (James)
1846-1928 . . . . **TCLC 5**
See also CA 104

O'Grady, Timothy 1951- . . . . **CLC 59**

O'Hara, Frank 1926-1966 . . . . . **CLC 2, 5, 13**
See also CA 9-12R; obituary CA 25-28R;
DLB 5, 16

O'Hara, John (Henry)
1905-1970 . . . . . . **CLC 1, 2, 3, 6, 11, 42**
See also CA 5-8R; obituary CA 25-28R;
DLB 9; DLB-DS 2

O'Hara Family
See Banim, John and Banim, Michael

O'Hehir, Diana 1922- . . . . **CLC 41**
See also CA 93-96

Okigbo, Christopher (Ifenayichukwu)
1932-1967 . . . . **CLC 25**
See also CA 77-80

Olds, Sharon 1942- . . . . **CLC 32, 39**
See also CANR 18; CA 101

Olesha, Yuri (Karlovich)
1899-1960 . . . . **CLC 8**
See also CA 85-88

Oliphant, Margaret (Oliphant Wilson)
1828-1897 . . . . **NCLC 11**
See also DLB 18

Oliver, Mary 1935- . . . . **CLC 19, 34**
See also CANR 9; CA 21-24R; DLB 5

Olivier, (Baron) Laurence (Kerr)
1907- . . . . **CLC 20**
See also CA 111

Olsen, Tillie 1913- . . . . **CLC 4, 13**
See also CANR 1; CA 1-4R; DLB 28;
DLB-Y 80

Olson, Charles (John)
1910-1970 . . . . . **CLC 1, 2, 5, 6, 9, 11, 29**
See also CAP 1; CA 15-16;
obituary CA 25-28R; CABS 2; DLB 5, 16

Olson, Theodore 1937-
See Olson, Toby

Olson, Toby 1937- . . . . **CLC 28**
See also CANR 9; CA 65-68

Ondaatje, (Philip) Michael
1943- . . . . **CLC 14, 29, 51**
See also CA 77-80; DLB 60

Oneal, Elizabeth 1934-
See Oneal, Zibby
See also CA 106; SATA 30

Oneal, Zibby 1934- . . . . **CLC 30**
See also Oneal, Elizabeth

O'Neill, Eugene (Gladstone)
1888-1953 . . . . **TCLC 1, 6, 27**
See also CA 110; DLB 7

Onetti, Juan Carlos 1909- . . . . **CLC 7, 10**
See also CA 85-88

O'Nolan, Brian 1911-1966
See O'Brien, Flann

O Nuallain, Brian 1911-1966
See O'Brien, Flann
See also CAP 2; CA 21-22;
obituary CA 25-28R

Oppen, George 1908-1984 . . . . **CLC 7, 13, 34**
See also CANR 8; CA 13-16R;
obituary CA 113; DLB 5

Orlovitz, Gil 1918-1973 . . . . **CLC 22**
See also CA 77-80; obituary CA 45-48;
DLB 2, 5

Ortega y Gasset, Jose 1883-1955 . . . **TCLC 9**
See also CA 106

Ortiz, Simon J. 1941- . . . . **CLC 45**

Orton, Joe 1933?-1967 . . . . . . CLC 4, 13, 43
  See also Orton, John Kingsley
  See also DLB 13

Orton, John Kingsley 1933?-1967
  See Orton, Joe
  See also CA 85-88

Orwell, George
  1903-1950 . . . . TCLC 2, 6, 15, 31
  See also Blair, Eric Arthur
  See also DLB 15

Osborne, John (James)
  1929- . . . . CLC 1, 2, 5, 11, 45
  See also CANR 21; CA 13-16R; DLB 13

Osborne, Lawrence 1958- . . . . CLC 50

Osceola 1885-1962
  See Dinesen, Isak; Blixen, Karen
    (Christentze Dinesen)

Oshima, Nagisa 1932- . . . . CLC 20
  See also CA 116

Oskison, John M. 1874-1947 . . . . . . TCLC 35

Ossoli, Sarah Margaret (Fuller marchesa d')
  1810-1850
  See Fuller, (Sarah) Margaret
  See also SATA 25

Ostrovsky, Alexander
  1823-1886 . . . . NCLC 30

Otero, Blas de 1916- . . . . CLC 11
  See also CA 89-92

Ovid 43 B.C.-c. 18 A.D.
  See also PC 2

Owen, Wilfred (Edward Salter)
  1893-1918 . . . . TCLC 5, 27
  See also CA 104; DLB 20

Owens, Rochelle 1936- . . . . CLC 8
  See also CAAS 2; CA 17-20R

Owl, Sebastian 1939-
  See Thompson, Hunter S(tockton)

Oz, Amos 1939- . . . CLC 5, 8, 11, 27, 33, 54
  See also CA 53-56

Ozick, Cynthia 1928- . . . . . . CLC 3, 7, 28, 62
  See also CANR 28; CA 17-20R; DLB 28;
  DLB-Y 82

Ozu, Yasujiro 1903-1963 . . . . CLC 16
  See also CA 112

Pa Chin 1904- . . . . CLC 18
  See also Li Fei-kan

Pack, Robert 1929- . . . . CLC 13
  See also CANR 3; CA 1-4R; DLB 5

Padgett, Lewis 1915-1958
  See Kuttner, Henry

Padilla, Heberto 1932- . . . . CLC 38
  See also CA 123

Page, Jimmy 1944- . . . . CLC 12

Page, Louise 1955- . . . . CLC 40

Page, P(atricia) K(athleen)
  1916- . . . . CLC 7, 18
  See also CANR 4, 22; CA 53-56; DLB 68

Paget, Violet 1856-1935
  See Lee, Vernon
  See also CA 104

Palamas, Kostes 1859-1943 . . . . TCLC 5
  See also CA 105

Palazzeschi, Aldo 1885-1974 . . . . CLC 11
  See also CA 89-92; obituary CA 53-56

Paley, Grace 1922- . . . . CLC 4, 6, 37
  See also CANR 13; CA 25-28R; DLB 28

Palin, Michael 1943- . . . . CLC 21
  See also Monty Python
  See also CA 107

Palma, Ricardo 1833-1919 . . . . TCLC 29
  See also CANR 123

Pancake, Breece Dexter 1952-1979
  See Pancake, Breece D'J

Pancake, Breece D'J 1952-1979 . . . . CLC 29
  See also obituary CA 109

Papadiamantis, Alexandros
  1851-1911 . . . . TCLC 29

Papini, Giovanni 1881-1956 . . . . . . TCLC 22
  See also CA 121

Paracelsus 1493-1541 . . . . LC 14

Parini, Jay (Lee) 1948- . . . . CLC 54
  See also CA 97-100

Parker, Dorothy (Rothschild)
  1893-1967 . . . . CLC 15; SSC 2
  See also CAP 2; CA 19-20;
  obituary CA 25-28R; DLB 11, 45

Parker, Robert B(rown) 1932- . . . . . . CLC 27
  See also CANR 1, 26; CA 49-52

Parkin, Frank 1940- . . . . CLC 43

Parkman, Francis 1823-1893 . . . . . NCLC 12
  See also DLB 1, 30

Parks, Gordon (Alexander Buchanan)
  1912- . . . . CLC 1, 16
  See also CANR 26; CA 41-44R; SATA 8;
  DLB 33

Parnell, Thomas 1679-1718 . . . . LC 3

Parra, Nicanor 1914- . . . . CLC 2
  See also CA 85-88

Pasolini, Pier Paolo
  1922-1975 . . . . CLC 20, 37
  See also CA 93-96; obituary CA 61-64

Pastan, Linda (Olenik) 1932- . . . . . . CLC 27
  See also CANR 18; CA 61-64; DLB 5

Pasternak, Boris
  1890-1960 . . . . CLC 7, 10, 18, 63
  See also CA 127; obituary CA 116

Patchen, Kenneth 1911-1972 . . . CLC 1, 2, 18
  See also CANR 3; CA 1-4R;
  obituary CA 33-36R; DLB 16, 48

Pater, Walter (Horatio)
  1839-1894 . . . . NCLC 7
  See also DLB 57

Paterson, Andrew Barton
  1864-1941 . . . . TCLC 32

Paterson, Katherine (Womeldorf)
  1932- . . . . CLC 12, 30
  See also CLR 7; CA 21-24R; SATA 13, 53;
  DLB 52

Patmore, Coventry Kersey Dighton
  1823-1896 . . . . NCLC 9
  See also DLB 35

Paton, Alan (Stewart)
  1903-1988 . . . . CLC 4, 10, 25, 55
  See also CANR 22; CAP 1; CA 15-16;
  obituary CA 125; SATA 11

Paulding, James Kirke 1778-1860 . . NCLC 2
  See also DLB 3, 59, 74

Paulin, Tom 1949- . . . . CLC 37
  See also CA 123; DLB 40

Paustovsky, Konstantin (Georgievich)
  1892-1968 . . . . CLC 40
  See also CA 93-96; obituary CA 25-28R

Paustowsky, Konstantin (Georgievich)
  1892-1968
  See Paustovsky, Konstantin (Georgievich)

Pavese, Cesare 1908-1950 . . . . TCLC 3
  See also CA 104

Pavic, Milorad 1929- . . . . CLC 60

Payne, Alan 1932-
  See Jakes, John (William)

Paz, Octavio
  1914- . . . . . CLC 3, 4, 6, 10, 19, 51; PC 1
  See also CA 73-76

Peacock, Molly 1947- . . . . CLC 60
  See also CA 103

Peacock, Thomas Love
  1785-1866 . . . . NCLC 22

Peake, Mervyn 1911-1968 . . . . CLC 7, 54
  See also CANR 3; CA 5-8R;
  obituary CA 25-28R; SATA 23; DLB 15

Pearce, (Ann) Philippa 1920- . . . . . . CLC 21
  See also Christie, (Ann) Philippa
  See also CLR 9; CA 5-8R; SATA 1

Pearl, Eric 1934-
  See Elman, Richard

Pearson, T(homas) R(eid) 1956- . . . . CLC 39
  See also CA 120

Peck, John 1941- . . . . CLC 3
  See also CANR 3; CA 49-52

Peck, Richard 1934- . . . . CLC 21
  See also CLR 15; CANR 19; CA 85-88;
  SAAS 2; SATA 18

Peck, Robert Newton 1928- . . . . CLC 17
  See also CA 81-84; SAAS 1; SATA 21

Peckinpah, (David) Sam(uel)
  1925-1984 . . . . CLC 20
  See also CA 109; obituary CA 114

Pedersen, Knut 1859-1952
  See Hamsun, Knut
  See also CA 104, 109

Peguy, Charles (Pierre)
  1873-1914 . . . . TCLC 10
  See also CA 107

Pepys, Samuel 1633-1703 . . . . LC 11

Percy, Walker
  1916- . . . . CLC 2, 3, 6, 8, 14, 18, 47
  See also CANR 1; CA 1-4R; DLB 2;
  DLB-Y 80

Perec, Georges 1936-1982 . . . . CLC 56

Pereda, Jose Maria de
  1833-1906 . . . . TCLC 16

Perelman, S(idney) J(oseph)
  1904-1979 . . . CLC 3, 5, 9, 15, 23, 44, 49
  See also CANR 18; CA 73-76;
  obituary CA 89-92; DLB 11, 44

Peret, Benjamin 1899-1959 . . . . TCLC 20
  See also CA 117

Peretz, Isaac Leib 1852?-1915 . . . . . TCLC 16
  See also CA 109

Rodgers, W(illiam) R(obert)
  1909-1969 . . . . **CLC 7**
  See also CA 85-88; DLB 20

Rodriguez, Claudio   1934- . . . . **CLC 10**

Roethke, Theodore (Huebner)
  1908-1963 . . . . . . **CLC 1, 3, 8, 11, 19, 46**
  See also CA 81-84; CABS 2; SAAS 1;
  DLB 5; CDALB 1941-1968

Rogers, Sam   1943-
  See Shepard, Sam

Rogers, Thomas (Hunton)   1931- . . . . **CLC 57**
  See also CA 89-92

Rogers, Will(iam Penn Adair)
  1879-1935 . . . . **TCLC 8**
  See also CA 105; DLB 11

Rogin, Gilbert   1929- . . . . **CLC 18**
  See also CANR 15; CA 65-68

Rohan, Koda   1867-1947 . . . . **TCLC 22**
  See also CA 121

Rohmer, Eric   1920- . . . . **CLC 16**
  See also Scherer, Jean-Marie Maurice

Rohmer, Sax   1883-1959 . . . . **TCLC 28**
  See also Ward, Arthur Henry Sarsfield
  See also CA 108; DLB 70

Roiphe, Anne (Richardson)
  1935- . . . . **CLC 3, 9**
  See also CA 89-92; DLB-Y 80

**Rolfe, Frederick (William Serafino Austin
  Lewis Mary)**   1860-1913 . . . . . . **TCLC 12**
  See also CA 107; DLB 34

Rolland, Romain   1866-1944 . . . . **TCLC 23**
  See also CA 118

Rolvaag, O(le) E(dvart)
  1876-1931 . . . . **TCLC 17**
  See also CA 117; DLB 9

Romains, Jules   1885-1972 . . . . **CLC 7**
  See also CA 85-88

Romero, Jose Ruben   1890-1952 . . . **TCLC 14**
  See also CA 114

Ronsard, Pierre de   1524-1585 . . . . **LC 6**

Rooke, Leon   1934- . . . . **CLC 25, 34**
  See also CANR 23; CA 25-28R

Roper, William   1498-1578 . . . . **LC 10**

Rosa, Joao Guimaraes   1908-1967 . . . **CLC 23**
  See also obituary CA 89-92

Rosen, Richard (Dean)   1949- . . . . **CLC 39**
  See also CA 77-80

Rosenberg, Isaac   1890-1918 . . . . **TCLC 12**
  See also CA 107; DLB 20

Rosenblatt, Joe   1933- . . . . **CLC 15**
  See also Rosenblatt, Joseph

Rosenblatt, Joseph   1933-
  See Rosenblatt, Joe
  See also CA 89-92

Rosenfeld, Samuel   1896-1963
  See Tzara, Tristan
  See also obituary CA 89-92

Rosenthal, M(acha) L(ouis)   1917- . . . **CLC 28**
  See also CAAS 6; CANR 4; CA 1-4R;
  DLB 5

Ross, (James) Sinclair   1908- . . . . **CLC 13**
  See also CA 73-76

Rossetti, Christina Georgina
  1830-1894 . . . . **NCLC 2**
  See also SATA 20; DLB 35

Rossetti, Dante Gabriel
  1828-1882 . . . . **NCLC 4**
  See also DLB 35

Rossetti, Gabriel Charles Dante   1828-1882
  See Rossetti, Dante Gabriel

Rossner, Judith (Perelman)
  1935- . . . . **CLC 6, 9, 29**
  See also CANR 18; CA 17-20R; DLB 6

Rostand, Edmond (Eugene Alexis)
  1868-1918 . . . . **TCLC 6, 37**
  See also CA 104, 126

Roth, Henry   1906- . . . . **CLC 2, 6, 11**
  See also CAP 1; CA 11-12; DLB 28

Roth, Joseph   1894-1939 . . . . **TCLC 33**

Roth, Philip (Milton)
  1933- . . . . . . **CLC 1, 2, 3, 4, 6, 9, 15, 22,
                                              31, 47**
  See also CANR 1, 22; CA 1-4R; DLB 2, 28;
  DLB-Y 82

Rothenberg, James   1931- . . . . **CLC 57**

Rothenberg, Jerome   1931- . . . . **CLC 6**
  See also CANR 1; CA 45-48; DLB 5

Roumain, Jacques   1907-1944 . . . . . . **TCLC 19**
  See also CA 117

Rourke, Constance (Mayfield)
  1885-1941 . . . . **TCLC 12**
  See also YABC 1; CA 107

Rousseau, Jean-Baptiste   1671-1741 . . . **LC 9**

Rousseau, Jean-Jacques   1712-1778 . . . **LC 14**

Roussel, Raymond   1877-1933 . . . . . **TCLC 20**
  See also CA 117

Rovit, Earl (Herbert)   1927- . . . . **CLC 7**
  See also CANR 12; CA 5-8R

Rowe, Nicholas   1674-1718 . . . . **LC 8**

Rowson, Susanna Haswell
  1762-1824 . . . . **NCLC 5**
  See also DLB 37

Roy, Gabrielle   1909-1983 . . . . . . **CLC 10, 14**
  See also CANR 5; CA 53-56;
  obituary CA 110; DLB 68

Rozewicz, Tadeusz   1921- . . . . **CLC 9, 23**
  See also CA 108

Ruark, Gibbons   1941- . . . . **CLC 3**
  See also CANR 14; CA 33-36R

Rubens, Bernice   192?- . . . . **CLC 19, 31**
  See also CA 25-28R; DLB 14

Rudkin, (James) David   1936- . . . . . . **CLC 14**
  See also CA 89-92; DLB 13

Rudnik, Raphael   1933- . . . . **CLC 7**
  See also CA 29-32R

Ruiz, Jose Martinez   1874-1967
  See Azorin

Rukeyser, Muriel
  1913-1980 . . . . **CLC 6, 10, 15, 27**
  See also CANR 26; CA 5-8R;
  obituary CA 93-96; obituary SATA 22;
  DLB 48

Rule, Jane (Vance)   1931- . . . . **CLC 27**
  See also CANR 12; CA 25-28R; DLB 60

Rulfo, Juan   1918-1986 . . . . **CLC 8**
  See also CANR 26; CA 85-88;
  obituary CA 118

Runyon, (Alfred) Damon
  1880-1946 . . . . **TCLC 10**
  See also CA 107; DLB 11

Rush, Norman   1933- . . . . **CLC 44**
  See also CA 121, 126

Rushdie, (Ahmed) Salman
  1947- . . . . **CLC 23, 31, 55, 59**
  See also CA 108, 111

Rushforth, Peter (Scott)   1945- . . . . . **CLC 19**
  See also CA 101

Ruskin, John   1819-1900 . . . . **TCLC 20**
  See also CA 114; SATA 24; DLB 55

Russ, Joanna   1937- . . . . **CLC 15**
  See also CANR 11; CA 25-28R; DLB 8

Russell, George William   1867-1935
  See A. E.
  See also CA 104

Russell, (Henry) Ken(neth Alfred)
  1927- . . . . **CLC 16**
  See also CA 105

Russell, Willy   1947- . . . . **CLC 60**

Rutherford, Mark   1831-1913 . . . . . . **TCLC 25**
  See also CA 121; DLB 18

Ruyslinck, Ward   1929- . . . . **CLC 14**

Ryan, Cornelius (John)   1920-1974 . . . **CLC 7**
  See also CA 69-72; obituary CA 53-56

Rybakov, Anatoli   1911?- . . . . **CLC 23, 53**
  See also CA 126

Ryder, Jonathan   1927-
  See Ludlum, Robert

Ryga, George   1932- . . . . **CLC 14**
  See also CA 101; obituary CA 124; DLB 60

**Sévigné, Marquise de Marie de
  Rabutin-Chantal**   1626-1696 . . . . . **LC 11**

Saba, Umberto   1883-1957 . . . . **TCLC 33**

Sabato, Ernesto   1911- . . . . **CLC 10, 23**
  See also CA 97-100

Sachs, Marilyn (Stickle)   1927- . . . . . **CLC 35**
  See also CLR 2; CANR 13; CA 17-20R;
  SAAS 2; SATA 3, 52

Sachs, Nelly   1891-1970 . . . . **CLC 14**
  See also CAP 2; CA 17-18;
  obituary CA 25-28R

Sackler, Howard (Oliver)
  1929-1982 . . . . **CLC 14**
  See also CA 61-64; obituary CA 108; DLB 7

Sade, Donatien Alphonse Francois, Comte de
  1740-1814 . . . . **NCLC 3**

Sadoff, Ira   1945- . . . . **CLC 9**
  See also CANR 5, 21; CA 53-56

Safire, William   1929- . . . . **CLC 10**
  See also CA 17-20R

Sagan, Carl (Edward)   1934- . . . . **CLC 30**
  See also CANR 11; CA 25-28R

Sagan, Francoise
  1935- . . . . **CLC 3, 6, 9, 17, 36**
  See also Quoirez, Francoise
  See also CANR 6

Sahgal, Nayantara (Pandit)   1927- . . . **CLC 41**
  See also CANR 11; CA 9-12R

Sciascia, Leonardo
1921-1989 . . . . CLC 8, 9, 41
See also CA 85-88

Scoppettone, Sandra 1936- . . . . CLC 26
See also CA 5-8R; SATA 9

Scorsese, Martin 1942- . . . . CLC 20
See also CA 110, 114

Scotland, Jay 1932-
See Jakes, John (William)

Scott, Duncan Campbell
1862-1947 . . . . TCLC 6
See also CA 104

Scott, Evelyn 1893-1963 . . . . CLC 43
See also CA 104; obituary CA 112; DLB 9, 48

Scott, F(rancis) R(eginald)
1899-1985 . . . . CLC 22
See also CA 101; obituary CA 114

Scott, Joanna 19??- . . . . CLC 50
See also CA 126

Scott, Paul (Mark) 1920-1978 . . . . CLC 9, 60
See also CA 81-84; obituary CA 77-80;
DLB 14

Scott, Sir Walter 1771-1832 . . . . . NCLC 15
See also YABC 2

Scribe, (Augustin) Eugene
1791-1861 . . . . NCLC 16

Scudery, Madeleine de 1607-1701 . . . . . LC 2

Sealy, I. Allan 1951- . . . . CLC 55

Seare, Nicholas 1925-
See Trevanian; Whitaker, Rodney

Sebestyen, Igen 1924-
See Sebestyen, Ouida

Sebestyen, Ouida 1924- . . . . CLC 30
See also CA 107; SATA 39

Sedgwick, Catharine Maria
1789-1867 . . . . NCLC 19
See also DLB 1

Seelye, John 1931- . . . . CLC 7
See also CA 97-100

Seferiades, Giorgos Stylianou 1900-1971
See Seferis, George
See also CANR 5; CA 5-8R;
obituary CA 33-36R

Seferis, George 1900-1971 . . . . CLC 5, 11
See also Seferiades, Giorgos Stylianou

Segal, Erich (Wolf) 1937- . . . . CLC 3, 10
See also CANR 20; CA 25-28R; DLB-Y 86

Seger, Bob 1945- . . . . CLC 35

Seger, Robert Clark 1945-
See Seger, Bob

Seghers, Anna 1900-1983 . . . . CLC 7, 110
See also Radvanyi, Netty Reiling
See also DLB 69

Seidel, Frederick (Lewis) 1936- . . . . . CLC 18
See also CANR 8; CA 13-16R; DLB-Y 84

Seifert, Jaroslav 1901-1986 . . . . . CLC 34, 44

Sei Shonagon c. 966-1017? . . . . CMLC 6

Selby, Hubert, Jr. 1928- . . . . . CLC 1, 2, 4, 8
See also CA 13-16R; DLB 2

Senacour, Etienne Pivert de
1770-1846 . . . . NCLC 16

Sender, Ramon (Jose) 1902-1982 . . . . CLC 8
See also CANR 8; CA 5-8R;
obituary CA 105

Seneca, Lucius Annaeus
4 B.C.-65 A.D. . . . . CMLC 6

Senghor, Léopold Sédar 1906- . . . . . . CLC 54
See also CA 116

Serling, (Edward) Rod(man)
1924-1975 . . . . CLC 30
See also CA 65-68; obituary CA 57-60;
DLB 26

Serpieres 1907-
See Guillevic, (Eugene)

Service, Robert W(illiam)
1874-1958 . . . . TCLC 15
See also CA 115; SATA 20

Seth, Vikram 1952- . . . . CLC 43
See also CA 121

Seton, Cynthia Propper
1926-1982 . . . . CLC 27
See also CANR 7; CA 5-8R;
obituary CA 108

Seton, Ernest (Evan) Thompson
1860-1946 . . . . TCLC 31
See also CA 109; SATA 18

Settle, Mary Lee 1918- . . . . CLC 19, 61
See also CAAS 1; CA 89-92; DLB 6

Sevigne, Marquise de Marie de
Rabutin-Chantal 1626-1696 . . . . . LC 11

Sexton, Anne (Harvey)
1928-1974 . . . CLC 2, 4, 6, 8, 10, 15, 53;
PC 2
See also CANR 3; CA 1-4R;
obituary CA 53-56; CABS 2; SATA 10;
DLB 5; CDALB 1941-1968

Shaara, Michael (Joseph) 1929- . . . . CLC 15
See also CA 102; obituary CA 125;
DLB-Y 83

Shackleton, C. C. 1925-
See Aldiss, Brian W(ilson)

Shacochis, Bob 1951- . . . . CLC 39
See also CA 119, 124

Shaffer, Anthony 1926- . . . . CLC 19
See also CA 110, 116; DLB 13

Shaffer, Peter (Levin)
1926- . . . . CLC 5, 14, 18, 37, 60
See also CANR 25; CA 25-28R; DLB 13

Shalamov, Varlam (Tikhonovich)
1907?-1982 . . . . CLC 18
See also obituary CA 105

Shamlu, Ahmad 1925- . . . . CLC 10

Shammas, Anton 1951- . . . . CLC 55

Shange, Ntozake 1948- . . . . . . CLC 8, 25, 38
See also CA 85-88; DLB 38

Shapcott, Thomas W(illiam) 1935- . . CLC 38
See also CA 69-72

Shapiro, Karl (Jay) 1913- . . CLC 4, 8, 15, 53
See also CAAS 6; CANR 1; CA 1-4R;
DLB 48

Sharp, William 1855-1905 . . . . TCLC 39

Sharpe, Tom 1928- . . . . CLC 36
See also CA 114; DLB 14

Shaw, (George) Bernard
1856-1950 . . . . TCLC 3, 9, 21
See also CA 104, 109, 119; DLB 10, 57

Shaw, Henry Wheeler
1818-1885 . . . . NCLC 15
See also DLB 11

Shaw, Irwin 1913-1984 . . . . . . CLC 7, 23, 34
See also CANR 21; CA 13-16R;
obituary CA 112; DLB 6; DLB-Y 84;
CDALB 1941-1968

Shaw, Robert 1927-1978 . . . . CLC 5
See also CANR 4; CA 1-4R;
obituary CA 81-84; DLB 13, 14

Shawn, Wallace 1943- . . . . CLC 41
See also CA 112

Sheed, Wilfrid (John Joseph)
1930- . . . . CLC 2, 4, 10, 53
See also CA 65-68; DLB 6

Sheffey, Asa 1913-1980
See Hayden, Robert (Earl)

Sheldon, Alice (Hastings) B(radley)
1915-1987
See Tiptree, James, Jr.
See also CA 108; obituary CA 122

Shelley, Mary Wollstonecraft Godwin
1797-1851 . . . . NCLC 14
See also SATA 29

Shelley, Percy Bysshe
1792-1822 . . . . NCLC 18

Shepard, Jim 19??- . . . . CLC 36

Shepard, Lucius 19??- . . . . CLC 34

Shepard, Sam
1943- . . . . CLC 4, 6, 17, 34, 41, 44
See also CANR 22; CA 69-72; DLB 7

Shepherd, Michael 1927-
See Ludlum, Robert

Sherburne, Zoa (Morin) 1912- . . . . . . CLC 30
See also CANR 3; CA 1-4R; SATA 3

Sheridan, Frances 1724-1766 . . . . LC 7
See also DLB 39

Sheridan, Richard Brinsley
1751-1816 . . . . NCLC 5

Sherman, Jonathan Marc 1970?- . . . . CLC 55

Sherman, Martin 19??- . . . . CLC 19
See also CA 116

Sherwin, Judith Johnson 1936- . . . CLC 7, 15
See also CA 25-28R

Sherwood, Robert E(mmet)
1896-1955 . . . . TCLC 3
See also CA 104; DLB 7, 26

Shiel, M(atthew) P(hipps)
1865-1947 . . . . TCLC 8
See also CA 106

Shiga, Naoya 1883-1971 . . . . CLC 33
See also CA 101; obituary CA 33-36R

Shimazaki, Haruki 1872-1943
See Shimazaki, Toson
See also CA 105

Shimazaki, Toson 1872-1943 . . . . TCLC 5
See also Shimazaki, Haruki

Sholokhov, Mikhail (Aleksandrovich)
1905-1984 . . . . CLC 7, 15
See also CA 101; obituary CA 112;
SATA 36

Sholom Aleichem   1859-1916 .... TCLC 1, 35
   See also Rabinovitch, Sholem

Shreve, Susan Richards   1939- ...... CLC 23
   See also CAAS 5; CANR 5; CA 49-52;
   SATA 41, 46

Shue, Larry   1946-1985 .... CLC 52
   See also obituary CA 117

Shulman, Alix Kates   1932- ...... CLC 2, 10
   See also CA 29-32R; SATA 7

Shuster, Joe   1914- .... CLC 21

Shute (Norway), Nevil   1899-1960 ... CLC 30
   See also Norway, Nevil Shute
   See also CA 102; obituary CA 93-96

Shuttle, Penelope (Diane)   1947- ..... CLC 7
   See also CA 93-96; DLB 14, 40

Siegel, Jerome   1914- .... CLC 21
   See also CA 116

Sienkiewicz, Henryk (Adam Aleksander Pius)
   1846-1916 .... TCLC 3
   See also CA 104

Sigal, Clancy   1926- .... CLC 7
   See also CA 1-4R

Sigourney, Lydia (Howard Huntley)
   1791-1865 .... NCLC 21
   See also DLB 1, 42, 73

Siguenza y Gongora, Carlos de
   1645-1700 .... LC 8

Sigurjonsson, Johann   1880-1919 ... TCLC 27

Sikelianos, Angeles   1884-1951 ..... TCLC 39

Silkin, Jon   1930- .... CLC 2, 6, 43
   See also CAAS 5; CA 5-8R; DLB 27

Silko, Leslie Marmon   1948- .... CLC 23
   See also CA 115, 122

Sillanpaa, Franz Eemil   1888-1964 ... CLC 19
   See also obituary CA 93-96

Sillitoe, Alan
   1928- .... CLC 1, 3, 6, 10, 19, 57
   See also CAAS 2; CANR 8, 26; CA 9-12R;
   DLB 14

Silone, Ignazio   1900-1978 .... CLC 4
   See also CAAS 2; CANR 26; CAP 2;
   CA 25-28, 11-12R,; obituary CA 81-84

Silver, Joan Micklin   1935- .... CLC 20
   See also CA 114, 121

Silverberg, Robert   1935- .... CLC 7
   See also CAAS 3; CANR 1, 20; CA 1-4R;
   SATA 13; DLB 8

Silverstein, Alvin   1933- .... CLC 17
   See also CANR 2; CA 49-52; SATA 8

Silverstein, Virginia B(arbara Opshelor)
   1937- .... CLC 17
   See also CANR 2; CA 49-52; SATA 8

Simak, Clifford D(onald)
   1904-1988 .... CLC 1, 55
   See also CANR 1; CA 1-4R;
   obituary CA 125; DLB 8

Simenon, Georges (Jacques Christian)
   1903-1989 ...... CLC 1, 2, 3, 8, 18, 47
   See also CA 85-88; DLB 72

Simenon, Paul   1956?-
   See The Clash

Simic, Charles   1938- .... CLC 6, 9, 22, 49
   See also CAAS 4; CANR 12; CA 29-32R

Simmons, Charles (Paul)   1924- ..... CLC 57
   See also CA 89-92

Simmons, Dan   1948- .... CLC 44

Simmons, James (Stewart Alexander)
   1933- .... CLC 43
   See also CA 105; DLB 40

Simms, William Gilmore
   1806-1870 .... NCLC 3
   See also DLB 3, 30

Simon, Carly   1945- .... CLC 26
   See also CA 105

Simon, Claude (Henri Eugene)
   1913- .... CLC 4, 9, 15, 39
   See also CA 89-92

Simon, (Marvin) Neil
   1927- .... CLC 6, 11, 31, 39
   See also CA 21-24R; DLB 7

Simon, Paul   1941- .... CLC 17
   See also CA 116

Simonon, Paul   1956?-
   See The Clash

Simpson, Louis (Aston Marantz)
   1923- .... CLC 4, 7, 9, 32
   See also CAAS 4; CANR 1; CA 1-4R;
   DLB 5

Simpson, Mona (Elizabeth)   1957- ... CLC 44
   See also CA 122

Simpson, N(orman) F(rederick)
   1919- .... CLC 29
   See also CA 11-14R; DLB 13

Sinclair, Andrew (Annandale)
   1935- .... CLC 2, 14
   See also CAAS 5; CANR 14; CA 9-12R;
   DLB 14

Sinclair, Mary Amelia St. Clair   1865?-1946
   See Sinclair, May
   See also CA 104

Sinclair, May   1865?-1946 ...... TCLC 3, 11
   See also Sinclair, Mary Amelia St. Clair
   See also DLB 36

Sinclair, Upton (Beall)
   1878-1968 .... CLC 1, 11, 15, 63
   See also CANR 7; CA 5-8R;
   obituary CA 25-28R; SATA 9; DLB 9

Singer, Isaac Bashevis
   1904- .... CLC 1, 3, 6, 9, 11, 15, 23, 38;
                                  SSC 3
   See also CLR 1; CANR 1; CA 1-4R;
   SATA 3, 27; DLB 6, 28, 52;
   CDALB 1941-1968

Singer, Israel Joshua   1893-1944 ... TCLC 33

Singh, Khushwant   1915- .... CLC 11
   See also CANR 6; CA 9-12R

Sinyavsky, Andrei (Donatevich)
   1925- .... CLC 8
   See also CA 85-88

Sirin, V.
   See Nabokov, Vladimir (Vladimirovich)

Sissman, L(ouis) E(dward)
   1928-1976 .... CLC 9, 18
   See also CANR 13; CA 21-24R;
   obituary CA 65-68; DLB 5

Sisson, C(harles) H(ubert)   1914- ..... CLC 8
   See also CAAS 3; CANR 3; CA 1-4R;
   DLB 27

Sitwell, (Dame) Edith   1887-1964 ... CLC 2, 9
   See also CA 9-12R; DLB 20

Sjoewall, Maj   1935-
   See Wahloo, Per
   See also CA 61-64, 65-68

Sjowall, Maj   1935-
   See Wahloo, Per

Skelton, Robin   1925- .... CLC 13
   See also CAAS 5; CA 5-8R; DLB 27, 53

Skolimowski, Jerzy   1938- .... CLC 20

Skolimowski, Yurek   1938-
   See Skolimowski, Jerzy

Skram, Amalie (Bertha)
   1847-1905 .... TCLC 25

Skrine, Mary Nesta   1904-
   See Keane, Molly

Skvorecky, Josef (Vaclav)
   1924- .... CLC 15, 39
   See also CAAS 1; CANR 10; CA 61-64

Slade, Bernard   1930- .... CLC 11, 46
   See also Newbound, Bernard Slade
   See also DLB 53

Slaughter, Carolyn   1946- .... CLC 56
   See also CA 85-88

Slaughter, Frank G(ill)   1908- ...... CLC 29
   See also CANR 5; CA 5-8R

Slavitt, David (R.)   1935- ...... CLC 5, 14
   See also CAAS 3; CA 21-24R; DLB 5, 6

Slesinger, Tess   1905-1945 .... TCLC 10
   See also CA 107

Slessor, Kenneth   1901-1971 .... CLC 14
   See also CA 102; obituary CA 89-92

Slowacki, Juliusz   1809-1849 ..... NCLC 15

Smart, Christopher   1722-1771 .... LC 3

Smart, Elizabeth   1913-1986 .... CLC 54
   See also CA 81-84; obituary CA 118

Smiley, Jane (Graves)   1949- .... CLC 53
   See also CA 104

Smith, A(rthur) J(ames) M(arshall)
   1902-1980 .... CLC 15
   See also CANR 4; CA 1-4R;
   obituary CA 102

Smith, Betty (Wehner)   1896-1972 ... CLC 19
   See also CA 5-8R; obituary CA 33-36R;
   SATA 6; DLB-Y 82

Smith, Cecil Lewis Troughton   1899-1966
   See Forester, C(ecil) S(cott)

Smith, Charlotte (Turner)
   1749-1806 .... NCLC 23
   See also DLB 39

Smith, Clark Ashton   1893-1961 .... CLC 43

Smith, Dave   1942- .... CLC 22, 42
   See also Smith, David (Jeddie)
   See also CAAS 7; CANR 1; DLB 5

Smith, David (Jeddie)   1942-
   See Smith, Dave
   See also CANR 1; CA 49-52

Smith, Florence Margaret   1902-1971
   See Smith, Stevie
   See also CAP 2; CA 17-18;
   obituary CA 29-32R

Smith, John   1580?-1631 .... LC 9
   See also DLB 24, 30

Taine, Hippolyte Adolphe
1828-1893 .... NCLC 15

Talese, Gaetano 1932-
See Talese, Gay

Talese, Gay 1932- .... CLC 37
See also CANR 9; CA 1-4R

Tallent, Elizabeth (Ann) 1954- ..... CLC 45
See also CA 117

Tally, Ted 1952- .... CLC 42
See also CA 120, 124

Tamayo y Baus, Manuel
1829-1898 .... NCLC 1

Tammsaare, A(nton) H(ansen)
1878-1940 .... TCLC 27

Tan, Amy 1952- .... CLC 59

Tanizaki, Jun'ichiro
1886-1965 .... CLC 8, 14, 28
See also CA 93-96; obituary CA 25-28R

Tarbell, Ida 1857-1944........... TCLC 40
See also CA 122; DLB 47

Tarkington, (Newton) Booth
1869-1946 .... TCLC 9
See also CA 110; SATA 17; DLB 9

Tasso, Torquato 1544-1595 .... LC 5

Tate, (John Orley) Allen
1899-1979 .... CLC 2, 4, 6, 9, 11, 14, 24
See also CA 5-8R; obituary CA 85-88;
DLB 4, 45, 63

Tate, James 1943-........... CLC 2, 6, 25
See also CA 21-24R; DLB 5

Tavel, Ronald 1940- .... CLC 6
See also CA 21-24R

Taylor, C(ecil) P(hillip) 1929-1981 .. CLC 27
See also CA 25-28R; obituary CA 105

Taylor, Edward 1644?-1729 .... LC 11
See also DLB 24

Taylor, Eleanor Ross 1920-......... CLC 5
See also CA 81-84

Taylor, Elizabeth 1912-1975 ... CLC 2, 4, 29
See also CANR 9; CA 13-16R; SATA 13

Taylor, Henry (Splawn) 1917-...... CLC 44
See also CAAS 7; CA 33-36R; DLB 5

Taylor, Kamala (Purnaiya) 1924-
See Markandaya, Kamala
See also CA 77-80

Taylor, Mildred D(elois) 1943-..... CLC 21
See also CLR 9; CANR 25; CA 85-88;
SAAS 5; SATA 15; DLB 52

Taylor, Peter (Hillsman)
1917- .... CLC 1, 4, 18, 37, 44, 50
See also CANR 9; CA 13-16R; DLB-Y 81

Taylor, Robert Lewis 1912-........ CLC 14
See also CANR 3; CA 1-4R; SATA 10

Teasdale, Sara 1884-1933.......... TCLC 4
See also CA 104; SATA 32; DLB 45

Tegner, Esaias 1782-1846........ NCLC 2

Teilhard de Chardin, (Marie Joseph) Pierre
1881-1955 .... TCLC 9
See also CA 105

Tennant, Emma 1937- .... CLC 13, 52
See also CAAS 9; CANR 10; CA 65-68;
DLB 14

Tennyson, Alfred 1809-1892 ..... NCLC 30
See also DLB 32

Teran, Lisa St. Aubin de 19??- ..... CLC 36

Terkel, Louis 1912-
See Terkel, Studs
See also CANR 18; CA 57-60

Terkel, Studs 1912- .... CLC 38
See also Terkel, Louis

Terry, Megan 1932-.............. CLC 19
See also CA 77-80; DLB 7

Tertz, Abram 1925-
See Sinyavsky, Andrei (Donatevich)

Tesich, Steve 1943?-.............. CLC 40
See also CA 105; DLB-Y 83

Tesich, Stoyan 1943?-
See Tesich, Steve

Teternikov, Fyodor Kuzmich 1863-1927
See Sologub, Fyodor
See also CA 104

Tevis, Walter 1928-1984 .... CLC 42
See also CA 113

Tey, Josephine 1897-1952 .... TCLC 14
See also Mackintosh, Elizabeth

Thackeray, William Makepeace
1811-1863 .... NCLC 5, 14, 22
See also SATA 23; DLB 21, 55

Thakura, Ravindranatha 1861-1941
See Tagore, (Sir) Rabindranath
See also CA 104

Thelwell, Michael (Miles) 1939-.... CLC 22
See also CA 101

Theroux, Alexander (Louis)
1939- .... CLC 2, 25
See also CANR 20; CA 85-88

Theroux, Paul
1941- .... CLC 5, 8, 11, 15, 28, 46
See also CANR 20; CA 33-36R; SATA 44;
DLB 2

Thesen, Sharon 1946-............. CLC 56

Thibault, Jacques Anatole Francois
1844-1924
See France, Anatole
See also CA 106

Thiele, Colin (Milton) 1920- ...... CLC 17
See also CANR 12; CA 29-32R; SAAS 2;
SATA 14

Thomas, Audrey (Grace)
1935- .... CLC 7, 13, 37
See also CA 21-24R; DLB 60

Thomas, D(onald) M(ichael)
1935- .... CLC 13, 22, 31
See also CANR 17; CA 61-64; DLB 40

Thomas, Dylan (Marlais)
1914-1953 ..... TCLC 1, 8; PC 2; SSC 3
See also CA 104, 120; SATA 60; DLB 13,
20

Thomas, Edward (Philip)
1878-1917 .... TCLC 10
See also CA 106; DLB 19

Thomas, John Peter 1928-
See Thomas, Piri

Thomas, Joyce Carol 1938-........ CLC 35
See also CA 113, 116; SATA 40; DLB 33

Thomas, Lewis 1913-............. CLC 35
See also CA 85-88

Thomas, Piri 1928-............... CLC 17
See also CA 73-76

Thomas, R(onald) S(tuart)
1913-.............. CLC 6, 13, 48
See also CAAS 4; CA 89-92; DLB 27

Thomas, Ross (Elmore) 1926-...... CLC 39
See also CANR 22; CA 33-36R

Thompson, Ernest 1860-1946
See Seton, Ernest (Evan) Thompson

Thompson, Francis (Joseph)
1859-1907 .... TCLC 4
See also CA 104; DLB 19

Thompson, Hunter S(tockton)
1939-.............. CLC 9, 17, 40
See also CANR 23; CA 17-20R

Thompson, Judith 1954-.......... CLC 39

Thomson, James 1834-1882...... NCLC 18
See also DLB 35

Thoreau, Henry David
1817-1862 .... NCLC 7, 21
See also DLB 1; CDALB 1640-1865

Thurber, James (Grover)
1894-1961 .... CLC 5, 11, 25; SSC 1
See also CANR 17; CA 73-76; SATA 13;
DLB 4, 11, 22

Thurman, Wallace 1902-1934 ...... TCLC 6
See also CA 104, 124; DLB 51

Tieck, (Johann) Ludwig
1773-1853 .... NCLC 5

Tillinghast, Richard 1940-........ CLC 29
See also CANR 26; CA 29-32R

Timrod, Henry 1828-1867 .... NCLC 25

Tindall, Gillian 1938-............. CLC 7
See also CANR 11; CA 21-24R

Tiptree, James, Jr. 1915-1987... CLC 48, 50
See also Sheldon, Alice (Hastings) B(radley)
See also DLB 8

Tocqueville, Alexis (Charles Henri Maurice
Clerel, Comte) de 1805-1859.. NCLC 7

Tolkien, J(ohn) R(onald) R(euel)
1892-1973 .... CLC 1, 2, 3, 8, 12, 38
See also CAP 2; CA 17-18;
obituary CA 45-48; SATA 2, 32;
obituary SATA 24; DLB 15

Toller, Ernst 1893-1939.......... TCLC 10
See also CA 107

Tolson, Melvin B(eaunorus)
1900?-1966.................. CLC 36
See also CA 124; obituary CA 89-92;
DLB 48, 124

Tolstoy, (Count) Alexey Nikolayevich
1883-1945 .... TCLC 18
See also CA 107

Tolstoy, (Count) Leo (Lev Nikolaevich)
1828-1910 .... TCLC 4, 11, 17, 28
See also CA 104, 123; SATA 26

Tomlin, Lily 1939-.............. CLC 17

Tomlin, Mary Jean 1939-
See Tomlin, Lily
See also CA 117

Tomlinson, (Alfred) Charles
1927- .... **CLC 2, 4, 6, 13, 45**
See also CA 5-8R; DLB 40

Toole, John Kennedy 1937-1969 .... **CLC 19**
See also CA 104; DLB-Y 81

Toomer, Jean
1894-1967 ..... **CLC 1, 4, 13, 22; SSC 1**
See also CA 85-88; DLB 45, 51

Torrey, E. Fuller 19??- .... **CLC 34**
See also CA 119

Tournier, Michel 1924- ...... **CLC 6, 23, 36**
See also CANR 3; CA 49-52; SATA 23

Townsend, Sue 1946- .... **CLC 61**
See also CA 119, 127; SATA 48, 55

Townshend, Peter (Dennis Blandford)
1945- .... **CLC 17, 42**
See also CA 107

Tozzi, Federigo 1883-1920....... **TCLC 31**

Trakl, Georg 1887-1914............ **TCLC 5**
See also CA 104

Transtromer, Tomas (Gosta)
1931- .... **CLC 52**
See also CA 117

Traven, B. 1890-1969.......... **CLC 8, 11**
See also CAP 2; CA 19-20;
obituary CA 25-28R; DLB 9, 56

Tremain, Rose 1943-.............. **CLC 42**
See also CA 97-100; DLB 14

Tremblay, Michel 1942-........... **CLC 29**
See also CA 116; DLB 60

Trevanian 1925- .... **CLC 29**
See also CA 108

Trevor, William 1928- ..... **CLC 7, 9, 14, 25**
See also Cox, William Trevor
See also DLB 14

Trifonov, Yuri (Valentinovich)
1925-1981 .... **CLC 45**
See also obituary CA 103, 126

Trilling, Lionel 1905-1975 .... **CLC 9, 11, 24**
See also CANR 10; CA 9-12R;
obituary CA 61-64; DLB 28, 63

Trogdon, William 1939-
See Heat Moon, William Least
See also CA 115, 119

Trollope, Anthony 1815-1882 ..... **NCLC 6**
See also SATA 22; DLB 21, 57

Trollope, Frances 1780-1863 ..... **NCLC 30**
See also DLB 21

Trotsky, Leon (Davidovich)
1879-1940 .... **TCLC 22**
See also CA 118

Trotter (Cockburn), Catharine
1679-1749 .... **LC 8**

Trow, George W. S. 1943-........ **CLC 52**
See also CA 126

Troyat, Henri 1911-.............. **CLC 23**
See also CANR 2; CA 45-48

Trudeau, G(arretson) B(eekman) 1948-
See Trudeau, Garry
See also CA 81-84; SATA 35

Trudeau, Garry 1948-............. **CLC 12**
See also Trudeau, G(arretson) B(eekman)

Truffaut, Francois 1932-1984....... **CLC 20**
See also CA 81-84; obituary CA 113

Trumbo, Dalton 1905-1976 .... **CLC 19**
See also CANR 10; CA 21-24R;
obituary CA 69-72; DLB 26

Trumbull, John 1750-1831....... **NCLC 30**
See also DLB 31

Tryon, Thomas 1926-........... **CLC 3, 11**
See also CA 29-32R

Ts'ao Hsueh-ch'in 1715?-1763....... **LC 1**

Tsushima Shuji 1909-1948
See Dazai Osamu
See also CA 107

Tsvetaeva (Efron), Marina (Ivanovna)
1892-1941 .... **TCLC 7, 35**
See also CA 104, 128

Tunis, John R(oberts) 1889-1975 ... **CLC 12**
See also CA 61-64; SATA 30, 37; DLB 22

Tuohy, Frank 1925- .... **CLC 37**
See also DLB 14

Tuohy, John Francis 1925-
See Tuohy, Frank
See also CANR 3; CA 5-8R

Turco, Lewis (Putnam) 1934- ... **CLC 11, 63**
See also CANR 24; CA 13-16R; DLB-Y 84

Turgenev, Ivan
1818-1883 .... **NCLC 21; SSC 7**

Turner, Frederick 1943-.......... **CLC 48**
See also CANR 12; CA 73-76; DLB 40

Tutuola, Amos 1920- .... **CLC 5, 14, 29**
See also CA 9-12R

Twain, Mark
1835-1910 ... **TCLC 6, 12, 19, 36; SSC 6**
See also Clemens, Samuel Langhorne
See also YABC 2; DLB 11, 12, 23, 64, 74

Tyler, Anne
1941-........ **CLC 7, 11, 18, 28, 44, 59**
See also CANR 11; CA 9-12R; SATA 7;
DLB 6; DLB-Y 82

Tyler, Royall 1757-1826......... **NCLC 3**
See also DLB 37

Tynan (Hinkson), Katharine
1861-1931 .... **TCLC 3**
See also CA 104

Tytell, John 1939- .... **CLC 50**
See also CA 29-32R

Tzara, Tristan 1896-1963......... **CLC 47**
See also Rosenfeld, Samuel

Uhry, Alfred 1947?-............. **CLC 55**
See also CA 127

Unamuno (y Jugo), Miguel de
1864-1936 .... **TCLC 2, 9**
See also CA 104

Underwood, Miles 1909-1981
See Glassco, John

Undset, Sigrid 1882-1949....... **TCLC 3**
See also CA 104

Ungaretti, Giuseppe
1888-1970 .... **CLC 7, 11, 15**
See also CAP 2; CA 19-20;
obituary CA 25-28R

Unger, Douglas 1952-............. **CLC 34**

Unger, Eva 1932-
See Figes, Eva

Updike, John (Hoyer)
1932-...... **CLC 1, 2, 3, 5, 7, 9, 13, 15,
23, 34, 43**
See also CANR 4; CA 1-4R; CABS 2;
DLB 2, 5; DLB-Y 80, 82; DLB-DS 3

Urdang, Constance (Henriette)
1922- .... **CLC 47**
See also CANR 9, 24; CA 21-24R

Uris, Leon (Marcus) 1924-....... **CLC 7, 32**
See also CANR 1; CA 1-4R; SATA 49

Ustinov, Peter (Alexander) 1921-.... **CLC 1**
See also CANR 25; CA 13-16R; DLB 13

Vaculik, Ludvik 1926-............. **CLC 7**
See also CA 53-56

Valenzuela, Luisa 1938-.......... **CLC 31**
See also CA 101

Valera (y Acala-Galiano), Juan
1824-1905 .... **TCLC 10**
See also CA 106

Valery, Paul (Ambroise Toussaint Jules)
1871-1945 .... **TCLC 4, 15**
See also CA 104, 122

**Valle-Inclan (y Montenegro), Ramon (Maria)
del** 1866-1936.............. **TCLC 5**
See also CA 106

Vallejo, Cesar (Abraham)
1892-1938 .... **TCLC 3**
See also CA 105

Van Ash, Cay 1918-.............. **CLC 34**

Vance, Jack 1916?-.............. **CLC 35**
See also DLB 8

Vance, John Holbrook 1916?-
See Vance, Jack
See also CANR 17; CA 29-32R

**Van Den Bogarde, Derek (Jules Gaspard
Ulric) Niven** 1921-
See Bogarde, Dirk
See also CA 77-80

Vandenburgh, Jane 19??-.......... **CLC 59**

Vanderhaeghe, Guy 1951- .... **CLC 41**
See also CA 113

Van der Post, Laurens (Jan) 1906-... **CLC 5**
See also CA 5-8R

Van de Wetering, Janwillem
1931- .... **CLC 47**
See also CANR 4; CA 49-52

Van Dine, S. S. 1888-1939........ **TCLC 23**

Van Doren, Carl (Clinton)
1885-1950 .... **TCLC 18**
See also CA 111

Van Doren, Mark 1894-1972..... **CLC 6, 10**
See also CANR 3; CA 1-4R;
obituary CA 37-40R; DLB 45

Van Druten, John (William)
1901-1957 .... **TCLC 2**
See also CA 104; DLB 10

Van Duyn, Mona 1921-....... **CLC 3, 7, 63**
See also CANR 7; CA 9-12R; DLB 5

Van Itallie, Jean-Claude 1936- ...... **CLC 3**
See also CAAS 2; CANR 1; CA 45-48;
DLB 7

Van Ostaijen, Paul 1896-1928..... **TCLC 33**

Van Peebles, Melvin 1932- ...... **CLC 2, 20**
See also CA 85-88

Literary Criticism Series
Cumulative Topic Index

This index lists all topic entries in the Gale Literary Criticism Series *Contemporary Literary Criticism, Literature Criticism from 1400 to 1800, Nineteenth-Century Literature Criticism,* and *Twentieth-Century Literary Criticism.*

TCLC Cumulative Nationality Index

Nationality Index

Title Index